'Books of collected geographical readings, so common of fashion. This carefully chosen selection by Agnew, how useful a role the "readings" once played in underg edited anthology deserves to reverse the trend.'

Professor Peter Haggett, University of Bristol

'This book will become the key reader for human geography students. Why? First, because the editors – each of them acknowledged leaders in the discipline – have tried to tell a story of modern human geography which is not just the winners' story. Second, because the choice of readings is correspondingly wise, striking a balance between "standards" and lesser known but equally important works. Third, because the editors have provided introductions to the volume and to each of its sections which are important summary statements in their own right. Just excellent.'

Professor N.J. Thrift, University of Bristol

'An exciting and well-conceived approach to geographic thought. In contrast to views that foreground great men or so-called paradigms this book breathes new life into the way geographers see their field. There is absolutely nothing like it. The word "essential" in the title is no mere decoration.'

Kevin R. Cox, Professor of Geography, The Ohio State University

HUMAN GEOGRAPHY

AN ESSENTIAL ANTHOLOGY

EDITED BY
JOHN AGNEW,
DAVID N. LIVINGSTONE
& ALISDAIR ROGERS

WILEY Blackwell

Human Geography: An Essential Anthology

Authorised reprint by Wiley India Pvt. Ltd., 4435-36/7, Ansari Road, Daryaganj, New Delhi-110002.

Reprint: 2016

Printed at: Radha Offset Press, Delhi.

ISBN: 978-81-265-6034-9

CONTENTS

ACKNOWLEDGEMENTS

Composing an 'essential anthology' for human geography has been no easy task. The three co-editors have had to collaborate over long distances and make difficult decisions over what to include. We have benefitted from the advice and counsel of a large number of prominent human geographers with different views of their field. We value their efforts while recognizing our own limitations in heeding in full so many informed opinions. In such a project you cannot please everyone, although we have tried to do justice to all. We would particularly like to thank the following for their assistance on the form and contents of the anthology: Denis Cosgrove, Kevin Cox, Peter Dicken, Felix Driver, Derek Gregory, Peter Haggett, David Harvey, Peter Jackson, Ron Johnston, Glenda Laws, Doreen Massey, Linda McDowell, Donald Meinig, Eric Sheppard, Neil Smith, Susan Smith, David Stoddart, Nigel Thrift, Richard Walker and Michael Watts. Special gratitude is due to Peter Gould for the care with which he scrutinized our proposal. Our thanks go to Tony Grahame for the speed and efficiency with which he copy-edited a difficult manuscript; and to Hilary Frost for her work on obtaining permissions. The *primum mobile* of the anthology has been John Davey. His wisdom and experience have guided our labours while his friendship and hospitality have rewarded them in equal measure.

John Agnew, David N. Livingstone, Alisdair Rogers

The authors and publishers wish to thank the following for permission to use copyright material:

Arnold, a member of the Hodder Headline Group for R. J. Johnston, 'Paradigms and Revolution or Evolution? Observations on Human Geography since the Second World War', *Progress in Human Geography*, 2, 2, 1978; and material from Yi-Fu Tuan, 'Space and Place: Humanistic Perspectives', *Progress in Human Geography*, 6, 1974, pp. 233–52.

Association of American Geographers for material from Richard Hartshorne, *The Nature of Geography*, reprint edition, 1961, pp. 436–44.

Blackwell Publishers Ltd for material from David Harvey, *The Urbanization of Capıtal,* 1985, pp. 32–4, 51–61; Horacio Capel Institutionalization of Geography and Strategies of Change' in *Geography, Idealogy and Social Concern,* ed. David R. Stoddart, 1981, pp. 37–69.

Blackwell Publishers Inc for material from Neil Smith and Phil O'Keefe, 'Geography, Marx and the Concept of Nature', *Antipode,* 12, 1980, pp. 30–9; Fred Schaefer, 'Exceptionalism in Geography: a Methodological Examination', *Annals, Association of American Geographers,* 43, 3, 1953, pp. 226–9, 231–49; David Harvey, 'On the History and Present Condition of Geography: an Historical Materialist Manifesto', *Professional Geographer,* 3, 1, 1981.

Cambridge University Press and the Open University for material from L. McDowell and D. Massey, 'A Woman's Place?' in *Geography Matters,* ed. Doreen Massey and John Allen, 1984.

Economic Geography for material from Allan Pred, 'The Choreography of Existence: Comments on Hagerstrand's Time-Geography and its Usefulness', *Economic Geography,* 53, 1977, pp. 207–11, 213–16, 217–19;

Feminist Studies, Inc for Donna Haraway, 'Situated Knowledges: The Science Question in Feminism and the Privilege of Partial Perspective', *Feminist Studies,* 14, 3, Fall 1988, c/o Women's Studies Program, University of Maryland.

The Geographical Association for A. J. Herbertson, 'Regional Environment, Heredity and Consciousness', *Geographical Teacher,* 9, 1961.

Harvard University Press for George H. T. Kimble, 'The Inadequacy of the Regional Concept' in *London Essays in Geography: Rodway Jones Memorial Volume,* ed. L. Dudley Stamp and S.W. Wooldridge. Copyright © 1951 by the President and Fellows of Harvard University Press.

Macmillan Press Ltd and Barnes and Noble Books for material from Derek Gregory, 'Areal Differentiation and Post-Modern Human Geography' in *Horizons in Human Geography,* ed. Derek Gregory and Rex Walford, 1989, pp. 67–72, 78–96.

Michigan Academy for J. Nystuen, 'Identification of Some Fundamental Spatial Concepts', *Papers of the Michigan Academy of Science, Arts and Letters,* 48, 1963.

Oxford University Press, Inc for material from Aldo Leopold, *A Sand County Almanac: And Sketches Here and There,* pp. 201–26 (in commemorative 1989 issue). Copyright © 1949, 1977 by Oxford University Press, Inc.

Pion Ltd for Rao Openshaw, 'A View on the GIS Crisis in Geography', *Environment and Planning A,* 23, 1991, pp. 621–8.

Regional Studies Association for Doreen Massey, 'In What Sense a Regional Problem?', *Regional Studies,* 13, 1979.

Gillian Rose for her essay, 'Geography as a Science of Observation: the Landscape, the Gaze and Masculinity' in *Nature and Science: Essays in the History of Geographical Knowledge, Historical Geography Research Series,* 28, ed. Felix Driver and Gillian Rose, Feb. 1992.

Routledge for material from Stephen Daniels, 'Marxism, Culture and the Duplicity of Landscape' in *New Models in Geography: The Political-Economy Perspective,* vol. 2, ed. Richard Peet and Nigel Thrift, pp. 196–220, Unwin & Hyman, 1989;

and with Pantheon Books, a division of Random House, Inc, for material from Edward W. Said, *Orientalism*, pp. 1–4, 54–8. Copyright © 1978 by Edward W. Said.

Royal Geographical Society for material from Halford Mackinder, 'The Geographical Pivot of History', *Geographical Journal*, 23, 4, 1904, pp. 421–37; and Halford Mackinder, 'On the Scope and Methods of Geography', *Proceedings of the Royal Geographical Society*, 9, 2, March 1887, pp. 141–60.

Royal Scottish Geographical Society for Friedrich Ratzel, 'The Territorial Growth of States', *Scottish Geographical Magazine*, 12, 1986; and table from H. J. Fleure, 'Human Regions', *Scottish Geographical Magazine*, 35, 1919, p. 103.

Scientific Research Society for Karl W. Butzer, 'Civilizations: Organisms or Systems?', *American Scientist*, 68, Sept.–Oct. 1980.

University of California Press for material from Carl O. Sauer, 'The Morphology of Landscape', *University of California Publications in Geography*, 2, 2, Oct. 1925, pp. 19–54; and Clarence J. Glacken, *Traces on the Rhodian Shore: Nature and Culture in Western Thought From Ancient Times to the End of the Eighteenth Century*, 1967, pp. vii–xii. Copyright © 1967 The Regents of the University of California.

University of Toronto Press for J. B. Harley, 'Deconstructing the Map', *Cartographica*, 26, 1989.

Verso/New Left Books for material from Edward W. Soja, *Postmodern Geographies*, 1990, pp. 118–31.

Yale University Press for material from John B. Jackson, *Discovering the Vernacular Landscape*, 1984, pp.3–8, 147, 148–57.

Every effort has been made to trace all the copyright holders but if any have been inadvertently overlooked the publishers will be pleased to make the necessary arrangement at the first opportunity.

GENERAL INTRODUCTION

This book provides you, as a student of human geography, with a vital resource, a collection – almost a mini-library – of writings critical to understanding the field as a whole, and which reveal the interaction of its component parts. It has been designed, with the aid and advice of scholars and teachers from all over the world, to give you ready access to articles and extracts from books that your studies are most likely to lead you to consult. We, the editors, hope that you will find the collection as revealing, challenging and enjoyable to read as we have found it to compile. Not least, we hope that its possession will save you hours of fruitless time lining up at the photocopying machine.

This general introduction has three aims: first, to explain the principles that have governed our organization of the book and our selection of its content; secondly, to give you a brief account of how we see the current state of the discipline; and thirdly, but not least, to show why human geography – indeed geography in general – is a subject worthy of your engagement – challenging, stimulating, puzzling, amusing or infuriating, but always rewarding.

Purpose

The purpose of this book is to provide the student of human geography and the interested general reader with a representative collection of significant writings critical to understanding the central concepts in the field. We have taken a long view of the subject, selecting readings from over the past 150 years. Often the central concepts are introduced in textbooks without much attention to the particular writings in which they were first put forward. This book should serve as a companion to such accounts or as a means of directly introducing the concepts that define the essential subject-matter of the field.

Human geography is a body of knowledge organized around a number of broad themes that distinguish it from other fields: the relationship between the natural and human worlds, the spatial distributions of human phenomena and how they come about, the social and economic differences between different parts of the world. The use of maps represents a method of study shared across all of these themes. Down the years there has been a wide range of different conceptual, empirical and methodological emphases. This diversity has frequently led to bouts of anxiety about the lack of unity to the field compared with the (apparent) unity of others. Yet, in its intellectual diversity may lie one of its strengths. The field is marked by a critical edge to inquiry producing bold and imaginative work that is usually subjected to careful scrutiny. A concern for the real problems faced by particular people has also always marked the field. More recently, its openness to the ideas of other disciplines and its focus on integrating these synthetically has put human geography at the heart of efforts to move beyond the disciplinary boundaries of the late nineteenth century in the direction of 'transdisciplinary inquiry'.

Three sets of concepts – nature, culture and landscape; region, place and locality; and space, time and space–time – are identified as defining the main ways in which human geography has been given intellectual coherence. These conceptual clusters are used to organize the anthology of original articles and book extracts we have selected as 'significant' for the field. Such writings are held to have been particularly important in the development of human geography. They also provide examples of the application of key concepts that could serve as the basis for classroom discussion.

The literature of modern human geography is a massive collection of books and of articles in scholarly journals. The amount of material is such that no single person can have command over it. Moreover, much of it is not readily available to the interested student. Even the English-language material is spread over a wide range of sources in a large number of the conventional library classification categories. This reflects the wide empirical scope and intellectual dynamism of human geography. Its substantive reach goes from detailed local studies of social and demographic change to examination of global economic and political trends. Such empirical issues are addressed from a whole variety of theoretical viewpoints. In this book we want to represent this reach and variety as fully as possible. The bias towards English-language material is justified partly in terms of our familiarity with it and with the needs of students in the English-speaking world but also in terms of the intellectual dominance on a world scale exercised over the past fifty years in particular by writing in the English language. It is important to note, however, that many of the concepts have roots in cultural contexts other than the Anglo-American. We have included, therefore, works by authors from other linguistic communities, such as Ratzel, Vidal de la Blache, Kropotkin, Boas and Hägerstrand, whose conceptual contributions have been very influential to the course of human geography in general.

There is an important educational value in attempting inclusion of all of the main concepts around which a subject has become organized when introducing it as an area of study. As already noted, human geography as a field is not readily restricted to a single empirical issue or theoretical viewpoint. There have been and are also strong differences of opinion about the nature of the subject and its concepts. This is a measure of the intellectual liveliness of the field, although, the extent of disagreement is sometimes taken as indicating weakness by those who value intellectual order (and 'their' version of concepts!) over intellectual competition.

Using original writings lends itself to encouraging inclusiveness and variety when introducing the field. Juxtaposing original writings covering a wide range of substantive and theoretical interests enables each piece of writing not only to reveal itself but also to say something about the other pieces as well. Each article and extract, therefore, can be thought of as a 'mirror' upon which others are reflected and cast in a new light. However ancient then, each item appears as a 'living' document, helping us to understand the others rather than simply being of a world unto itself.

The problem of 'access' to original writings, however, is not easy to resolve (see **Introduction to Part I: Recounting Geography's History**). One solution has been to identify 'key' figures in the history of the field, using their major writings as the resource for conceptual analysis (what we term *encyclopedism*). This approach to 'geographic thought' has had the drawback of putting attention solely on the so-called Big Thinkers and their lives rather than on their geographical ideas and how they relate to those of others. A perennial danger lies in slipping into a hagiography that misses the ideas through its obsession with the personality. A second solution has been to pigeon-hole writers in terms of their commitments to particular philosophies, methodologies and subject-matter. In this case, too, the geographical concepts get short shrift as attention shifts from substantive analysis to typologies of 'competing' philosophies or the claims of particular groups (white men, colonialists, etc.) as masked by philosophical differences (what we call *genealogy*).

This book proposes a third approach using 'clusters' of related concepts that have been at the heart of theoretical developments in human geography over the past 150 years. Together they define what we term the *tradition* of geography. The three clusters are: (1) nature, culture, and landscape; (2) region, place, and locality; and (3) space, time, and space–time. These three sets of three concepts have been closely related in the geographical literature so it makes considerable sense to examine them together. In each of the three sections devoted to the sets of concepts we provide an anthology of journal articles and book extracts selected to convey the main theoretical trajectories followed by the concepts over time, including, when we can, dead-ends, loose threads and rediscovered notions.

We frame the presentation of the clusters of geographical concepts with two introductory sections that provide specific responses, from over the years, to the following questions. (1) How has the conceptual development of human geography as a field of study been understood by geographers? (2) What is the subject-matter of human geography? These allow us to show that geographers have long been concerned about the nature and content of their field. Each generation has built on the efforts of previous ones. They also allow us to come to grips immediately with the central questions every new student has about a field: what is it about and, in brief, what is its history?

In the selection of items for all sections of the anthology we have chosen ones which we feel have had a continuing influence over time, that reflect the views of a number of writers in a period, or views which might have proved fruitful but did not, and items which rigorously focus on a key concept. We have tried not to select items simply on the basis of their authors' presumed greatness, their 'representativeness' of a presumed consensus during a particular period, or in terms of their fit into the boxes of a transcendental philosophical grid. We pay some attention to conceptual disputes that created tension in the field at the time they occurred (e.g. the so-called Schaefer/Hartshorne dispute in the 1950s). Our emphasis is also on what is geographical rather than the disciplinary affiliation of the writer *per se*, thus there are a number of items by 'non-geographers'. Many examinations of geographic thought confuse it with the history of university Geography and its professional associations. From our point of view geographers who do not use geographical concepts are doing something other than geography, however interesting it might be. Finally, stimulated by a number of careful readers of our original proposal for this book, we have attempted to survey a wide range of political and theoretical currents rather than follow our own narrower, if often conflicting, predilections. This is one case where more editors is definitely better than fewer.

We have tried to sample from throughout the past 150 years or so rather than focusing on the immediate past. This choice reflects our belief that the field has evolved over a long period of time and that many of the same questions keep coming up time and again only to be addressed in novel ways with the same concepts (if often with new meanings). In other words, what we do today builds, if only in opposition more than emulation, on what was done in the past.

Inevitably, we have not been able to include all that we would have liked. We have erred on the side of including items that have been influential but that are relatively hard to obtain, more than ones that are widely available. Our selection has not been driven by philosophical disputes (positivism vs. humanism vs. Marxism, etc.), although the items we have chosen do allow for insight into these disputes. Our concern has been more theoretical. We have wanted to trace how the concepts we have identified have changed in meaning and usage over time by presenting them in their original form rather than in a gloss provided by us.

The 'conceptual anthology' approach serves several purposes. One is to expose students beginning their studies to the rich theoretical heritage of human geography. Even leading practitioners often display an ignorance of past developments that leads them to over-emphasize current debates in framing their research. 'Knowing' the contemporary literature is not always enough. The past may have something to offer the present. Better knowledge of past positions might also encourage greater attention to the theoretical claims hidden in the seemingly most innocuous of terms adopted in the most empirical of work. The concepts used by practising geographers in selecting and interpreting their data are often an inheritance from the past. This does not make them 'untheoretical'; it may only be that they are connected to previous rather than current debates.

A purpose most appropriate to more advanced students involves helping students to place conceptual writings in their historical and geographical contexts. Often, scholars 'mine' past writings to lend the legitimacy of long dead disciplinary giants to their own endeavours or to point up the true novelty of the concepts they are using. Either everything has been said before or we are always starting from scratch. The danger is that students (and scholars) fail to appreciate ideas in terms of the changing social and political conditions under which they are produced. This can make them more, or less, relevant to present concerns but always interesting in their own right for what they say about the historical times and geographical settings in which they arose.

A particular issue in much contemporary theoretical debate in human geography involves the compression of past times into undifferentiated time-blocks such as 'before 1968' or in 'the 1950s'. Such labelling obscures the historical evolution of key concepts and encourages the almost pervasive sentiment that past human geography is an undifferentiated and static 'mass' that has little to say to a more dynamic present.

Finally, in many fields, such as economics or sociology, the 'sense' of their 'theoretical history' is an important part of education in them. Human geography has been lacking in this respect. The emphasis on either the 'biobibliographies' of Big Names or on 'potted philosophy' has led to a lack of focus on the central concepts of the field and, hence, on what it has had to contribute to knowledge in general. This encourages both a lack of recognition of a collective intellectual past, as opposed to individual writers and different philosophies, and a collective inferiority complex relative to other fields which, because they openly advertise their concepts, are then seen as more intrinsically theoretical than human geography.

Human Geography and Geographical Concepts

Before delving into the particular accounts of human geography and its development provided in the first two Parts of the book it may be useful to survey the peculiarities of the field as identified by some of its leading commentators. Critically examining five frequently expressed views about geography as a field of study – that it is 'empirical', 'practical', 'integrative' of physical and human domains, the field uniquely concerned with 'the geographical', and intellectually 'isolationist' – provides a backdrop for understanding the perspective on geographic thought and identifying the conceptual clusters used in this anthology.

A commonplace view of geography is that it is 'pre-eminently an empirical discipline, concerned with understanding the world and transmitting that understanding to a wide audience' (Johnston 1993, p. vii). How this distinguishes it from other fields is unclear, since most fields have empirical subject-matter. Perhaps what is meant is that geography addresses the *concrete* questions of where and under what conditions a wide range of phenomena connected to the Earth and its occupance occur. To do so, however, has required recourse to theoretical concepts including some that are explicitly geographical, i.e. relate directly to the geographical context and scope of the phenomenon in question. Some of these concepts are the subject-matter of this book. From this point of view geography is as intrinsically theoretical as most other fields of knowledge (except, perhaps, quantum physics).

Geography is also often seen as a uniquely 'practical' field. As one late nineteenth-century exponent expressed it, geography is 'the Science of Distances – the science of the merchant, the statesman, and the strategist' (Robertson 1900, p. 457). The basis for this view lay in the uses, commercial, political, and geopolitical, to which the accumulation of geographical knowledge could be put (see, for example, Godlewska and Smith 1994). This conception is still very much alive in contemporary debates in the United States over the contribution of geography to 'national competitiveness': understanding the features of competing national economies such as Japan, learning about potential markets for American goods, etc. But in fact many of the fields of knowledge defined by the emerging intellectual division of labour of the late nineteenth century could claim similar practical origins. Such fields, for example, as sociology, political science and economics had at their origins the practical interests of states in, respectively, social control, state management, and the national accumulation of wealth.

One peculiar feature of geography relative to many other fields has been its claim to provide knowledge integrative of the so-called physical and human domains even as the intellectual division of labour and the way universities are organized into discrete faculties of arts, science, and social science were institutionalized. The claim to useful knowledge, therefore, involved the concomitant claim that human activities could be understood only in relation to the physical environment. This claim (the 'geographical experiment', Livingstone (1992, p. 189) calls it) involved, for a time, a strong version of the relationship between the physical environment and the human occupance of the earth. Untainted by consideration of socio-economic causation, geography would attain its deserved status as a university 'subject' *only* 'by structuring human geography in terms of physical geography' (Gregory 1978, p. 17). A number of the authors included in this anthology subscribed to various versions of the physical environment–human occupance focus as what made geography unique as a field of study (e.g. Mackinder and Vidal de la Blache, **chapters 8 and 10** in Part II). But only as long as the human could be seen as a *direct* product of the physical did the claim about geography as an integrative field amount to more than mere rhetoric.

Indeed, the division of physical and human geography as distinctive fields dates from the time in the 1920s when a strong environmental determinism was largely abandoned by professional geographers. If later the methodological appeal of the natural sciences (in the form of positivism, at least) replaced the causal primacy of the natural world as the rhetorical glue for geography as a whole, as far as *research* was concerned the field itself had in fact come substantively unstuck into separate physical and human parts with little concrete or theoretical communality (Stoddart 1987; Johnston 1991). It is only in recent years that much attempt has been made at relaunching the relationship on substantive rather than rhetorical (or philosophical) grounds, largely as a result of the widespread sense of environmental crisis. Human geography now exists in practice as a separate field with its own readings of 'nature' and the physical environment. In physical geography philosophical and conceptual debates take place without much reference to those in human geography.

Less controversially than the intellectual division of geography, perhaps, geographical concepts have been seen as largely the province of the professional geographer. For the period 1920–1960 it certainly makes sense to talk, for example, of the 'devaluation' of geographical space and place by other fields, especially in the social sciences (Soja 1989; Smith 1992). Nevertheless, many other fields do rely on certain key geographical assumptions that, though taken-for-granted, indicate the extent to which the use of geographical concepts has not been the intellectual monopoly of geographers. For example, dominant intellectual strands in such fields as political sociology and international relations have adopted a *territorial* conception of space in which a modern 'national' culture is seen as increasingly displacing 'traditional' or 'local' ones (Agnew 1993). This is an implicit rather than an explicit concept, a 'hidden geography'. But just because it is not often written about very explicitly this does not mean that it does not exist in the practice of a field. The social sciences are filled with geographical assumptions about how social processes are bounded and take place. In an anthology such as this we cannot devote many of the limited pages at our disposal to examples of hidden geography, though one entry in Part IV on Region, Place, and Locality (Said, **chapter 26**) is so concerned. The major point here is to emphasize the importance of implicit geographical representations irrespective of the 'field' in which they occur.

Finally, geography in general and human geography in particular are often alleged to be 'isolationist', without significant links to the larger intellectual world. Their concepts are thus very much their own and without 'external' connections. This is obviously less the case now than it may have been in the past. There was a political 'quietism' to post-war Anglo-American geography marked by a 'fear' of the social sciences and a reluctance to engage with 'dangerous' issues that were engendered, perhaps, by the ideological bipolarity of the Cold War and the urge to give the field its legitimacy in terms of a modern intellectual birth that took place in Germany at the end of the nineteenth century but whose progeny was still of uncertain character (as in debates involving Sauer, Hartshorne and Schaefer). Above all, to many major figures politics was a doubtful business to be avoided by not talking about it. Certainly, many of the leading geographers in the United States had been, or were, government employees and this set limits to their potential involvement in politics. This intellectual conservatism, identified in Smith's (1989) essay on the logic and influence of Richard Hartshorne's *The Nature of Geography*, did lead to an internalist intellectual approach apparent in so many histories of geographic thought in which 'geography' appeared as if hermetically sealed from other fields.

This image of isolationism, certainly not accurate at the turn of the century, is even less true today. Geographers themselves have become voracious consumers of ideas from outside, as best can be measured using citations from journals in a range of fields (Bodman 1986). In recent times geographical terms have also begun to appear in the writings of such 'new' fields as cultural studies (e.g. Carter et al. 1993), indicating an affinity for geographical analysis that some have excitedly (and with a certain hubris given that usage is often metaphorical) labelled a 'geographical turn' in the social sciences (e.g. Soja 1989; Smith 1992; Dear 1994).

This book parts company, therefore, with some of the conventional views of geographic thought. This does not mean that they are 'false', only that they exaggerate certain features of the field and miss the central importance of certain key concepts to the development of human geography. To summarize in terms of the main consequences for the logic and organization of the anthology, we would make the following three points. First, human geography is no more or less theoretical than other fields with which it can be compared. Its characterization as uniquely empirical and practical is misleading, to say the least. Secondly, human geography is a meaningful label for a field of knowledge since, outside the realm of rhetoric, physical and human geography have become largely separated. Whether this *should* be the case or will always remain so are entirely different issues. We will refer to authors who over the years have tried to keep the connection alive. Thirdly, and finally, geographical concepts are not the special preserve of professional geographers. The intellectual practices of a wide range of fields are implicated in the origins and diffusion of geographical concepts. We cannot therefore restrict our attention to writings that are *sensu strictu* those of professional geographers alone.

History of Geographical Concepts

As the first section of articles and extracts makes clear, the history of geographical concepts has been understood usually in one or other of two ways. The first has been as a form of cumulative biography of 'leaders' in the discipline and their ideas, often organized under national 'schools': encyclopedism (e.g. James and Martin 1981). The second has been through identifying a series of 'paradigms' or philosophies that define the practices of the discipline (e.g. Johnston 1983 and **chapter 2**). Paradigms are defined as discrete bundles of phenomena, philosophies, and methods into which individuals are socialized by inclination and training. In the most rigid accounting, drawn from the historian of science Thomas Kuhn, one paradigm is seen as replacing another as the 'normal science' of the field. More typically, however, the argument is looser, drawing attention to competing paradigms rather than successive ones. Recently, such paradigms or research programmes (the usage is imprecise) have been seen as representing political interests rather than pure knowledge. This viewpoint can be labelled that of genealogy. In the first case it is the writers who are at centre stage, therefore, whereas in the second it is the paradigms or programmes. In neither case is it geographical concepts *per se*.

In contemporary intellectual history an important trend has been away from examining works solely in terms of the biographies of their authors or as parts of philosophical schools that compete for dominance within the field as a whole, and towards consideration of them as texts or as elements of discourses that persist over time and are rarely if ever displaced one by another. Viewing an article or a book as a text rests on the assumption, drawn from the French philosophers Barthes and Derrida, among others, that language is not a medium for conveying meaning but the producer of meaning. From this perspective emphasis falls on the 'performative' rather than the communicative aspect of writing. In contrast to the isolation of individual texts as presumably without connection to 'external' factors such as historical, social or biographical contexts, consideration of them as parts of discourses ties them very closely to context. In this frame of reference, what is written 'fits into a network that has its own history and conditions of existence' (Barrett 1991, p. 126). A discourse is defined by the appearance of regularity in the unity and dispersion of statements, concepts, and objects and by persistence over time. Edward Said (1988, p. 10), summarizing Michel Foucault's approach to discourse in a memorial essay, used the example of two professions or disciplines: 'what enables a doctor to practise medicine or a historian to write history is not mainly a set of individual gifts, but an ability to follow rules that are taken for granted as an unconscious a priori by all professionals'. A text only makes sense, therefore, in a context.

For us, however, a focus on concepts rather than texts makes more sense because then we can avoid selecting canonical works that only became important after their day (when canonized, so to speak), and we can connect the continuous emergence and disappearance of concepts to different historical eras. This is akin to the strategy of those scholars tracing the historical development of political concepts (Koselleck 1985; Richter 1990). The concepts we have identified as the focus for this anthology constitute key elements of 'geographical discourses' that have emerged historically over the past 150 years. There are no original or essential meanings to these concepts that can be privileged above others. Rather, meanings and the relative importance of concepts have evolved over time as the power relations forming the field of geographical knowledge have changed and as new meanings are enforced. 'Power relations' does not refer only to the social structure of the discipline or the wider society, but relates also to the power exercised by an *epistemic regime* (or system of knowing), which organizes the whole or part of the field through its dominant 'discursive practices' (favouring of certain concepts and allied meanings relative to others, association of concepts with others, modes of writing – narrative versus analysis, topics chosen for research, etc.).

The example of geographic thought suggests, however, that Foucault's insistence on discontinuity in discursive formations and the presumed absence of the volition of subjects (authors) from their construction are overstated. In particular, as this anthology makes clear, the same terms keep cropping up time after time even when invested with new meanings. There is an obvious linguistic continuity within the 'discursive streams' out of which the field is made. With respect to the second feature of Foucault's understanding of discourse, key authors have at crucial junctures led discursive innovations that would not have happened or achieved success but for their insight, energy and charisma. One thinks in this connection, for example, of authors such as Mackinder, Vidal de la Blache, Schaefer, Harvey and Massey, all of whom are represented in this anthology. This is not to say that an author is the single 'source of significations that fill a work' (Foucault 1979, p. 159), only that the author is more than a mere 'murmur' in a stream of discourse. The critique of that isolated genius, the bourgeois author, is all very well. But, as Raymond Williams (1977, p. 194) has pointed out, the danger lies in suppressing 'the living and reciprocal relationships of the individual and the social . . . in the interest of an abstract model of determinate social structures and their "carriers"'. Williams's complaint is addressed specifically to Marxist structuralists such as Althusser but in this context it also seems to apply reasonably well to Foucault.

This adoption of a modified 'discursive approach', perhaps more appropriately 'concepts in context', entails a number of points that bear stating here. In particular, from this point of view human geography does not have an 'essential' nature. Its nature changes over time as its concepts are invested with different meanings and significance. Consequently, theoretical concepts can only be understood in the social and intellectual circumstances in which they are deployed. Thus, it is always appropriate to ask of any concept or theory: 'why was it put forward? Whose interests did it advance or retard? In what kind of milieu was it conceived and communicated? How adapted was it to its cognitive and social environments?' (Livingstone 1992, p. 29). Finally, a radical distinction between concepts, texts and context is best avoided. Thoroughly contextualist and biographical approaches to intellectual history privilege the external setting in which texts are written to the exclusion of the texts themselves. So much of the so-called sociology of knowledge is of this type. But if concepts, texts and contexts co-exist discursively then contexts cannot *explain* texts, they are intrinsic to them. For example, the concepts used in a text have meanings particular to a specific context but over time the concepts change in meaning. Hence, the concepts in a text can only be understood contextually. 'The cognitive content of the very terms we employ is subject to historical change and cannot be appropriated with uncritical essentialist assumptions' (Livingstone 1992, p. 30).

Conceptual Clusters

A real dilemma for all approaches to human geography is that they must be written in terms of a 'present' that colours representation of the past. The main danger lies in making of the past a coherent path to the present. In doing so the history of a field is tidied up into 'schools' and 'paradigms' that flow unchanging and largely unhindered from their origins to the present day. The history then lies only in who has had most 'influence' institutionally and intellectually in which epoch; in who has been 'up' and who has been 'down'.

To avoid as best we can this caricaturing of the course of geographical knowledge we have chosen to focus on three sets of geographical concepts (nature, culture, landscape; region, place, locality; space, time, space–time) that have been at the heart of geographical analysis and dispute. These have been closely associated with one another over time, defining a series of geographical discourses, with, respectively, landscape, region, and space as the central geographical concepts in each cluster. Between them they define the main vocabulary of modern human geography.

The inspiration for this focus on clusters of concepts comes from a number of directions. In the first place, concepts provide a useful way of gaining access to the text–context nexus. By looking at usage over time in a selection of articles and book-extracts we can trace the emergence of new meanings or the return of old ones and connect them to changing circumstances. Most obvious of all, to those who know something about geography, each cluster is related to one of the 'three traditions' of geography that conventional approaches to geographic thought have seen as competing with one another: the cultural, regional, and spatial traditions.

In terms of the lineage of the field, as John K. Wright suggested in his classic article 'A plea for the history of geography' (reprinted in this anthology as **chapter 1** in Part I), a focus on geographical ideas, as we are resurrecting it here, involves tracing the 'geographical threads' that unite the intellectual past with the academic work of the present. This lends emphasis to the continuity in terminology that unites and divides the field and, hence, to its long theoretical heritage. *Contra* a fashionable obsession among many geographers with recent writing as the unique source of conceptual insight, 'theory' is not new to human geography but has a long heritage.

More revolutionary, the linguistic turn in intellectual history, signalled earlier in the discussion of concepts, texts and discourse, has drawn attention to the 'familiar' terms we use in our disciplinary practices and the need, if not to deconstruct them, at least to defamiliarize them so as the better to understand them or avoid taking them for granted as always given. From this point of view, the conceptual clusters constitute sets of 'keywords' around which the everyday work of geographers (and others) revolves.

Finally, a focus on concepts allows for a certain 'messiness' in the history of geographical knowledge through an alertness to paradox and contingency that is missing when the focus is on defining, and defending, schools and paradigms. This 'situated messiness' avoids our cleaning up intellectual history to make it smoother and more coherent than it really was (Livingstone 1992, p. 28).

We are aware that the approach is not without its own problems. The 'clusters' are not ones we would care to defend as involving necessary or inevitable relations between their constituent concepts. Our claim is merely one of the tendency for the concepts to occur empirically together. Other concepts such as diffusion, movement, circulation, and scale might also have been included. Our only response to this is that we have chosen those 'higher-order' geographical concepts that have had a persisting presence in the history of geographic thought. This is not to say that these other concepts are not important, only that they are derivative rather than fundamental. Finally, the conceptual clusters are an organizing device that we have imposed on the history of the field. They are an alternative to the tracking of schools and paradigms that involves a similar imposition of simplified models onto a more complex reality. Our only defence is that they may provide a better guide to understanding than do the alternative approaches, as elaborated previously.

The 'Politics' of Concepts

Alongside the shift to text–context and concepts–context interaction as the governing principles for fathoming the trajectory of geographic thought, there has grown in recent years an increasing sense of the limits of all theories and associated concepts for gaining purchase on reality. From one point of view 'reality' itself is drawn into question; nothing exists separate from our conceptions of it. From another it is more that theories and concepts are constructions that cannot be expected to give complete explanations. The critical issue is how helpful or disabling they are in relation to specific research problems. In both cases, however, there is an increasing sense of the 'malaise of theory in its disciplinary mode' (Seidman 1992, p. 72). Grand evolutionary narratives making universal causal claims such as those of Comte, Marx, Durkheim, and Spencer are now called into question not so much for their substantive deficiencies as for the goal they set themselves: universal objective knowledge.

Yet, despite the critique of 'totalizing' theory, there is still a constant use of concepts that have a universal reference by the very critics themselves. At the same time that a general suspicion of 'meta-narratives' or story-lines is expressed, the existence of 'patriarchy', 'capitalism', even 'racial cultures' is taken for granted. We cannot escape from using concepts as long as we try to practise human geography. To try otherwise is to become amateur philosophers, so obsessed by the words that we lose interest in the things to which they (problematically) refer.

Historical example suggests that crises of intellectual confidence are not new. In the aftermath of the time of religious disruption labelled later as the Reformation, for example, the poet John Donne thought that all coherence was gone. Following the Industrial Revolution in England the philosopher–revolutionary Karl Marx was sure that all that had been solid was melting into air. Of course, at least he had an intellectual system with which to make sense out of it. In the shadow of the Holocaust, George Steiner (1971, p. 81) noted pessimistically a whole series of 'losses' to Western civilization (not yet the idea itself!):

> *The loss of a geographic–sociological centrality, the abandonment or extreme qualification of the axiom of historical progress, our sense of the failure or severe inadequacies of knowledge and humanism in regard to social action – all these signify the end of an agreed hierarchic value-structure.*

Certainly in Europe and North America we live now in a time in which old certainties about political ideologies, political boundaries and national standards of living are coming into question. It is not surprising, therefore, that established knowledge, perhaps not so relevant to emerging conditions, is also called to account (for a good review of the contemporary 'post-modern' moment and its contradictions, see Thrift 1993).

And yet, as Galileo remarked at the time of his condemnation for heresy by Church authorities for his heliocentric theory of the solar system, 'Eppur si muove' (But it does move, all the same). The world exists however we happen to think of it. Trees fall in the forest whether we are there or not! From this perspective, even in the human realm it is not only ideas or our ideas about the world that make the world go round. Sexual desire, subsistence crises, and physical (military) power, for example, come to mind as important but largely non-discursive features of human existence.

A more modest take on the 'problem of theory' than that of the 'post-modern' alluded to above involves making two related points about what could be called the 'politics' of theory. This involves the claim that all concepts come with built-in assumptions and biases and can never be established as better or worse than one another on totally empirical grounds. The first point is to distinguish the *normative significance* from the *explanatory adequacy* of a given concept. Both are unavoidable features of concepts and theories (sets of concepts related to one another). While the latter can be established empirically to various degrees of satisfaction, however, the former cannot. This distinction, first made by the sociologist Max Weber, helps us to understand why conceptual commitments are so hard to break. Or, as the philosopher Russell Keat (1981, p. 53) puts it, 'theories are designed to solve problems, and the significance of these problems, which must ultimately be determined by normative criteria, is distinct from the adequacy of their proposed solutions, which in this case consists in providing explanations supported by evidence'. Without making this distinction it is impossible to evaluate what a particular concept is supposed to do in a specific text and, hence, to compare usage across texts/contexts and relative to other concepts.

The concept of landscape, for example, can refer normatively to a natural/human or to a human-built surface. Consequently it is confusing to use criteria of explanatory adequacy appropriate to the former to explain the latter, or vice versa. Yet much conceptual disputation and subsequent rehoning of conceptual definition is based precisely on this kind of confusion. More generally, and reaching across conceptual clusters, we may prefer a regional to a spatial account of a phenomenon such as personal incomes or level of manufacturing activity, invoking a mix of local and global factors rather than an explanation based on distance from large cities. This choice is essentially normative. We have an *a priori* commitment to a particular conceptual framing of the problem. Explanatory adequacy can only be established relative to this framing. Normative criticism (I prefer *this* concept or conceptual definition to *that* one) and empirical 'rejection' of a concept because it does not do what it is supposed to do *within its framing* are not the same, therefore. Consequently, concepts can fade or persist in usage irrespective of their explanatory adequacy.

The waxing and waning of discourses, what the idea of 'paradigm shift' has tried to capture, results in part from the outcome of conflicts over concepts that are preferred for *a priori* normative reasons. However, the use of empirical evidence is often part and parcel of conceptual disputes. It can never *finally* settle them but nevertheless consumes a tremendous amount of scholarly energy.

Secondly, normative commitments to concepts persist because concepts are always expressed from particular 'standpoints' (or subject-positions) and entangled within 'perspectives' or angles of vision which reflect those standpoints. The terminology is that of Mannheim (1936). In this construction, concepts in the social sciences are always 'loaded' politically in the sense that their 'authors' and users have particular social–geographical locations from which they define their research objectives (for one example of the historical geography of knowledge, the different receptions given by Belfast and Princeton Presbyterians in the 1870s to Darwin's *Origin of Species*, see Livingstone 1994, 1995; more generally, see Diesing 1982).

Research and writing are not neutral activities unaffected by social, professional, and global cultural/economic differences. Education and methodological training reinforce such social and intellectual differences (e.g. preference for numbers as evidence as against qualitative statements). This is why so many intellectual disputes and controversies take on such strongly emotional and polemical overtones. They are not arguments about the purchase that concepts give on reality so much as conflicts over political positions. Controversy, indeed much research and writing, is driven by adherence to such positions. Some perspectives survive and prosper in this environment. Others may disappear or be marginalized as their proponents fail to produce disciples or gain adequate levels of funding and disciplinary patronage in the form of jobs and grants. Perspectives are the 'driving force' behind persistence and change in the epistemic regimes (systems of knowing) that bring together normative commitments (a view of what the field should be about) with specific conceptual meanings and associated empirical work.

There is a danger, however, in pushing this argument too far. Perspectives can be rejected or modified in response to criticism. Geographic thought provides many examples of authors who have abandoned or adjusted their perspectives at one time or another during their careers (for example, Harvey, Massey, Johnston). This suggests the importance of retaining a concept of authorship such as that put forward previously. Geographical discourses are not simply self-perpetuating. Authorial intention is also at work, especially since proponents of particular concepts or meanings have become more conscious of the role of perspectives and standpoints in their research and writing!

Disputation over concepts, therefore, is neither a novel nor an episodic occurrence within human geography or other fields; it is perpetual. This is why we are able to supply such a large number of entries in this anthology (we could provide more) that indicate profound disagreement over the meaning and use of the same concepts or derivative ones. Some people find this disturbing. They would like to have a uniformity of opinion. However, the persisting failure to distinguish normative significance from explanatory adequacy and the presence of mutually exclusive standpoints and perspectives militates against the possibility that we shall ever be able to neatly define our key geographical concepts in terms agreeable to all. This is why it is important to survey a wide range of sources in order to understand what the field of human geography is all about.

Organization of the Book

The anthology is divided into five parts, each with a separate introduction which provides an overview of the articles and extracts that are included and the broad conception of human geography to which they correspond. Each article or extract is preceded by a brief introduction that says something about the work, its author and the historical–geographical context in which it was written. The book is designed to be read right through. In introductory courses, however, instructors may choose to be selective about what they require from the first two sections of the anthology. The core of the collection is to be found in the three parts that are focused on the sets of geographical concepts.

The first section of the anthology is concerned to lay out the ways in which the conceptual development of human geography has been thought of. The following section addresses the persisting dilemma of responses to the question: what is human geography? The bulk of the anthology, however, is taken up by the three sections that focus on the three sets of geographical concepts: (1) nature, culture and landscape (Part III); (2) region, place and locality (Part IV); and (3) space, time and space–time (Part V). It is upon these concepts that human geography has been built. It is fitting, therefore, that they provide the major sections around which this book is organized.

References

Agnew, J. A. 1993: Representing space: space, scale and culture in social science. In Duncan J. and Ley, D., editors, *Place/Culture/Representation*. London.

Barrett, M. 1991: *The politics of truth: from Marx to Foucault*. Stanford, CA.

Bodman, A. R. 1986: Geography on the circumference. *Journal of Geography* 85, 7–11.

Carter, E., Donald, J. and Squires, J., editors, 1993: *Space and place: theories of identity and location*. London.

Dear, M. 1994: Postmodern human geography: a preliminary assessment. *Erdkunde* 48, 2–13.

Diesing, P. 1982: *Science and ideology in the policy sciences*. New York.

Foucault, M. 1979: What is an author? In Harari, J. V., editor, *Textual strategies: perspectives in post-structural criticism*. Ithaca, NY.

Godlewska, A. and Smith, N., editors, 1994: *Geography and empire*. Oxford.

Gregory, D. 1978: *Ideology, science and human geography*. London.

James, P. E. and Martin, G. J. 1981: *All possible worlds: a history of geographical ideas* (2nd edition). New York.

Johnston, R. J. 1983: *Geography and geographers: Anglo-American human geography since 1945* (2nd edition). London.

Johnston, R. J. 1991: *A question of place: exploring the practice of human geography*. Oxford.

Johnston, R. J. 1993: A changing world: a changing discipline? An introduction. In Johnston, R. J., editor, *The challenge for geography. A changing world: a changing discipline*. Oxford.

Keat, R. 1981: *The politics of social theory: Habermas, Freud and the critique of positivism*. Chicago.

Koselleck, R. 1985: *Futures past: on the semantics of historical time*. Cambridge, MA.

Livingstone, D. N. 1992: *The geographical tradition: episodes in the history of a contested enterprise*. Oxford.

Livingstone, D. N. 1994: Science and religion: foreword to the historical geography of an encounter. *Journal of Historical Geography* 20, 367–83.
Livingstone, D. N. 1995: The spaces of knowledge: contributions towards a historical geography of science. *Environment and Planning D: Society and Space* 13, 5–34.
Mannheim, K. 1936: *Ideology and Utopia*, translated by L. Wirth and E. Shils. New York.
Richter, M. 1990: Reconstructing the history of political languages: Pocock, Skinner, and the *Geschichtliche Grundbegriffe*. *History and Theory* 29, 38–70.
Robertson, G. S. 1900: Political geography and the Empire. *Geographical Journal* 16, 447–57.
Said, E. 1988: Michel Foucault, 1926–1984. In Arac, J., editor, *After Foucault*. New Brunswick, NJ.
Seidman, S. 1992: Postmodern social theory as narrative with a moral intent. In Seidman, S. and Wagner, D., editors, *Postmodernism and social theory*. Cambridge, MA.
Smith, N. 1989: Geography as museum: private history and conservative idealism in 'The Nature of Geography'. In Entrikin, J. N. and Brunn, S., editors, *Reflections on Richard Hartshorne's 'The Nature of Geography'*. Washington, DC.
Smith, N. 1992: Geography, difference and the politics of scale. In Doherty, J., Graham, E. and Malek, M., editors, *Postmodernism and the Social Sciences*. New York.
Soja, E. 1989: *Postmodern geographies: the reassertion of space in critical social theory*. London.
Steiner, G. 1971: *In Bluebeard's castle: some notes towards the redefinition of culture*. New Haven.
Stoddart, D. R. 1987: To claim the high ground: geography for the end of the century. *Transactions of the Institute of British Geographers* NS 12, 327–36.
Thrift, N. 1993: The light fantastic: culture, postmodernism and the image. In Clark, G. L., Forbes, D. and Francis, R., editors, *Multiculturalism, difference and postmodernism*. Melbourne, Australia.
Williams, R. 1977: *Marxism and literature*. Oxford.

PART I

RECOUNTING GEOGRAPHY'S HISTORY

INTRODUCTION

There are many ways of telling the story of a life: some biographers sense continuity and cohesion, others perceive discontinuity and fragmentation; some look to external events, others focus on internal motivation; some happily chronicle progress, while others doubt the very possibility of truthfully telling the tale. So it is with the history of academic subjects. Ideas, disciplines and traditions of inquiry have biographies which may be told in radically different ways.

Geography has a story. But what *is* that story, and *how* is it to be told? In this section of the anthology we focus on ways of telling the story of geography as an academic discipline, or perhaps better, as a tradition of scholarly inquiry. But it is as well to remember that there are many other 'geographies' – folk geographies, fictional geographies, popular geographies – all of which have their own histories. Some of these are referred to in the opening piece by John Kirtland Wright (**chapter 1**) when he distinguishes the history of what he calls *scientific* geography from the non-professional geographical sensibilities of various ethnic groups, poets and novelists, painters and even musicians. By designating these as non-scientific, Wright does not mean to denigrate them. He merely means that such geographical ideas are not expressed in scientific or, rather more accurately, scholarly language. We concentrate on scholarly traditions of geography, not because the others are unimportant, but simply because this volume is addressed to modern students of geography as an academic discipline. We should note, however, that geographical motifs have featured increasingly prominently in other disciplines. This suggests that there is an important distinction to be drawn (even if it is exceedingly hard to map) between geography as a discipline and geography as a discourse (Gregory 1994).

This brief review of some of the main ways in which histories of geography have been written will not only pinpoint differences in their substance and shape, but will also raise some questions about the connections between knowledge, power and society that are of a vital interest in the contemporary cultural and intellectual landscape.

Standard Accounts

With few exceptions, conventional histories of geography have been dominated by an approach that stresses progress from a benighted past to an enlightened present. Not surprisingly the history of Western expansion, frequently referred to as the 'Voyages of Discovery', took pride of place in these works (Baker 1931; see also Boorstin 1983). Now we have come to suspect the rank Euro-centrism of such accounts; indeed there are those who contest the very term 'Discovery' urging that the Age of 'Conquest' or even 'Genocide' would better capture this historical moment. We will return to these alternative, post-colonial histories presently, but for the moment we only need to recall that the underlying assumption in these earlier works was that of cumulative progress.

These traditional histories had other distinguishing marks as well, of course. They were characterized all too frequently by partisan motivations: they were typically written to justify the author's vision of what geography ought to be. By securing the benediction of figures looming large in the subject's hagiography, such historians could thereby justify their own predilections. R. E. Dickinson (1969), for instance, saw geography as fundamentally the science of regional difference; for Preston James (1972), occupied space was the favoured definition; Richard Hartshorne (1939) focused on areal differentiation and described other visions as 'deviations' from the course of the discipline's proper historical development. Indeed Hartshorne's engagingly mistitled book might have been more appropriately subtitled *A Selective Survey of Past Thought in the Light of the Present*. Such works, whatever their industry and value, are geographical apologetics for particular viewpoints rather than sustained attempts to come to grips with the documents of the past in their own terms.

At least in part, it was because of the limitations of these histories that a number of voices began to be raised calling for a 'contextual' reading of the discipline's past. Because the standard texts seldom addressed issues of wider intellectual, social and political concern, preferring instead to read history with internalist spectacles, there were increasing calls for a 'contextual history' that would probe the significance of settings and situations rather than producing catalogues of people, dates and places (Livingstone 1979; Berdoulay 1981; Stoddart 1981; Barnes and Curry, 1983).

Newer Historiographies

In recent decades various new interpretative stances on the history of geographical knowledge have been forthcoming, partly from dissatisfaction with the standard accounts that were on offer (Aay, 1981), but also reflecting an awareness of moves being made within the history and philosophy of science, the sociology of knowledge, and social theory more generally. One of the earlier of such engagements was the encounter that some geographers made with Thomas Kuhn's notion of paradigms and paradigm shifts in the history of science. By 'paradigm' Kuhn roughly meant a tradition with historical exemplars. That is to say, for Kuhn, mature science takes place within a broad intellectual and social framework; this framework in turn sets the standards for relevant research, directs scientists to the current problems in need of solution, and initiates students into the ways of the tradition. Now, Kuhn went on, scientific revolutions occur when the accepted paradigm is replaced by another which gives rise to a completely new programme of research. Science history was thus seen to be a story of radical breaks and discontinuities, rather than a tale of linear progress.

Not surprisingly, geographers (no less than those in other disciplines) set out to identify a succession of geographical paradigms. To take just a single example, Harvey and Holly (1981) isolated five sacred texts – by Ratzel, Vidal, Sauer, Hartshorne, and Schaefer respectively – as enjoying paradigmatic status. Many other proposals were also forthcoming. But the difficulty of applying Kuhn's criteria to the social sciences in general, and to geography in particular was soon perceived. As Ron Johnston put it in 1978 (**chapter 2**), the 'failure to fit Kuhn's model to recent events in human geography with any conviction leads to the conclusion that the model is irrelevant to this social science'. Nevertheless even critics of the Kuhnian perspective remained fascinated by its elegance and potential explanatory power and so, as Mair (1986) astutely remarked, the flavour of his scheme lingered long among historians of the geographical enterprise, even among those seemingly assailing Kuhn's model.

There were, however, other links between geographical historiography and philosophical reflection. The turn to the centrality of language within philosophy also began to be registered among geographers. And here the cognitive role played by analogy and metaphor in human knowing attracted attention (Livingstone and Harrison 1982; Barnes and Duncan 1992). The idea was simply that geographers, in common with everyone else, resort to analogical thinking in the attempt to get a handle on the world's complexities. Just as physicists have thought of light as waves or particles, and cognitive scientists have conceived of the brain as a computer, so geographers have thought of the state as a 'living organism', of landscape change as a 'cycle', of the social world as a complex 'structure', and of the city as a 'text' to be read. Accordingly it seemed reasonable to suggest that the history of geography could be read as a succession of metaphorical visions changing in response to intellectual and social circumstances alike. In her 1982 article (**chapter 3**), Anne Buttimer, for example, elucidated what she called four 'root' metaphors whose influence on geographical thinking she believed was both pervasive and lasting.

Focusing on cognitive transformation, however, might well be seen as too 'intellectualist', too divorced from social life, too disengaged from mundane realities. Such suspicions have been expressed in a number of ways. Among historians of science one alternative strategy has been to take with renewed seriousness the institutional context within which scientific intercourse has been transacted. Such institutional arenas range from informal socio-scientific circles, networks, or what has been called 'invisible colleges', to formal scientific societies, university departments, and professional organizations. In this way the contexts within which knowledge is produced assume key importance.

Geography, of course, has also been transacted in the midst of a diverse range of institutional arenas. And, as Capel (**chapter 4**) has powerfully argued, these have shaped not only the organizational structure of the discipline, but also its cognitive claims. Indeed he goes so far as to suggest that the 'scientific community of geographers is an example of a scientific community constituted from clearly social factors, and not as a result of specific necessities in scientific knowledge. The presence of this science in programmes of primary and secondary education generated, from the nineteenth century, a need for geography teachers, which provoked in turn the university institutionalization of the science.'

Identifying the socio-scientific networks and institutional infrastructure within which geography has been practised does not exhaust the scope of sociological possibility. David Harvey (**chapter 5**), for instance, pressed on to a fully historical materialist interpretation of geography's 'history and present condition'. To him the structure, role and function of geography has always changed in direct response to the shifting desires and configurations of society. In large measure Harvey interprets modern academic geography's tale as one of an attempt to legitimate the very social conditions that created it in the first place. Such standard Victorian geographical practices as exploration, cartographic survey, regional inventory, geopolitical taxonomy, and resource compilation can thus only be understood in the context of imperial manipulation, management and exploitation. Accordingly both the form and substance of geography have been socially dictated.

Regardless of the details of Harvey's account, the import of his intervention has been to *situate* geographical knowledge in social, economic and political circumstance. Since then there has been an increasing realization that geographical knowledge is situated in other ways too. Consider, for example, the sequence of feminist interjections into the historiographical conversation. The argument here, at least in part, is either that geography's historians have elided the geographical work of women, or that what is seen as an unexamined masculinism has monopolized geographical thought and practice. Thus Mona Domosh (1991), for example, has called for the development of a distinctively feminist historiography, though the substance of her claim gravitates around the incorporation of the writings of women travellers into the corpus of the tradition. Alison Blunt (1994) has also sought to overcome what she sees as the 'masculinism' of various attempts to write the history of the geographical tradition by attending to the positionality – in terms of gender, class and ethnicity – of the travel writings of Mary Kingsley. Whether these pronouncements amount to a feminist *historiography* is another matter, of course, and perhaps the closest we have yet come to the cultivation of a distinctly feminist geographical philosophy is that from Gillian Rose, who, in *Feminism and Geography* (1993), subjects to feminist critique such cardinal methods – some might say tropes – in the geographical repertoire as observation and fieldwork.

Philosophically such work has drawn sustenance *inter alia* from the critiques of those like Donna Haraway (**chapter 6**) who have sought to dismantle the rationalist conception of knowledge as 'the view from nowhere' by taking seriously positioning in social space and the inescapably *situated* knowledge thereby necessarily produced. Partiality, rather than universalism, thus turns out to be not only unavoidable, but desirable. By the same token Haraway has sought to retrieve the notion of objectivity from certain feminist repudiations by arguing precisely for the coherence of what she calls 'positioned rationality'.

The writings of Blunt and Rose, and indeed Haraway, also call attention to other social and cognitive 'positionings'. Here connections between feminist challenges and what might be called the post-colonial turn are particularly prominent. The underlying concern here is to give expression to those who have been, for too long, on the receiving end of Western geographical surveillance, spatial discipline, and geopolitical power. The connection to issues of gender is therefore entirely understandable; post-colonialists and feminists have a shared concern to make audible the voice of 'the other' in the writing of history.

Drawing extensively, though certainly not always uncritically, on the insights of figures like Edward Said, who elegantly argued that the 'Orient' was constructed by the West 'politically, sociologically, militarily, ideologically, scientifically and imaginatively during the post-Enlightenment period' (1978, p. 3), some geographers have begun the task of disentangling the intricate webs of ideological practice connecting geography with empire (Driver 1992a; Godlewska and Smith 1994). Closely associated is the inspiration being drawn from the writings of Michel Foucault, whose exposure of the intimate associations between space, surveillance, power, and knowledge, have been used to open up new vistas to the history of geography by unmasking the pretended neutrality of spatial discourse in a variety of arenas both within and beyond the academy (Driver 1992b; Matless 1992; Philo 1992). At its most radical end, this stance can amount to a dismantling of the comfortable distinction between truth and falsity because both are embedded in discourses in particular time–space arenas – arenas which actually constitute the 'facts' to which interlocutors, both exploiter and exploited, both powerful and impotent, both oppressor and oppressed, appeal. In such circumstances the very idea of writing a history of geography is not just a contested undertaking, but a perverse one.

Taking Stock

A wide range of competing historiographical stances have plainly been on offer. But diverse though these are, it might well be argued that they can be reduced to three broad perspectives on the nature of historical writing, perspectives also articulated in the history of moral inquiry (MacIntyre 1990).

First, encyclopedism. In keeping with the encyclopedic style, the emphasis here has typically been on cumulative progress, great name history, and the cataloguing of people and publications. With such assumptions it never really entered the minds of such historians of geography to seek to locate past geographical pronouncements in their socio-intellectual circumstances, for the simple reason that thoughts were assumed to be independent of social forces and differences believed to be resolvable by rational consent. What was said was vital; who said it in what circumstances irrelevant.

Secondly, genealogy. The concern of the genealogist is to unmask the pretended neutrality of geographical concepts and practices, and to show these up for what they are, namely the agents of social power and exploitation. Of course genealogical stances come in a variety of styles. But whether they come from feminists seeking to uncover a deeply embedded (and sometimes not so deeply embedded) masculinism within geography, or from radical post-colonialists who suggest that the very idea of history is somehow or other a Western invention, the motif of exposing claims to truth as really the will to power comes clearly through.

Finally, tradition. The argument here is that geography is a tradition of inquiry, contested to be sure, but a tradition none the less (Livingstone 1992). By conceiving of tradition as 'an historically extended, socially embodied argument' (MacIntyre 1988, p. 350) and of geography as a tradition embodying continuities of conflict, this stance can be seen as occupying a mediating position between that of the encyclopedist and the genealogist.

The selections that follow are intended to exemplify just some of the perspectives that are discussed above. Their significance, however, is far from purely historical. They deal with matters that are not only at the heart of the history of geographical knowledge, but are to the forefront of debate within contemporary human geography and indeed the social sciences and cultural life more generally.

References

Aay, H. 1981: Textbook Chronicles: disciplinary history and the growth of geographic knowledge. In Blouet, B. W., editor, *The origins of academic geography in the United States*. Hamden, C.T., pp. 291–301.

Baker, J. N. L. 1931: *A history of geographical discovery and exploration*. London.

Barnes, T. and Curry, M. 1983: Towards a contextualist approach to geographical knowledge. *Transactions of the Institute of British Geographers*, N.S., 8, 447–82.

Barnes, T. J. and Duncan, J. S., editors, 1992: *Writing worlds: discourse, text and metaphor in the representation of landscape*. London.

Berdoulay, V. 1981: The contextual approach. In Stoddart, D. R., editor, *Geography, ideology and social concern*. Oxford, pp. 8–16.

Blunt, A. 1994: *Travel, gender, and imperialism: Mary Kingsley and West Africa*. New York and London.

Boorstin, D. 1983: *The discoverers. A history of man's search to know his world and himself*. New York.

Dickinson, R. E. 1969: *The makers of modern geography*. London.

Domosh, M. 1991: Towards a feminist historiography of geography. *Transactions of the Institute of British Geographers* N.S., 16, 95–104.

Driver, F. 1992a: Geography's empire: histories of geographical knowledge. *Environment and Planning D: Society and Space*, 10, 23–40.

Driver, F. 1992b: Geography and power: the work of Michel Foucault. In Burke, P. B., editor, *Critical essays on Michel Foucault*. Aldershot, pp. 147–156.

Godlewska, A. and Smith, N., editors, 1994: *Geography and empire*. Oxford.

Gregory, D. 1994: *Geographical Imaginations*. Oxford.

Hartshorne, R. 1939: *The nature of geography: a critical survey of current thought in the light of the past*. Lancaster, PA.
Harvey, M. E. and Holly, B. P. 1981: Paradigm, philosophy and geographic thought. In Harvey, M. E. and Holly, B. P., editors, *Themes in geographic thought*. London, pp. 11–37.
James, P. E. 1972: *All possible worlds. A history of geographical ideas*. Indianapolis.
Kuhn, T. S. 1970: *The structure of scientific revolutions*. Chicago.
Livingstone, D. N. 1979: Some methodological problems in the history of geographical thought. *Tijdschrift voor economische en sociale geografie*, 70, 226–31.
Livingstone, D. N. 1992: *The geographical tradition: episodes in the history of a contested enterprise*. Oxford.
Livingstone, D. N. and Harrison, R. T. 1982: Understanding in geography: structuring the subjective. In Herbert, D. T. and Johnston, R. J., editors, *Geography and the urban environment: progress in research and applications*, vol. 5. Chichester, pp. 1–39.
MacIntyre, A. 1988: *Whose justice? Which rationality?* Notre Dame, IN.
MacIntyre, A. 1990: *Three rival versions of moral enquiry: encyclopaedia, genealogy, and tradition*. Notre Dame, IN.
Mair, A. 1986: Thomas Kuhn and understanding geography. *Progress in human geography*, 10, 345–69.
Matless, D. 1992: An occasion for geography: landscape, representation, and Foucault's corpus. *Environment and Planning D: Society and Space*, 10, 41–56.
Philo, C. 1992: Foucault's geography. *Environment and Planning D: Society and Space*, 10, 137–61.
Rose, G. 1993: *Feminism and geography: the limits of geographical knowledge*. Oxford.
Said, E. W. 1978: *Orientalism: Western conceptions of the Orient*. London.
Stoddart, D. R. 1981: Ideas and interpretation in the history of geography. In Stoddart, D. R., editor, *Geography, ideology and social concern*. Oxford, pp. 1–7.

Further Reading

A review and critique of standard approaches to the history of geographical knowledge is available in Livingstone, D. 1992: *The Geographical tradition* (Oxford). Various contextual readings of aspects of geography's history appear in Stoddart, D. R., editor, 1981: *Geography, ideology and social concern* (Oxford). The sources of the newer historiographical currents are diverse. The rich body of material from the history and sociology of science is surveyed in Shapin, S. 1982: History of science and its sociological reconstructions, *History of Science* 20, 157–211. Other historiographical sources surface in the essays edited by Driver, F. and Rose, G., *Nature and science: essays in the history of geographical knowledge* (Historical Geography Research Series, number 28), and in the introduction to the collection of papers on *Geography and empire* (Oxford, 1994) edited by Godlewska, A. and Smith, N. Gillian Rose provides a feminist reading of the enterprise in *Feminism and geography: the limits of geographical knowledge* (Oxford, 1993).

1

A PLEA FOR THE HISTORY OF GEOGRAPHY

John K. Wright

John Kirtland Wright (1891–1969) was a pioneer of the history of geographical thought. He used his position as librarian and director of the American Geographical Society to compile many key bibliographies and undertake research across the full history of geography and cartography from medieval times onwards. His interests ranged from classics to theology and from literary criticism to statistics. This breadth of learning inclined him to what was, at the time, an original approach to the discipline's history. The article reprinted here appeared in *Isis*, making Wright one of the very few geographers to publish in this prestigious journal on the history of science. In it he argues that the history of geography is the history of geographical ideas, and not just of the works of professional or scientific geographers. Where relevant, this would include error, folly and emotion. What mattered most was what people believed at the time, because these beliefs would have their consequences. It would also involve reference to ideas in spoken and graphic form, in popular travel books, novels, paintings and music. Later he termed this body of knowledge 'geosophy' to distinguish it from geography, the study of realities. Wright's 'plea' was largely ignored at the time (the 1920s) but has been taken more seriously by later generations of historians of geography: Glacken's writings on the ideas of nature owe much to this perspective (**chapter 13**). Many of Wright's elegant and lucid writings on a diverse range of historiographical themes were collected together in the volume *Human nature in geography* (Cambridge, MA, 1966).

Source: A plea for the history of geography. *Isis* 8, 477–91, 1926.

The history of geography as a whole and in its wider bearings has been neglected in America, or at least it has not received the attention which an enthusiast may, perhaps, be permitted to regard as its due. Though they refer to very different matters, the terms 'history of geography' and 'historical geography' are often loosely employed even by geographers and historians themselves. Lest there be any confusion, at the outset a working definition may be given of each. 'Historical geography' is the study of geographical facts as they have existed in historical times, boundary changes, former distributions of population, the development of trade routes, and so on. The 'history of geography' on the other hand, is the history of geographical ideas.[1]

Historical Sketch of Studies of the History of Geography

Investigations into the history of the geographical ideas of earlier ages were made even in classical times. An academic controversy was waged over the reliability of the geographical data in Homer's 'Odyssey'.[2] Strabo, who believed the 'Odyssey' to be authentic and reliable, in a long and controversial passage levelled criticism against Eratosthenes for holding that Homer should be read as a poet and not as a scientific authority.[3] All through the Middle Ages students were interested in what classical writers had written on geographical subjects;[4] thus, in a certain sense, in the history of ancient geography. Ancient geography, however, was of little moment to medieval scholars from the historical point of view. They studied it, rather, for the light which it might shed on the geography of their own time. The revival of the Greek and Roman classics in the Renaissance brought with it enthusiasm not only for classical history, literature and archeology, but also for classical geography and geographers.[5] But this enthusiasm was more for the historical geography of antiquity than for the history of geography in antiquity. Ptolemy's treatise with the atlases based upon it and Strabo's great work were translated into Latin and published early in the fourteenth century.[6] The humanists, however, looked to Strabo and Ptolemy for what they actually told of classical lands and countries, not

[1] If we disregard the etymology of the word 'geography', conceiving it to mean the facts which are studied rather than what is written about these facts, we might coin the phrases 'geographology' to refer to doctrines about geography and 'geographography' to refer to what is written about geography. The 'history of geography' then would be the history of geographical facts, or the subject now conventionally covered by the term 'historical geography'; 'the history of geographology' would be the history of geographical ideas; and the 'history of geographography' (on the analogy of 'the history of historiography') would be the history of geographical ideas as they have been given written form. We do not, however, advocate the use of any such barbarisms.

[2] Hugo Berger, Geschichte der wissenschaftlichen Erdkunde der Griechen, 2nd edition, Leipzig, 1903, pp. 387–388, 443–453, 460, 504, 534–537, 576–577.

[3] Marcel Dubois, Examen de la géographie de Strabon, Paris, 1891, pp. 169–180; A. Thalamas, La géographie d'Ératosthène, Paris, 1921.

[4] See J. K. Wright, The Geographical Lore of the Time of the Crusades, (*American Geographical Society Research Series*, No. 15), New York, 1925, passim.

[5] The 'Italia illustrata' of Flavio Biondo, written about 1451 and published in 1471 was, perhaps, the first study in classical geography of any importance (see J. C. Husslein, Flavio Biondo als Geograph des Frühhumanismus, *Dissertation*, Würzburg, 1901). On the broader aspects of this subject see Siegmund Günther, 'Der Humanismus in seinem Einflusse auf die Entwicklung der Erdkunde', *Geographische Zeitschrift*, Vol. 7, 1900, pp. 65–89.

[6] The translation of Ptolemy's 'Geography' into Latin was begun by Emmanuel Chrysoloras and completed by Jacopus Angelus at the beginning of the fifteenth century. This translation was the basis of subsequent Latin editions of the fifteenth and sixteenth centuries. See A. E. Nordenskiöld, Facsimile Atlas to the Early History of Cartography, translated by J. A. Ekelof and Clements R. Markham from

for what they revealed of stages in the growth of geographical knowledge. As had been the case with Pliny, Aristotle, and others in the Middle Ages, Ptolemy's 'Geography' until the latter part of the sixteenth century was used as a source for geographical descriptions and as a basis for maps of the contemporary world.[7] Nevertheless, it was partly to the classical revival of the Renaissance that we may trace the origins of modern research in the history of geography. The interest in historical geography that was then kindled has lasted ever since and has led many students to delve into the geographical works of earlier times; and from the investigations thus inspired many of the data have been assembled upon which future studies in the history of geography may be based.

Researches in the history of geography during the Age of Discovery were also stimulated by the explorations themselves. The navigators of the time believed that the writings of earlier geographers contained information of practical value. Columbus was a serious student of the scientific opinions of Aristotle, Seneca and Ptolemy, and of the travels of Marco Polo. The acceptance of ancient theories of the distribution of land and water over the earth's surface persisted until as late as the middle of the eighteenth century. If Columbus' glory rests upon the discovery of continents not known to exist before his time, that of Captain Cook rests upon the sweeping away of an imaginary continent that for centuries had filled most of the southern hemisphere.[8]

Then again, the romantic interest of the great discoveries, no less than their political and commercial aspect, early led to the compilation of collections of voyages.[9] Among these those of Ramusio, De Bry, and the fascinating volumes of the English Hakluyt and Purchas are the best known. The work of compiling, editing, and commenting on the narrations of voyages has been continued ever since, and the results are now being embodied in such monumental series as the publications of the Hakluyt and Linschoten Societies, or the *Recueil de voyages et de mémoires* of the Société de Géographie, or the *Recueil de voyages et de documents pour servir à l'histoire de la géographie*, or the *Library of the Palestine Pilgrims Text Society*; and in America by the publications of the Champlain Society and Thwaites 'Jesuit Relations'.

Before the nineteenth century examination into the history of geography was devoted almost exclusively to the regional phases of the subject: to voyages and explorations; and indeed at all times this has been by far the most intensively cultivated portion of the field. The development of modern scientific geography in

the Swedish original, Stockholm, 1889, pp. 9–10; Justin Winsor, A Bibliography of Ptolemy's Geography (*Library of Harvard University, Bibliographical Contributions* No. 18), Cambridge, Mass., 1884.

Strabo's 'Geography' was translated into Latin by the famous Guarino of Verona and Gregory Tiferna and appeared in 1470. See Dubois, *op. cit.*, pp. 7–8.

7 The impress upon cartography of Ptolemy's overestimate of longitudes persisted until the close of the seventeenth century. See O. Peschel, Geschichte der Erdkunde bis auf Alexander von Humboldt und Carl Ritter, 2nd edition, edited by Sophus Ruge, Munich, 1877, pp. 654–655; Christian Sandler, Die Reformation der Kartographie um 1700, Munich und Berlin, 1905, p. 8.

8 See especially Armand Rainaud, Le continent austral: hypothèses et découvertes, Paris, 1893.

9 See Max Böhme, Die grossen Reisesammlungen des 16. Jahrhunderts und ihre Bedeutung, Strassburg, 1904.

Europe, however, has been accompanied by a growth of interest on the part of a relatively few students in the evolution of geographical theories and methods: in the history, that is, of mathematical and physical geography, cartography, and of bio- and anthropogeography.[10]

The nineteenth and twentieth centuries have also seen the production of a limited number of synthetic works by European scholars relating to the development of geographical knowledge and belief as a whole and over long periods of time. Among these Oscar Peschel's 'Geschichte der Erdkunde', 1877, [11] should be given the first place as the only really adequate and satisfactory work in existence in which the attempt is made to trace the entire development of geography. Thoroughly documented, written in a pleasing style, giving due weight to the scientific as well as to the exploratory phases of the subject, this volume would seem to be a model of what a study in the history of science should be; but unfortunately it is now old and seems to be little known outside of Germany. Siegmund Günther's compact 'Geschichte der Erdkunde', 1904,[12] is more in the nature of a reference work, encyclopedic in its style and full of bibliographical notes. Vivien de St. Martin, in his otherwise admirable 'Histoire de la Géographie',[13] which appeared at about the same time as the work of Peschel, tended to neglect the scientific side of the subject. In English the only history of the whole of geography is that of Scott Keltie and Howarth,[14] satisfactory as far as it goes but too short to serve as more than a brief and sketchy introduction.[15]

Thus we see that in European scholarship, particularly on the continent, histor-

[10] There is no general bibliography of the studies that have been devoted to the history of these phases of geography. For a discussion of the outstanding works dealing with their development in classical antiquity and during the Middle Ages, see Wright, *op. cit.*, pp. 496–502. Summaries of the progress of studies that were made between about 1880 and 1907 in the history of geography and cartography since the Middle Ages will be found in *Geographisches Jahrbuch*, Vols. 17, 18, 20, 23, 26, and 30. Detailed current bibliographies of the history of geography will also be found in *Bibliotheca géographica* (for 1891 to 1912 only) and in the *Bibliographie géographique* formerly published in the *Annales de Géographie* and now by the Association de Géographes Français.

Siegmund Günther, Geschichte der Erdkunde, Leipzig and Vienna, 1904, gives many valuable references to special studies on the history of geography down to the beginning of the nineteenth century.

[11] See above, note 7.

[12] See above, note 10.

[13] Louis Vivien de St-Martin, Histoire de la géographie et des découvertes géographiques depuis les temps les plus reculés jusqu'à nos jours, with atlas, Paris, 1873.

[14] J. Scott Keltie and O. J. R. Howarth, History of Geography, New York and London, 1913.

For the nineteenth century itself, Siegmund Günther, Entdeckungsgeschichte und Fortschritte der wissenschaftlichen Geographie im neunzehnten Jahrhundert, Berlin, 1902, and Otto Nordenskiöld, Jordklodens Udforskning: geografisk forskning og geografiske opdagelser i det nittende aarhundrede, Copenhagen, 1920, may be consulted.

[15] In addition to the above-mentioned general surveys, the volume of Karl Weule, Geschichte der Erdkenntnis und der geographischen Forschung: zugleich Versuch einer Würdiging beider in ihrer Bedeutung für die Kulturentwicklung der Menschheit, Berlin, etc., 1904, deserves mention. Geographical currents of thought in the seventeenth, eighteenth, and early nineteenth centuries especially are discussed by Emil Wisotzki, Zeitströmungen in der Geographie, Leipzig, 1897. An important series of articles on the development of geographical studies in different countries will be found in the Atti del

ical geography and the history of geography have long held honored places. One of the main reasons for this is the fact that geography has been associated in continental schools and universities with history and the humanities rather than with the physical and natural sciences. Indeed, Professor Emmanuel de Martonne of the Sorbonne, now one of the leading representatives of the modern French geographical school, would seem to regard the recent development of geography in France as something of an emancipation from the dominance of history.[16] In America, on the other hand, scientific geography has been evolved mainly out of geology and instruction in geography in the universities is usually given in close connection with geology departments.[17] Until the last few years our geographers have devoted less attention than foreign students to the human and historical phases of their subject and almost none to its history. Indeed, most American geographers have been so intent upon building up the newer aspects of their specialty and upon struggling for its recognition as a topic worthy of a dignified and independent place in university curricula, that they have had little opportunity to interest themselves in its past development. Yet, it is pleasing to note that a course in the history of geography is offered by Professor J. Paul Goode at the University of Chicago. So far as I know, this is the only college course in the field now given in the United States.

The beginnings of American history are but a chapter in the history of geographical exploration and consequently our historians have interested themselves not only in the history of the exploration of the Western Hemisphere but also – though to a lesser degree – in those earlier phases of the history of geography which bear directly or indirectly on the discovery of America. We need but mention the names of Winsor, Fiske, Thacher, Harrisse, and Vignaud (the last two American by birth but French by residence) among the older generation of students whose interest led them to investigate the relations of ancient and medieval ideas regarding the size and shape of the earth and distribution of land and water to the more immediate problems which faced Columbus and other navigators. An American, the late W. H. Tillinghast, had to his credit an unusually profound study of ancient geographical thought.[18] Moreover, the interest not only of genuine historians but of a formidable array of hack writers and cranks has at all times centered around Columbus and around the more nebulous questions of pre-Columbian voyages and cultural connections across the Atlantic and Pacific. The decade of the 1890s,

X Congresso Internazionale di Geografia, Roma MCMXIII, Rome, 1915. For the United States especially, see W. M. Davis, 'The Progress of Geography in the United States', *Annals of the Association of American Geographers*, Vol. 14, 1924, pp. 160–215. For Europe during the period immediately preceding 1922 see W. L. J. Goerg, 'Recent Geographical Work in Europe', *Geographical Review*, Vol. 12, 1922, pp. 431–484. (*Isis*, VI, 220.)

16 Emmanuel de Martonne, Geography in France (*American Geographical Society Research Series* N^O. 4a), New York, 1924 (reviewed in *Isis*, VII, 1925, pp. 153–155).

17 See Davis, op. cit.

18 W. H. Tillinghast, 'The Geographical Knowledge of the Ancients Considered in Relation to the Discovery of America' in: Justin Winsor, edit., Narrative and Critical History of America, Vol. 1, Boston and New York, 1889, ch. 1.

including as it did the centennial year, was notable for the vast volume then poured out of Columbian literature both good and bad. Probably one of the most important recent American contributions to Columbian studies is a volume on the geographical conceptions and aims of Columbus by a young Californian scholar, George E. Nunn.[19] A valuable service to the history of geography has been performed by the Hispanic Society of America in publishing many early maps and by Professor E. L. Stevenson in stressing the importance of maps as historical sources. California and Texas historians are doing very important work on the early Spanish discoveries. The publication of the 'Jesuit Relations' by Thwaites has opened the door to the history of explorations in the interior of North America. The 'Relations' were used, for instance, as the primary source for an investigation of the geographical knowledge acquired by the Jesuits, recently published by Nellis M. Crouse as a Cornell doctoral dissertation.[20] But on the whole, though much important special work has been done, almost no American historian has devoted himself to the history of geography as it bears upon other parts of the world than America or to its broader evolution.

The Scope of the History of Geography

The foregoing sketch of what has actually been accomplished in the history of geography must serve as the background for a statement of the possible scope of future studies in this field.

Brunhes asserts that the history of geography is nothing more than a part of the history of the sciences.[21] This is certainly true of the history of *scientific* geography. Yet, scientific geography is merely one of a large group of consciously geographical activities and interests, the history of which is an important element in intellectual and social history. I should include within the history of geography not only the history of scientific geography, but the history of these other geographical interests and activities as well. That many of the latter may be approached historically from wholly different points of view does not render them any less fitting subjects for examination from the point of view of the history of geography. Geography in its essence is a sphere of ideas relating to the regional groupings or phenomena on the earth's surface. The fact that it overlaps and borrows from other spheres of ideas bothers us no longer; we are fortunately outgrowing the tendency to mark off sharp and exclusive boundaries between the different domains of scholarship.

Human beings possess in varying degrees a geographical sense. The habit of thinking in geographical terms is widespread among many peoples. The Eskimos,

[19] G. E. Nunn, The Geographical Conceptions of Columbus: a Consideration of Four Problems (*American Geographical Society Research Series* N°. 14), New York, 1924 (*Isis*,VII, 541).

[20] Nellis, M. Crouse, Contributions of the Canadian Jesuits to the Geographical Knowledge of New France, 1632–1675, Ithaca, N.Y., 1924.

[21] Jean Brunhes, La géographie humaine, 3rd edition, 3 vols., Paris. 1925, Vol. 2, p. 921. See also H. E. Barnes, editor, The History and Prospects of the Social Sciences, New York, 1925, p. 100.

some of the Bedouins, some of the Polynesians, have truly marvelous topographical powers and are able to draw outline maps of very complicated tracts of country.[21A] There are a great many civilized individuals without notable geographical training and without any reason for professional interest in the subject who nevertheless find an atlas among the most absorbing of books[22] and enjoy works of travel quite as much for the geographical meat which they contain as for their exotic or adventurous substance. The geographical sense is an intellectual response to the environmental *milieu*. It leads to the acquisition of geographical ideas and to their expression in a multitude of forms. If the history of historiography be defined as the history of man's consciously expressed intellectual interpretations of events in their chronological order, the history of geography might be defined as the history of man's consciously expressed intellectual interpretations of his terrestrial environment; or, more simply, as the history of geographical ideas as they find spoken, graphic, or written expression. Nor need all these ideas be accurate, systematic, logical, or reasoned; for is not the history of error, folly, and emotion often as enlightening as the history of wisdom?

If we thus define the history of geography, what may we include within its limits?

We may include the consideration of ideas that for want of a better term we shall call 'scientific'. This does not mean that these ideas are necessarily 'scientific' in the modern, which some would consider the absolute, sense of the word: that is, that they are necessarily based on accurate observation, logically developed, and critically controlled. I use the term, rather, in a relative sense to mean ideas systematically worked out in conformity with the best intellectual standards of their age and that find expression in maps or formal scientific treatises. In addition to these, we may also include within the study of the history of geography the consideration of ideas that we shall call 'non-scientific'; not implying thereby that they are necessarily 'unscientific' or erroneous, but, rather, that they are not expressed in scientific form.

The Acquisition of Geographical Ideas

Before we turn to the character of geographical ideas, both scientific and non-scientific, a few words must be said about the manner in which they are acquired at first hand; for the history of thought can hardly be understood without some knowledge of its origins and stimuli.

Geographical ideas are obtained at first hand from what is usually called exploration when conducted in little known countries, and field work when conducted in the better known parts of the world – whether this exploration or field work be

21A See W. Dröber, Kartographie bei den Naturvölker, *Dissertation*, Erlangen, 1903; R. J. Flaherty, 'The Belcher Islands of Hudson Bay', *Geographical Review*, Vol. 5, 1918, pp. 440–458. The latter article, on p. 440, gives a facsimile of a remarkably accurate map drawn from memory by an eskimo.

22 See the altogether delightful little book of essays by W. P. James, The Lure of the Map, London, 1920.

strictly geographical, or geodetic, topographical, geological, ethnographical, or biological.

Only within the last two or three centuries have explorations and field work been carried out exclusively for scientific purposes. One of the first scientific expeditions of the modern type, accompanied by specialists, such as a botanist, a zoologist, a surveyor, an artist, was that of the Dane, Carsten Niebuhr, to the Yemen in 1761–1763.[23] Nearly all earlier explorations and most of the more recent ones have been undertaken primarily for commercial or political reasons, though incidentally geographical knowledge has been acquired through them. Adequately interpreted, the history of exploration should be more than a dry catalogue of dates and names and routes, or a romantic but unsubstantial chronicle of adventures. It should involve some examination of the complex factors that lie back of exploration in any given age or region; and in turn, it should throw some light on the effects of the expansion of regional knowledge in economic, political, social, spiritual, and intellectual conditions. The progress of exploration is meaningless unless viewed against a wider historical setting.

Non-scientific geographical ideas are derived at first hand through travel, whether it be for commercial, military, political, or administrative ends or whether it fall into the category of recreational travel. The latter may range from 'tripping' and 'joy riding' at the lower end of the scale up through various gradations of tourist travel, yachting, student-wandering, and so on, to those more serious levels, such as exploratory mountaineering, which merge into genuine field-work and scientific exploration. Travel in all its form is an enormously important social activity. Its history and philosophy have been all too little studied and interpreted.[24]

[23] 'Peter Forskall, a Swede by birth and a pupil of the great Linnaeus, was a physician with special knowledge of botany; Christian Charles Cramer, a surgeon and zoologist; Frederick Christian von Haven, a philologist and Oriental scholar; George William Baurenfeind, an artist; and lastly, Carsten Niebuhr, lieutenant of engineers, a mathematician and practical surveyor . . . Two of the party died in Yemen, one (and the Swedish servant) at sea on the voyage to India, and one on arrival there: none by violence, but all by the poison of the Yemen air. Niebuhr alone brought his report and the incomplete notes of his comrades to Denmark again'. D. G. Hogarth, The Penetration of Arabia, New York, 1904, pp. 39–40.

Vitus Bering's two voyages (1725–1730, 1733–1742) were also in the nature of scientific explorations (see F. A. Golder, Bering's Voyages (*American Geographical Society Research Series* N°. 1), 2 vols., New York, 1922, 1925, as were the famous French expeditions for the measurement of arcs of meridian in Peru and Ecuador and in Lapland (1736–1743). An interesting chapter on early scientific expeditions will be found in Peschel, *op. cit.*, pp. 535–640.

[24] The following recent publications should be of interest to students of the history of travel: W. W. Mooney, Travel Among the Ancient Romans, Boston, 1920; Jules Jusserand, English Wayfaring Life in the Middle Ages (XIVth Century), new and enlarged edition, New York, 1920; E. L. Guilford, Travellers and Travelling in the Middle Ages (*Texts for Students* N°. 38), London, 1924; Clare Howard, English Travellers of the Renaissance, London, 1914; Jean Bonnerot, Les routes de France, Paris, 1921; S. R. Roget, Travel in the Last Two Centuries of Three Generations, London, 1921; J. L. Mesick, The English Traveller in America, 1785–1835 (*Columbia University Studies in English and Comparative Literature*), New York, 1922; Wilhelm Lehner, Die Eroberung der Alpen, Munich, 1924. The last is a general history of mountaineering.

The Character and Expression of Geographical Ideas

Scientific geographical ideas

Now let us consider briefly something of the character and expression of geographical ideas themselves; and first of those that we call scientific.

It should be observed that scientific geographical ideas are not necessarily expressed exclusively through publications devoted in name to geography. One of the most interesting trends in modern scholarship is the ever increasing manifestation of the geographical spirit in all the natural and social sciences,[25] a development that no serious student of recent intellectual progress may well overlook. Nor in the study of earlier periods is it possible to avoid taking into consideration the geographical ideas revealed in non-geographical writings.[26]

Among the various media for the specifically geographical expression of geographical ideas, the map since very early days has been the most graphic. The history of cartography is an integral part of the history of geography. But the history of cartography should always be more than an antiquarian study. A comparative examination of maps of different ages gives a remarkably clear view of varying intellectual qualities and technical abilities. A medieval map often reveals an atmosphere of credulity and respect for authority, but withal a love of beauty in form and detail. What better way is there of grasping some of the essential differences between the spirit of medieval and of modern science than to set side by side maps of the two ages? The evolution of maps is intimately associated with the development of astronomy, geodetics, and trigonometry; with the growth of spherical geometry in the projections adopted; and with the evolution of the technical arts in the draftsmanship, engraving, and printing. The manner in which the subject matter on maps is selected and represented sheds light on the critical acumen of the map makers. The origin of most large-scale topographical maps of modern Europe is to be sought in military necessities and it is significant that nearly all the great topographical surveys have been made by war departments, except in the United States and Canada, where economic considerations have been foremost. The history of topographical maps should always be linked with the history of military or administrative economic policy.

The different characters that geographical ideas have assumed in different times and countries have been conditioned partly by environmental and partly by human factors.

The impress of geographical conditions themselves upon the nature of geographical thought is an alluring subject which has not been much investigated.[27]

[25] See especially Brunhes, *op. cit.*, Vol. 2, pp. 831–858; H. E. Barnes, The New History and the Social Studies, New York, 1925, pp. 55–75 (*Isis*, VIII, 380)

[26] Note, for example, Wright, *op. cit.*, pp. 88–115.

[27] See J. K. Wright, 'The History of Geography: a Point of View', *Ann. Assoc. Amer. Geogr.*, Vol. 15, 1925, pp. 192–201.

For instance, in parts of Greece, Dalmatia and Asia Minor, there are extensive limestone regions in which the process of solution has produced systems of subterranean caverns and watercourses. This not only gave rise to the old story that the River Alpheus in the Peloponnesus passes under the Ionian Sea to spring forth again in the fountain of Arethusa in Syracuse, but was the basis of a hydrographical theory that prevailed through the Middle Ages: the theory that the entire globe is seamed with watercourses which derive their ultimate source of supply either from vast interior reservoirs or from the sea.[28]

Another example of the same thing is to be found in the amazingly clear understanding of the processes of weathering and erosion held by certain Moslem and Persian writers of the Middle Ages, obviously facilitated by the aridity and bareness of the soil in the East, which permitted better observations of these processes than were possible in contemporary Europe.[29] Similarly, in our own west – where the physiographic nature of a region is frequently apparent even from the train window – aridity and lack of vegetation cover has contributed largely to the preeminence of American geographers in the study of land forms, or geomorphology.[30]

As a final example we may refer to the often obvious but often less apparent relation of geographical facts to the progress of exploration in the Age of Discovery. Nunn believes that Columbus deliberately chose a southern route sailing westward and a northern route sailing homeward in order to take advantage respectively of the north-easterly trade winds and the prevailing westerlies.[31]

More potent, however, than the direct effects of environmental conditions on the evolution of geographical ideas has been the influence of the general level of culture and intellectual life. The character of geographical writing in different countries and at different ages illustrates in a striking manner the outstanding qualities of contemporary or national thought. The scientific geography of the Greeks of the Hellenistic period is primarily speculative, theoretical, experimental; the geography of the Romans was essentially descriptive and practical. Early medieval geography was dominated by theology and based largely on scriptural exegesis. The geographical works of the Renaissance reveal the newly revived interest in classical antiquity and something of the humanist's pagan love of the world about him. Work of the modern French school of human geographers as represented by Vidal de la Blache and his followers reflects the severely critical quality of the French genius, its logical procedure of thought, its clarity and perfection of expression. The German anthropogeographers have been far more prone to build theoretical structures and systems. In Great Britain geographical interests (with notable exceptions) have tended to center on explorations and on economic geography.

[28] See Wright, Geographical Lore, passim.

[29] *Ibid.*, pp. 213, 446.

[30] See W. M. Davis, 'The Progress of Geography in the United States', *Annals of the Association of American Geographers*, Vol. 14, 1924, pp. 160–215, especially pp. 181–191.

[31] See Nunn, *op. cit.*, pp. 31–53.

Non-scientific geographical ideas

Geographical ideas of varying power and purity are expressed non-scientifically (and, alas, often unscientifically) in books and magazines of travel. The total number of these constitutes by no means an inconsiderable proportion of the total annual output of printed matter, other than newspapers and advertising, in all civilized states. Figures given in the *Publisher's Weekly* for January 31, 1925, show that 9012 books were produced in the United States in 1924. Of these, 1226 were fiction. Of the remaining 7786, 445 (or 4.9% of the grand total) are classified as geographical. They include, presumably, a small number of scientific treatises, a somewhat greater number of text books, and a preponderance of popular works of travel and description. The British statistics give an idea of the ratio of popular works of description and travel to works classified strictly as 'geography': in 1924, 574 of the former as against only 97 of the latter.

Nor is the popular book of travel anything new: we need but think of Megasthenes' 'Indica' or Giraldus Cambrensis' travels in Ireland and Wales, or Sir John Mandeville's delightful combination of fact and fancy. And one aspect of this almost universal interest in travel is the travelogue type of lecture so popular in the United States. It serves in this country much the same purpose served throughout parts of Europe by the local geographical society. Many of these are more like social clubs than like scientific institutions in the strict sense of the word: their primary purpose is for the bearing of talks on travel.

There are many men of letters in whom the geographical sense is highly developed. In the works of Ruskin there are some extraordinarily interesting analyses of the influence of geographical features – particularly mountains – on artistic expression.[32] The evolution of the love of nature, the development of the appreciation of landscape – particularly of wild landscape and mountains[33] – and the outpouring of the emotions aroused by the contemplation of nature in poems or prose, may be regarded as an expression of geographical ideas. Some novelists have had an even clearer vision for the facts of geography that are of most significance to the average man than professional writers on geographical subjects. One well-known bibliography by a geographer contains a list of geographical novels,[34] perhaps quite as valuable and even more reliable in their way than historical novels. The quest for local color in literature is also a quest for geographical

32 John Ruskin, Modern Painters, Vol. 4, containing Part 5, 'Mountain Beauty'.

33 See Francis Gribble, The Early Mountaineers, London, 1899; W. W. Hyde, 'The Development of the Appreciation of Mountain Scenery in Modern Times', *Geographical Review*, Vol. 3, 1917, pp. 107–118.

34 H. R. Mill, Guide to Geographical Books and Appliances, London, 1910, pp. 58–63; see also Miss D. Wharton, editor, Short List of Novels and Literary Works of Geographic Interest, Leeds Branch of the British Geographical Association, 1920. Septime Gorceix, Le miroir de la France: géographie littéraire des grandes régions françaises, Paris, 1923, is 'a selection . . . of excerpts from novels, poems, essays, and descriptions, chosen for the poignancy with which they depict the various *pays* and cities of France' (*Geographical Review*, Vol. 14, 1924, p. 660).

expression.[35] So is landscape painting, and it is perhaps not too far-fetched to say that even program-music may be of geographical interest provided one knows the title of the piece; Smetana's 'Moldau' brings to mind the sweep of a great river; Sibelius' 'Finlandia' evokes a vision of melancholy boreal moors. Ordinarily the approach to the study of the various ways in which the geographical sense has expressed itself is made – if made at all – through the study of the history of the *media* of expression – the history of science, literature, art, painting, or music. But will not the historian of civilization or the student of intellectual history find it possible and worth while also to approach these forms of expression from the geographical point of view?[36]

Conclusion

Some will think that this leads too far astray from the history of scientific geography, which, after all, is and should remain, the central core of the history of geography. And, indeed, the writer is fully conscious that he has wandered widely and seemed to arrogate to the history of geography what would certainly appear to be a miscellaneous mass of dissociated ideas. But this has been done deliberately. The purpose has been to give an extensive view of possibilities in this field. The miscellaneous material over which we have flitted, at least is united by a geographical thread. We are coming to recognize the importance of the 'history of science and civilization'; but taken as a whole, this is immense and uncoordinated. It cannot well be studied or taught unless some unifying threads be selected and consistently followed. Whichever threads one may choose – and different scholars naturally will choose different threads – they should in any case be connected with widely varied portions of the whole. The geographical threads at least fulfill this requirement.

[35] See Geographical Review, Vol. 14, 1924, pp. 659–661.

[36] Alexander von Humboldt in the second volume of 'Cosmos' deals with the history of the response of the mind to the contemplation of the physical universe. He devotes stimulating chapters to the analysis of 'incitements to the contemplation of nature' (i.e. to the history of poetic descriptions of nature in early and modern times, and to the history of landscape painting). These are followed by a broad and sweeping review of the growth of human knowledge of earth and heavens.

2

PARADIGMS AND REVOLUTION OR EVOLUTION?

R. J. Johnston

Rather than drawing on history for their models of geography's development (as Wright did, **chapter 1**), many geographers in the 1960s and 1970s turned towards ideas from the history and philosophy of science. Among the most prominent thinkers to which geographers looked was Thomas F. Kuhn. His argument in *The structure of scientific revolutions* (Chicago, 1962) was based not on what scientists ought to do – as Karl Popper had argued, for example – but on what they actually did do. Kuhn suggested that normal science passes through periods of stability, termed paradigms, interrupted by revolutions. An example of a revolution might be the shift from the Ptolemaic earth-centred view of the universe to the Copernican sun-centred view. But in the first serious examination of Kuhn's ideas by a geographer, Ron Johnston argues that they were largely irrelevant to social sciences, in which he includes human geography since 1945. Not only does he find that human geography is multi-paradigmatic, suggesting that few ideas are ever totally rejected, but he suggests that the discipline changes more by stealth than by sudden revolution. Even so, Johnston retains Kuhn's emphasis on the sociology of knowledge by highlighting the significance of the career structure for geography's development. This article forms part of Johnston's highly successful book *Geography and geographers: Anglo-American human geography since 1945* (London, 1979), in the later editions of which he discusses further the importance of external forces on geography and the ideas of other historians and philosophers of science.

Source: Paradigms and revolution or evolution? Observations on human geography since the Second World War. *Progress in Human Geography* 2, 189–206, 1978.

There has been confusion in the public mind for several decades about the nature of geography as an academic subject, a confusion which reflects both the lack of any clear consensus among geographers as to the aims and methods of their discipline and the many differences in what is taught as geography at various stages of the educational process. The last two and a half decades have been characterized by an almost continuous debate among human geographers concerning the nature of their discipline. No consensus seems ever to have been reached, and the continuing debate is reflected in the wide variety of course offerings at higher education institutions, both within and between individual departments.

The student of an academic subject needs a firm set of guiding principles which identifies the major characteristics of his chosen field; what sort of questions it asks; how it sets about answering them; and what use is made of its findings, for example. A newcomer to human geography will find such principles difficult to determine, unless his instruction in, and passage through, the subject's recent literature is myopic. It should be clear to even the most casual observer, let alone a student undertaking a course of several years' duration, that there is no consensus over major principles of the sort outlined above, despite numerous attempts to paper over the cracks. In order to make a decision as to where he stands with relation to current debates, therefore, the student needs an overview of their content. Such an overview is rarely provided, and it is extremely difficult to provide for oneself. Courses in, and books on, the history of geography pay relatively little attention to the contemporary period, no doubt because of the difficulties of participant observation. Nevertheless, it is the contemporary scene which is most relevant to current students, not least because virtually all the material that they must read has been produced in the period under review.

The aim of this paper is not to provide such an overview (that is attempted in a forthcoming volume: Johnson, 1979). Instead, the intention is to evaluate a model of the changes and debates which have taken place and which provides for some a framework for organizing the recent history of human geography. Such an evaluation requires a brief outline of the content of the debates, as well as a discussion of the model's relevance. In the latter context, the present paper moves further into the sociology of science than has been typical of other commentaries on the changing nature of human geography.

The Model, its Terminology, and its use in Human Geography

Argument about the nature of human geography is not new to the period being discussed here, and Hartshorne's classic *The nature of geography* (1939) was written in order to provide a coherent philosophy, based on a review of what was being done, in particular by German geographers. That not all agreed with his assessment is implicit in the title of a paper he published in 1948 ('On the mores of methodological discussion in American geography'). The nature of the debate did not surface in the published literature at that time, however, and it was only in the 1950s that Hartshorne's position was strongly challenged and even then, as will be indicated later, largely in a roundabout manner.

Evaluation of the changes which emerged in various parts of the United States during the 1950s included two major assessments; in one of these a new terminology was introduced, taken from the work of a historian-philosopher of science, Thomas Kuhn (1962). Haggett and Chorley (1967) adopted his concept of 'normal science', comprising a paradigm that sets the constraints within which a particular science operates; such a paradigm may be overthrown by a 'scientific revolution', and Haggett and Chorley perceived such a revolution taking place in human geography during the 1950s and 1960s.

A paradigm, according to Kuhn (1970), sets the framework within which a science proceeds, by indicating: first the accepted facts; second, the puzzles which remain to be solved; and third, the procedures by which solutions to the puzzles are sought. Normal science thus involves puzzle-solving activity, providing new facts on which further queries are based; its procedures and current status are reflected in textbooks. Some puzzles cannot be solved by the accepted procedures, however, and the solutions to others are at variance with the other parts of the framework, particularly the accepted facts. The results of such investigations are frequently set aside as anomalies which, as yet, the paradigm cannot account for. Eventually, however, either their bulk or their perceived salience is such as to throw general doubt on the whole paradigm and an alternative framework is sought which will incorporate both the acceptable and the unacceptable facts and will provide a set of procedures which allows the solution of the previously insoluble. Acceptance of the new paradigm involves a revolution in scientific thought.

Haggett and Chorley applied this model to contemporary geography, arguing the inability of the current paradigm to handle both the explosion of relevant data for geographical research and the increasing fragmentation and compartmentalization of the sciences. They proposed recognition of a new 'model-based' paradigm 'able to rise above this flood-tide of information and push out confidently and rapidly into new data-territories. It must possess the scientific habit of seeking for relevant pattern and order in information, and the related ability to rapidly discard irrelevant information' (p. 38). This was written for a British audience which was, even then (the mid 1960s), far from totally aware of the debates and changes of the preceding decade or so in the United States. As such, Haggett and Chorley were not so much initiating as diffusing a revolution.

Burton's (1963) paper appeared almost contemporaneously with Kuhn's (1962) book, and so was not directly influenced by it and its terminology. Nevertheless, his title included a 'Kuhnian' term – revolution – and his general argument is very similar in outline to Kuhn's more detailed model. Four years before the appearance of Haggett and Chorley's essay, Burton felt able to conclude that quantification was widely accepted by the geographical establishment and that a revolution – a theoretical and quantitative revolution – had taken place.

> *An intellectual revolution is over when accepted ideas have been overthrown or have been modified to include new ideas. An intellectual revolution is over when the revolutionary ideas themselves become a part of the conventional wisdom. When Ackerman, Hartshorne, and Spate are in substantial agreement about something, then we are talking about the conventional wisdom. Hence, my belief that the quantitative revolution is over and has been for some time. Further evidence may be found in the rate at which schools of geography in North America are adding courses in quantitative methods to their requirements for graduate degrees (p. 153)*

Burton was undoubtedly correct in saying that the erstwhile revolutionaries were now (1963) part of geography's establishment, but whether a true revolution had occurred remains to be assessed.

Kuhn's model of scientific progress was also used by Harvey (1973) in his attempt to initiate a revolution and the acceptance of a new paradigm for human geography. Attempts to introduce revolutionary theories and methods, he recognized, are rarely accepted immediately; most often they are opposed by counter-revolutionary theory produced by the supporters of the established paradigm. This poses two problems with regard to Kuhn's model: first, it does not indicate what conditions lead to the recognition of anomalies, the generation of crises, and the inception of revolutions; and second, it does not indicate how a new paradigm comes to be adopted, and what are the criteria for identifying such acceptance. The latter problem is crucial in the social sciences where revolutions in thought are frequently related to revolutions in practice, to social action as well as to social understanding. Thus knowledge in subjects like human geography cannot be abstracted from its material base, from the enveloping environment within which social scientific activity is conducted and which predisposes the attitudes of individual social scientists towards their subject matter.

Not all commentators are sure that revolutions have occurred within human geography since 1945. Chisholm (1975), for example, prefers an evolutionary interpretation, arguing that while there may have been a technical revolution in terms of analytical methods there has been much less change in terms of subject-matter studied (this raises again the question of what constitutes a revolution; can new puzzle-solving procedures be accepted within an existing paradigm?). Nor is Chisholm sure that a new paradigm is currently needed. Nevertheless, like the others he is prepared to discuss changes within human geography in the context of Kuhn's model. It is an assessment of the relevance of that model for describing the changes which occupies the rest of this paper.

The Paradigm Model; some Elaborations

Before assessing the validity of Kuhn's model for a description of the recent history of human geography, further inquiry into its characteristics are necessary. Two are crucial here: the nature of normal science – the accepted paradigm, and the nature of revolutions. Regarding the nature of normal science the key question is 'what is a paradigm?' To a considerable extent Kuhn is of little help in answering this, since, according to Masterman (1970), he uses the term in at least twenty-one different ways. These can be collapsed into three main types of usage, however: first, the metaphysical, in which the paradigm is a world view; second, the sociological, which is

> *a set of scientific habits. By following these, successful problem-solving can go on . . . research based upon one or more past scientific achievements that some particular community acknowledges for a time as supplying the foundation for its further practice (Masterman, 1970, 66);*

and third, the construct, a classic work which provides the tools and set of procedures by which puzzle-solving is approached. For the present purpose, the last two are relevant. They indicate that normal science involves working not only within a prescribed scientific framework but also in a given social structure. As will be argued later, the importance of this social structure is paramount.

Turning to the nature of revolutions, Harvey's problems with this part of Kuhn's model have already been noted. How is the model to be verified or falsified? What is acceptable evidence that one paradigm has been overthrown and replaced by another? Separate answers to these questions may be needed for the social sciences in which, much more so than in the natural sciences, interpretation of results is frequently influenced by the personal values of individual scholars and thus, in one sense of that word, is ideological. Right and wrong are not absolutes, so that, although Popper argues that the correct scientific method involves the search for events which falsify hypotheses, criteria of falsification are inherently fuzzy in much social science practice.

It is necessary to note that Kuhn recognized the existence of proto-sciences, particularly in the arts and philosophy, within which grouping human geography can be placed. These proto-sciences are, in Popper's term, 'revolution in permanence', with constant criticism of existing approaches and a proliferation of new modes of practice. Mature science has an established paradigm into which an individual researcher can key himself and from which he can derive puzzles to be solved which will advance knowledge within the paradigm; proto-science lacks such a paradigm and instead involves a set of conflicting 'schools of thought', each of which begins *de novo* and accepts little, if anything, of the established procedures and facts of its competitors.

Masterman (1970) has extended this proto-science/mature science dichotomy with a threefold classification. The first involves pre-paradigm science in which all facts are equally relevant and their collection is poorly structured. In this state (the equivalent of Kuhn's proto-science) different schools of thought interpret facts in their own way and use them to confront the interpretations of others. There is no consensus on either what is relevant or what should be done, and science does not progress with one set of discoveries providing the base for the next round of puzzle-solving. Second, there is multi-paradigm science. Again this involves several conflicting views, but these differ from those in the previous state in that work is undertaken within clearly established frameworks for puzzle-solving. Some of the applications may be technically advanced but they are usually substantively narrow and increasingly trivial, focusing on minor puzzles and lacking overall depth and a centralizing, unifying paradigm. Finally, she identifies dual paradigm science, in which two major views are competing in a revolutionary/counter-revolutionary setting. In addition, of course, there is the single paradigm state, within a universal consensus regarding aims and methods.

Change, Ever More Change; the Content of Human Geography Since 1945

Using Kuhn's model, it is common for three separate paradigms to be recognized within academic geography in the period up to 1950 (James, 1972; Herbert and Johnston, 1978); exploration, environmental determinism, and regionalism. Although elements of the first two remained, it was the last which dominated human geographical practice at the outset of the period being discussed here. Since then, three further paradigms are again recognized (Johnston, 1977; Herbert and Johnston, 1978); spatial science, behaviouralism, and radical/structural. Whether these are indeed separate, which would imply at least two revolutions, is to be assessed here.

The first 'revolution' had multiple origins in North American human geography. It was, to a considerable extent, a revolution by stealth, involving separate schools at Iowa (under McCarty and Schaefer), Madison (under Robinson), Seattle (under Garrison), and Princeton (under Stewart and Warntz – the 'social physics' school). The Iowa group published two major 'revolutionary' treatises (Schaefer, 1953; McCarty, 1954) arguing, explicitly in the first and implicitly in the second, for the adoption of the scientific method of the Vienna school of logical positivists. The social physicists also published programmatic statements, arguing their case for a macrogeography (Stewart and Warntz, 1958): all that the Wisconsin group produced was a series of technical communications on aspects of map comparison. The Seattle group was much more prolific, though again it lacked any clear paradigmatic statement. Evaluation of their publications (many of which remained in discussion paper form only), and particularly Garrison's trilogy on the spatial structure of the economy (Garrison, 1959a; 1959b; 1960), indicates that their main interest was the description of various types of spatial pattern which could be evaluated against ideal patterns (models) constructed from assumptions regarding rational economic behaviour.

The examples set by these four groups were followed and modified by many other workers, mostly of the latest generation of human geographers. Some aspects of their approaches were debated publicly, notably those relating to quantification (Burton, 1963; Taylor, 1976); the related aspect of scientific theory and laws received much less attention. Nevertheless, the widespread acceptance of work in this new genre and adoption of its methods within a decade and without major published debate (as Taylor, 1976, suggests, much of the 'debate' came after the 'revolution' was over), indicates the introduction of a new paradigm by the side door, if not by the back. Nevertheless, it is apparent that the full force of the positivist position was far from realized by many of those who embraced the revolution; the first presentation of it in its entirety was only published in 1969 (Harvey, 1969), by which time British geography, too, had largely acceded to the quantifiers.

The major change of the 1950s and early 1960s, then, was in procedures, and many of the 'revolutionaries' were at pains to emphasize the continuity in the ultimate objectives of human geography (Berry, 1964). The use of statistics for the making of relatively precise statements was generally accepted, although the related use of mathematics in modelling received much less attention. Similarly, many accepted the general argument that the main contribution of human geographers to the social sciences lay in their emphasis on the role of the spatial variable as an influence on human behaviour, although again there were no major programmatic statements arguing this view (Nystuen, 1968, got wide circulation relatively late). But the subject seemed to fragment into a series of separate, if not independent, branches. Urban, agricultural, transport, industrial and other geographies shared common methods, but worked independently in terms of subject matter. Despite attempts to provide a unifying, spatial overview (notably in Haggett, 1965), disciplinary cohesion was not marked. The various branches themselves comprised separate sub-branches (central-place studies and social-area analyses within urban geography, for example), while certain other branches, notably historical and cultural geography, remained more or less outside the revolution.

Although the new orientation was widely accepted, therefore, it was not universally acclaimed, and criticism developed with regard to the independence of the spatial viewpoint (May, 1970; Sack, 1972). The normative models such as those of Christaller and Von Thünen, on which Garrison and his associates based their work, were also criticized in terms of their value as attempts to understand the 'real world', and a positive approach based on observation of decision-making behaviour about spatial patterns and processes was propounded as an alternative (e.g. Pred, 1967; 1969). What was studied in this 'behavioural mould', and how the results were analysed and interpreted, was strongly influenced by work in the spatial science field, and the methods were often identical. The contribution probably involved setting up further branches in a developing multi-paradigm situation, and although to some a behavioural revolution was heralded, the nature of the change was very slight overall.

A second attempt at behavioural revolution promised to be much more far-reaching. The logical positivist approach was criticized both for ignoring the anomalies which its puzzle-solving had produced and for failing to establish exact criteria for the verification of hypotheses (Guelke, 1974). The alternative offered was a return to the pre-positive scientific method, formerly apparently unknown to human geographers, which emphasizes the characteristics of man as a thinking being, as opposed to the inanimate subject matter of the natural sciences. Hermeneutic approaches such as phenomenology and idealism were proposed, which investigate the worlds in which men live and act rather than impose hypothetical worlds on their actions, as with the positivist method. Despite several programmatic statements, however, and a few examples relating to landscape experience (Tuan, 1974; Relph, 1976) and landscape change (Powell, 1970; Prince, 1971), little substantive work has been reported in this genre, and it is hard to identify it as a major force in contemporary human geography yet.

The growth of what some identify as a further paradigm has been active since about 1968. What to call it is not clear; the term structural/radical introduced earlier really refers to only about half of the change, and a case could be made for the recognition of two new competing paradigms. Human geographers, like almost all social scientists, have always been involved in applied work, both because society expects it of them and because of the variety of rewards it brings to the individual. (For a review of the British tradition see House, 1973.) In the late 1960s there developed in many countries of the Western world a deep and widespread concern with various aspects of capitalist society, notably its wars (Vietnam), its inability to solve the problems of poverty and deprivation at home and abroad, its racism and its destructive exploitation of shrinking natural resources. Human geographers soon became enmeshed in this concern, both as individual citizens and as groups of researchers.

Initially, the concern was indicated by calls for action, both to diagnose and to offer cures for societal ills (e.g. Zelinsky, 1970). Geography and public policy became a major catch-phrase (Coppock, 1974) and the image was developed of geographers as applied social scientists actively influential in the corridors of power. The research so generated in large part involved relatively minor modifications of the positivist methods of the spatial science school, as in the humane, or welfare-oriented approaches espoused, *inter alia*, by Bunge (1973) and Smith (1973; 1977), although arguments were also put that humanitarian concerns could only be properly achieved by hermeneutic approaches which involved the improvement of man's self-awareness (Buttimer, 1976).

By the early 1970s, the view was growing that such humane human geography, which was dubbed liberal, offered little hope of any real amelioration of the problems of capitalist society (Peet, 1977). A more radical approach was proposed based on various structuralist arguments that parts could not be considered independently of wholes. In particular, the Marxist position that questions of distribution could not be separated from those of production attracted attention. One of the leaders of this school was Harvey (1973) who was led to ask 'what kind of geography for what kind of public policy?' (Harvey, 1974). A liberal versus radical debate was conducted in the pages of *Antipode* (a newly founded journal for radical geography) and in the book review section of the *Annals of the Association of American Geographers*. Meanwhile, others organized their research within this new mould, as with the group of postgraduates at Cambridge who investigated the managerial policies used in several types of capitalist institution to produce spatially-segregated housing markets. To many, this new school introduced for the first time an overt political element to geographical research and action, which was contrary to the conventional wisdom that science is neutral and apolitical.

This very brief review of changes in human geography over about three decades has been able to provide little more than a series of cartoons. Nevertheless, the major reorientations in terms of both methods and approaches to subject matter have been made clear. Whether these involved a series of revolutions remains to be discerned, but first it is necessary to outline the external and internal constraints to change.

The Environments of Change

As has already been noted, academic disciplines respond to the demands of their enveloping societies with regard to the orientation of their work. Thus the adoption of logical positivism by human geographers in the 1950s and 1960s reflects the conditions of the times. The Second World War was the war of the scientist, who also dominated the cold war that followed it, the succeeding space race, and the 'white-hot technological revolution' which Harold Wilson promised Britain in the early 1960s. Science was 'in', it was reputable to be a scientist and to be contributing to the national ethos. And this did not apply to the natural sciences only. Economics had won its spurs with the Keynesian revolution; social psychology has proved very useful in wartime personnel evaluation; scientific survey research was proving a boon to politicians and to marketeers; and so on. For geographers, then, the scientific analysis of spatial patterns was a respectable undertaking. Its use was assured by the growth of town and regional planning, and its later branch of transport planning, in which many trained geographers found career outlets.

If the 1950s and the early 1960s can be characterized as an era of 'hard science', the decade that followed can probably be associated with at least a questioning of science, even pronounced 'anti-science' attitudes. Increasingly, too, people began to resent the impersonal big organizations of the public and private sectors, within which the individual was submerged. Planning by these large bureaucracies did not seem to be solving the problems of the many deprived groups and societies, and science and technology were, if anything, widening the disparities within society. Thus a concern grew for more recognition of the position of the individual within mass society. President Johnson's 'Great Society' reflected such concern at a wider scale, and its attempts to correct many of the deprivations of capitalist society, with such techniques as social accounting, undoubtedly helped to generate the attempts to fashion a more humane human geography. Its manifest failures, notably in the protection of civil rights for blacks and in Vietnam, led to the deeper questioning of the values of capitalist society and the rejection of liberal reforms by radical groups in most social sciences.

An academic discipline may reflect in its concerns and work the issues of contemporary society, but it is also a society itself, with its own norms of scholarly behaviour that determine how members react to the demands from the external environment. Research and publication are the means to several ends: one of these is the advancement of knowledge; another, frequently of more immediate importance, is the advancement of the individual scientist's career. Although until recently contracts have been vague and sanctions few, academics are expected to conduct original research and to publish their findings in reputable outlets.

The accepted outlets for the findings of academic research, the major journals, are usually conservative in their operation. Editors and the referees they employ prefer to publish material which conforms to the norms of the current paradigm, and so steady progress through the academic career structure involves the production of a stream of reputable papers and books, which solve (or attempt to solve) the puzzles thrown up by the accepted paradigm. Attempts to foment a revolution with works that challenge the accredited normal science are frequently thwarted by the conservatism of the system. As a consequence, 'would-be revolutionaries' are unable to publish their ideas and findings in reputable places and are forced either to use informal outlets (such as departmental discussion papers) or, more rarely and usually only in the case of an established 'heretical' group, to found their own journals. The former are usually not recognized by the relevant academic establishment as conforming to their conservative norms, and thereby reputable, whereas the latter may find it difficult to establish a scholarly reputation among the sceptics.

Many of the prizes of an academic career involve the researcher becoming a bureaucrat, with major administrative responsibilities for a department or its equivalent, and perhaps also for a wider academic community. Power in bureaucracies is very much contingent on size and growth rates; political power in a university tends to be centred in the departments with large and growing student numbers. To obtain resources, growth is often necessary, and so expansion is seen as the *sine qua non* of both individual and departmental strength. Revolutions threaten such bureaucracies, for they can imply splits and departmental division. Student applicants may be discouraged, thereby limiting size, growth and power. Departmental survival requires the quiet consensus of normal science whenever possible.

The conservatism of the academic career structure and the bureaucracy which runs it is far from conducive to revolution, therefore. Change must come, however, if society requires it. The internal environment then usually adapts to the external. Individuals who have conformed to the norms of the system and progressed some distance within it perceive the necessity for a reorientation. They are able to lead a younger generation of workers towards the formulation of a new paradigm, to give them respectability and hence an entrée to the system. Bureaucratically, the system must be maintained. Thus, as Taylor (1976) points out, those arguing for change must phrase their demands so that they appear to be altering the general direction of the discipline's development but slightly, and not to be threatening total annihilation of all that went before. The conservative 'old guard' will then react by seeking a compromise, realizing that cooption is the best form of defence for the health of the subject and its bureaucracy. Some will argue stridently against anything new, but few will actually stand against it, even though they probably fail to understand it. Youth is to be 'given its head'; coopting it into the system will ensure, as does a mortgage, its eventual conservatism.

When changes are seen as necessary, for political as much as for academic reasons, they will be accepted grudgingly, therefore, so that new approaches (paradigms?) become respectable and the traditional publishing outlets are made available to them. Indeed, the new generation of workers will probably take the journals over. Research productivity, certainly as measured by the volume of publications, wanes rapidly as academics enter their 'middle age' and move on to the bureaucratic ladder. Attitudes change much less easily, however, and many if not most academics continue to favour the paradigm within which they were socialized in their early academic career. Thus in terms of research one gets generational differences, which are reflected in the fact that usually only one or two generations are publishing much at any one time. In periods of rapid change, however, several generations socialized through different paradigms may coexist uneasily in the same department, and the range of their course offerings will illustrate the lack of any real consensus about disciplinary aims and methods (Johnston, 1978).

An amalgamation of these views of the internal and external environments suggests that revolutions are rarely complete. Society requires change. Some post-graduate students may respond, but it is only when some established academics join them that the bureaucratic system accepts the necessity for change, because not to might endanger the major bureaucratic norms of system-maintenance which are most readily fostered by normal science. Thus in periods of rapid change, like the present, the academic response to flux in the external environment involves the fragmentation of a discipline, and departments come to comprise groups of teachers socialized under different paradigms. Some, like the Vicar of Bray, may seek to change with the times and remain *au fait* with the youngest generation, but the majority do not. As a consequence, the outsider and the incoming student are confused by the lack of a disciplinary consensus, a situation which does not occur when the external environment is stable over several generations and the academic community can remain snug in a single conception of normal science.

Human Geography and the Paradigm Model

How then can the content of human geography since the Second World War be evaluated in the context of Kuhn's paradigm model? There seems to be little doubt that the mature science concept of the model must be rejected, for there is little evidence either of large-scale disciplinary consensus for any length of time about the merits of a particular approach or of any revolutions that have been entirely consummated (on this general point, see Watkins, 1970). Certainly the quantitative and theoretical developments have had a major impact, but there are many residuals of the earlier regionalism (Paterson, 1974). Others have found the spatial science paradigm wanting (e.g. Harris, 1971), so that although it has had many supporters (in part because of rapid growth in the academic world at the time of its greatest dominance so that a large generation of human geographers was socialized through it) the takeover by spatial science was far from complete.

As a consequence of the above argument, the dual paradigm model must be rejected also, unless it is argued that the period of time considered here is too short for the completion of an academic revolution. There is still some conflict between regionalism and spatial science, although it surfaces only rarely, while the radical/structural approach has been posed as an alternative to spatial science, in both its traditions and its more recent, liberal forms. In addition, there are the behavioural alternatives, both those which are in effect branches of the spatial science paradigm, and those which are much more critical of the dominant view and are based on hermeneutic approaches.

Rejection of the mature science and the dual paradigm models leaves the alternatives as multi-paradigm and pre-paradigm (proto-science). For the former to be accepted, it has to be shown that progress is occurring, albeit on relatively narrow fronts, built on the foundations of earlier research. The notion of progress in human geography has been reviewed recently by Wise (1977).

If the mass of research papers is considered a mark of progress, of cumulative development of knowledge within a paradigmatic framework, then it would seem that the proto-science alternative does not apply to recent human geography. Comparison of the first edition of *Locational analysis in human geography* (Haggett, 1965) with the second (Haggett et al., 1977), for example, clearly indicates that much work has been done in spatial science in general to qualify it as a paradigm, while investigation of the various parts (social area analysis, for example; Herbert and Johnston 1976a, 1976b) suggests sufficient progress in each for the multi-paradigm situation to be espoused. Some of the behavioural work builds on this progress, but other aspects appear to offer a very obvious alternative. The radical/structural approach also builds to some extent on spatial science, taking its descriptions and offering alternative interpretations of the observed spatial forms; to some extent it could be said to offer an overarching framework that ties together the many relatively shallow paradigms of spatial science which are typical of a multi-paradigm state, with technical progress but a lag in theoretical understanding.

It has been outside the brief of this paper to investigate whether the regionalism approach which preceded the development of spatial science was itself a paradigm. Certainly there was still a debate in Britain during the 1950s over the earlier environmentalism which regionalism replaced (to some it was a development of environmentalism, displaying in its typical 'physical environment before human occupance' organization format much of the determinist viewpoint). Nevertheless, there was probably considerable agreement with Hartshorne (1939; 1948), Wooldridge and East (1951), and others about the aims and methods of human geography; it is argued by some that these aims at least still apply, and it is only in the application of more sophisticated methods that spatial science has departed from the accepted norms. Whether spatial science is a new paradigm or a continuation of regionalism, however, there would seem to be little doubt that many anomalies have been identified in the last decade, especially over explanation of spatial patterns, a topic for which neither regionalism nor spatial science has ever indicated much strength. One could then argue that regionalism/spatial science comprised a multi-paradigm state; that the recent recognition of anomalies has created a revolutionary situation; and that the current behavioural and radical/structural approaches represent a pre-paradigm contest within that revolution. But the revolution is not proceeding very far, very fast, which suggests that the model itself is not particularly valid to this relatively chaotic situation.

An Alternative

The above failure to fit Kuhn's model to recent events in human geography with any conviction leads to the conclusion that the model is irrelevant to this social science, and perhaps to social science in general. There can be little doubt that in many aspects society is changing more rapidly today, and more frequently in its orientation, than ever before, except perhaps at times of major revolutions (Toffler, 1970). Academic disciplines are involved in this change, because society is their paymaster and more and more of its members are involved in higher education. The disciplines are likely to lag somewhat behind the change, however, because of their conservative structures. And they are unlikely to embrace any change fully: bureaucratic norms require the cooption of change and the preservation of the current disciplinary system by which academia is organized. And so in the interaction between external environment and academic discipline a multi-paradigm situation is all that can be expected, and a model is needed which can describe this.

The model to be essayed here is extremely tentative in form. It is based on a general notion of academic generations in social sciences, and has the following outline:

1 The external environment sets the requirements for the activities of social science disciplines.
2 At certain times, the nature of this environment and its requirements change. The new demands are embraced by a minority of established members of the social science disciplines, and by associated members of the youngest generation of research workers.
3 Together, this grouping creates a new 'school of thought' or, in some cases, opposing 'schools of thought' presenting alternative reactions to the changed environment.
4 The new school(s) are coopted into the career system of the social sciences, occupying most of the new appointments as the 'establishment' recognizes the need to embrace the changes and make courses in them available to their students.
5 Because of the relationship between age/position in the career structure and publication rates of research material, the new school(s) take over the academic journals, with occasional ripostes from the older generations (usually in relatively privileged forms, such as presidential addresses to scholarly societies).
6 Paradigm unease is apparent in the teaching activities of the disciplines, as students face course offerings from various philosophies which indicate a lack of consensus and the uneasy accommodation made by the schools to each other.
7 Over time, the adherents of the new school(s) reach positions of seniority within the establishment and, as the older generations retire and die, they come to dominate their discipline.

Application of this model to human geography since the Second World War suggests the identification of two main eras. The first is that of scientific endeavour, of the rise of quantification, theorizing and spatial science. This had taken hold in North America by the end of the 1950s and, because the ensuing decade was one of very rapid growth in higher education, moved quickly into stages 4 and 5 of the model during the first half of the 1960s; by the middle of the decade, the leaders of spatial science were moving into positions of eminence within the geographical establishment although, because of the rapidity of the change, the paradigm unease indicated in stage 7 of the model was not diminishing through the retirement of the preceding generation.

The second era is that of anti-science, which began in the mid-1960s and received a major boost by the events of 1968. Whereas the reaction to the demands of the scientific era by geographers were relatively uniform (the four American 'schools' identified earlier did not differ on fundamentals), two major alternatives developed among this new generation: one is reductionist, suggesting adoption of behavioural methods which study man as an independent decision-maker; the other is generalist, and ideological to many who oppose it, concerned with man in an environment highly constrained by the forces of the mode of production, the analysis of which requires a reorientation of the formerly independent concerns of the separate social sciences.

Unlike the period of the first change, when spatial science rapidly moved to dominance within the research, and later the organizational, activities of human geography, the onset of this era of anti-science coincided with a period of crisis in the external environment and a lack of major growth in academia. As a consequence, the opportunities for expansion of the two alternatives to spatial science have been relatively slight. Spatial science continues to dominate the publication scene and adherents of the new schools find it hard to obtain permanent academic positions. The consequence of this is a confused situation within the discipline. The rapidity and nature of environmental change within the last three decades have led the academic bureaucracy in human geography to coopt, if not to embrace, a variety of postures and schools of thought. All are given opportunities to represent their ideas to student audiences, a reflection of the concept of academic freedom which produces an anarchic outcome (Johnston, 1976) and a catholic formlessness to curricula (Johnston, 1978).

Conclusions

The major aim of this essay has been to evaluate a model of scientific development which has been favoured by some observers as a reasonable account of events in human geography. The model has been found wanting, and it probably would be if applied to other social sciences for the same period. In common with the earlier suggestions of Harvey (1973), the problems of definition – of a paradigm, of a revolution, and of an anomaly, for example – made it extremely difficult to account for changes in a discipline which was reacting to rapid changes in its external environment. Furthermore, although Kuhn's concept of a paradigm is in part sociological, it pays little attention to the nature of conflict within an academic discipline, and how such conflict, notably that between generations socialized into different schools of thought (paradigms?), is countered and accommodated. To come closer to the social reality of a social science, the present essay offers an alternative model. This incorporates the notion of a paradigm, as an accepted method of working on particular types of problem, but does not argue that such paradigms 'take over' disciplines through revolutionary activity. Instead, their takeover occurs by stealth and often relatively slowly. A change in the external environment generates a change in academic methods. To maintain disciplinary unity, this change is allowed, though not accepted, by the establishment, and its adherents gradually move to positions of prominence within the career structure. Meanwhile, the discipline offers a confused picture of its activities to its students.

This model seems better able to account for the changes in human geography since the Second World War than does Kuhn's and would appear to offer a reasonable base for further investigation of the discipline's contemporary history. As indicated by recent events, however, the occurrence of a new environmental change before an earlier one has completely worked its way through the system is likely to increase the confusion, especially when this change stimulates alternative interpretations of what a 'new' human geography should comprise, and constraints on career development inhibit their academic recognition. The model allows for such confusion, since it does not propose, as does Kuhn, complete paradigm replacement through revolution (nor do many senior academics, who favour eclecticism: Wilson, 1977). Indeed, if environmental change continues to be rapid and each generation of academics offers at least one alternative approach, confusion, chaos, and anarchy are likely to become endemic conditions.

References

Berry, B. J. L. 1964: Approaches to regional analysis; a synthesis. *Annals of the Association of American Geographers* 54, 2–11.

Bunge, W. 1973: The geography of human survival. *Annals of the Association of American Geographers* 63, 275–95.

Burton, I. 1963: The quantitative revolution and theoretical geography. *Canadian Geographer* 7, 151–62.

Buttimer, A. 1976: Grasping the dynamism of lifeworld. *Annals of the Association of American Geographers* 66, 277–92.

Chisholm, M. 1975: *Human geography: evolution or revolution?* Harmondsworth: Penguin.

Coppock, J. T. 1974: Geography and public policy: challenges, opportunities and implications. *Transactions of the Institute of British Geographers* 63, 1–16.

Garrison, W. L. 1959a: Spatial structure of the economy I. *Annals of the Association of American Geographers* 49, 232–9.

1959b: Spatial structure of the economy II. *Annals of the Association of American Geographers* 49, 471–82.

1960: Spatial structure of the economy III. *Annals of the Association of American Geographers* 50, 357–73.

Guelke, I. 1974: An idealist alternative in human geography. *Annals of the Association of American Geographers* 64, 193–202.

Haggett, P. 1965: *Locational analysis in human geography*. London: Edward Arnold.

Haggett, P. and Chorley, R. J. 1967: Models, paradigms and the new geography. In Chorley R. J. and Haggett P., editors, *Models in geography*, London: Methuen, 19–42.

Haggett, P., Cliff, A. D. and Frey, A. 1977: *Locational analysis in human geography*, second edition, London: Edward Arnold.

Harris, C. 1971: Theory and synthesis in historical geography. *Canadian Geographer* 15, 157–72.

Hartshorne, R. 1939: *The nature of geography*. Lancaster, Pennsylvania: Association of American Geographers.
1948: On the mores of methodological discussion in American geography. *Annals of the Association of American Geographers* 38, 492–504.
Harvey, D. 1969: *Explanation in geography*. London: Edward Arnold.
1973: *Social justice and the city*. London: Edward Arnold.
1974: What kind of geography for what kind of public policy? *Transactions of the Institute of British Geographers* 53, 18–24.
Herbert, D. T. and Johnston, R. J., editors, 1976a: *Social areas in cities: Volume 1 Spatial processes and form*. London: John Wiley.
1976b: *Social areas in cities: Volume 2 Spatial perspectives on problems and policies*, London: John Wiley.
Herbert, D. T. and Johnston, R. J. 1978: Geography and the urban environment. In Herbert, D. T. and Johnston, R. J., editors, *Geography and the urban environment, Volume 1*, London: John Wiley, 1–33.
House, J. W. 1973: Geographers, decision-takers, and policy-makers. In Chisholm, M. and Rodgers, B., editors, *Studies in human geography*, London: Heinemann, 272–305.
James, P. E. 1972: *All possible worlds*. Indianapolis: The Odyssey Press.
Johnston, R. J. 1976: Anarchy, conspiracy, apathy: the three conditions of geography. *Area* 8, 1–3.
1977: Urban geography: city structures. *Progress in Human Geography* 1, 118–29.
1978: Further observations on the structure of British education and the role of geography. *Journal of Geography in Higher Education* 2, 3–8.
1979: *The making of modern geography: a history of Anglo-American human geography since 1945*. London: Edward Arnold.
Kuhn, T. S. 1962: *The structure of scientific revolutions*. Chicago: University of Chicago Press.
1970: Reflections on my critics. In Lakatos, I. and Musgrave, A., editors, *Criticism and the growth of knowledge*, Cambridge: Cambridge University Press, 231–78.
McCarty, H. H. 1954: An approach to a theory of economic geography. *Economic Geography* 30, 95–101.
Masterman, M. 1970: The nature of a paradigm. In Lakatos, I. and Musgrave, A., editors, *Criticism and the growth of knowledge*, Cambridge: Cambridge University Press, 59–90.
May, J. A. 1970: *Kant's concept of geography and its relation to recent geographical thought*. University of Toronto, Department of Geography, Research publication 4.
Nystuen, J. D. 1968: Identification of some fundamental spatial concepts. In Berry, B. J. L. and Marble, D. F., editors, *Spatial analysis*, Englewood Cliffs, New Jersey: Prentice Hall, 35–41.
Paterson, J. H. 1974: Writing regional geography. In Board, C. *et al.*, editors, *Progress in Geography* 6, London: Edward Arnold, 1–26.
Peet, J. R. 1977: The development of radical geography in the United States. *Progress in Human Geography* 1, 240–63.
Powell, J. M. 1970: *The public lands of Australia Felix*. Melbourne: Oxford University Press.
Pred, A. R. 1967: *Behaviour and location I*. Lund: Gleerup.
1969: *Behavior and location II*. Lund: Gleerup.
Prince, H. C. 1971: Real, imagined and abstract worlds of the past. In Board, C. *et al.*, editors, *Progress in Geography* 3, London: Edward Arnold, 1–86.
Ralph, E. 1976: *Place and placelessness*. London: Pion.
Sack, R. D. 1972: Geography, geometry, and explanation. *Annals of the Association of American Geographers* 62, 61–78.

Schaefer, F. K. 1953: Exceptionalism in geography: a methodological examination. *Annals of the Association of American Geographers* 43, 226–49.

Smith, D. M. 1973: *The geography of social well being in the United States.* New York: McGraw-Hill.

1977: *Human geography: a welfare approach.* London: Edward Arnold.

Stewart, J. Q. and Warntz, W. 1958: Macrogeography and social science. *Geographical Review* 48, 167–84.

Taylor, P. J. 1976: An interpretation of the quantification debate in British geography. *Transactions of the Institute of British Geographers,* New series 1, 129–42.

Toffler, A. 1970: *Future shock.* New York: Random House.

Tuan, Y.-F. 1974: Space and place: humanistic perspective. In Board, C. *et al.*, editors, *Progress in Geography* 6, London: Edward Arnold, 211–52.

Watkins, J. W. N. 1970: Against 'normal science'. In Lakatos, I. and Musgrave, A., editors, *Criticism and the growth of knowledge,* Cambridge: Cambridge University Press, 25–38.

Wilson, A. G. 1977: *Mathematical education for geographers,* School of Geography, University of Leeds, *Working Paper* 211.

Wise, M. J. 1977: On progress and geography. *Progress in Human Geography* I, 1–11.

Wooldridge, S. W. and East, W. G. 1951: *The spirit and purpose of geography,* London: Hutchinson.

Zelinsky, W. 1970: Beyond the exponentials: the role of geography in the great transition. *Economic Geography* 46, 499–535.

3

MUSING ON HELICON: ROOT METAPHORS AND GEOGRAPHY

Anne Buttimer

What lies behind the adoption of particular paradigms and perspectives in geography? Following her involvement in the International Dialogue Project, in which geographers and others reflected upon their knowledge and experience through autobiography, Annette Buttimer suggests that the reasons might be found in root metaphors. Following S. C. Pepper, four metaphors – formism, mechanism, organicism and contextualism – are identified as the deep underpinnings of views of reality, or the parents of paradigms. Buttimer argues that they are sedimented in language and lore and may structure the universal geographical experiences of humankind. By exploring them she hopes to establish the grounds for communication and mutual understanding among geographers. The metaphors allow her to examine the aesthetic and ideological grounds for privileging one paradigm over another. For example, she suggests that both spatial science and its radical or Marxist critique share the metaphor of mechanism. Buttimer's exposition is in keeping with her commitment to humanistic geography, which she shares with Tuan (**chapters 28**) and Ley (**chapter 11**) and of which she was an early proponent. It is also informed by her knowledge of the classical sources of science, humanities and geography. These themes are further explored in *Geography and the human spirit* (Baltimore, 1993).

Source: Musing on Helicon: root metaphors and geography. *Geografiska Annaler* 64B, 89–96, 1982.

On Mount Helicon dwelt the nine Muses, each presiding over a special art: Clio (history), Melpomene (tragedy), Calliope (epic poetry), Erato (lyric poetry), Thalia (comedy and pastoral poetry), Euterpe (music), Polhymnia (rhetoric and mime), Terpsichore (dance and choral singing), and Urania (astronomy). It was told that the beautiful Narcissus, in his sixteenth year, first saw his reflection on one of the many fountains of Helicon. He did not listen to the Muses; rather he fell in love with his own reflection and was transformed into a flower.

Know Thyself – Delphic and Socratic dictum

A recent upsurge of "humanistic" interest in Euro-America has evoked curiosity about connections between *Geo*graphic thought and the universal *geo*graphical experiences of humankind. With it comes a fresh perspective on the history of ideas, a somewhat belated response to John K. Wright's invitation to "the most fascinating *terrae incognitae* of all – those that lie within the minds and hearts of men" (Wright, 1947). Given certain characteristic values of the West, however, for instance, the sovereignty of intellect, it is to the minds of men that attention has been drawn: to those technical and ideological constructs deemed significant in shaping the face of the earth. Whatever there may be of emotion, intuition, faith or fancy in the hearts of men remains largely sub rosa.

The point in the Helicon story is to dramatize those starkly contrasting outcomes of self-reflection: the Narcissist and the Socratic. Narcissus fell in love with his own reflection while Socrates persisted on the journey toward critical self knowledge and emancipation from all that might impede the full adventure of reason (*logos*). So appealing indeed were the lofty claims of Reason, and so apparently triumphant its technology and power, that a-Musement too could be logically (rationally) organized. Nation States would readily create Chairs, curricula, and eventually Muse-ums. Among the twentieth century devotees of Clio and Urania, however, one finds again the countervailing moods of Narcissus and Socrates. What if, on this visit to Helicon, one were really to listen to the Muses? Might one not recognize how persistently Thalia, Melpomene, Polhymnia and the others have been playing in human descriptions of the earth and narratives of human experience? De-veiling the masks of alleged "objectivity" and absolutist claims to truth, would the open-minded pilgrim not recognize the poetic, the tragic or comic, the moral and symbolic modes of understanding life which have all the time been serving the interests of Reason?

The fountains most commonly visited on Helicon today yield distinct and only partially relatable reflections. Some encourage *epistemological* clarity, a critique of knowledge presuppositions unfettered by constraints assumed during the Positivist era when virtually exclusive preoccupation with method flourished. (Gregory, 1978; Smith, 1979; Sack, 1980). Meanwhile modernist philosophers cast doubts on the very notion of foundations for knowledge (Feyerabend, 1961, 1962; Rorty, 1979; Schrag, 1980). Others point to social or *sociological* enquiry, exploring the material and ideological conditions within which thought has been produced and reproduced, a route allegedly "liberated" from the discourse of instrumental action and favoring mutual understanding and improved communication (Habermas, 1968, 1979; Gadamer, 1975). Others still would focus on language itself, jostle with lexical as well as logical nuance, seeking evidence for the *archeological* foundations of inherited epistemes – at least those expressed in three major vernaculars, French, German, and English (Foucault, 1969, 1977; Wittgenstein, 1960, 1969; Olsson, 1979; Claval, 1980). The collage of all these and other reflections, however, does not seem to yield any whole picture. Could it be that one has not listened to the Muses at all?

It sounds like a truism in our day to remark that underlying most scientific theories and *chef d'oeuvres* of art and literature in Western history there are implicit hypotheses or beliefs about the nature of the world, time, fate, society and the physical earth (Glacken, 1968; Galtung, 1981; Nakamura, 1980). One could even claim that the bulk of Western scholarly energy, stirred by the Socratic dream, has been devoted to rendering such beliefs and myths *cognitively* credible, or at least aesthetically or ideologically acceptable (Barrett, 1962; Ricoeur, 1975; Merleau-Ponty, 1973). Scholars have, of course, quite explicitly acknowledged how culturally diverse are images of Nature and resources; geographers have documented the landscape correlates of different world views. But how successful have we really been in promoting better communication between or mutual understanding of essentially contrasting world views – even at home? Perhaps one has not explored deeply enough?

William William-Olsson once asked "Hur skall världen se ut?" sketching a map of Europe on aximuthal projections based in Beijing (China), Moscow (USSR), Urbana, Ill. (USA), and Johannesburg (S. Africa) in order to show how ethnocentric and myopic ordinary pictures of the world are (William-Olsson, 1975). A whole generation of geographers has explored "mental maps", perceptions and cognitions of space and environment (Moore and Golledge, 1976). Slowly but surely it is dawning on us that there is more to the experience of world than the visual and the cartographic. Humans, it seems, not only see and cognitively schematize their "world views"; they feel, believe, hope, love and hate certain symbols of the world. In fact, if Cassirer, Langer, and others are right, this propensity to make symbolic transformations of reality is the most characteristically human activity of all, and it expresses itself in languages and cultures, nations and states, boundaries and fences, institutions and art forms. "The development of civilisations" one writer claims, "is essentially a progression of metaphors" (Doctorow, 1977, 231–2).

If one were to identify some of those key metaphors of world which have become sedimented in the conventional language and lore of groups and nations, and most especially if we could get to the roots of our own, we might be in a better position to learn something from this encounter with our *terrae incognitae*.

Metaphor, it has been claimed, touches a deeper level of understanding than "paradigm", for it points to the process of learning and discovery – to those analogical leaps from the familiar to the unfamiliar which rally imagination and emotion as well as intellect. Variously defined as "the dreamwork of language" (Davidson, 1978), "the intellectual link between language and myth" (Cassirer, 1946), as literary trope (Jakobson, 1960), as "mode of argument" (White, 1973), metaphor has aroused curiosity and excitement in art, philosophy, music, history as well as in the social sciences (Shibles, 1971; Sacks, 1978; Morgan, 1980; Harrison and Livingstone, 1981). In fact, the volume of prose recently generated around this theme may soon lead to the kind of semantic inflation which threatened to banalize the notions of image and theory in the sixties and paradigm in the seventies. Scientists and philosophers of science have no doubt a primary interest in the cognitive import of metaphor (Black, 1962; Leatherdale, 1974), and each discipline will selectively screen out whatever meaning may be appropriate for its own stated ends, but social scientists and geographers may indeed have a lot to lose by simply following this bias toward the exclusively cognitive. "Squeezing out the cognitive juices" (Pepper, 1942), and ignoring the mytho-poetic and heuristic aspects of metaphor may simply be the modern day expression of what Heidegger refers to as the "technification" of thought, for whatever lofty aims this process is directed (Heidegger, 1971; Schrag, 1980).

Geographic language is thoroughly metaphorical. Have we not described the "face" of the earth in terms of "eyes", "nose", "mouth", "neck" and "profile", named and claimed its physiognomy with every conceivable analogy to the human anatomy and society? Regions and hamlets have been likened to "organisms", roadways and canals to "arteries of circulation", industrial complexes as "growth poles" and "generators" of economic development. Once these expressions become sedimented and common place in textbooks and atlases one forgets the metaphor and ascribes a literal meaning to these same words. Foolhardy it would be in this short essay to even touch on that vast panorama of insight which could be gleaned from semiotic and semantic scrutiny of language in geography. Wise, however, it might be to ask if there are enduring gestalt-type metaphors of the world as a whole which could be discerned in the traditions of the discipline in Western countries. One major opinion on such world gestalts may suffice to illustrate the direction in which research and reflection could be entertained.

Stephen Pepper (1942) claimed that there were really only four relatively adequate world hypotheses which have stood the test of time and intellectual scrutiny in the West: Formism, Mechanism, Organicism, and Contextualism. Even if this list is not exhaustive, or even if one may seriously question the grounds on which others are dismissed, it may serve a heuristic function to ask how these key world theories have found expression in Western geography.

This adventure may at least serve to illustrate the value of looking at some of the root differences underlying contrasting modes of analysis and description which have been cultivated in the discipline. It may also illustrate how limited is any study which directs attention exclusively to the cognitive aspects of metaphor.

Underlying each of these world hypotheses, Pepper claims, is a root metaphor which generates its analytical categories and substantiates its claims to truth. Formism grounds itself on the common sense experience of similarity; its cognitive claims rest on a *correspondence theory of truth* (Pepper, 151–185). In geography this metaphor expresses itself most typically in "mapping" – chorology and morphology, cartographic and mathematical representations of patterns in space. Its world picture is a dispersed one: each form may be analyzed and explained in terms of its own nature and appearance (de Geer, 1923; Hettner, 1927; Hartshorne, 1939; de Jong, 1955). Mechanism takes the common sense experience of the machine as its root metaphor. Our midcentury enthusiasm for "spatial systems" and "functional mechanisms" may well qualify as the geographic expression of this metaphor (Berry, 1964; Boulding, 1960; von Bertalanffy, 1968). Mechanism offers an integrated world view while also affording guidelines for detailed analysis. Its claims to cognitive validity rest on a *causal adjustment theory of truth* (Pepper, 221–231). Organicism also offers an integrated picture of the world, its aims synthetic rather than analytical. It tends to regard every event in the world as more or less concealed process, all eventually reaching maturation (and transcendence) in the organic whole. Throughout the nineteenth and twentieth centuries geographers have been attracted or repelled by the notion of "organism" (von Humboldt, 1845–62; Herbertson, 1905; Thomas, ed., 1956; see also Stoddart, 1967; Berdoulay, 1980, Harrison and Livingstone, 1981). Cognitive claims of an organicist world view rest on a *coherence theory of truth* (Pepper, 280–314). Contextualism sees the world as an "arena" of unique events, and tries to unravel the textures and strands of processes operative in, or associated with, particular events. Its world view is thus also a dispersed one, although its descriptive style is synthetic; it espouses an *operational theory of truth* (Pepper, 268–279; see also Dewey, 1925; James, 1940; Schutz, 1973). The contextual approach is most clearly evident among cultural and historical geographers (Wright, 1966; Lowenthal, 1961; Tuan, 1977; Harris, 1978) but the term "arena" can evidently have other connotations as well (Hägerstrand, 1975; Törnquist, 1981).

It should immediately be noted that rarely, if ever, are particular authors identifiable with one of these root metaphors. Most creative thinkers play quite freely with a variety of metaphorical styles, and with the exception of dogmatists, most thinkers feel at home with more than one; many indeed have been eclectic and inconsistent. Metaphors, as I am using the term here, could perhaps best be regarded as the *Dramatis Personae* of Western intellectual history, the actual narrative and plot of particular pieces staged in the material and ideological contexts in which scholars thought and practiced their professions.

These four root metaphors do not, of course, exhaust the full range of world conceptions evident in geographic research and teaching (Buttimer, 1981). They do, however, offer a useful macro perspective within which to note the convergence of theory and praxis in different branches of the field. I have found it pedagogically useful to look at the record of urban geography, for instance, from the vantage point of these metaphors. The city as "organism" was a favored image among scholars who described the social experience of immigrant groups, patterns of competition, succession, and *anomie*, being considered as critical indicators of people's levels of adaptation to new milieux (Park & Burgess, 1925). Designers of Garden City movements have been the most overt devotées of organic analogies (Howard, 1897; Geddes, 1915) but visionaries of centralized communications systems within the city have also used biological and cybernetic analogies (Meier, 1960). The city as "mechanism" may be even more readily recogniseable to students of post-war urban geography (Berry & Horton, 1970). Within each activity, be it manufacturing, retail, or service delivery, one assumed that there were mechanisms at work which would lead toward an optimal spatio-temporal articulation of life via central-place hierarchies of production or supply points. But the older, and perhaps more deeply revered, habit of mapping spatial form has always characterized the work of geographers and planners – formal patterns of space-time occupation, rather than functions generating topological surfaces. For this formal tradition the whole picture, if any, was a map: a mosaic of zones, sectors, and discretely bounded regions, each circumscribed by legal or physical limits on what activities could or should be housed therein (Murphy, 1966; Mayer, 1954). Finally, the city as arena of unique events was frequently found among writers of liberal or laissez-faire orientation (Jacobs, 1961; Clay, 1974). One sought to show how the urban context affected life styles, values, and attitudes, emphasis resting on the unique rather than the general, the spontaneous rather than the planned (Eliot Hurst, 1975).

Now each of these metaphors spells a distinct design for the physical and functional arrangements of space, time, and activities on the ground; their often incompatible demands eventually becoming legible in the texts and textures of urban life. Which metaphor, or combination of metaphors, will endure or dominate at any particular moment will, of course, be a function of economic and political power interests; but at any moment, if one had the eyes to see, then the urban landscape could be read as a text, or as a "mirror" of the civilization which produced it (Vidal de la Blache, 1922).

Looking at geographic thought now, would it not be interesting to explore particular milieux and the values of particular periods and settings in order to understand why, for example, the "map" became a favored metaphor at one period, "mechanism" at another, why "organism" evoked such acclaim or disdain, and why the world as "arena" has, by and large, been the metaphor of only a few?

I suggest that each metaphor, when faced with the challenges of particular values and milieux, undergoes a kind of adaptive radiation into three discrete forms: (1) *rhetorica* (diplomatic or philosophical rationale and "prose"), (2) *techne* (mode of instrumentation in analysis and presentation), and (3) *praxis* (relationship to societal interests and problem-solving). The metaphor as a whole will be evaluated, rejected or accepted, in terms of how the profession at a particular moment ranks these three sets of interests. In fact, each of these forms can develop a narrative of its own – pry itself loose from the root metaphor – depending on the overriding demands of a particular discipline. A few examples from American experience may illustrate the point.

Consider the twenties, a time when American geographers sought to establish disciplinary identity in an otherwise rather indifferent milieu. High ranking values were disciplinary autonomy, rejection of environmental determinism, some democracy of effort, and especially relevance to practical problem-solving in the optimistic business-entrepreneurial spirit of Bowman's *New World*. Of our four root metaphors, the "map" – chorology and morphology – seemed the best candidate for satisfying all requirements. Imported organicist rhetorica may have appealed for Presidential Addresses or as preamble for school textbooks, but did it not contain elements which were ideologically offensive? Besides, where in all of North America could one find the kind of *pays* or *Gemeinschaft* for which "organism" might be an appropriate metaphor? More importantly, "organism" did not prove tractable in terms of *techne* or *praxis*, both of which were deemed so crucial in the emerging criteria of "science" at the time. So chorology and morphology could begin their own narrative emphasizing *techne* – an emphasis later to be bolstered by Positivist conceptions of science and eventually outshining (even ridiculing) any possible critique of its own knowledge presuppositions. By the time of World War II, however, the "map" itself became transformed. The world from the air opened up new vistas, and postwar reconstruction/development interests demanded more powerful techne and praxis. "Mechanism", a metaphor which had proved itself so effective in operations research during wartime, (Morse and Kimball, 1951) gained appeal for the rational reconstruction of economic and technological process in a postwar world.

In terms of favored root metaphors, American (possible Anglo-American-Nordic) experience suggests a general preference for the categorial frameworks of Formism and Mechanism, two analytically oriented world hypotheses which complement each other and are most amenable to technical and instrumental human interests. Their convergence in the 1960's could be regarded as the key to geography's "new paradigm" (Haggett, 1965; Davies, 1972). So deeply did "map" and "mechanism" evidently impress themselves that a generation later rebel voices would still use these metaphors in their critique of the "establishment" and in proposals for alternatives. Marxist, Structuralist and Materialist critique tended to use the categories of mechanism (Harvey, 1972; Peet, 1977; Castells, 1977) whereas humanistic and phenomenological critique often favored the categories of formism (Ley and Samuels, 1978). But in the post-1968 period questions of *techne* were less interesting than those of *praxis*: cognitive issues rendered almost incidental to an overriding ethical concern for justice or revolution (Harvey, 1973; Santos, 1975; Smith, 1979). One wonders why contextualism – so closely akin to American Pragmatism – made so little headway? Was it that it did not promise direct response to the demands of disciplinary autonomy, practical problemsolving, or that from the beginning it demonstrated relatively greater adequacy with the unique event rather than the general pattern?

Although proponents and opponents of different approaches to geography have generally couched their arguments in epistemological or methodological terms, it seems obvious that questions of aesthetic and ideological choice, of cultural and social values, have entered quite influentially into the formation of disciplinary prose. Some parallels with the field of history may be instructive here. Popper's invective against organicist and mechanicist interpretations of history could find echoes within geography (Popper, 1961). No doubt an Anglo-Saxon penchant for empiricism could go a long way to explain the overriding preference for mapping and the disdain expressed for such "continental" abstractions as organism and mechanism during the first half of the twentieth century. But such cognitive preferences do not help explain the popularity of mechanist thinking among the post World War II generation.

Hayden White's study of four nineteenth century master historians (Ranke, Michelet, de Toqueville and Burckhardt) probes some of the implicit pre-critical grounds on which authors later built their theoretical constructs (White, 1973). He uses the notion of literary trope – metaphor, metonymy, synecdoche and irony – as the most appropriate way to describe an author's mode of "prefiguring" the historical field (cf. Jakobson, 1960; Levi-Strauss, 1966). Within any one of these major tropes, an author may achieve explanatory effect by combining logical argument, style of narrative, and ideological implication. He refers to Pepper's scheme of world hypotheses as "mode of argument", and adds two further considerations, viz., mode of employment in Romantic, Comic, Tragic, or Satirical style (cf. Frye,

1957; Burke, 1969) and mode of ideological implication in Anarchist, Radical, Conservative, or Liberal tone (cf. Mannheim, 1946). However one is to regard this juxtaposition of schemata, his conclusion is indeed plausible: "the best grounds for choosing one perspective on history rather than another are ultimately aesthetic or moral rather than epistemological" (White, 1973 xii, 426–434).

Meta-schemes, like Helicon, may be appealing for some and repulsive for others. White's theory of tropes raises provocative questions about disciplinary prose style and also about consistencies between ideology and root metaphor. It has been observed, for example, that radical arguments for societal change and/or rational reconstruction have often been couched in mechanistic language, and that conservative writers often emphasize the uniqueness of things and the randomness of events (White, 1973, 21). Both anarchists and conservatives have shown preferences for organicist conceptions of world reality. Romantic writers may play with varieties of Comedy and Tragedy, all of which are taboo to the Satirist (ibid., 7–11). At the meta-level, however, one is dealing with abstractions and a style of reading texts which still bears the stamp of *Herrschaftswissen*: they will no doubt reflect back whatever one's a priori curiosities pose to them.

To review permutations and combinations of symbolic, aesthetic, and ideological features of Western geography serves only to re-iterate the more fundamental issue of contrasting and hostile world views and does not necessarily lead to mutual understanding. But metaphor, however faded, can point beyond itself. If one were to read those same texts hermeneutically, the language and nature of interpretations might also become more emancipated. Imaginations could be directed toward those mythical and cosmological sources from which conventional explanations of reality spring. If one were to discern those Greek and Vedic sources of our four root metaphors perhaps one could more readily understand the enduring hold of Helicon on Western thought. One might then appreciate why so many contemporary humanists stake their orthodoxy claims on citations from Graeco-Roman and Enlightenment myths of humanness, and their doggedly hostile attitudes toward science and technology.

Is it not time one moved beyond the faded metaphors and jaded jargon of Helicon? Instead of breast-beating over the fragmentation of expertise, and tiresome *mea culpa* on the Midas touch of applied science and technology, why not instead seek new metaphors, revive or discover other values to guide humanity's relationship to earth and world? Could the encounter with *terrae incognitae* not be an occasion for such discovery and emancipation from those technical interpretations of thought which have been cultivated in the West since Socratic times (Gadamer, 1975; Heidegger, 1971). In the journey itself we may discover a world as "event" rather than "picture", in the encounter with contrasting myths/values we may learn how to discover the world.

The root metaphor approach can, I believe, afford an opening for this journey. It can help elucidate some of the connections between descriptive and normative practice, and thus help us transcend some of the impasses of communication between generations and practitioners of different styles at this moment in geography. It can also affirm a plurality of potential stances on the diversity of geographical experience by affording an opportunity to observe simultaneously the social, epistemological, and material contexts in which certain type of consenses have been reached within the discipline. And if we succeed in reaching some clarity on our own taken-for-granted traditions in the West, perhaps we may then be in a better position to ask about the root metaphors and myths of other civilizations.

Hur skall världen se ut? Who knows, the question we may be able to discuss with other civilizations is Hur skall världen vara?

References

Barrett, W., 1958: *Irrational Man*. Doubleday, New York.

Berry, B. J. L., 1964: Approaches to regional analysis: A synthesis. *Annals of the Association of American Geographers*, 54, pp. 2–11.

Berry, B. J. L. and R. E. Horton, 1970: *Geographic Perspectives on Urban Systems*. Prentice Hall, Englewood, N.J.

Black, M., 1962: *Models* and *Metaphors*. Cornell University Press, Ithaca.

Boulding, K., 1965: General systems theory – the skeleton of science. *Management Science*, 2, pp. 197–208.

1980: Science: Our common heritage, *Science*, 207, pp. 831–836.

Burke, K., 1969: *A Grammar of Motives*. University of California Press, Berkeley, Cal.

Buttimer, A., 1981: Socialité et temps vécu. *Temps Libre*, 3. pp. 69–86.

Cassirer, E., 1946: *Language and Myth*. Harper & Bros, New York.

1955: *Philosophy of Symbolic Forms*. Yale University Press, New Haven, Conn.

Castells, M., 1977: *The Urban Question*. Edward Arnold, London.

Claval, P., 1980: *Les mythes fondateurs des sciences sociales*. Presses Universitaires de France, Paris.

1981: Methodology and geography, *Progress in Human Geography*, 5, pp. 97–104.

Clay, G., 1974: *Close-Up: How to Read the American City*. Doubleday, New York.

Davidson, D., 1979: What metaphors mean, in Sacks, S. (ed.) *On Metaphor*, University of Chicago Press, Chicago and London, pp. 29–46.

Davies, W. K. D., 1972: *The Conceptual Revolution in Geography*. Rowman and Littlefield, New Jersey.

Dewey, J., 1925: *Experience and Nature*. Open Court, Chicago.

De Geer, S., 1923: On the definition, method, and classification of geography, *Geografiska Annaler*, 5, pp. 1–37.

de Jong, G., 1955: *Het karakter van de geografische totaliteit*. J. B. Wolters, Groningen. Translated (1962) as *Chorological Differentiation as the Fundamental Principle of Geography*. J. B. Wolters, Groningen.

Doctorow, E. L., 1977: False documents, *American Review*, 29, pp. 231–232.

Duncan, J. S., 1980: The superorganic in American cultural geography, *Annals of the Association of American Geographers*, 70, 2, pp. 181–198.

Eliot Hurst, M. E., 1975: *I came to the City. Essays and Comments on the Urban Scene*. Houghton-Mifflin, Boston.

Feyerabend, P., 1961: *Knowledge Without Foundations*. Oberlin College Press, Oberlin, Ohio.

Feyerabend, P., 1962: Problems of microphysics, in Colodny, R. G. (ed.) (1964) *Frontiers of Science and Philosophy*, George Allen & Unwin Ltd., London, pp. 189–284.

Firey, W., 1960: *Man, Mind and Land*. Free Press, Glencoe, III.
Foucault, M., 1969: *L'archéologie du savoir*. Gallimard, Paris.
1977: *Language, Counter-Memory, Practice*. Basil Blackwells', Oxford.
Frye, N., 1957: *The Anatomy of Criticism. Four Essays*. Princeton University Press, Princeton, N.J.
Gadamer, H.G., 1975: *Truth and Method*. Seabury Press, New York.
Gale, S. and G. Olsson, (eds.), 1979: *Philosophy in Geography*, Reidel, Dordrecht.
Galtung, J., 1981: Sivilisasjon, kosmologi, fred og utvikling. *Det Norske Videnskapsakademi Årsbok*, pp. 130–153.
Glacken, C., 1968: *Traces on the Rhodian Shore*. University of California Press, Barkeley, Cal.
Gregory, D., 1978: *Ideology, Science, and Human Geography*. Hutchinson, London.
Habermas, J., 1968: *Knowledge and Human Interests*. Beacon Press, Boston.
1979: *Communication and the Evolution of Society*. Beacon Press, Boston.
Haggett, P., 1965: *Locational Analysis in Human Geography*. Edward Arnold, London.
Hartshorne, R., 1939: *The Nature of Geography: A Critical Survey of Current Thought in the Light of the Past*. Association of American Geographers, Lancaster, Pa.
Harvey, D., 1972: Revolutionary and counter-revolutionary theory in geography and the problem of Ghetto-formation, *Antipode*, 4, pp. 1–12.
1973: *Social Justice and the City*. Edward Arnold, London.
Hägerstrand, T., 1975: Survival and arena. On the life-history of individuals in relation to their geographical environment, *Monadnock*, 49, pp. 9–27.
Heidegger, M., 1971: Letter on humanism, translated and reprinted in Languilli, N. (ed.) *The Existentialist Tradition: Selected Writings*. Anchor Books, New York, pp. 205–248.
Hettner, A., 1927: *Die Geographie: ihre Geschichte, ihre Wesen und ihre Methoden*. F. Hirt, Beslau.
Herbertson, A. J., 1905: The major natural regions: An essay in systematic geography, *Geographical Journal*, 25, pp. 3–12.
Howard, E., 1897, 1951: *Garden Cities for Tomorrow*. Faber, London.
Jacobs, J., 1961: *The Death and Life of Great American Cities*. Vintage Books, New York.
Jakobson, R., 1960: Linguistics and poetics, in Seboek, Thomas A. (ed.) *Style in Language*. Technology Press of M. I. T., Cambridge, Mass.
James, W., 1922, 1940: *Pragmatism*. Longmans' Green Co, London.
James, P. E. and G. Martin, 1979: *The Association of American Geographers: The First Seventy Five Years*, Association of American Geographers, Washington, D.C.
Leatherdale, W. H., 1974: *The Role of Analogy, Model, and Metaphor in Science*. North Holland Publishing Company, Amsterdam and Oxford.
Levi-Strauss, C., 1966: *The Savage Mind*. Weidenfeld and Nicholson, London.
Livingstone, D. and R. T. Harrison, 1981: Meaning through metaphor: Analogy as epistemology, *Annals of the Association of American Geographers*, 71, pp. 95–107.
Lowenthal, D and M. J. Bowden, (eds.) 1976: *Geographies of the Mind*. Oxford University Press, New York.
Lowenthal, D., 1961: Geography, experience and imagination: Towards a geography epistemology. *Annals of the Association of American Geographers*, 51, pp. 241–260.
Mayer, H., 1954: Geographers in city and regional planning, *Professional Geographer*, 6, pp. 7–12.
Meier, R. L., 1960: *A Communications Theory of Urban Growth*. M. I. T. Press, Cambridge, Mass.
Mannheim, K., 1946: *Ideology and Utopia: An Introduction to the Sociology of Knowledge*. Harcourt Brace and World, New York.
Merleau-Ponty, M., 1973: *The Prose of the World*. Northwestern University Press, Evanston, Ill.

Moore, G. and R. G. Golledge, (eds.) 1976: *Environmental Knowing: Theories, Research, and Methods*. Hutchinson and Ross, Stroudsburg, Penn.
Morgan, G., 1980: Paradigms, metaphors, and puzzle-solving in organization theory. *Administrative Science Quarterly*, 25, pp. 605–622.
Morse, P.M. and G. E. Komball, 1951: *Methods of Operations Research*. J. Wiley & Sons, Inc., New York.
Murphy, R., 1966: *The American City. An Urban Geography*. McGraw Hill, New York.
Nakamura, H., 1980: The idea of nature East and West, Encyclopedia Brittanica: *The Great Ideas Today*, pp. 235–304.
Newman, O., 1973: *Defensible Space: Crime Prevention Through Urban Design*: Collier, New York.
Norberg-Schulz, C., 1971: *Existence, Space*, and *Architecture*. Praeger, New York.
Olsson, G., 1979: Social science and human action, or hitting your head against the ceiling of language, in Gale, S. and G. Olsson (eds.), (op. cit. 1979) pp. 287–308.
Park, R. E. and E. Rugess, 1925: *The City*. University of Chicago Press, Chicago.
Peet, R., 1977: The development of radical geography in the United States, *Progress in Human Geography*, 1, pp. 240–263.
Pepper, S., 1942: *World Hypotheses*. University of California Press, Berkeley, Cal.
Popper, K. R., 1961: *The Poverty of Historicism*. Routledge & Kegan Paul, London.
Ricoeur, P., 1975: *La metaphore vive*. Seuil, Paris. Translated (1977) as *The Rule of Metaphor*, University of Toronto Press, Buffalo and Toronto.
1978: The metaphorical process as cognition, imagination, and feeling, in Sacks, (ed.) op. cit., pp. 141–158.
Rorty, R., 1979: *Philosophy and the Mirror of Nature*. Princeton University Press, Princeton, N.J.
Sack, R., 1980: Conceptions of geographic space, *Progress in Human Geography*, 4, pp. 315–345.
Sacks, S., ed., 1978: *On Metaphor*. University of Chicago Press, New York and London.
Schrag, C.O., 1980: *Radical Reflection and the Origin of the Human Sciences*. Purdue University Press.
Schütz, A., 1973: *Structures of the Life World*. Northwestern University Press, Evanston, Ill.
Shibles, W. A., 1971: *Metaphor: An Annotated Bibliography and History*. Whitewater, Wis.
Smith, N., 1979: Geography, science, and post-positivist modes of explanation, *Progress in Human Geography*, 3, pp. 357–383.
Stoddart, D. R., 1967: Organism and ecosystem as geographical models, in Chorley, R. J. and P. Haggett (eds.) *Models in Geography*. Methuen, London, pp. 511–548.
Thomas, W. L., ed. 1956: *Man's Role in Changing the Face of the Earth*. University of Chicago Press, Chicago.
Törnquist, G., 1981: Om arenan och system, *Svensk Geografisk Årsbok*, 57, pp. 209–222.
Tuan, Yi-fu, 1977: *Space* and *Place: The Perspective of Experience*. University of Minnesota Press, Minneapolis.
Vidal de la Blache, P., 1922: *Principes de géographie humaine*. Colin, Paris. Translated as *Principles of Human Geography*. Henry Holt, New York.
von Bertalanffy, L., 1968: *General Systems Theory*. Braziller, New York.
von Humboldt, A., (1845–62) *Kosmos. Entwurf einer physischen Weltbeschreibung*. Cotta, Stuttgart and Tübingen. Translated as *Cosmos: Sketch of a Physical Description of the Universe*, 4 vols.
William-Olsson, W., 1975: Vår världsbild, *Ymer*, 95, pp. 174–188.
White, H., 1973: *Metahistory. The Historical Imagination in Nineteenth Century Europe*. John Hopkins Press, Baltimore, Md.

Wittgenstein, L., 1960: *Philosophical Investigations.* Basil Blackwells', Oxford.
1969: *On Certainty.* Basil Blackwells', Oxford.
Wright, J. K., 1947: Terrae incognitae: The place of the imagination in geography, *Annals of the Association of American Geographers*, 37, pp. 1–15.
1966: *Human Nature in Geography. Fourteen Papers. 1925–1965.* Harvard University Press, Cambridge, Mass.

4

INSTITUTIONALIZATION OF GEOGRAPHY AND STRATEGIES OF CHANGE

Horacio Capel

While Johnston (**chapter 2**) addresses the internal battles of geography over paradigms, the Spanish geographer Horacio Capel delves into the external and institutional struggles of the discipline to establish itself in the academic division of labour. He argues that geography was in decline in the mid-nineteenth century and owed its revival to the need to produce geography teachers. The mushrooming of school geography, in turn, reflected the desire of European states to spread nationalist sentiments among their populations and to inform them of the possibilities provided by colonial empires. Capel provides statistical evidence of the role played by geographical societies in this process. He also details the various strategies by which societies and key individuals fought against other disciplines – notably geology, geophysics, cartography and meteorology – to create a cognitive and institutional space for geography. Since there was no essential discipline called geography, these parties had to lay claims for its conceptual territory. Reviewing the foundation of geography in France, Germany, Britain, the USA and Russia, Capel identifies common strategies. These include its appeals to scientific value, its utility and its distinctiveness from other disciplines. Although Capel concentrates on the late nineteenth century, this same struggle for academic territory is evident today. The readings in Part II can be interpreted as such claims for disciplinary space.

Source: Institutionalization of geography and strategies of change. In Stoddart, D. R., editor, *Geography, ideology and social concern*. Oxford: Basil Blackwell, pp. 37–69, 1981.

One of the characteristic traits of current social science is the generalized awareness of crisis and, in particular, the crisis of existing disciplinary divisions.[1] The unsatisfactory character of the acknowledged limits between the distinct scientific specialities is revealed through the efforts made within each discipline to surpass these limits and incorporate theories, methods or points of view derived from

[1] This paper was translated from Spanish into English by Kirk Mattson.

neighbouring disciplines, thus establishing connections that until recently were totally unsuspected. The recent evolution of our science after the discovery of the wide field of perception and behavioural geography, and the establishment of connections between geography and psychology are examples of the above, among others which could be cited.

It is increasingly evident that a reorganization of the fields of knowledge and of the limits between distinct specialized branches of the science is taking place. Some scientists believe that it is necessary to combine many existing branches of science with a view towards a reorganization of the disciplinary fields, to make possible a freer, more imaginative scientific viewpoint in the solution of concrete problems.

In such a situation, the study of the process of institutionalization of the sciences may prove particularly fruitful. If we can come to understand the factors that lead to the institutionalization of some sciences and the failure of the embryonic sciences that could facilitate alternative frameworks of scientific development, perhaps we would be able to understand their later evolution and proceed more easily to a reorganization of the fields of knowledge.

From this perspective, an investigation of the process of institutionalization of geography, and of the appearance of the scientific community of geographers, is particularly interesting. But the analysis of the origins and evolution of this science and the history of geographic thought must not be done apologetically – as is common in the histories of geography and, in fact, in the greater part of the histories of the different sciences – but rather set forth general problems relevant to the distinct social sciences, to which geographers can contribute the knowledge and experience of their own science.

The essential argument of this paper can be summarized thus: despite the antiquity of the term 'geography', the geography of the twentieth century has little to do with that of the nineteenth. Today's geography has its origins in the process of institutionalization that from the mid nineteenth century, and after a period of decline, leads to the appearance of the scientific community of geographers, extending without interruption to the present time. The factors which lead to the institutionalized existence of this community are directly related to the presence of geography in primary and secondary education at the time when the European countries begin the rapid process of diffusion of elementary education; the necessity to train geography teachers for primary and middle schools was the essential factor which led to the institutionalization of geography in the university and the appearance of the scientific community of geographers.

The emergence of the community depended upon the support of governments, geographical societies and of some scientists, and met with violent opposition from a good number of scientists from other fields. In the struggle for recognition, the members of the new community (whom we shall call geographers) had to strive to demonstrate the specific character of their science, arguing its objective and defining its limits with respect to the sciences practised by other scientific communities (geologists, historians, ethnographers, ecologists, sociologists, etc.). Later, the growth of the community and/or the blockage of traditional teaching careers – as a result of, for example, the competition of naturalists and historians in secondary education – led to the search for new professional opportunities for the members of the community; this influenced the appearance of new directions in the discipline and their corresponding theoretical justifications. The members of the scientific community of geographers possessed, thus, some specific interests and objectives; as a result some very coherent and permanent strategies can be found in the scientific texts produced by the community. This paper will demonstrate some of these strategies, analysing the process of institutionalization and the theoretical writings of some national communities of geographers. The necessity to introduce the perspective of the sociology of science in the study of the history of geographical thought is defended as a complement to other, now more usual approaches.

The Decline of a Science

The most specifically geographical texts produced during the first two centuries of the Modern age were either geographies or cosmographies that followed the Ptolemaic conception and constituted, in essence, a localization of toponyms for the use of navigators and astronomers, or descriptive geographies that contained narrations on the characteristics of the lands, customs and social organization of different countries, and that responded to the interest and curiosity of a wide public.

The *Geographia Generalis* of Varenius (1650) represented an attempt to develop a general geography that would permit the subject to be considered a science, and would facilitate the later development of regional or special studies. For Varenius, this general geography, which 'considers the earth in its entirety', was solely physical, mathematical and astronomical, while the human phenomena, which he affirmed as 'less pertinent to geography', entered into consideration only in the study of regions, and only then because, as he wrote, 'something must be conceded to the habit and usefulness of those that study geography' (Capel, 1974).

During the Modern age there frequently existed an instrumental and practical relationship between history and geography, particularly in their chorographical aspects. Geography and chronology were considered the basic columns of history, so that geography became an auxiliary science of history. This union between geography and history, based upon tradition and practical considerations, was elevated to the theoretical level towards the end of the eighteenth century by Kant, who considered that the two sciences are separated in the scientific system because they study unique phenomena in time, or in space. 'History and Geography', writes Kant, 'could be denominated thus, as description, with the difference that the first is a description in time and the second a description in space' (Schaefer, 1953).

In the European centres of higher education, the relationship between geography and history was close until well into the nineteenth century, and on many occasions geography was considered a simple auxiliary of history, as demonstrated by the existence of professors of geography and chronology in some universities as late as the middle of the century. And, in a way, it is to this relationship that is owed the geography of K. Ritter, considered one of the fathers of modern geographical science. When the University of Berlin, founded in 1810, called on Ritter as professor of geography, he still could not decide between the one subject and the other (having been professor of history at Frankfurt). Ritter was, of course, a geographer through his university activities as such, but his interests lie as much in history as in geography.

A case very distinct from Ritter's is that of A. von Humboldt, who can only with difficulty be considered a geographer in the strict sense of the word. Undoubtedly he consciously tried to create an earth science, the physics of the globe, in which he was influenced by the ideas about the unity of nature dominant in the Germany of his youth and particularly by the thought of Goethe (Beck, 1959–61). It is this unitary conception which led him to make observations in such diverse fields and which, without doubt, is at the root of his voyage to America. He considered this to be something more than a scientific expedition with first rate astronomical instruments; as he says in a letter written the day of his departure for America:

> *All of this is not, however, the principal objective of my journey. My eyes must always be fixed upon the combined action of the forces, the influences of inanimate creation upon the animal and vegetal world, upon this harmony. (Letter to Von Moll, 5 June 1799, cited by Minguet, 1969, 61)*

It is an idea that he maintained all his life, and that motivated the production of such different works as the 'Historical relation of the voyage to the equatorial regions of the new continent' (1818) – where he affirms that

> *the major problem of the Physics of the world is to determine . . . the external bonds that connect the life phenomena to those of inanimate nature*

– or the great work of his maturity, the *Cosmos*. Hence came the variety and richness of his observations, from geomagnetism to archaeology, and thus his work may be viewed as the foundation of diverse specialized sciences such as botany, meteorology, and geophysics. Humboldt was, above all, a naturalist of a rigorous scientific spirit and a defender of the empirical method, but imbued with the natural philosophy and the romantic ideas of his era. His work was valued by all interested in the earth sciences, and by 'geographers' of the epoch, essentially through geographical societies with a naturalist membership of botanists and geologists such as Murchison or Somerville.

Despite the existence of such a figure as Ritter, numerous accounts show that in all Europe, geography was a science in profound crisis and even upon the point of disappearance during the first half of the nineteenth century. This occurred as much in its academic status as in its popular esteem.

1. In Germany, the historians of geography habitually point out that the ten years that followed the death of Humboldt was a decade of crisis. Kretschmer (1930) has written that after the death of Humboldt in 1859 came 'a period of paralysation': 'Grand person-

alities did not exist, nor were there, properly speaking, schools; the seventh decade of the century forms a gap in the constant development of geography, a vacuum only interrupted by a few sensational discoveries.' This point of view is shared by Hettner (1898) and following him, Hartshorne (1959, 29). A similar opinion is held by Paul Claval (1974), alluding explicitly to the crisis of 1860–70, and by G. R. Crone (1970, 32) who indicates that 'after the death of Ritter, the impetus given by him gradually died away and for a time geographical theory received little attention in Germany.'

2. In France during the first two thirds of the nineteenth century, geography passed through a profound crisis, contrasting with the great development of the science in the preceding centuries. Contrary to the high esteem it enjoyed during the eighteenth century, and contrary to the awareness of its usefulness for navigation and commerce – translated into schemes such as the creation of a Geographical Museum during the Revolution (Broc, 1974) – the nineteenth century represents a 'long purgatory' which 'is aided by a recess of curiosity, a true regression' (Broc, 1974, 25). The accounts of this regression are varied, and some have been put together by Numa Broc (1976, 227) who insists that 'in the first half of the nineteenth century, geography does not enjoy high consideration', and demonstrates how the best-known geographers of the epoch, such as Malte-Brun and Balbi, scientists and public authorities considered geography a 'descriptive science', 'of facts and not of speculation', 'of the exclusive dominion of the memory', a science, in short, 'that must not try to go back to the cause and to explain', because 'although these be speculations of great importance, they are outside the domain of geography' (Broc, 1976, 227–8). After analysing these accounts, Broc concludes that for most of the authors cited, 'geography is not a science . . . but simply a practical discipline, appropriate for supplying the diplomat, the soldier, the merchant, with immediately useful information. In the schools it was considered no more than one of the "two eyes of history", beside chronology' (Broc, 229). Proof also of this slight esteem is the fact that in the logical classifications of science from the end of the eighteenth century, geography disappears or is found divided: 'nowhere appears the idea that the characteristic of geography could be, precisely, to integrate the physical and political facts' (Broc, 1976, 230).

In fact geography was studied alongside history, and provided the background necessary to understand historical events, principally of classical history. Thus it happened that the only university professorship in geography that existed at the Sorbonne from 1809 (under the title Geography and History till 1812) was occupied by historians, who according to L. Dussieux in 1883, confined themselves 'with a pedantic solemnity to the geography of Homer and of Herodotus' (cited by Broc, 1976, 225).

At the popular level geography had some impact through the publication of geographical encyclopaedias and informative magazines for the general public. The work of the Danish Malte-Brun, *Précis de Géographie Universelle* (1810–29) constituted, in this sense, the fundamental geographical work for many years. The curiosity of the general public for the exotic countries reflects itself above all in enterprises of illustrated journalism like the *Journal des Voyages* created by Malte-Brun in 1808 (Meynier, 1969), or *La Tour du Monde* or the *Lectures Géographiques*, to cite a few of the more expressive titles.

The works of Humboldt and Ritter did not have immediate impact, despite the fact that the former lived for a time in Paris, published much of his research in French, maintained throughout his life an intense exchange of letters with French scientists, especially with Arago, and influenced the creation of the Geographical Society of Paris (1821). One can, however, indicate one work comparable to that of Humboldt's *Cosmos* in Eugène Cortambert's *Physiographie: Description générale de la nature pour servir d'introduction aux sciences géographiques* (1836), in which the author tried to combine 'the general notions isolated in the special treatises of geology, geography, botany and meteorology.' With this work, Cortambert anticipated ideas of the *Cosmos* (Freeman, 1961, 32), although in a lesser way, permitting Broc to qualify this work as a 'poor man's *Cosmos*' (Broc, 1976, 229).

3. In Great Britain geography also seems to enter into crisis during the first half of the nineteenth century, above all from the fourth decade on. At the University of Oxford, geography had been taught from the sixteenth century to the eighteenth, 'but the changes in the educational system of the university led to the decline of geography in the nineteenth century' (Scargill, 1976, 440). In fact, in the first half of the century, courses in mathematical geography were given at only one college 'for a small audience' and among historians 'geography hardly received better treatment'. The reorganization of the course outlines in 1850 made possible the reconsideration of geography, theoretically, now that it had 'confirmed itself in its old place in classical studies and was made reference to in the regulations for the natural sciences (in the form of physical geography) and for modern history' (Scargill, 1976, 440). But the professorships remained unoccupied, and geography continued undeveloped.

In London, in 1833, a professorship in geography at University College was established, awarded to Captain Maconochie, then secretary of the Royal Geographical Society. But the post was occupied for only a short time, as its holder left for overseas, and it remained vacant because geography 'does not seem to be considered a part of general education. Not even the acknowledged distinction of the late Professor could obtain a numerous class' (cited by Crone, 1970, 28).

During the first half of the nineteenth century, the distinct branches of the natural sciences developed so much more rapidly than geography, that the latter, particularly physical geography, came to be considered part of one of these disciplines. Very significant, in this respect, is the change in section 'C' of the British Association, which was originally entitled 'Geography and Geology' but was changed to 'Geology and Physical Geography' in 1839. Later, however, in 1851, the section 'Geography and Ethnology' was created and survived until 1878 (Baker, 1948; cited by Freeman, 1961, 38).

The close relationship between physical geography and geology is revealed in the work of R. I. Murchison (1792–1871), a geologist of international repute and director of the Museum of Applied Geology, who was one of the founders of the Royal Geographical Society and later its president. Throughout his life, Murchison considered physical geography and geology as two 'inseparable scientific twins' and held a view of geography that would hardly be shared by today's community of geographers: on one hand he valued above all the *Cosmos* of Humboldt and on the other, considered Ritter rather as a historian (Crone, 1970, 30).

The need to establish relationships between separate phenomena, as shown by Humboldt in Germany, appears explicitly in the work of Mary Somerville (1780–1872), considered 'the first English geographer, by publishing the first textbook on physical geography written in English' (Sanderson, 1974, 410). In 1836 she published a work on the connection between the different physical sciences, and in 1848 her famous *Physical Geography*, which had been through seven editions by 1877. The work is inspired by the same spirit as Humboldt's, as shown by Somerville's use of Bacon's aphorism: 'no natural phenomena may be studied by itself, but, to be understood, must be considered in connection with all of nature.' The same point is demonstrated by her definition of physical geography as 'the description of the earth, the sea and the air, with its animal and vegetable inhabitants, of the distribution of these organized beings and the causes of this distribution' (cited by Sanderson, 1974). The inclusion of man in works of physical geography was a common practice in the epoch and persisted occasionally until the end of the nineteenth century, although 'there was no a clear conception of what a "geography of man" should embrace apart from the "distributions"' (Dickinson, 1976, 12).

4. The situation of geography in Italy during the first half of the nineteenth century was not very brilliant either. Geography was, in fact, during these years, simply an adjunct to history. Towards the end of the century C. Bertacchi alludes clearly to this fact, writing of:

a time in which geography was considered almost a dependency of history, and did not have value other than as illustration of the historical facts. Thus, as Chronology demonstrates the distribution of facts in time, Geography, which we will call more specifically historical, demonstrates their distribution in space. Yesterday's geography was, before all, an historical geography, that extended to the present has converted itself into political and statistical geography. (Bertacchi, 1892, 571)

The names which the Italian geographical histories customarily cite as principal figures of this epoch (Adriano Balbi, Emanuelle Repetti, Marmochi, De la Luca, Zucagni Orlandini) were not really specialized geographers, but authors who could belong to various social sciences. This shows that in mid-century Italy 'geography does not appear well individualized as a science' (Almagìa, 1961, 419), while Pracchi (1964, 575) considers that if one examines publications in this country between 1800 and 1890, one observes that 'during the greater part of the century, a vague and uncertain concept of geography dominated ... always intertwining itself with history, statistics or with other disciplines.'

Among the Italian scientists of the epoch, geography does not seem to have been held in high esteem. Thus, although in the congress of Italian scientists held in Milan in 1844 an autonomous section for geography was created, through the influence of A. Balbi, this autonomy 'disappeared in successive congresses, and geography was again associated with other sciences, above all those of the statistical-historical type or simply humanistic'. This explains why the Casati law of 1859 placed geography among the disciplines of the Faculty of Arts (Almagìa, 1961, 420). Everything seems to indicate that during the greater part of the nineteenth century, geography in Italy was for the most part a little valued subject of 'Arts'. As late as 1892, C. Bertacchi could give himself the objective of 'stripping this science of the character of literary exercise that until now it has been given in most of our schools', since 'a geography like this has no reason to exist'; and he could refer to the case of 'a well known personality who had declared jokingly that he did not "believe" in geography' or that of a politician who considered geography 'among the useless literaries' (Bertacchi, 1892, 572).

5. Russian geography had been forged during the eighteenth century through the expeditions organized for the study of the resources of an immense, little known country. In this sense, the expansionist politics of the Czars during the eighteenth and nineteenth centuries constituted an essential factor that led to the organization of a systematic plan of exploration. M. V. Lomonosov, director from 1758 of the department of geography of the Academy of Science of St. Petersburg, worked on this project in the last year of his life, and it was according to his plan that the important expeditions of the Academy (1768–74) were organized. The department of geography of the Academy played an important role in the collection of information and cartographic systematization and elaboration until the 1860s; but from this date, the creation of specialized organizations (like the official land registry, the cartographic services of the army and navy) made it

> lose importance. It was abolished in 1800, at the same time as were created sections of the social sciences (statistics, political economy, history). The Academy of Science continued organizing scientific expeditions during the nineteenth century, which contributed greatly to knowledge of the Russian territory and the development of the earth sciences, but it was the more specialized scientists, not geographers, who played the essential roles.
>
> From mid-century the Russian Geographical Society, founded in 1845, actively contributed to the organization of expeditions, as well as to the study of theoretical questions, man-nature relations (a theme accredited to K. M. Behr) and the study and fixing of the geographical terminology (Valskaya, 1976, 50). It was also important as a vehicle of new ideas through exchanges and discussions with other European centres and scientists (Matveyeva, 1976).
>
> Despite all this, during the first half of the nineteenth century geographers as such did not exist in Russia (Sukhova, 1976, 64), and it was other specialists (geologists, biologists, botanists) who made the most important contributions which today are collected in the geographical histories and who, in particular, studied the problem of the relations between natural phenomena (Sukhova, 1976).
>
> It was also these 'naturalist specialists' who accepted and utilized in the first place, from 1860, the ideas of Darwin (like those of Lyell before him) and contributed to the adoption of a new perspective for the study of the interdependencies between phenomena upon the surface of the earth. In particular, the biologists (botanists and zoologists) concentrated upon the study of interaction and also 'made attempts at biogeographical and zoogeographical spatial divisions, using such terms 'when such a notion did not exist in geography' (Sukhova, 1976, 64), smoothing the way for the development of the work and ideas of another naturalist, V. V. Dokuchayev, on genetic pedology.
>
> With regard to human and economic geography, during the nineteenth century 'it did not exist' (Gerasimov, 1976, 103). Their subject matter was studied in statistics – from 1804, departments of geography and statistics existed at the university according to Gerasimov (1976, 91) – and towards the end of the century in economics and political economy. In fact, it could be said that 'the military-statistical descriptions made by the General Staff were perhaps the nearest things to the economic-geographical investigations at that time' (Gerasimov, 1976, 103).

These accounts all demonstrate the profound decline of geographical science during the first half of the nineteenth century. In them, geography frequently appears as a science on the point of disappearance, lacking academic interest – except for historians – forgotten or impugned by many scientists and appreciated solely by the general public because of the descriptions of exotic countries that it contained.

The decline of geography is comprehensible if we take into account that the first half of the nineteenth century is a time in which a series of sciences that deepened the study of our planet were emerging. What Humboldt called the 'Physics of the globe' or 'Theory of the earth' was developing into a series of specialized scientific branches and began a process of institutionalization and professionalization. The economic transformations experienced in Europe to the middle of the eighteenth century, and especially the industrial revolution, pushed the earth sciences in new directions and provoked unprecedented scientific development. While in earlier epochs, maritime commerce had stimulated the development of science, the needs of industry now promoted diverse scientific branches. The exploitation of new mineral resources and the opening of new means of terrestrial transport (canals, roads, and railways) strongly promoted the development of geology, particularly in the period 1775–1825, when geology began to be considered worthy of specialized scientific study, and thus appeared the profession of geologist (Hall, 1976, 211, 232). The publication of Lyell's *Principles of Geology* (1830–36) was a decisive step in the development of geology, Lyell's definition of which doubtlessly affected geography, since it occupied a field which geography could pretend – and in fact, later claimed – to occupy. Geology is defined as a

> *science which investigates the successive changes that have taken place in the organic and inorganic kingdoms of nature; it enquires into the causes of these changes and the influence which they have exerted in modifying the surface and internal structure of our planet. (Lyell, 1830; cited by Hall, 1976, 234)*

In a parallel direction, geophysics began to emerge from Physics and the study of geomagnetism received a strong impulse from the development of maritime navigation and the introduction of iron-clad ships. At the same time there developed international cooperation – for example, the creation of the Magnetic Union of Göttingen, organized by F. Gauss in 1834, at the instigation of A. von Humboldt – and the profession of geophysicist, operating the network of observatories created from 1840 (Hall, 1976, 252).

Cartographic studies became a specialized scientific field because of their importance in exploration for resources and in navigation; geodesy also received a strong impulse, and the exact determinations of gravity and curvature became a basic prerequisite for adequate mapping. Mineralogical investigations led physicists and geologists to lively discussion of the problem of the earth's interior (Hall, 1976, 262). The organization of national networks of meteorological stations gave a clear impetus to the study of meteorology and climatology, but one made by specialists, not geographers. In another related direction, botanists and zoologists were modifying their old taxonomies before the appearance of new ideas that would result in the Darwinian revolution. And an equally rapid evolution is found in the field of the sciences of man.

In this emergent phase of the specialized scientific branches, the problems of articulation of distinct knowledge ceased when the unitary conception of nature with its idealist roots entered into crisis. Thus, as Dickinson has indicated (following G. R. Crone):

> *the study of the earth's surface forms as an integrated field was divided among the various sciences that sought to examine processes by reference to individual categories of earthbound phenomena. The concept of natural unities (*Länder*) together with their people, as envisaged by Forster and Pallas and developed by Humboldt and Ritter, was neglected by the scientists. (Dickinson, 1969, 52; Crone, 1951, 1970, 32).*

These are the circumstances that explain the profound crisis of geography during the first half of the nineteenth century, a crisis that, despite some suggestions otherwise, also seems to be shown, as we will see, by the evolution of the geographical societies.

The Institutionalization of the 'New Geography'

In contrast to the sombre panorama presented towards the mid nineteenth century, fifty years later geography appears extraordinarily vigorous and expansive in many countries. It is taught in a great number of universities and is present in all primary and secondary education programmes; it receives theoretical contributions from an active community of scientists who edit specialized journals and attend national and international conferences, and are consciously practising a 'new geography'.

The contrast between these situations is striking, and raises questions about the factors which led to the institutionalization and development of a science which only fifty or sixty years before was scarcely appreciated, and about the measure of continuity between this 'new' geography and the 'old' science.

The diffusion of education during the nineteenth century

The essential factor that leads to the institutionalization of geography and the appearance of the scientific community of geographers is the presence of this science in primary and secondary education by the middle of the nineteenth century. The tradition of teaching children elementary notions about our planet through 'geography', and the old relationship between geography and history, probably contributed to the inclusion of the course 'geography' in primary and secondary education programmes, in a residual fashion and generally united with history, at the beginning of the process of diffusion of elementary education all over Europe.

During the nineteenth century, once the debates, frequent at the end of the eighteenth and early nineteenth centuries, on the advisability of teaching the 'inferior classes' were over (Cipolla, 1969), elementary education began to spread and its spectacular results constituted one of the most important social advances of contemporary history. Around 1850, half of the adult European population did not know how to read (60 per cent if one includes Russia), and another 25 or 30 per cent read badly or did not understand what they read; one hundred years later, the proportion of illiterate adults in Europe had been reduced to less than ten per cent (Cipolla, 1969).

The growth of the number of schoolchildren was considerable, as much in absolute terms as in relative. Many European countries doubled the number in the second half of the century. From mid-century to 1910, the number of schoolchildren grew by some 5 million in Germany, 4 million in Great Britain, 2.5 million in France and Italy and close to 1 million in Spain (see table 4.1).

Table 4.1 [orig. table 4.1] Extension of primary and secondary education in various European countries (number of students in thousands).

	Primary education				*Secondary education*				
	Germany	*France*	*Italy*	*Great Britain*	*Germany*	*France*	*Italy*		*Great Britain*
1850	–	3 322	–	2 100	–	47.9	–	–	
1860	–	4 437 (1865)	1 009 (1861)	–	–	55.9	15.8(1861)	–	
1870	4 100 (Prussia)	4 610 (1875)	1 605	3 100	–	73.9 (1875)	23.2	–	
1880	–	5 049	2 003	3 274	–	86.8	32.5	–	
1890	–	5 594	2 419	4 288	–	90.8	63.5	–	
1900	8 966	5 526	2 708	5 387	–	98.7	91.6	–	
1910	10 310	5 655	3 309	6 114	1 016	126.0		164.0	180.5

Source: Mitchell, B. R. 1975: *European historical statistics 1750–1950 (London), 749–70.*

For figures in italics, the source is Cipolla, C. 1969: *Literacy and development in the West* (Harmondsworth), table 12.

Table 4.2 [orig. table 4.2]
Extension of primary education in various European countries (number of teachers in thousands).

	Germany	*France*	*Italy*	*Great Britain*
1850		*60.0* (1837)		
1860		*109.0* (1863)	28.2	7.6 (not Scotland)
1870			41.0	16.8
1880		123.0	48.3	50.7
1890	*120.0*	146.0	59.0	86.6
1900	147.0	158.0	65.0	132.9
1910	187.0	157.0	72.8	184.0

Sources: as Table 4.1

This growth of schooling required a parallel increase in the number of teachers in public and private institutions (table 4.2). Some countries, such as Germany and France, made considerable progress in this direction in a very short time. In Germany, it was prohibited by law to give work to children younger than nine years who had not attended school for at least three years (Cipolla, 1969), and this greatly affected the creation of public schools. Hence it was in Germany (and in Switzerland) that there first appeared a general interest in educational questions. In France, a notable effort had been made in secondary education during the Napoleonic era, although only in 1833 was obligatory basic education established, charged to the municipalities with aid from the state. But it was not until the defeat of 1870 that a concern for the reorganization of teaching methods was felt. Other small European countries (Switzerland, Netherlands, Sweden) had a great number of public schools and teachers by the mid-nineteenth century. In Great Britain, on the other hand, the conditions of the industrial revolution meant that 'popular education remained stagnant (in the first decades of the nineteenth century), whilst the economy expanded and wealth mounted now that the proportion of disposable income destined to education diminished progressively. Accumulated wealth was more often employed in contracting growing masses of children in factories than in sending them to schools' (Cipolla, 1969). In Britain, education was still in the hands of the municipalities and parishes, or philanthropic societies that created the 'mutual education' of Bell and Lancaster. Only from the fourth or fifth decade was Great Britain conscious of the necessity to systematize education with state intervention. The relatively late state intervention in this country, in comparison with other European countries, would have an effect upon the process of institutionalization of some sciences and especially upon geography.

During the nineteenth century, the impact of the work of Enrico Pestalozzi (1746–1827) contributed to the spread throughout Europe of a concern for the change of pedagogical methods and for an active education, not a pedantic one, in which the child would substitute his own personal experience for books. Form (drawing and geometry), number (arithmetic) and name (language, vocabulary) were for Pestalozzi the basic elements of the effective 'intuition' of things: the study of the sciences, geometry, mathematics, drawing and language would be basic in the Pestalozzi centres. Along with these, contact with nature, clearly of Rousseauian and Physiocratic roots, became another of the basic principles of the new pedagogy, also prompted – accentuating the idea of the profound unity of the real – by the work of Friedrich Fröbel, the great pedagogue of German romanticism (Abbagnano and Visalberghi, 1957, 466–87). Both authors are found at the root of the development of the *Heimatkunde*, which had such an effect upon the teaching of geography.

Linked with the above currents, from the middle of the century, was the influence of positivism in pedagogy which led to an insistence on attentive and scrupulous observation, on experiment, and on the generalization of methods that proceeded from the particular to the general.

Geography, one of the sciences that traditionally formed part of the teaching programmes, was affected by this pedagogic innovation; through the practice of concerned teachers it became active education, centred upon observation. And, as a science which taught basic notions about our planet, it was particularly to incorporate these new ideas and apply them to the study of the home territory of the child, as a first stage in the study of the earth as a whole.

Geography was thus reinforcing its own position in the educational realm, and becoming a worthy subject for teaching programmes when state intervention and administrative centralization began to formalize these programmes, converting them into legal texts in the greater part of the European countries. The presence of geography in these programmes was also supported in secondary education by the traditional union of geography and history, and by the historians' interest in giving knowledge of the 'theatre' in which developed the historic acts.

Geography and nationalism

Despite enjoying the support of tradition and despite the innovation in teaching methods, geography had clear rivals that aspired to its function. The development in Great Britain around 1870 of the *Physiography* of Thomas Huxley, a naturalist who had felt the impact of the Darwinian revolution (Stoddart, 1975a), is a good example of this threat.

It is reasonable to imagine that during the nineteenth century, geography could have been displaced in primary and secondary education and been substituted by various social and natural sciences. Contrary to what one is accustomed to think, the permanence of geography in teaching programmes is by no means inevitable, and as we have seen, it was, in general, a science little esteemed by scientists during the first half of the nineteenth century and even later. The reasons why geography continued to figure in the programmes, despite the direct rivalry of other sciences which were not able to introduce themselves into basic education (one thinks of physiography or ecology, and in the social sciences economics or later sociology, a science of a strong development and high prestige), needs explanation.

Among the reasons that explain the triumph of geography over rival disciplines, there is one of great importance: the function assigned to geography in the shaping of a feeling of nationalism.

The development of European nationalism during the nineteenth century is related to innumerable factors (the influence of the French Revolution, romanticism, discontent among small agricultural landowners and the emerging middle class, etc.). It is evident, nevertheless, that to a great extent nationalism also coincides, above all after 1848, with the interests of the growing European bourgeoisie, at a time when national markets were united and the bourgeoisie began dismantling the structures of the old régime and of rationalization and homogenization of their respective territories of influence.

In the development of the feeling of nationality, the idea of 'patria', or knowledge of the history and geography of one's own country, was an indispensible element. 'One only loves what one knows' would be an idea shared by politicians and pedagogues. This explains why both sciences could enter the basic education programmes with the strong support of the state, in that their presence corresponded with political interests.

Geography fulfilled a role which – like that of history – was absolutely essential in the epoch of the appearance of the European nationalism. And it fulfilled it not only through teaching, transmitting to the populace ideas of the 'unity within diversity' of the national territory, but also by way of 'scientific' and popular works about their countries, works whose suggestive titles (like *La Patria*) left little doubt about their objectives. When, in the second half of the century, geographers began to consider their science as a discipline concerned with the relations between man and environment, the magnification of the ties and dependencies that united man and territory would only reinforce the role of geography.

Thus, geography, during the second half of the nineteenth century, increasingly developed into a science at the service of governmental interests, of the nationalist European bourgeoisie, who gave generous support to successive ministries of public education. Despite this support, the official geography (there also existed a marginal geography) created a new group of adversaries: those who advocated the suppression of frontiers and international solidarity. The following passage of the geographer Marcel Dubois, delivered at the Sorbonne in the presence of eminent French officials during the inaugural lecture of the colonial geography course in 1893, is sufficiently clear in this respect.

> *I know that there exists a group, happily small, of historians that with difficulty pardon geography the fact that it marks a link between man and the soil, because this same idea of localization, of mutual influence, is something similar to the idea of 'patria', upon which they have declared war. Doubtlessly, geography molests their propaganda; because the chimera of the suppression of frontiers and homelands collides with the reality of the causes that keep groups of men separate. Because in reality, geography has the bad, although I would prefer to say the good, fortune to obstruct the path of these declared or dissimulated enemies of the idea of 'patria'. They have sworn to demonstrate that a certain sociology could completely substitute the role of geography; because they need, for their combinations that have nothing to do with science, an abstract man, always the same, removed from the action of the complex influences of nature; and I like to hear, from the mouths of those that ordinarily do not reproach*

themselves for their excesses of religious or moral orthodoxy, that geography is accused of being no more than a school of materialism and fatalism. (Dubois, 1893, 129)

One can rarely read such a clear description of the role played by the official geographical science and of the nature of the opposition and polemic that on occasion confronted geographers with social scientists of a left ideology and internationalist ideas (which frequently, although not always, went hand in hand).

To this it must be added that in the epoch of European imperialism, geography fulfilled another important function, spreading knowledge of the colonial empires. The detailed study of the colonies was an indispensable and fairly extensive part of the courses dedicated to 'universal descriptive geography'. The reasons for this outstanding presence are clear, if one takes into account the words of Emile Levasseur – the principal instigator of educational reform in France after 1870 – in the paper which he presented to the International Geographical Conference of London in 1895. To justify his ideas on the teaching of geography at the primary and secondary levels, Levasseur insisted that:

It is very important that the student has a precise knowledge, if not detailed, of the colonies, that it is necessary that he considers them an integral part of his country; the more familiar he is with this idea, the more willing he will be to serve in them or inhabit them without feeling an expatriate. (Levasseur, 1895; cited by Torres Campos, 1896, 217)

Once more, the submission of geography to the interests of the dominant classes in the Europe of the end of the century is manifest, and in this case, significantly, from the mouth of one of the main authors of the institutionalization of French geography. This substantially explains, we believe, the support of governments for this science, so little valued by other scientists, and its presence in all the programmes of primary and secondary education.

Thus, geography had the privilege to be one of the sciences favoured in the movement for educational reform and expansion. To provide teachers, geography became institutionalized in the university. And thus was born the scientific community of geographers, to teach geography to those who had to teach geography.

The role of the geographical societies

In the process of institutionalization of geography in the university, other secondary factors also had effect. One of these factors stands out – the pressure of the geographical societies for recognition of the academic status of geographical science. But this only reinforces the idea of the close relationship between the institutionalization of geographical science and the interests of the dominant classes, in that the development of the geographical societies is very much linked to the process of European imperial expansion.

The appearance of these societies follows the pattern of the expansionist politics of the European states. As a clear forerunner, one can point to the African

Association for Promoting the Discovery of the Interior Parts of Africa, created in London in 1788. The first societies founded were the Société Géographique de Paris (1821) which survived half-heartedly until mid-century, the Gesellschaft für Erdkunde of Berlin (1821) and the Royal Geographical Society of London (1830), which numbered from the start 460 members (Freeman, 1961, 50). Despite these early beginnings, the number of geographical societies grew slowly from the foundation of the first in 1821 to 1865, when there existed only 16 societies. From 1865, however, their growth in number was spectacular. From year to year, new societies were created in a great number of countries: in 1873 alone five new ones appeared; seven in 1876, four the following year and eight in 1878. By then there existed a total of fifty societies, according to a study made in that year and listed in the *Boletin de la Sociedad Geográfica de Madrid* (1879, no. 1). The total membership of these 50 societies was 21,263, the largest being the Royal Geographical Society of London with 3,334 members; most however had a membership of less than 1,000 (table 4.3)

Table 4.3 [orig. table 4.3]
Classification of geographical societies existing in.1878, according to membership

Members in individual societies	*Number of societies*	*Total number of members*
More than 2,000	1	3,334
From 1,000 to 2,000	4	5,420
From 500 to 1,000	10	7,002
From 100 to 500	17	4,759
Under 100 members	18	748
Total	50	21,263

Source: Elaborated from the figures of the *Boletin de la Sociedad Geográfica de Madrid*, 1879, No. 1, 273–6.

The figures on the evolution of the number of members of some societies demonstrates the existence of a period of crisis, which reached its peak in the decade 1840–50, and which coincides with the situation of general crisis of geography that we have described above; it is from the years 1865–70 that interest in geography really seems to increase. Thus the Geographical Society of Paris, which shortly after its foundation had 378 members (in 1827), experienced later a process of decline that lowered its membership to 100 in 1850, reaching 200 in 1860; from this date there was uninterrupted growth: 640 members in 1870, 800 in 1872, 1150 in 1875 and 1700 in 1877 (Broc, 1974, 550–51). A similar evolution took place in the Royal Geographical Society of London, which after a brilliant beginning, decayed noticeably until the decade of 1840, coinciding with the British social and economic crisis, when it seemed to be on the point of dissolution. Only after 1851, during the second presidency of R. I. Murchison, it began a trend that increased its membership from 600 to 2,000 towards 1870 (Crone, 1970, 29–30).

In the years following 1878, the founding of geographical societies continued with greater intensity all over the world, coinciding with the period of the apogee of European imperialism. Around 1885, there existed 94 geographical societies (of which 80 were European), with a total of 50,000 members. In 1896, the number of societies had risen to 107; of these, 48 were in France, 42 in Germany and 15 in Great Britain (Freeman, 1961, 53).

Between 1890 and 1920, geographical societies were formed at a slower pace, although in the decade 1920–30, the movement reached a last moment of splendour, with the creation of 30 new societies (see table 4.4).

Table 4.4 [orig. table 4.4]
Pattern of the creation of geographical societies

Period	*Number of societies founded*
1820–1829	2
1830–1839	4
1840–1849	2
1850–1859	6
1860–1869	6
1870–1879	34
1880–1889	28
1890–1899	10
1900–1909	11
1910–1919	10
1920–1929	30
1930–1940	2
Total	145

Sources: To 1878: Behn in *Geographisches Jahrbuch* (cited in *Boletin de la Sociedad Geográfica de Madrid*). From 1879: Sparn, E. in *Gaea, Boletin de la Sociedad Argentina de Estudios Geográficos* No. 22 (cited by J. Gavira, 1948).
Notes: The data from Sparn refers to the societies existing in 1945, which explains the differences that exist between the data of Behn and Freeman.

The curve showing the number of societies existing from 1821 to 1835 has a clear configuration of a graded logistical type (figure 4.1), which is so characteristic of scientific growth in general (Price, 1963; Crane, 1972). A period of slow growth between 1821 and 1870 is succeeded by two decades of exponential growth in which the number of societies is doubled approximately every 10 years. In 1869 there were 20 societies, in 1877 there were 40, and in 1889 their number exceeded 80. There followed a new period of slow growth in which the curve approaches the limit of saturation. This phase is interrupted by a new period of rapid growth, that nevertheless does not reach the same intensity as that of the period 1870–90. To interpret this intensification in the pattern of growth, one must take into account two facts: the societies created from 1910 appear in non-European countries (11 societies of a 'classical type'); and on the other hand, we are now dealing with

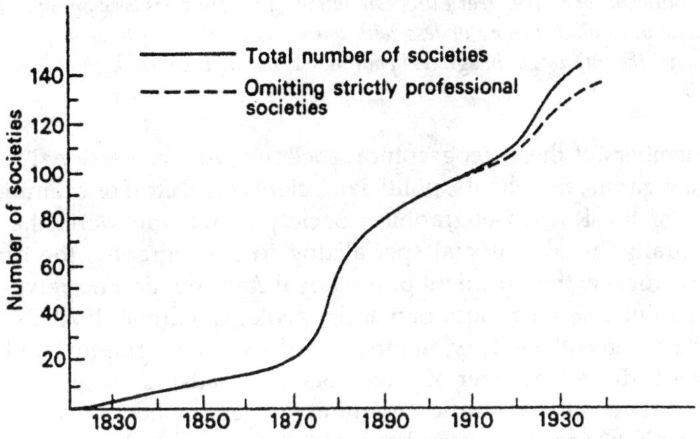

Figure 4.1 [orig. figure 4.1] Evolution of the number of geographical societies 1821–1935

professional associations (societies of geography teachers, of academics, of scientists specialized in various branches) and which therefore possess a very different character from the geographical societies of the nineteenth-century 'classical' type.

Most of these societies originated in European countries, but from the nineteenth century they also began to appear in the new American nations or in the territories under direct European rule. Towards 1935, the 136 societies in existence were distributed as shown in table 4.5.

Table 4.5 [orig. table 4.5]
Distribution of geographical societies by continents (1935).

Continents	*Number of societies*	*Number of members*
Europe	91	76,182
America	25	17,527
Asia	13	4,026
Africa	5	3,959
Oceania	2	2,018
Total	136	102,712

Source: Sparn, E., cited by Gavira, J., 1948, 300.

European imperialism was without doubt a driving force for this extraordinary growth of geographical societies in the period after 1870. As Lord Aberdare said in 1885:

to the politicians of all the great European nations, the period has been one of intense interest and anxiety, connected more or less with questions of vast territorial requisitions. To the geographer the interest, although less painful, has hardly been less keen. (Cited by Freeman, 1961, 58)

The members of these geographical societies were professional soldiers, naturalists, navigators, merchants, politicians, clergymen, etc. For example, among the founders of the Royal Geographical Society of London were: the Secretary of the Admiralty, a navy official specializing in hydrography, the director of the Ordnance Survey, the president of the Royal Astronomical Society, a diplomat, a botanist, a linguist, an antiquarian and a geologist (Crone, 1970, 27). Only at the end of the nineteenth century, in other words when geography had become institutionalized, did the number of professors and academics begin to be significant. Relations between the scientific community of geographers, once established, and the geographical societies, were, however, generally less than cordial.

The objectives of these societies were much wider than what today is understood as geographical, and included not only the organization of exploration and the development of commerce, but also the creation of meteorological stations, the making of astronomical observations, ethnographic studies, etc. To achieve their goals, some societies had access to large budgets from their membership fees and many enjoyed direct state economic support. But state support could also take other forms: aid for their publications, subscriptions to journals by official organizations, financing for particular projects, etc. The active participation of some politicians (ministers, senators, etc.) in the societies assured a valuable channel of communication for getting this support. And the interest of the politician in the work of the societies was doubtlessly great because, as the motto which headed one geographical magazine declared, 'The Earth will belong to he that knows it best.'

The societies acted through the organization of conferences, the concession of prizes and medals (large medals for explorers, and prizes for books or scholars that stood out), the organization of exploration or the granting of aid to make them possible, defending and supporting the idea of colonial expansion (applauding all the campaigns of expansion, for example). They were also the place where explorers were obliged to publicize the results of an expedition. The activity of the societies was shown in their periodical publications (magazines or bulletins) and in the series of scientific publications that they edited or patronized.

The idea of contributing to the expansion of civilization (European, of course) was accepted by all and was an ideological justification of the exploration ventures that preceded those of conquest and civilization. As Freeman correctly writes,

the need to spread civilizing influence over the more barbarous parts of the world was widely accepted by public opinion at this time. Geographical societies not only satisfied a natural curiosity about the more savage aspects of nature and society, but also cast a shrewd glance at the eventual possibilities of trade and colonial expansion. (Freeman, 1961, 51)

Thus, it is from these societies that geographical science received strong support in its institutionalization process. In a good number of European countries, the geographical societies actively pressurized governments for the university institutionalization of the science. This happened, for example, in France, where the national congresses of geographical societies repeatedly voted for this purpose (Broc, 1974). Similarly, in Great Britain, after the report by John Scott Keltie on the state of geographical teaching in Europe, the Royal Geographical Society offered aid to the universities of Oxford and Cambridge for the creation of posts for geography professors (Scargill, 1976; Stoddart, 1975b). And the Italian Geographical Society likewise played an equally decisive role, as we shall later see, as did the Geographical Society of Madrid, which from 1880 made repeated reports to the Ministry of Public Instruction on the convenience of creating university professors of geography.

The growth of the community of geographers

Because of the factors indicated, during the second half of the nineteenth century the institutionalization of geography proceeded and the scientific community of geographers appeared. Here, not in Humboldt or Ritter, is to be found the origin of modern geography; from this period it became possible to produce and reproduce scientific knowledge at a social scale, which does *not* necessarily imply that the science produced possessed an internal coherence.

The creation of university posts allowed this process of institutionalization to continue. From the description above, one can expect the existence of a close relationship between the growth of basic schooling and the corresponding demand for geography teachers and the creation of university chairs. Although this is a theme that requires more investigation, the available data seems to indicate that this correlation exists.

Thus, the early development of university geography in Germany and Switzerland may be interpreted in the light of the fact that these countries were those which first declared elementary education obligatory, and achieved important advances in popular education from the beginning of the nineteenth century. In France, the defeat of 1870 by the Germans revealed not only the potency of German industry and army, but also the power of German science and culture. The idea then spread that 'it was the German teacher who won the war' (Meynier, 1969, 8) and this contributed to the start of profound educational reform that is found at the root of the development of French geography. These three countries were the first foci of the development of modern geography and in 1875 there existed chairs in this science in seven German universities, seven French and three Swiss, according to a report of the Royal Geographical Society (Stoddart, 1975b).

The decade that followed 1875 saw the appearance of a great number of new university chairs. Another British report, that of John Scott Keltie in 1886, indicates that the number of chairs existing on the continent rose to 45. At that time there still did not exist a chair of geography in the British universities, which perhaps can be seen as a consequence of the delay in the process of public education. In any case, the slow university institutionalization of geography in Great Britain invalidates the interpretation that relates the development of modern geography to colonial exploratory activity: if any country had colonial interests it was Great Britain in the nineteenth century, which makes it difficult to understand, from this point of view, the delay of British geography.

During the 10 or 15 years following, university institutionalization of geography took place in Great Britain and the United States. In the latter, despite the early foundation of the American Geographical Society (1851), the real foundation of modern geography took place in the decade of 1890, coinciding with a wide movement of reform of secondary education (Dickinson, 1976, 184).

The decade of the 1890s may be considered that of the coming of age of the scientific community of geographers, reflected in the International Geographical Congresses that they held. That of Bern (1891) was the congress in which the geography professors, the real members of the scientific community of geographers, are found for the first time in the majority at an international congress of geography.

The participants of the first congresses of geography belonged in fact to various socio-professional groups: travellers and explorers, cartographers, meteorologists, professors, journalists, soldiers, and historians. At first, geography interested very definite social groups (the military, politicians, explorers) and scholars who had not yet formed their own institutionalized scientific communities. A statistical analysis made by J. J. Dubois (Union Géographique International, 1972) demonstrates the variety of the socio-professional composition of the participants (table 4.6).

The first congresses were characterized by the presence of relatively few geography teachers (secondary and higher education), which was to be expected in those years of the relatively weak institutionalization of the science. Politicians and the military constituted the largest proportion in the congress, together with merchants and industrialists and students of related sciences (cartographers, topographers, meteorologists, hydrologists, statisticians, historians, and economists; the proportion of the last group diminished, however, through their integration into other institutionalized scientific communities or through their conversion into professionals of the geographical science (geologists who became geographers, etc.). Under the heading 'various' (table 4.6) are included: liberal professions, journalists, museum curators, archivists, librarians; among them were also found editors (in the Congress of Bern, 1891, 41 persons out of a total of 293 whose professions are known), which demonstrates the interest they had in a science that always has had widespread popular demand (travel books, encyclopaedias, etc.), and the growing market for textbooks through geography's presence in the curricula of primary and secondary schools.

The proportion of geography teachers was increasing and became a majority in 1891. The tendency continued, with some oscillations, in the later congresses in which the proportion reached 85 per cent in the XX Congress held in London (1964). This confirms, from another perspective, the almost exclusively academic character of the scientific community of geographers.

Table 4.6 [orig. table 4.6]
Socio-professional categories of participants in the International Congresses of Geography (per cent).

		Professors	*Geographical Society members*	*Explorers*	*Related sciences*	*Engineers*	*The military, diplomats, ministers*	*Merchants financiers, industrialists*	*Various*	*Total*
I	Amberes, 1871	22.1	–	4.2	18.2	8.3	30.8	16.4	–	100
II	Paris, 1875	18.2	–	3.2	13.5	13.8	34.5	17.1	–	100
III	Venice, 1881	32.5	28.8	–	5.6	3.2	15.6	–	14.3	100
V	Bern, 1891	57.4	–	–	5.7	5.7	19.3	–	51.9	100
XX	London, 1964	85.3	–	–	7.9	0.6	4.4	–	1.8	100

Source: Dubois, J. in Union Géographique International, 1972, 50–4.

Note: The percentages have been calculated from the number of participants whose professions are known. For some categories information is not available for all the congresses.

Strategies of the community of geographers: towards a model

The institutionalization of geography in the university posed problems of recruitment of new professionals, since geographers did not at that time exist. For this reason, the university professors of the newly institutionalized science – those who became the founders and, in time, 'leaders' of the new community – came from diverse disciplines: historians, geologists, ethnographers, zoologists, naturalists. Perhaps some suddenly realized that it was worth devoting their energies to this new and attractive science. Others, undoubtedly numerous, came to geography after a careful evaluation of the professional opportunities that it offered. The study of the motivations that influenced these 'conversions' to geography and the entry into the scientific community of geographers constitutes an urgent task, although it is not hazardous to state that, in many cases, professional opportunity was the decisive element – similar to what also occurred in the development of other disciplines (see, for example, Ben-David and Collins, 1966). Faced with the traditional hagiographic interpretation that customarily shows the conversions as the fallen on the trip to Damascus, as sudden revelations of a new and marvellous science – a vision revealed at times during a voyage undertaken with other ends – the impartial reading of personal testimonies permits a different version. And this not only applies to second-rate geographers, but also includes the dominant figures. Sufficient, as an example, are the words of Ratzel, recorded by Jean Brunhes.

> *Professor Ratzel himself told me, in January 1904, a few months before his death, the characteristic evolution of his career, in these terms: 'I have travelled, drawn, described, which led me to the* Naturschilderung. *Meanwhile, I returned from America and* they told me that they needed geographers. *Thus, I collected and coordinated all the facts I had observed and collected on the Chinese immigration to California, Mexico and Cuba and wrote my work on Chinese immigration, which was my practical thesis. (Brunhes, 1912, 43; emphasis added)*

The case of Ratzel is very similar to that of Richtofen, Vidal de la Blache and so many other geographers who in the last three decades of the nineteenth century occupied university chairs of a geographical science which offered clear professional opportunities.

Once within the community, the newly arrived doubtless experienced a crisis of identity, and they were concerned, in some cases, to mark clear distances with respect to their former colleagues, emphasizing that which was distinctive in gerography with respect to the science which they had left. This explains why, surprisingly, some of the new geography professors tended to work on aspects of geography totally different from those of their prior education: ethnographers or historians became physical geographers, geologists developed the human aspects of the new science, etc. Others adapted a different strategy, tending to assert the knowledge of their initial training to create a place of prestige for themselves in the heart of the community of geographers; this would, however, need careful balancing, as it was always necessary to justify the new science and emphasize the differences between it and their old one.

In any case, the scientific community of geographers all began working hard to justify their science, trying on the one hand to emphasize its excellence and utility and on the other to delimit it unequivocally from neighbouring disciplines, with whom it had maintained close relations in the past (like history or geology) or with respect to other emergent sciences whose object was partially similar (for example, physiography or ecology). In this task of self-affirmation, geographers saw themselves forced to insist on the intermediate position of geography , on its character of a bridge discipline between the natural and social sciences.

Unlike historians and social scientists, geographers insisted on the 'natural' character of their discipline, and physical geography became the 'soul of geography', following an expression used by French geographers at various times in their disputes with the historians. Unlike the naturalists on the other hand, geography was presented as a science that also must include human data in its descriptions, and later, as an historical and social science. This led to the defence of a conception of geography in which it was given a 'real and proper coordinating function for scientific notions', as an Italian geographer said in 1895, while defending the indispensable role of geography in elementary education, alleging that 'knowledge that could not enter by the door (through specialized sciences absent at this level of education) will enter through the window, by way of geography' (see Capel, 1977, 14). The problems which geographers considered had to be the object of theoretical discussion, and generate scientific output which would show – with more or less success – the coherence of the new science. This scientific output could be interpreted as a justifying and rationalizing theoretical development, achieved from an acquired socio-professional position, which it had no intention of renouncing.

Naturally, this theoretical output developed using scientific and philosophical ideas found in the cultural medium in which it occurred. At the time of institutionalization of geography, these ideas were positivism, as a scientific method, and Darwinian evolutionism. Geography therefore shaped itself as a positive science. In that period, traditions were also created (accepted ideas about the object of geography and methods of work), that made it conserve this character for several decades, with the modifications and adaptions that historicism imposed on the discipline at the end of the century.

From the beginning of the twentieth century, the community of geographers appears, generally, consolidated and recognized within the scientific community. The principal task was to defend geography from other developing rival sciences. It is the period in which the polemics of geographers with other scientific communities that try to deprecate geography (like the sociologists or ecologists), acquired great virulence. The struggle with these rival communities is not a simple theoretical question. It is also – perhaps above all – a struggle to dominate other professional fields. When the encounters did not lead to the annihilation of one of the communities, one arrived at a situation of respect for respective professional fields of interest. This normally generates continuous scientific output tending to carefully delimit the respective sciences. That a diploma qualifies one for such and such profession can be at the base of hairsplitting discussions on the subtle differences between neighbouring sciences, differences which are, in truth, often nonexistent to a reasonable observer, who is not affected by the socio-professional implications of the discussion.

The invasion of some of the socio-professional fields of influence by rival communities generally provokes violent opposition in the affected community, translated into scientific articles dedicated, in one way or another, to this theme. Two types of reactions take place in the violated community: defensive reactions, which try to deprecate the rivals and show that they are not capable of performing the pretended function; and offensive reactions, that tend to find new professional outlets, although this may provoke new confrontations with another community. The polemic of the years 1920–30 sustained between geographers and specialists in the natural sciences as to who should teach it, is an example of the first kind of reaction; while the inclination towards land use and 'applied geography' after 1930 can be interpreted as an offensive reaction, which would lead geographical science through new paths.

The constant battle with neighbouring disciplines generates concern that the science should not be revealed as backward and deprecated in front of others. This would lead to the incorporation of ideas, methods or theories from other sciences, without the scientific community of geographers seeming to worry about the fact that these new ideas were not coherent with conceptions previously held.

Finally, one must take into account that the same scientific community is subject to violent tensions, as a result of the implacable struggle for prestige and – ultimateiy – for power. The confrontations between different scientific ideas or between distinct scientific paradigms can be the occasion in which these oppositions come to light and give place to defensive strategies or strategies of rejection – as Taylor (1976) has detected regarding the quantitative debate in British geography.

One can identify these strategies (strategies of self-affirmation, of delimitation of fields; of searches for new professional outlets of assimilation of the advances of other sciences; and of the struggle for power) from a re-reading of the theoretical output and the words of the members of the scientific community of geographers. The analysis of various national schools permits the checking of the validity of the model presented.[2]

Conclusion

The scientific community of geographers is an example of a scientific community constituted from clearly social factors, and not as a result of specific necessities in scientific knowledge. After a period in which geography had entered into profound crisis, suffering a process of depreciation related to the appearance of more specialized branches, the presence of this science in programmes of primary and secondary education generated, from the mid-nineteenth century, a need for

[2] We omit here the analysis of the case of Italy, which may be found in Capel, 1977: *Geo Critica*, 9.

geography teachers, which provoked in turn the university institutionalization of the science.

This is the origin of the scientific community of geographers, which may be considered fully constituted and recognized in many countries from the end of the nineteenth century. Institutionalization generated a process of development of geographical science similar to that of other disciplines. As Sklair (1973) has pointed out, 'when a social activity, like a science, institutionalizes itself, it experiences very significant changes in its scale, internal relations and in relations it possesses with other spheres or important institutions in the society.'

A large proportion of the members of the new community came to it after a clear appreciation of the socio-professional opportunities, and not for any 'inner call' or vocation towards the science. Although later, certain 'heroic myths' (Taylor, 1976), like that of vocation and sacrifice for the science, can be spread and accepted by the whole community.

Every scientific community, once institutionalized, establishes its own norms and value systems, which become a cohesive and stabilizing element of it. Increasingly, before becoming part of an institutionalized community (here geography), a period of training, of disciplining, is demanded, for the inculcation of those norms and values that were close to the science's heart, of knowledge of the relevant problems and methods of approaching them, of precedents and the work of the founding fathers (von Humboldt and Ritter).

The established community employs strategies tending to reproduce and amplify itself. Never will it opt for self-liquidation: the community will defend its survival, even if other communities of scientists investigate similar problems with like method, or if the logical incoherence of the conceptions that they defend is revealed. One can express the hypothesis that entire communities have rested, at times, upon hardly coherent conceptions, sometimes incoherent, without the community's members having thought for a moment to question their existence. The case of the scientific community of geographers (like that of the anthropologists) could, perhaps, be formulated from this perspective. Everything will be sacrificed for the reproduction and growth of the community, including the coherence of the very conception of the discipline: different conceptions can defend themselves in distinct moments or even simultaneously, without putting into doubt the continuity of the science practised.

In the heart of the community, hierarchically structured, the struggle for prestige and power creates, on occasions, strong internal tensions and more competition than cooperation. Despite this, the members of the group appear united by strong ties of solidarity facing rival communities.

It seems clear that at least some scientific communities, like that of the geographers, have been strongly influenced by social factors. Despite all, communities segregate their own traditions and solidarities and become social structures of a certain autonomy, which can react rigidly before external pressure or defend themselves through adaptive processes.

The thesis of this paper is that the strategies of the scientific communities can be detected through the 'scientific' output of its members. But also that *the same scientific output – as much theoretical as of specific research – can be likewise interpreted as results of the same strategies and not only as the logical and inevitable product of the development of scientific knowledge.* The 'internalist' conception of science, that considers it as an autonomous intellectual result of purely cognitive processes – the concept that appears in the works of Weber, of Popper, of Koyré and, in a lesser way, of Kuhn – must be modified. The evolution of 'scientific knowledge' is not only the result of the contrast and verification of theories and hypotheses, of the rigorous critique of scientific conceptions, that produce the devaluation of some and the triumph of others, of the battle between alternative paradigms. It is also the result of socio-professional interests of the members of the scientific community and of the strategies that they use to defend their interests against those of rival communities, and also of the struggle for power in the heart of the community. The confrontations of rival, alternative paradigms and the choice between them can be not only a battle between scientific conceptions that, for better or for worse, resolve determinate problems, but also a time of confrontations in the very heart of the community. The reasons why a scientist adheres to or rejects certain theories or conceptions is a question which one probably must answer by alluding not only to scientific reasons, but also socio-professional motivation. The production and the evaluation of scientific knowledge also relate – along with other factors – to the social structure of the science.

In the debate on the theory and sociology of science, the accent is frequently placed on the triumph of new and innovative ideas. But the persistence of old and unsustainable conceptions also deserves attention. As much in the triumph of new ideas as in the persistence of the old, factors of a social character seem to have an important influence. For this, the analysis of the social structure and of the strategies of the scientific communities and the relation of scientific output with these strategies, is a theme of great significance for the future, in that it can throw light on the ways in which scientific knowledge is produced.

References

Abbagnano, N. and Visalberghi, A. 1957: *Linee di storia della pedagogia* (Turin).

Almagìa, R. 1961: *La geografia in Italia dal 1860 al 1960* ('L'Universo', Instituto Geográfico Militar, Florence), 419–32.

Beck, H. 1959–61: *Alexander von Humboldt*. 2 vols. (Wiesbaden).

Ben David, J. and Collins, R. 1966: Social factors in the origins of a new science: the case of psychology. *American Sociological Review* 31, no. 4, 451–65.

Bertacchi, C. 1892: Delle vicende e degli ordinamenti dell' insegnamento geografico nelle scuole secondarie, dalla costituzione del Regno; e proposte dei mezzi per migliorarlo. In *Atti del Primo Congress Geografico Italiano* (Genoa), vol. 2, part 2, 551–83.

Broc, N. 1974: L'établissement de la géographie en France: diffusion, institutions, projets (1870–1890). *Annales de Géographie* 83, 545–68.

Broc, N. 1976: La pensée géographique en France au XIX siècle: continuité ou rupture? *Revue Géographique des Pyrenées et du Sud-Ouest*, 47, 225–47.

Brunhes, J. 1912: *La géographie humaine, essai de classification positive, principes et exemples* (Paris).

Capel, H. 1974: La personalidad geográfica de Varenio. In Varenio, B., *Geografia general en la que se explican las propriedades generales de la Tierra* (Barcelona), 11–84.
Capel, H. 1977: Institucionalización de la geografía y strategias de la comunidad cientifica de los geografos. *Geo Critica* (Barcelona) 8 and 9.
Cipolla, C. 1969: *Literacy and development in the West* (London).
Claval, P. 1964: *Essai sur l'évolution de la géographie humaine* (Paris).
Crane, D. 1972: *Invisible colleges: diffusion of knowledge in scientific communities* (Chicago).
Crone, G. R. 1970: *Modern geographers. An outline of progress since AD 1800* (Royal Geographical Society, London).
Dickinson, R. E. 1969: *The makers of modern geography* (London).
Dickinson, R. E. 1976: *Regional concept. The Anglo-American leaders* (London).
Dubois, M. 1894: Méthode de la Géographie coloniale. Leçon d'ouverture du cours de Géographie coloniale, Faculté des Lettres (1893). *Annales de Géographie* 3, 121–37.
Freeman, T. W. 1961: *A hundred years of geography* (London).
Gavira, J. 1948: Las sociedades geográficas. *Estudios Geográficos*, 309–15.
Gerasimov, I. editor, 1976: *A short history of geographical science in the Soviet Union* (Moscow).
Hall, D. H. 1976: *History of the earth sciences during the Scientific and Industrial Revolutions, with special emphasis on the physical geosciences* (Amsterdam).
Hartshorne, R. 1959: *Perspectives on the nature of geography* (Chicago).
Hettner, A. 1898: Die Entwicklung der Geographie im 19 Jahrhundert. *Geographische Zeitschrift* 4, 305–320.
Kretshmer, K. 1930: *Historia de la Geografia* (Barcelona).
Matveyeva, T. P. 1976: Documentary sources for the study of the development of geographical thought. In *History of Geographical Thought* (Abstracts of Papers, Leningrad, International Geographical Union), 55–9.
Meynier, A. 1969: *Histoire de la pensée géographique en France (182–1969)* (Paris).
Minguet, C. 1969: *Alexandre de Humboldt, Historien et géographe de l'Amérique espagnole (1799–1804)* (Paris).
Pracchi, R. 1964: Studi generali sull'Italia e monografie regionali. In *Un sessantenio di ricerca geografica italiana, Memorie della Società Geografica Italiana*, XVI, 575–600.
Price, D. J. de Solla 1963: *Little science, big science* (New York).
Sanderson, M. 1974: Mary Somerville: her work in physical geography. *Geographical Review* 64, 410–20.
Scargill, D. I. 1976: The R.G.S. and the foundations of geography at Oxford. *Geographical Journal* 142, 438–61.
Schaefer, F. K. 1953: Exceptionalism in geography: a methodological examination. *Annals of the Association of American Geographers* 43, 226–249.
Sklair, L. 1973: *Organized knowledge* (London).
Stoddart, D. R. 1975a: 'That Victorian Science': Huxley's *Physiography* and its impact on geography. *Transactions of the Institute of British Geographers* 66, 17–40.
Stoddart, D. R. 1975b: The R.G.S. and the foundations of geography at Cambridge. *Geographical Journal* 141, 216–39.
Sukhova, N.G. 1976: The idea of interaction between natural phenomena on Earth's surface and the development of geography in Russia. In *History of Geographical Thought* (Abstracts of Papers, Leningrad, International Geographical Union) 62–5.
Taylor, P. J. 1976: The quantification debate in British geography. *Transactions of the Institute of British Geographers* new series 1, 129–42.
Torres Campos, R. 1896: *La geografía en 1895. Memoria sobre el VI Congreso Internacional de Ciencias Geográficas celebrado en Londres* (Madrid).

Union Géographique International (1972): *La géographie à travers un siècle des Congrès Internationaux* (Caen).

Valskaya, B. A. 1976: The development of geographical thought in Russia in the first half of the 19th century. *History of Geographical Thought* (Abstracts of Papers, Leningrad, International Geographical Union), 46–51.

5

ON THE HISTORY AND PRESENT CONDITION OF GEOGRAPHY: AN HISTORICAL MATERIALIST MANIFESTO

David Harvey

The history of geography is inseparable from the history of society. Indeed, modern academic geography may be an attempt to bring legitimacy to the very social conditions which make the subject possible. This is the argument pursued by the leading Marxist geographer David Harvey (**chapter 37** for an example of his work). More so than Capel (**chapter 4**) or Johnston (**chapter 2**), he stresses the external forces acting upon geography. He challenges what he calls 'bourgeois geography' for its past complicity in imperialism, racism and the exploitation of both resources and labour. Harvey offers a principled and political critique of geography's past as well as its present. Its over-specialization, excessive concern for quantification and close involvement with corporations and governments are all faulted. To Harvey the purpose of exploring geography's history is not to glorify past achievements and celebrate worthy individuals. Although he does commend the work of dissidents such as Reclus and Kropotkin (**chapter 7**), he is generally critical of the discipline's record. In its place he proposes a more radical geography, one which is rigorous and committed and does not have pretensions to neutrality. The task of a geographer thus turns out to be a political project concerned with the transition from capitalism to socialism. As Harvey claims, 'geography is too important to be left to geographers' alone.

Source: On the history and present conditions of geography: an historical materialist manifesto. *Professional Geographer* 3, 1–11, 1984.

The present condition of Geography and proposals for its transformation must be firmly grounded in an understanding of history. The roles and functions of geographical knowledge, together with the structures of that knowledge, have changed over time in relation to and in response to shifting societal configurations and needs. The history of our discipline cannot be understood independently of the history of the society in which the practices of geography are embedded. The rise of merchant, and later industrial and finance forms of capitalism in the West, paralleled as it was by increasing spatial integration of the world economy under Western politico-economic hegemony, demanded and depended upon the crystallization of new forms of geographical knowledge within an increasingly fragmented professional and academic division of labor. The difficulties and alternatives geographers now face are likewise rooted in conflictual processes of societal transformation. Proposals for the transformation or stabilization of our discipline are, whether we like it or not, positions taken in relation to grander processes of social change. Awareness of that basic fact must inform debate over where our discipline is going and how it is to be restructured to meet contemporary challenges and needs.

On the History of Geography and Society

Geographical knowledge records, analyzes and stores information about the spatial distribution and organization of those conditions (both naturally occurring and humanly created) that provide the material basis for the reproduction of social life. At the same time it promotes conscious awareness of how such conditions are subject to continuous transformation through human action.

The form and content of such knowledge depends upon the social context. All societies, classes, and social groups possess a distinctive "geographical lore," a working knowledge of their territory, of the spatial configuration of use values relevant to them, and of how they may intervene to shape the use values to their own purposes. This "lore," acquired through experience, is codified and socially transmitted as part of a conceptual apparatus with which individuals and groups cope with the world. It may take the form of a loosely-defined spatial and environmental imagery or of a formal body of knowledge – GEOGRAPHY – in which all members of society or a privileged elite receive instruction. This knowledge can be used in the struggle to liberate peoples from "natural" disasters and constraints and from external oppression. It can be used in the quest to dominate nature and other peoples and to construct an alternative geography of social life through the shaping of physical and social environments for social ends.

The form and content of geographical knowledge cannot be understood independently of the social basis for the production and use of that knowledge. Pre-capitalist societies, for example, produced highly sophisticated geographical understandings but often of a particular and localized sort, radically different from geography as we know it [*15, 25*]. The trading empires of Greece, Rome, Islam, and China all produced elaborate geographies of the world as they knew it [*19, 21, 31, 42*]. These geographies typically mirrored the movement of commodities, the migrations of peoples, the paths of conquest, and the exigencies of administration of empire.

The transformation from feudalism to capitalism in Western Europe entailed a revolution in the structures of geographic thought and practice. Geographical traditions inherited from the Greeks and Romans, or absorbed from China and above all Islam, were appropriated and transformed in the light of a distinctively Western Europe experience. Exchange of commodities, colonial conquest and settlement formed the initial basis, but as capitalism evolved, so the geographical movement of capital and labor power became the pivot upon which the construction of new geographical knowledge turned. Six aspects of geographical practice stand out in the bourgeois era:

(1) Concern for accuracy of navigation and the definition of territorial rights (both private and collective) meant that mapping and cadastral survey became basic tools of the geographer's art [*3, 40*]. In the imperialist era, for example, the cartographic basis was laid for the imposition of capitalist forms of such rights in areas of the world (Africa, the Americas, Australia and much of Asia) that had previously lacked them. Such activity laid the basis for exclusive class-based privileges and rights to the appropriation of the fruits of both nature and labor within well-defined spaces. On the other hand, it also opened up the possibility for the rational organization of space and nature for the universal welfare of humankind.

(2) The creation of the world market meant "the exploration of the earth in all directions" in order to discover "new, useful qualities of things" and the promotion of "universal exchange of the products of all alien climates and lands" [*30, p. 409*]. Working in the tradition of natural philosophy, geographers such as Alexander von Humboldt [*20*] and Carl Ritter [*37*] set out to construct a systematic description of the earth's surface as the repository of use values, as the dynamic field within which the natural processes that could be harnessed for human action had their being. The accurate description of physical and biotic environments has remained central to geography ever since.

(3) Close observation of geographical variations in ways of life, forms of economy and social reproduction has also been integral to the geographer's practice. This tradition degenerated (particularly in the commercial geography of the late nineteenth century) into the mere compilation of "human resources" open to profitable exploitation through unequal or forced exchange, the imposition of wage labor through primitive accumulation, the redistribution of labor supplies through forced migration, and the sophisticated manipulation of indigenous economies and political power structures to extract surpluses. Geographical practices were deeply affected by participation in the management of Empire, colonial administration, and the exploration of commercial opportunities [*8*]. The exploitation of nature under capitalism evidently often went hand in hand with the exploitation of peoples. On the other hand, the construction of such knowledge in the spirit of liberty and respect for others, as for example in the remarkable work of Elisée Reclus [*36*], opened up the possibility for the creation of alternative forms of geographical practice, tied to principles of mutual respect and advantage rather than to the politics of exploitation.

(4) The division of the world into spheres of influence by the main capitalist powers at the end of the nineteenth century raised serious geopolitical issues. The struggle for control over access to raw materials, labor supplies, and markets was struggle for command over territory. Geographers like Friedrich Ratzel [*35*] and Sir Halford Mackinder [*28*] confronted the question of the political ordering of space and its consequences head on, but did so from the standpoint of survival, control, and domination. They sought to define useful geographical strategies in the context of political, economic and military struggles between the major

capitalist powers , or against peoples resisting the incursions of empire or neo-colonial domination. This line of work reached its nadir with Karl Haushoffer, the German geopolitician who actively supported and helped shape Nazi expansionist strategies [*12*]. But geopolitical thinking continues to be fundamental within the contemporary era, particularly in the pentagons of military power and amongst those concerned with foreign policy. By force of historical circumstance, all national liberation movements must define themselves geopolitically if they are to succeed.

(5) Concern with the use of "natural and human resources" and spatial distributions (of population, industry, transport facilities, ecological complexes, etc.) led geographers to consider the question of "rational" configurations of both. This aspect of geographical practice, which emerged strongly with the early geological, soil, and land use surveys, has increased markedly in recent years as the capitalist state has been forced to intervene more actively in human affairs [*11*]. Positive knowledge of actual distributions (the collection, coding and presentation of information) and normative theories of location and optimization have proved useful in environmental management and urban and regional planning. To a large degree these techniques entailed acceptance of a distinctively capitalist definition of rationality, connected to the accumulation of capital and the social control of labor power. But such a mode of thought also opened up the possibility for planning the efficient utilization of environments and space according to alternative or multiple definitions of rationality.

(6) Geographical thought in the bourgeois era has always preserved a strong ideological content. As science, it treats natural and social phenomena as things, subject to manipulation, management and exploitation. As art, it often projects and articulates individual and collective hopes and fears as much as it depicts material conditions and social relations with the historical veracity they deserve. For example, geographical literature often dwells upon the bizarre and quaint at the expense of dealing openly with the legitimate aspirations of peoples. Although it aspires to universal understanding of the diversity of life on earth, it often cultivates parochialist, ethnocentric perspectives on that diversity. It can be an active vehicle for the transmission of doctrines of racial, cultural, sexual, or national superiority. Ideas of "geographical" or "manifest" destiny, of "natural" geographical rights (e.g., United States control over the Panama Canal), of the "white man's burden" and the civilizing mission of the bourgeoisie or of American democracy, are liberally scattered in geographical texts and deeply embedded in popular geographical lore [*5, 10, 43*]. Cold War rhetoric, fears of "orientalism," and the like, are likewise pervasive [*38*]. Furthermore, the "facts" of geography, presented often as facts of nature, can be used to justify imperialism, neo-colonial domination, and expansionism. Geographical information also can be presented in such a way as to prey upon fears and feed hostility (the abuse of cartography is of particular note in this regard). But there is a brighter side to all of this. The geographical literature can express hopes and aspirations as well as fears, can seek universal understandings based on mutual respect and concern, and can articulate the basis for human cooperation in a world marked by human diversity. It can become the vehicle to

express utopian visions and practical plans for the creation of alternative geographies [22, 36].

The Rise of Geography as an Academic Discipline Within a Professional Division of Labor

Academic geographers sought to combine experience gained from these diverse practices into a coherent discipline within an academic division of labor that crystallized towards the end of the nineteenth century. They have not been altogether successful in this project. To begin with, they often remained eclectic generalists (posing grand questions on such topics as environmental determinism, the social relation to nature, the role of geography in history, etc.) in an academia increasingly dominated by professional analytic expertise. Also, rejecting historical materialism as a basic frame of reference, they lacked methods to achieve synthesis and overcome the innumerable dualisms within their subject, between, for example, physical and human geography, regional specialization and systematic studies of global variation, unique and generic perspectives, quantitative and qualitative understandings. The dominant institutions within the discipline (such as the Royal Geographical Society) were more concerned with the practices of discovery and subordination of nature and the techniques of management of empire than they were with the creation of a coherent academic discipline [8]. Academic geography, as a consequence, posed grand questions but all too frequently trivialized the answers.

In the face of external pressures and internal disarray, geography has tended to fragment in recent years and seek salvation in a far narrower professionalization of its parts. But the more successful it has been in this direction, the more its method has coalesced into a monolithic and dogmatic positivism and the more easily the parts could be absorbed into some cognate analytic discipline (physical geographers into geology, location theorists into economics, spatial choice theorists into psychology, etc.). Geographers thereby lost their *raison d'être* as synthesizers of knowledge in its spatial aspect. The more specialized they became, also, the more they distanced themselves from the processes of construction of popular geographical knowledge. What was once an important preserve for the geographer fell into the hands of popular magazines and the producers of commercial travelogues and brochures, television films, news, and documentaries. The failure to help build appropriate popular understandings to deal with a world undergoing rapid geographical integration was a startling abrogation of responsibility.

Caught between lack of academic identity and profundity on the one hand and a weak popular base on the other, academic geography failed to build a position of power, prestige, and respectability within the academic division of labor. Its survival increasingly depended upon cultivation of very specialized techniques (such as remote sensing) or the production of specialized knowledges for powerful special interests. Big government, the corporation, and the military provided a series of niches into which geographers might conveniently crawl. The academic evolution of the discipline is now threatened by total submission to the dictates of powerful special interests.

Yet to be conscious of the facts of geography has always meant to exercise responsibility with respect to them [*7, 18, 33, 39, 41*]. How that responsibility is expressed depends upon the social context and the individual and collective consciousness of geographers. Some, in the name of academic freedom and objectivity, have sought to raise the study of geography up onto some universal plane of knowledge, to create a positivist science above the influence of any mundane special interest. Others sought to confront the relation between power and knowledge directly, to create antidotes to what they see as one-sided geographical understandings and so become advocates for the legitimate aspirations of indigenous peoples or oppressed groups. Still others have struggled to help build an historical materialist science of human history in its geographical aspect, to create a knowledge that would help subject peoples, classes, and groups gain closer control over and the power to shape their own history.

The failing credibility of positivism in the late 1960s opened the way to attempts to create a more directly radical or Marxist tradition. Geographers were faced with a peculiar mix of advantages and disadvantages. Old-style geography – global, synthetic, and dealing with ways of life and social reproduction in different natural and social milieus – lent itself easily to historical materialist approaches, but was dominated by establishment thinkers attached to the ideology of empire or actively engaged in the service of national interests. A radical element lurked within this rather stuffy tradition. Reclus [*36*] and Kropotkin [*22*] brought anarchism and geography together to express their common social concerns in the late nineteenth century. More recently, writers like Owen Lattimore [*23*] and Keith Buchanan [*4*] tried to portray the world not from the standpoint of the superpowers, but from that of indigenous peoples (*From China Looking Outwards* is a typical Lattimore title). The active repression of such thinkers, particularly during the Cold War and McCarthyism [*32*], led many progressive geographers thereafter to express their social concerns behind the supposed neutrality of "the positivist shield." The main line of battle in the late 1960s, therefore, was over whether social concerns could be adequately expressed from behind the positivist shield or whether that shield was indeed as neutral as at first sight it appeared.

The radical and Marxist thrust in geography in the late 1960s concentrated on a critique of ideology and practice within the positivism that then reigned supreme [*34*]. It sought to penetrate the positivist shield and uncover the hidden assumptions and class biases that lurked therein. It increasingly viewed positivism as a manifestation of bourgeois managerial consciousness given over at worst to manipulation and control of people as objects and at best capable of expressing a paternalistic benevolence. It attacked the role of geographers in imperialist endeavors, in urban and regional planning procedures designed to facilitate social control and capital accumulation. It called into question the racism, sexism, ethnocentrism, and plain political prejudice communicated in many geographical texts.

But the critics also had to create geographical thought and practice in a new image. Marxism [*33, 34*], anarchism [*1, 2, 34*], advocacy [*9*], "geographical expeditions" [6] and humanism [26] became some of the rallying points for those seeking alternatives. Each had then to identify and preserve those facets of geography relevant to their project. The more mundane techniques, such as mapping, information coding, and resource inventory analysis, appeared recuperable if not unavoidable to any reconstitution of geographic practice. The problem was to shake them free from their purely positivist presentation and integrate them into some other framework. Bourgeois geographers had also long sought to understand how different peoples fashion their physical and social landscapes as a reflection of their own needs and aspirations. They had also shown that different social groups (children, the aged, social classes, whole cultures) possess distinctive and often incomparable forms of geographical knowledge, depending upon their experience, position, and traditions. These ideas also seem recuperable as the basis for fresh geographical practice. Historical and cultural geographers, insofar as they had paid attention to the processes of spatial integration, regional transformation, and changing geographical configurations through time, provided relevant raw materials.

From the initial fumblings and searchings, a new agenda for geography emerged, rooted deep in tradition yet original and breathtaking in scope, exhilarating if often frustrating in its practice [*17*]. The study of the active construction and transformation of material environments (both physical and social) together with critical reflection on the production and use of geographical knowledge within the context of that activity, could become the center of concern. The focus is on the process of *becoming* through which people (and geographers) transform themselves through transforming both their natural and social milieus. For the humanists, this process of becoming could be viewed religiously or secularly through the philosophical lenses of Heidegger and Husserl [*7*]. The Marxists had to look no further than Marx's characterization of human labor as a process through which human beings, in acting on the external world and changing it, at the same time changed their own natures [*29, p. 177*]. Anarchists could appeal to Reclus who argued that "humankind is nature becoming conscious of and taking responsibility for itself" [*36, Vol. 1, p. 106*]. Those actively engaged in advocacy could feel they were integral to processes of social transformation.

While the commonality of the new agenda was frequently masked by bitter backbiting amongst the participants, there could be no question as to the common core of concern. But there were deeper problems that inhibited its execution and threatened it with early extinction, crushed under the overwhelming critical silence of a positivist reaction. The problems are in part external to the profession, the product of a societal condition that does not favor experimentation, innovation, and intellectual debate but which seeks to discipline unruly academics to more narrowly based immediate and practical concerns as defined by powerful special interests. But the problems are also internal. Advocates for community cannot justify a stance of "community right or wrong" if one community's gain is another's loss any more than environmentalists can reasonably proceed oblivious of employment consequences. Humanists, if they are to avoid the trap of narcissistic radical subjectivism, need a more powerful theory than agency and structure to grapple with macro-problems of money power, inflation, and unemployment. Anarchists, while sensitized to ecological and communitarian concerns, lack the social theory to understand the dynamics of capitalism in relation to state power. Marxists come armed with a powerful theory but find it hard to cope with ecological issues or with a subject matter in which highly differentiated activities of individuals and social groups within the particularities of space and place are of paramount concern.

What is lacking is a clear context, a theoretical frame of reference, a language which can simultaneously capture global processes restructuring social, economic and political life in the contemporary era and the specifics of what is happening to individuals, groups, classes, and communities at particular places at certain times. Those who broke out from behind the safety of the positivist shield ruptured the political silence within geography and allowed conscience and consciousness freer play. But they spoke with many voices, generated a veritable cacophony of competing messages, and failed to define a common language to voice common concerns.

Between the safety of a positivist silence and the risk of nihilistic disintegration lies the passage to a revitalized geography, an intellectual discipline that can play a vital, creative, and progressive role in shaping the social transformations that beset us. How to negotiate that passage is *our* dilemma of *this* time.

The Present Condition of Geography

Geography is too important to be left to geographers. But it is far too important to be left to generals, politicians, and corporate chiefs. Notions of "applied" and "relevant" geography pose questions of objectives and interests served. The selling of ourselves and the geography *we* make to the corporation is to participate directly in making *their* kind of geography, a human landscape riven with social inequality and seething geopolitical tensions. The selling of ourselves to government is a more ambiguous enterprise, lost in the swamp of some mythic "public interest" in a world of chronic power imbalances and competing claims. The disenfranchised (and that includes most of us when it comes to interest rates, nuclear strategy, covert operations, and geopolitical strategizing) must be heard through the kind of geography we make, no matter how unpopular that voice within the corridors of power or with those who control our purse strings. There is more to geography than the production of knowledge and personnel to be sold as commodities to the highest bidder.

The geography we make must be a peoples' geography, not based on pious universalisms, ideals, and good intents, but a more mundane enterprise that reflects earthly interests, and claims, that confronts ideologies and prejudice as they really are, that faithfully mirrors the complex weave of competition, struggle, and cooperation within the shifting social and physical landscapes of the twentieth century. The world must be depicted, analyzed, and understood not as we would like it to be but as it really is, the material manifestation of human hopes and fears mediated by powerful and conflicting processes of social reproduction.

Such a peoples' geography must have a popular base, be threaded into the fabric of daily life with deep taproots into the well-springs of popular consciousness. But it must also open channels of communication, undermine parochialist world views, and confront or subvert the power of dominant classes or the state. It must penetrate the barriers to common understandings by identifying the material base to common interests. Where such a material base does not exist, it must frankly recognize and articulate conflict of equal and competing rights that flows therefrom. To the degree that conflicting rights are resolved through tests of strength between contending parties, so the intellectual force within our discipline is a powerful weapon and must be consciously deployed as such, even at the expense of internalizing conflicting notions of right within the discipline itself. The geographical studies we make are necessarily a part of that complex of conflictual social processes which give birth to new geographical landscapes.

Geographers cannot remain neutral. But they can strive towards scientific rigor, integrity and honesty. The difference between the two commitments must be understood. There are many windows from which to view the same world, but scientific integrity demands that we faithfully record and analyze what we see from any one of them. The view from China looking outwards or from the lower classes looking up is very different from that from the Pentagon or Wall Street. But each view can be represented in a common frame of discourse, subject to evaluation as to internal integrity and credibility. Only in this way the myriad masks of false conflict be stripped away and the real structure of competing rights and claims be exposed. Only in this way too, can we insure that the geography we make is used and not abused in the struggles of our time.

The intellectual task in geography, therefore, is the construction of a common language, of common frames of reference and theoretical understandings, within which conflicting rights and claims can be properly represented. Positivism undermines its own virtues of objective materialism by spurious claims to neutrality. Historical materialism, though appropriate, is too frequently held captive within the rigidities of some political orthodoxy that renders windows on the world opaque and substitutes subjectively conceived political fantasy for hard-nosed objective materialism. Under such conditions the construction of a common discourse for describing and theorizing becomes a tough task.

But the very nature of the intellectual baggage accumulated these past years makes the geographers' contributions potentially crucial. For example, the insertion of concepts of space, place, locale, and milieu into any social theory has a numbing effect upon that theory's central propositions. Microeconomists working with perfect competition find only spatial monopoly, macroeconomists find as many economies as there are central banks and a peculiar flux of exchange relations between them, and Marxists looking to class relations find neighborhoods, communities, and nations. Marx, Marshall, Weber, and Durkheim all have this in common: they prioritize time over space and, where they treat the latter at all, tend to view it unproblematically as the site or context for historical action. Whenever social theorists of whatever stripe actively interrogate the meaning of geographical categories and relations, they are forced either to make so many *ad hoc* adjustments to their theory that it splinters into incoherency, or else to abandon their theory in favor of some language derived from pure geometry. The insertion of spatial concepts into social theory has not yet been successfully accomplished. Yet social theory that ignores the materialities of actual geographical configurations, relations, and processes lacks validity [*13, 14*].

The temptation then exists to abandon theory, retreat into the supposed particularities of place and moment, resort to naive empiricism, and produce as many *ad hoc* theories as there are instances. All prospects for communication then break down save those preserved by the conventions of common language. The ambiguities of the latter masquerade as theory and theory itself is lost in a swamp of ambiguous meanings. Ambiguity may be preferable to rigid and uncompromising orthodoxy, but it is no basis for science. Retreat from explicit theory is retreat from the challenge to make conscious and creative interventions in the construction of future geographies. The junction between geography and social theory, therefore, is one of the crucial flash-points for the crystallization of new conceptions of the world and new possibilities for active intervention.

The political implications of a resolution of such real and highly charged intellectual dilemmas between geography and social theory are legion. Consider, for example, the clash between anarchist and Marxist perspectives both politically and within the history of geography. Reclus and Kropotkin, geographers both, were impressed by the remarkable diversity of life, culture, community, and environment revealed by their geographical studies. They respected that diversity and sought to preserve it through a political project that linked the peoples of the earth into some vast federation of autonomous self-governing communities. This entailed a highly decentralized and profoundly geographical vision of how an alternative society should look. It has helped fuel a political tradition concerned with worker self-management, community control, ecological sensitivity, and respect for the individual. Is it accidental that the radical urge in nineteenth century geography was expressed through anarchism rather than through Marxism? The sensitivity to issues of place, ecology, milieu, and geographical peculiarities still makes the anarchist vision appealing. Yet it is seriously flawed by the absence of any powerful theory of the dynamics of capitalism. Reclus [*36*] in his last work recognized that the intriguing geographical variety for which he had such respect was even then being swept away, crushed under the homogenizing heel of the circulation and accumulation of capital. The universality of that experience demands a global political response born out of more powerful universal understandings of the dynamics of capitalism than Reclus constructed. His political vision and his intellectual contribution are undermined by this crucial absence.

Marx, for his part, occupies the pinnacle of social theoretic power at the expense of excluding geographical variation as an "unnecessary complication" [*29*, Vol. 2, p. 470; see also *29*, Chapter 13]. From that highpoint he can proclaim a politics of universal class struggle founded on universal proletarian consciousness and solidarity. To be sure, Marx frequently admits of the significance of space and place within both his theory and his practice (the opposition between English and Irish working class interests parallels oppositions in his theoretical work between town and country, inner and outer transformations, and the like). But none of this is thoroughly integrated into theoretical formulations that are powerful with respect to time but weak with respect to space. His political vision and theoretical contribution founder on his failure to build a systematic and distinctively geographical dimension into his thought. This was the "error" that Lenin and the theorists of imperialism sought to rectify. They opened up the possibility of an alternative rhetoric within the Marxist tradition in which centers exploit peripheries, the first world subjugates the third, and capitalist powers compete for domination of protected space (markets, labor power, raw materials). People in one place exploit and struggle against those in another place. *Ad hoc* concessions to spatial structure provoke redefinitions of exploitation that coexist uneasily with Marx's view of a capitalist dynamic powered by the exploitation of one class by another. The theoretical foundations of Marxism-Leninism are thereby rendered ambiguous, sparking savage disputes over the right to national self-determination, the national question, the prospects for socialism in one country, the significance of geographical decentralization in political practice [*10, 16, 24, 27*].

There is more to the split between anarchists and Marxists (or divisions within the latter camp) than their respective approaches to geographical questions. But the Marxists, while proclaiming in principle the significance of geographical uneven development, have had a hard time integrating space or evolving a sensitivity to place and milieu within otherwise powerful social theories. The anarchist literature abounds with such sensitivity but founders on lack of theoretical and political coherence. All of which provokes the intriguing though somewhat idle thought: what would our political and intellectual world be like if Marx had been a better geographer and the anarchists better social theorists? That rhetorical question underlines the contemporary political importance of a theoretical project dedicated to the unification of geographical sensitivities and understandings with the power of general social theories formulated in the tradition of historical materialism. Such a theoretical project is more than just a tough academic exercise. It is fundamental to our thinking on the prospects for the transition to socialism.

An Historical Materialist Manifesto

The tasks before us can now be more clearly defined. We must:

1. Build a popular geography, free from prejudice but reflective of real conflicts and contradictions, capable also of opening new channels for communication and common understanding.
2. Create an applied peoples' geography, unbeholden to narrow or powerful special interests, but broadly democratic in its conception.
3. Accept a dual methodological commitment to scientific integrity and non-neutrality.
4. Integrate geographical sensitivities into general social theories emanating from the historical materialist tradition.
5. Define a political project that sees the transition from capitalism to socialism in historico-geographical terms.

We have the power through our collective efforts as geographers to help make our own history and geography. That we cannot do so under historical and geographical circumstances of our own choosing is self-evident. In part our role is to explore the limits imposed by the deadweight of an actually-existing geography and an already-achieved history. But we must define, also, a radical guiding vision: one that explores the realms of freedom beyond material necessity, that opens the way to the creation of new forms of society in which common people have the power to create their own geography and history in the image of liberty and mutual respect of opposed interests. The only other course, if my analysis of the trajectory of contemporary capitalism is correct [*16*], is to sustain a present geography founded on class oppression, state domination, unnecessary material deprivation, war, and human denial.

Literature Cited

1 Breitbart, M. M., ed. "Anarchism and Environment." *Antipode*, 10, No. 3: 11, No. 1 (Special Issue, 1979).

2 ——"Peter Kropotkin, the Anarchist Geographer." In *Geography, Ideology and Social Concern*, pp. 134–153. Edited by D. Stoddart. Oxford: Basil Blackwell, 1981.

3 Brown, L. A. *The Story of Maps*. Boston: Little Brown, 1949.

4 Buchanan, K. *The Transformation of the Chinese Earth*. New York: Praeger, 1970.

5 ——"Reflections on a 'Dirty Word.' " *Dissent*, 31 (1974), 25–31.

6 Bunge, W. "The First Years of the Detroit Geographical Expedition." In *Radical Geography*, pp. 31–39. Edited by R. Peet. Chicago: Maaroufa, 1977.

7 Buttimer, A. *Values in Geography*. Resource Paper No. 24. Washington: Association of American Geographers, 1974.

8 Capel, H. "Institutionalization of Geography and Strategies of Change." In *Geography, Ideology and Social Concern*, pp. 37–69. Edited by D. Stoddart. Oxford: Basil Blackwell, 1981.

9 Corey, K. "Advocacy in Planning: a Reflective Analysis." *Antipode*, 4 (1972), 46–63.

10 Davis, H. *Toward a Marxist Theory of Nationalism*. New York: Monthly Review, 1978.

11 Dear, M. and A. Scott, eds. *Urbanization and Urban Planning in Capitalist Society*. New York: Methuen, 1981.

12 Dorpalen, A. *The World of General Haushofer*. New York: Farrar and Rinehart, 1942.

13 Giddens, A. *A Contemporary Critique of Historical Materialism*. London: MacMillan, 1981.

14 Gregory, D. and J. Urry, eds. *Social Relations and Spatial Structures*. London: MacMillan, 1984.

15 Hallowell, A. I. *Culture and Experience*. Philadelphia: University of Pennsylvania Press, 1955.

16 Harvey, D. *The Limits to Capital*. Oxford: Basil Blackwell, 1983.

17 ——and N. Smith. "From Capitals to Capital." In *The Left Academy*, Vol. 2. Edited by B. Ollman and E. Vernoff. New York: Praeger, forthcoming.

18 *Hérodote: Stratégies, Géographies, Idéologies*. Paris: Maspero, 1975.

19 Herodotus. *The Histories*. Translated by A. Selincourt. Harmondsworth, Middlesex: Penguin, 1954.

20 Humboldt, A. von. *Cosmos*. Translated by O. Otté. London: H. G. Bohn, 1849–1852.

21 Ibn Khaldûn. *The Muqaddima*. Translated by F. Rosenthal. London: Routledge and Kegan Paul, 1958.

22 Kropotkin, P. *Fields, Factories and Workshops*. London: Nelson, 1898.

23 Lattimore, O. *Studies in Frontier History, Collected Papers, 1928–1958*. London: Oxford University Press, 1962.

24 Lenin, V. I. "The Right of Nations to Self-Determination." In *Selected Works*, Vol. 1, pp. 595–648. Moscow: Progress Publishers, 1970.

25 Levi-Strauss, C. *The Savage Mind*. Chicago: Chicago University Press, 1966.

26 Ley, D. and M. Samuels, eds. *Humanistic Geography: Prospects and Problems*. Chicago: Maaroufa, 1978.

27 Luxemburg, R. *The National Question: Selected Writings*. Edited by H. Davis. New York: Monthly Review Press, 1976.

28 Mackinder, H. *Democratic Ideals and Reality*. New York: Norton, 1962.

29 Marx, K. *Capital* (three volumes). New York: International Publishers, 1967.

30 ——*Grundrisse*. Harmondsworth, Middlesex: Penguin, 1973.

31 Needham, J. *Science and Civilization in China*. Cambridge: Cambridge University Press, 1954.

32 Newman, R. "Owen Lattimore and His Enemies." *Antipode* (forthcoming).

33 Peet, R. ed. *Radical Geography*. Chicago: Maaroufa, 1977.

34 Quaini, M. *Geography and Marxism*. Totowa, NJ: Barnes and Noble, 1982.

35 Ratzel, F. *Politische Geographie*. Munich: R. Oldenburg, 1923.

36 Reclus, E. *L'Homme et La Terre*. Paris: Maspero, 1982.

37 Ritter, C. *Die Erdkunde*. Berlin: Raimer, 1822–1859.

38 Said, E. *Orientalism*. New York: Vintage Books, 1979.

39 Sayer, A. "Defensible Values in Geography: Can Values be Science Free?" In *Geography and the Urban Environment*, vol. 4, pp. 29–56. Edited by D. T. Herbert and R. J. Johnston. New York: John Wiley, 1981.

40 Skelton, R. A. *Explorer's Maps: Chapters in the Geographic Record of Geographical Discovery*. New York: Praeger, 1958.

41 Stoddart, D., ed. *Geography, Ideology and Social Concern*. Oxford: Basil Blackwell, 1981.

42 Strabo. *The Geography of Strabo*. Translated by H. C. Hamilton and W. Falconer. London: G. Bell. 1903–1906.

43 Weinberg, A. K. *Manifest Destiny*. Chicago: Quadrangle Books, 1963.

6

SITUATED KNOWLEDGES: THE SCIENCE QUESTION IN FEMINISM AND THE PRIVILEGE OF PARTIAL PERSPECTIVE

Donna Haraway

This section concludes with a view from outside geography. Donna Haraway is Professor of the History of Consciousness Board at the University of California, Santa Cruz. She has explored the boundaries between feminism, biology, technology and primatology in a series of challenging essays. While Wright (**chapter 1**) and Harvey (**chapter 5**) note the existence of different geographies associated with civilizations and classes respectively, Haraway uses insights from the feminist critique of science to argue that all knowledge is situated and necessarily a partial perspective. This position is intermediate between the claims to absolute objectivity and value-neutrality on the one hand, and relativism – the proposition that it is not possible to find some external yardstick with which to decide among rival knowledge-claims – on the other. She arrives at this position by considering the centrality of vision in claims about truth in science. Haraway rejects the claim that there can be a 'view from nowhere' and then examines the means by which we do see. Vision is not a passive biological process, but an active and enabling practice which must take account of the technological and political contexts of seeing: read Openshaw (**chapter 41**) on Geographical Information Systems for an example of the kind of knowledge-claims she is questioning, and compare her argument with Rose's (**chapter 20**) critique of landscape as a masculine way of seeing. By addressing the connections between space, power and knowledge Haraway points towards a history of geography which focuses as much on the sites of the production of geography as on the objects of its attention. These and similar ideas also open up the possibility of a feminist historiography of geography.

Source: Situated knowledges: the science question in feminism and the privilege of partial perspective. In *Simians, cyborgs and women: the reinvention of nature*. London: Free Association Books, pp. 183–201, 1991. (Originally published in *Feminist Studies* 14, 575–600, 1988.)

[1] This chapter originated as a commentary on Harding (1986), at the Western Division meetings of the American Philosophical Association, San Francisco, March 1987. Support during the writing of this paper was generously provided by the Alpha Fund of the Institute for Advanced Study, Princeton, New

Academic and activist feminist enquiry has repeatedly tried to come to terms with the question of what *we* might mean by the curious and inescapable term 'objectivity'. We have used a lot of toxic ink and trees processed into paper decrying what *they* have meant and how it hurts *us*. The imagined 'they' constitute a kind of invisible conspiracy of masculinist scientists and philosophers replete with grants and laboratories; and the imagined 'we' are the embodied others, who are not allowed *not* to have a body, a finite point of view, and so an inevitably disqualifying and polluting bias in any discussion of consequence outside our own little circles, where a 'mass'-subscription journal might reach a few thousand readers composed mostly of science-haters. At least, I confess to these paranoid fantasies and academic resentments lurking underneath some convoluted reflections in print under my name in the feminist literature in the history and philosophy of science. We, the feminists in the debates about science and technology, are the Reagan era's 'special interest groups' in the rarefied realm of epistemology, where traditionally what can count as knowledge is policed by philosophers codifying cognitive canon law. Of course, a special interest group is, by Reaganoid definition, any collective historical subject which dares to resist the stripped-down atomism of Star Wars, hypermarket, postmodern, media-simulated citizenship. Max Headroom doesn't have a body; therefore, he alone *sees* everything in the great communicator's empire of the Global Network. No wonder Max gets to have a naïve sense of humour and a kind of happily regressive, pre-oedipal sexuality, a sexuality which we ambivalently – and dangerously incorrectly – had imagined was reserved for lifelong inmates of female and colonized bodies, and maybe also white male computer hackers in solitary electronic confinement.

It has seemed to me that feminists have both selectively and flexibly used and been trapped by two poles of a tempting dichotomy on the question of objectivity. Certainly I speak for myself here, and I offer the speculation that there is a collective discourse on these matters. On the one hand, recent social studies of science and technology have made available a very strong social constructionist argument for *all* forms of knowledge claims, most certainly and especially scientific ones.[2] In these tempting views, no insider's perspective is privileged, because all drawings of inside–outside boundaries in knowledge are theorized as power

Jersey. Thanks especially to Joan Scott, Rayna Rapp, Judy Newton, Judy Butler, Lila Abu-Lughod, and Dorinne Kondo.

2 For example, see Knorr-Cetina and Mulkay (1983); Bijker et al. (1987); and especially, Latour (1984, 1988). Borrowing from Michel Tournier's Vendredi (1967), Latour's brilliant and maddening aphoristic polemic against all forms of reductionism makes the essential point for feminists: 'Méfiez-vous de la pureté; c'est le vitriol de l'âme' (Labour, 1984, p. 171). Latour is not otherwise a notable feminist theorist, but he might be made into one by readings as perverse as those he makes of the laboratory, that great great machine for making significant mistakes faster than anyone else can, and so gaining world-changing power. The laboratory for Labour is the railroad industry of epistemology, where facts can only be made to run on the tracks laid down from the laboratory out. Those who control the railroads control the surrounding territory. How could we have forgotten? But now it's not so much the bankrupt railroads we need as the satellite network. Facts run on lightbeams these days.

moves, not moves towards truth. So, from the strong social constructionist perspective, why should we be cowed by scientists' descriptions of their activity and accomplishments; they and their patrons have stakes in throwing sand in our eyes. They tell parables about objectivity and scientific method to students in the first years of their initiation, but no practitioner of the high scientific arts would be caught dead *acting on* the textbook versions. Social constructionists make clear that official ideologies about objectivity and scientific method are particularly bad guides to how scientific knowledge is actually *made*. Just as for the rest of us, what scientists believe or say they do and what they really do have a very loose fit.

The only people who end up actually *believing* and, goddess forbid, acting on the ideological doctrines of disembodied scientific objectivity enshrined in elementary textbooks and technoscience booster literature are non-scientists, including a few very trusting philosophers. Of course, my designation of this last group is probably just a reflection of residual disciplinary chauvinism from identifying with historians of science and too much time spent with a microscope in early adulthood in a kind of disciplinary pre-oedipal and modernist poetic moment when cells seemed to be cells and organisms, organisms. *Pace*, Gertrude Stein. But then came the law of the father and its resolution of the problem of objectivity, solved by always already absent referents, deferred signifieds, split subjects, and the endless play of signifiers. Who wouldn't grow up warped? Gender, race, the world itself – all seem just effects of warp seeds in the play of signifiers in a cosmic force field. All truths become warp speed effects in a hyperreal space of simulations. But we cannot afford these particular plays on words – the projects of crafting reliable knowledge about the 'natural' world cannot be given over to the genre of paranoid or cynical science fiction. For political people, social constructionism cannot be allowed to decay into the radiant emanations of cynicism.

In any case, social constructionists could maintain that the ideological doctrine of scientific method and all the philosophical verbiage about epistemology were cooked up to distract our attention from getting to know the world *effectively* by practising the sciences. From this point of view, science – the real game in town, the one we must play – is rhetoric, the persuasion of the relevant social actors that one's manufactured knowledge is a route to a desired form of very objective power. Such persuasions must take account of the structure of facts and artefacts, as well as of language-mediated actors in the knowledge game. Here, artefacts and facts are parts of the powerful art of rhetoric. Practice is persuasion, and the focus is very much on practice. All knowledge is a condensed node in an agonistic power field. The strong programme in the sociology of knowledge joins with the lovely and nasty tools of semiology and deconstruction to insist on the rhetorical nature of truth, including scientific truth. History is a story Western culture buffs tell each other; science is a contestable text and a power field; the content is the form.[3]

[3] For an elegant and very helpful elucidation of a non-cartoon version of this argument, see White (1987). I still want more; and unfulfilled desire can be a powerful seed for changing the stories.

Period. The form in science is the artefactual-social rhetoric of crafting the world into effective objects. This is a practice of world-changing persuasions that take the shape of amazing new objects – like microbes, quarks, and genes.

But whether or not they have the structure and properties of rhetorical objects, late twentieth-century scientific entities – infective vectors (microbes), elementary particles (quarks), and biomolecular codes (genes) – are not Romantic or modernist objects with internal laws of coherence.[4] They are momentary traces focused by force fields, or they are information vectors in a barely embodied and highly mutable semiosis ordered by acts of recognition and misrecognition. Human nature, encoded in its genome and its other writing practices, is a vast library worthy of Umberto Eco's imagined secret labyrinth in *The Name of the Rose* (1980). The stabilization and storage of this text of human nature promise to cost more than its writing. This is a terrifying view of the relationship of body and language for those of us who would still like to talk about *reality* with more confidence than we allow the Christian right's discussion of the Second Coming and their being raptured out of the final destruction of the world. We would like to think our appeals to real worlds are more than a desperate lurch away from cynicism and an act of faith like any other cult's, no matter how much space we generously give to all the rich and always historically specific mediations through which we and everybody else must know the world.

So, the further I get with the description of the radical social constructionist programme and a particular version of postmodernism, coupled to the acid tools of critical discourse in the human sciences, the more nervous I get. Like all neuroses, mine is rooted in the problem of metaphor, that is, the problem of the relation of bodies and language. For example, the force field imagery of moves in the fully textualized and coded world is the matrix for many arguments about socially negotiated reality for the postmodern subject. This world-as-code is, just for starters, a high-tech military field, a kind of automated academic battlefield, where blips of light called players disintegrate (what a metaphor!) each other in order to stay in the knowledge and power game. Technoscience and science fiction

[4] In her analysis exploring the fault line between modernism and postmodernism in ethnography and anthropology – in which the high stakes are the authorization or prohibition to craft comparative knowledge across 'cultures', from some epistemologically grounded vantage point either inside, outside, or in dialogical relation with any unit of analysis – Marilyn Strathern (1987a) made the crucial observation that it is not the written ethnography that is parallel to the work of art as object-of-knowledge, but the culture. The Romantic and modernist natural-technical objects of knowledge, in science and in other cultural practice, stand on one side of this divide. The postmodernist formation stands on the other side, with its 'anti-aesthetic' of permanently split, problematized, always receding and deferred 'objects' of knowledge and practice, including signs, organisms, systems, selves, and cultures. 'Objectivity' in a postmodern frame cannot be about unproblematic objects; it must be about specific prosthesis and translation. Objectivity, which at root has been about crafting comparative knowledge (how to name things to be stable and to be like each other), becomes a question of the politics of redrawing of boundaries in order to have non-innocent conversations and connections. What is at stake in the debates about modernism and postmodernism is the pattern of relationships between and within bodies and language.

collapse into the sun of their radiant (ir)reality – war.[5] It shouldn't take decades of feminist theory to sense the enemy here. Nancy Hartsock (1983b) got all this crystal clear in her concept of abstract masculinity.

I, and others, started out wanting a strong tool for deconstructing the truth claims of hostile science by showing the radical historical specificity, and so contestability, of *every* layer of the onion of scientific and technological constructions, and we end up with a kind of epistemological electro-shock therapy, which far from ushering us into the high stakes tables of the game of contesting public truths, lays us out on the table with self-induced multiple personality disorder. We wanted a way to go beyond showing a bias in science (that proved too easy anyhow), and beyond separating the good scientific sheep from the bad goats of bias and misuse. It seemed promising to do this by the strongest possible constructionist argument that left no cracks for reducing the issues to bias versus objectivity, use versus misuse, science versus pseudo-science. We unmasked the doctrines of objectivity because they threatened our budding sense of collective historical subjectivity and agency and our 'embodied' accounts of the truth, and we ended up with one more excuse for not learning any post-Newtonian physics and one more reason to drop the old feminist self-help practices of repairing our own cars. They're just texts anyway, so let the boys have them back. Besides these textualized postmodern worlds are scary, and we prefer our science fiction to be a bit more utopic, maybe like *Women on the Edge of Time* or even *Wanderground*.

Some of us tried to stay sane in these disassembled and dissembling times by holding out for a feminist version of objectivity. Here, motivated by many of the same political desires, is the other seductive end of the duplicitous objectivity problem. Humanistic Marxism was polluted at the source by its structuring ontological theory of the domination of nature in the self-construction of man and by its closely related impotence to hisoricize anything women did that didn't qualify for a wage. But Marxism was still a promising resource in the form of epistemological feminist mental hygiene that sought our own doctrines of objective vision. Marxist starting points offered tools to get to our versions of standpoint theories, insistent embodiment, a rich tradition of critiques of hegemony without disempowering positivisms and relativisms, and nuanced theories of mediation. Some versions of psychoanalysis aided this approach immensely, especially anglophone object relations theory, which maybe did more for US socialist-feminism for a time than anything from the pen of Marx or Engels, much less Althusser or any of the late pretenders to sonship treating the subject of ideology and science.[6]

Another approach, 'feminist empiricism', also converges with feminist uses of

[5] Zoe Sofoulis (1988) has produced a dazzling (she will forgive me the metaphor) theoretical treatment of technoscience, the psychoanalysis of science fiction culture, and the metaphorics of extra-terrestrialism, including a wonderful focus on the ideologies and philosophies of light, illumination, and discovery in Western mythics of science and technology. My essay was revised in dialogue with Sofoulis's arguments and metaphors in her PhD dissertation.

[6] Crucial in this discussion are Harding (1985), Hartsock (1983a, 1983b), Flax (1983, 1987), Keller and Grontkowski (1983), H. Rose (1986), Haraway (1985; this vol. pp. 149–81, and Petchesky (1987).

Marxian resources to get a theory of science which continues to insist on legitimate meanings of objectivity and which remains leery of a radical constructivism conjugated with semiology and narratology (Harding, 1986, pp. 24–6, 161–2). Feminists have to insist on a better account of the world; it is not enough to show radical historical contingency and modes of construction for everything. Here, we, as feminists, find ourselves perversely conjoined with the discourse of many practising scientists, who, when all is said and done, mostly believe they are describing and discovering things *by means of* all their constructing and arguing. Evelyn Keller has been particularly insistent on this fundamental matter, and Harding calls the goal of these approaches a 'successor science'. Feminists have stakes in a successor science project that offers a more adequate, richer, better account of a world, in order to live in it well and in critical, reflexive relation to our own as well as others' practices of domination and the unequal parts of privilege and oppression that make up all positions. In traditional philosophical categories, the issue is ethics and politics perhaps more than epistemology.

So, I think my problem and 'our' problem is how to have *simultaneously* an account of radical historical contingency for all knowledge claims and knowing subjects, a critical practice for recognizing our own 'semiotic technologies' for making meanings, *and* a no-nonsense commitment to faithful accounts of a 'real' world, one that can be partially shared and friendly to earth-wide projects of finite freedom, adequate material abundance, modest meaning in suffering, and limited happiness. Harding calls this necessary multiple desire a need for a successor science project and a postmodern insistence on irreducible differences and radical multiplicity of local knowledges. *All* components of the desire are paradoxical and dangerous, and their combination is both contradictory and necessary. Feminists don't need a doctrine of objectivity that promises transcendence, a story that loses track of its mediations just where someone might be held responsible for something, and unlimited instrumental power. We don't want a theory of innocent powers to represent the world, where language and bodies both fall into the bliss of organic symbiosis. We also don't want to theorize the world, much less act within it, in terms of Global Systems, but we do need an earth-wide network of connections, including the ability partially to translate knowledges among very different – and power-differentiated – communities. We need the power of modern critical theories of how meanings and bodies get made, not in order to deny meaning and bodies, but in order to live in meanings and bodies that have a chance for a future.

Natural, social, and human sciences have always been implicated in hopes like these. Science has been about a search for translation, convertibility, mobility of meanings, and universality – which I call reductionism, when one language (guess whose) must be enforced as the standard for all the translations and conversions. What money does in the exchange orders of capitalism, reductionism does in the powerful mental orders of global sciences: there is finally only one equation. That is the deadly fantasy that feminists and others have identified in some versions of objectivity doctrines in the service of hierarchical and positivist orderings of what can count as knowledge. That is one of the reasons the debates about objectivity matter, metaphorically and otherwise. Immortality and omnipotence are not our goals. But we could use some enforceable, reliable accounts of things not reducible to power moves and agonistic, high status games of rhetoric or to scientistic, positivist arrogance. This point applies whether we are talking about genes, social classes, elementary particles, genders, races, or texts; the point applies to the exact, natural, social, and human sciences, despite the slippery ambiguities of the words *objectivity* and *science* as we slide around the discursive terrain. In our efforts to climb the greased pole leading to a usable doctrine of objectivity, I and most other feminists in the objectivity debates have alternatively, or even simultaneously, held on to both ends of the dichotomy, which Harding describes in terms of successor science projects versus postmodernist accounts of difference and I have sketched in this chapter as radical constructivism versus feminist critical empiricism. It is, of course, hard to climb when you are holding on to both ends of a pole, simultaneously or alternately. It is, therefore, time to switch metaphors.

The Persistence of Vision[7]

I would like to proceed by placing metaphorical reliance on a much maligned sensory system in feminist discourse: vision. Vision can be good for avoiding binary oppositions. I would like to insist on the embodied nature of all vision, and so reclaim the sensory system that has been used to signify a leap out of the marked body and into a conquering gaze from nowhere. This is the gaze that mythically inscribes all the marked bodies, that makes the unmarked category claim the power to see and not be seen, to represent while escaping representation. This gaze signifies the unmarked positions of Man and White, one of the many nasty tones of the world *objectivity* to feminist ears in scientific and technological, late industrial, militarized, racist and male dominant societies, that is, here, in the belly of the monster, in the United States in the late 1980s. I would like a doctrine of embodied

[7] John Varley's science fiction short story called 'The Persistence of Vision' is part of the inspiration for this section. In the story, Varley constructs a utopian community designed and built by the deaf-blind. He then explores these people's technologies and other mediations of communication and their relations to sighted children and visitors (Varley, 1978). In 'Blue Champagne', Varley (1986) transmutes the theme to interrogate the politics of intimacy and technology for a paraplegic young woman whose prosthetic device, the golden gypsy, allows her full mobility. But since the infintely costly device is owned by an intergalactic communications and entertainment empire for which she works as a media star making 'feelies', she may keep her technological, intimate, enabling, other self only in exchange for her complicity in the commodifications of all experience. What are her limits to the reinvention of experience for sale? Is the personal political under the sign of stimulation? One way to read Varley's repeated investigations of finally always limited embodiments, differently abled beings, prosthetic technologies, and cyborigan encounters with their finitude despite their extraordinary transendence of 'organic' orders is to find an allegory for the personal and political in the historical mythic time of the late twentieth century, the era of techno-biopolitics. Prosthesis is semiosis, the making of meanings and bodies, not for transcendence but for power-charged communication.

objectivity that accommodates paradoxical and critical feminist science projects: feminist objectivity means quite simply *situated knowledges*.

The eyes have been used to signify a perverse capacity – honed to perfection in the history of science tied to militarism, capitalism, colonialism, and male supremacy – to distance the knowing subject from everybody and everything in the interests of unfettered power. The instruments of visualization in multinationalist, postmodernist culture have compounded these meanings of dis-embodiment. The visualizing technologies are without apparent limit; the eye of any ordinary primate like us can be endlessly enhanced by sonography systems, magnetic resonance imaging, artificial intelligence-linked graphic manipulation systems, scanning electron microscopes, computer-aided tomography scanners, colour enhancement techniques, satellite surveillance systems, home and office VDTs, cameras for every purpose from filming the mucous membrane lining the gut cavity of a marine worm living in the vent gases on a fault between continental plates to mapping a planetary hemisphere elsewhere in the solar system. Vision in this technological feast becomes unregúlated gluttony; all perspective gives way to infinitely mobile vision, which no longer seems just mythically about the god-trick of seeing everything from nowhere, but to have put the myth into ordinary practice. And like the god-trick, this eye fucks the world to make techno-monsters. Zoe Sofoulis (1988) calls this the cannibal-eye of masculinist extra-terrestrial projects for excremental second birthing.

A tribute to the ideology of direct, devouring, generative and unrestricted vision, whose technological mediations are simultaneously celebrated and presented as utterly transparent, the volume celebrating the 100th anniversary of the National Geographic Society closes its survey of the magazine's quest literature, effected through its amazing photography, with two juxtaposed chapters. The first is on 'Space', introduced by the epigraph, 'The choice is the universe – or nothing' (Bryan, 1987, p. 352). Indeed. This chapter recounts the exploits of the space race and displays the colour-enhanced 'snapshots' of the outer planets reassembled from digitalized signals transmitted across vast space to let the viewer 'experience' the moment of discovery in immediate vision of the 'object'.[8] These fabulous objects come to us simultaneously as indubitable recordings of what is simply there and as heroic feats of techno-scientific production. The next chapter is the twin of outer space: 'Inner Space', introduced by the epigraph, 'The stuff of stars has come alive' (Bryan, 1987, p. 454). Here, the reader is brought into the realm of the infinitesimal, objectified by means of radiation outside the wave lengths that 'normally' are perceived by hominid primates, i.e., the beams of lasers and scanning electron microscopes, whose signals are processed into the wonderful full-colour snapshots of defending T cells and invading viruses.

But of course that view of infinite vision is an illusion, a god-trick. I would like to suggest how our insisting metaphorically on the particularity and embodiment

[8] I owe my understanding of the experience of these photographs to Jim Clifford, University of California at Santa Cruz, who identified their 'land ho!' effect on the reader.

of all vision (though not necessarily organic embodiment and including technological mediation), and not giving in to the tempting myths of vision as a route to disembodiment and second-birthing, allows us to construct a usable, but not an innocent, doctrine of objectivity. I want a feminist writing of the body that metaphorically emphasizes vision again, because we need to reclaim that sense to find our way through all the visualizing tricks and powers of modern sciences and technologies that have transformed the objectivity debates. We need to learn in our bodies, endowed with primate colour and stereoscopic vision, how to attach the objective to our theoretical and political scanners in order to name where we are and are not, in dimensions of mental and physical space we hardly know how to name. So, not so perversely, objectivity turns out to be about particular and specific embodiment, and definitely not about the false vision promising transcendence of all limits and responsibility. The moral is simple: only partial perspective promises objective vision. This is an objective vision that initiates, rather than closes off, the problem of responsibility for the generativity of all visual practices. Partial perspective can be held accountable for both its promising and its destructive monsters. All Western cultural narratives about objectivity are allegories of the ideologies of relations of what we call mind and body, of distance and responsibility, embedded in the science question in feminism. Feminist objectivity is about limited location and situated knowledge, not about transcendence and splitting of subject and object. In this way we might become answerable for what we learn how to see.

These are lessons which I learned in part walking with my dogs and wondering how the world looks without a fovea and very few retinal cells for colour vision, but with a huge neural processing and sensory area for smells. It is a lesson available from photographs of how the world looks to the compound eyes of an insect, or even from the camera eye of a spy satellite or the digitally transmitted signals of space probe-perceived differences 'near' Jupiter that have been transformed into coffee table colour photographs. The 'eyes' made available in modern technological sciences shatter any idea of passive vision; these prosthetic devices show us that all eyes, including our own organic ones, are active perceptual systems, building in translations and specific *ways* of seeing, that is, ways of life. There is no unmediated photograph or passive camera obscura in scientific accounts of bodies and machines; there are only highly specific visual possibilities, each with a wonderfully detailed, active, partial way of organizing worlds. All these pictures of the world should not be allegories of infinite mobility and interchangeability, but of elaborate specificity and difference and the loving care people take to learn how to see faithfully from another's point of view, even when the other is our own machine. That's not alienating distance; that's a *possible* allegory for feminist versions of objectivity. Understanding how these visual systems work, technically, socially, and psychically ought to be a way of embodying feminist objectivity.

Many currents in feminism attempt to theorize grounds for trusting especially the vantage points of the subjugated; there is good reason to believe vision is better from below the brilliant space platforms of the powerful (Hartsock, 1983a; Sandoval, n.d.; Harding, 1986; Anzaldúa, 1987). Linked to this suspicion, this chapter is an argument for situated and embodied knowledges and against various forms of unlocatable, and so irresponsible, knowledge claims. Irresponsible means unable to be called into account. There is a premium on establishing the capacity to see from the peripheries and the depths. But here lies a serious danger of romanticizing and/or appropriating the vision of the less powerful while claiming to see from their positions. To see from below is neither easily learned nor unproblematic, even if 'we' 'naturally' inhabit the great underground terrain of subjugated knowledges. The positionings of the subjugated are not exempt from critical re-examination, decoding, deconstruction, and interpretation; that is, from both semiological and hermeneutic modes of critical enquiry. The standpoints of the subjugated are not 'innocent' positions. On the contrary, they are preferred because in principle they are least likely to allow denial of the critical and interpretative core of all knowledge. They are savvy to modes of denial through repression, forgetting, and disappearing acts – ways of being nowhere while claiming to see comprehensively. The subjugated have a decent chance to be on to the god-trick and all its dazzling – and, therefore, blinding – illuminations. 'Subjugated' standpoints are preferred because they seem to promise more adequate, sustained, objective, transforming accounts of the world. But *how* to see from below is a problem requiring at least as much skill with bodies and language, with the mediations of vision, as the 'highest' techno-scientific visualizations.

Such preferred positioning is as hostile to various forms of relativism as to the most explicitly totalizing versions of claims to scientific authority. But the alternative to relativism is not totalization and single vision, which is always finally the unmarked category whose power depends on systematic narrowing and obscuring. The alternative to relativism is partial, locatable, critical knowledges sustaining the possibility of webs of connections called solidarity in politics and shared conversations in epistemology. Relativism is a way of being nowhere while claiming to be everywhere equally. The 'equality' of positioning is a denial of responsibility and critical enquiry. Relativism is the perfect mirror twin of totalization in the ideologies of objectivity; both deny the stakes in location, embodiment, and partial perspective; both make it impossible to see well. Relativism and totalization are both 'god-tricks' promising vision from everywhere and nowhere equally and fully, common myths in rhetorics surrounding Science. But it is precisely in the politics and epistemology of partial perspectives that the possibility of sustained, rational, objective enquiry rests.

So, with many other feminists, I want to argue for a doctrine and practice of objectivity that privileges contestation, deconstruction, passionate construction, webbed connections, and hope for transformation of systems of knowledge and ways of seeing. But not just any partial perspective will do; we must be hostile to easy relativisms and holisms built out of summing and subsuming parts. 'Passionate detachment' (Kuhn, 1982) requires more than acknowledged and self-critical partiality. We are also bound to seek perspective from those points of view, which can never be known in advance, which promise something quite extraordinary, that is, knowledge potent for constructing worlds less organized by axes of domination. In such a viewpoint, the unmarked category would *really* disappear – quite a difference from simply repeating a disappearing act. The imaginary and the rational – the visionary and objective vision – hover close together. I think Harding's plea for a successor science and for postmodern sensibilities must be read to argue that this close touch of the fantastic element of hope for transformative knowledge and the severe check and stimulus of sustained critical enquiry are jointly the ground of any believable claim to objectivity or rationality not riddled with breath-taking denials and repressions. It is even possible to read the record of scientific revolutions in terms of this feminist doctrine of rationality and objectivity. Science has been utopian and visionary from the start; that is one reason 'we' need it.

A commitment to mobile positioning and to passionate detachment is dependent on the impossibility of innocent 'identity' politics and epistemologies as strategies for seeing from the standpoints of the subjugated in order to see well. One cannot 'be' either a cell or molecule – or a woman, colonized person, labourer, and so on – if one intends to see and see from these positions critically. 'Being' is much more problematic and contingent. Also, one cannot relocate in any possible vantage point without being accountable for that movement. Vision is *always* a question of the power to see – and perhaps of the violence implicit in our visualizing practices. With whose blood were my eyes crafted? These points also apply to testimony from the position of 'oneself'. We are not immediately present to ourselves. Self-knowledge requires a semiotic-material technology linking meanings and bodies. Self-identity is a bad visual system. Fusion is a bad strategy of positioning. The boys in the human sciences have called this doubt about self-presence the 'death of the subject', that single ordering point of will and consciousness. That judgement seems bizarre to me. I prefer to call this generative doubt the opening of non-isomorphic subjects, agents, and territories of stories unimaginable from the vantage point of the cyclopian, self-satiated eye of the master subject. The Western eye has fundamentally been a wandering eye, a travelling lens. These peregrinations have often been violent and insistent on mirrors for a conquering self – but not always. Western feminists also *inherit* some skill in learning to participate in revisualizing worlds turned upside down in earth-transforming challenges to the views of the masters. All is not to be done from scratch.

The split and contradictory self is the one who can interrogate positionings and be accountable, the one who can construct and join rational conversations and fantastic imaginings that change history.[9] Splitting, not being, is the privileged

[9] Joan Scott reminded me that Teresa de Lauretis (1986a, pp. 14–15) put it like this:

> Differences among women may be better understood as differences within women . . . But once understood in their constitutive power – once it is understood, that is, that these differences not only constitute each woman's consciousness and subjective limits but all together define the female subject of feminism in its very specificity, its inherent and at least for now irreconcilable contradiction – these differences, then, cannot be again collapsed into a fixed identity, a sameness of all women as Woman, or a representation of Feminism as a coherent and available image.

image for feminist epistemologies of scientific knowledge. 'Splitting' in this context should be about heterogeneous multiplicities that are simultaneously necessary and incapable of being squashed into isomorphic slots or cumulative lists. This geometry pertains within and among subjects. The topography of subjectivity is multi-dimensional; so, therefore, is vision. The knowing self is partial in all its guises, never finished, whole, simply there and original; it is always constructed and stitched together imperfectly, and *therefore* able to join with another, to see together without claiming to be another. Here is the promise of objectivity: a scientific knower seeks the subject position not of identity, but of objectivity; that is, partial connection. There is no way to 'be' simultaneously in all, or wholly in any, of the privileged (subjugated) positions structured by gender, race, nation, and class. And that is a short list of critical positions. The search for such a 'full' and total position is the search for the fetishized perfect subject of oppositional history, sometimes appearing in feminist theory as the essentialized Third World Woman (Mohanty, 1984). Subjugation is not grounds for an ontology; it might be a visual clue. Vision requires instruments of vision; an optics is a politics of positioning. Instruments of vision mediate standpoints; there is no immediate vision from the standpoints of the subjugated. Identity, including self-identity, does not produce science; critical positioning does, that is, objectivity. Only those occupying the positions of the dominators are self-identical, unmarked, disembodied, unmediated, transcendent, born again. It is unfortunately possible for the subjugated to lust for and even scramble into that subject position – and then disappear from view. Knowledge from the point of view of the unmarked is truly fantastic, distorted, and so irrational. The only position from which objectivity could not possibly be practised and honoured is the standpoint of the master, the Man, the One God, whose Eye produces, appropriates, and orders all difference. No one ever accused the God of monotheism of objectivity, only of indifference. The god-trick is self-identical, and we have mistaken that for creativity and knowledge, omniscience even.

Positioning is, therefore, the key practice grounding knowledge organized around the imagery of vision, as so much Western scientific and philosophic discourse is organized. Positioning implies responsibility for our enabling practices. It follows that politics and ethics ground struggles for the contests over what may count as rational knowledge. That is, admitted or not, politics and ethics ground struggles over knowledge projects in the exact, natural, social, and human sciences. Otherwise, rationality is simply impossible, an optical illusion projected from nowhere comprehensively. Histories of science may be powerfully told as histories of the technologies. These technologies are ways of life, social orders, practices of visualization. Technologies are skilled practices. How to see? Where to see from? What limits to vision? What to see for? Whom to see with? Who gets to have more than one point of view? Who gets blinkered? Who wears blinkers? Who interprets the visual field? What other sensory powers do we wish to cultivate besides vision? Moral and political discourse should be the paradigm of rational discourse in the imagery and technologies of vision. Sandra Harding's claim, or observation, that movements of social revolution have most contributed to improvements in science might be read as a claim about the knowledge consequences of new technologies of positioning. But I wish Harding had spent more time remembering that social and scientific revolutions have not always been liberatory, even if they have always been visionary. Perhaps this point could be captured in another phrase: the science question in the military. Struggles over what will count as rational accounts of the world are struggles over *how* to see. The terms of vision: the science question in colonialism; the science question in exterminism (Sofoulis, 1988); the science question in feminism.

The issue in politically engaged attacks on various empiricisms, reductionisms, or other versions of scientific authority should not be relativism, but location. A dichotomous chart expressing this point might look like this:

universal rationality	ethnophilosophies
common language	heteroglossia
new organon	deconstruction
unified field theory	oppositional positioning
world system	local knowledges
master theory	webbed accounts

But a dichotomous chart misrepresents in a critical way the positions of embodied objectivity which I am trying to sketch. The primary distortion is the illusion of symmetry in the chart's dichotomy, making any position appear, first, simply alternative and, second, mutually exclusive. A map of tensions and resonances between the fixed ends of a charged dichotomy better represents the potent politics and epistemologies of embodied, therefore accountable, objectivity. For example, local knowledges have also to be in tension with the productive structurings that force unequal translations and exchanges – material and semiotic – within the webs of knowledge and power. Webs *can* have the property of systematicity, even of centrally structured global systems with deep filaments and tenacious tendrils into time, space and consciousness, the dimensions of world history. Feminist accountability requires a knowledge tuned to resonance, not to dichotomy. Gender is a field of structured and structuring difference, where the tones of extreme localization, of the intimately personal and individualized body, vibrate in the same field with global high tension emissions. Feminist embodiment, then, is not about fixed location in a reified body, female or otherwise, but about nodes in fields, inflections in orientations, and responsibility for difference in material-semiotic fields of meaning. Embodiment is significant prosthesis; objectivity cannot be about fixed vision when what counts as an object is precisely what world history turns out to be about.

How should one be positioned in order to see in this situation of tensions, resonances, transformations, resistances, and complicities? Here, primate vision is not immediately a very powerful metaphor or technology for feminist political-epistemological clarification, since it seems to present to consciousness already processed and objectified fields; things seem already fixed and distanced. But the visual metaphor allows one to go beyond fixed appearances, which are only the end products. The metaphor invites us to investigate the varied apparatuses of visual production, including the prosthetic technologies interfaced with our biological eyes and brains. And here we find highly particular machineries for processing regions of the electro-magnetic spectrum into our pictures of the world. It is in the intricacies of these visualization technologies in which we are embedded that we will find metaphors and means for understanding and intervening in the patterns of objectification in the world, that is, the patterns of reality for which we must be accountable. In these metaphors, we find means for appreciating simultaneously *both* the concrete, 'real' aspect and the aspect of semiosis and production in what we call scientific knowledge.

I am arguing for politics and epistemologies of location, positioning, and situating, where partiality and not universality is the condition of being heard to make rational knowledge claims. These are claims on people's lives; the view from a body, always a complex, contradictory, structuring and structured body, versus the view from above, from nowhere, from simplicity. Only the god-trick is forbidden. Here is a criterion for deciding the science question in militarism, that dream science/technology of perfect language, perfect communication, final order.

Feminism loves another science: the sciences and politics of interpretation, translation, stuttering, and the partly understood. Feminism is about the sciences of the multiple subject with (at least) double vision. Feminism is about a critical vision consequent upon a critical positioning in inhomogeneous gendered social space.[10] Translation is always interpretative, critical, and partial. Here is a ground for

[10] Harding (1986, p. 18) suggested that gender has three dimensions, each historically specific: gender symbolism, the social-sexual division of labour, and processes of constructing individual gendered identity. I would enlarge her point to note that there is no reason to expect the three dimensions to co-vary or co-determine each other, at least not directly. That is, extremely steep gradients between contrasting terms in gender symbolism may very well not correlate with sharp social-sexual divisions of labour or social power, but may be closely related to sharp racial stratification or something else. Similarly, the processes of gendered sujbect formation may not be directly illuminated by knowledge of the sexual division of labour or the gender symbolism in the particular historical situation under examination. On the other hand, we should expect mediated relations among the dimensions. The mediations might move through quite different social axes of organization of both symbols, practice, and identity, such as race. And vice versa. I would suggest also that sicence, as well as gender or race, might usefully be broken up into such a multi-part scheme of symbolism, social practice, and subject position. More than three dimensions suggest themselves when the parallels are drawn. The different dimensions of, for example, gender, race, and science might mediate relations among dimensions as a parallel chart. That is, racial divisions of labour might mediate the patterns of connection between symbolic connections and formation of individual subject positions on the science or gender chart. Or formations of gendered or racial subjectivity might mediate the relations between scientific social divison of labour and scientific symbolic patterns.

The chart below begins an analysis by parallel dissections. In the chart (and in reality?), both gender and science are analytically asymmetrical; i.e., each term contains and obscures a structuring hierarchicalized binarism, sex/gender and nature/science. Each binarism orders the silent term by a logic of appropriation, as resource to product, nature to culture, potential to actual. Both poles of the binarism are constructed and structure each other dialectically. Within each voiced or explicit term, further asym-

conversation, rationality, and objectivity – which is power-sensitive, not pluralist, 'conversation'. It is not even the mythic cartoons of physics and mathematics – incorrectly caricatured in anti-science ideology as exact, hyper-simple knowledges – that have come to represent the hostile other to feminist paradigmatic models of scientific knowledge, but the dreams of the perfectly known in high-technology, permanently militarized scientific productions and positionings, the god-trick of a Star Wars paradigm of rational knowledge. So location is about vulnerability; location resists the politics of closure, finality, or, to borrow from Althusser, feminist objectivity resists 'simplification in the last instance'. That is because feminist embodiment resists fixation and is insatiably curious about the webs of differential positioning. There is no single feminist standpoint because our maps require too many dimensions for that metaphor to ground our visions. But the feminist standpoint theorists' goal of an epistemology and politics of engaged, accountable positioning remains eminently potent. The goal is better accounts of the world, that is, 'science'.

Above all, rational knowledge does not pretend to be disengagement: to be from everywhere and so nowhere, to be free from interpretation, from being represented, to be fully self-contained or fully formalizable. Rational knowledge is a process of ongoing critical interpretation among 'fields' of interpreters and decoders. Rational knowledge is power-sensitive conversation (King, 1987a):

> knowledge:community::knowledge:power
> hermeneutics:semiology::critical interpretation:codes.

Decoding and transcoding plus translation and criticism; all are necessary. So

metrical splittings can be excavated, as from gender, masculine to feminine, and from science, hard sciences to soft sciences. This is a point about remembering how a particular analytical tool works, willy nilly, intended or not. The chart reflects common ideological aspects of discourse on science and gender and may help as an analytical tool to crack open mystified units like Science or Woman.

Gender	Science
symbolic system	symbolic system
social divison of labour (by sex, by race, etc.)	social division of labour (by craft, industrial, or post-industrial logics)
individual identity/subject position	individual identity/subject position
(desiring/desired; autonomous/relational)	(knower/known; scientist/other)
material culture (gender paraphernalia and daily gender technologies: the narrow tracks on which sexual difference runs)	material culture (laboratories: the narrow tracks on which facts run)
dialectic of construction and discovery	dialectic of construction and discovery

science becomes the paradigmatic model not of closure, but of that which is contestable and contested. Science becomes the myth not of what escapes human agency and responsibility in a realm above the fray, but rather of accountability and responsibility for translations and solidarities linking the cacophonous visions and visionary voices that characterize the knowledges of the subjugated. A splitting of senses, a confusion of voice and sight, rather than clear and distinct ideas, becomes the metaphor for the ground of the rational. We seek not the knowledges ruled by phallogocentrism (nostalgia for the presence of the one true Word) and disembodied vision, but those ruled by partial sight and limited voice. We do not seek partiality for its own sake, but for the sake of the connections and unexpected openings situated knowledges make possible. The only way to find a larger vision is to be somewhere in particular. The science question in feminism is about objectivity as positioned rationality. Its images are not the products of escape and transcendence of limits, i.e., the view from above, but the joining of partial views and halting voices into a collective subject position that promises a vision of the means of ongoing finite embodiment, of living within limits and contradictions, i.e., of views from somewhere.

Objects as Actors: The Apparatus of Bodily Production

Throughout this reflection on 'objectivity', I have refused to resolve the ambiguities built into referring to science without differentiating its extraordinary range of contexts. Through the insistent ambiguity, I have foregrounded a field of commonalities binding exact, physical, natural, social, political, biological, and human sciences; and I have tied this whole heterogeneous field of academically (and industrially, for example, in publishing, the weapons trade, and pharmaceuticals) institutionalized knowledge production to a meaning of science that insists on its potency in ideological struggles. But, partly in order to give play to both the specificities and the highly permeable boundaries of meanings in discourse on science, I would like to suggest a resolution to one ambiguity. Throughout the field of meanings constituting science, one of the commonalities concerns the status of any object of knowledge and of related claims about the faithfulness of our accounts to a 'real world', no matter how mediated for us and no matter how complex and contradictory these worlds may be. Feminists, and others who have been most active as critics of the sciences and their claims or associated ideologies, have shied away from doctrines of scientific objectivity in part because of the suspicion that an 'object' of knowledge is a passive and inert thing. Accounts of such objects can seem to be either appropriations of a fixed and determined world reduced to resource for the instrumentalist projects of destructive Western societies, or they can be seen as masks for interests, usually dominating interests.

For example, 'sex' as an object of biological knowledge appears regularly in the guise of biological determinism, threatening the fragile space for social constructionism and critical theory, with their attendant possibilities for active and transformative intervention, called into being by feminist concepts of gender as socially, historically, and semiotically positioned difference. And yet, to lose authoritative biological accounts of sex, which set up productive tensions with its binary pair, gender, seems to be to lose too much ; it seems to be to lose not just analytic power within a particular Western tradition, but the body itself as anything but a blank page for social inscriptions, including those of biological discourse. The same problem of loss attends a radical 'reduction' of the objects of physics or of any other sciences to the ephemera of discursive production and social construction.[11]

But the difficulty and loss are not necessary. They derive partly from the analytical tradition, deeply indebted to Aristotle and to the transformative history of 'White Capitalist Patriarchy' (how may we name this scandalous Thing?) that turns everything into a resource for appropriation, in which an object of knowledge is finally itself only matter for the seminal power, the act, of the knower. Here, the object both guarantees and refreshes the power of the knower, but any status as *agent* in the productions of knowledge must be denied the object. It – the world – must, in short, be objectified as thing, not as an agent; it must be matter for the self-formation of the only social being in the productions of knowledge, the human knower. Zoe Sofoulis (1988) identified the structure of this mode of knowing in technoscience as 'resourcing' – the second-birthing of Man through the homogenizing of all the world's body into resource for his perverse projects. Nature is only the raw material of culture, appropriated, preserved, enslaved, exalted, or otherwise made flexible for disposal by culture in the logic of capitalist colonialism. Similarly, sex is only the matter to the act of gender; the productionist logic seems inescapable in traditions of Western binarisms. This analytical and historical narrative logic accounts for my nervousness about the sex/gender distinction in the recent history of feminist theory. Sex is 'resourced' for its representation as gender, which 'we' can control. It has seemed all but impossible to avoid the trap of an appropriationist logic of domination built into the nature/culture binarism and its generative lineage, including the sex/gender distinction.

It seems clear that feminist accounts of objectivity and embodiment – that is, of a world – of the kind sketched in this chapter require a deceptively simple manoeuvre within inherited Western analytical traditions, a manoeuvre begun in dialectics, but stopping short of the needed revisions. Situated knowledges require that the object of knowledge be pictured as an actor and agent, not a screen or a ground or a resource, never finally as slave to the master that closes off the dialectic in his unique agency and authorship of 'objective' knowledge. The point is paradigmatically clear in critical approaches to the social and human sciences, where the agency of people studied itself transforms the entire project of producing social

[11] Evelyn Keller (1987) insists on the important possibilities opened up by the construction of the intersection of the distinction between sex and gender, on the one hand, and nature and science, on the other. She also insists on the need to hold to some non-discursive grounding in 'sex' and 'nature', perhaps what I am calling the 'body' and 'world'.

theory. Indeed, coming to terms with the agency of the 'objects' studied is the only way to avoid gross error and false knowledge of many kinds in these sciences. But the same point must apply to the other knowledge projects called sciences. A corollary of the insistence that ethics and politics covertly or overtly provide the bases for objectivity in the sciences as a heterogeneous whole, and not just in the social sciences, is granting the status of agent/actor to the 'objects' of the world. Actors come in many and wonderful forms. Accounts of a 'real' world do not, then, depend on a logic of 'discovery', but on a power-charged social relation of 'conversation'. The world neither speaks itself nor disappears in favour of a master decoder. The codes of the world are not still, waiting only to be read. The world is not raw material for humanization; the thorough attacks on humanism, another branch of 'death of the subject' discourse, have made this point quite clear. In some critical sense that is crudely hinted at by the clumsy category of the social or of agency, the world encountered in knowledge projects is an active entity. In so far as a scientific account has been able to engage this dimension of the world as object of knowledge, faithful knowledge can be imagined and can make claims on us. But no particular doctrine of representation or decoding or discovery guarantees anything. The approach I am recommending is not a version of 'realism', which has proved a rather poor way of engaging with the world's active agency.

My simple, perhaps simple-minded, manoeuvre is obviously not new in Western philosophy, but it has a special feminist edge to it in relation to the science question in feminism and to the linked questions of gender as situated difference and of female embodiment. Ecofeminists have perhaps been most insistent on some version of the world as active subject, not as resource to be mapped and appropriated in bourgeois, Marxist, or masculinist projects. Acknowledging the agency of the world in knowledge makes room for some unsettling possibilities, including a sense of the world's independent sense of humour. Such a sense of humour is not comfortable for humanists and others committed to the world as resource. Richly evocative figures exist for feminist visualizations of the world as witty agent. We need not lapse into an appeal to a primal mother resisting becoming resource. The Coyote or Trickster, embodied in American Southwest Indian accounts, suggests our situation when we give up mastery but keep searching for fidelity, knowing all the while we will be hoodwinked. I think these are useful myths for scientists who might be our allies. Feminist objectivity makes room for surprises and ironies at the heart of all knowledge production; we are not in charge of the world. We just live here and try to strike up non-innocent conversations by means of our prosthetic devices, including our visualization technologies. No wonder science fiction has been such a rich writing practice in recent feminist theory. I like to see feminist theory as a reinvented coyote discourse obligated to its enabling sources in many kinds of heterogeneous accounts of the world.

Another rich feminist practice in science in the last couple of decades illustrates particularly well the 'activation' of the previously passive categories of objects of knowledge. The activation permanently problematizes binary distinctions like sex and gender, without however eliminating their strategic utility. I refer to the reconstructions in primatology, especially but not only women's practice as primatologists, evolutionary biologists, and behavioural ecologists, of what may count as sex, especially as female sex, in scientific accounts (Haraway, 1989b). The *body*, the object of biological discourse, itself becomes a most engaging being. Claims of biological determinism can never be the same again. When female 'sex' has been so thoroughly re-theorized and revisualized that it emerges as practically indistinguishable from 'mind', something basic has happened to the categories of biology. The biological female peopling current biological behavioural accounts has almost no passive properties left. She is structuring and active in every respect; the 'body' is an agent, not a resource. Difference is theorized *biologically* as situational, not intrinsic, at every level from gene to foraging pattern, thereby fundamentally changing the biological politics of the body. The relations between sex and gender have to be categorically reworked within these frames of knowledge. I would like to suggest this trend in exploratory strategies in biology as an allegory for interventions faithful to projects of feminist objectivity. The point is not that these new pictures of the biological female are simply true or not open to contestation and conversation. Quite the opposite. But these pictures foreground knowledge as situated conversation at every level of its articulation. The boundary between animal and human is one of the stakes in this allegory, as well as that between machine and organism.

So I will close with a final category useful to a feminist theory of situated knowledges: the apparatus of bodily production. In her analysis of the production of the poem as an object of literary value, Katie King offers tools that clarify matters in the objectivity debates among feminists. King suggests the term 'apparatus of literary production' to highlight the emergence of what is embodied as literature at the intersection of art, business, and technology. The apparatus of literary production is a matrix from which 'literature' is born. Focusing on the potent object of value called the 'poem', King applies her analytic frame to the relation of women and writing technologies (King, 1987b). I would like to adapt her work to understanding the generation – the actual production and reproduction – of bodies and other objects of value in scientific knowledge projects. At first glance, there is a limitation to using King's scheme inherent in the 'facticity' of biological discourse that is absent from literary discourse and its knowledge claims. Are biological bodies 'produced' or 'generated' in the same strong sense as poems? From the early stirrings of Romanticism in the late eighteenth century, many poets and biologists have believed that poetry and organisms are siblings. *Frankenstein* may be read as a meditation on this proposition. I continue to believe in this potent proposition, but in a postmodern and not a Romantic manner of belief. I wish to translate the ideological dimensions of 'facticity' and 'the organic' into a cumbersome entity called a 'material-semiotic actor'. This unwieldy term is intended to highlight the object of knowledge as an active, meaning-generating axis of the apparatus of bodily production, without *ever* implying immediate presence of such objects or, what is the same thing, their final or unique determination of what can count as objective knowledge at a particular historical juncture. Like King's objects called 'poems', which are sites of literary production where language also is an actor independent of intentions and authors, bodies as objects of knowledge are material-semiotic generative nodes. Their *boundaries* materialize in social interaction. Boundaries are drawn by mapping practices; 'objects' do not pre-exist as such. Objects are boundary projects. But boundaries shift from within; boundaries are very tricky. What boundaries provisionally contain remains generative, productive of meanings and bodies. Siting (sighting) boundaries is a risky practice.

Objectivity is not about dis-engagement, but about mutual *and* usually unequal structuring, about taking risks in a world where 'we' are permanently mortal, that is, not in 'final' control. We have, finally, no clear and distinct ideas. The various contending biological bodies emerge at the intersection of biological research and writing, medical and other business practices, and technology, such as the visualization technologies enlisted as metaphors in this chapter. But also invited into that node of intersection is the analogue to the lively languages that actively intertwine in the production of literary value: the coyote and protean embodiments of a world as witty agent and actor. Perhaps the world resists being reduced to mere resource because it is – not mother/matter/mutter – but coyote, a figure for the always problematic, always potent tie of meaning and bodies. Feminist embodiment, feminist hopes for partiality, objectivity and situated knowledges, turn on conversations and codes at this potent node in fields of possible bodies and meanings. Here is where science, science fantasy, and science fiction converge in the objectivity question in feminism. Perhaps our hopes for accountability, for politics, for ecofeminism, turn on revisioning the world as coding trickster with whom we must learn to converse.

References

Anzalduá, Gloria (1987) *Borderlands/La Frontera*. San Francisco: Spinsters/Aunt Lute

Bijker, Wiebe E., Hughes, Thomas P., and Pinch, Trevor, eds (1987) *The Social Construction of Technological Systems*. Cambridge, MA: MIT Press

Bryan, C.D.B. (1987) *The National Geographic Society: 100 Years of Adventure and Discovery*. New York: Abrams.

de Lauretis, Teresa (1986a) 'Feminist studies/critical studies: issues, terms, and contexts', in de Lauretis (1986b), pp. 1–19.

ed. (1986b) *Feminist Studies/Critical Studies*. Bloomington: Indiana University Press.

Eco, Umberto (1983) *The Name of the Rose*, William Weaver, trans. New York: Harcourt Brace Jovanovich.

Flax, Jane (1983) 'Political philosophy and the patriarchal unconscious: a psychoanalytic perspective on epistemology and metaphysics', in Harding and Hintikka (1983), pp. 245–82.

(1987) 'Postmodernism and gender relations in feminist theory', *Signs* 12(4): 621–43.

Haraway, Donna (1985) 'Manifesto for cyborgs: science, technology, and socialist feminism in the 1980s', *Socialist Review* 80: 65–108.

(1989b) *Primate Visions: Gender, Race, and Nature in the World of Modern Science*. New York: Routledge.

Harding, Sandra (1986) *The Science Question in Feminism*. Ithaca: Cornell University Press.

and Hintikka, Merrill, eds (1983) *Discovering Reality: Feminist Perspectives on Epistemology, Metaphysics, and Philosophy of Science*. Dordrecht: Reidel.

Harstock, Nancy (1983a) 'The feminist standpoint: developing the ground for a specifically feminist historical materialism, in Harding and Hintikka (1983), pp. 283–310.

(1983b) *Money, Sex, and Power*. New York: Longman.

Keller, Evelyn Fox (1985) *Reflections on Gender and Science*. New Haven: Yale University Press.

(1987) 'The gender/science system: or, is sex to gender as nature is to science?', *Hypatia* 2(3): 37–49.

and Grontkowski, Christine (1983) 'The mind's eye', in Harding and Hintikka (1983), pp. 207–24.

King, Katie (1987a) 'Canons without innocence', University of California at Santa Cruz, PhD thesis.

(1987b) *The Passing Dream of Choice . . . Once Before and After: Andre Lourde and the Apparatus of Literary Production*, book prospectus, University of Maryland at College Park.

Knorr-Cetina, Karin and Mulkay, Michael, eds (1983) *Science Observed: Perspectives on the Social Study of Science*. Beverly Hills: Sage.

Kuhn, Annette (1982) *Women's Pictures: Feminism and Cinema*. London: Routledge & Kegan Paul.

Latour, Bruno (1984) *Les microbes, guerre et paix, suivi des irreductions*. Paris: Métailié

(1988) *The Pasteurization of France, followed by Irreductions: A Politico-Scientific Essay*. Cambridge, MA: Harvard University Press.

Mohanty, Chandra Talpode (1984) 'Under western eyes: feminist scholarship and colonial discourse', *Boundary* 2, 3 (12/13): 333–58.

Petchesky, Rosalind Pollack (1987) 'Fetal images: the power of visual culture in the politics of reproduction', *Feminist Studies* 13(2): 263–92.

Rose, Hilary (1986) 'Women's work: women's knowledge', in Juliet Mitchell and Ann Oakley, eds, *What is Feminism? A Re-Examination*. New York: Pantheon, pp. 161–83.

Sandoval, Chela (n.d.) Yours in Struggle: Women Respond to Racism, a Report on the National Women's Studies Association. Oakland, CA: Center for Third World Organizing.

Sofoulis, Zoe (1988) 'Through the lumen: Frankenstein and the optics of re-originiation', University of California at Santa Cruz, PhD thesis.

Strathern, Marilyn (1987a) 'Out of context: the persuasive fictions of anthropology', *Current Anthropology* 28(3): 251–81.

Tournier, Michel (1967) *Vendredi*. Paris: Gallimard.

Varley, John (1978) 'The persistence of vision', in *The Persistence of Vision*. New York: Dell, pp. 263–316.

(1986) 'Blue champagne', in *Blue Champagne*. New York: Berkeley, pp. 17–70.

White, Hayden (1987) *The Context of the Form: Narrative Discourse and Historical Representation*. Baltimore: Johns Hopkins University Press.

PART II

THE ENTERPRISE

INTRODUCTION

Although geography has existed as a more or less discrete sphere of scholarly investigation since ancient times, it has undergone numerous transformations. Just as species experience change, so disciplines undergo 'evolutionary' transmutation (Hull 1988). If we were to look at what passed for geography in Ptolemy's time, and then in the late Middle Ages, and then today, we would be struck by the differences. In classical times geography was intimately associated with astronomy, and we can easily see why Ptolemy has been described as the father of both geography and astronomy. In the late Middle Ages geography was part of a larger field called cosmography that included astrology and fields that today we might be inclined to dismiss as hocus-pocus. In the mid-twentieth century, by contrast, a good deal of academic geography concerned itself with spatial science, or locational analysis as it was also called, in which a variety of statistical models was developed in the attempt to account for spatial patterns.

Now if we were to look at these three moments in isolation from each other, what would undoubtedly strike us is the disparity between them. The diverse beliefs and practices that geography embodied at these different points in time seem scarcely related to each other even by the remotest family resemblance. But they *are* connected historically in that there are ties linking them together in just the same way as a foetus is connected to a human adult, or primitive organisms are linked in an evolutionary chain to contemporary life forms. The identity of geography, as with any discipline, is to be found precisely in its history. This implies, of course, that there is no transcendent or universal definition of 'geography' that will pass muster for all times and places. As Friedrich Nietzsche (1967, p. 80) once tellingly observed: 'only that which has no history is definable'.

To all this we must add that just as the discipline of geography changes historically, it also changes geographically, that is, from place to place. What it was to be a geographer in, say, Nazi *Germany* was different from what it was in Jeffersonian *America*, or Enlightenment *France*, or inter-war *Britain*: just as there is a history of geography, so there is an historical geography of geography, and of course both are connected in significant ways. But attending to the spatial components of knowledge points to the significance of national context in the production of geographical claims. And this is not the only scale at which the spatial context matters; regional and sub-regional differences may well mean that, for example, geography in Victorian times manifests itself rather differently in Edinburgh and in London, or in Boston and Charleston. Clearly period *and* place both matter in enunciations of what the geographical enterprise has meant.

Pre-professional Elaborations

Because the selections in this section of the anthology deal with various conceptions of the geographical enterprise over the past century or so, it is worth pausing to reflect on just some of the earlier ways in which geography was conceived prior to its becoming a 'professional' field of intellectual endeavour during the second half of the nineteenth century. Here we will provide only the barest outline of this earlier trajectory. These episodes have been more fully treated elsewhere (Glacken 1967; Livingstone 1992), and our focus is substantially on the more recent periods. Reviewing these earlier conceptualizations is an important aspect of this section nonetheless. It will give some historical depth to our understanding of the geographical enterprise prior to the changes in the structure of scholarship that took place just over a century ago, when scholarly endeavour was carved up into what were regarded as a set of discrete 'disciplines'. The forces that led to this new organization of knowledge had a huge bearing on the way in which the different fields became defined. The academic division of labour forced practitioners of various scholarly traditions to seek for a piece of conceptual and empirical territory over which they had more or less exclusive rights. In the pre-professional period different forces were at work.

In the ancient world, geography (literally geographia, earth-writing or earth-description) embodied a number of related, if distinct, practices – geometry (whose literal meaning is earth-measurement), cartography, maritime travel writing, and historical description. Of course in different places different emphases were apparent. In Miletus between the seventh and fifth centuries BC, for example, figures like Thales, Anaximander, and Hecataeus focused on geometrical and astronomical questions concerning the earth's shape and position among the heavenly bodies. Here the use of practical mathematics was evidently crucial.

The Greek maritime tradition which cultivated a taste for regional description and that arose from overseas travel was markedly different. The *Periplus of Hanno*, recording the voyage in 500 BC of a Carthaginian Admiral down the coast of West Africa, is representative of this travel literature. Different yet again were the historical contributions of figures such as Herodotus in the fifth century BC, for whom geography provided the stage on which the human drama was played out. These variant practices were all represented in the magisterial statement of the nature of geography made by Strabo who, in the first century AD, worked in the great library of Alexandria. For Strabo geography was a truly synthetic pursuit embracing both the philosophical and the practical, the mathematical and the descriptive. And yet the mathematical came through most strongly when Strabo wrote that for the 'fundamental principles of his science, the geographer must rely upon the geometricians who have measured the earth as a whole; and in their turn the geometricians must rely upon the astronomers' (Kish 1978, §29).

The mathematical emphasis was perpetuated by Claudius Ptolemy in the second century AD (Thomson 1965; Nicolet 1991), who distinguished between geography and chorography. The former, as a mathematical pursuit, dealt with the earth as a whole, the latter encompassed studies of particular portions of its surface. For Ptolemy the distinction was like that between drawing a whole head and the sketching of an eye: 'The aim of chorography is a consideration of the parts as would be the case for someone depicting just the ear or eye; but the aim of geography is a consideration of the whole, as it is for those (to use the same analogy) who depict the entire head' (quoted in Dilke 1987, p. 183).

These classical conceptions of geography exercised immense cognitive authority in the West right up to the sixteenth century. Peter Apian, for example, in his 1551 *Cosmographia*, illustrated the continuing cogency of the Ptolemaic conception by presenting a *mappamundi* (a map of the world) alongside a portrait of a whole head, and a city-view adjacent to a drawing of an ear (see Alpers 1983). The survival of these and other classical elements owed much to Islamic scholars who perpetuated the Ptolemaic system during the Middle Ages, and left an immense legacy of independent geographical work. The cartographic contributions of al-Idrisi and his successors in the twelfth century show the lingering influence of Ptolemy, while the maps emanating from the al-Balkī school in the tenth century and the production of Qibla charts owe much more to inspiration from within Islam itself (see Harley and Woodward 1992). Principles of regional interrogation were laid down by al-Muqaddasi, and impressive geodetic calculations were carried out by al-Biruni (see Kish 1978, §53, §57). Later in the fourteenth century, the travel writings of Ibn-Battuta and Ibn-Khaldun further contributed to Islam's geographical heritage.

The extensive voyages undertaken by Europeans during the fifteenth and sixteenth centuries induced serious reservations about much of the heritage of classical geography. The central significance attached to eye-witness observation and direct experience began to triumph over scholastic authority (Grafton 1992; Pagden 1993). Geographical empiricism questioned and subverted received dogma: experience could be, and was, cast as 'the mistress of all' (Lestringant 1994; also Cormack 1992). We can make too much of this empirical turn however, for geographical information was frequently harnessed to serve the needs of astrologers and other magical practitioners (Livingstone 1988). At the same time we should note that the cultivation of a taste for exotic depictions of other people and places (Campbell 1988) did much to construct the whole ideology of what may be called 'the-West-and-the-Rest-syndrome'.

During the scientific revolution of the seventeenth century many of the challenges to the classical heritage were confirmed. A number of key statements on the nature of the 'new' geography were forthcoming, but the structure of the old Ptolemaic framework for geography remained in place. In early seventeenth-century Germany, Keckermann spoke of the fundamental distinction between

Geographica Generalis and Geographica Specialis – a distinction drawn from Ptolemy's own discrimination of geography from chorology (Bowen 1981). In the English-speaking world, in his two-volume *Geography Delineated Forth,* Nathanael Carpenter repudiated the subservience to classical scholastic authority that characterized much of the geographical enterprise, and lauded the work of those relying on experience and observation. Yet for all that, the self-same dichotomy that Ptolemy had postulated surfaced in Carpenter's explicit resort to Keckermann's juxtaposition of General and Special Geography, as it also did in Varenius's 1650 *Geographia Generalis* (see Livingstone 1992).

These same structural oppositions continued to characterize the elucidation of the nature of geography during the Enlightenment. In the celebrated *Encyclopédie* of Diderot and d'Alembert, for example, geography was divided into 'universelle' and 'particulière', both of which were subsumed under the larger enterprise of cosmography (Withers 1993).

Such taxonomic considerations aside, the late eighteenth, and early nineteenth, centuries witnessed some of the most extensive treatments of geographical science – textually at least. In Alexander von Humboldt the conception of geography as *the* grand synthesizing science found the fullest expression. Indeed the powerful scientific thrust of his geography led Cannon to argue that the label 'Humboldtian science' characterized the scientific style of the pre-Darwinian era. This was a geographical species of science in which the 'accurate, measured study of widespread but interconnected real phenomena' held pride of place (Cannon 1978, p. 105). A similar emphasis on the interconnectedness of things was, concurrently, the leitmotif of Carl Ritter's geography, although in Ritter's case this conviction was suffused with teleological assurances about God's design in the universe – a theme that had dominated much English-speaking geography between the seventeenth and nineteenth centuries (Livingstone 1992).

Professional Pronouncements

Throughout the first half of the nineteenth century geography was seen largely either as an adjunct to overseas imperialism or as a doxological and universal science in which the natural and political orders were seen as manifestations of divine providence. The Victorian era of empire-building did much to confirm the practical and political power of the geographer's craft. But in the aftermath of Darwin's theory of evolution and with the increasing specialization of learning that accelerated the rise of the accredited expert, it became increasingly difficult to maintain a conception of geography as universal science. A variety of efforts to provide a chastened definition was soon forthcoming.

In different national contexts, the cause of geography was championed by different individuals (Livingstone 1992). In 1880s Germany, for example, Friedrich Ratzel sought to lay out the conceptual foundations of a new discipline – *Anthropogeographie,* a human geography. Ratzel's main concern was to situate this new enterprise in the framework of naturalistic science. He thus brought evolutionary principles to bear on a cluster of related issues – migration, diffusion and space – which in turn explained the spatial arrangements and social functionings of human cultures. Of central importance was his idea of the *Lebensraum*, the living space within which human cultures develop – an idea later to achieve notoriety in Nazi Germany.

In the United States, William Morris Davis did much to secure the establishment of geography as a university discipline. He too understood the subject as linked to nature and sought to discover the ways in which the physical features of the earth's surface had conditioned human responses to environmental challenges. Conceiving it on evolutionary principles, Davis depicted the study of geography as the relationship between what he termed 'inorganic controls and organic responses' (Davis 1906). Davis meant by this that living beings were directly acted upon by the physical environment, which determined many aspects of their behaviour.

In Britain, the chief apologist for university geography was Halford Mackinder, who outlined his thoughts on the nature of the enterprise in his famous 1887 address to the Royal Geographical Society 'On the Scope and Method of Geography' (**chapter 8**). Here Mackinder conceived geography as the 'meeting point' between the natural and cultural sciences, something which he felt was increasingly absent because of the professionalizing impulses of his day. Here was unoccupied academic territory the geographer could colonize at a time of mushrooming specialisms each with their own 'imperialist' agendas. Mere regional description was no longer good enough; what was needed was a 'scientific' geography in which the causal connections between the physical environment and human society could be traced. For Mackinder (in truly environmental determinist fashion) 'no *rational* political geography can exist which is not built upon and subsequent to physical geography'. This experiment in linking nature and culture and in exploring the connections between environment and society privileged the first over the second. It was to exercise a long and lasting influence.

Mackinder's geography, of course, was intimately connected with his geopolitical aspirations. As a strategist and an active politician, he was eager to bring geographical principles to bear on matters of concern to the British Empire. Indeed geography, in his mind, was a special kind of imperial envisioning. And so over the years he published a sequence of papers dealing, in one way or another, with issues of political power, the control of land, and global *Realpolitik* (Toal 1992). The Victorian ties that kept geography and imperialism as intimate partners found in Mackinder a willing accomplice.

Not all, however, were enamoured of the nineteenth-century imperial moment and with the complicity of geographers in its flourishing. Peter Kropotkin, formerly a Russian prince but now a leading anarchist, gave voice to an altogether different conception of geography's potential, although no less based on evolutionary thinking. In 1885 (**chapter 7**), Kropotkin outlined what he believed geography *ought* to be. For him it afforded the possibility of greater humanitarianism. Rather than furthering the ends of nationalistic exploitation, geography – properly conceived – could confirm the universal brotherhood and sisterhood of humankind. Instead of serving the desires of warmongers, Kropotkin hoped it could be 'a means of dissipating these prejudices and of creating other feelings more worthy of humanity'. For all that, Kropotkin continued to espouse a fundamentally naturalistic conception of geography, a stance no doubt derived from his Lamarckian interpretation of evolutionary theory (that socially or environmentally acquired characteristics are inheritable) and his long-standing interest in the direct impact of the environment on plants and animals.

Environmental determinism as a cardinal geographical principle did not go uncontested. In the United States one of its staunchest opponents was the anthropologist Franz Boas, who maintained a life-long interest in geography. In 1887 (**chapter 9**), Boas turned his attention to the methodological quandary that the discipline of geography faced in its efforts to combine scientific and historical modes of inquiry. The positivist ambition to reduce all phenomena to universal laws failed to do justice to the integrity of the particular and the individual. Thus Boas counterposed the 'scientific' spirit of Comte to the descriptive reverence of Humboldt. The attempt to elaborate a set of causal laws for geography (as the determinists typically did), he argues, was simply misguided; for geography was much more closely connected with what he called the 'affective impulse'. Especially for human geography, understanding rather than explanation was the appropriate mode of inquiry – a distinction Boas had imbibed from the philosopher Wilhelm Dilthey. Not surprisingly, in his later career as an anthropologist Boas steadfastly repudiated environmental determinism and espoused historical particularism, a stance that found ample expression in the cultural geography of Carl Sauer (an example of whose work may be seen in **chapter 17**).

In France, the querying of a crude necessitarianism owed much to the contributions of Vidal de la Blache and his successors. For Vidal, geography was fundamentally the study of the ways in which a variety of natural realms provided the milieux in which human life-styles – *genres de vie* – were produced. In Vidal's mind these different social aggregations had powerfully transformed the physical environment to produce a variegated mosaic of geographical regions (Buttimer 1971). In his famous *Tableau de la Géographie de la France* (1903) he demonstrated how the physiognomy of his native France was the product of a synthesis of nature and culture. And yet, for all that, as the introduction to his *Principles of Human Geography* (**chapter 10**) makes plain, Vidal thought of the subject in naturalistic terms, deriving inspiration from ecological principles and their potential application to human geography. Later enthusiasts in different circumstances and with a different agenda, intent on rediscovering an anti-positivist lineage, have all too frequently ignored this crucial element in the Vidalian corpus.

By now a variety of stances on how the physical and social might be interconnected, ranging from determinism to possibilism, were available to geographers. Yet proponents of both extremes could still agree that the subject-matter of the newly professionalized geography lay in its elucidation of regional variation. This view was championed in the English-speaking world by Richard Hartshorne who in 1939 (**chapter 24**) drew extensively on the writings of German theoreticians – notably Alfred Hettner – to justify this conception. The volume proved to be extremely influential and its cardinal regional principle came through in the widely-read *Spirit and Purpose of Geography* published in 1951 by S. W. Wooldridge and W. Gordon East. The portrayal of regional character thus formed the fulcrum of their assessment of 'The philosophy and purpose of geography'. For them Humboldt, Ritter, Hettner, Vidal, Sauer and Hartshorne could all be called as witnesses to their elaboration of geography as essentially concerned to answer the question 'how and why does one part of the earth's surface differ from another?.

Written at the dawn of the 1950s, the regional stance here promulgated was soon to be severely contested by those seeking to make geography a *science* of spatial analysis (see Part V). To advocates of this model, regional description was too impressionistic, lacking in rigour, and scarcely to be dignified by the term 'discipline'. The champions of this new geography turned for inspiration to the techniques of quantification and for philosophical sustenance to certain 'positivist' strands in the philosophy of science. Whether the latter was truly inspirational or mere retrospective philosophical justification is an open question. But that geography, like other social sciences, underwent a substantial quantitative transformation during the 1950s and the 1960s, bolstered by the language of positivism, is beyond doubt.

Paradoxically, perhaps, some of the key criticisms of statistical infatuation in geography were to come from the pens of some of its erstwhile enthusiasts. Of special note is the disaffection expressed by David Harvey, whose *Explanation in Geography* (1969) had done so much to give philosophical sustenance to positivist claims. A political awakening through the encounter with Marxist social theory alerted Harvey to the philosophical bankruptcy of positivism and led him to call for a radical geography committed to political transformation. Soon other critical voices were also to be heard. Some felt, for example, that the *human* in human geography had been elided in the search for spatial laws and locational models. Thus David Ley (**chapter 11**) sought to retrieve a more 'humanistic' heritage by reinstating the centrality of the human agent and deploying philosophical and moral arguments in support of his critique. The collection of essays, *Humanistic Geography* (1978), that Ley and Samuels had just edited, spelled out something of what a humanistic programme might look like.

These efforts at humanistic redress, however, have not been without criticism, not least from those urging that the humanists' conception of the human agent was much too autonomous, too disengaged from the realities of economic, social and political life. Thus Derek Gregory (1981) argued the case for treating human agency and social structure as reciprocally constituted in space. Drawing inspiration from Anthony Giddens, Gregory, Thrift, Pred and others have sought to locate geographical concerns at the heart of social theory by showing how the engagements between the individual and the social are always played out in particular arenas – places, domains, locales. This reassertion of particularities, of specifics, of places resonates with a post-modern mood suspicious of grand theories and of all-encompassing narratives. In such a cultural climate, a geography taking areal differentiation with renewed seriousness has found its admirers (for example, Soja

1989 and **chapter 38**). Thus Gregory's 'Areal Differentiation and Post-Modern Human Geography' (**Chapter 12**) deliberately deploys the old formula of Richard Hartshorne – areal differentiation – and attempts to retrieve its localist thrust at an entirely different philosophical and cultural moment.

The selection of materials we have chosen to depict recent conceptions of the geographical enterprise are not representative of every definitional transformation that modern geography has undergone. They are illustrative rather than exhaustive, suggestive rather than comprehensive. Yet they do illustrate how conceptions of the character of geography have changed in different social and intellectual contexts. A vital tradition is one in which there are continuities of conflict precisely over what constitutes the tradition itself: the geographical tradition has displayed a remarkable vitality since classical times – and continues to do so.

References

Alpers, S. 1983: *The art of describing. Dutch Art in the seventeenth century*. Chicago.

Bowen, M. 1981: *Empiricism and geographical thought: from Francis Bacon to Alexander von Humboldt*. Cambridge.

Buttimer, A. 1971: *Society and milieu in the French geographic tradition*. Chicago.

Campbell, M. B. 1988: *The witness and the other world. Exotic European travel writing, 400–1600*. Ithaca.

Cannon, S. F. 1978: *Science in culture: the early Victorian period*. New York.

Cormack, L. 1992: 'Good fences make good neighbors': Geography as self-definition in early modern England. *Isis* 82, 639–61.

Davis, W. M. 1906: An inductive study of the content of geography. *Bulletin of the American Geographical Society* 38, 67–84.

Dilke, O. A. W. 1987: The culmination of Greek cartography in Ptolemy. In Harley, J. B. and Woodward, D., editors, *The history of cartography. Volume 1: Cartography in prehistoric, ancient, and medieval Europe and the Mediterranean*. Chicago.

Glacken, C. J. 1967: *Traces on the Rhodian Shore. Nature and culture in Western thought from ancient times to the end of the eighteenth century*. Berkeley.

Grafton, A. 1992: *New worlds, ancient texts. The power of tradition and the shock of discovery*. Cambridge, MA.

Gregory, D. 1981: Human agency and human geography. *Transactions of the Institute of British Geographers*, n.s. 6, 1–18.

Harley, J. B. and Woodward, D., editors, 1992: *The history of cartography. Volume 2, Book 1: Cartography in the traditional Islamic and South Asian societies*, associate editors: Joseph E. Schwartzberg and Gerald R. Tibbetts, assistant editor: Ahmet T. Karamustafa. Chicago.

Hull, D. 1988: *Science as a process. An evolutionary account of the social and intellectual development of science*. Chicago.

Kish, G., editor, 1978: *A source book in geography*. Cambridge, MA: Harvard University Press.

Lestringant, F. 1994: *Mapping the Renaissance world. The geographical imagination in the age of discovery*. Cambridge.

Livingstone, D. N. 1988: Science, magic and religion: a contextual reassessment of geography in the sixteenth and seventeenth centuries. *History of Science* 26, 269–94.

Livingstone, D. N. 1992: *The geographical tradition: episodes in the history of a contested enterprise*. Oxford.
Nicolet, C. 1991: *Space, geography, and politics in the early Roman Empire*. Ann Arbor.
Nietzsche, F. 1967 (originally published 1874): *On the genealogy of morals*, edited with commentary by Walter Kaufmann. New York.
Pagden, A. 1993: *European encounters with the New World: from Renaissance to Romanticism*. New Haven.
Soja, E. 1989: *Postmodern geographies: the reassertion of space in critical social theory*. London.
Thomson, J. O. 1965: *History of ancient geography*. New York.
Toal, G. [O'Tuathail, G.] Putting Mackinder in his place: material transformations and myth. *Political Geography* 11,100–18.
Withers, C. W. J. 1993: Geography in its time: geography and historical geography in Diderot and d'Alembert's *Encyclopédie*. *Journal of Historical Geography* 19, 252–64.
Wooldridge, S. W. and East, W. G. 1951: *The spirit and purpose of geography*. London.

Further Reading

By far the most comprehensive survey of geographical knowledge up to the end of the eighteenth century is that by Glacken, C. J. 1967. A variety of episodes in the history of geography since the fifteenth century is available in Livingstone, D. N. 1992. D. R. Stoddart's *On geography* (Oxford, 1986) draws together a number of the author's key articles on the development of the subject. General overviews of the discipline are provided in Martin, G. J. and James, P. E. 1993: *All possible worlds: a history of geographical ideas*, 3rd edition (Indianapolis) and Unwin, T. 1992: *The place of geography* (Harlow). Human geography since the Second World War is the subject of Johnston, R. J. 1991: *Geography and geographers. Anglo-American human geography since 1945*, 4th edition (London). An accessible introduction to different perspectives on the contemporary geographical enterprise is provided in Cloke, P., Philo, C. and Sadler, D. 1991: *Approaching human geography: an introduction to contemporary theoretical debates* (London). For the importance of cartography in the history of the geographical tradition the series on *The history of cartography* (Chicago) edited by J. B. Harley and David Woodward – of which three volumes have now been published – is unsurpassed.

7

WHAT GEOGRAPHY OUGHT TO BE

Peter Kropotkin

Peter Kropotkin (1842–1922) is best known as one of the founding thinkers of anarchism, but he was also an active and leading geographer. Born a Russian aristocrat, his political views led him to be gaoled in Russia and France and banished from Switzerland before finding refuge in Britain. Gaining acceptance from the Royal Geographical Society (RGS), despite his radicalism, he delivered his views on geography to a wide audience. His thinking was shaped by his experiences in two expeditions across Siberia and the Russian Far East in 1864 and 1865. In contrast to the prevalent ideas of Social Darwinism, Kropotkin observed and stressed the role of co-operation and mutual aid in both organic evolution and peasant society. He opposed political centralization and economic concentration and favoured small-scale, self-sufficient social units living in greater harmony with their natural surroundings. His vision of geography was at odds with the prevailing emphasis on imperialism, militarism, national chauvinism and racism. Kropotkin considered school geography dull and uninspiring, yet believed it could appeal to a child's imagination concerning both local knowledge and travel to far-off places. Instead of the rote learning of facts, he called for greater self-instruction and discovery. The study of dry classics should be replaced by more learning about the folklores of other countries. Although these views were expressed as part of an RGS inquiry into school education, they proved too radical for the times. And despite his return to Russia after the 1917 revolution his political views made little impact on Bolshevism. Even so, fifty years after his death many radical geographers have sought inspiration from Kropotkin's dissident voice (for example, Harvey, **chapter 5**).
Source: What geography ought to be. *The Nineteenth Century* 18, 940–56, 1885.

It was easy to foresee that the great revival of Natural Science which our generation has had the happiness to witness for thirty years, as also the new direction

1 *Geographical Education.* Report to the Council of the Royal Geographical Society, by J. Scott Keltie. London, 1885.

given to scientific literature by a phalanx of prominent men who dared to bring up the results of the most complicated scientific researches in a shape accessible to the general reader, would necessarily bring about a like revival of Geography. This science, which takes up the laws discovered by its sister-sciences, and shows their mutual action and consequences with regard to the superficies of the globe, could not remain an outsider to the general scientific movement; and we see now an interest awakened in Geography which very much recalls the general interest taken in it by a preceding generation during the first half of our century. We have not had among us so gifted a traveller and philosopher as Humboldt was; but the recent Arctic voyages and deep-sea explorations, and still more the sudden progress accomplished in Biology, Climatology, Anthropology, and Comparative Ethnography, have given to geographical works so great an attraction and so deep a meaning that the methods themselves of describing the earthball have undergone of late a deep modification. The same high standard of scientific reasoning and philosophical generalisations which Humboldt and Ritter had accustomed us to, reappear again in geographical literature. No wonder, therefore, if works both of travel and of general geographical description are becoming again the most popular kind of reading.

It was quite natural also that the revival of taste for geography should direct the public attention towards geography in schools. Inquiries were made, and we discovered with amazement that of this science – the most attractive and suggestive for people of all ages – we have managed to make in our schools one of the most arid and unmeaning subjects. Nothing interests children like travels; and nothing is dryer and less attractive in most schools than what is christened there with the name of Geography. True that the same could be said, with almost the same words, and with but a few exceptions, with regard to Physics and Chemistry, to Botany and Geology, to History and Mathematics. A thorough reform of teaching in all sciences is as needful as a reform of geographical education. But while public opinion has remained rather deaf with regard to the general reform of our scientific education – notwithstanding its having been advocated by the most prominent men of our century – it seems to have understood at once the necessity of reforming geographical teaching: the agitation recently started by the Geographical Society, the above-mentioned Report of its Special Commissioner, its exhibition, have met with general sympathies in the Press. Our mercantile century seems better to have understood the necessity of a reform as soon as the so-called 'practical' interests of colonisation and warfare were brought to the front. Well, then, let us discuss the reform of geographical education. An earnest discussion will necessarily show that nothing serious can be achieved in this direction, unless we undertake a corresponding, but much wider, general reform of all our system of education.

Surely there is scarcely another science which might be rendered as attractive for the child as geography, and as powerful an instrument for the general development of the mind, for familiarising the scholar with the true method of scientific reasoning, and for awakening the taste for natural science altogether. Children are not great admirers of Nature itself as long as it has nothing to do with Man. The artistic feeling which plays so great a part in the intellectual enjoyments of a naturalist is yet very feeble in the child. The harmonies of nature, the beauty of its forms, the admirable adaptations of organisms, the satisfaction derived by the mind from the study of physical laws, – all these may come later, but not in early childhood. The child searches everywhere for man, for his struggles against obstacles, for his activity. Minerals and plants leave it cold; it is passing through a period when imagination is prevailing. It wants human dramas, and therefore tales of hunting and fishing, of sea-travels, of struggles against dangers, of customs and manners, of traditions and migrations, are obviously one of the best means of developing in a child the desire of studying nature. Some modern 'pedagogues' have tried to kill imagination in children. Better ones will understand what a precious auxiliary imagination is to scientific reasoning. They will understand what Mr. Tyndall tried once to impress on his hearers – namely, that no deeply-going scientific reasoning is possible without the help of a greatly-developed imaginative power; and they will utilise the child's imagination, not for stuffing it with superstitions, but for awakening the love of scientific studies. The description of the Earth and its inhabitants surely will be one of the best means for reaching that aim. Tales of man struggling against hostile forces of nature – what can be better chosen for inspiring a child with the desire of penetrating into the secrets of these forces? You may very easily inspire children with a 'collecting' passion and transform their rooms into curiosity-shops, but, at an early age, it is not easy to inspire them with a desire of penetrating the laws of nature; while nothing is easier than to awaken the comparative powers of a young mind by telling it tales of far countries, of their plants and animals, of their scenery and phenomena, as soon as plants and animals, whirlwinds and thunderstorms, volcanic eruptions and storms are connected with man. This is the task of geography in early childhood: through the intermediary of man, to interest the child in the great phenomena of nature, to awaken the desire of knowing and explaining them.

Geography must render, moreover, another far more important service. It must teach us, from our earliest childhood, that we are all brethren, whatever our nationality. In our time of wars, of national self-conceit, of national jealousies and hatreds ably nourished by people who pursue their own egotistic, personal or class interests, geography must be – in so far as the school may do anything to counterbalance hostile influence – a means of dissipating these prejudices and of creating other feelings more worthy of humanity. It must show that each nationality brings its own precious building-stone for the general development of the commonwealth, and that only small parts of each nation are interested in maintaining national hatreds and jealousies. It must be recognised that, apart from other causes which nourish national jealousies, different nationalities do not yet sufficiently know one another; the strange questions which each foreigner is asked about his own country; the absurd prejudices with regard to one another which are spread on both extremities of a continent – nay, on both banks of a channel – amply prove that even among whom we describe as educated people geography is merely known by its name. The small differences we notice in the customs and manners of different nationalities, as also the differences of national characters which appear especially among the middle classes, make us overlook the immense likeness which exists among the labouring classes of all nationalities – a likeness which becomes the more striking at a closer acquaintance. It is the task of geography to bring this truth, in its full light, into the midst of the lies accumulated by ignorance, presumption, and egotism. It has to enforce on the minds of children that all nationalities are valuable to one another; that whatever the wars they have fought, mere short-sighted egotism was at the bottom of all of them. It must show that the development of each nationality was the consequence of several great natural laws, imposed by the physics and ethnical characters of the region it inhabited; that the efforts made by other nationalities to check its natural development have been mere mistakes; that political frontiers are relics of a barbarous past; and that the intercourse between different countries, their relations and mutual influence, are submitted to laws as little dependent on the will of separate men as the laws of the motion of planets.

This second task is great enough; but there is a third one, perhaps still greater: that of dissipating the prejudices in which we are reared with regard to the so-called 'lower races' – and this precisely at an epoch when everything makes us foresee that we soon shall be brought into a much closer contact with them than ever. When a French statesman proclaimed recently that the mission of the Europeans is to civilise the lower races by the means he had resorted to for civilising some of them – that is, by bayonets and Bac-leh massacres – he merely raised to the height of a theory the shameful deeds which Europeans are doing every day. And how could they do otherwise when from their tenderest childhood they are taught to despise 'the savages,' to consider 'the very virtues of pagans as disguised crime, and to look upon the 'lower races' as upon a mere nuisance on the globe – a nuisance which is only to be tolerated as long as money can be made out of it. One of the greatest services rendered of late by ethnography has been to demonstrate that these 'savages' have understood how to develop highly in their societies the same humane sociable feelings which we Europeans are so proud to profess, but so seldom practise; that the 'barbarous customs' which we readily scoff at, or hear of with disgust, are either results of a rough necessity (an Esquimaux mother kills her new-born child, so as to be able to nourish the others, whom she cherishes and nurses better than millions of our European mothers do), or they are forms of life which we, the proud Europeans, are still living through, after having slowly modified them; and that the superstitions we find so amusing when we see them amidst 'savages,' are as alive with us as with them, the names alone having been changed. Until now the Europeans have 'civilised the savages' with whiskey, tobacco, and kidnapping; they have inoculated them with their own vices; they have enslaved them. But the time is coming when we shall consider ourselves bound to bring them something better – namely, the knowledge of the forces of Nature, the means of utilising them, and higher forms of social life. All this, and many other things, have to be taught by geography if it really intends becoming a means of education.

The teaching of geography must thus pursue a treble aim: it must awaken in our children the taste for natural science altogether; it must teach them that all men are brethren, whatever be their nationality; and it must teach them to respect the 'lower races.' Thus understood, the reform of geographical education is immense: it is nothing less than a complete reform of the whole system of teaching in our schools.

It implies, first, a complete reform in the teaching of all exact sciences. These last, instead of the dead languages, must be made the basis of education in our schools. We have already too long paid our tribute to the mediæval scholastic system of education. It is time to inaugurate a new era of *scientific* education. It is obvious, indeed, that so long as our children spend three-quarters of their school-time in the study of Latin and Greek, there can remain no time for a serious study of natural sciences. A mixed system would be necessarily a failure. The requirements of a scientific education are so large that a serious study of the exact sciences alone would absorb all the time of the scholar, not to mention the needs of technical education, or rather of the education of a near future – the so-called *instruction intégrale.* If a bastard system, combining the classical education with the scientific one, were adopted, our boys and girls would receive an education much worse than they are receiving now in classical lyceums.

Without, however, entering into the endless debate between the two systems of education, two remarks must be made, as they directly concern geographical education. Everybody knows now the two chief arguments of the defenders of classical studies, and surely no naturalist will underestimate them. We are told, first, that the study of dead languages is a powerful instrument for leading the pupil to self-thought, to self-inquiry, to self-reasoning, and that the study of natural sciences does not afford a like means of education; and, secondly, it is alleged that the study of Roman and Greek antiquity gives instruction a humanitarian character which cannot be given by natural sciences alone.

The first of these two objections has already received a brilliant answer from the naturalists – not only on paper, but in the school. They are already reforming their methods of teaching so as to render natural science the most powerful instrument of self-studies. Of course, if we give a pupil the book of Euclid – which is a summary of a painfully elaborate knowledge, from which all preliminary work of searching, of inquiry, has been eliminated – it is the same as if we gave our children a translation of Cicero, and asked them to learn it by heart, without inducing them to discover for themselves the meaning of each separate sentence. But there is already another geometry – that by means of which Mr. Tyndall once interested his pupils; that which is already in partial use in Germany and elsewhere: the geometry which consists in stating *only* gradual problems and which leads the scholar to *discover* the demonstrations of all theorems, instead of trying to commit to memory the demonstrations discovered by other people than himself. I have tried this method several times and obtained quite unexpected results, both for the seriousness of knowledge and the rapidity of teaching, especially if I was happy enough to find a boy or a girl who never had learned geometry on the usual mnemonic method. The rapidity of teaching on the 'problems' method is something really astonishing. If you have not pressed your pupil at the beginning; if you have had the patience to wait until he has discovered for himself the solution of a few simpler problems (each theorem obviously may be treated as a problem), you see him master the remainder of geometry (on the plane and in the space) in a very few months, and resolve the most complicated problems relative to the circles and tangents with an ease which makes you regret having been ever taught otherwise. What has been done for geometry, is already being done for natural science altogether. The time is not far off when in physics and chemistry, in botany and zoology, the scholar will no more learn from memory, but will be brought to discover himself the physical law and the functions of organs, as he already discovers the relations which exist between the sides of a triangle and the perpendicular drawn from one of its summits to the base.

So far – in these preliminary steps – natural sciences surely are not behind the study of languages as a means of accustoming the children to self-reasoning and self-inquiry. But where they are infinitely in advance, is in opening to our youths an immense field of *new* researches, of *new* inquiries. However limited the knowledge acquired in natural sciences – provided only it be a serious knowledge – young men, at every stage of their development, are enabled to make new inquiries, to collect new data, to discover, or to prepare the materials for the discovery of, new valuable facts. Professor Partsch at Breslau has already achieved with his students a most valuable work, certainly worth being published.[2] But the same could be done everywhere, even in the best-explored countries, even with scholars far less advanced than Professor Partsch's students.

As to the sudden progress made by a young man or girl in their intellectual development, as soon as they have made their first independent inquiry – Who has not observed it on somebody, or on himself? The reasoning deepens with a striking rapidity; it becomes wider and surer – and more cautious at the same time. I shall never forget the case of a young man of twenty, who had made, hammer and barometer in hand, his first independent geological inquiry. His elder brother, who closely watched his development, seeing his intellect suddenly taking a new strain, could not help exclaiming one day: – 'How rapidly you are increasing in intelligence, even in a few months! You must have studied hard the German *résumé* of Mill's Logic which I gave you!' – Yes, he had; but in the field, amidst the complicated stratification of rocks.

The second of the two above-mentioned objections stands, however, untouched. The humanitarian character of the study of antiquity; its stimulating influence on the development of humanitarian feelings and of artistic taste (this last being a powerful means for the development of the former); its importance in making the scholars reason about human societies and human relations – all these, we are told, are not given by natural sciences. Of course, neither physics nor mineralogy touch these important factors of human development. But surely there is not a single naturalist who would ask the exclusion from the school of all sciences dealing with man, for the benefit of those which deal with the remainder of organic and inorganic matter. On the contrary, he would ask a far more important part to be given to the study of history and literature of all nationalities than they have had hitherto. He would require the extension of natural science to man and human societies. He

2 *Geographical Education*, Appendix P, p. 135.

would ask a fair place in education for a comparative description of all human inhabitants of the Earth. In such an education, geography would take its right place. Remaining a natural science, it would assume, together with history (history of art as well as of political institutions), the immense task of caring about the humanitarian side of our education – as far as the school is able to forward it.

No more, of course; for humanitarian feelings cannot be developed from books, if all the life outside school acts in an opposite direction. To be real and to become active qualities, the humanitarian feelings must arise from the daily practice of the child. The *rôle* of teaching proper is very limited in this direction. But, however limited, nobody would recklessly refuse even this modest help. We have so much to achieve in raising the moral development of the majority to the high level reached by a few, that no means can be neglected, and surely we will not deny the importance of the mythical element of our education for approaching this aim. But why limit, then, this element to Roman and Greek tales? Have we not tales to tell and retell from our own life – tales of self-devotion, of love for humanity, not invented but real, not distant but near at hand, which we may see every day around us? And, if it be established that folk-lore better impresses the childish mind than the stories of our daily life, why are we bound to limit ourselves to Roman and Greek traditions? As a means of education, no Greek myth – almost always too sensual – will supersede the finely artistical, the chaste, the highly humanitarian myths and songs of, say, the Lithuanians or the Finns; while in the folk-lore of the Turco-Mongols, the Indians, the Russians, the Germans – in short, of all nationalities – we find such artistic, such vigorous, such broadly human tales, that one cannot see without regret our children fed on Greek and Roman traditions, instead of making them familiar with the treasures concealed in the folk-lore of other nationalities. In fact, rightly understood, ethnography hardly could be compared with anything else, as an instrument for developing in children and youths the love to mankind as a whole, the feelings of sociability and solidarity with every human creature, as well as self-devotion, courage, and perseverance – in a word, all the best sides of human nature. It removes, in my opinion, the last objection that might be produced in favour of an education based on the study of Greek and Latin antiquities. It introduces education by the natural sciences the necessary into humanitarian element.

If such a meaning be given to geography, it will cover, both in the inferior schools and in the universities, four great branches of knowledge, sufficiently wide to constitute in the higher instruction four separate specialities, or even more, but all closely connected together. Three of these branches – orogeny, climatology, and the zoo- and phyto-geography – would correspond, broadly speaking, to what is described now as physical geography; while the fourth, embodying some parts of ethnology, would correspond to what is partly taught now under the head of political geography; but they would so widely differ from what is at present taught under these two heads, both as to their contents and their methods, that the very names would soon be replaced by other and more suitable ones.

The very right of geography to be considered a separate science has often been contested, and Mr. J. S. Keltie's Report mentions some of the objections raised.

Even those, however, who make these objections will certainly recognise that there *is* a separate branch of knowledge – that which the systematic French mind describes as *Physique du Globe*, and which, though embodying a variety of subjects closely connected with other sciences, must be cultivated and taught separately for the mutual advantage of itself and of the other sister-sciences. It prosecutes a definite aim: that of disclosing the laws of the development of the globe. And it is not a mere descriptive science – not a mere *graphy*, as it has been said by one well-known geologist,[3] but a *logy*; for it discovers the *laws* of a certain class of phenomena, after having described and systematised them.

Geography should be, first, a study of the laws to which the modifications of the Earth's surface are submitted: the laws – for there are such laws, however imperfect our present knowledge of them – which determine the growth and disappearance of continents; their present and past configurations; the directions of different upheavals – all submitted to some telluric laws, as the distribution of planets and solar systems is submitted to cosmical laws. To take but one instance out of hundreds: when we consider the two great continents of Asia and North America, the part played in their structure by colossal table-lands, the antiquity of these table-lands, the series of ages during which they remained continents, and the direction of their axes and narrow extremities pointed towards a region in the vicinity of the Behring Strait; when, moreover, we take into consideration the parallelism of the chains of mountains and the perseverance with which two chief directions of upheavals (the north-western and north-eastern) are repeated in Europe and Asia throughout a series of geological ages; when we remark the present configuration of the continents having their narrow extremities pointed towards the South Pole – we must recognise that some telluric laws have presided at the formation of the great swellings and plaitings of the Earth's crust. These laws have not yet been discovered: the orography itself of four great continents is in an embryonic state; but we already perceive a certain harmony in the great structural lines of the Earth, and we may already guess about its causes. This wide subject touches, of course, that part of geology which has received of late the name of dynamic geology; but the two do not coalesce: the orogeny still remains a separate branch, too widely different from the former not to be dealt with separately. We may even say, without hurting either geographers or geologists, that the backward state of orogeny is due precisely to the circumstance that geographers too much relied on geologists for treating it, and that it has not been sufficiently treated by a separate kind of specialists – by geographers quite familiar with geology; while the backward state of dynamic geology proper (the unsettled state of the Quaternary period gives a sufficient right to make this assertion) is due to the circumstance that the number of geologists who were also geographers has never been sufficiently great, and that too many geologists neglected this branch abandoning it to geographers. Geographers have thus to take over the whole of the work, supplying geology with the data which it may be in need of.

3 *Geographical Education*, p. 21.

Geography has, secondly, to study the consequences of the distribution of continents and seas, of altitudes and depressions, of indentations and great masses of water on climate. While meteorology discovers, with the help of physics, the laws of oceanic and aërial currents, that part of geography which could be described as climatology has to determine the influence of local topographical causes on climate. In its general parts, meteorology has recently made an immense progress; but the study of local climates and of a variety of secondary, geographical and topographical causes influencing climate – climatology proper – remains to be made. This branch also requires its own specialists, that is, meteorologist-geographers, and the work already done a few years ago by MM. Buchan, Mohn, Hahn, Woyeikoff, and many others, in that direction, shows well what remains to be done.

A third immense branch, also requiring its own specialists, is that of zoo- and phyto-geography. As long as botany and zoology were considered as mere descriptive sciences, they could incidentally touch the distribution of plants and animals on the surface of the earth. But new fields of research have been opened. The origin of species would remain unexplained if the geographical conditions of their distribution are not taken into account. The adaptations of species to the medium they inhabit; their modifications; their mutual dependence; their slow disappearance and the appearance of new ones – the study of all these phenomena meets every day with insuperable obstacles precisely on account of the subject not having been treated from a sufficiently geographical point of view. Wallace, Hooker, Griesbach, Peschel, and so many others, have indicated the lines to be followed in that branch. But to do it, we must have again a special combination of capacities, in men who unite a wide geographical with botanical and zoological knowledge. Far from doubting the necessity of a special science for studying the laws of development of the globe and the distribution of organic life on its surface, we are thus brought to recognise that there is room for three separate sciences, which have special aims to pursue, but must remain more closely connected together than with any other science. The physics of the globe must be, and will be, raised to the height of a science.

And now there remains the fourth great branch of geographical science – that which deals with human families on the earth's surface. The distribution of human families; their distinctive features and the modifications undergone by these features under various climates; the geographical distribution of races, beliefs, customs, and forms of property, and their close dependency upon geographical conditions; the accommodation of man to the nature that surrounds him, and the mutual influence of both; the migrations of stems, in so far as they are dependent upon geological causes; the aspirations and dreams of various races, in so far as they are influenced by the phenomena of nature; the laws of distribution of human settlements in each country, displayed by the persistency of settlements at the very same places since the Stone Age until our own times; the raising of cities and the conditions of their development; the geographical subdivision of territories into natural manufacturing 'basins,' notwithstanding the obstacles opposed by political frontiers: all these are a wide series of problems which have recently grown up before us. If we consult the works of our best ethnologists, if we remember the attempts of Riehl and Buckle, as also those of several of our best geographers; if we realise the data accumulated and the hints scattered in ethnographical, historical, and geographical literature for the solution of these problems – we surely shall not hesitate to recognise that here also there is a broad place for a separate, most important science, and not merely for a *graphy*, but for a *logy*. Of course, here also the geographer will tax many kindred sciences in collecting his data. Anthropology, history, philology will be called upon. Many specialities will arise, some of them more closely connected with history, and others with physical sciences; but it is the true duty of geography to cover *all* this field at once and to combine in *one* vivid picture all separate elements of this knowledge: to represent it as an harmonious whole, all parts of which are consequences of a few general principles and are held together by their mutual relations.

As to the technical part of the instruction to be given in geography – the pedagogic methods of, and the appliances for, teaching geography – I shall limit myself to a few remarks. However low the level of geographical education in most of our schools, there are isolated teachers and institutions which have already elaborated excellent methods of teaching and highly perfect appliances for use in schools. A mere selection has to be made of the best of them, and the best way to that is the way chosen by the Geographical Society: an exhibition of geographical appliances, and a congress of teachers held in connection with it. Modern pedagogy is already in an excellent way for elaborating the easiest methods of teaching, and if inspired with the high aims of geographical education just mentioned, it will not fail to discover the best means for reaching these aims. There is now in pedagogy – we must recognise that – a tendency towards taking too minute a care of the child's mind, so as to check independent thought and restrain originality; and there is also a tendency towards too much sweetening the learning, so as to disaccustom the mind from intellectual strain, instead of accustoming it gradually to intellectual efforts. Both these tendencies exist; but they must be considered rather as a reaction against methods formerly in use, and surely they will be but transitory. More freedom for the intellectual development of the child! More room left for independent work, with no more help on behalf of the teacher than the strictly necessary! Fewer school-books, and more books of travel; more descriptions of countries written in all languages by our best authors, past and present, put in the hands of our scholars – these chief points never ought to be lost sight of.

It is obvious that geography, like other sciences, must be taught in a series of concentric courses, and that in each of them most stress must be laid on those departments which are most comprehensible at different ages. To subdivide geography into *Heimatskunde* for the earlier age, and into geography proper for an advanced age is neither desirable nor possible. One of the first things a child asks his mother is: 'What becomes of the sun when it goes down?' and as soon as he has read two descriptions of travel, in polar and in tropical countries, necessarily he will ask 'why palms do not grow in Greenland.' We are bound thus to give notions of cosmography and physical geography from the earliest childhood. Of course, we cannot explain to a child what the ocean is, if we do not show it a pond or a lake close by; and what a gulf is, if we do not point out to it a creek on the banks of a river. It is only on minor inequalities of ground around us that we can give children an idea of mountains and table-lands, of peaks and glaciers; and it is only on the map of its own village, or town, that the child can be brought to understand the conventional hieroglyphs of our maps. But the favourite reading of a child will always be a book of distant travel, or the tale of Robinson Crusoe. The creek of a pond, the rapids of a streamlet will acquire interest in a child's imagination only when it can imagine in the creek a wide gulf, with ships at anchor and men landing upon an unknown coast; and in the rapids of the streamlet, the rapids of a Canadian *fjärden* with the emaciated Dr. Richardson who throws himself in the *fjärden* to land a rope on the other bank.

Things near at hand are very often less comprehensible for the child than things far away. The traffic on our own rivers and railways, the development of our own manufactures and our shipping trade are, without comparison, less comprehensible and less attractive at a certain age than the hunting parties and customs of distant primitive stems. When I revert to my boyhood, I discover that what made me a geographer and induced me at the age of eighteen to inscribe myself in a regiment of Cossacks of the Amur, instead of the Horse Guards, was not the impression left by the excellent lessons of our excellent teacher in Russian geography, whose textbook I fully appreciate only now, but much more the great work of Defoe in my earlier years, and later on – first of all, above all – the first volume of Humboldt's *Cosmos*, his *Tableaux de la Nature*, and Karl Ritter's fascinating monographs on the tea-tree, the camel, and so on.

Another remark which ought to be impressed on the minds of all those who make schemes of reform for geographical education is, that no sound instruction can be given in geography as long as the instruction given in mathematical and physical sciences remains what it is now in most of our schools. What is the use of giving brilliant lessons in advanced climatology if the pupils never have had a *concrete* conception of surfaces and angles of incidence, if they never have *made* themselves surfaces and have not drawn lines to meet them at different angles? Can we make our hearers understand the motion of masses of air, of currents and whirlwinds, as long as they are not quite familiar with the principal laws of mechanics? To do this would simply mean to spread that kind of instruction which unhappily spreads too speedily, the knowledge of mere words and technical terms, without any serious knowledge beneath. The instruction given in exact sciences must be far wider than it is now, and go deeper. And it must be also rendered more concrete. Can we expect to find in our pupils mindful hearers when speaking of the distribution of plants and animals on the Earth's surface, of human settlements, and so on, if they have not been accustomed to make for themselves a complete geographical description of some limited region, to map it, to describe its geological structure, to show the distribution of plants and animals on its surface, to explain why the inhabitants of the villages have settled there and not higher up the valley, and, above all, to compare their own description with like ones made of other regions in other countries? However excellent the relief-maps of continents which we put into the hands of our children, we shall never accustom them to a concrete comprehension and a love for maps, if they have not made maps themselves – that is, as long as we have not put a compass into their hands, brought them to an open country and said: 'There is a landscape; in your compass and in your path you have all you need for mapping it; go and map it.' It is necessary to say what a pleasure it is for a boy of fifteen to wander thus alone in the woods, on the roads, and on the banks of rivers, and to have them all – forests, roads, and rivers – drawn on his sheet of paper; or to say how easily these results are obtained (I know it from my own school experience) if geometrical knowledge has been rendered concrete by applying it to measurements in the field?

Another feature to be introduced in our schools ought to be mentioned here. I mean the exchange, between schools, of correspondence on geographical subjects and of their natural science collections. This feature, already introduced in several schools of the United States by the 'Agassiz Association,' cannot be too warmly advocated. It is not enough to collect specimens of rocks, plants, and animals, from its own limited regions. Each village school ought to have collections from everywhere: not only from all parts of its own country, but from Australia and Java, from Siberia and the Argentine Republic. It cannot purchase them: but it may have, it can have, them in exchange for its own collections, from schools scattered everywhere on the surface of the globe.

Such is the great idea which presided at the creation of the 'Agassiz Association' – an association of schools which has already seven thousand members and six hundred 'Chapters,' or sections.[4] The children of this Association are accustomed to study natural sciences in the field, amidst nature itself; but they do not keep their treasuries to themselves. They write to other branches of the Association: they exchange with them their observations, their ideas, their specimens of minerals, plants, and animals. They write about the scenery of Canada to friends in Texas. Their Swiss friends (for something similar exists also in Switzerland) send them the *Edelweiss* of the Alps, and their English friends instruct them in the geology of England. Shall I add that in proportion as the existence of the Association becomes known, specialists, professors and *amateur*-naturalists hasten to offer their services to their young friends for lecturing before them, for determining their specimens, or for climbing with them on the hills in geological and botanical excursions? No need to say that: there is plenty of good-will among those who have instruction in anything; it is only the spirit of initiative which is wanting for utilising their services. Is it necessary to insist on the benefits of the 'Agassiz Association,' or to show how it ought to be extended? The greatness of the idea of establishing a lively connection between all schools of the Earth is too clear. Everybody knows that it is sufficient to have a friend in a foreign country – be it Moscow or Java – to begin to take some interest in that country. A newspaper paragraph entitled 'Moscow' or 'Java' will henceforth attract his attention. The more so if he is in a lively intercourse with his friend, if both pursue the same work and communicate to one another the results of their explorations. More than that. Let English children be in

4 *Handbook of the Agassiz Association*, by Harlam H. Ballard. Lenox, Mass. 1884.

a continuous exchange of correspondence, collections, and thoughts with Russian children; and be sure that after some time neither English nor Russians will so readily grasp at guns for settling their misunderstandings. The 'Agassiz Association' has a brilliant future; similar ones will surely extend all over the world.

Yet this is not all. Even if all our education were based on natural sciences, the results achieved would be still very poor if the general intellectual development of our children were neglected. The final aim of all our efforts in education ought to be precisely this 'general development of the intellect;' and, notwithstanding that, it is the last thing which is thought of. We may see, for instance, in Switzerland, real palaces for sheltering schools; we can find there the choicest exhibitions of pedagogical appliances; the children are very advanced in drawing; they perfectly know historical data; they point out, without hesitation, on the map, any town of importance; they easily determine the species of many flowers; they know by heart some *maximes de Jean-Jacques Rousseau,* and repeat some criticisms of the 'theories of Lassalle;' and at the same time they are utterly devoid of 'general development;' in that respect the great bulk are behind very many pupils of the most backward old-system schools.

So little attention is given to the general development of the scholar that I am not even sure of being rightly understood in what I say, and had better refer therefore to an example. Go, for instance, to Paris, Geneva, or Bern; enter a *café,* or a *brasserie,* where students are in the habit of meeting together, and join in their conversation. About what subjects will it be? About women, about dogs, about some peculiarity of some professor, perhaps about rowing; or – at Paris – about some political event of the day, a few sentences taken from leading newspapers being exchanged. And go now to a students' room in the Vassili Ostrov at St. Petersburg, or in the famous 'Sivtseff's Ravine' at Moscow. The scenery will be changed, and still more the subjects of conversation. The questions discussed there will be, first, the *Weltanschauung* – the Philosophy of the Universe – painfully elaborated by each student separately and by all together. For a Russian student may have no boots in which to go to the University, but he must have his own *Weltanschauung*. Kant, Comte, and Spencer are quite familiar to them, and while innumerable glasses of tea, or rather of tea-water, are consumed, the relative importance of these philosphical systems is carefully discussed. The economical and political *Anschauungen* may differ at Vassili Ostrov and in the Sivtseff's Ravine, but here and there Rodbertus, Marx, Mill, and Tchernyshevski will be discussed and boldly criticised. Be sure that Spencer's 'Evolutionist Moral' is already a quite familiar book in Sivtseff's Ravine, and that it is considered there a shame not to be acquainted with it. This example shows what I mean by 'general development:' the capacity and the taste for reasoning about subjects far above the meannesses of our daily life; the broader development of mind; the capacity of perceiving the causes of phenomena, of reasoning thereon.

Wherefore the difference? Are we better taught in our Russian schools? Certainly not! Pushkin's words: 'We all have learned not too much, and in a haphazard way,' are as true with regard to the Vassili Ostrov students as to those of the Boulevard St. Michel and Lake Leman. But Russia is living in a phase of its life when much stress is laid upon the general development of a young man. A student of the University, or of the higher classes of a lyceum, who would limit his readings only to class-books, would be despised by his comrades and find no respect in society. In consequence of a peculiar phase of intellectual awakening which we are now going through, the life outside the school imposes this condition. We have been brought to revise all forms of our previous life; and all social phenomena being closely connected together, we cannot do it without looking at all of them from a higher point of view. The school, in its turn, has responded to this need by elaborating a special type of teacher – the teacher in Russian literature. The *utchitel slovesnosti* is a quite peculiar and most sympathetic type of the Russian school. To him nearly all Russian writers are indebted for the impulse given to their intellectual development. He gives the scholars what none of the other teachers can give in his special classes: he sums up the knowledge acquired; he throws a philosophical glance on it; he makes his pupils reason about such subjects as are not taught in school. Thus, when speaking, for instance, of the Russian folk-lore, he will not spend all his time in analysing the form of the popular poetry, but he will make an excursion into the domain of æsthetics in general; he will speak of epic poetry as a whole, of its meaning, and of the influence of Greek poetry on the general intellectual development of Europe; Draper's theories and Quinet's *Merlin l'Enchanteur* will be mentioned; the ethics of Russian folk-lore, and ethics in general, its development in the course of centuries, will be discussed; and so on, without limiting himself by an official programme, and always speaking in accordance with his own inspiration, his own tastes. And so on each occasion throughout his 'course.' One easily understands what an influence a sincere and inspired teacher can exercise on young men when he speaks of these and like subjects, and what an impulse is given to thought by these lectures on the philosophy of the intellectual development of humanity, delivered in connection with the Russian literature. No matter that many points of the lecture will not be understood in their fulness by boys of fourteen to sixteen. The charm of it is perhaps yet greater therefor; and one must have seen a class of turbulent boys hanging on the lips of their teacher, whose inspired voice alone is heard amidst an absolute silence to understand the intellectual and moral influence exercised by such men.

As to the necessity of such lectures for the intellectual development of the young people, it is obvious. At each period of the development of the young man somebody must help him to sum up the knowledge acquired, to show the connection existing between all various categories of phenomena which are studied separately, to develop broader horizons before his eyes, and to accustom him to scientific generalisations.

But the teacher of literature perforce deals with only one category of philosophical instruction – the psychological world; while the same generalisations, the same philosophical insight must be given in respect of the natural sciences altogether. The natural sciences must have their own *utchitel slovesnosti*, who would also show the relations which exist between all the phenomena of the physical world, and develop before the eyes of his hearers the beauty and harmony of the *Cosmos*. The philosophy of nature will surely be considered one day as a necessary part of education; but in the present state of our schools, who could better undertake this task than the teacher of geography? It is not in vain that the *Cosmos* was written by a geographer. While describing the globe – this small spot lost amidst an immeasurable space – while showing the variety of mechanical, physical, and chemical agents at work modifying its surface, setting in motion aërial and aqueous oceans, raising continents and digging abysses; while speaking of the wonderful variety of organic forms, of their co-operation and struggles, of their admirable adaptations; while describing Man in intercourse with Nature – Who could better bring the young mind to exclaim with the poet –

Du hast mir nicht umsonst
Dein Angesicht im Feuer zugewendet,
Gabst mir die herrliche Natur zum Königreich,
Kraft sie zu fühlen, zu geniessen. Nicht
Kalt staunenden Besuch erlaubst du nur,
Vergönnest mir in ihre tiefe Brust,
Wie in den Busen eines Freunds, zu schauen.

Where to find teachers for performing the immense task of education? That is, we are told, the great difficulty which lies across all attempts at school-reform. Where to find, in fact, some hundred thousand of Pestalozzis and Fröbels, who might give a really sound instruction to our children? Surely not in the ranks of that poor army of schoolmasters whom we condemn to teach all their life, from their youth to the grave; who are sent to a village, deprived there of all intellectual intercourse with educated people, and soon accustomed to consider their task as a curse. Surely not in the ranks of those who see in teaching a salaried profession and nothing more. Only exceptional characters can remain good teachers throughout their life, until an advanced age. These precious men and women must therefore constitute, so to say, the elder brethren of the teaching army, the ranks and files of which must be filled with volunteers who are guided in their work by those who have consecrated all their life to the noble task of pedagogy. Young men and women consecrating a few years of their life to teaching – not because they see in teaching a profession, but because of their being inspired with the desire to help their younger friends in their intellectual development; people in more advanced age who are ready to give a number of hours to teaching in the subjects they best like – such will be probably the teachers' army in a better-organised system of education. At any rate, it is not by making teaching a salaried profession that we can obtain a good education for our children, and maintain among our pedagogues the freshness and openness of mind which are necessary for keeping pace with the ever-growing needs of science. The teacher will be a real teacher only when inspired with a real love both for children and for the subject he teaches, and this inspiration cannot be maintained for years if teaching is a mere profession. People ready to consecrate their powers to teaching, and quite able to do so, are not wanting even in our present society. Let us only understand how to discover them, to interest them in education, and to combine their efforts; and in their hands, with the aid of more experienced people, our schools will very soon become quite different from what they are now. They will be places where the young generation will assimilate the knowledge and experience of the elder one, and the elder one will borrow from the younger new energy for a common work for the benefit of humanity.

8

ON THE SCOPE AND METHODS OF GEOGRAPHY

Halford J. Mackinder

Two years after Kropotkin (**chapter 7**) had failed to steer geography in a radical and humanitarian direction, the young Halford Mackinder (1861–1947) delivered a paper to the Royal Geographical Society that was to prove a turning point in British geography. Before becoming known for his writings on geopolitics (see **chapter 33**), Mackinder was active in lecturing to audiences around the country on his vision of geography. On the strength of his views he was appointed to a position at Oxford University, becoming the first of a new generation of academic geographers and a vocal supporter of geographical education. *Scope and methods* coincided with the views of a faction within the RGS which backed the creation of a more scientific geography in place of its traditional emphasis on exploration and discovery. The lecture and the manoeuvres surrounding it can therefore be read as a good example of what Capel (**chapter 4**) describes as a strategy for claiming intellectual space. What part Mackinder's fine rhetoric or his felicitous timing played in the institutionalization of British geography cannot be known, but his model of a scientific geography was found appealing. To become a discipline rather than a mere body of information, the subject had to bridge the natural sciences and the humanities and take as its core 'the interaction of man in society and so much of his environment as varies locally'. Mackinder's version of the geographical experiment held physical and human geography together in an evolutionary perspective, while stressing the utility of the subject for teachers, scientists, statesmen and merchants alike. His views have often been recalled in debates as to whether human and physical geography should be kept together.

Source: On the scope and methods of geography. *Proceedings of the Royal Geographical Society* 9, 141–60, 1887.

What is geography? This seems a strange question to address to a Geographical Society, yet there are at least two reasons why it should be answered, and answered now. In the first place geographers have been active of late in pressing the claims of their science to a more honoured position in the curriculum of our schools and

Universities. The world, and especially the teaching world, replies with the question, "What is geography?" There is a touch of irony in the tone. The educational battle now being fought will turn on the answer which can be given to this question, Can geography be rendered a discipline instead of a mere body of information? This is but a rider on the larger question of the scope and methods of our science.

The other reason for now pressing this matter on your notice comes from within. For half a century several societies, and most of all our own, have been active in promoting the exploration of the world. The natural result is that we are now near the end of the roll of great discoveries. The Polar regions are the only large blanks remaining on our maps. For a time good work will be done in New Guinea, in Africa, in Central Asia, and along the boundaries of the frozen regions. For a time a Greely will now and again receive the old ringing welcome, and will prove that it is not heroes that are wanting. But as tales of adventure grow fewer and fewer, as their place is more and more taken by the details of Ordnance Surveys, even Fellows of Geographical Societies will despondently ask, "What is geography?"

It is needless to say that this paper would not be written were it my belief that the Royal Geographical Society must shortly close its history – a corporate Alexander weeping because it has no more worlds to conquer. Our future work is foreshadowed by papers such as those by Mr. Wells on Brazil, Mr. Buchanan on the Oceans, and Mr. Bryce on the Relation of History and Geography. Nevertheless, there will be great advantages in guiding our way into the new groove with our eyes to some extent, at any rate, open. A discussion of the question at the present moment will probably have the further incidental advantage of giving us new weapons in our educational struggle.

The first inquiry to which we must turn our attention is this: Is geography one, or is it several subjects? More precisely, Are physical and political geography two stages of one investigation, or are they separate subjects to be studied by different methods, the one an appendix of geology, the other of history? Great prominence has recently been given to this question by the President of the Geographical Section of the British Association. In his address at Birmingham he took up a very definite position. He said,–

"It is difficult to reconcile the amalgamation of what may be considered 'scientific' geography with history. One is as thoroughly apart from the other as geology is from astronomy."

It is with great reluctance and diffidence that I venture to oppose so justly esteemed an authority as Sir Frederic Goldsmid. I do so only because it is my firm conviction that the position taken up at Birmingham is fatal to the best prospects of geography. I take notice, moreover, of Sir Frederic Goldsmid's declaration that he is quite ready to abandon the conclusion at which he has arrived, before the arguments of sounder reason. In so difficult a discussion it would be extremely presumptuous, were I to assume that *mine* are arguments of sounder reason. I put them forward only because so far as I can see, they have not been met and overthrown in the address in question. Perhaps Sir Frederic Goldsmid has but expressed the vague views of the subject current in most men's minds. This is the more probable, because in his own statement he has used arguments going to support a view opposed to that which he himself formulates.[1]

On the same page as that from which our quotation is taken will be found a paragraph expressing the highest approval of Mr. Bryce's "Geography in its relation to History." The central proposition of Mr. Bryce's lecture is that man is largely "the creature of his environment." The function of political geography is to trace the interaction between man and his environment. Sir Frederic Goldsmid requires of political geography that it shall impart to our future statesmen a "full grasp" of "geographical conditions." So far no exception can be taken to his views. But he seems to imagine that the "full grasp" of which he speaks may be obtained from what remains after "physical and scientific" geography have been eliminated.

Before proceeding further, it will be well to see whether we cannot refine on our definition with advantage. Physiology would answer to the definition of the science which traces the interaction of man and his environment. It is the function of physiology, of physics, and of chemistry to trace the action of forces irrespective for the most part of precise locality. It is especially characteristic of geography that it traces the influence of locality, that is, of environment varying locally. So far as it does not do this it is merely physiography, and the essential topographical element has been omitted. I propose therefore to define geography as the science whose main function is to trace the interaction of man in society and so much of his environment as varies locally.[2]

Before the interaction can be considered, the elements which are to interact must be analysed. One of these elements,[3] is the varying environment, and the analysis of this is, I hold, the function of physical geography. Thus we are driven to a position in direct antagonism to current notions. We hold that no *rational* political geography can exist which is not built upon and subsequent to physical geography. At the present moment we are suffering under the effects of an irrational political geography, one, that is, whose main function is not to trace causal relations, and which must therefore remain a body of isolated data to be committed to memory. Such a geography can never be a discipline, can never, therefore, be honoured by the teacher, and must always fail to attract minds of an amplitude fitting them to be rulers of men.

But it may be retorted – For the purposes of political geography cannot you rest

1 Sir Frederic Goldsmid has written a very courteous answer to this paragraph. From it I gather that I have not attached the meaning to his words which he intended. For that I am sorry. I leave the paragraph standing, however, as I believe that mine is not an unnatural meaning to attach to the words. They might easily be quoted against the geographers, and with the more weight because they come from a known friend of geography.

2 For another definition from a rather different standpoint see my speech in opening the discussion, *infra*, p. 160 [Not included in this extract].

3 The other element is, of course, man in society. The analysis of this will be shorter than that of the environment. It may best be considered on the lines of Bagehot's 'Physics and Politics.' The communities of men should be looked on as units in the struggle for existence, more or less favoured by their several environments. See p. 11 for definition of "community" and "environment."

satisfied with a more superficial and more easily learned analysis than that furnished by physical geography? In reply, we take up our lowest position. Such analyses have been tried, and have been found wanting. It is practically easier to learn the profound analysis of science, raising and satisfying as it does at every point the instincts which drive us for ever to ask the question "why?" than to acquire a sufficient amount of information from the name-lists of the old school-books or the descriptions of so-called descriptive geography. Topography, which is geography with the "reasons why" eliminated, is almost unanimously rejected both by masters and pupils.

There are other reasons for our position of even higher importance than practical convenience in teaching. I will mention three. The first is this. If you learn what the old geographers term "the physical features" in their causal relations, advance becomes ever easier and easier. New facts fit in an orderly way into the general scheme. They throw a new light on to all previously obtained knowledge, and that knowledge in turn illuminates them from many points. When, however, the method of description has been adopted, and still more that of enumeration, each additional fact adds an ever-increasing amount to the burden to be borne by the memory. It is like throwing another pebble on to a heap of gravel. It is like learning mathematics by trying to remember formulæ instead of grasping principles.

Our second reason is shortly this. A superficial analysis is likely to lead into error: on the one hand by failing to go beneath the superficial similarity of things essentially differing; on the other hand by failing to detect the essential similarity of things superficially unlike.

The third reason is this. The mind which has vividly grasped in their true relations the factors of the environment is likely to be fertile in the suggestion of new relations between the environment and man. Even if there be no design of advancing the science, the same conditions will lead to a rapid, a vivid, and therefore a lasting appreciation of the relations which have been detected by others.

It will be well here to pause and to sum up our position in a series of propositions.

1. It is agreed that the function of political geography is to detect and demonstrate the relations subsisting between man in society and so much of his environment as varies locally.

2. As a preliminary to this the two factors must be analysed.

3. It is the function of physical geography to analyse one of these factors, the varying environment.

4. Nothing else can adequately perform this function.

Because –

> No other analysis can exhibit the facts in their causal relations and in their true perspective.

Therefore –

> No other analysis will –
>
> > Firstly, Serve the teacher as a discipline;
> > Secondly, Attract the higher minds among the pupils;
> > Thirdly, Economise the limited power of memory;

Fourthly, Be equally trustworthy; and
Fifthly, Be equally suggestive.

Here we must expect the observation that, granting the desirability of what we ask, we are none the less asking what is impossible. Our reply will be that it has not been tried. Physical geography has usually been undertaken by those already burdened with geology, political geography by those laden with history. We have yet to see the man who taking up the central, the geographical position, shall look equally on such parts of science and such parts of history as are pertinent to his inquiry. Knowledge is, after all, one, but the extreme specialism of the present day seems to hide the fact from a certain class of minds. The more we specialise the more room and the more necessity is there for students whose constant aim it shall be to bring out the relations of the special subjects. One of the greatest of all gaps lies between the natural sciences and the study of humanity. It is the duty of the geographer to build one bridge over an abyss which in the opinion of many is upsetting the equilibrium of our culture. Lop of either limb of geography and you maim it in its noblest part.

In speaking thus we are not blind to the necessity of specialism within geography itself. If you would do original work in the science you must specialise. But for this purpose either physical or political geography would be as unwieldy as the entire subject. Moreover, your special subject need not fall entirely within the realm of one or other branch; it may lie across the frontier. Geography is like a tree which early divides into two great branches, whose twigs may none the less be inextricably interwoven. You select a few adjacent twigs, but they may spring from different branches. As a subject of education, however, and as a basis for all fruitful specialism within the subject, we insist on the teaching and the grasping of geography as a whole.

This question of possibility leads us naturally into an inquiry as to the relations of geography to its neighbour sciences. We cannot do better than adopt Mr. Bryce's rough classification of the environment. First, we have the influences due to the configuration of the earth's surface; secondly, those belonging to meteorology and climate; and thirdly, the products which a country offers to human industry.

First, then, as to the configuration of the earth's surface. We have here a bone of contention between the geographers and the geologists. The latter hold that the causes which have determined the form of the lithosphere are dealt with by their science, and that there is neither room nor necessity for the physical geographer. The geographer has in consequence damaged his science by refusing to include among his data any but the barest results of geology. The rivalry must be well known to all here present. It has been productive of nothing but evil to geography. Two sciences may have data in part identical, yet there ought to be no bickering in consequence, for the data, though identical, are looked at from different points of view. They are grouped differently. Least of all should the geologist exhibit such weakness. At every step in his own department he is dependent on his scientific brethren. Palæontology is the key to the relative age of strata, but it is irrational apart from biology. Some of the most difficult problems of physics and chemistry lie within the realm of mineralogy, especially, for instance, the causes and methods of metamorphism. The best attempt to find a common measure of geological and historical time lies in Dr. Croll's astronomical interpretation of recurrent glacial epochs. But enough of this. The true distinction between geology and geography seems to me to lie in this: the geologist looks at the present that he may interpret the past; the geographer looks at the past that he may interpret the present. This line has already been traced for us by one of the greatest of the geologists.

In his 'Text-book of Geology,' Dr. Archibald Geikie gives the following lucid determination of it:[4]–

"An investigation of the geological history of a country involves two distinct lines of inquiry. We may first consider the nature and arrangement of the rocks that underlie the surface, with a view to ascertaining from them the successive changes in physical geography and in plant and animal life which they chronicle. But besides the story of the rocks, we may try to trace that of the surface itself, the origin and vicissitudes of the mountains and plains, valleys and ravines, peaks, passes, and lake basins, which have been formed out of the rocks. The two inquiries traced backwards merge into each other, but they become more and more distinct as they are pursued towards later times. It is obvious, for instance, that a mass of marine limestone which rises into groups of hills, trenched by river gorges and traversed by valleys, presents two sharply contrasted pictures to the mind. Looked at from the side of its origin, the rock brings before us a sea-bottom over which the relics of generations of a luxuriant marine calcareous fauna accumulated. We may be able to trace every bed, to mark with precision its organic contents, and to establish the zoological succession of which these superimposed sea-bottoms are the records. But we may be quite unable to explain how such sea-formed limestone came to stand as it now does, here towering into hills, and there sinking into valleys. The rocks and their contents form one subject of study, the history of their present scenery another."

The same idea is indorsed by Professor Moseley in his lecture on "The Scientific Aspects of Geographical Education." We quote the following passage from among many others in the same strain:[5] –

'Regarding physical geography as a part of geology to be separated from it:– The reason why such a separation should be effected is that there is thus formed and brought together for special treatment a subject which is far more necessary and suitable for general educational purposes than the whole of geology itself, which will attract far more students and act as a lever for promoting the study of other branches of science as special studies, and certainly of geology itself.

"The principal argument that is always brought against the establishment of professorships of physical geography at the Universities is that the subject is already covered by the professors of geology; but Prof. Geikie evidently does not

[4] Archibald Geikie, 'Text-book of Geology,' 1882, p. 910.
[5] 'R. G. S. Educational Reports,' 1886, p. 228, Professor Moseley.

take that view, and points out in his letter already referred to, 'Geology is every day increasing in its scope, which is already too vast for the physical powers of even the most indefatigable teacher.' "

In this passage Prof. Moseley advocates the establishment of a chair of physical geography. It must not be concluded from this that he is opposed to the unity of geography. This is made clear by other portions of his lecture.

"Possibly, although at the present moment it may not be possible to secure the representation of geography as a whole, because of the apparent vagueness of its bounds and the attacks on all sides to which it is in consequence liable, there may be a chance of success if the attempt be made to press the claims of physical geography."

And again:–

"Ought not physical geography to form part of every liberal education as being a subject specially adapted for purposes of general learning, and as the only true basis on which can be founded a knowledge of what is termed political geography?"

Perhaps nowhere is the damage done to geography by the theory which denies its unity better seen than in the case of physical geography. The subject has been abandoned to the geologists, and has in consequence a geological bias. Phenomena such as volcanoes, hot springs, and glaciers, have been grouped into chapters, irrespective of the regions in which they occur. From the geologist's point of view this is sufficient – he is looking at his Rosetta stone; the understanding of the individual hieroglyphics is of great importance, but the meaning of the entire passage, the account of the event recorded, is, for the purpose of interpreting other records, unimportant. But such a science is not really physical geography, and Dr. Archibald Geikie tells us plainly in his 'Elements of Physical Geography'[6] that he is using the words as equivalent to physiography. True physical geography aims at giving us a causal description of the distribution of the features of the earth's surface. The data must be regrouped on a topographical basis. If I may venture to put the matter somewhat abruptly – Physiography asks of a given feature, "Why is it?" Topography, "Where is it?" Physical geography, "Why is it there?" Political geography, 'How does it act on man in society, and how does he react on it?' Geology asks, "What riddle of the past does it help to solve?" Physiography is common ground to the geologist and the geographer. The first four subjects are the realm of the geographer. The questions come in sequence. You may stop short of any one of them, but it is my contention that you cannot with advantage answer a later one unless you have answered those which precede it. Geology proper, in its strict sense, is unnecessary to the sequence of the argument.

We will give two illustrations of the inadequacy for geographical purposes of the present (geological) physical geographies even when considered as physiographies.

The first is the undue prominence given to such subjects as volcanoes and

[6] New edition, 1884, p. 3.

glaciers. To this my attention has been several times drawn by your Assistant-Secretary, Mr. Bates. It is perfectly natural in books written by geologists. Volcanoes and glaciers are phenomena which leave most marked and characteristic traces behind them. Therefore, from a geological point of view they are most important, and are worthy of special study. But the result resembles a book on biology written by a palæontologist. In it we should expect to find the snail's shell, for instance, described in the greatest detail, but to the comparative neglect of the far more important soft white parts within.

My other illustration is a practical one, which must appeal to the experience of all thoughtful travellers. Let us say that you go for a trip up the Rhine; you must be strangely wanting in curiosity if you do not ask yourself such questions as the following:– Why is it that after passing over many miles of flat land through which the Rhine meanders almost on a level with the surrounding country, we come suddenly to a part of its course in which it passes through a gorge? Why, when we reach Bingen, does that gorge still more suddenly cease, its place taken by a lake-like valley bounded by parallel ranges of mountains? No ordinary physical geography that I have seen adequately answers such questions as these. If you happen to have a special knowledge of the subject, you may know that if you look into the 'Journal of the Geological Society' you will find a delightful paper on this subject by Sir Andrew Ramsay. But this implies the time and opportunity for research among original authorities, and even then your reward will be slight. It is only a few isolated regions which have been so treated.

I will close this portion of the subject with a constructive attempt. I shall select a region familiar to all, that your attention may be concentrated on the method rather than the matter. Let us take the south-east of England. The usual method of treating the geography of such a region would be to describe from a physical point of view first the coast and then the surface. The capes and inlets of the one and the hills and valleys of the other would be enumerated in order. You would then have a list of the political divisions, and a further list of the chief towns, stating the rivers on whose banks they stand. In some cases a few interesting but isolated facts would be added, mental pegs on which to hang the names. The political portion of such a work even at best rises no higher than to the rank of a good system of mnemonics. As for the physical portion, all the text-books agree in committing what is, from my point of view, a fundamental error. They separate the descriptions of the coast and the surface. This is fatal to the demonstration in due perspective of the chain of causes and effects. The accidents of the surface and of the coast are alike the results of the interaction of two forces, the varying resistance of the rock strata and the varying erosive powers of atmosphere and sea. The erosive powers, whether superficial or marginal, act on one and the same set of rocks. Why should there be a Flamborough Head? Why should there be a Yorkshire Wold? They are but two edges of the rim of one and the same mass of uptilted chalk-strata.

Let us try to construct a geography of South-eastern England which shall exhibit a continuous series of causal relations. Imagine thrown over the land like a white tablecloth over a table, a great sheet of chalk. Let the sheet be creased with a few simple folds, like a tablecloth laid by a careless hand. A line of furrow[7] runs down the Kennet to Reading, and then follows the Thames out to sea. A line of ridge passes eastward through Salisbury Plain and then down the centre of the Weald. A second line of furrow follows the valley of the Frome and its submarine continuations, the Solent and Spithead. Finally, yet a second line of ridge is carried through the Isle of Purbeck and its now detached member the Isle of Wight. Imagine these ridges and furrows untouched by the erosive forces. The curves of the strata would be parallel with the curves of the surface. The ridges would be flat-topped and broad. The furrows would be flat-bottomed and broad. The Kennet-Thames furrow would be characterised by increasing width as it advanced eastward. The slopes joining the furrow-bottom to the ridge-top would vary in steepness. It is not pretended that the land ever exhibited such a picture. The upheaving and the erosive forces have always acted simultaneously. As with the Houses of Parliament, the process of ruin commenced before the building was complete. The elimination of erosion is merely an expedient to show the simple arrangement of the rocks, which simplicity is masked by the apparent confusion of the ruin. Add one more fact, that above and below the hard chalk lie strata of soft clay, and we have drawn on geology for all that we require.

The moulder's work is complete; the chisel must now be applied. The powers of air and sea tear our cloth to tatters. But as though the cloth had been stiffened with starch as it lay creased on the table, the furrows and ridges we have described have not fallen in. Their ruined edges and ends project stiffly as hill ranges and capes. The furrow-bottoms, buried beneath the superincumbent clay, produce lines of valley along the London and Hampshire basins. Into the soft clay the sea has eaten, producing the great inlet of the Thames mouth, and the narrower but more intricate sea-channels which extend from Poole Harbour through the Solent to Spithead, and which ramify into Southampton Water and Portsmouth, Langstone, and Chichester Harbours. The upturned edge of the chalk-sheet produces the long range of hills, which, under the various names of Berkshire Downs, Chiltern, and Gogmagog Hills, and East Anglian Heights, bounds the Kennet-Thames basin to the north-west. The North and South Downs stand up facing each other, the springs of an arch from which the key-stone has been removed. The same arch forms Salisbury Plain, and its eastward prolongation in the chalk uplands of Hampshire; but here the key-stone, though damaged, has not been completely worn through. Beachy Head and the North and South Forelands are but the seaward projections of the Down ranges. The fact that the North Downs end not in a single promontory, like Beachy Head, but in a long line of cliff, the two ends of which are marked by the North and South Forelands, may serve to draw attention to a relation which frequently exists between the slope of the surface and the dip of the strata. A few sentences back, we mentioned the fact, that if our simple ridge and furrow system really obtained, the slopes connecting the ridge-tops and

[7] Furrow and ridge are here used in the sense of syncline and anticline. They must be carefully distinguished from valley and hill. The two are often causally related, as I point out in this paper, but they are far from identical.

the furrow bottoms would vary in steepness. By remembering the position of a hill-range in the "restored" ruin, we shall remember not merely its direction, but also the relative steepness of its two faces. One will be produced by the dipping strata, the other will be the escarpment where the strata have been cut short. On the dip of the strata will depend very much whether when we have climbed the escarpment, we see in front of us a sharp descent or an undulating upland. Contrast in this respect the two chalk uplands which form the broad projections of East Anglia and Kent with the narrow ridges, the Chilterns and the Hog's Back. The north-west escarpment of the Chilterns is continuous with the western scarped face of East Anglia. The south-eastern dip-slope of the Chilterns is continuous with the dip-slope which forms the broad uplands of Norfolk. The dip is steep in the case of the Chilterns, slight in that of Norfolk. Similarly the Kentish uplands are a prolongation of the Hog's Back. The southern scarped faces differ but little, whereas the northern dip-slope of the Hog's Back is steep, though its continuation in Kent is only gently inclined. This terminal expansion of the hill-ranges has been of great importance in English history, as will be seen presently. The expansions may be considered as dependent on the eastward widening of the Kennet-Thames basin. It will be noticed that the shores of the Thames estuary are on the whole parallel with the hill-ranges which mark the lips of the basin, the northern shore parallel with the curve traced by the hills from Hunstanton Point to the Chilterns, the southern parallel with the straighter range of the North Downs.

The rivers of the district fall naturally into three classes. First, we have those which flow down the dip-slope of East Anglia. As a consequence, they are numerous and roughly parallel. They do not combine to form one large stream presenting a tree-like appearance on the map. Secondly, we have those which flow down the great furrows, the Kennet and the Thames below Reading on the one hand, the Frome with its submarine prolongation by the Solent and Spithead on the other. The many tributaries of the Thames are obvious, but the tree-like character of the Frome is not obvious unless its submarine continuation be taken into account. Then the Frome, the Stour, the Avon, the Test, the Itchen, and the Medina, would combine to form one great stream, having its mouth east of the Isle of Wight. Such a river may very probably have actually existed. Lastly, there are the streams which pass by ravines through the chalk ranges, the Thames above Reading, and the various small rivers of the Weald. This circumstance is incomprehensible, unless we suppose that the strata arches were formerly complete. Then these streams would flow down the even slope of the ridge, following the ordinary hydrostatic laws. The only prominent feature of our area which would require a special explanation apart from the flexure of the rocks is the shingle bank which forms Dungeness.[8]

This being the general anatomy of the land, what has been its influence on man?

[8] I have omitted in this sketch to account for Leith Hill and the Forest Range of Sussex. They, too, depend on the flexure of the rocks; but to explain their cause would take up too much space in a paper which purports only to indicate methods, and not to exhaust its topic.

In the midst of forest and marsh three broad uplands stood out in early days, great openings in which man could establish himself with the least resistance from nature. In the language of the Celts they were known as "Gwents," a name corrupted by the Latin conquerors into "Ventæ." They were the chalk uplands with which we were familiar, the arch-top of Salisbury Plain and Hampshire, and the terminal expansions of the chalk ranges in East Anglia and Kent. In East Anglia was Venta Icenorum; in Kent and Canterbury[9] we still have relics of another Gwent. The first syllable of Winchester[10] completes the triplet. In later, but still early times, they were the first nests of the three races which composed the German host. The Angles settled in Norfolk and Suffolk, the Jutes in Kent, the Saxons in Hampshire. In still later England, Winchester, Canterbury, and Norwich were among the chief of mediæval cities. To this day the isolation of two of these regions at least has left its traces in the marked characteristics of their populations. The Fens cut off Norfolk, the Weald forests shut in Kent. Their people have taken distinct positions in our history. The "men of Norfolk" and the "men of Kent" have been of a remarkably rebellious disposition.

There were four great cities in the east and south; we have mentioned three. The fourth was London. Geographical conditions have determined the greatness of the metropolis. The map will make it clear at once, that the Fens and the Weald would compel the lines of communication from Norfolk and Kent on the one hand, and the rest of England on the other to pass in the general direction of London. Kent lies nearest to the Continent, and hence Watling Street was not merely the Kentish road, but also the road to Flanders. Where the hills narrow the Thames marshes most there is the natural crossing of Watling Street, first a ferry, then a bridge. This point lies between Tower Hill and the heights of Dulwich and Sydenham. Bermondsey, the isle of Bermond, was a dry spot, rising like a stepping-stone from among the surrounding marshes. The existence of solid ground on the immediate banks of the deep water, which is necessary, as the "take-off" for a bridge or ferry, is also necessary for a landing-place. Here then we have a crossing of natural ways on a spot which is a natural halting-place for both, hence a point at which a city is certain to rise. That city will be the more important if one way is by land and the other by water, for it is then a place of transhipment. It will be still more important if it is the necessary meeting-point of river and sea traffic. Even more pregnant with meaning is the position of the Thames mouth relatively to that of the Scheldt. It determines the linked greatness of London and Antwerp, and also much of the Continental policy of England. Thus many causes conspire to maintain the greatness of London. This is a fact to be marked. It is the secret of its persistent growth from the earliest times. The importance of a given geographical feature varies with the degree of man's civilisation. A city which

[9] So J. R. Green would have it, 'Making of England,' 1882, p. 9. But Isaac Taylor derives Kent from *Cenn*, a Gadhelic form of the Cymric *Pen* = a head, a projection – 'Words and Places,' 1885, p. 148.

[10] Venta Belgarum.

depends on one physical advantage my fall at any moment. A single mechanical discovery may effect the change.[11]

So much for the cities. Lastly as to the political divisions. There are two types of political divisions, neutral and arbitrary. The contrast presented by the old division of France into provinces and the revolutionary division into departments will serve to indicate the distinction. The one is the result of an unconscious process, such as the accretion of smaller states to a larger state. The other is the product of conscious legislation. In England we have the two kinds side by side. In the midlands we have arbitrary divisions, counties named after their chief towns, and supposed to have originated from the partition of Mercia.[12] In the east and south, on the other hand, the counties are of natural growth, and bear names indicating their distinct origin. In the case of arbitrary divisions the frontiers are also likely to be arbitrary. The frontiers of natural divisions will usually be natural, and may be of two kinds. Immigrants spread from a centre, either until they meet physical obstacles or until they meet with the opposition of other centrifugal settlements. In the region we are dealing with we see some excellent examples of this last. The inhabitants of Surrey, Kent, and Sussex would establish themselves on the chalk hills and uplands, and then push slowly into the forest until their advanced guards met in the centre. The frontier-lines of those counties are exactly what we should expect under these circumstances. With this we may compare the frontier dividing Berkshire and Hampshire from Surrey and Sussex. It crosses a region of commons, lying largely on the Bagshot sands. Such sterile land would be unworthy of occupation until the better land had been filled up. Take again the region of the Fens. Five counties send tongues into these marshes.

Time forbids our going further into this subject. The broad results are these. From a consideration of the folding of the chalk and of its hardness as compared with the strata above and below it, may be demonstrated the causes of the two great promontories, the two great inlets, and the three great upland openings which have determined the positions, the number, and the importance of the chief cities and divisions of South-eastern England. The same processes of reasoning might be continued to any required degree of detail. The geography of any other region might be treated in a similar way. Further, having once mastered the few simple geological ideas involved, a graphic and precise conception of a land may be conveyed in a few sentences. The effort required to grasp the first application of the method may be greater than that called for by the older methods. Its beauty lies in the fact that every fresh conquest gives increased ease of acquisition.

[11] In this account of the "greatness" of London I have not indicated the full significance of Tower Hill. The "dun" or hill-fort no doubt decided the precise locality of London; but other causes, as given above, have determined its greatness.

[12] Consider J. R. Green, 'Conquest of England,' 1883, p. 141, note. But compare Isaac Taylor, 'Words and Places,' 1885, p. 179.

We will sum up our results bearing on the relation of geology to geography in the form of propositions:–

1. It is essential to know the form of the lithosphere.
2. This can only be accurately and vividly remembered by grasping the causes which have determined it.
3. One of these causes is the relative hardness and arrangement of the rocks.
4. But no geological data or reasoning must be admitted unless it be pertinent to the geographical argument. It must help to answer the question, "Why is a given feature where it is?"

Mr. Bryce's two remaining classes of environment factors call for less remark. The distinction between meteorology and geography must be a practical one. So much of meteorology, and it is much, as deals with weather-forecasting cannot be required by the geographer. Average or recurrent climatic conditions alone come within his ken. Even here he must be content very often to adopt the results of meteorology as data, just as meteorology itself accepts the results of physics. It is a mistake, especially of the Germans, that they include too much in geography. Geography has bearings on many subjects, but it does not bodily include those subjects. Even the great Peschel includes in his 'Physische Erdkunde'[13] a discussion on the barometer and a demonstration of the formulæ needed in barometric corrections. Such digressions are the cause of the often repeated charge that geographers are merely dabblers in all the sciences. It is our contention that geography has a separate sphere of work. Its data may overlap those of other sciences, but its function is to point out certain new relations between those data. Geography must be a continuous argument, and the test of whether a given point is to be included or not must be this – Is it pertinent to the main line of argument? How far digressions with the view of proving data are allowable must of course be a practical question. As a rule they should be excluded if it is the function of any other science to prove them.

Mr. Bryce's last category includes the productions of a region. The distribution of minerals is obviously incidental to the rock-structure, and we need refer to it only to give another tap to the nail at which we have been hammering previously. As regards the distribution of animals and plants, we must apply the test to which we referred in the last paragraph – How far is it pertinent to the main line of geographical argument? So far as the animals and plants in question form an appreciable factor in man's environment, so far their distribution is very pertinent. So far also as that distribution gives evidence of geographical changes, such as the separation of islands from continents or a retirement of the snow-line, so far it is also pertinent. But the study of the distribution of animals and plants in detail and as an aid to the understanding of the evolution of those beings, is in no sense a part

[13] Vol. ii. pp. 118–127, 2nd edit.

of geography. It is a part of zoology or botany, for the proper study of which a preliminary study of geography is necessary.

The truth of the matter is that the bounds of all the sciences must naturally be compromises. Knowledge, as we have said before, is one. Its division into subjects is a concession to human weakness. As a final example of this we will deal with the relation of geography to history. In their elementary stages they must obviously go hand in hand. In their higher stages they diverge. The historian finds full occupation in the critical and comparative study of original documents. He has neither the time nor usually the turn of mind to scan science for himself with a view to selecting the facts and ideas which he requires. It is the function of the geographer to do this for him. On the other hand, the geographer must go to history for the verification of the relations which he suggests. The body of laws governing those relations, which might in time be evolved, would render possible the writing of much "prehistoric" history. John Richard Green's 'Making of England' is largely a deduction from geographical conditions of what must have been the course of history.

It remains that I should set out what I conceive to be the main line of geographical argument. I will do this in two stages. The first will be general, such as might be gathered from the syllabus of a university course of lectures or from the table of contents at the beginning of a text-book. The second will be a special application of this to the solution of a definite problem – the reasons why Delhi and Calcutta should have been respectively the old and the new capitals of India.

We presuppose a knowledge of physiography. We would then start from the idea of a landless globe, and build up a conception of the earth on the analogy of mechanics. First, the laws of Newton are demonstrated in their ideal simplicity on the hypothesis of absolute rigidity. It is not until these are fixed in the mind that the counteracting tendencies of elasticity and friction are introduced. So would we attack the study of geography. Imagine our globe in a landless condition, composed that is of three concentric spheroids – atmosphere, hydrosphere, and lithosphere. Two great world-wide forces would be in action – the sun's heat and the earth's rotation on its axis. Obviously the trade-wind system would have unimpeded away. Next introduce the third set of world-wide forces – the inclination of the earth's axis to the plane of its orbit and the revolution of the earth round the sun. The result would be an annual march from tropic to tropic of the calm zone separating the trades. The fourth and last of the causes which we have termed world-wide would be the secular variation in the ellipticity of the earth's orbit and in the obliquity of its axis. This would produce similar variations in the annual march and in the intensity of the trade-wind system.

Thus far we have steered clear of longitudinal variations. Given the latitude, the altitude, the season of year, and the year in the secular period, and the climatic conditions are deducible from very few data. Now we abandon our primary hypothesis. Conceive the world as it is, as heated, as cooling, as shrinking, as wrinkling. It was heated, it is cooling, therefore it is shrinking, and the outer more chilled crust is in consequence wrinkling. The lithosphere is no longer concentric with the atmosphere and the hydrosphere. The bed of the ocean is thrown into ridges and furrows. The ridges project into the hydrosphere, and through the hydrosphere into the atmosphere. They act as obstacles in the way of the world-currents. They may be compared to the stones in the bed of a rapid stream on which the currents impinge and are diverted. They either leap over them or are spilt upon them. This purely mechanical action is well seen in the splitting of the Southern Equatorial Drift on Cape San Roque. Cape San Roque has a distinct influence on the climate of England. The "leaping-over" action is visible in the case of winds rising over mountain-chains, and as a consequence covering their slopes with moisture. But, in addition to the mechanical, there are thermal causes of variation, due mainly to the different specific heats of land and water – hence the monsoons. The lie of the great wrinkles has a special meaning. Were the continents extended east and west instead of in three great bands across the Equator, climate would be approximately indexed by latitude.

Thus may we steadily progress in the analysis of the world's surface. Conceive the world as landless, and you will see the motor-powers of air- and water-circulation. Replace your conception by one of a wrinkled world, and you will grasp how by mechanical obstruction and thermal irregularity your simple currents are differentiated into currents of almost infinite but still orderly complexity.

But we must advance a stage further. The form of the lithosphere is not fixed. The shrinkage is still in progress. Old wrinkles are raised and new wrinkles come into existence. As they rise their destruction commences. The currents ever work at the removal of the obstacles which obstruct their course. They tend to achieve the ideal simplicity of circulation. Thus the features of the earth's surface are constantly changing. Their precise form is determined by their past history as well as by their present conditions. Recent changes are the subject of one of the most fascinating chapters in geography. Plains are built by the accumulation of débris. Continents give birth to islands. The evidence is drawn from a hundred sources – from the lines of migration of birds, the distribution of animals, or the depths of the neighbouring seas.

Each successive chapter postulates what has gone before. The sequence of argument is unbroken. From the position of the obstacles and the course of the winds may be deduced the distribution of rain. From the form and distribution of the wrinkle-slopes and from the distribution of the rainfall follows the explanation of the drainage-system. The distribution of soils is mainly dependent on the rock-structure, and on a consideration of soil and climate follows the division of the world into natural regions based on vegetation. I am not here referring to the distribution of botanical species, but to that of the broad types of what may be called the vegetable clothing of the world – the polar and tropical deserts, the temperate and tropical forests, and the regions which may be grouped together as grass-plains.

Passing now to the second stage of the investigation, it will be well to make use of two technical terms. "An environment" is a natural region. The smaller the area included the greater tends to be the number of conditions uniform or nearly uniform throughout the area. Thus we have environments of different orders, whose extension and intension, to borrow a logical phrase, vary inversely. So with communities. "A community" is a group of men having certain characteristics in common. The smaller the community, the greater tends to be the number of common characteristics. Communities are of different orders – races, nations, provinces, towns – the last two expressions used in the sense of corporate groups of men. By the use of these two terms precision can be given to such discussions as the effects of exposing two communities to one environment, and one community to two environments. For instance, this – How have geographical conditions differentiated the English race in the three environments, Britain, America, and Australia?

Everywhere political questions will depend on the results of the physical inquiry. Certain conditions of climate and soil are needed for the aggregation of dense populations. A certain density of population seems necessary to the development of civilisation. In the light of such principles would be discussed such problems as the contrast between the ancient upland civilisations of the New World, Peru and Mexico, and the ancient lowland civilisations of the Old World, Egypt and Babylon. Again, comparatively undisturbed strata usually underlie wide plains, and wide plains seem specially favourable to the development of homogeneous races, like the Russians and the Chinese. Yet again, the distribution of animal, vegetable, and mineral products has done much to determine the local characteristics of civilisation. Consider in this respect the series presented by the Old World, the New World, and Australia in the matter of comparative wealth in cereals and beasts of burden.

One of the most interesting chapters would deal with the reaction of man on nature. Man alters his environment, and the action of that environment on his posterity is changed in consequence. The relative importance of physical features varies from age to age according to the state of knowledge of of material civilisation. The improvement of artificial lighting has rendered possible the existence of a great community at St. Petersburg. The discovery of the Cape route to India and of the New World led to the fall of Venice. The invention of the steam engine and the electric telegraph have rendered possible the great size of modern States. We might multiply such instances greatly. We might group them into categories, but our object to-day is merely to indicate the possibilities of the subject. One thing, however, must always be borne in mind. The course of history at a given moment, whether in politics, society, or any other sphere of human activity, is the product not only of environment but also of the momentum acquired in the past. The fact that man is mainly a creature of habit must be recognised. The Englishman, for instance, will put up with many anomalies until they become nuisances of a certain degree of virulence. The influence of this tendency must always be kept in mind in geography. Milford Haven, in the present state of things, offers far greater physical advantages than Liverpool for the American trade; yet it is improbable that Liverpool will have to give way to Milford Haven, at any rate in the immediate future. It is a case of *vis inertiæ*.

We propose passing now to the special illustration which we have promised. We will start from the fountain-head. From the sun's heat and the earth's rotation we demonstrate the trade-wind system. From the influence of that heat on the vast mass of Asia we deduce the monsoon variation of the system. Within the monsoon area are collected some seven hundred out of the eight hundred millions of Asia. Right athwart the south-west monsoon extends the Himalaya. The moisture of the Indian Ocean in consequence deluges its southern face. Thus the full importance of the direction of the mountain-chain is brought out. The rains have washed down from the mountains the débris which forms the fertile plain at their base. Hence, along the southern foot of the Himalaya we have a belt of country possessing the conditions of climate and soil needed to sustain a large population. In effect we find two-fifths of the population of the entire peninsula concentrated in the provinces of Bengal, the North-west, and the Punjab, although these three provinces have but little more than one-sixth the area. Moreover, the abundant moisture of the monsoon coupled with the height of the Himalaya (the height is a consequence of the comparative newness of the wrinkle) produce an abundant glacial system from above the snowline. One result of this is that the rivers of the plain are perennial, and constantly navigable. Thus we have two conditions favourable to the development of civilisation, density of population, and ease of communication.

A wealthy civilised community is a region tempting to the conqueror. Now conquerors are of two kinds – land-wolves and sea-wolves. How would these respectively gain access to their prey in the Ganges valley? Consider first the landward frontier of India. On the north-east the Himalaya is practically impassable to a host.[14] On the north-west is the Sulaiman range, pierced by many passes. From the Iranian uplands of which this range is the boundary wall have swept down successive waves of conquerors. But within the mountain line is a far more effective obstacle, the Thar or great Indian desert, with its continuation the Rann of Katch. This barrier extends parallel to the Sulaiman Mountains from the sea almost to the Himalaya. Between the desert and the foot of the Himalaya the fertile belt is narrowest. Through that gate must pass whoever would gain access to the Ganges valley. Alexander advanced to its entrance. When he swerved to the right and followed the Indus, India was saved. Close to the eastern end of the pass is Delhi. It stands at the head of the Jumna-Ganges navigation, the place of transhipment from land to water carriage. It is therefore a natural centre of commerce. It is also the natural base of operations for the Asiatic conqueror, his left flanked by the mountains, his right by the desert, his line of communications secure to the rear. The strategic importance of the region has not escaped the British. Here is Simla, the summer capital of India. Here also the army cantonments are most thickly sown. Here are the fields of many battles. So much for Delhi. Now for Calcutta. From the sea India is singularly inaccessible. The eastern shore is beaten by a heavy surf. We have had to construct a harbour at Madras at great expense. The western coast has many good harbours, but in its rear rises the steep slope of the Western Ghats. Drenched by the monsoon, they are densely clothed with forests, which to this day are the abode of some of the most savage races of the world. Behind Bombay railways have now been carried over the mountains, but until recently they must have been a

14 Only one exception is recorded by history. A Chinese army once succeeded in reaching Nepaul.

most effectual barrier to communication. The Portuguese settled at Goa, and could not advance. The English possession at Bombay was our earliest in India,[15] yet the Presidency of Bombay was the last to grow. The one great natural water-gate is by the mouth of the Ganges. Here, on the Hoogly, the British established themselves at Calcutta. It is the place of junction of river and sea shipping, and therefore a commercial centre. It is also the natural basis of operations for the conquerors from over the sea. From it they have extended their influence far and wide. The old presidencies of Bombay and Madras have each been succeeded by a single province, but the Presidency of Bengal has begotten Bengal, the North-west, the Punjab, and the Central Provinces; we might almost add Assam and Burma. Thus, to sum up, at the two ends of the fertile belt are the two gates of India – the Khaibar Pass and the Hoogly. Along that belt the great highway is the Jumna-Ganges. At either end of the river navigation stands strategical and commercial capital, Delhi on the one hand, Calcutta[16] on the other.

Thus we complete our survey of the methods and scope of geography. I believe that on lines such as I have sketched a geography may be worked out which shall satisfy at once the practical requirements of the statesman and the merchant, the theoretical requirements of the historian and the scientist, and the intellectual requirements of the teacher. Its inherent breadth and manysidedness should be claimed as its chief merit. At the same time we have to recognise that these are the very qualities which will render it "suspect" to an age of specialists. It would be a standing protest against the disintegration of culture with which we are threatened. In the days of our fathers the ancient classics were the common element in the culture of all men, a ground on which the specialists could meet. The world is changing, and it would seem that the classics are also becoming a speciality. Whether we regret the turn which things have taken or whether we rejoice at it, it is equally our duty to find a substitute. To me it seems that geography combines some of the requisite qualities. To the practical man, whether he aim at distinction in the State or at the amassing of wealth, it is a store of invaluable information; to the student it is a stimulating basis from which to set out along a hundred special lines; to the teacher it would be an implement for the calling out of the powers of the intellect, unless indeed to that old-world class of schoolmaster who measure the disciplinary value of a subject by the repugnance with which it inspires the pupil. All this we say on the assumption of the unity of the subject. The alternative is to divide the scientific from the practical. The result of its adoption will be the ruin of both. The practical will be rejected by the teacher, and will be found indigestible in after life. The scientific will be neglected by most men, because it lacks the element of utility in every-day life. The man of the world and the student, the scientist and the historian, will lose their common platform. The world will be the poorer.

15 Our earliest possession. We had factories at Surat and at Fort St. George somewhat earlier.

16 Calcutta = Kali Katta – the village of the goddess Kali. This suggests the question, Why should this particular village have risen to be a metropolis rather than any other village? I would propose the term "geographical selection" for the process on the analogy of "natural selection."

9

THE STUDY OF GEOGRAPHY

Franz Boas

Franz Boas (1858–1942) received an education in physics and geography in his native Germany, but following ethnographic expeditions to Baffin Island and Vancouver Island he settled in the USA and became one of the founders of modern anthropology. His ideas were opposed to the environmental determinism widely espoused by contemporary geographers (compare him with Semple, **chapter 14**, for example), and did not receive widespread influence within the discipline until taken up by Carl Sauer (**chapter 17**) in the 1920s and 1930s. Sauer appreciated his emphasis on cultural diffusion rather than unilinear evolution, the significance of perception and the methodological concept of the culture area. Boas's anthropological research also led him to reject the common use of racial classifications and the prevailing taxonomy of racial types. His encounters with Eskimos (Inuit) convinced him that, even when people were living in the most extreme physical environments, culture could not be attributed simply to geographical surroundings. His writings, including the article reproduced here, dealt with the tensions between geographical determinism and historical particularism in the search for a more active conception of culture. In contrast with the leading American and British geographers of the time, Boas looked to historical understanding rather than natural science laws as the template for geography. The tension between explanation and understanding was to run through geography until the present day.

Source: The study of geography. *Science* 9, 137–41, 1887.

It is a remarkable fact, that, in the recent literature of geography, researches on the method and limits of that science occupy a prominent place. Almost every distinguished geographer has felt the necessity of expressing his views on its aim and scope, and of defending it from being disintegrated and swallowed up by geology, botany, history, and other sciences treating on subjects similar to or identical with those of geography. If the representatives of a science as young as geography spend a great part of their time in discussions of this kind, though the material for investigations is still unlimited; if they feel compelled to defend their field of research against assaults of their fellow-workers and outsiders, – the reason for this fact must be looked for in a deep discrepancy between their fundamental views of science and those of their adversaries.

Formerly, when the greater part of the earth's surface was undiscovered, and European vessels sailed only over their well-known routes from continent to continent, careful not to stray from the old path and fearing the dangers of unknown regions, the mere thought of these vast territories which had never been sighted by a European could fill the mind of geographers with ardent longing for extended knowledge; with the desire of unveiling the secrets of regions enlivened by imagination with figures of unknown animals and peoples. But the more completely the outlines of continents and islands became known, the stronger grew the desire to *understand* the phenomena of the newly discovered regions by comparing them with those of one's own country. Instead of merely extending their study over new areas, scientists began to be absorbed in examining the phenomena more intently, and comparing them with the results of observations already made. Thus Humboldt's admirable works and Karl Ritter's comparative geography arose out of the rapidly extending knowledge of the earth.

The fact that the rapid disclosure of the most remote parts of the globe coincided with the not less rapid development of physical sciences has had great influence upon the development of geography; for while the circle of phenomena became wider every day, the idea became prevalent that a single phenomenon is not of great avail, but that it is the aim of science to deduce laws from phenomena; and the wider their scope, the more valuable they are considered. The descriptive sciences were deemed inferior in value to researches which had hitherto been outside their range. Instead of systematical botany and zoölogy, biology became the favourite study; theoretical philosophy was supplanted by experimental psychology; and, by the same process, geography was disintegrated into geology, meteorology, etc.

Ever since, these sciences have been rapidly developed, but geography itself has for a long time been almost overshadowed by its growing children. However, we do not think they can fill its place, and wish to prove that its neglect cannot be remedied by the attentive cultivation of those sciences separately.

Those accustomed to value a study according to the scope of the laws found by means of it are not content with researches on phenomena such as are the object of geography. They consider them from a physical stand-point, and find them to be physical, meteorological, or ethnological; and, after having explained them by means of physical, physiological, or psychological laws, have finished their work. It is very instructive to consider thoroughly their definition of geography. They declare that the domain of this science comprises neither magnetical and meteorological nor geological phenomena and processes. They generously grant it the study of the distribution of animals and plants, as far as physiologists and evolutionists will permit; but all agree that anthropo-geography – the life of man as far as it depends on the country he lives in – is the true domain of geography.

It is not difficult to discover the principle on which this segregation is founded. Physical phenomena are subject to physical laws which are known, or which will assuredly be found by the methods used in discovering those that are known. Physiological, and, to a still higher degree, psychological, laws are not so well known as to allow their being treated in the same way as physical laws. The conditions of the phenomena are generally so complicated, that, even if the most general laws were known, a strict conclusion cannot easily be drawn. But were those auxiliary sciences just as far developed as physics, no doubt the same scientists who at the present time concede them willingly to geography would not hesitate to claim them for physiology and psychology. It is evident that there is no middle way: geography must either be maintained in its full extent or it must be given up altogether.

As soon as we agree that the purpose of every science is accomplished when the laws which govern its phenomena are discovered, we must admit that the subject of geography is distributed among a great number of sciences; if, however, we would maintain its independence, we must prove that there exists another object for science besides the deduction of laws from phenomena. And it is our opinion that there *is* another object, – the thorough understanding of phenomena. Thus we find that the contest between geographers and their adversaries is identical with the old controversy between historical and physical methods. One party claims that the ideal aim of science ought to be the discovery of general laws; the other maintains that it is the investigation of phenomena themselves.

It is easily understood, therefore, why in geography the contest between these views is particularly lively. Here naturalists and historians meet in a common field of work. A great number of modern geographers have been educated as historians, and they must try to come to an agreement with the naturalists, who, in turn, must learn to accommodate their views to those of the historians. It is evident that an answer to this fundamental question on the value of historical and physical science can only be found by a methodological investigation of their relation to each other.

All agree that the establishment of facts is the foundation and starting-point of science. The physicist compares a series of similar facts, from which he isolates the general phenomenon which is common to all of them. Henceforth the single facts become less important to him, as he lays stress on the general law alone. On the other hand, the facts are the object which is of importance and interest to the historian. An example will explain our meaning more satisfactorily than a theoretical discussion.

When Newton studied the motion of the planets, the distribution of those celestial bodies in space and time were the means, not the object, of his researches. His problem was the action of two bodies upon each other, and thus he found the law of gravitation. On the other hand, Kant and Laplace, in studying the solar system, asked the question, Why is every one of the bodies constituting the solar system in the place it occupies? They took the law as granted, and applied it to the phenomena from which it had been deduced, in order to study the history of the solar system. Newton's work was at an end as soon as he had found the law of gravitation, which law was the preliminary condition of Kant's work.

Here is another example: according to Buckle's conception, historical facts must be considered as being caused by physiological and psychological laws.

Accordingly, he does not describe men and their actions as arising from their own character and the events influencing their life, but calls our attention to the laws governing the history of mankind. The object of the historians is a different one. They are absorbed in the study of the facts, and dwell admiringly on the character of their heroes. They take the most lively interest in the persons and nations they treat of, but are unwilling to consider them as subject to stringent laws.

We believe that the physical conception is nowhere else expressed as clearly as in Comte's system of sciences. Setting aside astronomy, which has been placed rather arbitrarily between mathematics and physics, all his sciences have the one aim, to deduce laws from phenomena. The single phenomenon itself is insignificant: it is only valuable because it is an emanation of a law, and serves to find new laws or to corroborate old ones. To this system of sciences Humboldt's 'Cosmos' is opposed in its principle. Cosmography, as we may call this science, considers every phenomenon as worthy of being studied for its own sake. Its mere existence entitles it to a full share of our attention; and the knowledge of its existence and evolution in space and time fully satisfies the student, without regard to the laws which it corroborates or which may be deduced from it.

Physicists will acknowledge that the study of the history of many phenomena is a work of scientific value. Nobody doubts the importance of Kant's researches on the solar system; nobody derogates from that of investigations upon the evolution of organisms. However, there is another class of phenomena the study of which is not considered of equal value, and among them are the geographical ones. In considering the geography of a country, it seems that the geological, meteorological, and anthropo-geographical phenomena form an incidental conglomerate, having no natural tie or relation to one another, while, for instance, the evolutionist's subject of study forms a natural unity. We may be allowed to say that the naturalist demands an objective connection between the phenomena he studies, which the geographical phenomena seem to lack. Their connection seems to be subjective, originating in the mind of the observer.

Accordingly there are two principal questions which must be answered: first, the one referring to the opposition between physicists and cosmographers, i.e., Is the study of phenomena for their own sake equal in value to the deduction of laws? second, Is the study of a series of phenomena having a merely subjective connection equal in value to researches on the history of those forming an objective unity?

We shall first treat on the difference of opinion between physicists and cosmographers. The two parties are strongly opposed to each other; and it is a hard task to value justly the arguments of opponents whose method of thinking and way of feeling are entirely opposed to one's own. An unbiassed judgment cannot be formed without severe mental struggles which destroy convictions that were considered immovable, and had become dear to us. But those struggles lead to the grander conviction that both parties, though in a permanent state of conflict, aspire to the same end, – to find the eternal truth.

The origin of every science we find in two different desires of the human mind, – its aesthetic wants, and the feelings, which are the sources of the two branches of science. It was an early desire of developing mankind to arrange systematically the phenomena seen by the observer in overwhelming number, and thus to put the confused impressions in order. This desire must be considered an emanation of the aesthetical disposition, which is offended by confusion and want of clearness. When occupied in satisfying this desire, the regularity of the processes and phenomena would attain a far greater importance than the single phenomenon, which is only considered important as being a specimen of the class to which it belongs. The clearer all the phenomena are arranged, the better will the aesthetic desire be satisfied, and, for that reason, the most general laws and ideas are considered the most valuable results of science.

From this point of view, the philosophical ideas of Epicurus are very interesting, as they may be considered the extreme opinion to which this aesthetical desire can lead if the pleasure one enjoys in arranging phenomena in a clear system is the only incentive. He considered any explanation of a phenomenon sufficient, provided it be natural. It does not matter, he taught, if an hypothesis is true; but all probable explanations are of the same value, and the choice between them is quite insignificant. We believe this opinion is called to a new life by a number of modern scientists, i.e., by those who try to construct the evolution of organisms in details which, at the present time at least, can neither be proved nor refuted. If, for instance, Müller describes the history of the evolution of flowers, he gives only a probable way of development, without any better proof than that it seems to be the simplest and therefore the most probable. But this construction of a probable hypothesis as to the origin of these phenomena gives a satisfaction to our aesthetical desire to bring the confusion of forms and species into a system. But it should be borne in mind that a theory must be true, and that its truth is the standard by which its value is measured. Therefore naturalists are always engaged in examining the truth of their theories by applying them to new phenomena, and in these researches those phenomena are the most important which seem to be opposed to the theories. As soon as the question whether the theory is applicable to the class of phenomena is solved, the whole class is of little further interest to the investigator.

While physical science arises from the logical and aesthetical demands of the human mind, cosmography has its source in the personal feeling of man towards the world, towards the phenomena surrounding him. We may call this an 'affective' impulse, in contrast to the aesthetic impulse. Goethe has expressed this idea with admirable clearness: 'It seems to me that every phenomenon, every fact, itself is the really interesting object. Whoever explains it, or connects it with other events, usually only amuses himself or makes sport of us, as, for instance, the naturalist or historian. But a single action or event is interesting, not because it is explainable, but because it is true' (*Unterhaltungen deutscher Ausgewanderten*).

The mere occurrence of an event claims the full attention of our mind, because we are affected by it, and it is studied without any regard to its place in a system. This continuous impulse is the important counterbalance against the one-sidedness of a science arisen from merely aesthetic impulses. As the truth of every phenomenon causes us to study it, a true history of its evolution alone can satisfy the investigator's mind, and it is for this reason that Epicurus's probable or possible explanation is not at all satisfactory for science, but that every approach to truth is considered a progress by far superior to the most elaborate system which may give proof of a subtile mind and scrupulous thought, but claims to be only one among many possible systems.

Naturalists will not deny the importance of every phenomenon, but do not consider it worthy of study for its own sake. It is only a proof or a refutation of their laws, systems, and hypotheses (as they are deduced from true phenomena), which they feel obliged to bring as near the truth as possible. The deductions, however, are their main interest; and the reward of the indefatigable student is to review, from the summit of his most general deductions, the vast field of phenomena. Joyfully he sees that every process and every phenomenon which seem to the stranger an irregular and incomprehensible conglomerate is a link of a long chain. Losing sight of the single facts, he sees only the beautiful order of the world.

The cosmographer, on the other hand, holds to the phenomenon which is the object of his study, may it occupy a high or a low rank in the system of physical sciences, and lovingly tries to penetrate into its secrets until every feature is plain and clear. This occupation with the object of his affection affords him a delight not inferior to that which the physicist enjoys in his systematical arrangement of the world.

Our inquiry leads us to the conclusion that it is in vain to search for an answer to the question, 'Which of the two methods is of a higher value? as each originates in a different desire of the human mind. An answer can only be subjective, being a confession of the answerer as to which is dearer to him, – his personal feeling towards the phenomena surrounding him, or his inclination for abstractions; whether he prefers to recognize the individuality in the totality, or the totality in the individuality.

Let us now turn to the discussion of the second point. We have seen that physicists are inclined to acknowledge the value of a certain class of cosmographical studies. It is the characteristic quality of those phenomena that they are the result of the action of incidental causes upon one group of forces, or upon the elements of phenomena. The physicist does not study the whole phenomenon as it represents itself to the human mind, but resolves it into its elements, which he investigates separately. The investigation of the history of these elements of phenomena leads to a systematical arrangement, which gives to the aesthetical desire as much satisfaction as the formulation of laws. The end which evolutional and astronomical researches tend to is the best proof of this fact. A study of groups of phenomena, which seem to be connected only in the mind of the observer, and admit of being resolved into their elements, cannot lead to a similar result, and is therefore considered of inferior value. However, we have tried to prove that the source of cosmographical researches is an affective one. If this be right, we cannot distinguish between complex and simple phenomena, as the physicist tries to do, and neglect their subjective unity, – the connection in which they appear to the mind of the observer. The whole phenomenon, and not its elements, is the object of the cosmographer's study. Thus the physiognomy of a country is of no interest to the physicist, while it is important to the cosmographer.

From the stand-point we occupy, a discussion as to the value of these researches is of just as little avail as that on the value of the two branches of science, for the judgment will be founded on the mental disposition of the judge, and be only a confession as to which impulse predominates, the aesthetic or the affective. However, one fact appears from our inquiry: cosmography is closely related to the arts, as the way in which the mind is affected by phenomena forms an important branch of the study. It therefore requires a different treatment from that of the physical sciences.

We will apply these results to the study of geography. Its objects are, the phenomena caused by the distribution of land and water, by the vertical forms of the earth's surface, and by the mutual influence of the earth and its inhabitants upon each other.

What does the physicist do with this object of study? He selects a single element out of phenomena which are observed at a certain point of the earth's surface, and compares it with another one found at another place. He continues in this way searching for similar phenomena, and loses sight altogether of the spot from which he started. Thus he becomes the founder of the sciences into which geography has gradually been resolved, as his studies are either directed to geological phenomena alone, or to meteorological, botanical, or whatever it may be. The most general deductions which can be reached in the pursuit of these studies still have a close connection with the single object, as they cannot be carried farther than to the most general geographical ideas, as mountain-ranges, running water, oceans, etc. The most general results of his investigations will therefore be a general history of the earth's surface. If he brings these results into a system, he acts, as it seems to us, against the cosmographical character of the science. For instance, a system of all possible actions of water as forming the earth's surface seems to us of little value, except from a practical stand-point as being useful in studying the geological history of a district or of the earth's surface. Therefore these systems must be considered as important auxiliary sciences, but they are not geography itself. Their value is founded only on their applicability to the study of geography. The invention of geographical systems, so far as they do not serve this purpose, must be considered as useless, and classifications must be made only as far as geographical phenomena of a similar kind must be explained by different causes.

But there is another branch of geography besides this, equal to it in value, – the physiognomy of the earth. It cannot afford a satisfactory object of study to the physicist, as its unity is a merely subjective one; and the geographer, in treating these subjects, approaches the domain of art, as the results of his study principally affect the feeling, and therefore must be described in an artistic way in order to satisfy the feeling in which it originated.

Our consideration leads us to the conclusion that geography is part of cosmography, and has its source in the affective impulse, in the desire to understand the phenomena and history of a country or of the whole earth, the home of mankind. It depends upon the inclination of the scientist towards physical or cosmographical method, whether he studies the history of the whole earth, or whether he prefers to learn that of a single country. From our point of view, the discussion whether geology or meteorology belongs to geography is of little importance, and we are willing to call all scientists geographers who study the phenomena of the earth's surface. We give geology no preference over the other branches of science, as many modern scientists are inclined to do. The study of the earth's surface implies geological researches as well as meteorological, ethnological, and others, as none of them cover the scope of geography, to delineate the picture of the earth's surface.

Many are the sciences that must help to reach this end; many are the studies and researches that must be pursued to add new figures to the incomplete picture; but every step that brings us nearer the end gives ampler satisfaction to the impulse which induces us to devote our time and work to this study, gratifying the love for the country we inhabit, and the nature that surrounds us.

10

MEANING AND AIM OF HUMAN GEOGRAPHY

Paul Vidal de la Blache

Paul Vidal de la Blache (1845–1918) was the founding father of French geography. Following his appointment to the Chair of Geography at the Sorbonne, Paris, in 1898, his methods and views were widely adopted, not least because he either taught or supervised most of the next generation of leading French geographers. His position was comparable to that of W. M. Davis in the USA and of H. J. Mackinder (**chapter 8**) in Britain, marking a period when key individuals exerted a greater influence over national schools of geography than could be the case today. However, he led more by example than through methodological writings, and his most complete statement of what geography should be – *Principles of human geography* – was not published until after his death. Later generations of French and foreign geographers often turned to his ideas on genres de vie, particularly in search of a more humanistic geography (see Ley, **chapter 11**). Yet, as this extract from *Principles* demonstrates, Vidal saw geography as a natural science concerned with terrestrial unity in much the same way as did other geographers of the time – including Ratzel. Even so, his emphasis was more on historical change and humans as a geographic factor than on environmental determinism. Unlike Semple (**chapter 14**), Vidal did not stress natural laws, and repeatedly emphasized how societies had humanized nature for their own ends. His optimistic belief in the powers of human change led him to look favourably upon colonization and the volume includes a long chapter devoted to the progressive nature of human civilization.

Source: Introduction: meaning and aim of human geography. In *Principles of human geography* (translated by Millicent T. Bingham). London: Constable, 1926 (original French publication in 1921). Extract from pp. 3–24.

Critical Examination of the Concept of Human Geography

Human geography is a recent sprout from the venerable trunk of geographical science. If it were merely a question of terms nothing could be less novel, for the human element is an essential part of all geography. Man is interested in his own kind more than in anything else. As soon as the age of travel and distant voyages opened, it was the discovery of social as well as environmental differences which chiefly excited his interest. What Ulysses retained from his travels was "the knowledge of cities and the customs of many men." To most of the early authors who wrote about geography the notion of country was inseparable from that of inhabitants, – the food-supply and the appearance of the population were no less curiously foreign and unaccustomed than the mountains, deserts, and rivers which made up their environment.

Human geography, therefore, is not to be contrasted with a geography from which human interests are excluded. Indeed such has never existed except in the minds of specialists. But our science offers a new conception of the interrelationships between earth and man, – a conception resulting from a more synthetic knowledge of the physical laws governing our earth and of the relations between the living beings which inhabit it.

Human geography is the expression of a growth of ideas rather than the immediate, one might almost say material, result of discovery and the extension of geographical knowledge.

It would seem as if the new light shed upon the entire surface of the earth during the sixteenth century might have given rise to human geography in the real sense of the word. But such was not the case. Manners and customs, to be sure, do play a large part in the narrations and compilations which that age has bequeathed to us. But emphasis was laid upon the extraordinary and bizarre, when not upon mere anecdote. There was no principle of geographical classification underlying the various types of societies described. Those who try to reconstruct pictures or "mirrors" of the world by using data of such a nature are no more dependable than Strabo. In regard to human phenomena necessarily included in descriptions of countries, Bernhard Varenius, – whose *Geographia generalis,* written in 1650, was the most remarkable work up to the time of Ritter, – used phrases showing an almost contemptuous condescension on his part. And so, though knowledge about the most varied types of peoples had been increasing throughout two centuries of discovery, nothing resulted which was either clear-cut or satisfying from the point of view of scientific classification.

Nevertheless, scientific thought had long been attracted by the influences of the physical world upon human society. It would be unjust to a line of scholars reaching from the first Greek philosophers to Thucydides, Aristotle, Hippocrates and Eratosthenes, to forget the ingenious and often profound ideas which are often expressed in their writings. How could the varied and ever-widening spectacle of the external world fail, after reasonable reflection upon the progress of human societies, to awaken an echo in the philosophical schools that sprang up along Ionian shores? There were certain sages who, like Heraclitus, true predecessor of

Bacon that he was, thought that man, rather than confine the search for truth to the contemplation of "his own microcosm," would do very well to widen his horizon and seek truth from the "great world" of which he is a part.[1]

These wise men began by seeking in physical environment the explanation of whatever was particularly striking in the character of the inhabitants. Then, as observations on the march of events and of societies accumulated with the passage of time and broadened in scope, it became more and more evident just how much importance should be attached to geographical causes. The reflections of Thucydides upon archaic Greece, and of Strabo upon the location of Italy, are traceable to the same intellectual traits as certain chapters of the *Esprit des lois* or of Henry Thomas Buckle's *History of Civilisation in England.*

Ritter is also inspired by similar ideas in his *Erdkunde,* but he writes more as a geographer. Though he assigns a special rôle to each great continental country because of traces of historical bias, he nevertheless does regard the interpretation of nature as pivotal. For most historians and sociologists, on the other hand, geography exists only for purposes of consultation. One starts from man in order to come back by a detour to man once more. One pictures the earth as "the stage upon which man's activities take place," without reflecting that the stage itself is alive. The problem consists in enumerating the influences affecting man, in an attempt to discover in how far a certain kind of determinism is operative in the events of history. Important and interesting questions, surely. But answers to them require a knowledge of the world wider and more profound than any available until recently.

The Principle of Terrestrial Unity and the Conception of Environment

The dominant idea in all geographical progress is that of terrestrial unity. The conception of the earth as a whole, whose parts are coördinated, where phenomena follow a definite sequence and obey general laws to which particular cases are related, had early entered the field of science by way of astronomy. In the words of Ptolemy, geography is "the sublime science which sees in the heavens the reflection of earth." But the conception of terrestrial unity was long confined to the domain of mathematics. It did not become part of other branches of geography until our own day, and then largely through the knowledge of circulation of the atmosphere which governs climatic laws. More and more we have come to accept certain generalisations with reference to the world organism. Friedrich Ratzel very wisely insists on such a conception, making it the corner-stone of his *Anthropogeographie.*[2] The phenomena of human geography are related to terrestrial unity by

[1] Francis Bacon, *De Dignitate et Augmentis Scientiarum,* Book 1, § 43.

[2] *Anthropogeographie, Zweiter Teil, Die Hologaïsche Erdansicht,* Stuttgart, 1891.

means of which alone can they be explained. They are everywhere related to the environment, itself the creature of a combination of physical conditions.

Botanical geography has been largely responsible for light thrown upon such a conception of environment, but the light reaches far beyond, embracing the geography of all living creatures. Alexander von Humboldt, with his usual foresight, pointed out how important is the appearance of vegetation in determining the character of a landscape, and when H. Berghaus, inspired by him, published in 1836 the first edition of his *Physikalischer Atlas*,[3] the close relationship between climate and vegetation was clearly brought out. This fertile idea opened the way for a new series of researches. Classification of species became less important than a survey of the entire plant life of a region, made in such a way as to show how the influence of environmental conditions such as soil, temperature and humidity, manifests itself.

The general appearance of vegetation is certainly the most characteristic feature of a region. Absence of it is striking. When we try to recall a long-forgotten landscape, no particular plant such as palm or olive-tree comes to mind, but the ensemble of all the various plants which make up vegetation as a whole. They not only accentuate land-forms, but give to the landscape by their shape, colour, bulk and manner of grouping, a common, individual character. Steppe, savanna, silva, park lands, open forest and gallery forest (sparse woods skirting streams in steppe-areas) are collective terms which give an idea of such an ensemble. It is not a question of a mere pictorial impression, but rather of a certain character resulting from the very functions of the plants as well as from their physiological requirements.

This fact has been demonstrated by analysis and by comparison from mere observation and from experimental research in botanical geography, especially since such research has been extended to include different altitudes in both tropical and temperate regions. The rivalry of plants among themselves is so active that only those best adapted to the environment are able to survive. Even so, only a state of unstable equilibrium is maintained. Adaptation finds expression in different ways, in the height, size, and position of leaves, hairy covering, fibrous tissue, root development, etc. Not only does each plant provide as best it can for the carrying on of its own vital activity, but many different plant-associations are formed so that one may profit by the proximity of the other. Whatever the variety of species living side by side, whatever the external differences in processes of adaptation, the entire plant population has a common stamp not to be mistaken by a trained eye.

Such is the lesson of ecology, for which we are indebted to researches in botanical geography: ecology, or in words of the author of the term,[4] the science of "the correlations between all organisms living together in one and the same locality and their adaptation to their surroundings." For it is obvious that these relations include not plants alone. Animals, of course, with their powers of locomotion and

[3] 3d. edition, Gotha, 1892.

[4] Ernst Haeckel, *The History of Creation*, New York, 1876, Vol. II, p. 354.

man with his intelligence are better able than plants to cope with the environment. But, when one considers all that is implied in this word "environment," and all the unsuspected threads of which the fabric which enfolds us is woven, how could any living organism possibly escape its influence?

In conclusion, these researches result in an essentially geographical concept: that of environment as composite, capable of grouping and of holding together heterogeneous beings in mutual vital interrelationships. This idea seems to be the law governing the geography of living creatures. Every region is a domain where many dissimilar beings, artificially brought together, have subsequently adapted themselves to a common existence. If the zoölogical elements which have entered into the formation of a regional fauna are considered, its heterogeneous character is clearly apparent; it is composed of representatives of widely different types, which circumstances, – always difficult to define with accuracy, but inherent in the struggle for existence, – have brought to the region. And yet these organisms have adapted themselves to it; and if, among themselves, they are more or less hostile, they are none the less dependent upon one another for their very existence. Even islands, if they are sufficiently large, are no exception to the rule. Zoö-geographers use such expressions as "community of life" or even "faunal association," significant terms, which show that for animals as for plants, every area with a given relief, location and climate, is a composite environment where groups of elements, – indigenous, ephemeral, migratory or surviving from former ages, – are concentrated, diverse but united by a common adaptation to the environment.

How far are these facts applicable to human geography? We shall try to discover an answer to this question.

Man and Environment

But before proceeding further, one point must be briefly considered. Botanical geography is based upon an imposing array of observations and researches: zoölogical geography, although far less advanced, has profited by much fruitful exploration. What facts are at the disposal of human geography? What is their source of origin? Are they numerous enough to warrant conclusions of which we have already had a glimpse?

In the study of relations between earth and man the perspective has changed. We are looking at them from a greater distance.

Heretofore, only historic times have been under consideration, which include merely the last act of the human drama, a period of time exceedingly short in comparison with the life and activities of man on earth. Prehistoric research has shown that man has been established since time immemorial in widely diverse parts of the globe, equipped with fire and fashioning tools; and however rudimentary his industries, the modifications that the face of the earth has undergone because of them cannot be ignored. The paleolithic hunter and earliest neolithic agriculturists destroyed certain species of animals and plants and favoured others. That these hunters and agriculturists operated independently of one another, in different localities, is proved by the various methods of making fire still in use. Man has influenced the living world longer and more generally than has been supposed.

Because the human race was so early and so widely distributed, there are many degrees of adaptation. Each group discovered helps as well as obstacles in the particular environment where it had to establish itself; the different ways of meeting them represent just so many local solutions of the problem of existence. But at a moment when continental interiors were being made accessible and scientific explorers were systematically observing their inhabitants, a heavy curtain fell and concealed the various developments. The influences of environment are seen only through masses of historical events which enshroud them.

Direct observance of forms of life closely in touch with their environment is a recent result of systematic observation of the most isolated and backward families of the human race. The services rendered to botanical geography by analysis of extra-European floras, as we have seen, are precisely the same as those to which human geography is indebted through knowledge of peoples still close to nature – the *Naturvölker*. However much weight is given to exchanges, there is always, nevertheless, a marked endemic quality which explains how certain individuals, under certain definite natural conditions, went about organising their existence according to their own lights. Is it not upon such foundations that civilisations, which are, after all, only accumulated experience, have been built? While developing and becoming more complicated, they have not entirely lost contact with their origins.

Many of these primitive forms of life are ephemeral; many are extinct or in process of extinction. True. But they leave as witnesses products of local industries, – weapons, implements, clothing, etc., – all the various objects in which their relation to surrounding nature materialises, so to speak. It has been wise to collect such objects, to found special museums for them, where they can be grouped and geographically coördinated. An isolated object means very little; but collections from a given locality have a common stamp, and give a direct and vital impression of the environment. So ethnographical museums such as that founded at Berlin by the indefatigable enthusiasm of Bastian, or those of Leipzig and other cities, are veritable archives where man may study himself, not in the abstract, but by means of concrete examples.

Another sign of progress is that we are better informed at present as to the distribution of our kind, we know more accurately how large the populations in different parts of the earth really are. I would not say that there is an exact census of the human race, and that the figure 1,700,000,000 accurately represents the sum-total of our fellow-creatures; but it is certain that thanks to soundings made almost everywhere in the human ocean, thanks to frequent censuses and to trustworthy estimates, figures are available which are accurate enough to use as a basis for inference.

Considering the instability of relations between living beings, the numbers and territorial distribution of each species has great scientific value. It throws light upon the evolution of occupation. Human population is a constantly changing phenomenon. This is most plainly in evidence when, in addition to statistics with reference to particular states, general distribution throughout the world is taken into account. There are regions so over-populated that the inhabitants seem to have utilised all possible space. There are others where population has remained small and scattering, when neither soil nor climate seems to justify the anomaly. How can such differences be explained except as the result of currents of immigration which originated in prehistoric times and of which only geography can discover a trace? And naturally these neglected areas are becoming a focus of attraction for present day migrations.

One of the most suggestive relationships is that between number of inhabitants and any given area, in other words, density of population. If detailed statistics of population are compared with equally detailed maps, such as are available in almost all the principal countries of the world today, it is possible, by analysis, to find a connexion between human groups and physical conditions. Here we touch upon one of the basic problems of human occupation. For the existence of a dense population, – a large group of human beings living together in the smallest space consistent with certainty of a livelihood for the entire group, – means, if one stops to think of it, a victory which can only be won under rare and unusual circumstances.

Today transportation facilities minimize the difficulties which our forebears encountered in forming compact groups where they happened to be. And yet, most existing groups were formed in ancient times; an analysis of them reveals their genesis. In reality the population of a region is composed, as Levasseur has well shown,[5] of a certain number of scattered nuclei, surrounded by concentric zones of decreasing intensity. It gathers about centres or along lines of attraction. Population did not spread like a drop of oil; in the beginning it grew in clumps, like corals. Reefs of population collected at certain points by a sort of crystallisation process. These populations, by their intelligence, increased the natural resources and the value of such places, so that other men, whether voluntarily or under compulsion, came to share in the advantages of the inheritance, and successive layers accumulated on the chosen spot.

We now have anthropological data in regard to some of the countries where human alluvium has been thus deposited. Central Europe, the Mediterranean basin and British India[6] are for different reasons examples from which it is possible to gain some idea of the composition of peoples. In a general way, their complexity strikes us most. When an attempt is made, with the most trustworthy anthropological data available, to discover the elements of the population, not only of a large region, but even of a small one, lack of homogeneity is found to be the rule almost without exception. In France anthropologists have discovered very ancient elements dating back to prehistoric times, side by side with recent arrivals, often within a single region or even a single department. Why some places should contain more heterogeneous elements than others is easily explained by their

[5] E. Levasseur, *La répartition de la race humaine* (*Bulletin de l'institut intern. de statistique*, XVIII, 2, p. 56).

[6] *Le peuple de l'Inde d'après la série des recensements* (*Annales de Géographie*, XV, 1906, pp. 353–375 and 419–442).

nature and location. But in the present stage of development of human occupation, regions which seem to have entirely escaped waves of invasion that have swept over the surface of the earth are very exceptional, – only a few distant archipelagoes and mountain-fastnesses. Even in the African jungle tall Negroes and lighter-skinned pygmies live side by side in mutual relationships. In spite of current usage which confuses the terms "people" and "race," the fundamental distinction between them can henceforth be considered established. Beneath similarities of language, religion and nationality, the specific differences implanted in us by an ancient descent never cease to be operative.

Nevertheless, all such heterogeneous groups blend in a social organisation which makes of the population of a country a unit when looked at in its entirety. It sometimes happens that each of the elements of this composite whole is well established in a certain mode of life; some as hunters, others agriculturists, others shepherds; if such is the case, they coöperate with and supplement one another. It most often happens, except for certain obstinately refractory units within our European societies, such as gypsies, gitanos, zingani, etc., that the sovereign influence of environment has forced all into similar occupations and customs. There is material evidence of this uniformity. Such is the coalescing power which blots out original differences and blends them in a common type of adaptation. Human societies, like those of the vegetable and animal world, are composed of different elements subject to the influence of environment. No one knows what winds brought them together, nor whence, nor when; but they are living side by side in a region which has gradually put its stamp upon them. Some societies have long been part of the environment, but others are in process of formation, continuing to recruit members and to be modified day by day. Upon such, in spite of all they can do, surrounding conditions leave their impress, and in Australia, at the Cape, or in America, these people are slowly becoming saturated with the influence of the regions where their destinies are to unfold. Are not the Boers one of the most remarkable examples of adaptation?

Man as a Geographical Factor

As a result of the particularism of the earlier geography, certain broad, general concepts in regard to the relationships between earth and man are beginning to appear. Population distribution has been guided in its development by the proximity of land masses to one another. Ocean solitudes long divided inhabited countries (*oikoumenes*) and kept them in ignorance of one another. Throughout the continents widely separated groups met with physical obstacles which only time could overcome; mountains, forests, marshes, waterless regions, etc. Civilisation recapitulates the struggles against such obstacles. The peoples which surmounted them were enabled to profit by the results of a collective experience gained in a variety of environments. Other communities, on the other hand, because of prolonged isolation, lost the initiative which had inspired their early progress. Incapable of raising themselves by their own efforts above a certain level, they suggest certain animal communities which seem to have completed the utmost progress of which they are capable. Today all parts of the earth are interrelated. Isolation is an anomaly which seems like a challenge. Contacts are no longer between contiguous or neighbouring areas, as heretofore, but between widely separated regions.

Physical causes, whose value geographers have been fond of pointing out, are not without influence on this account; it is always necessary to note the effect of climate and relief, as well as of continental or insular position, on human societies. But we should observe their effects on man and on the whole of the living world conjointly.

In this way we are in a position to better appreciate the rôle which should be assigned to man as a geographical factor. He is at once both active and passive. For, according to the well-known phrase, "*natura non nisi parendo vincitur.*"

An eminent Russian geographer, Woeïkof, has noted that the objects over which man has control are chiefly what he calls "movable bodies".[7] Upon that part of the earth's crust modified by the mechanical action of surface agencies such as running water, frost, winds, the roots of plants, the transference of particles by animals and the constant tread of their feet, lies a residue, the result of decomposition, constantly being renewed and prepared for use, capable of being modified and of taking on different forms. In the most thankless wastes of the Sahara the dunes still show traces of vegetation and of life. Human activity finds greater opportunity in regions where this movable material is abundant than in those where a calcareous carapace, for example, or a clayey crust, has made the surface hard and sterile.

But it must be remembered that the earth itself, to use Berthelot's phrase, is "*quelque chose de vivant.*" Under the influence of light and of forces whose mechanical action is unknown, plants absorb and decompose chemical substances, and bacteria fix the nitrogen of the atmosphere in certain plants. Life, transformed as it passes from organism to organism, circulates through multitudes of living beings: some manufacture the substances by which others are nourished; some carry germs of diseases which destroy other species. Man utilises not only inorganic agencies in his work of transformation. He is not content merely to make use of the products of decomposition in the soil by ploughing, nor to utilise the waterfalls, the force of gravity brought into play by inequalities of relief. He further collaborates with all living forces grouped together by environmental conditions. He joins in nature's game.

The game is not free from chance. It is important to note that in many parts of the world, if not in all, climatic conditions are not as fixed as the means printed on maps would seem to indicate. Climate is a resultant of various forces and oscillates about a mean rather than holding to it. The still far from complete data in our possession have at least made clear the fact that such oscillations seem to be periodic in character, in other words, that the swing continues for several consecutive years, first in one direction, then in another. Series of rainy years alternate with dry

7 A. Woeïkof, *De l'influence de l'homme sur la terre* (*Annales de Géographie*, X, 1901, p. 98).

series; and even though these variations do not cause great damage in regions where rainfall is sufficient, the reverse is true in regions with only the necessary minimum. The implication in this remark is clear, for man by his intervention can reinforce the positive factor, establish, as it were, a permanent state upon a temporary one, – permanent, at least, until a new order of things.

For example: from North Africa to central Asia observers are struck by scenes of desolation in contrast to remnants of cultures and ruins which give evidence of ancient prosperity. The latter rested upon the fragile support of irrigation-works, thanks to which man was able to obtain a constant supply of water. If the beneficent function were interrupted for a while, all the enemies vanquished by irrigation would regain control. And what is far more serious, processes of adaptation would take another course. Other customs would prevail among men; their existence would depend on other means of livelihood, on other creatures with other territorial requirements. The forest has no greater adversary than the shepherd, while dykes and canals have an implacable enemy in the Bedouin, whose wanderings they obstruct.

Man's activities gain their chief effectiveness from the allies they mobilise in the living world – cultivated plants and domestic animals; for, in this way, inherent energy is freed, which, thanks to man, finds an outlet and proceeds to act. Most of the plants assembled by agriculture are species which formerly were widely scattered: such, for instance, as plants clinging to sunny slopes or along the banks of streams, overpowered by competition with more numerous, vigorous species, and allowed to remain only in certain places. From the favourable stronghold where they were thus entrenched, these plants, destined some day to receive the blessing of grateful men, lay waiting for the moment when new circumstances should allow them more space. Man, by making them part of his own clientèle, did them this service by setting them free. But simultaneously he opened the way to a whole procession of uninvited plants and animals. New groups took the place of those which had occupied the space before his arrival.

Without man's help, cultivated plants, at present characteristic of certain parts of the earth, would never have been able to win from rival species the space which they now occupy. Should it be inferred that if man withdrew his support, the species at whose expense the present incumbents have gained ground would once more assert their rights? Nothing could be less certain. For it may be that a new natural economy has had time to replace the old. When tropical forests disappear they are succeeded by brushland; and this change, by modifying light conditions, eliminates in part the creatures living in the forest, especially formidable insects (*Glossinae*) which kept away other species. Elsewhere great areas of underbrush such as *maqui* or *garigue*[8] have replaced forests. Other trains of events have taken place, transforming the living environment as well as economic conditions. A new field, almost illimitable in extent, seems to open for observation and perhaps for experiment. In studying the influence of man upon the earth, and the scars which

[8] See *Oecology of Plants*, Eug. Warming, Oxford Press, 1909, p. 304.

occupation, often of very long standing, has already made on its surface, human geography has a double aim. It not only has to take account of the destruction in which man may or may not have shared, one which has enormously reduced the number of great animal species since the Pliocene period, it is finding also, by a more intimate knowledge of the relationships which make a single unit of the entire living world, a means of thoroughly investigating the transformations taking place at the present time as well as those which can be foreseen in the future. In this respect, present and future undertakings of man, henceforth master of distances, armed with all that science places at his disposal, will far exceed any influence that our remote ancestors could exert. Let us congratulate ourselves, because the task of colonisation which constitutes the glory of our age would be only a sham if nature set definite, rigid boundaries, instead of leaving a margin for the work of transformation or reparation which it is within man's power to perform.

11

GEOGRAPHY WITHOUT HUMAN AGENCY: A HUMANISTIC CRITIQUE

David Ley

From the 1960s onwards geographers experimented with a number of new ideas, including spatial science, behavioural geography, radical and Marxist geography. Although these so-called 'paradigms' (see Johnston, **chapter 2**) were usually presented as distinctive departures from conventional wisdom and from one another, according to some they shared a common flaw. David Ley argues that they all subverted the central and active role of human agency, a fault he traces back to the nineteenth-century exchanges between Vidal de la Blache (**chapter 10**) and the French sociologist Emile Durkheim. Ley claims that this error is epistemological, theoretical, existential and moral. It glosses over the subjectivity of the observer, devalues the powers of human consciousness and encourages technical solutions to human problems. It also threatens to turn humans into the passive and mechanical entities that appear in geographical theories. Ley's most celebrated empirical work is a pioneering study entitled *The black inner city as frontier outpost* (Washington, DC, 1974), in which he was one of the first modern geographers to employ participant observation in an urban context (part of which he cites in the essay). In this and later works, he sought to retrieve the 'human' in human geography by representing people as creative, active and intentioned agents. His view of geography is a strongly normative and moral one. Along with Buttimer (**chapter 3**) and Tuan (**chapter 28**), Ley was one of the leading figures in humanistic geography and a noted critic of what he termed structural Marxism. [Note: at the author's request the editors have amended language concerned with gender to reflect contemporary sensibilities on the subject.]

Source: Geography without man: a humanistic critique. School of Geography Research Paper 24, Oxford University, 1980.

Introduction

As an undergraduate, a leading question raised several times as a stimulant for discussion in seminars or tutorials was, Can there be a geography of the moon? At that period, with relatively little human debris littered over the lunar surface, the discussion would invariably reach a consensus that without the significant presence of people there could not be a credible lunar geography. A geomorphology, perhaps, but not a geography, in the absence of the geographic agent.

The view of geography underpinning this conclusion was that the discipline was the 'study of the earth as the home of man'. This was the perspective of several major schools early in the twentieth century, including the classical French regional tradition identified with Paul Vidal de la Blache. It was a definition that incorporated an object with its own physical processes (the earth), a subject who was an active agent (society), and a place (the home) which represented a conflation or synthesis of the two. As such, place had both materialist and idealist attributes; it was both a thing and an idea. Within this balanced interpretation of society and environment, the two were inseparable, as interrelated it has been said, as a snail and its shell.[1] The French school has, of course, been subject to criticism on a number of grounds, some of them well founded. It has been accused of an overly limited view of environment which disregarded political and economic forces, of indifference towards generalisation and theory-building, of absorption within the dominant ideologies of the day including a belief in European imperialism, and of an attraction towards disappearing rural societies to the exclusion of emerging urban culture.[2] But despite these flaws its posing of a dialectical relationship between society and environment would continue to be regarded by many geographers as the core of their discipline.

However, often without our realising it, this dialectic has been disembodied over the past fifty years as major geographic schools, some of them claiming philosophical sophistication, have become geographies without actors. The geographic subject has been lost. As we now gainsay determinism as a quaint concept that has had its day, the true state of affairs is that in theoretical discussion the determinists are often in the ascendancy. Consider the following extracts, illustrative of two methodological turns which have been influential in human geography since 1965. Firstly, from spatial analysis:

> *Reduce all social relations to relations of space and it would be possible to apply to human relations the fundamental logic of the natural sciences.*[3]

[1] E. Wrigley, "Changes in the philosophy of geography," pp. 3–20 in R. Chorley and P. Haggett (eds.), *Frontiers in Geographical Teaching*. London: Methuen, 1965.

[2] Anne Buttimer, *Society and Milieu in the French Geographic Tradition*, AAG Monograph No. 6. Chicago: Rand McNally, 1971; idem, "Charism and context: the challenge of La Géographie Humaine", pp. 58–76 in David Ley and Marwyn Samuels (eds.), *Humanistic Geography*. London: Croon Helm, 1978.

[3] Robert Park, "Human ecology," *American Journal of Sociology* 42 (1936), pp. 1–15.

Though this statement was made by Robert Park in 1936 in a discussion of human ecology, it represents a project which geography set itself to achieve in the 1960's as it was reconstituted by writers like William Bunge and David Harvey as the geometric science of spatial relations.[4] But as Park recognised, the gain of scientific method would be at the cost of a faithful representation of social relations. Naturalism involved reductionism, as the human agent was abstracted away in the methodological interests of a supposedly superior logic. More recently in structuralism, the abstraction of the human agent has become not an unfortunate side-effect, but the object of a self-conscious quest. In the words of Lévi-Strauss:

I believe the ultimate goal of the human sciences is not to constitute man but to dissolve him.[5]

And yet a major movement in human geography in the 1970's has drawn theory to the realm of structures. Exemplified amongst others by Manuel Castells and David Harvey's reformulated position, structural marxism has taken over from positivism in suggesting a new philosophical and theoretical frontier.[6] But as we will see, in this geography of structures there is no place for human agency. It is dissolved.

These two statements illustrate the major proposition of this paper: that significant traditions in human geography have passed from a study of the contextual relations between society and environment to a study of the logical relations between things in an abstracted space or structure. This is a proposition which might yield a number of questions, though this essay will consider only two. It is concerned, firstly, to elaborate the thesis of the loss of the geographic agent, and secondly to identify some important shortcomings of this development in geographic theory and methodology.

The Loss of the Geographic Subject

The erosion of an active view of humans was already beginning in the heyday of the French school itself. There was a fascinating academic debate at the turn of the twentieth century between Vidal's group in regional geography and the followers of the great French sociologist, Émile Durkheim.[7] In the debate Durkheim and the sociologists were usually cast as the aggressors; the most effective respondent was

[4] William Bunge, *Theoretical Geography*. University of Lund Studies in Geography, Series C, no. 1. Lund, Sweden: Gleerup, 1966; David Harvey, *Explanation in Geography*. London: Arnold, 1969.

[5] C. Lévi-Strauss, *The Savage Mind*. Cited in Mark Poster, *Existential Marxism in Postwar France*. Princeton, N.J.: Princeton University Press, 1975, p. 319.

[6] Manuel Castells, *The Urban Question: A Marxist Approach*. London: Arnold, 1977; David Harvey, *Social Justice and the City*. London: Arnold, 1973.

[7] Vincent Berdoulay, "The Vidal-Durkheim debate," pp. 77–90 in Ley and Samuels (eds.), *Humanistic Geography* (note 2).

the historian Lucien Febvre who was deeply impressed by Vidalian scholarship. There were several grounds for this interdisciplinary rivalry, not least it seems being professional jealousy amongst the sociologists of the professional status and institutional success of Vidal's school.

But of more significance were two other facets of the debate. Durkheim's interest in Comte's positivist methodology and epistemology placed him in opposition to Vidal's more interpretative ventures at understanding. Durkheim was sympathetic to a naturalist position which would extend to social science the methods of natural science. His concern was with measurable, observable facts, not intangible values and motivations. To follow the Comtean positivist model the phenomena under study should be objective rather than subjective, and be defined by quantity rather than quality, by form rather than by meaning.

A second but related point of departure was at a more theoretical level. Durkheim's epistemology did not allow a theoretically active role for human agency. His mode of explanation emphasised the power of "social facts" external to humans and human consciousness, and the expression of an overarching *conscience collective*. Questions of motivation and human will do not enter such a formulation. Rather social facts are characterised by "the coercive power which they impose upon each individual independent of the person's will."[8] This position, as geographers well know, was counter to Vidal's more active view of human agency, embodied in the concept of possibilism where, in Febvre's famous phrase, there are no necessities but everywhere possibilities, and where man as master of the possibilities is judge of their use.

Interwar developments

During the interwar years geography moved towards the position of Durkheim rather than Vidal. The finely woven dialectic of subject and object in the concept of place was prised apart and succeeded by phenomenalism, a materialist concern with objects and forms. Jean Brunhes reinterpreted human geography in terms of its "essential facts" – house types, agrarian systems, settlement shapes and the like. Possibly this may have been a direct response to Durkheim's identification of social facts as the proper content of sociology. Certainly Brunhes was following Durkheim and Comte in setting out an identity for a human science in terms of distinctive phenomena, its own subject matter.

The direction indicated by Brunhes was refined in subsequent work characterised by increasing abstraction, first Demangeon's quantitative coding of rural settlements and culminating in Christaller's central place theory in the 1930's. By then human geography was well on the way to becoming the geometry of space and form, an abstract science of the spatial relations of objects. But in the transition from place to space, the geographic accent had disappeared. The richness of human encounter with the environment was reduced, in central place theory, to the single

[8] Russell Keat and John Urry, *Social Theory as Science*. London: Routledge and Kegan Paul, 1975, p. 83.

behavioural assumption of rational activity expressed in distance minimisation in the journey to shop and trade.

The diminution of human agency led to a redefinition of the respective roles of society and environment in the new formulations. With the disintegration of the Vidalian symbiosis, human agency was reduced to a frail spectre faced with an overarching and overpowering environmental presence, reminiscent of Durkheim's *conscience collective.* A passive view of humanity was not limited to the more obvious physical and economic conceptualisations of the environment. Duncan has recently suggested that Carl Sauer's landscape school in cultural geography was also drawn to an anonymous and overarching interpretation of culture.[9] This so-called superorganic conception of culture was derived from the anthropologist Alfred Kroeber whose career at Berkeley overlapped with that of Sauer. Like Durkheim, Kroeber was anxious to identify a separate subject matter for his discipline, and in culture he claimed a content to anthropology which could not be reduced to sociology or psychology. Like Durkheim, therefore, individuals were suppressed in favour of a superorganic concept, in this case of culture, which in itself directed human behaviour. Culture could not be reduced to the individual, discrete groups, or consciousness, for it incorporated a self-contained model of mechanism. It was its own determination. This is a message from which contemporary cultural geography has yet to disassociate itself. Wilbur Zelinsky, a leading spokesman of recent cultural geography, has observed:

> *following in the footsteps of Alfred Kroeber and with some mental reservations those of Leslie White . . . culture is to a large extent an autonomous, virtually "super-organic" system that functions and evolves according to its own internal logic and presumed set of laws.*[10]

Six years later in 1973, Zelinsky presented this conviction no less strongly, arguing that culture was "superorganic and supra-individual in nature, an entity with a structure, set of processes, and momentum of its own . . ."[11]

To culture is ascribed causal power. It has its own internal laws, a life of its own. It has become reified, and needs people merely to act as its passive carriers, bearing a burden they cannot resist.

A deterministic conception of environment was of course more commonly applied to the physical rather than to the cultural milieu, and in this form it lingered on into the 1930's. In its darwinian organismic form, it reappeared in the Nazi ideology of *lebensraum,* living space, which evoked the logic of nature to justify territorial expansion, an amazing extension of naturalism into human life. More mundanely, physical determinism was popularised by geographers like Ellsworth Huntington and Stephen Visher, with their imaginative portrayal of the

[9] James Duncan, "The superorganic in American cultural geography: a critical commentary," Unpublished paper, Department of Geography, University of British Columbia, 1979.
[10] Cited in Duncan, op. cit. (note 9).
[11] *Ibid.*

dominance of the physical environment in human affairs. In one particularly bold sortie in an interdisciplinary journal (under the embarrassing title of "Social Geography"), Visher claimed to find causal chains between physical phenomena and such human domains as the incidence of labour disputes, leading to the grand conclusion that "Democracy is interfered with by exceptionally fertile soil."[12]

But by the 1930's this was becoming a relict argument, for with the development of industrial society the salient environment was increasingly being defined according to economic rather than physical gradients. The way forward was suggested in Harlan Barrows' perceptive interpretation of geography as human ecology in 1923. He commented that "upon economic geography for the most part the other divisions of the subject must be based", while the status of social geography would remain more equivocal. To the extent that the material of social geography is "intangible . . . this body of relationships appears to form a potential field for geography rather than an assured one."[13] Note the conjunction: research pursuing intangible, that is subjective or intersubjective relations, would have an uncertain existence, whereas the objective and phenomenal realm of economic factors would provide the leading theoretical sector.

From human ecology to spatial analysis

Barrows' prediction was strikingly accurate, for economics has provided the primary directive to human geography over the past half century. Within this hegemony the derivative and unassured status of social geography is intimated by its association with human ecology, surely the least social branch of sociology. For Park's alternative title for human ecology was biological economics, a label which points to its essentially mechanistic and *non-social* nature. A biological model is concerned with ethology not culture, with instincts not perceptions, and with physiology not consciousness. Questions of values and culture do not belong in such a formulation. Similarly, an economic model is individualistic and competitive, with its shrunken view of 'rational economic man.' Once again people are reduced to passive agents before a powerful environment, for the origins of human ecology have a consistent root: "To a large extent the model may be seen as one of economic determinism."[14]

[12] Stephen Visher, "Social geography," *Social Forces* 10 (1932), pp. 351–4.

[13] Harlan Barrows, "Geography as human ecology," *Annals, Association of American Geographers* 13 (1923), pp. 1–14.

[14] Duncan Timms, *The Urban Mosaic*. Cambridge: Cambridge University Press, 1971. This may seem an unlikely interpretation of a tradition which contained such classics of urban social psychology as Frederic Thrasher's *The Gang*, Harvey Zorbaugh's *The Gold Coast and the Slum*, and Louis Wirth's *The Ghetto*. But the social psychological and biological economic components of the Chicago School were never fully synthesised. Their divorce was complete as early as the 1940's when authors such as Firey and Jonassen complained of the total neglect of socio-cultural variables in human ecology. Moreover, as was clear from Harlan Barrows' reading of human ecology, only the biological economic component was influential in human geography.

Essentially the same model undergirds geography's recent spatial school though it is more sophisticated and free of the cruder biological analogies of human ecology. Mackenzie's definition of human ecology captures much of the flavour of the spatial school: "Human ecology deals with the spatial aspects of the symbiotic relations of human beings and human institutions."[15] More confusing is Park's differentiation of human ecology as seeking to emphasise not so much geography as space, a differentiation which serves to accentuate the undifferentiated state of the disciplines by the 1960's when human geography had itself claimed the mantle of the science of spatial relations.[16] This convergence reasserts the continuity with earlier trends in the discipline when we recall that human ecology is regarded as a North American variant of Durkheim's social morphology. Again the course of intellectual history in human geography has favoured Durkheim rather than Vidal as the society-environment dialectic has been compromised by a naturalism which reduces human agency, while conceiving of a potent environment with a set of mechanistic processes operating in spite of society and human purposes and actions.

The connections between theory and epistemology remain close. A theoretical position which suppresses human agency is accompanied by a positivist epistemology highly sceptical of the subjective and intersubjective realms. The language of spatial analysis accommodates variables which may be specified precisely, and are therefore objective and measurable. But this is to disqualify another set of variables not because they may be theoretically unimportant, but only because they do not fit the particular and restrictive language of spatial analysis. Such variables are those representing the subjective and inter-subjective domains, the lifeworld of values and meaning where ambiguity, contingency, and non-linear changes through time confound conventional positivist categories. As Gunnar Olsson has observed:

> *Whereas our past strategy assumed that spatial relations and human actions obey the same extensional rules of arithmetic, the new strategy must recognise that in the oblique realm of intentions, hopes and fears, two times two is not always equal to four.*[17]

The creative and emergent world of values and meaning is not reducible to the fixed categories of positivist inquiry.

This epistemological impasse has been recognised by perceptive adherents to both human ecology and spatial analysis. In a response to criticisms directed

[15] R. Mackenzie, "Human ecology," *Encyclopedia of Social Sciences* 5 (1931), p. 314.

[16] R. Park, "The urban community as a spatial pattern and a moral order," pp. 3–18, in E. Burgess (ed.), *The Urban Community*. Chicago: University of Chicago Press, 1926.

[17] Gunnar Olsson, "The dialectics of spatial analysis," *Antipode* 6, no. 3 (1974), pp. 50–62. In more recent papers Olsson has suggested that not even language is supple enough to represent meaning: idem, "Social science and human action or on hitting your head against the ceiling of language," pp. 287–307 in S. Gale and G. Olsson (eds.), *Philosophy in Geography*. Dordrecht, Holland: D. Reidel, 1979. Despite Olsson's imaginative experimentation with surrealism, he seems to have now encountered an impasse from which there can be no exit.

against the mechanistic ecological processes evoked by Burgess' concentric land use model, the ecologist Quinn acknowledged that:

> *Attitudes, sentiments, motivations and the like are omitted from considerations* not because they are unimportant, but because the assumptions and point of view of human ecology are not adapted to their treatment.[18]

This observation was paralleled by William Alonso's candid introduction to his influential theory of urban land value, one of the most quoted works of the spatial school.

> . . . *from this wealth of subject matter only a pallid skeleton will emerge. Both the Puerto Rican and the Madison Avenue advertising man will be* reduced *to that uninteresting individual, economic man . . . we shall assume that the city sits on a featureless plain . . . what it does not have are such features as hills, low land, beautiful views, social cachet, or pleasant breezes.* These are undoubtedly important, but no way has been found to incorporate them into the type of theory that will be presented.[19]

The convergence of these conclusions by a sociologist and an economist a generation apart provides a forceful illustration of the inability of ecological or economic categories to incorporate satisfactorily the untidy realm of cultural values in their treatment of urban land use. Both Burgess and Alonso resolved the problem only by denying it, by reducing the actor to an anaemic figure while raising the economic environment to the level of the superorganic.

The behavioural movement has represented one attempt by positivist social scientists to recover the subjective. Though there is not space here to present a full critique of behavioural geography,[20] it is symptomatic that behaviouralism is usually regarded as simply a less extreme form of behaviourism, which rejected the subjective out of hand in one infamous phrase as "the phlogiston of the social sciences."[21] Even in behavioural approaches, the commitment to naturalism leads to a reduced view of the human agent. Behaviouralism cannot but be embarrassed by intersubjectivity for positivist method calls for the rigorous study of observable and repetitive phenomena rather than meaningful experiences, which are left in the dubious realm of the metaphysical. As one commentator has noted: "the behaviourally oriented sociologist finds it difficult to speak in terms of values, attitudes, consciousness . . ."[22]

[18] J. Quinn, "The Burgess zonal hypothesis and its critics," *American Sociological Review* 5 (1940), pp. 210–218 (my emphasis).

[19] William Alonso, *Location and Land Use*. Cambridge, Mass.: M.I.T. Press, 1965, pp. 1, 17 (my emphasis).

[20] A fuller critical discussion of behaviouralism appears in David Ley, "Behavioural geography and the philosophies of meaning," in K. Cox and R. Golledge (eds.), *Behavioural Geography Revisited*. London: Methuen, 1980.

[21] G. Lundberg, *Foundations of Sociology*. New York: D. McKay, 1964, p. 17.

[22] A. Brittan, *Meanings and Situations*. London: Routledge and Kegan Paul, 1973, p. 20.

The similarity of this assessment with the statements of the ecologist Quinn and the economist Alonso reminds us of behavioural geography's close association with spatial analysis and its positivist methodology. And, as we have already argued, such methodology is not subtle enough to incorporate the ambiguity, contingency, and non-linear changes which constitute the commonplace of relations within the lifeworld. In the quest for replicable method and generalisation, behavioural studies abstract away from the contexts of spontaneous everyday life; the student sample and methodological formalism are two expressions of this abstraction. But such rigour has its cost, for precision may only be won at the cost of accuracy. The sceptic might well suspect that the precise factor analysis output of semantic differential scales may provide only a polite fiction of real perceptions of an urban neighbourhood or some other geographic phenomenon.[23] The challenge by the phenomenologist Alfred Schutz of an earlier generation of behaviouristic psychologists has not lost its currency: "The safeguarding of the subjective point of view is the only but sufficient guarantee that the world of social reality will not be replaced by a fictional non-existing world constructed by the scientific observer."[24]

Marxian structuralism

In the 1970's a new paradigm of marxian structuralism has entered geography with claims no less sweeping than the positivism of the 1960's. In Harvey's uncompromising words:

> *The* only *method capable of uniting disciplines in such a fashion that they can grapple with issues such as urbanization, economic development and the environment, is that founded in a properly constituted version of dialectical materialism as it operates within a structured totality in the sense that Marx conceived of it.*[25]

And yet, despite such claims, the continuities are as visible as the departures between spatial analysis and geographic marxism as it has been developed by Harvey and Manuel Castells, the two most influential radical writers on the

[23] The shortcomings of formal research instruments in assessing the perceptions by consumers of a shopping centre are manifest in Roger Downs, "The Cognitive Structure of an Urban Shopping Center." *Environment and Behavior* 2 (1970), pp. 13–39. This journal contains examples of yet more rigid laboratory methodologies imposed far more uncritically upon studies of perceptions of the built environment. One experiment attached an overhead camera to a car driver's head by means of a dental bite bar in order to examine the roadside features that the driver noticed "spontaneously" on a "normal" drive on an urban motorway!

[24] Alfred Schutz, *On Phenomenology and Social Relations*, (ed.) H. Wagner. Chicago: University of Chicago Press, 1970, p. 271.

[25] Harvey, *Social Justice and the City*, p. 302, my emphasis (note 6). An expanded critique appears in D. Ley, "Ideology, theory and empirical study in marxian approaches to urban geography." Paper presented to the Anglo-French symposium on Geography and Ideology, Cambridge, March 1979.

geography of the western city. Marxian analysis in geography has maintained a model of mechanism in which the actors themselves have no say: they become puppets who dutifully act out the roles prepared for them by the theorist.

Like locational analysis, marxian structuralism does not escape a fundamentally economic and rationalist view of the world. When Harvey produced his famous answer to the ghetto problem, it was an answer which remained within the conceptual realm of land economics. As Olsson pointed out, to make the von Thunen or Alonso model *not* true as Harvey wanted is not to escape their categories and view of the world.[26] So too Richard Walker's materialist analysis of the relationship between business cycles and urban development revives the study of the same relationship by the conservative economist Paul Samuelson thirty years earlier.[27] The point here is that to reverse the categories of conservative political economy is not to transcend them, an argument that has been presented vigorously by the radical French writer, Jean Baudrillard:

> *Marx's theory of historical materialism . . . is too conservative, too rooted in the assumptions of political economy, too dependent on the system of ideas that it seeks to overthrow.*[28]

The result is an analysis that does not escape what Baudrillard has called "the phantom of production". One is reminded of the observation of Theodor Adorno, a founder of critical theory, that Marx wanted to make the whole world over into a giant workhouse. In light of the intellectual continuity we have suggested, it comes as no surprise that Manuel Castells is able to integrate human ecology into his own materialist analysis as he develops

> *a theoretical front that integrates the ecological, materialist-based problematic in a sociological analysis . . . whose foundation is the structural web that creates the problematic of any society.*[29]

Indeed, on a more speculative note, we might compare the social darwinism of human ecology with Marx's own teleology of historical progress, the role that naturalism plays in his argument, and his respect for Darwin as a theoretician who had

[26] "Our objective is to eliminate ghettos . . . The mechanism in this case is very simple – competitive bidding for the use of the land. If we eliminate this mechanism, we will presumably eliminate the result. This is immediately suggestive of a policy for eliminating ghettos." Harvey, *Social Justice and the City*, p. 137 (note 6); G. Olsson, "On reason and reasoning," *Antipode* 4 (July 1972), pp. 26–31.

[27] Richard Walker, "The transformation of urban structure in the nineteenth century and the beginnings of suburbanization," pp. 165–212 in K. Cox (ed.), *Urbanization and Conflict in Market Societies*. Chicago: Maaroufa, 1978: P. Samuelson, 'The business cycle and urban development,' pp. 6–17 in G. Greer (ed.), *The Problem of the Cities and Towns*. Cambridge, Mass.: Harvard University Press, 1942.

[28] Mark Poster, "Translator's introduction," in Jean Baudrillard, *The Mirror of Production*. St Louis: Telos, 1975, p. 17.

[29] Castells, *The Urban Question*, p. 122 (note 6).

developed a thesis essentially parallel with his own, a respect so deep that he offered to dedicate the first volume of *Capital* to him.[30]

The second major point that warrants discussion is the preoccupation of geographic marxism with structures. Again Harvey's text is unequivocal: "When we attempt to view society as a totality, then ultimately *everything* has to be related to the structures in the economic basis of society."[31] Marxian authors are suspicious of empirical studies for behind and beneath superficial urban facts they see a deeper reality with its own inherent logic, "hidden in the deep structure that lies below the commonly accepted social relations of capitalist society."[32] What is this hidden essence of which facts are merely an appearance? It is quite simply the compulsive logic of the mode of production, "that the material economic base of society determines the superstructure of social, legal and political institutions."[33]

Once again some hidden transcendental phenomenon is regarded as directing the course of human society. The mode of production, and the logic of capital assume a privileged theoretical status operating according to their own internal rules in a supra-human manner. Marx allowed capital such a privileged status, calling it "the alienated power of humanity", and this theme has been developed in much contemporary analysis. Harvey makes the strong claim that "I regard the channels through which surplus value circulates as the arteries through which course *all* of the relationships which define the *totality* of society."[34] Before this assessment cultural relations are once more granted a predictably derivative status. Humans again assume an essentially passive form. Perceptions and preferences are described as "purely epiphenomenal", and the notion of urban sub-cultures which exercise real effects is dismissed as "a myth rather than a specific social process."[35] In Althusser's brand of structuralism even historic transformations are accomplished through the autonomous unfolding of structures without reference to human action; it is a case of "revolution without rebels."[36]

Before the transcendental object man disappears. Indeed, it seems as if such is the intention of structuralism. The aim of Lévi-Strauss to dissolve the human was part of the reductionist style of structural anthropology with its project to eliminate any allusion to lived experience before an all-embracing scientism. Like

[30] This detail is recorded in Anthony Giddens, *Capitalism and Modern Social Theory*. Cambridge: Cambridge University Press, 1971, p. 66, note 4. For a reference to the naturalism within the marxist argument note the commentary by Habermas on a passage from the *1844 Manuscripts*: "This demand for a natural science of man, with its positivist overtones, is astonishing." Jurgen Habermas, *Knowledge and Human Interests*. Boston: Beacon Press, 1971, p. 46.

[31] Harvey, *Social Justice and the City*, p. 292, my emphasis (note 6).

[32] S. Roweis and A. Scott, *The Urban Land Question*. Toronto: University of Toronto, Department of Urban and Regional Planning, Research Paper No. 10, 1976.

[33] C. Pickvance, "Introduction," pp. 1–32 in C. Pickvance (ed.), *Urban Sociology: Critical Essays*. London: Tavistock, 1976.

[34] Harvey, *Social Justice and the City*, p. 312, my emphasis (note 6).

[35] Roweis and Scott, *The Urban Land Question* (note 32); Castells, *The Urban Question*, p. 95 (note 6).

[36] Poster, *Existential Marxism in Postwar France*, p. 340 (note 5).

Durkheim, Lévi-Strauss was committed to the style of positive science, and like him he used the vehicle of a transcendental object, namely structures which were inherited not created and of which mere people were the unaware, unknowing, carriers. In the science of structures, human consciousness, human values, and human culture are a distraction. The authorless nature gives a mechanical view of society and a passive view of humanity. This extreme view of the autonomy of structures, developed by the marxist intellectual Louis Althusser, has been appropriated in particular by Castells in his urban analysis. Althusser is preoccupied with the logic of abstract structures, untied necessarily to real events, as history is interpreted as the relentless unfolding of the systemic logic of structures; there is no place for human agents for

> *The true subjects . . . are not . . . 'concrete individuals' – 'real men' – but the definition and distribution of these places and functions. The true 'subjects' are these definers and distributors: the relations of production (and political and ideological social relations).*[37]

The agents of the historical process are not persons but abstractions, the relations of production. People simply play out roles prescribed for them not by themselves, or by any other people but by the functional necessity of a structural logic.

In review

At the cost of considerable over-generalisation it might be worth summarising the argument to this point. In reviewing the contributions to human geography made by Durkheim, Sauer's landscape school, the physical determinists, the economic determinists of human ecology and spatial analysis, and finally the structuralists, several repetitive features have been observed. The posing of a reified transcendental object, a superorganic causal factor, has been accompanied by the reduction of the geographic agent, and in a number of these traditions a naturalism which aspires after the methods of the natural sciences. Through this progression there has been a steady divorce between theory and empirical study, until with Althusser and marxian structuralism empirical studies themselves are distrusted because they do not reveal the concealed essence, the logic of the structure. In confronting the self-confidence of these developments, what Habermas has called the "dogma of the sciences' belief in themselves", it is pertinent to heed Berger and Luckmann's warning:

> *a purely structural sociology is endemically in danger of reifying social phenomena. Even if it begins by modestly assigning to its constructs merely heuristic status, it all too frequently ends by confusing its own conceptualisations with the laws of the universe.*[38]

[37] L. Althusser and E. Balibar, *Reading Capital*. Cited in Keat and Urry, *Social Theory as Science*, p. 136 (note 8).

[38] Peter Berger and Thomas Luckmann, *The Social Construction of Reality*. Garden City, N.Y.: Doubleday, 1966, p. 186.

The Necessity for an Active View of Humanity

In the preceding review of the erosion of human agency in several geographic traditions the analysis has taken an implicitly critical form. In this section the critique will become more explicit as four separate short-comings of a geography without human agency will be examined. I will suggest that such a development is flawed at the levels of epistemology, theory, existence and, perhaps more speculatively, at the level of morality.

The epistemological error

The denial or suppression of the subjective is an epistemological error for it glosses over the subjectivity of the theorist making the claim. In his reaction against behaviourism with its total rejection of subjectivity, Alfred Schutz mused how "It is not then quite understandable why an intelligent individual should write books for others or even meet others in congresses where it is reciprocally proved that the intelligence of the other is a questionable fact."[39] To complete Habermas' sentence cited above, through its dogmatic self-confidence "positivism assumes the prohibitive function of protecting scientific inquiry from epistemological self-reflection."[40] The wrenching of knowledge from human interests has hidden the ideological content of scientific knowledge, that it is knowledge derived by a subject and for a subject. There is a clear need in the human sciences for the impenetrable appearance of objectivity to be demystified to illuminate the shifting anthropocentric presuppositions masked by the firm categories and rigorous procedures.[41] There are already some edifying precedents. Reviewing the research of white American social scientists on the black family, the black sociologist Andrew Billingsley has remarked that "American social scientists are much more American than social and much more social than scientific."[42] Subjective in-group values have invaded objective research revealing as much about the researcher as about his research object.

Marxian structuralism is particularly vulnerable to such epistemological criticism, for its claim to a transcendent materialism is in fact a posture for a mundane idealism. The dependence of a materialist programme on an intellectual vanguard is an instructive contradiction, showing that material ideas remain, nonetheless, ideas.[43] It is only through reification that the *idea* of the structure takes on a reality of its own as it does in Althusser's strange world where it is the concept, the thought object, that has reality while the real object, the empirical situation, is a mere appearance. The position is reminiscent of a neo-Kantian

[39] Schutz, *On Phenomenology and Social Relations*, p. 266 (note 24).

[40] Habermas, *Knowledge and Human Interests*, p. 67 (note 30).

[41] For an example, see D. Ley, "Social geography and social action," pp. 41–57 in Ley and Samuels (eds.), *Humanistic Geography* (note 2).

[42] A. Billingsley, "Black families and white social science," *Journal of Social Issues* 26 (1970), pp. 127–142.

[43] A. Gouldner, "Marxism and social theory," *Theory and Society* 1 (1974), pp. 17–35.

idealism where it is the concept, the theory, that creates the facts. As Castells has it, following Althusser, theory is "a means of production of scientific facts." Consequently it is the theory that must be defended against the barbs of the real world. This leads Castells to the dangerous conclusion that "I prefer to take the risk of a certain empirical margin of error in order to clarify the ideas in the perspective I have outlined."[44] Reality, even material reality, must not it seems be allowed to confound thought.

The primary task of marxian structuralism then becomes not the clarification of the experience of social reality, but the preservation of a purely intellectual model of mechanism. Its unreflexive rejection of subjectivity is a supreme irony, for its own fundamental objective is the defence of consciousness, a subjective idealism.

The theoretical error

Secondly, the reduction of human agency is a theoretical error because it devalues the power of human consciousness and human action to redirect the course of events. It limits the creative power of human intentionality. Geographic facts are not fatalistically predetermined; they are the outcome of both constraint and choice, of processes of negotiation by geographic agents. Redirecting the deterministic form of a physical or economic environment is the spontaneity of the socio-cultural lifeworld, a world which is not simply derivative of its environment but has real autonomy of its own. So too the political arena is more than the expression of dominant economic interests. A more appropriate theoretical formulation would recognise the interdependence but also the autonomy of the different components of society. There is a growing consensus in the social sciences that adequate explanation of human actions must include both the limits defined by social and physical structures and the creative spontaneity of the lifeworld. To cite one example from many in contemporary social theory: "The primary problem is how to develop theories that satisfactorily synthesise the structural analysis of different social formations, and the explanation of human action in terms of subjective states and meanings."[45]

An illustration of the proposition of the importance of both meanings and constraints, both the agent's viewpoint and contextual factors, will be presented from a theoretically unpromising setting, the deprived world of inner city adolescents in the United States. During research in an inner city neighbourhood in North Philadelphia it became clear that a dominant meaning of the local environment to its residents was a place of fear; the environment was a multi-dimensional stressor.[46] The major component of stress identified by community residents was the

[44] Castells, *The Urban Question*, p. 200 (note 6).

[45] Keat and Urry, *Social Theory as Science*, p. 229 (note 8). A similar position is shared, amongst others, by A. Giddens, *New Rules of Sociological Method*. London: Hutchinson, 1977; Derek Gregory, *Ideology, Science and Human Geography*. London: Hutchinson, 1978.

[46] This account is taken from D. Ley, *The Black Inner City as Frontier Outpost: Images and Behavior of a Philadelphia Neighborhood*. Monograph Series No. 7. Washington D.C.: Association of American Geographers, 1974.

adolescent gang and delinquency problem. Why were the gangs active, violent, and predatory? A few months before field research had begun, a gang killing had occurred in the neighbourhood which was succinctly reported in a police incident file. The incident began with the arrival of two young outsiders, O. and M., at a local street gang party. The police file continued:

> *While there O. and M. reportedly bragged they were a "hit and wheel man team" meaning that O. could drive a vehicle while M., a passenger, could aim a shotgun at the window.*
>
> *A few of the gang members (39–Sutton) asked the two visitors, as a favor, to drive around the streets, locate and kill some members of an enemy gang in the area (45–Richmond).*
>
> *L.H., 22, a member of 39–S street gang, O. and M. drove around the west side of the 46th Street for some time but could find no potential victims.*
>
> *It was suggested that the trip cross to the east side of 46th Street. As they approached Bates and Malcolm Streets, they spotted A. and R. who were walking towards R.'s home . . .*

A. and R. were members of the rival 45th and Richmond gang. Both were shot from a passing car and one later died from his wounds.

Here is an outrageous action, but an action which is an integral part of the neighbourhood milieu. It is an action irrational in a conventional sense, not only in the doing but also in its consequences, for the arrest and conviction rate is very high in gang homicides. But such irrationality is not isolated; between 1962 and 1971 there occurred 203 gang-related killings in Philadelphia. An understanding of such actions required access to the gang culture, a contextual sensitivity to the social world of male adolescents in the ghetto. The interpretation which emerged emphasised the importance of competitive status-seeking; a significant component of gang culture is a search for 'rep', for peer group endorsement and prestige. In the words of one gang member:

> *Some people try to stay out of gangs . . . They stay in their house all the time, but they get tired of it. They don't want to stay in and be nothin'. When you're in a gang you're somethin' man. You've got respect.*

So an examination of the subjective meaning contexts of inner city gang members suggested a thesis of status-seeking, a trait not limited to any particular social world, or indeed to any particular historic era. But why in the inner city case did the quest for status assume such a perverse form?

Here it is necessary to go beyond the meaning contexts of the actors to broader contexts that may well be hidden from the actors themselves. The structural levels of North American society offer unequal opportunities, a skewed distribution of life chances. In mainstream society status may more usually be won legitimately, but in the deprived world of the inner city options are more limited. The gang culture is a social construction by inner city youth to wrench some glory from a miserly social structure. In their world, though, with limited access to legitimate outlets, status comes from being bad, and the badder an adolescent can be the higher the stakes in status gains and losses. That is why there was no backing down for the hit and wheel man team, for amidst a competitive peer group they were claiming too much of a scarce resource. In the intensity of the moment the boast was challenged and the two found themselves unable to retreat without a severe loss of face.

Before leaving this illustration of the combined effects of meanings and constraints in producing actions, it is worth considering more carefully the skewed distribution of life chances confronting inner city adolescents, for they are the result of a multidimensional definition of marginality. Inner city youth suffer not only economic marginality in the market place, but other forms of marginality as well. In as much as they suffer from racial prejudice they experience social marginality; as recent migrants or immigrants they may be penalised by cultural marginality; as adolescents who are usually high school dropouts they suffer both life cycle and intellectual marginality. There is some evidence they may exhibit personality disorders and to this extent they also endure personality marginality.[47] The different forms of marginality, though interlocking, form separate dimensions which cannot be collapsed into a single category (for example, capitalism). At the level of constraints (and disregarding for now the realm of meanings) the seeking of a one-dimensional "cause" is illusory. Confusing a one-dimensional analysis still further is the existence of related social groupings in earlier modes of society, for example the Sicilian mafia or Chinese secret societies. It could therefore be argued that "capitalism" is neither a sufficient nor even a necessary antecedent to the emergence of gang-related social groupings. Consequently it is an extremely speculative line of reasoning that asserts unequivocally, "The question is: What is necessary and unavoidable with a given system of production."[48] The conflation of constraints into a single dimension, so characteristic of abstract theoretical arguments posing a single transcendental object, is compromised by detailed, contextual analysis.

The existential error

The theoretical reduction of human agency is also an existential error for it falsely presents questions of meaning as questions of technique, inappropriately prescribing technical solutions for human problems. In planning for example, physical approaches too often pre-empt social approaches, setting up a tension between design for objects compared with design for people. The tower blocks of the 1950's and 1960's were a technically efficient solution to the housing crisis, but the 1970's have revealed their failings at the level of experience. So too on the maps of traffic engineers urban motorways represented an effective solution within the technical domain of system flows, capacities, and linkages. But in the experience of urban residents, increased air and noise pollution, and the costs to a community ravaged by a motorway alignment, suggested that other solutions would be less

[47] L. Yablonsky, *The Violent Gang*. Baltimore: Penguin, 1970.

[48] Marx, cited by Richard Peet, "Inequality and poverty: a marxist-geographic theory." *Annals, Association of American Geographers* 65 (1975), pp. 564–571.

destructive on the ground. Administrative reorganisation provides a third example, for the centralisation of public services to promote administrative rationalisation and efficiency has frequently been accompanied by a decline in the quality of services as an increasingly distant chain of control increases the sense of alienation amongst staff while reducing morale and the level of individual commitment and responsibility.

The determination of policy priorities according to a purely technical basis for assessment has invariably penalised social and cultural arguments. Cost-benefit analysis has, until very recently, proceeded by dismissing such considerations as "intangibles" beyond the scope of quantitative assessment and therefore excluded from the decision-making formula. The assumption that everything of importance may also be counted is a false rationalism which disqualifies the realm of experience from serious consideration and guarantees the extension of positivist reductionism into the corridors of power. Practical life problems are invaded by uncritical systems of technical control. Moreover, this "technocratic consciousness reflects not the sundering of an ethical situation, but the repression of 'ethics' as such as a category of life."[49]

The moral error

That is one reason why the reduction of human agency is, finally, a moral error. Conceptual reductionism might well give rise to an existential reductionism, as people may actually assume the role of the uncomplimentary puppets that the state's theorists model and its social engineers plan for. In such a setting (which is far from hypothetical) ethical and moral issues are themselves appropriated into the domain of the technical. Under the continuous extension of this formidable technical and managerial hegemony, even the expression of such basic human freedoms as free speech, free assembly and freedom to worship my be disqualified as incompatible with rational systems of control.

The secularisation of humanity and its relegation to class beings who respond to environmental stimuli in some conditioned manner provides a milieu in which much of what it is to be human will be lost, as traits such as spontaneity and creativity are usurped before the conditioned responses of mass man. Humanistic philosophers this century from Husserl to Habermas have traced the relationship between the theoretical reduction of human agency in social science and his existential reduction in everyday life. The suppression of humanity in theory first reflects and then justifies its suppression in practice. In the dialectic of theory and society, the theoretical proposition of an overwhelming environment, a transcendental object, is matched by the existential state of human passivity. Or, conversely, a passive theory of people justifies an ideology of domination.

In the western nations, so long as consumption standards are maintained, it appears that the public might be prepared to cede its integrity without a struggle.

[49] J. Habermas, *Towards a Rational Society*. Boston: Beacon Press, 1970, p. 112.

For Kierkegaard the true person was the individual who made authentic decisions for him- or her-self, but in the Copenhagen of his day he saw a mass society where people voluntarily gave up their integrity to others. So too Harold Pinter (in *The Dwarfs*) poses the moral dilemma of contemporary identity. Is the modern individual's authenticity no more than a reflection of environment?

> *The point is who are you? Not why or how, not even what. I can see what, perhaps, clearly enough. But who are you? . . . You're the sum of so many reflections. How many reflections? Whose reflections? Is that what you consist of?*

Perhaps Daniel Bell in his review of the impressionable consciousness of emerging western society may not be too far wrong in his observation that "The lack of a rooted moral belief system is the cultural contradiction of the society, the deepest challenge to its survival."[50]

In Conclusion

It is beyond the scope of this essay to outline in any detail the nature of a reconstituted human geography which would treat as problematic the status of the geographic subject.[51] There are clearly valid precedents from the past and to these should be added important developments of the 1970's – a revived interest in anthropocentric geographies, the experience of place, and an examination for the first time of the geographic relevance of the philosophies of meaning, including such philosophic traditions as existentialism, phenomenology, and pragmatism. In each of these research areas the issue of human agency emerges as a central theoretical question. But although this literature has engaged some important empirical questions, has re-opened lines of communication between geography and the humanities, and has provided a much needed philosophical antithesis to the uncritical positivism which threatened to overwhelm the discipline in the 1960's, it also contains the seeds of its own excess, the excess of idealism. Such a tendency is nourished in the 'stream of consciousness' predilection of popular culture and already a formal declaration has been made for an idealistic human geography.[52]

But such a geography would be as incomplete as the forms of reductionism we have criticised. The uninhibited hegemony of consciousness and subjectivity is as misleading as any reductionism, for notions of pure consciousness are as much an abstraction from human experience as any isotropic plain. The realities of

[50] Daniel Bell, *The Coming of Post-Industrial Society*. New York: Basic Books, 1976, p. 480.

[51] Indications of the possibilities (and problems) of such a geography are presented by the essays in Ley and Samuels (eds.), *Humanistic Geography* (note 2).

[52] Leonard Guelke, "An idealist alternative in human geography," *Annals, Association of American Geographers* 64 (1974), pp. 193–202.

everyday living confirm that ideas do not run free of context, of concrete time-space relations. If there is to be a geographic synthesis in the 1980's, it will be a synthesis which will incorporate both the symbolic and the structural, both the realm of constraints and the realm of meanings, where values and consciousness are seen as embedded and grounded in their contexts, and where environments are treated as contingent before emerging forms of human creativity.

12

AREAL DIFFERENTIATION AND POST-MODERN HUMAN GEOGRAPHY

Derek Gregory

Although Capel (**chapter 4**) describes how geography distanced itself from other subjects in its formative period, the discipline has also constantly renewed itself by borrowing from other fields of learning. Between *Ideology, science and human geography* (London, 1978) and *Geographical imaginations* (Oxford, 1994), Derek Gregory has led explorations into social theory and philosophy in search of new ideas. In the latter volume he sketches out a map of geography's intellectual landscape. From the eighteenth to the mid-twentieth centuries geography has been shaped by encounters with, in turn, anthropology, sociology and economics. Since then, he charts a return move through political economy, social theory and cultural studies which together constitute a post-modernization of geography. This chapter reviews the major developments in each of these fields, while retaining a commitment to an established geographical theme, that of areal differentiation. Gregory's aim is not therefore to dissolve geography and abandon all that came before, but to retrieve traditional concerns by entering into dialogues with adjacent disciplines. His reassertion of the central significance of areal differentiation, however, is not a call to reappropriate the past, but an effort to reconceptualize it in the light of recent social theory. He defines post-modernism in terms of its suspicion of total explanations, its rejection of monopolies on truth and deep structures, and its accent on difference, heterogeneity, particularity and disorder. But he prefers to examine the tensions between modern and post-modern geography rather than side with one or the other.

Source: Areal differentiation and post-modern human geography. In Gregory, D. and Walford, R., editors, *Horizons in human geography*. London: Macmillan, 67–96, 1989.

Searching for an epigraph to his Philosophical Investigations, Ludwig Wittgenstein considered using a quotation from King Lear: 'I'll teach you differences.' 'Hegel,' he once told a friend, 'always seems to me to be wanting to say that things which look different are really the same. Whereas my interest is in showing that things which look the same are really different.' – Terry Eagleton, Against the Grain.

Post-Modernism

If my title seems strange, so much the better. In this essay I want to explore some fragments of the contemporary intellectual landscape and to suggest some of the ways in which they bear upon modern human geography: and all of this will, I suspect, be unsettling. (Or, at any rate, if I can convey what is happening successfully then it ought to be unsettling.)

I use 'post-modernism' as a short-hand for a heterogeneous movement which had its origins in architecture and literary theory. The relevance of the first of these for human geography must seem comparatively straightforward – especially if the interpretative arch is widened to span the production of the built environment or, wider still, the production of space[1] – but the second is, as I will seek to show, every bit as important for the future of geographical inquiry. The converse may also be true: Frederic Jameson, one of the most exhilarating literary critics writing today, claims that 'a model of political culture appropriate to our own situation will necessarily have to raise spatial issues as its fundamental organizing concern'.[2]

Post-modernism is, of course, much more than these two moments. It has spiralled way beyond architecture and literary theory until it now confronts the terrain of the humanities and social sciences *tout court*. But whatever its location, I shall argue that post-modernism raises urgent questions about place, space and landscape in the production of social life.

Post-modernism is, in its fundamentals, a critique of what is usually called 'the Enlightenment project'. The European Enlightenment of the eighteenth century provided one of the essential frameworks for the development of the modern humanities and social sciences. It was, above all, a celebration of the power of reason and the progress of rationality, of the ways in which their twin engines propelled modernity into the cobwebbed corners of the traditional world. Both 'reason' and 'rationality' were given highly specific meanings, however, and a number of thinkers have been disturbed by the triumph of the particular vision of knowledge which those terms entailed. The more radical of them have sought to overthrow its closures and its supposed certainties altogether. Their critique has, for the most part, been conducted at high levels of abstraction – the exchanges between Habermas and Lyotard are of just such an order[3] – but one of the most concrete illustrations of what is at stake has been provided by David Ley in a remarkable essay on the politico-cultural landscapes of inner Vancouver.

[1] See Michael Dear, 'Postmodernism and planning' *Environment and Planning D: Society and Space*, 4 (1986) pp. 367–384.

[2] Frederic Jameson, 'Postmodernism, or the cultural logic of late capitalism', *New Left Review*, 146 (1984) pp. 53–92.

[3] See Richard Rorty, 'Habermas and Lyotard on Postmodernity', in Richard J. Bernstein (ed.) *Habermas and Modernity* (Cambridge: Polity Press, 1985) pp. 161–175; Peter Dews, 'From post-structuralism to postmodernity: Habermas's counter-perspective', *ICA Documents* 4 (1986) pp. 12–16.

Ley contrasts two redevelopment projects on either side of False Creek. To the north, 'an instrumental landscape of neo-conservatism': high-density, high-rise buildings whose minimalist geometric forms provide the backdrop for the spectacular structures of a sports stadium, conference centre, elevated freeway and rapid transit system and the towering pavilions of Expo '86. To the south, an 'expressive landscape of liberal reform': low-density groupings of buildings, diverse in design and construction, incorporating local motifs and local associations and allowing for a plurality of tenures, clustered around a lake which opens up vistas across the waterfront to the downtown skyline and the mountain rim beyond. The north shore is a monument to modern technology, to the internationalisation of 'rational' planning and corporate engineering: one of Relph's 'placeless' landscapes. The south shore, by contrast, is redolent of what Frampton calls a critical regionalism, a post-modern landscape attentive to the needs of people rather than the demands of machines and (above all) sensitive to the specificities of particular places.[4]

The contrast is, of course, emblematic of others, not least between different styles of human geography. But, as I must now show (and as the term itself suggests), post-modernism is no traditionalist's dream of recovering a world we have lost. It is a movement *beyond* the modern and, simultaneously, an invitation to construct our *own* human geographies. I will build my argument on three of its basic features.

Firstly, post-modernism is, in a very real sense, 'post-paradigm': that is to say, post-modern writers are immensely suspicious of any attempt to construct a system of thought which claims to be complete and comprehensive. In geography, of course, there have been no end of attempts of this kind, and many of those who have – in my view, mistakenly – made use of Kuhn's notion of a paradigm have done so *prescriptively*. They have claimed the authority of 'positivism', 'structuralism', 'humanism' or whatever as a means of legislating for the proper conduct of geographical inquiry and of excluding work which lies beyond the competence of these various systems. Others have preferred to transcend these, to them partial, perspectives and to offer some more general ('meta-theoretical') framework in which all these competing claims are supposed to be reconciled.

For over a decade this was usually assumed to be some kind of systems approach and now, apparently, it is the philosophy of realism (perhaps coupled with some version of Habermas's critical theory) which holds out a similar promise. But post-modernism rejects all of these manoeuvres. All of these systems of thought are – of necessity – incomplete, and if there is then no alternative but to pluck different elements from different systems for different purposes this is not a licence for an uncritical eclecticism: patching them together must, rather, display a sensitivity

[4]David Ley, 'Styles of the times: liberal and neo-conservative landscapes in inner Vancouver, 1968–1986', *J. Hist. Geogr.*, 13 (1987) pp. 40–56; see also Edward Relph, *Place and Placelessness* (London: Pion, 1976) and Kenneth Frampton, 'Towards a critical regionalism: six points for an architecture of resistance', in Hal Foster (ed.) *The Anti-aesthetic: Essays on Postmodern Culture* (Port Townsend: Bay Press, 1983) pp. 16–30.

towards the differences and disjunctures between them.[5] And 'sensitivity' implies that those different integrities must be respected and retained: not fudged. The certainties which were once offered by epistemology – by theories of knowledge which assumed that it was possible to 'put a floor under' or 'ground' intellectual inquiry in some safe and secure way – are no longer credible in a post-modern world.[6]

Secondly, this implies, in turn, that post-modern writers are hostile to the 'totalizing' ambitions of the conventional social sciences (and, for that matter, those of the humanities). Their critique points in two directions. First, they reject the notion that social life displays what could be called a 'global coherence': that our day-to-day social practices are moments in the reproduction of a self-maintaining social system whose fundamental, so to speak 'structural' imperatives necessarily regulate our everyday lives in some automatic, pre-set fashion. These writers do not, of course, deny the importance of the interdependencies which have become such a commonplace of the late twentieth-century world, and neither do they minimise the routine character of social reproduction nor the various powers which enclose our day-to-day routines. (These are, on the contrary, some of the most salient foci of their work). But they do object to the concept of totality which informs much of modern social theory, because it tacitly assumes that social life somehow adds up to (or 'makes sense in terms of') a coherent system with its own superordinate logic.

Second, and closely connected to this, these writers reject the notion that social life can be explained in terms of some 'deeper' structure. This was one of the premises of structuralism, of course, and it still surfaces in some of the cruder versions of realism. It is largely through this opposition that post-modernism is sometimes identified with 'post-structuralism' and, put like this, I imagine that the post-modern critique will seem to echo the complaints of those who saw in structuralism a displacement of the human subject. In human geography as elsewhere, many commentators were dismayed by the way in which various versions of structuralism replaced the concrete complexities of human agency by the disembodied transformations of abstract structures.[7] But post-modernism is not another humanism. It objects to structuralism because its sharpened concept of structure points towards a 'centre' around which social life revolves, rather like a kaleidoscope or a child's mobile; but it objects to humanism for the very same reason. Most forms of humanism appeal to the human subject or to human agency as the self-evident

[5] It is to the disclosure of these differences and disjunctures that 'deconstruction' is directed. I have found the following introductions particularly helpful: Terry Eagleton, *Literary Theory: An Introduction* (Oxford: Basil Blackwell, 1983) pp. 127–50; Christopher Norris, *Deconstruction: Theory and Practice* (London: Methuen, 1982); Michael Ryan, *Marxism and Deconstruction: A Critical Articulation* (Baltimore: Johns Hopkins University Press, 1982) Chapter 1.

[6] This thesis is argued with a special clarity in Richard Rorty, *Philosophy and the Mirror of Nature* (Oxford: Basil Blackwell, 1980); see also Richard J. Bernstein, *Beyond Objectivism and Relativism: Science, Hermeneutics and Praxis* (Oxford: Basil Blackwell, 1983).

[7] James Duncan and David Ley, 'Structural Marxism and human geography: a critical assessment', *Ann. Ass. Am. Geogr.*, 72 (1982), pp. 30–59.

centre of social life. And yet we are now beginning to discover just how problematic those terms are. Concepts of 'the person', for example, differ widely over space and through time and so, paradoxically, it is their very importance which ensures that they cannot provide a constant foundation for the human sciences. They are the *explanandum* not the *explanans*.

Thirdly, the accent on 'difference' which dominates the preceding paragraph is a *leitmotiv* of post-modernism. One of the distinguishing features of post-modern culture is its sensitivity to heterogeneity, particularity and uniqueness. To some readers this insistence on 'difference' will raise the spectre of the idiographic, which is supposed to have been laid once and for all (in geography at any rate) by the Hartshorne-Schaefer debate in the 1950s and by the consolidation of a generalising spatial science during the 1960s. To be sure, the caricature of Hartshorne as a crusty empiricist, indifferent to the search for spatial order, blind to location theory and ignorant of quantitative methods could never survive any serious reading of *The Nature of Geography*. There were, as several commentators have emphasised, deep-seated continuities between the Hartshornian orthodoxy and the prospectus of the so-called 'New Geography'. But Schaefer's clarion call for geography as a nomothetic science, compelled to produce morphological laws and to disclose the fundamental geometries of spatial patterns, undoubtedly sounded a retreat from areal differentiation which was heard (and welcomed) in many quarters. Specificity became eccentricity, and the new conceptual apparatus made no secret of its confinement: it was, variously, a 'residual'; background 'noise' to be 'filtered out'; a 'deviation' from the 'normal'. And yet in the 1980s other writers in other fields have given specificity a wider resonance. In philosophy, Lyotard claims that 'post-modern knowledge . . . refines our sensitivity to differences'; in social theory de Certeau wants to fashion 'a science of singularity . . . that links everyday pursuits to particular circumstances'; and in anthropology Geertz parades 'the diversity of things' and seeks illumination from 'the light of local knowledge'.[8]

In geography too there has been a remarkable return to areal differentiation. But it is a return with a difference. When Harvey speaks of the 'uneven development' of capitalism, for example, or when (in a radically different vocabulary) Hägerstrand talks about 'pockets of local order' (I shall have more to say about both of these in due course) they – and now countless others like them – are attempting much more than the recovery of geography's traditional project. For they herald not so much the reconstruction of modern geography as its *deconstruction*. I mean this to be understood in an entirely positive and specifically technical sense: not as a new nihilism, still less as the enthronement of some new orthodoxy, but as the transformation of the modern intellectual landscape as a whole. I should admit at once that it is still barely possible to map that new landscape – not least because it

[8] Jean-François Lyotard, *The Postmodern Condition: A Report on Knowledge* (Manchester: Manchester University Press, 1984); Michel de Certeau, *The Practice of Everyday Life* (Berkeley: University of California Press, 1984); Clifford Geertz, *Local Knowledge: Further Essays in Interpretative Anthropology* (New York: Basic Books, 1983). I cite these three texts as examples, not because I accept their particular theses.

is radically unstable – but in what follows I will try to put some preliminary markers around what Soja calls the 'post-modernization' of geography.[9]

Two disclaimers are immediately necessary. First, to work within disciplinary boundaries is obviously open to objection – and I am as uneasy about doing so as anyone else – but I have retained the conventional enclosures because I want to show that 'geography' has as much to contribute to post-modernism as it has to learn from it. In so far as social life cannot be theorised on the point of a pin, then, so it seems to me, the introduction of concepts of place, space and landscape must radically transform the nature of modern social theory. Second, to say that geography has re-opened the question of areal differentiation is to invite the response that, for many, it was never closed. I accept that it would be wrong to minimise the continuing power of traditional regional geographies which, at their very best, have always provided remarkably sensitive evocations of the particular relations between people and the places in which they live. And I insist on this not as a politeness to be pushed to one side as soon as possible. On the contrary, the 'problem of geographical description' with which so many of these writers struggle is, as I will show, part of a more general 'crisis of representation' throughout the contemporary human sciences. This realisation, pregnant with consequences at once theoretical and practical, has also played its part in changing the modern intellectual landscape: so much so that we need new, theoretically-informed ways of conveying the complexities of areal differentiation if we are to make sense of the post-modern world.

I realise that many readers will be uncomfortable at my emphasis on theory, and some of them will object to yet more intellectual baggage being strapped to the heads of the credulous. But hostility to theory, as Eagleton remarks in another context, 'usually means an opposition to other people's theories and an oblivion to one's own'.[10] Even so, I can understand how anyone, assaulted by the abstract technologies of spatial science and then bloodied by the philosophical critique of positivism, can yearn for an end to geography's alienation from – well, *geography*. Let me make it plain, therefore, that I have no interest in theory for its own sake. To be sure, one can derive genuine pleasure from theoretical work: and why not? But exercises of this sort cannot be justified by intellectual hedonism alone, and the theories that I propose to discuss demand, by their very nature, an engagement with the world rather than an estrangement from it: they are, in other words, profoundly critical, political constructions.

It will make things much clearer, I hope, if I sketch out the emerging relations between geography and three other disciplines: political economy, sociology and anthropology. This is, very roughly, the order in which cross-fertilisation has occurred in the post-war decades, but it also corresponds to a movement in the direction of post-modernism . . . [The following section, 'Geography as Political

[9] Edward Soja, 'What's new? A review essay on the postmodernization of geography', *Ann. Ass. Am. Geogr.*, 77 (1987) pp. 289–293. Cf. Michael E. Eliot Hurst, 'Geography has neither existence nor future.' In R. J. Johnston (ed.) *The Future of Geography* (London and New York: Methuen, 1985) pp. 59–61.

[10] Eagleton, *op. cit.*, p. vii.

Economy' has been omitted. It discusses work by Harvey and Massey, whose views may be found in chapter 25 and 37.]

Geography and Sociology

In the immediately post-war decades the relations between geography and sociology were, with one or two exceptions, far from close. In one sense this is not surprising. The a-social cast of spatial science made any engagement with the concerns of sociology unlikely. But in another sense it is strange, because before the Second World War sociology was not silent about questions of spatial structure. Georg Simmel was perhaps the first to propose a 'sociology of space', which (though its terms were different to Harvey's) also addressed the fleeting, fragmentary and contradictory social world of the modern metropolis and showed how this was embedded in the volatile circulation of money over space and through time. Across the Rhine, Emile Durkheim's early work on the division of labour in society prompted him to give a central place to concepts of spatial structure in his preliminary programme for sociology: but it was, of course, this occupation of part of the field of *géographie humaine* which prompted many champions of Vidal de la Blache to insist on the integrity of the pre-existing intellectual division of labour. The barricades went up. The story was much the same on the other side of the Atlantic. The doyen of the Chicago School of urban sociology, Robert Park, drew a sharp distinction between a supposedly 'idiographic' human geography and his own avowedly 'nomothetic' human ecology.[14]

Towards the end of the 1970s, however, a new dialogue was opened between geography and sociology. Like the continuing conversation between geography and political economy, this was distinguished by its historical sensitivity. Indeed, one of the most obvious features of late twentieth-century sociology has been the revival of historical sociology. But, just as significant, this has (in many cases) been accompanied by the rediscovery of concepts of spatial structure. Although this too echoes the geographical reconstruction of political economy, some of the most exciting work has in fact been stimulated by the *shortcomings* of historico-geographical materialism. Much the most important has been its failure to overcome the tension between what is sometimes called the 'two Marxisms': one celebrating the power of conscious and collective human agency, the other preoccupied with the structural logic of the mode of production. 'On this score,' Perry Anderson once concluded, 'classical Marxism, even at the height of its powers, provided no coherent answer.' And, as other commentators have noted, these two basic orientations have reappeared throughout the subsequent history of modern Marxism.[15]

[14] See Peter Jackson and Susan Smith, *Exploring Social Geography* (London: Allen & Unwin, 1984).

[15] Perry Anderson, *In the Tracks of Historical Materialism* (London: Verso, 1983), p. 34; Rick Roderick, *Habermas and the Foundations of Critical Theory* (London: Macmillan, 1986) pp. 142–3. Habermas's writings are particularly instructive on these questions, though he is sharply critical of both post-structuralism and post-modernism: see Note 3.

Historico-geographical materialism has proved to be no exception: or at any rate not much of one.[16]

To be sure, the same oppositions surface throughout non-Marxist social theory as well, and it is perfectly possible to speak of 'two sociologies' or 'two geographies' in broadly similar terms. But it is undoubtedly the Marxist tradition which has been the single most important source for the development of a critique seeking to transcend the dualism between human agency and social structure. And, as I now want to show, the incorporation of time-space relations has proved to be a strategic moment in the development of this 'post-Marxist' theory of structuration. For its principal author, Anthony Giddens, insists that '[the] spatial configurations of social life are just as much a matter of basic importance to social theory as are the dimensions of temporality' and that 'there are no logical or methodological differences between human geography and sociology'.[17]

The time–space constitution of social life

The compass of Giddens's writings is extraordinarily wide, but Figure 12.1 is a simple sketch of one of the basic frameworks of his theory of structuration.[18]

In Giddens's view, societal integration – however precarious and partial it might be – depends upon the 'binding' of time and space into the conduct of social life. To say more than this entails an analytical distinction between social integration and system integration.

Social integration The continuity of day-to-day life depends, in large measure, on routinised interactions between people who are *co-present* in time and space. This is what 'society' meant before the eighteenth century: simply the company of others. Giddens suggests that Hägerstrand's time-geography provides a notation through which the characteristic shapes of *time–space routinisation* can be captured (Figure 12.2). Thus each day we meet other people and part from them at particular times and at particular places ('stations') in order to fulfil particular purposes ('projects'). In doing so, we necessarily trace out 'paths' in time and space. From this perspective, therefore, time and space are, in effect, resources which have to be drawn upon in the conduct of everyday

[16] Nigel Thrift, 'On the determination of social action in space and time', *Environment and Planning D: Society and Space*, 1 (1983) pp. 23–57; Edward Soja, 'The spatiality of social life: towards a transformative retheorisation', in Derek Gregory and John Urry (eds) *Social Relations and Spatial Structures* (London: Macmillan, 1985) pp. 90–127.

[17] Derek Gregory, 'Space, time and politics in social theory: an interview with Anthony Giddens.' *Environment and Planning D: Society and Space*, 2 (1984) pp. 123–32; Anthony Giddens, *The Constitution of Society: Outline of the Theory of Structuration* (Cambridge: Polity Press, 1984) p. 368.

[18] The discussion which follows is largely based on Giddens, *op. cit.*; idem, *A Contemporary Critique of Historical Materialism* Volume 1: *Power, Property and the State* (London: Macmillan, 1981) Chapters 4–7; Derek Gregory, *The Geographical Imagination: Social Theory and Human Geography* (London: Hutchinson, forthcoming).

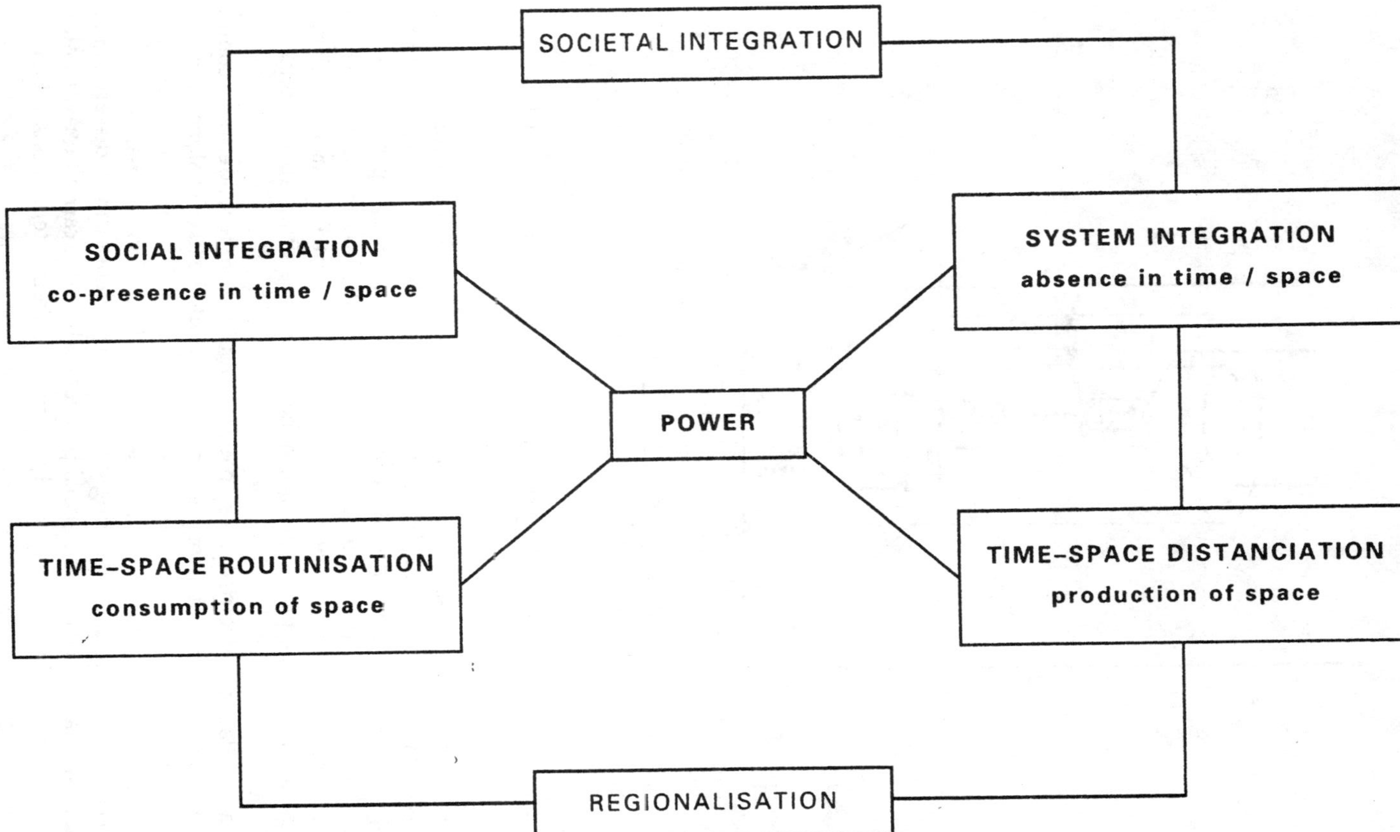

Figure 12.1 Gidden's theory of structuration [orig. Figure 1.4.3]

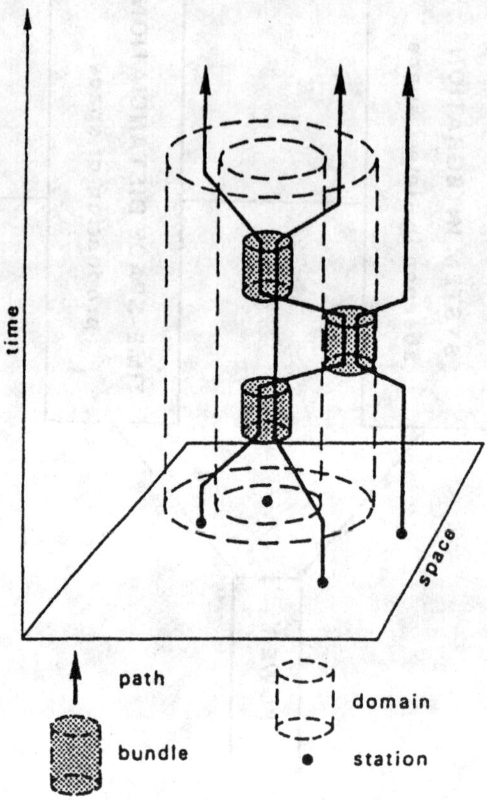

Figure 12.2 The notation of time–geography (after Hägerstrand) [orig. Figure 1.4.4]

life. It is for this reason that Hägerstrand sometimes describes his work as a time-space ecology. But this is much more than a metaphor: one of Hägerstrand's central concerns is the competitive struggle between people and projects for open paths. It is this 'jockeying for position' which is implied by the very concept of space he uses – in Swedish *rum* – for which the closest English equivalent is perhaps 'room'. The pattern of paths can then be seen as a time-space template of *power*.

For a population, of course, those patterns would seem bewilderingly complicated: imagine what the paths for just ten people would be like, let alone a hundred or a thousand! And then try to visualise them not just for a single day but for a whole year. Even so, Hägerstrand believes that if one looks closer (and thinks harder) then a fleeting and flickering time–space coherence can be discerned.

This arises partly because the social practices which are carried forward along those paths are, as I've said, typically routinised; their intersections repeatedly form knots of social activity in time and space ('bundles') which are tied and retied over and over again. But it also arises because those social practices are shaped by – and in turn themselves shape – wider structural features of the social systems in which they are implicated. Those structures can be glimpsed in concrete form in the various institutions which regulate access to constellations of stations and stipulate modes of conduct within them. Hägerstrand calls these constellations 'domains' – and there you can surely hear the distant echoes of the geopolitics of *domination* which so exercised Harvey. Although Giddens is critical of several of Hägerstrand's theoretical claims, and in my view rightly so, the time–space relations between power and domination constitute one of the main axes of structuration theory.[19]

System integration In so far as routinised social practices are recognisably the same over varying spans of time and space, then Giddens argues that they flow from and fold back into structural relations which reach beyond the 'here and now' to define interactions with other who are *absent* in time or space. This is what 'society' came to mean after the eighteenth century: the larger world stretching away from the human body and the human being. Giddens suggests that a basic task of structuration theory is therefore to show how 'the limitations of individual "presence" are transcended by the stretching of social relations across time and

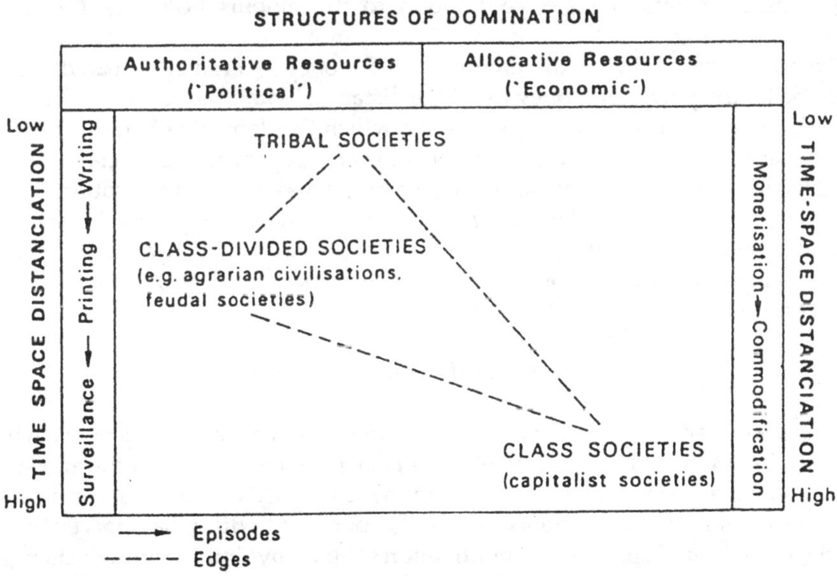

Figure 12.3 The developing historical geography of domination (after Giddens) [orig. Figure 1.4.5]

[19] For a critique of time-geography, see Derek Gregory, 'Suspended animation: the stasis of diffusion theory', in Derek Gregory and John Urry (eds) *Social Relations and Spatial Structures* (London: Macmillan, 1985) pp. 296–336.

space'. This sounds metaphysical, even mystical, but it turns out to be much more ordinary. What Giddens is talking about is, in effect, a developing historical geography of domination (Figure 12.3). In his view, structures of domination depend on resources which sustain dominion either over the social world ('authoritative' resources: roughly speaking, the 'political') or over the material world ('allocative' resources: roughly speaking, the 'economic'). These take different forms in different societies, of course, but more important is the fact that they connect in different ways in different types of society. For it is through these connections – through the differential mobilisation of authoritative and allocative resources – that different social systems 'stretch' across time and space in different ways. Giddens calls this process of 'stretching' *time–space distanciation*.

Giddens sorts some of the most powerful media of time–space distanciation into two sets (though there are undoubtedly others). The first set includes the emergence of writing, which was almost everywhere closely identified with the origins of the state and the formation of class societies, and which opened up spheres of interaction far beyond the spoken circles of oral cultures and traditional tribal societies and the diffusion of printing and other communications technologies, which dramatically enhanced the surveillance capabilities of the state and allowed it to penetrate much more deeply into the day-to-day lives of its subject populations. These various changes correspond to the mobilisation of authoritative resources.

The second set includes the emergence of money – Simmel repeatedly drew attention to 'the power of money to bridge distances' – and the subsequent universalisation of a convulsive money economy, which Giddens (like Marx) regards as the cutting edge of the so-called 'commodification' of everyday life in class-divided capitalist societies. These various changes correspond to the mobilisation of allocative resources. In the late twentieth century these two sets intersect in innumerable ways, perhaps most obviously in the way in which, as Harvey notes, credit transfers 'can move around the world as quickly as information and instructions concerning their use will allow'.[20]

The dissolution of the social

Gidden's work advances beyond Hägerstrand's in a number of directions. Where Hägerstrand puts the accent on the *consumption* of space, in which time and space are conceived as resources drawn upon in the realisation of individual and collective projects, structuration theory is equally concerned with what Harvey would call the *production* of space – the 'annihilation of space by time' – through changing modes of time–space distanciation. And where Hägerstrand emphasises the creation of 'pockets of local order', structuration theory is equally attentive to what Massey would call the changing systems of interdependence in which they are embedded. These couplets both find common ground in *regionalisation*. Giddens

[20] Harvey, Limits *op. cit.*, Chapter 9.

regards this as a phenomenon of decisive importance for social theory. 'No single concept helps more to redress the misleading divisions between "micro-[scale]" and "macro-[scale]" research,' he argues, and 'no single concept helps more to counter the assumption that a "society" is always a clear-cut unity with precisely defined boundaries to it.'[21]

The last point is put most sharply by Michael Mann. Against the grain of conventional sociology, he writes:

> *Societies are not unitary. They are not social systems (closed or open); they are not totalities . . . Because there is no whole, social relations cannot be reduced 'ultimately', 'in the last instance' to some systemic property of it – like the [mode of production] . . . Because there is no bounded totality, it is not helpful to divide social change or conflict into 'endogenous' and 'exogenous' varieties . . . Societies are much* messier than our theories of them.[22]

Like Giddens (though unlike him in other respects), Mann conceives the constitution of social life in terms of multiple sociospatial networks of power. This is not to say that social life can be fully accounted for in these terms, of course, but they are nevertheless of strategic importance to any post-modern social theory. 'A whole history remains to be written of spaces,' Michel Foucault once wrote, 'from the great strategies of geopolitics to the little tactics of the habitat.' And he made it plain that a project of this sort would have to be, at the very same time, 'a history of powers', 'Space,' he declared, 'is fundamental to the exercise of power'.[23] It is also critical for the construction of post-modern social theory.

The last paragraphs have drawn parallels between the geographical reconstruction of political economy and the geographical reconstruction of sociology. No doubt I have exaggerated them; a more nuanced account would evidently have to say much more about the contrasts between them (and the silences within them). But it is at least plausible to suggest that the 'disorganization of capitalism' – the tense and turbulent landscapes of production portrayed by Harvey and Massey – and the 'dissolution of the social' – the splintering of sociology's master-concept prefigured by Giddens and Mann – are bound together in some way. [24] In the most general terms, one might say that both of them seek to capture a wider nexus of overlapping, intersecting and contending relations through which actions in pockets of local order ricochet off one another in a constant play of difference. If that is indeed the case, then one of the most exacting problems in post-modern social theory turns on what a previous generation called 'the problem of geo-

21 Giddens, Constitution, *op. cit.*, p. 365.

22 Michael Mann, The *Sources of Social Power Volume 1: A History of Power from the Beginning to A.D. 1760* (Cambridge: Cambridge University Press, 1986) pp. 1–4.

23 Michel Foucault, *Power/Knowledge: Selected Interviews and Other Writings* (edited by Colin Gordon) (Brighton: Harvester, 1980) p. 149. I have provided a detailed discussion of Foucault's analytics of space in *Imagination*, op. cit.

24 Cf. Scott Lash and John Urry, 'The dissolution of the social?', in Mark Wardell and Stephen Turner (eds) *Sociological Theory in Transition* (Boston: Allen & Unwin, 1986) pp. 95–109.

graphical description'. For how can we convey all this in our writing? Some preliminary answers can be found in the developing relations between geography and anthropology.

Geography and Anthropology

Post-war geography in Britain was strangely indifferent to the achievements of anthropology, and yet the two could claim a common lineage reaching back to the eighteenth and nineteenth centuries. Geography emerged, so Stoddart claims, 'as Europe encountered the rest of the world, and indeed itself, with the tools of the new objective science, and all other geographical traditions are necessarily derivative and indeed imitative of it'. What 'made our own subject possible,' in his view, was 'the extension of scientific methods of observation, classification and comparison to peoples and societies'. Among these extensions Stoddart numbers 'a new concern for realism in illustration and description', through which 'places came to be seen as objects which could be recorded and related to each other in an objective manner, rather than simply as triggers to mood and to expression'.[25] Anthropology can claim much the same history (though one usually written in less triumphal terms). Yet – with the exception of Daryll Forde, H. J. Fleure and a handful of other geographers – the relations between anthropology and geography have, for most of the twentieth century, been much closer on the other side of the Atlantic. Cultural geography is still a much more prominent feature of the North American intellectual landscape, where it has even been suggested that one of Carl Sauer's most far-reaching achievements was the 'amalgamation' of the two.[26]

Ethnography and writing cultures

I mention Sauer not only because of his central role in the development of cultural geography. His writings are especially illuminating because they were animated by two traditions. The first derived from the work of Alfred Kroeber and Robert Lowie. These two Berkeley anthropologists saw culture as a coherent totality: as what Kroeber called a 'superorganic' collectivity which transcended the actions of individual human beings. This was a powerful and, as it turned out, an influential talisman: hence, presumably, Sauer's belief that human geography 'is a science that has nothing to do with individuals but only with . . . cultures'. It continued to be an article of faith in cultural geography (and elsewhere) for many decades. At the beginning of the 1980s, however, this totalising vision was subjected to a critique which, though it was scarcely confined to Sauer's particular formulations, nevertheless did much to re-direct some of the most interesting work in cultural

[25] D. R. Stoddart, *On Geography and its History* (Oxford: Basil Blackwell, 1986) pp. 35, 39.

[26] W. W. Speth, 'Berkeley geography 1923–33', in Brian W. Blouet (ed.), *The Origins of Academic Geography in the United States* (Hamden: Archon, 1981) p. 231.

geography towards a more 'interpretative' (which is not to say an individualistic) anthropology.[27]

The writings of Clifford Geertz have been of particular importance in this movement (and, in my judgement, are likely to become more so). 'The force of our interpretations,' Geertz insisted in one of his most famous essays, 'cannot rest, as they are now so often made to do, on the tightness with which they hold together'. For 'nothing has done more to discredit cultural analysis than the impeccable depictions of formal order in whose actual existence nobody can quite believe'. This could stand as an indictment of geography as easily as anthropology; but there is more.

> *If anthropological interpretation is constructing a reading of what happens, then to divorce it from what happens – from what, in this time or that place, specific people say, what they do, what is done to them, from the whole vast business of the world – is to divorce it from its implications and render it vacant.*

It is largely for this reason that Geertz commends *ethnography*, a research process in which one seeks to describe the day-to-day lives of people in other, particular cultures through a sustained encounter with them and the multiplicity of contexts in which they live. Its purpose is 'thick description': rendering the layers of meaning in which their social actions are embedded less opaque, less refractory to our own (no less particular) sensibilities, yet without destroying altogether the 'strangeness' which drew us to them in the first place.[28]

This is the impulse which now informs many descriptions of the geography of everyday life and, by extension, many de-codings of the cultural landscape. These developments have done much to blunt the prescriptions which Stoddart derived from the natural sciences, and they have, I suggest, extended the boundaries of 'realism' far beyond the confines of objects and objectivities. But they have not, in any substantial sense, challenged its *textual conventions*. And this matters more than you might think. For what do ethnographers do? *They write*, says Geertz. And ethnography is now not confined to anthropology (if it ever was): we all write. Yet we don't seem to have a developed understanding of the modes of representation which we deploy, let alone a willingness to experiment with them.[29]

This brings me to the second tradition which surfaces through Sauer's cultural geography. For this was suffused with the idealism of the Romantics who contested the unqualified naturalism of the Enlightenment. Foremost among them was

[27] See James Duncan, 'The superorganic in American cultural geography', *Ann. Ass. Am. Geogr.*, 70 (1980), pp. 181–98; cf. Note 7.

[28] Clifford Geertz, *The Interpretation of Cultures: Selected Essays* (New York: Basic Books, 1973) p. 18.

[29] These days we don't only write, of course, and the importance of film and video should be kept constantly in mind. Even so, the discussion which follows is confined to written texts, and although Geertz has noted the various ways in which the text can serve as a model for many other means of cultural expression, including landscapes, I do not mean to suggest that graphic images do not present their own, distinctive potentials (and problems).

Goethe. 'The foundation of Sauer's metatheory [about the morphology of the cultural landscape] rests,' so Speth argues, 'on Goethe's conception of morphological change'.[30] Goethe sought to reconcile the scientific and the artistic imaginations through the study of morphology, the ceaseless transformation of living forms, and to convey, in the same moment, 'both . . . the form produced and . . . the process of formation'. Sauer's morphology was perfectly consistent with this, of course; so too, for that matter, were elements of locational analysis. But what is of special interest is that, according to two commentators, Goethe's conception of form 'pervades all his writings, verse as well as prose, not only in the sense that conceptual statements of it are incorporated into his philosophical poems; *it is implicit in the structural relations of the language itself.*' There was thus in Goethe (but not, I think, in Sauer) a self-conscious attention to linguistic forms and textual conventions. One finds there, in part in consequence, a tension between order and chaos. Hence Goethe's anguished presentiment of 'a world bereft of forms, when time and place shivered to atoms and the normal congruence between self and surroundings snapped, found its precipitate . . . in his poetry'.[31]

I am not, of course, claiming that Goethe prefigures post-modernism: but the importance of linguistic forms and textual conventions is surely clear enough. It is this which Geertz accentuated; and it is this which is being explored, in a different register, by various experiments in post-modern ethnography.

Experiments in ethnography

I have already referred to the problem of geographical description.[32] 'Elevated to a central concern of theoretical reflection,' George Marcus and Michael Fischer propose, 'problems of description become problems of representation'. There is now, in their view, a crisis of representation throughout the human sciences. It is one which has demanded serious theoretical reflection about particular textual strategies (whose consequences, it so happens, reach far beyond the text), but it has also occasioned a series of practical experiments in writing ethnographies. Marcus and Fischer accentuate that what is important in all this 'is not experimentation for its own sake, but the theoretical insight that the play with writing technique brings to consciousness.'[33] This needs emphasis, I think, because in geography there have been rather too many calls for 'plain writing' by commentators who signally fail to understand the consequences of conventional genres and modes of representation. Those who dismiss the work of Gunnar Olsson, for example, need to see that the giving of descriptions is never a purely empirical exercise. It is not only that all

[30] Speth, *op. cit.*, pp. 233–4.

[31] E. M. Wilkinson and L. A. Willoughby, *Goethe: Poet and Thinker* (London: Edward Arnold, 1962) pp. 182–3.

[32] The classic paper is H. C. Darby, 'The problem of geographical description', *Trans. Inst. Br. Geogr.*, 30 (1962) pp. 1–14.

[33] George Marcus and Michael Fischer, *Anthropology as Cultural Critique: The Experimental Moment in the Human Sciences* (Chicago: University of Chicago Press, 1986) pp. 9, 42.

observations are inescapably 'theory-laden' (a leading theorem of virtually all postpositivist philosophies of science) but that the very act of stringing them together – of structuring the accounts in which they are placed – is *itself* an irredeemably theoretical practice. Olsson has in fact made this point in the most telling way possible: his theoretical reflections *on* discourse are themselves deliberate experiments *in* discourse.[34]

For all that, however, there have been pitifully few experiments in writing contemporary geography. There have been countless injunctions to exercise the geographical imagination, but these have usually been disciplined by the established conventions of (literary) realism. It may well be true that we are not trained to be painters or poets but, like Pierce Lewis, I don't think we should boast about it. For if we cannot evoke landscapes, if we cannot provide descriptions of the relations between people and places 'so vivid that they move our emotions', then – to adapt a phrase from Geertz – we radically 'thin' our geographies.[35] Consider the following:

> *My love affair with those Michigan dunes . . . had everything to do with violent immediate sensations: the smell of October wind sweeping in from Lake Michigan, sun-hot sand that turned deliciously cool when your foot sank in, the sharp sting of sand blown hard against bare legs, the pale blur of sand pluming off the dune crest against a porcelain-blue sky. Lake Michigan a muffled roar beyond the distant beach, a hazy froth of jade and white. As I try to shape words to evoke my feelings about that far-off place and time, I know why the Impressionists painted landscapes as they did – not literally, but as fragments of colour, splashes of pigment, bits of shattered prismatic light.*

Is that geography? Or is it an extract from a novel?[36] If you can give a straight answer to the question, then I must suppose you can draw a clear distinction between the two. But on what basis? And *why*?

In fact, one of the most important elements in the movement towards a post-modern ethnography has been a serious consideration of the textual strategies of contemporary fiction. For ethnographies *are* fictions, in the literal sense of *fictio* – 'something made'. And there are no end of ways in which they can be 'made'. What is more, some of the most interesting experiments in ethnographic writing derive from the Impressionism (and post-Impressionism) registered in the passage I have just cited; from the multiple voices and multiple perspectives which shatter the convention of a single author, outside the text and surveying, with a single gaze, all that happens inside its frame.[37] For it is this blurring of inside and outside which

[34] See Gunnar Olsson, *Birds in Egg/Eggs in Bird* (London: Pion, 1980) for an early example.

[35] Geertz, *Interpretation op. cit.*

[36] It does in fact come from Pierce Lewis's Presidential Address to the Association of American Geographers: 'Beyond Description', *Ann. Ass. Am. Geogr.*, 75 (1985) pp. 465–77.

[37] Cf. Stephen Kern, *The Culture of Time and Space 1880–1918* (Cambridge, Mass: Harvard University Press, 1983), pp. 140–43.

is one of the most arresting developments in post-modern fiction (think of John Fowles's *The French Lieutenant's Woman* or Christopher Priest's *The Glamour*): and it also distinguishes some of the very best experimental ethnography. As James Clifford sees it, the 'ground' from which conventional representations of the world have issued has been transformed.

> *A conceptual shift, 'tectonic' in its implications, has taken place. We ground things, now, on a moving earth. There is no longer any place of overview (mountaintop) from which to map human ways of life, no Archimedean point from which to represent the world. Mountains are in constant motion. So are islands: for one cannot occupy, unambiguously, a bounded cultural world from which to journey out and analyze other cultures. Human ways of life increasingly influence, dominate, parody, translate and subvert one another. Cultural analysis is always enmeshed in global movements of difference and power.*[38]

That was the real lesson of Europe's encounter with the rest of the world, but we have been astonishingly slow to grasp its implications. Eric Wolf makes things a good deal clearer when he censures traditional ethnographies for clinging leech-like to the myth of the pristine primitive, closed off from a wider nexus of political and economic relationships stretching across time and space. 'Europeans and Americans would never have encountered these supposed bearers of a pristine past,' he writes, 'if they had not encountered one another, in bloody fact, as Europe reached out to seize the resources and populations of the other continents.' And not only Europe (and America). 'Has there ever been a time,' he wonders, 'when human populations have existed in independence of larger encompassing relationships, unaffected by larger fields of force?' Wolf doubts it. Hence his conclusion:

> *Once we locate the reality of society in historically changing, imperfectly bounded, multiple and branching social alignments . . . the concept of a fixed, unitary and bounded culture must give way to a sense of the fluidity and permeability of cultural sets. In the rough-and-tumble of social interaction, groups are known to exploit the ambiguities of inherited forms, to impart new evaluations or valences to them, to borrow forms more expressive of their interests, or to create wholly new forms to answer changed circumstances. Furthermore, if we think of such interaction not [only] as causative in its own terms but as responsive to larger economic and political forces, the explanation of cultural forms must take account of the larger context, that wider field of force.*[39]

It is not just that, as Marcus and Fischer insist, 'experience has always been more complex than the representation of it that is permitted by traditional techniques of description and analysis'. Of course that is true, and experimental writing can properly be regarded as 'a radicalization of concern with how cultural difference

[38] James Clifford, 'Introduction: partial truths', in James Clifford and George Marcus (eds) *Writing Cultures: The Poetics and Politics of Ethnography* (Berkeley: University of California Press, 1986) p. 22.
[39] Eric Wolf, *Europe and the People without History* (Berkeley: University of California Press, 1982) pp. 18, 387.

is to be represented in ethnography'. But it is also the case that we need, somehow, to show how that very complexity derives from the way in which the day-to-day lives of particular people in particular places are in part shaped through their involvement in larger systems which stretch beyond the immediacies of the 'here and now' (or the 'there and then'): that 'the "outside" ... [is] an integral part of the construction and constitution of the "inside" '. Recognising this, Marcus and Fischer continue, experimental ethnographies are concerned

> *to capture more accurately the [historico-geographical] context of [their] subjects, and to register the constitutive workings of impersonal international political and economic systems on the local level where fieldwork usually takes place. These workings can no longer be accounted for as merely external impacts upon local, self-contained cultures. Rather, external systems have their thoroughly local definition and penetration, and are formative of the symbols and shared meanings within the most intimate life-worlds of ethnographic subjects.*[40]

These are, so it seems to me, substantially the same concerns which exercised Harvey and Giddens. But they are also the concerns which animate Fowles and Priest.

And yet, when set alongside the variety of textual strategies encompassed by the contemporary novel – changes in perspective, jump-cuts and cross-cuts between scenes, dislocations of chronology and composition, commentaries on the construction of the text by author and reader, and so on – the conservative character of many of the most radical geographies is truly astonishing.[41] Let me repeat: this is not an argument for experimentation for the sake of experimentation. It is instead a recognition that the form which we give to our texts materially affects what we say through them. Narrative, to take just one example, is not an innocent genre. It makes a series of strategic assumptions, usually unremarked, about closure and coherence. Stories are supposed to 'hang together', to make sense in a particular way; loose ends have to be tied up and a sense of finitude achieved. But what entitles us to represent the world – to 'make' sense of it – in this *particular* way? And, make no mistake, it is a particular way; other textual strategies are possible and, to some critics, even preferable.

Frederic Jameson contends that narrative is a 'socially symbolic act' which belongs to everyday life 'as lived on the social surface'. His thesis, as I understand it, is that the 'comprehensible order' of the conventional narrative conceals a much more tense and fundamentally contradictory social reality. Similarly, Hayden White suggests that the value we usually ascribe to narrative in the representation of 'what happened' arises 'out of a desire to have real events display the coherence, integrity, fullness and closure of an image of life that is and can only be imaginary'. For both writers, therefore, conventional narratives are structurally implicated in

[40] Marcus and Fischer, op. cit., 39, 43.

[41] Exceptions are now beginning to appear, though few of them have the freshness or immediacy of the best contemporary travel writing: and in my view they *ought* to.

the construction of highly *specific* ideologies.[42] Post-modernism is, in part, a challenge to those conventions and an exploration of other possibilities.

It is not my purpose to debate these claims here: but they *ought* to be debated if we are to be vigilant about our work. One of the reasons Harvey's *Limits to Capital* is so different – so much more schematic, so much more systematised – than his later *Consciousness and the Urban Experience*, for example, is to do with the formal differences between the two texts: the one a sustained theoretical critique with, as I have shown, a central object and a master-narrative directed towards the urbanisation of capital, the other a collection of essays with a looser structure and an episodic, almost fragmentary evocation of the urbanisation of consciousness. This is to overstate the contrast, I know: Harvey has still not broken with the totalising vision of modern Marxism. But the change in textual strategy evident in his extraordinary essay on the historical geography of Paris is, I think, indicative of a growing tension in his work. Theory construction, he says, 'does not proceed in isolation from reflection, speculation and historical-geographical experience. But it does proceed rather differently.' And he admits that his thinking 'has been as much influenced by Dickens, Balzac, Zola, Gissing, Dreiser, Pynchon, and a host of others' as it has been by 'dry-as-dust science'.[43] And that influence, I suggest, extends beyond their evocations of urban experience to the modes of representation which they deploy.

In sum, I believe we might profitably attend to the poetics of our descriptions as much as to their poetry: to the textual strategies which shape what we say as much as to the words we use.[44] Put like that, then for those who worry about these things geography is an 'art' (it is a 'science' too); *but the 'arts' are every bit as 'theoretical' in their sensibilities as the 'sciences'*. Poetics is about the theoretical scrutiny of textual strategies in whatever medium and in whatever field they are used, and the modes of representation which we deploy in our texts surely deserve our most careful theoretical reflection. There *is* a poetics of geography, for geography *is* a kind of writing – and writing, along with reading, is still the most difficult of all the skills we have to learn.

42 Frederic Jameson, *The Political Unconsciousness: Narrative as a Socially Symbolic Act* (Ithaca: Cornell University Press, London; Methuen, 1980); Hayden White, 'The value of narrativity', in W. J. T. Mitchell (ed.) *On Narrative* (Chicago: University of Chicago Press, 1981) pp. 1–23. See also Wallace Martin, *Recent Theories of Narrative* (Ithaca and London: Cornell University Press, 1986). An important geographical essay which is sensitive to these questions (though not as critical of conventional narrative as I would want to be) is Stephen Daniels, 'Arguments for a humanistic geography', in R. J. Johnston (ed.) *The Future of Geography* (London and New York: Methuen, 1985) pp. 143–58.

43 David Harvey, *Consciousness and the Urban Experience* (Oxford: Basil Blackwell, 1985) pp. xv–xvi.

44 For a brilliant demonstration of what I have in mind, which shows just how constrained Darby's conception of the problem of geographical description really was, see John Barrell, 'Geographies of Hardy's Wessex', *J. Hist. Geogr.*, 8 (1982) pp. 347–61.

Post-Modernism?

There is an irony in all this. I said at the very start that post-modernism was suspicious of master-narratives, of systems with centres, of stories that claimed coherence and completeness. And yet my own account has been shaped by a conventional chronology, in which the successive cross-fertilisations of geography and political economy, sociology and anthropology have moved towards a post-modernism haunted by a central theme. There is probably comedy too: not only post-modernism but post-positivism, post-structuralism, post-Marxism, post-Impressionism . . . Where will it all end?

But the tragedy would be to treat the developments I have described here as symptomatic of yet another 'revolution', one more sea-change to roll with or roll back. These are, instead, ideas to think about and to work with – critically, vigilantly, constructively. One way of measuring the distance between them and modern human geography is, perhaps, to reverse one of the catch-phrases of spatial science: that there is more *disorder* in the world than appears at first sight is not discovered until that disorder is looked for.[45] That is more than mere word-play; it may be that one of the most ideological impulses of all – the 'commonsense' response to the complexity of the world – is to impose a coherence and a simplicity which is, at bottom, illusory.

Even so, I would not wish this essay to be taken as an unqualified manifesto for post-modernism. I am well aware that post-modernism can be read in a number of different ways, some of them acutely conservative as well as insistently radical; that there are all sorts of difficulties in its formulations which I have had no space to consider here; and that some of its own criticisms (of Habermas, for example) are wide of the mark. That said, the various themes which I have pulled together raise questions which, in my view, cannot be ignored. For, like Eagleton, I suspect that we are presently strung out between notions of social totality which are plainly discreditable and a 'politics of the fragment or conjuncture' which is largely ineffectual.[46] And to go *beyond* these limitations, I suspect, we need, in part, to go *back* to the question of areal differentiation: but armed with a new theoretical sensitivity towards the world in which we live and to the ways in which we represent it. Whether we focus on 'order' or 'disorder' or on the tension between the two – and no matter how we choose to define those terms – we still have to 'look'. We are still making geography.

[45] The original phrase was Sigwart's, cited in P. Haggett and R. J. Chorley, 'Models, paradigms and the New Geography', in R. J. Chorley and P. Haggett (eds) *Models in Geography* (London: Methuen, 1967) p. 20.

[46] Terry Eagleton, *Against the Grain: Selected Essays* (London: Verso, 1986) p. 5.

Acknowledgements

I am grateful to Michael Dear, Felix Driver, Peter Jackson, David Ley, Chris Philo, Ed Soja, Nigel Thrift and Rex Walford for discussing the themes of this essay with me and for their comments on an early draft. I am also indebted to Denis Blackburn and Stella Gutteridge for preparing the illustrations.

PART III

NATURE, CULTURE AND LANDSCAPE

INTRODUCTION

Modern geography began as an experiment in holding together nature and society in a single explanatory framework (Part II), a position which was not shared by related disciplines. Both economics and demography, for example, dispensed with land as a constraint on economic and population growth (Wrigley 1987). The Industrial Revolution, and particularly the development of inorganic energy sources, released human productivity from its complete dependence on the sun. Urbanization unlocked the close local connections between place, food and materials supply, and community. That geography should combine what other knowledges separated left it with a difficult legacy of evolutionary thinking and environmental determinism. Yet, in the late twentieth century, when environmental crisis and resource management have become pressing issues, geography is well-placed to supply both scientific and critical theoretical perspectives. So central are the relations between humanity and nature that they involved geographers in many of the major scientific, ethical and political debates of the twentieth century. As Glacken (**chapter 13**) indicates, it proves difficult to isolate thinking about nature from the whole of human thought.

In his magisterial survey of ideas of nature in European history from ancient times to the late eighteenth century, Glacken extracts three recurring questions: Is the earth designed for humans? Do variations in the physical world account for variations in human beings? What impacts have humans had upon the physical world? Although his inquiries halt before the complexities of the Industrial Revolution, these themes find echoes today. The popular ideas of Gaia suggest that life itself 'guides' the environment, with biotic, climatic and inorganic systems linked in a single homeostatic state. The earth might then be considered as a single organism which designs itself. Neo-Malthusian ideas of a finite earth and an impending resource scarcity suggest that nature acts as a final control on humans. Although widely dismissed by economists, such sentiments have widespread intuitive appeal. Finally, the dominant theme now, and more so than ever, is that humans are having substantial and frequently negative effects on the physical world. Although their emphases and methods may be different, geographers today are engaged with the same issues as in times past. There may be advances in scientific understanding, but there are also returns to older ideas. Cosgrove (1990) finds strong parallels between Renaissance environmentalism and post-modern thought. In contrast with modernism, both believe in a balance between 'techne' – science and technology – and 'poesis' – 'a wonder at the deeply felt sense of moral order in nature' (p. 356). They possess a strong sense of spirituality, metaphorical correspondence and enchantment in contrast with modernism's hard distinctions between spirit and matter, humans and nature, subject and object.

These comments raise a key distinction in the speculations about nature and society. Some thinking stresses the fundamental unity of human and non-human, while other ideas imply a dualistic separation of them. Smith and O'Keefe (**chapter 16**, also Smith 1984) summarized these ideas as either universal or external conceptions. While Cosgrove stresses the alignment of each view with historical periods, Glacken, and Smith and O'Keefe regard these social constructions of nature as co-existing. In capitalist societies, nature is conceptualized as both everything there is and all that is not human. Such a position is not logically possible, of course. At any time and in any place one should not expect ideas of nature and society to be strictly coherent and consistent. Smith traces the contradiction to the objectification of nature in the production process. Human beings are subject to the laws of nature, but, in transforming the material world, alienate themselves from it and come to regard this external nature as hostile and requiring domination.

While Smith and O'Keefe rely on Marx's historical materialism, Glacken offers a more idealist account of the labours of intellectuals. Neither directly address what one might call a social history of nature, nor do they delve into what ordinary people think. These subjects are gaining importance, notably in the growing interest in environmental history (for example, Cronon 1983; Thomas 1983; Worster 1992, 1994). Furthermore, according to Harrison and Burgess (1994), while it is possible to identify distinct views of the environment, people may hold more than one at a time or shift between them. In their study of a land-use conflict in southern England, they found that lay persons did not really share the view of either developers or conservationists, but tended to see nature as unpredictable and capricious. Burgess's related research on parks, open spaces and media images of the environment has done much to reveal the differences between intellectual speculation and lay understanding. Much of modern Western environmental debate often claims the interdependence of earth and humanity, but then focuses on distant phenomena such as ozone layers and rainforests. The intimate connections between nature and society in everyday life – of the kind that Leopold (**chapter 21**) was intensely aware of – are thereby lost.

One way of recovering this intimacy is to take a step back and consider a question prior to those raised by Glacken and others. Instead of asking what the relationship between nature and society is, one might ask where the boundary between them lies. If one follows the distinction between universal and external nature, then it appears that the boundary runs through our very bodies. To be human is to be both part of and apart from nature at the same time. Theology, law and science have, in the Western tradition, provided systematic separations and classifications of nature and society. For example, Christian theologians distinguished humans by their possession of souls; Linnaeus's taxonomy of plants replaced local and vernacular names of plants and animals by universal ones; and sixteenth-century England passed injunctions against bestiality. They all maintained a boundary between human and other forms of organic life. And yet one does not have to look to pre-capitalist societies to find countless examples of humans breaching this boundary in their everyday life. We give some animals names and talk to them, we decorate our houses with plants, and we protest against the harsh treatment of farm animals. Haraway (1985) argues that the boundaries between humans and animals, organisms and machines, and the physical and non-physical are breaking down. In an age of genetic engineering, nothing convincingly settles the boundary between humans and animals, not language, tool use or social behaviour. This is no bad thing, maintains Haraway. The nexus of technology, humanity and biology now informs everything from the politics of human reproduction to the fantasies of modern weaponry. We are all cyborgs, hybrids of machines and organisms, and the goal is to explore these dissolving boundaries without fear, seeking kinship with animals and machines instead of control.

Haraway's imaginative speculations are a far cry from Glacken's studious excavation of Western thought. Both might seem detached from what geographers do. But in holding society and humanity together, geographers have entered a difficult philosophical terrain. Two themes have predominated in their responses: determination and synthesis. We turn to these next, and then consider political and ethical issues.

Determination

If geography must include within its subject-matter both natural and social phenomena, then it must do so without collapsing one onto the other completely. Yet keeping them apart raises awkward questions of causation and determination which have strong philosophical, ethical and political consequences. Glacken's second core question addresses one half of this issue. It asks if the earth's climates, its relief and the configuration of its continents have influenced the moral and social character of individuals and cultures. An affirmative answer is found in the various ideas grouped together as environmental determinism, which represented the dominant position in modern geography's formative period.

Although it had critics at the time, such as Kropotkin and Boas (see Part II), with hindsight geographers have frequently denounced such views as complicit with imperialism, racism and oppression (Harvey, **chapter 5**). Among those singled out for attack were Semple, Huntington and Taylor (Livingstone 1992). If one reads just the opening paragraph of Semple's book (**chapter 14**) then it is not hard to see why. She writes that 'Man is the product of the earth's surface', which would seem to deny all possibility of human ingenuity and creativity and assert the natural basis of racial hierarchies. Yet Semple, like many others, hedged such claims with provisos, cautioning against speaking of control or single-factor determination. Lewthwaite (1966) calls such thinkers 'indeterminate determinists', adding to the terminological confusion which surrounds such writing. He attempts to clarify things by distinguishing between two kinds of determinism. There are those like Mackinder (**chapter 8**) and W. M. Davis, who assert the unity of physical and human geography but argue that everything must start with the former. This weaker form survives in the tendency to begin regional geography texts with accounts of geology or climate, or the common practice of setting physical geography examination papers before human ones. Then there are those who, despite pronouncements to the contrary, in their writings consistently ascribe a strong measure of final control to the physical environment. After all, Semple does claim that desert plains produce monotheism.

If this reduction of the social to the natural was finally unacceptable, then the converse reduction of the natural to the social could be equally problematic. In the 1930s Stalin sought to distance Soviet from American geography and stress the independence of the laws of social development from the physical environment (Hooson 1959; Matley 1966). The 1948 Plan for the Transformation of Nature included bold schemes for changing the environment to meet human needs, which some have argued lay behind later environmental disasters. Furthermore, in the USSR human geography declined because of its association with physical geography. When Anuchin attacked such indeterminism in the 1960s he still faced intense opposition from the geographical establishment. Geography's association with determinism also caused problems in the USA. The failure to provide an alternative and coherent intellectual position was one of the factors behind the closure of Harvard's department in the 1940s (Smith 1987).

The geographical experiment therefore faced an intellectual problem of how to combine nature and society without according either one the dominant or sole control. Put this way, there were two kinds of resolution increasingly adopted after the 1920s. The first was suggested by the geographer-turned-anthropologist C. Daryll Forde. He wrote that 'between the physical environment and human activity there is always a middle term . . . a cultural pattern' (1934, p. 463). Like Sauer, Forde included in his idea of culture components of change, diffusion and exchange which meant that peoples' cultures were not direct reflections of just their local physical environment. While Semple looked for, and found, similarities of human response to like environments, Forde stressed the differences. There were other possible middle terms. In French geography under Vidal de la Blache (**chapter 10**), history or the passage of time itself could be something which transformed both sides of the equation. In Europe (and unlike much of the USA) a long period of settlement and agriculture meant that people and their local environments moulded one another like a snail and its shell. It was pointless trying to give ultimate priority to one side or the other.

A third middle term was found in the powers of human labour, both in Herbertson's Lamarckian view (**chapter 22**) and in the early work of Marxist geographer Karl Wittfogel (see Peet 1988). Labour is a social process which transforms both humans and the material environment. Smith and O'Keefe (**chapter 16**) write of labour as producing a second nature out of first nature, one which combines use and exchange values along with cultural meanings of nature. This nature is not freed from physical laws, but it does respond to the laws of capital accumulation. That something can be both natural and socio-historical at the same time avoids the terminological debates of searching for a boundary between them. Labour, or the experience of working the land, is also central to the radical views of landscape espoused by Berger and Williams (in Daniels, **chapter 19**).

A quite different solution was suggested by Kirk (1963). Drawing upon insights from gestalt psychology, he attempted to close the gap between nature and mind by making a distinction between the Phenomenal and Behavioural Environments. The former includes all material things, making no division between natural and human-made. People are physically connected to the Phenomenal Environment, but are only ever aware of some of it. This perceived or Behavioural Environment is the one which is relevant to understanding human activity. It stands between the external world and the internal or mental world and allows for historical and cultural differences in relations with the physical environment (Livingstone 1992). Such writing was influential in the study of behaviour and perception (see Brookfield 1969). A good example of this approach is Saarinen's study of drought in the Great Plains of the USA. He established that farmers do not adapt to the 'objective' facts of drought incidence, but adapt to what they know of drought, which knowledge does not match completely the climatic record (Saarinen 1966).

Culture, history, labour and perception have all served as middle terms between nature and society. The second means of resolving this dualism – and not incompatible with the first – is to stress the multiplicity of causal factors. Although this is what Semple claims she does, the overwhelming impression from her book is that she does not. Sauer (**chapter 17**) objected to environmental determinism because it starts with the assumption that the environment is the major control, instead of demonstrating scientifically that it is so. It is dogma, says Sauer. Semple was scientific in the thinking of her time, but the canons of science changed towards deductive methods and hypothesis testing. While she scoured the whole of human history in search of instances which confirmed her laws, later geographers were more concerned to formulate deductive tests. This might mean working from the assumption that the physical environment may be one among many independent variables or necessary conditions. Herbertson (**chapter 22**) ascribes equal significance to environment and heredity, in which he includes the past in terms of traditions and cultures. Butzer adopts a multiple causal perspective in his account of Egyptian civilization (**chapter 15**). Here and elsewhere (1976) he questions Wittfogel's thesis that irrigation leads to authoritarian power (Wittfogel 1956). He suggests that environment, technology and population may all be regarded as independent variables, with social organization and differentiation as the dependent variable. In this case, throughout Egypt's long history the balance of 'external' physical and 'internal' human factors changed from period to period.

Any causal system is determinate in a mathematical sense (Harvey 1969). The weakness of environmental determinism, and of Stalinist triumphalism, was partly that they began with an assumption that one cause mattered more than any other.

None of the critics above dispense altogether with a notion of determination, although they do differ as to what can be considered as cause and effect. Some of the research of the likes of Semple – on Appalachian communities – and Huntington – on the reconstruction of past climates in Central Asia – does stand as good science in some respects. But their thinking was so entangled with ethical and political consequences that these efforts were obscured.

Synthesis

According to Langton (1988) there are two main traditions in geographical thought. One is systematic, scientific, analytical and has concentrated on spatial relations. The other is synthetic, integrative, ecological and more akin to the humanities. Questions of determination are more prominent in the former, those of interpretation and understanding feature in the latter. In this tradition a number of concepts and devices have been used by geographers to keep nature and society together. These include landscape, place and region, often embodying organic metaphors of wholeness or functional inter-relation. But such concepts as the ecosystem and devices like GIS (Geographical Information Systems) have also been ecological and integrative and sometimes analytical as well.

Organic analogies are common in the history of geographical thought. Many of the selections in this volume make use of them. Mackinder, Vidal, Sauer and Herbertson (**chapters 8, 10, 17, and 22**) stress the unity of the subject, on the basis of the organic unity of the environment and humanity. Ratzel (**chapter 32**) represents states and the relationship between people and land in similar terms, although Semple (1911) argues that such analogies are only scaffolding for his thought and can be discarded. In such views, geographers should not pull apart what has been put together in reality. In more recent times, this sentiment is expressed in the repeated call to integrate human and physical geography. Butzer makes a distinction between organic analogies of society and civilization, which can be found in the ideas of Spengler, Spencer and Toynbee, and his own more systematic approach. The problem with such analogies is that they offer a superficial semblance of unity and bring together large amounts of data, but do not pose analytical or scientific questions (Stoddart 1967). This clash between synthetic and analytic perspectives is apparent in the differences between Clements and Tansley's views of the ecosystem (Bowler 1992). Working mainly with American grassland ecologies, Clements viewed the plant community almost as a superorganism, obeying laws of its own. It would reach a natural climax, a state of perfect balance and harmony. The British ecologist Tansley stressed instead the more mechanical and analytical view of nature, one more in keeping with the evidence of the Dust Bowl in the 1930s. Their differences, between holism and a lingering sense of ultimate design on the one hand, and a more materialist or reductionist stance which allowed for no final stages, might characterize many of the debates within geography. In contrast with the idea that civilizations rise and fall according to some notion of design or evolutionary law (perhaps an analogy with plant communities and climax), Butzer's research emphasizes the open-ended and unpredictable course of societal history.

The ecosystem could smuggle in ideas of design and organic unity, but it could also serve as an apparently natural standard against which to assess the sustainability of social systems. Both Leopold (**chapter 21**) and Butzer draw upon ideas of trophic levels, niches, energy flows, food chains etc. both to comment on the stability of certain kinds of society and to measure the disruptive power of the human impact. Leopold observes that human action opens local ecosystems into longer and more complex energy flows, and wider spatial transfers. The rate at which it does so exceeds the natural evolutionary order with the result that, although some biota are stable, others – such as in the south-western USA – are rendered unstable. In this view the impact of industrialization is not to free humanity from nature, but to make the connections less local. Butzer argues that 'steep-sided' social systems, such as occurred at times in Egypt, are more vulnerable. Further, the more complex inter-relations that exist, the more likely it is that negative factors can come together to undermine social systems. The result of such complexity, Butzer claims, is to make societal change less teleological and more stochastic.

Both these writers demonstrate the heuristic significance of likening human societies to ecosystems. The drawbacks of extending the comparison too far are revealed in comments by Chorley (1973). He notes that 'the ecosystem model is of geographical significance in so far as Man can be considered to operate in the same manner as other life forms, the model is inappropriate in so far as Man stands apart from Nature' (p. 160). Such human phenomena as capital and information cannot be readily reduced to energy or matter. It will be no surprise then if, from an ecosystemic perspective, human action always appears disruptive. We are back to the basic problem of nature as both external and universal, and the analytical difficulties of placing humans in nature and outside of it at the same time. In cultural ecology it is not unexpected that analytical studies should focus on food availability and on historical or Third World contexts (Butzer 1990). The awkward questions of industrialization and urbanization, forces responsible for stretching the food chains and energy transfers, are kept at arm's length.

The difference of emphasis between the synthetic and the analytic is also apparent in contrasting approaches to defining landscape. Both Sauer and J. B. Jackson (**chapter 18**) try to isolate a clear meaning of landscape, the latter by tracing its etymological roots. By contrast, Daniels (**chapter 19**) is more willing to admit to its ambiguities or, in his phrase, the duplicity of landscape. To him, the value of landscape lies precisely in its ability to combine the symbolic and material dimensions, a position he supports by reference to the writings of Berger and Williams. While Sauer alludes to the importance of aesthetic understanding, he is hesitant about it and falls back on the centrality of the material and observable record of humans upon the landscape. For Daniels, whose own research has been into painters such as Turner and Constable (Daniels 1993), the aesthetic qualities of landscape as distributed across various 'texts' are central. Although he shares the metaphor of landscape-as-text with those geographers who have turned to literary theory to decode the rhetorical constructions of landscape (such as Duncan and Duncan 1988), Daniels holds on more to its materiality. The contrast between Sauer and Daniels is also apparent in their interpretations of what is natural. The former recognizes a pristine, pre-human nature which is then transformed into a cultural landscape by human action. The latter allows for the social and cultural construction of the meanings of nature, reversing the emphasis. One might ask of Sauer what constitutes pristine nature, given that the exact origins of the human species itself are by no means certain or precise. To Daniels, a painting such as Gainsborough's 'Mr and Mrs Andrews' is interesting because it contains a number of different social definitions of the natural. In other words, it is what constitutes beauty or aesthetic value at any time and place which matters.

In their own ways, Jackson and Leopold share this concern. Throughout Jackson's writings he expresses a love of those landscapes and landscape features normally overlooked by the dominant tradition, such as commercial strips, centre-pivot irrigated fields, and mobile-home parks. These vernacular places are often small, irregular and subject to rapid change in use and ownership. They are where mobility and impermanence, features he associates with a distinctive American landscape, are worked into the landscape. Leopold farmed an area of Wisconsin regarded as largely worthless because of its low agricultural potential and its lack of natural wonder. Here, however, he found beauty and value, a place in which he could dream of a land ethic which maintained both the biological stability and the pleasure of nature. It is interesting to note that John Berger also found inspiration in an overlooked or left-over landscape, in Haute Savoie, France.

That landscape has not been the sole preserve of geography has been recently demonstrated by the eminent historian Simon Schama, whose *Landscape and Memory* (1995) gives credit to the work of geographers such as Tuan, Daniels and Cosgrove. Neither Jackson nor Leopold, nor, for that matter, Berger and Williams, wrote as geographers. Their concerns, for the politics, ethics and aesthetics of land and landscapes, have become more significant in geographical work and especially in a cultural geography, which has sought to find alternatives to Sauer's more natural scientific integration of society and the environment. The ecosystem – and cultural ecology – are examples of how the insights of biological sciences can still inform a synthesizing geography. By contrast, landscape explores the connections between geography and the humanities, with a greater emphasis on the non-material components of the society–nature relation. The geographical experiment continues.

Politics and Ethics

Questions about the relationship between nature and society are always political and ethical. There are three main reasons for this. First, different people have different ideas about what nature or the environment is. A developer sees a piece of land as waste ground and ripe for construction, but local people see it as a valuable community resource for rest and education. Secondly, it follows that nature is a contested term; the land cannot be both developed and a nature area and it is likely that there will be conflict as to its proper use. Finally, all human societies have tended to see themselves in nature and vice versa; nature and society resonate. If Darwin's evolutionary theories informed Social Darwinist ideas of the superiority of some races and classes over others, it is partly because he found part of his inspiration in Malthus's views on population. Thinkers of both left and right have looked to nature for support of their views. Ideas of climatic or environmental determinism once supported the doctrine that races were 'naturally' superior and inferior to one another. Kropotkin, by contrast, saw in his observations of plants and animals confirmation of his anarchistic notions of mutual aid and co-operation as 'natural'. There may be no values actually inherent in nature (Harvey 1993), but plenty of geographers, political philosophers and others have sought them relentlessly.

It follows therefore that geographical writings on these themes generally bear the marks of their social and historical contexts. The ideas on heredity and environment informing the geographical experiment's origins (including Darwinism, neo-Lamarckianism, eugenics, scientific racism, natural theology and ecology) addressed two principal concerns of the time. The first related to colonialism, for example the right of Europeans to possess other parts of the world, and the problems of acclimatization. Semple (1903) provided a reasoning for American imperialism based on the operation of natural laws. The second focused on domestic issues, such as the control of the working classes and the basis of middle-class hegemony. The geographer Francis Galton, among others, devised statistical tests to demonstrate the inheritance of intelligence, many of which are still used. Griffith Taylor was obliged to leave his native Australia when his deterministic views on the natural limits to settlement and the inadvisability of further white immigration clashed with the government's views. Karl Wittfogel's historical materialism began as a challenge to German geopolitics, but he revised his ideas on hydraulic societies to assault Stalinism. After environmental determinism waned, the predominant geographical view was of nature-as-resource, itself perhaps grounded in Adam Smith's economics. Questions of resource availability and management were central to industrialization at home and abroad, while the problems arising from such exploitation encouraged the adoption of technical and managerial methodologies such as ecosystems. The less dominant view, a more ecological one, received impetus from the environmental and economic disaster of the Dust Bowl (see Glacken, **chapter 13**). It was in the early 1930s, for example, that Aldo Leopold began to sketch out his land ethic.

Modern geographical debates on the environment are fuelled by a sense of impending ecological crisis, but they also owe much to earlier writers such as Leopold. In 'The Land Ethic', he introduces two themes which still excite interest. The first is 'sustainable development', or the idea that the value of the environment can be measured in economic terms. Leopold had worked for the US Forest Service, which was concerned with maintaining nature for profit as much as pleasure. In more recent times, the World Bank and the United Nations and many Western governments have adopted environmental economics as one means of resolving the damage done by environmental exploitation. By cost–benefit analysis, pollution taxes, tradable permits and privatization measures they hope to prevent the over-exploitation of resources which comes about when their users do not pay their real monetary value. By measuring and maintaining the economic worth of the stock of resources from one generation to the next they hope to make economies more sustainable. This monetization of nature does bring it into a realm that most people can understand, which is universal and which is recognizable to powerful corporations and governments (Harvey 1993). But Leopold does not think it will work; no more than 5 per cent of Wisconsin's species have any economic value, for instance.

For this reason Leopold goes on to advocate a land ethic, the other idea which holds interest today (Merchant 1992; Nash 1989). Many of the writers on landscape note the connections between dominant aesthetic views of nature and ownership of it in the form of property (see Daniels, Jackson and Rose, **chapters 18–20**). To own land meant that one could dispose of its features and inhabitants, arrange them at will, and then have that power confirmed by a landscape painting. Jackson links the Renaissance aesthetics of landscape, the Jeffersonian ideal of a small-farmers' democracy, and the federal land subdivisions of the United States government. Against this ethic of possession Leopold advances a land ethic in which the community is enlarged to include non-human life and the land itself. Humans would cease being conquerors of the land, and instead become citizens with it. He comes close to proposing a biocentric view of nature, one in which the human interest is not paramount. This view has spread in the years since his death, and has been taken up by much of the ecological movement (Nash 1989). What this might mean in practice is harder to say. Leopold was a landowner himself. Judging by his writings, he attempted to exercise husbandry over his property, using it for his needs but also trying to learn its deep history, its natural cycles and the inter-connections among its species. While Berger and Williams sought to find the intimate human histories of landscapes as a way of getting past the bourgeois culture of ownership, Leopold looked for kinship-like relations with the plants and animals of his territory.

To many readers of 'The Sand County Almanac', however, his evident pleasure in shooting birds and animals for sport as well as for food seems like hypocrisy. Furthermore, his journals and writings convey an impression of the lone, male individual (sometimes with his dog) getting back to nature. His emphasis upon the etiquette of killing and the exercise of 'virile and primitive' skills could be regarded as a singularly masculine ethic of nature. If this is the case, then his land ethic might only be a partial improvement on outright ownership. Rose (**chapter 20**) argues that the visual pleasure in landscape is a specifically sexual one which has passed largely unacknowledged by geographers. The cold and detached view of science and the aesthetic gaze of painting are equally male pleasures in her argument. The dominant metaphor of Nature in Western thought is feminine (Smith 1984). Semple (**chapter 14**) writes of 'Mother Earth' nurturing and guiding a masculine and childlike humanity, which is one side of this metaphorical resemblance. The other side consists of representations of both nature and women as chaotic, threatening and requiring taming or domination. The correspondence of nature and females in Western and masculine scientific thought results in their dual objectification as either outside or beneath humanity – external and universal. The true social relationships between men and women and between humans and their environment are thereby obscured. But it is not only women who are so placed. There lingers in geographical thought at least a sense that Third World peoples are 'closer to nature'. If this was once underpinned by ideas of racial hierarchy and environmentalism, then today it persists in the neo-Malthusian view that the world's poor are doomed to suffer the brunt of natural disasters.

In a century of modern geography the interest in the relationships between nature and society has been a constant feature, albeit one overshadowed at times by the more analytical and systematic focus on space and region (Parts IV andV). The dominant view of nature has shifted from determinism to resource and then to environment and socially constructed meanings. That modern debates echo earlier ones, as Glacken was aware, suggests that the history of geographical thought contains much that is instructive and challenging. The writings selected here are but a small part of an increasingly important field of knowledge.

References

Bowler, P. J. 1992: *The Fontana history of the environmental sciences*. London.

Brookfield, H. C. 1969: On the environment as perceived. *Progress in Geography* 1, 51–80.

Butzer, K. W. 1976: *Early hydraulic civilization in Egypt: a study in cultural ecology*. Chicago.

Butzer, K. W. 1990: The realm of cultural-human ecology: adaptation and change in historical perspective. In Turner, B. L. II et al., editors, *The Earth as transformed by human action*. Cambridge, pp. 685–701.

Chorley, R. J. 1973: Geography as human ecology. In Chorley, R. J., editor, *Directions in geography*. London, pp. 155–70.

Cosgrove, D. 1990: Environmental thought and action: pre-modern and post-modern. *Transactions of the Institute of British Geographers* 15, 344–58.

Cronon, W. 1983: *Changes in the land: Indians, colonists and the ecology of New England*. New York.

Daniels, S. 1993: *Fields of vision: landscape imagery and national identity in England and the United States*. Cambridge.

Duncan, J. and Duncan, N. 1988: (Re)reading the landscape. *Environment and Planning D: Society and Space* 6, 117–26.

Forde, C. D. 1934: *Habitat, economy and society: a geographical introduction to ethnology*. London.

Haraway, D. 1985: A manifesto for cyborgs: science, technology and socialist feminism in the 1980s. *Socialist Review* 15, 65–107.

Harrison, C. M. and Burgess J. 1994: Social constructions of nature: a case study of conflicts over the development of Rainham Marshes. *Transactions of the Institute of British Geographers* 19, 291–310.

Harvey, D. 1969: *Explanation in geography*. London.

Harvey, D. 1993: The nature of the environment: the dialectics of social and environmental change. In Miliband, R. and Panitch, L., editors, *Socialist register 1993*. London.

Hooson, D. J. M. 1959: Some recent developments in the content and theory of Soviet geography. *Annals of the Association of American Geographers* 49, 73–82.

Kirk, W. 1963: Problems of Geography. *Geography* 48, 357–71.
Langton, J. 1988: The two traditions of geography: historical geography and the study of landscapes. *Geografiska Annaler* 70B, 17–25.
Lewthwaite, G. R. 1966: Environmentalism and determinism: a search for clarification. *Annals of the Association of American Geographers* 56, 1–23.
Livingstone, D. 1992: *The geographical tradition: episodes in the history of a contested enterprise.* Oxford.
Matley, I. M. 1966: The Marxist approach to the geographical environment. *Annals of the Association of American Geographers* 56, 97–111.
Merchant, C. 1992: *Radical ecology: the search for a livable world.* New York.
Nash, R. 1989: *The rights of nature: a history of environmental ethics.* Madison.
Peet, R. 1988: Wittfogel on the nature–society dialectic. *Political Geography Quarterly* 7, 81–3.
Saarinen, T. F. 1966: *Perception of the drought hazard on the Great Plains.* Chicago.
Schama, S. 1995: *Landscape and memory.* New York.
Semple, E. C. 1903: *American history and its geographic conditions.* Boston.
Semple, E. C. 1911: *Influences of the geographic environment.* New York.
Smith, N. 1984: *Uneven development: nature, capital and the production of space.* Oxford.
Smith, N. 1987: 'Academic war over the field of geography': the elimination of geography at Harvard, 1947–1951. *Annals of the Association of American Geographers* 77, 155–72.
Stoddart, D. R. 1967: Organism and ecosystem as geographical models. In Chorley, R. J. and Haggett, P., editors, *Models in Geography.* London, pp. 511–48.
Thomas, K. 1983: *Man and the natural world: changing attitudes in England 1500–1800.* London.
Wittfogel, K. 1956: The hydraulic civilizations. In Thomas, W. L., editor, *Man's role in changing the face of the earth.* Chicago, pp. 152–64.
Worster, D. 1992: *Under western skies: nature and history in the American West.* New York.
Worster, D. 1994: *Nature's economy: a history of ecological ideas.* Cambridge.
Wrigley, E. A. 1987: Geography and demography. Mackinder Centenary Lecture, School of Geography, Oxford University.

Further Reading

On the history of western ideas of nature: Bowler 1992; Clacken 1967: *Traces on the Rhodian Shore* (Berkeley, CA); Thomas 1983; Worster 1994. On ethical and political issues of society and nature: Haraway 1985; Harvey 1993; Merchant 1992; Nash 1989. On sustainable development and environmental economics: Pearce, D., Markandaya, A. and Barbier, E. 1989: *Blueprint for a green economy* (London). A classical example of environmental determinism: Huntington, E. 1907: *The pulse of Asia* (London). On the more spiritual side of geography: Cosgrove 1990; Matless, D. 1991: Nature, the modern and the mystic: tales from the early twentieth century. *Transactions of the Institute of British Geographers* 16, 272–86. On the integration of spatial and ecological themes: Cronon, W. 1991: *Nature's metropolis: Chicago and the great west* (New York); Fitzsimmons, M. 1989: The matter of nature, *Antipode* 21, 106–20. On landscape, compare the approaches found in: Cosgrove, D. 1993: *The Palladian landscape* (Leicester); Daniels 1993; Duncan, J. 1990: *The city as text: the politics of landscape interpretation in the Kandyan kingdom* (Cambridge); Meinig, D. 1969: *Imperial Texas* (Texas). Exchanges on whether human and physical geography should be integrated can be found in: *Transactions of the Institute of British Geographers* 11, 441–67, 1986; *The Canadian Geographer* 38, 291–313, 1994.

13

TRACES ON THE RHODIAN SHORE

Clarence J. Glacken

Clarence J. Glacken (1909–1989) was an American geographer who worked for the US government in the relief of migrant farmworkers fleeing the Dust Bowl to California and in the post-war administration of occupied Korea before taking up an academic post at the University of Berkeley, California (where he joined Carl Sauer). He travelled the world in 1937, including East Asia and the Mediterranean, and had life-long interests in both conservation and the history of ideas. These experiences, described in the Preface, made *Traces on the Rhodian shore* one of the century's finest examples of geographical scholarship. His concern was to uncover the variety and complexity of thinking on nature and culture in the Western tradition and to show how contemporary interests in conservation had long histories. Published in 1967, the volume predated the resurgence of interest in environmentalism in America. In the extract reprinted here Glacken suggests three key questions which informed this history (see Introduction to Part III). There was to be another volume bringing these themes up to date but it was not completed by the time of his death. He describes his life in 'A late arrival in academia' in A. Buttimer, editor, *The practice of geography* (London, 1983).

Source: *Traces on the Rhodian shore: nature and culture in Western thought from ancient times to the end of the eighteenth century*. Berkeley: University of California Press, 1967. Extract from Preface, pp. vii–xii.

In the history of Western thought, men have persistently asked three questions concerning the habitable earth and their relationships to it. Is the earth, which is obviously a fit environment for man and other organic life, a purposefully made creation? Have its climates, its relief, the configuration of its continents influenced the moral and social nature of individuals, and have they had an influence in molding the character and nature of human culture? In his long tenure of the earth, in what manner has man changed it from its hypothetical pristine condition?

From the time of the Greeks to our own, answers to these questions have been and are being given so frequently and so continually that we may restate them in the form of general ideas: the idea of a designed earth; the idea of environmental influence; and the idea of man as ageographic agent. These ideas have come from the general thought and experience of men, but the first owes much to mythology, theology, and philosophy; the second, to pharmaceutical lore, medicine, and weather observation; the third, to the plans, activities, and skills of everyday life such as cultivation, carpentry, and weaving. The first two ideas were expressed frequently in antiquity, the third less so, although it was implicit in many discussions which recognized the obvious fact that men through their arts, sciences, and techniques had changed the physical environment about them.

In the first idea, it is assumed that the planet is designed for man alone, as the highest being of the creation, or for the hierarchy of life with man at the apex. The conception presupposes the earth or certain known parts of it to be a fit environment not only for life but for high civilization.

The second idea originated in medical theory. In essence, conclusions were drawn by comparing various environmental factors such as atmospheric conditions (most often temperature), waters, and geographical situation with the different individuals and peoples characteristic of these environments, the comparisons taking the form of correlations between environments and individual and cultural characteristics. Strictly speaking, it is incorrect to refer to these early speculations as theories of climatic influence, for there was no well-developed theory of weather and climate; it would be more correct to refer to them as theories of airs, waters, and places in the sense in which these terms are used in the Hippocratic corpus. Although environmentalistic ideas arose independently of the argument of divine design, they have been used frequently as part of the design argument in the sense that all life is seen as adapting itself to the purposefully created harmonious conditions.

The third idea was less well formulated in antiquity than were the other two; in fact, its full implications were not realized until Buffon wrote of them, and they were not explored in detail until Marsh published *Man and Nature* in 1864. Like the environmental theory, it could be accommodated within the design argument, for man through his arts and inventions was seen as a partner of God, improving upon and cultivating an earth created for him. Although the idea of environmental influences and that of man as a geographic agent may not be contradictory – many geographers in modern times have tried to work out theories of reciprocal influences – the adoption by thinkers of one of these ideas to the exclusion of the other has been characteristic of both ancient and modern times; it was not perceived, however, until the nineteenth century that the adoption of one in preference to the other led to entirely different emphases. One finds therefore in ancient writers, and in modern ones as well, ideas both of geographic influence and of man's agency in widely scattered parts of their work without any attempt at reconciling them; since Greek times the two ideas have had a curious history, sometimes meeting, sometimes being far apart.

The main theme of this work is that, in Western thought until the end of the eighteenth century, concepts of the relationship of human culture to the natural environment were dominated – but not exclusively so – by these three ideas, sometimes by only one of them, sometimes by two or even the three in combination:

Man, for example, lives on a divinely created earth harmoniously devised for his needs; his physical qualities such as skin and hair, his physical activity and mental stimulation are determined by climate; and he fulfills his God-given mission of finishing the creation, bringing order into nature, which God, in giving him mind, the eye, and the hand, had intended that he do. This group of ideas and certain subsidiary ideas which gathered around them were part of the matrix from which in modern times the social sciences have emerged; the latter of course have deep roots as well in the history of theology, ethics, political and social theory, and philosophy. In Western civilization these three ideas have played an important role in the attempt to understand man, his culture, and the natural environment in which he lives. From the questions they have posed have come the modern study of the geography of man.

One does not easily isolate ideas for study out of that mass of facts, lore, musings, and speculations which we call the thought of an age or of a cultural tradition; one literally tears and wrenches them out. There is nothing disembodied about them, and the cut is not clean. They are living small parts of complex wholes; they are given prominence by the attention of the student.

These simple truths introduce a more difficult problem. Where and when does one stop? Let me give some examples. Everyone recognizes that a striking shift in the attitude toward nature occurred in the Latin Middle Ages during the twelfth and thirteenth centuries. The designed world of that era was more complex than was that of the early Church Fathers, and it bore a lighter load of symbolism. More attention was given to everyday matters and to secondary causes. But in exploring this theme one quickly becomes involved in realism versus nominalism, in modern ideas concerning the origins of science, in changes in religious art such as the portrayal of the Crucifixion, the Ascension, and the Virgin and Child, in the role of the Franciscan order in nature study, in the implications of Etienne Tempier's condemnation of 1277, and in the more realistic approaches to the study of botany – and indeed of the human form. These subjects comprise another work; yet they are suggested by themes in this one.

Galileo – to take a second illustration – pushed aside secondary qualities in his methodology. It proved to be the correct way to make discoveries in theoretical science. This procedure, which could have cleared the way for a purposive control over nature through applied science, contributed less to the development of natural history, whose students found it hard to simplify the variety and individuality of life which were clearly apparent to the senses. Smells and colors were important. In the eighteenth century Buffon in his criticism of Descartes realized the limitations of abstract thought. Natural history requires description, study of detail, of color, smell, environmental changes, of the influence of man whether his acts are or are not purposive. Modern ecology and conservation also need this kind of examination, for many of their roots lie in the old natural history. So we have another book contrasting the history of methodology in physics with that of natural history and biology, noting the obvious fact that teleology continued as a working scientific principle far longer in the latter than it did in physics. We should contrast also the purposive control over nature through applied science with the unlooked for, perhaps unconscious and unperceived, changes that men perpetually make in their surroundings.

Large related bodies of thought thus appear, at first like distant riders stirring up modest dust clouds, who, when they arrive, reproach one for his slowness in recognizing their numbers, strength, and vitality. One thinks of the history of ideas concerned with gardens, sacred landscapes, and nature symbolism.

Only rarely can one look at a landscape modified in some way by man and say with assurance that what one sees embodies and illustrates an attitude toward nature and man's place in it. Landscape painting presents similar difficulties. What indeed are we to make of Pieter Bruegel the Elder's *Fall of Icarus*? An exception, in my opinion, is the history of the garden, whether it is English, Chinese, or Italian. In gardens, one can almost see the embodiment of ideas in landscapes. Is art imitating nature, or is nature opposed to art? Is the garden like a lesson in geometry, are its lawns well raked, or does it suggest soft rolling meadows? And what does it say about the attitudes men should have not only to their surroundings but to themselves? But this theme would require yet another book; one can see the possibilities in the writings of Siren and in Clifford's *A History of Garden Design*.

In the world as a whole, there are few more inviting themes for the historian of attitudes toward the earth than the role of the sacred. Today the best illustrations come from non-Western cultures, but the history of Western civilization is rich in them too. One thinks of Scully's study of Greek sacred architecture and its landscapes, the possible origins of Roman centuriation in cosmic speculation, the celestial city and the heavenly Jerusalem, cathedral siting in the Middle Ages, sacred groves, and nature symbolism. Indeed, gardens, sacred landscapes, religious and esthetic attitudes toward environmental change by man, entice one into studies with profound human meaning which are not easily exhausted.

There are many illustrations in this work of that separation between man and nature which occurs so frequently in Western thought, and conversely of the union of the two as parts of live and indivisible wholes. The dichotomy has plagued the history of geographical thought (for example, the distinction, which many would now abandon, between the natural and the cultural landscape) and contemporary ecological discussions concerned with man's disturbance of the balance of nature. Essays confidently begin with assertions that man is part of nature – how could he be otherwise? – but their argument makes sense and gains cogency only when human cultures are set off from the rest of natural phenomena. I cannot claim to have clarified this difficult subject. In Western thought, it is too involved in other histories of ideas – in the philosophy of man, in theology, in the problem of physical and moral evil.

Did the distinction between man and nature begin in primordial times when man saw himself, so clearly like the animals in many respects, but able nevertheless to assert his will over some of them? Was it enshrined in Western thought by the Jewish teaching that man, sinful and wicked as he is, is part of the creation but distinct from it too because he is the one living being created in the image of God? Was it in the ancient consciousness of artisanship that men felt themselves superior to other living and nonliving matter? Prometheus was considered to be a supreme craftsman and was worshipped as such, particularly in Attica.

Is another phase of the problem the distinction between the ways in which men have lived their lives, some in the country, some in the town or the city, the former closely identified with what is natural, the latter with the artificial, the creation of man? Did not Varro say that "divine nature made the country, but man's skill the towns," illustrating the old distinction between nature and art? Did this deep-lying conviction gain added strength and incontrovertible proof through the theoretical accomplishments of seventeenth century science and the practical mastery to which they led, awareness so vividly expressed in the writings of Leibniz? What the Arab scientists, the medieval alchemists, Bacon, Paracelsus, Descartes, Leibniz himself had hoped for was now being realized: man had reached the point at which he could be confident of his progressive ability to control nature.

My first awareness of the existence and importance of the history of ideas came to me as a young Berkeley undergraduate when, over thirty years ago, I took Professor Teggart's course on the Idea of Progress. Today I still remember these lectures vividly and possess the classroom notes. Frederick J. Teggart was a man of enormous learning and a superlative lecturer. The *Prolegomena to History*, the *Processes of History*, the *Theory of History*, his review of Spengler's *Decline of the West*, opened up fields of scholarship I scarcely knew existed.

To the reader it must seem that the present work is exclusively a product of the library. Actually, the early stimulus to study these ideas came also from personal experience and from observations which pointed to the role of ideas and values in understanding the relationships of culture to the environment. During the depression years, as I worked with resident and transient families on relief, with migratory farm workers who had come from the Dust Bowl, I became aware – as did countless thousands of others – of the interrelationships existing between the Depression, soil erosion, and the vast migration to California.

In 1937 I spent eleven months traveling in many parts of the world. The yellow dust clouds high over Peking, the dredging of pond mud along the Yangtze, the monkeys swinging from tree to tree at Angkor Vat, a primitive water-lifting apparatus near Cairo, the Mediterranean promenade, the goat curd and the carob of Cyprus, the site of Athens and the dryness of Greece, the shrubs, the coves, the hamlets, and the deforestation of the Eastern Mediterranean, the shepherds of the Caucasus, the swinging swords of Central Asians in the markets of Ordzhonikidze, the quiet farms of Swedish Skåne – these and many other observations made me realize as part of my being the commonplace truth that there is a great diversity both of human cultures and of the physical environments in which they live. It is the difference between knowing about the midnight sun and spending a summer night on the Arctic circle. One is continually asking questions about the circumstances which stimulate human creativity, about the effect of religious belief, about the custom and tradition which men have soaked into their soils. And although I have used abstract words like "man" and "nature" as a convenience, it is really human culture, natural history, the relief of the land that I mean.

Phrases like "man and nature" are useful as titles, as a shorthand to express far more complex sets of ideas.

In 1951, living in three small Okinawan villages and studying their way of life, I could see the profound importance of the Chinese family system, altered of course by the Japanese and the Okinawans themselves, and the influence of the system of inheritance on the use and the appearance of the land. In such circumstances, it seems natural to see differences in traditions concerning culture and the environment, to see the ideas developed in Western civilization merely as a few of many possibilities.

Finally during a year spent in Norway in 1957, visiting its old towns, especially those of the Gudbrandsdal, its farms, an occasional *seter*, and reading about the history of its forests, I saw more clearly and vividly how deep is the European interest in the history of landscapes, the Norwegian interest in the history of farms, the *seter*, place names – in all aspects of rural life. The water-driven saws from the eighteenth century at the open-air museums at Bygdøy in Oslo and at Elverum on the Glomma made me read the literature on environmental change in the Middle Ages with new attentiveness because this important invention was first illustrated in the *Album* of Villard de Honnecourt in the thirteenth century.

In many places one can see evidences of a relationship between religious attitudes towards the earth and the appearance of a landscape, of limitations imposed by a local environment, of the historical depth of changes made in the physical environment by human culture.

14

INFLUENCES OF GEOGRAPHIC ENVIRONMENT

Ellen C. Semple

Ellen C. Semple (1863–1932) was the foremost female geographer of her time and a leading exponent of environmental determinism. Both *Influences* and an earlier book, *American history and its geographic conditions* (1903) were the result of her admiration for the work of Friedrich Ratzel (**chapter 32**), whose lectures she attended at Leipzig in 1891. She describes her book as more than a translation of his ideas for the 'Anglo-Celtic mind'. It was also an extension and confirmation of his geographical laws by the inclusion of extensive evidence based on her own travels and wide reading. Its more than 600 pages include chapters on general geographical relationships, geographical factors such as movement, location and boundary, and then chapters dedicated to certain kinds of locations such as coasts, oceans, islands and mountains. For each topic she sketches out a general relationship between the physical environment and human culture, including ideas and race characteristics, drawing on both ancient and modern history for supporting evidence. According to J. K. Wright [Miss Semple's 'Influences of geographic environment': notes towards a biobibliography, *Geographical Review* 52, 346–61], the book was very well received at first and only attacked in the 1920s, mainly by the French historian, Lucien Febvre. Her views may also be contrasted with those of the anthropologist, Franz Boas (**chapter 9**). The notoriety of environmental determinism perhaps obscured the fact that the book does contain a wealth of interesting geographical observation, as well as untested and untestable assertions.

Source: *Influences of geographic environment on the basis of Ratzel's system of anthropogeographie*. New York: Henry Holt, 1911. Extract from pp. vii (the Preface) and chapter 1, 1–32.

The writer's own method of research has been to compare typical peoples of all races and all stages of cultural development, living under similar geographic conditions. If these peoples of different ethnic stocks but similar environments manifested similar or related social, economic or historical development, it was reasonable to infer that such similarities were due to environment and not to race.

Thus, by extensive comparison, the race factor in these problems of two unknown quantities was eliminated for certain large classes of social and historical phenomena.

The writer, moreover, has purposely avoided definitions, formulas, and the enunciation of hard-and-fast rules; and has refrained from any effort to delimit the field or define the relation of this new science of anthropo-geography to the older sciences. It is unwise to put tight clothes on a growing child. The eventual form and scope of the science, the definition and organization of its material must evolve gradually, after long years and many efforts of many workers in the field. The eternal flux of Nature runs through anthropo-geography, and warns against precipitate or rigid conclusions. But its laws are none the less well founded because they do not lend themselves to mathematical finality of statement. For this reason the writer speaks of geographic factors and influences, shuns the word geographic determinant, and speaks with extreme caution of geographic control. . . .

Man is a product of the earth's surface. This means not merely that he is a child of the earth, dust of her dust; but that the earth has mothered him, fed him, set him tasks, directed his thoughts, confronted him with difficulties that have strengthened his body and sharpened his wits, given him his problems of navigation or irrigation, and at the same time whispered hints for their solution. She has entered into his bone and tissue, into his mind and soul. On the mountains she has given him leg muscles of iron to climb the slope; along the coast she has left these weak and flabby, but given him instead vigorous development of chest and arm to handle his paddle or oar. In the river valley she attaches him to the fertile soil, circumscribes his ideas and ambitions by a dull round of calm, exacting duties, narrows his outlook to the cramped horizon of his farm. Up on the wind-swept plateaus, in the boundless stretch of the grasslands and the waterless tracts of the desert, where he roams with his flocks from pasture to pasture and oasis to oasis, where life knows much hardship but escapes the grind of drudgery, where the watching of grazing herd gives him leisure for contemplation, and the wide-ranging life a big horizon, his ideas take on a certain gigantic simplicity; religion becomes monotheism, God becomes one, unrivalled like the sand of the desert and the grass of the steppe, stretching on and on without break or change. Chewing over and over the cud of his simple belief as the one food of his unfed mind, his faith becomes fanaticism; his big spacial ideas, born of that ceaseless regular wandering, outgrow the land that bred them and bear their legitimate fruit in wide imperial conquests.

Man can no more be scientifically studied apart from the ground which he tills, or the lands over which he travels, or the seas over which he trades, than polar bear or desert cactus can be understood apart from its habitat. Man's relations to his environment are infinitely more numerous and complex than those of the most highly organized plant or animal. So complex are they that they constitute a legitimate and necessary object of special study. The investigation which they receive in anthropology, ethnology, sociology, and history is piecemeal and partial, limited as to the race, cultural development, epoch, country or variety of geographic conditions taken into account. Hence all these sciences, together with history so far as history undertakes to explain the causes of events, fail to reach a satisfactory solution of their problems largely because the geographic factor which enters into them all has not been thoroughly analyzed. Man has been so noisy about the way he has "conquered Nature" and Nature has been so silent in her persistent influence over man, that the geographic factor in the equation of human development has been overlooked.

In every problem of history there are two main factors, variously stated as heredity and environment, man and his geographic conditions, the internal forces of race and the external forces of habitat. Now the geographic element in the long history of human development has been operating strongly and operating persistently. Herein lies its importance. It is a stable force. It never sleeps. This natural environment, this physical basis of history, is for all intents and purposes immutable in comparison with the other factor in the problem – shifting, plastic, progressive, retrogressive man.

History tends to repeat itself largely owing to this steady, unchanging geographic element. If the ancient Roman consul in far-away Britain often assumed an independence of action and initiative unknown in the provincial governors of Gaul, and if, centuries later, Roman Catholicism in England maintained a similar independence towards the Holy See, both facts have their cause in the remoteness of Britain from the center of political or ecclesiastical power in Rome. If the independence of the Roman consul in Britain was duplicated later by the attitude of the Thirteen Colonies toward England, and again within the young Republic by the headstrong self-reliance, impatient of government authority, which characterized the early Trans-Allegheny commonwealths in their aggressive Indian policy, and led them to make war and conclude treaties for the cession of land like sovereign states; and if this attitude of independence in the over-mountain men reappeared in a spirit of political defection looking toward secession from the Union and a new combination with their British neighbor on the Great Lakes or the Spanish beyond the Mississippi, these are all the identical effects of geographical remoteness, made yet more remote by barriers of mountain and sea. This is the long reach which weakens the arm of authority, no matter what the race or country or epoch.

As with geographical remoteness, so it is with geographical proximity. The history of the Greek peninsula and the Greek people, because of their location at the threshold of the Orient, has contained a constantly recurring Asiatic element. This comes out most often as a note of warning; like the *motif* of Ortrud in the opera of "Lohengrin," it mingles ominously in every chorus of Hellenic enterprise or pæan of Hellenic victory, and finally swells into a national dirge at the Turkish conquest of the peninsula. It comes out in the legendary history of the Argonautic Expedition and the Trojan War; in the arrival of Phœnician Cadmus and Phrygian Pelops in Grecian lands; in the appearance of Tyrian ships on the coast of the Peloponnesus, where they gather the purple-yielding murex and kidnap Greek women. It appears more conspicuously in the Asiatic sources of Greek culture; more dramatically in the Persian Wars, in the retreat of Xenophon's Ten Thousand, in Alexander's conquest of Asia, and Hellenic domination of Asiatic trade through Syria to the Mediterranean. . . .

If the factor is not one of geographical location, but a natural barrier, such as a mountain system or a desert, its effect is just as persistent. . . . The Alps long retarded Roman expansion into central Europe, just as they delayed and obstructed the southward advance of the northern barbarians. Only through the partial breaches in the wall known as passes did the Alps admit small, divided bodies of the invaders, like the Cimbri and Teutons, who arrived, therefore, with weakened power and at intervals, so that the Roman forces had time to gather their strength between successive attacks, and thus prolonged the life of the declining empire. So in the Middle Ages, the Alpine barrier facilitated the resistance of Italy to the German emperors, trying to enforce their claim upon this ancient seat of the Holy Roman Empire.

It was by river-worn valleys leading to passes in the ridge that Etruscan trader, Roman legion, barbarian horde, and German army crossed the Alpine ranges. Today, well-made highways and railroads converge upon these valley paths and summit portals, and going is easier; but the Alps still collect their toll, now in added tons of coal consumed by engines and in higher freight rates, instead of the ancient imposts of physical exhaustion paid by pack animal and heavily accoutred soldier. Formerly these mountains barred the weak and timid; to-day they bar the poor, and forbid transit to all merchandise of large bulk and small value which can not pay the heavy transportation charges. . . .

As the surface of the earth presents obstacles, so it offers channels for the easy movement of humanity, grooves whose direction determines the destination of aimless, unplanned migrations, and whose termini become, therefore, regions of historical importance. Along these nature-made highways history repeats itself. The maritime plain of Palestine has been an established route of commerce and war from the time of Sennacherib to Napoleon.[1] The Danube Valley has admitted to central Europe a long list of barbarian invaders, covering the period from Attila the Hun to the Turkish besiegers of Vienna in 1683. The history of the Danube Valley has been one of warring throngs, of shifting political frontiers, and unassimilated races; but as the river is a great natural highway, every neighboring state wants to front upon it and strives to secure it as a boundary.

The movements of peoples constantly recur to these old grooves. The unmarked path of the voyageur's canoe, bringing out pelts from Lake Superior to the fur market at Montreal, is followed to-day by whaleback steamers with their cargoes of Manitoba wheat. To-day the Mohawk depression through the northern Appalachians diverts some of Canada's trade from the Great Lakes to the Hudson, just as in the seventeenth century it enabled the Dutch at New Amsterdam and later the English at Albany to tap the fur trade of Canada's frozen forests. Formerly a line of stream and portage, it carries now the Erie Canal and New York Central Railroad.[2] Similarly the narrow level belt of land extending from the mouth of the

[1] George Adam Smith, Historical Geography of the Holy Land, pp. 149–157. New York, 1897.

[2] A. P. Brigham, Geographic Influences in American History, Chap. I. Boston, 1903.

Hudson to the eastern elbow of the lower Delaware, defining the outer margin of the rough hill country of northern New Jersey and the inner margin of the smooth coastal plain, has been from savage days such a natural thoroughfare. Here ran the trail of the Lenni-Lenapi Indians; a little later, the old Dutch road between New Amsterdam and the Delaware trading-posts; yet later the King's Highway from New York to Philadelphia. In 1838 it became the route of the Delaware and Raritan Canal, and more recently of the Pennsylvania Railroad between New York and Philadelphia.[3] . . .

Geographical environment, through the persistence of its influence, acquires peculiar significance. Its effect is not restricted to a given historical event or epoch, but, except when temporarily met by some strong counteracting force, tends to make itself felt under varying guise in all succeeding history. It is the permanent element in the shifting fate of races. Islands show certain fundamental points of agreement which can be distinguished in the economic, ethnic and historical development of England, Japan, Melanesian Fiji, Polynesian New Zealand, and pre-historic Crete. The great belt of deserts and steppes extending across the Old World gives us a vast territory of rare historical uniformity. From time immemorial they have borne and bred tribes of wandering herdsmen; they have sent out the invading hordes who, in successive waves of conquest, have overwhelmed the neighboring river lowlands of Eurasia and Africa. They have given birth in turn to Scythians, Indo-Aryans, Avars, Huns, Saracens, Tartars and Turks, as to the Tuareg tribes of the Sahara, the Sudanese and Bantu folk of the African grasslands. But whether these various peoples have been Negroes, Hamites, Semites, Indo-Europeans or Mongolians, they have always been pastoral nomads. The description given by Herodotus of the ancient Scythians is applicable in its main features to the Kirghis and Kalmuck who inhabit the Caspian plains to-day. The environment of this dry grassland operates now to produce the same mode of life and social organization as it did 2,400 years ago; stamps the cavalry tribes of Cossacks as it did the mounted Huns, energizes its sons by its dry bracing air, toughens them by its harsh conditions of life, organizes them into a mobilized army, always moving with its pastoral commissariat. Then when population presses too hard upon the meager sources of subsistence, when a summer drought burns the pastures and dries up the water-holes, it sends them forth on a mission of conquest, to seek abundance in the better watered lands of their agricultural neighbors. Again and again the productive valleys of the Hoangho, Indus, Ganges, Tigris and Euphrates, Nile, Volga, Dnieper and Danube have been brought into subjection by the imperious nomads of arid Asia, just as the "hoe-people" of the Niger and upper Nile have so often been conquered by the herdsmen of the African grasslands. Thus, regardless of race or epoch – Hyksos or Kaffir – history tends to repeat itself in these rainless tracts, and involves the better watered districts along their borders when the vast tribal movements extend into these peripheral lands.

[3] R. H. Whitbeck, Geographic Influences in the Development of New Jersey, *Journal of Geography*, Vol. V, No. 6. January, 1908.

Climatic influences are persistent, often obdurate in their control. Arid regions permit agriculture and sedentary life only through irrigation. The economic prosperity of Egypt to-day depends as completely upon the distribution of the Nile waters as in the days of the Pharaohs. The mantle of the ancient Egyptian priest has fallen upon the modern British engineer. Arctic explorers have succeeded only by imitating the life of the Eskimos, adopting their clothes, food, fuel, dwellings, and mode of travel. Intense cold has checked both native and Russian development over that major portion of Siberia lying north of the mean annual isothern of 0 degree C. (32 degrees F.); and it has had a like effect in the corresponding part of Canada. It allows these sub-arctic lands scant resources and a population of less than two to the square mile. Even with the intrusion of white colonial peoples, it perpetuates the savage economy of the native hunting tribes, and makes the fur trader their modern exploiter, whether he be the Cossack tribute-gatherer of the lower Lena River, or the factor of the Hudson Bay Company. The assimilation tends to be ethnic as well as economic, because the severity of the climate excludes the white woman. In the same way the Tropics are a vast melting-pot. The debilitating effects of heat and humidity, aided by tropical diseases, soon reduce intruding peoples to the dead level of economic inefficiency characteristic of the native races. These, as the fittest, survive and tend to absorb the new-comers, pointing to hybridization as the simplest solution of the problem of tropical colonization.

The more the comparative method is applied to the study of history – and this includes a comparison not only of different countries, but also of successive epochs in the same country – the more apparent becomes the influence of the soil in which humanity is rooted, the more permanent and necessary is that influence seen to be. Geography's claim to make scientific investigation of the physical conditions of historical events is then vindicated. "Which was there first, geography or history?" asks Kant. And then comes his answer: "Geography lies at the basis of history." The two are inseparable. History takes for its field of investigation human events in various periods of time; anthropo-geography studies existence in various regions of terrestrial space. But all historical development takes place on the earth's surface, and therefore is more or less molded by its geographic setting. Geography, to reach accurate conclusions, must compare the operation of its factors in different historical periods and at different stages of cultural development. It therefore regards history in no small part as a succession of geographical factors embodied in events. Back of Massachusetts' passionate abolition movement, it sees the granite soil and boulder-strewn fields of New England; back of the South's long fight for the maintenance of slavery, it sees the rich plantations of tidewater Virginia and the teeming fertility of the Mississippi bottom lands. This is the significance of Herder's saying that "history is geography set into motion." What is to-day a fact of geography becomes to-morrow a factor of history. The two sciences cannot be held apart without doing violence to both, without dismembering what is a natural, vital whole. All historical problems ought to be studied geographically and all geographic problems must be studied historically. Every map has its date. Those in the Statistical Atlas of the United States showing the distribution of population from 1790 to 1890 embody a mass of history as well as of geography. A map of France or the Russian Empire has a long historical perspective; and on the other hand, without that map no change of ethnic or political boundary, no modification in routes of communication, no system of frontier defences or of colonization, no scheme of territorial aggrandizement can be understood.

The study of physical environment as a factor in history was unfortunately brought into disrepute by extravagant and ill-founded generalization, before it became the object of investigation according to modern scientific methods. And even to-day principles advanced in the name of anthropo-geography are often superficial, inaccurate, based upon a body of data too limited as to space and time, or couched in terms of unqualified statement which exposes them to criticism or refutation. Investigators in this field, moreover, are prone to get a squint in their eye that makes them see one geographic factor to the exclusion of the rest; whereas it belongs to the very nature of physical environment to combine a whole group of influences, working all at the same time under the law of the resolution of forces. In this plexus of influences, some operate in one direction and some in another; now one loses its beneficent effect like a medicine long used or a garment outgrown; another waxes in power, reinforced by a new geographic factor which has been released from dormancy by the expansion of the known world, or the progress of invention and of human development.

These complex geographic influences cannot be analyzed and their strength estimated except from the standpoint of evolution. That is one reason these half-baked geographic principles rest heavy on our mental digestion. They have been formulated without reference to the all-important fact that the geographical relations of man, like his social and political organization, are subject to the law of development. Just as the embryo state found in the primitive Saxon tribe has passed through many phases in attaining the political character of the present British Empire, so every stage in this maturing growth has been accompanied or even preceded by a steady evolution of the geographic relations of the English people.

Owing to the evolution of geographic relations, the physical environment favorable to one stage of development may be adverse to another, and *vice versa*. For instance, a small, isolated and protected habitat, like that of Egypt, Phœnicia, Crete and Greece, encourages the birth and precocious growth of civilization; but later it may cramp progress, and lend the stamp of arrested development to a people who were once the model for all their little world. Open and wind-swept Russia, lacking these small, warm nurseries where Nature could cuddle her children, has bred upon its boundless plains a massive, untutored, homogeneous folk, fed upon the crumbs of culture that have fallen from the richer tables of Europe. But that item of area is a variable quantity in the equation. It changes its character at a higher stage of cultural development. Consequently, when the Muscovite people, instructed by the example of western Europe, shall have grown up intellectually, economically and politically to their big territory, its area will become a great national asset. Russia will come into its own, heir to a long-withheld inheritance.

Many of its previous geographic disadvantages will vanish, like the diseases of childhood, while its massive size will dwarf many previous advantages of its European neighbors. . . .

Meanwhile, local geographic advantages in the old basins remain the same, although they are dwarfed by the development of relatively greater advantages elsewhere. The broken coastline, limited area and favorable position of Greece make its people to-day a nation of seamen, and enable them to absorb by their considerable merchant fleet a great part of the trade of the eastern Mediterranean,[10] just as they did in the days of Pericles; but that youthful Aegean world which once constituted so large a part of the *oikoumene,* has shrunken to a modest province, and its highways to local paths. The coast cities of northern Germany still maintain a large commerce in the Baltic, but no longer hold the pre-eminence of the old Hanse Towns. The glory of the Venetian Adriatic is gone; but that the sea has still a local significance is proven by the vast sums spent by Austria and Hungary on their hand-made harbors of Trieste and Fiume.[11] The analytical geographer, therefore, while studying a given combination of geographic forces, must be prepared for a momentous readjustment and a new interplay after any marked turning point in the economic, cultural, or world relations of a people.

Skepticism as to the effect of geographic conditions upon human development is apparently justifiable, owing to the multiplicity of the underlying causes and the difficulty of distinguishing between stronger and weaker factors on the one hand, as between permanent and temporary effects on the other. We see the result, but find it difficult to state the equation producing this result. But the important thing is to avoid seizing upon one or two conspicuous geographic elements in the problem and ignoring the rest. The physical environment of a people consists of all the natural conditions to which they have been subjected, not merely a part. Geography admits no single blanket theory. The slow historical development of the Russian folk has been due to many geographic causes – to excess of cold and deficiency of rain, an outskirt location on the Asiatic border of Europe exposed to the attacks of nomadic hordes, a meager and, for the most part, ice-bound coast which was slowly acquired, an undiversified surface, a lack of segregated regions where an infant civilization might be cradled, and a vast area of unfenced plains wherein the national energies spread out thin and dissipated themselves. The better Baltic and Black Sea coasts, the fertility of its Ukraine soil, and location next to wide-awake Germany along the western frontier have helped to accelerate progress, but the slow-moving body carried too heavy a drag. . . .

Every country forms an independent whole, and as such finds its national history influenced by its local climate, soil, relief, its location whether inland or maritime, its river highways, and its boundaries of mountain, sea, or desert. But it is also a link in a great chain of lands, and therefore may feel a shock or vibration imparted at the remotest end. The gradual desiccation of western Asia which took

10 Hugh Robert Mill, International Geography, p. 347. New York, 1902.

11 Joseph Partsch, Central Europe, pp. 228–230. London, 1903.

a fresh start about 2,000 years ago caused that great exodus and displacement of peoples known as the *Völkerwanderung*, and thus contributed to the downfall of Rome; it was one factor in the Saxon conquest of Britain and the final peopling of central Europe. The impact of the Turkish hordes hurling themselves against the defenses of Constantinople in 1453 was felt only forty years afterward by the far-off shores of savage America. Earlier still it reached England as the revival of learning, and it gave Portugal a shock which started its navigators towards the Cape of Good Hope in their search for a sea route to India. The history of South Africa is intimately connected with the Isthmus of Suez. It owes its Portuguese, Dutch, and English populations to that barrier on the Mediterranean pathway to the Orient; its importance as a way station on the outside route to India fluctuates with every crisis in the history of Suez.

The geographic factors in history appear now as conspicuous direct effects of environment, such as the forest warfare of the American Indian or the irrigation works of the Pueblo tribes, now as a group of indirect effects, operating through the economic, social and political activities of a people. These remoter secondary results are often of supreme importance; they are the ones which give the final stamp to the national temperament and character, and yet in them the causal connection between environment and development is far from obvious. They have, therefore, presented pitfalls to the precipitate theorizer. He has either interpreted them as the direct effect of some geographic cause from which they were wholly divorced and thus arrived at conclusions which further investigation failed to sustain; or seeing no direct and obvious connection, he has denied the possibility of a generalization.

Montesquieu ascribes the immutability of religion, manners, custom and laws in India and other Oriental countries to their warm climate.[17] Buckle attributes a highly wrought imagination and gross superstition to all people, like those of India, living in the presence of great mountains and vast plains, knowing Nature only in its overpowering aspects, which excite the fancy and paralyze reason. He finds, on the other hand, an early predominance of reason in the inhabitants of a country like ancient Greece, where natural features are on a small scale, more comprehensible, nearer the measure of man himself.[18] The scientific geographer, grown suspicious of the omnipotence of climate and cautious of predicating immediate psychological effects which are easy to assert but difficult to prove, approaches the problem more indirectly and reaches a different solution. He finds that geographic conditions have condemned India to isolation. On the land side, a great sweep of high mountains has restricted intercourse with the interior; on the sea side, the deltaic swamps of the Indus and Ganges Rivers and an unbroken shoreline, backed by mountains on the west of the peninsula and by coastal marshes and lagoons on the east, have combined to reduce its accessibility from the ocean. The effect of such isolation is ignorance, superstition, and the early

[17] Montesquieu, Spirit of the Laws, Book XIV, chap. IV.
[18] Henry Buckle, History of Civilization in England, Vol. I, pp. 86–106.

crystallization of thought and custom. Ignorance involves the lack of material for comparison, hence a restriction of the higher reasoning processes, and an unscientific attitude of mind which gives imagination free play. In contrast, the accessibility of Greece and its focal location in the ancient world made it an intellectual clearing-house for the eastern Mediterranean. The general information gathered there afforded material for wide comparison. It fed the brilliant reason of the Athenian philosopher and the trained imagination which produced the masterpieces of Greek art and literature.

Heinrich von Treitschke, in his recent "Politik," imitates the direct inference of Buckle when he ascribes the absence of artistic and poetic development in Switzerland and the Alpine lands to the overwhelming aspect of nature there, its majestic sublimity which paralyzes the mind.[19] He reinforces his position by the fact that, by contrast, the lower mountains and hill country of Swabia, Franconia and Thuringia, where nature is gentler, stimulating, appealing, and not overpowering, have produced many poets and artists. The facts are incontestable. They reappear in France in the geographical distribution of the awards made by the Paris *Salon* of 1896. Judged by these awards, the rough highlands of Savoy, Alpine Provence, the massive eastern Pyrenees, and the Auvergne Plateau, together with the barren peninsula of Brittany, are singularly lacking in artistic instinct, while art flourishes in all the river lowlands of France. Moreover, French men of letters, by the distribution of their birthplaces, are essentially products of fluvial valleys and plains, rarely of upland and mountain.[20]

This contrast has been ascribed to a fundamental ethnic distinction between the Teutonic population of the lowlands and the Alpine or Celtic stock which survives in the isolation of highland and peninsula, thus making talent an attribute of race. But the Po Valley of northern Italy, whose population contains a strong infusion of this supposedly stultifying Alpine blood, and the neighboring lowlands and hill country of Tuscany show an enormous preponderance of intellectual and artistic power over the highlands of the peninsula.[21] Hence the same contrast appears among different races under like geographic conditions. Moreover, in France other social phenomena, such as suicide, divorce, decreasing birth-rate, and radicalism in politics, show this same startling parallelism of geographic distribution,[22] and these cannot be attributed to the stimulating or depressing effect of natural scenery upon the human mind.

Mountain regions discourage the budding of genius because they are areas of isolation, confinement, remote from the great currents of men and ideas that move along the river valleys. They are regions of much labor and little leisure, of poverty to-day and anxiety for the morrow, of toil-cramped hands and toil-dulled brains.

[19] Heinrich von Treitschke, *Politik*, Vol. I, p. 225. Leipzig, 1897. This whole chapter on *Land and Leute* is suggestive.

[20] W. Z. Ripley, Races of Europe, pp. 524–525. New York, 1899.

[21] *Ibid.*, 526.

[22] *Ibid*, 517–520, 533–536.

In the fertile alluvial plains are wealth, leisure, contact with many minds, large urban centers where commodities and ideas are exchanged. The two contrasted environments produce directly certain economic and social results, which, in turn, become the causes of secondary intellectual and artistic effects. The low mountains of central Germany which von Treitschke cites as homes of poets and artists, owing to abundant and varied mineral wealth, are the seats of active industries and dense populations,[23] while their low reliefs present no serious obstacle to the numerous highways across them. They, therefore, afford all conditions for culture.

Let us take a different example. The rapid modification in physical and mental constitution of the English transplanted to North America, South Africa, Australia and New Zealand has been the result of several geographic causes working through the economic and social media; but it has been ascribed by Darwin and others to the effect of climate. The prevailing energy and initiative of colonists have been explained by the stimulating atmosphere of their new homes. Even Natal has not escaped this soft impeachment. But the enterprise of colonials has cropped out under almost every condition of heat and cold, aridity and humidity, of a habitat at sea-level and on high plateau. This blanket theory of climate cannot, therefore, cover the case. Careful analysis supersedes it by a whole group of geographic factors working directly and indirectly. The first of these was the dividing ocean which, prior to the introduction of cheap ocean transportation and bustling steerage agents, made a basis of artificial selection. Then it was the man of abundant energy who, cramped by the narrow environment of a Norwegian farm or Irish bog, came over to America to take up a quarter-section of prairie land or rise to the eminence of Boston police sergeant. The Scotch immigrants in America who fought in the Civil War were nearly two inches taller than the average in the home country.[24] But the ocean barrier culled superior qualities of mind and character also – independence of political and religious conviction, and the courage of those convictions, whether found in royalist or Puritan, Huguenot or English Catholic.

Such colonists in a remote country were necessarily few and could not be readily reinforced from home. Their new and isolated geographical environment favored variation. Heredity passed on the characteristics of a small, highly selected group. The race was kept pure from intermixture with the aborigines of the country, owing to the social and cultural abyss which separated them, and to the steady withdrawal of the natives before the advance of the whites. The homogeneity of island peoples seems to indicate that individual variations are in time communicated by heredity to a whole population under conditions of isolation; and in this way modifications due to artificial selection and a changed environment become widely spread.

Nor is this all. The modified type soon becomes established, because the abundance of land at the disposal of the colonists and the consequent better conditions of living encourage a rapid increase of population. A second geographic factor of

23 Joseph Partsch, Central Europe, pp. 256–257, 268–271. London, 1903.

24 W. Z. Ripley, Races of Europe, p. 89. New York, 1899.

mere area here begins to operate. Ease in gaining subsistence, the greater independence of the individual and the family, emancipation from carking care, the hopeful attitude of mind engendered by the consciousness of an almost unlimited opportunity and capacity for expansion, the expectation of large returns upon labor, and, finally, the profound influence of this hopefulness upon the national character, all combined, produce a social rejuvenation of the race. New conditions present new problems which call for prompt and original solution, make a demand upon the ingenuity and resourcefulness of the individual, and therefore work to the same end as his previous removal from the paralyzing effect of custom in the old home country. Activity is youth and sluggishness or paralysis is age. Hence the energy, initiative, adaptability, and receptivity to new ideas – all youthful qualities – which characterize the Anglo-Saxon American as well as the English Africander, can be traced back to the stimulating influences, not of a bracing or variable climate, but of the abundant opportunities offered by a great, rich, unexploited country. Variation under new natural conditions, when safe-guarded by isolation, tends to produce modification of the colonial type; this is the direct effect of a changed environment. But the new economic and social activities of a transplanted people become the vehicle of a mass of indirect geographic influences which contribute to the differentiation of the national character.

The tendency to overlook such links between conspicuous effects and their remote, less evident geographic causes has been common in geographic investigation. This direct rather than indirect approach to the heart of the problem has led to false inferences or to the assumption that reliable conclusions were impossible. Environment influences the higher, mental life of a people chiefly through the medium of their economic and social life; hence its ultimate effects should be traced through the latter back to the underlying cause. But rarely has this been done. Even so astute a geographer as Strabo, though he recognizes the influence of geographic isolation in differentiating dialects and customs in Greece,[25] ascribes some national characteristics to the nature of the country, especially to its climate, and the others to education and institutions. He thinks that the nature of their respective lands had nothing to do with making the Athenians cultured, the Spartans and Thebans ignorant; that the predilection for natural science in Babylonia and Egypt was not a result of environment but of the institutions and education of those countries.[26] But here arise the questions, how far custom and education in their turn depend upon environment; to what degree natural conditions, molding economic and political development, may through them fundamentally affect social customs, education, culture, and the dominant intellectual aptitudes of a people. It is not difficult to see, back of the astronomy and mathematics and hydraulics of Egypt, the far off sweep of the rain-laden monsoons against the mountains of Abyssinia and the creeping of the tawny Nile flood over that river born oasis. . . .

In all democratic or representative forms of government permitting free

25 Strabo, Book VII, chap. I, 2.

26 Strabo, Book II, chap. III, 7.

expression of popular opinion, history shows that division into political parties tends to follow geographical lines of cleavage. In our own Civil War the dividing line between North and South did not always run east and west. The mountain area of the Southern Appalachians supported the Union and drove a wedge of disaffection into the heart of the South. Mountainous West Virginia was politically opposed to the tidewater plains of old Virginia, because slave labor did not pay on the barren "upright" farms of the Cumberland Plateau; whereas, it was remunerative on the wide fertile plantations of the coastal lowland. The ethics of the question were obscured where conditions of soil and topography made the institution profitable. In the mountains, as also in New England, a law of diminishing financial returns had for its corollary a law of increasing moral insight. In this case, geographic conditions worked through the medium of direct economic effects to more important political and ethical results.

The roots of geographic influence often run far underground before coming to the surface, to sprout into some flowering growth; and to trace this back to its parent stem is the necessary but not easy task of the geographer.

The complexity of this problem does not end here. The modification of human development by environment is a natural process; like all other natural processes, it involves the cumulative effects of causes operating imperceptibly but persistently through vast periods of time. Slowly and deliberately does geography engrave the sub-titles to a people's history. Neglect of this time element in the consideration of geographic influences accounts equally for many an exaggerated assertion and denial of their power. A critic undertakes to disprove modification through physical environment by showing that it has not produced tangible results in the last fifty or five hundred years. This attitude recalls the early geologists, whose imaginations could not conceive the vast ages necessary in a scientific explanation of geologic phenomena.

The theory of evolution has taught us in science to think in larger terms of time, so that we no longer raise the question whether European colonists in Africa can turn into negroes, though we do find the recent amazing statement that the Yankee, in his tall, gaunt figure, "the colour of his skin, and the formation of his hair, has begun to differentiate himself from his European kinsman and approach the type of the aboriginal Indians."[28] Evolution tells the story of modification by a succession of infinitesimal changes, and emphasizes the permanence of a modification once produced long after the causes for it cease to act. The mesas of Arizona, the earth sculpture of the Grand Canyon remain as monuments to the erosive forces which produced them. So a habitat leaves upon man no ephemeral impress; it affects him in one way at a low stage of his development, and differently at a later or higher stage, because the man himself and his relation to his environment have been modified in the earlier period; but traces of that earlier adaptation survive in his maturer life. Hence man's relation to his environment must be looked at through the perspective of historical development. It would be impossible to explain the history and national character of the contemporary English solely by

[28] Hans Helmolt, History of the World, Vol. II, pp. 244–245. New York, 1902–1906.

their twentieth century response to their environment, because with insular conservatism they carry and cherish vestiges of times when their islands represented different geographic relations from those of today. Witness the wool-sack of the lord chancellor. We cannot understand the location of modern Athens, Rome or Berlin from the present day relations of urban populations to their environment, because the original choice of these sites was dictated by far different considerations from those ruling to-day. In the history of these cities a whole succession of geographic factors have in turn been active, each leaving its impress of which the cities become, as it were, repositories.

The importance of this time element for a solution of anthropo-geographic problems becomes plainer, where a certain locality has received an entirely new population, or where a given people by migration change their habitat. The result in either case is the same, a new combination, new modifications superimposed on old modifications. And it is with this sort of case that anthropo-geography most often has to deal. So restless has mankind been, that the testimony of history and ethnology is all against the assumption that a social group has ever been subjected to but one type of environment during its long period of development from a primitive to a civilized society. Therefore, if we assert that a people is the product of the country which it inhabits at a given time, we forget that many different countries which its forbears occupied have left their mark on the present race in the form of inherited aptitudes and traditional customs acquired in those remote ancestral habitats. The Moors of Granada had passed through a wide range of ancestral experiences; they bore the impress of Asia, Africa and Europe, and on their expulsion from Spain carried back with them to Morocco traces of their peninsula life.

A race or tribe develops certain characteristics in a certain region, then moves on, leaving the old abode but not all the accretions of custom, social organization and economic method there acquired. These travel on with the migrant people; some are dropped, others are preserved because of utility, sentiment or mere habit. For centuries after the settlement of the Jews in Palestine, traces of their pastoral life in the grasslands of Mesopotamia could be discerned in their social and political organization, in their ritual and literature. Survivals of their nomadic life in Asiatic steppes still persist among the Turks of Europe, after six centuries of sedentary life in the best agricultural land of the Balkan Peninsula. One of these appears in their choice of meat. They eat chiefly sheep and goats, beef very rarely, and swine not at all.[29] The first two thrive on poor pastures and travel well, so that they are admirably adapted to nomadic life in arid lands; the last two, far less so, but on the other hand are the regular concomitant of agricultural life. The Turk's taste to-day, therefore, is determined by the flocks and herds, which he once pastured on the Trans-Caspian plains. . . .

The origin of Roman political institutions is intimately connected with conditions of the naturally small territory where arose the greatness of Rome. But now, after two thousand years we see the political impress of this narrow origin spreading to the governments of an area of Europe immeasurably larger than the

[29] Roscher, *National-oekonomik des Ackerbaues*, p. 33, note 3. Stuttgart, 1888.

region that gave it birth. In the United States, little New England has been the source of the strongest influences modifying the political, religious and cultural life of half a continent; and as far as Texas and California these influences bear the stamp of that narrow, unproductive environment which gave to its sons energy of character and ideals. . . .

A people may present at any given time only a partial response to their environment also for other reasons. This may be either because their arrival has been too recent for the new habitat to make its influence felt; or because, even after long residence, one overpowering geographic factor has operated to the temporary exclusion of all others. Under these circumstances, suddenly acquired geographic advantages of a high order or such advantages, long possessed but tardily made available by the release of national powers from more pressing tasks, may institute a new trend of historical development, resulting more from stimulating geographic conditions than from the natural capacities or aptitudes of the people themselves. Such developments, though often brilliant, are likely to be short-lived and to end suddenly or disastrously, because not sustained by a deep-seated national impulse animating the whole mass of the people. They cease when the first enthusiasm spends itself, or when outside competition is intensified, or the material rewards decrease. . .

The history and culture of a people embody the effects of previous habitats and of their final environment; but this environment means something more than local geographic conditions. It involves influences emanating from far beyond the borders. No country, no continent, no sea, mountain or river is restricted to itself in the influence which it either exercises or receives. The history of Austria cannot be understood merely from Austrian ground. Austrian territory is part of the Mediterranean hinterland, and therefore has been linked historically with Rome, Italy, and the Adriatic. It is a part of the upper Danube Valley and therefore shares much of its history with Bavaria and Germany, while the lower Danube has linked it with the Black Sea, Greece, the Russian steppes, and Asia. The Asiatic Hungarians have pushed forward their ethnic boundary nearly to Vienna. The Austrian capital has seen the warring Turks beneath its walls, and shapes its foreign policy with a view to the relative strength of the Sultan and the Czar.

The earth is an inseparable whole. Each country or sea is physically and historically intelligible only as a portion of that whole. Currents and wind-systems of the oceans modify the climate of the nearby continents, and direct the first daring navigations of their peoples. The alternating monsoons of the Indian Ocean guided Arab merchantmen from ancient times back and forth between the Red Sea and the Malabar coast of India.[33] The Equatorial Current and the northeast trade-wind carried the timid ships of Columbus across the Atlantic to America. The Gulf Stream and the prevailing westerlies later gave English vessels the advantage on the return voyage. Europe is a part of the Atlantic coast. This is a fact so significant that the North Atlantic has become a European sea. The United States also is a part

33 Bunbury, History of Ancient Geography, Vol. II, pp. 351, 470–471. London, 1883.

of the Atlantic coast: this is the dominant fact of American history. China forms a section of the Pacific rim. This is the fact back of the geographic distribution of Chinese emigration to Annam, Tonkin, Siam, Malacca, the Philippines, East Indies, Borneo, Australia, Hawaiian Islands, the Pacific Coast States, British Columbia, the Alaskan coast southward from Bristol Bay in Bering Sea, Ecuador and Peru.

As the earth is one, so is humanity. Its unity of species points to some degree of communication through a long prehistoric past. Universal history is not entitled to the name unless it embraces all parts of the earth and all peoples, whether savage or civilized. To fill the gaps in the written record it must turn to ethnology and geography, which by tracing the distribution and movements of primitive peoples can often reconstruct the most important features of their history.

Anthropo-geographic problems are never simple. They must all be viewed in the long perspective of evolution and the historical past. They require allowance for the dominance of different geographic factors at different periods, and for a possible range of geographic influences wide as the earth itself. In the investigator they call for pains-taking analysis and, above all, an open mind.

15

CIVILIZATIONS: ORGANISMS OR SYSTEMS?

Karl W. Butzer

Karl Butzer was born in Germany but went to North America, eventually holding chairs in Anthropology and Geography at the University of Chicago and then at the University of Texas, Austin. His research has exemplified the sub-discipline of cultural ecology, a combination of anthropology, ecology and geography which addresses the interlocking nature of society and the environment through both systems of ideas and detailed case studies. The short article reprinted here draws on his book *Early hydraulic civilization in Egypt* (Chicago, 1976), which combines data from archaeology, hydrology, geomorphology and demography to challenge the over-simplified explanations of ancient Egyptian society suggested by Karl Wittfogel's oriental despotism thesis. He also rejects the simple organic analogies for social systems as put forward by thinkers such as Spencer, Toynbee and Spengler, who were preoccupied with the rise and fall of civilizations during the peak of imperial power. Instead, he views civilizations as adaptive systems, allowing for chance, combinations of causal factors, and fluctuating states of stability and instability. The breadth of his sources and influences places Butzer among the most important geographers writing in the synthetic tradition.

Source: Civilizations: organisms or systems? *American Scientist* 68, 517–23, 1980.

Oswald Spengler's *Decline of the West* (1926) regarded societies as organisms, with an inevitable life cycle of youth, maturity, and decay. This organic analogy had earlier been formulated by Herbert Spencer in his *Study of Sociology* (1872), and was subsequently adapted in a less deterministic fashion in A. J. Toynbee's *Study of History* (1934). Toynbee emphasized the role of creative individuals in the growth of civilizations, and attributed breakdown and disintegration to the failure of creative power among the dominant minority, to alienation of the masses, and to pressures of foreign peoples.

The model of ascendance, climax, and retrogression entered American anthropology with the writings of Julian Steward in the 1940s, and was then formalized in archaeology by the historical-development scheme of G. R. Willey and P. Phillips

(*Method and Theory in American Archaeology*, 1958). David Clarke (1968) has formulated this model of birth, growth and death as one of "culture system ontogeny," with formative (florescent), coherent (classic climax), and postcoherent (postclassic) stages, by incorporating Spencer's long-neglected insight that a society is an interdependent system of specialized parts.

A Systemic Alternative

The integration of the developmental and systemic models represents a significant improvement in analyzing the apparently rhythmic rise and fall of civilizations. But the emphasis remains on ontogeny, and therefore presumes a sequential interplay of predictable processes. In fact, cultures can be more advantageously examined as ecological systems, in which human populations interact with the biophysical environment, as well as among themselves. Such a systemic model is more suitable to explain the archaeological record of relatively simple hunting-gathering "cultures" that responded to repeated internal or external inputs by minor or major transformations, although the basic character of their adaptive system remained unchanged over many thousands of years. The records of such prehistoric systems suggest a steady-state (rather than homeostatic) equilibrium (Figure 15.1).

More complex cultures frequently responded to novel inputs by relatively sudden equilibrium shifts, leading to more fundamental sociopolitical transformations, with or without a change of adaptive strategy. It appears that the time trajectories of "high" civilizations, in particular, have tended to resemble a metastable equilibrium pattern marked by thresholds at which "positive" or "negative" shifts of equilibrium level have taken place (Fig. 15.1). Whereas the established, developmental model for civilizations generally assumes a succession of ever-higher homeostatic plateaus, followed by abrupt collapse, the systemic model proposed here can do justice to both the steady-state and metastable equilibrium concepts, while also allowing for long-term, nondisjunctive directional trends (dynamic equilibrium).

It is therefore possible to view civilizations as ecosystems that emerge in response to sets of ecological opportunities, that is, econiches to be exploited. Over a span of time, a variety of internal (social) and external (environmental) adjustments will inevitably take place; some of these will be "successful," leading to demographic expansion, others "retrograde," requiring demographic curtailment. These demographic trends are commonly associated with, and parallel to, the ups and downs of political power, although this is not always the case. However, political structures generally are less durable than either cultural identity or ethnic consciousness, and these in turn are less persistent than the basic adaptive system on which they are predicated. This is consistent with the ecosystem analogy, since the structural components of a population are devices to ensure adaptive success and not the other way around.

The processes integral to "ascendancy" and "retrogression" are reconcilable

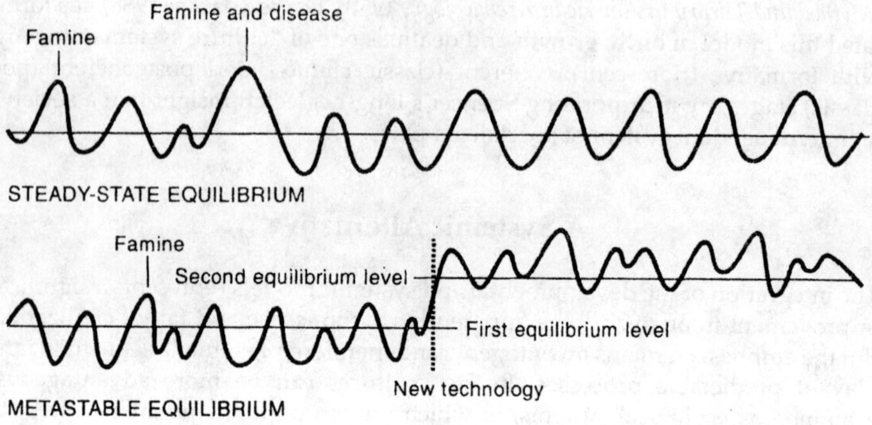

Figure 15.1 [orig Fig. 1] Demographic curves express the quality of human adaptation. One common type of equilibrium is steady-state (top), in which recurrent famine and epidemic diseases lead to repeated population fluctuations without long-term directional change. In more complex societies, new adaptive strategies may allow one or more jumps in equilibrium level (metastable equilibrium, *below*), and subsequent demographic oscillations may be of smaller amplitude; negative social or environmental inputs can also have a reversed impact. (Equilibrium curves based on Chorley and Kennedy 1971.)

with a systemic model. Ascendancy can be identified as a sociopolitical transformation in which structural organization favors an optimal flow of energy within the system. A useful ecological concept is that of trophic levels among biotic communities, in which organisms with similar feeding habits, such as photosynthetic producers, herbivores, and carnivores, define successive tiers interlinked in a vertical food chain. An efficient social hierarchy comprises several "trophic" levels arranged in a low-angle pyramid, supported by a broad base of agricultural producers and linked to the central, administrative apex by a reasonable number of middle-echelon bureaucratic agencies (see Figure 16.2). The vertical structures serve to channel food and information, and an "efficient" energy flow would imply conditions allowing each trophic level to flourish in a steady state or even a dynamic equilibrium.

A flatter pyramid with little or no vertical structure would provide less information flow and so limit the potential productivity of the substrate. This version of the model allows for growth, with new technological or organizational devices, of external or internal origin, favoring expanded energy generation at lower trophic levels. On the other hand, a steeper pyramid, with a top-heavy bureaucracy, would place excessive demands on the producers and so jeopardize the food chain. The steep pyramid model represents a system prone to metastable equilibrium, with external or internal inputs liable to undermine the productive substrate and so to destroy the nonproductive superstructure; the probable result would be a much-simplified pyramid.

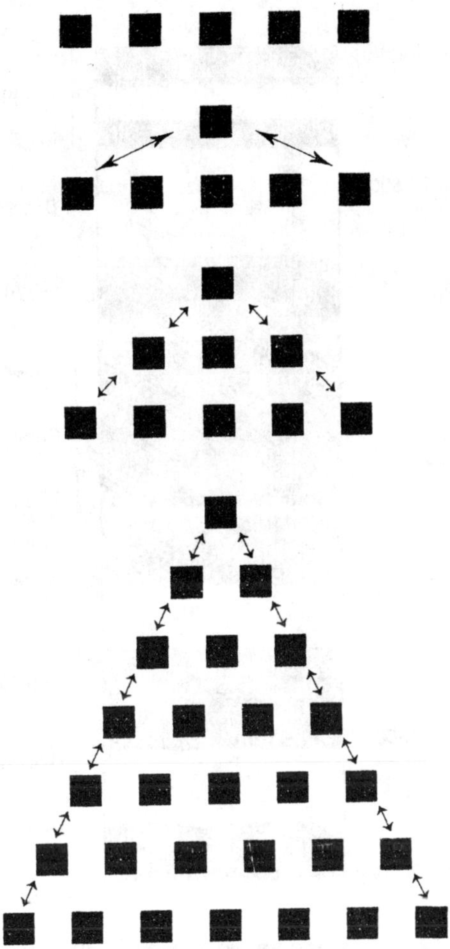

Figure 15.2 [orig. fig. 2] Sociopolitical hierarchies, whether simple of complex, can be compared with the organization of trophic levels in a food chain. These schematic models show different modes of energy and information flow for increasingly complex sociopolitical hierarchies in preindustrial societies. The first model shows no vertical structure, with horizontal but no vertical information flow, and slow change. The second model indicates limited vertical structure, with some vertical information flow, and increased dynamism. The third model depicts elaborate vertical structure, characterized by efficient energy and information flow, with each level as well as the whole system in steady-state or dynamic equilibrium. The fourth model represents a top-heavy vertical structure, with impeded information flow, increased energy expenditure for system maintenance, excessive demands on the productive substrate, and a metastable equilibrium.

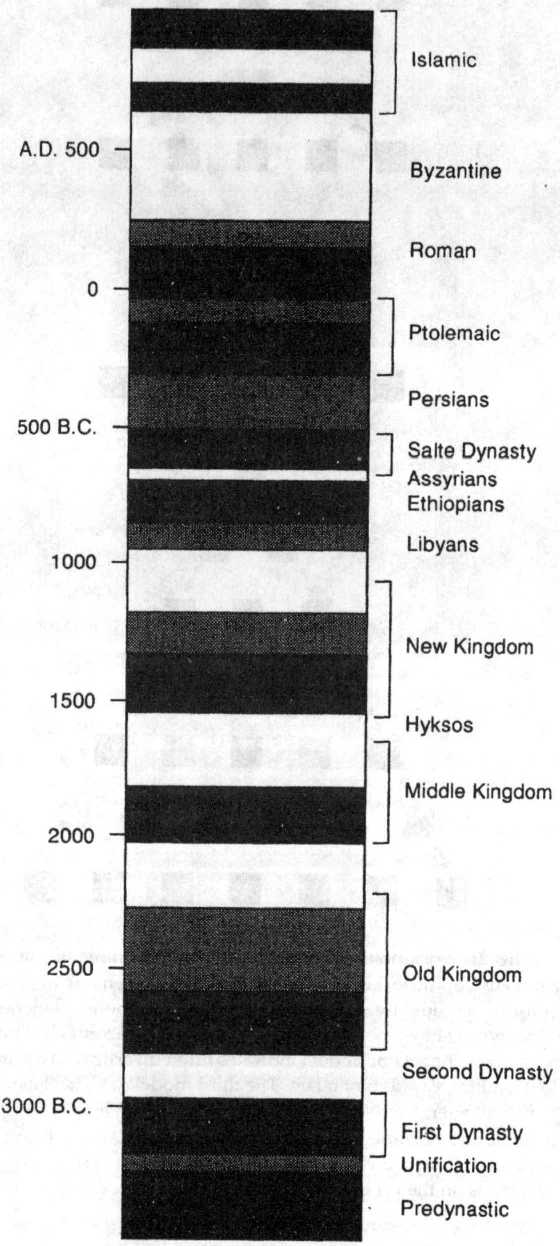

Figure 16.3 [orig. fig. 3] On this Egyptian time-line, periods of increasing population are shown in black, those of decreasing population are in white, and periods of stable population are in gray.

Processes of Growth

Both the advantages and difficulties of this ecosystemic view of civilizations can be illustrated and then elaborated with specific reference to ancient Egypt (Butzer 1976, 1980).

The political history of Egypt has traditionally been organized in several cycles: the Old Kingdom (ca. 2760–2225 B.C.), the Middle Kingdom (2035–1668 B.C.), and the New Kingdom (1570–1070 B.C.). Each reached its apex in an episode of strong, central government, followed by a long period of stagnation and eventual decline. The First Dynasty (ca. 3170–2970 B.C.) represents another such culmination of a less clearly delineated protohistoric development. Each phase of political devolution was accompanied by economic deterioration and temporary or substantial demographic decline (see Figure 15.3). The greatest population density prior to the radical technological improvements of the last one hundred years was achieved during early Roman times.

We can first examine the processes of growth. Episodes of growth in Egypt were made possible by such innovations as improved irrigation organization, devices for controlled water distribution during bad flood years, lift mechanisms to allow cultivation of marginal areas or several crops per year, as well as new cultigens better suited for poorer or drier soils and for summer cultivation – in an agricultural system originally geared only to postflood, winter crops. These innovations represent the basic range of human impact on an environment that, thanks to the river, remained undegraded until the construction of the Aswan High Dam.

1. The First Dynasty was preceded by several centuries during which political power was consolidated, a rudimentary bureaucracy organized, and controlled flood irrigation begun. The final unification of Egypt marshalled all resources at the direct or indirect disposal of the pharaoh.
2. The early Old Kingdom saw a strengthening of bureaucratic structures; there was also conscious "development" of the central Delta (see Figure 15.4) and its desert margins for stock-raising and high-productivity plantations, including orchards and vineyards.
3. The founding administrators of the Middle Kingdom responded to several centuries of repetitive Nile failure by greater government intervention in food redistribution, to feed the productive population in times of famine. Large-scale internal colonization now focused on draining and settling parts of the Faiyum Depression.
4. A major introduction of the New Kingdom was the *shaduf*, a work-saving bucket-and-lever device to raise water a meter or so from wells or ditches, to water market gardens or tree crops on large estates. The eastern Delta was systematically developed, as a hinterland to the new administrative capital of Pi-Ramesse.The center of demographic gravity now shifted from the narrow Nile Valley to the broad Delta (see Figure 15.5), and the new Asiatic dependencies generated additional wealth for Egypt.
5. Colonization of the marshy, northern Delta and the Maryut Depression began 650–525 B.C. during a brief revival of pharaonic power, and resumed after 300 B.C. under the Ptolemies. This foreign dynasty maximized its economic resources by creating efficient administrative centers in each provincial capital, with a formal harbor authority to regulate exchange on the internal waterways. In the Faiyum they completed drainage and achieved a showpiece of agricultural productivity, made possible by a ring of high-lying

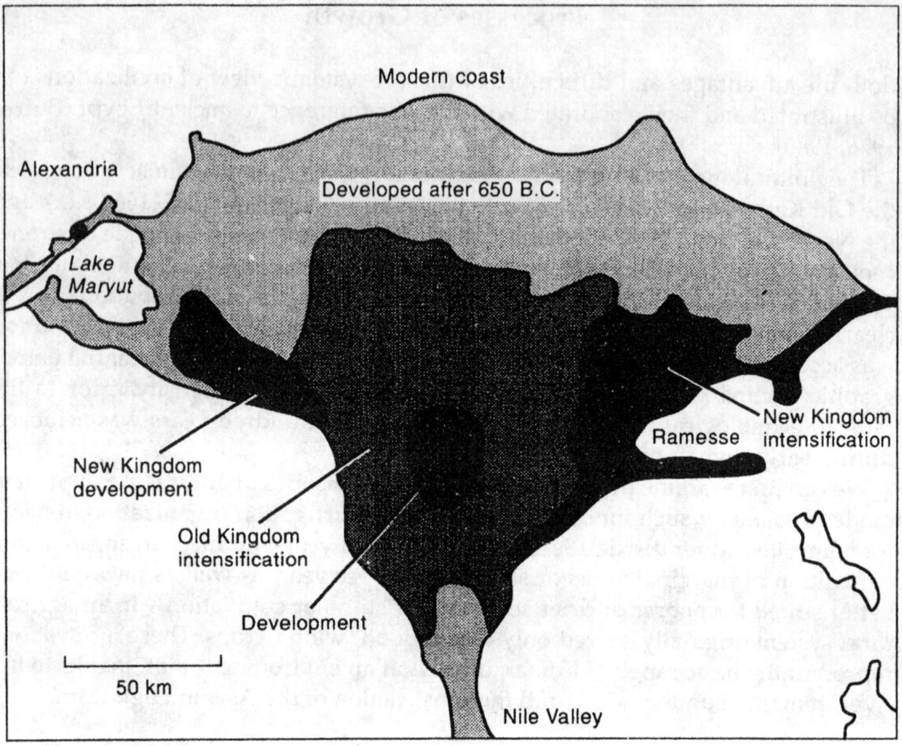

Figure 15.4 [orig. fig. 4] Land use on the central Nile Delta was intensified during the Old Kingdom, when many new villages were founded. Settlement expanded along the sandy margins of the Delta during the New Kingdom; the marshy northern Delta was opened up to large-scale settlement only after 650 B.C. (Waterways of the Nile Delta, which repeatedly changed in number and position, are not shown on this map.)

canals fed by a Nile branch and in turn supplying a string of new cities (see Figure 15.6), largely settled by Macedonian colonists. The animal-drawn waterwheel (*saqiya*) began to make possible two crops a year on prime lands, and summer crops such as sorghum were introduced.

The basic impact of such improved organizational efficiency, new technology, or expansion and intensification of agriculture was to increase both the labor force and national productivity. In response, it is probable that the population of Egypt increased from less than a million under the First Dynasty to about five million in the second century B.C.

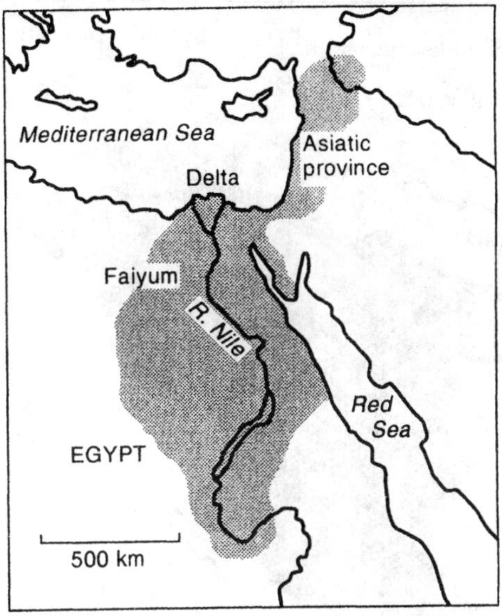

Figure 15.5 [orig. fig. 5] This overview map of New Kingdom Egypt shows the relative locations of the Nile Delta, the Faiyum Depression, and the Asiatic Province.

Processes of Decline

It has commonly been assumed that floodplain irrigation provides an ecosystem that is uniquely productive and predictable, one in which environmental inputs do not generate significant change. In fact, however, this is a gross oversimplification.

Predynastic, Old Kingdom, and Middle Kingdom agriculture was based on no more than a rudimentary flood-basin irrigation that lacked the lift technology essential to (1) cultivate the entire floodplain, (2) guarantee a reasonable minimum of food during poor flood years, or (3) allow more than a single crop per plot per year, except in gardens watered by hand. Pharaonic agriculture was extensive, rather than intensive, with perhaps half the agricultural lands used for grazing or in fallow in 2000 B.C., and large parts of the potentially fertile floodplain were still underdeveloped in the eleventh century B.C..

Irrigation was organized not centrally, but locally. Food storage facilities were limited to private domains until the New Kingdom, and even then public redistribution in times of need was ineffective. A substantial body of data shows that flood levels declined drastically during the Second Dynasty (ca. 2970–2760 B.C.), that catastrophic Nile failures recurred at least several times at the end of the Old Kingdom (ca. 2250–2000 B.C.), that equally catastrophic, aberrantly high floods marked the second half of the Middle Kingdom (1840–1770 B.C.), and that major, negative readjustment of Nile hydrology took place over several generations

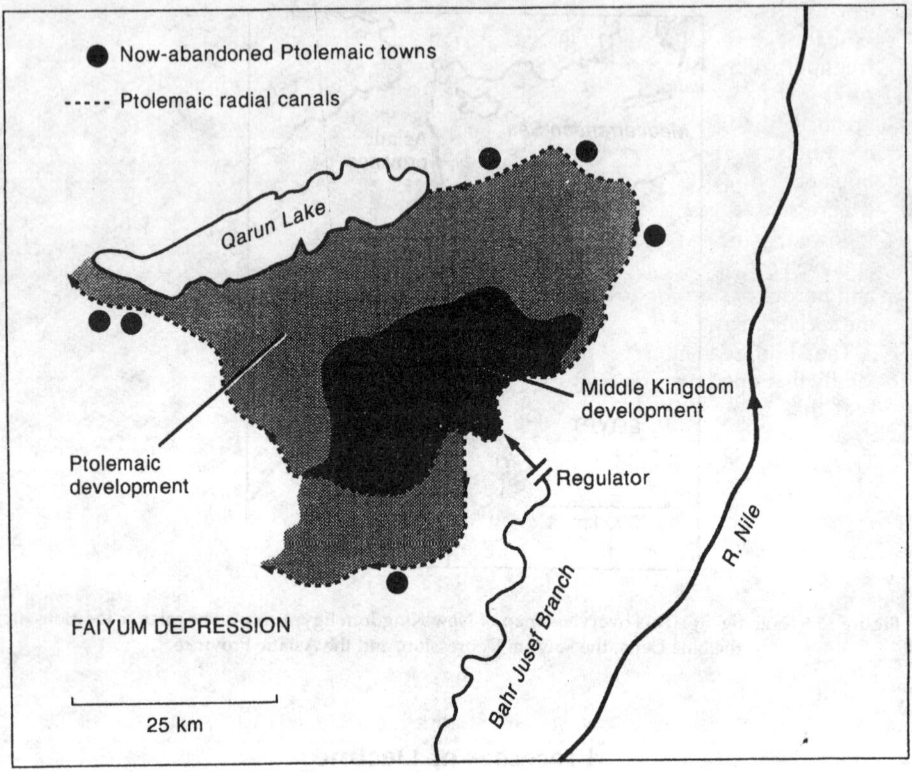

Figure 15.6 [orig. fig. 6] Colonization of the higher parts of the Faiyum Depression took place during the Middle Kingdom; a sophisticated drainage and irrigation system covering the greater part of the Depression was completed under the Ptolomies in the third century B.C. Water was fed into a ring of high-lying canals that supplied a network of local feeders and allowed towns to flourish in the former desert

shortly after 1200 B.C., when the Nubian floodplain was no longer inundated by the Nile and had to be abandoned.

These facts provide a different perspective for evaluation of the long intervals of economic stagnation, demographic decline, and political discontinuity in pharaonic Egypt. We can now attempt to identify these phases and processes of decay.

1. The Second Dynasty was an era of political instability, revolts, reduced foreign trade, and probable impoverishment. Nile floods declined by an overall 30%, and in some years failed entirely.
2. Cheops (ca. 2638–2613 B.C.), builder of the Great Pyramid, controlled more personal power and wealth than any other pharaoh, and later royal tombs progressively diminished in size or elaboration. The Fifth Dynasty kings (ca. 2541–2407 B.C.) had to compete

with the power of the temples, while the uneconomical policy of setting up perpetual tax-free mortuary foundations began to withdraw extensive agricultural lands and their produce from the tax base. Under the Sixth Dynasty (ca. 2407–2255 B.C.), the burgeoning aristocracy and upper-level bureaucracy shared in more of the wealth, eventually creating rival power bases in the provinces. But an overall reduction in the size and opulence of funerary architecture, both in the capital and in the provinces, documents progressive economic decline during the Sixth Dynasty. Two centuries of political chaos followed, with periods of civil war, anarchy, catastrophic Nile failures, repeated famines, and even cannibalism. Food stores were plundered, the estates of the rich dispossessed, and hordes of starving people roamed the countryside, threatening the foundations of the social order.

3. The Middle Kingdom pharaohs after 1794 B.C. were reduced to puppets of a powerful family that ruled as prime ministers but failed to keep the country unified. Records indicate that from 1840–1770 B.C. one flood out of three was exceptionally high and destructive (2–4 m above normal), capable of destroying the entire irrigation system several times every decade. But literary sources tell us nothing about the actual process of decline. Then, in 1668 B.C., the Asiatic Hyksos conquered Egypt and held it for a century.

4. The New Kingdom saw the temple of Amun acquire great wealth and power, and the unsuccessful reaction under Akhenaten (ca. 1350–1334 B.C.) shook Egypt, endangering the Asiatic empire. A reasonable degree of prosperity was eventually restored, but invasion attempts by several barbarian peoples were barely staved off in 1207, 1177, and 1171 B.C., and the Asiatic provinces were lost. Grain prices, compared with prices of non-food products, increased rapidly to as much as 24 times the standard price. Together with at least six verified food riots or strikes and indications that the government granaries were empty, this documents a severe food shortage between 1153 and 1105 B.C. The agricultural abandonment of the Nubian floodplain, now no longer inundated by the annual floods, ties in these years of starvation with long-term reduced Nile discharge and falling lake levels in sub-Saharan Africa. The government was rife with corruption and could no longer maintain public order. After 1120 B.C. desert marauders terrorized the overtaxed and depopulated countryside. Eventually the high priest of Amun displaced the impotent king, and four centuries of weak priestly or foreign rulers barely held the country together.

5. Egypt stagnated again under intermittent and ineffective Persian rule from 525 to 332 B.C., and the immense social problems of the overcrowded Delta can be inferred from Herodotus's description of about 450 B.C. Following the apex of economic revitalization under the early Ptolemies, Roman rule initially restored stability while population peaked near 5.5 million, despite a policy of calculated exploitation. Government became grossly inefficient by A.D. 200, with overtaxation and a brutal, arbitrary tax-farming system that drove cultivators off the land. In combination with violent religious and civil strife, and the monastic movement, dramatic depopulation reduced Egypt to an underdeveloped economy by the fifth century. Totally demoralized by a millennium of foreign exploitation, the Egyptian people accepted their own particularist version of Christianity and disowned their cultural traditions. After seven centuries of Islamic rule, beginning A.D. 641, they also lost their Coptic Egyptian language and became linguistic Arabs.

The common denominator of each period of decline was rural depopulation and decreasing economic productivity. The responsible processes were complex and involved at least two of three major factors: excessive demands on the productive population; a high incidence of poor or destructively high Nile floods; and insecurity due to political instability, foreign rule, or invasion. Each retrograde phase coincided with negative social developments within, as well as negative environmental or social interventions from without.

In the case of the Old and New Kingdoms, internal social evolution was unfavorable for at least three centuries prior to political breakdown, suggesting that external inputs may have triggered drastic readjustment of a sociopolitical system already in a state of metastable equilibrium. However, for the First to Second Dynasties and the Middle Kingdom there is no tangible evidence of overtaxation; instead breakdown takes place within a century of the first hints of political weakness, arguing for a severe and unpredictable stress exerted on an otherwise functional system. Strong oscillations of productivity since the eighth century B.C. are less coherent, as a result of recurrent foreign intervention.

Identifying Systemic Variables

Several key variables can be identified in this analysis of the periods of growth and decline. First, a potent but not universal factor is a progressive social pathology, linked to our model of a top-heavy and metastable sociopolitical pyramid. Karl Wittfogel (1957) has described this as progressive overexploitation of the masses by a growing unproductive elite, with resulting social disequilibrium and eventual politicoeconomic collapse. This process can be discerned in the case of the Old and New Kingdoms, as well as during the late Roman and the Byzantine periods. It is not verifiable during the Second Dynasty nor during the decline of the Middle Kingdoms.

The importance of leadership, then as now, is equally apparent as a second key variable. The case is best made in reference to strong leadership, since ineffectual leadership speaks for itself. Strong leadership in ancient Egypt is well documented in the case of Ramesses III (1182–1151 B.C.), the last competent ruler of the New Kingdom. Despite two centuries of social stress he marshalled sufficient support to beat off powerful foreign invaders who had destroyed the other kingdoms of the eastern Mediterranean world. He still managed to maintain internal order through the first years of a growing, Nile-related food shortage. His death (possibly by assassination) 2 years after the first food riots then opened the doors to general chaos, unchecked rural depopulation, and economic disaster. Earlier, the Old Kingdom had been subject to 250 years of socioeconomic stagnation or even decline prior to Pepi II (ca. 2350–2260 B.C.), who experimented with three different approaches to the sharing of centralized authority during a 90-year reign. That authority collapsed only after his death. As another example of strong government, the first Ptolemies and the early Roman emperors managed to milk Egypt according to a calculated cost-benefit strategy, while allowing the totally disenfranchised population to maintain a phenomenal demographic peak for some 500 years.

Foreign intervention is a third critical variable. The military effectiveness of the Assyrian, Persian, Macedonian, Roman, and Arab armies is well known. The

Hyksos were equally formidable, as recent evidence shows – powerful, well-armed and armored warriors, using swift, horse-drawn chariots. The Egyptians were only able to dislodge the Hyksos with difficulty, after modernizing their own armies. (Other peripheral peoples never managed to upset the system, and the "Libyan" and "Ethiopian" dynasties, 946–656 B.C., were rooted among immigrants or conquered people already acculturated.) Unlike the Hyksos invasion, Egyptian society had been remarkably self-sufficient and had functioned to some degree as an approximation to a closed system; after the Hyksos invasion the New Kingdom Empire resembled an open system, and with the first Assyrian incursion in 664 B.C., Egypt became a subsystem of a much larger socioeconomic network that embraced the Near East, and ultimately the whole Mediterranean world.

A fourth critical variable is ecological stress, as a result of Nile behavior. The co-agency of Nile failure in the New Kingdom collapse is beyond question, and in the disintegration of the Old Kingdom, plausible. In Second Dynasty and late Middle Kingdom times, aberrant Nile behavior is not only the single external variable in evidence but the most prominent agent overall. This does not attribute the role of a determinant to Nile behavior. Instead, at a given level of technology, the Nile ecosystem provides a set of opportunities and constraints to agricultural productivity, varying from season to season, as well as from year to year.

The key variables singled out in this Egyptian example are more or less specific to Egypt. A fuller roster of potential variables for consideration would include agricultural productivity and access to resources (Butzer, in press), technology, settlement aggregation, exchange networks for food, raw materials, and finished goods, demography, socioeconomic structures, warfare, as well as political structures and leadership. Together these define a complex set of interrelationships, with a full range of transition from "dependent" to "independent" variables.

Civilizations as Adaptive Systems

These systemic variables all contribute to the explication of the interaction between society and environment. Collectively, they help define adaptive systems (in the sense of Buckley 1968), which are characterized by a body of community behavior that reflects perception of the bio-physical environment and that adjusts in response to external as well as internal changes.

In terms of general evaluation, it can be argued that complex societies are buffered from external variables by multiple "layers" of technology, social organization, and exchange networks. The instability threshold for such systems is increasingly high, in proportion to the number of negative feedback mechanisms that can absorb or counteract the impact of external variables, particularly on a short-term basis. But over the longer term, complex, "steep-sloped" systems are not stable (for similar views, based on different arguments, see May 1977 and Rappaport 1978). The very multiplicity of systemic components increases the probability of a chance concatenation of negative inputs. For example, the unexpected coincidence of poor leadership, social pathology, external political stress, and environmental perturbation can trigger a catastrophic train of mutually reinforcing events (Figure 15.7) that the system is unable to absorb.

A systemic model has a substantial advantage over the ontogenetic approach because it is nondeterministic and allows for chance. In fact, given the plethora of interlinked variables, transformations in a highly structured, vertical, and metastable system tend to be stochastic rather than teleological. It is a matter of probability, not of organismic inevitability, that cultural systems, like all human institutions, will eventually collapse given a sufficiently long span of time.

A systemic, ecological model can be applied to more than functional or synchronic interpretation. The model proposed here includes synchronic components (Fig. 15.2) as well as temporal and diachronic dimensions (Figs. 15.1 and 15.7). It can therefore accommodate a cyclic alternation between centuries when population and productivity increase and other intervals of demographic decline and political devolution. These periodicities are interpreted not as organic cycles of growth and senescence, but as readjustments among the processual variables that maintain the adaptive system.

Civilizations are indeed a type of adaptive system that can be objectively studied, as Adams (1978) has done in evaluating the impact of de facto, long-term or short-term maximization strategies for sustained adaptive equilibrium. Equally so, the discontinuities simulated by systemic collapse can be examined without recourse, to traditional, subjective, and often moralistic interpretations such as "decadence."

The long course of Egyptian history exemplifies the dynamism of an adaptive system, characterized by a flexible but persistent social adjustment that was intimately linked to its floodplain environment. Major crises, external or internal, were successively overcome by reorganization of the political and economic superstructure, permitting new leases on national power or at least on economic productivity. Through all of this, the essential components of the sociocultural and

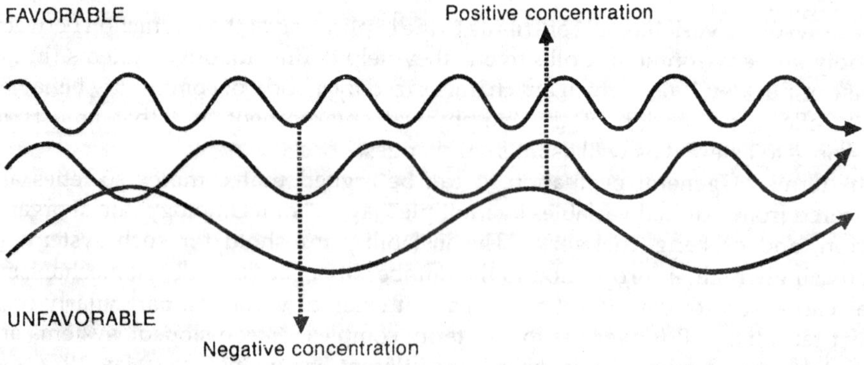

Figure 15.7 [orig. fig. 7] Several processes with varying periodocites may occasionally coincide, reinforcing one another and creating an overall tendency that is strongly unfavourable (low point of trends) or favourable (high point) to the system.

environmental adaptation survived more or less intact until the nineteenth century A.D., even though the political, and ultimately also the ethnic, identity was transformed. In other words, Egyptian civilization did not "die" during times of political discontinuity. It survived as a flexible adaptive system, and the success of that adaptation is demonstrated in the fundamental continuities that link ancient and modern Egypt.

The adaptive system is of a far more basic character than the artistic and political achievement of a civilization. In this sense it is at the level of the adaptive system that processual studies can probably be implemented with the greatest profit.

References

Adams, R. M. 1978. Maximization, stability, and resilience in Mesopotamian society, settlement, and agriculture. *Proc. Amer. Phil. Soc.* 122:329–335.

Buckley, W. 1968. Society as a complex adaptive system. In *Modern Systems Research for the Behavioral Sciences*, ed. W. Buckley. Aldine, pp. 490–513.

Butzer, K. W. 1976. *Early Hydraulic Civilization in Egypt*. Univ. of Chicago Press.

1980. Long-term Nile flood variation and political discontinuities in Pharaonic Egypt. In *The Causes and Consequences of Food Production in Africa*, eds. J. D. Clark and S. A. Brandt. Univ. of California Press.

In press. Rise and fall of Axum, Ethiopia: a Geo-archaeological perspective. *Am. Antiquity*.

Chorley, R. J., and B. A. Kennedy. 1971. *Physical Geography: A Systems Approach*. Prentice-Hall.

Clarke, D. L. 1968. *Analytical Archaeology*, rev. by B. Chapman 1978. Columbia Univ. Press.

May, R. M. 1977. Thresholds and breakpoints in ecosystems with a multiplicity of stable states. *Nature* 269:471–477.

Rappaport, R. A. 1978. Maladaptation in social systems. In *The Evolution of Social Systems*, ed. J. Friedman and M. J. Rowlands. Univ. of Pittsburgh Press, pp. 49–72.

Wittfogel, Karl. 1957. *Oriental Despotism*. Yale Univ. Press.

16

GEOGRAPHY, MARX AND THE CONCEPT OF NATURE

Neil Smith and Phil O'Keefe

When Marxist geography emerged in the 1970s it focused its attack mainly on the spatial tradition of geography. In particular, radical geographers addressed issues of urban crisis, poverty, inequality, and regional and global development. This article by Smith and O'Keefe was among the first to explore what Marxism had to say about society and nature. Although Plekhanov and Wittfogel had trodden this path long before, Smith and O'Keefe based their thoughts mainly on Marx himself. They acknowledge Glacken's contribution (see **chapter 13**) but they suggest that, as an intellectual history, his book left out the concrete relations of humans with nature. To understand these one must consider the labour process as that social act which transforms both humans and nature and dissolves the intellectual dualism. Nature is produced, they argue, but this does not mean that humans simply dominate it nor that the material world ceases to have significance in an industrial capitalist society. As an example of how their approach differs from the mainstream, they criticize natural hazards research for its neglect of class and social context. A longer treatment of these ideas was made by Smith in *Uneven development* (Oxford, 1984).

Source: Geography, Marx and the concept of nature. *Antipode* 12, 30–9, 1989.

Although "nature" is one of the most commonly invoked concepts in science (natural or social), it has in recent years been the subject of surprisingly little methodological discussion. An understanding of nature is fundamental to the manner in which science sees and conducts itself, yet the concept is generally taken for granted. Even the current enthusiasm to write introspective philosophies, sociologies and histories, science has left the stone of "nature" unturned. The neglect is not too difficult to explain; it is wholly consistent with the contemporary practice and self-image of science. Though not exclusive, the positivist tradition dominates orthodox science and positivism presupposes (among other things) that nature exists in and for itself, external to human activity. Thus we can know nature only by perceiving its facts and eventually discovering its laws. Nature is constituted as an external repository of facts that live according to autonomous natural laws. Mystery exists in nature only to the extent that science has not yet discovered these facts and laws.

The Concept of Nature in Social Science

With difficulty has social science adopted this rather stark conception of nature. Intimately connected with human *nature*, the nature that social scientists study is far harder to view as external. As social scientists internalize the positivist paradigm in larger and larger numbers, therefore, they gradually expose beneath the concept's calm exterior a turbulent core; beneath its taken-for-grantedness they reveal a dual conception of nature. On the one hand, nature is external, non-human reality, pure and god-given; on the other, nature is more abstract, incorporating human as well as non-human spheres of reality. In practice, this dual conception of nature is contradictory within positivism. At the same time as it is strictly non-human, "nature" is expected to be simultaneously human and non-human. Practicing scientists tend to adopt one or the other concept of nature, sometimes adopting both consecutively but rarely simultaneously.

The contradiction within the positivist conception of nature is usually dealt with in one of three ways:

1) Natural science studies nature, social science does not; it studies society which has nothing to do with nature. To talk of "human nature" or the *nature* of a certain society is therefore only metaphor or linguistic accident, according to this interpretation. But this is unsatisfactory because metaphors and linguistic "accidents" have a historical habit of referring to something objectively real. It is therefore no accident that we talk of "human nature" or the "nature of human societies".[1] Such usage of "nature" is not trivial. Is not human physiology every bit as "natural" as animal physiology, and are not human psychology and human physiology thoroughly intertwined making "human nature" a genuine rather than accidental concept? The contradiction within the positivist conception of nature cannot be ignored by banishing one side of it in theory while it remains in practice.

2) The second way of dealing with the contradiction is the assertion that social science like natural science does study nature but that the nature it studies is different from that studied by natural science. The "nature" of natural science is deemed autonomous from human activity while that of social science is seen as socially created. Insofar as the contradiction within the concept of nature is perceived, this is a popular solution, but it relies on displacing the contradiction from the concept itself into the nature to which the concept refers; nature as a unified concept refers to a bifurcated reality. Thus there remains a contradiction between this actual nature, which incorporates the separation of human and non-human, and the concept "nature," which refers to this opposition as a unity.

1 For a sketchy account of the way in which "nature" came historically to be applied to the social realm, see Louis Althusser's discussion of Montesquieu in *Politics and History*. (London: New Left Books, 1972). Paradoxically, the concept of nature is conspicuously absent from the rest of Althusser's work.

3) The third solution dissolves human nature into external nature. According to this solution, human behavior is regulated according to the same body of laws as the lowest artropod. The difference between them is simply one of scale and complexity within a single nature. Social Darwinism and much contemporary behaviorism hold this view of nature. Such a "solution" dissolves the contradiction in nature theoretically, but leaves it unsolved practically. In practice, human societies prove themselves able to appropriate the "laws of nature" for their own purposes, and this appropriation along with its purposes are not ruled by "natural law".

Geography has been particularly resistant to simplistic, contradictory concepts of nature. Mainly concerned with the relationship between human kind and nature ("Man-Nature" or "Man-Environment" relations, as they used to be called), geographers have generally been more sensitive to the complexity of "nature" and less willing to see it in simple dualistic terms. But even they, in recent years, have succumbed, as positivism tempted geographers with the promise of relevance, apparent sophistication, and the resulting social prestige. There have been exceptions, of course, among whom Glacken stands out. His *Traces on the Rhodian Shore* is a remarkable intellectual history of the idea of nature. . . .

Writing explicitly about the *idea* of nature, Glacken was also concerned to relate the historical currency of these ideas to the concrete material relation of societies with nature. He notes that the Greeks were able, for the first time in history, to conceive of nature as modified by human activity because their productive forces were sufficiently developed to demonstrate human power over nature.[3] Nonetheless, intellectual history was Glacken's primary concern. It will be our purpose here to examine in part what Glacken left aside. First, we shall emphasize not the idea of nature, but the concrete relation of human beings with nature. For it is this alone which can give Glacken's history a material and historical grounding. Second, in contradistinction to Glacken, we shall look (however historically) at the contemporary period. For good reason, Glacken restricted his account to pre-eighteenth century societies; the coming of capitalism heralded a new relation of human society with nature. In Glacken's own words:[4]

> *With the eighteenth century there ends in Western civilization an epoch in the history of man's relationship to nature. What follows is of an entirely different order, influenced by the theory of evolution, specialization in the attainment of knowledge, acceleration in the transformation of nature.*

As has been pointed out elsewhere, Marx was also concerned to view nature in historical terms.[5] More than any other historical period, capitalism wrenches

[3] Glacken, *Traces on the Rhodian Shore.* (Berkeley: University of California Press, 1967). p. 117.

[4] Glacken, *op. cit.*, footnote 3, p. 705.

[5] Neil Smith, "Geography, Science and Post-Positivist Modes of Explanation: A Critical Review." *Progress in Human Geography* 3, 3 (September 1979), pp. 356–383.

history from its socket in nature, and vice versa. It is therefore of special importance to make their connection explicit:[6]

> *In the whole conception of history up to the present this real basis of history [the material relations of human societies with nature] has either been totally neglected or else considered as a minor matter quite irrelevant to the course of history . . . The real production of life seems to be primeval history, while the truly historical appears to be separated from ordinary life, something extra-superterrestrial. With this the relation of man to nature is excluded from history and hence the antithesis of nature and history is created.*

This unity (but not identity) of nature with history underlies all of Marx's work, which ought, for that reason alone, to be of critical interest to social scientists. But in addition, Marx offers an alternative, unified and non-contradictory conception of nature. Positivism's contradictory concept of nature was developed (most recently) out of eighteenth and early nineteenth century philosophical materialism, and Marx's critique of this tradition remains relevant in terms of contemporary positivism.

Glacken, succumbing to an all too common mythology, dismissed Marx as teleological.[7] Collingwood, for his part, was so concerned to dismiss Marx on the first page that he had to resort to a mechanical misinterpretation of Hegel's famous "owl of Minerva." This should offer itself as a recommendation not a deterrent.

The Concept of Nature in Historical Materialism

Marx provided no systematic theory of nature, but in his, as in every other, attempt at science, a concept of nature is implied. By way of a critique of classical political economy, his primary concern was to outline a theory of capitalist society. This theory is now generally referred to as historical materialism, and as its name suggests, it attempts a historical explanation of how capitalism works, focusing on the social structures the society creates for sustaining its material existence. It is in this context that Marx discusses nature, but as an explication of "nature" *per se* these discussions remain fragmented and incomplete. At the same time, however, an understanding of "nature" is clearly central to Marx's project, and a concept is implied in his work though is never more than implicit. When teased out, elaborated and developed this concept reveals an insightful theoretical basis on which to build scientific theory.

[6] Karl Marx and Friedrich Engels, *The German Ideology* (New York: International Publishers, 1970 edn.) p. 59.
[7] Glacken, *op. cit.*, footnote 3 pp. 550, 649.

Nature as a unity: first and second nature

Nature separate from society had no meaning for Marx; nature is always related to societal activity. He meant this materially as well as ideally; the entire earth bears on its face the stamp of human activity. Writing as long ago as the 1840s, when Africa was still known as the Dark Continent, Marx and Engels could conclude that a "nature [which] preceded human history . . . no longer exists anywhere (except perhaps on a few Australian coral-islands of recent origin).[8] Though somewhat iconoclastic 135 years ago, this idea is orthodox geographic wisdom today. Historically and practically, the relation with nature is at the centre of human activity since people rely on nature for the fulfillment of fundamental needs. Theoretically, therefore, to conceive of nature as separate from society is a false abstraction: "the idea of *one* basis for life and another for science is from the outset a lie."[9] In a more ideal sense, to posit nature as external to society is absurd since this very act of positing implies a prior awareness of our *knowledge relation* with nature. We cannot know nature as external; we can know it only by entering into a relation with it. This latter, rather ideal, assumption hardly tells us a lot, but is utterly practical in so far as it reminds us that science cannot in good faith treat nature as external. Yet this is exactly what positivism attempts: it ignores the inescapability of this relation with nature, assumes nature to be an external thing-in-itself, and then by proceeding to gather knowledge about this nature, contradicts itself at every turn.

Nature and society are not two totally separate parts of reality as, in common parlance, they are often assumed to be. Rather, there is a unity of nature that is differentiated within. Thus Marx views capitalism as operating according to "natural laws," and declares as the "ultimate aim" of *Capital* the attempt to "lay bare the economic law of motion of modern society." The laws of its own operation and development are embedded in the structure of capitalist society, and this society cannot, by purely individual or even legislative effort, remove "the obstacles offered by the successive phases of its normal development."[10] "Men make their own history, but they do not make it just as they please; they do not make it under circumstances chosen by themselves, but under circumstances directly encountered, given and transmitted from the past."[11]

The laws that regulate the development of Marx's "second nature" are not at all the same kind of laws, that the physicist finds in the "first nature." They are not invariant and universal laws because the societies they describe are in flux, constantly changing and developing. According to Thomas, "Marx's analyses do not subordinate society to permanent laws like those of physics, because society is

[8] Marx and Engels, *op. cit.*, footnote 6, p. 63.

[9] Karl Marx, *Early Writings*. (Harmondsworth: Penguin, 1975), p. 355.

[10] Karl Marx, *Capital*. (New York: International Publishers, 1967 edn.) Vol. 1, p. 10.

[11] Karl Marx, *The 18th Brumaire of Louis Bonaparte*. (New York: International Publishers, 1963 edn.), p. 15.

seen by Marx as being in transition, as moving toward a new arrangement in which the 'laws' of classical economics *will no longer apply.*"[12]

The "economic laws of motion" which Marx sought were the laws (themselves historically mutable) which were responsible for this social transition. It is a law of capitalist society, for example, that to survive, individual capitalists must expand and accumulate larger and larger quantities of capital. But as a side effect of this *individual* necessity to expand, capitalism *as a whole* produces the conditions for its own decline and transformation into something different. By this "Marx does not intend to prove that the process was historically necessary. On the contrary: only after he has proved from history that in fact the process has partially already occurred, and partially must occur in the future, he in addition characterizes it as a process which develops in accordance with a definite dialectical law."[13] Obviously, Marx's dialectic is a quite different mode of thought from the formal logic of positivist science, and it is symptomatic of the narrow-mindedness of the latter that its adherents often cannot even conceive of different logics. Logic for them is simply logic, just as nature is nature; when Marx discusses natural laws in connection with the second nature, the positivist consciousness imagines these as *identical* with natural laws about the first nature (laws of physics, for example) and therefore imagine Marx to be a determinist of one shade or another. But when Marx discusses natural law, there is no implication of determinate inevitability, that much is a projection of the positivist consciousness. What Marx alludes to in calling social laws natural is not the society in and for itself, but the internal relationship between society and the people living under it. Thus Engels concludes that "the laws of economics confront men in all . . . planless incoherent production as objective laws over which they have no power, therefore in the form of laws of nature."[14] Far from being inevitable, these laws are socially created and can be socially abolished. While they remain, people are constrained in their social actions; they can abolish the laws responsible for this constraint not by isolated individual action but only by deliberate, collective social action.

Dialectics of nature?

The idea of second nature is not new. Glacken traces it back to Cicero, and it reappears in a more modern guise in Hegel. For them, the idea of a second nature was connected with the idea of a designed nature.[15] It was left for Marx to separate the concept from this teleology, and in so doing he "stood Hegel's dialectic on its

12 Paul Thomas, "Marx and Science." *Political Studies*. Vol. 24. (1976), pp. 1–23. 20. Alfred Schmidt. *The Concept of Nature in Marx* (London: New Left Books). Ch. 4.

13 Friederich Engels, *Anti-Duhring*. (London: Lawrence and Wishart, 1975 edn.), p. 161.

14 Engels, quoted in Schmidt, *op. cit.*, footnote 12, p. 43.

15 Glacken, *op. cit.*, footnote 3. Glacken never discusses Hegel's second nature but see G. W. F. Hegel, *The Philosophy of Right*. (London: Oxford University Press, 1952 edn.), p. 20.

head." But this dialectical comprehension of the second nature, together with Marx's insistence on a unified conception of nature, misses the question first posed by Engels of the role of the dialectic in comprehending the first nature. Engels posed the question as follows:[16]

> *Empirical natural science has accumulated such a tremendous mass of positive material for knowledge that the necessity of classifying it in each separate field of investigation systematically and in accordance with its inner interconnection has become absolutely imperative.*

Establishing these "inner inter-connections" required converting the formal logic of natural science into the dialectic. This Engels did by trying to show that the dialectic was inherent in nature, a property of all material relations, and his "dialectic of nature" became an integral part of Soviet ideology under Stalin. But ultimately, Engels commits the same metaphysical sin as the scientists whose theory he attempts to inject with the dialectic. He treats nature as something external, existing in itself, and quite separate from its human appropriation. If in Lukacs' philosophical language we accept the dialectic to be a relation of Subject and Object, it is clear that by separating nature from its human appropriation, Engels has attempted to find the dialectic within the Object itself.[17] The so-called "dialectic of nature" is not inherent in nature but rather, as we shall see, it is embedded in the human relation with nature. The dialectic, separate from human beings, has no meaning. . . .

Production in general

In his initial, abstract introduction to the topic in *Capital*, Marx depicts production as a process by which the form of nature is altered. The producer "can work only as nature does, that is by changing the form of matter. Nay more, in this work of changing the form he is constantly helped by natural forces." By "his industry," the producer "changes the forms of the materials furnished by nature, in such a way as to make them useful to him. The form of wood, for instance, is altered, by making a table out of it. Yet, for all that, the table continues to be that common, everyday thing, wood."[26]

In so far as labor produces useful commodities that fulfill human needs, "it is an eternal nature-imposed necessity, without which there can be no material exchanges between men and nature, and therefore no life."[27] But labor effects more than just a simple change in the form of matter; it produces a simultaneous change

[16] F. Engels, *The Dialectics of Nature* (Moscow: Progress Publishers, 1972 edn.). p. 42.

[17] Georg Lukacs, *History and Class Consciousness*. (Cambridge. Mass: MIT Press, 1971).

[26] Marx, *op. cit.*, footnote 10, pp. 43, 71. In this edition of *Capital* "Nature" is sometimes capitalized in translation, but we have decided to retain the lower case, since it is always capitalized in the German original by dint of its being a noun and for no other apparent reason. This is in keeping with other translations.

[27] Marx, *op. cit.*, footnote 10, p. 43.

in the labourer, and it is from this abstract definition of the relation with nature that a unified marxist theory of nature can be constructed.

> *Labour is, in the first place, a process in which both man and nature participate, and in which man of his own accord starts, regulates, and controls the material re-actions between himself and nature. He opposes himself to nature as one of her own forces, setting in motion arms and legs, head and hands, the natural forces of his body, in order to appropriate nature's productions in a form adapted to his own wants. By thus acting on the external world and changing it, he at the same time changes his own nature.*[28]

Like Adam Smith, but unlike contemporary neo-classical economists for whom utility and value are synonymous, Marx distinguished two ways of viewing a commodity: as an embodiment of useful attributes and qualities which supply the commodity with a *use-value;* and as an embodiment of a certain quantity of labor time, which supplies it with an *exchange-value.* Use-values are the material substratum of exchange-values, and in so far as nature can be equated with the realm of use-values as Schmidt claims, we can view it in similar terms. Nature then becomes the material which has its form altered by productive labor, becoming also the material embodiment of exchange value; the wood is made into a commodity, the table. Things are produced, we assume, because they are needed, and the "relation with nature" is thereby a use-value relation. Natural material is qualitatively altered by being brought into human productive activity, and human activity is simultaneously worked into natural material outside itself.

Since Marx was initially concerned to explain the inner workings of the capitalist economy, he tended to abstract from the sphere of use-values, focusing on exchange-values. Thus his notion of nature did not explicitly proceed beyond this rather abstract equation of nature with use-value. Given this abstract formulation it is possible to see how a dual conception of nature could be read into Marx, since like Schmidt, he has only at this point asserted the unity of nature without deriving it practically, i.e. logically and historically. In reality, Schmidt has failed to go beyond Marx in any substantive way; what he has articulated is a rationalization for the dual conception he implicitly reads into Marx. Yet this dual conception contradicts Marx's larger project.

Production for exchange

Few contemporary societies do not produce goods for an exchange economy, and given such an arrangement, our understanding of the "relation with nature" can be further refined. In short, it can no longer be seen as a purely use-value relation since if things are produced for exchange, direct need is no longer the sole determinant of what is produced. Exchange-value is what the immediate producer seeks

[28] Marx, *op. cit.*, footnote 10, p. 177.

when he or she produces for exchange. This exchange-value generally appears in material form as money which mediates the exchange of commodities.

With an exchange system we begin to see not a homogeneous relation with nature, but rather the production of a second nature out of the first, the development of a set of social institutions to carry out and regulate this exchange. Although the second nature is composed of (and circulates) products produced out of the first nature, it is for the most part only indirectly related to it through the production process. This separation of first and second natures Schmidt conveys well because his intellectual mentors (Kant and Hegel predominantly) lived and wrote in a time when precapitalist exchange economies had developed fully and were in the process of giving birth to capitalism. The unreconciled dualisms in Schmidt's concept of nature, particularly the idea of a second versus a first nature, are more truly and practically representative of this historical period – a period of developing exchange economies – than any other. Schmidt set off to "determine more exactly the position of Marx between Kant and Hegel," and this is precisely what he has done. He has abstracted from the historically different mode of production that has developed since Kant and Hegel, and which preoccupies Marx. He has treated Marx as an amalgamation of, rather than a movement beyond, Kant and Hegel.[29]

Capitalist production

Based on private property, capitalism differs from other exchange economies in this: it produces on the one side a class which possess the means of production for the whole society yet who do no labour, and on the other side a class that possess only their own labor power, which they must sell to survive.[30] Compared to its predecessors, the capitalist mode of production is inherently progressive and revolutionary. As it developed internationally, capitalism swept before it all other modes of production. These were forcibly subordinated to the dictates of capitalism which, since it had achieved a higher level of productiveness than all preceding modes of production, had the political and military, as well as the economic, wherewithall to enforce its expansion. Hence the growth of colonial empires among the more advanced capitalist nations of Europe and the fierce competition between these nations leading to sporadic imperial wars.

Under capitalism, the relation with nature is a use-value relation only in the most subordinate sense. Before anything else it is an exchange-value relation. "Expansion," "growth," "progress" and "development" refer primarily to economic change (the necessary accumulation of greater and greater quantities of capital) upon which all other kinds of change are made dependent. At a day to day level, these changes are particularly apparent in the spheres of reproduction and consumption. Witness, for example, the constant barrage of nostalgia for

[29] Schmidt, *op. cit.*, footnote 12, p. 12.
[30] Marx, *op. cit.*, footnote 10, p. 570.

uncommercialized art and culture, or the perpetual Christmas time complaints about the commercialization of religion. This commercialization is in reality a *capitalization*, an extension of the capitalist commodity structure into realms of life and experience that had previously been "sacred," that is, had survived independently in the realm of use values. Now, however, art, religion and culture are in the process of becoming commodities much as scientific knowledge already is, and their exchange-value label (price) comes to dominate their use-value.

But it is not just this "second nature" that is increasingly produced as part of the capitalist mode of production. The "first nature" is also produced. Indeed the "second nature" is not longer produced *out of* the first nature, but rather the first is produced *by* and within the confines of the second. Whether we are talking about the laborious conversion of iron ore into steel and eventually into automobiles or the professional packaging of Yosemite National Park, nature is produced. In a quite concrete sense, this process of production transcends the ideal distinction between a first and a second nature. The form of all nature has been altered by human activity, and today this production is accomplished not for the fulfillment of needs in general but for the fulfillment of one particular "need:" profit.

Over forty years ago, this exchange-value relation with nature was intuitively recognized and unwittingly encapsulated by that great imperial geographer, Isaiah Bowman, who declared that human beings "cannot move mountains" – not, that is, without first "floating a bond issue."[31]

To say that nature is produced does not imply that every atom of some tree, mountain or desert is humanly created, any more than that every atom of the Empire State Building is humanly created; matter is neither created nor destroyed. It does mean the human activity is responsible to a greater or lesser extent for the form of matter; the size and shape of the buildings, the hybrid or location of the tree, the physiognomy of the mountain, the spatial extent of the desert. The abstract difference between Schmidt's first and second natures is transformed into a difference of degree, and the unity of nature becomes practically realized in production. Behind the vague and mechanical "domination of nature" we find in reality the *production* of nature.

There will be those who see this theory of nature centered on the nature of production as a crude violation of the inherent beauty, sanctity and mystery of nature. The meaning of nature to them is not only sacred; it transcends such vulgar considerations as production. Yet those are the same people who drive their campers to Yellowstone to see Yogi Bear, who gladly use the beauty salon in the wilderness of Yosemite, and who capture the wildest nature on film so they can *reproduce* it in their living room. No less than nature itself, the cultural meaning of nature is socially produced. This is not to diminish the genuine insights that an imaginative phenomenology (as opposed to humanism) can offer; rather it is to understand the limits as well as the possibilities of this form of discourse.[32] The

31 Isaiah Bowman, *Geography in Relation to the Social Sciences* (New York: Charles Scribner. 1974).

32 For an assessment of phenomenology in geography and the distinction between humanism and phenomenology see Smith, *op. cit.*, footnote 5.

"realm of freedom actually begins only where labour which is determined by necessity . . . ceases." The "true realm of freedom . . . can blossom forth only with this realm of necessity as its basis."[33]

Implications

Science

"We know only a single science," wrote Marx and Engels, "the science of history. One can look at history from two sides and divide it into the history of nature and the history of men. Both sides are dependent on each other so long as men exist."[34] This unity of science was not an abstract principle for Marx but the eventual product of a concrete social development: "Natural Science will in time subsume the science of man just as the science of man will subsume natural science; there will be *one* science."[35] Or as Wilbur Zelinsky rather unwittingly explains: "I entertain the wicked suspicion that when our vision of science has graduated to a higher level, we shall discover, to our surprise, that the precociously adolescent natural sciences must be consumed within a larger, essentially social science of which they form a peculiar special subset." This after describing Marxism as a luxuriating religion.[36]

On the basis of this historical understanding of the unification of science, it is possible to recast Engels unfortunate attempt to inject the dialectic into nature. Contemporary "natural science" is an historical relic. It originated in the sixteenth and seventeenth centuries with the need to appropriate nature through industry, and reflects this need concretely by continuing to posit nature as wholly external to human activity. By so doing, science could provide capitalism with the technology through which nature could be socialized. At the precise moment when nature was being theorised as external, however, the last vestiges of this externality were being practically destroyed; nature became increasingly produced. The unity of science therefore demands nothing so simple as the injection of nature with the dialectic. That dialectic already exists in the *relation* to nature exemplified by natural science. The issue is not to inject the dialectic but to retrieve it.

By holding nature as external to society, the Object as wholly outside the Subject, natural science constitutes itself as rigorously non-dialectical. It makes itself deliberately blind to the other side of relation with nature. Yet as it maintains this externality of nature, it at the same time appropriates nature, brings it within itself,

33 Marx, *op. cit.*, footnote 10, Vol. 3, p. 820. For a more elaborate version of this argument, see Smith, N. 'The Production of Nature' John Hopkins, Mimeo.

34 Mars & Engels, *Feuerbach.* (London: Lawrence and Wishart, 1973), p. 15.

35 Marx, *op. cit.*, footnote 9, p. 355.

36 Wilbur Zelinsky, "The Demigod's Dilemma," *Annals of the Association of American Geographers*, Vol. 65, (1975), pp. 140, 125, c.f. also: "the natural sciences are in a pre-social state," David Harvey, *Social Justice and the City.* (Baltimore: John Hopkins University Press, 1973), p. 127.

in order to produce knowledge of it. This very project is clearly contradictory; nature is assumed external but made internal. This and other contradictions arise from the way natural scientists relate to nature, but they are ignored or rather displaced and externalized. They do not long remain external, however; they resurface in quite tangible form and are becoming more and more difficult to conceive as externalities: the production of deficient soils and the general degradation of much agricultural land; the production of culturally deficient landscapes; pollution and the erratic availability of resources; the politics of nuclear energy; internal scientific revolutions.[37]

Burgess notes appropriately that "geographical theory, at the heart of which must stand a concept of nature, oscillates between a generality that would appall even a diplomat and an ecelecticism that would frighten a scientologist."[38] The foregoing sketch of a theory of nature offers a more coherent focus for scientific research. It suggests two things: first, the relation of human societies and individuals with nature is the inescapable context or problematic for science; second, the unity of this relation is contradicted by the arbitrariness of disciplinary boundaries. Geography is not unique in its concern to produce a "science of man's relation to nature;" all science is concerned to a greater or lesser extent with this relation.

It is possible to illustrate this argument more concretely with reference to natural hazard research. Typically, this research displays the three major ways of dealing with the contradiction within the positivist conception of nature (see above). Thus the physical science paradigm deems nature as totally separate from human activity, and it is this interpretation that dominates natural hazards research.[39] The hazard event (landslide, flood, earthquake, etc.) is seen as the result of the natural and inevitable operation of internal physical processes ranging from the geological to the climatological. This interpretation accepts hazards as natural, meaning in effect that they are "acts of God" – beyond the realm of societal influence. It is not surprising, then, that most government research money is channeled into the search for "natural" causes, rather than an examination of human vulnerability in hazards, for the assumption of the autonomy of nature provides plausible depoliticized explanations for the distribution of the disaster's effect throughout the population. And these "act of God" explanations are then used by insurance companies to avoid liability – an astute use of feudal scientific categories by finance capital.

[37] On the degradation of cultural landscapes, see E. Relph, *Place and Placelessness*, Pion, London, 1976. On science's reaction to its own occasional sterility, consider the reaction to Thomas Kuhn's *The Structure of Scientific Revolutions*, U. of Chicago Press, 1962. That this book was ecstatically received is due to the relatively sophisticated way in which Kuhn explained scientific revolutions as the product of a dialectical process of development within science. But he managed to do so purely as an exercise in intellectual history, without threatening the cherished autonomy of science from other human activity. Neither did he impose external social reality on the transubstantial psyches of practicing scientists, nor did he for a moment entertain the dangerous idea that the dialectic had a place in natural scientific inquiry itself, as opposed to the history of it.

[38] Rod Burgess, "The concept of Nature in Geography and Marxism." *Antipode*, Vol. 10.2, (1978), p. 4.

[39] For a statement of this approach see E. A. Keller, *Environmental Geology* (Columbus: Merrill, 1976).

A second approach to natural hazards has been pioneered by geographers, who have likewise asserted the separation of natural and social events, but who place this separation under a larger umbrella concept of nature; natural and social science study different natures. At best this interpretation understands disaster occurrence as an inter-face between a vulnerable population and an extreme event. This dualism does not surpass the subject–object distinction of nature and society and so reduces scientific inquiry to an examination of two forms whose essential *natures* are given. More frequently, disaster vulnerability is analysed as if nature is neutral so that the environment is hazardous *only* when it "intersects with people."[40] But behind this posited neutrality of nature with respect to society is a clear technocratic agenda that seeks to control "natural" hazards by extending the human domination of a supposedly external nature.

The third approach to hazards which reflects the third method for dealing with the contradiction in the positivist concept of nature amounts to the dissolution of human nature into external nature. Virtually Malthusian in outlook, this approach notes that the poor are worst affected in most disasters, and attributes this not only to the lack of resources commanded by the poor, but especially to a tendency for the poor to breed too fast. This approach is a classic example of blaming the victim, and the policy recommendations accompanying it make this clear. The Malthusian logic leads to a triage policy – the "logical" selection of which victims should be assisted after the event.[41]

In capitalist society, it is the material production of nature that unifies the previously separate social and natural realms, but it does so without, at the same time, making them identical – without dissolving one into the other. This offers a superior framework within which to view disasters. It emphasizes not nature or society as such, but primarily the relation *with* nature (first *and* second nature); it is this relation that is responsible for shaping both nature and society in the production process. It is a social relation which in capitalist society means a class relation. Thus vulnerability to disaster is, as the Malthusian approach recognizes, a class relation, but the reasons for this are not to be found in the individual incapabilities of the working class, peasantry or whatever: "*nature* does not produce on the one side owners of money or commodities, and on the other men possessing nothing but their own labour power. This relation has no natural basis, neither is its social basis one that is common to all historical periods."[42] The division of labor, which

[40] The paradigmatic work in this approach is I. Burton, R. W. Kates, and G. F. White, *The Environment as Hazard*. (New York: Oxford University Press, 1978).

[41] Among adherents to this approach see Garrett Hardin, "The Tragedy of Commons," *Science*, Vol. 162, (1968), pp. 1243–8. For a critique of Malthusian population doctrine see David Harvey, "Population, Resources, and the Ideology of Science." *Economic Geography*, Vol. 50, (1974), pp. 256–77.

[42] Marx, *op. cit.*, footnote 10, Vol. 1, p. 169 (emphasis added). After the 1976 earthquake in Guatemala City there occurred an interesting illustration of the class relation with nature. Residents stopped talking of an earthquake and called it a "classquake." See also P. Susman, P. O'Keefe, and B. Wisner, "Global Disasters: A Radical Approach," in K. Hewitt, ed., *Approaches to National Hazard*. (Waterloo, Ontario; Wilfred Laurier University Press), forthcoming.

achieves a qualitatively different significance with the coming of capitalist society, ensures differential access to nature, and this is equally the case with so-called natural disasters. Exposure to the environment produced under capitalism is universal, but the consequence of this exposure are far from uniform. . . .

Conclusion

The capitalist mode of production can continue to produce nature – and, as a by-product, space – only so long as it can continue to produce its own "natural" basis: Labor on the one side, Capital on the other. To grasp scientifically this relation with nature, it will be necessary to do as Marx did: "through the critique of . . . Science to bring . . . science to the point where it can be presented dialectically."[47] By thus retrieving the dialectic, science will also retrieve the politics of class struggle which rightfully permeate its subject-matter, but which, under orthodox bourgeois conceptions of science, are ideologically displaced.

[47] Marx in a letter to Engels, February, 1858, quoted in Schmidt, *op. cit.*, footnote 14, p. 52.

17

THE MORPHOLOGY OF LANDSCAPE

Carl O. Sauer

One of the century's most eminent geographers, Carl Sauer (1889–1975) was associated with the University of California, Berkeley, for most of his academic life. While a graduate student at Chicago he had attended lectures by Ellen Semple (**chapter 14**) but came to reject her brand of environmentalism as dogmatic. In one of his few methodological statements, 'Morphology' presented a coherent alternative derived from mainly German geographical influences, many of which he shared with Hartshorne (**chapter 24**) despite their evident clashes over the question of time. Geography could not be defined as an abstract relationship, it had to have a substantive content, the cultural landscape. This emphasized the material record of humans upon the landscape and the areal association of physical and cultural phenomena, excluding customs and beliefs. The essay was well received by his contemporaries but Sauer's own work in Mexico and Latin America rarely stuck to this programme. He figured prominently in studies of the origins of agriculture, the diffusion of plants and animals, and the impact of conquest upon indigenous American societies. Sauer was a prime mover of the Princeton symposium on Man's Role in Changing the Face of the Earth, in 1955, and a long-time advocate of a less destructive attitude towards the environment. But many later geographers (for example, Daniels, **chapter 19**) have criticized his methodological statements for containing an inadequate or determinist concept of culture.

Source: The Morphology of landscape. *University of California Publications in Geography* 2, 2, 19–54, 1925.

Introduction

Diverse opinions regarding the nature of geography are still common. The label, geography, as is the case with history, is no trustworthy indication as to the matter contained. As long as geographers disagree as to their subject it will be necessary, through repeated definition, to seek common ground upon which a general position may be established. In this country a fairly coherent series of viewpoints has been advanced, especially through presidential addresses before the Association of American Geographers, which may be accepted as mirror and mould of geographic opinion in America. They are sufficiently clear and well known that they need not be restated.[1] In European geography a somewhat different orientation appears to be developing. In various quarters significant activity is being displayed, probably in some measure influenced by anti-intellectualist currents. At any rate a shaking up of some vigor is under way. It may therefore be appropriate to reëxamine the field of geography, keeping current views abroad especially in mind, in order to attempt a working hypothesis that may serve to illuminate in some degree both the nature of the objective and the problem of systematic method.

The Field of Geography

The phenomenologic view of science. – All science may be regarded as phenomenology,[2] the term science being used in the sense of organized process of acquiring knowledge, rather than in the common restricted meaning of a unified body of physical law. Every field of knowledge is characterized by its declared preoccupation with a certain group of phenomena, which it undertakes to identify and order according to their relations. These facts are assembled with increasing knowledge of their connection; the attention to their connection denotes scientific approach. "A fact is first determined when it is recognized as to limits and qualities, and it is understood when it is viewed in its relations. Out of this follows the necessity of predetermined modes of inquiry and of the creation of a system that makes clear the relation of the phenomena. . . . Every individual science is naïve as a special discipline, in so far as it accepts the section of reality which is its field *tel quel* and does not question its position in the general scene of nature; within these limits, however, it proceeds critically, since it undertakes to determine the connection of the phenomena and their order."[3] According to such definition of the grounds of knowledge, the first concern is with the phenomena that constitute the "section of reality" which is occupied by geography, the next with the method of determining their connection.

Geography as a 'naïvely given section of reality.' – Disagreement as to the content of geography is so great that three distinct fields of inquiry are usually designated as geography: (1) The study of the earth as the medium of physical processes, or

[1] In particular the following addresses are notable expressions of leading opinion: Davis, W. M., "An Inductive Study of the Content of Geography," Bull. Am. Geog. Soc., vol. 38, pp. 67–84 (1906); Fenneman, N. M., "The Circumference of Geography," Ann. Assoc. Am. Geog., vol. 9, pp. 3–12 (1919); Barrows, H. H., "Geography as Human Ecology," *ibid.*, vol. 13, pp. 1–14 (1923).

[2] v. Keyserling, H., Prolegomena zur Naturphilosophie, p. 11 (1910).

[3] *Ibid.*, pp. 8 and 11.

the geophysical part of cosmologic science; (2) the study of life-forms as subject to their physical environment, or a part of biophysics, dealing with tropisms; and (3) the study of the areal or habitat differentiation of the earth, or chorology. In these three fields there is partial accordance of phenomena, but little of relation. One may choose between the three; they may hardly be consolidated into one discipline.

The great fields of knowledge exist because they are universally recognized as being concerned with a great category of phenomena. The experience of mankind, not the inquiry of the specialist, has made the primary subdivisions of knowledge. Botany is the study of plants, and geology that of rocks, because these categories of fact are evident to all intelligence that has concerned itself with the observation of nature. In the same sense, area or landscape is the field of geography, because it is a naïvely given, important section of reality, not a sophisticated thesis. Geography assumes the responsibility for the study of areas because there exists a common curiosity about that subject. The fact that every school child knows that geography provides information about different countries is enough to establish the validity of such a definition.

No other subject has preëmpted the study of area. Others, such as historians and geologists, may concern themselves with areal phenomena, but in that case they are avowedly using geographic facts for their own ends. If one were to establish a different discipline under the name of geography, the interest in the study of areas would not be destroyed thereby. The subject existed long before the name was coined. The literature of geography in the sense of chorology begins with parts of the earliest sagas and myths, vivid as they are with the sense of place and of man's contest with nature. The most precise expression of geographic knowledge is found in the map, an immemorial symbol. The Greeks wrote geographic accounts under such designations as periplus, periodos, and periegesis long before the name geography was used. Yet even the present name is more than two thousand years old. Geographic treatises appear in numbers among the earliest printed books. Explorations have been the dramatic reconnaissances of geography. The great geographic societies justly have accorded a place of honor to explorers. "Hic et ubique" is the device under which geography has stood always. The universality and persistence of the chorologic interest and the priority of claim which geography has to this field are the evidences on which the case for the popular definition may rest.

We may therefore be content with the simple connotation of the Greek word which the subject uses as its name, and which means most properly areal knowledge. The Germans have translated it as *Landschaftskunde* or *Länderkunde*, the knowledge of landscape or of lands. The other term, *Erdkunde*, the science of the earth in general, is falling rapidly into disuse.

> *The thought of a general earth science is impossible of realization; geography can be an independent science only as chorology, that is as knowledge of the varying expression of the different parts of the earth's surface. It is, in the first place, the study of lands; general geography is not general earth science, rather it presupposes the general properties and processes*

of the earth, or accepts them from other sciences; for its own part it is oriented about their varying areal expression.[4]

With this preference of synthetic areal knowledge to general earth science the entire tradition of geography is in agreement.

The interdependence of areal phenomena. – Probably not even the adherents of other, recent schools of geography would deny place for such a view of the subject, but they deem this naïvely given body of facts inadequate to establish a science, or at the most would consider it an auxiliary discipline which compiles fragmentary evidence, to find its place ultimately in a general geophysical or biophysical system. The argument then is shifted from the phenomenal content to the nature of the connection of the phenomena. We assert the place for a science that finds its entire field in the landscape on the basis of the significant reality of chorologic relation. The phenomena that make up an area are not simply assorted but are associated, or interdependent. To discover this areal "connection of the phenomena and their order" is a scientific task, according to our position the only one to which geography should devote its energies. The position falls only if the non-reality of area be shown. The competence to arrive at orderly conclusions is not affected in this case by the question of coherence or incoherence of the data, for their characteristic association, as we find them in the area, is an expression of coherence. The element of time is admittedly present in the association of geographic facts, which are thereby in large part non-recurrent. This, however, places them beyond the reach of scientific inquiry only in a very narrow sense, for time as a factor has a well-recognized place in many scientific fields, where time is not simply a term for some identifiable causal relation. . . .

Summary of the objective of geography. – The task of geography is conceived as the establishment of a critical system which embraces the phenomenology of landscape, in order to grasp in all of its meaning and color the varied terrestrial scene. Indirectly Vidal de la Blache has stated this position by cautioning against considering "the earth as 'the scene on which the activity of man unfolds itself,' without reflecting that this scene is itself living."[8] It includes the works of man as an integral expression of the scene. This position is derived from Herodotus rather than from Thales. Modern geography is the modern expression of the most ancient geography.

The objects which exist together in the landscape exist in interrelation. We assert that they constitute a reality as a whole which is not expressed by a consideration of the constituent parts separately, that area has form, structure, and function, and hence position in a system, and that it is subject to development, change, and completion. Without this view of areal reality and relation, there exist only

[4] Hettner, A., "Methodische Zeit und Streitfragen," Geog. Ztschr., vol. 29, p. 37 (1923). Hettner is cited here in the latest statement of the position he has defended ably for many years. To American geographers Fenneman's address of 1919, cited above, is ever memorable for its spirited declaration of the same thesis.

[8] Principes de la géographie humaine, p. 6 (1922).

special disciplines, not geography as generally understood. The situation is analogous to history, which may be divided among economics, government, sociology, and so on; but when this is done the result is not history.

The Content of Landscape

Definition of landscape. – The term 'landscape' is proposed to denote the unit concept of geography, to characterize the peculiarly geographic association of facts. Equivalent terms in a sense are 'area' and 'region.' Area is of course a general term, not distinctively geographic. Region has come to imply, to some geographers at least, an order of magnitude. Landscape is the English equivalent of the term German geographers are using largely and strictly has the same meaning, a land shape, in which the process of shaping is by no means thought of as simply physical. It may be defined, therefore, as an area made up of a distinct association of forms, both physical and cultural.[9]

The facts of geography are plain facts; their association gives rise to the concept of landscape. Similarly, the facts of history are time facts; their association gives rise to the concept of period. By definition the landscape has identity that is based on recognizable constitution, limits, and generic relation to other landscapes, which constitute a general system. Its structure and function are determined by integrant, dependent forms. The landscape is considered, therefore, in a sense as having an organic quality. We may follow Bluntschli in saying that one has not fully understood the nature of an area until one "has learned to see it as an organic unit, to comprehend land and life in terms of each other."[10] It has seemed desirable to introduce this point prior to its elaboration because it is very different from the unit concept of physical process of the physiographer or of environmental influence of the anthropogeographer of the school of Ratzel. The mechanics of glacial erosion, the climatic correlation of energy, and the form content of an areal habitat are three different things.

Landscape has generic meaning. – In the sense here used, landscape is not simply an actual scene viewed by an observer. The geographic landscape is a generalization derived from the observation of individual scenes. Croce's remark that "the geographer who is describing a landscape has the same task as a landscape painter"[11] has therefore only limited validity. The geographer may describe the individual landscape as a type or possibly as a variant from type, but always he has in mind the generic, and proceeds by comparison.

An ordered presentation of the landscapes of the earth is a formidable undertaking. Beginning with infinite diversity, salient and related features are selected

[9] Sölch, J., Auffassung der natürlichen Grenzen (1924), has proposed the term 'Chore' to designate the same idea.

[10] "Die Amazonasniederung als harmonischer Organismus," Geog. Ztschr., vol. 27, p. 49 (1921).

[11] Quoted by Barth, P., Philosophie der Geschichte (ed. 2), p. 10.

in order to establish the character of the landscape and to place it in a system. Yet generic quality is non-existent in the sense of the biologic world. Every landscape has individuality as well as relation to other landscapes, and the same is true of the forms that make it up. No valley is quite like any other valley; no city the exact replica of some other city. In so far as these qualities remain completely unrelated they are beyond the reach of systematic treatment, beyond that organized knowledge that we call science. "No science can rest at the level of mere perception. . . . The so-called descriptive natural sciences, zoology and botany, do not remain content to regard the singular, they raise themselves to concepts of species, genus, family, order, class, type."[12] "There is no idiographic science, that is, one that describes the individual merely as such. Geography formerly was idiographic; long since it has attempted to become nomothetic, and no geographer would hold it at its previous level."[13] Whatever opinion one may hold about natural law, or nomothetic, genetic, or causal relation, a definition of landscape as singular, unorganized, or unrelated has no scientific value.

Element of personal judgment in the selection of content. – It is true that in the selection of the generic characteristics of landscape the geographer is guided only by his own judgment that they are characteristic, that is, repeating; that they are arranged into a pattern, or have structural quality, and that the landscape accurately belongs to a specific group in the general series of landscapes. Croce objects to a science of history on the ground that history is without logical criteria: "The criterion is the choice itself, conditioned, like every economic art, by knowledge of the actual situation. This selection is certainly conducted with intelligence, but not with the application of a philosophic criterion, and is justified only in and by itself. For this reason we speak of the fine tact, or scent, or instinct of the learned man."[14] A similar objection is sometimes urged against the scientific competence of geography, because it is unable to establish complete, rigid logical control and perforce relies upon the option of the student. The geographer is in fact continually exercising freedom of choice as to the materials which he includes in his observations, but he is also continually drawing inferences as to their relation. His method, imperfect as it may be, is based on induction; he deals with sequences, though he may not regard these as a simple causal relation.

If we consider a given type of landscape, for example a North European heath, we may put down notes such as the following:

The sky is dull, ordinarily partly overcast, the horizon is indistinct and rarely more than a half-dozen miles distant, though seen from a height. The upland is gently and irregularly rolling and descends to broad, flat basins. There are no long slopes and no symmetrical patterns of surface form. Watercourses are short, with clear brownish water, and perennial. The brooks

[12] Barth, *op. cit.*, p. 11.

[13] *Ibid.*, p. 39.

[14] On History, pp. 109, 110. The statement applies to the history that has the goal simply of "making the past live again." There is, however, also a phenomenologic history, which may discover related forms and their expression.

end in irregular swamps, with indistinct borders. Coarse grasses and rushes form marginal strips along the water bodies. The upland is covered with heather, furze, and bracken. Clumps of juniper abound, especially on the steeper, drier slopes. Cart traces lie along the longer ridges, exposing loose sand in the wheel tracks, and here and there a rusty, cemented base shows beneath the sand. Small flocks of sheep are scattered widely over the land. The almost complete absence of the works of man is notable. There are no fields or other enclosed tracts. The only buildings are sheep sheds, situated usually at a distance of several miles from one another, at convenient intersections of cart traces.

The account is not that of an individual scene, but a summation of general characteristics. References to other types of landscape are introduced by implication. Relations of form elements within the landscape are also noted. The items selected are based upon "knowledge of the actual situation" and there is an attempt at a synthesis of the form elements. Their significance is a matter of personal judgment. Objective standards may be substituted for them only in part, as by quantitative representation in the form of a map. Even thus the personal element is brought only under limited control, since it still operates in choosing the qualities to be represented. All that can be expected is the reduction of the personal element by agreeing on a "predetermined mode of inquiry," which shall be logical.

Extensiveness of areal features. – The content of landscape is something less than the whole of its visible constituents. The identity of the landscape is determined first of all by conspicuousness of form, as implied in the following statement: "A correct representation of the surface form, of soil, and of surficially conspicuous masses of rock, of plant cover and water bodies, of the coasts and the sea, of areally conspicuous animal life and of the expression of human culture is the goal of geographic inquiry."[15] The items specified are chosen because the experience of the author has shown their significance as to mass and relation. The chorologic position necessarily recognizes the importance of areal extensiveness of phenomena, this quality being inherent in the position. Herein lies an important contrast between geography and physiography. The character of the heath landscape described above is determined primarily by the dominance of sand, swamp, and heather. The most important geographic fact about Norway, aside from its location, probably is that four-fifths of its surface is barren highland, supporting neither forests nor flocks, a condition significant directly because of its extensiveness.

Habitat value as a basis for the determination of content. – Personal judgment of the content of landscape is determined further by interest. Geography is distinctly anthropocentric, in the sense of value or use of the earth to man. We are interested in that part of the areal scene which concerns us as human beings because we are part of it, live with it, are limited by it, and modify it. Thus we select those qualities of landscape in particular that are or may be of use to us. We relinquish those features of area that may be significant to the geologist in earth history but are of no concern in the relation of man to his area. The physical qualities of landscape then are those that have habitat value, present or potential.

[15] Passarge, Grundlagen der Landschaftskunde, vol. 1, p. 1 (1920).

The natural and the cultural landscape. – "Human geography does not oppose itself to a geography from which the human element is excluded; such a one has not existed except in the minds of a few exclusive specialists."[16] It is a forcible abstraction, by every good geographic tradition a tour de force, to consider a landscape as though it were devoid of life. Because we are interested primarily in "cultures which grow with original vigor out of the lap of a maternal natural landscape, to which each is bound in the whole course of its existence,"[17] geography is based on the reality of the union of physical and cultural elements of the landscape. The content of landscape is found therefore in the physical qualities of area that are significant to man and in the forms of his use of the area, in facts of physical background and facts of human culture. A valuable discussion of this principle is given by Krebs under the title "Natur- und Kulturlandschaft."[18]

For the first half of the content of landscape we may use the designation 'site,' which has become well established in plant ecology. A forest site is not simply the place where a forest stands; in its full connotation, the name is a qualitative expression of place in terms of forest growth, usually for the particular forest association that is in occupation of the site. In this sense the physical area is the sum of all natural resources that man has at his disposal in that area. It is beyond his power to add to them; he may 'develop' them, ignore them in part, or subtract from them by exploitation.

The second half of landscape viewed as a bilateral unit is its cultural expression. There is a strictly geographic way of thinking of culture; namely, as the impress of the works of man upon the area. We may think of people as associated within and with an area, as we may think of them as groups associated in descent or tradition. In the first case we are thinking of culture as a geographic expression, composed of forms which are part of geographic phenomenology. In this view there is no place for a dualism of landscape.

The Application of the Morphologic Method

Form of induction. – The systematic organization of the content of landscape proceeds with the repression of a priori theories concerning it. The massing and ordering of phenomena as forms that are integrated into structures and the

[16] Vidal de la Blache, P., *op. cit.*, p. 3.

[17] Spengler, O., Untergang des Abendlandes, vol. 1, p. 28 (1922–23): "Kulturen die mit urweltlicher Kraft aus dem Schoose einer mütterlichen Landschaft, an die jede von ihnen im ganzen Verlauf ihres Daseins streng gebunden ist, erblühen."

[18] Ztschr. Gesell. f. Erdkunde, Berlin (1923), p. 83. He states the content of geography as being "in the area (Raum) itself with its surfaces, lines, and points, its form, circumference, and content. The relations to geometry, the pure areal science, become even more intimate, when not only the area as such, but its position with reference to other areas is considered."

comparative study of the data as thus organized constitute the morphologic method of synthesis, a special empirical method. Morphology rests upon the following postulates: (1) that there is a unit of organic or quasi-organic quality, that is, a structure to which certain components are necessary, these component elements being called 'forms' in this paper; (2) that similarity of form in different structures is recognized because of functional equivalence, the forms then being 'homologous'; and (3) that the structural units may be placed in series, especially into developmental sequence, ranging from incipient to final or completed stage. Morphologic study does not necessarily affirm an organism in the biologic sense as, for example, in the sociology of Herbert Spencer, but only organized unit concepts that are related. Without being committed in any sense to a general biogenetic law, the organic analogy has proved most useful throughout the fields of social inquiry. It is a working device, the truth of which may perhaps be subject to question, but which leads nevertheless to increasingly valid conclusions.[19]

The term 'morphology' originated with Goethe and expresses his contribution to modern science. It may be well to recall that he turned to biologic and geologic studies because he was interested in the nature and limits of cognition. Believing that there were things "accessible and inaccessible" to human knowledge, he concluded: "One need not seek for something beyond the phenomena; they themselves are the lore (Lehre)." Thus originated his form studies, and especially those of homology of form. His method of scientific inquiry rested on a definite philosophic position.

If therefore the morphologic method appears unpretentious to the student who is eager to come to large conclusions, it may be pointed out that it rests upon a deliberate restraint in the affirmation of knowledge. It is a purely evidential system, without prepossession regarding the meaning of its evidence, and presupposes a minimum of assumption; namely, only the reality of structural organization. Being objective and value-free, or nearly so, it is competent to arrive at increasingly significant results. . . .

Preparatory Systematic Description

The first step in morphologic study. – Historically "geography commenced by describing and registering, that is as a systematic study. It proceeded thereupon to . . . genetic relation, morphology."[24] The geographic study is still thus begun. The description of observed facts is by some predetermined order that represents a preliminary grouping of the material. Such systematic description is for the purpose of morphologic relation and is really the beginning of morphologic synthesis. It is therefore distinguishable from morphology not at all in principle

[19] The assumption 'as if,' advanced by Vaihinger as "Philosophie des Als Ob."
[24] Krebs, *op. cit.*, p. 81.

but in that it lies at a lower critical level. The relation is not dissimilar to that between taxonomy and biologic morphology.

Descriptive terminology. – The problem of geographic description differs from that of taxonomy principally in the availability of terms. The facts of area have been under popular observation to such an extent that a new terminology is for the most part not necessary. Salisbury held that the forms of landscape had generally received serviceable popular names and that codification might proceed from popular parlance without the coining of new terms. Proceeding largely in this manner, we are building up a list of form terms, that are being enriched from many areas and many languages. Very many more are still awaiting introduction into geographic literature. These terms apply as largely to soil, drainage, and climatic forms as they do to land surface. Also popular usage has named many vegetational associations and has prepared for us a still largely unprospected wealth of cultural form terms. Popular terminology is a fairly reliable warrant of the significance of the form, as implied in its adoption. Such names may apply to single form constituents, as glade, tarn, loess. Or they may be form associations of varying magnitude, as heath, steppe, piedmont. Or they may be proper names to designate unit landscapes, as, for example, the regional names that are in use for most parts of France. Such popular nomenclature is rich in genetic meaning, but with sure chorologic judgment it proceeds not from cause but from a generic summation; namely, from form similarities and contrasts.

If systematic description is a desideratum for geography, we are still in great need of enlarging our descriptive vocabulary. The meagerness of our descriptive terms is surprising by comparison with other sciences. Contributing causes may be the idiographic tradition of unrelated description, and the past predilection for process studies which minimized the real multiplicity of forms.

The predetermined descriptive system. – The reduction of description to a system has been largely opposed by geographers and not entirely without cause. Once this happens the geographer is responsible within those limits for any areal study he undertakes; otherwise he is free to roam, to choose, and to leave. We are not concerned here with geography as an art. As a science it must accept all feasible means for the regimentation of its data. However excellent the individualistic, impressionistic selection of phenomena may be, it is an artistic, not a scientific desideratum. The studies in geomorphology, in particular those of the school of Davis, represent perhaps the most determined attempt to oppose uncontrolled freedom of choice in observation by a strict limitation of observations and of method. Different observations may be compared as to their findings only if there is a reasonable agreement as to the classes of facts with which they deal. The attempt at a broad synthesis of regional studies by employing our existing literature immediately runs into difficulties, because the materials do not fit together. Findings on the most important theme of human destructiveness of natural landscape are very difficult to make because there are no adequate points of reference. Some observers note soil erosion systematically, others casually, and still others may pay no attention to it. If geography is to be systematic and not idiosyncratic, there must be increasing agreement as to items of observation. In particular this should mean a general descriptive scheme to be followed in the collection of field notes.[25]

A general descriptive scheme, intended to catalogue areal facts broadly, without proceeding at this stage from hypothetical origins and connections, has been recently proposed by Passarge under the name *Beschreibende Landschaftskunde.*[26] It is the first comprehensive treatment of this subject since v. Richthofen's Führer für Forschungsreisende, written just prior to the most flourishing period of geomorphology (1886). The work of Passarge is somewhat rough-hewn and it is perhaps excessively schematic, yet it is the most adequate consideration by far that the whole matter of geographic description has had. Its express purpose is "first of all to determine the facts and to attempt a correct presentation of the significant, visible facts of area without any attempt at explanation and speculation."[27] The plan provides

> *for the systematic observation of the phenomena that compose the landscape. The method resembles most closely the Chrie, a device for the collection of material in theme writing. It helps to see as much as possible and to miss as little as possible and has the further advantage that all observations are ordered. If earlier geographers had been familiar with a method of systematic observation of landscape, it would have been impossible for the characteristic red color of tropical residual soils to have escaped attention until v. Richthofen discovered that fact.*[28]

Passarge proceeds with an elaborate schedule of notes covering all form categories of the landscape, beginning with atmospheric effects and ending with forms of habitation. From these he proceeds to a descriptive classification of form associations into larger areal terms. For the further elaboration of the plan the reader is referred to the volume in question, as worthy of careful consideration.

The author has applied his system elsewhere to the 'pure' as against the 'explanatory' description of areas, as for example in his characterization of the Valley of the Okavango, in the northern salt steppe of the Kalahari.[29] That he succeeds in giving to the reader an adequate picture of the composition of area will probably be admitted.

One may note that Passarge's supposedly purely descriptive procedure is actually based on large experience in areal studies, through which a judgment as to the significant constituents of landscape has been formed. These are really determined through morphologic knowledge, though the classification is not genetic, but properly based on the naïvely generic forms. The capacious dragnet which Passarge has fashioned, though disclaiming all attempt at explanation, is in reality a device fashioned by experienced hands for catching all that may be wanted in an a real morphology and for deferring explanation until the whole material is sorted.

25 Sauer, C. O., "The Survey Method in Geography," Ann. Assoc. Am. Geog., vol. 14, pp. 19 ff. (1924).
26 Grundlagen der Landschaftskunde, vol. 1.
27 *Ibid.*, p. vi.
28 *Ibid.*, p. 5.
29 Hamburg Mitt. geog. Gesell, 1919, no. 1.

Forms of Landscape and Their Structure

The division between natural and cultural landscapes. – We cannot form an idea of landscape except in terms of its time relations as well as of its space relations. It is in continuous process of development or of dissolution and replacement. It is in this sense a true appreciation of historical values that has caused the geomorphologists to tie the present physical landscape back into its geologic origins, and to derive it therefrom step by step. In the chorologic sense, however, the modification of the area by man and its appropriation to his uses are of dominant importance. The area prior to the introduction of man's activity is represented by one body of morphologic facts. The forms that man has introduced are another set. We may call the former, with reference to man, the original, natural landscape. In its entirety it no longer exists in many parts of the world, but its reconstruction and understanding are the first part of formal morphology. Is it perhaps too broad a generalization to say that geography dissociates itself from geology at the point of the introduction of man into the areal scene? Under this view the prior events belong strictly in the field of geology and their historical treatment in geography is only a descriptive device employed where necessary to make clear the relationship of physical forms that are significant in the habitat.

The works of man express themselves in the cultural landscape. There may be a succession of these landscapes with a succession of cultures. They are derived in each case from the natural landscape, man expressing his place in nature as a distinct agent of modification. Of especial significance is that climax of culture which we call civilization. The cultural landscape then is subject to change either by the development of a culture or by a replacement of cultures. The datum line from which change is measured is the natural condition of the landscape. The division of forms into natural and cultural is the necessary basis for determining the areal importance and character of man's activity. In the universal, but not necessarily cosmologic sense, geography then becomes that part of the latest or human chapter in earth history which is connected with the differentiation of the areal scene by man. . . .

Diagrammatic representation of the morphology of the natural landscape. – We may now attempt a diagram of the nature of physical morphology to express the relation of landscape, constituent forms, time, and connecting causal factors [see Figure 17.1]. The thing to be known is the natural landscape. It becomes known through the totality of its forms. These forms are thought of not for and by themselves, as a soil specialist would regard soils, for example, but in their relation to one another and in their place in the landscape, each landscape being a definite combination of form values. Behind the forms lie time and cause. The primary genetic bonds are climatic and geognostic, the former being in general dominant and operating directly as well as through vegetation. The 'X' factor is the pragmatic 'and,' the always unequated remnant. These factors are justified as a device for the connection of the forms, not as the end of inquiry. They lead toward the concept of the natural landscape which in turn leads to the cultural landscape. The character of the landscape is determined also by its position on the time line. Whether

FACTORS		FORMS	
Geognostic Climatic Vegetational X	——TIME——→	Climate Land surface soil drainage mineral resource Sea and coast Vegetation	NATURAL LANDSCAPE

Figure 17.1 [orig. unnumbered]

this line is of determinate or infinite length does not concern us as geographers. In some measure, certainly, the idea of a climax landscape is useful, a landscape that, given a constancy of impinging factors, has exhausted the possibilities of autogenous development. Through the medium of time the application of factor to form as cause and effect relation is limited; time itself is a great factor. We are interested in function, not in a determination of cosmic unity. For all chorologic purposes the emphasis of the diagram lies at its right hand; time and factor have only an explanatory descriptive rôle.

This position with reference to the natural landscape involves a reaffirmation of the place of physical geography, certainly not as physiography nor geomorphology as ordinarily defined, but as physical morphology which draws freely from geology and physiography certain results to be built into a view of physical landscape as a habitat complex. This physical geography is the proper introduction to the full chorologic inquiry which is our goal. . . .

Summary of the form relations in the natural landscape. – The large emphasis on climate in the previous statements does not mean that geography is to be transformed into climatology. The physical area is fundamental to any geographic study because it furnishes the materials out of which man builds his culture. The identity of the physical area rests fundamentally on a distinctive association of physical forms. In the physical world, generic character of area and its genesis are coupled so closely that the one becomes an aid to the recognition of the other. In particular, climate, itself an areal form, largely obscure as to origin, so largely controls the expression of the other physical forms that in many areas it may be considered the determinant of form association. An express disclaimer may be entered, however, against the notion of the necessity of a genetic bond in order to organize the phenomenology of the natural landscape. The existence of such bonds has been determined empirically. By regarding the relationship of forms we have discovered an important light on "the obscurity of their descent," but as geographers we are not enjoined to trace out the nature of this descent. This remains the problem of geomorphology, which indeed now appears more complicated than ever, the validity of climatic control and of great secular changes of climate being accepted.

Thus far the way is pretty well marked. We know the 'inorganic' composition of landscape fairly well, and, except for a somewhat excessive aloofness existing

properly cared for.

The extension of morphology in the cultural landscape. – The natural landscape is being subjected to transformation at the hands of man, the last and for us the most important morphologic factor. By his cultures he makes use of the natural forms, in many cases alters them, in some destroys them.

The study of the cultural landscape is, as yet, largely an untilled field. Recent results in the field of plant ecology will probably supply many useful leads for the human geographer, for cultural morphology might be called human ecology. In contrast to the position of Barrows in this matter, the present thesis would eliminate physiologic ecology or autecology and seek for parallels in synecology. It is better not to force into geography too much biological nomenclature. The name ecology is not needed: it is both morphology and physiology of the biotic association. Since we waive the claim for the measurement of environmental influences, we may use, in preference to ecology, the term morphology to apply to cultural study, since it describes perfectly the method that is involved.

Among geographers in America who have concerned themselves with systematic inquiry into cultural forms, Mark Jefferson, O. E. Baker, and M. Aurousseau have done outstanding pioneering. Brunhes' "essential facts of geography" represent perhaps the most widely appreciated classification of cultural forms.[40] Sten DeGeer's population atlas of Sweden[41] was the first major contribution of a student who has concentrated his attention strictly on cultural morphology. Vaughan Cornish introduced the concepts of 'march,' 'storehouse,' and 'crossroads' in a most valuable contribution to urban problems.[42] Most recently, Geisler has undertaken a synthesis of the urban forms of Germany, with the deserved subtitle: "A contribution to the morphology of the cultural landscape."[43] These pioneers have found productive ground; our periodical literature suggests that a rush of homesteaders may soon be under way.

Diagrammatic representation of the morphology of the cultural landscape. – The cultural landscape is the geographic area in the final meaning (*Chore*). Its forms are all the works of man that characterize the landscape. Under this definition we are not concerned in geography with the energy, customs, or beliefs of man but with man's record upon the landscape [see Figure 17.2]. Forms of population are the phenomena of mass or density in general and of recurrent displacement, as seasonal migration. Housing includes the types of structures man builds and their grouping, either dispersed as in many rural districts, or agglomerated into villages or cities in varying plans (*Städtebild*). Forms of production are the types of land utilization for primary products, farms, forests, mines, and those negative areas which he has ignored.

The cultural landscape is fashioned out of a natural landscape by a culture group. Culture is the agent, the natural area is the medium, the cultural landscape

40 Brunhes, J., Human Geography (1910: Am. ed., 1920).

41 Befolkningens Fördeliing i Sverige (Stockholm, 1917).

42 The Great Capitals (London, 1923).

43 Die deutsche Stadt (Stuttgart, 1924).

FACTOR		MEDIUM	FORMS	
Culture	→ TIME →	Natural Landscape	Population density mobility Housing plan structure Production Communication XX	CULTURAL LANDSCAPE

Figure 17.2 [orig. unnumbered]

group. Culture is the agent, the natural area is the medium, the cultural landscape the result. Under the influence of a given culture, itself changing through time, the landscape undergoes development, passing through phases, and probably reaching ultimately the end of its cycle of development. With the introduction of a different, that is, alien culture, a rejuvenation of the cultural landscape sets in, or a new landscape is superimposed on remnants of an older one. The natural landscape is of course of fundamental importance, for it supplies the materials out of which the cultural landscape is formed. The shaping force, however, lies in the culture itself. Within the wide limits of the physical equipment of area lie many possible choices for man, as Vidal never grew weary of pointing out. This is the meaning of adaptation, through which, aided by those suggestions which man has derived from nature, perhaps by an imitative process, largely subconscious, we get the feeling of harmony between the human habitation and the landscape into which it so fittingly blends. But these, too, are derived from the mind of man, not imposed by nature, and hence are cultural expressions.

Morphology as Applied to the Branches of Geography

The consolidation of the two diagrams gives an approximation of the total scientific content of geography on the phenomenologic basis by which we have proceeded.[44] They may readily be expressed so as to define the branches of geography. (1) The study of the form categories per se in their general relation, the system of the forms of landscape, is morphology in the purely methodologic sense and is the equivalent of what is called, especially in France and Germany, general geography, the propaedeutic through which the student learns to work with his materials. (2) Regional geography is comparative morphology, the process of placing individual landscapes into relation to other landscapes. In the full chorologic sense, this is the ordering of cultural, not of natural landscapes. Such a critical

[44] The conclusions presented in this paper are substantially in agreement with Sten DeGeer's article "On the Definition, Method, and Classification of Geography," Geog. Annaler, 1923, pp. 1–37, with the contrast that a 'concrete' *landscape* takes the place of DeGeer's 'abstract' *areal relation*.

has thereby nearly rounded out a critique of the entire field of geography.[45] (3) Historical geography may be considered as the series of changes which the cultural landscapes have undergone and therefore involves the reconstruction of past cultural landscapes. Of special concern is the catalytic relation of civilized man to area and the effects of the replacement of cultures. From this difficult and little touched field alone may be gained a full realization of the development of the present cultural landscape out of earlier cultures and the natural landscape. (4) Commercial geography deals with the forms of production and the facilities for distribution of the products of areas.

Beyond Science

The morphologic discipline enables the organization of the fields of geography as positive science. A good deal of the meaning of area lies beyond scientific regimentation. The best geography has never disregarded the aesthetic qualities of landscape, to which we know no approach other than the subjective. Humboldt's 'physiognomy,' Banse's 'soul,' Volz's 'rhythm,' Gradmann's 'harmony' of landscape, all lie beyond science. They seem to have discovered a symphonic quality in the contemplation of the areal scene, proceeding from a full novitiate in scientific studies and yet apart therefrom. To some, whatever is mystical is an abomination. Yet it is significant that there are others, and among them some of the best, who believe, that having observed widely and charted diligently, there yet remains a quality of understanding at a higher plane which may not be reduced to formal process.[46]

Divergent Views of Geography

The geographic thesis of this article is so largely at variance with certain other views of the subject that it may be desirable to set forth in summary form what has been expressed and implied as to contrast in the several positions.

Geomorphology as a branch of geography. – German geographers in particular tend to regard geomorphology as an essential division of geography, and use largely the term *Oberflächengestaltung*, or the record of development of surficial form. The forms considered are ordinarily topographic only. The content of geomorphology has been most broadly defined by Penck,[47] who included the following forms: plains, hill surfaces, valleys, basins, mountains, cavernous forms, sea-coasts,

[45] Vergleichende Landschaftskunde (Berlin, 1923); Landschaftsgürtel der Erde (Breslau, 1923).

[46] A good statement of current searchings in this field is by Gradmann, R., "Das harmonische Landschaftsbild," Ztschr. Gesell. Erdk., Berlin, 1924, pp. 129–147. Banse has been publishing since 1922 a non- or antiscientific journal, Die Neue Geographie, in which numerous good items are enclosed in a repellently polemic shell.

[47] Morphologie der Erdoberfläche (1894), vol. 2.

seafloors, islands. These descriptive topographic terms are studied by geomorphology as to their derivation, not as to use significance.

Geomorphology being the history of topography, it derives present surfaces from previous forms and records the processes involved. A study of the geomorphology of the Sierra Nevada is a history of the sculpturing of the mountain massif, concerned with the uplift of the earth block, and the stages of modification in which erosional processes, secondary deformations, and structural conditions are in complex relations. Relief features in this sense are the result of the opposition of orogenic and degraditional processes through geologic periods of time. Certain features, such as peneplains and terrace remnants, thus have high diagnostic value in reading the record of modification of surface. These elements of the landscape, however, may be of little or no significance in the chorologic sense. To geomorphology the peneplain has been extremely important; the trend of geography has not been notably affected by its discovery. Out of the topographic complex the geomorphologist may select one body of facts illustrative of earth history, the geographer will use a largely different set of facts which have habitat significance.

The geomorphologist, therefore, is likely to be a specialized historical geologist, working on certain, usually late, chapters of earth history. Conventional historical geology is mostly concerned with the making of rock formations. The geomorphologist directs attention to erosional and deformational surfaces in the record of the rocks. To such an extent has this been the American orientation that we have in our country little geomorphologic work of recent date that is consciously geographic in purpose, that is, descriptive of actual land surfaces.

The geomorphologist can and does establish a connection between the fields of geography and geology and his labors further our own work. He advances our studies of landscape materially where he has preceded the geographer, and we properly regard him potentially as much a collaborator in geography as in geology. One of the present needs in American geography is a greater familiarity with and application of geomorphologic studies.

Physiography and physical geography. – When Huxley reapplied the term physiography he disclaimed expressly the desire to reform physical geography. He was not lecturing, he said, "on any particular branch of natural knowledge, but on natural phenomena in general."[48] The subtitle of his treatise read: "An Introduction to the Study of Nature." He chose the Basin of the Thames as the area for his demonstration, not through chorologic interest, but in order to show that any area contained abundant material for the demonstration of the general laws of physical science. Huxley said:

> *I endeavored to show that the application of the plainest and simplest processes of reasoning to any of these phenomena, suffices to show, lying behind it, a cause, which will again suggest another; until, step by step, the conviction dawns upon the learner that, to attain to even an elementary conception of what goes on in his parish he must know something about the*

[48] Physiography (1877), p. vi.

universe; that the pebble he kicks aside, would not be what it is and where it is, unless a particular chapter of the earth's history, finished untold ages ago, had been exactly what it was.[49]

The two central ideas in his mind were the unity of physical law as shown by the features of the earth and the evolutionary march of the geologic record. It was the bright hour of dawn in scientific monism, with Huxley officiating at the observation of the lands. Physiography served in such a canonical rôle in elementary scientific education until a later age of machinery sent it into the discard in favor of 'general science.'

Physiography is still the general science of the earth, and concerns itself with the physical processes that operate at the surface of the earth and in the earth's crust. We still find the captions that Huxley introduced into his text: the work of rain and rivers, ice and its work, the sea and its work, earthquakes and volcanoes. These things have chorologic expression but they are studied as general processes. As an investigator the physiographer must be above all things a physicist, and increasing demands are made on his physical and mathematical knowledge. The way of the development of physiography as research is through geophysical institutes. Academically it fits in best as a part of dynamic geology. The geographer probably needs to know little more of it than he should know of historical geology.

One may question, therefore, the propriety of such terms as regional physiography and physiographic regions. They contradict the essential meaning of the subject and ordinarily mean rather a loose form of geomorphology, which of necessity has areal expression. Physiography was conceived as a purely dynamic relation and is categorically incapable of consistent areal expression unless it becomes also a name applied to physical geography or to geomorphology.

Geographic morphology vs. 'geographic influences.' – The study of the physical environment as an active agency has recently been subjected to trenchant criticism by L. Febvre, with an equally incisive foreword by Henri Berr.[50] Both thoroughly relish the chance to riddle this geographic ambition. Geography as they see it is "to give an example of the true task of synthesis. . . . The effort of synthesis is a directed activity; it is not a premature realization.'[51] Questions of environment "may have for the geographer their interest; but they are not his end. He must guard well against acclaiming as 'scientific' verities theories of adaptation 'simpliste' in character which more competent people are in process of completing or correcting.'[52] "What is, then, the commendable attitude in human geography? It can consist only in searching for the relations which exist between earth and life, the rapport which exists between the external milieu and the activity of the

[49] *Ibid.*, pp. vii, viii.
[50] La terre et l'évolution humaine (Paris, 1922).
[51] *Ibid.*, p. ix.
[52] *Ibid.*, p. 11.

occupants."[53] Vidal de la Blache's thesis that in the relation of man to the earth there exists less of necessary adaptation than of 'possibilisme' is worked out with skill and conviction. Excepting for their spirited devotion to the master of French geography, the authors are not really familiar with geographic thought. They do not fairly represent the tenets of geography because they know chiefly the publicists of environmentalism, against whom they consider Vidal as the outstanding bulwark. Vidal will have an honored place in the history of geography, but we are no longer much impressed by his concern to establish decently good relations with rationalistic thought. Rationalism has seen better days than these; we no longer need to come to terms with it by diplomatic compromise. In spite of the deficient orientation in geographic thought, the volume directs a quality of dialectic at one geographic school which entitles it to high rank in geographic criticism.

In this country the theme that geography is the study of natural environment has been dominant in the present generation. It has come to be advertised abroad that such is the American definition of geography.[54] The earliest term was 'environmental control.' This was succeeded by 'response,' 'influence,' 'adjustment,' or some other word that does not change the meaning, but substitutes a more cautious term for the ringing declaration of control. All these positions are mechanistic. In some way they hope to measure the force that physical environment exerts over man. The landscape as such has no interest for them, but only those cultural features for which a causal connection with the physical environment can be established. The aim, therefore, is to make of geography a part of biophysics, concerned with human tropisms.

Geographic morphology does not deny determinism, nor does it require adhesion to that particular faith in order to qualify in the profession. Geography under the banner of environmentalism represents a dogma, the assertion of a faith that brings rest to a spirit vexed by the riddle of the universe. It was a new evangel for the age of reason, that set up its particular form of adequate order and even of ultimate purpose. The exposition of the faith could proceed only by finding testimonials to its efficacy. To the true believer there were visible evidences of the existence of what he thought should be, which were not to be seen by those who were weak in the faith. Unless one has the proper temperament, the continued elaboration of this single thesis with the weak instruments at his hand becomes dreadfully monotonous. In such a study one knows beforehand that one will encounter only variants of the one theme of 'influence.'

The narrowly rationalistic thesis conceives of environment as process and of some of the qualities and activities of man as products. The agency is physical nature; man responds or adapts himself. Simple as the thesis sounds, it incurs continually grave difficulties in the matching of specific response to specific stimulus or inhibition. The direct influence of environmental stimuli is purely somatic. What happens to man through the influence of his physical surroundings is

[53] *Ibid.*, p. 12.

[54] Van Valkenburg, Amsterdam Tijdschr., K. Ned. Aardr. Gesell., vol. 41, pp. 138, 139 (1924).

beyond the competence of the geographer; at most he may keep informed as to physiologic research in that field. What man does in an area because of tabu or totemism or because of his own will involves use of environment rather than the active agency of the environment. It would, therefore, appear that environmentalism has been shooting neither at cause nor at effect, but rather that it is bagging its own decoys.[55]

Conclusion

In the colorful reality of life there is a continuous resistance of fact to confinement within any 'simpliste' theory. We are concerned with "directed activity, not premature realization" and this is the morphologic approach. Our naïvely selected section of reality, the landscape, is undergoing manifold change. This contact of man with his changeful home, as expressed through the cultural landscape, is our field of work. We are concerned with the importance of the site to man, and also with his transformation of the site. Altogether we deal with the interrelation of group, or cultures, and site, as expressed in the various landscapes of the world. Here are an inexhaustible body of fact and a variety of relation which provide a course of inquiry that does not need to restrict itself to the straits of rationalism.[56]

[55] Kroeber, A. L., Anthropology (1923), pp. 180–193, 502–503, scrutinizes the ex parte nature of environmentalist tenets in their relation to culture.

[56] Wissler, Clark, Ecology, vol. 5, p. 311 (1924): "While the early history of the concept is probably lost to us forever, there are not wanting indications that the ecological idea was conceived in the same atmosphere as the theory of design, or of purposeful adaptation. However that may be, the effort on the part of later professors of ecology has been to eschew all such philosophies except the fundamental assumption that plants and the rest of nature are intimately interdependent one upon the other." Thus "the anthropologist is not only trying to show what all the forms and forces of nature have done to man, but even with more emphasis what man has done to nature" (p. 312). This definition of anthropology includes a very large part of the social field, and is also a good definition for geography. At present anthropology is the study of culture per se. If our studies of man and of his work have large success in synthesis, a gradual coalescence of social anthropology and of geography may represent the first of a series of fusions into a larger science of man.

18

DISCOVERING THE VERNACULAR LANDSCAPE

John B. Jackson

Geographers are not the only people to write about landscape. John Brinckerhoff Jackson was educated in history and literature at Harvard University before working in wartime intelligence and then trying his hand at ranching in the south-western USA. Prevented from continuing by an accident, he instead started a journal, Landscape, in 1951. Unlike Sauer (**chapter 17**), Jackson was interested in the contemporary and vernacular American landscape and, less so, its European antecedents. He was also concerned with urban places, roads, mining towns and sites normally overlooked by both planners and intellectuals, such as mobile-home parks and back-yards. His writing is closer to the architectural classic *Learning from Las Vegas* by R. Venturi, D. Scott Brown and S. Izenour (Cambridge, MA, 1972) than to the work of most geographers. In *Discovering the vernacular landscape* he discusses landscapes of circular irrigated fields, commercial strips in small towns, and the American tradition of moveable dwellings as well as the medieval and Renaissance roots of moral and political landscapes. These two general themes are brought together in his argument about the three Landscapes that have characterized America and how planning needs to be sensitive to the real needs of people for mobility as well as stability, for recreational nature as well as wilderness. In contrast perhaps to Leopold (**chapter 21**), Jackson likes many of the new landscape features and, unlike Sauer, he does not desire a return to some pre-industrial past.

Source: *Discovering the vernacular landscape*. New Haven: Yale University Press, 1984. Extracts from pp. 3–8, 147–57.

Why is it, I wonder, that we have trouble agreeing on the meaning of *landscape*? The word is simple enough, and it refers to something which we think we understand; and yet to each of us it seems to mean something different.

What we need is a new definition. The one we find in most dictionaries is more than three hundred years old and was drawn up for artists. It tells us that a landscape is a "portion of land which the eye can comprehend at a glance." Actually when it was first introduced (or reintroduced) into English it did not mean the view itself, it meant a *picture* of it, an artist's interpretation. It was his task to take the forms and colors and spaces in front of him – mountains, river, forest, fields, and so on – and compose them so that they made a work of art.

There is no need to tell in detail how the word gradually changed in meaning. First it meant a picture of a view; then the view itself. We went into the country and discovered beautiful views, always remembering the criteria of landscape beauty as established by critics and artists. Finally, on a modest scale, we undertook to make over a piece of ground so that it resembled a pastoral landscape in the shape of a garden or park. Just as the painter used his judgment as to what to include or omit in his composition, the landscape gardener (as he was known in the eighteenth century) took pains to produce a stylized "picturesque" landscape, leaving out the muddy roads, the plowed fields, the squalid villages of the real countryside and including certain agreeable natural features: brooks and groves of trees and smooth expanses of grass. The results were often extremely beautiful, but they were still pictures, though in three dimensions.

The reliance on the artist's point of view and his definition of landscape beauty persisted throughout the nineteenth century. Olmsted and his followers designed their parks and gardens in "painterly" terms. "Although three-dimensional composition in landscape materials differs from two-dimensional landscape painting, because a garden or park design contains a *series* of pictorial compositions," the *Encyclopaedia Britannica* (13th edition) informs us, ". . . nevertheless in each of these pictures we find the familiar basic principles of unity, of repetition, of sequence and balance, of harmony and contrast." But within the last half century a revolution has taken place: landscape design and landscape painting have gone their separate ways. Landscape architects no longer turn to Poussin or Salvator Rosa or Gilpin for inspiration; they may not even have heard of their work. Knowledge of ecology and conservation and environmental psychology are now part of the landscape architect's professional background, and protecting and "managing" the natural environment are seen as more important than the designing of picturesque parks. Environmental designers, I have noticed, avoid the word *landscape* and prefer *land* or *terrain* or *environment* or even *space* when they have a specific site in mind. *Landscape* is used for suggesting the esthetic quality of the wider countryside.

As for painters, they have long since lost interest in producing conventional landscapes. Kenneth Clark, in his book *Landscape into Painting*, comments on this fact. "The microscope and telescope have so greatly enlarged the range of our vision," he writes, "that the snug, sensible nature which we can see with our own eyes has ceased to satisfy our imaginations. We know that by our new standards of measurement the most extensive landscape is practically the same as the hole through which the burrowing ant escapes from our sight."[1]

This does not strike me as a very satisfactory explanation of the demise of traditional landscape painting. More than a change in scale was responsible. Painters

[1] Kenneth Clark, *Landscape Into Painting* (New York, 1950), p. 140.

have learned to see the environment in a new and more subjective manner: as a different kind of experience. But that is not the point. The point is, the two disciplines which once had a monopoly on the word – landscape architecture and landscape painting – have ceased to use it the way they did a few decades ago, and it has now reverted as it were to the public domain.

What has happened to the word in the meantime? For one thing we are using it with much more freedom. We no longer bother with its literal meaning – which I will come to later – and we have coined a number of words similar to it: roadscape, townscape, cityscape, as if the syllable *scape* meant a space, which it does not; and we speak of the wilderness landscape, the lunar landscape, even of the landscape at the bottom of the ocean. Furthermore the word is frequently used in critical writing as a kind of metaphor. Thus we find mention of the "landscape of a poet's images," "the landscape of dreams," or "landscape as antagonist" or "the landscape of thought," or, on quite a different level, the "political landscape of the NATO conference," the "patronage landscape." Our first reaction to these usages is that they are farfetched and pretentious. Yet they remind us of an important truth: that we always need a word or phrase to indicate a kind of environment or setting which can give vividness to a thought or event or relationship; a background placing it in the world. In this sense *landscape* serves the same useful purpose as do the words *climate* or *atmosphere,* used metaphorically. In fact *landscape* when used as a painter's term often meant "all that part of a picture which is not of the body or argument" – like the stormy array of clouds in a battle scene or the glimpse of the Capitol in a presidential portrait. In the eighteenth century, *landscape* indicated scenery in the theater and had the function of discreetly suggesting the location of the action or perhaps the time of day. As I have suggested elsewhere, there is no better indication of how our relation to the environment can change over the centuries than in the role of stage scenery. Three hundred years ago Corneille could write a five-act tragedy with a single indication of the setting: "The action takes place in the palace of the king." If we glance at the work of a modern playwright we will probably find one detailed description of a scene after another, and the ultimate in this kind of landscape, I suppose, is the contemporary movie. Here the set does much more than merely identify the time and place and establish the mood. By means of shifts in lighting and sound and perspective the set actually creates the players, identifies them, and tells them what to do: a good example of environmental determinism.

But these scenic devices and theater landscapes are mere imitations of real ones: easily understood by almost everyone, and shared. What I object to is the fallacy in the metaphorical use of the word. No one denies that as our thoughts become complex and abstract we need metaphors to give them a degree of reality. No one denies that as we become uncertain of our status we need more and more reenforcement from our environment. But we should not use the word *landscape* to describe our private world, our private microcosm, and for a simple reason: a landscape is a concrete, three-dimensional shared reality. . . .

Nevertheless the formula *landscape as a composition of man-made spaces on the land* is more significant than it first appears, for if it does not provide us with a definition it throws a revealing light on the origin of the concept. For it says that a landscape is not a natural feature of the landscape but a *synthetic* space, a man-made system of spaces superimposed on the face of the land, functioning and evolving not according to natural laws but to serve a community – for the collective character of the landscape is one thing that all generations and all points of view have agreed upon. A landscape is thus a space deliberately created to speed up or slow down the process of nature. As Eliade expresses it, it represents man taking upon himself the role of time.

A very successful undertaking on the whole, and the proof, paradoxically enough, is that many if not most of these synthetic organizations of space have been so well assimilated into the natural environment that they are indistinguishable and unrecognized for what they are. The reclamation of Holland, of the Fens, of large portions of the Po Valley are familiar examples of a topographical intervention producing new landscapes. Less well known are the synthetic landscapes produced simply by spatial reorganization. Historians are said to be blind to the spatial dimension of history, which is probably why we hear so little about the wholesale making of agricultural landscapes throughout seventeenth-century Europe.

It is not a coincidence that much of this landscape creation took place during a period when the greatest gardens and parks and the most magnificent of city complexes were being designed. A narrow and pedantic taxonomy has persuaded us that there is little or nothing in common between what used to be called civil engineering and garden or landscape architecture, but in fact from an historical perspective their more successful accomplishments are identical in result. The two professions may work for different patrons, but they both reorganize space for human needs, both produce works of art in the truest sense of the term. In the contemporary world it is by recognizing this similarity of purpose that we will eventually formulate a new definition of *landscape*: a composition of man-made or man-modified spaces to serve as infrastructure or background for our collective existence; and if *background* seems inappropriately modest we should remember that in our modern use of the word it means that which underscores not only our identity and presence, but also our history.

It is not for me to attempt to elaborate on this new definition. My contribution would in any event be peripheral, for my interest in the topic is confined to trying to see how certain organizations of space can be identified with certain social and religious attitudes, especially here in America. This is not a new approach, for it has long been common among architectural and landscape architectural historians; and it leaves many important aspects of the contemporary landscape and contemporary city entirely unexplored. But it has the virtue of including the visual experience of our everyday world and of allowing me to remain loyal to that old-fashioned but surprisingly persistent definition of *landscape*: "A portion of the earth's surface that can be comprehended at a glance." . . .

Often a disconcerting thought has come to me and given me pause. It is this: Whatever I may have fondly supposed, all that I have been writing and saying over the past years has in the last analysis dealt with a single topic – how to define (or redefine) the concept *landscape*. The *concept*; not landscape as phenomena, as environments; these I have been able to handle without much difficulty. What everyone likes to hear is that the landscape where they live is unique of its kind, worthy of the closest study, and so one has only to emphasize its *unique* characteristics to give full satisfaction. Yet an unforeseen complication has arisen. The greater the number of landscapes I explored, the more it seemed that they all had traits in common and that the essence of each was not its uniqueness but its similarity to others. It occurred to me that there might be such a thing as a prototypal landscape, or more precisely landscape as a primordial idea, of which all these visible landscapes were merely so many imperfect manifestations. It then became a question of defining that idea or concept, after which the defining of the individual landscape would be plain sailing. . . .

It may be that I am here on the track of that elusive landscape concept: the ideal landscape defined not as a static utopia dedicated to ecological or social or religious principles, but as an environment where permanence and change have struck a balance. Few landscapes have achieved this and fewer still have managed to maintain it for any length of time. But all of them, it seems to me, have sought it; all of them in one manner or another, that is to say, have acknowledged the existence of landscape as idea. The world being what it is, it is far easier to find examples of imbalance than of landscape balance. The two examples of the former I offer are worth studying not merely for their cautionary value – for one shows the perils of mobility, the other the perils which come with too great a regard for *position* in the landscape – but also because they are both related, though indirectly, to our own American landscape and its future.

I have elsewhere explained the original meaning of the word *landscape*, so it is enough to say that it meant a collection, a "sheaf" of lands, presumably interrelated and part of a system. A land was a defined piece of ground, and we can assume that in the medieval world it was most often used to indicate a patch of plowed or cultivated ground, that being the most valuable kind. Landscape therefore must have been a word much used by villagers and peasants and farmhands; it described their own small world. But how much was it used by other elements in society? It rarely occurs in legal documents of the period. The Domesday Book, a remarkable inventory of land holdings compiled by order of William the Conqueror in the eleventh century, was, to be sure, written in Latin, but no translation ever mentioned landscape, and indeed the word itself seems to have fallen into disuse. Two centuries after the conquest a new term, imported from France, though of Latin origin, took its place. *Country* or *countryside* came to indicate a much more extensive, though less precisely defined area; the territory of a community of people all speaking the same dialect, all engaged in the same kind of farming, all subjects of the same local lord, all conscious of having customs and traditions of their own and of possessing certain ancient rights and privileges. It was not until modern times that the word *country* came to indicate *nation*.

It is here, in the usage of the two words *landscape* and *country*, that we are confronted with the distinction between the vernacular and the aristocratic or political concepts of space. In the view of the noblemen and clergy, of the larger landowners, *landscape* was merely a vernacular or peasant term describing a cluster of small, temporary, crudely measured spaces which frequently changed hands and even changed in shape and size. It was, in fact, a fragment of a larger feudal estate, a right or series of rights granted to its occupants but ultimately the property of the lord or of the crown. It was a term current only in small villages. The aristocratic concept of space was entirely different. The estate of a nobleman or of a bishop, the barony or domain of the knight, the forest of the king, not to mention his kingdom, all had a definite, almost sacred origin, their boundaries vouched for by treaty or charter. Those who held them not only had the right to administer justice, but to bequeath them to their descendants. Aristocratic space, in the medieval world, was thus permanent and relatively autonomous. It was the creation of political or legal decisions.

Although the two kinds of space were intermingled, the difference between the two ways of seeing the world and of organizing the space was profound, and insofar as we are exploring the early usage of the word *landscape* it is the *vernacular* landscape which concerns us. The current tendency to associate the word *vernacular* with a local form of speech and a local form of art and decoration entitles us to use the word to describe other aspects of local culture. The word derives from the Latin *verna*, meaning a slave born in the house of his or her master, and by extension in Classical times it meant a native, one whose existence was confined to a village or estate and who was devoted to routine work. A vernacular culture would imply a way of life ruled by tradition and custom, entirely remote from the larger world of politics and law; a way of life where identity derived not from permanent possession of land but from membership in a group or super-family.

It follows, I think, that there can be such a thing as a vernacular landscape: one where evidences of a political organization of space are largely or entirely absent. I have already mentioned several features of the political landscape: the visibility and sanctity of boundaries, the importance of monuments and of centrifugal highways, the close relationship between status and enclosed space. By *political* I mean those spaces and structures designed to impose or preserve a unity and order on the land, or in keeping with a long-range, large-scale plan. Under that heading we should include such modern features as the interstate highway, the hydroelectric dam, the airport and power transmission lines, whether we happen to care for them or not.

A vernacular landscape reveals a distinct way of defining and handling time and space. In the United States there is a series of vernacular landscapes of a particularly pure type in the Pueblo Indian communities of the Southwest, and whenever we see one we are likely to find it confusing and all but impossible to interpret in our conventional European–American terms. The medieval landscape is scarcely easier to understand, even though in the course of centuries it gradually acquired several political components: castles, manors, king's highways, and chartered cities. Those are what enable us to see its evolution. Yet underneath those symbols of permanent political power there lay a vernacular landscape – or rather thousands of small and impoverished vernacular landscapes, organizing and using spaces in their traditional way and living in communities governed by custom, held together by personal relationships. We learn something about them by investigating the topographical and technological and social factors which determined their economy and their way of life, but in the long run I suspect no landscape, vernacular or otherwise, can be comprehended unless we perceive it as an organization of space; unless we ask ourselves who owns or uses the spaces, how they were created and how they change. Often it is the legal aspects of the landscape that give us the clearest insight, especially into the relationship between the peasant or villager and the piece of land he works.

"It is very rare, during the whole of the feudal era," Marc Bloch remarks,

> *for anyone to speak of ownership, either of an estate or an office. . . . [T]he word ownership as applied to landed property would have been almost meaningless . . . for nearly all land and a great many human beings were burdened at this time with a multiplicity of obligations differing in their nature, but all apparently of equal merit. None implied the fixed proprietary exclusiveness which belonged to the concept of ownership in Roman law. The tenant who – from father to son, as a rule – ploughs the land and gathers in the crop; his immediate lord to whom he pays dues and who, in certain circumstances, can resume possession of the land; the lord of the lord, and so on, right up the feudal ladder – how many persons there are who can say, each with as much justification as the other "that is my field!"*[2]

Spaces in this vernacular landscape thus indicate personal relationships, and they indicate in no less complicated manner the involved and often conflicting traditions of the community: who controls the vast number of "waste spaces" – some as extensive as a whole moor or marsh, others no larger than the margin of a road or a lane. Is the road itself a waste? Given a new use, a space changes its name: a "land" grown to grass becomes a "ley"; waste, preempted by the crown, becomes a royal forest with its own set of laws. Maitland, the legal historian, endeavoring to make legal sense of the landscape of medieval Cambridge, reminds us of its hopeless complexity and bids us "think of the grantor [King John] and his royal rights, of the grantees and their complex interests, of the strips in the fields and the odds and ends of sward, of the green commons of the town, of the house covered nucleus of the patchwork of fiefs, the network of rents"[3] – and from this confusion we are somehow to deduce a coherent spatial pattern.

At the present state of our studies of the vernacular landscape as a type all that we can say is that its spaces are usually small, irregular in shape, subject to rapid change in use, in ownership, in dimensions; that the houses, even the villages themselves, grow, shrink, change morphology, change location; that there is always a vast amount of "common land" – waste, pasturage, forest, areas where natural resources are exploited in a piecemeal manner; that its roads are little more than paths and lanes, never maintained and rarely permanent; finally that the vernacular landscape is a scattering of hamlets and clusters of fields, islands in a sea of

2 *Bloch, Feudal Society*, vol. 1, p. 116.
3 F. W. Maitland, *Township and Borough* (Cambridge, 1898), p. 81.

waste or wilderness changing from generation to generation, leaving no monuments, only abandonment or signs of renewal.

Mobility and change are the key to the vernacular landscape, but of an involuntary, reluctant sort; not the expression of restlessness and search for improvement but an unending patient adjustment to circumstances. Far too often these are the arbitrary decisions of those in power, but natural conditions play their part and so do ignorance and a blind loyalty to local ways, and so does the absence of long-range objectives: the absence of what we would call a sense of future history. A vernacular landscape, both in the Southwest and in medieval Europe, is an impressive display of devotion to common customs and of an inexhaustible ingenuity in finding short-term solutions.

At the same time, we cannot overlook what to us is the cultural poverty of such a landscape, its lack of any purposeful continuity. It thinks not of history but of legends and myths. Well into the Renaissance and even later, the inhabitants of vernacular landscapes in Europe still half-believed in heathen divinities, adorned their houses with heathen symbols, and observed heathen rites and holidays. Even historical figures, like Charlemagne or Barbarossa, historical events like the Crusades or the actual settlement of a town or city, were transformed into fairy tales. They lived in a landscape of ancient villages, ruined castles, churches built on the site of temples, yet the only monuments they recognized were miraculous springs, magic rocks, and trees, the only event they understood was the sound of Odin with his pack of hounds rushing through the forest by night. A landscape without visible signs of political history is a landscape without memory or forethought. We are inclined in America to think that the value of monuments is simply to remind us of origins. They are much more valuable as reminders of long-range, collective purpose, of goals and objectives and principles. As such even the least sightly of monuments gives a landscape beauty and dignity and keeps the collective memory alive.

Let us call that early medieval landscape Landscape One. There is another landscape (which we may call Landscape Two), which began to take shape in the latter part of the fifteenth century and which we can associate with the Renaissance; and since we are giving them names, let us identify a Landscape Three, which we can see in certain aspects of contemporary America.

I am tempted to think that Landscape Three is already beginning to show some of the characteristics of Landscape One, but before I offer evidence let me say something about Landscape Two, which was in many ways the reverse of Landscape One. We are in fact very familiar with Landscape Two. Artists and architects and landscape designers spend much time studying it, and they copy it in their professional work; and all of us who write about it travel to Europe to see it at firsthand. So I merely mention the ways in which it differs from Landscape One. Its spaces, rural and urban, are clearly and permanently defined and made visible by walls and hedges or zones of open greenery or lawn. They are designed to be self-contained and shapely and beautiful. Landscape Two sets great store on visibility; that is why we have that seventeenth-century definition of landscape as "a vista or view of scenery of the land" – landscape as a work of art, as a kind of supergarden. Unlike Landscape One, which mixed all kinds of uses and spaces together, Landscape Two insists on spaces which are homogeneous and devoted to a single purpose. It makes a distinction between city and country, between forest and field, between public and private, rich and poor, work and play; it prefers the linear frontier between nations rather than the medieval patchwork of intermingled territories. As for the distinction between mobility and immobility, it clearly believes that whatever is temporary or short-lived or movable is not to be encouraged.

But the essential characteristic of Landscape Two is its belief in the sanctity of *place.* It is place, permanent position both in the social and topographical sense, that gives us our identity. The function of space according to this belief is to make us visible, allow us to put down roots and become members of society. Land in Landscape One meant being a member of a working community; it was a temporary symbol of relationships. In Landscape Two land means property and permanence and power.

Landscape Two started to evolve at a time in European history when the old customary farm community with its disposable parcels of land and its confusion of rights and obligations was being abandoned in favor of the individual ownership and operation of farms: private holdings composed of single-purpose permanent fields with the homestead of the owner in the center of the property. There was a time when men were discovering the natural environment and its many variations in climate and soil and topography, and when the challenge to agriculture was to define all varieties of land and put them to their appropriate use. It was in consequence a time when the forest was discovered as a distinct environment, with distinct economic and ecological characteristics; an environment worth preserving and improving.

There is little new to be said about the beauty and order of Landscape Two. It remains to this day the most successful landscape, esthetically speaking, that there has ever been in the Western world, one which we will always try to imitate when we want to produce landscapes for delight and inspiration. Americans have a special reason for admiring it, for it is here in the United States that we see the largest and most impressive example of neo-classic spatial organization. Our national grid system, devised by the Founding Fathers, represents the last attempt to produce a Classical political landscape, one based on the notion that certain spaces – notably the square and the rectangle – were inherently beautiful and therefore suited to the creation of a just society. It is, to be sure, a landscape with few dramatic beauties and much monotony, but it is a landscape which conforms to Winckelmann's definition of Classical perfection: one of noble simplicity and quiet grandeur.

What we enjoy about the early-nineteenth-century American landscape is the ease with which it can be read and interpreted. The farm stands in the midst of its fields and clearly reveals its degree of prosperity and contentment. Each church has a white steeple, each public square has a monument, each field its fence, each straight road its destination. It is a landscape of rectangular fields, green woodlands, white houses, and red brick towns. It is like a luminous painting: vivid, carefully composed, appealing to the emotions, and reassuringly stable.

Yet it did not last for long: scarcely a half century, and a number of reasons can be given for its rapid decay: the coming of the railroad, the opening up of newer land further West, the invention of the balloon frame and of horse-drawn farm equipment, the growth of manufacturing in the East, the influx of settlers from Europe – all these developments affected the spatial organization of Landscape Two in America and in a few decades made it obsolete. Yet I cannot help feeling that even from the start Landscape Two was not entirely suited to us. It never produced those politically active farm communities that Jefferson and his colleagues dreamt of, never really persuaded us to put down roots and stay put in one place. Instead of being a blueprint for the ideal Classical democratic social order, the grid system became simply an easy and effective way of dividing up the land and of encouraging the settlement of the Midwest. The question which we will eventually have to confront is whether Landscape Two ever belonged in the English-speaking New World. (I say *English-speaking* advisedly, because it *did* take hold in Latin America.)

The settlement of Anglo-Americans can best be understood as a belated episode in the history of Landscape One: a last titanic wave of mobility, of immigrants leaving the vanishing vernacular landscape of rural England. Once settled here, the predominantly young, blue-collar population produced a colonial version of Landscape One – but lacking in one important traditional feature: the farm village. New England tried to produce it, the authorities in London tried to produce it in Virginia, but new ways of farming, new kinds of land ownership, and a new kind of freedom frustrated every attempt, and by the time of the Revolution even in New England the farm village was out of date. What survived of that early colonial vernacular culture was its mobility, its adaptability, its preference for the transitory, the ephemeral: the short-lived log cabins, the brief exploitation of the environment; the ad hoc community of the frontier and the trading post, even while the grid of Landscape Two stood waiting for Jefferson's Classical farm villages to appear.

It would be wrong to imply that modern America is entirely the product of that vernacular culture, or that we do not possess a vast and rich landscape, urban as well as rural, dedicated to stability and history and established landscape values. My concern is that these two landscapes do not always recognize what each has to offer to the other and that Landscape Three may fail to achieve a balance between them. I do not believe that the Establishment – political, intellectual, artistic – is aware of the vitality and extent of that vernacular element, and I do not believe that we recognize the danger of having two distinct sublandscapes, one dedicated to stability and place, the other dedicated to mobility. Such was the case in Landscape One. Our vernacular landscape has unparalleled vitality and diversity, but it resembles Landscape One in its detachment from formal space, its indifference to history, and its essentially utilitarian, conscienceless use of the environment. We cannot say that we are returning to the Dark Ages, but the similarity between Landscape Three and Landscape One is based on an important circumstance: both lack the humanist tradition of the Renaissance. Both are ignorant of Landscape Two and what it stood for.

As I travel about the country, I am often bewildered by the proliferation of spaces and the uses of spaces that had no counterpart in the traditional landscape: parking lots, landing fields, shopping centers, trailer courts, high-rise condominiums, wildlife shelters, Disneyland. I am bewildered by our casual use of space: churches used as discotheques, dwellings used as churches, downtown streets used for jogging, empty lots in crowded cities, industrial plants in the open country, cemeteries used for archery practice, Easter sunrise services in a football stadium. I am confused by the temporary spaces I see: the drive-in, fast-food establishments that are torn down after a year, the fields planted to corn and then to soya beans and then subdivided; the trailer communities that vanish when vacation time is over; the tropical gardens in shopping malls that are replaced each season; motels abandoned when the highway moves. Because of my age my first reaction to these new spaces is dismay; they are not the kind of spaces I was accustomed to in the Landscape Two of my youth. But my second and (I hope) more tolerant reaction is that all this is part of our culture, that it can be treated with respect and that here is a new and challenging field of environmental design.

I would like to think that in the future the profession of landscape architecture will expand beyond its present confines (established by Landscape Two) and involve itself in making mobility orderly and beautiful. This would mean knowing a great deal about land, its uses, its values, and the political and economic and cultural forces affecting its distribution. The environmental designer should be concerned with the spatial changes taking place. It is precisely in the field of land use and community planning that a trained imagination, an awareness of environment and habitat can be of the greatest value. What has been done in the way of producing new landscapes, new wilderness areas, farms and factories and cities in Holland and Israel could serve as a model. Environmental design is not simply a matter of protecting nature as it is, but of creating a new nature, a new beauty. It is finally a matter of defining landscape in a way that includes both the mobility of the vernacular and the political infrastructure of a stable social order.

In matters having to do with the natural environment we are most of us children of Landscape Two. From that parent we have learned not only to study the world around us but also to lavish upon it and bring it to a state of lasting perfection. It was Landscape Two that taught us that the contemplation of nature can be a kind of revelation of the invisible world, and of ourselves.

But it was also Landscape Two that impressed upon us the notion that there can be only *one* kind of landscape: a landscape identified with a very static, very conservative social order, and that there can be only one true philosophy of nature: that of Landscape Two.

The first heritage of love and wonder is still with us, stronger perhaps than ever. It is that other heritage, that clinging to obsolete forms and attitudes, that threatens the emergence of a truly balanced Landscape Three. We no longer live in the country, we no longer farm, we no longer derive our identity from possession of land. Like the harassed peasant of Landscape One, though to a far greater degree, we derive our identity from our relationship with other people, and when we talk about the importance of *place*, the necessity of belonging to a *place*, let us be clear that in Landscape Three place means the people in it, not simply the natural environment. For political and economic reasons Landscape Two greatly exaggerated the importance of belonging to a community. But the agricultural community was what was meant, the tightly organized hierarchy of landowners and masters and workers. Not every applicant was admitted, and the conditions attached to membership were strict and arbitrary; final acceptance was slow in coming. In Landscape Three the reverse is the case, and the ease with which a stranger can be assimilated, the speed with which a new community can come into being are both extraordinary phenomena. It may not be entirely accurate to say (as a developer once said to me) that "people follow plumbing," meaning that utilities are the infrastructure of any residential community. It is nevertheless true that we have abandoned the old political procedures of creating places. The forming of a new community now calls for little more than the gregarious impulse of a dozen families attracted by certain elementary public services. This is the kind of new community that we are seeing all over America: at remote construction sites, in recreation areas, in trailer courts, in the shanty towns of wetbacks and migrant workers; the emergence of what we may call vernacular communities – without political status, without plan, ruled by informal local custom, often ingenious adaptations to an unlikely site and makeshift materials, destined to last no more than a year or two, and working as well as most communities do. They would be better and last longer if they were properly designed and serviced. They could acquire dignity if the political landscape made a gesture of recognition. Yet very little is needed to give those new communities a true identity: a reminder, a symbol of permanence to indicate that they too have a history ahead of them.

One reason for paying more attention to this aspect of Landscape Three is that these settlements will in time serve as nuclei for small-scale landscapes. For that is always how landscapes have been formed; not only by topography and political decisions, but by the indigenous organization and development of spaces to serve the needs of the focal community: gainful employment, recreation, social contacts, contacts with nature, contacts with the alien world. In one form or another, these are the ends which all landscapes serve, and that is why they are all fundamentally versions of the primal *idea* of landscape.

My search for a definition has led me back to that old Anglo-Saxon meaning: landscape is not scenery, it is not a political unit; it is really no more than a collection, a system of man-made spaces on the surface of the earth. Whatever its shape or size it is *never* simply a natural space, a feature of the natural environment; it is *always* artificial, always synthetic, always subject to sudden or unpredictable change. We create them and need them because every landscape is the place where we establish our own human organization of space and time. It is where the slow, natural processes of both growth and maturity and decay are deliberately set aside and history is substituted. A landscape is where we speed up or retard or divert the cosmic program and impose our own. "By conquering nature," Mircea Eliade writes, "man can become Nature's rival without being the slave of time. . . . Science and industry proclaim that man can achieve things better and faster than nature if he, by means of his intelligence, succeeds in penetrating to her secrets."[4]

When we see how we have succeeded in imposing our own rhythm on nature in the agricultural landscape, how we have altered the life cycle of plants and animals and even transposed the seasons, we become aware of how dangerous a role we have assumed, and there are many who say that the salvation of Landscape Three depends on our relinquishing this power to alter the flow of time and on our returning to a more natural order. But the new ordering of time should affect not only nature, it should affect ourselves. It promises us a new kind of history, a new, more responsive social order, and ultimately a new landscape.

[4] Eliade, *The F rge and the Crucible*, p. 169.

19

MARXISM, CULTURE AND THE DUPLICITY OF LANDSCAPE

Stephen Daniels

An alternative route from Marxism to geography from the one taken by Smith and O'Keefe (**chapter 16**) is being taken by a number of cultural geographers, including Stephen Daniels. Their intellectual sources include leading theorists of cultural studies such as Raymond Williams, John Berger and Stuart Hall. In contrast to Sauer's emphasis upon the material record in the landscape (**chapter 17**), Daniels turns towards more metaphorical concepts of landscape, as distributed among a number of 'texts'. These include novels and paintings, a feel for the symbolic and aesthetic dimensions of landscapes as well as the material. While Sauer tended to regard culture as something acting upon people, Daniels follows Williams's view of culture as a medium of social power, something which is contested. This does not mean that culture can be reduced to economics, however. Both Berger and Williams find spaces for morality, tradition and experience, especially the experience of working the land. Like Daniels, they are aware of both the politics and the poetics of landscape.

Source: Marxism, culture and the duplicity of landscape. In Peet, R. and Thrift, N., editors, *New models in geography, volume II*. London: Unwin Hyman, 1987. Extract from pp. 196–220.

Landscape is a concept of high tension, declares Inglis, because it 'stands at the intersection of concepts a social scientist would strain to hold apart: "institution", "product", "process" and "ideology"' (Inglis 1977, p. 489). We might further observe that this tension between landscape as an élitist (and illusory) 'way of seeing' and landscape as a vernacular (and realistic) 'way of life' is rooted in the very complications of the idea of culture I discussed earlier. Landscape may be seen, as Adorno sees culture generally, as a 'dialectical image', an ambiguous synthesis whose redemptive and manipulative aspects cannot finally be disentangled, which can neither be completely reified as an authentic object in the world nor thoroughly dissolved as an ideological mirage (Jay 1984, pp. 111–60). What can be done is to explore this duplicity of landscape – which has been sensed since the first use of the word landscape in English in the 17th century (Daniels & Cosgrove 1987) – in particular contexts.

Adorno himself sketches the notion of landscape as a dialectical image in some remarks on 'the domain of what the Germans call Kulturlandschaft' – old architecture in local materials arranged around a square or church. Because such *Kulturlandschaften* are now encountered 'mainly in ads promoting festivals of organ music and phoney togetherness', are co-opted by market society as the 'ideological complement of itself' because 'they do not visibly bear [its] stigmata', the joy we might feel at seeing them 'is spoiled by a guilty conscience'. Even so 'that joy has survived the objection which tries to make it suspect.' The factor that gives *Kulturlandschaften* 'the most validity, and therefore staying power, is their specific relation to history . . . [they] bear the imprint of history as expression and of historical continuity as form. They dynamically integrate these elements in ways similar to artistic production. What commands aesthetic attention in them is the manner in which they give expression to human suffering. It is only just that the image of a limited world should make us happy, provided we do not forget the repression that went into making it. In this sense, that image is a reminder' (Adorno 1984, pp. 94–7). And to press the dialectic further, we might add that the image is also a forgetting.

The power of landscape as a concept resides, to use Inglis's phrase, in the 'field of force' which its oppositional meanings generate. In the remainder of this chapter I will explore and exploit this field of force as it is generated in the works of the two British Marxist cultural critics most concerned with geographical experience and imagination, Williams and Berger. This will involve considering the pressure exerted upon landscape in their works by cognate concepts such as country, region, land, and nature and the counterveiling pressure which landscape exerts upon them.

Raymond Williams

'A working country is hardly ever a landscape', declares Williams in *The country and the city* (1973) 'the very idea of landscape implies separation and observation'. Landscape is an 'elevated sensibility' fundamentally one of patrician control, which is reproduced in 'internal histories of landscape painting, landscape writing, landscape gardening and landscape architecture' and sentimentalized as 'part of an elegy for a lost way of life'. Such ideological histories, Williams maintains, should be connected to and exposed by the 'real history . . . the common history of a land and its society' (Williams 1973, pp. 120–1). The defining feature of this real history and one which is masked by the conventions of patrician landscape, is the condition and experience of those who worked the land. When considering the 18th-century writers who questioned patrician taste Williams is more sympathetic to a poet like Crabbe who professed to give 'a real picture of the poor' and who for Williams 'restore[d] the facts of labour to the idyllic landscape' than he is to a poet like Goldsmith whose nostalgic evocation of an independent and leisurely peasantry Williams accused of dissolving 'the lives and work of others into an image of the past' (Williams 1987). As Barrell points out, this appraisal misses the repressive force of Crabbe's insistence on toil, and the egalitarian implications of Goldsmith's celebration of leisure: Goldsmith disengaged the labourer from his 'proper', 'natural' identity as a labourer, as a man born to toil, and suggested that he could be 'as free to dispose of his time as other poets insisted only the richman or the shepherd was free to do' (Barrell 1989, p. 78). In recovering the peasant village as an 'image of the past', overlaid by the park of an engrossing landlord, Goldsmith affirmed that the landscape and its poor inhabitants had a past that was qualitatively different from the present and, by implication, a future that might be so too. In the historicity of the landscape lay its potential liberation from, and resistance to, the actuality of present toil and hardship. Williams is aware of this historical dimension to landscape but locates it not in the narratives of 18th-century poetry but in the narratives of Victorian novels.

While acknowledging the Victorian novel's potential for a more adequate representation of land and society, Williams notes the residual power of 18th-century sensibilities. So although George Eliot 'restores the real inhabitants of rural England to their places in what had been a socially selective landscape she does not get further than restoring them *as a landscape*' (Williams 1973, p. 168; emphasis in original). Williams credits Thomas Hardy with more fully developing the novel as a 'knowable community' in a tradition to which Williams himself as a novelist subscribes. Hardy country is not for Williams so much a location as a relationship, a sometimes tense dialectic of dwelling and detachment expressed for many most forcibly in *The return of the native*:

> *At the same time the separation of the returned native is not only a separation from the standards of the educated and affluent world 'outside'. It is also, to some degree inevitably, a separation from the people who have not made the journey; or more often a separation which can mask itself as a romantic attachment to a way of life in which people are merely instrumental: figures in a landscape . . . [So] the real Hardy country, we soon come to see, is that border country so many of us have been living in: between custom and education, between work and ideas, between love of place and experience of change (Williams 1973, pp. 203, 196).*

Border country is the title of Williams's first, autobiographically informed novel published in 1960 and I want to consider this book, the first in a trilogy, and *The fight for Manod* (1979a), the final book, because they forcefully disclose the shifting status of landscape in Williams's thought.

In an interview Williams maintained that in *Border country* he was trying to realize the potential of the Victorian realist novel, especially as written by Hardy, in accounting for 'the experience of work' and (against the trend of modern fiction) trying to recover some of its formal devices in giving characters and places 'a whole network of history'. So a place becomes 'not just the site of an event . . . but the materialization of a history which is often quite extensively retracted'. This, for Williams, 'was the highest moment of bourgeois cultural engagement: a moment from which historical materialism is itself a development' (Williams 1979a, pp. 276, 275). At the beginning of *Border country* Matthew Price, son of a railway signalman, and a university lecturer in economic history, returns, when his father suffers a stroke, to the Welsh valley of his upbringing:

> *He had felt empty and tired, but the familiar shape of the valley and the mountains held and replaced him. It was one thing to carry its image in his mind, as he did, everywhere, never a day passing but he closed his eyes and saw it again, his only landscape. But it was different to stand and look at the reality. It was not less beautiful; every detail of the land came up with its old excitement. But it was not still, as the image had been. It was no longer a landscape or a view, but a valley that people were using. He realized, as he watched, what had happened in going away. The valley as landscape had been taken, but its work forgotten (Williams 1960, p. 75).*

Price finds this narrowly scenic notion of landscape as blunt an instrument for understanding the valley as the demographic concepts and techniques he deploys in his research on 19th-century migration into the industrial valleys of South Wales. But by the end of the novel, after its narration of the social experience of his father's generation (centrally the General Strike and its connections well beyond the valley), Price enjoys a more comprehensive view of the valley, sitting above a black rock, the Kestrel:

> *It was strange to be up there alone, with the valley so quiet. The people he had lived with, the voices he had listened to, were all there under his eyes, in the valley. But all he could see from this height were the fields and orchards; the houses white under the sun; the grey farm buildings; the occasional train, very small under its plume of smoke . . . The station was out of sight, hidden in its cutting. Work went on there, in the ordinary routine, but from here it might not have existed, and the trains might have been moving themselves, with everyone gone from the valley (Williams 1960, pp. 290–1).*

But on remaining there, sitting 'very still' Price looks below the Kestrel, 'in legend . . . the guardian, the silent watcher over this meeting of the valleys', and he focuses in:

> *He could see the detail of oak and elm, in the full hedgerows. There, in an orchard, was an old tedder turned on its side, and the littered straw round a half-eaten potato clamp. He saw the long white wall of a farmhouse, and the end wall, at a curious angle, was crossed by a melting violet shadow. And here, on the high-banked road, was a cart moving, and a dog barked somewhere, insistently, not too far away. This, seen close, was his actual country. But lift with the line of the Kestrel, and look far out. Now it was not just the valley and the village, but the meeting of valleys, and England blue in the distance. In its history the country took on a different shape (Williams 1960, pp. 290–1).*

Price looks in each direction, turning from 'the decayed shape of violence' of Norman dominion 'confused in legend with the rockfall of the Holy mountain, where the devil's heel had slipped as he strode westward into our mountains' to a limestone scarp where 'along the outcrop had stood the ironmasters, Guest,

Crawshay, Bailey, Homfray, and this history had stayed'. His witness over, Price descends to the valley:

> *On the way down the shapes faded and the ordinary identities returned. The voice in his mind faded, and the ordinary voice came back. Like old Bailey asking, digging his stick in the turf. What will you be reading Will [Price's local nickname]. Books, sir? No, better not. History, sir. History from the Kestrel, where you sit and watch memory move, across the wide valley. That was the sense of it: to watch, to interpret, to try to get clear (Williams 1960, pp. 292–3).*

This profound conception of landscape and observation is then characterized by a deep sense of the past – historic, prehistoric, geological, mythical – a sense which diminishes the lives of those in the present, and enlarges them too. This conception of landscape is characteristic of Hardy. In novels like *Tess of the d'Urbervilles* and *Jude the Obscure* the landscape as a densely textured record of history, community, and personal experience is counterposed to these forces of progress and mobility which threaten to erase it, to reduce it to a scenic or utilitarian resource. It is a conception of landscape which has this century powerfully informed many popular and academic narratives of the English countryside, notably Hoskins's *The making of the English landscape* (1970). It subverts narrowly scenic conceptions of landscape both in its detailed focus and in its scope which can best be called regional. For Williams, it is the regional dimension of the English novel which provides the potential to resist patrician or bourgeois forms of rural description. While the notion of region still carries its original implication of subordination and underdevelopment, it can also, in a more modern derivation, denote a countermovement to a centralized, sophisticated notion of culture, carrying the 'implications of a valuably distinctive way of life'. Williams admits that some of Hardy's novels like *Under the greenwood tree* are regional 'in an encapsulating and enclosing sense' – they contribute to his reputation 'as a regional novelist because he wrote about Wessex – that strange, particular place – rather than about London or the Home Counties' yet other novels like *Tess* 'are set even more deeply in their region but . . . are not in any limiting sense "regional": what happens in them, internally and externally – those two abstractions in a connected process – involves a very wide and complex, a fully extended and extensive, set of relationships' (Williams 1983, pp. 265–6; 1984b, pp. 231–2). Williams wrote *Border country* seven times to find this regional form and in the *The fight for Manod*, the final novel of the trilogy, he 'found that form very consciously and explicitly' (Williams 1984b, p. 231).

Whereas *Border country* was for Williams 'the present, including and trying to focus an immediate past', *The fight for Manod* was 'a present trying to include and focus a future' (Williams 1979a, p. 292). In the language of landscape it is a novel of prospect. Matthew Price, still an industrial historian, is employed as a consultant on a proposal to build a city in mid-Wales. Price's brief is to produce a 'lived inquiry', to dwell in the locality of the proposal for as long as it takes to understand the feelings and needs of local people. The city is conceived similarly, 'in post-industrial terms . . . a city of small towns, a city of villages almost. A city settling into its country' (Williams 1979b, pp. 15, 13). The fight for Manod is a fight for the different meanings of Manod although, as some leftist critics have pointed out, there is 'surprisingly little actual fight demonstrated in the narrative itself . . . the absence of collective scenes is striking. There is no equivalent of the solidarity [in *Border country*] of the railway line' (Williams 1979a, p. 294). This 'thinning out' (as these critics called it) of the experience of labour is accompanied by a 'thickening' of Price's own experience of Manod, notably his experience of the natural world.

As in *Border country*, Price's sensibilities are initially imprisoned within élitist conventions. Looking at the plans at a ministerial office

> *he had caught the familiar smell of a world of arrangements beyond him; of things happening, planned, brought about, without people even being told. He stared through the window at the railway yard, the office tower, the streets climbing the hill. By narrowing his eyes he could see the window and the city beyond it as a framed picture. It reminded him of the map on the opposite wall (Williams 1976b, p. 17).*

Approaching the valley by car he sensed the physical shape of the land and in 'the long folds, the sudden scarps, the deep watercourses' he found it 'so much his own country: solid, remote, self contained'. Then looking down from a ridge upon the town to be transformed, 'its history stood out very sharply, as if on a slide.' He recalls 'The Kestrel, the watcher' and 'seeing the history of his country in the shapes of the land', but tries now to imagine it inscribed with a future, 'scrawls and projections, lines on glass, over known places, the embedded lives'. 'It is easy to reject it for the warmth, the heaviness, of a known past: a green past, in which lives have been lived and completed . . . this projection and outline of a future. Seen from above, from the height of the Kestrel. From this ridge below the Daren, it must be like this always. It is history past and future, an extended landscape' (Williams 1979b, pp. 29, 36, 38).

As it turns out the 'extended landscape' remains barely realized, torn between, on one hand, a calculating conception of location and, on the other, a sensual conception of land. For the post-industrial city turns out, upon investigation by Price's fellow consultant Peter Owen to be a corrupt speculation by a multinational corporation, 'its local reproduction'. And while Owen, a late 1960s radical sociologist, surgically delineates the circuits of capital, Price fights for words to express the sensory pull of the land. Together they look down at the rush of water under a bridge:

> *"You feel it here, do you?", Matthew asked.*
> *"Feel what?"*
> *"Something different. Something other. Some altered physical sense."*
> *"You grew up in this sort of country, Matthew. You're remembering that."*
> *"Yes, I know when I remember it. And I try to understand it as a memory. But sometimes I think it's a different experience. Something that actually alters me."*
> *"No", Peter said, "I don't get that."*
> *"It only comes occasionally. Some particular shape: the line of a hedge, the turn of a path round*

a wood, or in movement sometimes, the shadow of a cloud that bends in a watercourse, or then again a sound, the wind in wires, wind tearing at a chimney."
"Moments of heightened attention."
"Yes, but attention to what? What I really seem to feel is these things as my body. As my own physical existence, a material continuity in which there are no breaks. As if I was feeling through them, not feeling about them."
Peter stared down at the river.
"I can hear that you feel it. But . . . ."
"Yes. But. There's usually nothing to be said" (Williams 1979b, pp. 97–8).

This dialogue specifies Williams's concept of 'structure of feeling', the 'area of tension' between articulation and experience, and an area in which Williams often finds himself. He can feel the 'sensory pull' of some monumental buildings like cathedrals and yet be aware of the way they inscribe social dominion in their physical fabric, in their reproduction as 'heritage', and in precisely the kind of powerful feelings which they were designed to induce. 'I find it even more difficult when I take the problem across to the very strong feelings which I have about land . . . I don't fully understand them, partly because I've never had any training in this kind of visual discrimination' (Williams 1979a, p. 348). Berger, primarily concerned with the visual arts not literature, has developed this kind of visual discrimination to a remarkably high degree and it is to his interrogation of landscape that I now turn.

John Berger

If for Williams 'we learn to see a thing by learning to describe it' (Williams 1965, p. 39), for Berger 'seeing comes before words' (Berger 1972, p. 7). Berger has probed the varieties of visual experience – looking, scanning, ogling, imagining – in a variety of visual media, notably painting and photography. Moreover, Berger is a highly visual writer, in his figures of speech and in his tendency to display arguments (in epigrammatic sentences, sometimes with pictures) rather than develop them prosaically. It is then not surprising that landscape with its irreducibly visual dimension is more central to Berger's work than it is to Williams's. It is more troubling for Berger too. For putting pressure on his visual sensibility is Berger's increasing commitment to narrative. Indeed, Berger's work can be seen to explore the territory between image and narrative, between, in his phrases, 'ways of seeing' and 'ways of telling' (Dyer 1986, pp. 118–42). At the beginning of his 1967 documentary essay on a country doctor, *A fortunate man* (Berger & Mohr 1967), and over a photograph of the doctor's district by his collaborator Jean Mohr, Berger declared 'Landscapes can be deceptive. Sometimes a landscape seems to be less a setting for the life of its inhabitants than a curtain behind which their struggles, achievements and accidents take place.' In his endeavour to get 'behind the curtain' Berger next describes an incident mixing qualities that contradict the tranquil view Mohr had photographed – the doctor rushing to minister to an agonized woodcutter crushed beneath a tree (Berger & Mohr 1967, pp. 12–13, 17–19). Nevertheless, many of

Mohr's subsequent photographs still show views of the countryside and Berger continues to describe how it looks, but now as part of an attempt to represent landscape as something lived in not just looked at, and to make it express the experiences and knowledge of those who live in it. Berger & Mohr focus again on the drama of woodcutting in a more recent attempt to realize a more adequate notion of landscape, *Another way of telling* (1982), a book documenting life in the peasant village in the Haute Savoie (where Berger now lives) and intending to represent 'the way peasants look at themselves'. One sequence of photographs is commissioned by a woodcutter's wife to commemorate her husband if he should be killed in the forest and is permitted by the husband 'on condition that they show what the *work* is like', centrally the critical and dangerous moment when the tree falls. The sequence shows, from many angles and from many focal lengths, the process of felling a tree, culminating with a landscape, a view of the woodcutter in a clearing burying his axe in the log, posed against the background of the wooded slopes. In opposition to picturesque renderings of the peasantry and their countryside, it is an image that attempts to make 'appearances become the language of a lived life' (Berger & Mohr 1982, pp. 84, 59–70, 288). But it is not an image that is independent of a tradition of rural painting. Indeed, the photograph of the woodcutter burying his axe in a log recalls a painting of a woodcutting by Millet, the *Woodsawyers* (1848). And the recollection is surely not accidental, for, according to Berger, it was Millet who 'destroy[ed] the traditional language for depicting scenic landscape' by 'representing the close, harsh, patient physicality of a peasant's labour *on*, instead of *in front of*, the land' (Berger 1980, p. 77).

Much of Berger's analysis of the media of landscape representation has been concerned with their potential both to obscure and to articulate lived experience. As an existentialist Marxist, whose interpretations of the experience of woodcutting owe as much to Heidegger as to Marx or to the woodcutters themselves (Berger 1980, pp. 79–86), Berger is as sensitive to the self-consciousness of those who make landscapes on canvas or paper as he is to that of those who make them on the ground. Not surprisingly, this double sense of lived experience can be a source of tension. For example, in an essay of 1966 'Painting a landscape', he questions why he should feel both innocent pleasure and philosophical significance in 'making lustreless marks upon a tiny canvas in front of a landscape that has been cultivated for centuries and in view of the fact that such cultivation has and still demands lives of the hardest labour' especially when 'any peasant born in the village knows it a thousand times better'. Reasoning that since Cubism has 'broken' the genre of landscape as the replication of appearances he feels free to explore a psychoanalytical dimension of painting. In painting this landscape his sense of mastery is in imagining a world from above and he likens this to 'the experience of every child who imagines he is able to fly', for 'the sexual content assumed to exist in dreams about flying is closely connected to the sexual content of the landscape' (Berger 1972b, pp. 172–7).

In *Ways of seeing* (1972a), a television series and a book, Berger locates the repressive aspect of this pictorial mastery in realistic conventions of landscape painting, as part of his thesis on the complicity of the realistic tradition of Western painting with capitalist strategies of economic, social, and sexual appropriation and control. Linear perspective, centring 'everything on the eye of the beholder', and oil paint, 'reduc[ing] everything to the equality of objects' made the model of this tradition 'not so much a framed window open on to the world as a safe let into the wall, a safe in which the visible has been deposited'. So the point of Gainsborough portraying Mr and Mrs Andrews in the setting of their estate was to give them 'the pleasure of seeing themselves depicted as landowners and this pleasure was enhanced by the ability of oil paint to render their land in all its substantiality' (Berger 1972a, pp. 16, 87, 109, 108). Yet even in *Ways of seeing* the notion of landscape escapes bourgeois appropriation. At the beginning of the book Berger uses it as a metaphor for the kind of social-historical knowledge he himself uses to contextualize and criticize a painting like *Mr and Mrs Andrews* and indulgent interpretation of it; 'when we "see" a landscape, we situate ourselves in it. If we "saw" the art of the past, we would situate ourselves in history.' Indeed, Berger maintains that of all the categories of oil painting, landscape is the one to which his thesis of a proprietorial way of seeing applies the least, for 'landscape painting begins with the problems of painting sky and distance [and] the sky has no surface and is intangible; the sky cannot be turned into a thing or given a quantity.' Furthermore, it was innovative landscape painters like Turner and Monet who subverted the tradition of oil painting by leading it 'progressively away from the substantial and tangible towards the indeterminate and intangible' (Berger 1972a, pp. 11, 105). Nevertheless, this celebration of artists who dematerialize may be seen to be consistent with another thesis of *Ways of seeing*, that derived from Walter Benjamin, that the transformation of painting by modern means of reproduction into a more ephemeral 'language of images' is potentially liberating and consistent also with his photomontagist strategy of placing on a print of *Mr and Mrs Andrews* a sign saying 'Trespassers keep out'.

Subsequent to *Ways of seeing* Berger has further questioned the complicity of oil painting with bourgeois attitudes towards property; indeed he has argued that the very substance of oil paint offers a potential space in which to resist these attitudes, not in dissolving the material world but in reconstituting it in ways inimical to bourgeois versions of materialism. So to explain the subversive power of Courbet's very substantive oil paintings, Berger offers what he calls a 'geographical interpretation' to 'ground, give material, visual substance to, the social-historical one'. This is based on the 'need to interrogate the landscape' Courbet grew up in and painted throughout his life – the valley of the Loue on the western side of the Jura mountains – to 'visualize the mode of appearances in such a landscape in order to discover the perceptual habits it might encourage'. These appearances include dense forests, steep slopes and waterfalls, and fundamentally the outcrops of limestone 'which create the presence of the landscape'; where so much is in shadow and 'the visible . . . has to be grasped when it does make its appearance', the perceptual habits encouraged are 'the eyes of a hunter'. Painted on dark ground and with little atmospheric perspective there is 'no hierarchy of appearances' in Courbet's landscapes: 'Courbet painted everything – snow, flesh, hair, fur, clothes, bark – as he would have painted it had it been a rock face.' And it is in giving life to this landscape 'in which the visible is both lawless and irreduceably real' (as much as in articulating the hard lives of those work in such a landscape) that Berger sees the subversive power of Courbet's art. Proudhon, who came from the same area, wrote: 'I am pure Jurassic limestone.' Courbet, boastful as always, said that in his paintings, 'I even make stones think.' Berger suggests this physiographic interpretation of painting might be extended: 'The Thames developed Turner. The cliffs around Le Havre were formative in the case of Monet' (Berger 1980, pp. 134–41).

In signifying the realistic, historical, and material interconnections they made between land and life, Berger's admiration for Courbet's and Millet's sense of landscape (as against Gainsborough's) corresponds to Williams's admiration for Hardy's sense of landscape (as against Goldsmith's and Jane Austen's). And the correspondence goes further than this. Like Williams, Berger in his recent writings distances himself from semiological varieties of Marxist cultural theory in emphasizing a materialism which is biophysical as well as historical (Berger & Mohr 1982, pp. 111–16). Referring both to bourgeois and to revolutionary theory Berger declares that 'the nineteenth-century discovery of history as the terrain of human freedom inevitably led to an underestimation of the ineluctable and continuous.' Also underestimating it has been 'the new reductionism of revolutionary theory'. So he attacks *Art history and class struggle* (1978) by Hadjinicolaou for its reduction of all paintings to ideology, likening it to the way the culture of capitalism reduces them to commodities or to advertisements for other commodities: 'Both eliminate art as a potential model of freedom.' Resisting Hadjinicolaou's conception of painting as the reproduction of 'visual ideology' and the pleasure of looking at painting to a further reproduction of that visual ideology, Berger emphasizes the energy in the 'work' of art, the energy used by 'every painter since palaeolithic times onwards' to 'push' against the limits of his materials. This 'will to push' is for Berger 'intrinsic to the activity, to rendering the absent present, of cheating the visible, of making images'.

> *Ideology partly determines the finished result but it does not determine the energy flowing through the current. And it is with this energy that the spectator identifies. Every image used by a spectator is a* going further *than he could have achieved alone, towards a prey, a Madonna, a sexual pleasure, a landscape, a face, a different world (Berger 1985, pp. 197–204).*

Berger's notion of the imagination as a kind of craft is here deployed against the reproductive ideology of image-making in the mass media. In a recent essay, Berger upholds Van Gogh as an artist who closed the space between the acts of painting things and of making them, in his pictures of chairs, beds, and boots, but also in his landscapes, if 'before a landscape the process required was far more complicated and mysterious'. 'If one imagines God creating the world from earth and water, from clay, his way of handling it to make a tree or a cornfield might well resemble the way Van Gogh handled paint when he painted that tree or cornfield.' The religious metaphor is not meant here, or elsewhere in Berger's recent work, to question the materialism of nature or of painting but to restore the spiritual implications of creation to the material world. When Van Gogh 'painted a road, the roadmaker was there in his imagination. When he painted the turned earth of a ploughed field, the gesture of the blade turning the earth was included in his own act . . . when he painted a small peartree in flower, the act of the sap rising, of the bud forming, the bud breaking, the flower forming, the styles thrusting out, the stigmas becoming sticky, these acts were present for him in the act of painting.' The artist whose paintings are perhaps most subject to capitalist commodification – in the number of photographic reproductions, in the enormous prices for his works – Van Gogh, in the original, 'takes us as close as any man can . . . to that permanent process by which reality is produced' (Berger 1985, pp. 176–281).

Berger then closes the space between the aesthetics of art and the aesthetics of nature. While 'the social use to which an aesthetic emotion may be put changes according to the historical moment', he acknowledges, 'yet there seem to be certain constants which all cultures have found "beautiful": among them – certain flowers, trees, forms of rock, birds, animals, the moon, running water . . .'. And the 'aesthetic moment' of finding such things beautiful 'offers hope', it means 'that we are less alone, that we are more deeply inserted into existence than the course of a single life would lead us to believe'. 'Several years ago', recalls Berger, 'when considering the historical face of art, I wrote that I judged a work according to whether or not it helped men in the modern world to claim their social rights. I hold to that. Art's other, transcendental face raises the question of man's ontological rights' (Berger 1985, pp. 8–9). . . .

References

Adorno, T. 1984: *Aesthetic theory*. London: Routledge & Kegan Paul.

Barrell, J. 1980: *The dark side of the landscape: the rural poor in English painting 1730–1840*. Cambridge: Cambridge University Press.

Berger, J. 1972a: *Ways of seeing*. London: Harmondsworth.

Berger, J. 1972b: *Selected essays and articles: the look of things*. Harmondsworth: Pelican.

Berger, J. 1980: *About looking*. London: Writers & Readers Publishing Co-operative.

Berger, J. 1985: *The sense of sight*. New York: Pantheon Books.

Berger, J. and Mohr, J. 1967: *A fortunate man*. Harmondsworth: Penguin.

Berger, J. and Mohr, J. 1982: *Another way of telling*. London: Writers & Readers Publishing Co-operative.

Daniels, S. and Cosgrove, D. E. 1987: Iconography and landscape. In *The iconography of landscape*, D. E. Cosgrove and S. Daniels (eds). Cambridge: Cambridge University Press.

Hadjinicolaou, N. 1978: *Art history and class struggle*. London: Pluto Press.

Hoskins, W. G. 1970: *The making of the English landscape*. Harmondsworth: Pelican.

Inglis, F. 1977: Nation and community: a landscape and its morality. *Sociological Review* NS 25, 489–514.

Jay, M. 1984: *Adorno*. London: Fontana.

Williams, R. 1960: *Border country*. London: Chatto & Windus.

Williams, R. 1965: *The long revolution*. Harmondsworth: Penguin.

Williams, R. 1973: *The country and the city*. London: Chatto & Windus.
Williams, R. 1979a: *The fight for Manod*. London: Chatto & Windus.
Williams, R. 1979b: *Politics and letters*. London: New Left Books.
Williams, R. 1983: *Keywords*. London: Fontana.
Williams, R. 1984b: *Writing in society*. London: Verso.
Williams, R. 1987: The practice of possibility. *New Statesman*, 10–15, 7 August.

20

GEOGRAPHY AS A SCIENCE OF OBSERVATION: THE LANDSCAPE, THE GAZE AND MASCULINITY

Gillian Rose

Feminist geographers, like Marxist geographers, mostly begin their critique by attacking the spatial tradition. The turn towards the nature-society tradition eventually drew upon ideas from anthropology, environmental history and, as here, psychoanalysis and film theory. Gillian Rose confronts what Sauer (**chapter 17**), Daniels (**chapter 19**) and others take for granted, namely the pleasure of looking that often accompanies both fieldwork and landscape study. This gaze has roots not only in the landowner's possession of landscape but also in the masculine desire for, and fear of, a feminine nature. Like nature, women in Western society have been, and still are, coded as passive and nurturing on the one hand and wild and uncontrollable on the other. In both cases they are objects of knowledge, not the makers of it. Rose argues that cultural geographers should explore these feelings. One might note that Glacken (**chapter 13**) says almost nothing about the near universal gendering of ideas of nature, for example. These thoughts are elaborated in Rose's important and challenging book *Feminism and geography* (Cambridge, 1993), while her views on the politics of vision complement those of Haraway (**chapter 6**).

Source: Geography as the science of observation: the landscape, the gaze and masculinity. In Driver, F. and Rose, G., editors, *Nature and science: essays in the history of geographical knowledge*. Historical Geography Research Series, number 28, pp. 8–18, 1992.

> *In the course of fieldwork or on a summer holiday we have all climbed a mountain and gazed over uninhabited or unfamiliar country . . . In the contemplative mood that mountain tops induce, we have brooded over the view, speculated on the lay of the land, experienced a pleasurable sense of the mysterious – perhaps felt even a touch of the sinister. We have heard the Sirens' voices. (Wright, 1947, p. 2)*

One of the most important expressions of the relationship between power and knowledge in the discipline of geography in the Western academy is the exclusion of women and their experiences as both subjects and objects of research. Their marginality to hegemonic definitions of geography has been well-documented (Domosh, 1991; Monk and Hanson, 1982; Peake, 1989). There has, however, been relatively little discussion of its implications for the kinds of knowledge through which the discipline defines itself; feminist geographers have, until very recently, been more concerned to make women and gender relations a part of geographical knowledge than to question the epistemology and ontology of the geographical project (but see Domosh, 1991; Johnson, 1987).

Identifying the under-representation of women in geography is not to suggest, however, that femininity is absent from geographical knowledge; on the contrary, as this chapter will argue, the feminine is present in geography's texts. The chapter looks at one of the key concepts of Western geographical knowledge – landscape – and argues that the unknown and unknowable in landscape is implicitly represented by geographers as feminine. In order to understand why, the work of Le Doueff (1980) is helpful. In the context of her study of Western philosophical texts, she argues that their meaning depends on an internal contrast with what is meaningless (see Grosz, 1989). This dualism is gendered; masculine knowledge defines itself in contrast to a feminine unknowable. The work the feminine performs in geography is similarly epistemological, for the feminine presence is that against which the meaningfulness of masculine knowledge is established. My task then is not to put women back into the historiography of the discipline, but rather to examine the masculinism of its central categories and ways of knowing.[1] Clearly this is an ambitious project, and only an extremely schematic start can be made here.

Landscape is one of geography's most resilient terms because it refers to one of the discipline's most abiding interests: the relationship between the natural environment and human society. Landscape developed as a concept in geography in nineteenth-century Germany as *Landschaft*, which literally translates as *the shape of the land*. By studying the morphology of scenery it was argued that geographers could formulate systematic and scientific theories of societies' interaction with the physical environment around them, in particular by relating the environment to the social, economic and cultural activity in the area over a period of time. Landscape then was never a self-evident object in geography. A theoretical framework always structured its interpretation; it was an analytic concept which afforded objective understanding. As a reviewer of interwar landscape studies insisted, although 'literally [the landscape] is the scene within the range of the observer's vision', the view demanded analysis and interpretation in order to gain an objective understanding of the landscape in its entirety (Dickinson, 1939, p. 1).

The practice of fieldwork was crucial to this scientific understanding of landscape; its purpose was to observe directly the synthesis of land, flora, fauna and people. The eye held the landscape together as a unit and the geographer then

[1] I use the term 'masculinism' because it avoids the universalist connotations of 'patriarchy' and the often purely linguistic reference of the term 'phallocentrism'.

analysed the view, selecting the features requiring elucidation, and fieldwork is still of central importance to the discipline. As a manual on fieldwork for school-teachers puts it, 'when we train and seek to inspire a new generation of geographers we must by precept and by example remind them that the great discoveries and advances made in geography have been made by men who went to look *and think* in the field' (Jones, 1968, p. 1, my emphasis). Every schoolchild and student is taken on visits to the field, and undergraduate field trips are the initiation ritual of the discipline. Field trips instill the ethos of geographical knowledge into its students, and it is an ethos of science triumphant:

> *In the discipline a major approach has been through field study, in which geographers go directly to the original source of all geographical knowledge and confront the raw and undisturbed phenomena with which they have to deal. Field study [is] . . . an endless effort to bridge the gap between raw data and penetrating comprehensive knowledge (Platt, 1959, p. 1).*

The real geographer faces wild nature for the sake of rational science; as Stoddart proudly tells us, 'on uninhabited Pacific atolls, sailing alone the barrier reefs of Australia and Belize, in the mangrove swamps of Bangladesh, on English coastal marshes, I have been concerned with making sense of nature' (Stoddart, 1986, p. ix). This heroism continues today too, with the organisers of field trips to the museums and cafes of Venice forced to legitimate themselves by referring to Sauer and Wooldridge as antecedents (Cosgrove and Daniels, 1989, p. 179).

The analytic look was thus a crucial part of field research. But the gaze also gave pleasure to the geographer. It offered him the gorgeous scene, the enlightening detail, the beauty of diversity and the breathtaking view (Stoddart, 1986), and a past president of the Association of American Geographers has claimed that 'many of us are in geography because it involves using our eyes, and for the latitude it allows for wonderment at the world around us' (Parsons, 1977, p. 2). Such pleasure in and awe of landscape is often celebrated by geographers, but with hesitation, even treated with suspicion. Pleasure in the landscape was often seen as a threat to the scientific gaze, and it was often argued that the geographer should not allow himself to be seduced by what were described as 'the sirens of *terrae incognitae*' (Wright, 1947, p. 1).[2] This need for a certain analytical distance from the aesthetic pleasures of the view is repeated in much more recent accounts of landscape (Meinig, 1979; Cosgrove, 1985).

In the rest of the paper, I want to explore some connections between this ambivalent pleasure in looking at landscape and the scientist-as-hero ethos of fieldwork. The next section examines some more recent studies of landscape by cultural geographers, and suggests that pleasure in looking is again acknowledged but repressed unexamined. In order to explicate the ambivalent fantasies which structure the masculine gaze of the geographer, discussions of the discursive and visual encoding of nature as feminine follow. These suggest that the landscape which

[2] I would like to thank Steve Daniels and Peter Sunley for helpful comments here.

geographers hope to know but whose pleasures escape their mastery is a construct of masculine power and desire.

The Critique of Landscape by the New Cultural Geography

In 1987, a paper by Cosgrove and Jackson heralded 'new directions' in cultural geography. It marked the development of a rich and subtle literature in which, among other things, the concept of 'landscape' has undergone a major critique. Central to its arguments is the visuality of the landscape idea, and the following brief account focusses on this aspect of the new work.

Cosgrove has problematised the term landscape through a study of the concept as it first emerged in Renaissance Italy (Cosgrove, 1985). He understands landscape not as a material expression of a particular relationship between a society and an environment, observable in the field by the objective gaze of the geographer, but rather as a concept which makes sense of a particular relationship between society and land. In particular, geographers have stressed the construction of the look at landscape and have argued that landscape is a way of seeing which we learn: 'a landscape is a cultural image, a pictorial way of representing, structuring or symbolising surroundings' (Daniels and Cosgrove, 1988, p. 1). A landscape's meanings draw on the cultural codes of the society for which it was made. These codes are embedded in social power structures, and theorisation of the relationship between culture and society by these 'new' cultural geographers has so far drawn on the humanist marxist tradition which sees the material and symbolic dimensions of the production and reproduction of society as inextricably intertwined (see Daniels, 1989). Cosgrove, for example, says culture is:

> *symbolisation, grounded in the material world as symbolically appropriated and produced. In class societies, where surplus production is appropriated by the dominant group, symbolic production is likewise seized as hegemonic class culture to be imposed on all classes (Cosgrove, 1983, p. 5).*

Cosgrove places the development of landscape painting in the context of an emerging bourgeoisie which, while it was buying land in the countryside and constantly searching for new markets, was also improving various means of depicting and thus controlling these spaces. Surveying and map-making increased both its knowledge of and power over space and people. Cosgrove stresses the importance of the technique of three-dimensional perspective to this material/cultural process, a technique which enabled artists to render depth realistically. In so doing they established a particular viewpoint for the spectator of a landscape view: a single, fixed point which sees the property of the bourgeois individual spread out before it. Cosgrove concludes that landscape is a way of seeing which is patrician because it is seen and understood from the social position of the landowner: it is a 'visual ideology' made hegemonic (Cosgrove, 1985, p. 47), and the pleasure if offers is merely the bourgeois pleasure in possession.

Although by the twentieth century landscape painting was no longer necessarily perspectival, the power of images of landscape remains as strong as ever. Its continuing significance has been connected not only to its ideological dominance but also to its emotive power in an important essay by Daniels (1989) which elaborates and complicates Cosgrove's arguments. Daniels advocates a sense of landscape as not merely ideological, but duplicitous. Pleasure in landscape could be used by the bourgeoisie in ways explored by Cosgrove, but its enduring intensity suggests to Daniels that it also expresses something profound and constant about the human condition.

I want now to look briefly at the mid-eighteenth century double portrait of *Mr and Mrs Andrews* by Thomas Gainsborough, an image often used to exemplify these arguments about class and property and English landscape. For Berger, for example, and, by implication, for Cosgrove, pleasure in the right hand side of the canvas – its intense green fields, the heaviness of the sheaves of corn, the English sky threatening rain – is made problematic by the two figures on the left: Mr and Mrs Andrews, the improvers of the land. 'They are landowners and their proprietary attitude towards what surrounds them is visible in their stance and their expressions' (Berger, 1972, p. 107). The perspective in this image allows our gaze to wander freely across the land in the way only landowners of the time could, and its use supports Cosgrove's claim that landscape painting is a form of visual ideology. The fact that this couple owned the fields and trees about them is central to the painting's creation and therefore to its meaning, and so any pleasure we feel must be tainted by theirs. However, following Daniels's insistence on the duplicity of landscape, our pleasure in its representation of the countryside remains real and enables the shock of Steve Bell's cartoon for CND in which Mr and Mrs Andrews are replaced by Reagan and Thatcher and Cruise missiles litter the fields obscenely (Bell, n.d.). The landscape here, in its desecration, works against the power which the two figures represent.

Daniels's essay is highly innovatory in its frank admission of visual pleasure; as this chapter has already noted, geographers have traditionally been careful not to over-respond to the pleasures of their observed landscape. Tuan, for example, simply says that when confronted with the emotional pull of art, 'the proper response is silence' (Tuan, 1979, p. 422). In Daniels's essay, however, there remains another kind of refusal to engage critically with this expressive power, partly enabled by his claim that it is a universal, transcendental pleasure and therefore unproblematic. Its impact is also kept at bay by the reiteration of a quotation from Berger about visual pleasure which is repeated almost like a talisman against the power of which it speaks; for the spectator, pleasure is 'a going further than he [sic] could have achieved alone, towards a prey, a Madonna, a sexual pleasure, a landscape, a face, a different world' (Daniels, 1989, p. 203 and p. 215). It seems that the function of repeating the text which represents visual pleasure is to mark the ground of an apparently unspeakable pleasure; to delimit it, to render it bounded, a definition against which a stable system of interpretation is erected. The new cultural geography then seems as ambivalent about the apparently disruptive power of the visual as the old. But why is this power characterised in terms of a

Madonna, and in terms of sexual pleasure? Let's take a second look at Mr and Mrs Andrews.

The Discourse of Feminine Nature

It is possible to differentiate between Mr and Mrs Andrews. For although both figures are relaxed and share the sense of partnership so often found in eighteenth-century portraits of husband and wife, their unity is not entire; they are given rather different relationships to the land around them. Mr Andrews stands, gun in arm, ready to leave his pose and go shooting; his hunting dog is at his feet already urging him away. Mrs Andrews meanwhile sits impassively, rooted to her seat with its wrought iron branches and tendrils, her upright stance echoing that of the tree directly behind her. If Mr Andrews seems at any moment able to stride off into the vista, Mrs Andrews looks planted to the spot. Through a discussion of this difference, I want first to establish the way it draws on a discursive association of women with nature, and then to think about what this means for geographers' ambivalent visual pleasure in landscape.

Many feminists have argued that the discursive construction of femininity as closer to nature than masculinity is the source of women's oppression, and in the mid-1970s anthropologists attempted a cross-cultural theorisation of patriarchy by suggesting that the naturalisation of women's childbearing role confined women to the domestic arena and excluded them from the public world of the polity, economy and culture (Rosaldo and Lamphere, 1974). Feminist historians have begun to specify this process both substantively and theoretically in Euro-America, and their work offers part of an explanation for Mrs Andrews's difference from Mr Andrews.

The notion that culture was separate from nature was made in classical times in Europe, but its gendering was elaborated in the seventeenth and eighteenth centuries. The discourses of that era in various and complex ways hardened the already-existing division between abstract and rational man who could pursue universal knowledge unencumbered by the limitations of a body placed in a particular period and place, and relational, emotional woman closely bound to the particular instincts, rhythms and desires of her fleshly, located body. With the development of mechanical theories of the world in the seventeenth century, women were seen as the repositories of natural laws and, like nature tamed by man, women too could be examined by male science and made intelligible. Science represented nature as passive and therefore female: a set of discrete functioning mechanisms which could be known and controlled (Merchant, 1980). Political theorists pointed to the closeness of women to nature in their arguments against women's participation in the polity (Okin, 1979). The expression of such themes in legal discourse meant that only Mr Andrews was a landowner when Gainsborough painted him, and this suggests one reason why Mrs Andrews is denied the mobility of her husband and represented more as part of the landscape. Moreover, the shadow of the oak tree over Mrs Andrews refers to the family tree she was expected to propagate and nurture (Daniels, 1988); like the field she sits beside, her role was to produce. As Bermingham (1987, pp. 14–16) notes, these references to trees and fields also serve to naturalise Mrs Andrews's function as a mother.

The comparison between women and nature was a complex one, though, for women were both the passive and nurturing mother nature of organic theories of the self and cosmos, as well as tempestuous and uncontrollable wild nature; medical discourse argued that both woman's fecundity and her lust placed her closer to nature than man (Moscucci, 1990; Poovey, 1989). Woman as both mother and whore was constructed as natural. And in many landscape paintings with women, not least in numerous images from the second half of the nineteenth century when geography was emerging as a discipline, Nature is discursively represented as feminine, both maternal and seductive. French genre scenes of that period often demonstrate the presumed naturalness of peasant women's maternal role by their visual equivalence of the women with the animals and land they tend (Nochlin, 1980). Woman's sexuality as well as her fertility was explored in images of classical, fantastical or allegorical women surrounded by wild nature; they are found in fields and woods throughout late nineteenth-century art, entwining themselves as nymphs or dryads in trees, or lying on the leaf-covered earth, languid, vulnerable, so that, according to Dijkstra's somewhat over-emphatic account, 'we can almost hear them call to us like animals waiting to be fed' (Dijkstra, 1986, p. 99). In a final iconographic twist, women become allegories of nature herself, for the seasons, for weather, for the time of day, for flowers.

It is this transcending of the complex meanings of woman and nature which begins to suggest an explanation of geographers' suspicion about visual pleasure. The first French encounter with Tahiti is described by Stoddart (1986, p. 35) as one of the founding moments of scientific geography. Jordanova claims that by the eighteenth century, 'science [was] a sexual activity in its relationship to nature' (Jordanova, 1980, p. 66), and the specific encounter Stoddart chooses to elaborate is a sexual one; the cook jumps ship to find Tahitian women. The new land to be explored, mapped, penetrated and known is thus shown as feminine and desirable, not an uncommon trope in the language of geographic exploration (Kolodny, 1975; Said, 1978); at a later colonial moment, Gauguin's paintings of Tahiti fused beautiful, sexual, fertile women with a gorgeous, generous, lush land. In Stoddart's tale however the women are also threatening; the cook returns and says that whatever punishment his captain chooses for him could not be more terrible than them. Daniels too confirms the sinister and seductive sexuality of pleasure in landscape in his repeated attempt to contain its disruption through a conflation of hunting, a virgin, the single male orgasm and landscape. We are now in a position to understand this ambivalent pleasure in terms of the discursive construction of nature as both a nurturing mother and a seductive and dangerous mistress.

In its stress on the discursive construction of nature, however, this argument does not fully address the *visual* pleasure geographers find in landscape. Many feminist art historians and cultural critics have suggested that 'the specificity of visual performance and address has . . . a privileged relation to issues of sexuality' (Pollock, 1988, p. 123), so I want now to suggest that visual pleasure in landscape is specifically sexual; there is a gendered logic of the gaze (Bryson, 1983). I want to connect geographers' ambivalence towards 'the landscape of the reclining torso' (Armstrong, 1986, p. 237) to the imagined and desired sexuality of the feminine which is offered to the *spectator* of landscape, as well as to the discursive representation of nature as both maternal and sexual.

Visual Pleasures and Fears

To summarise crudely a large and complex feminist literature which draws to some extent on Lacanian psychoanalysis 'looking implies subjects who arrange things into images and who are themselves produced by looking' (Deutsche, 1991, p. 10); there is a 'complex identificatory investment in images' (Grosz, 1989, p. 22). But in a phallocracy, not everyone can look equally; woman is image and man is bearer of the look (Mulvey, 1989, p. 19). The active look is masculine, and the passivity of being looked at is constituted as the feminine position. Mulvey's (1989) comments on Hollywood cinema suggest that these positions are established through images of landscape especially. She argues that films re-enact some of the earliest moments of self-identification when the subject sees its image reflected in a mirror, and so we see ourselves on the screen, ourselves as we would like to be, heroic. The use of landscape structured through Renaissance perspective is central to this process, because 'the active male figure . . . demands a three-dimensional space corresponding to that of the mirror recognition in which the alienated subject internalised his own representation of his . . . existence" (Mulvey, 1989, p. 20). Movie heroes are the coherent, active subjects in which subjectivity is first recognised in the mirror; and Mulvey notes that women who identify with the hero are taking up masculine positions. Here then lies part of the satisfaction of fieldwork for geographers; they see themselves as the masculine hero in a landscape, and fulfilling themselves through their attempts to understand feminine nature.

The masculine gaze is also characterised by Mulvey as one of desire, a search for something that is lost, and the pleasure which both men and women find in visual images has been argued to rest in part on their ability to partially and temporarily assuage our sense of loss. In particular, images of women, of nature, of mother nature and the 'maternal natural landscape', to quote Sauer (1963, p. 325), can offer plenitude and pleasure and suspend the fear of lack (Pointon, 1990).

However, alienation is also a necessary consequence of the importance of the mirror to identity, for the image in the mirror is separate from the subject who sees it/himself. This implies that voyeurism is also part of subjectivity, and the analytical distance upon which the protocols of fieldwork insist is a kind of voyeurism: investigative and controlling, instituting a distance from and mastery over the image. Such boundaries are needed, and visual pleasure is deeply ambivalent, because if images of women and the feminine can disavow lack, they also threaten to overwhelm the masculine subject. Dijkstra (1986) charts these anxieties in the nineteenth-century paintings of mermaids, sirens, sphinxes and Medusas, and studies of the exploration of North America and Africa have revealed the ways in which the terrors of the overwhelming unknown were seen in terms of maternal suffocation (Kolodny, 1975; Stott, 1989). Landscape can then signify visually not the welcoming topography of a nurturing mother or peepshow tease, but terrifying swamps, floods, seas. Geographers' ambivalence about landscape is therefore also part of the desires and fears which mediate their gaze and the image.

Looking and Knowing

Geographers' profound ambivalence toward the landscape they desire so much must be seen as part of geography's 'erotics of knowledge' (De Certeau in Deutsche, 1990, p. 11). I have suggested that the feminine unknown is represented in cultural geography by visual pleasure, and that the geographers' gaze at landscape is structured by a distinction between nature (the feminine scene, to be interpreted) and science (the masculine look, the interpreter). The complexity of the feminisation of nature in the West, and the complexities of sexually-differentiated interpretation of geographical knowledge needs the specificities of historical geography often missing from psychoanalytic accounts of the visual, and the work of the new cultural geography is clearly valuable here. But its repressive refusal to explore its own pleasures only continues to deny and simultaneously to display its masculinity.

References

Bell, S. (n.d.) *Old Masters No. 2: After Mr and Mrs Andrews* (Leeds, Leeds Postcards).
Berger, J. (1972) *Ways of Seeing* (London, British Broadcasting Corporation).
Bermingham, A. (1987) *Lancscape and Ideology: The English Rustic Tradition 1740–1860* (London, Thames & Hudson).
Bryson, N. (1983) *Vision and Painting* (Basingstoke, Macmillan).
Cosgrove, D. (1983) 'Towards a radical cultural geography: problems of theory', *Antipode* 15, pp. 1–11.
Cosgrove, D. (1985) 'Prospect, perspective and the evolution of the landscape idea', *Transactions of the Institute of British Geographers* 10, pp. 45–62.
Cosgrove, D. and S. Daniels (1989) 'Fieldwork as theatre', *Journal of Geography in Higher Education* 13, pp. 169–83.
Daniels, S. (1989) 'Marxism, culture and the duplicity of landscape', in R. Peet and N. Thrift, (eds), *New Models in Geography Volume 2* (London, Unwin Hyman), pp. 196–220.
Daniels, S. and D. Cosgrove (1988) 'Introduction: the iconography of landscape' in D. Cosgrove and S. Daniels (eds), *The Iconography of Landscape* (Cambridge, Cambridge University Press) pp. 43–82.
Deutsche, R. (1991) 'Boys town', *Environment and Planning D: Society and Space* 9, pp. 5–30.
Dickinson, R. E. (1939) 'Landscape and society' *Scottish Geographical Magazine* 55, pp. 1–14.
Dijkstra, B. (1986) *The Idols of Perversity* (New York, Oxford University Press).
Domosh, M. (1991) 'Towards a feminist historiography of geography', *Transactions of the Institute of British Geographers* 16, pp. 95–104.
Grosz, E. (1989) *Sexual Subversions: Three French Feminists* (Sydney, Allen and Unwin).

Johnson, L. (1987) '(Un)realist perspectives: patriarchy and feminist perspectives in geography', Antipode 19, pp. 210–15.

Jones, P. A. (1968) *Field Work in Geography* (London, Longman's Green).

Jordanova, L. (1980) 'Natural facts: a historical perspective on science and sexuality' in C. MacCormack and M. Strathern (eds), *Nature, Culture and Gender* (Cambridge University Press), pp. 42–69.

Kolodny, A. (1975) *The Lay of the Land: Metaphor as Experience and History in American Life and Letters* (Chapel Hill, North Carolina University Press).

Le Doeuff, M. (1980) *Recherches sur L'Imaginaire Philosophique* (Paris, Payot).

Meinig, D. (ed.) (1979) *The Interpretation of Ordinary Landscapes* (Oxford, Oxford University Press).

Merchant, C. (1980) *The Death of Nature: Women, Ecology and the Scientific Revolution* (San Francisco, Harper & Row).

Monk, J. and S. Hanson (1982) 'On not excluding half of the human in human geography', *Professional Geographer* 34, pp. 11–23.

Moscucci, O. (1990) *The Science of Woman: Gynaecology and Gender in England 1800–1929* (Cambridge, Cambridge University Press).

Mulvey, L. (1989) *Visual and Other Pleasures* (Basingstoke, Macmillan).

Nochlin, L. (1980) 'The *Cribleuses de Blé*: Courbet, Millet, Breton, Kollwitz and the image of the working woman' in *Malerei und Theorie: Das Courbet-Colloquium 1979* (Frankfurt, Staatlische Galerie in Stadelschen Kunstinstitut), pp. 49–74.

Okin, S. M. (1979) *Women in Western Political Thought* (Princeton, Princeton University Press).

Peake, L. (ed.) (1989) 'The challenge of feminist geography', *Journal of Geography in Higher Education* 13, pp. 85–121.

Parsons, J. J. (1977) 'Geography as exploration and discovery', *Annals of the Association of American Geographers* 67, pp. 1–16.

Platt, R. S. (1959) *Field Study in American Geography* (University of Chicago Geography Department Research paper no. 6).

Pointon, M. (1990) *Naked Authority: The Body in Western Painting 1830–1908* (Cambridge, Cambridge University Press).

Pollock, G. (1988) *Vision and Difference* (London, Routledge).

Poovey, M. (1989) *Uneven Developments: The Ideological Work of Gender in Mid-Victorian England* (London, Virago).

Rosaldo, M. Z. and L. Lamphere, (eds) (1974) *Women, Culture and Society* (Stanford, Stanford University Press).

Said, E. W. (1978) *Orientalism: Western Conceptions of the Orient* (London, Routledge and Kegan Paul).

Sauer, C. O. (1963) in J. Leighley, (ed.) *Land and Life* (Berkeley, California University Press).

Stoddart, D. R. (1986) *On Geography and its History* (Oxford, Basil Blackwell).

Stott, R. (1989) 'The dark continent: Africa as female body in Haggard's adventure fiction', *Feminist Review* 32, pp. 69–89.

Tuan, Y. F. (1979) 'Sight and pictures', Geographical Review 69, pp. 411–22.

Wright, J. K. (1947) 'Terrae incognitae: the place of the imagination in geography', *Annals of the Association of American Geographers* 37, pp. 1–15.

21

THE LAND ETHIC

Aldo Leopold

A sand county almanac is one of the classic texts of US environmental thinking, although it was published after the death of its author and was not widely read until the 1960s. Aldo Leopold (1887–1947) began his career with the US Forest Service and was responsible for managing Carson National Forest, New Mexico, during a period in which utilitarianism informed US conservation. He was party to the virtual war waged on wolves and other predators, designed to maintain the stock of deer for hunters. But during the 1930s he began to realize that wolves were a vital part of the ecosystem and he questioned the ethics of game management. In 1933 he took up a post at the University of Wisconsin and bought a small farm in the sand counties in the north of the state. There he fused detailed observation of nature with philosophical speculation on the relationship between humans and the environment. He thus joined a succession of naturalist–philosophers like Gilbert White, Henry Thoreau and John Muir, who based their thoughts on the intimate knowledge of particular landscapes. The *Almanac* includes a nature diary of his land in the course of the year in which poetic and scientific appreciation are combined. The land ethic, the idea that we should be citizens with the land rather than conquerors of it, therefore developed from the kind of close geographical observation admired by Sauer and Jackson.

Source: *A sand county almanac and sketches here and there.* Oxford: Oxford University Press, 1949. Extract from pp. 201–26, special commemorative edition, Oxford, 1989.

When god-like Odysseus returned from the wars in Troy, he hanged all on one rope a dozen slave-girls of his household whom he suspected of misbehavior during his absence.

This hanging involved no question of propriety. The girls were property. The disposal of property was then, as now, a matter of expediency, not of right and wrong.

Concepts of right and wrong were not lacking from Odysseus' Greece: witness the fidelity of his wife through the long years before at last his black-prowed galleys clove the wine-dark seas for home. The ethical structure of that day covered wives, but had not yet been extended to human chattels. During the three thousand years which have since elapsed, ethical criteria have been extended to many fields of conduct, with corresponding shrinkages in those judged by expediency only.

The Ethical Sequence

This extension of ethics, so far studied only by philosophers, is actually a process in ecological evolution. Its sequences may be described in ecological as well as in philosophical terms. An ethic, ecologically, is a limitation on freedom of action in the struggle for existence. An ethic, philosophically, is a differentiation of social from anti-social conduct. These are two definitions of one thing. The thing has its origin in the tendency of interdependent individuals or groups to evolve modes of co-operation. The ecologist calls these symbioses. Politics and economics are advanced symbioses in which the original free-for-all competition has been replaced, in part, by co-operative mechanisms with an ethical content.

The complexity of co-operative mechanisms has increased with population density, and with the efficiency of tools. It was simpler, for example, to define the anti-social uses of sticks and stones in the days of the mastodons than of bullets and billboards in the age of motors.

The first ethics dealt with the relation between individuals; the Mosaic Decalogue is an example. Later accretions dealt with the relation between the individual and society. The Golden Rule tries to integrate the individual to society; democracy to integrate social organization to the individual.

There is as yet no ethic dealing with man's relation to land and to the animals and plants which grow upon it. Land, like Odysseus' slave-girls, is still property. The land-relation is still strictly economic, entailing privileges but not obligations.

The extension of ethics to this third element in human environment is, if I read the evidence correctly, an evolutionary possibility and an ecological necessity. It is the third step in a sequence. The first two have already been taken. Individual thinkers since the days of Ezekiel and Isaiah have asserted that the despoliation of land is not only inexpedient but wrong. Society, however, has not yet affirmed their belief. I regard the present conservation movement as the embryo of such an affirmation.

An ethic may be regarded as a mode of guidance for meeting ecological situations so new or intricate, or involving such deferred reactions, that the path of social expediency is not discernible to the average individual. Animal instincts are modes of guidance for the individual in meeting such situations. Ethics are possibly a kind of community instinct in-the-making.

The Community Concept

All ethics so far evolved rest upon a single premise: that the individual is a member of a community of interdependent parts. His instincts prompt him to compete for his place in that community, but his ethics prompt him also to co-operate (perhaps in order that there may be a place to compete for).

The land ethic simply enlarges the boundaries of the community to include soils, waters, plants, and animals, or collectively: the land.

This sounds simple: do we not already sing our love for and obligation to the land of the free and the home of the brave? Yes, but just what and whom do we love? Certainly not the soil, which we are sending helter-skelter downriver. Certainly not the waters, which we assume have no function except to turn turbines, float barges, and carry off sewage. Certainly not the plants, of which we exterminate whole communities without batting an eye. Certainly not the animals, of which we have already extirpated many of the largest and most beautiful species. A land ethic of course cannot prevent the alteration, management, and use of these 'resources,' but it does affirm their right to continued existence, and, at least in spots, their continued existence in a natural state.

In short, a land ethic changes the role of *Homo sapiens* from conqueror of the land-community to plain member and citizen of it. It implies respect for his fellow-members, and also respect for the community as such.

In human history, we have learned (I hope) that the conqueror role is eventually self-defeating. Why? Because it is implicit in such a role that the conqueror knows, *ex cathedra*, just what makes the community clock tick, and just what and who is valuable, and what and who is worthless, in community life. It always turns out that he knows neither, and this is why his conquests eventually defeat themselves.

In the biotic community, a parallel situation exists. Abraham knew exactly what the land was for: it was to drip milk and honey into Abraham's mouth. At the present moment, the assurance with which we regard this assumption is inverse to the degree of our education.

The ordinary citizen today assumes that science knows what makes the community clock tick; the scientist is equally sure that he does not. He knows that the biotic mechanism is so complex that its workings may never be fully understood.

That man is, in fact, only a member of a biotic team is shown by an ecological interpretation of history. Many historical events, hitherto explained solely in terms of human enterprise, were actually biotic interactions between people and land. The characteristics of the land determined the facts quite as potently as the characteristics of the men who lived on it.

Consider, for example, the settlement of the Mississippi valley. In the years following the Revolution, three groups were contending for its control: the native Indian, the French and English traders, and the American settlers. Historians wonder what would have happened if the English at Detroit had thrown a little more weight into the Indian side of those tipsy scales which decided the outcome of the colonial migration into the cane-lands of Kentucky. It is time now to ponder the fact that the cane-lands, when subjected to the particular mixture of forces represented by the cow, plow, fire, and axe of the pioneer, became bluegrass. What if the plant succession inherent in this dark and bloody ground had, under the impact of these forces, given us some worthless sedge, shrub or weed? Would Boone and Kenton have held out? Would there have been any overflow into Ohio, Indiana, Illinois, and Missouri? Any Louisiana Purchase? Any transcontinental union of new states? Any Civil War?

Kentucky was one sentence in the drama of history. We are commonly told what the human actors in this drama tried to do, but we are seldom told that their success, or the lack of it, hung in large degree on the reaction of particular soils to the impact of the particular forces exerted by their occupancy. In the case of Kentucky, we do not even know where the bluegrass came from – whether it is a native species, or a stowaway from Europe.

Contrast the cane-lands with what hindsight tells us about the Southwest, where the pioneers were equally brave, resourceful, and persevering. The impact of occupancy here brought no bluegrass, or other plant fitted to withstand the bumps and buffetings of hard use. This region, when grazed by livestock, reverted through a series of more and more worthless grasses, shrubs, and weeds to a condition of unstable equilibrium. Each recession of plant types bred erosion; each increment to erosion bred a further recession of plants. The result today is a progressive and mutual deterioration, not only of plants and soils, but of the animal community subsisting thereon. The early settlers did not expect this: on the ciénegas of New Mexico some even cut ditches to hasten it. So subtle has been its progress that few residents of the region are aware of it. It is quite invisible to the tourist who finds this wrecked landscape colorful and charming (as indeed it is, but it bears scant resemblance to what it was in 1848).

This same landscape was 'developed' once before, but with quite different results. The Pueblo Indians settled the Southwest in pre-Columbian times, but they happened *not* to be equipped with range livestock. Their civilization expired, but not because their land expired.

In India, regions devoid of any sod-forming grass have been settled, apparently without wrecking the land, by the simple expedient of carrying the grass to the cow, rather than vice versa. (Was this the result of some deep wisdom, or was it just good luck? I do not know.)

In short, the plant succession steered the course of history; the pioneer simply demonstrated, for good or ill, what successions inhered in the land. Is history taught in this spirit? It will be, once the concept of land as a community really penetrates our intellectual life.

The Ecological Conscience

Conservation is a state of harmony between man and land. Despite nearly a century of propaganda, conservation still proceeds at a snail's pace; progress still consists largely of letterhead pieties and convention oratory. On the back forty we still slip two steps backward for each forward stride.

The usual answer to this dilemma is 'more conservation education.' No one will debate this, but is it certain that only the *volume* of education needs stepping up? Is something lacking in the *content* as well?

It is difficult to give a fair summary of its content in brief form, but, as I understand it, the content is substantially this: obey the law, vote right, join some organizations, and practice what conservation is profitable on your own land; the government will do the rest.

Is not this formula too easy to accomplish anything worth-while? It defines no right or wrong, assigns no obligation, calls for no sacrifice, implies no change in the current philosophy of values. In respect of land-use, it urges only enlightened self-interest. Just how far will such education take us? An example will perhaps yield a partial answer.

By 1930 it had become clear to all except the ecologically blind that southwestern Wisconsin's topsoil was slipping seaward. In 1933 the farmers were told that if they would adopt certain remedial practices for five years, the public would donate CCC labor to install them, plus the necessary machinery and materials. The offer was widely accepted, but the practices were widely forgotten when the five-year contract period was up. The farmers continued only those practices that yielded an immediate and visible economic gain for themselves.

This led to the idea that maybe farmers would learn more quickly if they themselves wrote the rules. Accordingly the Wisconsin Legislature in 1937 passed the Soil Conservation District Law. This said to farmers, in effect: *We, the public, will furnish you free technical service and loan you specialized machinery, if you will write your own rules for land-use. Each county may write its own rules, and these will have the force of law.* Nearly all the counties promptly organized to accept the proffered help, but after a decade of operation, *no county has yet written a single rule.* There has been visible progress in such practices as strip-cropping, pasture renovation, and soil liming, but none in fencing woodlots against grazing, and none in excluding plow and cow from steep slopes. The farmers, in short, have selected those remedial practices which were profitable anyhow, and ignored those which were profitable to the community, but not clearly profitable to themselves.

When one asks why no rules have been written, one is told that the community is not yet ready to support them; education must precede rules. But the education actually in progress makes no mention of obligations to land over and above those dictated by self-interest. The net result is that we have more education but less soil, fewer healthy woods, and as many floods as in 1937.

The puzzling aspect of such situations is that the existence of obligations over and above self-interest is taken for granted in such rural community enterprises as the betterment of roads, schools, churches, and baseball teams. Their existence is not taken for granted, nor as yet seriously discussed, in bettering the behavior of the water that falls on the land, or in the preserving of the beauty or diversity of the farm landscape. Land-use ethics are still governed wholly by economic self-interest, just as social ethics were a century ago.

To sum up: we asked the farmer to do what he conveniently could to save his soil, and he has done just that, and only that. The farmer who clears the woods off a 75 per cent slope, turns his cows into the clearing, and dumps its rainfall, rocks, and soil into the community creek, is still (if otherwise decent) a respected member of society. If he puts lime on his fields and plants his crops on contour, he is still entitled to all the privileges and emoluments of his Soil Conservation District. The District is a beautiful piece of social machinery, but it is coughing along on two cylinders because we have been too timid, and too anxious for quick success, to tell the farmer the true magnitude of his obligations. Obligations have no meaning without conscience, and the problem we face is the extension of the social conscience from people to land.

No important change in ethics was ever accomplished without an internal change in our intellectual emphasis, loyalties, affections, and convictions. The proof that conservation has not yet touched these foundations of conduct lies in the fact that philosophy and religion have not yet heard of it. In our attempt to make conservation easy, we have made it trivial.

Substitutes for a Land Ethic

When the logic of history hungers for bread and we hand out a stone, we are at pains to explain how much the stone resembles bread. I now describe some of the stones which serve in lieu of a land ethic.

One basic weakness in a conservation system based wholly on economic motives is that most members of the land community have no economic value. Wildflowers and songbirds are examples. Of the 22,000 higher plants and animals native to Wisconsin, it is doubtful whether more than 5 per cent can be sold, fed, eaten, or otherwise put to economic use. Yet these creatures are members of the biotic community, and if (as I believe) its stability depends on its integrity, they are entitled to continuance.

When one of these non-economic categories is threatened, and if we happen to love it, we invent subterfuges to give it economic importance. At the beginning of the century songbirds were supposed to be disappearing. Ornithologists jumped to the rescue with some distinctly shaky evidence to the effect that insects would eat us up if birds failed to control them. The evidence had to be economic in order to be valid.

It is painful to read these circumlocutions today. We have no land ethic yet, but we have at least drawn nearer the point of admitting that birds should continue as a matter of biotic right, regardless of the presence or absence of economic advantage to us.

A parallel situation exists in respect of predatory mammals, raptorial birds, and fish-eating birds. Time was when biologists somewhat overworked the evidence that these creatures preserve the health of game by killing weaklings, or that they control rodents for the farmer, or that they prey only on 'worthless' species. Here again, the evidence had to be economic in order to be valid. It is only in recent years that we hear the more honest argument that predators are members of the community, and that no special interest has the right to exterminate them for the sake of a benefit, real or fancied, to itself. Unfortunately this enlightened view is still in the talk stage. In the field the extermination of predators goes merrily on: witness the impending erasure of the timber wolf by fiat of Congress, the Conservation Bureaus, and many state legislatures.

Some species of trees have been 'read out of the party' by economics-minded foresters because they grow too slowly, or have too low a sale value to pay as timber crops: white cedar, tamarack, cypress, beech, and hemlock are examples. In Europe, where forestry is ecologically more advanced, the non-commercial tree species are recognized as members of the native forest community, to be preserved as such, within reason. Moreover some (like beech) have been found to have a valuable function in building up soil fertility. The interdependence of the forest and its constituent tree species, ground flora, and fauna is taken for granted.

Lack of economic value is sometimes a character not only of species or groups, but of entire biotic communities: marshes, bogs, dunes, and 'deserts' are examples. Our formula in such cases is to relegate their conservation to government as refuges, monuments, or parks. The difficulty is that these communities are usually interspersed with more valuable private lands; the government cannot possibly own or control such scattered parcels. The net effect is that we have relegated some of them to ultimate extinction over large areas. If the private owner were ecologically minded, he would be proud to be the custodian of a reasonable proportion of such areas, which add diversity and beauty to his farm and to his community.

In some instances, the assumed lack of profit in these 'waste' areas has proved to be wrong, but only after most of them had been done away with. The present scramble to reflood muskrat marshes is a case in point.

There is a clear tendency in American conservation to relegate to government all necessary jobs that private landowners fail to perform. Government ownership, operation, subsidy, or regulation is now widely prevalent in forestry, range management, soil and watershed management, park and wilderness conservation, fisheries management, and migratory bird management, with more to come. Most of this growth in governmental conservation is proper and logical, some of it is inevitable. That I imply no disapproval of it is implicit in the fact that I have spent most of my life working for it. Nevertheless the question arises: What is the ultimate magnitude of the enterprise? Will the tax base carry its eventual ramifications? At what point will governmental conservation, like the mastodon, become handicapped by its own dimensions? The answer, if there is any, seems to be in a land ethic, or some other force which assigns more obligation to the private landowner.

Industrial landowners and users, especially lumbermen and stockmen, are inclined to wail long and loudly about the extension of government ownership and regulation to land, but (with notable exceptions) they show little disposition to develop the only visible alternative: the voluntary practice of conservation on their own lands.

When the private landowner is asked to perform some unprofitable act for the good of the community, he today assents only with outstretched palm. If the act cost him cash this is fair and proper, but when it costs only forethought, open-mindedness, or time, the issue is at least debatable. The overwhelming growth of land-use subsidies in recent years must be ascribed, in large part, to the government's own agencies for conservation education: the land bureaus, the agricultural colleges, and the extension services. As far as I can detect, no ethical obligation toward land is taught in these institutions.

To sum up: a system of conservation based solely on economic self-interest is hopelessly lopsided. It tends to ignore, and thus eventually to eliminate, many elements in the land community that lack commercial value, but that are (as far as we know) essential to its healthy functioning. It assumes, falsely, I think, that the economic parts of the biotic clock will function without the uneconomic parts. It tends to relegate to government many functions eventually too large, too complex, or too widely dispersed to be performed by government.

An ethical obligation on the part of the private owner is the only visible remedy for these situations.

The Land Pyramid

An ethic to supplement and guide the economic relation to land presupposes the existence of some mental image of land as a biotic mechanism. We can be ethical only in relation to something we can see, feel, understand, love, or otherwise have faith in.

The image commonly employed in conservation education is 'the balance of nature.' For reasons too lengthy to detail here, this figure of speech fails to describe accurately what little we know about the land mechanism. A much truer image is the one employed in ecology: the biotic pyramid. I shall first sketch the pyramid as a symbol of land, and later develop some of its implications in terms of land-use.

Plants absorb energy from the sun. This energy flows through a circuit called the biota, which may be represented by a pyramid consisting of layers. The bottom layer is the soil. A plant layer rests on the soil, an insect layer on the plants, a bird and rodent layer on the insects, and so on up through various animal groups to the apex layer, which consists of the larger carnivores.

The species of a layer are alike not in where they came from, or in what they look like, but rather in what they eat. Each successive layer depends on those below it for food and often for other services, and each in turn furnishes food and services to those above. Proceeding upward, each successive layer decreases in numerical abundance. Thus, for every carnivore there are hundreds of his prey, thousands of their prey, millions of insects, uncountable plants. The pyramidal form of the system reflects this numerical progression from apex to base. Man shares an intermediate layer with the bears, racoons, and squirrels which eat both meat and vegetables.

The lines of dependency for food and other services are called food chains. Thus soil–oak–deer–Indian is a chain that has now been largely converted to soil–corn–cow–farmer. Each species, including ourselves, is a link in many chains. The deer eats a hundred plants other than oak, and the cow a hundred plants other than corn. Both, then, are links in a hundred chains. The pyramid is a tangle of chains so complex as to seem disorderly, yet the stability of the system proves it to be a highly organized structure. Its functioning depends on the co-operation and competition of its diverse parts.

In the beginning, the pyramid of life was low and squat; the food chains short and simple. Evolution has added layer after layer, link after link. Man is one of thousands of accretions to the height and complexity of the pyramid. Science has given us many doubts, but it has given us at least one certainty: the trend of evolution is to elaborate and diversify the biota.

Land, then, is not merely soil; it is a fountain of energy flowing through a circuit of soils, plants, and animals. Food chains are the living channels which conduct energy upward; death and decay return it to the soil. The circuit is not closed; some energy is dissipated in decay, some is added by absorption from the air, some is stored in soils, peats, and long-lived forests; but it is a sustained circuit, like a slowly augmented revolving fund of life. There is always a net loss by downhill wash, but this is normally small and offset by the decay of rocks. It is deposited in the ocean and, in the course of geological time, raised to form new lands and new pyramids.

The velocity and character of the upward flow of energy depend on the complex structure of the plant and animal community, much as the upward flow of sap in a tree depends on its complex cellular organization. Without this complexity, normal circulation would presumably not occur. Structure means the characteristic numbers, as well as the characteristic kinds and functions, of the component species. This interdependence between the complex structure of the land and its smooth functioning as an energy unit is one of its basic attributes.

When a change occurs in one part of the circuit, many other parts must adjust themselves to it. Change does not necessarily obstruct or divert the flow of energy; evolution is a long series of self-induced changes, the net result of which has been to elaborate the flow mechanism and to lengthen the circuit. Evolutionary changes, however, are usually slow and local. Man's invention of tools has enabled him to make changes of unprecedented violence, rapidity, and scope.

One change is in the composition of floras and faunas. The larger predators are lopped off the apex of the pyramid; food chains, for the first time in history, become shorter rather than longer. Domesticated species from other lands are substituted for wild ones, and wild ones are moved to new habitats. In this world-wide pooling of faunas and floras, some species get out of bounds as pests and diseases, others are extinguished. Such effects are seldom intended or foreseen; they represent unpredicted and often untraceable readjustments in the structure. Agricultural science is largely a race between the emergence of new pests and the emergence of new techniques for their control.

Another change touches the flow of energy through plants and animals and its return to the soil. Fertility is the ability of soil to receive, store, and release energy. Agriculture, by overdrafts on the soil, or by too radical a substitution of domestic for native species in the superstructure, may derange the channels of flow or deplete storage. Soils depleted of their storage, or of the organic matter which anchors it, wash away faster than they form. This is erosion.

Waters, like soil, are part of the energy circuit. Industry, by polluting waters or obstructing them with dams, may exclude the plants and animals necessary to keep energy in circulation.

Transportation brings about another basic change: the plants or animals grown in one region are now consumed and returned to the soil in another. Transportation taps the energy stored in rocks, and in the air, and uses it elsewhere; thus we fertilize the garden with nitrogen gleaned by the guano birds from the fishes of seas on the other side of the Equator. Thus the formerly localized and self-contained circuits are pooled on a world-wide scale.

The process of altering the pyramid for human occupation releases stored energy, and this often gives rise, during the pioneering period, to a deceptive exuberance of plant and animal life, both wild and tame. These releases of biotic capital tend to becloud or postpone the penalties of violence.

* * *

This thumbnail sketch of land as an energy circuit conveys three basic ideas:

(1) That land is not merely soil.
(2) That the native plants and animals kept the energy circuit open; others may or may not.
(3) That man-made changes are of a different order than evolutionary changes, and have effects more comprehensive than is intended or foreseen.

These ideas, collectively, raise two basic issues: Can the land adjust itself to the new order? Can the desired alterations be accomplished with less violence?

Biotas seem to differ in their capacity to sustain violent conversion. Western Europe, for example, carries a far different pyramid than Caesar found there. Some large animals are lost; swampy forests have become meadows or plowland; many new plants and animals are introduced, some of which escape as pests; the remaining natives are greatly changed in distribution and abundance. Yet the soil is still there and, with the help of imported nutrients, still fertile; the waters flow normally; the new structure seems to function and to persist. There is no visible stoppage or derangement of the circuit.

Western Europe, then, has a resistant biota. Its inner processes are tough, elastic, resistant to strain. No matter how violent the alterations, the pyramid, so far, has developed some new *modus vivendi* which preserves its habitability for man, and for most of the other natives.

Japan seems to present another instance of radical conversion without disorganization.

Most other civilized regions, and some as yet barely touched by civilization, display various stages of disorganization, varying from initial symptoms to advanced wastage. In Asia Minor and North Africa diagnosis is confused by climatic changes, which may have been either the cause or the effect of advanced wastage. In the United States the degree of disorganization varies locally; it is worst in the Southwest, the Ozarks, and parts of the South, and least in New England and the Northwest. Better land-uses may still arrest it in the less advanced regions. In parts of Mexico, South America, South Africa, and Australia a violent and accelerating wastage is in progress, but I cannot assess the prospects.

This almost world-wide display of disorganization in the land seems to be similar to disease in an animal, except that it never culminates in complete disorganization or death. The land recovers, but at some reduced level of complexity, and with a reduced carrying capacity for people, plants, and animals. Many biotas currently regarded as 'lands of opportunity' are in fact already subsisting on exploitative agriculture, i.e. they have already exceeded their sustained carrying capacity. Most of South America is overpopulated in this sense.

In arid regions we attempt to offset the process of wastage by reclamation, but it is only too evident that the prospective longevity of reclamation projects is often short. In our own West, the best of them may not last a century.

The combined evidence of history and ecology seems to support one general deduction: the less violent the man-made changes, the greater the probability of successful readjustment in the pyramid. Violence, in turn, varies with human population density; a dense population requires a more violent conversion. In this respect, North America has a better chance for permanence than Europe, if she can contrive to limit her density.

This deduction runs counter to our current philosophy, which assumes that because a small increase in density enriched human life, that an indefinite increase will enrich it indefinitely. Ecology knows of no density relationship that holds for indefinitely wide limits. All gains from density are subject to a law of diminishing returns.

Whatever may be the equation for men and land, it is improbable that we as yet know all its terms. Recent discoveries in mineral and vitamin nutrition reveal unsuspected dependencies in the up-circuit: incredibly minute quantities of certain substances determine the value of soils to plants, of plants to animals. What of the down-circuit? What of the vanishing species, the preservation of which we now regard as an esthetic luxury? They helped build the soil; in what unsuspected ways may they be essential to its maintenance? Professor Weaver proposes that we use prairie flowers to reflocculate the wasting soils of the dust bowl; who knows for what purpose cranes and condors, otters and grizzlies may some day be used?

Land Health and the A-B Cleavage

A land ethic, then, reflects the existence of an ecological conscience, and this in turn reflects a conviction of individual responsibility for the health of the land. Health is the capacity of the land for self-renewal. Conservation is our effort to understand and preserve this capacity.

Conservationists are notorious for their dissensions. Superficially these seem to add up to mere confusion, but a more careful scrutiny reveals a single plane of cleavage common to many specialized fields. In each field one group (A) regards the land as soil, and its function as commodity-production; another group (B) regards the land as a biota, and its function as something broader. How much broader is admittedly in a state of doubt and confusion.

In my own field, forestry, group A is quite content to grow trees like cabbages, with cellulose as the basic forest commodity. It feels no inhibition against violence; its ideology is agronomic. Group B, on the other hand, sees forestry as fundamentally different from agronomy because it employs natural species, and manages a natural environment rather than creating an artificial one. Group B prefers natural reproduction on principle. It worries on biotic as well as economic grounds about the loss of species like chestnut, and the threatened loss of the white pines. It worries about a whole series of secondary forest functions: wildlife, recreation, watersheds, wilderness areas. To my mind, Group B feels the stirrings of an ecological conscience.

In the wildlife field, a parallel cleavage exists. For Group A the basic commodities are sport and meat; the yardsticks of production are cipher of take in pheasants and trout. Artificial propagation is acceptable as a permanent as well as a temporary recourse – if its unit costs permit. Group B, on the other hand, worries about a whole series of biotic side-issues. What is the cost in predators of producing a game crop? Should we have further recourse to exotics? How can management restore the shrinking species, like prairie grouse, already hopeless as shootable game? How can management restore the threatened rarities, like trumpeter swan and whooping crane? Can management principles be extended to wildflowers? Here again it is clear to me that we have the same A-B cleavage as in forestry.

In the larger field of agriculture I am less competent to speak, but there seem to be somewhat parallel cleavages. Scientific agriculture was actively developing before ecology was born, hence a slower penetration of ecological concepts might be expected. Moreover the farmer, by the very nature of his techniques, must modify the biota more radically than the forester or the wildlife manager. Nevertheless, there are many discontents in agriculture which seem to add up to a new vision of 'biotic farming.'

Perhaps the most important of these is the new evidence that poundage or tonnage is no measure of the food-value of farm crops; the products of fertile soil may be qualitatively as well as quantitatively superior. We can bolster poundage from depleted soils by pouring on imported fertility, but we are not necessarily bolstering food-value. The possible ultimate ramifications of this idea are so immense that I must leave their exposition to abler pens.

The discontent that labels itself 'organic farming,' while bearing some of the earmarks of a cult, is nevertheless biotic in its direction, particularly in its insistence on the importance of soil flora and fauna.

The ecological fundamentals of agriculture are just as poorly known to the public as in other fields of land-use. For example, few educated people realize that the marvelous advances in technique made during recent decades are improvements in the pump, rather than the well. Acre for acre, they have barely sufficed to offset the sinking level of fertility.

In all of these cleavages, we see repeated the same basic paradoxes: man the conqueror *versus* man the biotic citizen; science the sharpener of his sword *versus* science the searchlight on his universe; land the slave and servant *versus* land the collective organism. Robinson's injunction to Tristram may well be applied, at this juncture, to *Homo sapiens* as a species in geological time:

Whether you will or not
You are a King, Tristram, for you are one
Of the time-tested few that leave the world,
When they are gone, not the same place it was.
Mark what you leave.

The Outlook

It is inconceivable to me that an ethical relation to land can exist without love, respect, and admiration for land, and a high regard for its value. By value, I of course mean something far broader than mere economic value; I mean value in the philosophical sense.

Perhaps the most serious obstacle impeding the evolution of a land ethic is the fact that our educational and economic system is headed away from, rather than toward, an intense consciousness of land. Your true modern is separated from the land by many middlemen, and by innumerable physical gadgets. He has no vital relation to it; to him it is the space between cities on which crops grow. Turn him loose for a day on the land, and if the spot does not happen to be a golf links or a 'scenic' area, he is bored stiff. If crops could be raised by hydroponics instead of farming, it would suit him very well. Synthetic substitutes for wood, leather, wool, and other natural land products suit him better than the originals. In short, land is something he has 'outgrown.'

Almost equally serious as an obstacle to a land ethic is the attitude of the farmer for whom the land is still an adversary, or a taskmaster that keeps him in slavery. Theoretically, the mechanization of farming ought to cut the farmer's chains, but whether it really does is debatable.

One of the requisites for an ecological comprehension of land is an understanding of ecology, and this is by no means co-extensive with 'education'; in fact, much higher education seems deliberately to avoid ecological concepts. An understanding of ecology does not necessarily originate in courses bearing ecological labels; it is quite as likely to be labeled geography, botany, agronomy, history, or economics. This is as it should be, but whatever the label, ecological training is scarce.

The case for a land ethic would appear hopeless but for the minority which is in obvious revolt against these 'modern' trends.

The 'key-log' which must be moved to release the evolutionary process for an ethic is simply this: quit thinking about decent land-use as solely an economic problem. Examine each question in terms of what is ethically and esthetically right, as well as what is economically expedient. A thing is right when it tends to preserve the integrity, stability, and beauty of the biotic community. It is wrong when it tends otherwise.

It of course goes without saying that economic feasibility limits the tether of what can or cannot be done for land. It always has and it always will. The fallacy the economic determinists have tied around our collective neck, and which we now need to cast off, is the belief that economics determines *all* land-use. This is simply not true. An innumerable host of actions and attitudes, comprising perhaps the bulk of all land relations, is determined by the land-users' tastes and predilections, rather than by his purse. The bulk of all land relations hinges on investments of time, forethought, skill, and faith rather than on investments of cash. As a land-user thinketh, so is he.

I have purposely presented the land ethic as a product of social evolution because nothing so important as an ethic is ever 'written.' Only the most superficial student of history supposes that Moses 'wrote' the Decalogue; it evolved in the minds of a thinking community, and Moses wrote a tentative summary of it for a 'seminar.' I say tentative because evolution never stops.

The evolution of a land ethic is an intellectual as well as emotional process. Conservation is paved with good intentions which prove to be futile, or even dangerous, because they are devoid of critical understanding either of the land, or of economic land-use. I think it is a truism that as the ethical frontier advances from the individual to the community, its intellectual content increases.

The mechanism of operation is the same for any ethic: social approbation for right actions: social disapproval for wrong actions.

By and large, our present problem is one of attitudes and implements. We are remodeling the Alhambra with a steam-shovel, and we are proud of our yardage. We shall hardly relinquish the shovel, which after all has many good points, but we are in need of gentler and more objective criteria for its successful use.

PART IV

REGION, PLACE AND LOCALITY

INTRODUCTION

Rather than the visual and concrete landscape or the abstract and intangible space, an important intellectual current in human geography has privileged the role of discrete units of geographical space (in particular, the 'region') which are seen either as defining distinct clusters of human-physical phenomena or as maximizing the differences between areas in relation to one or more phenomena. However, both landscape and region are often seen as 'integrative' or 'synthetic' concepts as distinct from the 'analytical' way in which spatial concepts (such as space, distance, territory, etc) are used.

Geographic units such as regions are sometimes distinguished from one another as the inventions of an observer, and at other times they are presumed to 'exist in nature', so to speak, rather than being purely mental constructs. Either way, geographical understanding is served by drawing boundaries around geographical areas to distinguish them in terms of either single or multiple criteria of difference. Terms such as 'region', 'place' and 'culture area' are applied to the resulting spatial units, often irrespective of the geographical scale – local, within-state, continental or world-wide – at which spatial division has taken place.

Although observers cannot claim to 'engage' or 'feel' a region in the sense they can a landscape, the focus on geographic units does represent a compromise between the polarized appeal of, on the one hand, an apparently concrete landscape and, on the other hand, the abstract/continuous space beyond much everyday experience. A region, place or locality offers a *real* piece of space that can still be thought of theoretically as resulting from the division of an enveloping space that transcends the particular attributes of any specific unit.

The relationship of the 'particulars' characteristic of different regions to the 'universals' driving the partition of geographical space into regions can be thought of as similar to the problem of classification or taxonomy engaged in throughout the natural and the social sciences. In this perspective not only can specific regions be related to general principles but they can also be viewed as existing in a nested hierarchy of regions extending from the most local to the most global in geographical scale.

Regions or places, however, can also be viewed as expressing a sense of belonging or lived experience for the people who inhabit them. From this point of view, the region or place is a locus of identity; while living their lives people invest their surroundings with meaning and can develop a 'sense of place'. So places can be construed as representing an aspect of human subjectivity as much as or more than an observer's attempt at dividing geographical space into units that can be used 'objectively' to classify a wide range of phenomena.

In this section a range of articles and extracts is presented to survey usage of the three concepts over the past one hundred years. The introduction provides an overview of the logic that lay behind the selection, presents a discussion of the incidence and usage of the three terms, and identifies some of the tensions that have plagued development and interpretation of the concepts down the years.

Areal Differentiation

The three main concepts that have been deployed over the years to define geographical units – region, place and locality – share a common heritage in the study of the areal differentiation of the Earth's surface. This is the oldest Western conception of geographical inquiry, tracing its beginnings to the Greeks Hecateus of Miletus and Strabo. The geographer, according to Strabo, is 'the person who describes the parts of the Earth'. But the task was not one of mere inventory. The purpose of geography was to understand those features of 'parts' of the Earth that were of importance to political and military activities. This focus was lost somewhat once Ptolemy's (AD 100–178) view of geography as a field concerned only with measuring the shape and dimensions of the entire Earth – geodesy and cartography – came to exercise greater influence.

European expansionism after 1500 gave a boost to defining and surveying regions, as new territories came under colonial dominion. The need to draw administrative boundaries and to make inventories of assets was also felt at home in Europe. As the modern states system came into existence so did attempts at showing the natural regions out of which states were made, and the cultural identity of the whole state territory as growing out of the parts. The 'classic' epoch of regional geography, to use Claval's (1993, p. 15) phrase, was reached in the late nineteenth and early twentieth centuries when much of the conceptual debate in geography was devoted to the nature of the region. The Frenchman Paul Vidal de la Blache and the German Alfred Hettner are only the most well known of the contributors to this debate. One of the main issues concerned the relative weight to be given to natural or cultural factors in defining and describing regions.

This period was one in which the desire to claim more space (in the form of imperialism) came up against the supposed 'closing' of the frontier of European expansion and the 'leveling of traditional spatial hierarchies' (Kern 1983, p. 8). Nationalism and the creeping secularization of life undermined conventional political and religious hierarchies. This was manifest, for example, in German and Italian unification, the slow collapse of the Ottoman Empire in the Balkans, and the strains inside the Austro-Hungarian Empire. The division of 'horizontal' space, so to speak, into regions out of which states were made and administrative units wrested, became a powerful means of making sense of the new 'territorial challenge' facing the European states. States could now enhance their power only through deepening the attachment of 'their' regions to the state and, if possible, expanding into regions around their edges (see Ratzel, **chapter 32**). Vidal de la Blache's famous monograph on *France de l'Est*, for example, was written during the time of the German occupation and annexation of Alsace-Lorraine. Vidal attempted to show that the region was a unique *pays* tied to France rather than to Germany (Gregory 1993).

So even as regional differences were celebrated they were accounted for by common units of comparison and methods that implied an underlying communality. As Patriarca (1994, p. 364) remarks with respect to the regions widely used in late nineteenth-century Italy, statistical categories were particularly important in this process: 'The language of numbers actually helped conceive the national space by constructing it as a homogenous surface in which differences appeared only as a matter of quantity.' The typical usage of the term region as indicating a within-state meso-scale unit is intimately tied to its administrative role in state formation. Such contemporary derivatives of this usage as 'regional development' and 'regional policy' reflect this past.

Drawing strongly from Hettner, the American geographer Richard Hartshorne (**chapter 24**) offered an academic justification for the focus on meso-scale regions. In his *The Nature of Geography* (1939) he claimed that the region provided the means for realizing geography's integrative or synthetic purpose. It was not the unique character of regions that was of interest so much as the differential co-variation of phenomena manifested in different regions. In the 1950s and 1960s, however, this was not the reading given by critics of Hartshorne who, in furthering their own spatial agenda, pinned the label of uniqueness or areal particularity onto his argument for regional geography (Agnew 1989). Whatever the merits of this claim, regional geography was institutionalized as the centre-piece of geographical endeavour. For example, the first substantive chapter of *American Geography: Inventory and Prospect* (1954) was devoted to 'The Regional Concept and the Regional Method' (Whittlesey 1954).

Hartshorne's argument should be distinguished from much practice in regional geography. This was largely concerned with defining boundaries between regions and establishing the essential differences between them, working from the natural environment to the human features (Johnston 1990, p. 122). Most critics attacked this descriptive regional geography not only for its implicit environmental determinism but also as outdated in a modern world in which 'it is the *links* in the landscape . . . rather than the breaks that impress' (Kimble, **chapter 31**). Or, as Haggett (1965) put it later, 'areal differentiation had dominated geography at the expense of areal integration'. Missing from these critiques, however, has been an appreciation of the variety of work that was conducted under the regional rubric. The 'regional surveys' inspired by Patrick Geddes (e.g. 1898), for example, drew on the previous writing of Herbertson (**chapter 22**) and Fleure (**chapter 23**) to consider regional 'consciousness', the need for new local knowledge and the link between local knowledge and citizenship (Matless 1992). This was hardly the arid exercise in regional inventory that many recent accounts of traditional regional geography would lead one to expect.

The term region, however, was never a monopoly of 'regional' geographers (see, for example, Jensen 1951). In other hands the term preserved much of its older, looser meaning from before the nineteenth century. In this usage region could refer to a vast tract of land such as 'Amazonia' in South America, an ocean basin such as the Mediterranean Basin, or the 'heartland' of Eurasia and its surrounding 'insular crescents' (see Mackinder, **chapter 33**), as well as to the sections of the United States (such as 'the South'), areas of specialized economic activity (e.g., industrial regions), or port-cities and their hinterlands. Indeed, entire literatures in political and economic history, regional sociology and international relations grew up around these alternative definitions of region.

Particularly important in recent years have been schemes dividing the world into West and East (see Said, **chapter 26**), colonial and colonizer (see Pratt 1992), the Three Worlds of development (a free, developed First World; a communist, developed Second World; and a traditional, underdeveloped Third World) (Pletsch 1981), and developed 'North'/underdeveloped 'South'. These 'top-down' global regions have provided an alternative to the state-centred regionalism of the 'bottom-up' regional geography practised by Vidal de la Blache and have found widespread use in a number of different academic fields.

Within human geography, however, Said's discussion of the 'imaginative geography' that inspires much popular and intellectual thinking about global cultural differences has been assimilated to the field's historic preference for the 'local', losing the global context in reference to which it was proposed (Rogers 1992, p. 517). Although, in general, the major problem with all of the global regionalizations is their single-minded focus on the global scale even when they aspire, as does Said, for example, to 'expose the false universality and hegemony of imperial expansion and modernization, [but] seem unwilling themselves to renounce the aspiration of theorizing globally on the basis of particular strands in European philosophy' (Thomas 1994, p. x) (see also Harley, **chapter 27**).

In the 1970s and 1980s the areal differentiation tradition underwent something of a revival among geographers. Although sometimes referred to as the 'new' regional geography, there is little or no connection to the central canons of Hettner's or Vidal's perspectives or to the practices of descriptive regional geography (although this still has its proponents, such as Hart 1982). Intellectual inspiration has come from a number of directions, none of which are directly connected to old debates about areal differentiation or use the same terminology as the others. What they all share is a disaffection from the spatial tradition that became intellectually hegemonic in academic geography in the 1960s and 1970s and an insistence on the need to reformulate regions as places or localities which provide the contextual units in which the dramas of individual and social life are played out. To articulate their perspectives they also draw conceptually (if not usually at the same time!) from writing in such disparate fields as phenomenology, microsociology, world-systems theory and Marxist political economy.

The positivist philosophy of science associated with the spatial tradition, searching for 'laws' of spatial behaviour or activity usually expressed in terms of the impact of distance on some activity such as shopping, voting or commuting, reached its zenith during the optimistic years of the 1960s when, in the United States and other Western countries, there was a widely held belief that human behaviour could be predicted and regulated, at least in those countries that followed the American/Western path to modernization. In the 1970s a reaction set in as a number of movements in various academic fields – 'humanism' and Marxism, for example – argued that this was neither possible nor positive. One reaction of some geographers, potentially justifiable in terms of the heritage of the field, was to re-invent the areal differentiation tradition, only this time in conjunction with 'external' influences from other fields – world-systems theory (Wallerstein 1983) and structuration theory (Giddens 1981) in sociology, and regional-systems theory in anthropology (Skinner, see Smith 1976), for example – actively searching for a resolution to their intellectual dilemmas and now claiming explanatory or hermeneutic understanding rather than descriptive significance for their work using regional or place concepts.

This intellectual trend did not just drop out of a clear blue sky. A variety of economic and political changes on a number of geographical scales, such as deindustrialization, the growth of the Newly Industrializing Countries (NICs), the globalization of production and finance and the gentrification of previously neglected and marginalized neighbourhoods, prompted the sense of a world in the throes of major geographical reorganization (see Cooke, **chapter 30**). The context of the times and the places – the 1970s and 1980s in North America and Western Europe – was ripe for a rejuvenation of a hitherto largely moribund geographical tradition.

Three major intellectual roots of the revival of areal differentiation can be identified. The first is that of a phenomenology which emphasizes the connection between 'being in the world' and the sense of place associated with living in specific places (e.g. Tuan, **chapter 28**; Entrikin 1991). The second is that of an analysis of the uneven development of capitalism and the geography of layers of investment associated with changes in the spatial division of labour (e.g. Massey, **chapter 25**). The third root is that of attempts in sociology and human geography to create a contextual theory of human action in which place or region (usage varies) is viewed as geographically mediating between human agency and social structure to produce geographical sameness and difference, (e.g. Agnew 1987; Entrikin 1991; also see Hägerstrand, **chapter 40** and Pred, **chapter 39**). This approach has often been distinguished from a research tradition, common to the social sciences, in which 'compositional analysis' (analysis of nationally-defined categories such as those from the census relating to social class, gender, age, etc.) has been privileged over examination of the influences of the contexts (including the geographical) in which human activities are realized.

The third of these could be seen as potentially integrating the other two, but this would be misleading. There are important philosophical differences between all three. For instance, the first tends to privilege the human subjective experience of place whereas the others view the division of space in terms of objective social-spatial processes. The second and third part company over the second's insistence on separating abstract (general) processes from local contingencies. The third sees no necessary conflict between the abstract and the local.

The Three Terms

The term *region* is now typically used in any one of three main ways. One is as in traditional regional geography. Here a premium is placed on describing the character of a region, usually as a means of teaching students about the essential differences that exist between different parts of a country or world-region (Farmer 1973; Hart 1982). A second usage has a more self-conscious theoretical accent in which a region is viewed as part of a process of political-economic or social structuration. From this point of view a region is the unit of space that defines a setting for social interaction or economic production, or in which human subjectivities are defined, from a room to a locality to a state. What is meant by a region, therefore, is not separable from the specific theoretical process that is implicated in its definition (see, for example, Gilbert 1988; Pudup 1988; Taylor 1988; Thrift 1991). The final usage is technical-methodological. In this perspective regions, both those based on the presence or absence of distinguishing features within a discrete block of space (formal regions) and those based on spatial routes and flows between centres or cities and their peripheries or hinterlands (functional regions), provide a way of mapping and describing the outcome of processes of political-economic and demographic polarization and marginalization. This approach is popular with those who see geography, in the form of the regional concept, as providing a methodology to address questions concerning state-building, economic development, social-class formation and urbanization (see, for example, Andreucci and Pescarolo 1989; Bergeron 1992; Hochberg and Earle 1996; Terlouw 1994).

In the 1970s a series of streams of thought in geography, referred to collectively as 'humanistic geography', used the term *place* to refer to the specific geographical settings or locales in which a sense of place is established by knowing and sentient human beings (e.g. Tuan, **chapter 28**). This usage was explicitly opposed to that which saw place solely as location, as one place among many on a spatial surface, and can be seen as a reaction against the positivist philosophy of the spatial science of the 1960s. During the 1980s interest in the concept of place grew outside of humanistic geography. Economic geographers such as Massey (1984) and McDowell and Massey (**chapter 29**), for example, sought to define place as the geographical manifestation of specificity built up historically in a wider web of general processes producing economic restructuring and uneven development. The insights of both of these perspectives have been taken further by writers such as Agnew (1987), Pred (1990) and Sack (1992). In different ways they have all tried to show how place is implicated in the reproduction of social relations and the production of meaning. Agnew, for example, identified three dimensions to place: the locale, or settings in which social relations are constituted; location, the geographical area encompassing the settings and defined by the social and economic processes operating at a wider scale; and a sense of place, or local 'structure of feeling' associated with a place.

The term *locality* emerged as a synonym for place or region in debates in Britain in the 1980s over the impact of economic restructuring on local areas and their populations. Of course, such usage is by no means totally new. But one source of the term's new popularity was a government-sponsored research initiative. The British Economic and Social Research Council (ESRC) organized a number of research programmes that focused around the impact of restructuring on specific local areas (see, for example, Cooke 1989; Bagguley et al. 1990). These locality studies involved collecting detailed empirical information about the nature, causes and outcomes of restructuring. Most used local labour-market areas or local government areas as their basic units. A number of debates sprang up among the geographers and sociologists who were the main participants in the localities research effort and with some outsiders. One debate has concerned the extent to which localities can be construed as actors or forces having effects on wider processes (e.g. Cooke, **chapter 30**; Duncan and Savage 1989). Another has involved the contention that a focus on localities necessarily implies a lack of interest in general theory (Smith 1987). A final chord of dissent has come from those disturbed that the research programmes out of which the term has evolved have tended to stress economic production at the expense of communal relations and local cultures (e.g. Jackson 1991).

The three terms, therefore, even though they overlap in meaning and intellectual genealogy, have acquired distinctive uses and defined different literatures between which there is not much cross-citation. Unsurprisingly, given the history of areal differentiation, region is the most general, the least well-defined and the most used of the three. A number of persisting conceptual tensions limit the possibility of rapid synthesis, irrespective of the political and intellectual commitments that also continue to separate protagonists.

Conceptual Tensions

We can only outline the main controversies and definitional disputes that have wracked the literature on areal differentiation down the years. We make no pretense at comprehensiveness in our review, let alone at resolving the conflicts. The first concerns the classic contrast drawn between the idiographic and the nomothetic, a distinction that was once commonly made but about which there has been increasing confusion. This revolves around the claim sometimes made that locations and places are totally different or unique, and is opposed by the view that locations are homogeneous or interchangeable. Alternatively, the contrast can be drawn between the particular aspects of things and their general aspects.

Dispute between proponents and opponents of these two positions was important in the 1950s in arguments that the advocates of a spatial perspective directed towards those they saw as defenders of traditional regional geography. The language of the distinction dates to the beginning of the twentieth century when neo-Kantians and positivists argued about the possibility of describing human events in terms similar to those of physical events, the former disagreeing and the latter being enthusiastically in favour. Much of the recent theorizing in geography about regions and places explicitly denies the relevance of this old distinction (e.g. Smith 1979; Gregory 1981; Agnew 1987). They have redefined the problem as one of the global and the local rather than of the particular and the general. Although Entrikin (1991) organizes his claim for the experiential importance of place around the distinction, showing that there is intellectual mileage in it yet.

A second controversy has involved the intimate bonds between physical and human phenomena that traditional regional geography accepted as intrinsic to the character of regional units. From one point of view, regional geography surreptitiously perpetuated a commitment to environmental determinism that was often hidden behind a vocabulary of regional difference. Chapter One in most regional texts would be on geology and/or climate. More recently, the ecological niches that such a framework could express in human terms have become rather an attractive feature of regional geography. The systemic quality of human-environmental relations has found one of its expressions in the idea, for example, of 'bioregionalism': intimate familiarity with one's ecological surroundings (see Leopold, **chapter 21**). But to those wary of the 'determinist' potential of even *considering* the human-environmental interface, such ideas are profoundly troubling (Gregory 1981).

A more rarified dispute has been directed at the language of region, place and locality and how the terms should be used (e.g. Duncan and Savage 1989). Some people worry that these terms can be imbued with a misplaced concreteness that betrays a 'spatial fetishism', in which the areas to which they refer take on a life of their own. Critics remind us that regions and localities do not act or do things to one another. Of course, municipal or regional governments may well act. The problem then is of precision in the use of labels for the governments as opposed to those for the localities or regions themselves. More generally, all theoretical terms suffer from the danger of misplaced concreteness. It is not a problem unique to geographical terminology.

A less noted controversy has involved the degree to which a place or region is seen as specific to a particular phenomenon (politics, economics, literature), or totalistic, covering a wide range of different but somehow linked phenomena (Agnew 1989). Although the trend has been away from multiple-phenomena towards single-phenomenon regions, the classic defences of regional geography have usually justified the purpose of regions in terms of the need to synthesize across a number of phenomena. This raises the question of what is of primary interest: a region itself or the region-as-a-concept that helps us to understand another substantive phenomenon (Johnston 1990)?

Perhaps the most contentious of disputes has been that over the ontology of region and place (Gregory 1981; also **chapter 12**). This refers to the issue of what kind of 'thing' are regions or places. The main division has been between those who endorse a simple physicalist conception of them as objects like any other, say a table or a chair, and those who view them either as mental constructs through which the world is engaged or as purely mental without any correspondence to a world independent of conceptions of it. This is also a problem that has arisen in connection with other concepts, such as space and space-time.

The dispute is an old one going back to before Herbertson (**chapter 22**). The old terminology was that of regions as 'wholes' or 'organisms' versus the region as an idea or intellectual concept (on this see, for example, Paul 1989). Recently, the debate has taken a new, post-modern turn. A long-standing agnosticism about ontological commitments has been replaced by an obsession with them to the extent that attention has turned from theorizing with such concepts as region, place and locality to debate about its difficulty or impossibility (e.g. Dear 1994).

Finally, the question of geographical scale in relation to region and place has come to occupy an increasingly important part of debate over the concepts themselves. This connects up with debates over space and space-time (see Part V). Two themes have predominated: (1) The scale of geographical *difference*. Are regions and places fixed at one scale for all time or are boundaries forever merging and splitting to produce variations in the scale of aggregation over time (see, for example, Agnew 1989)? (2) The scale of geographical *explanation*. At what scale(s) of abstraction – global, national, local – are the social and economic relationships that produce particular regions and places thought to be operating? In his critique of locality studies Smith (1987, 1992) has noted how scale is produced historically rather than given naturally. In other words, socio-economic processes produce scale, so the processes can be mis-specified if a particular scale (such as the local) is privileged *a priori*. Of course, many people continue to use the terms without much apparent concern for these considerations.

The Selection

The selection of articles and extracts proposing various understandings of region, place and locality moves from the early twentieth century to the present. We start with extracts from Herbertson and Fleure – two British geographers whose work had a wide influence, particularly on the growth of regional surveys. Their arguments also recapitulate those of others during their epoch. The extract from Hartshorne's *The Nature of Geography*, on the 'character' of regional geography, completes the older sources used in the selection.

Tuan was an important figure in the specification of a concept of place that was one part of the revival of areal differentiation in the 1970s. A section of his 1974 paper on 'Space and place: a humanistic perspective' is included for this reason. Massey provided a very different source of renewed interest and her widely referenced 1979 paper on 'In what sense a regional problem?' is included because of this.

Inside and outside of 'professional geography' in the 1970s and 1980s there was also a renewal of interest in regions at the global geographical scale. This was combined with a sense of these regions as features of 'imagined geographies' which gave understanding and meaning to the world for both intellectuals and ordinary folk. The extract from Said's *Orientalism* captures one aspect of this: the separation of east (Orient) from west around which so much knowledge-production revolves. The article by Harley gives an example from the history of map-making that pursues further the globalist understanding of areal differentiation.

The two other conceptual innovations of the 1980s were the refinement of concepts of place and the emergence of the literature on localities. The article by McDowell and Massey is an interesting example of the former, relying on a series of vignettes about women's work and place. The article by Cooke captures the 'spirit' of the localities initiative. Finally, Kimble's chapter provides an early (1951) example of hostility to the way in which the regional concept had been used. This animosity helps explain why it was not until the 1970s that there was a revival of conceptual interest in areal differentiation.

References

Agnew, J. A. 1987: *Place and politics: the geographical mediation of state and society*. London.

Agnew, J. A. 1989: Sameness and difference: Hartshorne's *The Nature of Geography* and geography as areal variation. In Entrikin, J. N., and Brunn, S., editors, *Reflections on Richard Hartshorne's 'The Nature of Geography'*. Washington, DC.

Andreucci, F. and Pescarolo, A., editors, 1989: *Gli spazi del potere: aree, regioni, Stati, le coordinate territoriali della storia contemporanea*. Florence

Bagguley, P. et al. 1990: *Restructuring: place, class and gender*. London.

Bergeron, L., editor, 1992: *La croissance régionale dans l'Europe méditerranéenne*. Paris.

Claval, P. 1993: *Initiation à la géographie régionale*. Paris.

Cooke, P. 1989: *Localities: the changing face of urban Britain*. London.

Dear, M. 1994: Postmodern human geography: a preliminary assessment. *Erdkunde* 48, 2–13.

Duncan, S. S. and Savage, M. 1989: Space, scale and locality. *Antipode* 21, 179–206.

Entrikin, J. N. 1991: *The betweenness of place: towards a geography of modernity*. Baltimore.

Farmer, B. H. 1973: Geography, area studies and the study of area. *Transactions of the Institute of British Geographers* 60, 1–16.

Geddes, P. 1898: The influence of geographical conditions on social development. *Geographical Journal* 12, 580–7.

Giddens, A. 1981: *A contemporary critique of historical materialism. Volume 1: Power, property and the state*. Berkeley, CA.

Gilbert, A. 1988: The new regional geography in English and French speaking countries. *Progress in Human Geography* 12, 208–28.

Gregory, D. 1981: Human agency and human geography. *Transactions of the Institute of British Geographers* 6, 1–18.

Gregory, D. 1993: *Geographical imaginations*. Oxford.

Haggett, P. 1965: *Locational analysis in human geography*. London.

Hart, J. F. 1982: The highest form of the geographer's art. *Annals of the Association of American Geographers* 72, 1–29.
Hochberg, L. and Earle, C., editors, 1996: *Geographical perspectives on social change*. Stanford, CA.
Jackson, P. 1991: Mapping meanings: a cultural critique of locality studies. *Environment and Planning A* 23, 215–28.
Jensen, M., editor, 1951: *Regionalism in America*. Madison, WI.
Johnston, R. J. 1990: The challenge for regional geography. In Johnston, R. J., Hauer, J. and Hoekveld, G. A., editors, *Regional geography: current developments and future prospects*. London.
Kern, S. 1983: *The culture of time and space, 1880–1918*. Cambridge, MA.
Massey, D. 1984: *Spatial divisions of labour*. London.
Matless, D. 1992: Regional survey and local knowledges: the geographical imagination in Britain, 1918–39. *Transactions of the Institute of British Geographers* 17, 464–80.
Patriarca, S. 1994: Statistical nation building and the consolidation of regions in Italy. *Social Science History* 18, 359–76.
Paul, L. J., editor, 1989: *Post-war development of regional geography, with special attention to the United Kingdom, Belgium and the Netherlands*. Amsterdam/Utrecht.
Pletsch, C. 1981: The Three Worlds, or the division of social scientific labor, circa 1950–1975. *Comparative Studies in Society and History* 23, 565–90.
Pratt, M. L. 1992: *Imperial eyes: travel writing and transculturation*. London.
Pred, A. 1990: *Making histories and constituting human geographies: the local transformation of practice, power relations, and consciousness*. Boulder, CO.
Pudup, M. 1988: Arguments within regional geography. *Progress in Human Geography* 12, 369–90.
Rogers, A. 1992: The boundaries of reason: the world, the homeland and Edward Said. *Environment and Planning D: Society and Space* 10, 511–26.
Sack, R. D. 1992: *Place, modernity, and the consumer's world: a relational framework for geographical analysis*. Baltimore.
Smith, C., editor, 1976: *Regional analysis*, 2 volumes. New York.
Smith, N. 1979: Geography, science and post-positivist modes of explanation. *Progress in Human Geography* 3, 356–83.
Smith, N. 1987: Dangers of the empirical turn: some comments on the CURS initiative. *Antipode* 19, 59–68.
Smith, N. 1992: Geography, difference and the politics of scale. In J. Doherty et al., editors, *Postmodernism and the social sciences*. New York.
Taylor, P. 1988: World systems analysis and regional geography. *Professional Geographer* 40, 259–65.
Terlouw, C. P., editor, 1994: *Methodological exercises in regional geography: France as an example*. Utrecht/Amsterdam.
Thomas, N. 1994: *Colonialism's culture: anthropology, travel and government*. Princeton, NJ.
Thrift, N. 1991: For a new regional geography. *Progress in Human Geography* 15, 456–65.
Wallerstein, I. 1983: *The politics of the world-economy*. Cambridge.
Whittlesey, D. 1954: The regional concept and the regional method. In James, P. and Jones, C. F., editors, *American geography: inventory and prospect*. Syracuse, NY.

Further Reading

On the history of areal differentiation: Entrikin 1991; Whittlesey 1954; Minshull, R. 1967: *Regional geography: theory and practice*. London. On disputes over the concept of region: Hart 1982; Johnston 1990; Paul 1989. On the influence and heritage of Hartshorne: Entrikin, J. N. and Brunn, S. B., editors, 1989: *Reflections on Richard Hartshorne's 'The Nature of Geography'*. Washington, DC. On place as a 'mediating' concept: Agnew 1987; Entrikin 1991. On locality studies; Bagguley et al. 1990; Cooke 1989: Smith 1987. On recent disputes over the 'concreteness' of regions, places and localities: Gregory 1993; Thrift 1991.

22

REGIONAL ENVIRONMENT, HEREDITY AND CONSCIOUSNESS

A.J. Herbertson

The heyday of regional geography in the early twentieth century saw the region concept used as a means of bringing together all those factors thought of as influencing the differences among humankind. This synthesis is evident in the article by Andrew J. Herbertson (1865–1915), a British geographer educated at the Universities of Edinburgh and Freiburg (Germany) who taught at Oxford from 1899 to 1915. His early work was naturalistic and determinist, drawing from Patrick Geddes and influenced by Halford Mackinder (**chapter 8**). Thus his popular book *Man and His Work* (London, 1899) was organized around a series of environmentally determined regions from which various ethnic 'modes of life' were seen as emanating. Though purportedly importing the French sociologist Le Play's scheme of 'work – place – society' into geography, Herbertson tended towards a regional geography of races in which climate exercised a powerful influence. However, in the long run Herbertson's writing departed strongly from such materialist reductionism. In his posthumously published article (reprinted here) a holistic sense of the material and affective links between 'man' and 'environment' pervades the entire narrative. While displaying a set of humanistic sentiments concerning 'regional consciousness' and the *genius loci* of places, Herbertson also retained an attachment to a number of neo-Lamarckian motifs inherited from Geddes: a criticism of strict hereditarianism as applied to humans, a tendency to invoke learned adaptation, and a commitment to the complexity of social evolution. A persisting theme across his work was the importance of regional mediation to the intersection of human and environment relations.

Source: Regional environment, heredity and consciousness. *Geographical Teacher* 8, 147–53, 1916.

To set a form upon that digest
So shapeless and so rude.

There is a fascination for most of us in comparing the present with the past. The cynic loves to show that there is nothing new under the sun, the chauvinist sees that his country has been specially favoured of heaven and is the best of all countries, and the sentimentalist feels that better times succeed the former and all is for the best in this the best of all possible worlds. The sober historian is more concerned to analyse the differences as well as the resemblances between past and present, to discover the life history of communities, and to apply this knowledge to the guidance of present conduct in political and economic affairs.

There is an equal fascination for some of us in comparing different countries and communities in the present world. Cynics, chauvinists and sentimentalists can also select the aspects which support their theses from such comparisons. The sober geographer, like his historical colleague, is more concerned to analyse the resemblances and differences between the various lands and their peoples, to see how far the conditions of one correspond with those of another and whether or not solutions of problems suitable for one country are necessarily suitable for another, as our politicians too often assume they must be.

Such comparisons yield analogies, suggestive if we remember their limitations, but misleading if we forget them. We must not expect them to solve all our problems. For instance, the British and the Roman Empires are often compared, and the fate of the former deduced from that of the latter. Sir Charles Lucas has recently done a great service in pointing out the fallacies in this assumption, and from his intimate knowledge of the one and of the history of both he has given us a valuable corrective to such current speculation. We can learn much from Roman experience, but it does not follow that Rome's history will be ours.

So it is also with geographical comparisons. Japan is frequently termed the Britain of the East, and some assume that Japan may become in the Pacific Ocean what Britain has been in the Atlantic and Indian Oceans. Miss Semple has analysed very fully the significance of island empires and paid much attention both to British and Japanese conditions. No one can deduce the history of the latter from that of the former, though the Japanese have learned much from British experience, and we have also learned some things from the Japanese.

Another set of fascinating comparisons is made between the life histories of communities and individuals. A state grows slowly, from a sapling to a stately tree, which may flourish for centuries before it decays and disappears. Those who expect this to be our inevitable course are engrossed in discovering the stage which the British Empire has now reached.

The modern biologist has much subtler comparisons. Instead of the old view that the life of a people is that of one of its individuals on a larger scale, he shows us that the life of the individual is but a recapitulation of that of the race. Much has taken place in the womb of time before a nation is born. The cycle of individual form and life is fixed within very narrow limits. That of the race is not necessarily the same, it is slow, it may be progressive, it is not necessarily retrogressive, it may gradually change to something far more different than youth is from age in the individual.

The long cycle from protozoa to man is not to be represented by a circle but by an expanding spiral. The same thing never happens again in precisely the same way. When one form of life grows in vigour and occupies the earth it is adapted to its environment, and until something fitter is evolved to do this it dominates. This something fitter may be itself if it possesses the power of adaptability.

It is germane to our subject to consider for a moment the question of heredity and environment. These fascinating problems have also been mishandled by those who explain everything by race, and by those for whom all is determined by environment. Mr. and Mrs. Whetham, sound eugenists, pour scorn on the simple faith of many social reformers and politicians, who cite diminished death rates and other statistical evidence of the value of improved material conditions of life. The eugenists reply, 'true, but you are merely preserving the unfit who breed most quickly, and it is by the elimination of the unfit that progress is obtained.' It is obvious that no matter how fit any organism is, unless it lives in optimum conditions it cannot achieve the best results.

The quarrel is endless until we realise that for society, as distinct from the individual man, heredity and environment have not the simple meanings we often give them. The inheritance of a society is transmitted in a much more complex way than by continuity of germ plasm. Convection and radiation as well as conduction are as it were at work. There is not merely the transference of tradition from father and mother to child, not merely that from living man to living man, but also that from dead men, whose works live after them, to living men.

Environment, too, is not merely the physical circumstances among which we live, important though those are. It, too, is found to be more complex and more subtle the more we examine it. There is a mental and spiritual environment as well as a material one. It is almost impossible to group precisely the ideas of a community into those which are the outcome of environmental contact, and those which are due to social inheritance.

Environment is not constant, but changes, even physically, *e.g.* when a new drainage or irrigation or railway system is constructed. Social tradition is not constant. In fact, heredity and environment are very convenient ideas for analysis. Abstract either element from the whole – and it is less than the whole, – and the whole cannot be understood.

It is no doubt difficult for us accustomed to these dissections to understand that the living whole, while made up of parts with different structures and functions, is no longer the living whole when it is so dissected, but something dead and incomplete. The separation of the whole into man and his environment is such a murderous act. There are no men apart from their environment. There is a whole for which we have no name, unless it is a country, of which men are a part. We cannot consider men apart from the rest of the country, nor an inhabited country apart from its inhabitants without abstracting an essential part of the whole. It is like studying a human being without his nervous system, and his nervous system apart from the rest of him. It may be a useful form of analysis at a particular stage of our investigation, but it is inadequate and misleading until we have once more considered the complete man.

So it is with a country, a region, a district – whatsoever name we care to give it.

In its present form and activities man is an essential element of it, and man cannot be considered apart from the rest of it without limiting our study to something less than the whole. The analogy with an individual man is no doubt useful. There are specialists skilled in the knowledge of healthy and diseased conditions of the bones, the muscles, the digestive system, the eye, the brain, and so on; but the wise physician must know something of all of these, and as a rule his conception of the whole man is more complete and truer than that of the specialist. So with the higher natural whole or region, tinker, tailor, soldier, sailor and the thousand and one necessary specialists do not replace the wise man who knows the countryside thoroughly, and thinks of it and loves it naturally as a whole.

When we take such a complex whole as a valley or a countryside, we find the present conditioned by the past. The structure and surface forms of the land bear evidences of a long history, and we can speak of inheritance from the past, as definite and apparently as inevitable as in the case of the skeleton inherited by the individual man. When we look at its surface covering of soil and plants, and the animals living in and around them, we also find elements which have been inherited, some apparently unalterable, others capable of modification. Even the human beings themselves have the same mixture of fixed and variable characters, for nothing is more impressive than the persistence of the same stocks in most countrysides which are without minerals or manufactures to attract outsiders. Excluding the consideration of such industrial areas for the moment, we find in most others a very large element which is relatively stable and fixed – the rocks, the soil these make, the climate, the general character of plants and animals including the human inhabitants. There are also variable elements. Leaving out of account secular changes of land forms and of climate, there are minor adjustments of plants and animals to each other, and to modifications in the surface conditions due to floods, droughts, etc., and even to the minor variations of seasons, [1] and there are also the more conscious efforts of man to alter the conditions as far as they can be changed for his advantage.

Nowhere is there unchanging permanence, nowhere is there unrestricted change.

A number of common thoughtless phrases obscure the truth. We are assured that progress is through the struggle for existence and that the strongest is victor. The people who have to struggle the hardest for existence, such as the Eskimo, have little time for anything else. We hear of man's conquest of nature – a misleading phrase, man's disciplining of himself would be nearer the truth: the so called conquest of nature is due to a more intimate knowledge of nature's ways, and the use of certain natural forces to overcome certain natural obstacles. The man who uses natural products without payment, who takes the goods the gods provide without any return, is the hunter and fisher, the wanderer on the face of the earth, whose hand is against every other man's, who fights and sleeps and feasts and

[1] An autumn of good beechnuts, as in 1912, followed by an open winter leads to an enormous increase of mice in the Chiltern Hills. See also W. A. Cabot's 'In Northern Labrador,' pp. 287–292.

starves alternately. He tries to use nature without return. He is parasitic on the countryside, and in some regions of the world a limited number of such parasites can be supported.

Human progress has been bound up with more and more intimate association of man and the earth, man giving more and more of himself. Far from geography becoming less important as society becomes more complex, it becomes more important. The geographical divisions are the real divisions which form a whole, and all other groups are incomplete. The more important the human element becomes in a region, the more important that region becomes geographically. It grows more complex, it becomes a higher type.

Perhaps this is most obvious in such cases as the draining of the Fens or the building and keeping in repair of the dykes of Holland. Here, man, by well planned, patient, constant labour, keeps out excess of water and makes his district productive. He gives himself for his countryside, he puts into it the thought of his brain and the work of his hands, he makes himself a part of it in an essential way, and as long as he maintains that intimate union, he transforms it and himself into something different, something more complex, nobler, higher than before. He has had to give in order to get. It is impossible to think of either apart from the other. Man and nature here are obviously one and indissoluble. Should any change come into their intimate relations, both alter and the country is not what it was.

The resources of many regions are very varied and some of these resources may be more important in one stage of development than in another. The changes from bison hunting grounds to bonanza farms, from poor rural to busy mining industrial districts in many coalfields are obvious. The character of the region changes. Its structure and climate have not altered, but they are bound up with man in a new way and we rightly class the district in a different category. A migration of men may modify a district as well as the district may modify the immigrants.

The remarkable development of means of transport (of ideas and aspirations as well as of men and materials) is sometimes said to have annihilated space and time. It has not annihilated space, it has not altered the soil or the seasons, but it has allowed man to bring in and use more easily materials for improving the soil, to make more of the favourable seasons and to guard against the disasters of unfavourable seasons. It allows a more intimate union of man and space. It allows man to use one part of space to better advantage and to supplement its deficiencies from other parts of space which have also been more intimately understood and utilised by their inhabitants.

Information and even ideas can be transmitted almost instantaneously. But the movement of ideas is not dependent on cables or wireless apparatus alone. There must be the society fit to receive them as well as the society capable of producing them. These are not instantaneously shaped. Only within very narrow limits can we hurry growth, and all our efforts for higher education show that we strive to lengthen rather than to shorten the most actively growing period.

Before roads and railways, telegraphs and telephones, newspapers and books penetrated everywhere, each district was more or less self supporting and isolated; each person living in it was an intimate part of it. It had its good years and its bad years, its joys and its sorrows, in which all shared; but these were little affected by the world beyond and rarely stirred by outside events, hardly by great ones such as the catastrophe of some war or the ferment of some religious inspiration.

Each district as it becomes less self supporting does not become less important to itself, but it has to consider more than its own needs. It has to take into account the conditions of the world around it and decide what it is best fitted for. It may have to look far beyond its neighbouring districts even to the other side of the world. The agricultural depression of England was the first outcome of the expansion of railways across the American prairies. The agricultural regeneration which is now going on in England is based on a better knowledge of each district of its own conditions and capacities, a better knowledge of other districts and their needs and capacities for serving them. The farmers are developing a regional consciousness. As they come to grasp this for their own region they will begin to grasp it for others.

This new regional consciousness differs from the old one when each region was almost independent of the outer world, because it is bound to take the outer world into consideration. No doubt each region must consider and decide how far it should become self supporting, or how far it should produce the most of the best and seek other things in accessible markets. In either case the best results will depend in the long run on the conscious activity of each individual, knowing his neighbourhood and its needs, and sure of his own part in it.

* * *

There will be people who know intimately every square yard of some part of the land and how to keep it in a healthy condition capable of yielding good returns year after year. This intimate union must be personal and local. Production for the best results must be individualized. On the other hand matters of collection and distribution are more communal than individual. They must be communised. The proportion of men needed for this service, however, will always be smaller than that of the producers, but this question and that of the distribution of human activities within a region are too large to be discussed in the present article; and so are the obvious application of these ideas to many current political problems.

This has been written to make it clear that for the understanding of history, or economics, or politics, or any study of mankind, it is necessary (i) to realise that the wholes which are greater than the individual are geographical, (ii) to grasp the idea of a region and the need for a feeling of regional consciousness. It is not enough to know where certain mountains and rivers are, where towns or boundaries are or have been, not enough to know in what parts of the world wheat or cotton or rubber can be had, not enough to distinguish between protectorates and colonies, or to appreciate the situation of naval stations and fortified camps. A regional consciousness is not obtained in this way. The region must be recognised

Note. The asterisks mark a passage where in the author's MS. an intended interpolation had not been made at the time of his lamented death. – (*Acting Editor, G.T.*)

as a whole, composed of different parts, each with its own character and role. Its essential elements may not alter, but in the course of human history its surface has changed and man has been incorporated in it in very different ways. It is necessary to understand the permanent elements, the phases of development the region has passed through, and something of its potentialities. It is not merely a passive environment, a theatre of human action of which we must know the stage properties. It is something alive, active, not merely letting man act on it, but vigorously reacting on man.

No one who has read any description of the retreat from Moscow can ever think of environment as passive, but neither can anyone who has understood the huertas of Spain or the terraced vineyards of the Rhine.

The historian must be able to recognise a natural region when he sees one, to know its present characters, to distinguish between those which are permanent and those which are relatively transient, and to trace the sequence of changes of the latter. The economist must evaluate the wealth of the district, not merely actual but also potential. The statesman must so measure the forces of the present transition period, for all periods are times of transition, that he can guide the changes to a finer issue.

This involves no purely materialistic interpretation of history or of geography. The geographer is no more confined to materialistic considerations than the historian. There is a *genius loci* as well as a *Zeitgeist* – a spirit of a place as well as of a time. No social psychology is worth much that is not also regional psychology, and no regional psychology is possible without a loving familiarity with the region. The regional psychology is not the same at all periods of the region's history – though no doubt we can speak of the spirit of the mountains, the fascination of the desert, and so on. The spirit of a place changes with the spirit of the time; it alters with man's relation to the region. The historian has to reckon with both changes in his great cycle, the geographer has to consider both in trying to understand the present regional consciousness.

It is not safe therefore to argue from the present regional psychology to the past without intimate historical knowledge of the region. It is not safe to apply conclusions from the social psychology of one region to those of another, without understanding the differences in their regional characters.

For all the problems of man the two studies of history and geography, of heredity and environment, are essential. They cannot be separated with impunity. They have both to become more discerning and catholic. No simple chronicle suffices for the historian, no superficial geographical inventory suffices for the geographer – and economists, statesmen, and everyone concerned in more than his own individual life has to become regionally conscious, to know intimately his own region and its history, and, through the sympathetic understanding of this, to appreciate other regions and their histories, and their relations to his own region and to each other.

23

HUMAN REGIONS

H.J. Fleure

A major challenge to the idea that geographical regions were defined and determined by natural conditions came from H. J. Fleure. Like Herbertson (**chapter 22**), H. J. (Herbert John) Fleure (1877–1969) was also influenced by Geddes's interest in evolutionary biology and the region as a geographical context for the environmental differentiation of human groups. Unlike Herbertson, Fleure was never sympathetic to determinism. His career, spent largely at the University College of Wales, Aberystwyth, saw him move, successively, from geology to zoology and, finally, to a chair in geography and anthropology in 1917. Fleure injected greater attention to human experience into geography through his conception of regions as products of human energy as well as environmental endowments. Thus, he wrote of regions of difficulty, of privation, of nomadism, and so on. In his 1917 paper 'Régions Humaines', published in the French journal *Annales de Géographie*, Fleure fused Herbertson's naturalistic system with this more humane set of categories. A revised, English-language version of this paper was published two years later and it is from this version that the table reprinted here is taken. Fleure emphasized not only the interdependence of people and place but also the shifting people-people relations as contact zones led to the exchange of cultural influences. Throughout Fleure's work there was an explicit concern for cultural diversity and international understanding. But his suspicion of urban-industrial society led him to an enthusiasm for rural values and to a dalliance with such exercises as anthropometric typing (measurement of human body types and ascription of types to areas) that led back to racial categorization rather than to a more thoroughly humanistic regional geography. Fleure's long-term influence on others (such as Estyn Evans and Darryle Forde), however, lay more in his evocation of regional 'character' than in racial or environmental categorization.

Source: Human regions. *Scottish Geographical Magazine* 35, table p. 103, 1919.

Class	Physical Characters	Human Activities	Examples
I. REGIONS OF HUNGER	Extreme cold or isolated deserts	Hunting and collection of plant products	Arctic Regions, Deserts of Australia and S. Africa.
II. REGIONS OF DEBILITATION	Equatorial rains, Tierra Caliente, overheated islands.	Collection of plant products, hunting, sometimes a little gardening and fishing.	Amazon lands, Congo Tierra Caliente generally, parts of Guinea, Madagascar Lowlands, E. Coast of Africa, parts of monsoon lands, several Pacific islands.
III. REGIONS OF INCREMENT.	Climate with sufficiency and regular alternation of sun and rain.	Fruit cultivation, gardening, rice-growing, commerce, cities, aesthetics, engineering work, such as roads, bridges, etc.	Parts of Mediterranean Coast, Colchis, Kuban, California, S.E. United States, part of Chili and Brazil, parts of E. Coast of Australia, parts of New Zealand, of India, and of the E. Indies, of Indo-China, of China and Japan. Some highlands in Mexico, Brazil, Uganda, Abyssinia, Madagascar. Some oases are intermediate between this and the next group.
IV. REGIONS OF EFFORT.	Usually temperate climate, without too great changes. Moisture at most seasons.	Corn-growing, states organised for defence, privileges of property. Much energy for exploitation of resources.	France, British Isles, Germany, S. Scandinavia, central parts of Russian plain where not too wet, parts of the Balkans, Transvaal, Rhodesia, Manchuria, parts of Siberia, of the Sudan, most of the U.S.A., parts of the east of Central Australia, most of New Zealand.
V. INDUSTRIALISED REGIONS.	Up to the present, temperate climate, and some natural source of industrial power. Facilities for communication.	Manufacturing, usually with intense specialisation, Agriculture threatened, but sometimes maintained by special effort (Germany). Invention and organisation. Finance.	Portions of England and of Central Lowlands of Scotland, Belfast district, N. France, and Belgium, parts of Germany, especially near the 'Fall-Line', Bohemian districts, parts of Poland and Russia. Scandinavian and Alpine regions thanks to hydro-electric power. Japan, and parts of the U.S.A. and Canada. Possibilities in India, China, New Zealand, etc.

Class	Physical Characters	Human Activities	Examples
VI. REGIONS OF LASTING DIFFICULTY.	High valleys of temperate regions. Plateaux with cold winters.	Small farming, stock raising, herding with transhumance, exportation of men, especially for manual labour and the Mercantile Marine.	Alpine valleys, Pyrenees, Tatra, parts of Balkan Peninsula, Caucasus, Armenia, Spanish Meseta, Plateau Central, several parts of Wales, Scotland, and Scandinavia, Afghanistan, parts of Sudan, etc.
VII. REGIONS OF WANDERING.	Great variations of temperature, seasonal drought.	Herding and, in parts, hunting.	Large areas in W. and Central Asia, in Africa, in Patagonia, in U.S.A. east of the Rockies. In each case the application of the resources of civilisation acquired especially in IV. is now being foreshadowed.

24

THE CHARACTER OF REGIONAL GEOGRAPHY

Richard Hartshorne

The American geographer Richard Hartshorne's *The nature of geography*, from which this extract is taken, is the major statement in modern English-language professional geography justifying regional studies as the centre-piece of the field. Hartshorne (1899–1992) based his claim on an interpretation of scholarly writing, particularly that of nineteenth- and early twentieth-century German geographers. The writings of the German geographer Hettner, and precursors such as Kant and Humboldt, figure prominently in *The nature of geography*. From them Hartshorne took the idea that the region was a mental construct for analysis and not a natural or pre-given entity. Originally published in 1939, *The nature of geography* was for many years the major text identifying the essential principles of the field as understood by an unabashed 'regionalist'. This is not to say that it went unchallenged. Far from it. Its author became an important participant in controversy over the direction of the field, especially in his exchanges over the posthumously published article of Schaefer (see **chapter 35**). Eventually *The Nature* came to be regarded more as a 'window for looking into a geographic past' (J. N. Entrikin, Introduction: *The Nature of Geography* in perspective. In J. N. Entrikin and S. D. Brunn, editors, *Reflections on Richard Hartshorne's The Nature of Geography*. Washington, DC, 1989, p. 2) than as a guide to how to combine a sense of the empirical differences between places with a perspective based on the 'objective view' of the scientist. Hartshorne still has his champions and there are those who believe that his views have been lampooned by his critics, but the revival of interest in place and regional geography in the 1980s owed little if anything to the influence of Hartshorne's arguments. Whether Hartshorne's ideas are necessarily antithetical to the new ones is an entirely different question.

[We have silently changed the author's system of referencing, to the Harvard system.]

Source: The character of regional geography. *In The Nature of Geography: a Critical Survey of Current Thought in Light of the Past.* (Association of American Geographers, Washington, DC, 1939), extract from 1961 reprint edition, pp. 436–44.

The development of geography during the past thirty-odd years has been marked by an increasing interest in regional geography. Under the leadership of Vidal in France, of Hettner, Penck, Gradmann, Passarge, and many others in Germany, European geographers gradually shifted away from the concentration on systematic geography, which had been a natural result of the emphasis on universals in all science. Likewise, in this country, the programmatic papers of Barrows (1923) and Sauer (1925), however divergent in other respects, agreed in the emphasis on regional studies as the core of geography. Though Pfeifer (1938) is correct in noting the similarity of these, the two most influential methodological statements in current American geography, he over-estimates their importance in determining the course of current thought in American geography by failing to note the major degree to which, like the earlier methodological pronouncements of the presidents of this association, they simply "mirror . . . geographic opinion in America" [94]. As Platt has pointed out, the roots of the current movement, in particular of the tendency for detailed studies of small areas, reach back to geological field courses before the World War and military mapping during the War.[105] It is neither possible nor necessary to determine even approximately what forces or what individuals have been responsible for this development. Mention should certainly be made of the influence that Bowman (1934), as Director of the American Geographical Society, exerted towards intensive regional studies. Possibly most important of all has been the personal influence exerted by the group of Midwestern geographers whose annual field conferences, in the years 1923 and following, concentrated the attention of a much larger number of workers on the problems of regional mapping [note, for example, the report of the joint conclusions of this group (see the bibliography for its members), which Jones and Finch published in 1925, as well as the significant studies of Finch (1933, 1934), Hall (1935), Jones (1930, 1934a, 1934b), Whitaker (1932), Whittlesey (1929, 1935a, 1935b), James (1934)].

If geography, in America as well as in Europe, may be said to have returned, in a certain sense, to the point of view that was common with Humboldt and Ritter (see Sec. II D), its long period of concentration on systematic studies has enabled it to return far better equipped with generic concepts and principles with which to interpret the findings of regional geography – though unfortunately this equipment is relatively deficient in respect to human or cultural features, both in geographic literature and in the training of most of its students.

Many geographers who have accepted this shift in emphasis evidently have done so under the provisional assumption that regional geography is to be made as "scientific" as systematic geography has been, that somehow it must be raised to the plane on which scientific principles may be constructed. We have noted a

[105] In a paper read before the association at the recent meetings, 1938. Specifically Platt notes that the first publication cited by Pfeifer as containing "proposals made by Sauer" [footnote 12] actually consisted of proposals, presented without distinction of authorship, of both its co-authors (as well as of other unnamed members of a seminar group at the University of Chicago): W. D. Jones and C. O. Sauer: "Outlines of Field Work in Geography," BULL. AM. GEOGR. SOC., 47 (1915), 520–5.

number of difficulties into which this ambition has led. In our final consideration of regional geography it is necessary to understand clearly certain limitations imposed upon the student that are not found in systematic geography.

After a number of unsuccessful attempts to express the special nature of regional study in words, I find it can be most clearly presented if we may use mathematical symbols, though we shall not, of course, find it possible to express such complicated problems in any real mathematical formulae or equations.

Any particular geographic feature, z, varying throughout a region, might theoretically be represented as a function, $f(x, y)$, x and y representing co-ordinates of location. As a function of two variables, any such feature that we are able to measure mathematically – such as slope, rainfall, or crop yield – can be represented concretely by an irregular surface. Such a surface would then present the actual character of that feature for the whole region; it would, theoretically, be correct for every point, and for every small district. Furthermore, if the function involved were not too complicated, the theory of integral calculus would permit us to integrate the total of that feature for any limited section, as well as for any individual point. In a sense, part of our work in systematic geography corresponds to this form of presentation.

Likewise, the relation of any two or three geographic factors to each other within a region – *e.g.*, the relation of crop yield to rainfall and humus content of soil – might be represented as a functional equation involving that many variables: $z_3=f'(z_1z_2)$. The concrete representation of this relation would require again a surface form. More commonly, in systematic geography, we consider only the relation of one factor to but one other, which we may then represent as a curve on a plane surface. Each of these factors, z, is of course a different function, $f(x, y)$, and the more complex equation, $z_3 = f'(z_1, z_2)$ holds true only if z_3 is unaffected by other z factors, or if those which affect it are constant throughout the region under consideration. Neither of these conditions is strictly true: almost any geographic element we may consider is affected by more than two of the natural elements, and may also be affected by incommensurable, or quite unknown, human factors; and all of the factors considered vary to some extent no matter how small the area considered. Consequently, we have introduced a degree of distortion of reality even at this step in systematic geography.

We may introduce a further step by establishing element-complexes, u, each representing functions of many z elements, varying, by more or less regular rules, with the variations in a smaller number of those elements. Thus, given certain conditions of soil, slope, temperature, and rainfall we may presume within a wide margin of both inaccuracy and uncertainty, certain conditions of natural vegetation and wild animal life, and we may express the total of all these z elements by one u element-complex. If it were conceivable that we could express this feature, u, arithmetically, its character over an area would likewise form an irregular surface that would indicate its character for any limited part. From the nature of these element-complexes, however, it is obvious that any such representation would have a high degree of unreliability.

In regional geography, however, we are concerned with a vastly more complicated function of the location co-ordinates. It cannot be expressed as the function of any one element or element-complex, but rather of various semi-independent element-complexes, u, and of additional semi-independent elements, z'. Thus, the total geography, w, at any point, might be expressed by the function, $F(u_1, u_2 \ldots u_n, z'_2 \ldots z'n)$. If we could have accurate and complete information concerning the form of the function, F, and every one of the element-complexes, u – each as a function of various z elements – and of the semi-independent elements z', the function would be so complicated that we could not hope to represent it by any concrete form, even in terms of n-dimensional space. We would have a function that could be solved only for each point, x, y, in the region, but could not be correctly expressed for any small part larger than a point. In other words, we could study the geography of the area only from the study of the geography of the infinite number of points within it. This task, being infinite, is impossible. The problem of regional geography, as distinct from a geography of points, is how to study and present the geography of finite areas, within each of which the total complex function involved depends on so many complex functions, complexely interrelated, as to permit of no solution by any theory of integration.

Consequently we are forced to consider, not the infinite number of points at each of which w is in some degree different, but a finite number of small, but finite, areal divisions of the region, within each of which we must assume that all the factors are constant. In order, then, to cover an entire region we will need but a finite number of resultants, w, each representing the geography of a small unit of area rather than of a point. This method is legitimate only if one remembers that it inevitably distorts reality. The distortion can be diminished by taking ever smaller unit areas, but it cannot be eliminated entirely; no matter how small the unit, we know that the factors which we assume to be constant within it are in fact variable. In practice, the smallest units that we can commonly take time to consider are sufficiently large to permit of a marked degree of variation, and therefore of a significant distortion of reality in our results.

To express our conclusion in more common terms, in any finite area, however small, the geographer is faced with an interrelated complex of factors, including many semi-independent factors, all of which vary from point to point in the area with variations only partially dependent on each other. He cannot integrate these together except by arbitrarily ignoring variations within small units of area, *i.e.*, by assuming uniform conditions throughout each small, but finite unit. He may then hope to comprehend, by analysis and synthesis, the interrelated phenomena within each particular unit area.

Although the studies of all the unit areas added together will constitute an examination of the entire region, this does not complete the regional study. As Penck has emphasized, it is not sufficient to study individual "chores" (approximately homogeneous districts) and to establish types of chores. "Above all geography must consider the manner in which these are fitted together to form larger units, just as the chemist does not limit himself merely to studying the atoms, but investigates also the manner of their situation beside each other in individual combinations. The comprehension of geographic forms (*Gestalten*) has scarcely been taken into consideration by the new geography." Just as a mosaic cannot be comprehended, Penck (1926) continues, by classifying and studying the individual stones of which it is made, but requires also that we see the arrangement and grouping of the individual pieces, so the study of the arrangement of the "chores"[106] will present different structural forms of significance [in part also in his address given in Philadelphia and published in English, (1927) 640].

Our second step – in a theoretical approach to regional geography – is to relate the unit areas to each other to discover the structural and functional formation of the larger region. Since all the factors concerned, and therefore the resultants, have been made arbitrarily constant for each small unit, it may be permissible to speak of functional relations between one factor in one unit and another in another unit, as though these were functional relations between the units themselves – provided that we understand that this is not strictly true. Further, the regional structure produced by this method will have the character of a mosaic of individual pieces, each of which is homogeneous throughout, many of them so nearly alike that in any actual method of presentation they will appear as repetitions in different parts of the region. But we are not to be deceived into regarding this mosaic which we have made as a correct reproduction of reality. It is simply the device by which finite minds can comprehend the infinitely variable function of many semi-independent variable factors. The fiction involved is threefold: we have arbitrarily assumed each small unit area to be uniform throughout; we have delimited it from its neighbours arbitrarily, as a distinct unit (individual); and we have arbitrarily called very similar units identical in character.

There are certain other fundamental limitations that must be insisted upon if we are to compare the face of the earth, even in the more or less distorted form in which the geographer must present it, to a mosaic. We may say that there is a similarity in the detail of technique but, unless we are to return to some telelogical principle, we cannot liken the face of the earth to any work of art, for we cannot assume that it is the organized product of a single mind. On the contrary, if we may transfer Hettner's analogy of a building built by several architects working independently to Huntington's picture of "The Terrestrial Canvas," we may say that the face of the earth has been produced by the interrelated combination of different color designs each applied by different artists working more or less independently, and each changing his plan as he proceeded. In systematic geography one might say,

[106] This is the word that Sölch (1924) introduced as a term for a unit area. As he defined it the concept is independent of size; the chore is simply an area of land determined by the relative degree of homogeneity of all geographical factors – "geo-factors." A chore established on any particular scale could be divided into smaller chores each of which would presumably show a higher degree of homogeneity; the limit of such a process is, of course, the perfectly homogeneous unit, which can only be a point. In adopting this term Penck has used it in a different meaning, according to which the "chores" appear as the smallest land units, indivisible cells, so to speak, which he adds up to form larger "forms." We do not follow this usage, not only because it changes the meaning of the term as the inventor defined it, but also because there can be no smallest land units. As Penck himself elsewhere has recognized, we may continue the process of division indefinitely and our subdivisions are no less (and no more) real units than those we divided.

we attempt to separate each of the individual designs in order to understand its form and its relation to the others and, thereby, to the total picture. Since the total pictures were not produced simply by superimposing different color plates in printing, but are, to some extent, causally related to each other, this separation involves the analysis of the causal and functional relations of each design to the others. In regional geography we first reduce the subtle gradations which the different artists of nature have applied and intermixed on the face of the earth, to the stiff and arbitrary form of the mosaic technique. When we then survey the formation of the mosaic pieces, we are not to expect some unified organized pattern such as every work of art must have. On the other hand, neither need we expect mere chaos, or a kaleidoscope; for we know, from our studies in systematic geography, that there were principles involved in the individual designs, and if our determination of the unit areas of homogeneity has not been purely arbitrary, but has been based on the combination of careful measurement and good judgement, we may expect the combinations of these designs to show more or less orderly, though complex patterns. Further, whatever the explanation of these patterns may be, their form is significant to each of the parts, since the development in each unit part is affected by that in the others.

The last thought leads us finally to another major respect in which any analogy of the earth surface to a work of art is inadequate, namely, the fact that, while the latter is static, consisting of motionless forms, the face of the earth includes moving objects that are constantly connecting its various parts. (To attempt to introduce the artist's special use of such terms as "lines of force," "movement," "opposite forces," etc., would merely add to confusion here.) In other words, the geographer must consider function as well as form. In establishing our arbitrary small unit areas we not only assume that each is uniform throughout in character, but also in function. Likewise, in combining these units into larger regional divisions our problem is complicated by the fact that we must consider the functional relations of the units to one another as well as their form. For example, if two neighboring areal units are so similar that we have painted them as much alike as two pieces of mosaic of the same color, but one of them is functionally related to a city center in one region, the other to a city center in another, are we to include them in the different regions, or, if in the same region, in which? Any answer to this question can only be more or less intelligent: there can be no one "correct answer."

Just as it is necessary to know the arrangement of units areas in a region, it is likewise necessary to understand the arrangement of regions to each other. Both Penck and Granö (who follows a similar line of thought (1929) 28–31) would carry the process on to larger units; the size of the areas concerned is immaterial. Regional geography, therefore, studies the manner in which districts are grouped and connected in larger areas, the manner in which these larger areas are related in areas of greater scale, and so on, until one reaches the final unit, the only real unit area, the world.

There is, however, one important difference at the different levels of integration. Both Penck and Granö appear to ignore the fact that the small, but fundamental, element of fiction in the assumption of homogeneity of the smallest units of area increases progressively as one advances to larger divisions. Consequently, the determination of these larger divisions requires increasingly arbitrary distortions of fact.

Assuming the first step, the establishment of "homogeneous units" of area, we may proceed to the second by enclosing in a continuous area which we call a region, the greatest possible number of "homogeneous units" that we judge to be nearly similar, together with the smallest number of dissimilar units. Our judgment of similarity will involve subjective judgment as to which characteristics of the homogeneous units are of greater importance than others, so that, at best, the determination of the region is in a sense arbitrary.

Furthermore we seldom find in reality such a simple solution as that described. Though some geographic features vary but gradually from place to place, the irregular and steep variations of others – such as soils, slopes in mountainous areas, urban settlement, and all the features of essentially linear form, rivers, roads, and railroads – will force us to include in any region, "units" of quite different character. It is necessary therefore to determine which kinds of units are, either in actual interrelation or merely in juxtaposition, characteristic of the region as approximately considered, and then so determine it as to include the greatest number of those several kinds of similar units, with the smallest number of units of other kinds.

In considering any large area in which we have first recognized "homogeneous units" and are attempting to form them into regions, which we can briefly characterize in terms of similarities or relations among some of those units, we may find the task relatively simple in parts of the area, where perhaps the great majority of the units are notably similar. But it may be extremely difficult in parts between these, which may be characterized by units that are, in some respects, similar to units on one side of them, in other respects, to units on another side. Further, we will find areas containing such a variety of different kinds of units that we cannot see where to include them. In some cases, to be sure, we may recognize such areas as transition zones, but that merely postpones the fundamental problem without solving it. Likewise, to call them "characterless areas," or areas of "general" or "mixed" types is simply to dodge the problem entirely.

The individual student, no doubt, would gladly wipe such troublesome areas off the map, but he is not granted that privilege. Neither is a science which seeks to know what the world is like permitted to ignore more difficult areas and confine itself to those easier to organize into its body of knowledge. Since these doubtful areas are commonly not merely narrow borders of transition, but areas of wide extent, perhaps as great or greater than those more clearly classified, there is no basis for assuming that they are of less importance in the total picture of the larger area, or of the world, than the areas whose character we can more readily describe. Fenneman's statement with reference to the different parts of geography applies even more literally to parts of an area – "there is no more inherent worth in a center than in a border."

Consequently, when we divide any given area into parts which we call regions, so determined that those characteristics that we have judged to be most important may be most economically stated for each region, we cannot avoid many decisions based on judgment rather than on measurement. We must, therefore, acknowledge that our regions are merely "fragments of land" whose determination involves a considerable degree of arbitrary judgment. On the other hand, if all possible objective measures have been used, and the arbitrary decisions are based on the student's best judgment, we may properly regard his regions as having more validity than is expressed by the bare phrase "arbitrarily selected." On the other hand, the view of various writers previously noted, that geographers could be expected to come to approximate agreement on the specific limits of regions – or even on their central cores – appears, in view of all the difficulties listed, overly optimistic.

It hardly needs to be added that the conclusion that geography cannot establish any precise objective basis for regional division does not permit it to shirk the task of organizing regional knowledge into areal divisions determined by the best judgment possible. In order to utilize the generic concepts and principles developed in systematic geography to interpret the finding of regional geography, the latter must be organized into parts that are as significant as is possible. In the present state of development of the field – if not indefinitely – we do not have what would be the simplest solution, namely, a single standardized and universally accepted division and subdivision of the world into regions. Therefore, each student of regional geography has imposed upon him the task of standardizing his own system of regional division – unless he can utilize that of some colleague. "Standardized" is used here to indicate that the regional system is based on certain standards specifically stated, so that other students may know precisely what the organization is.

The complete organization of regional knowledge in geography requires – whether as a final or as a primary step – the division of the whole world. In whichever direction the process is carried on – and we noted that it requires consideration in both directions – the completed system must provide a regional division of the world in which our knowledge of each small part may be logically placed. For this extremely difficult problem we found two different methods of solution. Geographical knowledge may be logically arranged in systems of areas classified according to certain characteristics of the areas. Though this method has distinct utility for comparative purposes, it does not permit organizing all regional knowledge into one system, but requires several independent systems. Furthermore, it does not present the actual relations of areas as parts of larger areas. These relations can be included only in a realistic division of the world into a system of specific regions, in which all regional knowledge may be incorporated in a single logical system. Such a system unfortunately is not provided the geographer by any natural division present in reality, nor by anything corresponding to the simple division of organic forms. It must be developed and constantly modified by geographers as a result of research, at the same time that it is being used, always in tentative form, as the organizing structure of regional research.

We have suggested, in very general terms, the manner in which the problem of delimiting regions may be met, in order that geographic knowledge may be organized intelligently in regional units. What kind of knowledge is to be included within the regional study itself? So far as the nature of the material is concerned, we have previously indicated that a complete geography of a region includes all the kinds of phenomena that are included in systematic geography – insofar as they may be present in the particular region. The only field of geography that is not included in regional geography, as well as in systematic geography, is historical geography. As there was a different geography in every past period. there may be any number of independent historical geographies, each including its own systematic and regional divisions.

References

H.H. Barrows, 1923: Geography as human ecology, *Annals of the Association of American Geographers* 13, 1–14.

I. Bowman, 1934: *Geography in Relation to the Social Sciences*. New York.

V.C. Finch, 1933: Montfort, a study in landscape types in southwestern Wisconsin. *Geographical Society of Chicago, Bulletin* 9.

— 1934a: Conventionalizing geographic investigation and presentation; a symposium, *Annals of the Association of American Geographers* 24, 77–122.

— 1934b: Written structures for presenting the geography of regions, *Annals of the Association of American Geographers* 24, 113–20.

J. G. Granö, 1929: Reine Geographie: eine methodologische Studie beleuchtet mit Beispielen aus Finnland und Estlund, *Acta Geographica*, 2, No. 2 (Helsinki). Review by H. Hassinger, *Geogr. Ztschr.* 36 (1930), 293–6.

R. B. Hall, 1935: The geographic region: a resumé, *Annals of the Association of American Geographers* 25, 122–36.

P. E. James, 1934: The terminology of regional description, *Annals of the Association of American Geographers* 24, 77–86.

W. D. Jones, 1930: Ratios and isopleth maps in regional investigation, *Annals of the Association of American Geographers* 20, 177–95.

— 1934: Procedures in investigating human occupance of a region, *Annals of the Association of American Geographers* 24, 93–107.

— and V. C. Finch, 1925: Detailed field mapping in the study of the economic geography of an agricultural area, *Annals of the Association of American Geographers* 15, 148–57.

A. Penck, 1926: Geographie und Geschichte, *Neue Jahrbücher f. Wissench. u. Jugenbildg.* 2, 47–54. Abstract in *Ztschr. f. Ges. f. Erdk.*, Berlin, 60 (1925), 384.

— 1927: Geography among the Earth's Sciences, *Proceedings American Philosophical Society* 66, 621–44.

G. Pfeifer, 1938: Entwicklungstendenzen in Theorie und Methode der regionalen Geographie in den Vereingten Staaten, nach dem Kriege, *Ztsch. d. Ges f. Erdk.*, Berlin, 93–125. Abstract by J. Leighley, *Geographical Review* 28, (1938), 679.

C. O. Sauer, 1926: The morphology of landscape, *University of California Publications in Geography* 2, 19–53.

J. Sölch, 1924: *Die Auffassung der "natürlichen Grenzen" in der Wissenschaftlichen Geographie*. Innsbruck. Review by R. Sieger, *Peterm. Mitt.* 71 (1925), 57–9.

R. Whitaker, 1932: Regional interdependence, *Journal of Geography* 31, 164.

D. Whittlesey, 1929: Sequent occupance, *Annals of the Association of American Geographers* 19, 162–65.

— 1935a: The impress of effective central authority upon the landscape, *Annals of the American Association of Geographers* 34, 85–97.

— 1935b: A conference on regions, *Annals of the Association of American Geographers* 25, 121–74.

25

IN WHAT SENSE A REGIONAL PROBLEM?

Doreen Massey

In the 1980s human geographers renewed their interest in the region for two reasons. One reason was disillusionment with the focus on spatial distributions that had come to dominate a large part of human geography. This focus had led to an understanding of geographical differences in employment or industrial composition as being the result of relative spatial centrality or marginality, which could be righted through the correct mix of policies. The second reason was the perceived breakdown of the (large-scale) Fordist production system in countries such as Britain and the United States, which was seen as shaking up the conventional maps of economic geography. In the new view, the relationships of particular geographical areas to the ever-changing character of economic activity – in particular, shifts in the spatial division of labour – were identified as a more profound source of geographical disequilibrium than deviations from a national norm in standards of employment or industrial composition. As a result of increased competition across national boundaries production was now less organized within regions, as it had been under Fordism, than across them. Doreen Massey's writing was at the forefront of redefining the 'regional problem' (differences in average incomes, unemployment rates and industrial growth between geographical areas) in this way. The article reprinted here is one of the earlier statements of Massey's argument for a spatial division of labour producing regional inequality through the organization of economic production. This perspective was later expressed to great effect in one of the most cited books of modern human geography, *Spatial divisions of labour* (London, 1984), in which Massey elaborated on her claim that production arrangements across regions, and the historical pattern of regional investment and emergent social structures, jointly condition the formation and character of regions themselves. The logic of this perspective bears a close relationship to that represented in **chapter 29** (McDowell and Massey) and served as one of the inspirations for locality studies (Cooke, **chapter 30**). It also demonstrates an alternative Marxism to the 'spatializations' of Marx represented by Harvey (**chapter 37**) and Soja (**chapter 38**), in which geographical organization is built into capitalist production rather than being a single strategy among many (the 'spatial fix' of Harvey) or always manifesting a particular spatial form (such as the 'core' and 'periphery' of Soja).

Source: In what sense a regional problem? *Regional Studies* 13, 233–43, 1979.

Introduction

The aim of this paper is to raise some questions about common conceptions of 'regional problems' within capitalist societies. Some of the points to be made are well known, others are raised less frequently; some challenge explicit positions in the established theory, others implicit assumptions in methodology. The hope is that, by collecting these points together, and indicating some of their interrelationships, the implications of each one may be taken more seriously.

Regional Differentiation and the Concept of the Spatial Division of Labour

This section of the paper presents a framework for the analysis of regional differentiation. Such a framework will, of necessity, be rather abstract at this stage, but later sections will attempt to put more flesh on the bones.

One thing should be made clear from the start, and that is that there always has been spatial (or regional) inequality. This is a historical statement, and the kind of general framework to be introduced here is a framework for the analysis of real historical processes. It is only in formal models that one starts with the featureless equality of a clean sheet.

A second point, however, is what one means in such a context as 'inequality'. The word tends to get used indiscriminately in the literature in two rather different ways. First, there is inequality in the degree of attractiveness of a particular area to the dominant form of economic activity; secondly, there is inequality in terms of various indicators of social well-being (rate of unemployment, *per capita* income, degree of external control of production, for example). The two are evidently not necessarily the same. In a crude sense, one is a cause and the other an effect. It is the first with which this paper is concerned at this point – that is: regional inequality in the degree of attractiveness to, and suitability for, economic activity. At any point in time, in other words, there is a given uneven geographical distribution of the conditions necessary for profitable, and competitive, production.

A third point is that such geographical inequality is a historically-relative phenomenon. It is historically-relative (in other words, it will change) as a result of two processes. On the one hand it will respond to changes in the geographical distribution of the requirements of production – which are frequently called changes in the spatial, or locational, surface – such things as actual changes in the distribution of the population or of resources, or changes in relative distances caused by developments in transport and communication. On the other hand, the pattern of spatial inequality may change as a result of changes in the requirements of the production process itself, in other words because of changes in the locational demands of profitable economic activity. In turn, such changes in the requirements of production are themselves a result, not of neutral technical advance, but of the imperatives of the overall process of accumulation.

However, in any particular period, new investment in economic activity will be geographically distributed in response to such a given pattern of spatial differentiation. A fourth question then arises, however, as to what 'in response to' means, and it is here that I want to introduce the term *'spatial division of labour'*. The term is introduced in order to make a point. The normal assumption is that any economic activity will respond to geographical inequality in the conditions of production, in such a way as to maximise profits. While this is correct, it is also trivial. What it ignores is the variation in the way in which different forms of economic activity incorporate or use the fact of spatial inequality *in order* to maximise profits. This manner of response to geographical unevenness will vary both between sectors and, for any given sector, with changing conditions of production. It may also vary with, for instance, the structure of ownership of capital (depending on, for example, the size and range of production under single ownership). The determination of this manner of response will itself be a product of the interaction between, on the one hand the existing characteristics of spatial differentiation, and on the other hand the requirements at that time of the particular process of production. Moreover, if it is the case that different industries will use spatial variation in different ways, it is also true that these different modes of use will subsequently produce/contribute to different forms of geographical inequality. Different modes of response by industry, implying different spatial divisions of labour within its overall process of production, may thus generate different forms of 'regional problem'.

One schematic way of approaching this as a historical process is to conceive of it as a series of 'rounds' of new investment, in each of which a new form of spatial division of labour is evolved. In fact, of course, the process of change is much more diversified and incremental (though certainly there are periods of radical redirection). Moreover, at any given historical moment a whole number of different spatial divisions of labour may be being evolved, by different branches of industry. In any empirical work, therefore, it is necessary both to analyse this complexity and to isolate and identify those particular divisions which are dominant in reshaping the spatial structure. The geographical distribution of economic activity which results from the evolution of a new form of division of labour will be overlaid on, and combined with, the pattern produced in previous periods by different forms of division of labour. This combination of successive layers will produce effects which themselves vary over space, thus giving rise to a new form and spatial distribution of inequality in the conditions of production, as a basis for the next 'round' of investment. 'The economy' of any given local area will thus be a complex result of the combination of its succession of roles within the series of wider, national and international, spatial divisions of labour.

Different Forms of the Spatial Division of Labour in the United Kingdom

As a way of illustrating some of the points already made, and as a basis for discussion in later sections, it is worth at this point running briefly through two forms of spatial division of labour which have been, or are, significant components of the 'regional problem' in the United Kingdom.

The first of these examples is so well known as to warrant only brief attention. It is that form of the spatial division of labour which structured the spatial organisation of the UK during much of the nineteenth century (McCrone, 1969, p. 16), and which took the form of sectoral spatial specialisation. It was the UK's early dominance of the growth of modern industry, its consequent commitment both to retaining that dominance through free trade and to its own specialisation in manufacturing within the international division of labour, which enabled the burgeoning growth up to the First World War of major exporting industries based on coal, shipbuilding, iron and steel, and textiles. In establishing their spatial pattern of production *within* the UK these industries were not faced with an undifferentiated geographical surface. The aspects of differentiation which were significant to these industries at that stage of development were such things as access to ports for export, and for import of raw materials (e.g. cotton), a supply of skilled labour, and, to some extent still, access to coal. The form of spatial division of labour to which this conjunction of production requirements and geographical differentiation gave rise was, as already stated, that of sectoral spatial specialisation. The different sectors simply concentrated all their capacity in the areas most propitious in terms of their requirements for production. Moreover, because these were among the dominant industries in terms of new investment and growth in output and employment, they were the structuring elements in the new emerging pattern of regional differentiation. 'Thus Clydeside meant ships and heavy engineering, the North East meant export coal, iron and steel, ships and heavy engineering, Lancashire meant cotton and some engineering; the West Riding meant coal and woollens; South Wales meant export coal and iron and steel' (Hall, 1974, p. 84). From the point of view of the individual localities involved, this led to a situation in which 'several of the major industrial regions had based their prosperity on a very limited economic base' (Hall, p. 83).

The subsequent effects of this particular form of the spatial division of labour are well known, but it is important to emphasise a number of points. First, in itself such a pattern of industrial distribution was not necessarily problematical, in the sense of producing geographical inequality. On the contrary, secondly, the resulting regional *problem* was precipitated by changes in the relation of the UK economy as a whole, and of these particular industries, to the international division of labour. 'It is really to the collapse of this policy (of international specialisation based on industrial dominance and free trade) that the regional problem, at any rate in the industrial areas, owes it origin. The over-valuation of the pound in the 1920s, the emergence of economic blocs in the 'thirties, changes in technology and competition from lower-wage countries, all combined to produce a secular decline in the traditional export industries' (McCrone, 1969, p. 16). The 'regional problem' which emerged was thus produced by the effects on the spatial division of labour within these industries of the change in imperial relationships and the decline of the United Kingdom as a dominant world capitalist economy. Third, this process produced a specific form of regional problem. Sectoral decline brought with it specifically *regional* decline, and the indices on which the consequent regional inequality were measured were the well-known ones of rate of unemployment, amount of manufacturing employment, *per capita* earnings, and out-migration.

It has been this form of spatial division of labour which has frequently been analysed as being the root-cause of the 'regional problem' (at least the industrial-region problem) of the UK. Thus the UK background paper for its submission to the European Regional Development Fund announces: 'The United Kingdom's regional problem is primarily one of decline in employment in the traditional industries – coal, steel, shipbuilding, textiles and agriculture, the reasons for the decline varying from industry to industry. Most of these industries are concentrated in a small number of areas and these are, therefore, disproportionately hard hit by their contraction' (Trade and Industry, 1977, p. 358). Much present thinking and a number of continuing policy-preoccupations (in particular, for instance, a general commitment to sectoral diversification as a basis for stability) reflect the experience of this early period. Indeed, there are intimations in a number of writings that the demise of this form of spatial division may herald the end (or at least the beginning of the end) of regional problems: 'Yet as time goes on, the structure of the problem regions is gradually becoming more favourable; the declining industries cannot decline for ever, and new industries are playing a larger part in the regional economies. As this process continues the problem should get easier' (McCrone, 1969, p. 166). And clearly there have been signs of change. On the one hand, many studies indicate a generally declining degree of sectoral specialisation (see, for instance, Chisholm and Oeppen, 1973; Dixon and Thirlwall, 1975). On the other hand, there have been changes in the comparative rating of the regions on the indices relevant to this form of regional problem. Thus in a recent article, Keeble (1977) writes 'the period since about 1965, and in fact particularly since 1970, has witnessed striking convergence of nearly all these different indices of regional economic performance towards the national average' (p. 4). The indices referred to are share of manufacturing employment, unemployment rate, earnings, and net migration.

Yet, even as this 'convergence' (though admittedly around lower national norms) is being registered, other indices are being pointed to which imply, not the end of spatial differentiation, but its existence in a different form, in terms both of the nature of spatial inequality and of its geographical base. The new indices refer, for instance, to the degree of external ownership, to the effects of hierarchies of control, and to differentiation in employment type. Westaway (1974) points to a developing spatial hierarchy of ownership and control, and to its consequences for employment-type, with the increasing dominance of multi-plant companies; and the work of North and Leigh (1976) and of Massey (1976) indicates the effects of hierarchisation produced in recent years by the increasing degree of industrial concentration (see also MASSEY and MEEGAN, forthcoming). FIRN (1975) examines evidence on the degree and type of external ownership and control of Scottish manufacturing; the work of McDERMOTT (1976) is in the same vein. In terms of the changing *geographical* basis of 'spatial problems', it is of course the combination of regional 'convergence' with the new prominence of inner city areas which is the dominant aspect of change.

In a paper of this length there can obviously be no pretence of producing a complete analysis of this spatial restructuring, but it is appropriate briefly to describe one emerging form of spatial division of labour which appears to be at least a contributory component.[1] While based in certain aspects (though not all) on the impact of the division already described, this form of spatial division of labour is completely different from that of sectoral spatial specialisation. In particular, and perhaps ominously, the 'inequalities' inherent in this division do not appear only on its demise – they are integral to the form of spatial organisation itself. Nor are the evolution and effects of this form dependent only on the ups and downs of whole sectors of the economy; they result also from changes in the form of organisation of production *within* sectors.

Following the framework outlined in the last section, it is first necessary to specify the characteristics and requirements of production which, in combination with particular spatial conditions, form the basis of the development of a new division of labour. Such characteristics and requirements include the increasing size of individual firms, and of individual plants (see, for example, DUNFORD, 1977), the separation and hierarchisation of technical, control, and management functions (see WESTAWAY, 1974), and the division, even within production, into separately-functioning stages (see MASSEY, 1976; LIPIETZ, 1977). Within the production process itself, there have also been considerable changes. On the one hand, the growing intensity of competition in recent years has led to increased pressure to cut labour costs and increase productivity, and this in turn has produced an apparent acceleration of the processes of standardisation of the commodities produced (thus reducing both the number of workers for any given level of output, and the levels of skill required of them), of automation (with effects similar to standardisation), and of the introduction of systems such as numerical-control machine tools (again reducing, in general, the number and skill-requirements of the direct labour force, but also needing a small number of more qualified technicians). In terms of the bulk of workers, then, a deskilling process of some significance seems to have been in operation (see, for instance, MASSEY and MEEGAN, forthcoming). At the other end of the scale, both the changing balance between sectors of the economy, and the nature of competition (particularly the reliance on fast rates of technological change) in the newly dominant sectors, such as electronics, have increased the relative importance within the national employment structure of research and development.

[1] It must be emphasised that this spatial division of labour *only characterises certain sectors,* but sectors which appear to be important in the present establishment of new aggregate geographical patterns of economic activity.

Where such developments are occurring in countries in which there is already some degree of spatial differentiation in levels of skill (both within the production workforce, and between them and technical and scientific workers), in the wage levels of the relevant (i.e. increasingly only semi-skilled) sections of production workers, in the degree of organisation and militancy of the labour movement, and in the level of presence of, for instance, the banking, commercial and business-service sectors, a new form of spatial division of labour has, in the last decade or so, begun to take root. Such is the case in most countries of Western Europe, and in the USA.

And it is precisely the changing conditions of production which are enabling industry to take advantage of spatial differentiation in this manner. For one typical 'use' by industry of this particular form of spatial differentiation is increasingly based on the geographical separation of control and R & D functions from those processes of direct production still requiring skilled labourers, and of these in turn from the increasingly important element of mass-production and assembly work for which only semi-skilled workers are needed. The expanding size of individual companies is central to this process. On the other hand it is necessary in order to finance the huge costs of research and development (see MASSEY, 1976; NEDO, 1972; NEDO, 1973) and on the other hand it increases the number of products within a firm which are produced at a scale sufficient to warrant some degree of automation, and therefore in turn to enable reductions in aggregate labour costs and increases in individual labour productivity. Finally, of course, it is the greater size of individual units which increases the feasibility of separate locations for the different stages in the overall process of production, and consequently enables the establishment of locational hierarchies taking advantage of spatial inequality.

Taking the 'bottom' end of the hierarchy first, the mass-production and assembly stages of production are located increasingly in areas where semi-skilled workers are not only available, but where wages are low, and where there is little tradition amongst these workers of organisation and militancy. Very frequently this will mean location in areas where there are workers with little previous experience of waged work. These may be areas suffering from the collapse of a previously-dominant industrial sector, such as the former coal-mining areas of Northumberland, or the coal or shale-mining areas of Scotland. In such cases, the labour drawn upon will not mainly be that previously employed in the former specialisation, but more typically the women of the area. Other areas favoured for this stage of production include those where workers (again mainly women) do not become totally dependent upon (nor organised around) waged work. Seaside resorts with seasonal or part-time self-employment in tourism are typical of this second type of area. Although the introduction of this new investment in production facilities into such (frequently depressed) areas is new, and often hailed as beneficial, its positive effects may well be small. Wages and skills remain low, and it is not even necessarily the case that much new employment will result – one of the major characteristics of such factories is that they have few local links and stimulate little locally in terms of association production (see, for instance,

McDermott, 1976; Lipietz, 1977; Dunford, 1977; and hints in McCrone, 1975). Firn (1975), after documenting the extent and form of occurrence of external control in the Scottish economy, draws some preliminary conclusions about its likely effects. These closely parallel those implied by the argument above. Thus, Firn hypothesises, it is likely that existing disparities in the type of labour available will be exacerbated. Such investment will not expand the local technical, research or managerial strata. Moreover the lack of a R & D component will also, given the presently-dominant nature of formation of new companies, reduce the likelihood of the internal generation of new firms. Again the division of labour exacerbates existing inequalities, in this case further reducing the degree of local control in such regions. Firn's hypotheses also accord with our own evidence (Massey and Meegan, forthcoming) on the effects on the direct workforce and on *per capita* income. Thus he writes, 'The nature of new jobs provided by external plants has been principally orientated towards female, semi-skilled assembly operations in, for example, electronics plants, whereas the jobs lost have been mainly of male, highly paid, skilled craftsmen. Therefore there seems to have been a net wage reduction per new job provided, as well as an element of deskilling, although this assertion remains to be proved' (p. 411). Finally, in these regions, this form of spatial division of labour 'will express itself in terms of a very open regional economy, with a high degree of integration with other economic systems' (Firn, 1975, p. 411). Dunford (1977) and Lipietz (1977) give similar evidence on this from Italy and from France.

The 'second-stage' of production (that is, those processes not yet automated, reduced to assembly-work, or producing standardised products) is still typically located in the old centres of skilled labour – primarily nineteenth century industrial towns and cities. The critical characteristic of this stage, however, is its decreasing quantitative importance. More and more, the de-skilling processes already referred to are enabling industry to be locationally freed from its old ties to skilled labour and (consequently, one might add, from well-unionised workers). The effect of the relationship between such changes in the production process and the possibilities open to industry *as a result of* the spatial differentiation of labour, is one component of the present industrial decline of the inner cities (see Community Development Project, 1977; Massey and Meegan, 1978).

Finally, at the 'top' of the hierarchy, the central metropoles (which still include European cities such as London and Paris) are typified by the presence of control functions (including the allocation of production to other regions), research, design and development, and by the significant presence of managerial and technical strata (it is this presence, rather than the absence of manual work, which is distinctive).

In order to clarify the content of the term 'spatial division of labour' it is worth elaborating in what ways this is a different form of use by capital of spatial differentiation from the form described as sectoral spatial specialisation. First, and most obviously, it is not a sectoral geographical division. It is an intra-sectoral division of labour within the overall process of production of an individual capital. Second, as already mentioned, regional inequality is inherent in its very nature, and not merely a consequence of its demise, as was the case with sectoral spatial specialisation.

Third, and most importantly, its effects are different. Thus, although some of the 'indices of inequality' to which we have become accustomed may still be relevant, not all of them will be, and it may be necessary to devise others to capture the effects of this new form of differentiation. The important aspects of disparities in skill, control and wage-levels have already been referred to. Perhaps the effect most commonly cited, however, is that, as a result of the high degree of external control at the 'bottom' end of the locational hierarchy, such regions have extremely 'open' economies. There are a number of implications of this openness. The first is that the regional economy is at the mercy of external economic changes. This is often argued to be a new effect, but in fact, as the 1930's showed, internally-controlled sectoral specialisation has similar implications. But in two other ways, the effects of openness in this spatial division of labour *are* very different from in the case of sectoral spatial specialisation. Moreover, both are related to the fact that openness is here as a result of external control. The first is the likelihood of a very low local employment multiplier effect. The second is the probability of remissions of interest, profits and dividends to a parent plant outside the region of production.

The fourth way in which this form of spatial division differs from the first is that it implies a rather different geographical configuration of 'problem-areas' – as has been mentioned, it is a component of the present collapse of inner-cities, both within and outside of the assisted areas.

Fifthly, and finally, a similarity: the development of this new spatial division of labour is once again a product of changes in production which are themselves a response to wider economic forces. The present crises of profitability and of markets have considerably reinforced both the pressure to increase the size of individual companies (with the implications already mentioned) and the pressure to reduce the costs of labour (see MASSEY, 1976; MASSEY and MEEGAN, forthcoming).

Some Implications

It is quite possible that what has been discussed so far seems unexceptionable. However, if such an approach is taken seriously, it would appear to have substantial implications for certain assumptions commonly made at the moment about the nature and causes of 'regional problems'.

Perhaps the major point to be made is that questions of regional problems and policy are normally analysed as problems solely of geographical distribution. The previous framework and examples, however, emphasised their basis in the form and level of the process of *production*, and its relation to the existing pattern of geographical inequality. The normal emphasis simply on geographical distributional outcome goes along with a predisposition for analysis to concentrate only on space, on spatial differentiation, and on changes in the spatial surface. In fact, while spatial changes are most certainly important, the foregoing discussion has indicated that one should not assume that the rest of the relevant world remains constant over time. The requirements of production also change – in response to the pressures of the international and national economic system – and, therefore, so does the relevance to production of any given form of spatial differentiation.

An example is in order, so as to avoid any impression that only straw people are being attacked here. We shall concentrate on the issue of 'convergence' already referred to (and documented in KEEBLE, 1976; 1977). As has already been said, such convergence refers only to certain indicators, and by no means foreshadows the end of the regional problem, but clearly some changes are underway. Why?

In fact, most studies which cover this period (mid-1960's to early 1970's) are absolutely clear on the matter – the convergence was due to regional policy. Now, while I do *not* wish to argue that policy did not have an effect, it is interesting to examine a bit more closely how this conclusion is frequently reached. A common procedure is to project through time some notion of 'what would have happened', and then to analyse deviations from this putative behaviour pattern. The variable which is projected in this way is normally industrial location behaviour – or some effect of it, such as the inter-regional distribution of manufacturing employment – with appropriate proxy adjustments, for instance for cyclical variations in pressure of demand. The question asked is: did this effect of locational behaviour show any significant change around the mid-1960's – in other words at the period when regional policy was strengthened?

The method of enquiry, therefore, is couched entirely in terms of an explanation of changes in the locational behaviour of industry which relies on changes, not in industry itself, but only in the environment within which the locational decision takes place (the locational surface). Insofar as production is considered, it is dealt with by trend-projections. Such a method does not allow for account to be taken of any structural shifts within the economy. Neither does quantitative trend projection yield any information on the mechanisms underlying those trends. But it is precisely those mechanisms which may imply significant changes in the locational requirements of industry.[2] In contrast, the application of regional policy is seen as having increased in intensity relatively suddenly in the mid-1960's.

Now regional policy *was* certainly increased in intensity in the mid-1960's, and it certainly did alter the locational surface – for instance by changing the distribution of costs. But it is also true that over this period enormous changes have taken place within industry itself. Moreover, some of these changes increased in importance in the mid-1960's – precisely the period from which the phases both of intensive regional policy, and of convergence, also date. There have been structural changes both in the world economy and in the UK's relation to it. Competition has

[2] This criticism applies also to the normal method of assessing the effect on regional employment distribution of the absolute decline in manufacturing employment. This decline is normally considered simply as a quantitative constraint (for instance on the availability of mobile manufacturing employment). In fact it is itself only a reflection, but a reflection of important underlying changes – of increasingly critical conditions facing manufacturing industry, and of its response in terms both of declining rate of growth of output and of relatively increasing growth of labour productivity – with all the attendant implications for production and locational requirements.

become more severe. There has been a collapse of profitability and a decline of markets. There is at the present moment in the UK the most serious economic crisis since the 1930's. It can hardly be expected that these events would fail to have an effect on production. The relevant point here is that these developments have increased the relative importance of changes within the production processes of a number of sectors of industry. Moreover, our own research indicates clearly that these changes in production have in turn changed the locational requirements of the sectors concerned, and changed them in a manner which would indicate some tendency, quite independent of regional policy, towards convergence (see, for a detailed report on this, MASSEY and MEEGAN, forthcoming; and MASSEY, 1976). The 'labour factor' is a case in point. Thus, as already indicated in the consideration of spatial divisions of labour, recent changes in production in some sectors have tended to reduce the general level of skill-requirements, and thus to free industry from former locational constraints. Relatively, availability and low cost of labour are increasing in importance for many direct-production processes, in comparison with skill and adaptability. And it is in availability and low cost that peripheral regions have an advantage (see the review of evidence presented in KEEBLE, 1976, ch. 4). In other words, as well as the spatial surface changing, the response of certain industries to a *given* form of regional inequality – the nature of their spatial division of labour – may be being redefined. Given that some of the sectors affected in this way are quantitatively significant in the present evolution of spatial employment patterns, such changes could well be important components of the process of convergence which has been registered on certain indices of employment and unemployment.

The changes in regional distribution of employment, therefore, could be being contributed to, not only by regional policy, but also by the effects of the present crisis on industry's requirements. But many approaches to regional policy evaluation do not even include this as a possibility. Regional policy – i.e. the spatial surface – emerges as the only explanation because it is the only explanatory factor which is allowed to vary over time. The demands of industry are held constant. In fact, from the evidence I have examined, I should argue that it is likely that the *combination* of changes, in industry and in policy has been mutually reinforcing.[3] But the point which really emerges out of this illustrative example is that, commonly, the regional distribution of employment (and consequently the 'regional problem') is not just seen as a spatial *phenomenon*, it is also (if only implicitly) interpreted as being the result of purely spatial *processes*.

Something of an aside is necessary here. It should not be thought that the above discussion is intended to present an alternative analysis of changing regional

[3] By 'mutually-reinforcing' is meant more than simply the operation of industry and policy changes as additive factors. In particular, changes in production may have been one of the pre-conditions for advantage to be taken of regional policy. It is also possible, of course, as a number of authors argue, that the combination worked also the other way around – that regional policy (through the grants available at a period of restricted company liquidity) in turn encouraged or even enabled some of the investment in new processes of production.

patterns. It merely indicates an important component not considered by most current approaches. The changing use of space by a number of important sectors, and the emergence of new forms of spatial division of labour, has not on its own produced the considerable changes in spatial pattern at present under way. It has been combined with other effects of the economic crisis. In particular, it has been increased in relative importance – and consequently in its impact – by the slackening of the rate of growth of a number of sectors of manufacturing output. In such a situation, while new investment in capacity embodying new technology may continue, in response to competitive pressures to reduce costs, it will now – more than in a period of fast growth – be 'compensated for' by the scrapping of the least profitable capacity. (In a period of fast growth, in contrast, such new investment could simply add to capacity.) There is thus a double spatial effect. The new technology embodied in the new investment may enable, and require, a changed location, while employment is lost at the original point of production. Empirical investigation of such behaviour, and a detailed formal framework for its analysis is at present being elaborated in work by the present author and Richard Meegan at CES. The points to note in relation to the present argument are the following. First, *even* if the new investment is located in Development Areas entirely as a result of regional policy (which the previous argument about production technology would at least throw open to question) it is not this alone which would account for convergence. If the original location is in a Development Area there will of course not necessarily *be* convergence. And if the original location is in a non-assisted part of the country, it is not the location of the new investment alone, but its combination with a loss of jobs in the non-assisted area, which produces convergence. Second, it is necessary, if such phenomena are occurring, to be careful about the claims made for the effect of regional policy (or, in other words, purely spatial changes). While it will be true, on these assumptions, that the Development Areas will have more jobs than otherwise, this is not the same as regional policy accounting for convergence. Still less does it mean that regional policy has been a success. The regional problem continues. But third, and most important, is that such developments are crucially a result of changes, not in spatial configuration within the UK, but in the relation of the UK to the world economy as a whole.

In summary, I am not at all arguing that regional policy has had no effect (and certainly not that it should be discontinued). It is, however, important that assessments of this effect do not fail to take account of the changes going on in industry itself. Too many current interpretations of changing regional patterns ignore this relation to production and to the overall economic system. Too frequently spatial distribution is given its own autonomous existence. The fact that each form of distribution is the result of specific forms of production, is lost. This, in turn, enables problems which are in fact direct results of the productive system to be treated as matters entirely of spatial arrangement. The second thread of what is being argued is that, in any case, the convergence of regions on certain indices does not *in any way* imply an end to regional inequality. It is not merely that this is a convergence in a context of overall decline, but that, with the emergence of new forms of use of spatial unevenness by industry, the very *form* of regional inequality may to some degree be changing.

In what sense, then, are 'regional' problems *regional* problems? Clearly such inequalities do not result from a simple absolute deficiency. They are, rather, the outcome of the changing relationship between the requirements of private production for profit and the spatial surface. Again, while such a statement may appear as the essence of the obvious, its implications are frequently ignored. How many times has the 'inner city problem' been 'explained' in terms of characteristics totally internal to those areas? – to a supposed lack of skilled labour (the bulk of the evidence being to the contrary – see, for instance, MASSEY and MEEGAN, 1978), to the actions of planners (hardly likely, anyway, to be a dominant cause), or, worst of all, to the psychological propensities and sociological characteristics of their inhabitants? In fact, the reasons have changed over time, but the recent dramatic decline has resulted from pressures similar to those already mentioned – pressures for rationalisation and restructuring which derive from the crisis of the economy as a whole (see also FALK and MARTINOS, 1975). Again, how often are the problems of peripheral regions laid at the door of 'a lack of native entrepreneurship', a 'deficiency of atmosphere of growth'? But these are effects, not causes (and indeed if they are causes the policy implications are hard to imagine); FIRN (1975) gives some hints of the mechanisms involved.

By this means, regional problems are conceptualised, not as problems *experienced by* regions, but as problems for which, somehow, those regions are to blame. Moreover, this subtle substitution of geographical distribution alone for its combination with the changing requirements of production has a political effect. As with all purely 'distributional struggles', it is divisive: it sets one region against another, the inner cities against the peripheral regions, when the real problem lies at the aggregate level, in an overall deficiency of jobs, for instance, or an overall problem of deskilling.

A further, and rather different, point is that the conceptualisation of spatial differentiation as a 'spatial division of labour' challenges the frequent disaggregation of the regional problem into structural and locational components. Strictly, this disaggregation is merely a statistical exercise and may well help to disentangle processes, and suggest further questions. But frequently its status is extended – into summarising the regional problem, identifying it, even analysing it. Thus, to quote one example, but one which does offer a very clear definition: 'If one is to consider the ways in which regional policy might be developed so as to become more effective . . . the right starting point is to consider the underlying causes of the problem . . . inadequate growth may be thought to be the problem. But why should growth be inadequate? . . . There are two alternative hypotheses . . . According to the traditional view . . . the prime cause of the problem is that the regions have inherited an unfavourable economic structure, and that there is no reason why other industries should not be established in these regions to provide the necessary growth . . . Alternatively, it could be suggested that the problem regions, because of some endemic disadvantage such as their peripheral situation as regards the centre of the British economy, do not provide a satisfactory environment for the modern growth industries, that this is why these industries did not establish themselves in these areas in the first place and why it requires so much effort to persuade them to go there now' (McCRONE, 1969, p. 169). Clearly, the first spatial division of labour discussed, that of sectoral spatial specialisation, does conform to the structural component of such a disaggregation (it might even be the case that the preoccupation with this form of disaggregation may stem from here). Evidently, too, there are still elements of this form of problem in many regional economies – see the TOOTHILL REPORT, 1961; ODBER, 19655; BROWN, 1967 (all quoted in McCRONE, 1969). It is equally clear, however, that the second form of spatial division of labour, that based on locational hierarchies of production, can *not* be encapsulated in either of these products of statistical manipulation. Plants may be established within all regions in the hierarchy by a single company-division (certainly falling within one Minimum List Heading). This is evidently not a problem of sectoral industrial structure. Such a hierarchy is, moreover, likely to be established precisely in 'the modern growth industries' referred to by McCrone. Neither, therefore, is it a problem of this aspect of the locational component. Finally, because of the existence of such a hierarchy, it is unlikely that simple inter-regional comparisons of sectoral rates of growth will have much meaning.

The aim of this discussion is not, however, simply to point to some disadvantages of the structural/locational dichotomy, but to indicate that once again commonly-used statistical procedures fail even to address questions of the organisation of production, or of the dynamic of the economic system.

For what is at issue is the changing form of creation, and of use, by industry of specific types of spatial differentiation. Regional inequality is not a frictional or abnormal outcome of capitalist production. As the first example of a spatial division of labour indicated, the process of capital investment has historically normally been one of the opening up of some areas, and the desertion of others. The inner cities, at this moment, are being deserted. They are, moreover, being deserted for reasons relating directly to the requirements of internationally competitive and profitable production. THE COMMUNITY DEVELOPMENT PROJECT (1977) put it well:

> *It is clear that there are similarities between the way in which the urban problem is being discovered, defined and tackled now and the way the regional problem was taken up during and after the depression. Both are ways of defining particular problems of capital as problems of certain spatial areas, due to the characteristics of those areas. The importance of this technique is that it diverts attention from the way in which the problems that appear in particular places are really particular manifestations of general problems – problems of the way the economic system operates.*
>
> *Such an approach also puts across the problems of these areas, regions, inner cities and so on, so that they seem marginal – not in the sense of unimportant, but certainly peculiar to these areas; while things in general, of course, are fundamentally alright and "normal". All that remains to be done is to equalise indices of deprivation, achieve a "balanced" population, and so on. (p. 55)*

I would suggest, however, that the problem goes deeper than that. For it is also the case that spatial inequality may be positively *useful* for unplanned private production for profit. It may be the fact of spatial separation which enables the preservation for a longer period than otherwise of certain favourable conditions of production – low wages and lack of militancy may be easier to ensure in isolated areas, dependent maybe on only one or two sources of employment. The ability of a firm to move, say from an area in which labour is well-organised to an area in which it is not, may well make easier – for the firm – the introduction of new production methods which involve a change of workforce. The analysis by SECCHI (1977) of the Italian 'regional problem' reports on work which argues that 'the existence and growth of regional inequalities made the Italian economic system more flexible in terms of labour supply than it would have been in a better-balanced regional situation, given an equal rate of employment in the various sectors of the economy; or, in other words, that it gave the Italian economic system the possibility of a higher rate of technical progress for a given investment rate, than would have occurred in a well-balanced regional situation' (p. 36).

Finally, some comments on policy. While clearly the analysis so far indicates that the problem is not simply soluble, neither does that mean one can do nothing. First, at the simplest level of all, it is important to recognise that the problem will change – in nature and in geography. My contention is that something of that order is happening now. But it will only be possible to get to grips with analysing what is happening now if an effort is made to go beyond essentially statistical techniques and distributional outcomes to understand theoretically the mechanisms behind the numbers. Second, if the 'regional problem' is not a problem produced by regions, but by the organisation of production itself, neither is its solution simply a technical question. If production for profit may actually both imply and require such inequality, the issue of policy must be 'who pays?' There is a need to make explicit, political choices. Finally, the implication of this analysis is that intervention in spatial distribution cannot be divorced from issues of intervention at the level of production. To see regional policy and regional problems as simply questions of spatial distribution is completely inadequate.

Acknowledgements

I would particularly like to acknowledge the help of Richard Meegan, Centre for Environmental Studies, with whom much of the background research relevant to the arguments in this paper has been done. This paper was originally presented to a Regional Studies Association Conference, entitled, 'The Death of Regional Policy'.

References

Brown A. J. (1967) The Green Paper on the Development Areas, *National Institute Economic Review*, May, pp. 26–29

Chisholm M. and Oeppen J. (1973) *The Changing Pattern of Employment: Regional Specialisation and Industrial Localisation in Britain.* Croom Helm, London.

Community Development Project (1977) *The Costs of Industrial Change.*

Dixon R. J. and Thirwall A. P. (1975) *Regional Growth and Unemployment in the United Kingdom.* Macmillan, London.

Dunford M. F. (1977) 'Regional policy and the restructuring of capital', Sussex University: Urban and Regional Studies, Working Paper 4.

Falk N. and Martinos H. (1975) *'Inner City'*, Fabian Research Series 320, May.

Firn, J. (1975) External control and regional development: the case of Scotland, *Envir. Plann. A* 7, 393–414.

Hall P. (1974) *Urban and Regional Planning.* Penguin Books, Geography and Environmental Studies, Harmondsworth, Middlesex.

Keeble D. (1976) *Industrial Location and Planning in the United Kingdom,* Methuen, London.

Keeble D. (1977) Spatial policy in Britain: regional or urban? *Area* 9, 3–8.

Lipietz A. (1977) *Le Capital et Son Espace,* Maspero. Economie et Socialisme, p. 34.

Massey D. B. (1976) 'Restructuring and regionalism: some spatial effects of the crisis'. Paper presented to American Regional Science Association. Centre for Environmental Studies, Working Note 449.

Massey D. B. and Meegan R.A. (1978) 'Restructuring vs the cities', *Urban Studies,* 15.

Massey D.B. and Meegan R.A. The geography of industrial reorganisation: the spatial effects of the restructuring of the electrical engineering sector under the Industrial Reorganisation Corporation, *Progress in Planning,* Pergamon, Oxford.

McCrone G. (1969) *Regional Policy in Britain,* Unwin, University of Glasgow: Social and Economic Studies, 15.

McCrone G. (1975) 'The determinants of regional growth rates' in *Economic Sovereignty and Regional Policy* (Vaizey, J. Ed.) pp. 63–79. Gill and Macmillan, Dublin.

McDermoyy P. J. (1976) Ownership, organisation and regional dependence in the Scottish electronics industry, *Reg. Studies,* 10, 319–335.

Nedo Electronics EDC (1972) Annual Statistical Survey of the Electronics Industry, HMSO, London.

Nedo (1973) Industrial Review to 1977: Electronics, HMSO, London

North D. and Leigh R. (1976) Reflections on the micro-behavioural approach to regional analysis. Paper presented to the ninth annual conference of the Regional Science Association, mimeo.

Odber A. J. (1965) 'Regional policy in Great Britain' in: *Area Redevelopment Policies in Britain and the Countries of the Common Market,* pp. 410–421. US Department of Commerce and Area Redevelopment Administration.

Secchi B. (1977) Central and peripheral regions in a process of economic development: The Italian case, in *Alternative Frameworks for Analysis* (Massey D. B. and Batey P. W. J. Eds). London Papers in Regional Science, Vol. 7. Pion, London.

Toothill Report (1962) Report of the Committee of Enquiry on the Scottish Economy, Scottish Council (Development and Industry).

Trade and Industry (1977) Regional Development Programme for the United Kingdom, *Trade and Industry,* 11 February, pp. 358–362.

Westaway J. (1974) 'The spatial hierarchy of business organisations and its implications for the British urban system' *Reg. Studies* 8, 145–155.

26

FROM *ORIENTALISM*

Edward Said

As a Palestinian and Professor of English and Comparative Literature (at Columbia University, New York), Edward Said has set himself the task of relating the two aspects of his self: the 'colonized' subject and the authority on the literature of a (former) major imperial state. He has partly done so through a series of books that relate the history of Western imperialism to the representations of the rest of the world found in English (and other European) literature, music, historiography, and social science. His most influential book – from which the extracts reproduced here are taken – is probably *Orientalism*, first published in 1978. In these extracts Said points out how the geography of the world in the Western discourse of 'Orientalism' has been organized around a series of oppositions based on the essential difference between the West and the Rest. In Said's view this 'imaginative geography' serves both to regionalize the world and to discipline it – since knowledge flows from power. All of the smaller divisions of space conventionally used to break down the world into its parts follow from the primary division of West and East. Such regions are not natural or pre-given, but depend upon and reproduce imperial and neo-colonial power. Said's initial exploration of the historical roots of global geographical divisions remains an immensely influential rendering of the process whereby Western history, geography and social science have come to reproduce a set of 'commonsensical' understandings that stand in need of constant interrogation by those who study the 'regions' of the world. After Said, regionalization at whatever geographical scale can never again be regarded as an entirely 'innocent' or apolitical exercise.
Source: *Orientalism*. New York: Vintage, 1978, pp. 1–4, 54–8.

On a visit to Beirut during the terrible civil war of 1975–1976 a French journalist wrote regretfully of the gutted downtown area that "it had once seemed to belong to . . . the Orient of Chateaubriand and Nerval."[1] He was right about the place, of

[1] Thierry Desjardins, *Le Martyre du Liban* (Paris: Plon, 1976), p. 14.

course, especially so far as a European was concerned. The Orient was almost a European invention, and had been since antiquity a place of romance, exotic beings, haunting memories and landscapes, remarkable experiences. Now it was disappearing; in a sense it had happened, its time was over. Perhaps it seemed irrelevant that Orientals themselves had something at stake in the process, that even in the time of Chateaubriand and Nerval Orientals had lived there, and that now it was they who were suffering; the main thing for the European visitor was a European representation of the Orient and its contemporary fate, both of which had a privileged communal significance for the journalist and his French readers.

Americans will not feel quite the same about the Orient, which for them is much more likely to be associated very differently with the Far East (China and Japan, mainly). Unlike the Americans, the French and the British – less so the Germans, Russian, Spanish, Portuguese, Italians, and Swiss – have had a long tradition of what I shall be calling *Orientalism,* a way of coming to terms with the Orient that is based on the Orient's special place in European Western experience. The Orient is not only adjacent to Europe; it is also the place of Europe's greatest and richest and oldest colonies, the source of its civilizations and languages, its cultural contestant, and one of its deepest and most recurring images of the Other. In addition, the Orient has helped to define Europe (or the West) as its contrasting image, idea, personality, experience. Yet none of this Orient is merely imaginative. The Orient is an integral part of European *material* civilization and culture. Orientalism expresses and represents that part culturally and even ideologically as a mode of discourse with supporting institutions, vocabulary, scholarship, imagery, doctrines, even colonial bureaucracies and colonial styles. In contrast, the American understanding of the Orient will seem considerably less dense, although our recent Japanese, Korean, and Indochinese adventures ought now to be creating a more sober, more realistic "Oriental" awareness. Moreover, the vastly expanded American political and economic role in the Near East (the Middle East) makes great claims on our understanding of that Orient.

It will be clear to the reader (and will become clearer still throughout the many pages that follow) that by Orientalism I mean several things, all of them, in my opinion, interdependent. The most readily accepted designation for Orientalism is an academic one, and indeed the label still serves in a number of academic institutions. Anyone who teaches, writes about, or researches the Orient – and this applies whether the person is an anthropologist, sociologist, historian, or philologist – either in its specific or its general aspects, is an Orientalist, and what he or she does is Orientalism. Compared with *Oriental studies* or *area studies,* it is true that the term *Orientalism* is less preferred by specialists today, both because it is too vague and general and because it connotes the high-handed executive attitude of nineteenth-century and early-twentieth-century European colonialism. Nevertheless books are written and congresses held with "the Orient" as their main focus, with the Orientalist in his new or old guise as their main authority. The point is that even if it does not survive as it once did, Orientalism lives on academically through its doctrines and theses about the Orient and the Oriental.

Related to this academic tradition, whose fortunes, transmigrations, specializations, and transmissions are in part the subject of this study, is a more general meaning for Orientalism. Orientalism is a style of thought based upon an ontological and epistemological distinction made between "the Orient" and (most of the time) "the Occident." Thus a very large mass of writers, among whom are poets, novelists, philosophers, political theorists, economists, and imperial administrators, have accepted the basic distinction between East and West as the starting point for elaborate theories, epics, novels, social descriptions, and political accounts concerning the Orient, its people, customs, "mind," destiny, and so on. *This* Orientalism can accommodate Aeschylus, say, and Victor Hugo, Dante and Karl Marx. A little later in this introduction I shall deal with the methodological problems one encounters in so broadly construed a "field" as this.

The interchange between the academic and the more or less imaginative meanings of Orientalism is a constant one, and since the late eighteenth century there has been a considerable, quite disciplined – perhaps even regulated – traffic between the two. Here I come to the third meaning of Orientalism, which is something more historically and materially defined than either of the other two. Taking the late eighteenth century as a very roughly defined starting point Orientalism can be discussed and analyzed as the corporate institution for dealing with the Orient – dealing with it by making statements about it, authorizing views of it, describing it, by teaching it, settling it, ruling over it: in short, Orientalism as a Western style for dominating, restructuring, and having authority over the Orient. I have found it useful here to employ Michel Foucault's notion of a discourse, as described by him in *The Archaeology of Knowledge* and in *Discipline and Punish*, to identify Orientalism. My contention is that without examining Orientalism as a discourse one cannot possibly understand the enormously systematic discipline by which European culture was able to manage – and even produce – the Orient politically, sociologically, militarily, ideologically, scientifically, and imaginatively during the post-Enlightenment period. Moreover, so authoritative a position did Orientalism have that I believe no one writing, thinking, or acting on the Orient could do so without taking account of the limitations on thought and action imposed by Orientalism. In brief, because of Orientalism the Orient was not (and is not) a free subject of thought or action. This is not to say that Orientalism unilaterally determines what can be said about the Orient, but that it is the whole network of interests inevitably brought to bear on (and therefore always involved in) any occasion when that peculiar entity "the Orient" is in question. How this happens is what this book tries to demonstrate. It also tries to show that European culture gained in strength and identity by setting itself off against the Orient as a sort of surrogate and even underground self.

Historically and culturally there is a quantitative as well as a qualitative difference between the Franco-British involvement in the Orient and – until the period of American ascendancy after World War II – the involvement of every other European and Atlantic power. To speak of Orientalism therefore is to speak mainly, although not exclusively, of a British and French cultural enterprise, a project whose dimensions take in such disparate realms as the imagination itself, the whole of India and the Levant, the Biblical texts and the Biblical lands, the spice trade, colonial armies and a long tradition of colonial administrators, a formidable scholarly corpus, innumerable Oriental "experts" and "hands", an Oriental professorate, a complex array of "Oriental" ideas (Oriental despotism, Oriental splendor, cruelty, sensuality), many Eastern sects, philosophies, and wisdoms domesticated for local European use – the list can be extended more or less indefinitely. My point is that Orientalism derives from a particular closeness experienced between Britain and France and the Orient, which until the early nineteenth century had really meant only India and the Bible lands. From the beginning of the nineteenth century until the end of World War II France and Britain dominated the Orient and Orientalism; since World War II America has dominated the Orient, and approaches it as France and Britain once did. Out of that closeness, whose dynamic is enormously productive even if it always demonstrates the comparatively greater strength of the Occident (British, French, or American), comes the large body of texts I call Orientalist . . .

Imaginative Geography and Its Representations: Orientalizing the Oriental

It is perfectly possible to argue that some distinctive objects are made by the mind, and that these objects, while appearing to exist objectively, have only a fictional reality. A group of people living on a few acres of land will set up boundaries between their land and its immediate surroundings and the territory beyond, which they call "the land of the barbarians." In other words, this universal practice of designating in one's mind a familiar space which is "ours" and an unfamiliar space beyond "ours" which is "theirs" is a way of making geographical distinctions that *can be* entirely arbitrary. I use the word "arbitrary" here because imaginative geography of the "our land–barbarian land" variety does not require that the barbarians acknowledge the distinction. It is enough for "us" to set up these boundaries in our own minds; "they" become "they" accordingly, and both their territory and their mentality are designated as different from "ours." To a certain extent modern and primitive societies seem thus to derive a sense of their identities negatively. A fifth-century Athenian was very likely to feel himself to be nonbarbarian as much as he positively felt himself to be Athenian. The geographic boundaries accompany the social, ethnic, and cultural ones in expected ways. Yet often the sense in which someone feels himself to be not-foreign is based on a very unrigorous idea of what is "out there," beyond one's own territory. All kinds of suppositions, associations, and fictions appear to crowd the unfamiliar space outside one's own.

The French philosopher Gaston Bachelard once wrote an analysis of what he called the poetics of space.[28] The inside of a house, he said, acquires a sense of intimacy, secrecy, security, real or imagined, because of the experiences that come to

[28] Gaston Bachelard, *The Poetics of Space*, trans. Maria Jolas (New York: Orion Press, 1964).

seem appropriate for it. The objective space of a house – its corners, corridors, cellar, rooms – is far less important than what poetically it is endowed with, which is usually a quality with an imaginative or figurative value we can name and feel: thus a house may be haunted, or homelike, or prisonlike, or magical. So space acquires emotional and even rational sense by a kind of poetic process, whereby the vacant or anonymous reaches of distance are converted into meaning for us here. The same process occurs when we deal with time. Much of what we associate with or even know about such periods as "long ago" or "the beginning" or "at the end of time" is poetic – made up. For a historian of Middle Kingdom Egypt, "long ago" will have a very clear sort of meaning, but even this meaning does not totally dissipate the imaginative, quasi-fictional quality one senses lurking in a time very different and distant from our own. For there is no doubt that imaginative geography and history help the mind to intensify its own sense of itself by dramatizing the distance and difference between what is close to it and what is far away. This is no less true of the feelings we often have that we would have been more "at home" in the sixteenth century or in Tahiti.

Yet there is no use in pretending that all we know about time and space, or rather history and geography, is more than anything else imaginative. There are such things as positive history and positive geography which in Europe and the United States have impressive achievements to point to. Scholars now do know more about the world, its past and present, than they did, for example, in Gibbon's time. Yet this is not to say that they know all there is to know, nor, more important, is it to say that what they know has effectively dispelled the imaginative geographical and historical knowledge I have been considering. We need not decide here whether this kind of imaginative knowledge infuses history and geography, or whether in some way it overrides them. Let us just say for the time being that it is there as something *more* than what appears to be merely positive knowledge.

Almost from earliest times in Europe the Orient was something more than what was empirically known about it. At least until the early eighteenth century, as R. W. Southern has so elegantly shown, European understanding of one kind of Oriental culture, the Islamic, was ignorant but complex.[29] For certain associations with the East – not quite ignorant, not quite informed – always seem to have gathered around the notion of an Orient. Consider first the demarcation between Orient and West. It already seems bold by the time of the *Iliad*. Two of the most profoundly influential qualities associated with the East appear in Aeschylus's *The Persians*, the earliest Athenian play extant, and in *The Bacchae* of Euripides, the very last one extant. Aeschylus portrays the sense of disaster overcoming the Persians when they learn that their armies, led by King Xerxes, have been destroyed by the Greeks. The chorus sings the following ode:

Now all Asia's land
Moans in emptiness.

[29] R. W. Southern, *Western Views of Islam in the Middle Ages* (Cambridge, MA; Harvard University Press, 1962), p. 14.

Xerxes led forth, oh oh!
Xerxes destroyed, woe, woe!
Xerxes' plans have all miscarried
In ships of the sea.
Why did Darius then
Bring no harm to his men
When he led them into battle,
That beloved leader of men from Susa?[30]

What matters here is that Asia speaks through and by virtue of the European imagination, which is depicted as victorious over Asia, that hostile "other" world beyond the seas. To Asia are given the feelings of emptiness, loss, and disaster that seem thereafter to reward Oriental challenges to the West; and also, the lament that in some glorious past Asia fared better, was itself victorious over Europe.

In *The Bacchae*, perhaps the most Asiatic of all the Attic dramas, Dionysus is explicitly connected with his Asian origins and with the strangely threatening excesses of Oriental mysteries. Pentheus, king of Thebes, is destroyed by his mother, Agave, and her fellow bacchantes. Having defied Dionysus by not recognizing either his power or his divinity, Pentheus is thus horribly punished, and the play ends with a general recognition of the eccentric god's terrible power. Modern commentators on *The Bacchae* have not failed to note the play's extraordinary range of intellectual and aesthetic effects; but there has been no escaping the additional historical detail that Euripides "was surely affected by the new aspect that the Dionysiac cults must have assumed in the light of the foreign ecstatic religions of Bendis, Cybele, Sabazius, Adonis, and Isis, which were introduced from Asia Minor and the Levant and swept through Piraeus and Athens during the frustrating and increasingly irrational years of the Peloponnesian War."[31]

The two aspects of the Orient that set it off from the West in this pair of plays will remain essential motifs of European imaginative geography. A line is drawn between two continents. Europe is powerful and articulate; Asia is defeated and distant. Aeschylus *represents* Asia, makes her speak in the person of the aged Persian queen, Xerxes' mother. It is Europe that articulates the Orient; this articulation is the prerogative, not of a puppet master, but of a genuine creator, whose life-giving power represents, animates, constitutes the otherwise silent and dangerous space beyond familiar boundaries. There is an analogy between Aeschylus's orchestra, which contains the Asiatic world as the playwright conceives it, and the learned envelope of Orientalist scholarship, which also will hold in the vast, amorphous Asiatic sprawl for sometimes sympathetic but always

30 Aeschylus, *The Persians*, trans. Anthony J. Podleck (Englewood Cliffs, N. J.: Prentice-Hall, 1970), pp. 73–4.

31 Euripides, *The Bacchae*, trans. Geoffrey S. Kirk (Englewood Cliffs, N. J.: Prentice-Hall, 1970), p.3. For further discussion of the Europe-Orient distinction see Santo Mazzarino, *Fra oriente e occidente: Ricerche di storia greca arcaica* (Florence: La Nuova Italia, 1947), and Denys Hay, *Europe: The Emergence of an Idea* (Edinburgh: Edinburgh University Press, 1968).

dominating scrutiny. Secondly, there is the motif of the Orient as insinuating danger. Rationality is undermined by Eastern excesses, those mysteriously attractive opposites to what seem to be normal values. The difference separating East from West is symbolized by the sternness with which, at first, Pentheus rejects the hysterical bacchantes. When later he himself becomes a bacchant, he is destroyed not so much for having given in to Dionysus as for having incorrectly assessed Dionysus's menace in the first place. The lesson that Euripides intends is dramatized by the presence in the play of Cadmus and Tiresias, knowledgeable older men who realize that "sovereignty" alone does not rule men;[32] there is such a thing as judgment, they say, which means sizing up correctly the force of alien powers and expertly coming to terms with them. Hereafter Oriental mysteries will be taken seriously, not least because they challenge the rational Western mind to new exercises of its enduring ambition and power.

But one big division, as between West and Orient, leads to other smaller ones, especially as the normal enterprises of civilization provoke such outgoing activities as travel, conquest, new experiences. In classical Greece and Rome geographers, historians, public figures like Caesar, orators, and poets added to the fund of taxonomic lore separating races, regions, nations, and minds from each other; much of that was self-serving, and existed to prove that Romans and Greeks were superior to other kinds of people. But concern with the Orient had its own tradition of classification and hierarchy. From at least the second century B.C. on, it was lost on no traveler or eastward-looking and ambitious Western potentate that Herodotus – historian, traveler, inexhaustibly curious chronicler – and Alexander – king warrior, scientific conqueror – had been in the Orient before. The Orient was therefore subdivided into realms previously known, visited, conquered, by Herodotus and Alexander as well as their epigones, and those realms not previously known, visited, conquered. Christianity completed the setting up of main intra-Oriental spheres: there was a Near Orient and a Far Orient, a familiar Orient, which René Grousset calls "l'empire du Levant,"[33] and a novel Orient. The Orient therefore alternated in the mind's geography between being an Old World to which one returned, as to Eden or Paradise, there to set up a new version of the old, and being a wholly new place to which one came as Columbus came to America, in order to set up a New World (although, ironically, Columbus himself thought that he discovered a new part of the Old World). Certainly neither of these Orients was purely one thing or the other: it is their vacillations, their tempting suggestiveness, their capacity for entertaining and confusing the mind, that are interesting.

Consider how the Orient, and in particular the Near Orient, became known in the West as its great complementary opposite since antiquity. There were the Bible and the rise of Christianity; there were travelers like Marco Polo who charted the trade routes and patterned a regulated system of commercial exchange, and after

[32] Euripides, *Bacchae*, p. 52.

[33] René Grousset, *L'Empire du Levant: Histoire de la question d'Orient* (Paris: Payot, 1946).

him Lodovico di Varthema and Pietro della Valle; there were fabulists like Mandeville; there were the redoubtable conquering Eastern movements, principally Islam, of course; there were the militant pilgrims, chiefly the Crusaders. Altogether an internally structured archive is built up from the literature that belongs to these experiences. Out of this comes a restricted number of typical encapsulations: the journey, the history, the fable, the stereotype, the polemical confrontation. These are the lenses through which the Orient is experienced, and they shape the language, perception, and form of the encounter between East and West. What gives the immense number of encounters some unity, however, is the vacillation I was speaking about earlier. Something patently foreign and distant acquires, for one reason or another, a status more rather than less familiar. One tends to stop judging things either as completely novel or as completely well known; a new median category emerges, a category that allows one to see new things, things seen for the first time, as versions of a previously known thing.

27

DECONSTRUCTING THE MAP

J. B. Harley

The division of the world into the regions Said (**chapter 26**) sees as emerging out of the East-West opposition is typically rendered by mapping and naming the regional units. Until recently the study of cartography has been concerned largely with the technical and professional practices association with map-making. In the 1970s the history of cartography suddenly began to explore the modern beginnings of map-making in the context of European state-formation and imperial expansion rather than simply in terms of the national histories of important cartographers, explorers, and mapping organizations. Although there were isolated precursors, such as H. R. Wilkinson's remarkable book *Maps and politics: a review of the ethnographic cartography of Macedonia* (Liverpool, 1951), the leader of this critical turn in the history of cartography was J. B. (Brian) Harley (1932–1991), a British geographer who moved to the United States in the early 1980s to work with the American Geographical Society library at the University of Wisconsin, Milwaukee. In a spate of writings Harley interrogated the connections between maps, knowledge, and power, suggesting that maps have long been important, if neglected, instruments of nationalism and imperialism. In the article reproduced here he presents a general overview of his perspective. Particularly important to Harley throughout his work was the role of maps in 'normalizing' the division of space into states and other administrative units. As part of a political 'sign system' maps provide one of the most intellectually powerful ways in which the world is divided up into the geographic units that then pass into common use as 'natural' features of the world. From this point of view, maps serve a mediating function between the deployment of power, on the one hand, and the construction of knowledge, on the other. This is a geographical elaboration on points made previously about the disciplining influence of apparently simple and 'innocent' technocratic activities, by writers such as Michel Foucault.

Source: Deconstructing the map. *Cartographica* 26, 1–20, 1989.

A map says to you, "Read me carefully, follow me closely, doubt me not." It says, "I am the earth in the palm of your hand. Without me, you are alone and lost."

And indeed you are. Were all the maps in the world destroyed and vanished under the direction of some malevolent hand, each man would be blind again, each city be made a stranger to the next, each landmark become a meaningless signpost pointing to nothing.

Yet, looking at it, feeling it, running a finger along its lines, it is a cold thing, a map, humourless and dull, born of calipers and a draughtsman's board. That coastline there, that ragged scrawl of scarlet ink, shows neither sand nor sea nor rock; it speaks of no mariner, blundering full sail in wakeless seas, to bequeath, on sheepskin or a slab of wood, a priceless scribble to posterity. This brown blot that marks a mountain has, for the casual eye, no other significance, though twenty men, or ten, or only one, may have squandered life to climb it. Here is a valley, there a swamp, and there a desert; and here is a river that some curious and courageous soul, like a pencil in the hand of God, first traced with bleeding feet.

Beryl Markham, 1983[1]

The pace of conceptual exploration in the history of cartography – searching for alternative ways of understanding maps – is slow. Some would say that its achievements are largely cosmetic. Applying conceptions of literary history to the history of cartography, it would appear that we are still working largely in either a 'premodern,' or a 'modern' rather than in a 'postmodern' climate of thought.[2] A list of individual explorations would, it is true, contain some that sound impressive. Our students can now be directed to writings that draw on the ideas of information theory, linguistics, semiotics, structuralism, phenomenology, developmental theory, hermeneutics, iconology, marxism, and ideology. We can point to the names in our footnotes of (among others) Cassirer, Gombrich, Piaget, Panofsky, Kuhn, Barthes and Eco. Yet despite these symptoms of change, we are still, willingly or unwillingly, the prisoners of our own past.

My basic argument in this essay is that we should encourage an epistemological shift in the way we interpret the nature of cartography. For historians of cartography, I believe a major roadblock to understanding is that we still accept uncritically the broad consensus, with relatively few dissenting voices, of what *cartographers* tell us maps are supposed to be. In particular, we often tend to work from the premise that mappers engage in an unquestionably 'scientific' or 'objective' form of knowledge creation. Of course, cartographers believe they have to say this to remain credible but historians do not have that obligation. It is better for us to begin from the premise that cartography is seldom what cartographers say it is.

As they embrace computer-assisted methods and Geographical Information Systems, the scientistic rhetoric of map makers is becoming more strident. The 'culture of technics' is everywhere rampant. We are told that the journal now

[1] Beryl Markham, *West with the Night*. New York: North Point Press, 1983.

[2] For these distinctions see Terry Eagleton, *Literary Theory: An Introduction*. Minneapolis: University of Minnesota Press, 1983; for an account situated closer to the direct concerns of cartography see Maurizio Ferraris, "Postmodernism and the Deconstruction of Modernism," *Design Issues* 4/1 and 2, Special Issue, 1988: 12–24.

named *The American Cartographer* will become *Cartography and Geographical Information Systems*. Or, in a strangely ambivalent gesture toward the nature of maps, the British Cartographic Society proposes that there should be two definitions of cartography, "one for professional cartographers and the other for the public at large." A definition "for use in communication with the general public" would be "Cartography is the art, science and technology of making maps": that for 'practicing cartographers' would be "Cartography is the science and technology of analyzing and interpreting geographic relationships, and communicating the results by means of maps."[3] Many may find it surprising that 'art' no longer exists in 'professional' cartography. In the present context, however, these signs of ontological schizophrenia can also be read as reflecting an urgent need to rethink the nature of maps from different perspectives. The question arises as to whether the notion of a progressive science is a myth partly created by cartographers in the course of their own professional development. I suggest that it has been accepted too uncritically by a wider public and by other scholars who work with maps.[4] For those concerned with the history of maps it is especially timely that we challenge the cartographer's assumptions. Indeed, if the history of cartography is to grow as an interdisciplinary subject among the humanities and social sciences, new ideas are essential.

The question becomes how do we as historians of cartography escape from the normative models of cartography? How do we allow new ideas to come in? How do we begin to write a cartographic history as genuinely revisionist as Louis Marin's 'The King and his Geometer' (in the context of a seventeenth-century map of Paris) or William Boelhower's 'The Culture of the Map' (in the context of sixteenth-century world maps showing America for the first time)?[5] These are two studies informed by postmodernism. In this essay I also adopt a strategy aimed at the deconstruction of the map.

The notion of deconstruction[6] is also a password for the postmodern enterprise. Deconstructionist strategies can now be found not only in philosophy but also in localized disciplines, especially in literature, and in other subjects such as architecture, planning and, more recently, geography.[7] I shall specifically use a

[3] Reported in *Cartographic Perspectives: Bulletin of the North American Cartographic Information Society* 1/1, 1989: 4.

[4] Others have made the same point: see, especially, the trenchantly deconstructive turn of the essay by Denis Wood and John Fels "Designs on Signs/Myth and Meaning in Maps," *Cartographica* 23/3, 1986: 54–103.

[5] Louis Marin, *Portrait of the King*, trans. Martha M. Houle, *Theory and History of Literature* 57. Minneapolis: University of Minnesota Press, 1988: 169–79; William Boelhower, *Through a Glass Darkly: Ethnic Semiosis in American Literature*. Venezia: Edizioni Helvetia, 1984: esp. 41–53. See also, Boelhower's "Inventing America: A Model of Cartographic Semiosis," *Word and Image* 4/2, 1988: 475–97.

[6] Deriving from the writings of Jacques Derrida: for exposition see the translator's Preface to Jacques Derrida, *Of Grammatology*, trans. Gayatri Chakratvorty Spivak. Baltimore: The John Hopkins University Press, 1976: ix-lxxxvii; Christopher Norris, *Deconstruction: Theory and Practice*. London: Methuen, 1982; and Christopher Norris, *Derrida*, Cambridge, Mass.: Harvard University Press, 1987.

[7] On architecture and planning see, for example, *The Design Professions and the Built Environment*, ed.

deconstructionist tactic to break the assumed link between reality and representation which has dominated cartographic thinking, has led it in the pathway of 'normal science' since the Enlightenment, and has also provided a ready-made and 'taken for granted' epistemology for the history of cartography. The objective is to suggest that an alternative epistemology, rooted in social theory rather than in scientific positivism, is more appropriate to the history of cartography. It will be shown that even 'scientific' maps are a product not only of "the rules of the order of geometry and reason" but also of the "norms and values of the order of social . . . tradition."[8] Our task is to search for the social forces that have structured cartography and to locate the presence of power – and its effects – in all map knowledge.

The ideas in this particular essay owe most to writings by Foucault and Derrida. My approach is deliberately eclectic because in some respects the theoretical positions of these two authors are incompatible. Foucault anchors texts in socio-political realities and constructs systems for organizing knowledge of the kind that Derrida loves to dismantle.[9] But even so, by combining different ideas on a new terrain, it may be possible to devise a scheme of social theory with which we can begin to interrogate the hidden agendas of cartography. Such a scheme offers no 'solution' to an historical interpretation of the cartographic record, nor a precise method or set of techniques, but as a broad strategy it may help to locate some of the fundamental forces that have driven map-making in both European and non-European societies. From Foucault's writings, the key revelation has been the omnipresence of power in all knowledge, even though that power is invisible or implied, including the particular knowledge encoded in maps and atlases. Derrida's notion of the rhetoricity of all texts has been no less a challenge.[10] It demands a search for metaphor and rhetoric in maps where previously scholars had found only measurement and topography. Its central question is reminiscent of Korzybski's much older dictum "The map is not the territory"[11] but deconstruction goes further to bring the issue of how the map represents place into much sharper focus.

Deconstruction urges us to read between the lines of the map –"in the margins of the text" – and through its tropes to discover the silences and contradictions that

Paul L. Knox. London: Croom Helm, 1988; Derek Gregory, "Postmodernism and the Politics of Social Theory," *Environment and Planning D: Society and Space* 5, 1987: 245–48; on geography see Michael Dear, "The Postmodern Challenge: Reconstructing Human Geography," *Transactions, Institute of British Geographers* (New Series), 13, 1988: 262–74.

[8] Marin, *Portrait of the King*, 173, the full quotation appears later in this article.

[9] As an introduction I have found to be particularly useful Edward W. Said, "The Problem of Textuality: Two Exemplary Positions," *Critical Inquiry* 4/4, Summer 1978: 673–714; also the chapters 'Jacques Derrida' by David Hoy and 'Michel Foucault' by Mark Philp in Quentin Skinner, ed., *The Return of Grand Theory in the Human Sciences*. Cambridge: Cambridge University Press, 1985: 41–64: 65–82.

[10] On the other hand, I do not adopt some of the more extreme positions attributed to Derrida. For example, it would be unacceptable for a social history of cartography to adopt the view that nothing lies outside the text.

[11] Alfred Korzybski, *Science and Sanity: An Introduction to Non-Artistotelian Systems and General Semantics*, 3rd ed. with new pref. Lakeville, Connecticut: The International Non-Aristotelian Library Pub. Co., 1948: 58, 247, 498, 750–51.

challenge the apparent honesty of the image. We begin to learn that cartographic facts are only facts within a specific cultural perspective. We start to understand how maps, like art, far from being "a transparent opening to the world," are but "a particular human way . . . of looking at the world."[12]

In pursuing this strategy I shall develop three threads of argument. First, I shall examine the discourse of cartography in the light of some of Foucault's ideas about the play of rules within discursive formations. Second, drawing on one of Derrida's central positions I will examine the textuality of maps and, in particular, their rhetorical dimension. Third, returning to Foucault, I will consider how maps work in society as a form of power-knowledge.

The Rules of Cartography

One of Foucault's primary units of analysis is the discourse. A discourse has been defined as "a system of possibility for knowledge."[13] Foucault's method was to ask, it has been said,

> *what rules permit certain statements to be made; what rules order these statements; what rules permit us to identify some statements as true and others as false; what rules allow the construction of a map, model or classification system . . . what rules are revealed when an object of discourse is modified or transformed . . . Whenever sets of rules of these kinds can be identified, we are dealing with a discursive formation or discourse.*[14]

The key question for us then becomes, "What type of rules have governed the development of cartography?" Cartography I define as a body of theoretical and practical knowledge that map-makers employ to construct maps as a distinct mode of visual representation. The question is, of course, historically specific: the rules of cartography vary in different societies. Here I refer particularly to two distinctive sets of rules that underlie and dominate the history of Western cartography since the seventeenth century.[15] One set may be defined as governing the technical production of maps and are made explicit in the cartographic treatises and writings of the period.[16] The other set relates to the cultural production of maps. These must be understood in a broader historical context than either scientific procedure or technique. They are, moreover, rules that are usually ignored by cartographers so that they form a hidden aspect of their discourse.

12 H. G. Blocker, *Philosophy and Art*, New York: Charles Scribner's Sons, 1979: 43.

13 Mark Philp, 'Michel Foucault,' *In* Skinner, *The Return of Grand Theory*: 69.

14 *Ibid.*

15 'Western cartography' is defined as the types of survey mapping first fully visible in the European Enlightenment and which then spread to other areas of the world as part of European overseas expansion.

16 The history of these technical rules has been extensively written about in the history of cartography, though not in terms of their social implications nor in Foucault's sense of discourse: see, for example, the later chapters of G. R. Crone, *Maps and Their Makers: An Introduction to the History of Cartography*, 1st ed., 1953, 5th ed. Folkestone, Kent: Dawson; Hamden, Conn.: Archon Books, 1978.

The first set of cartographic rules can thus be defined in terms of a scientific epistemology. From at least the seventeenth century onward, European map-makers and map users have increasingly promoted a standard scientific model of knowledge and cognition. The object of mapping is to produce a 'correct' relational model of the terrain. Its assumptions are that the objects in the world to be mapped are real and objective, and that they enjoy an existence independent of the cartographer; that their reality can be expressed in mathematical terms; that systematic observation and measurement offer the only route to cartographic truth; and that this truth can be independently verified.[17] The procedures of both surveying and map construction came to share strategies similar to those in science in general: cartography also documents a history of more precise instrumentation and measurement; increasingly complex classifications of its knowledge and a proliferation of signs for its representation; and, especially from the nineteenth century onward, the growth of institutions and a 'professional' literature designed to monitor the application and propagation of the rules. [18] Morever, although cartographers have continued to pay lip service to the 'art and science' of mapmaking, [19] art, as we have seen, is being edged off the map. It has often been accorded a cosmetic rather than a central role in cartographic communication.[20] Even philosophers of visual communication – such as Arnheim, Eco, Gombrich, and Goodman[21] – have tended to categorize maps as a type of congruent diagram – as analogs, models, or 'equivalents' creating a similitude of reality – and, in essence, different from art or painting. A 'scientific' cartography (so it was believed) would be untainted by social factors. Even today many cartographers are puzzled by the suggestion that political and sociological theory could throw light on their practices. They will probably shudder at the mention of deconstruction.

17 For a discussion of these characteristics in relation to science in general see P. N. Campbell, "Scientific Discourse," *Philosophy and Rhetoric* 6/1, 1973: also Steve Woolgar, *Science: The Very Idea*. Chichester, Sussex: Ellis Horwood, 1988, esp. Chapter 1, and R. Hooykaas, "The Rise of Modern Science: When and Why?" *The British Journal for the History of Science* 20/4, 1987; 453–73, for a more specifically historical context.

18 For evidence see John A. Wolter, "The Emerging Discipline of Cartography," Ph.D. Diss., University of Minnesota, 1975; also, "Cartography – an Emerging Discipline," *The Canadian Cartographer*, 12/2, 1975: 210–216.

19 See, for example, the definition of cartography in International Cartographic Association, *Multilingual Dictionary of Technical Terms in Cartography*, ed. E. Meynen. Wiesbaden: Franz Steiner Verlag, 1973, 1, 3: or, more recently, Helen M. Wallis and Arthur H. Robinson, eds. *Cartographical Innovations: An International Handbook of Mapping Terms to 1900*. Tring, Herts: Map Collector Publications and International Cartographic Association, 1987, xi, where cartography "includes the study of maps as scientific documents and works of art."

20 See the discussion in J. Morris, "The Magic of Maps: The Art of Cartography," M. A. Diss., University of Hawaii, 1982.

21 Rudolf Arnheim, "The Perception of Maps," *In* Rudolf Arnheim, *New Essays on the Psychology of Art*. Berkeley: University of California Press, 1986: 194–202; Umberto Eco, *A Theory of Semiotics*. Bloomington: Indiana University Press, 1976: 245–57; E. Gombrich, "Mirror and Map: Theories of Pictorial Representation," *Philosophical Transactions of the Royal Society of London*, Series B, vol. 270, Biological Sciences, 1975: 119–49; and Nelson Goodman, *Languages of Art: An Approach to a Theory of Symbols*. Indianapolis and New York: Bobbs-Merrill, 1968: 170–171; 228–30.

The acceptance of the map as 'a mirror of nature' (to employ Richard Rorty's phrase[22]) also results in a number of other characteristics of cartographic discourse even where these are not made explicit. Most striking is the belief in progress: that, by the application of science ever more precise representations of reality can be produced. The methods of cartography have delivered a "true, probable, progressive, or high confirmed knowledge."[23] This mimetic bondage has led to a tendency not only to look down on the maps of the past (with a dismissive scientific chauvinism) but also to regard the maps of other non-Western or early cultures (where the rules of mapmaking were different) as inferior to European maps.[24] Similarly, the primary effect of the scientific rules was to create a 'standard' – a successful version of 'normal science'[25] – that enabled cartographers to build a wall around their citadel of the 'true' map. Its central bastions were measurement and standardization and beyond there was a 'not cartography' land where lurked an army of inaccurate, heretical, subjective, valuative, and ideologically distorted images. Cartographers developed a 'sense of the other' in relation to nonconforming maps. Even maps such as those produced by journalists, where different rules and modes of expressiveness might be appropriate, are evaluated by many cartographers according to standards of 'objectivity,' 'accuracy,' and 'truthfulness.' In this respect, the underlying attitude of many cartographers is revealed in a recent book of essays on *Cartographie dans les médias.*[26] One of its reviewers has noted how many authors attempt to exorcise from

> *the realm of cartography any graphic representation that is not a simple planimetric image, and to then classify all other maps as 'decorative graphics masquerading as maps' where the 'bending of cartographic rules' has taken place . . . most journalistic maps are flawed because they are inaccurate, misleading or biased.*[27]

Or in Britain, we are told, there was set up a 'Media Map Watch' in 1984. "Several hundred interested members [of cartographic and geographic societies] submitted several thousand maps and diagrams for analysis that revealed [according to the rules] numerous common deficiencies, errors, and inaccuracies along with misleading standards."[28] In this example of cartographic vigilantism the 'ethic of

[22] Richard Rorty, *Philosophy and the Mirror of Nature*, Princeton, 1979.

[23] Larry Laudan, *Progress and Its Problems: Toward a Theory of Scientific Growth*. Berkeley: University of California Press, 1977: 2.

[24] For a discussion of these tendencies in the historiography of early maps see J. B. Harley. "L'Histoire de la cartographie comme discours," *Préfaces* 5 December 1987–January 1988: 70–75.

[25] In the much-debated sense of Thomas S. Kuhn, *The Structure of Scientific Revolutions*. Chicago: The University of Chicago Press, 1962. For challenges and discussions, see Imre Lakatos and Alan Musgrave, eds., *Criticism and the Growth of Knowledge*. Cambridge: Cambridge University Press, 1970.

[26] *Cartographie dans les médias*, ed M. Gauthier. Québec: Presses de l'Université du Québec, 1988.

[27] Sona Karentz Andrews, review of *Cartography in the Media* in *The American Cartographer*, 1989, forthcoming.

[28] W. G. V. Balchin, "The Media Map Watch in the United Kingdom," in *Cartographie dans les médias*, 1988: 33–48.

accuracy' is being defended with some ideological fervor. The language of exclusion is that of a string of 'natural' opposites: 'true and false'; 'objective and subjective'; 'literal and symbolic' and so on. The best maps are those with an "authoritative image of self-evident factuality."[29]

In cases where the scientific rules are invisible in the map we can still trace their play in attempting to normalize the discourse. The cartographer's 'black box' has to be defended and its social origins suppressed. The hysteria among leading cartographers at the popularity of the Peters' projection,[30] or the recent expressions of piety among Western European and North American map-makers following the Russian admission that they had falsified their topographic maps to confuse the enemy give us a glimpse of how the game is played according to these rules. What are we to make of the 1988 newspaper headlines such as "Russians Caught Mapping" (*Ottawa Citizen*), "Soviets Admit Map Paranoia" (*Wisconsin Journal*) or (in the *New York Times*) "In West, Map makers Hail 'Truth' " and "The rascals finally realized the truth and were able to tell it, a geographer at the Defense Department said"?[31] The implication is that Western maps are value free. According to the spokesman, our maps are not ideological documents, and the condemnation of Russian falsification is as much an echo of Cold War rhetoric as it is a credible cartographic criticism.

This timely example also serves to introduce my second contention that the scientific rules of mapping are, in any case, influenced by a quite different set of rules, those governing the cultural production of the map. To discover these rules, we have to read between the lines of technical procedures or of the map's topographic content. They are related to values, such as those of ethnicity, politics, religion, or social class, and they are also embedded in the map-producing society at large. Cartographic discourse operates a double silence toward this aspect of the possibilities for map knowledge. In the map itself, social structures are often disguised beneath an abstract, instrumental space, or incarcerated in the coordinates of computer mapping. And in the technical literature of cartography they are also ignored, notwithstanding the fact that they may be as important as surveying, compilation, or design in producing the statements that cartography makes about the world and its landscapes. Such an interplay of social and technical rules is a

[29] The phrase is that of Ellen Lupton, "Reading Isotype," *Design Issues* 3/2, 1986, 47–58 (quote on page 53).

[30] Arno Peters, *The New Cartography*, New York, Friendship Press, 1983. The responses included John Loxton, "The Peters Phenomenon," *The Cartographic Journal* 22/2, 1985: 106–8; "The So-called Peters Projection," in *ibid.*, 108–10; A. H. Robinson, "Arno Peters and His New Cartography," *American Cartographer 12, 1985:* 103–11; Phil Porter and Phil Voxland, "Distortion in Maps: The Peters' Projection and Other Devilments," *Focus* 36, 1986: 22–30; and, for a more balanced view, John P. Snyder, "Social Consciousness and World Maps," *The Christian Century*, February 24th, 1988: 190–92.

[31] "Soviet Aide Admits Maps Were Faked for 50 Years" and "In West, Map Makers Hail 'Truth'," *The New York Times*, September 3, 1988; "Soviets Admit Map Paranoia," *Wisconsin State Journal* Saturday, September 3, 1988; "Soviets Caught Mapping!" *The Ottawa Citizen* Saturday, September 3, 1988; "Faked Russian Maps Gave the Germans Fits," *The New York Times* September 11, 1988; and "National Geoglasnost?" *The Christian Science Monitor* September 12, 1988.

universal feature of cartographic knowledge. In maps it produces the "order" of its features and the "hierarchies of its practices."[32] In Foucault's sense the rules may enable us to define an *episteme* and to trace an archaeology of that knowledge through time.[33]

Two examples of how such rules are manifest in maps will be given to illustrate their force in structuring cartographic representation. The first is the well-known adherence to the 'rule of ethnocentricity' in the construction of world maps. This has led many historical societies to place their own territories at the center of their cosmographies or world maps. While it may be dangerous to assume universality, and there are exceptions, such a rule is as evident in cosmic diagrams of pre-Columbian North American Indians as it is in the maps of ancient Babylonia, Greece or China, or in the medieval maps of the Islamic world or Christian Europe.[34] Yet what is also significant in applying Foucault's critique of knowledge to cartography is that the history of the ethnocentric rule does not march in step with the 'scientific' history of map-making. Thus, the scientific Renaissance in Europe gave modern cartography coordinate systems, Euclid, scale maps, and accurate measurement, but it also helped to confirm a new myth of Europe's ideological centrality through projections such as those of Mercator.[35] Or again, in our own century, a tradition of the exclusivity of America was enhanced before World War II by placing it in its own hemisphere ('our hemisphere') on the world map.[36] Throughout the history of cartography ideological 'Holy Lands' are frequently centered on maps. Such centricity, a kind of "subliminal geometry,"[37] adds geopolitical force and meaning to representation. It is also arguable that such world maps have in turn helped to codify, to legitimate, and to promote the world views which are prevalent in different periods and places.[38]

32 Michel Foucault, *The Order of Things: An Archaeology of the Human Sciences*. A Translation of *Les mots et les choses*. New York: Vintage Books, 1973, xx.

33 *Ibid.*, xxii.

34 Many commentators have noted this tendency. See, for example, Yi-Fu Tuan, *Topophilia. A Study of Environmental Perception, Attitudes, and Values*. Englewood Cliffs, New Jersey: Prentice-Hall, 1974, Chapter 4, "Ethnocentrism, Symmetry, and Space," 30–44. On ancient and medieval European maps in this respect see J. B. Harley and David Woodward, eds., *The History of Cartography*, vol. 1, *Cartography in Prehistoric, Ancient, and Medieval Europe and the Mediterranean*. Chicago: The University of Chicago Press, 1987. On the maps of Islam and China see J. B. Harley and David Woodward, eds., *The History of Cartography*, vol. 2, *Cartography in the Traditional Islamic and Asian Societies*, Chicago: The University of Chicago Press, forthcoming.

35 Arno Peters, *The New Cartography, passim.*

36 For the wider history of this 'rule' see Arthur P. Whitaker, *The Western Hemisphere Idea: Its Rise and Decline*. Ithaca, New York: Cornell University Press, 1954; also S. Whittemore Boggs, "This Hemisphere," *Department of State Bulletin* 12/306, May 6, 1945: 845–50; Alan K. Henrikson, "The Map as an 'Idea': The Role of Cartographic Imagery During the Second World War," *The American Cartographer* 2/1, 1975: 19–53.

37 J. B. Harley, "Maps, Knowledge, and Power," in *The Iconography of Landscape*, ed. Denis Cosgrove and Stephen Daniels, Cambridge: Cambridge University Press, 1988: 289–90.

38 The link between actually mapping, as the principal source of our world vision, and *mentalité* still has to be thoroughly explored. For some contemporary links see Alan K. Henrikson "Frameworks for

A second example is how the 'rules of the social order' appear to insert themselves into the smaller codes and spaces of cartographic transcription. The history of European cartography since the seventeenth century provides many examples of this tendency. Pick a printed or manuscript map from the drawer almost at random and what stands out is the unfailing way its text is as much a commentary on the social structure of a particular nation or place as it is on its topography. The map-maker is often as busy recording the contours of feudalism, the shape of a religious hierarchy, or the steps in the tiers of social class,[39] as the topography of the physical and human landscape.

Why maps can be so convincing in this respect is that the rules of society and the rules of measurement are mutually reinforcing in the same image. Writing of the map of Paris, surveyed in 1652 by Jacques Gomboust, the King's engineer, Louis Marin points to "this sly strategy of simulation-dissimulation":

> *The knowledge and science of representation, to demonstrate the truth that its subject declares plainly, flow nonetheless in a social and political hierarchy. The proofs of its 'theoretical' truth had to be given, they are the recognisable signs; but the economy of these signs in their disposition on the cartographic plane no longer obeys the rules of the order of geometry and reason but, rather, the norms and values of the order of social and religious tradition. Only the churches and important mansions benefit from natural signs and from the visible rapport they maintain with what they represent. Townhouses and private homes, precisely because they are private and not public, will have the right only to the general and common representation of an arbitrary and institutional sign, the poorest, the most elementary (but maybe, by virtue of this, principal) of geometric elements; the point identically reproduced in bulk.*[40]

Once again, much like 'the rule of ethnocentrism,' this hierarchicalization of space is not a conscious act of cartographic representation. Rather it is taken for granted in a society that the place of the king is more important than the place of a lesser baron, that a castle is more important than a peasant's house, that the town of an archbishop is more important than that of a minor prelate, or that the estate of a landed gentleman is more worthy of emphasis than that of a plain farmer. Cartography deploys its vocabulary accordingly so that it embodies a systematic social inequality. The distinctions of class and power are engineered, reified and legitimated in the map by means of cartographic signs. The rule seems to be 'the more powerful, the more prominent.' To those who have strength in the world shall be added strength in the map. Using all the tricks of the cartographic trade – size of

the World," Preface in Ralph E. Ehrenberg, *Scholars' Guide to Washington, D.C. for Cartography and Remote Sensing Imagery*. Washington, D.C.: Smithsonian Institution Press, 1987, viii-xiii. For a report on research that attempts to measure this influence in the cognitive maps of individuals in different areas of the world see Thomas F. Saarinen, *Centering of Mental Maps of the World*. Department of Geography and Regional Development, Tucson, Arizona, 1987.

39 For a general discussion see Harley, "Maps, Knowledge, and Power," 292–94; in my essay on "Power and Legitimation in the English Geographical Atlases of the Eighteenth Century," in *Images of the World: The Atlas Through History*, ed. John A. Wolter. Washington, D.C.: Library of Congress, forthcoming, these 'rules of the social order' are discussed in the maps of one historical society.

40 Marin, *Portrait of the King*, 173.

symbol, thickness of line, height of lettering, hatching and shading, the addition of color – we can trace this reinforcing tendency in innumerable European maps. We can begin to see how maps, like art, become a mechanism "for defining social relationships, sustaining social rules, and strengthening social values."[41]

In the case of both these examples of rules, the point I am making is that the rules operate both within and beyond the orderly structures of classification and measurement. They go beyond the stated purposes of cartography. Much of the power of the map, as a representation of social geography, is that it operates behind a mask of seemingly neutral science. It hides and denies its social dimensions at the same time as it legitimates. Yet whichever way we look at it the rules of society will surface. They have ensured that maps are at least as much an image of the social order as they are a measurement of the phenomenal world of objects.

Deconstruction and the Cartographic Text

To move inward from the question of cartographic rules – the social context within which map knowledge is fashioned – we have to turn to the cartographic text itself. The word 'text' is deliberately chosen. It is now generally accepted that the model of text can have a much wider application than to literary texts alone. To non-book texts such as musical compositions and architectural structures we can confidently add the graphic texts we call maps.[42] It has been said that "what constitutes a text is not the presence of linguistic elements but the act of construction" so that maps, as "constructions employing a conventional sign system,"[43] become texts. With Barthes we could say they "presuppose a signifying consciousness" that it is our business to uncover.[44] 'Text' is certainly a better metaphor for maps than the mirror of nature. Maps are a cultural text. By accepting their textuality we are able to embrace a number of different interpretative possibilities. Instead of just the transparency of clarity we can discover the pregnancy of the opaque. To fact we can add myth, and instead of innocence we may expect duplicity. Rather than working with a formal science of communication, or even a sequence of loosely related technical processes, our concern is redirected to a history and anthropology of the image, and we learn to recognize the narrative

[41] Gifford Geertz, "Art as a Cultural System" in *Local Knowledge: Further Essays in Interpretive Anthropology*. New York: Basic Books, 1983, 99.

[42] This is cogently argued by D. F. McKenzie, *Bibliography and the Sociology of Texts*. London: The British Library, 1986, esp. 34–39, where he discusses the textuality of maps. Robinson and Petchenik, 1976, p. 43, reject the metaphor of map as language: they state that 'the two systems, map and language are essentially incompatible," basing their belief on the familiar grounds of literality that language is verbal, that images do not have a vocabulary, that there is no grammar, and the temporal sequence of a syntax is lacking. Rather than isolating the differences, however, it now seems more constructive to stress the *similarities* between map and text.

[43] McKenzie, *Bibliography*: 35.

[44] Roland Barthes, *Mythologies: Selected and Translated from the French by Annette Lavers*. London: Paladin, 1973: 110.

qualities of cartographic representation[45] as well as its claim to provide a synchronous picture of the world. All this, moreover, is likely to lead to a rejection of the neutrality of maps, as we come to define their intentions rather than the literal face of representation, and as we begin to accept the social consequences of cartographic practices. I am not suggesting that the direction of textual enquiry offers a simple set of techniques for reading either contemporary or historical maps. In some cases we will have to conclude that there are many aspects of their meaning that are undecidable.[46]

Deconstruction, as discourse analysis in general, demands a closer and deeper reading of the cartographic text than has been the general practice in either cartography or the history of cartography. It may be regarded as a search for alternative meanings. "To deconstruct," it is argued,

> *is to reinscribe and resituate meanings, events and objects within broader movements and structures; it is, so to speak, to reverse the imposing tapestry in order to expose in all its unglamorously dishevelled tangle the threads constituting the well-heeled image it presents to the world.*[47]

The published map also has a 'well-heeled image' and our reading has to go beyond the assessment of geometric accuracy, beyond the fixing of location, and beyond the recognition of topographical patterns and geographies. Such interpretation begins from the premise that the map text may contain "unperceived contradictions or duplicitous tensions"[48] that undermine the surface layer of standard objectivity. Maps are slippery customers. In the words of W. J. T. Mitchell, writing of languages and images in general, we may need to regard them more as "enigmas, problems to be explained, prison-houses which lock the understanding away from the world." We should regard them "as the sort of sign that presents a deceptive appearance of naturalness and transparence concealing an opaque, distorting, arbitrary mechanism of representation."[49] Throughout the history of modern cartography in the West, for example, there have been numerous instances of where maps have been falsified, of where they have been censored or kept secret, or of where they have surreptitiously contradicted the rules of their proclaimed scientific status.[50]

As in the case of these practices, map deconstruction would focus on aspects of

45 The narrative qualities of cartography are introduced by Denis Wood in "Pleasure in the Idea: The Atlas as Narrative Form," in *Atlases for Schools: Design Principles and Curriculum Perspectives*, ed. R. J. B. Carswell, G. J. A. de Leeuw and N. M. Waters, *Cartographica* 24/1, 1987: 24–45 [Monograph 36].

46 The undecidability of textual meaning is a central position in Derrida's criticism of philosophy: see the discussion by Hoy, "Jacques Derrida" *In* Skinner, *The Return of Grand Theory*, 1985: 54–58.

47 Terry Eagleton, *Against the Grain*. London: Verso, 1986: 80. Quoted in Edward W. Soja, *Postmodern Geographies*. London: Verso, 1989, 12.

48 Hoy, "Jacques Derrida," 540.

49 W. J. T. Mitchell, *Iconology: Image, Text, Ideology*. Chicago: The University of Chicago Press, 1986: 8.

50 J. B. Harley, "Silences and Secrecy: The Hidden Agenda of Cartography in Early Modern Europe," *Imago Mundi* 40, 1988: 57–76.

maps that many interpreters have glossed over. Writing of "Derrida's most typical deconstructive moves," Christopher Norris notes that

> *deconstruction is the vigilant seeking-out of those 'aporias,' blindspots or moments of self-contradiction where a text involuntarily betrays the tension between rhetoric and logic, between what it manifestly means to say and what it is nonetheless constrained to mean. To 'deconstruct' a piece of writing is therefore to operate a kind of strategic reversal, seizing on precisely those unregarded details (casual metaphors, footnotes, incidental turns of argument) which are always, and necessarily, passed over by interpreters of a more orthodox persuasion. For it is here, in the margins of the text – the 'margins', that is, as defined by a powerful normative consensus – that deconstruction discovers those same unsettling forces at work.*[51]

A good example of how we could deconstruct an early map – by beginning with what have hitherto been regarded as its 'casual metaphors' and 'footnotes' – is provided by recent studies reinterpreting the status of decorative art on the European maps of the seventeenth and eighteenth centuries. Rather than being inconsequential marginalia, the emblems in cartouches and decorative titlepages can be regarded as *basic* to the way they convey their cultural meaning[52], and they help to demolish the claim of cartography to produce an impartial graphic science. But the possibility of such a revision is not limited to historic "decorative" maps. A recent essay by Wood and Fels on the Official State Highway Map of North Carolina[53] indicates a much wider applicability for a deconstructive strategy by beginning in the 'margins' of the contemporary map. They also treat the map as a text and, drawing on the ideas of Roland Barthes of myth as a semiological system,[54] develop a forceful social critique of cartography which though structuralist in its approach is deconstructionist in its outcome. They begin, deliberately, with the margins of the map, or rather with the subject matter that is printed on its verso:

> *One side is taken up by an inventory of North Carolina points of interest – illustrated with photos of, among other things, a scimitar horned oryx (resident in the state zoo), a Cherokee woman making beaded jewelry, a ski lift, a sand dune (but no cities) – a ferry schedule, a message of welcome from the then governor, and a motorist's prayer ("Our heavenly Father, we ask this day a particular blessing as we take the wheel of our car . . ."). On the other side, North Carolina, hemmed in by the margins of pale yellow South Carolinas and Virginias, Georgias and Tennessees, and washed by a pale blue Atlantic, is represented as a meshwork of*

[51] Christopher Norris, *Derrida*. Cambridge, Mass.: Harvard University Press, 1987: 19.

[52] Most recently, C. N. G. Clarke, "Taking Possession: The Cartouche as Cultural Text in Eighteenth-Century American Maps," *Word and Image* 4/2, 1988: 455–74; also Harley, "Maps, Knowledge, and Power," esp. 296–99 and J. B. Harley, "Meaning and Ambiguity in Tudor Cartography," in *English Map-Making, 1500–1650: Historical Essays*, ed. Sarah Tyacke. London: The British Library Reference Division Publications, 1984: 22–45; and "Power and Legitimation in the English Geographical Atlases of the Eighteenth Century," in *Images of the World: The Atlas Through History*, ed, John A. Wolter, Washington, D.C.: Library of Congress, Center for the Book, forthcoming.

[53] Wood and Fels, "Designs on Signs", 1986.

[54] Roland Barthes, "Myth Today," *In* Barthes, *Mythologies*: 109–59.

> *red, black, blue, green and yellow lines on a white background, thickened at the intersections by roundels of black or blotches of pink . . . To the left of . . . [the] title is a sketch of the fluttering state flag. To the right is a sketch of a cardinal (state bird) on a branch of flowering dogwood (state flower) surmounting a buzzing honey bee arrested in midflight (state insect).*[55]

What is the meaning of these emblems? Are they merely a pleasant ornament for the traveler or can they inform us about the social production of such state highway maps? A deconstructionist might claim that such meanings are undecidable, but it is also clear that the State Highway Map of North Carolina is making other dialogical assertions behind its mask of innocence and transparence. I am not suggesting that these elements hinder the traveler getting from point A to B, but that there is a second text within the map. No map is devoid of an intertextual dimension and, in this case too, the discovery of intertextuality enables us to scan the image as more than a neutral picture of a road network.[56] Its 'users' are not only the ordinary motorists but also the State of North Carolina that has appropriated its publication (distributed in millions of copies) as a promotional device. The map has become an instrument of State policy and an instrument of sovereignty.[57] At the same time, it is more than an affirmation of North Carolina's dominion over its territory. It also constructs a mythic geography, a landscape full of 'points of interest,' with incantations of loyalty to state emblems and to the values of a Christian piety. The hierarchy of towns and the visual dominating highways that connect them have become the legitimate natural order of the world. The map finally insists "that roads really *are* what North Carolina's all about."[58] The map idolizes our love affair with the automobile. The myth is believable.

A cartographer's stock response to this deconstructionist argument might well be to cry 'foul.' The argument would run like this: "Well after all it's a state highway map. It's designed to be at once popular and useful. We expect it to exaggerate the road network and to show points of interest to motorists. It is a derived rather than a basic map."[59] It is not a scientific map. The appeal to the ultimate scientific map is always the cartographers' last line of defence when seeking to deny the social relations that permeate their technology.

It is at this point that Derrida's strategy can help us to extend such an interpre-

55 Wood and Fels, "Designs on Signs", 1986: 54.

56 On the intertextuality of all discourses – with pointers for the analysis of cartography – see Tzvetan Todorov, *Mikhail Bakhtin: The Dialogical Principle,* trans. Wlad Godzich. Minneapolis: University of Minnesota Press, 1984: 60–74; also M. M. Bakhtin, *The Dialogic Imagination: Four Essays,* ed. Michael Holquist, trans. Caryl Emerson and Michael Holquist. Austin: University of Texas Press, 1981. I owe these references to Dr. Cordell Yee, History of Cartography Project, University of Wisconsin at Madison.

57 Wood and Fels, "Designs on Signs", 1986: 63.

58 *Ibid.*, 60.

59 The 'basic' and 'derived' division, like that of 'general purpose' and 'thematic,' is one of the axiomatic distinctions often drawn by cartographers. Deconstruction, however, by making explicit the play of forces such as intention, myth, silence and power in maps, will tend to dissolve such an opposition for interpretive purposes except in the very practical sense that one map is often copied or derived from another.

tation to all maps, scientific or non-scientific, basic or derived. Just as in the deconstruction of philosophy Derrida was able to show "how the supposedly literal level is intensively metaphorical"[60] so too we can show how cartographic 'fact' is also symbol. In 'plain' scientific maps, science itself becomes the metaphor. Such maps contain a dimension of 'symbolic realism' which is no less a statement of political authority and control than a coat-of-arms or a portrait of a queen placed at the head of an earlier decorative map. The metaphor has changed. The map has attempted to purge itself of ambiguity and alternative possibility.[61] Accuracy and austerity of design are now the new talismans of authority culminating in our own age with computer mapping. We can trace this process very clearly in the history of Enlightenment mapping in Europe. The topography as shown in maps, increasingly detailed and planimetrically accurate, has become a metaphor for a utilitarian philosophy and its will to power. Cartography inscribes this cultural model upon the paper and we can examine it in many scales and types of maps. Precision of instrument and technique merely serves to reinforce the image, with its encrustation of myth, as a selective perspective on the world. Thus maps of local estates in the European *ancien regime*, though derived from instrumental survey, were a metaphor for a social structure based on landed property. County and regional maps, though founded on scientific triangulation, were an articulation of local values and rights. Maps of the European states, though constructed along arcs of the meridian, served still as a symbolic shorthand for a complex of nationalist ideas. And world maps, though increasingly drawn on mathematically defined projections, nevertheless gave a spiralling twist to the manifest destiny of European overseas conquest and colonization.[62] In each of these examples we can trace the contours of metaphor in a scientific map. This in turn enhances our understanding of how the text works as an instrument operating on social reality.

In deconstructionist theory the play of rhetoric is closely linked to that of metaphor. In concluding this section of the essay I will argue that notwithstanding 'scientific' cartography's efforts to convert culture into nature, and to 'naturalize' social reality,[63] it has remained an inherently rhetorical discourse. Another of the lessons of Derrida's criticism of philosophy is "that modes of rhetorical analysis, hitherto applied mainly to literary texts, are in fact indispensable for reading *any* kind of discourse."[64] There is nothing revolutionary in the idea that cartography is an art of persuasive communication. It is now commonplace to write about the rhetoric of the human sciences in the classical sense of the word rhetoric.[65] Even

[60] Hoy, "Jacques Derrida" *In* Skinner, *The Return of Grand Theory*, 1985: 44.

[61] I derive this thought from Eagleton, *Literary Theory*, 135, writing of the ideas of Roland Barthes.

[62] These examples are from Harley, "Maps, Knowledge, and Power", 1988: 300.

[63] Eagleton, *Literary Theory*, 1983: 135–36.

[64] Christopher Norris, *Deconstruction*, 19.

[65] See, for example, Donald N. McCloskey, *The Rhetoric of Economics*. Madison: The University of Wisconsin Press, 1985; and *The Rhetoric of the Human Sciences: Language and Argument in Scholarship and Public Affairs*, ed. John S. Nelson, Allan Megill, and Donald N. McCloskey. Madison: The University of Wisconsin Press, 1987.

cartographers – as well as their critics – are beginning to allude to the notion of a rhetorical cartography but what is still lacking is a rhetorical close-reading of maps.[65]

The issue in contention is not whether some maps are rhetorical, or whether other maps are partly rhetorical, but the extent to which rhetoric is a universal aspect of all cartographic texts. Thus for some cartographers the notion of 'rhetoric' would remain a pejorative term. It would be an 'empty rhetoric' which was unsubstantiated in the scientific content of a map. 'Rhetoric' would be used to refer to the 'excesses' of propaganda mapping or advertising cartography or an attempt would be made to confine it to an 'artistic' or aesthetic element in maps as opposed to their scientific core. My position is to accept that rhetoric is part of the way all texts work and that all maps are rhetorical texts. Again we ought to dismantle the arbitrary dualism between 'propaganda' and 'true', and between modes of 'artistic' and 'scientific' representation as they are found in maps. All maps strive to frame their message in the context of an audience. All maps state an argument about the world and they are propositional in nature. All maps employ the common devices of rhetoric such as invocations of authority (*especially* in 'scientific' maps[67]) and appeals to a potential readership through the use of colors, decoration, typography, dedications, or written justifications of their method.[68] Rhetoric may be concealed but it is always present, for there is no description without performance.

The steps in making a map – selection, omission, simplification, classification, the creation of hierarchies, and 'symbolization' – are all inherently rhetorical. In their intentions as much as in their applications they signify subjective human purposes rather than reciprocating the workings of some "fundamental law of cartographic generalisation."[69] Indeed, the freedom of rhetorical manoeuvre in cartography is considerable: the mapmaker merely omits those features of the world that lie outside the purpose of the immediate discourse. There have been no limits to the varieties of maps that have been developed historically in response to different purposes of argument, aiming at different rhetorical goals, and embodying different assumptions about what is sound cartographic practice. The style of maps is neither fixed in the past nor is it today. It has been said that "The rhetorical code appropriates to its map the style most advantageous to the myth it intends to propogate."[70] Instead of thinking in terms of rhetorical versus

[66] For a notable exception see Wood and Fels, "Designs on Signs", 1986. An interesting example of cartographic rhetoric in historical atlases is described in Walter Goffart, "The Map of the Barbarian Invasions: A Preliminary Report" *Nottingham Medieval Studies* 32, 1988: 49–64.

[67] In *ibid.* p. 99, the examples are given for topographical maps of reliability diagrams, multiple referencing grids, and magnetic error diagrams; on thematic maps "the trappings of F-scaled symbols and psychometrically divided greys" are a similar form of rhetorical assertion.

[68] The 'letter' incorporated into Gomboust's map of Paris, as discussed by Marin, *Portrait of the King*, 169–74, provides an apposite example.

[69] This is still given credence in some textbooks: see, for example, Arthur H. Robinson, Randall D. Sale, Joel L. Morrison and Phillip C. Muehrcke, *Elements of Cartography*, 5th ed. New York: John Wiley & Sons, 1984, 127.

[70] Wood and Fels, "Designs on Signs", 1986, 71.

non-rhetorical maps it may be more helpful to think in terms of a theory of cartographic rhetoric which accommodated this fundamental aspect of representation in all types of cartographic text. Thus, I am not concerned to privilege rhetoric over science, but to dissolve the illusory distinction between the two in reading the social purposes as well as the content of maps.

Maps and the Exercise of Power

For the final stage in the argument I return to Foucault. In doing so I am mindful of Foucault's criticism of Derrida that he attempted "to restrict interpretation to a purely syntactic and textual level,"[71] a world where political realities no longer exist. Foucault, on the other hand, sought to uncover "the social practices that the text itself both reflects and employs" and to "reconstruct the technical and material framework in which it arose."[72] Though deconstruction is useful in helping to change the epistemological climate, and in encouraging a rhetorical reading of cartography, my final concern is with its social and political dimensions, and with understanding how the map works in society as a form of power-knowledge. This closes the circle to a context-dependent form of cartographic history.

We have already seen how it is possible to view cartography as a discourse – a system which provides a set of rules for the representation of knowledge embodied in the images we define as maps and atlases. It is not difficult to find for maps – especially those produced and manipulated by the state – a niche in the "power/knowledge matrix of the modern order."[73] Especially where maps are ordered by government (or are derived from such maps) it can be seen how they extend and reinforce the legal statutes, territorial imperatives, and values stemming from the exercise of political power. Yet to understand how power works through cartographic discourse and the effects of that power in society further dissection is needed. A simple model of domination and subversion is inadequate and I propose to draw a distinction between *external* and *internal* power in cartography. This ultimately derives from Foucault's ideas about power-knowledge, but this particular formulation is owed to Joseph Rouse's recent book on *Knowledge and Power*,[74] where a theory of the internal power of science is in turn based on his reading of Foucault.

The most familiar sense of power in cartography is that of power *external* to maps and mapping. This serves to link maps to the centers of political power. Power is

[71] Hoy, "Jacques Derrida" *In* Skinner, *The Return of Grand Theory*, 1985: 60; for further discussion see Norris, *Derrida*, 1987: 213–20.

[72] Hoy, 'Jacques Derrida': 60.

[73] Philp, "Michel Foucault," *In* Skinner, *The Return of Grand Theory*, 1985: 76.

[74] Joseph Rouse, *Knowledge and Power: Toward a Political Philosophy of Science*. Ithaca: Cornell University Press, 1987.

exerted *on* cartography. Behind most cartographers there is a patron; in innumerable instances the makers of cartographic texts were responding to external needs. Power is also exercised *with* cartography. Monarchs, ministers, state institutions, the Church, have all initiated programs of mapping for their own ends. In modern Western society maps quickly became crucial to the maintenance of state power – to its boundaries, to its commerce, to its internal administration, to control of populations, and to its military strength. Mapping soon became the business of the state: cartography is early nationalized. The state guards its knowledge carefully: maps have been universally censored, kept secret and falsified. In all these cases maps are linked to what Foucault called the exercise of 'juridical power.'[75] The map becomes a 'juridical territory': it facilitates surveillance and control. Maps are still used to control our lives in innumerable ways. A mapless society, though we may take the map for granted, would now be politically unimaginable. All this is power *with* the help of maps. It is an external power, often centralized and exercised bureaucratically, imposed from above, and manifest in particular acts or phases of deliberate policy.

I come now to the important distinction. What is also central to the effects of maps in society is what may be defined as the power *internal* to cartography. The focus of inquiry therefore shifts from the place of cartography in a juridical system of power to the political effects of what cartographers do when they make maps. Cartographers manufacture power: they create a spatial panopticon. It is a power embedded in the map text. We can talk about the power of the map just as we already talk about the power of the word or about the book as a force for change. In this sense maps have politics.[76] It is a power that intersects and is embedded in knowledge. It is universal. Foucault writes of

> *The omnipresence of power: not because it has the privilege of consolidating everything under its invincible unity, but because it is produced from one moment to the next, at every point, or rather in every relation from one point to another. Power is everywhere; not because it embraces everything, but because it comes from everywhere.*[77]

Power comes from the map and it traverses the way maps are made. The key to this internal power is thus cartographic process. By this I mean the way maps are compiled and the categories of information selected; the way they are generalized, a set of rules for the abstraction of the landscape; the way the elements in the landscape are formed into hierarchies; and the way various rhetorical styles that also reproduce power are employed to represent the landscape. To catalogue the world

[75] Michel Foucault, *Power/Knowledge: Selected Interviews and Other Writings*, 1972–1977, ed. Colin Gordon, trans. Colin Gordon, Leo Marshall, John Mepham, Kate Sopher. New York, Pantheon Books, 1980, 88; see also Rouse, *Knowledge and Power*: 209–10.

[76] I adapt this idea from Langdon Winner, "Do Artifacts have Politics?", *Daedalus* 109/1, 1980: 121–36.

[77] Michel Foucault, *The History of Sexuality: Vol I: An Introduction*, trans. Robert Hurley. New York: Random House, 1978: 93.

is to appropriate it,[78] so that all these technical processes represent acts of control over its image which extend beyond the professed uses of cartography. The world is disciplined. The world is normalized. We are prisoners in its spatial matrix. For cartography as much as other forms of knowledge, "All social action flows through boundaries determined by classification schemes."[79] An anology is to what happens to data in the cartographer's workshop and what happens to people in the disciplinary institutions – prisons, schools, armies, factories – described by Foucault:[80] in both cases a process of normalization occurs. Or similarly, just as in factories we standardize our manufactured goods so in our cartographic workshops we standardize our images of the world. Just as in the laboratory we create formulaic understandings of the processes of the physical world so too, in the map, nature is reduced to a graphic formula.[81] The power of the mapmaker was not generally exercised over individuals but over the knowledge of the world made available to people in general. Yet this is not consciously done and it transcends the simple categories of 'intended' and 'unintended' altogether. I am not suggesting that power is deliberately or centrally exercised. It is a local knowledge which at the same time is universal. It usually passes unnoticed. The map is a silent arbiter of power.

What have been the effects of this 'logic of the map' upon human consciousness, if I may adapt Marshall McLuhan's phrase ("logic of print")?[82] Like him I believe we have to consider for maps the effects of abstraction, uniformity, repeatability, and visuality in shaping mental structures, and in imparting a sense of the places of the world. It is the disjunction between those senses of place, and many alternative visions of what the world is, or what it might be, that has raised questions about the effect of cartography in society. Thus, Theodore Roszak writes

> *The cartographers are talking about their maps and not landscapes. That is why what they say frequently becomes so paradoxical when translated into ordinary language. When they forget the difference between map and landscape – and when they permit or persuade us to forget that difference – all sorts of liabilities ensue.*[83]

[78] Adapting Roland Barthes, "The Plates of the *Encyclopedia*," in *New Critical Essays*. New York: Hill and Wang, 1980: 27, who writes much like Foucault, "To catalogue is not merely to ascertain, as it appears at first glance, but also to appropriate." Quoted in Wood and Fels, "Designs on Signs", 1986: 72.

[79] Robert Darnton, *The Great Cat Massacre and Other Episodes in French Cultural History*. New York: Basic Books, 1984: 192–93.

[80] Rouse, *Knowledge and Power*: 213–26.

[81] Indeed, cartographers like to promote this metaphor of what they do: read, for example, Mark Monmonier and George A. Schnell, *Map Appreciation*. Englewood Cliffs, New Jersey: Prentice Hall, 1988: 15. "Geography thrives on cartographic generalization. The map is to the geographer what the microscope is to the microbiologist, for the ability to shrink the earth and generalize about it . . . The microbiologist must choose a suitable objective lens, and the geographer must select a map scale appropriate to both the phenomenon in question and the 'regional laboratory' in which the geographer is studying it."

[82] Marshall McLuhan, *The Gutenberg Galaxy: The Making of Typographic Man*. Toronto: University of Toronto Press, 1962, *passim*.

[83] Theodore Roszak, *Where the Wasteland Ends: Politics and Transcendence in Postindustrial Society*. New

One of these 'liabilities' is that maps, by articulating the world in mass-produced and stereotyped images, express an embedded social vision. Consider, for example, the fact that the ordinary road atlas is among the best selling paperback books in the United States[84] and then try to gauge how this may have affected ordinary Americans' perception of their country. What sort of an image of America do these atlases promote? On the one hand, there is a patina of gross simplicity. Once off the interstate highways the landscape dissolves into a generic world of bare essentials that invites no exploration. Context is stripped away and place is no longer important. On the other hand, the maps reveal the ambivalence of all stereotypes. Their silences are also inscribed on the page: where, on the page, is the variety of nature, where is the history of the landscape, and where is the space-time of human experience in such anonymized maps?[85]

The question has now become: do such empty images have their consequences in the way we think about the world? Because all the world is designed to look the same, is it easier to act upon it without realizing the social effects? It is in the posing of such questions that the strategies of Derrida and Foucault appear to clash. For Derrida, if meaning is undecidable so must be, *pari passu,* the measurement of the force of the map as a discourse of symbolic action. In ending, I prefer to align myself with Foucault in seeing all knowledge[86] – and hence cartography – as thoroughly enmeshed with the larger battles which constitute our world. Maps are not external to these struggles to alter power relations. The history of map use suggests that this may be so and that maps embody specific forms of power and authority. Since the Renaissance they have changed the way in which power was exercised. In colonial North America, for example, it was easy for Europeans to draw lines across the territories of Indian nations without sensing the reality of their political identity.[87] The map allowed them to say, "this is mine; these are the boundaries."[88] Similarly, in innumerable wars since the sixteenth century it has been equally easy for the generals to fight battles with colored pins and dividers rather than sensing the

York: Doubleday, 1972, 410; Roszak is using the map as a metaphor for scientific method in this argument, which again points to the widespread perception of how maps represent the world.

[84] Andrew McNally, "You Can't Get There from Here, with Today's Approach to Geography," *The Professional Geographer* 39, November, 1987: 389–92.

[85] This criticism is reminiscent of Rolande Barthes' essay on "The *Blue Guide,*" *Mythologies*: 74–77, where he writes of the *Guide* as "reducing geography to the description of an uninhabited world of monuments" (we substitute 'roads'). More generally, this tendency is also the concern of Janos Szegö, *Human Cartography: Mapping the World of Man,* trans. Tom Miller. Stockholm: Swedish Council for Building Research, 1987. See also Roszak, *Where the Wasteland Ends* 1972, where he writes p. 408, that "We forfeit the whole value of a map if we forget that it is *not* the landscape itself or anything remotely like an exhaustive depiction of it. If we do forget, we grow rigid as a robot obeying a computer program; we lose the intelligent plasticity and intuitive judgement that every wayfarer must preserve. We may then know the map in fine detail, but our knowledge will be purely academic, inexperienced, shallow."

[86] See *The Foucault Reader,* ed. by Paul Rabinow. New York: Pantheon Books, 1984: 6–7.

[87] J. B. Harley, "Victims of a Map: New England Cartography and the Native Americans." Paper read at the Land of Norumbega Conference, Portland, Maine, December, 1988.

[88] Boelhower, *Through a Glass Darkly,* 47, quoting François Wahl, "Le désir d'espace," in *Cartes et figures de la terre.* Paris: Centre Georges Pompidou, 1980: 41.

slaughter of the battlefield.[89] Or again, in our own society, it is still easy for bureaucrats, developers and 'planners' to operate on the bodies of unique places without measuring the social dislocations of 'progress.' While the map is never the reality, in such ways it helps to create a different reality. Once embedded in the published text the lines on the map acquire an authority that may be hard to dislodge. Maps are authoritarian images. Without our being aware of it maps can reinforce and legitimate the status quo. Sometimes agents of change, they can equally become conservative documents. But in either case the map is never neutral. Where it seems to be neutral it is the sly "rhetoric of neutrality"[90] that is trying to persuade us.

Conclusion

The interpretive act of deconstructing the map can serve three functions in a broad enquiry into the history of cartography. First, it allows us to challenge the epistemological myth (created by cartographers) of the cumulative progress of an objective science always producing better delineations of reality. Second, deconstructionist argument allows us to redefine the historical importance of maps. Rather than invalidating their study, it is enhanced by adding different nuances to our understanding of the power of cartographic representation as a way of building order into our world. If we can accept intertextuality then we can start to read our maps for alternative and sometimes competing discourses. Third, a deconstructive turn of mind may allow map history to take a fuller place in the interdisciplinary study of text and knowledge. Intellectual strategies such as those of discourse in the Foucauldian sense, the Derridian notion of metaphor and rhetoric as inherent to scientific discourse, and the pervading concept of power-knowledge are shared by many subjects. As ways of looking at maps they are equally enriching. They are neither inimical to hermeneutic enquiry nor anti-historical in their thrust. By dismantling we build. The possibilities of discovering meaning in maps and of tracing the social mechanisms of cartographic change are enlarged. Postmodernism offers a challenge to read maps in ways that could reciprocally enrich the reading of other texts.

Acknowledgements

These arguments were presented in earlier versions at 'The Power of Places' Conference, Northwestern University, Chicago, in January 1989, and as a 'Brown Bag' lecture in the

[89] For a modern example relating to Vietnam see Phillip C. Muehrcke, *Map Use: Reading, Analysis, and Interpretation*, 2nd ed. Madison: J. P. Publications, 1986, 394, where, however, such military examples are classified as 'abuse' rather than a normal aspect of action with maps. The author retains "maps mirror the world" as his central metaphor.

[90] There is a suggestive analogy to maps in the example of the railway timetable given by Robin Kinross, "The Rhetoric of Neutrality," *Design Issues*, 2/2, 1985: 18–30.

Department of Geography, University of Wisconsin at Milwaukee, in March 1989. I am grateful for the suggestions received on those occasions and for other helpful comments received from Sona Andrews, Catherine Delano Smith, and Cordell Yee. I am also indebted to Howard Deller of the American Geographical Society Collection for a number of references and to Ellen Hanlon for editorial help in preparing the paper for press.

28

SPACE AND PLACE: HUMANISTIC PERSPECTIVE

Yi-Fu Tuan

The humanistic critique of a singular spatial focus for geography in the 1970s led to an interest in articulating an alternative to it in the form of a concept of place. The most original and coherent contribution to this came from the Chinese/American geographer Yi-Fu Tuan. This extract is the second part of an article whose first part gives Tuan's views on space. From one point of view this concern with place represents a return to the human dimensions of region emphasized by Vidal de la Blache (**chapter 10**) and Fleure (**chapter 23**). But in fact there is a much stronger influence from such fields as architecture, anthropology and phenomenological sociology. Tuan sees place as combining the sense of position within society (the uses and symbolic significance of specific locations) with the sense of and identity with spatial location that comes from living in and associating with it. Place does not have any particular geographical scale associated with it, even though typical usage (at least in the English-speaking world) links it to the small or local. What is important is that places result from 'fields of care', which depend for their force on the emotional investments that people make in different places. Even the apparently objective spatial geography draws on the place experiences of particular students even as that geography reminds the humanistic geographer of the limits of human freedom. The identification of the latter with the understanding of the 'sense of place', however, provides a distinctively different cast to the geographical enterprise from that aspect pursued by the spatial geographer (Ley, **chapter 12**). Only later were there attempts, in the work of such geographers as Pred, Entrikin, and Agnew, to combine within a concept of place both spatial referents (such as location and locale) and the subjective sense of place.

Source: Space and place: humanistic perspective. *Progress in Geography* 6, 233–46, 1974.

Definition

In ordinary usage, place means primarily two things: one's position in society and spatial location. The study of status belongs to sociology whereas the study of location belongs to geography. Yet clearly the two meanings overlap to a large degree: one seems to be a metaphor for the other. We may ask, which of the two meanings is literal and which a metaphorical extension? Consider, first, an analogous problem the word 'close'. Is it primarily a measure of human relationship, in the sense that 'John and Joe are close friends', or is it primarily an expression of relative distance as, for example, when we say that 'the chair is close to the window'? From my discussion of space, it is clear that I believe the meaning of human relationship to be basic. Being 'close' is, first, being close to another person, on whom one depends for emotional and material security far more than on the world's non-human facts (Erickson, 1969). It is possible, as Marjorie Grene suggests, that the primary meaning of 'place' is one's position in society rather than the more abstract understanding of location in space (1968, 173). Spatial location derives from position in society rather than vice versa (Sorokin, 1964). The infant's place is the crib; the child's place is the playroom; the social distance between the chairman of the board and myself is as evident in the places we sit at the banquet table as in the places we domicile; the Jones's live on the wrong side of the tracks because of their low socio-economic position; prestige industries requiring skilled workers are located at different places from lowly industries manned by unskilled labour. Such examples can be multiplied endlessly. People are defined first by their positions in society: their characteristic life styles follow. Life style is but a general term covering such particulars as the clothes people wear, the foods they eat, and the places at which they live and work. Place, however, is more than location and more than the spatial index of socio-economic status. It is a unique ensemble of traits that merits study in its own right.

Meaning of Place

a *Spirit and personality*: A key to the meaning of place lies in the expressions that people use when they want to give it a sense carrying greater emotional charge than location or functional node. People talk of the 'spirit', the 'personality' and the 'sense' of place. We can take 'spirit' in the literal sense: space is formless and profane except for the sites that 'stand out' because spirits are believed to dwell in them. These are the sacred places. They command awe. 'Personality' suggests the unique: places, like human beings, acquire unique signatures in the course of time. A human personality is a fusion of natural disposition and acquired traits. Loosely speaking, the personality of place is a composite of natural endowment (the physique of the land) and the modifications wrought by successive generations of human beings. France, according to Vidal de la Blache (1903), Britain, according to Cyril Fox (1932), and Mexico, according to Carl Sauer (1941), have 'personality'. These regions have acquired unique 'faces' through the prolonged interaction between nature and man. Despite the accretion of experience the child is recognisable in the adult; and so too the structural lineaments of a region – its division into highland and lowland, north and south – remain visible through the successive phases of change.

Personality has two aspects: one commands awe, the other evokes affection. The personality that commands awe appears as something sublime and objective, existing independently of human needs and aspirations. Such is the personality of monumental art and holy places. Powerful manifestations of nature, like the Grand Canyon and the Matterhorn, are also commanding personalities. By contrast, a place that evokes affection has personality in the same sense that an old raincoat can be said to have character. The character of the raincoat is imparted by the person who wears it and grows fond of it. The raincoat is for use, and yet in time it acquires a personality, a certain wayward shape and smell that is uniquely its own. So too a place, through long association with human beings, can take on the familiar contours of an old but still nurturing nanny. When the geographer talks of the personality of a region, he may have both aspects in mind. The region can be both cozy and sublime: it is deeply humanised and yet the physical fundament is fundamentally indifferent to human purpose.

b A sense of place: Place may be said to have 'spirit' or 'personality', but only human beings can have a sense of place. People demonstrate their sense of place when they apply their moral and aesthetic discernment to sites and locations. Modern man, it is often claimed, has lost this sensitivity. He transgresses against the genius loci because he fails to recognise it; and he fails to recognise it because the blandness of much modern environment combined with the ethos of human dominance has stunted the cultivation of place awareness.

Sense, as in a sense of place, has two meanings. One is visual or aesthetic. The eye needs to be trained so that it can discern beauty where it exists; on the other hand beautiful places need to be created to please the eye. From one limited point of view, places are locations that have visual impact. On a flat plain, the buttes and silos are places; in a rugged karst landscape, the flat poljes are places. However, other than the all-important eye, the world is known through the senses of hearing, smell, taste, and touch. These senses, unlike the visual, require close contact and long association with the environment. It is possible to appreciate the visual qualities of a town in an afternoon's tour, but to know the town's characteristic odours and sounds, the textures of its pavements and walls, requires a far longer period of contact.

To sense is to know: so we say 'he senses it', or 'he catches the sense of it'. To see an object is to have it at the focus of one's vision; it is explicit knowing. I see the church on the hill, I know it is there, and it is a place for me. But one can have a sense of place, in perhaps the deeper meaning of the term, without any attempt at explicit formulation. We can know a place subconsciously, through touch and remembered fragrances, unaided by the discriminating eye. While the eye takes in a lovely street scene and intelligence categorises it, our hand feels the iron of the school fence and stores subliminally its coolness and resistance in our memory (Santmyer, 1962, 50). Through such modest hoards we can acquire in time a profound sense of place. Yet it is possible to be fully aware of our attachment to place only when we have left it and can *see* it as a whole from a distance.

Stability and Place

We shall not cease from exploration
And the end of all our exploring
Will be to arrive where we started
And know the place for the first time.
T.S. Eliot, *The Four Quartets*

An argument in favour of travel is that it increases awareness, not of exotic places but of home as a place. To identify wholly with the ambiance of a place is to lose the sense of its unique identity, which is revealed only when one can also see it from the outside. To be always on the move is, of course, to lose place, to be placeless and have, instead, merely scenes and images. A scene may be of a place but the scene itself is not a place. It lacks stability: it is in the nature of a scene to shift with every change of perspective. A scene is defined by its perspective whereas this is not true of place: it is in the nature of place to appear to have a stable existence independent of the perceiver.

A place is the compelling focus of a field: it is a small world, the node at which activities converge. Hence, a street is not commonly called a place, however sharp its visual identity. L'Etoile (Place de Charles de Gaulle) is a place but the Champs-Elysées is not: one is a node, the other is a through-way. A street corner is a place but the street itself is not. As we have noted earlier, a street is directed, historical space: on the horizontal plane, only non-directed homogeneous spaces can be places. When a street is transformed into a centre of festivities, with people milling around in no particular direction, it becomes non-directed space – and a place. A great ocean liner is certainly a small world, but it is not rooted in location; hence it is not a place. These are not arbitrary judgments. They are supported by the common use and understanding of language. It is a great wit who asks: 'When is this place (the *Queen Mary*) going to New York?'

Types of Place

In the discussion on the personality and sense of place, I distinguished between places that yield their meaning to the eye, and places that are known only after prolonged experience. I shall call the one type 'public symbols', and the other 'fields of care' (Wild, 1963, 47). Public symbols tend to have high imageability because they often cater to the eye. Fields of care do not seek to project an image to outsiders; they are inconspicuous visually. Public symbols command attention and even awe; fields of care evoke affection. It is relatively easy to identify places that are public symbols; it is difficult to identify fields of care for they are not easily identifiable by external criteria, such as formal structure, physical appearance, and articulate opinion (see Table 28.1).

Table 28.1 [orig. table 2]

Places as public symbols	*Places as fields of care*
(high imageability)	(low imageability)
sacred place	park
formal garden	home, drugstore, tavern
monument	street corner, neighbourhood
monumental architecture	marketplace
public square	town
ideal city	

Obviously, many – perhaps most – places are both public symbols and fields of care in varying degree. The Arch of Triumph is exclusively a symbol; the secluded farmstead, the focus of bustling rural activities, is exclusively a field of care. But the city may be a public (national) symbol as well as a field of care, and the neighbourhood may be a field of care and a public symbol, a place that tourists want to see. What do the Arch of Triumph and the secluded farmstead have in common so that both may be called places? I believe the answer to be that each is, in its own way, a small world, i.e., a centre of power and meaning relative to its environs. With a monument the question that arises is how a lifeless object can seem to be a vital centre of meaning. With a field of care the question is one of maintenance, that is, what forces in experience, function, and religion can sustain cohesive meaning in a field of care that does not depend on ostentatious visual symbols?

Public Symbols

In the ancient world, as well as among many non-literate peoples, the landscape was rich in sacred places (White, 1967). Let a thunderbolt strike the ground and the Romans regarded it as holy, a spot that emitted power and should be fenced off (Fowler, 1911, 36–7; Wissows, 1912, 467–8, 477, 515). In ancient Greece Strabo's description suggests that one could hardly step out of doors without meeting a shrine, a sacred enclosure, an image, a sacred stone or tree (Book 8, 3 : 12). Spirits populated the mountains and forests of China. Some were endowed with human pedigrees and carried official ranks (De Groot, 1892, 223). Although an entire landscape could embody power (Scully, 1962, 3), yet it was often the case that spirits lent numen to particular localities at which they received periodic homage. Examples of the holy place can be multiplied endlessly from all parts of the world. The essential point is that location, not necessarily remarkable in itself, nonetheless acquires high visibility and meaning because it harbours, or embodies, spirit (Eliade, 1963, 367–87; Van der Leeuw, 1963, 393–402). The belief system of many cultures encourages one to speak, literally, of the spirit of place. Modern secular society discourages belief in spirit, whether of nature or of the illustrious dead, but traces of it still linger in people's attitudes toward burial places, particularly those of national importance; and of course in the attitudes of ardent preservationists who tend to view wilderness areas, nature's cathedrals, as sacred. Wilderness areas in the United States are sacred places with well-defined boundaries, into which one enters with, metaphorically speaking, unshod feet.

Public monuments create places by giving prominence and an air of significance to localities (Figure 28.1). Monument building is a characteristic activity of all high civilisations (Johnson, 1968). Since the nineteenth century, however, monument building has declined and with it the effort to generate foci of interest (places) that promote local and national pride. Most monuments of modern times commemorate heroes, but there are important exceptions. St Louis' Gateway Arch (St Louis, United States), for example, commemorates a pregnant period in the city's, and

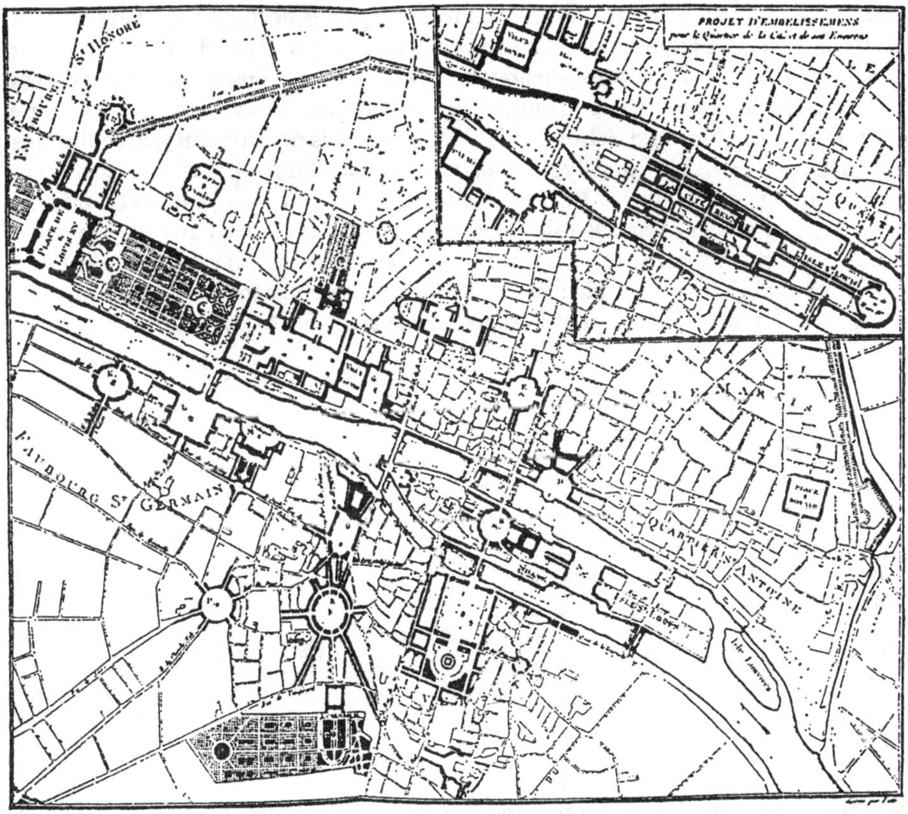

Figure 28.1 [orig. fig. 5] Place as highly visible public symbol, something that architects can create. M. Patte's prize-winning plan for the Paris of Louis XV, in which the *place royale* is extremely prominent. Each *place royale* has a statue of the monarch at the centre, and streets fanning out like rays. (*Based on Moholy-Nagy, 1968.*)

nation's, history. Public squares often display monuments and they are also a type of 'sacred area', in the sense that they may be dedicated to heroic figures and transcend purely utilitarian ends. Certain public buildings are also symbols: the Houses of Parliament, Chartres Cathedral, the Empire State Building, and, in the United States, the palatial railway stations. To modern geographers, it may seem lax usage to call monuments and buildings 'places', just like towns and cities, but this reflects our parochialism and distance from phenomenological reality. Elizabethan geographers of the early seventeenth century did not labour under such constraint and freely described towns and buildings at the same level of concreteness (Robinson, 1973). Cities are of course places, and ideal cities are also monuments and symbols. In the second world war, Coventry and Hiroshima were destroyed but Oxford and Kyoto were spared from aerial decimation (Lifton, 1967, 16). Thus the cultural and historical significance (the symbolic value) of Oxford and Kyoto was recognised even by the enemy. This recognition by the outsider is characteristic of places that are public symbols.

Monuments, artworks, buildings and cities are places because they can organize space into centres of meaning. People possess meaning and are the centres of their own worlds, but how can things made of stone, brick, and metal appear to possess life, wrap (so to speak) space around them and becomes places, centres of value and significance (Norberg-Schulz, 1971)? The answer is not difficult with buildings and cities for these are primarily fields of care, habitats for people who endow them with meaning in the course of time. Buildings and cities can, however, also be considered as works of art, as piles of stone that create places. How they are able to do this is the problem for philosophers of art: that they have this power is a matter for experience. A single inanimate object, useless in itself, can appear to be the focus of a world. As the poet Wallace Stevens (1965, 76) put it:

I placed a jar in Tennessee,
And round it was, upon a hill.
It made the slovenly wilderness
Surround that hill.

The wilderness rose up to it,
And sprawled around, no longer wild.
The jar was round upon the ground
And tall and of a port in air.

It took dominion everywhere.
The jar was gray and bare.
It did not give of bird or bush,
Like nothing else in Tennessee.

Only the human person can command a world. The art object can seem to do so because its form, as Susanne Langer (1953, 40) would say, is symbolic of human feeling. Perhaps this can be put more strongly. Personhood is incarnate in a piece of sculpture; and by virtue of this fact it seems to be the centre of its own world.

Though a statue is an object in our perceptual space, we see it as the centre of a space all its own. If sculpture is personal feeling made visible, then a building is an entire functional realm made visible, tangible, and sensible: it is the embodiment of the life of a culture. Thus monuments and buildings can be said to have vitality and spirit. The spirit of place is applicable to them, but in a sense different from holy places in which spirits are believed to dwell literally.

Some symbols transcend the bounds of a particular culture: for example, such large architectural forms as the square and the circle, used to delimit ideal (cosmic) cities, and such smaller architectural elements as the spire, the arch, and the dome, used in buildings with cosmic pretentions (Moholy-Nagy, 1968). Certain structures persist as places through aeons of time; they appear to defy the patronage of particular cultures. Perhaps any overpowering feature in the landscape creates its own world, which may expand or contract with the passing moods of the people, but which never completely loses its identity. Ayer's Rock in the heart of Australia, for example, dominated the mythical and perceptual field of the aborigines who lived there, but it remains a place for modern Australians who are drawn to visit the monolith by its awe-inspiring image. Stonehenge is an architectural example. No doubt it is less a place for British tourists than for its original builders: time has caused its dread, no less than its stones, to erode, but nonetheless Stonehenge is still very much a place (Dubos, 1972, 111–34; Newcomb, 1967). What happens is that a large monument like Stonehenge carries both general and specific import: the specific import changes in time whereas the general import remains. The Gateway Arch of St Louis, for example, has the general import of 'heavenly dome' and 'gate' that transcends American history (Smith, 1950), but it also has the specific import of a unique period in American history, namely, the opening of the West to settlement. Enduring places, of which there are very few in the world, speak to humanity. Most public symbols cannot survive the decay of their particular cultural matrix: with the departure of Britain from Egypt, the statues of Queen Victoria no longer command worlds but merely stand in the way of traffic. In the course of time, most public symbols lose their status as places and merely clutter up space.

Fields of Care

Public symbols can be seen and known from the outside: indeed, with monuments there is no inside view. Fields of care, by contrast, carry few signs that declare their nature: they can be known in essence only from within. Human beings establish fields of care, networks of interpersonal concern, in a physical setting (Wagner, 1972). From the viewpoint that they are places, two questions arise. One is, to what degree is the field of care emotionally tied to the physical setting? The other is, are the people aware of the identity and limit of their world? The field of care is indubitably also a place if the people are emotionally bound to their material environment, and if, further, they are conscious of its identity and spatial limit.

Human relationships require material objects for sustenance and deepening.

Personality itself depends on a minimum of material possessions, including the possession of intimate space. Even the most humble object can serve to objectify feelings: like words – only more permanent – they are exchanged as tokens of affective bond. The sharing of intimate space is another such expression. But these myriad objects and intimate spaces do not necessarily add up to place. The nature of the relationship between interpersonal ties on the one hand and the space over which they extend on the other is far from simple. Youth gangs have strong interpersonal ties, and they have a strong sense of the limits of space: gang members know well where their "turf" ends and that of another begins. Yet they have no real affection for the space they are willing to defend. When better opportunity calls from the outside world, the local turf – known to the gang members themselves for its shoddiness – is abandoned without regret (Eisenstadt, 1949; Suttles, 1968). Strong interpersonal ties require objects: English gypsies, for example, are avid collectors of china and old family photographs (Lynch, 1972, 40). But the resilience of the gypsies shows that the net of human concern does not require emotional anchoring in a particular locality for its strength. Home is wherever we happen to be, as all carefree young lovers know. Place is position in society as well as location in space: gypsies and young lovers are placeless in both senses of the word and they do not much care.

The emotion felt among human beings finds expression and anchorage in things and places. It can be said to create things and places to the extent that, in its glow, they acquire extra meaning. The dissolution of the human bond can cause the loss of meaning in the material environment. St Augustine left his birthplace, Thagaste, for Carthage when his closest friend died in young manhood. 'My heart was now darkened by grief, and everywhere I looked I saw death. My native haunts became a scene of torture to me, and my own home a misery. Without him everything we had done together turned into excruciating ordeal. My eyes kept looking for him without finding him. I hated all the places where we used to meet, because they could no longer say to me, "Look, here he comes", as they once did' (*Confessions*, Book 4:4–9). On the other hand, it is well known that the dissolution of a human bond can cause a heightening of sentimental attachment to material objects and places because they then seem the only means through which the dead can still speak. Sense of place turns morbid when it depends wholly on the memory of past human relationships.

What are the means by which affective bond reaches beyond human beings to place? One is repeated experience: the feel of place gets under our skin in the course of day-to-day contact (Rasmussen, 1962). The feel of the pavement, the smell of the evening air, and the colour of autumn foliage become, through long acquaintance, extensions of ourselves – not just a stage but supporting actors in the human drama. Repetition is of the essence: home is 'a place where every day is multiplied by days before it' (Stark, 1948, 55). The functional pattern of our lives is capable of establishing a sense of place. In carrying out the daily routines we go regularly from one point to another, following established paths, so that in time a web of nodes and their links is imprinted in our perceptual systems and affects our bodily expectations. A 'habit field', not necessarily one that we can picture, is thus established: in it we move comfortably with the minimal challenge of choice. But the strongest bond to place is of a religious nature. The tie is one of kinship, reaching back in time from proximate ancestors to distant semi-divine heroes, to the gods of the family hearth and of the city shrines. A mysterious continuity exists between the soil and the gods: to break it would be an act of impiety. This religious tie to place has almost completely disappeared from the modern world. Traces of it are left in the rhetoric of nationalism in which the state itself, rather than particular places, is addressed as 'father land' or 'mother land' (Gellner, 1973: Doob, 1964). Religion is maintained by rites and celebrations; these, in turn, strengthen the emotional links between people and sacred places. Celebrations as such demarcate time, that is, stages in the human life cycle, seasons in the year, and major events in the life of a nation; but notwithstanding this temporal priority celebrations, wherever they occur, lend character to place. The progressive decline in the sense of place, then, is the result of various factors, among them being: the demise of the gods; the loosening of local networks of human concern, with their intense emotional involvements that could have extended to place; the loss of intimate contact with the physical setting in an age when people seldom walk and almost never loiter; and the decline of meaningful celebrations, that is, those that are tinged with religious sentiment and tied to localities (James, 1961).

Unlike public symbols, fields of care lack visual identity. Outsiders find it difficult to recognise and delimit, for example, neighbourhoods which are a type of field of care (Keller, 1968). Planners may believe an area to be a neighbourhood, and label it as such on the ground that it is the same kind of physical environment and people come from a similar socio-economic class, only to discover that the local residents do not recognise the area as a neighbourhood: the parts with which they identify may be much smaller, for instance, a single street or an intersection (Gans, 1962, 11). Moreover, although the residents of an area may have a strong sense of place, this sense is not necessarily self-conscious. Awareness is not self-awareness. Total immersion in an environment means to open one's pores, as it were, to all its qualities, but it also means ignorance of the fact that one's place as a whole has a personality distinct from that of all other places. As Dardel puts it (1952, 47):

> *La réalité géographique exige une adhésion si totale du sujet, à travers sa vie affective, son corps, ses habitudes, qu'il lui arrive de l'oublier, comme il peut oublier sa propre vie organique. Elle vit pourtant, cachée et prête à se reveiller. L'éloignement, l'exil, l'invasion tirent l'environment de l'oublie et le font apparaître sous le mode de la privation, de la souffrance ou de la tendresse. La nostalgie fait apparaître le pays comme absence, sur le fond d'un dépaysement, d'une discordance profonde. Conflit entre le géographique comme intériorité, comme passé, et le géographique tout extérieur du maintenant.*

The sense of place is perhaps never more acute than when one is homesick, and one can only be homesick when one is no longer at home (Starobinski, 1966). However, the loss of place need not be literal. The threat of loss is sufficient. Residents not only sense but know that their world has an identity and a boundary when they feel threatened, as when people of another race wants to move in, or

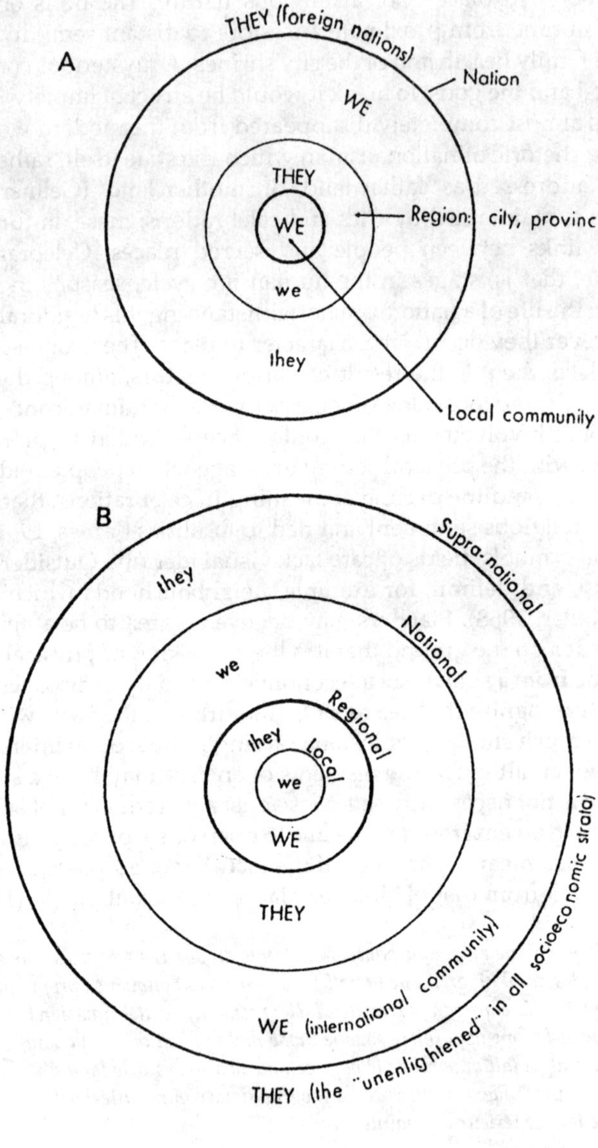

Figure 28.2 [orig. fig. 6] The 'we-they' syndrome in the definition of space. Among people of the lower middle socio-economic class: **A:** the 'we-they' distinctions tend to be clearly recognized at the local and national (superpatriotic) levels. The suspicion of strangers and foreigners extends to their lands. Among the cosmopolitan and highly educated types: **B:** the home base is broadened beyond the local neighbourhood to a region, and nationalism (national boundary) is transcended by familiarity with the international life style.

when the area is the target of highway construction or urban renewal (Suttles, 1972). Identity is defined in competition and in conflict with others: this seems true of both individuals and communities (Figure 28.2). We owe our sense of being not only to supportive forces but also to those that pose a threat. Being has a centre and an edge: supportive forces nurture the centre while threatening forces strengthen the edge. In theological language, hell bristles with places that have sharply drawn – indeed fortified – boundaries but no centre worthy of defence; heaven is full of glowing centres with the vaguest boundaries; earth is an uneasy compromise of the two realms.

What is a Place?

The infant's place is in the crib, and the place of the crawling child is under the grand piano. Place can be as small as the corner of a room or large as the earth itself: that earth is our place in the universe is a simple fact of observation to homesick astronauts. Location can become place overnight, so to speak, through the ingenuity of architects and engineers. A striking monument creates place; a carnival transforms temporarily an abandoned stockyard or cornfield into place; Disneylands are permanent carnivals, places created out of wholecloth. On the other hand, places are locations in which people have long memories, reaching back beyond the indelible impressions of their own individual childhoods to the common lores of bygone generations. One may argue that engineers create localities but time is needed to create place (Lowenthal, 1966; Lynch, 1972). It is obvious that most definitions of place are quite arbitrary. Geographers tend to think of place as having the size of a settlement: the plaza within it may be counted a place, but usually not the individual houses, and certainly not that old rocking chair by the fireplace. Architects think on a smaller scale. To many of them places are homes, shopping centres, and public squares that can be taken from the drawing boards and planted on earth: time, far from 'creating' place, is a threat to the pristine design of their handiworks. To poets, moralists, and historians, places are not only the highly visible public symbols but also the fields of care in which time is of the essence, since time is needed to accumulate experience and build up care. All places are small worlds: the sense of a world, however, may be called forth by art (the jar placed on the hill) as much as by the intangible net of human relations. Places may be public symbols or fields of care, but the power of the symbols to create place depends ultimately on the human emotions that vibrate in a field of care. Disneyland, to take one example, draws on the capital of sentiments that has accumulated in inconspicuous small worlds elsewhere and in other times.

References

Dardel, E. 1952: *L'homme et la terre: nature de la réalité géographique*. Paris: Presses Universitaires de France. (133 pp.)

DeGroot, J. J. M. 1892: *The religious system of China*. Leiden: Brill (360 pp.)

Doob, L. 1964: *Patriotism and nationalism: their psychological foundations*. New Haven: Yale University Press. (297 pp.)
Dubos, R. 1972: *A god within*. New York: Scribner. (325 pp.)
Eisenstadt, S. N. 1949: The perception of time and space in a situation of culture-contact. *Journal of the Royal Authropological Institute of Great Britain and Ireland* 79, 63–8.
Eliade, M. 1963: *Patterns in comparative religion*. Cleveland, Ohio: World Publishing Co. (484 pp.) Translation of *Traité d'histoire des religions*, Paris: Payot, 1953.
Erickson, S. A. 1969: Language and meaning. In Edie, J. M., Editor, *New essays in phenomenology*. Chicago: Quadrangle Books, 39–49.
Fowler, W. W. 1911: *The religious experience of the Roman people*. London: Macmillan. (504 pp.)
Fox, C. F. 1932: *The personality of Britain: its influence on inhabitant and invader in prehistoric and early historic times*. Cardiff: National Museum of Wales and the Press Board of the University of Wales. (84 pp.)
Gans, H. J. 1962: *The urban villagers*. New York: Free Press. (367 pp.)
Gellner, E. 1973: Scale and nation. *Philosophy of the social sciences* 3, 1–17.
Grene, M. 1968: *Approaches to a philosophical biology*. New York: Basic Books. (295 pp.)
James, E. O. 1961: *Seasonal feasts and festivals*. London: Thames and Hudson. (336 pp.)
Johnson, P. 1968: Why we want our cities ugly. In *The fitness of man's environment*, Washington, DC: Smithsonian Annual 2, 145–60.
Keller, S. I. 1968: *The urban neighborhood*. New York: Random House. (201 pp.)
Langer, S. K. 1953: *Feeling and form*. New York: Scribner. (431 pp.)
Lifton, R.J. 1967: *Death in life: survivors of Hiroshima*. New York: Random House. (594pp.)
Lowenthal, D. 1961: Geography, experience, and imagination: towards a geographical epistemology. *Annals of the Association of American Geographers* 51, 241–60.
1966: The American way of history. *Columbia University Forum* 9, 27–32.
Lynch, K. 1972: *What time is this place?* Cambridge, Mass.: MIT Press. (277 pp.)
Moholy-Nagy, S. 1968: *Matrix of man: an illustrated history of urban environment*. New York: Praeger. (317 pp.)
Newcomb, R. M. 1967: Monuments three millenia old – the persistence of place. *Landscape* 17, 24–6.
Norberg-Schulz, C. 1971: *Existence, space and architecture*. New York: Praeger. (120 pp.)
Rasmussen, S. E. 1962: *Experiencing architecture*. Cambridge: MIT Press. (245 pp.)
Santmyer, H. H. 1962: *Ohio town*. Columbus: Ohio State University Press. (309 pp).
Sauer, C. O. 1941: The personality of Mexico. *Geographical Review* 31, 353–64.
Scully, V. 1962: *The earth, the temple, and the gods*. New Haven and London: Yale University Press. (257 pp.)
Smith, E. B. 1950: *The dome, a study in the history of ideas*. Princeton, New Jersey: Princeton University Press. (164 pp.)
Sorokin, P. A. 1964: *Sociocultural causality, space, time*. New York: Russell and Russell. (246 pp).
Stark, F. 1948: *Perseus in the wind*. London: John Murray. (168 pp.)
Starobinski, J. 1966: The idea of nostalgia. *Diogenes* 54, 81–103.
Stevens, W. 1965: *Collected poems*. New York: Knopf. (534 pp.)
Suttles, G. D. 1972: *The social construction of communities*. Chicago: University of Chicago Press. (278 pp.)
Van der Leeuw, G. 1963: *Religion in essence and manifestation*. (2 vols., 714 pp.) Translation of *Phänomenologie der Religion*, Tübingen: Mohr 1933.
Vidal de la Blache, Paul 1903: La personnalité géographique de la France. In E. Lavisse, editor, *Histoire de France* I (I), Paris: Hachette.

Wagner, P. 1972: *Environments and peoples*. Englewood Cliffs, New Jersey: Prentice-Hall. (110 pp.)
White, L. 1967: The historical roots of our ecological crisis. *Science* 155, 1203–7.
Wild, J. 1963: *Existence and the world of freedom*. Englewood Cliffs, New Jersey: Prentice-Hall. (243 pp.)
Wissowa, G. 1912: *Religion und Kultur der Römer*. Munich: Beck'sche. (612 pp.)

29

A WOMAN'S PLACE?

Linda McDowell and Doreen Massey

In the 1980s there was not only a revival of geographies that were organized around concepts such as region and place, but also a new interest in questions of gender as they relate to the experience of place. Indeed, it could be argued that the concern of feminists for the different experiences of men and women was important among some geographers (and others) in the revival of interest in the specificities of places. In particular, the idea that patriarchy (the historical pattern of male social dominance) was perhaps manifested differently in different places because of differing articulations between it and local relations of production inspired Linda McDowell and Doreen Massey (then both at Britain's Open University) to write the article reproduced here. This theme is examined in a frame of reference drawn from Massey's previous work on spatial divisions of labour (**chapter 25**). What is most remarkable about it, however, may be the extent to which the focus on women's work experiences in different types of place provides a much more nuanced understanding of the particularities of places than does the more abstract argument to be found in Massey's previous work. In addition to its central concern with the impact on places of gender divisions of labour, this chapter points to the effects of place on the experience of gender. It could also be read as a reworking of regional geography's traditional concern with place, work and family. The contribution of this approach, therefore, extends well beyond the singular case of gender to other social divisions (such as class and ethnicity) that have rarely been well articulated in geographical writing.

Source: 'A woman's place?' In *Geography Matters!*, editors D. Massey and J. Allen, Cambridge: Cambridge University Press, 1984, pp. 128–47.

The nineteenth century saw the expansion of capitalist relations of production in Britain. It was a geographically uneven and differentiated process, and the resulting economic differences between regions are well known: the rise of the coalfields, of the textile areas, the dramatic social and economic changes in the organization of agriculture, and so forth. Each was both a reflection of and a basis for the period of dominance which the UK economy enjoyed within the nineteenth-century international division of labour. In this wider spatial division of labour, in other words, different regions of Britain played different roles, and their economic and employment structures in consequence also developed along different paths.

But the spread of capitalist relations of production was also accompanied by other changes. In particular it disrupted the existing relations between women and men. The old patriarchal form of domestic production was torn apart, the established pattern of relations between the sexes was thrown into question. This, too, was a process which varied in its extent and in its nature between parts of the country, and one of the crucial influences on this variation was the nature of the emerging economic structures. In each of these different areas 'capitalism' and 'patriarchy' were articulated together, accommodated themselves to each other, in different ways.

It is this process that we wish to examine here. Schematically, what we are arguing is that the contrasting forms of economic development in different parts of the country presented distinct conditions for the maintenance of male dominance. *Extremely* schematically, capitalism presented patriarchy with different challenges in different parts of the country. The question was in what ways the terms of male dominance would be reformulated within these changed conditions. Further, this process of accommodation between capitalism and patriarchy produced a different synthesis of the two in different places. It was a synthesis which was clearly visible in the nature of gender relations, and in the lives of women.

This issue of the synthesis of aspects of society within different places is what we examine in the following four subsections of this chapter. What we are interested in, in other words, is one complex in that whole constellation of factors which go to make up the uniqueness of place.

We have chosen four areas to look at. They are places where not only different 'industries' in the sectoral sense, but also different social forms of production, dominated: coal mining in the north-east of England, the factory work of the cotton towns, the sweated labour of inner London, and the agricultural gang-work of the Fens. In one chapter we cannot do justice to the complexity of the syntheses which were established in these very different areas. All we attempt is to illustrate our argument by highlighting the most significant lines of contrast.

Since the construction of that nineteenth-century mosaic of differences all these regions have undergone further changes. In the second group of sections we leap ahead to the last decades of the twentieth century and ask 'where are they now?'. What is clear is that, in spite of all the major national changes which might have been expected to iron out the contrasts, the areas, in terms of gender relations and the lives of women, are still distinct. But they are distinct in different ways now. Each is still unique, though each has changed. In this later section we focus on two threads in this reproduction and transformation of uniqueness. First, there have been different changes in the economic structure of the areas. They have been incorporated in different ways into the new, wider spatial division of labour, indeed the new international division of labour. The national processes of change in the UK economy, in other words, have not operated in the same way in each of the areas. The new layers of economic activity, or inactivity, which have been superimposed on the old are, just as was the old, different in different places. Second, however, the impact of the more recent changes has itself been moulded by the different existing conditions, the accumulated inheritance of the past, to produce distinct resulting combinations. 'The local' has had its impact on the operation of 'the national'.

The Nineteenth Century

Coal is our life: whose life?

Danger and drudgery; male solidarity and female oppression – this sums up life in the colliery villages of Co. Durham during much of the nineteenth century. Here the separation of men and women's lives was virtually total: men were the breadwinners, women the domestic labourers, though hardly the 'angels of the house' that featured so large in the middle class Victorian's idealization of women. The coal mining areas of Durham provide a clear example of how changes in the economic organization of Victorian England interacted with a particular view of women's place to produce a rigidly hierarchial and patriarchal society. These villages were dominated by the pits and by the mine owners. Virtually all the men earned their livelihood in the mines and the mines were an almost exclusively male preserve, once women's labour was forbidden from the middle of the century. Men were the industrial proletariat selling their labour power to a monopoly employer, who also owned the home. Mining was a dirty, dangerous and hazardous job. Daily, men risked their lives in appalling conditions. The shared risks contributed to a particular form of male solidarity, and the endowment of their manual labour itself with the attributes of masculinity and virility. The shared dangers at work led to shared interests between men outside work: a shared pit language, shared clubs and pubs, a shared interest in rugby. Women's banishment from the male world of work was thus compounded by their exclusion from the local political and social life.

Jobs for women in these areas were few. Domestic service for the younger girls; for married women poorly paid and haphazard work such as laundry, decorating or child care. But most of the families were in the same position: there was little cash to spare for this type of service in families often depending on a single source of male wages. For miners' wives almost without exception, and for many of their daughters, unpaid work in the home was the only and time-consuming option. And here the unequal economic and social relationships between men and women imposed by the social organization of mining increased the subordinate position of women. A miner's work resulted in enormous domestic burdens for his wife and family. Underground work was filthy and this was long before the installation of pithead showers and protective clothing. Working clothes had to be boiled in coppers over the fire which had to heat all the hot water for washing clothes, people and floors. Shift work for the men increased women's domestic work: clothes had to be washed, backs scrubbed and hot meals prepared at all times of the day and night:

> *I go to bed only on Saturday nights', said a miner's wife; 'my husband and our three sons are all in different shifts, and one or other of them is leaving or entering the house and requiring a meal every three hours of the twenty four. (Webb, 1921, pp. 71–2)*

An extreme example, perhaps, but not exceptional.

These Durham miners, themselves oppressed at work, were often tyrants in their own home, dominating their wives in an often oppressive and bullying fashion. They seem to have "reacted to [their own] exploitation by fighting not as a class against capitalism, but as a gender group against women – or rather within a framework of sex solidarity against a specific woman chosen and caged for this express purpose" (Frankenberg, 1976, p. 40). Men were the masters at home. Here is a Durham man, who himself went down the pits in the 1920s, describing his father:

> *He was a selfish man. If there was three scones he'd want the biggest one. He'd sit at the table with his knife and fork on the table before the meal was even prepared . . . Nobody would get the newspaper till he had read it. (Strong Words Collective, 1977, pp. 11–12)*

Thus gender relations took a particular form in these colliery villages. National ideologies and local conditions worked together to produce a unique set of patriarchal relations based on the extreme separation of men's and women's lives. Masculine supremacy, male predominance in every area of economic and social life became an established, and almost unchallenged, fact. Patriarchal power in this part of the country remained hardly disturbed until the middle of the next century.

Cotton towns: the home turned upside down?

The images of homemaker and breadwinner are of course national ones, common to the whole of capitalist Britain, and not just to coalfield areas. But they were more extreme in these regions, and they took a particular form; there were differences between the coalfields and other parts of the country.

The cotton towns of the north-west of England are probably the best-known example from, as it were, the other end of the spectrum, and a major element in this has been the long history of paid labour outside the home for women. It is often forgotten to what extent women were the first labour-force of factory-based, industrial capitalism. "In this sense, modern industry was a direct challenge to the traditional sexual division of labour in social production" (Alexander, 1982, p. 41). And it was in the cotton industry around Manchester that the challenge was first laid down.

Maintaining patriarchal relations in such a situation was (and has been) a different and in many ways a more difficult job than in Durham. The challenge was nonetheless taken up. Indeed spinning, which had in the domestic organization of the textile industry been done by women, was taken over by men. Work on the mule came to be classified as 'heavy', as, consequently, to be done by men, and (also consequently) as skilled (Hall, 1982). The maintenance of male prerogative in the face of threats from women's employment, was conscious and organized:

> *The mule spinners did not leave their dominance to chance . . . At their meeting in the Isle of Man in 1829 the spinners stipulated 'that no person be learned or allowed to spin except the son, brother, or orphan nephew of spinners'. Those women spinners who had managed to maintain their position were advised to form their own union. From then on the entry to the trade was very tightly controlled and the days of the female spinners were indeed numbered. (Hall, 1982, p. 22)*

But if men won in spinning, they lost (in those terms) in weaving. The introduction of the power loom was crucial. With it, the factory system took over from the handloom weavers, and in the factories it was mainly women and children who were employed. This did present a real challenge:

> *The men who had been at the heads of productive households were unemployed or deriving a pittance from their work whilst their wives and children were driven out to the factories. (Hall, 1982, p. 24)*

Nor was 'the problem' confined to weavers. For the fact that in some towns a significant number of married women went out to work weaving meant that further jobs were created for other women, doing for money aspects of domestic labour (washing and sewing, for example) that would otherwise have been done for nothing by the women weavers. Further, the shortage of employment for men, and low wages, provided another incentive for women to earn a wage for themselves (Anderson, 1971).

The situation caused moral outrage among the Victorian middle classes and presented serious competition to working-class men. There was "what has been described as 'coincidence of interests' between philanthropists, the state – representing the collective interests of capital – and the male working class who were represented by the trade union movement and Chartism – which cooperated to reduce female and child labour and to limit the length of the working day" (Hall, 1982, p. 25). In the same way, it was at national level that arguments about 'the family wage' came to be developed and refined as a further means of subordinating women's paid labour (for pin money) to that of men's (to support a family). The transformation from domestic to factory production, a transformation which took place first in the cotton towns,

> *provoked, as can be seen, a period of transition and re-accommodation in the sexual division of labour. The break-up of the family economy, with the threat this could present to the male head of household, who was already faced with a loss of control over his own labour, demanded a re-assertion of male authority. (Hall, 1982, p. 27)*

Yet in spite of that reassertion, the distinctiveness of the cotton areas continued. There were more women in paid work, and particularly in relatively skilled paid work, in the textile industry and in this part of the country, than elsewhere:

> *In many cases the family is not wholly dissolved by the employment of the wife, but turned upside down. The wife supports the family, the husband sits at home, tends the children, sweeps the room and cooks. This case happens very frequently: in Manchester alone, many hundred such men could be cited, condemned to domestic occupations. It is easy to imagine the wrath aroused among the working-men by this reversal of all relations within the family, while the other social conditions remain unchanged. (Engels, 1969 edn, p. 173)*

This tradition of waged-labour for Lancashire women, more developed than in other parts of the country, has lasted. Of the early twentieth century, Liddington writes "Why did so many Lancashire women go out to work? By the turn of the century economic factors had become further reinforced by three generations of social conventions. It became almost unthinkable for women *not* to work" (1979, pp. 98–9).

And this tradition in its turn had wider effects. Lancashire women joined trade unions on a scale unknown elsewhere in the country: "union membership was accepted as part of normal female behaviour in the cotton towns" (Liddington, 1979, p. 99). In the nineteenth century the independent mill-girls were renowned for their cheekiness; of the women of the turn-of-the-century cotton towns, Liddington writes: "Lancashire women, trade unionists on a massive scale unmatched elsewhere, were organized, independent and proud" (1979, p. 99). And it was from this base of organized working women that arose the local suffrage campaign of the early twentieth century. "Lancashire must occupy a special place in the minds of feminist historians. The radical suffragists sprang from an industrial culture which enabled them to organize a widespread political campaign for working women like themselves" (p. 98).

The radical suffragists mixed working-class and feminist politics in a way which challenged both middle-class suffragettes and working-class men. In the end, though, it was precisely their uniqueness which left them isolated – their uniqueness as radical trade unionists *and* women, and, ironically, their highly regionalized base:

> *The radical suffragists failed in the end to achieve the political impact they sought. The reforms for which they campaigned – of which the most important was the parliamentary vote – demanded the backing of the national legislature at Westminster. Thousands of working women in the Lancashire cotton towns supported their campaign, and cotton workers represented five out of six of all women trade union members. No other group of women workers could match their level of organization, their (relatively) high wages and the confidence they had in their own status as skilled workers. Their strength, however, was regional rather than national, and when they tried to apply their tactics to working-class women elsewhere or to the national political arena, they met with little success. Ultimately the radical suffragists' localised strength proved to be a long-term weakness. (Liddington, 1979, p. 110)*

The rag-trade in Hackney: a suitable job for a women?

But there were other industries in other parts of the country where women were equally involved in paid labour, where conditions were as bad as in the cotton mills, yet where at this period not a murmur was raised against their employment. One such area was Hackney, dominated by industries where sweated labour was the main form of labour-organization.

What was different about this form of wage relation for women from men's point of view? What was so threatening about women working? Hall (1982) enumerates a number of threads to the threat. The first was that labour was now *waged* labour. Women with a wage of their own had a degree of potential unsettling financial independence. But Lancashire textiles and the London sweated trades had this in common. The thing that distinguished them was the spatial separation of home and workplace. The dominant form of organization of the labour-process in the London sweated trades was homeworking. The waged-labour was carried out in the home; in Lancashire, birthplace of the factory-system, waged-labour by now meant leaving the house and going to the mill. It wasn't so much 'work' as 'going out to' work which was the threat to the patriarchal order. And this in two ways: it threatened the ability of women adequately to perform their domestic role as homemaker for men and children, and it gave them an entry into public life, mixed company, a life not defined by family and husband.

It was, then, a change in the social *and the spatial* organization of work which was crucial. And that change mattered to women as well as men. Lancashire women did get out of the home. The effects of homeworking *are* different: the worker remains confined to the privatized space of the home, and individualized, isolated from other workers. Unionization of women in cotton textiles has always been far higher than amongst the homeworking women in London.

Nor was this all. For the *nature* of the job also mattered in terms of its potential impact on gender relations:

> *Only those sorts of work that coincided with a woman's natural sphere were to be encouraged. Such discrimination had little to do with the danger or unpleasantness of the work concerned. There was not much to choose for example – if our criterion is risk to life or health – between work in the mines, and work in the London dressmaking trades. But no one suggested that sweated needlework should be prohibited to women. (Alexander, 1982, p. 33)*

Thinking back to the contrast between the coalfields and the cotton towns and the relationship in each between economic structure and gender relations and roles, it is clear that the difference between the two areas was not simply based on the presence/absence of waged labour. We have, indeed, already suggested other elements, such as the whole ideology of virility attached to mining. But it was also to do with the *kind* of work for women in Lancashire: that it was factory work, with machines, and outside the home. In the sweated trades of nineteenth-century London, capitalism and patriarchy together produced less immediate threat to men's domination.

There were other ways, too, in which capitalism and patriarchy interrelated in the inner London of that time to produce a specific outcome. The sweated trades in which the women worked, and in particular clothing, were located in the inner areas of the metropolis for a whole variety of reasons, among them the classic one of quick access to fast-changing markets. But they also needed labour, and they needed cheap labour. Homeworking, besides being less of an affront to patriarchal relations, was one means by which costs were kept down. But costs (wages) were also kept down by the very availability of labour. In part this was a result of immigration and the vulnerable position of immigrants in the labour market. But it was also related to the predominantly low-paid and irregular nature of jobs for men (Harrison, 1983, p. 42). Women in Hackney *needed* to work for a wage. And this particular Hackney articulation of patriarchal influences and other 'location factors' worked well enough for the clothing industry.

But even given that in Hackney the social organization and nature of women's work was less threatening to men than in the cotton towns, there were still defensive battles to be fought. The labour-force of newly arrived immigrants also included men. Clearly, were the two sexes to do the same jobs, or be accorded the same status, or the same pay, this would be disruptive of male dominance. The story of the emergence of a sexual division of labour within the clothing industry was intimately bound up with the maintenance of dominance by males in the immigrant community. They did not use the confused and contradictory criteria of 'skill' and 'heavy work' employed so successfully in Lancashire. In clothing *any* differentiation would do. Phillips and Taylor (1980) have told the story, of the establishment of the sexual division of labour in production, based on the minutest of differences of job, changes in those differences over time, and the use of them in whatever form they took to establish the men's job as skilled and the women's as less so.

Rural life and labour

Our final example is drawn from the Fenlands of East Anglia, where the division of labour and gender relations took a different form again. In the rural villages and hamlets of nineteenth-century East Anglia, as in the Lancashire cotton towns, many women 'went out to work'. But here there was no coal industry, no factory production of textiles, no sweated labour in the rag trade. Economic life was still overwhelmingly dominated by agriculture. And in this part of the country farms were large, and the bulk of the population was landless, an agricultural proletariat. The black soils demanded lots of labour in dyking, ditching, claying, stone-picking and weeding to bring them under the 'New Husbandry', the nineteenth-century extension of arable land (Samuel, 1975, pp. 12 and 18). Women were an integral part of this agricultural workforce, doing heavy work of all sorts on the land, and provoking much the same moral outrage as did the employment of women in mills in Lancashire:

> *. . . the poor wage which most labourers could earn forced their wives to sell their labour too, and continue working in the fields. In Victorian eyes, this was anathema for it gave women an*

independence and freedom unbecoming to their sex. 'That which seems most to lower the moral or decent tone of the peasant girls', wrote Dr. Henry Hunter in his report to the Privy Council in 1864, 'is the sensation of independence of society which they acquire when they have remunerative labour in their hands, either in the fields or at home as straw-plaiters etc. All gregarious employment gives a slang character to the girls appearance and habits, while dependence on the man for support is the spring of modest and pleasing deportment'. The first report of the Commissioners on The Employment of Children, Young Persons and Women in Agriculture in 1867, put it more strongly, for not only did landwork 'almost unsex a woman', but it 'generates a further very pregnant social mischief by unfitting or indisposing her for a woman's proper duties at home'. (Chamberlain, 1975, p. 17)

The social and spatial structure of the rural communities of this area also influenced the availability and the nature of work. Apart from work on the land, there were few opportunities for women to earn a wage. Even if they did not leave the village permanently, it was often necessary to travel long distances, frequently in groups, with even more serious repercussions in the eyes of the Victorian establishment:

The worst form of girl labour, from the point of view of bourgeois respectability, was the 'gang' system, which provoked a special commission of inquiry, and a great deal of outraged commentary, in the 1860s. It was most firmly established in the Fen districts of East Anglia and in the East Midlands. The farms in these parts tended to be large but the labouring population was scattered . . . The labour to work the land then had to be brought from afar, often in the form of travelling gangs, who went from farm to farm to perform specific tasks. (Kitteringham, 1975, p. 98)

There are here some familiar echoes from Lancashire. And yet things were different in the Fens. In spite of all the potential threats to morality, domesticity, femininity and general female subordination, 'going out to work' on the land for women in the Fens, even going off in gangs for spells away from the village, does not seem to have resulted in the kinds of social changes, and the real disruption to established ways, that occurred in Lancashire. In this area, women's waged-labour did not seem to present a threat to male supremacy within the home. Part of the explanation lies in the different nature of the work for women. This farm labour was often seasonal. The social and spatial organization of farmwork was quite different from that of factory work, and always insecure. Each gang negotiated wage rates independently with the large landowners, the women were not unionized, did not work in factories, were not an industrial proletariat in the same sense as the female mill workers in the cotton towns. Part of the explanation too, as in the colliery villages, lies in the organization of male work. Men, too, were predominantly agricultural labourers, though employed on an annual rather than a seasonal basis, and like mining, agricultural work was heavy and dirty, imposing a similar domestic burden on rural women.

A further influence was the life of the rural village, which was overwhelmingly conservative – socially, sexually and politically. Women on the land in this area did not become radicalized like women in the cotton towns. Relations between the sexes continued unchanged. Women served their menfolk, and both men and women served the local landowner; nobody rocked the boat politically:

> *When the Coatesworths ruled the village to vote Tory was to get and keep a job. The Liberals were the party of the unemployed and the undeserving . . . Concern over politics was not confined to men. The women took an interest, too. They had to. Their man's political choice crucially affected his employment, and their lives. (Chamberlain, 1975, p. 130)*

Where Are They Now?

What is life like in these areas now? Have the traditional attitudes about women's place in the home in the heavy industrial areas survived post-war changes? Have Lancashire women managed to retain the independence that so worried the Victorian middle class? In this century there have been enormous changes in many areas of economic and social life. The communications revolution has linked all parts of the country together, TV, radio, video and a national press have reduced regional isolation and increased the ease with which new ideas and attitudes spread. Changes in social mores, in the role of the family, in the labour process of domestic work, increased divorce rates and a rapid rise in women's participation in waged-labour between the Second World War and the end of the seventies have all had an impact. And yet, we shall argue here, regional differences remain.

There are, as we said in the introduction, two threads which we shall follow in this process of the reproduction of local uniqueness. The first concerns the geographically differentiated operation of national processes. Over 40% of the national paid labour-force in the UK now consists of women: a vast majority of them married. One of the consequences of this growth of jobs 'for women' has paradoxically been both an increase and a reduction in regional differences. The gender division of labour is changing in different ways in different areas, in part in response to previous patterns. Regional disparities in the proportion of women at work are closing, but the corollary of this, of course, is that the highest proportions of new and expanding jobs are in those very regions where previously few women have been involved in waged-labour. The four regions are being drawn in different ways into a new national structure of employment and unemployment. We cannot here attempt to explain this new spatial pattern. One thing we do hint at though, is that the form of gender relations themselves, and the previous economic and social history of women in each of these places, may be one, though only one, thread in that explanation.

The areas, then, have experienced different types of change in their economic structure. In many ways the growth of jobs for women has been of greater significance in the north-east and in East Anglia than in the cotton towns or in Hackney. But that is not the end of the story. For those changes have themselves been combined with existing local conditions and this has influenced their operation and their effect. The impact of an increase in jobs for women has not been the same in the Fens as it has been in the coalfields of the north-east. This, then, is the second thread in our discussion of the reproduction of local uniqueness.

In the rest of this chapter we try to show the links between past and present patterns, how changing attitudes to women and men's roles at work and in the family in different parts of the country (themselves related to previous economic roles) both influence and are influenced by national changes in the nature and organization of paid employment over time. The present gender division of labour in particular places is the outcome of the combination over time of successive phases. Space and location still matter. The structure of relationships between men and women varies between, and within, regions. Life in inner London is still not the same as in the Fenlands, in the coalfields of the north-east, as in the textile towns round Manchester. The current division of labour between women and men is different, paid employment is differently structured and organized, and even its spatial form varies between one part of the country and another.

Coal was our life?

The decline of work in the pits is a well-known aspect of post-war economic changes in Britain. How have the men and women of the north-east reacted to this decline in their traditional livelihood? Have the changes challenged or strengthened the traditional machismo of the north-eastern male? What is happening in the north-east today in many ways recalls some of the images – and the social alarm – generated by the cotton towns a hundred years earlier. It is now in the north-east that homes are being 'turned upside down' and patriarchy threatened by women going out to work. At the beginning of the 1960s, still something less than a quarter of all adult women in the old colliery areas worked outside their homes for wages. The figure has more than doubled since then. And part of the explanation lies in the local distinctiveness, the uniqueness of these areas that has its origins in the nineteenth century. The women of this area have no tradition of waged-labour, no union experience. It was, of course, these very features that proved attractive to the female-employing industries that opened branch plants in increasing numbers in Co. Durham in the sixties and seventies.

The new jobs that came to the north-east, then, were mainly for women. They were located on trading estates and in the region's two New Towns built to attract industrial investment and also to improve housing conditions. The women who moved into the New Towns of Peterlee and Washington provided a cheap, flexible, untrained and trapped pool of labour for incoming firms. And added to this, the loss of jobs for men together with the rent rises entailed by a move to new housing pushed women into the labour market.

Male antagonism to the new gender division of labour was almost universal. Outrage at women 'taking men's jobs', pleas for 'proper jobs', an assumption that the packing, processing and assembly line work that loomed ever larger in the economic structure of the area was an affront to masculine dignity: "I think a lot of men feel that assembly work wouldn't be acceptable; they'd be a bit proud about doing that type of work in this area. North East ideas are ingrained in the men in this area" (Lewis, 1983, p. 19). These assumptions appear to be shared by the new employers: "we are predominantly female labour orientated . . . the work is more suited to women, it's very boring, I suppose we're old-fashioned and still consider it as women's work . . . the men aren't interested".

This lack of interest plays right into the hands of the employers: once defined as 'women's work', the jobs are then classified as semi- or unskilled and hence low paid. An advantage that can be further exploited, as this factory director explains:

> *we changed from full-time to part-time women(!) . . . especially on the packing . . . because two part-timers are cheaper than one full-timer . . . we don't have to pay national insurance if they earn less than £27.00 a week, and the women don't have to pay the stamp . . . the hours we offer suit their social lifes. (Lewis, Ph.D., forthcoming)*

So if men aren't doing jobs outside the house, what are they doing instead? Are men here, like their Lancashire forebears, 'condemned to domestic occupations?'. Unlikely. An ex-miner's wife speaking on *Woman's Hour* in 1983 recalled that her husband would only reluctantly help in the home, pegging out the washing, for example, under cover of darkness!

Things *are* changing, though. Men are seen pushing prams in Peterlee, Newcastle-upon-Tyne Council has a women's committee, TV crews come to inquire into the progress of the domestication of the unemployed north-eastern male and the social and psychological problems it is presumed to bring with it. Working-class culture is still dominated by the club and the pub but even their male exclusivity is now threatened. The 1984 miners' strike seems set to transform gender relations even further. New battle lines between the sexes are being drawn. The old traditional pattern of relations between the sexes, which was an important condition for the new gender division being forged in the labour market, is now under attack.

Industry in the country?

How has life changed in the Fens? In some ways, continuity rather than change is the link between the past and present here. For many women, especially the older ones, work on the land is still their main source of employment:

> *hard work, in uncompromising weather, in rough old working clothes padded out with newspaper against the wind . . . Marriage for convenience or marriage to conform . . . Land-worker, home servicer. Poverty and exploitation – of men and women by the landowners, of women by their men. (Chamberlain, 1975, p. 11)*

Not much different from their grandmothers and great-grandmothers before them. Gangs are still a common feature and the nature of fieldwork has hardly changed either. Flowers are weeded and picked by hand. Celery and beet are sown and picked manually too. And this type of work is considered 'women's work'. It is poorly paid, seasonal and backbreaking. Male fieldworkers, on the other hand, have the status of 'labourers', relative permanence and the benefits associated with full-time employment. And they are the ones who have machinery to assist them.

Life *has* changed though. Small towns and rural areas such as the Fens have been favoured locations for the new branch plants and decentralizing industries of the sixties and seventies. Labour is cheap here – particularly with so few alternatives available – and relatively unorganized. Especially for younger women, the influx of new jobs has opened up the range of employment opportunities. It provides a means, still, both of supplementing low male wages, and of meeting people – of getting out of the small world of the village.

The impact of such jobs on women's lives, though, even the possibility of taking them, has been structured by local conditions, including gender relations. This is still a very rural area. The new jobs are in the nearby town. So unless factories provide their own transport (which a number do), access is a major problem. Public transport is extremely limited, and becoming more so. There are buses – but only once a week to most places. Not all families have a car, and very few women have daily use of one, let alone own 'their own' car. For many women, a bicycle is the only means of getting about.

This in turn has wider effects. For those who do make the journey to a factory job the effective working day (including travel time) can be very long. The time for domestic labour is squeezed, the work process consequently intensified. Those who remain in the village become increasingly isolated. The industrial workers, be they husbands or women friends, are absent for long hours, and services – shops, doctors, libraries – gradually have been withdrawn from villages.

It seems that the expansion of industrial jobs 'for women' has had relatively little impact on social relations in the rural Fens. In part, this is to do with the local conditions into which the jobs were introduced: the impact back of local factors on national changes. The Fenland villages today are still Conservative – politically and socially. Divorce, left-wing politics, women's independence are very much the exception.

Old cultural forms, transmitted, have remained remarkably intact:

> *Although love potions and true-lovers' knots made of straw have disappeared, Lent and May weddings are still considered lucky. The Churching of Women – an ancient post-natal cleansing ceremony – is still carried on, and pre-marital intercourse and the resulting pregnancy is as much a hangover from an older utilitarian approach to marriage as a result of the permissive society. In a farming community sons are important and there would be little point in marrying an infertile woman. (Chamberlain, 1975, p. 71)*

Attitudes to domestic responsibilities also remain traditional:

> *No women go out to work while the children are small – tho' there isn't much work anyway, and no facilities for childcare. Few women allow their children to play in the streets, or let them be seen in less than immaculate dress. Many men come home to lunch and expect a hot meal waiting for them. (p. 71)*

It takes more than the availability of a few jobs, it seems, substantially to alter the pattern of life for women in this area:

> *Although employment is no longer dependent on a correct political line, the village is still rigidly hierarchic in its attitudes, and follows the pattern of the constituency in voting solidly Conservative. And in a rigidly hierarchical society, when the masters are also the men, most women see little point in taking an interest in politics, or voting against the established order of their homes or the community as a whole . . . Most women must of necessity stick to the life they know. Their husbands are still the all-provider. The masters of their lives. (Chamberlain, 1975, pp. 130–1)*

Gender relations in East Anglia apparently have hardly been affected by the new jobs, let alone 'turned upside down'.

A regional problem for women?

The contrast with the cotton towns of Lancashire is striking. Here, where employment for women in the major industry had been declining for decades, was a major source of female labour, already skilled, already accustomed to factory work, plainly as dextrous as elsewhere. And yet the new industries of the sixties and seventies, seeking out female labour, did not come here, or not to the extent that they went to other places.

The reasons are complex, but they are bound up once again with the intricate relationship between capitalist and patriarchal structures. For one thing, here there was no regional policy assistance. There has, for much of this century, been massive decline in employment in the cotton industry in Lancashire. Declines comparable to those in coalmining, for instance, and in areas dominated by it. Yet the cotton towns were never awarded Development Area status. To the extent that associated areas were not designated on the basis of unemployment rates, the explanation lies at the level of taxes and benefits which define women as dependent. There is often less point in signing on. A loss of jobs does not necessarily show up, therefore, in a corresponding increase in regional unemployment. Development Areas, however, were *not* designated simply on the basis of unemployment rates. They were wider concepts, and wider regions, designated on the basis of a more general economic decline and need for regeneration. To that extent the non-designation of the cotton towns was due in part to a more general political blindness to questions of women's employment.

So the lack of regional policy incentives must have been, relatively, a deterrent to those industries scanning the country for new locations. But it cannot have been the whole explanation. New industries moved to other non-assisted areas – East Anglia, for instance. Many factors were in play, but one of them surely was that the women of the cotton towns were not, either individually or collectively in their history, 'green labour'. The long tradition of women working in factory jobs, and their relative financial independence, has continued. In spite of the decline of cotton textiles the region still has a high female activity rate. And with this there continued, in modified form, some of those other characteristics. Kate Purcell, doing research in the Stockport of the 1970s, found that:

> *It is clear that traditions of female employment and current rates of economic activity affect not only women's activity per se, but also their attitudes to, and experience of, employment. The married women I interviewed in Stockport, where female activity rates are 45 per cent and have always been high, define their work as normal and necessary, whereas those women interviewed in the course of a similar exercise in Hull, where the widespread employment of married women is more recent and male unemployment rates are higher, frequently made references to the fortuitous nature of their work. (Purcell, 1979, p. 119)*

As has so often been noted in the case of male workers, confidence and independence are not attributes likely to attract new investment. It may well be that here there is a case where the same reasoning has applied to women.

But whatever the precise structure of explanation, the women of the cotton towns are now facing very different changes from those being faced by the women of the coalfields. Here they are not gaining a new independence from men; to some extent in places it may even be decreasing. Women's unemployment is not seen to 'disrupt' family life, or cause TV programmes to be made about challenges to gender relations, for women do the domestic work anyway. Having lost one of their jobs, they carry on (unpaid) with the other.

Hackney: still putting out

What has happened in Hackney is an intensification of the old patterns of exploitation and subordination rather than the superimposition of new patterns. Here manufacturing jobs have declined, but the rag trade remains a major employer. The women of Hackney possess, apparently, some of the same advantages to capital as do those of the coalfields and the Fens: they are cheap and unorganized (less than 10% are in a union – Harrison, 1983, pp. 69–70). In Inner London, moreover, the spatial organization of the labour-force, the lack of separation of home and work, strengthens the advantages: overheads (light, heat, maintenance of machinery) are borne by the workers themselves; workers are not eligible for social security benefits; their spatial separation one from another makes it virtually impossible for them to combine to force up wage rates, and so on.

So given the clear advantages to capital of such a vulnerable potential workforce, why has there been no influx of branch plants of multinationals, of electronics assembly-lines and suchlike? Recent decades have of course seen the growth of new types of jobs for women, particularly in the service sector, if not within Hackney itself then within travelling distance (for some), in the centre of London. But, at the moment, for big manufacturing capital and for the clerical–mass production operations which in the sixties and seventies established themselves in the Development Areas and more rural regions of the country, this vulnerable labour of the capital city holds out few advantages. Even the larger clothing firms (with longer production runs, a factory labour process, locational flexibility and the capital to establish new plant) have set up their new branch plants elsewhere, either in the peripheral regions of Britain or in the Third World. So why not in Hackney? In part the women of Hackney have been left behind in the wake of the more general decentralization, the desertion by manufacturing industry of the conurbations of the First World. In part they are the victims of the changing international division of labour within the clothing industry itself. But in part, too, the reasons lie in the nature of the available labour. Homeworking does have advantages for capital, but this way of making female labour cheap is no use for electronics assembly-lines or for other kinds of less individualized production. The usefulness of this way of making labour vulnerable is confined to certain types of labour process.

The influx of service jobs in central London has outbid manufacturing for female labour, in terms both of wages and of conditions of work (see Massey, 1984, ch. 4). But working in service jobs has not been an option available to all. For women in one way or another tied to the home, or to the very local area, homeworking in industries such as clothing has become increasingly the only available option. Given the sexual division of labour in the home, homeworking benefits some women:

> *Homework when properly paid, suits many women: women who wish to stay at home with small children, women who dislike the discipline and timekeeping of factory work and wish to work at their own pace. Muslim women observing semi-purdah. (Harrison, 1983, p. 64)*

But homework seldom is 'properly paid'. Harrison again, on types of work and rates of pay in Hackney in 1982:

> *There are many other types of homework in Hackney: making handbags, stringing buttons on cards, wrapping greeting cards, filling Christmas crackers, assembling plugs and ballpens, sticking insoles in shoes, threading necklaces. Rates of pay vary enormously according to the type of work and the speed of the worker, but it is rare to find any that better the average female hourly earnings in the clothing trade in 1981, £1.75 an hour, itself the lowest for any branch of industry. And many work out worse than the Wages Council minimum for the clothing trade of £1.42 per hour (in 1982). Given these rates of pay, sometimes the whole family, kids and all, are dragooned in: . . . one mother had her three daughters and son helping to stick eyes and tails on cuddly toys. (Harrison, 1983, pp. 67–8)*

The involvement of all members of a family in homework or working as a team in small family-owned factories is not uncommon, especially among ethnic minorities. For small companies the extended family may be essential to survival:

> *the flexibility comes from the family: none of their wages are fixed. When times are good, they may be paid more. When they are bad, they are paid less. They get the same pay whether their hours are short or long.*

The fact that women are employed in the context of an extended family is important not only in the organization of the industry but also for the lives of the women themselves. They may have a wage, but they do not get the other forms of independence which can come with a job. They do not get out of the sphere of the family, they do not make independent circles of friends and contacts, nor establish a spatially separate sphere of existence. Within the family itself the double subordination of women is fixed through the mixing in one person of the role of husband or father with that of boss and employer.

But it is not that there have been no changes in recent decades for the homeworkers of Hackney. They too have been caught up in and affected by the recent changes in the international division of labour. The clothing industry of London in the second half of the twentieth century finds itself caught between cheap imports on the one hand and competition for labour from the better working conditions of the service sector on the other. The clothing firms with the ability to do so have long since left. For those that remain, cutting labour costs is a priority, and homeworking a means to do it. So an increasing proportion of the industry's work in the metropolis is now done on this social system while the amount of work overall, and the real wages paid, decline dramatically. For the women who work in this industry there is thus more competition for available work, increasing vulnerability to employers and intensification of the labour process. And this change in employment conditions brings increased pressures on home life too, though very different ones from those in the north-east, or the Fens. For these women in Hackney their workplace is also their home.

Here's Mary, a forty-five-year-old English woman with teenage children describing the pressures she feels:

> *I've been machining since I was fifteen, and with thirty years' experience I'm really fast now . . . But I'm having to work twice as hard to earn the money. The governors used to go on their knees to get you to take work if they had a rush to meet a delivery date. But they're not begging no more. It's take it or leave it. If you argue about the price they say we can always find others to do it. It's like one big blackmail. Three years ago we used to get 35p to 40p for a blouse, but now [1982] you only get 15p to 20p . . .*
>
> *I used to get my work done in five hours, now I work ten or twelve hours a day . . . The kids say, mum, I don't know why you sit there all those hours. I tell them, I don't do it for love, I've got to feed and clothe us. I won't work Sundays though. I have to think about the noise . . . I'm cooped up in a cupboard all day – I keep my machine in the storage cupboard, it's about three feet square with no windows. I get pains in my shoulders where the tension builds up. I've got one lot of skirts to do now, I've got to do sixteen in an hour to earn £1.75 an hour, that means I can't let up for half a second between each skirt. I can't afford the time to make a cup of tea. With that much pressure, at the end of the day you're at screaming pitch. If I wasn't on tranquillizers, I couldn't cope. I'm not good company, I lose my temper easily. Once I might have been able to tolerate my kids' adolescence, with this I haven't been able to, I haven't been able to help them – I need someone to help me at the end of the day.* (Harrison, 1983, pp. 65–7)

Reflected in this woman's personal experience, her sweated labour and family tensions, is a new spatial division of labour at an international scale. Low wage, non-unionized workers in Hackney are competing directly with the same type of low-technology, labour-intensive industries in the Third World. But it is precisely the history of the rag trade in Hackney, the previous layers of economic and social life, that have forced this competition on them. The intersection of national and international trends, of family and economic relationships, of patriarchy and capitalism have produced this particular set of relationships in one area of Inner London.

References

Alexander, S. (1982) 'Women's work in nineteenth-century London: a study of the years 1820–50', pp. 30–40 in E. Whitelegg *et al.* (eds.), *The Changing Experience of Women*, Martin Robertson, Oxford.

Anderson, M. (1971) *Family and Social Structure in Nineteenth-Century Lancashire*, Cambridge University Press, Cambridge.

Chamberlain, M. (1975) *Fenwomen*, Virago, London.

Engels, F. (1969 edn) *The Conditions of the Working Class in England*, Panther, St Albans.

Frankenberg, R. (1976) 'In the production of their lives, man (?) . . . sex and gender in British community studies', chapter 2, pp. 25–51 in D. L. Barker and A. Allen (eds.), *Sexual Divisions and Society: Process and Change*, Tavistock, London.

Hall, C. (1982) 'The home turned upside down? The working class family in cotton textiles 1780–1850', in E. Whitelegg *et al.* (eds.), *The Changing Experience of Women*, Martin Robertson, Oxford.

Harrison, P. (1983) *Inside the Inner City*, Penguin, Harmondsworth.

Kitteringham, J. (1975) 'Country work girls in nineteenth-century England', Part 3, pp. 73–138, in R. Samuel (ed.), *Village Life and Labour*, Routledge and Kegan Paul, London.

Lewis, J. (1983) 'Women, work and regional development', *Northern Economic Review*, no. 7. Summer, pp. 10–24.

Lewis, J. (forthcoming) Ph.D Thesis, Department of Geography, Queen Mary College, London.

Liddington, J. (1979) 'Women cotton workers and the suffrage campaign: the radical suffragists in Lancashire, 1893–1914', chapter 4, pp. 64–97, in S. Burman (ed.), *Fit Work for Women*, Croom Helm, London.

Massey, D. (1984) *Spatial Divisions of Labour: Social Structures and the Geography of Production*, Macmillan, London.

Phillips, A. and Taylor, B. (1980) 'Notes towards a feminist economics', *Feminist Review*, vol. 6, pp 79–88.

Purcell, K. (1979) 'Militancy and acquiescence amongst women workers', chapter 5, pp. 98–111, in S. Burman (ed.), *Fit Work for Women*, Croom Helm, London.

Samuel, R. (1975) *Village Life and Labour*, Routledge and Kegan Paul, London.

Strong Words Collective (1977) *Hello, are you working?* Erdesdun Publications, Whitley Bay.

Strong Words Collective (1979) *But the world goes on the same*, Erdesdun Publications, Whitley Bay.

Webb, S. (1921) *The Story of the Durham Miners*, Fabian Society, London.

30

THE CONTESTED TERRAIN OF LOCALITY STUDIES

Phil Cooke

One response to the sense that the 1970s and 1980s was an era of large-scale restructuring in economic and political life throughout the Western world was a revaluation of the 'local'. In this perspective the universalizing discourses represented by such grand theories as Marxism and neoclassical economics have run out of intellectual energy as the world has shifted away from the (modernist) modes of political-economic organization upon which their theoretical claims rested (see Gregory, **chapter 12**). This has produced an increased emphasis on disorder, difference, and flexibility as inherent features of the emergent political economy. In this context a number of scholars working in urban and regional studies laid a claim for the emerging significance of locality in the 'post-modern world' under (dis)organization. The intellectual fragmentation of society has been accompanied by an analogous geographical fragmentation. Philip Cooke's writing represents one of the most clear and careful renderings of this point of view. In the extract reprinted here Cooke offers two novel contributions as well as stating the general case for a major turning point in political-economic and intellectual organization. The first is the claim for the locality as a 'proactive' entity rather than as an outcome of larger structures. In this view localities can have a causal power when local groups endow the locality with their collective will. The second is to argue that the critique of universal discourses, on the one hand, and an ontological relativism that would deny the possibility of causal power to an entity such as a 'locality', on the other, do not necessarily go together. It is the key to Cooke's argument that one can combine the two main features of his article (a post-modern world and the relevance of locality to it) in a philosophically coherent manner. In his attempt to do so lies the originality of the article but also the potential for criticism from those who remain wedded to a universalizing discourse (such as Marxism) or those who see no possibility of any conceptual resolution in a world in which all coherence 'has melted into air'.

Source: The contested terrain of locality studies. *Tijdschrift voor Economische en Sociale Geografie* 80, 14–22, 27, 1989.

Introduction

One of the fascinating features in contemporary social science and the humanities is the way in which a jagged, but more or less continuous, fault has opened up across them in the recent past. This fault represents a break in the traditionally understood projects and even methods of reasoning in the disciplines in question. There appears to be a marked mood of exhaustion regarding the explanatory capacity of established 'ways of seeing' and a searching for alternatives, which, intriguingly, seem to share a new perspective – one in which notions of 'the local', 'the different', 'the combinable', even 'the reversible' are strong motifs. The key question is the extent to which the breaks that appear to be undermining our social knowledge are internal to that knowledge and so constitute merely a perspectival shift, or whether they are expressive of shifts in social reality that have made established perspectives effectively redundant, as a consequence of which social scientists in their dissatisfaction are reaching for new understandings.

I argue that the intellectual crises are expressive of contemporary social and economic change as well as contributing substantively to such change, so that the answer to the question just posed is – yes, to both parts. I hope to be able to sustain my argument with reference to knowledge generated in the recent study of change in the urban and regional system in the UK. This is not simply a matter of conveniently applying ideas from elsewhere to the field of urban studies; rather, change being experienced in the urban, regional and global networks of production, information and consumption is at the forefront of the more general change processes I wish, briefly, to describe. In particular, a fundamental shift in power relations consequent on the failure of centralised solutions and institutions to continue to remedy problems of social wellbeing, has led to a valorization of 'the local' both within and beyond the large city. The problem is that the emergent networks of power are held back by outmoded, centralist and modernist legal and organizational structures. These 'monopolitical monsters' of state and giant corporation as Lyotard (1987) calls them, now constitute severe blockages to the social development process. Despite this, new flexible social, political and economic ways are being developed to get around such blockages. Amongst them are post-Fordist modes of economic flexibility, the growth of movement or issue-based modes of political activity, and pluralistic social forms displayed particularly clearly in a revitalized urban culture of excessive consumption but also of popular expression (Boyer 1986; Castells 1983; Lipsitz 1987).

The argument of the article is, in brief, that recent theoretical developments in the social sciences have sought to come to terms with processes that seem to be undermining accepted perceptions of socio-spatial and politico-economic organization. First, there is in this readjustment of focus, a revaluation of the idea that *local* discourses and local powers are important, in part because universalising discourses and powers have been weakened. Second, there is a stress on the notion of *difference*, partly as a consequence of the decline of universalism, partly because of a growing segmentation and pluralism in cultural, social and political life. Third, restructuring and economic reorganization have produced a tendency towards the unravelling and, at the extreme, the *reversal* of motifs that have appeared fixed. These would include mass-production, mass-consumption and mass-culture amongst others. Eagleton (1986, p. 80) has expressed this deconstructive turn as the tendency:

> *. . . to reverse the imposing tapestry in order to explore in all its unglamorously dishevelled tangle the threads constituting the well-heeled image it presents to the world.*

As Eagleton, Ryan (1982) and Norris (1982) have shown, deconstructive thinking is itself a contested terrain. They use it as a rigorous instrument for preventing theory which itself purports to be radical from becoming a species of repressive rationality.

One key dimension around which the revaluation of these ideas can be focussed is that of the locality. If old certainties, such as the existence of an interventionary state, a mixed economy and a homogeneous society have been subjected to processes of fragmentation, there should be evidence of a growth in locally based activity. The article argues that there is a great deal of evidence for precisely this but that 'localism' is being controlled tightly by the UK state, and channeled away from municipal and towards private and voluntary-sector initiative.

Geography

One interesting shift in perspective amongst writers actually grappling with the disintegration of key aspects of their ways of thinking has been to recognise that a discourse of space and spatiality has begun to challenge the supremacy of the discourse of time and temporality. One of the progenitors, not so much of a wish to subsume history under spatiality as to even up the balance between the two, was Harvey (1982) with his call for a historico-geographical materialism in Marxist studies.

Jameson (1984) was one of the first to comment upon this revaluing of space in the context of his critique of the new downtown developments that have come to characterise the urban renaissance of American cities. More recently, Kroker & Cook (1986), citing Foucault for inspiration, have drawn attention to the following tendency:

> *As time loses its place in a culture that cannot produce the "high" values of the European past, the sense of the social begins to flee towards a spatial domain governed by movement.*

The architectural critic E. M. Farrelly (1986) sees this as mere aesthetic populism in which while:

> *. . . "giving the people what they want" may sound like all-too-rare architectural humility, it has with frightening rapidity become no more than the pretty plaything of rampant capitalism.*

The latter judgement is a common and mistaken reaction to contemporary innovation in the urban built environment. More sober judgement (e.g. Foster 1985; Arac 1986) sees it correctly as an essentially contested political terrain.

The question of the politics of contemporary spatial transformations has been subject to confusion in the geographical literature. David Harvey (1987), like Farrelly, equates postmodern architecture with political neoconservatism, and modernism with more progressive instincts. David Ley (1987) equates modernist cityscapes with neoconservatism and postmodern styles with liberalism. What is at fault with both authors is their cultural reductionism, of course. But their differing equations betoken the essentially contested nature of the political reality both seek to comprehend. A less restrictive geographical reading of the new currents, as they affect the discipline, is provided by Gregory (1987) and echoed by Soja (1987). Here the basic conclusion is that it is too early to say with precision quite what effect the restructuring of social space has had upon those whose disciplinary gaze must focus upon it, but that something significant has occurred both objectively and subjectively seems probable. For Gregory, space has necessarily been revalued as a constitutive element of contemporary social processes just as social anthropology and political economy have revivified the explanatory capacities of geography. It is this deconstruction of intellectual barriers that signifies a great advance, both intellectually and politically. For Soja too, the disintegrative impact of a consciousness of spatiality upon social and political-economic theory is to be welcomed, though the risks of reaction and neoconservatism have vigilantly to be guarded against.

In sum, therefore, it has become an unexceptionable practice to reinsert the spatial dimension into traditionally neglectful, aspatial social theory (see, for example, Giddens 1984; Mann 1986; Rustin 1987). This condition is a product of a certain balancing up of the spatial and temporal co-ordinates of contemporary existence. The cause of the latter is the profound, global restructuring of wide areas of social, political and economic life, consequent upon a failure of established historical modes of organization (e.g. imperialism, statism, corporatism) to deal with real-world crises. This has given rise to the search for successful models from present-day societies that are geographically distinct, even remote but increasingly being recombined into a global system of accumulative power.

Philosophy

The critique of philosophy has, of late, been sufficiently profound for a leading figure such as Putnam to wonder publicly whether or not the basic project of professional philosophy has reached a dead end (Putnam 1986). Richard Rorty, the leading American philosopher of the new generation, resigned from and refused appointments to any academic philosophy department on the grounds that his own neo-pragmatist perspective on philosophy made such a position untenable. He moved to a department of literary studies. And therein lies the source of the fault to which I have referred. For it was the work of the French post-structuralist

Derrida that contributed most to the crisis of philosophy's intellectual authority. The deconstructive turn introduced by Derrida revealed a weakness in Western metaphysics whereby metaphors, for example 'structure', tend to be deployed as aids to thought which are then, not entirely unconsciously, allowed to envelop thought and, indeed become the externalised object of thought. This *displacement* testifies to the circular logic lying at the foundation of a mode of reasoning which verifies itself internally while professing to a privileged discourse for equating subject and object. The problem for philosophy is that such technique is:

> *. . . ultimately a reflex image of the visual or spatial metaphors to which Western thought has so often resorted in its quest for understanding.*
>
> *To think without the aid of such figurative props may well be beyond the powers of mind.' (Norris 1982, pp. 79–80)*

Inevitably then, thought is itself localised (albeit on a continental cultural scale) because it draws on meanings intrinsic to particular contexts.

For Derrida, therefore, the only way of grasping truth is through the interrogation of texts which seek to articulate it. Texts – including philosophical texts – are literary forms, and the technical equipment approximate to the task of interrogating or deconstructing text are those of literary criticism rather than philosophy. This is a further development of the work of Wittgenstein who proposed, somewhat influentially, that philosophy always fails to discover the logical correspondence between language and the world it seeks to describe. Language was not to be understood as 'photography', but rather as a series of conventions or 'games' designed to facilitate a diversity of human practices.

Rorty takes this deconstructive formulation beyond the relativism implied by the notion of language games in his recovery of the pragmatic tradition in American philosophy. In a definitive paper (Rorty 1986) he distinguishes two traditions of persons conveying communicable truth. To put it in his own words:

> *The first is by telling the story of their contribution to a community . . . The second way is to describe themselves as standing in immediate relation to a nonhuman reality . . . I shall say that stories of the former kind exemplify the desire for solidarity, and that stories of the latter kind exemplify the desire for objectivity. (Rorty 1986, p. 3)*

Arguing, with Derrida and Wittgenstein, that objectivity is impossible, Rorty concludes that philosophical truth can only be the product of informed, pragmatic effort to reach consensus. Nor does this mean the victory to the loudest shouter; for Rorty at least, the fruits of the Enlightenment, in terms of the conventions of rational debate, are to be preferred to any other available criteria. Against the charge of ethnocentrism Rorty argues that it is unavoidable since we all speak principally to those who share enough of our beliefs to make conversation worthwhile.

Hence, it is philosophy's trans-cultural and trans-historical claims that have been put to the test by deconstruction and neo-pragmatism, and the logic of that critique is a renewed legitimacy to the claims of the local over the general.

Sociology

Rorty's appeal to consensus as the adjudicator of truth-claims implies an active-interactive community of informed participants in debate. However, it is precisely the possibility of generalising such social forms that the critique of Western metaphysics has placed in doubt. For Bauman (1987) we live in 'an age of noise', in a world overfilled with messages the interpretation of which is difficult because of the loss of a common sense of meaning hitherto supplied by 'authority'. The central value system which sociology claimed to have identified, (most elaborately in the work of Parsons) no longer dominates. Indeed, system-management seems little affected by the proliferation of diverse ideological preferences. The old, centralized organization of society derived from the hierarchy of world and imperial power; with the flattening of that hierarchy, and the undermining of its structure of internal social dominion, a new configuration of individual dependencies, in which negotiation and involvement are key features, has emerged. Compare even the contemporary authoritarian British government which has regularly to negotiate with its political equals in various spheres, to the high-handedness displayed only thirty or so years ago when its forces invaded Egypt at the time of the Suez crisis.

With the decline of older forms of authority, discursive exchange and rapproachement are the new bases of belief. Yet there are well-established obstacles to the achievement of democratic consensus, such as power asymmetries caused by inequality in resources whether of expression, education or economy. Into this vacuum, formerly occupied by a now-discredited philosophy, must enter the sociological arts of interrogating the nature of consensual truth by reference to the social conditions under which it may have been achieved. Pseudo-consensus, brought about by the asymmetrical exertion of power, can be no valid criterion of truth.

Thus, in Bauman's conception the changed world in which sociology operates calls forth a new function for sociology as the interpreter and consolidator of a fragmenting society. More pessimistically, Baudrillard and sympathetic interpreters of his work such as Kroker (1985) and Chen (1987), insist upon the 'death of the social' (Baudrillard 1983). In Baudrillard's view society is disappearing as the mechanisms which brought it into being – mass production, division of labour, use-value, etc. – recede into the background and a culture of consumption moves to centre stage. Society is rapidly becoming a nihilistic, individuated sign-system as a result of which social relations and interactions are *imploding* into a dense mass. As this signifying culture triumphs, so established social solidarities are replaced by simulated 'realities', or 'hyper-realities' as Eco (1987) calls them, provided by the mass-media.

The principal means of escape is through a re-engagement with the sign-system or *simulacrum* rather than a directly oppositional logic of resistance. Whereas dominant culture was meant, through museums, artworks etc., to incorporate, even anaesthetize, the dominated strata, it now creates popular spaces such as the Beaubourg (Baudrillard 1982) where official culture is transgressed by a sometimes stampeding 'critical mass' which absorbs it rather than being absorbed by it. But such 'hypersimulation', where the mass appropriates elite culture in the new, popular museum is, as Chen (1987) points out, not the only option. There is movement across space, there is consumption within the perspectival space of the sign-system and there is acceptance of the challenge to change the perspective contained in that space, by critical practices rooted in a recognition of local conditions of existence. Spatiality or the spatial variation in conditions of existence (Mann 1986), is the cause of one kind of death or 'dissolution of the social' (Lash & Urry 1987) in that it makes the concept of homogeneous 'society' redundant. But such variation, in the form of localised differences in consciousness, is the means of re-precipitating social solidarities.

Politics

Spatiality is also to the forefront in the work of Foucault (1980), who inquires into what he calls the 'genealogy' of power. In *Power/Knowledge* he argues that:

> *A whole history remains to be written of spaces – which would at the same time be the history of powers. (Foucault 1980, p. 149)*

What is meant by this is that, as in the celebrated case of the Panopticon – the perspectival space of social control in the prison – on which he places so much theoretical weight, power and knowledge are necessarily related. Moreover, that necessity is *locally* situated. Particular spaces, including domestic microspaces, and specific technologies are sites and means of the exercise of power. It is necessary, continues Foucault, to understand these local expressions of power in particular contexts and, further, to understand their articulation, prior to developing an explanation of more global forms of power. This is because the latter themselves derive from the segmentation of space into particular, controllable hierarchies of territory and property. These in turn serialise or render discontinuous modes of existence in everyday life. Power, exercised in this way, has its repressive but also a certain creative existence as it moulds subjects into actors in diverse local struggles. Many of these struggles are precisely against those forces which legitimize some kinds of knowledge while marginalizing or repressing others (Norris 1985, p. 199).

A related point is addressed by Jameson (1982) in commenting on the concept of 'the political'. He rejects the single-function definition of politics recognising that individuals operate in a multi-dimensional political space, each segment of which provides opportunities for a different kind of politics. Rejecting the politics of the programme he proposes that:

> *. . . the metaphysical question: what is politics . . . is worthwhile only when it leads to enumeration of all the possible options, and not when it lures you into following the mirage of the single great strategic idea. (Jameson 1982, p. 75)*

Jameson's tends to be a somewhat individualised conception of politics but in the public sphere of the state and law, his analysis holds good insofar as *issue* rather than *programme*-based politics proliferate. For example, reproduction, sexuality or gender are sub-bases for such diverse issues as abortion, personal rights, and labour market equality, and have become important components of movement-based politics, in this case the women's movement. Similar sub-divisions on issues within other movement-politics can now be identified quite easily. In the urban sphere alone there are issue-based struggles on a wide geographical scale around housing, employment, environmental protection, transport, pollution and community regeneration, and doubtless sub-divisions within those. As Castells (1983) has foreseen, the rhetoric of locally defined meanings is the energising force in contemporary politics in a context where that of class struggle has become occluded (see also Laclau & Mouffe 1985). In this context, the traditional monolithic parties capable of massing support behind a programme may be experiencing their greatest historical challenge in the face of an emergent politics of *difference*, represented with some force in, for example, the European Green movement.

Economics

Whether at the level of the firm or at the systemic scale, economic thought is being reworked in ways that bring theory more into line with a more fragmented, negotiated reality. With respect to the former scale, the contributions of Williamson (1975, 1985) are suggestive of a changing conception of the nature of the firm. In the Williamsonian perspective, firms are to be thought of not, as hitherto, in terms of production functions operating within hierarchically structured, preset boundaries, but rather as structures of governance, operating with variable boundaries. This viewpoint stresses the importance of the nature of *relationships* between economic institutions over *factors* of production because, it is argued, transactions precede, by determining resource allocations, production. The upshot of this is a revised view of the functions of the firm as a power centre confronted with the decision of whether to 'make or buy' and if the latter, whether to purchase in the market or by an interfirm agreement. The latter decision-choice, which is shown to be empirically on the increase, is resolved in terms of transaction cost differences (including non-monetary ones). In order for such a system to work there must be an increased level of local autonomy and negotiating capacity within and beyond the corporation. Such 'networking', it is argued, heralds the demise of Chandler's (1962) 'modern corporation' and the emergence of the 'postmodern corporation' (Teece & Pisano 1987). Key characteristics of the latter include: collaboration in innovation; shared R&D costs between firms; increased cross-licensing of technology between firms; increased sub-contracting of production; increased organizational decentralization; and a greater range and variety of inter-firm contractual negotiations.

At the macroeconomic level such phenomena as these are consistent with the emergent theory of *flexibility* which with its numerous suffixes, flexible specialisation (Piore & Sabel 9184); flexible manufacturing systems (Schonberger 1982); flexible employment (Boyer 1986) and now flexible accumulation (Harvey 1987) constitutes the conventional wisdom of the age. What these terms seek to comprehend is a paradigm shift within productive organization in Western economies provoked by the effects of harsh competition from the most successful countries, notably Japan. Thus, what came to be a dominant mode of organizing the key elements of the manufacturing economy, namely mass-production or Fordism, has been under challenge because of inbuilt rigidities. Fordism is perceived to be giving way to more flexible production methods, often with the character of local specialisation in spatially distinctive industrial districts such as Toyota City or the Third Italy.

The conceptual lineaments of the more flexible mode of production would seem to include the following at least:

a) the 'de-dedication' of assembly lines enabling a diversity of models of a product to be produced, using new technology;
b) the local integration of aspects of production hitherto separated within the corporate hierarchy, e.g. marketing, production and R&D;
c) the search for efficiency through cutting inventories and setting up local 'just-in-time' sub-contracting networks;
d) the forming of tactical and strategic alliances between firms to reduce marketing, distribution and R&D costs;
e) the restructuring of the labour force into a secure, multi-skilled 'core' and a casualised 'periphery'.

The reasons for the adoption, singularly or in combination, of these strategies include the need to reduce rigidity in an uncertain competitive climate, the need to increase choice and speed of response to change in market structures and level of demand, and the relative ease of satisfying such requirements in a context of growth in the small-firm sector and general slackness in national and local labour markets.

Hence, if one were to summarise the argument so far and, in the process, identify the parameters of the paradigm-shift in these intellectual disciplines and in the reality they seek to interpret, the following would need to be underscored.

First, there is an elevation of the status of the concept '*local*' in all these discourses. This accompanies a noticeable decline in the hegemony of other universalist concepts as, for example, in philosophy with the concept of universal reason, sociology with its master-concept 'society', politics in respect of 'the party', and in economics with regard to 'the firm'. Space and spatiality are important, though by no means exhaustive, dimensions of this valorization of the local; some meanings of 'local' are better-understood as 'particular': for example, the focus on particular political issues such as peace or the environment. But a substantial part of what has been discussed as the enhancing of the local does have directly spatial connotations: for example, in the localisation of decision-making in some hitherto centrally controlled parts of production, the recognition of spatiality as fatal to a homogeneous conception of society, and in the valorization of the local as a setting for the exercise of power.

Second, we see a new stress on the notion of *difference*. In Derrida's work, *difference* is given the double meaning of the differential play of meaning within language and the element of deferral of identity between symbol and the object it seeks to signify. In the context of post-analytic philosophy, difference in the legitimacy of truth-claims is accepted and a pragmatic, communicative means of intersubjective understanding is proposed. In sociology that consensus-seeking process is subject to its own complex deconstruction, while in politics and economics difference is celebrated and negotiated into workability.

The third dimension of this triangle of elements is what I will call the tendency towards *reversal*. It is cognate with the idea of deconstruction (in the sense of a spatial – not temporal – overturning of an established form) except that it is not only a critical technique but a social process. In sociology it is captured in Baudrillard's use of 'implosion' to describe a central element of what he sees as the death, and others the dissolution, of the social. There is a connection here with the reversal of economic processes, the loss of key structuring mechanisms involved in social production under Fordism. This entails a return to new versions of pre-modern productive practices, notably 'putting-out', artisanal production, small business, etc. There is, too, an apparent philosophical reversal to a specifically American, but undoubtedly older, tradition of pragmatism which was swamped in the twentieth century by the importation of European positivism and analytical philosophy. I will try to show in later sections of this article how, at the more mundane level of the city and locality, reversal is an emergent feature of the sociospatial development process at present.

One final, and extremely important, point needs to be made at this stage. Much of what I have been writing about, and to which most critics refer as the post-structuralist inheritance, is equated with at worst neoconservatism and at best a form of apolitical radicalism, the intent of which is, like Samson, to demolish the Enlightenment temple from within. I have sought to show that these critiques themselves constitute *a contested terrain*. It is no longer apparent, as Habermas (1985) claims, that writers such as Derrida and Lyotard are boundlessly subjective, non-radical and that deconstruction has the sole purpose of destabilising Western metaphysics or worse. In Derrida's case it remains unclear whether he sees himself as more than the interrogator of dominant cultural mores, though Eagleton (1986) sees him as retaining an ambiguous commitment to Marxism. Ryan (1982) cites the feminist and Italian autonomist movements as examples of the margins radicalizing a supposedly progressive theoretical tradition. Finally, Lyotard (1987) has made it clear that he rejects the labels neoconservative or neoliberal as 'illusions' in a society dominated by corporate and state megastructures, the demise of which he goes on to show that he welcomes.

From Locale to Proactive Localities

If, as poststructuralist thinking suggests, local phenomena are undergoing a revaluation, can the nature and powers of the denoted concept 'locality' be further specified? Drawing on geographical theory, Giddens (1984) introduces the concept of 'locale' to refer to the settings for routine social practices. These bases for social integration are said to be important in linking routine social integration processes to more wide-ranging system integration because they supply a degree of permanence to the institutions of which the system consists. More challengingly, Giddens suggests that locale is a key conduit by means of which new institutional arrangements can bring about change in the systemic structures of society. However, quite how this agency role works is never satisfactorily tackled. Instead, reference is made to change which is expressed, for example, in the institutions of the city, but the originating forces are not clearly specified. Locale seems to be, indeed, a rather passive setting or backdrop and one, moreover, whose scale can stretch from the living-room to the nation. Thus, having introduced this concept which, as we have seen, can have a distinctly destabilising effect upon traditional, universalist conceptions of 'society', Giddens seems only prepared to confer upon it a rather mysterious, contextuating position regarding questions of system change. 'Locale' in the sense of 'setting' is allowed more of a contribution to system stability than to system transformation.

This lopsidedness also appears in a recent attempt to theorise 'locality' from a realist standpoint (Savage, Barlow, Duncan & Saunders 1987). The analysis proceeds from the assumption that space does make some difference to the operation of social processes. The very existence of spatial variation in the character and incidence of phenomena such as cities, industrial areas, wilderness and so on is inexplicable in purely sociological terms. The non-sociological dimension introduced here is that of natural structures. Thus local resource endowments, while not in themselves responsible for the unevenness of, for example, population distribution, may, through interaction with a structural social process such as capitalist (or socialist) economic organization, give rise to a concentration of population in an industrial district or city. This outcome is contingent upon the resource in question having a market or social value. But the cause of local variation lies in the interaction between natural and social structures. Locality is thus a secondary effect of supralocal causes and contingencies.

However, over time, the interactions of these supralocal forces in space create effects which combine to give distinctive identity to the site in which they are found. The example of a local labour market is given to show that a contingent social entity may develop its own generative powers with respect, for instance, to workforce, gender or political composition. In this respect locality is beginning to take on a limited expressiveness of its own from the aggregation of secondary effects of which it is composed. If the labour market is proletarian, then more council than private housing may be built, for example. Finally, as an effect of this it is hypothesized, in turn, that these tertiary effects could possibly give rise to the quaternary one of the 'locality-effect' whereby members of the locality develop a locally distinctive way of thinking and acting, for example in terms of political preferences. But such local cultures are thought to be empirically unfounded.

Hence, this formulation shares much with that of Giddens in its, in this case explicit, reluctance to allow the concept of locality any real identity beyond that which is *exogenously* given by the causal powers and contingencies of supralocal structures and forces. Thus, from the initial assumption that space matters to the form taken by social processes, the analysis concludes that its importance lies in the way social processes leave a kind of extraneous residue on the landscape around which they have to negotiate their future course.

It is important to state that this analysis is incomplete rather than mistaken. There is clearly a sense in which exogenous forces exert their effect upon locality, nowhere more poignantly than in the way in which a global corporation may close its local operations somewhere because of other global forces such as competition, rather than any inadequacy in its local operator. However, this account severely underestimates the *proactive capacity* or initiative-taking ability contained within 'locality'. From a realist perspective 'locality' stands in a necessary relation to the more powerful social entity, 'nation'. This asymmetric, necessary relation is paralleled by that between the 'nation-state' and the 'local-state'. Both locality and nation are key vehicles for social mobilisation and political intervention (Cooke 1989).

The nature of this relationship is that of a citizenship-allegiance exchange. This mechanism confers rights on both entities: a variety of freedoms for citizens, such as those of association, combination and protection; a variety of obligations from them, for example conscription and representation (e.g. in war and law). Many, but not all, of these rights are expressed through the nation-state/local-state relationship, though, increasingly, local social movements may by-pass it and other sources of local effectivity, such as enterprise in the arts, voluntary services or business, may have nothing directly to do with it. Such proactive capacities frequently derive from bases in the locality and sometimes exert causal effects on non-local structures.

One need only think, in the arts, of the phenomenon of summer festivals which have proliferated following the success of that in Edinburgh, and which through 'fringe' activities have helped shift the axis of elite culture. In terms of local business enterprise the Rochdale Pioneers of the co-operative movement clearly had a massive supralocal effect, as did Manchester and Bradford textile barons or Pittsburgh steelmakers as entrepreneurs. In the voluntary sector, the local health schemes in coalmining areas such as South Wales became a model for Britain's National Health Service which in turn was admired worldwide. Many of these examples are historical precisely because the nation-state acquired an increasing role as universal regulator by appropriating local powers to itself. A salient political question is whether the limits of that encroachment have been reached and whether localities have begun to recalibrate their balance of proactive capacity vis à vis that of the nation-state. Clearly, under the control of the political Right, any offloading of responsibilities has been to the direct benefit of private property. But it is instructive that outside Britain (notably Denmark where local tax-raising powers have been limited, and Australia with the case of Sydney's loss of local government status) there has, of late, been national legislation to circumscribe local proactivity centred in the local state.

It might appear, particularly in the UK context, that local power is being snuffed out by a Conservative government intent on centralising large areas of power to minimise local discretion over spending because of its negatively perceived effects on the public expenditure and borrowing requirement levels. Certainly the Thatcher government has abolished some local, democratically elected bodies, especially in the largest cities (Duncan & Goodwin 1988). However, this can easily be seen to be a negative response to forms of local proactivity, some of which work with rather than against difference in a context of economic reversal. But, more to the point, it is a mistake to reduce 'the local' to just local government or the local state. There are numerous dimensions of local activity both alive and revivified in the context of the present restructuring. Some of these work against or outside central state constraints, others are stimulated into action precisely by that state with its strong emphasis upon private initiative within a so-called 'enterprise culture'.

'Locality' is a theoretical concept with a specificity derived from the interaction of exogenous and endogenous causal powers. Recent attempts to theorise it have stressed the former at the expense of the latter and have thereby missed the importance of the concept as a key social base and motive force in social change. Locality is to be understood as a spatial concentration of national subjects endowed with rights and capacities for proactivity. Local action, therefore, is the product of some degree of collective will to exercise these rights in specific circumstances. The nature and extent of that proactivity is influenced but not determined by the impact of supralocal effects originating in natural or social structural forces. In passing, it may be noted that this active sense of 'locality' further distances the concept from that of 'community', the latter being best understood as a *residual* social form in the sense deployed by Williams (1977).

One final point that this discussion raises but which cannot satisfactorily be resolved here is the metaphysical relationship between the poststructural neo-pragmatism which privileges 'the local' but which denies epistemology, i.e. considers the subject/object dichotomy a non-problem because language is the only cognisable source of truth, and realism, used to derive the theoretical status of 'locality', which claims privileged status in bridging that dichotomy. Of course realism is a form of discourse and its narrative is always open to a deconstructive reading. One weakness that such a reading would expose is the relativism implied in the notion of contingency (possibly 'necessity' too, given that more than one necessary relationship can exist vis à vis a single social entity). There are two candidate solutions: one is to take, with Ryan (1982), the deconstructive insight that there can be undecidability in a heterogeneous reality and recognise that the search for logical priority is a species of idealism. The other is to recognise that language is the means of interrogating as well as referring to truth-claims about reality and to seek a consensus about the undecidability or otherwise of causes in a form of realist pragmatism (Margolis 1986). Either way, the standoff between post-structuralism and realism need not imply a necessary relation of incompatibility (Norris 1985) . . .

From Metapowers to Local Powers?

In contemporary fiction the narrator often provides a choice of endings. This is certainly no fiction, but there is a formal choice (though most would not consider it so) between acquiescence and the taking of local power through the exercise of existing, though limited, democratic rights of assembly, deliberation and proposal. The alternative is to retreat in the face of the overweening power of a central state that daily seems to chip away, sometimes removing in large lumps, historically established democratic rights. The implication of that is the almost Henry Fordist promise that you can have any local policy you like as long as it is an Urban Development Corporation.

The principal lesson to be drawn from this account is that the active creation of local networks of power is a necessary protection against the overarching powers of state and global economy. More than that, such 'metapowers', as Foucault (1986) calls them, can only themselves operate on the basis of existing local power relations. Moreover, these metapowers do not occupy and totalise the range of prefigurative or existing models of economy, society or polity. The example of decentralised political and economic success from the so-called 'Third Italy' testifies to that (Cooke & Rosa Pires 1985). Clearly, local power operates in a hierarchical relationship to many other non-local forms of power, but these tend to be routine and often negative in nature, hence vulnerable to hard-edge critical thinking. Also, there is no necessary relation between a more generalised local proactivity and the negative conclusion that one locality's success is another one's failure. There are positive-sum as well as zero-sum games, so that to tackle local crises can, especially where there is co-operation, add up to more than the position of status quo ante.

The lesser conclusions are that two conditions that seem to be a common product of the ending of Fordist hegemony and the onset of a flexible future, these being *difference* and the tendency towards *reversal*, are as much contested terrains as the local power relations that seem to be developing in relation to them. Local network building as a bridge across pluralities is a necessary precondition of the successful use of proactive capacity. Finally, reversal, the spatial overturning of trajectories, is a condition of the 'creative destruction' implicit in capitalist development. The point is to build the protective networks that minimise the worst of those effects while remaining sufficiently flexible to take advantage of the opportunities that reversals open up for progressive initiative, such as that of the Swedish trade-union movement as described by Lash & Urry (1987), at local level and beyond.

Acknowledgements

This article arose from the UK Economic and Social Research Council's research programme 'The Changing Urban and Regional System in the UK' (CURS) for which I was Co-ordinator. I presented it in an earlier form at the invitation of the Sixth Urban Change and Conflict Conference, University of Kent at Canterbury, England in September 1987 and at the 'Declining Cities and Urban Politics' Symposium at the University of Bremen, FR Germany in October 1987. The article could not have been produced without the excellent collaborative work of the seven teams from: Gloucester College of Advanced Technology, CES Ltd., and the Universities of Kent, Bristol, Aston, Lancaster and Durham who undertook the locality studies element of CURS. The following people commented on various points of the original paper causing me to change or clarify aspects of it, I hope for the better: Nigel Thrift, John Urry, Derek Gregory, Doreen Massey, Ray Pahl, Roger Penn, David Harvey, Chris Hamnett, Rob Shields, Peter Saunders, Enzo Mingione, Hartmut Hausserman and Dieter Läpple. Many of them disagreed substantially with what I had to say and may well continue to do so. Some CURS colleagues also found aspects of my interpretation contentious. So, more than usually, the responsibility for the outcome is mine alone. I would like to thank Jan van Weesep for his special interest and assistance.

References

Arac, J. (1986), *Postmodernism & Politics*. Minneapolis, Minnesota: University of Minnesota Press.

Baudrillard, J. (1982), The Beaubourg-Effect: Implosion and Deterrence. *October* 20, pp. 3–13.

Baudrillard, J. (1983), *In the Shadow of the Silent Majorities*. New York: Semiotext(e).

Bauman, Z. (1987), The Philosopher in the Age of Noise: a Reading of Richard J. Bernstein's *Philosophical Profiles. Theory Culture and Society* 4, pp. 157–165.

Boyer, R. (1986), *La Flexibilité du Travail en Europe*. Paris: Editions La Decouverte.

Castells, M. (1983), *The City and the Grassroots*. London: Edward Arnold.

Chandler, A. (1962), *Strategy and Structure*. Cambridge: MIT Press.

Chen, K. -H. (1987), The Masses and the Media: Baudrillard's Implosive Postmodernism. *Theory, Culture and Society* 4, pp. 71–88.

Cooke, P., ed. (1989), *Localities*. London: Unwin Hyman.

Cooke, P. & A. de Rosa Pires (1985), Productive Decentralisation in Three European Regions. *Environment & Planning A* 17, pp. 527–544.

Duncan, S. & M. Goodwin (1988), *The Local State and Uneven Development*. Cambridge: Polity.

Eagleton, T. (1986), *Against the Grain*. London: Verso.

Eco, U. (1987), *Travels in Hyper-Reality*. London: Picador.

Farrelly, E. (1986), The New Spirit. *Architectural Review* 180, pp. 7–12.

Foster, H. (1985), Postmodernism: a Preface. *In*: H. Foster, ed., *Postmodern Culture*. London: Pluto.

Foucault, M. (1980), The Eye of Power. *In*: M. Foucault, *Power/Knowledge* (edited by C. Gordon). New York: Pantheon.

Foucault, M. (1986), Truth and Power. *In*: P. Rabinow, ed., *The Foucault Reader*. Harmondworth: Penguin.

Giddens, A. (1984), *The Constitution of Society*. Cambridge: Polity.

Gregory, D. (1987), Difference, Distance and Postmodern Geography (mimeo).

Habermas, J. (1985), Questions and Counterquestions. *In*: R. Bernstein, ed., *Habermas and Modernity*. Cambridge: Polity.

Harvey, D. (1982), *The Limits to Capital*. Oxford: Basil Blackwell.
Harvey, D. (1987), Flexible Accumulation through Urbanization: Reflections on 'Post-modernism' in the American City. *Antipode* 19, pp. 260–286.
Jameson, F. (1982), Interview. *Diacritics* 12, pp. 72–91.
Jameson, F. (1984), Postmodernism, or the Cultural Logic of Late Capitalism. *New Left Review* 146, pp. 53–94.
Kroker, A. (1985), Baudrillard's Marx. *Theory, Culture and Society* 2, pp. 69–84.
Kroker, A & D. Cook (1986), *The Postmodern Scene*. New York: St. Martin's Press.
Laclau, E. & C. Mouffe (1985), *Hegemony and Socialist Strategy: Towards a Radical Democratic Politics*. London: Verso.
Lash, S & J. Urry (1987), *The End of Organized Capitalism*. Cambridge: Polity.
Ley, D. (1987), Styles of the Times: Liberal and Neoconservative Landscapes in Inner Vancouver, 1968–1986. *Journal of Historical Geography* 13, pp. 40–56.
Lipsitz, G. (1987), Cruising Around the Historical Bloc – Postmodernism and Popular Music in East Los Angeles. *Cultural Critique* 5, pp. 157–178
Lyotard, J. (1987), Rules and Paradoxes and Svelte Appendix. *Cultural Critique* 5, pp. 209–219.
Mann, M. (1986), *The Sources of Social Power, Vol. I: a History of Power from the Beginning to A.D. 1760*. Cambridge: Cambridge University Press.
Margolis, J. (1986), *Pragmatism without Foundations: Reconciling Realism and Relativism*. Oxford: Blackwell.
Norris, C. (1982), *Deconstruction: Theory and Practice*. London: Methuen.
Norris, C. (1985), *The Contest of Faculties: Philosophy and Theory after Deconstruction*. London: Methuen.
Piore, M. & C. Sabel (1984), *The Second Industrial Divide*. New York: Basic Books.
Putnam, H. (1986), After Empiricism. *In*: J. Rajchman & C. West, eds., *Post-Analytic Philosophy*. New York: Columbia University Press.
Rorty, R. (1986), Solidarity or Objectivity? *In*: J. Rajchman & C. West, eds., *Post-Analytical Philosophy*. New York: Columbia University Press.
Rustin, M. (1987), Place and Time in Socialist Theory. *Radical Philosophy* 47, pp. 30–36.
Ryan, M. (1982), *Marxism and Deconstruction: a Critical Articulation*. Baltimore: Johns Hopkins University Press.
Savage, M., J. Barlow, S. Duncan & P. Saunders (1987), 'Locality Research': the Sussex Programme on Economic Restructuring, Social Change and the Locality. *The Quarterly Journal of Social Affairs* 3, pp. 27–51.
Schonberger, R. (1982), *Japanese Manufacturing Techniques*, London: Macmillan.
Soja, E. (1987), The Postmodernization of Geography: A Review. *Annals of the Association of American Geographers* 77, pp. 289–323.
Teece, D. & G. Pisano (1987), Collaborative Arrangements and Technology Strategy. School of Business Administration, University of California, Berkeley (mimeo).
Williams, R. (1977), *Marxism and Literature*. Oxford: Oxford University Press.
Williamson, O. (1975), *Markets and Hierarchies*. New York: The Free Press.
Williamson, O. (1985), *The Economic Institutions of Capitalism*. New York: The Free Press.

31

THE INADEQUACY OF THE REGIONAL CONCEPT

George H.T. Kimble

Conceptual critique is hardly new to human geography, although its intensity has certainly increased since the 1960s. George H. T. Kimble's 1951 article illustrates the fact that geographical concepts have not remained beyond explicit critique, and also indicates a long-standing unhappiness with use of the regional concept. Not surprisingly, Derwent Whittlesey's paean to mid-twentieth-century regional study by American geographers (in P. James and C. F. Jones, editors, *American geography: inventory and prospect*. Syracuse, 1954) fails to mention Kimble's critique. Kimble, an American geographer of English origin, traced the increasing dissatisfaction with the 'region' as a central geographical concept to doubts about how regions can be satisfactorily defined and the neglect of linkages or functional ties relative to internal homogeneity in most regional accounts. The essential arbitrariness of the regions used in mid-century geography is identified as a special problem. Although elements of Kimble's presentation have a period flavour to them (for example, the continued use of 'man' for human and the reference to agricultural 'belts' of one type or another), the general thrust of his argument is immediately relevant to the revival of regionalism in the 1980s. To what extent have recent claims about place and region dealt with the problems identified by Kimble? Are regions really present-day fictions left over from a time when they did exist (the European eighteenth century?), living on in the geographical imagination rather than in the real world? Are regional studies always personal portraits drawn by the scholar rather than definitive accounts of an actually-existing reality? To the extent that answers to these questions lead us back to Kimble's scepticism, they may also lead us towards the use of other concepts such as landscape or space. That indeed is what happened in the years after Kimble wrote. [We have included full references where the author refers to earlier citations.]

Source: The inadequacy of the regional concept. In *London Essays in Geography: Rodwell Jones Memorial Volume*, editors, L. Dudley Stamp and S. W. Wooldridge. London: Longmans, Green, 1951, pp. 151–74.

Introduction

We geographers are men of many creeds and tongues. We have plenty to say, but we seldom say it in unison or in harmony. Our labours of a generation notwithstanding, we are still without an agreed testament of faith. No doubt if we were asked for a single-sentence definition of our subject, most of us would talk of "regions" and contend that the highest form of geographical enquiry was a kind of "hunt-the-region" game, in which (provided we were offered enough clues) we were bound to discover that life in a given land or continent resolves itself into a neat pattern of cultural entities we call regions. But having said this much, we should need to add hastily that we were still debating the exact connotation of the term; that there were no less than one hundred definitions of it in our geographical literature, and that those who did agree about their terms and techniques were not altogether certain what to do with the region when they had eventually identified it and described it.

Unable (or unwilling?) to present a united front to the academic world, it is not altogether surprising that our external impact has so far been slight. Nor is it entirely surprising that some of our near neighbours in the other social sciences are beginning to ask us whether a phenomenon which has thus far escaped definition can have any real existence. And not our neighbours only. In the light of present social and economic trends, even some geographers are beginning to wonder whether the regional concept is in fact as satisfactory a mould for the fashioning of geographical studies as they have been wont to regard it.

The Meaning of the Concept

Reasons for this growing dissatisfaction are not hard to find. First, there is the historical fact that the region is an eighteenth-century concept (if, indeed, it is not much older): the world that fathered it now lies "mouldering in the grave," and it has yet to be shown that the ponderous ideological fashions of the eighteenth century become the much shrunken and infinitely more fleet-footed world of the twentieth.

It will be well for us, perhaps, to call to mind the original signification of the term. From the time of Strabo onwards, geographers repeatedly expressed concern over the treatment of earth knowledge on a basis of political divisions. Some writers, notably Varenius, had proposed alternative organizations of the subject, but before the eighteenth century none of them attracted any great following. However, in the second half of that century, Gatterer in Germany, following a lead given him by Buache in France, proposed a physical division of the world into lands and regions (*Gebiete*). This scheme was later taken up by Hommeyer, who developed the idea of a real unity based on a single phenomenon, namely, land-forms. The concept of a composite unity, the integration of all phenomena (natural and human) of an area into an individual unit distinct from those of neighbouring areas, did not appear before the nineteenth century. It finds emphatic expression about 1810 in the writings of Zeune and Butte. For Butte, the individual units were organisms which, like any organism, included a physical side – inanimate nature – and a psychical side – animate nature. "The unit areas (*Raüme*)," he averred, "assimilate their inhabitants, and the inhabitants strive no less constantly to assimilate their areas."

Needless to say, so radical a notion did not fail to arouse opposition. Wilhelmi and Selten, while ready to recognize the existence of the "natural" unit, both argued that its boundaries could not be determined on the basis of any one kind of phenomenon, and that, in those many instances where the boundaries were not clearly defined by nature, the selection of one would necessarily be arbitrary. The criticisms of Bücher were more fundamental. He claimed, and he supported the claim with an impressive array of material culled from some forty current text-books, that it was futile to look for "natural divisions," since nature had for the most part not thought it necessary to administer her affairs as neatly as civil servants. Systematic geography was, in his view, the important thing: areal studies on a unitary basis were "only needed for special purposes, for which the areas concerned could be arbitrarily bounded in any convenient way."

But, by and large, the critics of the new concept did not attract as much attention as the sponsors of it. Most of the "classical" and "post-classical" writers accepted the idea of the region without challenge, and even without curiosity. Indeed, Hartshorne (whose work on the origins of modern geography cannot be too highly regarded) goes so far as to say that in the century and a quarter since Butte first spoke of areas as organisms, nobody has seriously attempted to establish the organic character of a single region and in the century since Bücher's scientific integrity led him to announce his failure to establish a regional division of lands, no one has seriously attempted to show the error of his method or argument, or to produce what he found impossible. Yet many modern writers of geography text-books continue to predicate the existence of such organic units, and to assume that the whole world is tidily parcelled up into "unitary entities." Not to put too fine a point on it, this looks uncommonly like intellectual laziness – if not dishonesty!

Broadly speaking, present-day supporters of the regional concept are divided into two camps. Those who, following Herbertson, make the natural region serve as the plastercast of a specific kind of human economy: and those who focus attention on cultural distributions, and regard the region – to cite only two of the hundred-odd current definitions – as an area in which "a functionally coherent way of life dominates,"[1] or an area which is "dynamically homogeneous in respect of certain inter-related characteristics in the make-up of its society, whether past or present."[2] The first school of thought is not as influential as the second, possibly because of the difficulty it has in demonstrating that a climatico-vegetal region (or climax area) is capable of enslaving its inhabitants, whether in respect of their movements, occupations or *mores*. Too often in modern society, and in earlier societies as well, it is the State rather than the environment that does the enslaving!

[1] C. O. Sauer, "Foreword to Historical Geography," *Ann. Assoc. Amer. Geog.*, Mar. 1941, pp. 11–12.
[2] R. E. Dickinson, *The German Lebensraum*, p. 19.

As Dickinson shows in his *German Lebensraum*, there is absolutely no evidence for supposing that a natural region, even when possessed of the most clearly defined frontiers, gives rise to a corresponding unit in the human modes developed within it.

The trouble with the followers of the second school of thought is that they are united more by their general disagreements than by their beliefs. They are still hunting for a formula of words which will satisfy everybody's requirements. So far, the most common usages are the least meaningful. After all, who can tell us when an area is, or is not, "functionally coherent"? Is "coherence" a measurable quantity? Is it something that is achieved when the industrial output per man-hour reaches a certain level? Or when there is full employment? Or when local supplies of men, goods and services are exactly balanced by local demands? And if it is not measurable by unequivocal standards, how can its presence, or absence, be confirmed?

Similarly, how may we define "dynamic homogeneity" (or even "static homogeneity," for that matter), and what is the precise connotation of "inter-related characteristics" and "entities of circulation of goods and persons," to use another term favoured by Dickinson?[3] And precisely how stable is such an entity, or state of homogeneity? If an area is, at a given point of time, a homogeneous product of the fusion of various elements or element-complexes, then it must follow that as soon as one of those elements changes in time or place, the whole regional complex changes. And how often some of these elements – industrial output, export and import trade, supplies of raw materials, labour-management relations, etc. – do change! (Is the manufacturing belt of north-eastern U.S.A. "functionally coherent" when it lies palsied under the hand of John L. Lewis, or the Palestinian coast plain, when it is in the grip of a Terrorist campaign?)[3a] Unity and coherence can scarcely be more than an instantaneous condition of cultural relationships.

Again, how must we regard those areas which lack even this fleeting coherence? For we do not need to be told that there are plenty of regions in the world where there is no fundamentally coherent way of life, and no "sufficient concordance of common traits."[4] At the same time there are areas which have so many interwoven strands that they produce confusion rather than cohesion: colour in plenty, but little form: unlimited activity, but little pattern. (It has always seemed to us that the capital-heavy countries of the Southern Hemisphere are troubled in this way. With 75 per cent of its population cooped up in five cities, Australia is hardly a model of regional coherence: and much the same applies to South Africa and South America).

[3] Dickinson, op. cit., p. 172

[3a] This essay was written in 1946, before the creation of the state of Israel.

[4] C. O. Sauer, op. cit., p. 12. It is worthy of note in this connection that Rodwell Jones never once succumbed in his lectures or writings to the temptation of "regionalizing" the whole of a continent or country. In the preface to *North America* he and Dr Bryan put it on record that "though . . . regions exist, it by no means follows that a whole continent can be divided up into equally well-marked areas . . ." p. 41 (7th Edition).

At the same time, there is no reason to over-stress the significance of "homogeneity" and "common traits," etc. Not all homogeneity spells unity or coherence: the dominant historical quality of the Asiatic steppes has been uniformity rather than unity. *Per contra*, unity is frequently the product, not so much of *uniformity* of terrain, climate and resources, as of *contrasted* physical and economic conditions, integrated by commercial movements and/or by political ideals. This would certainly seem to be the case with the Paris Basin, and (in so far as it is possible to speak of nation-wide functional unity) with Nazi Germany and Soviet Russia as well.

With the academicians unable to agree upon the content of the word, it is little wonder that the general laity continue to think of "region" as little more than an alternative unit of area which can be administered with slightly less fuss than tiresome political units.

Our doubts about the adequacy of the regional concept increase when we come to look into the nature and constitution of the region, as represented in current geographical literature.

The Constitution of the Region

Consider in the first place the problem of delimiting regional boundaries.

Self-evidently, if there is such a thing as a real region, it must be capable of mensuration. Granted that there may be alternative ways of carrying out the measurement and of determining the exact lineaments of the region at any one instant, there can be no question of indeterminism. No amount of sophistry will ever persuade our critics that an "organism," a "coherent whole," a "unitary entity," etc., etc., can have substance without form, or quality without quantity. And it is no defence to say that we are dealing with dynamic boundaries, or zones which are not amenable to measurement, because it must surely be impossible to tell how dynamic the boundaries are unless we have a measured datum line. Nor is it of any avail to argue that the homogeneous centre of the region matters more than the diversified circumference. As geographers we are just as much concerned with diversity on the earth's surface as we are with homogeneity: and who shall say that the diversities of the boundary zones are less rich in meaning for us than the uniformity, or unity, within the region?[5]

But what tools can we use for the measuring operation? Contours? Isotherms? Population densities? Linguistic distributions, etc.? The truth of the matter is that the geographer's world is so full of a number of unlike things – some of them mobile, others incalculable, and nearly all of them sporadic in occurrence – that it is impossible to use a *universal* yardstick for the operation. A unit area as determined by one criterion does not necessarily coincide with a unit area as determined

[5] Sauer (op. cit.) has recently reminded us that the centres of culture areas are often near the *boundary* zones of physical regions.

by another. In one area, as, for instance, Southern California, it is the climate that seems to define the limits of the "region": in another, the Laurentian Shield, for example, the circumscribing feature would seem to be the rock structure: in yet a third, e.g. the Pacific North-west, we might argue that it is provided by the topography. The problem would not be so complex if the boundary lines of these natural phenomena coincided. But this is far from being always the case. A mountain crest line frequently lies astride a geological outcrop or a vegetation belt: in the Alps and Pyrenees, flocks and herds freely wander over the mountain-top pastures flanking *both* sides of the international boundary – to the perennial embarrassment of their owners.

Which brings to mind a further consideration, namely that, owing to their greater versatility, humans are wont to show even less regard for the significance of boundaries than nature. Were their actions ruled by respect for logic, for statistics and the niceties of ecological adjustment, no doubt they would have realized long before now that they were mere eddies in the stream of time, doomed to extinction the moment they wandered from the main channel of social evolution. But they have shown an amazing ability for "wandering," and for surviving the impact of new, and suddenly changed, conditions. If their native environment ever had such a thing as organic unity, of which they formed an integral part, they seldom seem to have noticed it – or its absence.

We have only to recall how hard it is to get any of the usual climatic and vegetation regions to "jibe" with human landscape types, with economic, ethnic, linguistic and commercial distributions in order to realize how little respect man has shown for his alleged organic unity with his environment. The truth would seem to be that none of these basic natural distributions is sufficiently determining to tether men in perpetuity to specific parts of the world and to specific modes of living. To superimpose two or more of the basic distributions may help the student to see broad correlations between place, people and their occupations, but the more elements he attempts to correlate, the greater, generally speaking, the fragmentation of the land into element patterns, few of which can be found to bear any close resemblance to the distribution of distinctive ways of human life. Indeed, we should be lucky to emerge from such an exercise with anything more than a "doodle" of intertwining boundaries. Attempts to reduce these to significant order would lead us into the field of arbitrary compromise, and be likely to give a manifestly false picture for a greater number of places than those for which the picture proved to be even approximately true. Regional boundaries cannot be fixed by ballot: no region is a region merely because a quorum of geographers have voted it to be so.

Nor do we fare much better by attempting to define regional boundaries with the aid of only those element complexes for which man is responsible, e.g. land-use patterns and settlement types. Thus the limits of the Cotton Belt are not coterminous with the "South": the *milieu* of the Kentucky cotton farmer is very different from that of the Texas cotton farmer. Similarly, the Corn Belt is not coterminous with the Midwest or with the distribution of any special brand of politics, religion or newspaper. If it is impossible to equate economy with culture in localities which have a dominant (almost homogeneous) economy, we need not expect to be able to do it in those far more numerous areas where men have elected *not* to use their land in any such unitary fashion: for example, in the Great Plains, where ranching (stock-raising) and grain farming intermingle, yet produce two distinctive and independent economies? Or where, in cases equally numerous, we find intrusive social features which fit oddly into the general picture, and which suggest a dichotomous, rather than a unitary organization of living patterns? Often, as Fleure has recently reminded us, the geographical features we observe are not responses to the present environment of the group studied, but instead are "imports": many aspect of Maori life and tradition indicate this clearly, as also does Islamic culture in Nigeria and the transplanting of European tradition to the new world and Australasia.[6] In such cases we can often define our boundaries between the intrusive and native groups with great precision, but that does not mean we have "corralled" a region in the sense of having isolated a unit whole, or a coherent economy.

We must face the fact that it is far more easy to devise seemingly logical systems of classification than it is to produce, from these systems, patterns of culture that have reality on the ground. And, furthermore, we must face the equally disturbing fact that natural boundaries can sometimes be less meaningful than man-made ones. For what proof is there that an isotherm or a contour is any more restrictive of human ways than a political frontier? Does the ten-inch isohyet act as more of a determinant in the economy of its contiguous areas than does the European frontier of the U.S.S.R.? To the best of our knowledge, traffic in ideas and commodities continues to move freely back and forth across the Great Plains. Nature's "curtains" are fashioned of more malleable material than iron!

To persist in making these classifications (whether political or natural), and endowing them with the authority of law, is to pay a lip service to the "logic of geography" for which the makers of history have so far shown much less regard than the writers of it, and to construct a strait-jacket which man has shown little or no inclination to wear. As Hettner observed years ago, the difficult question as to precisely which criterion should be selected for the determination of regions finds no answer in nature. The choice must be made by the individual geographer,

> *according to his subjective judgement of their importance. There is no universally valid regional division which does justice to all phenomena: we can only endeavour to secure a division with the greatest possible number of advantages and the least possible number of disadvantages.*

It is small wonder, then, that Hartshorne, viewing the labyrinth of so-called regional boundaries, should be constrained to admit that "our regions are merely fragments of land whose determination involves a considerable degree of arbitrary

[6] H.J. Fleure, "Geographical Thought in the Changing World," *Amer. Geog. Rev.*, Oct. 1944.

judgement"; that it would be unwarranted to expect geographers to come to even an approximate agreement on the specific limits of these fragments, or even on their central nuclei; and that, at best, we may only hope to contrive a fragmentation of land that has a little more significance than is expressed by the bare phrase "arbitrarily selected . . . Because the different areas of the world have not been separated (either as individuals or types) in their development, but rather the development of each particular characteristic of an area has been a part of the development of that element elsewhere, we know that this process has produced no simple system of classification of areas, whose general outline can be recognized on the basis of our present knowledge of the field."

Just how "unwarranted" it is to expect geographers to agree on such matters would quickly become apparent were they to do more of their travelling about by air. As a class, we geographers are still far from being air-minded. (Some of us do not yet regard aerial surveys and photographs as part of our stock-in-trade.) The more's the pity! For as Mary de Bunsen observes in a recent article, from the air it is possible to catch a glimpse of the larger pattern of man's life, and to gain an insight (not otherwise to be had) into the nature of man's ecological achievement. "From this viewpoint," she writes, "man is judged, not at his own valuation, but . . . as part of a universe which is greater than himself."[7] From the air, surface valuations of spatial phenomena are frequently invalidated. Having, in the course of the past two or three years, flown over many of the "textbook" examples of regions, I readily confess to experiencing real difficulty in locating from the air their precise position and lineaments. The Wheat Belt of the American prairies merges almost imperceptibly into the Hay and Dairy Belt to the east, and the Corn Belt to the south. The cotton economy of the Deccan is subtly woven into the rice economy of its north-eastern and western perimeters. In the Kenya Highlands, there is no telling where the zones of the white man's culture ends and the African's begins. Similarly, in Australia, there are no landmarks separating the sheep-ranching country from the desert.

From the air it is the *links* in the landscapes, the rivers, roads, railways, canals, pipe-lines, electric cables, rather than the *breaks* that impress the aviator: and if he flies low he cannot fail to be impressed by the animation of the "arteries" which couple area with area – by their solidarity, in fact. In India, during the past war, two of the commonest sights seen from the air were the endless files of people padding along the highways in search of employment, and the "hobo" encampments fringing airfields and factories under construction. Here, in the aggregate, were millions of displaced persons whose wanderings were fast disrupting such regional unity as India's economy had ever known.

Our suspicions that regional geographers may perhaps be trying to put boundaries that do not exist around areas that do not matter are further reinforced when we turn our attention from the circumference to the centre. For then it becomes apparent that, as far as present-day distributions are concerned, we are certainly

[7] *Geographical Mag.*, Aug., 1946, p. 158.

not dealing with a world of neatly articulated entities, unitary in nature and integrated in activity. Whatever degree of functional autonomy existed between one area and another before the advent of the Air Age, practically none survives today. The airplane has made the whole world a neighbourhood, and made it just about as private. The effects of the new mobility are legion, and none more significant than the accelerated tempo of cultural diffusion. The purveyors of culture – whether in the form of merchandise or ideas – are already storming the last strongholds of autarchy. Even Tibet is now open to the blandishments of foreigners selling everything from corrugated iron to ladies' slacks; while Solomon islanders chew gum and ride jeeps along tarmac roads where, until 1942, there was nothing but jungle paths; and Kabyles replace the immemorial burnous by Parisian modes, and make paper-knives for tourists instead of sabres for assassins.

Of no single part of the earth can it now be said that the pattern of living is a straightforward product of evolution brought about by local and internal forces. Rather is the pattern – if pattern it be – the interim product of partially related, and partially independent, changes set in motion by such forces as the will and energy of the people living both within and without the area, and by alterations in the individual natural elements composing the area. On balance these act more often in conflict with one another than in unity. In other words, a geographical area should perhaps be viewed more as a register of internal and external conditions, than as the derivative of a predestined evolution. We must, however, be wary of employing figures of speech in this connection. Thus the familiar analogy of a "terrestrial canvas" produced by the combination of different colour designs each applied by different artists working more or less independently and each changing his plan as he proceeded, does little to convey the dynamism of geographic reality. If anything, we are dealing with a "cinema," not a "canvas": the true complexity of our picture can never be apprehended by merely card-indexing the various colour designs and their combinations, or by determining the exact contribution and period of activity of the several artists. Geographic reality is not trapped by such naïve devices, any more than the reality of man is apprehended by an anatomical dissection of his body.

Naïvété should have no place in geographical research: yet, if we are frank with ourselves, we must confess that many of us are reluctant to credit geographical man – that is, man living in specific areal groups – with anything like as much wit and foresight, sophistication, artifice and irrationality as we know he manifests as an individual. Few of us would make so bold as to say that we *know* ourselves physically – let alone say that we have explored the "dark caverns of the mind" – yet we do not hesitate to set about the infinitely more complex task of knowing geographical areas, armed only with an eye for scenery, a head for figures, and unlimited enthusiasm. Despite many illustrations of the geographic complexity of even the smallest area, some of us still cling to the notion that one person, even a newly graduated student, is competent to study, understand and interpret all phases of a given locality. Not a little of our dogmatism concerning, and unquestioning acceptance of the reality of the "region" would seem to stem from the fact, as Ackerman points out in his indictment of amateurish tinkering with geography, that few of us have been properly apprenticed on the systematic side of our calling.

> *With the complexity that is now evident in the study of settlement forms, agricultural occupance, industrial location and governmental structure to mention only a few – we can hope for very little more than we have received from the single "regional" worker. He has not, and cannot report adequately on all phases of anything more than a very simple element complex. Where many elements are involved, he usually has an appreciation only of the more obvious features of each. The holistic investigator has even less foundation for the complete correlation which he seeks, since accurate correlation requires a deeper understanding than observation alone.*[8]

But the reality we are investigating is even more subtle and many-sided than this, since the whole life of a given area is greater than the sum of all the measurable parts, whether dynamic or static. Ideas cannot be measured or card-indexed or dissected, yet without doubt they can be a most potent force in shaping the geographical ensemble. An engineer conceives a plan, the upshot of which is the T.V.A., that not only alters the whole areal pattern from drainage schemes to settlement, but fires the imagination of people living in other areas, even in other continents. Or to take another instance. When the Italians moved out of Cyrenaica, the Arabs moved in: today they live in the same houses, farm the same land, raise the same crops, travel the same roads, buy and sell the same goods, as did their Fascist predecessors. But Arab Cyrenaica is a very different geographical phenomenon from Italian Cyrenaica. The Italians were intruders – aliens – and they lived in cultural isolation, and in contempt for native ways. The Arabs "belong," and today in spite of its Italian framework, Cyrenaica is, in culture, ideologies and loyalties, just another part of Islam.

Living, as we do, within the sound of the atomic bomb, it should not be difficult for us to realize that ideas and associations, memories and prospects, can be just as influential in energizing culture groups as they often are in fashioning individual lives: and that these ideas do not necessarily stem from environmental constraints or from biological inheritance. Nor are they subject, of necessity, to the ordinary geographical laws of movement: frequently they transgress political boundaries as freely as those of land and sea. So strong is the power of an idea that even a veiled threat of a shift in the political frontier or a change in the form of government can lead hundreds of thousands to live, in a sense, on both sides of a boundary – their homes on one side and their bank accounts on the other – a precaution that does nothing to promote functional harmony in the areas in question. Can we doubt, further, that the new post-war styles in European and Asiatic economy, indeed in the whole pattern of living relationships, are being tailored to fit ideological designs quite as much as geographical ones? So far the great powers have paid no particular heed to the words, or blueprints, of geographers: where security,

[8] "Geographic Training, Wartime Research and Immediate Professional Objectives," *Ann. Assoc. Amer. Geog.*, Dec. 1945.

diplomacy or strategy demand it, regional considerations are discarded. The partition of Germany, the amputation of Hungary, the Danubian reshuffle and the internationalizing of Trieste can more readily be rationalized by reference to power politics than geographical discernment. Trieste, in particular, demonstrates how intricately the web of ideas and associations has been woven into the woof of European geography, and how dismal is the prospect of achieving an abiding synthesis of habitat, economy and society in that troubled part of Central Europe. For how can an area possibly attain unity of work and outlook, all the time it is denied its national affiliations, and deprived of the right of self-determination, even of the use of its cultural symbols, but which at the same time is daily bombarded by the propagandist weapons of fascist and democrat, communist and catholic; and an area, furthermore, which is almost certain to be sidestepped commercially by its neighbours? The only unity it is likely to know is that of caged prisoners scheming their escape. And yet politicians (and even geographers?) continue to speak of geographical societies as though they were geological fossils. Unfortunately for their peace of mind, these "fossils" have a knack of hitting back!

This last consideration raises yet another question. Is it possible for an area possessing an appreciable degree of unity to co-exist alongside areas lacking even the very vestiges of it? That is, can we circumscribe areal unity to the extent of being able to say, for instance, that a lasting solution to the Trieste problem could be arrived at, without at the same time concerting the discordant geographical economies and ethnic distributions in its hinterland? All the evidence goes to show that geographical unity is one and indivisible. To deny a locality its national affiliations is to give it no greater expectation of life than that of a cut-flower. It may, so to speak, "live off its own fat" for a while, but sooner or later it will show symptoms of internal disorder, economic stringency, and sub-normal, ersatz living standards. Rather does geographical unity stem from an appreciation of the complementary nature of human environments – no single area has enough of all the ingredients of the good life for all its people all the time – and the consequent necessity of cultivating close "arterial" relations between differently endowed neighbours, each serving the other, and in turn being served by it. (In a sense, geographical unity represents the "climax association" of human activities, in that, like a plant climax, it is the end-product of a process of selection by elimination.) If neighbour areas are not organized on an optimum basis, if, for example, region A is not producing the grain crops for which it is better endowed than region B, and B is not producing the meat and wool for which it is better suited, the economy of both areas will suffer. "If one member of the body suffers, all the members suffer." In other words, it is impossible for optimum geographical relationships in one area – the prerequisite of regional unity – to co-exist with sub-optimum relationships (*alias* regional disunity) in another. Judging by the number of functionally unintegrated, characterless areas in the world today, it would seem either that we are still a very long way from organizing society on a regional basis, or that we gave up the attempt in the eighteenth century when the Industrial Revolution got out of hand.

Were it simply the tangible, measurable phenomena that were unintegrated, there would perhaps be good ground for believing in an ultimate regionalization of our world: but the present disunity and confusion arises quite as much from imponderable ideologies and feelings as from measurable economies. In many parts of Europe and the Near East the feelings of two or more nationalities about the same piece of land are seemingly irreconcilable: the French, we may take it, are never likely to "feel" as the Germans do about the Saar Basin: nor are the Arabs likely to "feel" the same way as the Jews do over the Jordan valley: or the Italians, as the Yugoslavs, in regard to Venezia Giulia. The overlapping sovereignties and remembered wrongs of the past effectively prevent the regional integration of activity in these areas. Which brings us to our next topic, namely, precisely how widespread is the occurrence of the region?

The Incidence of the Region

In their writings upon the subject, geographers frequently make two cognate assumptions: first, that the "region" is the ultimate, inevitable synthesis of all the folk-work-place relationships in a given unit area – much in the same way as Darwin regarded man as the consummation of a slow evolutionary process: second, that the whole world is organized (or in process of becoming so) on a "synthetic" regional basis, which it is the primary function of the geographer to identify, describe and explain.

Is such optimism justified? Is it possible to separate the whole world into neat areas exhibiting even the barest rudiments of "unity," "coherence" or "organic entity"? We must confess to a difficulty in naming and delimiting, unequivocally, a dozen such areas outside Europe and the British Isles. And even in Europe it is by no means easy to accommodate certain areas into a generally acceptable and meaningful scheme of regions, for some of those which are generally regarded as classic examples of regions, give the impression of being the product of a past, rather than a contemporary, synthesis. Their survival, in as far as they do survive, would appear to be due partly to the persistence of the earlier cultural *forms*, e.g. house and road patterns, after the decay of the cultural *modes;* and partly due to the momentum of the "going concern." To substantiate this thesis, it will be necessary to remind ourselves of some of the features of the European world during the epoch of its cultural differentiation.

As we noted earlier, the regional concept is of European provenance, and was first propounded to a world as yet untouched by the Industrial Revolution. As far as the general pattern of life was concerned, eighteenth-century France and Germany *looked* very little different from their sixteenth- or even fourteenth-century prototypes. The turnpike and the stagecoach were beginning to affect the tempo of life in the towns, but beneath this ripple of change the great currents of eighteenth-century society continued to flow on quietly in their mediaeval channels. What struck the writers of the time was the stability, even the permanence, of the cultural landscape: the unchanging farm practice – they could point to thousand-year-old triennial rotations: the Romano-Gallic origins of the farmsteads of Picardy and Flanders – farmsteads which had often been in the possession of the same family since Norman times. They were constantly impressed by the harmonies between land and economy: the localizations of dialect and of distinctive domestic and ecclesiastical architectural styles. Most communities in Germany, France, England, etc., were, from the continuing exigencies of communication, still practically self-supporting. They had to live "off the land" and the local land at that.[9] Roads were mostly paths and often impassable because of mud. (Even to this day the countless little hamlets in the southern half of the Massif Central, the farmsteads of the Basin of Rennes and of Brie are distributed quite independently of roads: they communicate with one another by means of a network of byways.) While this meant that the basic structure of society was much the same throughout Europe in as far as most areas needed to raise their own requirements of grain, fuel, and raw materials, there was plenty of local diversity: Beauce soon acquired a reputation for its grain; Berry, for its wool and meat; and so on. A further landscape differential was provided by the fact that these early communities, being substantially self-supporting in constitution, had to learn to fashion all their cultural artifacts out of local materials: farmsteads, churches, manors, as well as fences and bridges were built in the media most readily available. In the clay vales of the Severn and Thames it was brick: in the Cotswolds, stone: in the Weald, timber: on the Downlands, thatch and flint. Likewise only those industries could flourish which could draw upon local raw materials and local sources of power. Even in eighteenth-century Europe, mineral workings and factories serving more than their immediate localities were very few and far between. Neither the demand for coal and iron nor the technique of their production on a large scale yet existed. Similarly the trade of Europe was still almost entirely parochial in character, and small in amount. No efforts had then been made to provide suitably constructed roads for internal transport. As for the Roman roads, these for the most part had been plundered of their stone and allowed to fall into disuse. The remarkable sub-division of middle Europe into no less than three hundred distinct states involved the continual crossing of frontiers and payment of customs. Under these conditions, the movement of goods was bound to be costly: it is estimated, for instance, that wood for fuel could be economically carried by road for a distance of only ten to twelve miles.[10] It is perhaps impossible for us, living in an age of all pervading mobility, to appreciate how very small a world these little communities administered, and how ignorant of the outer

[9] In eastern France and in the agricultural plains of Germany it was possible until recently to see vestiges of this autarchical economy. "From a nucleus of farm houses, the fields, under a system of communal rotation, extended in long, parallel bands so that sowing, tilling, harvesting and consignment to pasture succeed one another in regular sequence, and are completed simultaneously. Originally there were village streets between them in the form of narrow strips, either grass-covered or lying fallow for the convenience of the peasant. This local system of communications is characteristic of a village community. It is sufficient unto itself. Roads may have been added later in order to communicate with the external world, but the social unity, the cell so organised has to be self-supporting, unless we already provide for its own circulation." Vidal de la Blache, *Principles of Human Geography*, pp. 280–1.

[10] *Vide*, W. G. East, *Historical Geography of Europe*, p. 406.

world they were. To find a modern-day parallel we should need to go far afield; for example, to Annam, concerning which country one twentieth-century writer has spoken as follows: "Because of the great variety of communal institutions, we Annamese imagine ourselves in China or America as soon as we leave our village."

Restricted severely in their external contacts by intervening forests and marshes, by the absence of roads and multiplication of political boundaries, European communities had early become distinguished from one another, in physical appearance, loyalties and outlooks, if not in the organization of their social life. This rudimentary regionalization of life owed much to the mediaeval Church. As the paramount influence in the community, the Church was able to direct the secular as well as the spiritual activities of her followers. Not only did she enforce regular attendance at mass and take tithes of the farmers' crops (thereby putting a premium upon sedentary habits and good husbandry, and a discount on landless nomadism), she also actively promoted land settlement. The widespread clearing of forests and founding of new villages in France in the twelfth century was to no small degree the effort of the Cistercian Order. With the consequent increase in rural population and the Cistercian-inspired improvements in methods of cultivation went a growth of the towns and a development of those industries needed to supply the elementary wants of the rural population. While the appearance of the artisan class did something to break down the self-sufficiency of the manor, it substantially strengthened the solidarity of the parish and diocese, in that it gave the inhabitants of town and country a sense of common cause – of being "workers together." This sense was assiduously fostered by the Church, which had no wish to promote the prosperity of the town at the expense of the countryside. On the contrary, she had early discovered that good Christians were more easily made from landed farming folk than from landless urban folk. Nomadism and paganism have long gone together; and even though it might be unkind to draw a parallel between the godlessness of the horse-riding Magyars and the car-driving, Sabbath-breaking New Yorkers, it remains a fact that itinerant souls have always presented a serious ecclesiastical problem.

So town and countryside came to be looked upon as a unit whole, with the town subserving the country. If need be, the country could do without the town, but not the town without the country. This mutuality of interest made for close liaison between the two, and did much to promote the feeling of local self-consciousness and local patriotism.

Over large parts of Europe this areal differentiation of the culture pattern can be traced far back into the Middle Ages.[11] By the time the eighteenth-century thinkers were beginning to enquire into its nature and origin, the mould had been set for centuries, and the dominant features of life had already acquired a strong traditional flavour. Many signs of this persistence of acquired characteristics survive until this day: indeed it would almost seem that the regionalization of Europe is

[11] In France, most of the *pays* were already well differentiated by the twelfth and 13th centuries: similarly with the German *gaus*.

most conspicuous in those areas where the hand of history lies most heavily. For if we call to mind almost any of the textbook examples of regions, such as the Weald of Kent and Sussex, the Fenlands, the Scottish Highlands, the Paris Basin and its constituent *pays*, the Bohemian Diamond or the Tyrol, what are the features that strike us most forcibly? The distinctive topography? Mountains have been laid low and valleys exalted, but not within recorded times. The characteristic weather pattern? There have been few significant changes (whether cyclical or non-periodic) in the European climate since the fourteenth century.[12] Is it the appearance of the cultural landscape? The general disposition of forests and farms, villages and roads has changed little in the last half millennium: many English fields and lanes are of more ancient lineage than England's nobility, while the clustered villages of Normandy, Artois and the middle Neckar, the dispersed hamlets of the Weald, the Cotentin Peninsula and the Allgäu, have retained the same basic morphology since the days of their founding. Is it the style of the secular and ecclesiastical architecture? Apart from those in the newer industrial and dormitory towns, most of Europe's churches were built before A.D. 1600, and her most typical farmsteads, inns and noble houses are of similar antiquity. Is it the social and human economy? Here again the distinctive features of local folk-lore, dress, dialect, music and art, and even of agricultural practice, have changed little since the late fourteenth or early fifteenth centuries. What interested Arthur Young most notably when he made his famous survey of European agriculture in the eighteenth century was its traditional and primitive character. The open field system and simple rotation of crops and fallow, was still general in the arable regions, and serfdom, in all but a few areas, was still the order of the day.

It is true, of course, that life in the Middle Ages had not entirely stagnated: that there had been periods of economic and social unrest, especially during the fourteenth and early fifteenth centuries, when there were popular uprisings in the Netherlands, in England and elsewhere: that there had been an increase in urban activity and in specialization of labour with a consequent increase in the role of capital and of the middle class; but as agencies of attrition upon a custom-controlled world, their influence was neither profound nor enduring. Feudal institutions, chivalric and autarchical ideals continued to be all-powerful in the life of the continent.

In other words, many of the most unequivocal, highly individualized geographical areas in Europe and Great Britain today are in the nature of historical survivals from the pre-industrial age – relics, as it were, from a world that was practically self-contained and self-supporting.

Is there any evidence that the Machine Age has produced a cultural pattern comparable in significance and coherence with those developed in feudal times? Some writers claim to see a new pattern of geographical areas crystallizing out

[12] The last major change seems to have taken place towards the end of that century, when "the ancient dry phase of British climate [gave place to] the present cool phase" (E. Huntington, *Mainsprings of Civilisation*, p. 595). That an agriculturally significant change did occur at that epoch is predicated, *inter alia*, by the disappearance of the grape, as an outdoor crop, from about A.D. 1350 to 1400 onwards.

from the crucible of industrialization. For instance, in place of old static entities, Dickinson saw emerging in pre-war Germany a new, more dynamic regional pattern, based on economic activity. These regions he called "entities of circulation and persons, with respect both to actual movements and to regional organization." But even if there were such a thing as "an entity of circulation" in Germany (which we take leave to doubt, for entity connotes functional independence and/or separate existence, and quite clearly the aim of Nazi Germany was to organize the *whole* Fatherland, rather than its component parts, on a unitary basis – thus the *Autobahn* system served national strategy rather than local economy), we cannot agree that the areas Dickinson chooses to call "circulation regions" had in fact anything more than a statistical existence. For what unitary quality did Silesia possess, with its three well-marked physical sub-divisions, set as it was in the midst of one of the most hotly-contested march-lands of Europe, with its borders on three sides arbitrarily fixed by treaty, not to speak of the ardent and opposing nationalisms of its peoples? And how can we regard the Rhine-Ruhr region as an "entity of circulation"? As every statesman in Europe now knows, this region is the very nerve ganglion of Germany, and has no more power of circulation, when severed from the rest of the body politic, than its human counterpart. If the only kind of regionalized unity possessed by modern (pre-war) Germany was its circulation pattern, then the day of the region is nearly at an end, since mobility is the catalyst of regional diversity, and must sooner or later dissolve the whole compartmental structure of our civilization.

It is not without interest to note in this connection that wherever men are sensible of the permeation of society by a monotype culture, they are busy organizing associations for the encouragement of the old regional ways. In France, where the differentiation of the country into *pays* (*alias* "regions") is probably more strongly accented than in any other part of the world, staunch endeavours are being made to resuscitate dying folk-habits, local dialects and traditional arts and crafts. The French know (who better?) that it is the "silent backward tracings", the feelings of cultural identity and group experiences surrounding place and home that compose the stuff by which regional consciousness is sustained and fostered.

We see, therefore, that the standard-model region is essentially a phenomenon of the European continent: that it was sired by feudalism and raised in the cultural seclusion of a self-sufficing environment, that it owed almost as much to history as to geography, and that it does not appear to thrive in the more turbulent atmosphere of modern times. This being so, are we justified in assuming that it will transplant freely in the radically different *milieux* of the Americas and Australasia?[13]

[13] By general consent, Asia has always been more conspicuous for the widespread uniformity of its cultural life and *mores*, than contrariwise. One reason for this may be, as Vidàl de la Blache opines, that "in China as in Japan and in India, there has been no methodical attack on new agricultural areas . . . Human establishments continue to be confined to particular zones . . . Europe is the most humanized part of the world. No other presents so rich a field with such a hierarchy of types" (*Principles of Human Geography*).

From a purely environmental point of view, Europe had a flying start over all the other continents in the matter of localization of culture patterns. Hume remarked upon this in the eighteenth century: "Of all parts of the earth, Europe is the most broken by seas, rivers and mountains, and . . . most naturally divided into several distinct governments."[14] Modern geographers might perhaps choose to express this implied relationship rather more academically, but they are unlikely to dissent from the general thesis that Europe's national and cultural fragmentation could not have persisted so long and been so radical, had it not been for the physiographic fission – to borrow a rather over-worked word – of that continent. The distribution of land and water, the dovetailing of plains and mountains, and the contiguity of steppes and forests all have had their share in producing a compartition of peoples and societies which no other region on earth possesses to the same degree.

Then, from the historical standpoint, it needs to be remembered that the ideologies which nourished Europe in the era of its cultural differentiation were already passing away, if not extinct, when the New World was being opened up. Not even the oldest settled parts of North America, with the possible exception of the Lower St. Lawrence Valley, succeeded in transplanting the regional idea in its pristine European likeness. From the time of the Pilgrims onwards (the very name Pilgrim is suggestive of a different attitude – one of detachment from regions and places), almost all the immigrants were animated by a sense of involvement in a new, un-European kind of life.[15] "A spirit of brotherhood," writes Commager, "transcending class, race and religion, a feeling that all dwellers within these states are partners in a common enterprise, is the peculiar quality that brought the American Republic into being."[16] At the Stamp Act Conference of 1765, a delegate declared: "There ought to be no New Englander, no New Yorker, known on this continent, but all of us Americans . . ." Seventeen years later St John de Crèvecoeur could write:

> *Individuals of all nations are melted into a new race of men, whose labours and posterity will one day cause great changes in the world . . . The Americans were once scattered all over Europe: here they are incorporated into one of the finest systems of population which has ever appeared, and which will hereafter become distinct . . .*[17]

To realize this new mode of life, it was soon found necessary to eschew thoughts of areal self-sufficiency; to do business with pagan Indian, Anglican Virginian and even catholic Cavalier; to welcome men, irrespective of their cultural and national prejudices, and, above all, to keep the frontier moving. Where the frontier rolled

14 *Of the Rise and Progress of Arts and Science.*

15 William Bradford put it – rather too pietistically, perhaps, for our modern ears – in these words: "So they left that goodly and pleasant city, which had been their resting place near twelve years: but they knew they were pilgrims, and looked not much at those things, but lifted up their eyes to the heavens, their dearest country, and quieted their spirits" (*Of Plimoth Plantation*).

16 *The Growth of the American Republic*, Vol. II, pp. 591–2.

17 *Letters from an American Farmer.*

back apace, and the immigrant flood ran strongly, as in the Midwest, Central California, and the Pacific Northwest, European regionalism never had a chance to take root.

> *The triumphant achievements of the great railways gave the continent physical unity and overcame the natural effects of geographical sectionalism . . . A single type of life spreading from a single centre created the economic unity of the country . . . Free trade over the whole area assimilated the mechanism of daily existence, the habits of the people, their food and dress. Wherever the immigrant went, he entered into the same kind of life and was caught up into its activities.*[18]

Is it not significant that almost the only parts of North America where distinctive, areally circumscribed modes of life still persist are those which were sidestepped by the highway and the railroad during the epoch of the retreating frontier? It is only in the comparatively quiet backwaters of the continent, like the Lower St Lawrence Valley, the higher Appalachians, the Ozarks and the Indian reserves that we can still see relics of a dissident cultural tradition, and of a distinctive regionalism. But every year sees a further shrinkage in the size and influence even of these "islands."

In the light of the foregoing, we need not wonder that it is the uniformity of American civilization, rather than the diversities of its peoples and countrysides, that impresses the modern traveller most deeply. When one hundred and fifty millions of people, enjoying, in the mass, a higher standard of well-being than any other people on earth, are coaxed into buying the same soap, eating the same canned goods, reading the same magazines, listening to the same radio programmes and joining the same service clubs, it is difficult to see how distinctive folk-habits, dialects and arts and crafts, which have in the past done so much to sustain regional self-consciousness, can possibly survive. Areal variations in the pattern of living, in all categories except perhaps land-use, modes of employment and population densities, would seem destined to attenuation, if not gradual extinction. Messrs. F. W. Woolworth, Henry Ford and Sears Roebuck have already gone quite a long way towards ensuring this end.

We have only to reflect upon the phenomenal achievements of the Tennessee Valley Authority to realize something of the efficacy of modern technology and propaganda in breaking down the barriers of cultural non-conformity. Some writers tend to regard the transformation newly wrought in the hills and valleys of Tennessee as merely the substitution of an antique regional pattern by a more modern pattern; but the T.V.A. has done far more than integrate the economy of the upper Tennessee Valley. It has altered the whole conception of group living in neighbouring states, and threatens to disrupt the balance of the agricultural economy even as far afield as Wisconsin. Thus we read in a recent article[19] that, thanks largely to cheap electricity, cheap fertilizers and almost year-round outdoor

[18] Benians, *Race and Nation in the U.S.*

[19] *New York Times*, Sunday, July 28, 1946.

grazing, dairy farming is expanding in Tennessee to such an extent that there is talk of moving a part of the vast dairy industry of Wisconsin to the Valley. So far from being a rather inconspicuous brick in the geographic fabric of the nation, it now bids fair to become the cornerstone of a new social and economic structure which may well alter the entire look of the continent. We should, therefore, be singularly out of step with the times to over-emphasize the significance of distinctive distributions of human modes and economies, whether localized in time or place.

As Dr Bowman reminded us in a recent paper,[20] scientific invention is a perpetually unsettling factor. Every time a new implement or machine is invented or a new technique is devised, a new appraisal must be made of every scrap of territory and the possibility of a new orientation of human activities be predicated. Areal distributions are essentially impermanent. Even while we are, so to speak, photographing it, the picture changes. The mechanism of civilization is so delicate that it can be disrupted almost over-night. Ancient desert civilizations like that of Palmyra (and what is a civilization but an expression of cultural unity over a given geographical area?) have vanished like the smoke of a nomad's fire when some internal tumult or foreign unrest has dislocated the organization of the caravan routes. Much the same is true of Tyre and Sidon, Petra and Ur, and a hundred other cultural centres of the past.

Modern civilizations manifest rather more resilience to disruptive forces than those of antiquity: it must be confessed, however, that this does not seem to have extended their expectation of life appreciably! None of the Axis empires lasted even a generation: Fascist Africa was destroyed almost as easily – and speedily – as Palmyra. But, thanks largely to the greater versatility of twentieth-century man, there has been no abandonment of the desolated lands to the wild beasts. Even the conservative, tradition-ridden Arab has learned to make himself almost as much at home in Benghazi as in a Bedouin encampment, and to be almost equally happy irrigating crops as watering flocks. Indeed, Miss Freya Stark contends, in her *East is West*, that "the desert . . . no longer gives the essential picture of Arabian life."[21]

What is happening in Islam is, of course, also happening (and has already happened) in many other parts of the world. The ferment of change is universal. What with the desolations of war, the imperfections of the peace treaties and the ever-accelerating pace of scientific progress, the structure of every human society is now in process of being rebuilt. The russification of Eastern Europe means, among other things, the introduction of collective farming and planned industrial economies in Poland, Eastern Germany and elsewhere. The transference of twelve million Germans and the liquidation of eight million Jews from Poland will do much more than alter the ethnic composition of the country: similarly the exchange of populations between Sudetenland and Saxony can hardly be achieved without making a major impress on the life of both regions. The peace treaties provide a

[20] *Foreign Affairs*, Jan., 1946.

[21] *East is West*, p. xiii.

new order in Italy's old African colonies; while the allied government of Germany is fashioning a very different kind of economic unity from that divined by writers a few years ago. And what is true of the Old World is also true of the New, for the process of renovating the environment to suit the cultural fashions of our day extends to the remotest isles of the Pacific.

Conclusion

We must, then, face the fact that the old order is changing, and that we should only be deceiving ourselves to say as the French have taught us to do: "Plus ça change, plus c'est la même chose." That epigram was coined before the invention of the internal combustion engine, sponsored radio programmes, totalitarian propaganda and jet-propelled bombs. Whatever the pattern of the new age may be, we can be sure that there will be no independent, discrete units in it – no "worlds within worlds." There will be no neatly demarcated "regions" where geographers (or economists or sociologists, for that matter) can study a "fossil" community. Man's "region" is now the world. This does not render superfluous the continued organization of geographical studies on a systematic areal basis. On the contrary: the very increase in the interpenetration of human modes would call for more, rather than fewer, such studies. But it does mean that we should be well advised, when making these studies, to refrain from searching for "unitary patterns of living," "entities of distribution," and from assuming, in the manner of determinists, that "regional unity" is the goal towards which civilized society is moving, and that if we but had the wit, we could not fail to see signs of it emerging. Let us rather admit that the ways of man, like those of his Maker, are frequently inscrutable, that while the regional idea may look very promising on paper, it does not enjoy the wholehearted support of the facts (any more than does the Darwinian idea of biological evolution with which the regional concept has obvious parental affinities). At best, a regional study can be only a personal work of art, not an impersonal work of science – a portrait rather than a blueprint. As such, it can have substantial value, but its value will lie in the realm of illumination and suggestion rather than of definitive analysis and synthesis. It will do well if it catches the dominant traits of the area: it cannot hope to carry out a distillation of all the compound elements (physical, economic, social and political) which are present. To presume otherwise would be grossly to under-estimate the complexity of our world. For the understanding of areal differentiations, we must, as a *sine qua non*, be able to draw upon the analyses provided by men trained in the several contributory disciplines. At present such analyses are woefully few in number, and flimsy in character. But even if this were not the case, it is still uncertain whether we could contrive to establish regional geography on a rigorously scientific foundation. With Finch we find ourselves inclining to the view that "the complexities of man and nature are too much for his abilities at rationalization."[22]

[22] V.C. Finch, "Geographical Science and Social Philosophy," *Ann. Assoc. Amer. Geog.*, March, 1939.

Instead of continuing to add to the already impressive pile of chorographic studies – many of which amount to little more than a laborious transferring of dead bones from one coffin to another – should we not rather devote our energies to the pursuit of more worthwhile, if more restricted, objectives? Ackerman has recently indicated where we shall find such objectives. "Human geography," he says, "will never be accepted as a mature scholarly discipline until a more thorough systematic literature begins to take shape in it."[23] And he reminds us that geomorphology, climatology, plant and soil geography are not the whole of systematic geography: that land-use, conservation, the geographies of manufacturing, transportation, settlement and resources are equally important, though in professional esteem (judging by the amount of attention they have received over the past twenty-five years) they are a bad second to the more physical disciplines. Carl Sauer has also recently indicated a number of worthwhile objectives: as, for example, the study of man as an agent of physiographic change, of dwelling patterns, house types and field systems, of "cultural climaxes," successions and receptivity. These, of course, put the emphasis on the more historical side of systematic geography.[24] Nor is this list in any way exhaustive: a reading of Van Burkalow's work on the distribution of fluorine in U.S. water supplies,[25] suggests almost unending possibilities for research in the geography of disease: while our current refugee problems should surely cause many of us to bestir ourselves in the neglected field of pioneer settlement and the geography of marginal areas.

Here are subjects worthy of our most earnest and sustained consideration: they bear closely on the social and political problems which bedevil our times: and what is more, they are, for the larger part, amenable to definitive treatment. To ignore them, and spend our days "regionalizing," is to chase a phantom, and to be kept continually out of breath for our pains.

[23]Ackerman, op. cit., p. 141.
[24]Sauer, op. cit., pp. 17 et seq.
[25]*Vide Geog. Rev.*, Apr., 1946.

PART V

SPACE, TIME AND SPACE-TIME

INTRODUCTION

In the interests of science, it is necessary over and over again to engage in a critique of these fundamental concepts [space and time], in order that we may not be unconsciously ruled by them. (Einstein, cited in N. Smith, 1984 p. 66)

As basic philosophical categories, time and space are particularly suitable as a framework for a general cultural history, because they are comprehensive, universal and essential. (S. Kern 1983 p. 2)

These quotations suggest at least two levels of analysis concerning the relations between geography and space and time. First, many geographers have explicitly theorized space and time, often doing so as a means of redirecting the discipline (for example, Nystuen and Soja, **chapters 36** and **38**). Secondly, as Kern suggests, one may find implicit assumptions about the nature of space and time in all geographical work. These are generally shared by other disciplines and wider public debates. Although writings do not always directly refer to philosophical issues, we can deduce what the authors' working assumptions and ideas may be. Readings by Mackinder and Openshaw (**chapters 33** and **41**) fit this description. According to the first line of inquiry, at various times space and time may be neglected or treated inadequately. Soja (1989), for example, criticizes both the devaluation of space in social theory and the insufficiently instrumental concept of space in geography throughout most of the twentieth century, including the era of spatial science (see General Introduction, p. 7). Yet the use of such concepts in geography's earlier decades should not be overlooked, including those when more natural or physical themes dominated. Whether through metaphor, borrowed theory or background assumption, ideas of time and temporality, space and spatiality were as present then as they were later. In this sense geographical enterprise has always grappled with a set of basic problems to do with space and time, even when they were addressed under other headings.

Basic Questions of Time and Space

There are at least four basic questions concerning space and time in geography which are addressed by the selected readings. The first, and perhaps the most prominent, is their 'true' nature, and particularly whether they are absolute or relative concepts. The concept of absolute space and time holds that they are apart from one another and from matter and energy, that they precede matter and exist as backdrops or containers of social life. In a stronger version, they may possess causal influence in themselves. Alternatively, and commonly within geography, space may be there waiting to be filled by human endeavour. The alternative view, that space and time are (variously) relative or relational, holds that they are neither separate from one another nor matter and energy, and that they have no independent causal powers. They could therefore be acted upon. If they are absolute and separate, then it might follow that different knowledges can treat either separately, which is a second basic question. This was the source of the dispute between Hartshorne, who argued that geography was a chorological science treating all objects in a spatial dimension, and Sauer, who insisted on the inclusion of temporal perspectives. Although he disagreed with Hartshorne on many points, Schaefer (**chapter 35**) shared the stress on geography as a pre-eminently spatial discipline. However, this could simply substitute spatial determinism for environmental determinism, implying that spatial forms are the outcome of other spatial forms and not social processes. The alternative view of relegating spatial patterns to the status of mere outcomes of social processes – which would seem to dispense with geography altogether – is hardly tenable either. The compromise view, which is shared in various epistemological ways by most of the authors of the significant volume edited by Gregory and Urry (1985), is that space is both the medium and the outcome of social relations: Soja (**chapter 38**) spells out the position in more detail.

Given that a powerful tradition in human geography rests upon separating space from time, and given that many theorists find this untenable, the problem remains of how to reintegrate them. There are at least four distinct resolutions to this third basic question. One is dialectical and, within human geography, best expressed by Harvey. He argues (in **chapter 37**) that geographical difference cannot be considered apart from the temporal dynamics of capitalism. The periodic crises of accumulation which beset capitalism can only be overcome by producing new spatial configurations, which, with further accumulation, themselves become obstacles to the process and are the source of new crises. Another resolution integrates time and space through the medium of social action, such as in Hägerstrand's time-geography. Pred (**chapter 39**) advances the basic spatial and temporal terms of a distinct and original geographical lexicon, such as path, domain and constraint, which are the necessary – but not sufficient – conditions for all social action. Such terms are derived from such simple observations as the fact that a body cannot be in two places at one time, or that time itself is a limited resource. Hägerstrand (**chapter 40**) uses the autobiography of his childhood to substantiate these ideas. A third way of reintegrating them, grounded more in experience, suggests that people do not live space and time separately. While times and spaces are joined by bodies tracking through them daily, in Hägerstrand's thinking, they are held together by such things as the body's senses – the realm of subjective meanings and the process of childhood learning and language in Tuan's (1974) more phenomenological perspective. Finally, and following in the tradition of spatial modelling of large data sets (see Clarke and Wilson 1985), Openshaw (**chapter 41**) argues that Geographical Information Systems (GIS) can further integrate spatial and temporal information.

The fourth basic question concerns the relationship between space, time and nature. The emphasis on spatial science in the 1960s encouraged the separation of physical and human geography (Guelke 1989). The facts of physical geography were lost in the isotropic planes of spatial analysis. Yet nature does reappear. In Tuan's thinking it takes the form of the corporeality of the body: up, down, left, right, behind and in front are all basic categories of experience deriving from the physical body. In Harvey, nature appears via the commodity, produced by human labour from the material world (also Smith and O'Keefe, **chapter 16**). Hägerstrand's 'situational ecology' introduces ecological rhythms and flows of energy into the time-geographies of his subjects, and emphasizes the 'being together' of the human and the physical in place.

The basic questions – outlined albeit briefly – demonstrate a series of connections between ontological problems such as the nature of space and time, methodological questions such as whether to include temporal analysis, and disciplinary questions of whether space alone can define a separate area of knowledge. They are recurrent within geographical thought, although rarely raised in exactly the same way twice. In order to further understand these ideas we now address three principal episodes in human geography: imperialism, the space age, and present times.

Geopolitics and Chronopolitics

In 1884 the International Meridian Conference made Greenwich Mean Time the world's standard time and established time zones. This new universal time was spatialized around lines of longitude, while minutes and seconds marked out both time and nautical distance. This episode marked a new turn in the space–time ordering of the world, completing what had perhaps begun in 1493–4 when Spain and Portugal divided the New World by a geometric act. Thrift (**chapter 34**) recounts the temporal regulation of local British times in the nineteenth century under the pressure of railways and postal services, and the same process of establishing a single public time continued in the imperial possessions. Many sacred spaces and places of pre-conquest American societies were actively subsumed into Christianity's sacred calendars (Wolf 1982). Later, within the West itself, sacred time gave way first to secular time and then to spatialized time, which is why Fabian (1983) declared 'chronopolitics' to be the ideological foundation of 'geopolitics'.

By the secularization and spatialization of time Fabian refers to the processes by which time came to be thought of as co-extensive with the world, and through which relationships between parts of the world could be understood as temporal relations. In anthropology this took a simple form: here (the West) was now, and there (the Rest) was then. This formed the basis for typological times such as civilized/primitive, modern/traditional etc. All societies were united in a single, progressive, one-way history that owed much to the ideas of evolutionary biology. If developments in technologies such as the telegraph, railway and telephone contributed to a strong and thickened sense of the present as a global simultaneity (Kern 1983), then the heavy emphasis on evolution and progress structured the world in the opposite direction, towards an absence of 'co-evalness' (Fabian's phrase). This contradiction can be found in contemporary geographical writings. Geopolitics enabled geographers to 'think big' and on a world-wide scale, while chronopolitics underscored the evolutionary typologies of the world's peoples.

This imperial world-view was not confined to scholarly works, and a pervasive 'structure of attitude and reference' pervaded the period's literature (Said 1994). This term indicates 'the way in which structures of location and geographical reference appear in cultural languages of literature, history, or ethnography, sometimes allusively and sometimes carefully plotted, across several individual works that are not otherwise connected to one another or to an official ideology of "empire"', (Said 1994, p. 61). This structure, says Said, has three main elements: the authority of the European observer; a hierarchy of spaces separating and joining 'home' and 'overseas territory'; and the relegation of non-Europeans to a secondary racial status (p. 71). The idea of Empire was deep in common-sense as well as in official pronouncements. It may not be actively expressed in geographical works, but is nonetheless present among unacknowledged conditions.

Thinking big was a feature of many key geographical ideas in the imperial period, 1870–1918. While geography was evidently the servant of imperialism, the connections were rarely simple and geographers partook in the many conflicting debates on the matter (Godlewska and Smith 1994). It is no surprise to find a strong notion of absolute space running through much of the writing, because it is a concept appropriate to social domination. The world space was there for Europeans to fill with their ideas of property, exclusive nation-states and homogeneous cultures bound to territories (Smith and Katz 1993). Some 85 per cent of the earth's land surface was claimed by European powers in 1914, not including the extensive Ottoman Empire (Said 1994). Mackinder's world maps, Herbertson's and Fleure's regions, were therefore apparently natural and scientific efforts to carve up and fill up the world in thought, without regard to the desires of the peoples living beyond their shores (**chapters 33, 22** and **23**).

Space was there not only to be colonized physically, but also to be viewed from a central point. Gregory (1994) names this view 'the world-as-exhibition'. This 'modern constellation of power, knowledge, and spatiality' (p. 5) can be found in cartography, the universal exhibitions, panoramas, dioramas, cinema houses and even, in the case of Second Empire Paris, in city layouts themselves. According to Gregory, this sense of visual command is also found in Paul Vidal de la Blache's

'Tableau de la géographie de France' (1903), in which the country is represented as a picture, a coherent composition which embodies the landscape and the French nation, to be seen as a whole.

If space is laid out to be occupied and seen like a picture, then it is because it is also framed. Kearns's (1984) comparison of Mackinder's 'pivot of history' thesis and F. J. Turner's frontier thesis suggests that both conceived of space as closed. For Mackinder the imminent charting of the poles marked the end of the Columbian era of exploration. For Turner, 1890 was the closing of the American frontier. Both drew upon biological analogies to establish the end of one evolutionary phase and the beginning of another. Future expansion could only be achieved in the struggle between existing states, necessitating a preparation for war. Ratzel (**chapter 32**) thought Europe was crowded and Mackinder regarded it as a vulnerable peninsula threatened by the Eurasian heartland. Ratzel extended organic analogies to the state – its need for growth and territory, the interdependencies among people, and the relationship between people and soil. States must grow, by the 'mechanical' means of territorial annexation and the 'organic' means of a closer union between people and land. European peoples were more advanced in evolutionary terms, had 'larger ideas of space' and must therefore expand or decay.

Geographical conceptions of space and time owed as much, if not more, to analogies from life sciences than to the physical sciences, which became more prominent as the century progressed. Life sciences also provided temporal concepts such as succession and climax communities in plant ecology, the Davisian cycle of erosion in landform study, the Chicago School's urban ecology and the rise and fall of races and civilizations, in the work of Huntington, Taylor and others (see Livingstone 1992, pp. 227–31). Even so, many of the concepts outlined above outlasted the imperial era and have lived on in the space age.

The Space Age

Derwent Whittlesey's article 'The Horizon of Geography' (1945) set the tone for a bold and confident post-war human geography in which 'the prime essence . . . is space' (p. 32). His new global sense of space was forged by the completion of polar expeditions, the conquest of the air and the mining of the depths. Adding time, Whittlesey described a four-dimensional space waiting to be filled by the possibilities of new technologies and by geographical research. This contrasted with the closed and crowded space which had preoccupied many of the imperial geographers. The future could be grasped confidently, unlike Mackinder's retrospective view of a geography partially trapped by history. In the following decade many of these technological dreams came true: the sound barrier was broken, the Mount Palomar reflecting telescope was built, atomic devices were exploded, B52s and nuclear-powered submarines entered service and exploration of the ocean floor revealed critical information about plate tectonics. In 1957 Sputnik was launched. But far from entering the space age – either in the skies above or through the imagined spaces of a revived science fiction – human geographers tended to keep their eyes down, fixed on the two dimensions of terrestrial space. However, that space provided plenty of material for the study of two principal themes, spatial patterns and spatial movement.

The emergence of human geography as a spatial science in the 1950s and 1960s has been written about extensively elsewhere (for example, Johnston 1991). A predominant notion of absolute space understood through basic spatial concepts (Nystuen, **chapter 36**) and geometric terms (Haggett 1965) rested upon the emulation of physical sciences. Analogies with gravity, gaseous behaviour, molecules, thermodynamic equilibrium, entropy-maximization, diffusion etc. informed many key ideas. They were deployed in understanding spatial patterns, of transport, cities, land-use, industrial location etc. Distance could be Euclidean, but also measured in time and cost terms or perceived by cognitive subjects. The other principal focus was on movement, mobility and circulation. The combination of Pax Americana, the Bretton Woods monetary institutions and the dismantling of imperial trade preferences opened up global spaces for trade and development, for spatial interaction and diffusion. Under the rubric of modernization theories the developing world could be subjected to a more systematic inquiry. At home, the expanding circulation of goods, commuters and ideas generated adequate material for spatial modelling. What then were the sources of the new geographical thinking, which, though never total in its dominance, seems to have close associations with the post-war condition?

Carter's (1988) unorthodox reinterpretation of Thomas Pynchon's novel 'Gravity's Rainbow' fixes on a single image to bring together social and technological change. The last V2 rocket launched from German soil traverses the post-war world until it is poised above a Los Angeles cinema 25 years later. Out of the chaos of middle Europe in 1945, the rocket delivers Germany's industrial and scientific knowledge and elements of its state apparatus, which Carter describes as a 'totalitarian engineering'. He suggests that Pynchon envisaged an America in which a new social order was based around both constraint and pleasure, in which war-making had become internalized throughout government (see Kirby 1994). As James Earl Webb, Administrator of NASA 1961–8, saw it, the moonshot programme was the direct descendant of Turner's frontier thesis; the final frontier.

Human geography followed something of this trajectory. Many American geographers found their way to Germany before 1939. Hartshorne's deliberations on 'The Nature of Geography' were made during the incipient chaos of middle Europe in the 1930s, when political boundaries were under threat. He returned with one vision of geography – areal differentiation – while the left-wing refugee F. K. Schaefer brought over another – spatial science (Hartshorne 1939: Schaefer, **chapter 35**; Entrikin and Brunn 1989). Most of the basic models that informed spatial science, such as those derived from Christaller, Von Thünen, Alfred Weber and Lösch, also came out of Germany, although they were often removed from their original political contexts. Wartime service brought many geographers into close contact with government agencies, with new skills and techniques such as air-photograph interpretation, and with poorly charted parts of the world (Kirby

1994). The war hastened the decline of regional and political geography, and elevated more systematic and technical studies.

The Second World War alone did not change geography, nor were geographers solely servants of a militarized state. There was a wider social context. Scott (1982) argues that the post-war capitalist state undertook the extensive management of the conditions of production and reproduction in an effort to control the crises which had struck pre-war society. This involved the question of the efficient allocation and spatial deployment of resources, which in turn demanded a technical and rational scientific approach – a total engineering. Geographical work on central place theory, land-use models, regional development, transportation networks, hydrological and soil systems, met this demand. Spatial science addressed questions of optimal location precisely because these were the management priorities. Post-war economics rested on Keynesian ideals of establishing stable equilibrium amidst potentially chaotic market processes at the national scale. But Scott argues that such management could never fully resolve either the crisis tendencies of capitalism (Harvey, **chapter 37**) or the human-resource problems that arose from managerial responses – notably urban unrest. Therefore, an alternative spatial interest in human conditions and subjectivity was a counterpart of the more technical interest. In this sense, therefore, there was one 'revolution' in human geography which produced both spatial science and its radical alternatives in Marxist and humanistic geography (compare Harvey and Tuan, **chapters 37** and **28**).

This argument suggests a reason why human geography generally eschewed temporal relations in favour of purely spatial ones. A managerial geography would have addressed short-term crises in land-use or transport planning, and not the rise and fall of entire civilizations. It is worth noting that, in so far as physical geography adopted the timeless ideas of dynamic equilibrium, displacing a Davisian model of stages by a more experimental science, then it too focused on short-term management problems and abandoned longer-term issues of environmental change (Kennedy 1993a). But, as the 1970s instilled a sense of deep crisis in capitalist societies, it became harder to ignore deeper shifts.

Transition to New Spaces

'The last few years have been marked by an inverted millenarianism, in which premonitions of the future, catastrophic or redemptive, have been replaced by senses of the end of this or that' (Jameson 1984, p. 53). Jameson was not alone in sensing that something big was happening; Harvey describes a 'sea-change in cultural as well as in political–economic practices since around 1972' (1989, p. vii). Since the mid-1980s, the idea of transition or rupture has become pervasive, in geography as elsewhere (Gregory and Cooke, **chapters 12** and **30**). The temporality of change may be disputed. Some focus on the 40–50–year Kondratieff long waves in economic growth, others on regimes of accumulation such as Fordism and flexible accumulation, or the end of the Cold War. Some address the more epochal break of modernism and post-modernism, others the long-term changes to the climate and biophysical systems consequent on the human impact. Harvey (1989) argues that there is a deepening round of time–space compression in which the sense and demands of speed or rapid turnover of capital become paramount. Kennedy (1993b) suggests our timescales of geophysical inquiry are extending, and distant (in time as in space) features of the universe are coming more into view. Geography is positioned near the centre of another round of space–time restructuring comparable in magnitude and complexity to that of the late nineteenth century (Kern 1983).

To unravel real changes from continuities can be difficult. Regarding human geography, there are some continuities with the age of chronopolitics and geopolitics. Geographical Information Systems extend the practices of rational management and surveillance – the world-as-exhibition – into higher levels of sophistication, drawing upon the explosion of information (Haraway and Openshaw, **chapters 6** and **41**). Said's 'structure of attitude and reference' survives in the Gulf War (Said 1994). Mackinder's heartland thesis finds favour in US foreign-policy circles (Ò Tuathail, 1994). By contrast, Fabian's model of imperial chronopolitical order has begun to break down. Increased travel, immigration, satellite television etc. have certainly brought peoples who were once far apart closer together and eroded the sense of temporal difference between civilized and primitive. Yet, many of the metaphors deployed to describe these new cultural patterns cannot shake off notions of absolute space (Smith and Katz 1993). A cultural mosaic suggests a multiplication of absolute spaces rather than a genuine transformation into new relative ones. But with a newfound emphasis on diasporas, creolization, hybridities and travelling cultures (Gregory 1994), many of the absolute and categorical ideas of socially homogeneous cultures neatly sorted into discrete territories are giving way. Fractals may be a more appropriate geometry than mosaics. What this suggests is that a firmer sense of epochal change is accompanied by a weaker sense of the spatial co-ordinate system in which peoples, regions and locations can be mapped.

In part, outlines of this co-ordinate system are provided by those geographers emphasizing uneven development or new spatial divisions of labour and the renewed debates on place and locality (see Part IV). By combining temporal and spatial changes they suggest a determined, but nonetheless unpredictable geography of development. The search for a final or transcendental answer about the nature of space or time seems to be over, and the door is opened to the possibility of many spaces, none of which may be said to be the sole cause of all others. This multiplication of spaces includes metaphorical spaces (Smith and Katz 1993), third-spaces (Soja and Hooper 1993), imaginative geographies (Said 1994), masculine and feminine spaces (Rose 1993).

A combination of determination and unpredictability also appears in the application of chaos thinking in the human and natural sciences. Like post-modernism in the cultural and social sciences, chaos emphasizes contingent outcomes, complex and non-linear determinations, differences, and challenges to the older scientific models of the neutral and objective observer (Best 1991). Although chaos and non-linear dynamics have so far found proponents mostly in physical geography (Phillips and Renwick 1992), their exponents point towards a concept of landscapes consisting of elements operating at a range of temporal scales and rates rather than a single equilibrium. In natural history, the strong sense of directed evolution which Darwinianism gave to geography has broken down (Gould 1989). In Gould's opinion, re-analysis of the astonishing breadth of life found in the Burgess Shale cannot fail to instil an enlarged sense of contingency in the life process itself. A similar observation can be made about social life. It may be pointless trying to define a single time, and more productive to examine the multitude of times in which humans live (Adam 1995). These include everyday, work and bodily rhythms, while events such as birth and death, and anxieties about planetary futures, indicate the mutual permeation of cultural and natural times.

Making sense of these plural spaces and times is challenging. One response, proposed by Harvey (1989), stresses underlying continuities of material process leading to discontinuities in experience and representation. Another replaces established epistemologies by post-modern insights (see Cooke, **chapter 30**). Soja (1989) and Gregory (1994) explore the tensions between established and newer ways of thinking. A different kind of compromise is suggested by Livingstone's (1992, p. 28) 'situated messiness' in the history of geographical thought or Mann's (1993) 'patterned mess' in the analysis of societal change. Like Gould, they search for the lines which separate laws in the background from contingency in the details. Finding this balance between determination and contingency, and connecting the plurality of social and natural times and spaces, would seem to describe the preoccupations of the present generation of geographical thinkers.

References

Adam, B. 1995: *Timewatch: the social analysis of time.* Cambridge.

Best, S. 1991: Chaos and entropy. *Science as Culture* 2, 188–226.

Carter, D. 1988: *The final frontier: the rise and fall of the American rocket state.* London.

Clarke, M. and Wilson, A. 1985: The dynamics of urban spatial structure: the progress of a research-program. *Transactions of the Institute of British Geographers* 10, 427–51.

Entrikin, J. N. and Brunn, S. D., editors, 1989: *Reflections on Richard Hartshorne's 'The Nature of Geography'*. Washington, DC.

Fabian, J. 1983: *Time and the Other: how anthropology makes its object.* New York.

Godlewska, A. and Smith, N., editors, 1994: *Geography and empire.* Oxford.

Gould, S. J. 1989: *Wonderful life: the Burgess Shale and the nature of history.* London.

Gregory, D. 1994: *Geographical imaginations.* Oxford.

Gregory, D. and Urry, J., editors, 1985: *Social relations and spatial structures.* London and Basingstoke.

Guelke, L. 1989: Intellectual coherence and the foundations of geography. *Professional Geographer* 41, 123–30.

Haggett, P. 1965: *Locational analysis in geography.* London.

Hartshorne, R. 1939: *The nature of geography.* Lancaster, PA.

Harvey, D. 1989: *The condition of postmodernity: an enquiry into the origins of cultural change.* Oxford.

Jameson, F. 1984: Postmodernism, or the cultural logic of late capitalism. *New Left Review* 145, 53–93.
Johnston, R. J. 1991: *Geography and geographers: Anglo-American human geography since 1945.* Third Edition London.
Kearns, G. 1984: Closed space and political practice: Frederick Jackson Turner and Halford Mackinder. *Environment and Planning D: Society and Space* 2, 23–34.
Kennedy, B. 1993a: The end of equilibrium? The William Vaughan Lewis Seminars, number 3, Department of Geography, University of Cambridge.
Kennedy, B. 1993b: '. . . no prospect of an end . . .' *Geography* 78, 124–36.
Kern, S. 1983: *The culture of time and space 1880–1918.* London.
Kirby, A. 1994: What did you do in the war daddy? In Godlewska, A. and Smith, N., editors, *Geography and empire.* Oxford, pp. 300–15.
Livingstone, D. 1992: *The geographical tradition.* Oxford.
Mann, M. 1993: *The sources of social power, Volume II: The rise of classes and nation-states, 1760–1918.* Cambridge.
Ò Tuathail, G. 1994: Problematizing geopolitics: survey, statesmanship and strategy. *Transactions, of the Institute of British Geographers* 19, 259–72.
Phillips, J. D. and Renwick, W. H., editors, 1992: *Geomorphic systems.* Amsterdam.
Rose, G. 1993: *Feminism and geography: the limits of geographical knowledge.* Cambridge.
Said, E. W. 1994: *Culture and imperialism.* London.
Sauer, C. O. 1941: Foreword to historical geography. *Annals of the Association of American Geographers* 31, 1–24.
Scott, A. J. 1982: The meaning and social origin of discourse on the spatial foundations of society. In Gould, P. and Olssen, G., editors, *In search of common ground.* London.
Smith, N. 1984: *Uneven development: nature, capital and the production of space.* Oxford.
Smith, N. and Katz, C. 1993: Grounding metaphor: towards a spatialized politics. In Keith, M. and Pile, S., editors, *Place and the politics of identity.* London.
Soja, E. W. 1989: *Postmodern geographies: the reassertion of space in critical social theory.* London.
Soja, E. W. and Hooper, B. 1993: The space that difference makes: some notes on the geographical margins of the new cultural politics. In Keith, M. and Pile, S., editors, *Place and the politics of identity.* London.
Tuan, Y-F. 1974: Space and place: a humanistic perspective. *Progress in Geography* 6, 211–52.
Whittlesey, D. 1945: The horizon of geography. *Annals, Association of American Geographers* 35, 1–36.
Wolf, E. R. 1982: *Europe and the people without history.* Berkeley, CA.

Further Reading

On theoretical and conceptual questions of space and time: Blaut, J, 1961: Space and process, *Professional Geographer* 13, 1–7: Gregory and Urry (1985); Harvey, D. 1973: *Social justice and the city.* London; Harvey, D. 1990: Between space and time, *Annals of the Association of American Geographers* 80, 418–34; Lefebvre, H. 1991: *The production of space.* Oxford; Smith (1984). A good review on the relations between social theory and space and time is:
Thrift, N. 1983: On the determination of social action in time and space, *Environment and Planning D: Society and Space 1*, 23–57. A good companion piece to Ratzel and Mackinder (**chapters 32 and 33**) and an interesting application of the frontier thesis are:
Turner, F. J. 1893: The significance of the frontier in American history, in 1920: *The frontier in American history.* New York; Melbin, M. 1978: The night as frontier, *American Sociological*

Review 43, 3–22. Typical examples of spatial science are: Bunge, W. 1966: *Theoretical geography* [Lund]; Haggett 1965; Janelle, D. 1969: Spatial organization: a model and concept, *Annals of the Association of American Geographers* 59, 348–64. More humanistic ideas can be found in: Buttimer, A. and Seamon, D., editors, 1980: *The human experience of space and place*. London. Openshaw's article (**chapter 41**) was followed by several comments and his reply in later issues of *Environment and Planning A*.

32

THE TERRITORIAL GROWTH OF STATES

Friedrich Ratzel

Friedrich Ratzel (1844–1904) was one of the founders of modern geography, a German scholar whose two-volume *Anthropogeographie* (1881 and 1891) was the link between the ecology of Darwin and Haeckel and the human geography of Vidal, Semple and Sauer (**chapters 10, 14** and **17**). In the 1890s his writing shifted towards a more political geography, consistent with his own active campaigning to persuade Germany to acquire overseas colonies and build up its naval fleet to challenge Britain. His thinking expressed the spatial consequences of the Darwinist struggle for survival. According to the 'laws' of territorial growth, states must expand to thrive, and higher forms of civilization must expand at the expense of lower. These laws were supposedly natural, but given the recent unification of Germany, the inter-state rivalry in Europe (General Schlieffen was already drawing up his plan for the invasion of France) and its empires (Africa was carved up at the Berlin Conference in 1884–5). Ratzel's views accorded with Germany's territorial designs. After his death and after the First World War, German geopoliticians revived Ratzel's ideas to suit their own ambitions and, as a result, his writings were condemned by Anglo-American geographers. Had Germany won the war then perhaps Mackinder (**chapter 33**) would have suffered in his stead.

Source: The territorial growth of states. *Scottish Geographical Magazine* 12, 351–61, 1896.

In political geography not only must the territory over which a nation holds complete sway be considered, but also the extension of its rule over the adjacent seas, and those various rights which encroach on the domain of one state to the advantage of another. Such is the acknowledgment of the Caspian Sea as a Russian lake, contained in the Russo-Persian treaties of 1813 and 1828. The inclusion of Luxemburg in the German Customs union, and the control of marine and sanitary

[1] Abstract of *Die Gesetze des räumlichen Wachstums der Staaten*, by Prof. Dr. F. Ratzel, in *Petermanns Mitt.*, Bd. xlii. No. 5.

regulations by Austria-Hungary along the coast of Montenegro, are also important in political geography. For modifications such as these usually occur at the borders of the domains of a state, and are the signs of an advance for which they prepare the way, or the remnant of a former extension. The territory of a state is no definite area fixed for all time – for a state is a living organism, and therefore cannot be contained within rigid limits – being dependent for its form and greatness on its inhabitants, in whose movements, outwardly exhibited especially in territorial growth or contraction, it participates. Political geography regards each people as a living body extending over a portion of the Earth's surface, and separated from other similar bodies by imaginary boundaries or unoccupied tracts. The peoples are constantly agitated by internal movements, which are transformed into external movement whenever a portion of the Earth's surface is occupied afresh, or one formerly occupied is surrendered. Thus, in a metaphor employed by more than one writer, a people resembles a fluid mass slowly ebbing and flowing. It has seldom occurred in history that such movements have taken place over unoccupied areas; as a rule they take the form of encroachment and usurpation, or small territories, with their inhabitants, are annexed to larger ones. Similarly these larger states fall to pieces, and this union and disintegration, expansion and contraction, constitute a great part of those historical movements which geographically are represented by a division of the surface into greater or smaller portions.

The extension of the geographical horizon, a consequence of the corporeal and mental efforts of numberless generations, has continually provided new domains for the territorial growth of nations. To obtain political control over these, to fuse them and keep them together, has demanded ever fresh forces, which could only be developed with the slow growth of civilisation. Civilisation constantly supplies new foundations and bonds by which the sections of a people may be built up into a connected whole, and increases the number of those who are knit together by a consciousness of their interdependence. Ideas and material possessions spread out from small centres, and gradually extend their domains. We see the close connection between religious and political expansions, but this is far surpassed by the immense influence of commerce, which now gives a mighty impulse to efforts of expansion. And all these motive forces derive new energy from the increased population, which must find room for itself, and leads to expansion after it has helped on the march of civilisation by its concentration.

Though the most civilised peoples have not always been the greatest founders of states – for state organisation is an application of the forces of civilisation under particular conditions – still, all the great states of the past and present have been those of civilised nations. This is evident at the present day, for the great states are situated in Europe and the European colonial territories. China is the only state of vast dimensions that belongs to a non-European civilisation, and of non-European civilisations the East Asiatic is the most highly developed. At the commencement of our own civilisation we find the largest states in its cradle around the Mediterranean Sea, where the lands, however, owing to their form and situation in a steppe zone, could not give rise to states of continental dimensions. Only when several of them were merged into the Persian Empire, did a state spring up, the area of which, some 2,000,000 square miles, could compare with European Russia. Egypt, with its desert lands, contains not more than 150,000 square miles, and the inhabited tracts of Assyria and Babylon not more than 50,000. During the short period of its greatest extension, Assyria ruled over a country only about three times as large as Germany. Of all the earlier world-empires only Persia deserved this title. The kingdom of Alexander the Great (1,700,000 square miles) and the Roman Empire (1,300,000 square miles at the death of Augustus) did not attain to its truly Asiatic dimensions. The empires of the Middle Ages were merely fragments of the Roman. The feudal system favoured the formation of small states, for the land was divided and subdivided into private estates, and hence the general dissolution of states in which the last remnant of the old Roman occupation passed away, after its other creations, science and commerce, had already perished. On the ruins new organisations arose, and in other continents, first in America and Asia, dominions sprang up in conjunction with the commerce, faith, and civilisation of Europe, which occupied twice and three times the area of the largest states hitherto founded. The rapid advance of geographical discovery allowed these new states to spread in three hundred years over America, Northern and Southern Asia, and Australia, and the practically continuous growth of population in Europe during the past two hundred years, together with the invention of new means of communication, furnished ever new material for, and inducements to, further expansion. The British Empire, the Russian Empire in Europe and Asia, the United States of America, China, and Brazil, are of a size never attained in the past.

Since the areas of states grow with their civilisation, people in a low state of civilisation are naturally collected in very small political organisations, and the lower their condition the smaller are the states. Before the Egyptian occupation Schweinfurth counted thirty-five – and probably there were more – in the Sandeh country, within an area estimated at about 53,000 square miles. In Junker's time a large state possessed a territory scarcely as large as a third of Baden (Ndoruma's covered some 1900 square miles), while most of them measured one to five square miles, being indeed merely villages with their lands. Hardly less was the subdivision in Roman times among the Rhaetians, Illyrians, Galls, and Germans.

Peoples also of more powerful organisation, who threatened with their locust-like swarms the infant colonies in North America and South Africa, founded only small states. They laid waste wide areas, but could not retain possession of them and weld them together. At the annexation Basutoland contained 12,000, Zululand 8,500 square miles, and, but for the interference of the Whites, these territories would have been still further disintegrated. The confederation of the Six Nations in the Alleghany country, which for a century was the most dangerous enemy of the young Atlantic colonies, held sway over, perhaps, 20,000 square miles, only partially inhabited, and in 1712 could send 2150 warriors into the field. The empires of Montezuma and of the Incas were not great states in respect of the size of their territories, nor were they firmly consolidated. The Incas at the arrival of Pizarro had not extended their conquests over as large an area as that of the Roman Empire in the time of Augustus, and their dominion was but a conglomeration of conquered states, barely a generation old, and beginning to fall to pieces even without the help of the Spaniards. Before Europeans and Arabs planted great states in America, Australia, Northern Asia, and Africa, these vast areas lay politically fallow. Politics, like agriculture, learned by degrees the resources hidden in the soil, and the story of each country is that of the progressive development of its geographical conditions. The attainment of political power by the union of small territories was introduced as a new idea into the divided lands of primitive peoples, and the struggle that naturally arose between the policies and needs of large and small state organisations is one of the chief causes of the deterioration of these peoples since they have come in contact with Europeans.

Accordingly the size of states diminishes with their age. Of the present great empires only China can be called old, and it has acquired the greater half of its territory within the last hundred years (Mongolia and Manchuria, Tibet, Yunnan, Western Sze-chuen and Formosa). All the others – the Russian Empire, Brazil, the United States, British North America, and Australia – have sprung up during the last three-quarters of a century on the territories of small native states. On the other hand, Andorra is more than ten centuries old, and Liechtenstein and some other small principalities of Germany are among the oldest in their part of the world; compared to them Prussia and Italy are in their first youth.

Certain developments have been alluded to which progress more rapidly than the state and prepare the way for it. Ranke lays stress on community of life among men. This lies in the ideas and wares which are passed on from one people to another. It is seldom that a state has been able to set limits to their wanderings; as a rule, indeed, they have drawn the states after them. Animated by the same impulse and following the same path, are frequently found together ideas and wares, missionaries and merchants, drawing peoples closer and assimilating them, and thus preparing the ground for political approach and union.

All old states and those in a low state of culture are theocracies. The spiritual world here not only controls the life of the individual, but also determines that of states. Every chief has priestly functions, every tribe its holy place, every dynasty prides itself on a divine origin. Over the universal political decay of Europe hovered the Church, preparing the way for new and greater states, while Islam undertook the same task in Western Asia and North Africa, and in Africa of to-day the powers of Islam and Christianity preside over political separation, while between lies paganism, with its smaller divisions.

Primitive states are national in a very restricted sense; their development is brought about by the removal of the barriers, and then they become again national in a more extended sense. The states of primitive peoples are family states, but their earliest growth is often due to the advent of strangers. Thus people of the same origin may indeed be brought together, as far as the territory of the race extends, but the union is not national, though the community of language and customs produced by intercourse independent of politics may facilitate political connection. In times of greater intellectual development these common possessions produce a feeling of nationality, and exercise an attractive and cohesive force. This feeling of nationality, however, does not spread with the rapidity of religion and commerce, and, therefore, comes sooner into conflict with the territorial extension of the state, which has always gained the final victory ever since the Roman Empire first strove after a cosmopolitan character. But the state recognises the value of national feeling, and seeks to convert it into political patriotism by helping on the fusion of peoples, and to use it for its own ends – Panslavism, for instance. The modern state, embracing a large area of territory, but truly national, is the peculiar product of this process. Between this and the restricted state of early times lie the numerous states of the past and present, which lack a civilisation sufficiently powerful to weld together the heterogeneous elements of the ethnographical foundation.

Commerce and traffic hurry on far in advance of politics, which follow in their footsteps and are never sharply separated from them. Peaceful intercourse is the condition of the growth of a state. Its primitive network of routes must be laid down beforehand. Knowledge of a neighbouring territory must precede its political annexation. When the state has commenced to expand, it shares with traffic in its interest for means of communication, and may even take the lead; the made roads of the Iranian and of the old American states owed their origin to political aims rather than commercial. Every route prepares the way for political influence, every waterway is a natural agent for state development, every confederation entrusts its traffic arrangements to the central power, every negro chief is the first, and if possible the only, trader in his land. The advance of the customs boundary precedes that of the political boundary; the customs union proclaimed the coming of the German Empire.

The connection of the enlargement of the geographical horizon with political expansion is too evident to need much discussion. Even in the present time the greatest results have been obtained through geographical exploration, of which the Russians in Central Asia have afforded the most brilliant examples.

The growth of states proceeds through the annexation of small territories to amalgamation, while at the same time the attachment of the people to the soil becomes ever closer. Out of the mechanical union of territories of varying size, population, and stages of culture, an organic growth is started by the approachment, mutual intercourse, and intermingling of the inhabitants. Growth which never goes beyond mere annexation creates only loose, easily dismembered conglomerations, which are only temporarily held together. The Roman Empire was constantly threatened with disintegration till the first century BC, when the military organisation necessary to hold it together was established, and the commercial supremacy was won for Italy, which made the fortunate peninsula in the middle of the Mediterranean the centre of a region traversed by excellent trade-routes.

This process of fusion of various tracts also indicates a closer connection of the people with the soil. The expansion of the state over the Earth's surface may also be accompanied by a downward growth which helps to fix it to the soil. It is not a mere metaphor to speak of a people taking root. A people is an organic body which in the course of its history is fixed more and more firmly in the soil on which it lives. As the individual contends with the virgin soil until he has converted it into cultivated land, so a people struggles with its territory and makes it ever more and more its own by shedding its sweat and blood on its behalf, until the two cannot even be thought of apart. We cannot think of the French apart from France, or of the Germans apart from Germany. But this union was not always so close, and there are states which even now are not so intimately associated with the land. There is a historical succession in the relation of states to their territory, as there is in their dimensions. We never meet with that complete severance from the soil which, according to the theories advanced by many speculators, is the mark of a primitive state of existence. But the further we go back, the looser becomes the connection. Men are more scattered, and their cultivation is more superficial and is lightly transferred from one field to another, and their social relations bind them so firmly together that their relation to the soil is comparatively weaker. And as the small states of this stage of culture are isolated from one another by uninhabited marches, etc., not only does a large tract, often more than the half of an extensive territory, lie politically fallow, but the emulation is wanting to develop what is politically of value in the country. Thus the large rivers are not used by Indians and Negroes as boundaries or waterways, while they immediately acquire inestimable value as soon as they are reached by Europeans.

Hence on the whole there is a decrease in the appreciation of the political value of the ground as we go back from the newer to the older states. It stands in close relationship to the decrease of political areas. The earlier observers of African life have remarked that the constant petty wars lead to no extension of territory, but are merely a means of obtaining slaves. This fact is of the greatest import in the history of the Africa of the Negroes; the slave raids decimate the population, and at the same time hinder the development of states. The state never rests, and the continual excursions across the frontiers makes it a centre for expeditions of conquest surrounded by a zone of depopulated and desolated country. The frontiers are not clearly defined, and evidently depend on the energy with which excursions are made. As soon as this energy declines the territory shrinks. There is no time for the people to take root on a particular area. Hence the usually short duration of these powers, of which examples may be found in south-east Africa, from the Zulus to the Wahehe. In the more advanced states of the Sudan this region of conquest, or rather of raiding expeditions, occupies only a part of the state; the position and extent of the Fulah states, in Bornu, Baghirmi, Wadaï, Darfur, remain for a long time unaltered, but vary continually where they come in contact with the subject heathen lands, that is, chiefly on the southern side. Nachtigal in the north, Crampel and Dybowski in the south, have shown how indefinite the position and extent of Wadaï is in those parts. Still more indefinite is the political value of the soil. The land-hunger of the conquering states of antiquity, especially of the Romans, so often mentioned, does not stand out clearly by any means. The acquisition of territory is only a secondary feature in the great political upheavals of antiquity. Power, slaves, treasure, are the prize, especially in the wars of the Asiatics; hence the ephermeral character of their growth. In Rome, after the wars with Pyrrhus, a struggle with the necessity of acquiring new territory may be observed, in which, as empire was desired, the system of alliances and of keeping one power in check by others, had to give way. Caesar's greatness lies in his having first given the state, together with extension of territory, a defined and secure boundary.

Territorial growth is effected on the periphery of the state by the displacement of the frontier. A state which aims at the possession of certain tracts sends out spurs which are filled with more vigorous life than the rest of the periphery. The outposts of Peshawur and Western Tibet, of Merv and Kokan, show even to those who do not know their history, that in these directions British India and Russia are pushing on with peculiar energy, endeavouring to possess themselves of all the advantages of the intervening lands, just as Rome, by the conquest of Gall, made haste to oppose the advance of the Germani. On its German and Italian frontiers, for centuries the scene of especially vigorous growth, France concentrates her forces with the object of regaining lost ground. The marches of Germany, as it expanded eastwards, were fortified and colonised bit by bit as they were conquered, and the same process was repeated in the United States of America and in Argentina, where in a few years large towns sprang up on the site of the primitive block-houses of the Indian frontiers. In the crowded state of Europe, such parts of the periphery are the most exposed to danger, and the most strongly fortified; the wounds they may receive are the most to be feared.

In the most primitive states the frontiers are so indistinct as to vanish altogether. The attempt to apply our notion of a frontier, as a well-defined line, to states which occupy no sharply delimited tract, has led to the worst misunderstandings, both in the Indian policy of the American states and in Africa. Lichtenstein spoke of the futile attempts to fix a definite boundary for the Kaffir territories, which neither party should cross without the special permission of the chiefs. Not lines, but positions, are the essential features in these cases. Contact is avoided, and the state draws itself together, surrounding itself with a politically empty zone. But if its people thrust themselves forward beyond these limits, they insinuate themselves in among their neighbours rather than displace them. The proprietary rights of the chiefs among primitive peoples are inextricably mixed up. Though the confusion has caused much perplexity to colonial offices, it has afforded conquering and colonising powers, bringing with them different notions of what a frontier is, excellent opportunities for interference and aggression. Combined with the different appreciation of the value of land politically, it has wonderfully accelerated the dispossession of the natives. Their policy was like their trade, for they recklessly gave away their most valuable possession, because they had no idea of its value. Long before, the isolation of one small state from another had made its disastrous consequences felt in causing stagnation, which on the arrival of Europeans turned into decay. At a higher stage – in the Sudan and Further India – the frontier is defined in many parts, mountains and watersheds being made use of, though the system of unoccupied marches is still retained. China had separated herself, till a few years ago, from Korea by such a frontier zone, which was, however, in contrast to the African and Further Indian, clearly defined.

The state in its growth selects the geographically advantageous positions, occupying the good lands before the bad, and, if its growth is accompanied by encroachment on the territory of another state, it takes possession of the important points, and then advances towards the less valuable parts. In new lands (colonies), the history of which is fully known, the new political organisations spread up from the sea, beside the streams and lakes, on the fruitful plains, while the older political organisations are thrust back into those parts of the interior which are difficult of access, and offer little temptation to the aggressor, into steppes and deserts, mountains and swamps. This is what has happened in North America, Siberia, Australasia, and South Africa. Pioneers of the same civilisation have on the whole the same notions with regard to the value of the land, and hence the harmony in the expansion of all the European colonies of the last century. But in other times different notions prevailed. The old Peruvians did not descend to the Amazons, but spread themselves over a small strip of plateau 2500 miles in length. The old Greeks did not seek for large fertile inland tracts, but, like the Phoenicians, islands and peninsulas, while the Turks occupied the elevated steppes of Asia Minor. Beside the stage of civilisation the force of habit plays an important *rôle*, and that is why political expansion proceeds as far as possible over regions where the conditions of life and work are the same. The Phoenicians settled on the coasts, the Dutch on islands, the Russians on river-banks. How much the landlocked character of the Mediterranean Sea contributed to the expansion of the Roman Empire was well known to the ancients. To both Greeks and Romans these lands were a most happily situated colonial sphere, where they could everywhere feel themselves at home, just as the Europeans of Central Europe do in America between 45° and 35° N. lat. The enclosure of politically advantageous points often determines the configuration of states. The extension of Germany along the North and Baltic Seas, the incorporation of the Meuse north of Sedan in France, and England's possession of the Channel Islands, are cases in point. Chile's northern frontier across the apparently worthless desert of Atacama, in lat. 24°, was pushed forward to the 23rd parallel as soon as the guano deposits in the bay of Mejillones were discovered, and the advance of Great Britain across the Orange river followed the discovery of diamonds on the Vaal river in 1867. At a lower stage states show a preference for trade-routes and the neighbourhood, as may be remarked in the Sudan and in Central Africa.

In many cases the growth of states preserves for long periods the same direction, with the object of obtaining political benefits, for there is an advantage in following the line of country most favourable to the movements, or rather succession of movements, by which this growth is effected. So people make for the coasts, pass along the rivers, and spread over plains. Others push their way up to the limits of the country accessible to man, the incentive being the advantage of filling up a territory with natural boundaries. Rome spread out in North Africa and West Asia along the desert. 222 B.C. it had reached the southern foot of the Alps, but it was not till two centuries later that it progressed further, when it had already spread eastwards and westwards far beyond the Alps. Bohemia filled its hollow before any neighbouring state had acquired fixed boundaries, and when it expanded further, it was towards Moravia, in the direction of the opening in its hollow. To the same group of cases belongs the growth in the direction of least political resistance. The spread of the states of Central Europe in the east, beginning with the first division of Poland, was a reflux of the political energy long in vain directed westwards.

A simple political body, if left to itself, renews and multiplies this body continually, but never creates another. The family is renewed in its offspring and creates new families. From the family tribe or the race another family tribe branches off, and so on. All these corporations become states through connection with the soil. As they increase, no larger state arises out of the small one, but a number of states of the same size. In order that the customary limit of growth may not be transgressed, the number of the population is kept down by every possible means, some being of the most ghastly description. Thus the state may be kept within manageable limits and be held in the grasp of one hand. As far as we are acquainted with the states of primitive peoples, their growth has always been brought about by external influence. Men from countries where larger ideas of space prevail, carry the conception of larger states into those where the ideas of space are more restricted. The stranger is superior to the native, who is only acquainted with one state, by the fact that he knows at least two. If we think of Africa before the foundation of European colonies, we find the large states all along the line where Negroes are in contact with Semitic and Hamitic peoples, and scarcely any where Negro states lie side by side or border on the sea. Where, moreover, Negro states exist in the interior, their foundation is always traditionally associated with a stranger. All states in Africa are due to conquest and colonisation. History exhibits again and again the quiet immigration and spread of a people which, at first only tolerated, has suddenly come to the front as rulers. Such has been the course of European colonisation in almost every case, thus the Chinese established their kingdoms in Borneo, and at the dawn of the Roman Empire we find, veiled indeed in mythical obscurity, the strangers whose advent gave to Rome, advantageously situated for trade and navigation, a preponderance over the other towns of Latium. In the whole of Melanesia at the advent of Europeans there was only one state formation, through immigrant Malays on the north-west coast of New Guinea, and similar cases may be found in America.

Where Europeans have not brought in the conception of an extensive dominion into the region of small states, its introducers have been sea, desert, and steppe peoples – Hamitic and Semitic, Mongols and Turks. If we further inquire whither the search after its origin leads us, we arrive at the shore of the eastern Mediterranean, where fruitful lands are situated amid extensive steppes. Egypt and Mesopotamia, Syria and Persia, are large oases favourable for the concentration of the people on a narrow area, and surrounded by regions which tempt the inhabitants to expand. As Lower Egypt has extended over Upper Egypt, China from its löss districts in all directions, all these regions have supplied men for armed incursions and slow conquest by colonisation. The political organisation of these masses, and the wide supremacy which knit together the individual lands, were the creations of the steppes, whence sprang the founders of large states in Egypt and Mesopotamia, Persia, India and China, and the African Sudan. The absence of pastoral peoples who once ruled the greater part of the Old World, deprived pre-European America of an ever-active political ferment, and hence is partly due the weakness of its state organisation.

The influence of nomad pastoral tribes on agricultural and industrial peoples is only one side of a deeper contrast. This is the fundamental fact which underlies the state foundation of the seafaring nations – the Phoenicians, Normans, and Malays – and of the most recent European colonies. We find it also in the universal tendency of settled peoples, and especially agriculturists, to withdraw or cut themselves off from political affairs. All purely agricultural colonisation, of the Achaeans in Grecia Magna, the Germans in Transylvania, and the Boers in South Africa, tends to stagnation, and the success of Rome lay in stimulating a sturdy peasantry by more mobile and experienced elements.

There is a difference in the historical progress of mankind. Some remain stationary, while others push on, and both conditions are favoured by the nature of the country, wherefore from seas and steppes, the regions of movement, state formation advances into the forest and arable lands, the regions of fixed settlement. In a stationary condition weakness and decay creep in, whereas aggression demands organisation, which among the Tartar hordes, as in the ships of the Vikings and Malays, accomplished great results with small forces. The most extreme cases exist in Africa, where a martially organised people, like the Zulus, is found side by side with a people that for generations has been falling to pieces, like the Mashona. They form part of a single whole, for the one people exists at the expense of the other.

As the appreciation of the political value of land becomes greater, territory becomes to a greater degree the measure of political strength and the prize towards which the efforts of a state are directed. That the relative areas of Austria-Hungary, Germany, France, and Spain may be represented by the figures 100, 86, 84, and 80, those of the Netherlands and Belgium by 100 and 90, of the United States and British North America by 100 and 96, is the result of slow development and a balance struck after many struggles. From the smallest beginnings of growth up to the mighty states of the present age we see the same struggle of small states to raise themselves to an equality with the larger, and of the larger to push themselves to the front. The impulse has been as strong in the village states of Sandehland as in the huge states which occupy half a continent. We see it now at work in continental Europe, which it has awakened to the necessity of combination, in commercial affairs at least, against the giants, Russia, North America, and the British Empire. And the same law has prevailed no less in the most recent colonial enterprises; in Africa there has been an eager competition among the powers for the acquisition of territory, and the east of New Guinea has been divided between Great Britain and Germany in the proportion of 125 : 100.

The end has been attained in very different ways. A small state has taken enough land from its neighbours to make it equal, or nearly so, to the largest of them. Or states develop side by side or in succession, the later comer appropriating as large an extent of land as the first has occupied – the United States and British North America, for instance. Again a state may split into two of nearly equal areas, as the Netherlands and Belgium. A state that has been reduced in area may annex in another direction enough land to make good the loss, as when Austria acquired 19,730 square miles in the Balkan peninsula to compensate for the loss of 17,110 square miles in the Apennine peninsula. Russia and China, finding themselves in a huge territory where it was impossible to remain stationary, have become the masters of Central Asia, the former having similar problems to solve with regard to the Turkish peoples, as the latter in dealing with the Mongols.

Naturally the efforts of nations are not confined to extension of territory. Even large states come into close contact at length. Neighbouring states share in the advantages of position and natural resources, and hence arises a uniformity of interests and modes of activity. Beside the lines of communication between the Atlantic and Pacific in the United States, Canada has constructed her Canadian Pacific railway, and the navigation of the great lakes is made available by canals on both sides, Throughout America the constitution and political life of the United States serve as a model, just as in the Sudan one form is observable through all the Mohammedan states, whether their founders were Fulahs or Arabicised Nubians.

In peaceful competition, as in armed contests, the rule is that the aggressor must advance on to the ground occupied by his opponent, and in overcoming him he assimilates himself to him. States bordering on steppes in their struggle with the inhabitants of the steppes must acquire so much of the same character as will enable them to avail themselves of the advantages the steppe affords. Russia and Central Asia and France in Algeria illustrate this principle.

33

THE GEOGRAPHICAL PIVOT OF HISTORY

Halford J. Mackinder

The year Ratzel (**Chapter 32**) died, the foremost British geographer, H. J. Mackinder (1861–1947), wrote an article which was still being read in US foreign-policy circles 80 years later. After 1900 Mackinder had switched his abundant energies from the cause of geographical education (**chapter 8**), moved to London, and sought to influence British domestic and imperial policy directly. He joined Joseph Chamberlain's campaign for imperial protectionism and against free trade, and from 1910 to 1922 represented a Glasgow constituency in the House of Commons. During that time he was British High Commissioner in Southern Russia, charged with preventing the region from falling to the Bolshevik armies. He failed, and therefore his 'pivot' paper became all the more topical. Two events persuaded him to write it: the British defeat in the Boer War (1902) and the imminent Russo-Japanese war, which surprisingly resulted in both land and sea victories for the Japanese. Taking Eurasia as his scope and regarding the world as a single, closed political system within which events reverberated, Mackinder considered the relationship between geographical facts and historical events. His analysis of the balance of sea and land power, Central Asian nomads and the settled peoples of the Eurasian margins throughout history led him to see the 'pivot' – that area inaccessible by maritime forces – as central to the fate of the continent. The thesis was amended in 1919 and 1943, and stood as a warning to the British government and its allies of the dangers of German and Russian expansion for world peace.

Source: The geographical pivot of history. *Geographical Journal* 23, 421–37, 1904.

When historians in the remote future come to look back on the group of centuries through which we are now passing, and see them foreshortened, as we to-day see the Egyptian dynasties, it may well be that they will describe the last 400 years at the Columbian epoch, and will say that it ended soon after the year 1900. Of late it has been a common-place to speak of geographical exploration as nearly over, and it is recognized that geography must be diverted to the purpose of intensive survey and philosophic synthesis. In 400 years the outline of the map of the world has been completed with approximate accuracy, and even in the polar regions the voyages of Nansen and Scott have very narrowly reduced the last possibility of dramatic discoveries. But the opening of the twentieth century is appropriate as the end of a great historic epoch, not merely on account of this achievement, great though it be. The missionary, the conqueror, the farmer, the miner, and, of late, the engineer, have followed so closely in the traveller's footsteps that the world, in its remoter borders, has hardly been revealed before we must chronicle its virtually complete political appropriation. In Europe, North America, South America, Africa, and Australasia there is scarcely a region left for the pegging out of a claim of ownership, unless as the result of a war between civilized or half-civilized powers. Even in Asia we are probably witnessing the last moves of the game first played by the horsemen of Yermak the Cossack and the shipmen of Vasco da Gama. Broadly speaking, we may contrast the Columbian epoch with the age which preceded it, by describing its essential characteristic as the expansion of Europe against almost negligible resistances, whereas mediaeval Christendom was pent into a narrow region and threatened by external barbarism. From the present time forth, in the post-Columbian age, we shall again have to deal with a closed political system, and none the less that it will be one of world-wide scope. Every explosion of social forces, instead of being dissipated in a surrounding circuit of unknown space and barbaric chaos, will be sharply re-echoed from the far side of the globe, and weak elements in the political and economic organism of the world will be shattered in consequence. There is a vast difference of effect in the fall of a shell into an earthwork and its fall amid the closed spaces and rigid structures of a great building or ship. Probably some half-consciousness of this fact is at last diverting much of the attention of statesmen in all parts of the world from territorial expansion to the struggle for relative efficiency.

It appears to me, therefore, that in the present decade we are for the first time in a position to attempt, with some degree of completeness, a correlation between the larger geographical and the larger historical generalizations. For the first time we can perceive something of the real proportion of features and events on the stage of the whole world, and may seek a formula which shall express certain aspects, at any rate, of geographical causation in universal history. If we are fortunate, that formula should have a practical value as setting into perspective some of the competing forces in current international politics. The familiar phrase about the westward march of empire is an empirical and fragmentary attempt of the kind. I propose this evening describing those physical features of the world which I believe to have been most coercive of human action, and presenting some of the chief phases of history as organically connected with them, even in the ages when they were unknown to geography. My aim will not be to discuss the influence of this or that kind of feature, or yet to make a study in regional geography, but rather to exhibit human history as part of the life of the world organism. I recognize that I can only arrive at one aspect of the truth, and I have no wish to stray into excessive materialism. Man and not nature initiates, but nature in large measure controls. My concern is with the general physical control, rather than the causes of universal history. It is obvious that only a first approximation to truth can be hoped for. I shall be humble to my critics.

The late Professor Freeman held that the only history which counts is that of the Mediterranean and European races. In a sense, of course, this is true, for it is among these races that have originated the ideas which have rendered the inheritors of Greece and Rome dominant throughout the world. In another and very important sense, however, such a limitation has a cramping effect upon thought. The ideas which go to form a nation, as opposed to a mere crowd of human animals, have usually been accepted under the pressure of a common tribulation, and under a common necessity of resistance to external force. The idea of England was beaten into the Heptarchy by Danish and Norman conquerors; the idea of France was forced upon competing Franks, Goths, and Romans by the Huns at Chalons, and in the Hundred Years' War with England; the idea of Christendom was born of the Roman persecutions, and matured by the Crusades; the idea of the United States was accepted, and local colonial patriotism sunk, only in the long War of Independence; the idea of the German Empire was reluctantly adopted in South Germany only after a struggle against France in comradeship with North Germany. What I may describe as the literary conception of history, by concentrating attention upon ideas and upon the civilization which is their outcome, is apt to lose sight of the more elemental movements whose pressure is commonly the exciting cause of the efforts in which great ideas are nourished. A repellent personality performs a valuable social function in uniting his enemies, and it was under the pressure of external barbarism that Europe achieved her civilization. I ask you, therefore, for a moment to look upon Europe and European history as subordinate to Asia and Asiatic history, for European civilization is, in a very real sense, the outcome of the secular struggle against Asiatic invasion.

The most remarkable contrast in the political map of modern Europe is that presented by the vast area of Russia occupying half the Continent and the group of smaller territories tenanted by the Western Powers. From a physical point of view, there is, of course, a like contrast between the unbroken lowland of the east and the rich complex of mountains and valleys, islands and peninsulas, which together form the remainder of this part of the world. At first sight it would appear that in these familiar facts we have a correlation between natural environment and political organization so obvious as hardly to be worthy of description, especially when we note that throughout the Russian plain a cold winter is opposed to a hot summer, and the conditions of human existence thus rendered additionally uniform. Yet a series of historical maps, such as that contained in the Oxford Atlas, will reveal the fact that not merely is the rough coincidence of European Russia with the Eastern Plain of Europe a matter of the last hundred years or so, but that in all earlier time there was persistent re-assertion of quite another tendency in the political grouping. Two groups of states usually divided the country into northern and southern political systems. The fact is that the orographical map does not express the particular physical contrast which has until very lately controlled human movement and settlement in Russia. When the screen of winter snow fades northward off the vast face of the plain, it is followed by rains whose maximum

Figure 33.1 [orig. fig. 1] Eastern Europe before the nineteenth century. (After Drude in Gerghaus' Physical Atlas)

occurs in May and June beside the Black sea, but near the Baltic and White seas is deferred to July and August. In the south the later summer is a period of drought. As a consequence of this climatic *régime*, the north and north-west were forest broken only by marshes, whereas the south and south-east were a boundless grassy steppe, with trees only along the rivers. The line separating the two regions ran diagonally north-eastward from the northern end of the Carpathians to a point in the Ural range nearer to its southern than to its northern extremity. Moscow lies a little to north of this line, or, in other words, on the forest side of it. Outside Russia the boundary of the great forest ran westward almost exactly through the centre of

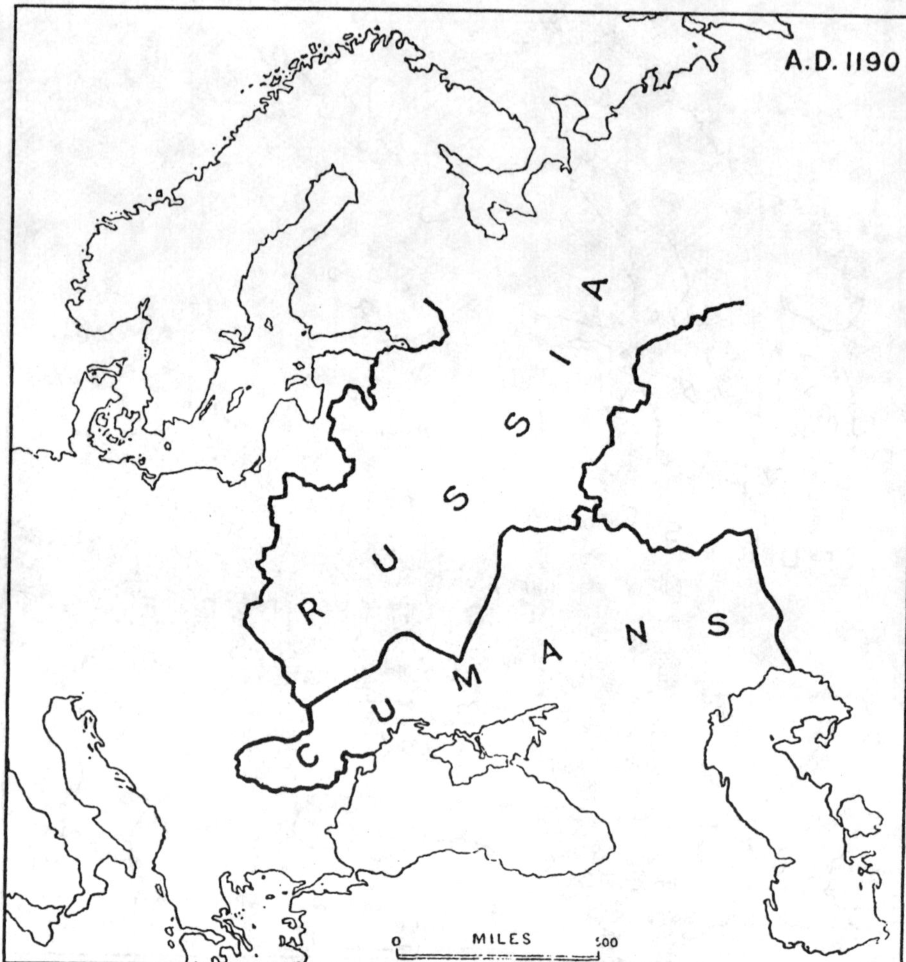

Figure 33.2 [orig. fig. 2] Political divisions of eastern Europe at the time of the Third Crusade. (After 'The Oxford Historical Atlas')

the European isthmus, which is 800 miles across between the Baltic and the Black seas. Beyond this, in Peninsular Europe, the woods spread on through the plains of Germany in the north, while the steppe lands in the south turned the great Transylvanian bastion of the Carpathians, and extended up the Danube, through what are now the cornfields of Roumania, to the Iron Gates. A detached area of steppes, known locally as Pusstas, now largely cultivated, occupied the plain of Hungary, ingirt by the forested rim of Carpathian and Alpine mountains. In all the west of Russia, save in the far north, the clearing of the forests, the drainage of the marshes, and the tillage of the steppes have recently averaged the character of the landscape,

Figure 33.3 [orig. fig. 3] Political divisions of eastern Europe at the accession of Charles V. (After 'The Oxford Historical Atlas')

and in large measure obliterated a distinction which was formerly very coercive of humanity.

The earlier Russia and Poland were established wholly in the glades of the forest. Through the steppe on the other hand there came from the unknown recesses of Asia, by the gateway between the Ural mountains and the Caspian sea, in all the centuries from the fifth to the sixteenth, a remarkable succession of Turanian nomadic peoples – Huns, Avars, Bulgarians, Magyars, Khazars, Patzinaks, Cumans, Mongols, Kalmuks. Under Attila the Huns established themselves in the midst of the Pusstas, in the uttermost Danubian outlier of the steppes, and thence dealt blows northward, westward, and southward against the settled peoples of Europe. A large part of modern history might be written as a commentary upon the changes directly or indirectly ensuing from these raids. The Angles and Saxons, it is quite possible, were than driven to cross the seas to found England in Britain. The Franks, the Goths, and the Roman provincials were compelled, for the first time, to stand shoulder to shoulder on the battlefield of Chalons, making common cause against the Asiatics, who were unconsciously welding together modern France. Venice was founded from the destruction of Aquileia and Padua; and even the Papacy owed a decisive prestige to the successful mediation of Pope Leo with Attila at Milan. Such was the harvest of results produced by a cloud of ruthless and idealess horsemen sweeping over the unimpeded plain – a blow, as it were, from the great Asiatic hammer striking freely through the vacant space. The Huns were followed by the Avars. It was for a marchland against these that Austria was founded, and Vienna fortified, as the result of the campaigns of Charlemagne. The Magyar came next, and by incessant raiding from his steppe base in Hungary increased the significance of the Austrian outpost, so drawing the political focus of Germany eastward to the margin of the realm. The Bulgarian established a ruling caste south of the Danube, and has left his name upon the map, although his language has yielded to that of his Slavonic subjects. Perhaps the longest and most effective occupation of the Russian steppe proper was that of the Khazars, who were contemporaries of the great Saracen movement: the Arab geographers knew the Caspian as the Khazar sea. In the end, however, new hordes arrived from Mongolia, and for two centuries Russia in the northern forest was held tributary to the Mongol Khans of Kipchak, or "the Steppe," and Russian development was thus delayed and biased at a time when the remainder of Europe was rapidly advancing.

It should be noted that the rivers running from the Forest to the Black and Caspian seas cross the whole breadth of the steppe-land path of the nomads, and that from time to time there were transient movements along their courses at right angles to the movement of the horsemen. Thus the missionaries of Greek Christianity ascended the Dnieper to Kief, just as beforehand the Norse Varangians had descended the same river on their way to Constantinople. Still earlier, the Teutonic Goths appear for a moment upon the Dneister, having crossed Europe from the shores of the Baltic in the same south-eastward direction. But these are passing episodes which do not invalidate the broader generalization. For a thousand years a series of horse-riding peoples emerged from Asia through the broad interval between the Ural mountains and the Caspian sea, rode through the open spaces of southern Russia, and struck home into Hungary in the very heart of the European peninsula, shaping by the necessity of opposing them the history of each of the great peoples around – the Russians, the Germans, the French, the Italians, and the Byzantine Greeks. That they stimulated healthy and powerful reaction, instead of crushing opposition under a widespread despotism, was due to the fact that the mobility of their power was conditioned by the steppes, and necessarily ceased in the surrounding forests and mountains.

A rival mobility of power was that of the Vikings in their boats. Descending from

Scandinavia both upon the northern and the southern shores of Europe, they penetrated inland by the river ways. But the scope of their action was limited, for, broadly speaking, their power was effective only in the neighbourhood of the water. Thus the settled peoples of Europe lay gripped between two pressures – that of the Asiatic nomads from the east, and on the other three sides that of the pirates from the sea. From its very nature neither pressure was overwhelming, and both therefore were stimulative. It is noteworthy that the formative influence of the Scandinavians was second only in significance to that of the nomads, for under their attack both England and France made long moves towards unity, while the unity of Italy was broken by them. In earlier times, Rome had mobilized the power of her settled peoples by means of her roads, but the Roman roads had fallen into decay, and were not replaced until the eighteenth century.

It is likely that even the Hunnish invasion was by no means the first of the Asiatic series. The Scythians of the Homeric and Herodotian accounts, drinking the milk of mares, obviously practised the same arts of life, and were probably of the same race as the later inhabitants of the steppe. The Celtic element in the river-names *Don*, *Don*etz, *Dn*eiper, *Dn*eister, and *Dan*ube may possibly betoken the passage of peoples of similar habits, though not of identical race, but it is not unlikely that the Celts came merely from the northern forests, like the Goths and Varangians of a later time. The great wedge of population, however, which the anthropologists characterize as Brachy-Cephalic, driven westward from Brachy-Cephalic Asia through Central Europe into France, is apparently intrusive between the northern, western, and southern Dolico-Cephalic populations, and may very probably have been derived from Asia.[1]

The full meaning of Asiatic influence upon Europe is not, however, discernible until we come to the Mongol invasions of the fifteenth century; but before we analyze the essential facts concerning these, it is desirable to shift our geographical view-point from Europe, so that we may consider the Old World in its entirety. It is obvious that, since the rainfall is derived from the sea, the heart of the greatest land-mass is likely to be relatively dry. We are not, therefore, surprised to find that two-thirds of all the world's population is concentrated in relatively small areas along the margins of the great continent – in Europe, beside the Atlantic ocean; in the Indies and China, beside the Indian and Pacific oceans. A vast belt of almost uninhabited, because practically rainless, land extends as the Sahara completely across Northern Africa into Arabia. Central and Southern Africa were almost as completely severed from Europe and Asia throughout the greater part of history as were the Americas and Australia. In fact, the southern boundary of Europe was and is the Sahara rather than the Mediterranean, for it is the desert which divides the black man from the white. The continuous land-mass of Euro-Asia thus included between the ocean and the desert measures 21,000,000 square miles, or half of all the land on the globe, if we exclude from reckoning the deserts of Sahara and Arabia. There are many detached deserts scattered through Asia, from Syria

[1] See 'The Races of Europe,' by Professor W. Z. Ripley (Keegan Paul, 1900).

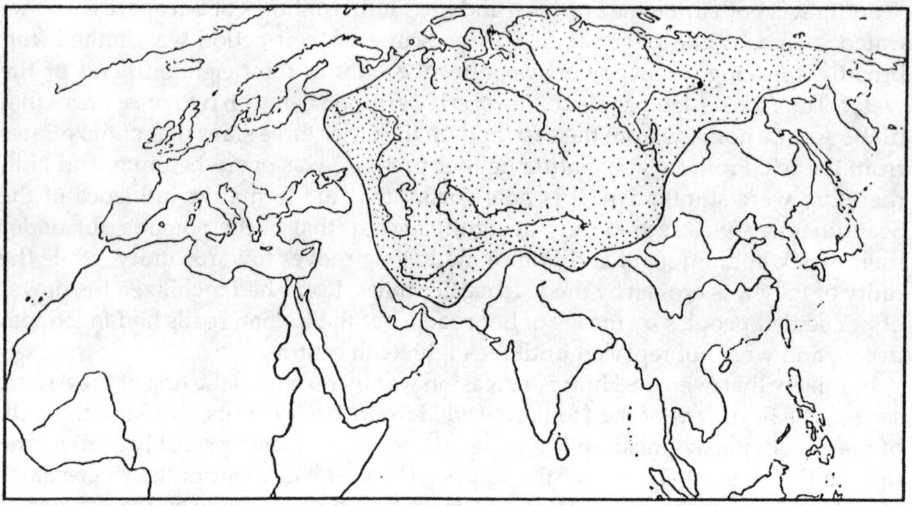

Figure 33.4 [orig. fig. 4] Continental and Arctic drainage. (Equal area projection)

and Persia north-eastward to Manchuria, but no such continuous vacancy as to be comparable with the Sahara. On the other hand, Euro-Asia is characterized by a very remarkable distribution of river drainage. Throughout an immense portion of the centre and north, the rivers have been practically useless for purposes of human communication with the outer world. The Volga, the Oxus, and the Jaxartes drain into salt lakes; the Obi, the Yenisei, and the Lena into the frozen ocean of the north. These are six of the greatest rivers in the world. There are many smaller but still considerable streams in the same area, such as the Tarim and the Helmund, which similarly fail to reach the ocean. Thus the core of Euro-Asia, although mottled with desert patches, is on the whole a steppe-land supplying a wide-spread if often scanty pasture, and there are not a few river-fed oases in it, but it is wholly unpenetrated by waterways from the ocean. In other words, we have in this immense area all the conditions for the maintenance of a sparse, but in the aggregate considerable, population of horse-riding and camel-riding nomads. Their realm is limited northward by a broad belt of sub-arctic forest and marsh, wherein the climate is too rigorous, except at the eastern and western extremities, for the development of agricultural settlements. In the east the forests extend southward to the Pacific coast in the Amur land and Manchuria. Similarly in the west, in prehistoric Europe, forest was the predominant vegetation. Thus framed in to the north-east, north, and north-west, the steppes spread continuously for 4000 miles from the Pusstas of Hungary to the Little Gobi of Manchuria, and, except in their westernmost extremity, they are untraversed by rivers draining to an accessible ocean, for we may neglect the very recent efforts to trade to the mouths of the Obi and Yenisei. In Europe, Western Siberia, and Western Turkestan the steppe-lands lie low, in some places below the level of the sea. Further to the east, in Mongolia, they extend over plateaux; but the passage from the one level to the other, over the naked, unscarped lower ranges of the arid heartland, presents little difficulty.

The hordes which ultimately fell upon Europe in the middle of the fourteenth century gathered their first force 3000 miles away on the high steppes of Mongolia. The havoc wrought for a few years in Poland, Silesia, Moravia, Hungary, Croatia, and Servia was, however, but the remotest and the most transient result of the great stirring of the nomads of the East associated with the name of Ghenghiz Khan. While the Golden Horde occupied the steppe of Kipchak, from the Sea of Aral, through the interval between the Ural range and the Caspian, to the foot of the Carpathians, another horde, descending south-westward between the Caspian sea and the Hindu Kush into Persia, Mesopotamia, and even into Syria, founded the domain of the Ilkhan. A third subsequently struck into Northern China, conquering Cathay. India and Mangi, or Southern China, were for a time sheltered by the incomparable barrier of Tibet, to whose efficacy there is, perhaps, nothing similar in the world, unless it be the Sahara desert and the polar ice. But at a later time, in the days of Marco Polo in the case of Mangi, in those of Tamerlane in the case of India, the obstacle was circumvented. Thus it happened that in this typical and well-recorded instance, all the settled margins of the Old World sooner or later felt the expansive force of mobile power originating in the steppe. Russia, Persia, India and China were either made tributary, or received Mongol dynasties. Even the incipient power of the Turks in Asia Minor was struck down for half a century.

As in the case of Europe, so in other marginal lands of Euro-Asia there are records of earlier invasions. China had more than once to submit to conquest from the north; India several times to conquest from the north-west. In the case of Persia, however, at least one of the earlier descents has a special significance in the history of Western civilization. Three or four centuries before the Mongols, the Seljuk Turks, emerging from Central Asia, overran by this path an immense area of the land, which we may describe as of the five seas – Caspian, Black, Mediterranean, Red, and Persian. They established themselves at Kerman, at Hamadan, and in Asia Minor, and they overthrew the Saracen dominion of Bagdad and Damascus. It was ostensibly to punish their treatment of the Christian pilgrims at Jerusalem that Christendom undertook the great series of campaigns known collectively as the Crusades. Although these failed in their immediate objects, they so stirred and united Europe that we may count them as the beginning of modern history – another striking instance of European advance stimulated by the necessity of reacting against pressure from the heart of Asia.

The conception of Euro-Asia to which we thus attain is that of a continuous land, ice-girt in the north, water-girt elsewhere, measuring twenty-one million square miles, or more than three times the area of North America, whose centre and north, measuring some nine million square miles, or more than twice the area of Europe, have no available water-ways to the ocean, but, on the other hand, except in the subarctic forest, are very generally favourable to the mobility of horsemen and camelmen. To east, south, and west of this heart-land are marginal regions, ranged in a vast crescent, accessible to shipmen. According to physical conformation, these regions are four in number, and it is not a little remarkable that in a general way they respectively coincide with the spheres of the four great religions – Buddhism, Brahminism, Mahometanism, and Christianity. The first two are the monsoon lands, turned the one towards the Pacific, and the other towards the Indian ocean. The fourth is Europe, watered by the Atlantic rains from the west. These three together, measuring less than seven million square miles, have more than 1000 million people, or two-thirds of the world population. The third, coinciding with the land of the Five Seas, or, as it is more often described, the Nearer East, is in large measure deprived of moisture by the proximity of Africa, and, except in the oases, is therefore thinly peopled. In some degree it partakes of the characteristics both of the marginal belt and of the central area of Euro-Asia. It is mainly devoid of forest, is patched with desert, and is therefore suitable for the operations of the nomad. Dominantly, however, it is marginal, for sea-gulfs and oceanic rivers lay it open to sea-power, and permit of the exercise of such power from it. As a consequence, periodically throughout history, we have here had empires belonging essentially to the marginal series, based on the agricultural populations of the great oases of Babylonia and Egypt, and in free water-communication with the civilized worlds of the Mediterranean and the Indies. But, as we should expect, these empires have been subject to an unparalleled series of revolutions, some due to Scythian, Turkish, and Mongol raids from Central Asia, others to the effort of the Mediterranean peoples to conquer the overland ways from the western to the eastern ocean. Here is the weakest spot in the girdle of early civilizations. for the isthmus of Suez divided sea-power into Eastern and Western, and the arid wastes of Persia advancing from Central Asia to the Persian gulf gave constant opportunity for nomad-power to strike home to the ocean edge, dividing India and China, on the one hand, from the Mediterranean world on the other. Whenever the Babylonian, the Syrian, and the Egyptian oases were weakly held, the steppe-peoples could treat the open tablelands of Iran and Asia Minor as forward posts whence to strike through the Punjab into India, through Syria into Egypt, and over the broken bridge of the Bosphorus and Dardanelles into Hungary. Vienna stood in the gateway of Inner Europe, withstanding the nomadic raids, both those which came by the direct road through the Russian steppe, and those which came by the loop way to south of the Black and Caspian seas.

Here we have illustrated the essential difference between the Saracen and the Turkish controls of the Nearer East. The Saracens were a branch of the Semitic race, essentially peoples of the Euphrates and Nile and of the smaller oases of Lower Asia. They created a great empire by availing themselves of the two mobilities permitted by their land – that of the horse and camel on the one hand, that of the ship on the other. At different times their fleets controlled both the Mediterranean as far as Spain, and the Indian ocean to the Malay islands. From their strategically central position between the eastern and western oceans, they attempted the conquest of all the marginal lands of the Old World, imitating Alexander and anticipating Napoleon. They could even threaten the steppe-land. Wholly distinct from Arabia as from Europe, India, and China were the Turanian pagans from the closed heart of Asia, the Turks who destroyed the Saracen civilization.

Mobility upon the ocean is the natural rival of horse and camel mobility in the heart of the continent. It was upon navigation of oceanic rivers that was based the Potamic stage of civilization, that of China on the Yangtse, that of India on the Ganges, that of Babylonia on the Euphrates, that of Egypt on the Nile. It was essentially upon the navigation of the Mediterranean that was based what has been described as the Thalassic stage of civilization, that of the Greeks and Romans. The Saracens and the Vikings held sway by navigation of the oceanic coasts.

The all-important result of the discovery of the Cape road to the Indies was to connect the western and eastern coastal navigations of Euro-Asia, even though by a circuitous route, and thus in some measure to neutralize the strategical advantage of the central position of the steppe-nomads by pressing upon them in rear. The revolution commenced by the great mariners of the Columbian generation endowed Christendom with the widest possible mobility of power, short of a winged mobility. The one and continuous ocean enveloping the divided and insular lands is, of course, the geographical condition of ultimate unity in the command of the sea, and of the whole theory of modern naval strategy and policy as expounded by such writers as Captain Mahan and Mr Spenser Wilkinson. The broad political effect was to reverse the relations of Europe and Asia, for whereas in the Middle Ages Europe was caged between an impassable desert to south, an unknown ocean to west, and icy or forested wastes to north and north-east, and in the east and south-east was constantly threatened by the superior mobility of the horsemen and camelmen, she now emerged upon the world, multiplying more than thirty-fold the sea surface and coastal lands to which she had access, and wrapping her influence round the Euro-Asiatic land-power which had hitherto threatened her very existence. New Europes were created in the vacant lands discovered in the midst of the waters, and what Britain and Scandinavia were to Europe in the earlier time, that have America and Australia, and in some measure even Trans-Saharan Africa, now become to Euro-Asia. Britain, Canada, the United States, South Africa, Australia, and Japan are now a ring of outer and insular bases for sea-power and commerce, inaccessible to the land-power of Euro-Asia.

But the land power still remains, and recent events have again increased its significance. While the maritime peoples of Western Europe have covered the ocean with their fleets, settled the outer continents, and in varying degree made tributary the oceanic margins of Asia, Russia has organized the Cossacks, and, emerging from her northern forests, has policed the steppe by setting her own nomads to meet the Tartar nomads. The Tudor century, which saw the expansion of Western Europe over the sea, also saw Russian power carried from Moscow through Siberia. The eastward swoop of the horsemen across Asia was an event almost as pregnant with political consequences as was the rounding of the Cape, although the two movements long remained apart.

It is probably one of the most striking coincidences of history that the seaward and the landward expansion of Europe should, in a sense, continue the ancient opposition between Roman and Greek. Few great failures have had more far-reaching consequences than the failure of Rome to Latinize the Greek. The Teuton was civilized and Christianized by the Roman, the Slav in the main by the Greek. It is the Romano-Teuton who in later times embarked upon the ocean; it was the

Graeco-Slav who rode over the steppes, conquering the Turanian. Thus the modern land-power differs from the sea-power no less in the source of its ideals than in the material conditions of its mobility.[2]

In the wake of the Cossack, Russia has safely emerged from her former seclusion in the northern forests. Perhaps the change of greatest intrinsic importance which took place in Europe in the last century was the southward migration of the Russian peasants, so that, whereas agricultural settlements formerly ended at the forest boundary, the centre of the population of all European Russia now lies to south of that boundary, in the midst of the wheat-fields which have replaced the more western steppes. Odessa has here risen to importance with the rapidity of an American city.

A generation ago steam and the Suez canal appeared to have increased the mobility of sea-power relatively to land-power. Railways acted chiefly as feeders to ocean-going commerce. But trans-continental railways are now transmuting the conditions of land-power, and nowhere can they have such effect as in the closed heart-land of Euro-Asia, in vast areas of which neither timber nor accessible stone was available for road-making. Railways work the greater wonders in the steppe, because they directly replace horse and camel mobility, the road stage of development having here been omitted.

In the matter of commerce it must not be forgotten that ocean-going traffic, however relatively cheap, usually involves the fourfold handling of goods – at the factory of origin, at the export wharf, at the import wharf, and at the inland warehouse for retail distribution; whereas the continental railway truck may run direct from the exporting factory into the importing warehouse. Thus marginal ocean-fed commerce tends, other things being equal, to form a zone of penetration round the continents, whose inner limit is roughly marked by the line along which the cost of four handlings, the oceanic freight, and the railway freight from the neighbouring coast, is equivalent to the cost of two handlings and the continental railway freight. English and German coals are said to compete on such terms midway through Lombardy.

The Russian railways have a clear run of 6000 miles from Wirballen in the west to Vladivostock in the east. The Russian army in Manchuria is as significant evidence of mobile land-power as the British army in South Africa was of sea-power. True, that the Trans-Siberian railway is still a single and precarious line of communication, but the century will not be old before all Asia is covered with railways. The spaces within the Russian Empire and Mongolia are so vast, and their potentialities in population, wheat, cotton, fuel and metals so incalculably great, that it is inevitable that a vast economic world, more or less apart, will there develop inaccessible to oceanic commerce.

[2] This statement was criticized in the discussion which followed the reading of the paper. On reconsidering the paragraph, I still think it substantially correct. Even the Byzantine Greek would have been other than he was had Rome completed the subjugation of the ancient Greek. No doubt the ideals spoken of were Byzantine rather than Hellenic, but they were not Roman, which is the point.

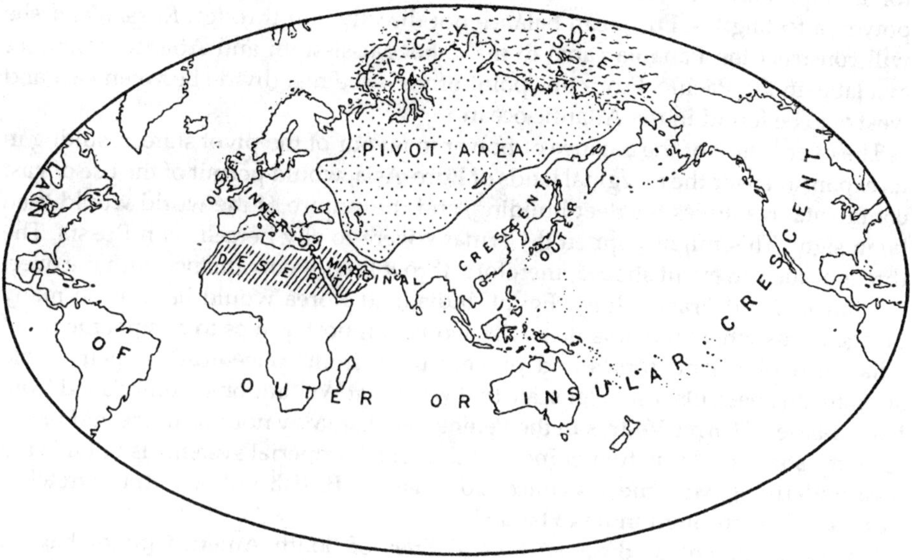

Figure 33.5 [orig. fig. 5] The Natural Seats of Power
Pivot area: wholly continental
Outer crescent: wholly oceanic
Inner crescent: partly continental, partly oceanic

As we consider this rapid review of the broader currents of history, does not a certain persistence of geographical relationship become evident? Is not the pivot region of the world's politics that vast area of Euro-Asia which is inaccessible to ships, but in antiquity lay open to the horse-riding nomads, and is to-day about to be covered with a network of railways? There have been and are here the conditions of a mobility of military and economic power of a far-reaching and yet limited character. Russia replaces the Mongol Empire. Her pressure on Finland, on Scandinavia, on Poland, on Turkey, on Persia, on India, and on China replaces the centrifugal raids of the steppe-men. In the world at large she occupies the central strategical position held by Germany in Europe. She can strike on all sides and be struck from all sides, save the north. The full development of her modern railway mobility is merely a matter of time. Nor is it likely that any possible social revolution will alter her essential relations to the great geographical limits of her existence. Wisely recognizing the fundamental limits of her power, her rulers have parted with Alaska; for it is as much a law of policy for Russia to own nothing over seas as for Britain to be supreme on the ocean.

Outside the pivot area, in a great inner crescent, are Germany, Austria, Turkey, India, and China, and in an outer crescent, Britain, South Africa, Australia, the United States, Canada, and Japan. In the present condition of the balance of power, the pivot state, Russia, is not equivalent to the peripheral states, and there is room for an equipoise in France. The United States has recently become an eastern power, affecting the European balance not directly, but through Russia, and she will construct the Panama canal to make her Mississippi and Atlantic resources available in the Pacific. From this point of view the real divide between east and west is to be found in the Atlantic ocean.

The oversetting of the balance of power in favour of the pivot state, resulting in its expansion over the marginal lands of Euro-Asia, would permit of the use of vast continental resources for fleet-building, and the empire of the world would then be in sight. This might happen if Germany were to ally herself with Russia. The threat of such an event should, therefore, throw France into alliance with the over-sea powers, and France, Italy, Egypt, India, and Korea would become so many bridge heads where the outside navies would support armies to compel the pivot allies to deploy land forces and prevent them from concentrating their whole strength on fleets. On a smaller scale that was what Wellington accomplished from his sea-base at Torres Vedras in the Peninsular War. May not this in the end prove to be the strategical function of India in the British Imperial system? Is not this the idea underlying Mr Amery's conception that the British military front stretches from the Cape through India to Japan?

The development of the vast potentialities of South America might have a decisive influence upon the system. They might strengthen the United States, or, on the other hand, if Germany were to challenge the Monroe doctrine successfully, they might detach Berlin from what I may perhaps describe as a pivot policy. The particular combinations of power brought into balance are not material; my contention is that from a geographical point of view they are likely to rotate round the pivot state, which is always likely to be great, but with limited mobility as compared with the surrounding marginal and insular powers.

I have spoken as a geographer. The actual balance of political power at any given time is, of course, the product, on the one hand, of geographical conditions, both economic and strategic, and, on the other hand, of the relative number, virility, equipment, and organization of the competing peoples. In proportion as these quantities are accurately estimated are we likely to adjust differences without the crude resort to arms. And the geographical quantities in the calculation are more measurable and more nearly constant than the human. Hence we should expect to find our formula apply equally to past history and to present politics. The social movements of all times have played around essentially the same physical features, for I doubt whether the progressive desiccation of Asia and Africa, even if proved, has in historical times vitally altered the human environment. The westward march of empire appears to me to have been a short rotation of marginal power round the south-western and western edge of the pivotal area. The Nearer, Middle, and Far Eastern questions relate to the unstable equilibrium of inner and outer powers in those parts of the marginal crescent where local power is, at present, more or less negligible.

In conclusion, it may be well expressly to point out that the substitution of some new control of the inland area for that of Russia would not tend to reduce the geographical significance of the pivot position. Were the Chinese, for instance, organized by the Japanese, to overthrow the Russian Empire and conquer its territory, they might constitute the yellow peril to the world's freedom just because they would add an oceanic frontage to the resources of the great continent, an advantage as yet denied to the Russian tenant of the pivot region.

34

OWNER'S TIME AND OWN TIME: THE MAKING OF A CAPITALIST TIME-CONSCIOUSNESS 1300-1800

Nigel Thrift

Alongside the geopolitics described by the likes of Ratzel and Mackinder (**chapters 32 and 33**), the late nineteenth century also saw the consolidation of a chronopolitics. At the global scale this involved the establishment of a universal public time based on the Greenwich meridian. At the national scale it meant the triumph of a new kind of time-consciousness, one based on economic rationality which was both measurable and capable of being used as a measure of work, leisure and social activity. Nigel Thrift explores the spread of clock-time, its placing within class struggles over the length of the working day, and its gradual dissolution of local, absolute times. He also shows how this new consciousness was made necessary by the heightened capacities for mobility implied by the spread of railways in England (see Harvey, **chapter 37**). Everyday life was colonized by new technologies and social practices of time-keeping and measurement until they became regarded as normal. His analysis of the relations between time and power can be compared with Foucault's examination of space and power in the panopticon [*Discipline and punish.* New York, 1979].

Source: Owners' time and own time; the making of a capitalist time-consciousness 1300–1880. In Pred, A., editor, *Space and time in geography: essays dedicated to Torsten Hägerstrand.* Lund, Sweden: CWK Gleerup, pp. 56–84, 1981.

Third Period: The Imprisoning, 1750–1880

Disembedded from human experience, its transcendent elements suppressed, time was now perceived as an objective force within which people were imprisoned. (F. Hearn, 1978)

For the English upper classes consciousness of the new time had come early. Old customs based on temporal inexactitude, for instance the system of lighting a taper in the window when callers were welcome and keeping a permanently laid table in case of callers,[27] gave way to the most rigid social timetabling and a fixed social calendar of an almost byzantine social complexity. Clock time was fetishized. Meal times, work times, dressing times, visiting times; all activities were made temporally exact and exacting since breaches of timekeeping "were treated as much a moral lapse as a breach of good taste" (Davidoff, 1973, p. 35). Gongs and house bells were first introduced into the upper class household in the early nineteenth century. Dressing for dinner had become common by the 1860s. In the matter of calls, the leaving of cards was used as the basis for a new, complex and precisely defined system of social interaction with very exact response times. In the early part of the nineteenth century such social timetables were relatively simple. For instance, "the official timetable for visiting was 3 p.m. to 4 p.m. for ceremonial calls, 4 p.m. to 5 p.m. for semi-ceremonial calls and 5 p.m. to 6 p.m. for closer friends and family. Sunday was traditionally a day for closer friends and family" (Davidoff, 1973, p. 43). By the latter part of the century these timetables had become far more elaborate.[28]

By contrast to this opulent and mannered lifestyle the agricultural worker's lot remained much as it always had been, or got worse. Weekly wage labor became more and more common and task-oriented piece-work less and less common. Complaints against time wasted at seasonal fairs, market days, and the annual parish feasts or "wakes" became a concerted attack on the farm worker's free time and certainly resulted in a drastic curtailment of wakes (Table 34.1).[29]

Table 34.1 [orig. table 1] *The Curtailment of Wakes in the Northampton Area.*

Period of Time	*1724*	*mid-1840s*
January to early May	1	1
Around Whit and Trinity Sundays	4	15
Late June to early July	38	31
Second half of July	20	6
Early August	1	6
Around 15 August	14	5
Late August/First half of September	22	0
Second half of September	–	16
Around Michaelmas	31	–
October	18	20
Around All Saints' Day	33	7
Rest of November and December	23	11
	205	118

[27] By contrast, according to Davidoff (1973), such customs were still in use in Moscow and St Petersburg in the 1860s and 1870s. See also Quinlan (1941).

[28] Of course this obsession with time dialectically spilled over into the literature of the age, cf. Meyerhoff (1955), Buckley (1967), Pocock (1971), Patrides (1976). The intellectual ideas of Darwin, Marx and others also gave, not coincidentally, the Victorian age a general obsession with time.

[29] The table is from Malcolmson (1973), p. 18. It is interesting in this context, to note one of Josiah

This diminution was not unconnected with the fact that, at the beginning of the period, most workshops were outside municipal limits and existed in what were rural areas where the old rhythmic time consciousness still persisted. Thomas Hardy, in *The Mayor of Casterbridge* (1886, p. 324), lets a farm laborer explain that the death of Henchard took place "about half-an-hour ago, by the sun; for I've got no watch to my name".

But it was in the industrial sphere with the rapid growth of an industrial work-force that time consciousness now decisively changed. In the cities enclosure did not, as in the country, take place just in space but also in time.

In the cities time became the nexus of class struggle, being invested now with not just a use value but an exchange value.[30] With the recasting of the worker's time sense assured by a new labor process relying on the all-pervasive clock, time became a formal, measurable quantity able to become a commodity. The increasing division of labor and associated deskilling allowed labor power to become a commodity measurable in units of clock time. But not only the sphere of instrumental action was affected. Gradually clock time would come to colonize the sphere of symbolic interaction as well. Work time would become the reference point and a gradual separation of work time from personal time would take place[31] in which, paradoxically, work time and "leisure" time would gradually become more alike.

The period of "manufacture" expanded the social productivity of labor by the multiplication of detailed functions, subordinating large areas of the country and many branches of production to the urban capitalist. The subsumption of labor to capital remained, however, external and formal. Production was only modified by subdivision of tasks; the labor process stood much as it had in the pre-capitalist period. With the advent of production based on machinery comes the period of "modern industry", real subsumption of labor and the factory system. Whilst the introduction of machinery into production took place in England from the last third of the eighteenth century, the period from that time until 1880 can now be seen to be a period of gradual adjustment to modern industry, with manufacture

Wedgewood's complaints, quoted in Pollard (1965), p. 182, about his workers "our men will go to the Wakes, if they were sure to go to the D . . . l next. I have not spared them in threats and I would have thrash'd them right heartily if I could." And, he added, in 1776: "Our men have been at play 4 days this week. I have rough'd and smooth'd them over, and promised them a long Xmass, but I know it is all in vain, for Wakes must be observed though the World was to end with them." The proximity of work-shops to the country parishes was a real threat to work discipline still at this time and may have been one of the causes of the protests. See also McKendrick (1961). The decline of markets and fairs is, of course, less easy to link to upper and middle class protest since growth of the railways, etc. led to many markets' economic decline.

30 The best source is still *Capital, Volume 1*, Marx (1976), Chapter 10, "The Working Day". Note also Marx's formula in Chapter 18:
surplus value/value of labour power = surplus labour time/necessary labour time = unpaid labour/paid labour time. For a discussion see Horvath (1981). It is not possible to pack all that is available on the changing time consciousness of the nineteenth century into the next few paragraphs. What follows is, of necessity, selective.

31 For a more detailed study of this theme cf. Pred (1981a).

and modern industry coexisting side by side and the latter only very gradually and unevenly subsuming the former according to branch of production and region.[32] Modern industry required the transformation, both technical and organizational, of the productive process with big cities as the main source of labor power. But, above all, modern industry required worker discipline if machine and man were to be integrated. This requirement, in turn, demanded that the worker be trained to take for granted a new time structure suited to this reorganization.[33]

The villager, the farmer and the outworker, none of these needed to confront the problem of compartmentalized and artificially regulated time. "The task and not the timepiece still regulated productive activity" (Thompson, 1967, p. 73). But, as human activity was geared to the machine synchronization or "entrainment" to the productive process was required. This process of retiming man's consciousness took place in two dimensions, that of instrumental action and that of symbolic interaction.

In the sphere of instrumental action the main need was for discipline.

> *What was needed was regularity and steady intensity in place of irregular spurts of work; accuracy and standardization in place of individual design; and care of equipment and material in place of pride in one's tools. (Pollard, 1964, p. 213)*

The old habit of leaving off work when enough money had been earned for the week had to be eradicated now that machinery was involved. Three basic methods of time discipline were used – deterrents, wage incentives and the formulation of a new work ethos (cf. Pollard, 1965; Thompson, 1963, 1967). Outright use of deterrents like dismissal, fines, and punishments were more usual at the beginning of the third period. At this time a number of innovations intended to promote "time-thrift" amongst the workers were introduced. At the scale of the day bad timekeeping was punished by devices such as severe fines. Often the gates of the factory were locked exactly at the start of the workday. By the mid-nineteenth century, however, wage incentives had become more common.

The formulation of a new work ethos was no more subtle. Apart from the moral blandishments of numerous Victorian clerics and the Samuel Smiles and Hannah Mores (Thompson, 1967), the main thrust was aimed at everywhere imposing the new temporality on people's consciousness. Clocks stared from walls, the factory hooter and the knocker-up cajoled and reminded. "Timetables" (a word peculiar to the nineteenth century) and lists of rules were prominent in all factories (and, in the last quarter of the nineteenth century, in the new offices).

32 Cf. Samuel (1977); Gregory (1978, 1981). It is doubtful that "modern industry" reached its real heyday until sometime after Marx's death. The fact that Samuel has now shown the large number of non-mechanized craft industries still left in the 1880s and 1890s explains the persistence of so many of the old time practices like Saint Monday beyond 1880. It might be noted that the very regularity of machinery probably contributed towards the time consciousness of those workers associated with it.

33 At the end of the century the new work discipline would reach into offices as well, cf. Braverman (1974).

But the more subtle conditioning took place in the sphere of communicative interaction, in particular in the areas of education and leisure. In education many of the new working class elementary schools and Sunday schools were quite explicitly "abstract machines"[34] aimed, amongst other things, at inculcating the habit of time discipline into children. In these schools "the division of time became increasingly minute; activities were governed in detail by orders that had to be obeyed immediately" (Foucault, 1977, p. 150). Just as in factories there were fines (and other corporal deterrents). There were even monetary incentives (note McCann, 1977; Jones and Williamson, 1979).

> *The drive for popular education at the end of the eighteenth and the beginning of the nineteenth centuries also gained some impetus from hopes that the elementary school could be used to break the labouring classes into those habits of work discipline now necessary for factory production. Sunday schools were commended for providing a spectacle of order and regularity: and for making workers both more 'tractable and obedient' and more punctual in their attendance. Putting little children to work at school for very long hours at very dull subjects was seen as a positive virtue, for it made them 'habituated, not to say naturalized, to labour and fatigue'. One effect on education of industrial capitalism was therefore to add support for the penal and disciplinary aspects of a school, which were seen by some largely as a system to break the will and to condition the child to routinized labour in the factory. Only later did it become apparent that an industrial society also needed the mass distribution of a wide range of intellectual skills which could only be acquired through education. (Stone, 1969, p. 92)*

In the area of leisure the problem of time discipline was part of the more general problem of how to keep order and discipline. Leisure time had to be put to *use* and related in some way to work, otherwise it might become a dangerous distraction. Of course, at first, the very length of the working day acted as a decisive authority constraint on recreation. But as a general decrease in working hours took place during the course of the nineteenth century considerable numbers of hours were opened up for recreational activities. But, at the end of the eighteenth and beginning of the nineteenth century a legal and moral assault of great ferocity had been made on popular (and boisterous) recreations limiting them in time and space, an assault only aided by the new built environment which had, for instance, few playing fields or other facilities at this time (e.g., Malcolmson, 1973). Thus, when time for recreation again became available, the almost empty stage enabled the rise of such organized and commercialized recreations as railway outings (first introduced during or even before 1844), new spectator variants of old sports (such as cricket or football), as well as activities like bible study groups. The new recreations were based on paying consumption rather than participating production and could be more easily confined to particular locations and precise time slots.[35]

[34] This term is from Foucault (1977).

[35] E.g., Meller (1976) on the moral dimension of the new recreation. The Football Association was founded in 1867 (Magoun, 1938). Later, working class activities like union meetings would be scheduled for precise times! See also Andersen (1961).

This truncation of traditional working class recreational habits was combined with a gradual undermining of the traditional working calendar and working week with the intent of making them, like the day, more regular. The richer fabric of the traditional holiday calendar with its associated wakes and pleasure fairs, was gradually worn away and replaced with a piece of shoddy. The working week was also made more regular. "Saint Monday" was one casualty.[36] Monday had been a customary holiday for workers in small scale domestic and outwork industries and in the pits. It was also common in some of the new manufacturing industries. The day, which was often portrayed by contemporary writers simply as a day of drinking and gambling,[37] had, by the mid-century, become a rather more staid affair as the old recreations gave way to new recreational pursuits, like cheap railway excursions, cricket, and so on. But a complete weekday off was obviously inconvenient to capitalists and the available evidence suggests that the institution of a Saturday half-holiday was used as a bargaining counter by employers to rid themselves of the Monday holiday.[38] The adoption of the new holiday, partly in place of the old, varied spatially and temporally[39] and was a function, at least in part, of local factors like worker resistance and strength of the indigenous half-day movement. It is interesting to note that Saint Monday was still in existence, therefore, in some trades which had unmechanized small workshop production in the late nineteenth and early twentieth century.[40]

There was, of course, worker resistance to all these moves but it tended to be fragmented. There were triumphs, however. The various shorter hours movements had considerable success with the result that over the half-century from 1836 to 1886 average hours were reduced by one fifth[41] with the Ten Hour Act of 1847 forming the most important milestone. The 1870s also saw important gains with the Bank Holiday acts of 1871 and 1875 establishing four days in the year (Boxing Day, Easter Monday, Whit Monday and the first Monday in August) as national (though unpaid) holidays.[42] Gradually relative replaced absolute surplus value.

[36] For details of "St Monday' see Thompson (1967) and Reid (1976). The attack on the traditional calendar came from another quarter in France. Cf. Zerubavel (1977).

[37] With some justification, it might be added.

[38] See especially Reid (1976). The new half-day holiday was usually made up for by longer hours the rest of the week. The 1867 Factory Act made Saturday a mandatory half holiday for women. It is interesting to note the connection with leisure patterns. In Birmingham by 1853 the busiest night of the week at the Theatre Royal was Saturday, in 1841 and 1842 this had not been the case. Cf. Reid (1976). See also Harrison (1967).

[39] Saturday half-day was adopted in Manchester in 1843, in Sheffield in the 1840s, in St Helens in 1857, in Nottingham in 1861 and in Barrow-in-Furness not until the late 1860s. Cf. Reid (1976).

[40] It is difficult to know when the Saturday half-day reached rural areas. George Sturt (1923, p. 16), who worked in a wheelwright's shop in Farnham, Surrey recalls that "it was probably in 1885 that we left off Saturdays at one o'clock instead of at four; and it may have been about the same time . . . that half-past five was substituted for six as the normal closing time." Banks (1973) notes, following Pimlott (1947), that no half-day was given to country-dwellers or shop assistants until the end of the century.

[41] Burnett (1974). On the significance of the 1847 act see Hearn (1978), p. 163, and de Grazia (1962).

[42] For the changing holiday calendar at this time cf. Pimlott (1947). Annual holidays did not appear until 1875 at the earliest, and were rare until 1884. Holidays with pay were all but unknown until the turn of the century.

But the shorter hours campaigns show the rub. For the workers were not now fighting against the new idea of time, only for adjustments to it (de Grazia, 1962). From now on they would win battles but the war was lost. Time was now money, not tasks.

By 1880 a new set of strategies of control had sprung up that gradually replaced the older strategies which were overwhelmingly based on simple coercion. Now that the foundations had been laid direct coercion or rule (Gramsi's "dominio") was replaced by a more pervasive and more effective hegemony relying on a culture based on economy. The idea of punishment was replaced by the idea of reform with an emphasis on self-improvement. In the sphere of instrumental action, as workers were socialized to the new work regime, a new terrain of class struggle was formed based upon the arrangement and length of work time and the rates for the job but not on the existence of work time itself. That a part of the day was called "work time" became part of the taken-for-granted world. The symbolic point for this occurrence may be the Ten House Act of 1847; in reality, of course, it was an uneven process of capitulation over space and in time, taking place at different rates in different regions (cf. Gregory, 1978, 1981).

In the sphere of symbolic interaction the same process of formation of a hegemonic control occurred. In education, there was a gradual replacement of schools that were essentially military regimens with policing functions in which time was simply a vacuum to be filled by disciplined, moral activity. This base could be built upon. For instance, the timetable of pauper schools now:

> *specified an alternation of religious and secular instruction, punctuated by outdoor exercise in the playground and, in the case of industrial and workhouse schools, interspersed with periods of supervised labour. This careful scheduling gave a moral value to time itself as a structured deployment of supervised activity. 'The moral training pervades every hour of the day, from the period when the children are marched from their bedrooms in the morning to that when they march back to their bedrooms at night'. (Jones and Williamson, 1979, p. 89)*

The schools were becoming increasingly "anthroponomic",[43] reorganized not just to produce workers but to produce and distribute different kinds of workers. There was a renewed emphasis on the three r's, and on the needs of an institutionally diversifying capitalism. The symbolic turning point was probably the year 1861, when the criteria applied by the inspectorate of state schools changed from simple inspections for "moral tenor" to consideration of levels of elementary skills as well. The question had changed – from the existence of the system itself to how the system might be refined. In the sphere of leisure, recreation also became increasingly ordered and confined in space and time. Games of fixed length took place in walled-off spaces. A number of symbolic dates might be given to the commencement of this process of consumption instead of production of leisure – the first railway excursions in the 1840s perhaps, or the founding of the Football

[43] This term comes from Bertaux (1977). See also Bourdieu and Passeron (1977, 1979).

Association in 1867 and the first professional clubs in the late 1870s. There are many claimants (cf. Magoun, 1937; Delaney, 1963; Keeton, 1972).

But perhaps the most important factor in terms of incorporation of the time sense of the working class was the new economic rationality. For, at some point, consumer demand, dialectically intertwined with the development of consumer industries, became a popular economic aspiration (Reid, 1976). Bishop Berkeley's "creation of wants" triumphed. Allied with this development were the growth of savings and credit institutions like building societies and insurance companies, and the appearance of new forms of usury like hire purchase. Consequently, a new importance was attached to regular wages and to "planning ahead". No more would workers turn up to work only until they had enough money for the week. The new economic calculation put a financial value on future time so that an objective future became a part of the habitus of the worker. Not only present but future time was now money. An indefinable but important cusp was reached similar to the one Bourdieu documents for Algerian workers in a later time period:

> *It appears that for a person to be able to take his destiny in hand by the organization of resources, by the establishment of a balance of assets and liabilities, thrift, the management of capital for investment or credit, or by improvement of productive techniques, it is necessary for him to retain a minimum of control over his present and over his environment. The demonstration of this was provided by a factory in Algeria in 1954. It was decided to raise wages by 20 per cent; the workers, containing to the logic of the traditionalist spirit, reduced their working time by one fifth. Wages were then doubled reaching 240 per cent of the initial rate. The consequences of this second increase were radically different from those of the first. As if a threshold had been broken, the workers showed a desire to work, to earn even more, to work overtime, to anticipate the future by thrift. It was as if the whole of their attitude toward the world had undergone a complete restructuring as a result of the modification of a single trait, as if, freed from his anxiety over subsistence, the individual suddenly discovered that he was capable of taking his own future in his hands. (Bourdieu, 1963, p. 71)*

Workers therefore both gained and lost in the exchange of a present for a future and culture for economy.

An Episode in the Development of Capitalist Time Consciousness: A Case Study of the Diffusion of Greenwich Mean Time[44]

> The railway and the telegraph time are
> here from 'Lunnon town';
> I wonder if the Lunnon time will
> be the next thing down.[45]

[44] This section relies heavily on Thrift (1977a), Parkes and Thrift (1979), Smith (1976), Ponsford (1978), and Howse (1980).

[45] *Woolmer's Exeter and Plymouth Gazette*, August 14th 1852, quoted in Ponsford (1978) p. 11.

This final section provides a case study of the interplay between the development of precise and co-ordinated timekeeping and time consciousness. Whilst the section shows the old pre-capitalist time in its death throes, it also shows that the process of diffusion was uneven. The transformation took place at different rates in different places depending upon a number of different factors (cf. Gregory, 1978, 1981).

It was only in the year 1784 that the first regular stage coach service was set up (between London and Bristol). But the innovation spread quickly and by 1785 regular stage coach services were in operation from London to 25 towns.[46] The new regularity had immediate social effects, for instance on some London working habits:

> *Incoming mail was formerly opened late in the morning, dealt with at leisure during the day, and the replies sent out in the evening; it did not matter that clerks worked late, so long as they caught the midnight post for which boxes closed at 11. Now all the mails left the GPO at 8 pm; the boxes closed at 7 and the clerks were then free. (Wright, 1968, p. 125)*

But the organization of the new regular stage coach services was not without attendant problems. In particular, the vagaries of local time began to tell, for most towns in Britain were still wrapped in their own "time zones". In 1792 it was agreed that communities in England should keep mean time but the time kept was based on the meridian of the place concerned. This meant that quite substantial variations in the time kept between places occurred. There was, for instance, a sixteen minute time difference between London and Plymouth. For the moment this variation did not matter. Stage coach travel was slow and adjustments could be made. The difference in time on the London to Bristol run, for instance, was accounted for by the coach guard who was responsible for monitoring the schedule. He would simply adjust his timepiece so that it lost twenty minutes on the "down" run to London and gained twenty minutes on the "up" run to Bristol. (Local Bristol time differed from London time by twenty minutes.)

But in 1825 the Stockton – Darlington line opened and with it the railway era. The increased speeds made possible by rail travel made synchronization of the towns in Britain to one time more and more imperative. At first the railways ran in a quite haphazard manner and made no great impact on other types of transport. In 1831, for instance, the Liverpool and Manchester railway published a combination of their time-tables with those of the coaches and steam-packets from Liverpool that connected with their trains. There were eight pages of coach times, two of shipping times, but only one quarter of a page of train times. Some of the current perceptions of time did nothing to help. For instance, when George Bradshaw was preparing his first time-tables for the Railway Companion in 1839, one railway company director refused to supply him with times of arrivals: "I believe that it would tend to make punctuality a sort of obligation" (Wright, 1968, p. 28).

However, in 1838 the railways started to carry the Royal Mail. This made the

[46] Bagwell (1970) and Wright (1968) are the chief sources for this section to 1840.

situation even more pressing. Although the mail coach tradition of a guard carrying an official timepiece was continued the allowances for easting and westing had to be foregone. The birth of the new telegraph companies (which were able to transmit time signals) only added to the problem of coordination. By the beginning of the 1840s at least three organizations in England were finding the problem of keeping different times at different places difficult; the Post Office, the railway companies and the telegraph companies.

The experience for the railway passenger of this period is difficult to imagine now.[47] Those passengers reading the Great Western timetable in 1841, for instance, were confronted with the following disconcerting statement:

> *London time is kept at all the Stations on the Railway, which is about 4 minutes earlier than Reading time; 5½ minutes before Steventon time; 7½ minutes before Cirencester time; 8 minutes before Chippenham time; and 14 minutes before Bridgewater time. (Great Western Railway, 1841)*

It is not surprising, therefore, that a number of Victorian railway travellers carried especially-made watches with two dials, one to show local time and one the time of the place the traveller was visiting.

Pressure was soon brought to bear for uniformity of time, especially in view of the rapid increase in railway mileage, the increasing volume of rail traffic, and new innovations like the first excursion trains. The first broad-side appears to have been fired by Abraham Osler in Birmingham in a talk to the Birmingham Philosophical Institute.[48] But it was Henry Booth, secretary of the Liverpool and Manchester Railway, who put the position for a standard time most clearly and eloquently in a pamphlet from 1847:

> *Now, contemplate the picture as it is. The parish clocks in some half a dozen hamlets or fishing towns in the extreme east in quick succession, commence the long and dissonant peal; Norwich and Yarmouth, Harwich and Ramsgate, with a few hundred clock and chimes ring vigorously; Canterbury, Colchester and Cambridge prolong the feu de joie; with a thousand intermediate towns, each with its parish clock or market bell proclaiming its own time . . . Westward the noise moves on, till it gains the suburbs of the huge metropolis; Poplar and Limehouse, Stepney and Bethnal Green, each with its clocks and bells . . . jar gratingly; while as the moving din reaches St Martins-le-Grand the great bell of St Paul's, with mournful voice, tolls ONE, in grave rebuke of the passing clamour. And still the din proceeds; still in its westward course – Brentford and Windsor, Reading and Oxford, Southampton and Salisbury, onward for a mortal hour, "by Shrewsbury clock"; while every city, town, or township, or "extra-parochial place" as the incessant roar sweeps over its head marking its particular Time, calls out – "That's my thunder!" (Booth, 1847, p. 11)*

[47] The closest parallel nowadays is travelling by air.

[48] Reported in the *Illustrated London News,* May 14th , 1842. Cited in Howse (1980).

And as he, and industrial capitalism, would like it, the uniformity of time thus:

The great bell of St Paul's strikes ONE, and, simultaneously, every City clock and village chime, from John of Groat's to the Land's End, strikes ONE, also. The finger of every watch or timepiece . . . points to the same hour! At one and the same moment, whether in London or Edinburgh, at Canterbury or Cardiff, the labourer returns to his toil from his hour of rest. The man of business keeps his appointment; and the traveller regulates his movements with the confidence of one who has no longer the fear of "the longitude" before his eyes. There is sublimity in the idea of a whole nation Stirred by one impulse; in every arrangement, one common signal regulating the movements of a mighty people![49]

The Great Western railway had kept *London* time (there is a 23 seconds time difference between London time and Greenwich time) at its stations and in its timetables since November 1840. Similarly, in 1846 the North-western railway introduced London time at the Manchester and Liverpool termini. This caused some difficulties of coordination. For instance, in November of 1846 "the late running of a train . . . was attributed to the fact that London time was kept on the line between Rugby and York (run by the Midland Railway) whereas local Rugby time was kept at Rugby Station (run by the North Western)" (Howse, 1980, p. 87).

It was the Railway companies who finally decided, therefore, through the mediation of the Railway Clearing House (a body set up in 1842 to coordinate a number of aspects of railway operation in Great Britain) to recommend "to each company to adopt Greenwich time at all their stations as soon as the Post Office permits them to do so" (Smith, 1976, p. 221; cf. McCrea, 1975). The Post Office seemed to have no qualms and within a year of the recommendation most railways had switched to Greenwich time, nearly all of them doing so on December 1st 1847. The January 1848 edition of *Bradshaw's Railway Guide* lists the London and South Western, London and North Western, Midland, Chester and Birkenhead, Lancaster and Carlisle, East Lancashire and York and North Midland railways as all keeping to Greenwich time. It is also known that the Great Western, South Eastern and Caledonian had switched to the new time.[50]

But if the railway stations had now changed to Greenwich time not all the surrounding towns had done so, with inevitable confusion.[51]

It should here be observed that the clocks at the various railway stations are universally set and regulated by "London time". For instance, most of our readers are aware that when it is twelve o'clock in the metropolis, it is either earlier or later than that hour elsewhere, according to the distance from London and the direction of the compass. Thus the clocks of a provincial town may point at five minutes to twelve, whereas it has already struck twelve in London, and the

[49] Booth (1847), pp. 10–11. Other such pamphlets do exist, for example Frodsham (1848).

[50] Howse (1980), p. 88. Howse also points out that in December, 1848, the Chester and Holyhead decided to regulate all its times by the Craig-y-don gun (16 minutes and 30 seconds after Greenwich time). The adoption of Greenwich time by the railway companies was therefore by no means uniform!

[51] It is interesting to note that at this time high church clocks and services still tended to be run on local time while nonconformist churches had already switched to London time.

Table 34.2 [orig. table 2]:
Times kept by public clocks in England, Wales and Scotland, February 17, 1852.

*Greenwich Time**	*Local Time*	*Greenwich Time**	*Local Time*
England		*Wales* (old boundaries)	
Banbury	Axminster	Cardiff	Brecon
Bedford	Basingstoke	Carmarthen	Milford Haven
Birmingham (1847)	Bath	Denbigh	
Bridgewater	Bodmin	Holyhead	
Buckingham	Bridport	Montgomery	
Burnham-on-Sea	Bristol	Newport	
Canterbury	Cambridge	Saint Asaph	
Carlisle	Chelmsford	Swansea	
Cheltenham	Colchester		
Chepstow	Crediton		
Chester	Dartmouth		
Chichester	Devizes	*Scotland*	
Collumpton	Dorchester		
Coventry	Ely	Aberdeen	Peebles
Cowes	Exeter	Berwick	
Derby	Falmouth	Dumfries	
Doncaster	Harwich	Dundee	
Dover	Ipswich	Edinburgh (1848)	
Droitwich	Launceston	Glasgow (1848)	
Durham	Margate	Greenock (1848)	
Folkestone	Newton Abbott	Inverary	
Gloucester	Norwich	Inverness	
Hastings	Oxford	Paisley	
Hereford	Penzance	Perth (1848)	
Hull	Portsmouth	Stirling (1848)	
Kendal	Plymouth		
Lancaster	Teignmouth		
Leeds	Totnes		
Leicester	Trowbridge		
Lichfield	Truro		
Lincoln	Wolverhampton		
Liverpool	Yarmouth		
London			
Lynn			
Manchester (1847)			
Monmouth			
Newbury			
Newcastle			
Newport			
Northampton			
Nottingham			
Oswestry			

Table 34.2 (continued)

*Greenwich Time**
Peterborough
Preston
Ramsgate
Reading
Ripon
Rochester
Salisbury
Scarborough
Sheffield
Shrewsbury
Southampton
Stafford
Stockport
Sunderland
Taunton
Tewkesbury
Tiverton
Tonbridge
Torquay
Wellington
Wells
Weston-super-Mare
Whitehaven
Wigan
Windsor
Worcester (1851)
York

*Dates in brackets are dates of changeover to Greenwich Time where known.

> *train appointed for departure at that hour has already started, when the unmindful traveller thinks that he has still a few minutes to spare. Bearing this fact in mind, it will be wise, upon alighting at a provincial station, to note the difference between the time registered there and London time, so that the discrepancy may be duly allowed for in the traveller's subsequent movements. (Simmons, 1971, p. 32; cf. Cockman, 1976)*

Owing to the publication of maps given by a firm of watch and clock makers, Henry Ellis and Son of Exeter, to all customers it is possible to draw up a directory of which towns and cities were on local and Greenwich time in 1852 (Table 34.2). In fact, some of these towns and cities had changed over to Greenwich time before the railways; for instance, Birmingham under the "leadership" of the indefatigable Osler.[52] Others, for instance Manchester, changed to Greenwich time on exactly the same date as the local railway:

The Committee for General Purposes, having considered a letter from the Lancashire and Yorkshire railway company on 1 December 1847 recommended that all clocks under the control of the Corporation, and that of the church wardens, should be adjusted by the necessary nine minutes, to conform with railway time; a symbolic act of homage by a mercantile and industrial community to the new masters of its traffic (Kellett, 1969, pp. 173–174).

In Scotland, the changeover to Greenwich time was somewhat later. Edinburgh, Glasgow, Greenock, Stirling and Perth all reset their public clocks to Greenwich time on January 29th, 1848.[53]

But there was some opposition to the changeover, most notably from towns on the farther extremities of the East–West axis who had the most time to lose (or gain).[54] Thanks to excellent documentation the debate in the South-west can be followed in some detail. In Exeter the first railway to the city opened on May 1st, 1844. From December, 1847 the Bristol and Exeter Railway ran to Greenwich (London) time but Exeter stuck steadfastly to local mean time. White's *Devonshire Directory* for 1850 gives railway users this advice:

London time, which is kept at all stations, is 11 minutes before Bath and Bristol, 14 minutes before Exeter, and 13 minutes before Plymouth. (Ponsford, 1978, p. 11)

Clocks were provided in the city showing both Greenwich and local time:

As a matter of great public convenience, a new dial affixed at St Johns Church, Fore Street Hill, in this city, exhibits as well as the correct time at Exeter, the railway time, which is several minutes in advance, and non attendance to this has sometimes placed parties in unpleasant situations. The railway time is shown by a silvered minute hand, the minute hand denoting the true time being gilt.[55]

And watches could be bought showing local and Greenwich time. In 1850 Exeter was 14 minutes 12 seconds slow of Greenwich. The campaign to have this discrepancy altered began in earnest, led by the aforementioned Henry Ellis, in 1851 at a town council meeting in which the Mayor was requested to desire the Dean of Exeter Cathedral (the site of the principal clock in the town) to change the clock to

[52] Howse (1980), p. 105 recounts how Osler simply switched Birmingham's town hall clock to Greenwich time one Sunday morning; no real dissent followed this move – all the town's clocks and watches were adjusted to the new time.

[53] Howse (1980), p. 106. This meant clocks had to be put forward 12.5 minutes in Edinburgh and 17 minutes in Glasgow. It is interesting to note that it is the new industrial communities that seem to switch over first to Greenwich time.

[54] It is difficult to know the strength of the opposition, or who the opposition were. Sir George Airy, Astronomer Royal, makes an interesting, if lofty comment, in a letter to Sir Stafford Northcote: "I think it possible that persons of the higher ranks who frequently travel on long lines and possess good watches see very clearly the merits of one side of the question: the far greater mass who are almost stationary are more likely to prefer the other" (cited in Smith, 1976).

[55] *Trewman's Exeter Flying Post*, October 16th, 1845, cited in Ponsford (1980, p. 11). The same device was used in Oxford at this time, according to Howse (1980). See also Davies (1978).

Greenwich time. A petition had been drawn up in favor the previous evening and it "had already received the signatures of the principal firms in the city" (Ponsford, 1978, p. 12). A lengthy debate followed in which it was pointed out that "in a dispute which arose as to a young lady being of age, owing to the Church clock saying she was of age and the Cathedral clock saying she was not, a court of law had decided that the Cathedral clock governed other clocks" (Ponsford, 1978, p. 12). The motion was carried by 16 votes to 5 but the Dean refused to countenance the alteration of the Cathedral clock.[56] This state-of-affairs and others like it prompted the *Athenaum* of the time to remark that it would surprise nobody "to find Bath, and Exeter in the list of places choosing their local right to keep in the rear of the world's great movement" (Ponsford, 1978, p. 13).

At the beginning of August 1852 the telegraph was completed to Exeter railway station causing further pressure for change. An editorial in the local newspaper, for instance, opined that:

> *as the public have become much more locomotive than in former years, every individual is made to feel the personal inconvenience arising from the fluctuation in the computation of time in the various towns . . . We trust the citizens of Exeter will endeavour to secure the advantages which must arise from the adoption of conformity of time, and which has been eagerly seized by a large number of important cities and towns in the UK.*[57]

The cause was taken up by Sir Stafford Northcote, who was instrumental in forming a committee to pressure for the adoption of Greenwich time in the West of England, Bristol, Bath and Exeter. On August 31st, 1852, the matter of conformity to Greenwich time was again raised in Exeter in a council meeting. This meeting was followed, on the 28th of October, by a Public Meeting at the Guildhall at which it was unanimously resolved that public clocks should be altered. The Dean finally gave way and, on November 2nd, 1852, the change to Greenwich time took place; only one day after the first regular time signal was sent down the telegraph lines to Exeter Station from Greenwich:

> *Notice is hereby given "That upon and after Tuesday, the second day of November next; the Cathedral clocks and other public clocks of this city will be set to and indicate Greenwich time."*[58]

[56]It is difficult to gauge the strength of popular opposition to the Greenwich Mean Time proposals in Exeter. The *Memoirs* of Henry Ellis, a private account of the local clockmaker's life meant only for his family (cited in Ponsford, 1978), note only that: "The difference between Railway Time (Greenwich) and Exeter mean time was nearly a quarter of an hour, which was found to be very inconvenient often occasioning the loss of the train. *Through much opposition* Henry succeeded in inducing the authorities here to adopt the former. Railway Time is I believe now general in every town in the Kingdom" (my italics).

[57]*Woolmer's Exeter and Plymouth Gazette*, August, 1852, cited in Ponsford (1978), p. 13.

[58]This notice was placed in the Exeter newspapers. Notice cited in letter to the *Western Morning News*, December 29th, 1936, p. 4, from Henry Harlow. It is interesting to note that the change took place a day later at Topsham, four miles away from Exeter. Was a hierarchical diffusion process in operation?

The change to Greenwich time had already taken place in Bristol at a meeting of the Council on the 14th of September, 1852 (Latimer, 1887). Plymouth followed shortly thereafter,[59] as did Bath and Devonport. The South West was now synchronized with the rest of the country.

By 1855 98 per cent of the public clocks in Great Britain were set to Greenwich Mean Time (Howse, 1980). There were still some problems. For instance, a decision by the Court of Exchequer in 1858 led to legal time being specified as local time (Howse, 1980; Davies, 1978). But on August 2nd, 1880 this final anomaly was ironed out when the Statutes (Definition of Time) Bill was given the Royal Assent. From this date in 1880 all activities in Great Britain were entrained to Greenwich Mean Time.[60]

Conclusions

The hegemony of the mediaeval period was based on two dimensions, culture and economy, intertwined. By the end of the nineteenth century a great restructuring had taken place in which economy became the major dimension of society. The restructuring took place in fits and starts – here progressing, there retreating and there digressing. But take place it did. Through the late eighteenth and most of the nineteenth century it took the form of simple coercion and crude ideological conditioning. But by the late nineteenth century the transformation to a new hegemony was complete. The preconditions for this new hegemony were many. One, on which this paper has concentrated, was a new consciousness of time as the domain of calculation; as an appropriation of the future. By 1880 the owners' time had become own time. The inward notation had become much the same as the outward. Time was now spent: it was no longer measured in tasks completed. Time was now inextricably tied to a future-oriented calculative rationality. For most people time and calculative rationality had become one and the same thing: stages in life's journey of accumulation.

The stage was now set for some of the excesses of twentieth century capitalism. At work – Taylorism, Fordism, even neo-Fordism,[61] at school – anthroponomy,

[59] From the Town Council debate in Plymouth, reported in the *Plymouth, Devonport and Stonehouse Herald*, Sept. 18th, 1852, p. 8, cited in Howse (1980), p. 113:
Mr W. MOORE disapproved of the movement, for workmen would thereby be enabled to leave work 16 minutes earlier every day, but he was sure employers would not be able to get them to come 16 minutes earlier in the morning (*a laugh*). Mr R. RUNDLE so far differed from the last speaker that he believed tradesmen and others would be very glad of a change which would establish an uniform time throughout the Kingdom . . . Mr W. F. COLLIER remarked it would be well if the Mayor could, at the same time, cause Railway trains to arrive at the hours which they were due (*hear, hear*).

[60] The same story can be written for the adoption of Standard time in the United States in the 1880s. Cf. Cottrell (1939), Corliss (1941), Korenbaum (1963), Howse (1980), and especially Abbe (1979).

[61] There is such a vast literature on Taylorism it cannot be cited. However, cf. Braverman (1979), who has been much criticized. On Fordism and neo-Fordism cf. Gramsci (1971), Palloix (1976), Aglietta (1979).

self-discipline (cf. Bourdieu and Passeron, 1977; Chamboredon and Prévot, 1975; Karabel and Halsey, 1977; Bernstein, 1975); at home – policing of the family and the conspicuous consumption of leisure time (cf. Donzelot, 1979; Pasquino, 1978; Knemeyer, 1980; Linder, 1970; Pred, 1981a). And the splitting-off of work, school, and leisure. And all this bound together by state and capital in a hopefully gordian knot of "governmentality"[62] and positivist science.

If there is a way to cut the knot part of the answer must lie in changing consciousness of time. But not through an unrestricted atavism. There must be a way to:

> *combine in a new synthesis elements of the old and of the new, finding an imagery based neither upon the seasons nor upon the market but upon human occasions. Punctuality in working hours would express respect for one's fellow workmen. And unpurposive passing of time would be behaviour which the culture approved. (Thompson, 1967, p. 96)*

Acknowledgments

The research on the adoption of Greenwich Mean Time would not have been possible without the help of Mr D. Howse (Head of Navigation and Astronomy, National Maritime Museum, Greenwich), Mr G. Ottley (Librarian, Leicester University), Mr C. N. Ponsford (Exeter), Mr M. M. Rowe (Area Archivist, Devon Record Office, Exeter) and Mr H. M. Smith (Former Head, Time Section, Greenwich Observatory, Herstmonceux).

References

Abbe, W. W. (1979): *The Arrival of Standard Time.* Paper presented to the 75th Annual Meeting of the Association of American Geographers, Philadelphia, April 25th, 1979.

Aglietta, M. (1979): *A Theory of Capitalist Regulation: The US Experience.* London: New Left Books.

Andersen, H. W. (1961): *Work and Leisure.* New York.

Bagwell, P. (1960): *The Transport Revolution from 1770.* London: Batsford.

Bernstein, B. (1975): *Class, Codes and Control: Vol 3, Towards a Theory of Educational Transmissions.* London: Routledge and Kegan Paul.

Bertaux, D. (1977): *Destins Personnels et Structure de Classe.* Paris: Presses Universitaires de France.

Bourdieu, P. (1963): "The Attitude of the Algerian Peasant Toward Time", in J. Pitt-Rivers (ed.), *Mediterranean Countrymen: Essays in the Social Anthropology of the Mediterranean.* Paris: Mouton.

Bourdieu, P. and Passeron, J. C. (1977): *Reproduction in Education, Society and Culture.* London: Sage.

Bourdieu, P. and Passeron, J. C. (1979): *The Inheritors: French Students and Their Relation to Culture.* Chicago: Chicago University Press.

Braverman, H. (1974): *Labor and Monopoly Capital: The Degradation of Work in the Twentieth Century.* New York: Monthly Review Press.

[62] I have taken this term from Foucault (1979). Most of Foucault's more recent work is relevant here.

Buckley, J. H. (1967): *The Triumph of Time: A Study of the Victorian Concepts of Time, History, Progress and Decadence.* Cambridge, Mass: Belknap Press.
Burnett, J. ed. (1974): *Useful Toil: Authobiographies of Working People From the 1820's to the 1920's.* London: Allen Lane.
Chamboredon, J. C. and Prévot, J. (1975): Changes in the Definition of Early Childhood and the New Forms of Symbolic Violence. *Theory and Society*, 2, 331–350.
Corliss, C. J. (1941): *The Day of the Two Noons.* Washington.
Cottrell, W. F. (1939): Of Time and the Railroader. *American Sociological Review*, 4, 190–198.
Davidoff, L. (1973): *The Best Circles: Society, Etiquette and the Season.* London: Croom Helm.
Davies, A. C. (1978): Greenwich and Standard Time. *History Today*, 28, 194–199.
De Grazia, S. (1962): *Of Time, Work, and Leisure.* New York: Twentieth Century Fund.
Delaney, T. (1963): *A Century of Soccer.* London: Heinemann.
Donzelot, J. (1979): *The Policing of Families.* New York: Pantheon.
Foucault, M. (1977): *Discipline and Punish: The Birth of the Prison.* London: Allen Lane.
Foucault, M. (1979): On Governmentality. *Ideology and Consciousness*, No. 5, 5–21.
Gramsci, A. (1971): *Selections from the Prison Note Books.* London: Lawrence and Wishart.
Great Western Railway (1841): *Timetable.* York: National Railway Museum.
Gregory, D. (1978): "The Process of Industrial Change 1730–1900", in R. A. Dodgshon and R. A. Butlin (eds.), *An Historical Geography of England and Wales.* London: Academic Press, pp. 291–311.
Gregory, D. (1981): *Regional Transformation and Industrial Revolution.* London: MacMillan.
Hardy, T. (1886): *The Mayor of Casterbridge.* London: Pan edition (1978).
Harrison, B. (1967): Religion and Recreation in Nineteenth Century England. *Past and Present*, no. 38, 98–125.
Hearn, F. (1978): *Domination, Legitimation, and Resistance. The Incorporation of the Nineteenth-Century English Working Class.* Westport, Connecticut: Greenwood Press.
Howse, D. (1980): *Greenwich Time and the Discovery of the Longitude.* Oxford: Oxford University Press.
Jones, K. and Williamson, K. (1979): The Birth of the School Room: A Study of the Transformation in the Discursive Conditions of English Popular Education in the First-Half of the Nineteenth Century. *Ideology and Consciousness*, no. 5, 59–110.
Karabel, J. and Halsey, A. H. eds. (1977): *Power and Ideology in Education.* New York: Oxford University Press.
Keeton, G. W. (1972): *The Football Revolution: A Study of the Changing Pattern of Association Football.* Newton Abbott: David and Charles.
Kellett, J. R. (1969): *The Impact of Railways on Victorian Cities.* London: Routledge and Kegan Paul.
Knemeyer, F. (1980): Polizei. *Economy and Society*. 9, 172–196.
Korenbaum, M. (1963): "Translator's Preface" in G. Gurvitch, *The Spectrum of Social Time.* Dordrecht: D. Reidel.
Latimer, J. (1887): *The Annals of Bristol in the Nineteenth Century.* Bristol.
Linder, S. B. (1970): *The Harried Leisure Class.* New York: Columbia University Press.
McCann, P. ed. (1977): *Popular Education and Socialization in the Nineteenth Century.* London: Methuen.
McCrea, W. H. (1975): *The Royal Greenwich Observatory.* London: HMSO.
McKendrick, N. (1961): Josiah Wedgewood and Factory Discipline. *Historical Journal*, 4, 30–55.
Magoun, F. P. Jr. (1938): *History of Football From the Beginnings to 1871.* Bochum Verlag Heinrich Pöpinghaus O.H.G.

Malcolmson, R. W. (1973): *Popular Recreations in English Society, 1700–1850.* Cambridge: Cambridge University Press.
Marx, K. (1976): *Capital, Volume 1.* Harmondsworth: Penguin/New Left Review.
Meller, H. (1976): *Leisure and the Changing City, 1870–1914.* London: Routledge and Kegan Paul.
Meyerhoff, N. (1955): *Time in Literature.* Berkeley: University of California Press.
Palloix, C. (1976): "The Labour Process: From Fordism to neo-Fordism" in *The Labour Process and Class Strategies.* Brighton: Conference of Socialist Economists.
Parkes, D. N. and Thrift, N. J. (1979): Time Spacemakers and Entrainment. *Transactions, Institute of British Geographers,* N.S. 4, 353–372.
Pasquino, P. (1978): Theatrum Politicum: The Genealogy of Capital-Place and the State of Prosperity. *Ideology and Consciousness,* no. 4, 41–54.
Patrides, C. A. ed. (1976): *Aspects of Time.* Manchester: Manchester University Press.
Pimlott, J. A. R. (1947): *The Englishman's Holiday: A Social History.* London: Faber and Faber (reprinted 1976, Hassocks: Harvester).
Pocock, J. G. A. (1971): *Politics, Language and Time: Essays on Political Thought and History.* London: Methuen.
Pollard, S. (1963): Factory Discipline in the Industrial Revolution. *Economic History Review,* Second Series, 16, 260–269.
Pollard, S. (1964): *The Genesis of Modern Management.* London: Edward Arnold.
Ponsford, C. N. (1978): *Time in Exeter: A History of 700 Years of Clocks and Clock-making in an English Provincial City.* Exeter: Heapwell Vale Books.
Pred, A. (1981a): Production, Family, and Free-time Projects: A Time-Geographic Perspective on the Individual and Societal Change in Nineteenth-Century U.S. Cities. *Journal of Historical Geography, 7, 3–36.*
Quinlan, M. J. (1941): Victorian Prelude: A History of English Manners 1700–1830. New York.
Reid, D. A. (1976): The Decline of Saint Monday: 1766–1876, *Past and Present,* no. 71, 76–101.
Samuel, R. (1977): Workshop of the World: Steam Power and Hand Technology in Mid-Victorian Britain. *History Workshop,* no. 3, 6–72.
Smith, H. M. (1976): Greenwich Time and the Prime Meridian. *Vistas in Astronomy,* 20.
Simmons, J. (ed.) (1971): *The Railway Traveller's Handy Book of Hints, Suggestions and Advice Before the Journey, on the Journey and After the Journey.* Bath: Adams and Dart (1862 edition).
Sturt, G. (1923): *The Wheelwright's Shop.* Cambridge: Cambridge University Press.
Thompson, E. P. (1963): *The Making of the English Working Class.* London: Gollancz.
Thompson, E. P. (1967): Time, Work-Discipline and Industrial Capitalism. *Past and Present,* 38, 56–97.
Thrift, N. J. (1977a): *The Diffusion of Greenwich Mean Time in Great Britain: An Essay on a Neglected Aspect of Social and Economic History.* (University of Leeds, School of Geography Working Paper 188.) Leeds.
Wright, L. (1968): *Clockwork Man.* London: Elek.
Zerubavel, E. (1977): The French Republican Calendar: A Case Study in the Sociology of Time. *American Sociological Review,* 42, 868–77.

35

EXCEPTIONALISM IN GEOGRAPHY: A METHODOLOGICAL EXAMINATION

F.K. Schaefer

The dominant methodological statement in American geography in the 1940s and 1950s was provided by Richard Hartshorne's volume *The nature of geography* (see **chapter 24**). Although it had many detractors (including Sauer), the first major challenge in print was this article by Schaefer. Much quantitative geography was already under way and many of the elements of the spatial scientific approach were developing anyway. But Schaefer's essay was widely regarded as a rallying point for a new generation of human geographers. It was equally dismissed as poor scholarship and irrelevant by others. The conditions of its publication added to the controversy surrounding it. Hartshorne was one of the most eminent US geographers of his day. Schaefer was a refugee who had fled Nazi Germany to the USA because of his left-wing politics and thought that the FBI was spying on him. The fact that he died before the article was fully finished and that the period was one of anti-communist witch-hunts may have added to the sense of martyrdom many geographers found in Schaefer. At the time, the exchange between the two raised strong passions. Hartshorne wrote a detailed line-by-line refutation of the article accusing it of misrepresenting both himself and his sources [*Annals of the American Association of Geographers* 45, 207–44, 1954; also *Perspective on the nature of geography*. Washington, DC, 1959]. But with hindsight it is clear that they shared much and that the differences between them were not as monumental as many then imagined. Both relied upon mainly German sources such as Kant, Humboldt and Hettner and both directed geographers towards spatial patterns. Even so, Schaefer was among the first geographers to teach the ideas of Christaller, Von Thünen and Lösch, which Hartshorne had not acknowledged but which were to become the mainstay of 1960s human geography. He also positioned human geography in the social

* I am much indebted to Professor Gustav Bergmann of the Philosophy Department of The State University of Iowa who has kindly read the manuscript and made many valuable suggestions.

** Editor's Note. Professor Fred K. Schaefer died on June 6, 1953. Galley for this article was read by Professor Gustav Bergmann.

sciences and its philosophical debates rather than the humanities or natural sciences. Geography, he argues, must be like other social sciences and not 'exceptional'.

Source: Exceptionalism in geography: a methodological examination. *Annals of the Association of American Geographers* 43, 226–49, 1953.

The methodology of a field is not a grab bag of special techniques. In geography such techniques as map making, "methods" of teaching, or historical accounts of the development of the field are still often mistaken for methodology. It is one of the purposes of the present paper to help dispel this confusion. Methodology proper deals with the position and scope of the field within the total system of the sciences and with the character and nature of its concepts.

Methodology thrives on change and evolution. In an active field concepts are continuously either refined or entirely discarded; laws and hypotheses are, as the case may be, confirmed or disconfirmed or, perhaps, reduced to the status of no longer satisfactory approximations. Methodology is the logic of this process. That is why, particularly in young disciplines, methodological debate is a sign of health. Seen in this light, the methodology of geography is too complacent. Some fundamental ideas have remained unchallenged for decades though there is ample reason to doubt their power. Some others, half forgotten, lie scattered around, exposed to slow erosion like the tells in the plain of Iraq. Spethmann[1] made this point when he complained in 1928 that the methodology Hettner[2] had just published was in the main a collection of articles twenty or thirty years old, at a time when virtually all the other sciences experienced almost hectic change and progress. Turning to America, one may add that Hartshorne[3] in 1939 restated many of Hettner's views with little change or criticism. Worse than that, Hartshorne's own work, undoubtedly an important milestone in the history of American geographical thought, went itself unchallenged through the thirteen years that have passed since its publication.

The methodological literature is small. Alexander von Humboldt, rightly called the father of scientific geography, was also the first relatively modern author to pay attention to the logic of its concepts. Two generations passed before the next major contribution was made by Hettner. But only two years after Hettner's book had appeared an Austrian philosopher of science, Viktor Kraft,[4] published an essay in the field which is as yet unexcelled in clarity and succinctness. Hartshorne's work in this country was the only other, and is so far the last major attempt. It will appear from the following discussion that while Hartshorne follows Hettner rather closely in some respects, Kraft may be said to continue more nearly the tradition of Humboldt.

[1] Hans Spethmann, *Dynamische Länderkunde*. Breslau, 1928. p. 119.

[2] Alfred Hettner, *Die Geographie, ihre Geschichte, ihr Wesen und ihre Methoden*. Breslau, 1927.

[3] Richard Hartshorne, "The Nature of Geography," *Annals of the Association of American Geographers*, XXIX (1939): 171–658. Reprinted in book form. Page references cited below are to the 4th edition (1951).

[4] Viktor Kraft, "Die Geographie als Wissenschaft," in *Enzyklopädie der Erdkunde*, ed. Oskar Kende. Leipzig, Wien, 1929.

I

Geographers writing on the scope and nature of geography often begin quite apologetically as if they had to justify its very existence. And strangely, or perhaps, psychologically speaking, not so strangely, they go on claiming too much. In such writings geography, together with history, emerges as *the* "integrating science," completely different from other disciplines, whose unique importance finds its expression in the special methods which it must use to reach its profound results. Unhappily, the actual results of geographical research, while not to be minimized, are somewhat lacking in those startling new and deeper insights which one is led to expect from such exuberant characterizations of the field. In fact, the progress of geography was slower than that of some other social sciences such as, for instance, economics. Some of this lag is perhaps due to the unrealistic ambitions fostered by the unclear idea of a unique integrating science with a unique methodology all its own. On the other hand, there is no need for the apologies which so often precede the exaggerated claims. The existence of a field is after all mainly the product of the division of labor; it needs no "methodological" justification. In this obvious sense geography is no doubt an important field.

With the development of the natural sciences in the eighteenth and nineteenth centuries it became apparent that mere description would not do. Description, even if followed by classification, does not explain the manner in which phenomena are distributed over the world. To explain the phenomena one has described means always to recognize them as instances of laws. Another way of saying the same thing is to insist that science is not so much interested in individual facts as in the patterns they exhibit. In geography the major pattern-producing variables are, of course, spatial. Humboldt, who had come from the natural sciences, and also Ritter, accepted the proposition that all natural relations and, therefore, all spatial relations, were governed by laws. For this new type of work tools had to be provided in the form of concepts and laws. Hence geography had to be conceived as the science concerned with the formulation of the laws governing the spatial distribution of certain features on the surface of the earth. The latter limitation is essential. For, with the successful rise of geophysics, astronomy, and geology, geography can no longer deal with the whole earth, but only the earth's surface and "with the earthly (irdischen) things that fill its spaces."[5]

Humboldt and Ritter thus recognized as the major concern of geography the manner in which the natural phenomena, including man, were distributed in space. This implies that geographers must describe and explain the manner in which things combine "to fill an area." These combinations change, of course, from area to area. Different areas contain different factors or the same factors in different combinations. These differences either in the combination of factors or in their arrangement from place to place underlie the common sense notion that areas differ. Following the Greek geographers, this viewpoint is called the chorographic or chorological one, depending on the level of abstraction. Geography, thus, must pay attention to the spatial arrangement of the phenomena in an area and not so

[5] Carl Ritter, *Über die historischen Elemente in der geographischen Wissenschaft*. Berlin, 1833. p. 45.

much to the phenomena themselves. Spatial relations are the ones that matter in geography, and no others. Nonspatial relations found among the phenomena in an area are the subject matter of other specialists such as the geologist, anthropologist, or economist. Of all the limitations on geography this one seems to be the most difficult for geographers to observe. To judge even from recent research they do not always clearly distinguish between, say, social relations on the one hand and spatial relations among social factors on the other. Actually, one may safely say that most of what we find in any given area is of primary interest to the other social scientists. For instance, the connections between ideology and political behaviour, or the lawful connections between the psychological traits of a population and its economic institutions do not concern the geographer. If he attempts to explain such matters the geographer turns into a jack of all trades. Like all others the geographer had better cultivate his speciality, the laws concerning spatial arrangements. But to say this is not to say that some of these "geographical" laws are not of interest to other disciplines.

Kraft, in discussing Humboldt and Ritter, agrees with them that geography is, at least potentially, a science trying to discover laws; that it is limited to the earth's surface; and that it is essentially chorological. Incidentally, he also feels that this suffices to set geography logically apart as a discipline of its own.

The chorological viewpoint presented geography with a problem that has caused more methodological controversy and misunderstanding than any other. The geographer's investigations, be he a physical, economic, or political geographer, are of two different types: either *systematic* or *regional*. A region contains, to be sure, a special, unique, yet in some ways uniform combination of kinds or categories of phenomena. The detail with which the regional geographer describes, lists, or catalogues these features at the outset of his investigation depends, of course, on the size of the region considered. Next he will want to gather information as to the spatial distribution of the individuals in each class. But this information, too, belongs to his data rather than his results. For it does not go beyond mere description. His proper task as a social scientist begins only at this stage. First,he must try to find those relations obtaining among the individuals and the classes by virtue of which the area considered has that unitary character that makes it a region. Second, he must identify the relations which obtain in this particular area as instances of the causal interrelations that hold, by virtue of general laws among such features, individuals, classes, or what have you, in all known circumstances. This second step amounts, therefore, to an application of systematic geography to the area in question. Only after both these steps have been taken can one say that a scientific understanding of the region has been achieved.

This brings us to systematic geography. Its procedure is in principle not different from that of any other social or natural science which searches for laws or, what amounts to the same thing, has reached the systematic stage. Spatial relations among two or more selected classes of phenomena must be studied all over the earth's surface in order to obtain a generalization or law. Assume, for instance, that two phenomena are found to occur frequently at the same place. A hypothesis may then be formed to the effect that whenever members of the one class are found in a place, members of the other class will be found there also, under conditions specified by the hypothesis. To test any such hypothesis the geographer will need a larger number of cases and of variables than he could find in any one region. But if it is confirmed in a sufficient number of cases then the hypothesis becomes a law that may be utilized to "explain" situations not yet considered. The present conditions of the field indicate a stage of development, well known from other social sciences, which finds most geographers still busy with classifications rather than looking for laws. We know that classification is the first step in any kind of systematic work. But when the other steps, which naturally follow, are not taken, and classifications become the end of scientific investigation, then the field become sterile . . .

Hettner, and even Kraft, speak of the two complementary emphases [systematic and regional] as founding a "dualism" which sets geography apart from all other disciplines. It should be already clear that there is, in fact, nothing unique or peculiar to geography in all this. If the term is meant to indicate opposition or conflict, then it is outright misleading. Yet, this so-called "dualism" has been cited in support of the claim that geography is a methodologically unique discipline. Nor is the complexity of the situation that faces the regional geographer in any sense out of the ordinary so that he would have a peculiarly difficult task of "integration," in another meaning of the glittering term. Quite to the contrary; he is at all fours with the other social scientists. When the economist applies his generalizations or laws to a given economic order, he deals not only with the complexity of the purely economic situation but takes account of the political, psychological, and social factors that influence it. This, after all, is the gist of so-called institutional economics. Similarly, a sociologist or anthropologist who analyzes a given primitive society, or a communist or agricultural one, deals with very complex situations In the pretentious language of some geographers, such a sociologist "integrates" not only heterogeneous phenomena but, clearly, also heterogeneous laws. To say that the task of those social scientists is less complex, or less integrative than that of the geographer makes no sense. If anything, it is even more complex. For, the geographer's specific task in the analysis of a region is limited to spatial relations only. Accordingly, even the most complete geographical analysis of any region gives only partial insight into it. After the geographer is done there is still much work left before one understands fully the social structure of that region. Obviously; for, how could such an understanding be attained without even considering such factors as the ecology, economics, institutions, and mores of the region. In a manner of speaking, the geographer provides only the setting for the further studies of the other social scientists. It is, therefore, absurd to maintain that the geographers are distinguished among the scientists through the integration of heterogeneous phenomena which they achieve. There is nothing extraordinary about geography in that respect. One may conjecture that this notion is a hangover from the time when there were no social sciences and not much natural science, and when such quaint and encyclopedic endeavors as natural history and cosmology still occupied their place.

We have seen that there is a whole group of ideas which are variations of a common theme: geography is quite different from all the other sciences, methodologically unique, as it were. Influential and persistent as this position is in its several variations, it deserves a name of its own. I shall call it *exceptionalism*, and, for the moment, inquire into some of its historical roots.

II

The father of exceptionalism is Immanuel Kant. Though undoubtedly one of the great philosophers of the eighteenth century, Kant was a poor geographer when compared with his contemporaries or even Bernhard Varenius who died more than one hundred and fifty years before him. Kant made the exceptionalist claim not only for geography but also for history. According to him history and geography find themselves in an exceptional position different from that of the so-called systematic sciences. This grouping of geography with history has tempted many subsequent writers to elaborate the alleged similarity in order to obtain some insight into the nature of geography. This is undoubtedly one of the roots of the historicist variant of the claim to uniqueness with which we shall have to deal presently. But let us first inquire into what Kant himself said.

Kant taught a course in physical geography all through his teaching career, almost fifty times. The text of these lectures or, rather, class notes, was published in 1802, two years before his death.[6] It is in this work that one finds the statement on geography and history that has been quoted so reverently again and again by those who make it the cornerstone of geographical method. Ritter[7] used it; so did Hettner and, eventually Hartshorne. Humboldt, interestingly, neither quotes Kant nor shares his views. Neither does Kraft. But now for the words of the master:

> *We can refer to our empirical perceptions either according to conceptions or according to time and space where they are actually found. The classification of perceptions according to concepts is the logical one, however, that according to time and space is the physical one. By the former we obtain a system of nature, such as that of Linnaeus, and by the latter a geographical description of nature.*
>
> *For example, if I say that cattle is included under the class of quadrupeds, or under the group of this class having cloven hooves, that is a classification that I make in my head, hence a logical classification. The system of nature is like a register of the whole; here I place each thing in its competent class even if they are found in different, widely separated places of the world.*
>
> *According to the physical classification, however, things are considered in their location on earth. The system of nature refers to their place in their class, but geographical description of*

[6] Immanuel Kant, *Physische Geographie*. Ed. F. T. Rink, Koenigsberg, 1802. In fairness to Kant it should be said that according to Adickes, the famous Kant scholar, the text as edited by Rink and used by Ritter, Hettner, and Hartshorne is of doubtful authenticity. Four fifths of the manuscript is not in Kant's handwriting. It probably consists of notes taken by students during the very first semester in which Kant gave that course. Also, editing was done shortly before Kant's death when, as Adickes points out, he was too ill to make any alterations in what he had written or dictated in class before 1756. Quite apart from this, Erich Adickes in his book *Untersuchungen zu Kant's physischer Geographie* (Tuebingen, 1911) is rather distressed about the geographical ignorance displayed by his philosophical idol.

[7] Hartshorne, *op.cit.*, p.136, maintains that Ritter 'does not appear to have stated the comparison as clearly as either Kant or Humboldt.'

nature shows where they are to be found on earth. Thus the lizard and the crocodile are basically the same animal. The crocodile is merely a tremendously large lizard. But they exist in different places. The crocodile lives in the Nile and the lizard on the land, also in this country. In general, here we consider the scene of nature, the earth itself and the places in which things are actually found, in contrast with the systems of nature where we inquire not about the place of birth but about the similarity of forms . . .

History and geography both could be called, so to speak, a description, with the difference that the former is a description according to time while the latter a description according to space. Hence, history and geography increase our knowledge in respect to time and space.

. . . Hence history differs from geography only in respect to time and space. The former is, as stated, a report of events which follow another in time.The other is a report of events which take place side by side in space. History is a narrative, geography is a description . . .

Geography is a name for a description of nature and the whole world. Geography and history together fill up the entire area of our perception: geography that of space and history that of time.[8]

Kant's gigantic achievements in his own field as well as the influence which this unfortunate statement has had in ours require careful criticism, systematic as well as historical. Systematic criticism proceeds along two main lines. *First,* the distinction as intended is untenable in itself. It is simply not true that such systematic disciplines as, say, physics abstract from or otherwise neglect the spatio-temporal coordinates of the objects they study. One only needs to think of Newtonian astronomy to see immediately how wrongheaded this idea is. For what are the "systematic" laws of astronomy, such as Kepler's laws, if not a set of rules to compute from the positions of the heavenly bodies at any given moment their positions at any other moment? The error is really so obvious that one must immediately ask for a plausible cause. The answer, I suggest, is historical. When Kant wrote the passage in his youth he had probably not yet undergone the full impact of Newtonian science. Accordingly, he thinks of systematic lawfulness as essentially classificatory in the style of Aristotle and Linnaeus rather than of the process law variety of Newton. For the "precritical" Kant of 1756 this makes sense, at least biographically. But one may well doubt whether he would still have written this passage during his critical period, in his maturity during the seventies and eighties of the eighteenth century, after he had undergone the full impact of Newton and Hume. Into this period, however,fall the achievements on which his authority rests. How unfortunate, then, that so many geographers kowtow to a patently immature idea of his youth.

Second, we noticed that the resulting notion of geography is descriptive in the narrowest sense of the term. Obviously, it does not follow that there are no laws either of geography or of the socio-historical process simply because Kant thought that there were none. The facts have long proved him wrong. Historically, one can again understand how he came to hold such views around the middle of the eighteenth century. The social sciences were virtually nonexistent at that time. Their place was taken either by narrative history or by moral reflections or by a

[8] Immanuel Kant, *Physische Geographie.* Ed. F. T. Rink, Königsberg, 1802. Vol. I. pp. 6–8.

mixture of these two. The pioneer work of Bodin was forgotten; Macchiavelli was hated or refuted as a diabolic tempter; Montesquieu was more often praised than understood; the great contributions of Voltaire, Hume and Adam Smith were either still in the future or had not yet penetrated into the academic precincts of provincial Koenigsberg. (One look into Kant's *Moral Geography* or, as we would now say, comparative anthropology, suffices to convince one that it is as crudely and clumsily classificatory and enumerative as his *Physical Geography*.) The biological disciplines were at that time still largely classificatory or, as one says in this case, taxonomic. So it was not unnatural after all, that Kant in 1756 conceived of geography exclusively as a catalogue of the spatial arrangement and distribution of taxonomic features. What he formulated was therefore not so much the methodological schema of what we now call geography but, rather, in unusually abstract terms, the pattern of the then fashionable cosmologies whose literary history goes back to the Middle Ages. Humboldt's "Kosmos" is the last and, because of its stylistic merits, the most famous specimen of this literary genre. So it is forgotten that Humboldt himself in his other writings distinguished very well between cosmological description on the one hand and geography on the other. The literary charm of "Kosmos" has, unfortunately, overshadowed this fact. Yet, to judge Humboldt as a geographer by what he says in "Kosmos" is like judging Darwin's contribution to biology from the diary that he kept on the Beagle. For that matter, even in the introductory chapter of "Kosmos" Humboldt[9] patiently explained to the general public the difference between science and cosmology. All sciences, according to him, search for laws, or, as the later term goes, are nomothetic. Cosmology is *not* a rational science but at best thoughtful contemplation of the universe. Such contemplation has its place. Whatever else assumes the "pretentious name of a system of nature" is nothing but taxonomy, a mere catalogue of phenomena. Having delivered himself briefly of these fundamental observations, Humboldt, naturally enough in the introduction to his own cosmology, goes on to discuss the field of cosmology, only occasionally touching on goegraphy. Cosmology is descriptive, something like an art. He advises it should not be studied without a good previous training in such systematic sciences as physics, astronomy, chemistry, anthropology, biology, geology, and *geography*. It is unfortunate that Hettner and, following him, Hartshorne, mistake this discussion for one of the methodology of geography. Humboldt is really not an authority properly cited in support of exceptionalism. One must not be misled by the circumstance that the great Kant in his day called geography what in Humboldt's terminology is *cosmology* . . .

III

Hettner's great prestige helped to perpetuate the confusion that has just been unraveled. Invoking the formidable authority of Kant, Hettner successfully

[9] Alexander von Humboldt, *Kosmos. Entwurf einer physischen Weltbeschreibung*. Stuttgart, Tuebingen, 1845. Vol I. p. 66.

impressed upon geography the exceptionalist claim in analogy to history. On this basic fallacy he built an elaborate argument. The principles of natural history or cosmology were forced upon geography. Spurious similarities between history and geography were constructed. Thus geography was laid open to the invasion of a whole host of nonscientific, not to say antiscientific ideas: the typically romantic argument from uniqueness; the hypostatization of the quite uncontroversial fact that variables must be expected to interact into an antianalytical holism; in connection with this the spurious claim for a specific integrating function of geography; and, finally, the appeal to the intuition and artistic touch of the investigator in preference to the sober objectivity of standard scientific method. Some at least of these points must now be taken up in detail.

Let us begin with a brief statement of Hettner's position in one of its two major aspects. Both history and geography are essentially chorological. History arranges phenomena in time, geography in space. Both, in contrast to the other disciplines, integrate phenomena heterogeneous among themselves. Also, these phenomena are unique. No historical event and historical period is like any other. In geography no two phenomena and no two regions are alike. Thus both fields face the task of explaining the unique. Such explanation, is therefore, unlike all scientific explanation which "explains" by subsumption under laws. But there are no laws for the unique; little use, then, in looking for historical or geographical laws or prediction. The best one can hope for is, in Dilthey's fashion, some sort of "understanding" or, more frankly, empathetic understanding. An idiomatic difference between German and English has been instrumental in obscuring the basically antiscientific bias of this doctrine. Hettner calls history "time-Wissenschaft" and geography "space-Wissenschaft." Hartshorne, as far as the dictionary goes quite correctly, translates this into "time science" and "space science." The point is that the German term Wissenschaft is much wider than the English "science" or, for that matter, the French "science." Wissenschaft for a German is *any* organized body of knowledge, not only what we call a science. Law is called Rechstiswissenschaft; literary criticism or even numismatics, if cultivated with the proper Teutonic thoroughness and erudition may acquire the status of Wissenschaften in their own right. That much for Hettner's position and terminology. Now for criticism.

The use of the term history in methodological discussion is tantalizingly ambiguous. For the sake of precision it will here for the moment be given a very narrow meaning. History or historical research is the ascertainment of events that occurred in the past. Of course, not all past events are of equal interest to the historian. What he cares for are such phenomena as, say, the movement of the American frontier during the nineteenth century, or the reception of Roman law at the end of the Middle Ages. However, there is no need to begin with a methodological distinction between these and other past events. Historically significant facts are simply those which interest the historian in view of the patterns into which he hopes to arrange them. It should be granted without argument that the ascertaining of past events, even if they are not as elusive as the thought and motives of dead people, is by no means a simple matter. Quite to the contrary. Many sciences and also the most elaborate "scientific method" of inference from traces and relics to what they are the traces and relics of, must be put into the service of this most difficult undertaking of ascertaining the historical course of events. In this noncontroversial, auxiliary sense history certainly makes use of science and its methods. But what it thus achieves is nevertheless mere description and, in the nature of things, a very selective description at that. Science or, perhaps, Wissenschaft begins only when the historian is no longer an historian in the narrow sense and tries to fit his facts into a pattern. This, whether they know it or not, is what all historians try to do. What then, logically speaking, are they doing? At this point the argument begins. A baffling variety of analyses has been proposed. Basically there are two views, the scientific approach and historicism.

The scientific view, which is here taken, claims that all the data, which the historian in the narrow sense of the term collects, are nothing but raw material for the social scientist. The historian, in constructing his pattern is, therefore, whether he knows it or not, a social scientist. In other words, apart from all the technical difficulties which were just mentioned, there is no difference in principle between a social scientist's use of the last census report on the one hand and his use of what historians have found out about the census variables in ancient Rome on the other. At this point, the terminological awkwardness of defining history as narrowly as it has been done for the sake of precision becomes obvious. For no worth-while "historian" will stop there. Assume, for instance, that he is interested in the market prices that prevailed in ancient Rome during a certain period. Naturally, he will first have to find out what they were. But then he will wish to go beyond that limited goal and try to find out how demand and supply interacted with each other and the other relevant social factors to produce those prices. The causal relations on which he draws for such "explanation" are *not* special historical laws but obviously, such as they are, the laws of economic theory. Similarly in all other instances. This is the point. With reference to geography, it follows that the historian who goes, as all historians do, beyond mere fact finding, is comparable to the regional geographer. In getting the facts the historian does what the regional geographer does in getting his. In trying to understand or, better, to explain them he does exactly what the regional geographer does in applying systematic geography to his region. In this broader sense of history, history is a science or, less ambiguously, history is social science applied to the conditions of a special "historical situation." Turned this way Hettner's analogy is acceptable. But then we have merely followed his words, not his meaning. What is this meaning? This brings us to the other view, historicism.

Historicism maintains that there is an alternative, radically different way of understanding the past or, for that matter, the present as a product of its past. The gist of it is the belief that by merely arranging the past events in their temporal order some sort of "meaningful" pattern, cyclic, progressive, or otherwise, will appear. To understand anything it is necessary and sufficient to know its history. Again, there is no argument if one takes that to mean that knowledge of the past state of a system *and of the laws of its development* leads to the knowledge of its present state. But what understanding can be gained merely from contemplating the successive stages of an unfolding process is hard to see. In other words, in the historicist interpretation the "genetic method" yields nothing.

For better or worse the antiscientific spirit of historicism was one of the major intellectual forces of the nineteenth century. Through Hettner it has penetrated geographical thought and, as we see it, powerfully affected its course. Characteristically, the very first sentence of Hettner's methodological work reads: "The present can always be understood only from the past." Also, his work on social and cultural geography exemplifies the genetic method applied to geography. And, as one would expect from a man of his breadth and vision, much of the material is not at all geographical but anthropological, cultural, or political.[10] To be sure, that makes for good reading. But Humboldt's *Kosmos*, too, makes good reading; yet it is not geography. Among American geographers, Carl Sauer is perhaps the outstanding representative of historicism, building his geography consistently on Hettner's premise stated above.

The argument for the uniqueness of the geographical material stems both logically and historically from historicism. The main protagonist of this line of thought in America is Hartshorne. So it is easily understood why he makes so much of the old Kantian parallelism between history and geography. If history, according to the historicist, deals with unique events and if geography is like history, then geography, too, deals with the unique and must try to "understand" rather than search for laws. The formal syllogism is beyond reproach. To refute it one must, as we have tried to do, attack its premise. So let us first turn to the uniqueness argument as such and only then to the use Hartshorne makes of it.

The main difficulty of the uniqueness argument is that, as Max Weber has pointed out, it proves too much. Are there really two stones completely alike in all minute details of shape, color, and chemical composition? Yet, Galileo's law of falling bodies holds equally for both. Similarly, limited as our present psychological knowledge is, it seems safe to say that no two people would register identical scores on all tests as yet devised. Does it follow that our psychologists have so far discovered not a single law? What it all comes down to is a matter of degree. In the physical sciences we have succeeded in discovering a set of variables such that if two objects or situations, no matter how different they are in other respects, agree in these variables or indices, then their future with respect to these indices will be the same and predictable. To what extent and how soon any other field will reach a state as satisfactory as this is a matter of fact, to be decided by trial and error, not to be prejudged by pseudomethodological argument. Of course, the social sciences are not as well developed as physics. This is, indeed, what we mean when we call them less developed. On the other hand, it is also true that sciences which are less developed in this sense often resort with remarkable success to the search for statistical laws. Whether this kind of lawfulness is a measure of our temporary ignorance or must be taken as ultimate is a purely speculative point. Surely, the recent development in physics should give pause to anybody who attempts to

[10] Alfred Hettner, *Vergleichende Länderkunde*. Vol. IV. Leipzig, Berlin, 1935; *Der Gang der Kultur über die Erde*. Leipzig, Berlin, 1929; *Das Europäische Russland*. Leipzig, Berlin, 1905.

deny on these ground the logical unity of the sciences. To apply all this to geography, the claim is, then, that the difference between the differences between two "unique" regions on the one hand and the equally numerous differences between our two stones, on the other, is again a matter of degree.

There is still another misunderstanding that prevents some from fully appreciating this point. Stones do not really, as Galileo's formula tacitly assumes, fall in a vacuum. And they fall differently according to the characteristics of the medium through which they travel. Airplanes, by the way, do not fall at all in the ordinary course of events. Does that mean that Galileo's law is false; or that there are as many laws as there are atmospheric conditions; and still another set of laws for airplanes? Obviously, this is not the way that science operates. What scientists do is, rather, this. *They apply to each concrete situation jointly all the laws that involve the variables they have reason to believe are relevant*. The rules by which these laws are combined, thus reflecting what is loosely called the interaction of the variables, are themselves among the regularities science tries to discover. In fact, these are among the most powerful laws of nature and their very existence refutes the exaggerated claims of various brands of holism or gestaltism. There is thus no point in challenging, as Hartshorne does, the social scientist to produce a single law that would explain as complex a situation as the geography of New York Harbor. Descriptively the situation is indeed unique in the obvious sense that there has and will never be a region or location exactly like New York Harbor with all the services it supplies for its hinterland. Nor will there ever be any law to account for it. For, what point would there be in a law that takes care of one and one case only? But, on the other hand, urban geographers do by now know a few systematic principles which, jointly applied to New York Harbor, do explain quite a bit though not all of its structure and functions. This is the point. Or shall we give up the attempt to explain because we cannot as yet explain everything? In this respect geography finds itself once more in the same boat with all other social sciences. Or should we really reject sociology because the prediction of election results is not yet as reliable as some wish; or because we cannot tell for sure whether the Argentine will be a dictatorship or democracy five years hence? Such councils of despair are now heard again. Surely, they are merely a sign of the intellectual crisis of the age.

Hartshorne, like all vigorous thinkers, is quite consistent. He does, in fact, reject all social science and is particularly sceptical of the future of sociology. With respect to uniqueness he says that, 'While this margin is present in every field of science, to greater or less extent, the degree to which phenomena are unique is not only greater in geography than in many other sciences, but the unique is of the very first practical importance.'[11] Hence generalizations in the form of laws are useless, if not impossible, and any prediction in geography is of insignificant value.[12] Thus he comes after lengthy discussions to the same conclusion as Kant. 'Both history and geography might be described as naive sciences, examining

[11] Hartshorne, *op. cit.*, p. 432.

[12] *Ibid.*, p. 433.

reality from a naive point of view, looking at things as they are actually arranged and related, in contrast to the more sophisticated but artificial procedure of the systematic sciences which take phenomena of particular kinds out of their real setting.'[13] One may say that Hartshorne goes Kant even one better. For Kant geography is description; for Hartshorne it is "naive science" or, if we accept his meaning of science, naive description. As one would expect from all this, and as has been mentioned before, regional studies are for Hartshorne the heart of geography. The terminology he uses stems in part from the German historicist philosopher Rickert who distinguishes between idiographic and nomothetic disciplines. The former describe the unique; the latter search for laws. Geography according to Hartshorne is essentially idiographic. Whenever laws are discovered or applied one is no longer in the area of geography. All it contributes is facts. "In its (geography's) naive examination of the interrelation of phenomena in the real world it discovers phenomena which the sophisticated academic view of the systematic sciences may not have observed, shows them to be worthy of study in themselves and thus adds to the field of the systematic studies."[14] In other words, Hartshorne takes permanently and systematically as narrow a view of geography as we have, temporarily and for the sake of the argument, taken of history.

Mainly through Hartshorne's efforts, American geographers have come to look at Hettner as the major recent authority in support of the idiographic conception of their field. Under these circumstances, it is important to point out that the picture Hartshorne paints of the German author is as one-sided as his quotations are selective. As has been hinted before, there is another side of Hettner's work. He could just as effectively be cited in support of the nomothetic position. Consider, for instance, the following excerpts from one of his earlier papers:

> *Therefore, if we assume in geography the necessity of relations and, as in the natural sciences, exceptions in these only as apparent ones, as gaps in our knowledge, then with the frequent appearance of similar conditions we obtain the possibility of establishing anthropogeographical laws.*
>
> *We cannot say that similar conditions produce everywhere and always the same effects. Such a statement would ignore the fact that people differ and therefore can act differently under similar natural conditions. Also wrong, of course, would it be to say that similar people act alike under different natural conditions. Anthropogeographical laws have to take into account the difference in conditions of existence as well as the difference among people. Of course, in reality there will never be a repetition of exactly the same condition. Each situation is individual, unique, as a result of which no law will be able to explain the totality of a given phenomenon as in the natural sciences. There will always be a rest which must be explained under a different law or will remain unexplainable . . .*
>
> *There are no absolute relations between man and environment which are valid for all time. With the development of mankind changes the nature of relationships between man and environment.*

[13] *Ibid.*, p. 373.
[14] *Ibid.*, p. 461.

The development of these relationships rests on the constancy of effects although the causes which produced these effects may have disappeared some time ago.[15]

Nor was this an incidental remark that did not fit into Hettner's final thought. In his main work of 1927 one can still find passages like the following:

> *As much as the individualizing method is appreciated and needed, one must say that geography received only through the generalizing method its stricter scientific character. Only the generic treatment which concentrated many properties and features into one word, made a concise and relatively short and easily conceived description possible. Thereby it created the basis for a more concise form of explanation resting on comparative investigation and leading to laws. In doing this, modern geography is far advanced over history.*[16]

One may agree or disagree with such passages which, as far as we know, have never before been translated into English. But one can hardly deny that, even taken by themselves, they amount to a programmatic declaration in favor of the conception of geography which is here advocated and which has been so vigorously opposed. Nor has this side of Hettner's thought been overlooked by all American geographers. Isaiah Bowman, for example, one of the pioneers of American geography, has declared that the search for laws and prediction based on laws is "the measure of a science."[17]

To emphasize this systematic side of Hettner is not to accuse Hartshorne of reading into him what is not there. Hettner undoubtedly advocated at different times and at different places the idiographic as well as the nomothetic conceptions of geography and, for all the complexity and subtlety of his thought, did not succeed in integrating them. This requires some comments, logical as well as historical. Logically, it must be noted again that there is in fact no conflict or opposition between the descriptive and systematic aspects of geography or, for that matter, of any other science, either physical or social. Difficulties arise only when the descriptive component is, in the German manner, rationalized into the idiographic method which is then conceived as coordinate with that of explanatory science. Historically, it seems plausible to say that the reason Hettner did not see this clearly is to be found in the preponderant historicism of his environment. The strength of historicism in German thought, academic or otherwise, ever since Hegel and up to the present is a matter of record. However, the German universities became during the same period one of the centers, perhaps the main center, of the rising natural sciences and, in connection with this, of what is sometimes called the positivistic philosophy of science, which stresses the search for laws and the methodological unity of all inquiry. These two philosophies have never been

[15] Alfred Hettner, "Die Geographie des Menschen," *Geographische Zeitschrift*, Leipzig, 1907.

[16] Alfred Hettner, *Die Geographie, ihre Geschichte, ihr Wesen und ihre Methoden*. Breslau, 1927. pp. 222–223.

[17] Isaiah Bowman, "Commercial Geography as a Science. Reflections on some recent Books," *Geographical Review*, XV (1925): 285–294. See also his: *Geography in Relation to the Social Sciences*. Report of the Commission on the Social Studies, Part V, American Historical Association, New York, 1934.

reconciled in the German mind. Nor is Hettner, and with him geography, the only victim of this sterile struggle. Perhaps the most tragic case, certainly the one with the most tragic and far-reaching consequences, is Karl Marx. There is no doubt that Marx made some historically important contributions to economics. In this respect he continued, characteristically, the work of the British classical economists, who thought of their field as a systematic discipline and were quite free from the Hegelian influence. Nor can it be denied that Marx's attempt to analyze the historical process, no matter how one-sided and biased his view of it may have been, represents a daring attempt to apply scientific thought to concrete situations. The historicist bias appears in Marx's conception of history as an "understandable" progression. From there it is but a small step to conceiving of history as a progress toward a desirable goal. In other words, history itself takes care of our aspirations. This is the basic teleology of historicism. Logically, this error is much more vitiating and, if you please, vicious than Marx's preoccupation with the economic variables . . .

IV

There is one major aspect in which geography does differ from the other social sciences. The latter, as they mature, concentrate more and more on the discovery of process laws, that is, to repeat, laws that are in one important aspect like the laws of Newtonian astronomy. Given the state of a system at a certain point in time, process laws allow for the prediction of the changes that will take place. Geography is essentially morphological. Purely geographical laws contain no reference to time and change. This is not to deny that the spatial structures we explore, are, like all structures anywhere, the result of processes. But the geographer, for most part, deals with them as he finds them, ready made. (As far as physical geography is concerned, the long-term processes that produce them are part of the subject matter of geology.) Let us in this connection consider Koeppen's Hypothetical Continent. The word hypothetical merely indicates that he neglected, for the purpose of his climatological generalization, all but a few variables. For the remaining ones he states a spatial correlation that is a morphological law. To call such comparatively crude correlations patterns rather than laws is perhaps laudable modesty. But to think that patterns, in this sense of pattern, are different from laws, would be a mistake. This absence of the time factor within physical geography is the source of a peculiar phenomenon within all branches of human geography. The "social process" is, as the very term indicates, a process in the logical sense; and this process interacts with geographical factors. Assume for the sake of the argument two regions to be alike in all relevant physical aspects. They may, and as a rule will, differ with respect to some or all of the variables that interest the economic or social geographer. The reason for this is that the populations of the two regions went through different processes. Settlement patterns, for instance, may vary according to the state of technology at the time of occupation. What we are faced with in this case is not a failure of geography as a social science nor, as some would have it, with a breakdown of "causality." What we have uncovered is, rather, the exact point where the geographer must cooperate with all the other social scientists if they are jointly to produce more and more comprehensive explanations. Whether the geographer should stick to strictly morphological work which he can do by himself or, on the proper occasion, cooperate with the other social scientists is not a theoretical but a practical question to which we shall return at the end of the paper . . .

Regions and other geographical entities have been considered by many geographers as wholes in the sense of the doctrine of holism or gestaltism. A whole, in this peculiar doctrine, is more than the sum of its parts; also, it is unique in the sense that its various properties cannot be accounted for by applying standard scientific methods to its compound parts and the relations that obtain among them. Hartshorne, in arguing against such holists, is rightly opposed to the use of that doctrine in the definition of the geographical area and the region.[19] But after this rejection he finds it necessary to reintroduce the doctrine into geography when, later on, he defines cultural regions and, by the way of example, farm units as "primary wholes" the parts of which can be understood only in terms of the whole.[20] This is, indeed, different from "the merely analytic method of Hettner" says Passarge as quoted by Hartshorne. Now, the complete logical analysis of holism is an elaborate matter and cannot be taken up here in detail.[21] What it all comes down to is this. Whenever the one side insists that it has a whole, the other side claims that we simply do not as yet know enough to explain its behaviour by standard scientific methods. In many crucial cases such explanation has actually come forth later on. One may, therefore, doubt whether there is such a thing as a whole in the holist's sense anywhere in nature. Within our field, the earlier discussion of the geography of New York Harbor is a case in point. Hartshorne who calls it unique, would consistently also have to call it a whole whose parts, like those of a farm unit, can only be understood from the whole. We, in turn, from our viewpoint, doubt whether any geographical entity, region or not, is a whole in this methodological sense.

Whoever rejects the scientific method in any area of nature, rejects in principle the possibility of prediction. In other words, he rejects what is also known as scientific determinism. The intellectual motif behind this attitude is in most cases some version of the metaphysical doctrine of free will. This may seem a far-fetched allegation in a field like geography. A look at some recent publications[22] should suffice to allay any such doubt. Generally, the many interrelations between the various holisms, uniqueness doctrines, and free will philosophies are a matter of record.

If determinism is taken to mean that nature is lawful throughout, permitting of

[19] Hartshorne, *op. cit.*, pp. 263–266.

[20] *Ibid.*, pp. 351.

[21] For a discussion of holism see: Gustav Bergmann, "Holism, Historicism, and Emergence," *Philosophy of Science*, XI (1944): 209–221. Also: "Theoretical Psychology," in *Annual Review of Psychology*, IV (1953), Stanford, by the same author.

[22] Robert S. Platt, "Determinism in Geography," *Annals of the Association of American Geographers*, XXXVIII (1948): 126–132; and by the same author: "Environmentalism versus Geography," *American Journal of Sociology*, LIII (1948): 351–358.

no "exceptions," then it is the common ground of all modern science. And if freedom of the will means that human decisions are not determined by their (physiological and/or socio-psychological) antecedents, then the will is indeed not free. At any rate, most scientists proceed on this assumption and are more than willing to leave the debate to the metaphysicians. However, the word determinism has still another meaning. Those, for instance, who blame Marx for his "economic determinism" do not need to reject the idea of universal lawfulness. What they reject is, rather, the doctrine that one who knows everything about the economic and technological conditions of a society, could in these terms alone predict its "super-structure" and its future development. Scientific determinism as such must therefore be carefully distinguished from the various determinisms with an adjective, such as economic determinism. These latter determinisms are specific scientific theories, to be accepted or rejected on the basis of the empirical evidence. Geography has been bedevilled by its own kind of determinism. Geographical determinism or environmentalism attributes to the geographical variables the same role in the social process as Marxism does to the economic ones. There is no good reason to believe that either of these two special determinisms is anything but a gross exaggeration of some admittedly valuable insights. There is nothing wrong with investigating the influence which the physical environment exercises, positively or as a limiting condition, on the social process. Most geographers would expect to find lawful connections in this area; that does not make them geographical determinists. Ratzel was the first to think originally and imaginatively along these lines. Like Marx, he was not quite as bad as some of his latter day disciples. In this country Semple was a student of Ratzel. In Ellsworth Huntington's writings geographical determinism reaches some of its dizziest heights. In France, Demolins insisted that if French history had to happen all over again it would essentially run the same course on account of the natural environment. The contemporary reaction against these exaggerations is understandably strong. But to fight them from the standpoint of science is one thing; to fight geographical determinism in order to fight science and its underlying idea of universal lawfulness is another thing.

We cannot and need not, as geographers, settle the future of science. But we may wonder what can reasonably be said about the future of geography as a discipline, an organized unit within the intricate division of intellectual labor. This is not strictly a methodological question and depends on many extraneous factors. Yet, it has a theoretical core that is not unrelated to methodology. So we shall venture a few remarks in conclusion. Science, to repeat once more, searches for laws. What then, one may ask, are the peculiarities of the laws we look for and which would make it advisable that they be kept together in one discipline? From this viewpoint, we believe, the laws of geography fall into three categories. Typical of the first are most of the laws of physical geography. These are not strictly geographical. Many of them are specializations of laws independently established in the physical sciences. These we take as we find them, apply them systematically to the various conditions that prevail on the surface of the earth and analyze them with particular attention to the spatial variables they contain. To be specific, the climatologist uses much physics (meteorology), the agricultural geographer, applied biology (agronomy).

Typical of the second category are many laws of economic geography, for instance, the now flourishing theory – for it has, indeed, reached the stage where one can speak of a theory in the strict sense of a whole group of deductively connected generalizations – of general location. As everybody knows, this theory investigates the spatial relations obtaining between the places at which the various economic factors, raw materials, producing units, means of communication, consumers, and so on, are to be found in any region. As far as they are morphological, these laws are genuinely geographic. The pioneer work in this area has, in fact, been done by economists, if we except Christaller who is a geographer.[23] But, as the theory is being refined, the geographer's skill will increasingly come into its own. For, he is more expert than others in the treatment of spatial factors and he knows from his rich store of experience with which others they typically interact. As far as these laws are not morphological, they belong to the third category.

This is a crucial point. We touched on it before when we used as an illustration two similar regions showing different settlement patterns because of the different processes their population had undergone. Let us try to state the case more generally. Mature social science looks for process laws. Knowing such laws one can ideally predict the whole course of history in a region, provided one also knows the influences that flow into it from without, if one knows its physical factors and the characteristics of the population that occupied it at a given time. Such laws are, of course, not geographical laws, nor do they belong entirely within any of the other now current divisions, such as anthropology or economics. The variables one must expect to occur in them extend over the whole range of systematic social science. Spatial variables are essentially and inevitably among them, but they are no more self-sufficient than those of economics or traditional sociology. It is our task to make explicit the role these geographical variables play in the social process. In other words, we must try to explore what else would be different in the future if, all other things being equal, the spatial arrangements in the present were different from what they actually are. To insist on this is, as we saw, not geographical determinism. The real danger here is geographical isolationism. For, we have also seen that the search for these laws can only proceed in cooperation with the other social sciences.

What may one infer from all this for the future of geography? It seems to me that as long as geographers cultivate its systematic aspects, geography's prospects as a discipline of its own are good indeed. The laws of all the three categories which we have distinguished are no doubt both interesting and important. And they all contain spatial factors to an extent that requires special skills and makes the professional cultivation of these skills well worth while. We, the geographers, are these

[23] Johann Heinrich von Thünen, *Der isolierte Staat*. Rostock, 1842. August Lösch, *Die räumliche Ordnung der Wirtschaft*. Jena, 1940. Edgar M. Hoover, *The Location of Economic Activity*. New York, 1948. Walter Christaller, *Die zentralen Orte in Süddeutschland*. Jena, 1933.

professionals. I am not so optimistic in case geography should reject the search for laws, exalt its regional aspects for its own sake and thus limit itself more and more to mere description. In this event the systematic geographer will have to move much closer and eventually attach himself to the systematic sciences.

36

IDENTIFICATION OF SOME FUNDAMENTAL SPATIAL CONCEPTS

John D. Nystuen

Schaefer's methodological treatise (**chapter 35**) alone could not provide the basis for a new spatial science. It was too abstract and vague as to the exact meaning of spatial relations. The foundations of a quantitative and systematic geography were instead laid by a small number of geographers in two or three US departments, among them the University of Washington in Seattle. From 1955, under the tutelage of William Garrison and Edward Ullman, a group of young geographers including John Nystuen, Richard Morrill, Brian Berry and Art Getis prepared the ground. They were encouraged by a visit from the Swedish geographer Hägerstrand (**chapter 40**) and by contacts with planners, mathematicians and philosophers of science. In contrast to Schaefer's philosophical argument, Nystuen's essay elaborates basic spatial concepts such as distance, pattern, relative position, site and accessibility. He cites Von Thünen but his choice of an isotropic surface upon which to base these concepts is a novel one, the interior of a mosque (an idea suggested by Hägerstrand). He thereby draws attention to the social organization of space and also argues that all forms of social inquiry are only complete when they consider spatial concepts. But by abstracting spatial relations from cultural ones he affirms a separate discipline of space – in the end, the mosque is merely a convenient device. Critics note that such strictly geometrical relationships hide the stories, biographies and intentions of human life.

Source: Identification of some fundamental spatial concepts. *Papers of the Michigan Academy of Science, Arts and Letters* 48, 373–84, 1963.

The objective of this paper is to consider how many independent concepts constitute a basis for the spatial point of view, that is, the geographical point of view. Geographers have a common subject matter which reveals itself in certain words used again and again. The problems found interesting and being investigated in all branches of the discipline are defined using this common set of words – the controversy over the definition of geography notwithstanding. These words describe spatial arrangements and associations of activities and processes in geographical space. We adopt a spatial point of view whether the problem considered is one of physiography, cultural diffusion, economic expansion, or any of the diverse problems found attractive to geographers. Some of the words I refer to are: *distance, pattern, relative position, site,* and *accessibility*. Many others come to mind. What subset of these common words are necessary and sufficient to employ the geographical point of view? Given such a subset, what meanings do the basic words have? Answers to these questions will set into bold relief the essential geographical nature of a problem or situation.

The Search for a Basis of the Geographical Point of View

The definitions of the words we employ to invoke a spatial point of view are tautological. We break the circle of definitions at some point and settle on a group of words which are accepted as undefined. We must, however, describe the properties of the concepts to which the undefined words refer. This is best done operationally by describing how the concept is observed. For example, distance is a fundamental concept in most geographical studies. But distance may have several properties. In one study it may be scaled off in miles, feet, or some other unit measure. In another circumstance the distances between elements under study may only be ranked as nearest, next nearest, and so on, without reference to a scalar measure. This is a different type of distance, and these differences have important bearing on understanding the differences between geographical problems. Different types of distances are only one example. The properties of all the basic concepts may vary in subtle but important ways. Operational definitions of the words and subsequent consistent use of the words representing the concepts in the particular context under study are necessary.

Each word in the basis is required for a complete description but does not duplicate the meaning of other words in the basis, that is, each word is necessary and independent. All other concepts will be compounds of this basic set. Obviously there can be more than one basis because synonyms of basic words may replace them, giving a new set of words which convey the same concepts. I will present one basis here, and I stand ready to enlarge it at your suggestions so long as the additions do not say the same thing using different words. What I am searching for is the complete minimum set of concepts necessary to the spatial point of view of geographers.

Advantages of Abstract Geographical Systems

Certain incentives prompt me in this search. The main purpose is to clarify my objectives in studying geography so that I may study geography in the abstract. I want to remove my investigations from real world subject matter but, at the same time, carry into abstract formulations just those concepts essential to the geographical point of view. To study a problem completely in the abstract has many advantages. The main ones are simplicity and clarity. The elements in an abstract system possess only the properties explicitly assigned to them. In the real world, behaviour of a variable is often due to causes not included in the explanation because they were not thought of or because chains of causes and effects are so involved they cannot be traced through. In considering a problem in the abstract, one can restrict the properties of the object under study to a bare minimum and allow only simple associations to exist. By doing this the problem may become simple enough to understand. The abstract systems which are of use to geographers are precisely those in which the elements in the systems retain some geographically significant properties.

Thünen understood this value of abstract systems when he implored the reader:

> *... not to be deterred by the initial assumptions which deviate from reality and not to consider them as arbitrary and without purpose. On the contrary, these assumptions are necessary in order to clearly understand the effect which a given variable has. In actual life we have only a vague idea of the effect and operation of any single variable because it appears always in conflict with other variables operating at the same time. This procedure has thrown light on so many problems in my life and seems to me to be so generally applicable that I consider it the most important feature of my work.*[1]

The work he spoke of was his study of an isolated state, in which he addressed himself to the question of how agriculture land use patterns would develop on farmland associated with a single market place in a plain that was flat, homogeneously fertile, and equal in every respect from place to place.

Geographers frequently recoil at such a landscape. A common reaction to the homogeneous plain assumption is to assert that there is no geography without variation from place to place. Indeed, geography has usually been defined as the "study of areal differentiation." See, for example, Hartshorne's chapter on areal differentiation in his *Perspective on the Nature of Geography.*[2] On page 14 of that work he cites four authorities employing this definition with slight variations and additions.

Hartshorne complains that none of the short statements defining geography reveals the background thinking out of which the definitions of geography have evolved.[3] As a counterpoise to the study of differences over the earth's surface he cites "special interest" in cases in which separate areas appear to be alike. Thus the study of areal differentiation becomes the study of like places when you understand the full breadth of the meaning of the term.

He also argues with Ullman's suggestion that "areal differentiation" be considered a sub-concept of geography as "spatial interaction." This seems to Hartshorne, "... to result from a misconception of the former term, if not also the latter."[4] He

[1] J. H. von Thünen, *Der isolierte Staat in Beziehung auf Landwirtschaft und Nationalökonomie,* in K. W. Kapp and L. L. Kapp, eds., *Readings in Economics* (New York: Barnes & Noble, Inc., 1949), p. 299.

[2] R. Hartshorne, *Perspective on the Nature of Geography* (Chicago: Rand McNally & Co., 1959), pp. 12 ff.

[3] *Ibid.*, pp. 14–15.

[4] *Ibid.*, p. 19. The article referred to is E. L. Ullman, "Human Geography and Area Research," *Annals, of the Association of American Geographers,* 43 (1953), 54–66.

implies that Ullman does not understand the fullness of the original term. This type of argument over semantics will be endless as long as the definitions of words such as "areal differentiation" remain flexible enough to include all aspects and nuances of geographical content simply by expanding the background thinking out of which the definition has evolved.

Clearly, if we are attempting to define an abstract system with the simplest geographical properties, we must use a set of simple words with clearly defined meanings rather than to invoke broad, compound, and complicated expressions in an attempt at being all inclusive in our definitions. Even Hartshorne admits to the difficulties of the all-embracing expressions. He concludes his chapter on areal differentiation:

> *If the phrase "areal differentiation" can be accepted as a label referring to that full description, rather than whatever the two words may appear to mean from dictionary definitions, it may be convenient – though perhaps risky – to continue to use the term as a shorthand label,* but only among professional colleagues who have learned what it is intended to represent.[5]

Under these circumstances, to say geography is the study of areal differentiation is to say geography is the study of geography.

There is a contrast here in the use of words which reflects one fundamental methodological difference between those who strive for a geography which is a complete explanation of place and those who strive to isolate only certain geographical aspects of a place for analysis. The systematic fields of geography consider only parts of regions. The urban and transportation geography which interested Ullman led to a theoretical geography, and beyond to an abstract geography. An abstract geography must use definitions which isolate certain geographical properties and consciously exclude other geographical properties.

Few geographers have advocated a completely abstract geography implied by an extreme of the latter approach. Yet even an extremely abstract approach has some merit. Ackerman extends a timid suggestion:

> *. . . a theoretical framework is probably as important at this time as definition of the earth's physical matrix for observation was at an earlier stage in the science. Geography thus far has been notably weak in its attention to this possible building block. While the science has a voluminous literature on methodology and procedure, geographers have done comparatively little toward considering their subject in the abstract . . .*[6]

An abstract geography will be an aid in generalization. We may expect essential similarities to emerge from extremely unlike circumstances. More penetrating and critical empirical studies may be planned based on suggestions from theoretical or abstract studies. New questions for empirical investigation will arise. I do not

[5] *Ibid.*, p. 21. (Emphasis mine.)

[6] E. A. Ackerman, *Geography as a Fundamental Research Discipline*, University of Chicago, Department of Geography, Research Paper No. 53 (1956), pp. 28–29.

anticipate that an abstract geography would drift from central themes of empirical investigations. Each complements and is an inspiration to the other. Empirical work is well developed in geography. Let it remain strong. Effort should also be made to build an abstract geography equally rich.

An Example of an Abstract Space – The Isotropic Plain

Hägerstrand uses the words "isotropic plain" for the elementary, abstract, geographical space that has no difference from place to place or in one direction to another; that is, not only are places the same, but movement effort is the same in all directions from every place. The isotropic plain is not, incidentally, one of my basic words. I will use the device, however, to show how spatial properties of elements emerge with great clarity in abstract systems.

Imagine a concrete example of an isotropic plain. The interior of a mosque will do. This analogy was suggested to me by Torsten Hägerstrand, and we subsequently developed it quite far in a casual conversation. A mosque is normally devoid of furniture, illuminated by a diffused light, and has a flat, highly polished tile floor – a good representation perhaps of an isotropic surface. Let me introduce a group of people to the mosque and let them be engaged in an activity – a teacher teaching the word of Allah and his attending pupils. The teacher settles himself on the polished floor, choosing no place in particular, nor does he face in any particular direction. The pupils, however, do not choose random positions. We can imagine they arrange themselves in a very determinate fashion. They settle close in front of the teacher – but not too close. The first row forms a half-circle. Before the first row extends very far around the teacher a second row begins to develop. It is more desirable to be in the second row directly in front of the teacher than in the first row far off to one side. The second row is probably staggered so that pupils in this position can see past the heads of the ones in the first row. The arc of the students and the number of rows grow in an interdependent fashion. This relationship will depend upon the teacher's voice, how loud it is, how well he enunciates, whether there is an advantage in seeing his mouth as he speaks, etc.

Another set of variables is also important. Each pupil occupies, with his flowing robes, a certain area – call it a unit area. Also, some distance separates each pupil from another to prevent crowding. Like the number of rows, this separation depends upon the number in the class. Crowding will occur if the class is very large. There is probably a greater tendency for crowding near the front than at the rear of the class. At some distance, the teacher's voice no longer carries the message distinctly. A certain amount of shuffling around occurs, some pupils look around or sit facing other directions. They might even start talking among themselves. Given my own experience as a teacher, I can conceive of some pupils [who] might even seek out a location in the last row and beyond the cover of the teacher's eye.

The size of the mosque relative to the size of the class might eventually become a factor too, but that complicates the picture with the difficult problem of the effects of boundaries. Usually the isotropic surface is unbounded. Are there any geographical elements in the scene described? I am sure you recognize some, even though I described a model of a region with no distinguishable features. All of the geography present is created by intragroup association.

Directional Orientation

There is a directional quality to the teacher's voice. In fact, the teacher and pupils sit face-to-face if possible. The human form has a natural orientation – a front and back – which defines a line of sight. A location or point and a line of sight or ray are necessary and sufficient to define orientation – one basic geographical property I recognize. If elements in the space have no intrinsic orientation, it is necessary and sufficient that two points exist and that direction be indicated from one to the other, perhaps by an arrow on the line connecting them.

Distance

The effectiveness of the teacher's voice falls with distance. Distance, or separation, is a fundamental geographical property also. Intensity of communication falling off continuously with distance is a property shared by many, but not all, phenomena. An example of the opposite effect of distance is a transportation cost which normally rises with distance. Other phenomena are invariant with distance – at least within some range. Legal jurisdiction is as binding at the borders of a state as in its center.

The distance between two points is usually defined as a geodesic, that is, the shortest path between two points in whatever space and unit measure being considered. There are many spaces and measures possible. These spaces are defined by assigning properties to the distance measure. I will not define a distance suitable for all geographical problems. There is none. The problem must be evaluated and then the properties of the distance measure specified. Distance might be measured by simple ranking, or it may be asymmetric, e.g., the distance from *a* to *b* is not the same as the distance from *b* to *a*. An example of the latter is travel on a one-way street system.

Distance in a metric space has several useful properties which will affect most activities in the space. One such property is the triangular inequality in which

$$d\ (ab) \leq d(ac) + d(cb)$$

where *a*, *b*, and *c* are points and *d*(*ab*) is the distance between *a* and *b*. To what extent properties of this type may be extended into different spaces is significant for geographical study because many familiar geographical problems seem to be associated with something other than the familiar Euclidean space. Using the example above, distances which separate points for a traveler on a one-way street system are non-Euclidean because of their lack of symmetry.

Connectiveness

We may remove measures of distance and direction from a geographical study and speak of connection only. Some other words for this property of space are adjacency, contiguity, or simply relative position. This is best thought of as a topological property of space. The properties of connectiveness may remain invariant under transformations which change direction and distance relations. A map of the United States may be stretched and twisted, but so long as each state remains connected with its neighbors, relative position does not change. Connectiveness is independent of direction and distance – all three properties are needed to establish a complete geographical point of view.

Functional Associations and Specifications of the Space Under Study

Important problems may be investigated when one or more of the above properties are not defined. In urban studies direction is often eliminated by drawing an average profile through the city center showing rent, traffic density, etc. The familiar diagram of decreasing intensity of activity with distance from the center of a city implies no differences in direction from the center. Circular isolines appear in the plane projection of the rotation of this function about its central axis and directional differences are eliminated.

Both distance and direction are eliminated in studies concerned with networks of connections only. A simple example are route maps on railroad schedules which show only the sequence of stops.

Connections need not be adjacent boundaries or physical links. They may be defined as functional associations. Functional associations of spatially separate elements are best revealed by the exchanges which take place between the elements. The exchanges may often be measured by the flows of people, goods, or communication. The term Ullman uses for these functional relations is "interaction."[7] He calls for a greater concentration of research on these connections between areas, and he is correct in his emphasis. In the absence of site characteristics, such as I described in the example of the mosque, with its perfectly flat, polished surface, the pattern or arrangement of the people depends entirely upon their functional associations. The exchange in this case is a flow of words. By specifying the properties of this functional relation and identifying each person's role, the geographical pattern of this group of people engaged in this activity may be anticipated. If the same group of people engage in another activity, for example, social dancing, or a tug-of-war, new arrangements would arise. To study relations abstractly requires explicit recognition of the properties of the relationship. One property mentioned above is symmetry. Many relations are not symmetrical. For

[7] E. Ullman, *op. cit.*

example, the largest flow of telephone calls from a small city may be to a large central city, but the largest flow of telephone calls of the large central city need not be to the smaller city. Mathematicians have studied such relations in great detail. It is very possible we can borrow many of their theorems to our advantage if we can specify the properties of the functional relation between spatially separate elements.

Elements and Processes in Geographical Space

In order to talk about the properties on an isotropic plane I introduced a subject matter – the teacher and his pupils – and specified a functional association between them – the reciprocal acts of teaching and learning. These steps are necessary in order to apply a geographical point of view. Activities or processes associating the elements in a study over space must be assumed.

There is one special case where elements in space are not related to one another in any fashion whatsoever or, what amounts to the same thing, the elements are associated in so many ways that no finite set of associations can describe the resulting pattern. The special case results in a random distribution in space. There are certain advantages in addressing ourselves to this special case, but we will not consider them here.

We are interested in those activities and processes which explain how the elements under study are arranged and associated in space. I use the words "activities" and "processes" as synonyms just to emphasize [that] I mean spatial association between groups of people as well as spatial association of all nonhuman elements or the interaction between both these classes of elements.

Site and situational characteristics

To return to my analogy once more, if I took the class out of the mosque and settled them down in a garden or out in a woods, site characteristics would modify the arrangement of the class. A wind blowing, or the direction of the sun, might shift the orientation of the pupils. The arrangement of rocks or benches would affect the arrangement also. All of the geographical elements present inside the mosque are still present, but their effects are modified by the characteristics of the site chosen.

The difference between these two sets of influences of geographical patterns is implied in the terms "site" and "situation" or in the terms "place" and "location." It is sometimes difficult to separate "site" from "situational properties." This is probably true because the classification is artificial and depends to some extent upon the scale of observation. Nevertheless I consider the distinction useful in clarifying the geographical features of a problem.

Basic Geographical Problems

Themes recur when defining the geographical elements of a study. Recognizing them helps to identify basic similarities between apparently unlike phenomena.

Historical tension

Certain site characteristics are extremely important. If my study group from the mosque are using benches of stone set down by a prior group for some other purpose, very likely they will accommodate themselves to the existing arrangement rather than take the effort of reorganizing the heavy benches. The benches represent the accumulated benefit and legacy of the past. In many studies this legacy from the past may be the single most important fact. Existing facilities and institutions will always be not quite suitable for the present because society is always creating new activities which, for greatest efficiency, require new arrangements. This tension of present activities with past arrangements is a fundamental geographical problem which arises again and again.

Dimensional tension

There are other tensions which create problems of great interest. Geographical elements may be characterized as points, lines, or areas. In fact, even more dimensions are added if we accept as significant such concepts as social distance. For example, there are geographical effects from the social distances separating races in our big cities.

Dimensional tension is created between point- and area-occupying activities. [On] a national scale, agricultural activities are area-occupying, whereas factories may be thought of as points. A dimensional tension is created by the fact we require association with, and the products of, both farm and factory. This is what central place theory is all about. Given the need to distribute a set of point-occupying functions over an area, what is the optimum arrangement of the points?

Time–space tension

Similarly there is a time-space tension which creates interesting geographical problems. When time is short, space is conserved. When an activity has a deadline associated with it, congestion in space is likely. This is essentially the problem of highway congestion in the journey-to-work hours. The concentration of the women's dress industry in New York City and the concentration of wholesale fresh fruit and vegetable markets in large urban areas are also examples of the time-space tensions.

Scale of observation and unit areas

There is undoubtedly great advantage in considering geographical elements as points, because this will very likely simplify the abstract relations. Whether it will be useful to do so or not will depend on the scale of observation and the relative scale of the elements under study to the entire study area. On a world-wide scale there is little error in considering cities as points. At a county level this same abstraction would cause great error. In my example of the class in the mosque, the area occupied by each person was important in establishing the arrangement of the class and could not be ignored. This unit area or internal dimension is of fundamental importance. Many terms used by geographers are compounds of this term with counts of other elements. Density, intensity crop yield, rent, or land value are calculated on this basis.

Summary

The terms which seem to me to contain the concepts of a geographical point of view are *direction* or *orientation, distance,* and *connection* or *relative position.* Operational definitions of these words are the axioms of the spatial point of view. Other words, such as pattern, accessibility, neighborhood, circulation, [etc.], are compounds of the basic terms. For abstract models, the existence of these elements and their properties must be specified. The properties such as a metric unit, unit area, symmetry, transitivity, and others depend upon the particular set of elements and their processes or activities under study. These subject matters must be in mind when deciding which properties the space will possess.

Spatial relationships will be clarified if a class of site or place phenomena is distinct from a class of situational or locational phenomena. Certain themes recur when applying a spatial point of view. They may be included in an abstract study or not, but a conscious choice of inclusion or omission will be very valuable in evaluating the results.

Common geographical problems may be thought of as a group of tensions: a dimensional tension between point line, and area activities; a time-space tension in current activities; or a tension between present activities and past facilities and institutions. The scale of the study cannot be ignored, nor can the relative scale of elements in the study, because upon these scale differences will depend the appropriateness of the abstractions used.

There may be fundamental concepts which I have omitted. I have not thought through the question of boundaries. Two questions arise in boundary considerations. First, how may the boundaries be defined, and second, what influence do the boundaries have on other activities and phenomena?

I feel boundaries should be included in this statement of the basis of the geographical point of view. If you see other omissions, I would appreciate your comments.

37

THE GEOGRAPHY OF CAPITALIST ACCUMULATION

David Harvey

Geographers working in the spatial science tradition generally sought different theories for different geographical facts such as industrial locations, central place patterns or regional development. David Harvey turned towards Marx's thoughts on capital accumulation to provide a way of bringing all of these together while at the same time restoring the link between human practice and conceptualizations of space (see also **chapter 5**). In doing so he also put space and geography into Marxism itself. After *Social justice and the city* (London, 1973) he developed his ideas until their full realization in *The limits to capital* (Oxford, 1982). The essay reproduced here is based on articles written in 1975 and 1981 for the radical journal Antipode. It contains many of his key insights, including one of the strongest theoretical statements made by a geographer in the 1970s, the concept of the spatial fix. For Harvey, geography does not just belong to the outcomes of capitalism – something which spatial scientists study – but is fundamental to its workings. The temporal dynamics and geographical difference of capitalist societies can be understood as aspects of a single process of capital accumulation, being produced by it and in turn shaping its subsequent states. The example he gives here relates to imperialism, but the main ideas can also be found in the urbanization process. This chapter can be compared with Massey (**chapter 25**) – another geographer who found inspiration in Marx – and is a demonstration of the profoundest thinking to be found in Marxist geography.

Source: *The urbanization of capital*. Oxford: Basil Blackwell, 1985. Extract from pp. 32–61. [David Harvey notes in the acknowledgements section of this book that "The Geography of Capitalist Accumulation: Toward a Reconstruction of the Marxian Theory", has been rewritten from two articles on that theme which earlier appeared in *Antipode* 7, No. 2 (1975), and 13, No. 3 (1981).']

The need of a constantly expanding market for its products chases the bourgeoisie over the whole surface of the globe. It must nestle everywhere, settle everywhere, establish connexions everywhere. . . . All old established national industries have been destroyed or are daily being destroyed. They are dislodged by new industries, whose introduction

> *becomes a life and death question for all civilized nations, by industries that no longer work up indigenous raw material but raw material drawn from the remotest zones; industries whose products are consumed, not only at home, but in every quarter of the globe. In place of the old wants, satisfied by the productions of the country, we find new wants, requiring for their satisfaction the products of distant lands and climes. In place of the old local and national seclusion and self-sufficiency, we have intercourse in every direction, universal inter-dependence of nations. (The Communist Manifesto,* 46–47)

The geographical dimension of Marx's theory of the accumulation of capital has for too long been ignored. This is, in part, Marx's own fault, since, in spite of the dramatic depiction of the global conquests of the bourgeoisie in *The Communist Manifesto*, his writings on the topic are fragmentary, casually sketched, and unsystematic. His intention was, apparently, not to leave matters in such an unordered state. But projected books on the state, the world market, and crisis formation were never given even serious consideration. Careful scrutiny of his works reveals, however, a scaffold of thought on the subject that can bear the weight of substantive theorizing and historical interpretation. My purpose is to give more explicit shape and substance to that scaffold and so to lay the basis for more profound theorizing about the spatial dynamics of accumulation. This will, I hope, help us elucidate and interpret the actual historical geography of capitalism.

The importance of such a step scarcely needs stressing. Phenomena as diverse as urbanization, uneven geographical development, interregional interdependence and competition, restructurings of the regional and international division of labor, the territoriality of community and state functions, imperialism, and the geopolitical struggles that flow therefrom all stand to be elucidated and incorporated into the grand corpus of theory that Marx bequeathed us. The trick is to unravel the relation between the temporal dynamics of accumulation of capital and the production of new spatial configurations of production, exchange, and consumption.

But the path to such an understanding is littered with all manner of obstacles. The theory that Marx did produce usually treats capitalism as a closed system. External space relations and internal spatial organization apparently play no role in shaping temporal dynamics. And most Marxists have followed Marx in this and so have produced an extraordinary bias within that tradition against any explicit theorization of space and space relations. How, then, can we rectify this omission and insert space and geography back into the argument? In what follows I shall insist that space and geography not be treated as afterthoughts, as mere appendages to already achieved theory. There is more to the problem than merely showing how capitalism shapes spatial organization, how it produces and continuously revolutionizes its geographical landscape of production, exchange, and consumption. I shall argue that space relations and geographical phenomena are fundamental material attributes that have to be present at the very beginning of the analysis and that the forms they assume are not neutral with respect to the possible paths of temporal development. They are to be construed, in short, as fundamental and "active moments" within the contradictory dynamics of capitalism. My grounds for this insistence are twofold.

First, I interpret Marx's method not as seeking firm and immutable conceptual building blocks from which to derive conclusions but as a process that moves dialectically and that, at each new phase, extends, revises, and expands our interpretations of the basic categories with which we commenced our investigations. The investigation of the dynamics of crisis formation, of the circulation of fixed capital, of the operations of the credit system, for example, all lead to significant reformulations of basic concepts like "use value" and "value" (Harvey 1982). The same proposition holds when we consider spatial dynamics and geographical phenomena. Withholding consideration of space and geography at the outset, as Marx tends to do, has no necessarily deleterious effects upon our final understandings – provided, therefore, that we take seriously the admittedly difficult task of reformulating our conceptual apparatus as we go.

Second, there is abundant evidence within Marx's own often fragmentary comments that this is exactly what he thought to do. To begin with, the first chapters of *Capital* incorporate several spatial concepts (community, place, world market, etc.), while spatial images abound (value is understood with the help of a geometric illustration and is then described as "crystals" – an image in which the transformation of spatial form and content are integral to each other – of some social substance). There is a sense, then, in which Marx does not exclude such issues even at the outset of his analysis. Furthermore, the phrases he uses throughout frequently indicate a close connection between spatial and geographical phenomena on the one hand and the basic conceptual apparatus on the other. In what follows we shall hit upon abundant examples of such a connection. But the point is important enough to warrant some preliminary demonstration.

Early in *Capital* (1:86–89), Marx notes that 'money is a *crystal*' formed 'of necessity' through 'the historical progress and *extension*' of exchange which 'develops the contrast, latent in commodities, between use value and value.' It then follows that 'the value of commodities more and more expands into an embodiment of human labour in the abstract' in 'proportion as exchange *bursts its local bonds*.' This is a familiar theme in Marx. It says that the growth of trade across the world market is fundamental to the use value/value distinction as well as to the distinction between concrete and abstract labor. To the degree that the latter distinction is 'the pivot upon which a clear comprehension of Political Economy turns,' who can doubt that the study of the geographical integration of market exchange and the circulation of capital, of changing space relations, has much to say about the interpretation to be put on value itself? And this is no isolated instance either. We find Marx arguing, for example, that transportation over space is 'productive of value,' that the capacity to overcome spatial barriers belongs to 'the productive forces,' that the detail and social division of labor depends upon the agglomeration of laborers and the concentration of productive force in space, that differentials in labor productivity have a 'basis' in natural differentiations, that the value of labor power varies according to geographical circumstances, and the like. Whenever spatial and geographical phenomena are introduced, the fundamental conceptual apparatus is usually not far behind. Such phenomena have therefore to be accorded a fundamental position in the overall theory.

Our task, then, is to bring spatial relations and geographical phenomena explicitly into the main corpus of Marxian theory and to trace the effects of such an insertion upon our interpretations of fundamental concepts. The first step is to search among the clues liberally sprinkled in Marx's own writings to get a sense of directions to take and paths to explore. The harder we push this kind of research, the closely we shall come to creating a theory with which to understand the central dynamics of capitalism's historical geography. And that, surely, is no mean agenda for research.

Transportation Relations, Spatial Integration, and the Annihilation of Space by Time

The *circulation of capital* in its standard form can be defined as a continuous process: money is used to buy commodities (labor power and means of production), which, when transformed through production, allows a fresh commodity to be thrown upon the market in exchange for the initial money outlay plus a profit. The *circulation of commodities*, however, refers simply to the patterns of market exchange of commodities. While there can be market exchange of commodities without the circulation of capital, the latter presupposes the former. For purposes of analysis, therefore, we can begin by isolating the exchange of commodities as a single transitional moment in the overall circulation of capital. By analyzing the conditions of the circulation of commodities, we can prepare the way for a more thorough understanding of the circulation of capital in space.

When mediated by money, the circulation of commodities 'bursts through all restrictions as to time, place, and individuals' (*Capital* 1:113). Selling in one place and buying in another while holding money in between becomes a normal social act. When aggregated, the innumerable acts of buying and selling define the circulation processes of both money and commodities. These processes entail costs of two sorts (*Capital* 2: chap. 6). What Marx calls the *'faux frais'* of circulation are regarded as necessary but unproductive costs, necessary deductions from surplus value created in production. These include costs of circulation such as storage, bookkeeping, and the labor expended and profit extracted from retailing, wholesaling, banking, legal and financial services, and the like. These costs contrast with the expenditure of labor power to move commodities, money, and information from one place to another.

An analysis of the separation between buying and selling in space leads directly, therefore, to a consideration of the role of transport and communications in the circulation of commodities and money, and, hence, of capital. Marx has a fair amount to say on this topic. The industry that 'sells change of location' as its product, he argues, is directly productive of value because 'economically considered, the spatial condition, the bringing of the product to market, belongs to the production process itself. The product is really finished only when it is on the market' (*Grundrisse*, 533–34; *Capital* 2:150). This means that capital can be productively invested to enhance the circulation of commodities across space. However, the industry has its own peculiar laws of production and realization, because transportation is itself produced and consumed simultaneously at the moment of its use, while it also typically relies heavily upon fixed capital (roadbeds, terminals, rolling stock, and the like). Although there is potential here for direct surplus value production, there are good reasons for capitalists not to engage in its production except under certain favorable circumstances. The state is often, therefore, very active in this sphere of production (*Grundrisse*, 533–34).

Any reduction in the cost of transportation is important, Marx argues, because 'the expansion of the market and the exchangeability of the product,' as well as the prices of both raw materials and finished goods, are correspondingly affected (loc cit.). The ability to draw in raw materials over long distances and to dispatch products to distant markets is obviously affected by these costs. Such cost reductions depend upon the production of "improved, cheaper and more rapid transportation" (*Capital* 2:142). Viewed from the standpoint of production in general, therefore, "the reduction of the costs of real circulation [in space] belongs to the development of the forces of production by capital" (*Grundrisse*, 533–34).

Put in the context of Marx's general proposition of the impulsion, under capitalism, to perpetually revolutionize the productive forces, this implies an inevitable trend toward perpetual improvements in transportation and communications. Marx provides some hints as to how pressure is brought to bear to achieve such improvements. "The revolution in the modes of production of industry and agriculture made necessary a revolution . . . in the means of communication and transport," so that they "became gradually adapted to the modes of production of mechanical industry, by the creation of a system of river steamers, railways, ocean steamers and telegraphs" (*Capital* 1:384).

Elsewhere, he advances the following general proposition: "the more production comes to rest on exchange value, hence on exchange, the more important do the physical conditions of exchange – the means of communication and transport – become for the costs of circulation. Capital by its nature drives beyond every spatial barrier. Thus the creation of the physical conditions of exchange . . . becomes an extraordinary necessity for it" (*Grundrisse*, 524). The consequent reduction in transport costs opens up fresh pastures for the circulation of commodities and, hence, of capital. "The direct product can be realized in distant markets in mass quantities," and new "spheres of realization for labor driven by capital" can be opened up (loc cit.).

But the movement of commodities over greater distances, albeit at lower cost, tends to increase the time taken up during circulation. The effect is to increase the turnover time of capital – defined as the production time plus the circulation time (*Capital* 2:248), unless there are compensating improvements in the speed of circulation. Since the longer the turnover time of a given capital the smaller its annual yield of surplus value, the speed of commodity circulation is just as important to the circulation of capital as the cost. Marx takes up this idea explicitly. Speeding up "the velocity of circulation of capital" in the spheres of both production and exchange contributes to the accumulation of capital. From the standpoint of the circulation of commodities, this means that "even spatial distance reduces itself to time: the important thing is not the market's distance in space, but the speed . . . with which it can be reached" (*Grundrisse*, 538). There is every incentive, therefore, to reduce the circulation time of commodities to a minimum (*Capital* 2:249). A dual need, to reduce both the cost and the time of movement, therefore arises out of the imperatives of accumulation of capital: "While capital must on one side strive to tear down every spatial barrier to intercourse, i.e., to exchange, and conquer the whole earth for its market, it strives on the other side to annihilate this space with time. . . . The more developed the capital . . . the more does it strive simultaneously for an even greater extension of the market, and for greater annihilation of space by time" (*Grundrisse*, 539).

The phrase "annihilation of space by time" is of great significance within Marx's thinking. It suggests that the circulation of capital makes time the fundamental dimension of human affairs. Under capitalism, after all, it is *socially necessary labor time* that forms the substance of value, *surplus labor time* that lies at the origin of profit, and the ratio of surplus labor time to *socially necessary turnover time* that defines the rate of profit and, ultimately, the average rate of interest (Harvey 1982, chaps. 9 and 10). Under capitalism, therefore, the meaning of space and the impulse to create new spatial configurations of human affairs can be understood only in relation to such temporal requirements. The phrase "annihilation of space by time" does not mean that the spatial dimension becomes irrelevant. It poses, rather, the question of how and by what means space can be used, organized, created, and dominated to fit the rather strict temporal requirements of the circulation of capital.

Consideration of that question leads Marx down a number of interesting paths. He argues, for example, that the continuity of flow across space and the regularity of delivery play significant roles in relation to turnover time – the reduction of reserve stocks and of inventories of all types reduces the quantity of capital necessarily kept idle within the overall turnover process. It follows that there is a strong need to organize the transport and communications system to guarantee regularity of delivery as well as speed and low cost (*Capital* 2:249–50).

But the temporal requirements of the circulation of capital prompt further important adjustments within the organization of capitalism to deal with the spatial barriers it encounters. Long-distance trade, because it separates production and consumption by a relatively long time interval, poses serious problems for the continuity of capital flow. Herein, in Marx's opinion, lies "one of the material bases" of the credit system (*Capital* 2:251–52). In the *Grundrisse* (535) Marx develops this argument at greater length in language that renders explicit the relations between time, space, and the credit system under capitalism:

> *Circulation appears as an essential process of capital. The production process cannot be begun anew before the transformation of the commodity into money. The constant continuity of this process, the unobstructed and fluid transition of value from one form into the other, or from one phase of the process into the next, appears as a fundamental condition for production based on capital to a much greater degree than for all earlier forms of production. [But] while the*

> *necessity of this continuity is given, its phases are separate in time and space. . . . It thus appears as a matter of chance . . . whether or not its essential condition, the continuity of the different processes which constitute its process as a whole, is actually brought about. The suspension of this chance element by capital itself is* credit.

The credit system in effect permits money to circulate in space independently of the commodities for which that money is an equivalent. The circulation of credit on the world market then becomes one of the chief mechanisms for the annihilation of space by time and dramatically enhances the capacity to circulate commodities (and hence capital) across space. In the process a certain power devolves upon the money capitalists vis-à-vis industrialists, while the contradictions inherent in the credit system also take on specific geographical expression (*Capital* 3:338–613; Harvey 1982, chaps. 9 and 10). This is a matter that I shall take up again shortly.

The efficiency with which commodities can be circulated over space depends also upon the activities of the merchant capitalists. Marx here contrasts the historical role of the merchant – buying cheap in order to sell dear; mediating between geographically dispersed producers at low levels of development; accumulating capital through profiteering, robbery, and violence; and forming the world market (*Capital* 3: chap. 20) – with the position of the merchant under a purely capitalist mode of production. In the latter instance, Marx argues, the merchant's role is to lower the cost and speed up the circulation of commodities (and hence of capital) by specializing in the marketing function (*Capital* 3: chaps. 16–19). Profits are to be had out of the efficient performance of such a role. But, like the money capitalists, the position of the merchants in the overall circulation process of capital gives them a certain power vis-à-vis the industrial capitalists and provides all too frequent opportunity for free expression of their penchant for speculation, profiteering, cheating, and excessive accumulation. Nevertheless, to the degree that the heart of the modern form of capitalism is shaped by "the imminent necessity of this mode of production to produce on an ever-enlarged scale" (*Capital* 3:333), so the formation of the world market can no longer be attributed to the activities of the merchant but must be traced back to its origins in capitalist production.

The direct relaxation of spatial constraints through revolutions that reduce the cost and time of movement and improve its continuity and efficiency can therefore be supplemented by the increasing efficiency of organization of the credit and marketing system. The latter helps to annihilate space with time and so increases the capacity for spatial integration between geographically dispersed producers. The industrial capitalists, however, can achieve much the same effect through their organization of production, their location decisions, and their technological choices. Let us see how Marx deals with such a possibility.

The capacity to procure surplus value is linked to the physical productivity of the labor employed. Capitalists can here exploit those variations that have their origin in nature (*Capital* 1:178, 511–15). Superior locations can similarly be exploited in trade. Under the coercive laws of competition, therefore, we might reasonably expect the location of production to be increasingly sensitive to natural variation and locational advantage. Marx rejects such an idea without, however, denying the basis of human activity in nature and location. He insists, first of all, that fertility, productivity, and location are *social* determinations, subject to direct modification through human action and equally subject to reevaluation through changing technologies of production: "Capital with its accompanying relations springs from an economic soil that is the product of a long process of development. The productiveness of labour that serves at [capital's] foundation and starting point is a gift, not of Nature, but of history embracing thousands of centuries" (*Capital* 1:512). Fertility can be built up in the soil, relative locations altered by transport improvements, and new productive forces embedded by human labor in the land itself (*Capital* 3:619, 651, 781). Furthermore, the advantage of access to, say, a waterfall as a power source can be eliminated overnight by the advent of the steam engine. Marx is primarily interested in the way in which transformations of this sort liberate capitalist production from natural constraints and produce a humanly created "second nature" as the arena for human action. And if circumstances arise (and Marx concedes this was frequently the case in the agriculture of his time) where natural fertility and location continue to give permanent advantages to privileged producers, then the benefit could be taxed away as ground rent.

The location of production cannot, therefore, be interpreted as a mere response to natural conditions but as the outcome of a social process in which modifications of nature, of locational advantage, and of the labor process are linked. The persistence of spatial and resource endowment constraints has then to be interpreted as an effect internal to the logic of capitalist development rather than as something that resides in external nature. And this brings us back to the idea that one of the principles internal to the logic of capitalist organization of production is the annihilation of space by time and the reduction of spatial barriers.

For example, when capitalists seeking relative surplus value strive to mobilize and appropriate labor's powers of cooperation, they do so by concentrating activity within a relatively smaller space (*Capital* 1:329). The reorganization of the detail division of labor for the same purpose demands that processes that were once successive in time "go on side by side in space" simultaneously (*Capital* 1:344). The application of machinery and the rise of the factory system consolidate this tendency toward the spatial concentration of labor and productive forces within a restricted space. This same principle carries over to questions of interindustry linkages within the social division of labor. The agglomeration of production within a few large urban centers, the workshops of capitalist production, is a tendency inherent in the capitalist mode of production (*Capital* 1:532; *Grundrisse*, 587; *The Communist Manifesto*, 47–48). In all of these instances we see that the rational organization of production in space is fundamental to the reduction of turnover time and costs within the circulation process of capital.

The tendency toward the agglomeration of population and productive forces in large urban centers is reinforced by a number of other processes of considerable significance. Technological innovations that liberate industry from close dependence upon a particular and localized raw material or energy source permit greater concentration of production in urban centers. This was precisely the importance of the steam engine, which "permitted production to be concentrated in towns" because it was "of universal application and, relatively speaking, little affected by its choice of residence by local circumstances" (*Capital* 1:378). Improvements in the means of transportation also tend "in the direction of the already existing market, that is to say, towards the great centers of production and population, towards ports of export, etc. . . . These particularly great traffic facilities and the resultant acceleration of capital turnover . . . give rise to quicker concentration of both the centers of production and the markets" (*Capital* 2:250).

The resultant "concentration of masses of men and capital thus accelerated at certain points" is even further emphasized because "all branches of production which by the nature of their product are dependent mainly upon local consumption, such as breweries, are . . . developed to the greatest extent in the principal centers of population" (loc. cit.). What Marx in effect depicts are powerful cumulative forces making for the production of urbanization under capitalism. And he helps us see these forces as part and parcel of the general processes seeking the elimination of spatial barriers and the annihilation of space by time.

But this process also requires the agglomeration of laborers, the concentration of population, within the restricted space of urban centers. "The more rapidly capital accumulates in an industrial or commercial town, the more rapidly flows the stream of exploitable human material" (*Capital* 1:661). This flow can arise out of "the constant absorption of primitive and physically uncorrupted elements from the country," which presupposes the existence there of "a constant latent surplus population" that can be dislodged by primitive accumulation – enclosures or other violent means of expropriation from the land (*Capital* 1:269, 642). The importation of Irish laborers into the industrial and commercial centers of England was of particular interest to Marx, for it not only provided a necessary flow of surplus laborers but did so in a way that divided the working-class movement (*Selected Correspondence*, 236–37). In the absence of such migrations, the expansion of the labor force depended upon the "rapid renewal" and "absolute increase" of a laboring population through fundamental and distinctively urban transformations in the social conditions of reproduction of labor power – earlier marriages, employment opportunities for children that encouraged laborers to "accumulate" children as their only source of wealth, and so on. And in the event of labor shortage, technological change tended to produce a "floating" industrial reserve army concentrated "in the centres of modern industry" (*Capital* 1:641). Even under conditions of technologically induced high unemployment, the capitalists could still leave the reproduction of labor power to "the labourer's instincts of self-preservation and of propagation" (*Capital* 1:572). The accumulation of capital in space goes hand in hand with "the accumulation of misery, agony of toil, slavery, ignorance, brutality, mental degradation," while children are raised in "conditions of infamy" (*Capital* 1:645).

Limits obviously exist to the progressive concentration of productive forces and laboring populations in a few large urban centers, even though such agglomeration may help reduce turnover times and circulation costs. Such concentrations of human misery form breeding grounds for class consciousness and organization, while overcrowding both in the factory and in the living space can become a specific focus of social protest (cf. *The Communist Manifesto*). But capital does not wait upon the emergence of such problems to set in motion its own quest for dispersal. The tendency to create the world market is, after all, "given in the concept of capital itself." The creation of surplus value at "one point requires the creation of surplus value at *another* point," which means "the production of a constantly widening sphere of circulation" through complementary tendencies to create new points of production and exchange. The exploration of "all nature in order to discover new, useful qualities of things," as well as to gain access to raw materials, entails "universal exchange of the products of all alien climates and lands" (*Grundrisse*, 407–10). The tendency toward agglomeration is partially offset, therefore, by an increasingly specialized "territorial division of labour which confines special branches of production to special districts of a country" coupled with the rise of a "new and international division of labour" responsive to the needs of modern industry (*Capital* 1:353, 445–51). And all of this is facilitated by new transport and credit systems that facilitate long-distance movement, reduce spatial barriers, and annihilate space by time.

The conception toward which Marx appears to be moving is of a geographical landscape beset by a pervasive tension between forces making for agglomeration in place and forces making for dispersal over space in the struggle to reduce turnover time and so gain surplus value. If there is any general structure to it all – and Marx is far from explicit on the point – it is that of a progressive concentration of forces of production (including labor power) at particular places together with rapid geographical expansion of market opportunities. With the accumulation of capital, Marx comments, 'flows in space' increase remarkably; while the 'market expands spatially, the periphery in relation to the center is circumscribed by a constantly expanding radius' (*Theories of Surplus Value*, pt. 3:288). Some sort of center-periphery relation, perhaps an echo of that original antithesis between town and country which lies at the origin of the social division of labor (*Capital* 1:352; *The German Ideology*, 69), appears almost certain to arise.

But such a structure is perpetually being recast in the restless quest for accumulation. The creation of absolute surplus value rests upon 'the production of a constantly widening sphere of circulation,' while the production of relative surplus value entails 'quantitative expansion of existing consumption: . . . creation of new needs by propagating existing ones in a wide circle' and 'production of new needs and discovery and creation of new use values' through 'the exploration of the earth in all directions.' Marx then goes on to integrate the rise of science, the definition of new social wants and needs, and the transformation of world culture into his general picture of the global transformations necessarily wrought through an expansionary capitalism powered by the impulsion of accumulation for accumulation's sake:

> *Capital drives beyond national barriers and prejudices as much as beyond nature worship, as well as all traditional, confined, complacent, encrusted satisfactions of present needs, and reproductions of old ways of life. It is destructive towards all of this and constantly revolutionizes it, tearing down all the barriers which hem in the development of the forces of production, the expansion of needs, the all-sided development of production, and the exploitation and exchange of natural and mental forces. (Grundrisse, 407–10)*

But to the degree that capitalist production "moves in contradictions which are constantly overcome but just as constantly posited," so we find contradictions internal to this overall expansionary dynamic. In particular, the search for "rational" geographical configurations of production and consumption runs up against the impulsion to revolutionize the productive forces in transport and communications. Expansion occurs in a context where transformations in the cost, speed, continuity, and efficiency of movement over space alter "the relative distances of places of production from the larger markets." This entails "the deterioration of old and the rise of new centres of production" and a perpetual "shifting and relocation of places of production and of markets as a result of the changes in their relative positions" (*Capital* 2:249–50). This instability is exacerbated by processes of technological and organizational change that either liberate production from specific locational requirements (access to particular raw material or energy supplies, dependence upon particular labor skills) or confirm the trend toward increasing specialization within a territorial division of labor. And the shifting physical and social capacity of the laborers to migrate (on a temporary or permanent basis) also enters into the picture (Results of the Immediate Process of Production, 1013–14).

The shifts in spatial configurations produced by such processes become problematic to the degree that capitalism requires fixed and immobile infrastructures, tied down as specific use values in particular places, to facilitate production, exchange, transportation, and consumption. Capitalism, after all, "establishes its residence on the land itself and the seemingly solid presuppositions given by nature [appear] in landed property as merely posited by industry" (*Grundrisse*, 740). The value embodied in such use values cannot be moved without being destroyed. Capital thus must represent itself in the form of a physical landscape created in its own image, as use values created through human labor and embedded in the land to facilitate the further accumulation of capital. The produced geographical landscape constituted by fixed and immobile capital is both the crowning glory of past capitalist development and a prison that inhibits the further progress of accumulation precisely because it creates spatial barriers where there were none before. The very production of this landscape, so vital to accumulation, is in the end antithetical to the tearing down of spatial barriers and the annihilation of space by time.

This contradiction grows with increasing dependence upon fixed capital (machinery, plant, physical infrastructures of all kinds). The problem arises because with "fixed capital the value is imprisoned within a specific use value" (*Grundrisse*, 728), while the degree of fixity increases with durability, other things being equal (*Capital* 2:160). Marx describes the conditions governing the circulation of fixed capital in the following terms: "The value of fixed capital is reproduced only insofar as it is used up in the production process. Through disuse it loses its value without its value passing on to the product. Hence the greater the scale on which fixed capital develops . . . the more does the continuity of the production process or the constant flow of reproduction become an externally compelling condition for the mode of production founded on capital" (*Grundrisse*, 703). The employment of fixed and immobile capital, in short, exerts a strong claim upon the future circulation of capital and the future deployment of labor power. Until the capital invested in such assets is amortized through use, capital and labor power are constrained geographically to patterns of circulation that help realize the value embodied in all improvements "sunk in the soil . . . every form in which the product of industry is welded fast to the surface of the earth" (*Grundrisse*, 739–40; Harvey 1982, chap. 8).

Capitalist development has to negotiate a knife-edge path between preserving the values of past capital investments embodied in the land and destroying them in order to open up fresh geographical space for accumulation. A perpetual struggle ensues in which physical landscapes appropriate to capitalism's requirements are produced at a particular moment in time only to be disrupted and destroyed, usually in the course of a crisis, at a subsequent point in time.

This contradiction hides an irony that is nowhere more apparent than in the transport industry itself. The elimination of spatial barriers and the annihilation of space by time requires "a growth of that portion of social wealth which, instead of serving as direct means of production, is invested in means of transportation and communication and in the fixed and circulating capital required for their operation" (*Capital* 2:351). In other words, the production of a fixed configuration of space (e.g., the rail, road, and port systems) is the only means open to capital to overcome space. At some point the impulsion to overcome space must render the initial investments obsolete and redundant, perhaps well before the value embodied in them has been realized through use.

The location theory in Marx (if we may call it that) is not much more specific than this (although there is much of peripheral interest in his analyses of rent and fixed capital formation – see Harvey 1982, chaps. 8 and 11). The virtue of his fragmentary remarks lies not in their sophistication but in the vision they project of the role of the production and restless restructuring of geographical landscapes and space relations as active moments within the dynamics of capital accumulation. Revolutions in the productive forces embedded in the land, in the capacity to overcome space and annihilate space with time, are not afterthoughts to be added on in the final chapter of some analysis. They are fundamental because it is only through them that we can give flesh and meaning to those most pivotal of all Marxian categories, concrete and abstract labor.

This last point is of sufficient importance to warrant reflection. The expenditure of human labor power "in a special form and with a definite aim" to produce use values in a given place and time is, as Marx puts it, "an eternal nature-imposed necessity, without which there can be no material exchanges between man and

Nature, and therefore no life." These different qualities of concrete labor are brought into relation with each other through exchange and, ultimately, through the circulation of capital. And that process of bringing different concrete labor activities into a general social relation gives that same labor process abstract qualities tied to value as socially necessary labor time, the labor time "required to produce an article under the normal conditions of production, and with the average degree of skill and intensity prevalent at the time" (*Capital* 1:39–46). The "normal conditions" and "average skill and intensity" cannot be specified, however, except with reference to a given space of exchange and capital circulation. The processes of formation of the world market, of spatial integration, of the international and territorial division of labor, of the geographical concentration of production (labor power and productive force), are therefore fundamental to understanding how a concrete labor process acquires abstract, universal qualities. For the geographer this must surely be one of Marx's most profound insights. For it not only puts the study of space relations and geographical differentiation into the heart of Marx's theorizing but it also points the way to a solution of the problem that has for so long bedeviled the geographical imagination: how to make universal generalizations about the evident unique particularities of space. The answer lies, of course, not in philosophical speculation but in a study of exactly how the processes of capital circulation bring the unique qualities of human action in given places and times into a framework of universal generality. And that, presumably, was exactly what Marx meant by that stunning conception that bears repeating: "Abstract wealth, value, money, hence abstract labour, develop in the measure that concrete labour becomes a totality of different modes of labour embracing the world market" . . .

The Geography of Crisis Formation and Resolution: The Search for a "Spatial Fix" for Capitalism's Internal Contradictions

Marx often specifically excludes foreign trade and geographical dimensions from his analysis of the dynamics of capitalist accumulation and crisis formation. Yet there are innumerable hints that he did not feel comfortable so doing. While he admits that "capitalist production does not exist at all without foreign commerce," he also argues that consideration of foreign trade merely confuses "without contributing any new elements of the problem [of accumulation], or of its solution" (*Capital* 2:470). While he accepts that foreign trade can counteract the tendency toward a falling rate of profit (and hence stave off crises), he hurriedly counters that this merely raises the rate of accumulation and so hastens the fall in the profit rate in the long run (*Capital* 3:237). While foreign trade evidently "transfers the contradictions [of capitalism] to a wider sphere and gives them greater latitude" (*Capital* 3:408), and while he also at one point anticipated a separate work on the world market and crises, he does not pay much attention in practice to such processes. For purposes of analysis, he argues, it is sufficient to proceed as if capitalism were a closed system: "in order to examine the object of our investigation in its integrity, free from all disturbing subsidiary circumstances, we must treat the world as one nation, and assume that capitalist production is everywhere established and has possessed itself of every branch of industry" (*Capital* 1:581).

Yet, in spite of these avowals, the very last chapter of the first volume of *Capital* takes up "the modern theory of colonization" and so opens up the whole question of foreign and colonial settlement and trade in a work that treats capitalism as a closed system. The position of the chapter is doubly odd in that it obscures what many would regard as a more natural culmination to Marx's argument in the penultimate chapter. There Marx announces, with a grand rhetorical flourish reminiscent of *The Communist Manifesto*, the death knell of capitalist private property and the inevitable expropriation of the expropriators (*Capital* 1:762–63).

The positioning and content of the final chapter reflects, I believe (cf. Harvey 1981), a desire on Marx's part to deal with a problem that Hegel had raised and left open in *The Philosophy of Right* (Hegel 1952, 149–52). Hegel there attributes the social unrest and evident instability of bourgeois civil society to the increasing polarization of the social classes – concentration of wealth in a few hands and the formation of a "rabble of paupers". This condition has its origin in the loss of property on the part of laborers and their consequent condemnation to an alienated existence, even though the laborers are the original source of all wealth. It also leads, for reasons that Hegel leaves obscure, to general crises of overproduction and underconsumption that civil society appears powerless to remedy. This "inner dialectic" forces civil society "to push beyond its own limits and seek markets, and so its necessary means of subsistence, in other lands that are either deficient in the goods it has overproduced, or else generally backward in industry." It must also found colonies and thereby permit a part of its unemployed population access to property and a return to an unalienated condition of existence while simultaneously supplying itself "with a new demand and field for its industry." Colonialism and imperialism are posited as necessary external resolutions to the internal contradictions of capitalism.

Much of Marx's *Capital* can be read as a transformation and materialist rendition of Hegel's idealist argument. Curiously, Marx avoided consideration of these questions in his *Critique of Hegel's Philosophy of Right*, but thirty years later, in an Afterword to *Capital* (1:19) admitted that his critique of Hegel had had a profound effect upon his mode of argumentation. The theme of increasing polarization of the social classes is writ large in Marx's "general law of capitalist accumulation." There Marx shows how and why capitalism reproduces "the capital relation on a progressive scale, more capitalists at this pole, more wage workers at that." Furthermore, the processes at work also produce a "relative surplus population," a "reserve army" of unemployed "set free" primarily through technological and organizational changes imposed by the capitalists. This reserve army helps drive wages down and control workers' movements. It is therefore a prime lever of accumulation. The effect, Marx observes in language deeply reminiscent of Hegel, is "the accumulation of wealth at one pole" and the "accumulation of misery, agony of toil, slavery, ignorance, brutality, mental degradation, at the opposite pole (*Capital* 1:630–45). Accumulation requires, then, that capitalists control both the demand for and supply of labor power. They must be able to create and maintain labor surpluses, either through the mobilization of "latent labor reserves" (women and children, peasants thrown off the land, etc.) or through the creation of technologically induced unemployment. Any threat to that control, Marx notes, is countered "by forcible means and State interference." In particular, capitalists must strive to check colonization processes that give laborers access to free land at some frontier (*Capital* 1:640). The colonial policies studied in the final chapter of *Capital* drive home Marx's argument with dramatic force – the powers of private property and the state were to be used to exclude laborers from easy access to free land in order to preserve a pool of surplus laborers for exploitation by capitalists.

There is, in this, a tacit answer to the question Hegel posed. If laborers can return to a genuinely unalienated life through migration to some frontier, then capitalist control over labor supply is undermined. Marx accepts the idea that higher wages and better conditions of life could exist in the United States precisely because of the laborer's access to a relatively open frontier. The survival of capitalism depends therefore upon the recreation of capitalist relations of private property and the associated power to appropriate the labor of others, even and especially at the open frontier. What Marx illustrates in his final chapter is the explicit bourgeois recognition of such a principle. He thereby signals a rejection of Hegel's proposition that there could be some "spatial fix" for capitalism's internal contradictions.

The same issue crops up again in Marx's consideration of crises. Polarization then takes the form of "unemployed capital at one pole, and unemployed worker population at the other." Can the formation of such crises be prevented or actual crises resolved through geographical expansion? Marx does not rule out the possibility that foreign trade can counteract the tendency toward a falling rate of profit in the short run (*Capital* 3:237–59). But how long is the short run? And if it extends over many generations, then what does this do to Marx's theory and its associated political practice of seeking revolutionary transformations in the heart of civil society in the here and now?

To answer this question we need a firmer interpretation of Marx's view of the "inner dialectics" of capitalism in crisis. This is not an uncontroversial matter, since rival interpretations of Marx's arguments abound. I shall work with a highly simplified version in which individual capitalists, locked in class struggle and coerced by competition, are forced into technological adjustments that destroy the prospects for balanced accumulation and so undermine the conditions of reproduction of both the capitalist and working classes. The end product of such a process is a condition of *overaccumulation of capital,* defined as an excess of capital in relation to opportunities to employ that capital profitably, and excess of labor power – widespread unemployment or underemployment (Harvey 1982, chap. 7). That capitalism should periodically produce such unemployable surpluses in the midst of such enormous human need was, for Marx, a tragic demonstration of the underlying irrationality of supposedly rational competitive market allocations. The "hidden hand" was by no means as benevolent as Adam Smith thought. That the only exit from such a state was the devaluation of both capital and labor power illustrates the destructive proclivities of bourgeois domination.

Is there, then, some way in which the surpluses of both capital and labor power generated in the course of crises can be successfully disposed of through geographical expansion? To answer that question we must first recognize that surpluses of capital can exist as money (a highly mobile form of capital), as commodities (variably mobile), or as idle productive capacity (hardly mobile at all). Marx's comments on the prospects for a spatial fix for capitalism's internal contradictions can then be assembled under three main headings.

External Markets and Underconsumption

In the course of a crisis,

> *the English, for example, are forced to lend their capital to other countries in order to create a market for their commodities. Overproduction, the credit system, etc., are means by which capitalist production seeks to break through its own barriers and to produce over and above its own limits.... Hence crises arise, which simultaneously drive it onward and beyond [its own limits] and force it to put on seven-league boots, in order to reach a development of the productive forces which could be achieved only very slowly within its own limits. (Theories of Surplus Value, pt. 3:122; cf. Grundrisse, 416)*

Such lending of excess money capital to a foreign country in order to allow the latter to buy up the excess commodities produced at home (so permitting the full employment of productive capacity and labor power at home) appears a neat way to deal with the overaccumulation problem. The difficulty is that it accelerates the development of the productive forces at home and so exacerbates the tendency toward overaccumulation. At the same time, it puts an undue debt burden on the foreign country which must at some point be paid. In the long run, therefore, the overaccumulation problem is merely intensified and spread out over a wider area. The collapse, when it comes, triggers an intricate sequence of events because of the gaps that exist between the imbalance of trade and the balance of payments. Marx describes a typical sequence this way:

> *the crisis may first break out in England, the country which advances most of the credit and takes the least, because the balance of payments . . . which must be settled immediately, is unfavourable, even though the general balance of trade is favorable. . . . The crash in England initiated and accompanied by a gold drain, settles England's balance of payments. . . . Now comes the turn of some other country . . .*
>
> *The balance of payments is in times of crisis unfavourable to every nation . . . but always to each country in succession, as in volley-firing. . . . It then becomes evident that all these nations have simultaneously over-exported (thus over-produced) and over-imported (thus over-traded), that prices were inflated in all of them, and credit stretched too far. And the same break-down takes place in all of them.*

The costs of devaluation are then forced back onto the initiating region by,

> *first, shipping away precious metals; then selling consigned commodities at low prices;*

> *exporting commodities to dispose of them or obtain money advances on them at home; increasing the rate of interest, recalling credit, depreciating securities, disposing of foreign securities, attracting foreign capital for investment in these depreciated securities, and finally bankruptcy, which settles a mass of claims. (Capital 3:491–92, 517)*

The sequence sounds dismally familiar. There is no prospect here, evidently, for a long-term spatial fix for capitalism's internal contradictions.

A more intriguing possibility arises with respect to trade with noncapitalist social formations. After all.

> *when an industrial people, producing on the foundation of capital, such as the English, e.g. exchange with the Chinese, and absorb value . . . by drawing the latter within the sphere of circulation of capital, then one sees right away that the Chinese do not therefore need to produce as capitalists. (Grundrisse, 729)*

Circumstances can then arise that make the development of capitalism "conditional on modes of production lying outside of its own stage of development." The degree of relief afforded thereby depends on the nature of the noncapitalist society and its capacity or willingness to integrate into the capitalist system in ways that absorb the excess capital. Crises, it transpires, can be checked only if the noncapitalist countries "consume and produce at a rate which suits the countries with capitalist production" (*Capital* 2:110; 3:257). And how can that be assured short of some form of political and economic domination? The current difficulties of East-West trade and the Polish debt form an excellent case in point. And even if such domination can be assured, the resolution is bound to be temporary. "You cannot continue to inundate a country with your manufactures," says Marx, "unless you enable it to give you some produce in return," Hence, "the more the [British] industrial interest became dependent on the Indian market, the more it felt the necessity of creating fresh productive powers in India" (*On Colonialism*, 52). And this broaches a whole new set of possible resolutions of the problem.

The Export of Capital for Production

Surplus capital can be lent abroad to create fresh productive powers in new regions. The higher rates of profit promised provide a "natural" incentive for such a flow and, if achieved, stand to increase the average rate of profit in the system as a whole (*Capital* 3:237, 256; *Theories of Surplus Value*, pt. 2:436–37). Crises are temporarily resolved. "Temporarily" because higher profits mean an increase in the mass of capital looking for profitable employment. The tendency toward overaccumulation is thereby exacerbated but now on an expanding geographical scale. The only escape lies in a continuous acceleration in the creation of fresh productive powers in new regions.

But when a particular civil society seeks to relieve its overaccumulation problem through the creation of fresh productive powers elsewhere, it thereby establishes a rival center of accumulation which, at some future point, will also run into problems of internal overaccumulation and seek refuge in some spatial fix. Marx thought he saw the first step down such a path as the British exported capital to India:

> *When you have once introduced machinery into the locomotion of a country, which possesses iron and coals, you are unable to withhold it from its fabrication. You cannot maintain a net of railways over an immense country without introducing all those industrial processes necessary to meet the immediate and current wants of railway locomotion, and out of which there must grow the application of machinery to those branches of industry not immediately connected with the railways. The railway system will therefore become, in India, truly the forerunner of modern industry . . . [which] will dissolve the hereditary divisions of labor, upon which rest the Indian castes, those decisive impediments to Indian progress and Indian power. . . . The bourgeois period of history has to create the material basis of the new world. . . . Bourgeois industry and commerce create these material conditions of a new world in the same way that geological revolutions have created the surface of the earth.* (On Colonialism, 85–87)

We here see that the capitalist imperative to overcome spatial barriers and annihilate space with time also necessitates revolutions in the productive forces in the spaces brought within the metabolism of global exchange. But the transition that Marx anticipated in India was blocked by a mixture of internal resistance to capitalist penetration and imperialist policies imposed by the British. The latter were, by and large, specifically geared to preventing the rise of India as a competitor, even to the point of destroying that country's industrial base in order to open up a market for British products. The transition was not blocked, however, in the United States, which was already becoming, as Marx noted in 1867, a new and independent center for capital accumulation.

These two contrasting examples hint at a more than trivial dilemma in the search for a spatial fix for overaccumulation through the export of capital. The dependent and constrained form of capitalist development in India avoided the problem of competition but quickly degenerated into a mere trading relation that, as we have seen, could do nothing for the long-run absorption of surplus capital and surplus labor power. The pace of growth and accumulation in India was not, in short, fast enough to absorb the ever-increasing surpluses emanating from Britain. The unconstrained development of capitalism in the United States, in contrast, absorbed far more excess British capital (and labor power) than India ever did, but the new productive forces created there posed a competitive threat to the initiating country.

While Marx does not make the point directly, we can quickly infer here the existence of a "Catch 22" of the following sort: if the new region is to absorb the surpluses from the home country effectively, then it must be allowed to develop freely into a full-fledged capitalist economy that is in turn bound to produce its own surpluses and so enter into competition with the home base. If, however, the new region develops in a constrained and dependent way, then competition with the home base is held in check but the rate of expansion is insufficient to absorb the burgeoning surpluses at home. Devaluation occurs no matter what. Unless, of course, still newer growth regions can be opened up. The effect, however, as Marx observes, is simply to spread the contradictions over ever wider geographical spheres and give them ever greater latitude of operation.

But, *nota bene,* capitalism can open up considerable breathing space for its own survival through this particular form of the spatial fix. It is rather as if, having sought to annihilate space with time, capitalism can then buy back time for itself out of the spaces it conquers. The geographical spread and intensification of capitalism is a long-drawn-out revolution accomplished over many years. While local, regional, and "switching" crises are normal grist for the working out of this process, the building of a truly global crisis of capitalism depends upon the exhaustion of possibilities for further revolutionary transformations along capitalist lines. And that depends upon the capacity to propagate new productive forces across the face of the earth, combined with the supply of fresh labor power open to exploitation as wage labor.

Primitive Accumulation and the role of the Labor Surplus

"An increasing population," wrote Marx, is a "necessary condition" if "accumulation is to be a steady continuous process." This idea is subsequently qualified to mean growth of population "freed" from control over the means of production; that is, growth in the wage labor force and the industrial reserve army. The faster the growth in these aggregates, the more crises will appear as pauses within an overall trajectory of expansion (*Grundrisse,* 608, 764, 771; *Theories of Surplus Value,* pt. 2:47).

The key role of labor surpluses in Marx's thought cannot be over-emphasized. Surpluses of labor must always be available if accumulation is to be sustained, while the processes of technological change which underlie crisis formation tend to produce surpluses of labor that cannot be absorbed. I concentrate for the moment on the prior process of production of the labor surplus. Where does this expansion in the exploitable population come from? In the "general law of capitalist accumulation," Marx divides the relative surplus population into three categories – latent, floating, and stagnant. The mobilization of latent reserves entails either primitive accumulation (the forcible separation of peasants, artisans, self-employed and independent producers, and even other capitalists from control over the means of production) or the substitution of family for individual labor (the employment of women and children in particular). A floating supply can be generated by any combination of sagging commodity production and labor-saving technological innovation. Taken in the context of natural population growth (itself not immune to the influence of capitalism's dynamic), these mechanisms must provide the fresh supplies of labor power to feed accumulation (the stagnant reserve army by virtue of its condition can play only a very small role).

Marx does not subject these processes to detailed scrutiny, but the flow of his logic points to certain conclusions. *Within* a particular civil society, viewed as a closed system, accumulation will accelerate until all latent elements are absorbed and the limits of natural population growth reached. Floating populations must then increasingly be relied upon as the source of an industrial reserve army. Society shifts from the trouble and turmoil of primitive accumulation and the destruction of precapitalist family relationships to the trauma of technologically induced unemployment. Both processes will be the focus of intense class struggles, though of a rather different sort. But resort to floating reserves is rather more problematic because it presupposes a strong dynamic of technological change, and this underlies, in the end, the tendency toward the overaccumulation of both capital and labor power. Though they may not be systematically aware of it, there is a distinct advantage to capitalists in exploiting latent rather than floating reserves. The more they depend on the latter, the deeper and more frequent crises will be.

To the degree that geographical expansion opens up access to fresh labor reserves, it can dampen the crisis tendencies of capitalism. Primitive accumulation on the exterior of civil society through the imposition of capitalist property relations by the state, the penetration of money relations and commodity exchange, and so forth, opens up new fields of action for overaccumulated capital. This was the main significance of the plantation economies, which capitalism brought under its sway, and the new systems of colonial exploitation built up. Conversely, the labor surpluses so created could be imported from abroad. This, for Marx, was the significance of Ireland to English capitalism (*Ireland and the Irish Question*). Primitive accumulation in the former place furnished labor surpluses that could be used in the latter place to fuel accumulation, depress wages, and undermine the organized power of English workers (*Selected Correspondence*, 228–38). In the absence of slavery (or something akin to slavery, such as an indenture system), however, the importation of labor surpluses has to depend upon the free geographical mobility of labor power, and this implies the "abolition of all laws preventing the laborers from transferring from one sphere of production to another and from one local center of production to another" (*Capital* 3:196; Results of the Immediate Process of Production, 1013). But if the privilege of geographical mobility is conferred on the laborers from the exterior, it is hard to deny it to the floating reserves generated at home. The latter may emigrate to some free frontier or to wherever the money wage is highest. The significance of Marx's last chapter on colonization now strikes home with redoubled force. Primitive accumulation at the frontier is just as important as primitive accumulation at home or in some well-developed noncapitalist social formation abroad. Only in this way can the capitalist class as a whole ensure control over both the demand for and the supply of labor power on a global scale.

The "golden chain" that binds labor to capital can evidently be stretched a little in either direction, but only within strict limits. When labor is scarce the conditions of life of the laborer can improve somewhat, but at the price of triggering those technological adjustments that render capitalism more and more unstable and crisis-prone. In contrast, accelerating accumulation and the moderation of capitalism's internal contradictions depend upon the rapid expansion of the wage labor force through global primitive accumulation, the international mobilization of latent labor reserves, and other processes deeply disruptive of qualities of life, community, and standards of material well-being of the mass of the labor force. In either case, of course, the capital-labor relation remains intact – which is another way of saying that the geographical expansion of wages labor simply projects *the* fundamental contradiction of capitalism over ever-wider spheres and gives it greater and greater latitude of operation.

The Geography of Capitalist Accumulation: Toward a Synthesis

The various programmatic sketches that Marx prepared before writing *Capital* invariably make reference to the geographical aspects of accumulation. In one such passage in the *Grundrisse*, for example, he begins with fundamental class relations, proceeds through topics such as town and country, the credit system, the "concentration of bourgeois society in the form of the state," and state debt, and concludes: "The colonies. Emigration. . . . The international relation of production. International division of labor. International exchange. Export and import. Rates of exchange. . . . The world market and crises" (108). Marx certainly thought that no theoretical account of capitalist development would be complete without integration of geographical aspects. And we have seen how he sporadically gestured in that direction. It remains, however, to evaluate the strengths and weaknesses of the ideas he did bequeath us and to move toward a more synthetic statement.

The implied synthesis can perhaps best be depicted as dual and intersecting contradictions that locate the underlying tensions that shape and propel the historical-geographical evolution of capitalism.

First Contradiction. Space can be overcome only through the production of space. We have encountered two rather different versions of this proposition. In the first we saw how the competitive thrust to diminish turnover time spills over into a compulsive pressure to break down spatial barriers and annihilate space with time. Close examination reveals how revolutions in the means of transportation and communications, how changes in the social division of labor and technology and in the locational requirements for capitalists and laborers, perpetually revolutionize space relations and the geographical landscapes of production, exchange, and consumption. Space cannot be overcome, however, without embedding productive forces in space. Tensions arise because the dead labor (capital) embedded in space ultimately becomes the barrier to be overcome. Capitalism has then no option but to destroy a part of itself in order to survive. The second version of this same proposition arises out of a consideration of foreign trade between communities (states) within the world market. The qualities of abstract labor come to dominate social life to the degree that different concrete labor processes in different communities are welded into a unity of global exchange. But concrete labor processes are perpetually modified in response to abstract requirements: "all old established national industries have been destroyed or are daily being destroyed," to be "dislodged by new industries whose introduction becomes a life and death question for all civilized nations." The circulation of capital in general and the creation of fresh productive forces within the community differentiate what simple exchange renders homogeneous. A permanent tension exists, therefore, between value as a representation of the universality of social labor and the particularities of concrete labor shaped as a competitive local response to the pressures exerted by competition in the world market. The homogenization of space through foreign trade is achieved, as it were, through processes that perpetually differentiate and transform the geographical division of labor.

Second Contradiction. The internal contradictions of capitalism can be resolved by a spatial fix, but in so doing capitalism transfers its contradictions to a wider sphere and gives them greater latitude. Overaccumulation of capital and labor power can be absorbed through geographical expansion, but this necessarily entails the reproduction of the social relations of capitalism in new geographical environments and spaces. Although capitalism can buy back time for itself out of the space it conquers, it cannot do so indefinitely nor avoid spreading the conditions for crisis formation over ever-wider spheres.

Intersection. The more fiercely capitalism is impelled to seek a spatial fix for its internal contradictions, the deeper becomes the tension of overcoming space through the production of space. The greater the overaccumulation and the faster the consequent pace of geographical expansion, the faster the pace of transformation of geographical landscapes. To the degree that those landscapes embody dead labor (capital) that has yet to be realized, so an increasing portion of that capital has to be destroyed in order to make way for new geographical configurations of production, exchange, and consumption. Capitalism requires increasing levels of self-destruction in order to survive. We here encounter the geographical dimension within Marx's basic proposition that "the universality towards which [capitalism] irresistibly strives encounters barriers in its own nature" (*Grundrisse*, 410).

Marx's stance with respect to the historical geography of capitalism has some distinctive virtues. The twin concepts of abstract and concrete labor for example, allow him to confront head-on a difficulty that has long bedeviled all forms of geographical enquiry: the relation between universal generalizations and the evident uniqueness of human activities and experience in particular places and time. A seemingly insuperable conceptual difficulty is thus transformed into a conceptual tension out of which theoretical elaborations can be evolved. Such a strategem is intuitively appealing, since it explicitly recognizes how we are simultaneously in and of the world. But is also appears powerful enough to bear quite extraordinary conceptual fruits, chief of which, in my judgement, is a pathway toward the integration of geography and space relations into the general social theory that Marx proposed. That the proper harvesting of such a rich theoretical perspective has for so long been denied is, surely, one of the extraordinary and outstanding failures of an otherwise powerful Marxist tradition.

Our task, then, is to take these basic propositions concerning the contradictions inherent in the production of space under capitalist social relations and put them to work so as to understand how the historical geography of capitalism takes on its own particular and peculiar qualities. It is only in such a context that we can begin to reconstruct more detailed theoretical understandings of phenomena such as urbanization, regional development, and the geopolitics of uneven geographical development.

References

WORKS BY MARX

Capital. 3 vols. International Publishers, New York, 1967.
Critique of Hegel's philosophy of right. Ed. J. O'Malley, Cambridge University Press, London, 1970.
Theories of surplus value. 3 vols. Lawrence and Wishart, London, pts. 1 and 2, 1969; pt. 3, 1972.
Grundrisse. Ed. M. Nicolaus. Penguin Publishers, Harmondsworth, Middlesex, 1973.

WORKS BY MARX AND ENGELS

Manifesto of the Communist Party. Progress Publishers, Moscow, 1952.
Selected Correspondence. Progress Publishers, Moscow, 1955.
The German Ideology. Ed. C. J. Arthur. International Publishers, New York, 1970.
On colonialism. International Publishers, New York, 1972.
Ireland and the Irish question. Prepared by L. I. Goldmand and V. E. Kumina. International Publishers, New York, 1972.

OTHER WORKS CITED

Harvey, D. 1981: The spatial fix: Hegel, von Thünen, and Marx, *Antipode* 13, no. 3: 1–12.
—— 1982: *The Limits to capital.* Oxford.
Hegel, G. W. [1821] 1952: *Philosophy of right.* Trans. T.M. Knox. Oxford.

38

REASSERTIONS: TOWARDS A SPATIALIZED ONTOLOGY

Edward W. Soja

In common with Harvey (**chapter 37**), Ed Soja has been concerned with the relationships between Western Marxism and geography. He has argued that modern geography has suffered from a weak, depoliticized concept of space because of its rejection of materialism after turning away from environmental determinism. He also claims that modern social theory has placed too much emphasis on time and history at the expense of space and geography. Hence the subtitle of the book from which this piece is taken, 'the reassertion of space in critical social theory'. Soja shares Harvey's desire to return space to social theory, but unlike Harvey he does not think that all the answers lie with Marx, in whom he detects a distrust of space. Soja's influences are therefore more from the twentieth century, including Poulantzas, Giddens, Foucault and, above all, Henri Lefebvre. Indeed, many of the ideas in this extract are taken directly from this French Marxist's influential text *The production of space* (1991, Oxford), first published in 1974. Space is socially produced (compare this with Smith and O'Keefe's discussion of the production of nature, **chapter 16**) and this spatiality combines both mental and material aspects. To separate it out into either objective or subjective space – something which is common to both spatial scientists and some of its critics – is labelled an illusion by Soja.

Source: *Postmodern geographies: the reassertion of space in critical social theory*. London: Verso, 1989, Extract from pp. 118–31.

> *For its part, Marxist research has up to now . . . considered that transformations of space and time essentially concern ways of thinking: it assigns a marginal role to such changes on the grounds that they belong to the ideological-cultural domain – to the manner in which societies or classes* represent *space and time. In reality, however, transformations of the spatio-temporal matrices refer to the materiality of the social division of labour, or the structure of the State, and of the practices and techniques of capitalist economic, political and ideological power; they are the* real substratum *of mythical, religious, philosophical or 'experiential' representations of space-time. (Poulantzas, 1978, 26)*

> *This primal material framework is the mould of social atomization and splintering, and it is embodied in the practices of the labour process itself. At one and the same time presupposition of the relations of production and embodiment of the labour process, this framework consists in the organization of a continuous, homogeneous, cracked and fragmented space-time such as lies at the basis of Taylorism: a cross-ruled, segmented and cellular space in which each fragment (individual) has its place, and in which each emplacement, while corresponding to a fragment (individual) must present itself as homogeneous and uniform; and a linear, serial, repetitive and cumulative time, in which the various moments are integrated with one another, and which is itself oriented toward a finished product – namely the space-time materialized* par excellence *in the production line. (Ibid., 64–65)*

With the publication of *State, Power, Socialism* (1978), the last of his major works, Nicos Poulantzas provided stirring evidence that he too had discovered a socio-spatial dialectic of sorts and was seeking to re-direct Marxist analysis toward a materialist interpretation of space and time, an explicitly historical geography of capitalism. Building in part upon the contributions of Lefebvre, he defined the spatial and temporal 'matrices' of capitalism, its material groundedness, as simultaneously presuppositions and embodiments of the relations of production. These intertwining matrices were not just the outcomes of a mechanical causality in which pre-existing relations of production give rise at some subsequent stage to a concrete history and a geography. 'Territory' and 'tradition', as Poulantzas labelled spatial and temporal matrices, were a *logical priority* (what Marx called *Voraussetzung*) and appear 'at the same time' as their presupposition. Neither were they to be seen, following the Kantian narrowing, only as ways of thinking, modes of representation. The creation and transformation of spatial and temporal matrices establish a primal material framework, the real substratum of social life.

These are complex and discomforting arguments which, like Lefebvre's introductory chapter in *La Production de l'espace*, assign to space what had so assertively been attached to time in the Marxist tradition: a fundamental materiality, a problematic social genealogy, a political praxis impelled through an indissoluble link to the production and reproduction of social life, and behind all this an ontological priority, an essential connection between spatiality and being. Without abandoning Marx, Poulantzas, again like Lefebvre, criticized Marxism for its persistent failure to see the material and ideological spatialization associated with the development and survival of capitalism, a spatialization intimately bound up with the social division of labour, the institutional materiality of the state, and the expressions of economic, political, and ideological power. At the same time he was clearly more comfortable with history than with the less familiar spatial matrix, a residual historical bias shared with Anthony Giddens and other social theorists who catch sight of the interpretive power of spatiality rather late in their careers. Nevertheless, Poulantzas joined with these other spatial envisionaries at the end of the 1970s in raising the call for a significant retheorization of the spatiality of social life.

Accompanying this call was another, more meta-theoretical project, a search for an appropriate ontological and epistemological location for spatiality, an active 'place' for space in a Western philosophical tradition that had rigidly separated time from space and intrinsically prioritized temporality to the point of expunging the ontological and epistemological significance of spatiality. Michel Foucault, an important contributor to this debate, recognized the philosophical invisibility of space relative to time (after being pushed to this realization by the interviewers from *Herodote*, 1980). His words are worth repeating: 'Space was treated as the dead, the fixed, the undialectical, the immobile. Time, on the contrary, was richness, fecundity, life, dialectic.' To recover from this historicist devaluation, to make space visible again as a fundamental referent of social being, requires a major rethinking not only of the concreteness of capitalist spatial practices but also of the philosophizing abstractions of modern ontology and epistemology.

Materiality and Illusion in the Conceptualization of Space

The generative source for a materialist interpretation of spatiality is the recognition that spatiality is socially produced and, like society itself, exists in both substantial forms (concrete spatialities) and as a set of relations between individuals and groups, an 'embodiment' and medium of social life itself.

As socially produced space, spatiality can be distinguished from the physical space of material nature and the mental space of cognition and representation, each of which is used and incorporated into the social construction of spatiality but cannot be conceptualized as its equivalent. Within certain limits (which are frequently overlooked) physical and psychological processes and forms can be theorized independently with regard to their spatial dimensions and attributes. The classical debates in the history of science over the absolute versus relative qualities of physical space exemplify the former, while attempts to explore the personal meaning and symbolic content of 'mental maps' and landscape imagery illustrate the latter. This possibility of independent conceptualization and inquiry, however, does not produce an unquestionable autonomy or rigid separation between these three spaces (physical, mental, social), for they interrelate and overlap. Defining these interconnections remains one of the most formidable challenges to contemporary social theory, especially since the historical debate has been monopolized by the physical–mental dualism almost to the exclusion of social space.

The assertion of (social) spatiality shatters the traditional dualism and forces a major reinterpretation of the materiality of space, time, and being, the constructive nexus of social theory. In the first place, not only are the spaces of nature and cognition incorporated into the social production of spatiality they are significantly transformed in the process. This social incorporation–transformation sets important limits to the independent theorizations of physical and mental space, especially with regard to their potential applicability to concrete social analysis and interpretation. In their appropriate interpretive contexts, both the material space of physical nature and the ideational space of human nature have to be seen as being socially produced and reproduced. Each needs to be theorized and understood, therefore, as ontologically and epistemologically part of the spatiality of social life.

Conversely, spatiality cannot be completely separated from physical and psychological spaces. Physical and biological processes affect society no matter how much they are socially mediated, and social life is never entirely free of such restrictive impingements as the physical friction of distance. The impress of this 'first nature' is not naively and independently given, however, for its social impact always passes through a 'second nature' that arises from the organized and cumulative application of human labour and knowledge. There can thus be no autonomous naturalism or social physics, with its own separate causal logic, in the materialist interpretation of human geography and history. In the context of society, nature, like spatiality, is socially produced and reproduced despite its appearance of objectivity and separation. The space of nature is thus filled with politics and ideology, with relations of production, with the possibility of being significantly transformed.

Neil Smith captures the meaning of this social production of nature in his recent work, *Uneven Development* (1984), revealingly subtitled 'Nature, Capital and the Production of Space'.

> *The idea of the production of nature is indeed paradoxical, to the point of sounding absurd, if judged by the superficial appearance of nature in capitalist society. Nature is generally seen as precisely that which cannot be produced; it is the antithesis of human productive activity. In its most immediate appearance, the natural landscape presents itself to us as the material substratum of daily life, the realm of use-values rather than exchange-values. As such it is highly differentiated along any number of axes. But with the progress of capital accumulation and the expansion of economic development, this material substratum is more and more the product of social production, and the dominant axes of differentiation are increasingly societal in origin. In short, when this immediate appearance of nature is placed in historical context, the development of the material landscape presents itself as a process of the production of nature. The differentiated results of this production of nature are the material symptoms of uneven development. At the most abstract level, therefore, it is in the production of nature that use-value and exchange-value, and space and society, are fused together. (Smith, 1984, 32)*

A similar argument can be made with respect to cognitive or mental space. The presentation of concrete spatiality is always wrapped in the complex and diverse re-presentations of human perception and cognition, without any necessity of direct and determined correspondence between the two. These representations, as semiotic imagery and cognitive mappings, as ideas and ideologies, play a powerful role in shaping the spatiality of social life. There can be no challenge to the existence of this humanized, mental space, a spatialized *mentalité*. But here too the social production of spatiality appropriates and recasts the representations and significations of mental space as part of social life, as part of second nature. To seek to interpret spatiality from the purview of socially independent processes of semiotic representation is consequently also inappropriate and misleading, for it tends to bury social origins and potential social transformation under a distorting screen of idealism and psychologism, a universalized and edenic human nature prancing about in a spaceless and timeless world.

Tied to this interpretation of the connections between physical, mental, and social space is a key assumption about the dynamics of spatiality and hence about the relations between (social) space and time, geography and history. Spatiality exists ontologically as a product of a transformation process, but always remains open to further transformation in the contexts of material life. It is never primordially given or permanently fixed. This may seem obvious when so simply stated, but it is precisely this transformative dynamic, its associated social tensions and contradictions, and its rootedness in active spatial praxis, that has been blocked from critical theoretical consciousness over the past hundred years. The spaces that have been seen are illusive ones, blurring our capacity to envision the social dynamics of spatialization.

Misplacing spatiality: the illusion of opaqueness

A confusing myopia has persistently distorted spatial theorization by creating illusions of opaqueness, short-sighted interpretations of spatiality which focus on immediate surface appearances without being able to see beyond them. Spatiality is accordingly interpreted and theorized only as a collection of things, as substantive appearances which may ultimately be linked to social causation but are knowable only as things-in-themselves. This essentially empiricist (but also occasionally phenomenological) interpretation of space reflects the substantive-attributive structure (Zeleny, 1980) that has dominated scientific thought since the philosophy of the Enlightenment, a powerful heritage of objective naturalism to which spatial and social theorists have repeatedly appealed for both insight and legitimacy.[1]

From this myopic perspective, spatiality is comprehended only as objectively measurable appearances grasped through some combination of sensory-based perception (a purview developed by Hume and Locke and later revised and codified by Comte and others in a much less sceptical form of positivism); Cartesian mathematical-geometric abstractions (extended to manifold non-Euclidian variations); and the mechanical materialism of a post-Newtonian social physics or a post-Darwinian sociobiology. A more contemporary cynosure of this spatial myopia, especially influential in the French philosophical and scientific tradition, was the *fin de siècle* figure of Henri Bergson. As we look back to the extraordinary devaluation and subordination of space (relative to time) that marked the last half of the nineteenth century, Bergson increasingly stands out as one of its most forceful instigators. For him, time, the vital realm of *durée* was the carrier of

1 Relevant here are the epistemological critiques of positivism arising from a group of realist philosophers and significantly influencing the contemporary retheorization of spatiality. See, for example, Bhaskar (1975 and 1979), Keat and Urry (1982), Sayer (1984), and, more directly applied to human geography, Gregory (1978).

creativity, spirit, meaning, feeling, the 'true reality' of our world and our consciousness. Space, in the form of the categorizing intellect, was seen as orienting the mind to quantity (versus quality), measurement (versus meaning). Space is thus seen as pulverizing the fluid flow of duration into meaningless pieces and collapsing time into its own physical dimensionalities. As Lefebvre frequently notes – most recently in an interview published in *Society and Space* (Burgel et al., 1987) – this Bergsonian view 'throws all sins onto space' and rigidly separates space and time as science versus philosophy, form versus life, a vindictive dichotomization that would influence Lukács and so many other historicizers throughout the twentieth century.[2]

In all these approaches, spatiality is reduced to physical objects and forms, and naturalized back to a first nature so as to become susceptible to prevailing scientific explanation in the form of orderly, reproduceable description and the discovery of empirical regularities (largely in the spatial co-variation of phenomenal appearances). Such a short-sighted approach to space has proved productive in the accumulation of accurate geographical information and seductive as a legitimization for a presumed science of geography. It becomes illusive, however, when geographical description is substituted for explanation of the social production of space and the spatial organization of society, in other words, when geographical appearances are asserted as the source of an epistemology of spatiality. Yet, as I have noted before, this is precisely how space has been theorized in mainstream social science and in the theoretical geography which took shape in the 1960s. Even when a narrow empiricism or positivism is eschewed, the 'spatial organization of society' is made to appear socially inert, a deadened product of the ordering discipline of the friction of distance, the relativity of location, the statistics of ecological covariation, and the axioms of geometry. Within this optical illusion, theories are constructed which always seem to mask social conflict and social agency, reducing them to little more than the aggregate expression of individual preferences which are typically assumed to be (naturally? organically?) given. Lost from view are the deeper social origins of spatiality, its problematic production and reproduction, its contextualization of politics, power, and ideology.

It is not surprising that the development and persistence of this illusion of opaqueness, with its submergence of social conflict in depoliticized geometries, has been interpreted (by those who can see beyond the myopic illusion) as an integral part of the evolution of capitalism. As one critic observed, 'Time and space assume . . . that character of absolute timelessness and universality which must mark the exchange abstraction as a whole and each of its features' (Sohn-Rethel 1978, quoted in Smith, 1984, 74). Time and space, like the commodity form, the competitive

[2] Bergson's key works on space and time are his *Essai sur les données immédiates de la conscience* (1889; see also Bergson, 1910) and *Matière et mémoire* (1896). For a contemporary paean to Bergson and his followers and to the privileging of time and history against the evils of spatialization, see David Gross, 'Space, Time, and Modern Culture', published in *Telos* (Winter 1981–82), 'a quarterly journal of radical thought'. So intense is the urge to maintain the prioritization of time over space in this journal that the front cover and each page-top of the Gross article states the title as 'Time, Space and Modern Culture'!

market, and the structure of social classes, are represented as a natural relation between things, explainable objectively in terms of the substantive physical properties and attributes of these things in themselves, rather than as a 'continuous, homogeneous, cracked and fragmented space-time' rooted in the capitalist labour process, to recall Poulantzas' incisive words. Illusions of opaqueness have pervaded 'normal' science, both physical and social, throughout the past several centuries, obscuring from view the problematic historical geography of capitalism.

Misplacing spatiality: the illusion of transparency

A similar interpretation can be made of a second source of illusion in the theorization of spatiality, one which evolves in a complex interaction with the first, often as its attempted philosophical negation.[3] Whereas the empiricist myopia cannot see the social production of space behind the opacity of objective appearances, a hypermetropic illusion of transparency sees right through the concrete spatiality of social life by projecting its production into an intuitive realm of purposeful idealism and immaterialized reflexive thought. Seeing is blurred not because the focal point is too far in front of what should be seen, inducing near-sightedness, but because the focal point lies too far away from what should be seen, the source of a distorting and over-distancing vision, hypermetropic rather than myopic. The production of spatiality is represented – literally re-presented – as cognition and mental design, as an illusive ideational subjectivity substituted for an equally illusive sensory objectivism. Spatiality is reduced to a mental construct alone, a way of thinking, an ideational process in which the 'image' of reality takes epistemological precedence over the tangible substance and appearance of the real world. Social space folds into mental space, into diaphanous concepts of spatiality which all too often take us away from materialized social realities.

The philosophical origins of this approach to theorization are probably Platonic. It was certainly boosted by Leibniz's assertion of the relativism of physical space, its existence as an idea rather than a thing. But its most powerful source of philosophical legitimacy and elaboration is Kant, whose system of categorical antinomies assigned an explicit and sustaining ontological place to geography and spatial analysis, a place which has been carefully preserved in a continuing neo-Kantian interpretation of spatiality. The Kantian legacy of transendental spatial idealism pervades every wing of the modern hermeneutic tradition, infiltrates Marxism's historical approach to spatiality, and has been central to the modern discipline of geography since its origins in the late nineteenth century. The vision of human geography that it induces is one in which the organization of space is projected from a mental ordering of phenomena, either intuitively given, or relativized into many different 'ways of thinking'. These ideas about space are then typically allocated to categorical structures of cognition such as human nature or

[3] The continuing historical 'see-saw' between the dominant naturalist/scientific current of positivism and empiricism on the one side, and its 'anti-naturalist hermeneutic foil' on the other, is vividly described in Bhaskar (1979).

culture at its most general, or biographical experience as its most specific, or alternatively to 'science', to the Hegelian 'spirit', to the structuralist Marxist 'ideological-cultural domain', to an almost infinite variety of possible ideational compartments and sources of consciousness in-between.

Exemplifying just such a neo-Kantian cognitive mapping is Robert Sack's work, appealingly titled *Conceptions of Space in Social Thought* (1980). Although it propounds a realist philosophy, and ventures far beyond the limits of pure spatial subjectivity, Sack's analysis of the 'elemental structures' of 'modes of thought' is virtually divorced from the specific influence of 'socio-material conditions', a subject which Sack, in consummate neo-Kantian fashion, assigns for possible future research. Instead, he packages the conceptualization of spatiality into a neat categorical dualism that opposes the 'sophisticated-fragmented' spatial meaning associated with the arts, sciences, and contemporary industrial society; to the 'unsophisticated-fused' conceptualization of the primitive and the child, of myth and magic. In many ways, this dichotomization of spatial concepts parallels and can be mapped into such equally procrustean dualisms of social theory as *Gemeinschaft* and *Gesellschaft*, mechanical and organic solidarity, Tradition and Modernity, the 'raw' and the 'cooked'.

Again, there are useful insights to be drawn from such approaches, but they also serve to reinforce a fundamental illusion that disguises the social production of space, especially when the ideation of spatiality is represented as a direct route towards understanding its problematic and politically-charged production and reproduction. Generic human conceptions of space may have some intrinsic and identifiable qualities worthy of further study, but if spatial fusion-fragmentation is indeed one of the elemental structures of social thought, it must be ground at all times in the material conditions of human life and not made to float as a timeless and placeless universal of human nature. Neither fusion nor fragmentation arise in this thin air of transcendental idealism.

As Lefebvre points out, and Poulantzas, Foucault, Giddens, Gregory, and others repeat in different ways, spatial fragmentation as well as the appearance of spatial coherence and homogeneity are social products and often an integral part of the instrumentality of political power. They do not arise from material spatiality or the mode of production in some simple, deterministic fashion, nor do they reflect back on society, once established, with simplistic determinacy of another kind. But conceptions or representations of space in social thought cannot be understood as projections of modes of thinking hypothetically (or otherwise) independent of socio-material conditions no matter where or when they are found, whether they emanate from the collective minds of a band of hunters and gatherers or from the institutionalized citizenry of the advanced capitalist state.

Refocusing on the elusive spatiality of capitalism

As I have argued, a peculiar anti-spatialism, rooted in part in Marx's reaction to Hegel, has stubbornly screened Western Marxism from an appropriate materialist interpretation of spatiality. Marx treated space primarily as a physical context, the sum of the places of production, the territory of different markets, the source of a crude friction of distance to be 'annihilated' by time and the increasingly unfettered operations of capital. It can be argued that Marx recognized the opacity of spatiality, that it can hide under its objective appearances the fundamental social relations of production, especially in his discussions of the relations between town and countryside. He also approached, if not so directly, the basic problematic of the socio-spatial dialectic: that social relations are simultaneously and conflictually space-forming and space-contingent. The spatial contingency of social action, however, was reduced primarily to fetishization and false consciousness and never received from Marx an effective materialist interpretation.

Arguments about the spatial contingency of social relations, that these social relations of production and class can be reconfigured and possibly transformed through the evolving spatiality which makes them concrete, are still perhaps the most difficult part of the materialist interpretation of space for contemporary Marxist scholars to accept. A continuing aversion to any hint of a geographical determination of social life makes it difficult to see that spatiality is itself a social product that is not independently imposed and that it is never either inert or immutable. The geography and history of capitalism intersect in a complex social process which creates a constantly evolving historical sequence of spatialities, a spatio-temporal structuration of social life which gives form to and situates not only the grand movements of societal development but also the recursive practices of day-to-day activity – even in the least capitalist of contemporary societies.

The production of spatiality in conjunction with the making of history can thus be described as both the medium and the outcome, the presupposition and embodiment, of social action and relationship, of society itself. Social and spatial structures are dialectically intertwined in social life, not just mapped one onto the other as categorical projections. And from this vital connection comes the theoretical keystone for the materialist interpretation of spatiality, the realization that social life is materially constituted in its historical geography, that spatial structures and relations are the concrete manifestations of social structures and relations evolving over time, whatever the mode of production. To claim that history is the materialization of social life would cause little controversy, especially amongst Marxist scholars. It is virtually axiomatic to historical materialist analysis. But it is at this fundamental, axiomatic, and ontological level that spatiality must be incorporated as a second materialization/contextualization of social being. The constitution of society is spatial and temporal, social existence is made concrete in geography and history.

The first explicit and systematically developed assertion of this fundamental premise comes from Lefebvre in *La Production de l'espace* (1974):

> *There remains one question that has not yet been posed: what exactly is the mode of existence of social relations? Substantiality? Naturality? Formal Abstraction? The study of space now allows us to answer: the social relations of production have a social existence only insofar as they exist spatially; they project themselves into a space, they inscribe themselves in a space*

while producing it. Otherwise, they remain in 'pure' abstraction, that is, in representations and consequently in ideology, or, stated differently, in verbalism, verbiage, words. (152–53, author's translation)

This 'discovery' is the wellspring for the major reconceptualization of postmodern critical social theory that has advanced significantly in the 1980s. Lefebvre, Poulantzas, Giddens, and many others who have begun to reconceptualize the spatiality of social life share several additional specific emphases: the instrumental power which adheres to the organization of space at many different scales, the increasing reach of this instrumental and disciplinary power into everyday life as well as into more global processes of capitalist development, the changing and often contradictory roles of the state in these power relations wherever they are implanted.

Whether seen as the formation of a spatial matrix or as spatial structuration, the power-filled social production of space under capitalism has not been a smooth and automatic process in which social structure is stamped out, without resistance or constraint, onto the landscape. From its origins, the development of industrial capitalism was rooted in a conflict-filled attempt to construct a socially transformative and encompassing spatiality of its own. The arenas of struggle were many: the destruction of feudal property relations and the turbulent creation of a proletariat 'freed' from its former means of subsistence; the related uprootings associated with the spreading enclosure and commodification of rural and urban land; the expansive geographical concentration of labour power and industrial production in urban centres (and the attendant if incomplete destruction of earlier forms of urbanization, industrialization, and rural life); the induced separation of workplace and residence and the equally induced patterning of urban land-uses and the built environment of urbanism; the creation of differentiated regional markets and the extension of the territorial role of the capitalist state; the beginnings of an expansion of capitalism on to a global scale. As Poulantzas argued (and Michel Foucault took up with such detail and insight in his *recherches*), 'the direct producers are freed from the soil only to become trapped in a grid – one that includes not only the modern factory, but also the modern family, school, army, the prison system, the city and national territory' (Poulantzas, 1978, 105). Poulantzas goes on to describe the paradoxical fragmentation and homogenization, spatial differentiation and levelling-off of differences, that lies behind the geographically uneven development of capitalism:

Separation and division in order to unify; parcelling out in order to encompass; segmentation in order to totalize; closure in order to homogenize; and individualization in order to obliterate differences and otherness. The roots of totalitarianism are inscribed in the spatial matrix concretized by the modern nation-state – a matrix that is already present in its relations of production and in the capitalist division of labor. (107)

The production of capitalist spatiality, however, is no once-and-for-all event. The spatial matrix must constantly be reinforced and, when necessary, restructured –

that is, spatiality must be socially reproduced, and this reproduction process is a continuing source of conflict and crisis.

The problematic connection of social and spatial reproduction follows straightforwardly. If spatiality is both outcome/embodiment and medium/presupposition of social relations and social structure, their material reference, then social life must be seen as both space-forming and space contingent, a producer and a product of spatiality. This two-way relationship defines – or perhaps, redefines – a socio-spatial dialectic which is simultaneously part of a spatio-temporal dialect, a tense and contradiction filled interplay between the social production of geography and history. To provide the necessary recomposition of Marx's familiar dictum: We make our own history and geography, but not just as we please; we do not make them under circumstances chosen by ourselves, but under circumstances directly encountered, given and transmitted from the historical geographies produced in the past.

The general argument I have presented can be briefly summarized in a sequence of linked premises:

1. Spatiality is a substantiated and recognizable social product, part of a 'second nature' which incorporates as it socializes and transforms both physical and psychological spaces.
2. As a social product, spatiality is simultaneously the medium and outcome, presupposition and embodiment, of social action and relationship.
3. The spatio-temporal structuring of social life defines how social action and relationship (including class relations) are materially constituted, made concrete.
4. The constitution/concretization process is problematic, filled with contradiction and struggle(amidst much that is recursive and routinized).
5. Contradictions arise primarily from the duality of produced space as both outcome/embodiment/product and medium/presupposition/producer of social activity.
6. Concrete spatiality – actual human geography – is thus a competitive arena for struggles over social production and reproduction, for social practices aimed either at the maintenance and reinforcement of existing spatiality or at significant restructuring and/or radical transformation.
7. The temporality of social life, from the routines and events of day-to-day activity to the longer-run making of history (*évènement* and *durée*, to use the language of Braudel), is rooted in spatial contingency in much the same way as the spatiality of social life is rooted in temporal/historical contingency.
8. The materialist interpretation of history and the materialist interpretation of geography are inseparably intertwined and theoretically concomitant, with no inherent prioritization of one over the other.

Taken together, these premisses frame a materialist interpretation of spatiality that is only now taking shape and affecting empirical research. They still have to be teaseu out of the current literature since, for the most part, they have remained implicit. Often research which brilliantly illuminates the arguments behind these premisses is not immediately recognized as such, even by the researchers themselves, as was noted in the case of Foucault. Or else, well-intentioned exemplifications end up clouding more of the arguments than they illuminate by falling back into the traps of spatial separatism.

Furthermore, powerful and persistent barriers still remain to accepting a materialist interpretation of spatiality and an assertive historical-geographical materialism aimed specifically at understanding and changing capitalist spatializations. The most rigid of these barriers arise from an unyielding Marxist, if not more generally post-Enlightenment, tradition of historicism which reduces spatiality either to the stable and unproblematic site of historical action or to the source of false consciousness, a mystification of fundamental social relations. Historicism blocks from view both the material objectivity of space as a structuring force in society and the ideational subjectivity of space as a progressively active part of collective consciousness. Stated somewhat differently, in terms that would take on new meaning in the debates of the 1980s on the restructuring of critical social theory. Western Marxism's conceptualization of the interplay between human agency and social structure has remained essentially historical, defined in the praxis of making history. Spatiality, as the praxis of creating human geography, still tends to be pushed into an epiphenomenal shadow as history's mirroring container. Historicism continues to be one of the most forceful nineteenth-century monuments that must be destroyed before critical social theory and Western Marxism can successfully envision the spatiality of contemporary social life.

Can Western Marxism be spatialized without inducing the aura of an antihistory? If so, how can the historical imagination be made to accommodate a space which is as rich and dialectical as time? These are challenging questions which have rarely, if ever, been asked before the present decade. One possible approach in response to these questions is through logical persuasion, the straightforward rational assertion of a socio-spatial dialectic, a historical and geographical materialism, a space-time structuration of social life. By now, this trajectory of theoretical assertion will be familiar to the patient reader. But it is not enough. A promising alternative path, which took me eventually to the study of urban restructuring in Los Angeles (and which will eventually take the reader there as well), is one of empirical demonstration, the application of a materialist interpretation of spatiality to contemporary 'real world' issues and politics. This turn to empirical research will undoubtedly be vital to the future development of an historical geographical materialism and a reconstructed postmodern critical social theory.

There is, however, another path, rarely followed these days, which departs from theoretical assertion in the opposite direction, looking at the 'backward linkages' rather than the empirical and political 'forward linkages' of theory formation. This is a path into the even more slippery and abstract realm of ontology, the meta-theoretical discourse which seeks to discover what the world must be like in order for knowledge and human action to be possible, what it means to *be* (Bhaskar, 1975). Assuming that there is little of importance left to discover in ontological discourse, with its characteristic distancing from praxis, most Western Marxists have been reticent to venture very far along this backward-looking path. But it is a worthwhile journey to take, for it can help us find some still-missing connections between space, time and being, and hence between the makings of history, human geography, and society.

References

Bergson, H. 1910: *Time and Free Will: An Essay on the Immediate Data of Consciousness*, trans. by F. Pogson, London: G. Allen; New York, Macmillan.
Bhaskar, R. 1979: *The Possibility of Naturalism*, Brighton: Harvester Press.
Bhaskar, R. 1975: *A Realist Theory of Science*, Leeds: Alma.
Burgel, Gallia, Burgel, G., and Dezes, M. 1987: 'An Interview with Henri Lefebvre', translated by E. Kofman, *Environment and Planning D: Society and Space*, 5, 27–38.
Foucault, M. 1980: 'Questions on Geography', in C. Gordon (ed.), *Power/Knowledge: Selected Interviews and Other Writings 1972–1977*, 63–77.
Gregory, D. 1978: *Ideology, Science and Human Geography*, London: Hutchinson.
Keat, R. and Urry, J. 1982: *Social Theory as Science*, London: Routledge and Kegan Paul.
Lefebvre, H. 1974: *La Production de l'espace*. Paris: Anthropos.
Poulantzas, N. 1978: *State, Power, Socialism*, London: Verso.
Sack, R. 1980: *Conceptions of Space in Social Thought*, Minneapolis: University of Minnesota Press.
Sayer, A. 1984: *Method in Social Science: A Realist Approach*, London: Hutchinson.
Smith, N. 1984: *Uneven Development*, Oxford: Basil Blackwell.
Zeleny, J. 1980: *The Logic of Marx*, Oxford: Oxford University Press.

39

THE CHOREOGRAPHY OF EXISTENCE: COMMENTS ON HÄGERSTRAND'S TIME-GEOGRAPHY AND ITS USEFULNESS

Allan Pred

Among the most influential geographers of the past 40 years is the Swede Torsten Hägerstrand (see **chapter 40**). As well as pioneering the study of innovation diffusion ana stochastic simulation in the 1950s, he developed the ideas and techniques of time-geography with a group of geographers at Lund University in the 1970s. Pred suggests that time-geography is an original geographical idea which might resolve many of the discipline's intellectual and methodological issues. Like Nystuen (**chapter 36**) it provides a basic set of concepts and terms applicable to a wide range of geographical problems – although it includes time as well as space. In his survey Pred indicates its relevance to landscape, regions, innovation, migration and the history of geography itself. In fact Pred has written about his own biography using time-geographic concepts [in 'The academic past through a time-geographic looking-glass', *Annals of the Association of American Geographers* 69, 175–80, 1979]. He was one of the many geographers to visit Sweden in the 1960s and learn from Hägerstrand. Because it holds together time and space, individual and society, ecology and place, time-geography addresses many of the dualisms which much modern social theory attempts to overcome. Pred's own writing, based on research on both the USA and Sweden in the nineteenth century, has done much to develop the methodological possibilities of time-geography into a coherent social theory of modernity and societal change.

Source: The choreography of existence: comments on Hägerstrand's time-geography and its usefulness. *Economic Geography* 53, 207–21, 1977.

Many, perhaps most, of the research efforts and themes which have proven highly fashionable among "modern" human geographers during the 1960s and 1970s have depended heavily upon other disciplines for their conceptual frameworks. At times, it has appeared as if individual geographers were less concerned with problems of intellectual substance than with the possible geographical ramifications of models, concepts, and techniques used by psychologists, economists, sociologists, and political scientists. The validity of employing conceptual frame-works developed by scholars in other fields is certainly not to be questioned *per se*, but the all too frequent placement of the borrowed-framework or borrowed-technique cart before the problem-defining horse would appear rather difficult to defend. In view of the haphazard groping and stumbling about for thematic foci which seems so characteristic of much contemporary Anglo-American human geography, it is perhaps high time to cease asking what other disciplines can provide us in the way of usable schema and to begin giving more emphasis to the intelligent definition of research problems and the employment of our own conceptual structures.

In this context, this article will suggest that human geography would stand to benefit greatly if a considerable volume of its research involved the application of concepts contained in Torsten Hägerstrand's time-geography.

Among other things, Hägerstrand's framework has the potential for shedding new light on some of the very different kinds of questions customarily posed by "old fashioned" regional and historical geographers, as well as "modern" human geographers. The time-geographic framework also holds the promise of identifying new questions of social and scholarly significance. It may also satisfy the longing shared by many for a more humanistically oriented geographic approach to some of the more complex and frustrating problems of modern society. In addition, insofar as time-geography has something to say about the deep structure of all interactions and transactions between man and man, man and elements of the natural environment, and man and man-made objects, it has the potential for enabling geographers to attain a new level of intellectual maturity. That is, through Hägerstrand's conceptual structure geographers may grow so bold as to seriously ask themselves what insights and assistance they can provide to researchers in the neighboring social and biological sciences.

The Contents of Hägerstrand's Time-Geography

There is little need to fully depict the main features of the time-geography framework which is still being refined and elaborated upon by Hägerstrand and his Lund associates. Although the bulk of the time-geography literature remains in Swedish, a number of partial statements and summaries are available in English [4; 8; 10; 16; 21; 23; 27; 28; 47] and several specific components of the framework have been introduced in articles appearing on earlier pages of this issue of *Economic Geography*. Consequently, only a crudely summarized statement of some of the principal characteristics of Hägerstrand's time-geography is provided as a backdrop.

At one level of analysis time-geography deals with the time-space "choreography" of the individual's existence at daily, yearly, or lifetime (biographical) scales of observation. Time and space are seen as inseperable. Each and every one of the actions and events which in sequence compose the individual's existence has *both* temporal and spatial attributes – not merely one or the other [*15; 33*]. More specifically, an individual's existence can be diagrammatically described as a trajectory, a "daily-" or "life-path" of movement – a weaving dance through time-space. The most significant elementary steps, or events, in such a "choreographic" depiction occur at physically fixed buildings or territorial units of observation – referred to as "stations" or "domains" – either when two or more individuals meet to form a group (or "activity bundle") or when such groups dissolve, with one or more of the participating individuals moving in space *and time* to eventually form other "activity bundles" at other "stations."[1] This choreographic point of view – by which the structure and process of outward physical existence become one – focusses on the constraints which in both obvious and subtle ways limit the individual's freedom to move from station to station and to choose activity bundles.

Three major classes of constraint to a considerable degree steer the action and event sequence, or score the choreography, of the individual's daily existence [*16*; *47*]. *Capability constraints* circumscribe activity participation by demanding that large chunks of time be allocated to physiological necessities (sleeping, eating, and personal care) and by limiting the distance an individual can cover within a given time-span in accord with the transportation technology available. *Coupling constraints* pinpoint where, when, and for how long the individual must join other individuals (or objects) in order to form production, consumption, social, and miscellaneous activity bundles. *Authority constraints* in some measure spring from the simple fact that space-occupation is exclusive and that all spaces have a limited packing capacity. Authority constraints subsume those general rules, laws, economic barriers, and power relationships which determine who does or does not have access to specific domains at specific times to do specific things. Several other general constraints impinge upon the individual's freedom of action, for example: the indivisibility of each individual (no person may be at two different places simultaneously); the limited ability of any human being to undertake more than one task at a time; the fact that station-to-station movement is always time-consuming; and "the fact that every situation is inevitably rooted in past situations" [*27*] (among other things, the time-geographic characteristics of each daily-activity choice limit the possible set of activity options for the remaining portion of the day).

The constraints which must be overcome in order to enable the formation of any single activity bundle or interaction are synonymous with the necessary (but not the sufficient) conditions which must be met for the occurrence of that activity bundle or interaction. In other words, time-geography can specify the necessary (but not the sufficient) conditions for virtually all forms of interaction – social and otherwise – involving human beings. Hence, the implications of Hägerstrand's time-geography spill well beyond the bordering ridges of human geography into the catchment basins of the various so-called social and behavioral sciences. Moreover, since the physical existence and "life-paths" of "individuals" belonging to

[1] Hägerstrand's station concept is a very flexible one. Since movement within a station is not observed or charted, the physical extent of a station depends upon one's temporal scale of observation. Thus, for example, an individual's city of residence may be regarded as a station at the life-path scale of observation, but at the daily scale of observation that city is broken up into a number of stations [*34*].

tool, machinery, building, manufactured good, vegetation, raw-material, and other non-human "populations" also can be traced in time-geographic terms, time-geography can: (1) specify the necessary (but not the sufficient) conditions for virtually all interaction between man and elements of the natural environment, and man and man-made objects; and (2) provide a bridge to cover the gap between human ecology and biological ecology [25].

The time-geography framework possesses the most unusual feature of being able to treat both the individual and society (or large segments thereof) as a whole. Thus, at a second level of analysis time-geography considers the physical existence of society within any specified bounded area by observing and analyzing the ceaseless matching process, or pairing-up ballet, that is played out between the "population" and "activity" systems of that area [*4; 17; 18*]. The "population system" of an area is made up of all its inhabitants and their household groupings, and its most important attribute is that is has a *finite supply of daily time resources*. These resources, quite plainly, are equal to 24 hours multiplied by the number of individuals involved.

An area's "activity system" includes all those activities within its borders which require direct human participation. Most significantly, in large measure the "activity system" consists of employment and other roles (e.g., shopper, meal-preparer, college student, soldier) which share the following characteristics: they have an independent existence in the sense that when they are not filled by one person they sooner or later must be filled by another person; they are generated by coalitions ranging in size from the family, to the business organization, to the state; and, they make *time demands* upon their holders, often at fixed temporal locations. The choreographic details of the population-system, activity-system matching process are mainly the result of: the indivisibility of each population-system member; the specific competency requirements of each role; the immobility of roads and buildings; the time requirements of interactivity spatial movement; and the fact that once all the roles of an activity bundle are staffed, the bundle becomes closed to additional participants.

The Intents of Hägerstrand's Time-Geography

It should be apparent from this considerably distilled summary that the time-geographic framework is at one and the same time disarmingly simple in composition and ambitious in design. The ambitiousness of the construct is fully in keeping with Hägerstrand's intentions, personal values, and aspirations.

For one thing, Hägerstrand is attempting to provide a way of thinking which will enable human geographers to get away from their overly "strong emphasis upon the spatial cross-sectional view" [22] of human phenomena and to focus a great deal more on time, while also paying more attention to people as physically existing individuals and to the concept of "finitude." ("Finitude" applies to space-packing capacities and limited time resources as well as limited natural resources and environmental tolerances [29]). The concern with time is not to be confused with the perspective of time-budget researchers. This is because in their preoccupation with daily and weekly time allocations they totally ignore the lifetime scale; because they unrealistically regard any sum of continuous time as a value-measure, much like money, which can be chopped into pieces and reassembled into use categories; and because they show little interest in the simultaneous time-groupings formed by different individuals [*17*]. Nor is the joint concern with time and space to be confused with the perspectives of those philosophers and physicists who treat space and time as a unified entity. Such writers restrict themselves almost entirely to questions associated with astronomical and sub-atomic scales of observation rather than with the very different scale at which the choreography of human existence occurs [*27*]. Instead, space and time are to be jointly treated by human geographers because "when events are seen located together in a block of space-time they inevitably expose relations which cannot be traced" if those events are "bunched . . . into classes and drawn . . . out of their place in the block," i.e., conventionally analyzed [*20*].

Hägerstrand's call for a time-geographic focus on people and, in particular, the event sequences which constitute the days and life of each individual person stems from a humanistic concern with the "quality-of-life" and everyday freedom of action implications *for individuals*" of both existing and alternative technologies, institutions, organizations, and urban forms. It is also based on the conviction that a common language – "a very general kind of space-time ecology" [*27*] – is needed to either assess or do something about these implications. Given his feeling that "it is not so much what people actually do as what they are free to do which it is most important to understand" [*23*] and his contention that there is a need to be "able to pinpoint the reasons for 'non-events,' that is, to trace barriers which prevent certain types of events and states from occurring" [*25*], it is perfectly logical that the spotlight of Hägerstrand's time-geography falls on the various types of constraint and finitude which wall-in the action alternatives of individuals. It should be realized that in choosing to develop a theoretical construct which reveals specific interactional and transactional constraints Hägerstrand is, in essence, rejecting any effort to directly predict individual behaviour [*27*].

From another point of view, the time-geographic framework represents a reaction to the tremendously specialized and fragmented manner in which systematic geography, the social sciences, and other disciplines treat human activities and experience. Whatever undeniable advantages there may be to subjecting tightly defined classes of activity and experience to the specially focussed analytic microscope of either, for example, population geography, economic geography, or cultural geography, or, for example, economics, sociology, demography, or psychology, they completely disintegrate when questions are raised regarding the *interdependence* of dissimilar and mixed activities.

Thus, one of the intentions behind the formulation of Hägerstrand's time-geography is the desire to develop a *contextual* rather than a *compositional* integrative approach to human activities and experiences [*24; 30*]. The *compositional* approach to synthesizing, as practiced by geographers and others, typically asks how given sets of phenomena, or systematic wholes, are divided into a hierarchy of component parts, and then proceeds to establish how the parts are joined together to form the whole. Compositional synthesis, in short, centers on form and structure. The *contextual* approach to synthesizing instead asks in what kind of situation is an included object or individual (or unit of observation) to be found and what connections exist between the object's or individual's characteristics and its (her) behavior in different situations or contexts. In Hägerstrand's case this means asking "how phenomena – irrespective of where their normal disciplinary home is taken to be – behave because they are closely co-existing in space and time" [*30*]. Hence, contextual synthesis centers on structure and *process*. And, in Hägerstrand's version of such synthesis, it is explicit that process ought to extend to general types of event sequences rather than just specific chains of occurrences [*26*].

Put yet another way, it is Hägerstrand's intention that his time-geographic framework should uncover "structural patterns and outcomes of processes which can seldom be derived from the laws of science as they are formulated today" [*29*]. This is to be accomplished by focussing on the *local connectedness* of real-world phenomena as well as the connections between spatially separate configurations of locally connected phenomena.[2] Hägerstrand is claiming, in other words, that existing scientific general principles simply cannot get at certain process outcomes because they ignore the "collateral" nature of processes involving the actions and experiences of "individuals," and because they fail to recognize that all such processes unfold in unbroken temporal and spatial continua, that all such processes entail *synchronization* and "*synchorization*." Finally, it is to be recognized that Hägerstrand's concern for local connections and the collateral processes which envelop different populations of individuals also amounts to a call for new links between human geography and biogeography [*29*] . . .

Applications Related to Traditional Research Themes in Human Geography

Owing to the circumstances under which it has developed, its contents, and its applications to date, there is a great danger that Hägerstrand's time-geographic framework will be mistakenly construed as nothing more than a planning tool. On the contrary, as initially suggested, the potential usefulness of the framework to geographers is of much greater range. No small part of this potential usefulness lies within or adjacent to areas which have been explored at length by human geographers.

[2]Hägerstrand's sensitive awareness of the local connectedness of phenomena is somewhat influenced by the hereto little known work of J. G. Granö and the comments made by his son Olavi Granö [*11*].

The Study of Regions and Landscape Evolution

Much traditional regional geography has taken the form of landscape inventory compilation – of cataloging individual components of the physical and human landscape – in the vain hope of somehow being able to create an integrated picture of the bounded region as a whole. Likewise, much traditional historical geography has sought to recreate the evolution of entire landscapes by constructing snapshot depictions of particular landscape elements at selected dates. Hägerstrand's time-geography actually provides a framework within which to view any one class of landscape components as part of an interdependent regional whole. The structure and process orientation of time-geography also enables one to see landscape evolution as an uninterrupted event sequence simultaneously involving both similar and dissimilar landscape – element classes. More precisely, Hägerstrand envisions a *new* regional geography and school of landscape evolution wherein the bounded region selected for observation is regarded as an interdependent set, or system, of human, natural, and technological "populations" each of whose "individuals," in "a kind of ballet," spins out a trajectory from that space-time "point when they come into being unto that point where they [either] become transformed" – as when a tree becomes a piece of furniture – or cease to exist [29]. The emphasis in such a rejuvenated regional and historical geography would not be upon " the understanding of unique areas of the world." It would instead seek the acquisition of "a deeper insight into the *principles of togetherness*," or the local connections of populations and individuals as expressed in "collateral processes," i.e., those processes which "have to accommodate themselves under the pressures and opportunities which follow from their common coexistence in terrestrial time and space" [29]. (It would, of course, be cumbersome or, more likely, impossible to empirically describe and handle the space-time trajectories of all individuals and populations except in the most narrowly defined of regions. Thus, in each study, seemingly appropriate populations would need to be singled out and certain aggregation procedures and simplifications – already employed by Hägerstrand and his associates – would have to be called into play.)

Were human geographers to turn to this new brand of regional and historical geography they would no longer have to totally abandon geography's once accepted preoccupation with the physical landscape of a region and the non-human living things upon it. Note, however, that time-geography based regional and historical geography would not necessarily be without its practical implications. As Hägerstrand has himself observed: "Landscapes or regions with their total content of connected natural and societal phenomena are again coming up on the agenda, if not for other reasons than the practical ones. Human undertakings have reached such a large scale and begun to encroach so visibly upon Nature and collective social life that landscape evolution as a wholesale problem is beginning to force itself upon the political arena" [29].

Ongoing work by Buttimer is not unrelated to Hägerstrand's envisioned regional geography. One of her more general aims is to create a dialogue between the phenomenological approach to human geography – with its concern for the relation of subjective perception and cognition to lived experience and the meaning of the everyday landscape upon which existence is set – and the spatial organization and systems approach to human geography – with its frequent concern for space in terms of "its objectively measurable character as context, rather than expression, of human experience" [2]. A somewhat more specific aim is to forge a link between knowing about places or regions as observer (or outsider) and knowing about them as resident experiencer (or insider) via studying their time-geographic centered "genre de vie." This is supposedly to be accomplished by examining the interplay – for both human individuals and local or regional society as a whole – between deeply rooted time-geographic routines and: (1) ideas, values, and symbols; (2) institutions; (3) technology; and (4) natural rhythms, or seasonal and biological rhythms.

Innovations

In no small measure because of the pioneering work of Hägerstrand [*14*], modern human geographers have devoted a tremendous volume of research to various aspects of the diffusion of innovations. However, given the concern of some social scientists and historians with "technology assessment," human geographers have allocated surprisingly little effort to the attainment of some understanding of the actual or potential impact of innovations. The following time-geographic based line of reasoning, or "socio-technical ecology" [*21*], would permit a study of such impacts in a humanistic manner sharply differing from the economic orientation typical of most current inquiries.

The use of virtually all technological and material innovations, whether adopted by persons, households, firms, organizations, or governments, necessitates at the very least that one human individual spend some time at a specific place. Unless the innovation is a time saving substitution for an already used innovation (e.g., a piece of agricultural machinery), this will require that some previous participation in a production, consumption, social, or leisure-time activity be foregone. (Such individual time and activity displacement may occur at daily, weekly, annual, or lifetime scales.) If use of the innovation is only possible at a "station" at which the user would not normally find herself, then some time would also have to be spent moving to and from that station, with the consequent sacrifice of additional time-consuming, space-specific activities. When the innovation is a time-saving substitution, it definitionally frees up time for interactivity travel and additional activity-participation or social-interaction combinations. In short, even at the single-person level, innovation use always sets in motion a string of time-geographic activity and experiential impacts.

Now, the use of technological and material innovations normally extends beyond one human individual. The use of such innovations usually involves the binding up of the time-space trajectories of several people and inanimate objects as well as information and energy. Frequently, all the participating "individuals" are not brought together at a single time-space niche, but – as in some kind of manufacturing process or agricultural production – in an orderly fashioned "project" sequence of different combinations at different moments and locations [*21*]. The synchronization and "synchorization" of innovation-use projects may preempt the use of space (*with its limited packing capacity*) as well as the activity-participation and interactivity-travel time of numerous "individuals." Thus, the constraint impacts on the formation of other activity bundles may spread rather far both temporally and spatially. This is especially so when some project inputs may themselves have originated in other innovation-use projects. Moreover, insofar as innovation-use projects have outputs that are to be absorbed or used by private persons, coalitions, and organizations, their influence on activity-bundle formation may extend temporally beyond the completion of each project iteration. On the other hand, the singular synchronization and "synchorization" requirements of any innovation-use project may conflict with the holding capacity of space-time, or with the existing time-geographic activity patters of *indivisible* potential project participants, to such a degree as to bar the innovation's successful adoption [*3; 7; 21*]. Thus, in order to fully fathom either the failure or impact of an innovation in a particular set of circumstances, something has to be established about the pre-existing time geography.

Three things are to be further realized in connection with innovations and time-geography. Firstly, the pre-use introduction or construction of some innovations, such as communications facilities and factories, in themselves constitute "projects" with time-geographic attributes and impacts. Secondly, the described line of reasoning is applicable to time – and space-utilizing non-technological and non-material innovations in, for example, social life, the arts, and religion [*21*]. Thirdly, the information circulation and exchange generally acknowledged to be so central to innovation diffusion processes is dependent upon the time capacity of people to transmit and receive and upon the bringing together of human trajectories in space and time [*5; 7; 9*].

The "socio-technical ecology" of innovations can also be analyzed from the vantage point of population-system, activity-system matching dynamics. This is so because each new technological innovation cropping up in the activity system of a place or region either appropriates some of the finite time resources of its corresponding population-system or releases time, often creating unemployment by substituting fixed capital for labor. This aggregate perspective is perhaps most relevant, since it facilitates an appreciation of some not otherwise graspable societal problems in modern "advanced economies" where the overall choreography of existence of entire local population systems is no longer being largely determined by natural rhythms and internal ideas, needs, and wishes, but instead mainly by both the technology of the local activity system and the decision-making units and technology of numerous nonlocal activity systems.

Hägerstrand is hopeful that if human geographers do pursue the application of time-geography to the study of innovation impacts, they will not become excessively concerned with obtaining sharp detail and precision about a great number of peculiar instances. "It would be illuminating enough if we were able to construct models of *types of cases*, representative of their kind, time and area" [*21*] . . .

Other Possible Uses

Since time-space trajectories are universal – being followed by all humans plus all natural and man-made phenomena – once one is deeply imbued with the time-geographic mode of thinking a whole new world of insights is apt to open itself up. It also becomes apparent that there are almost a countless number of opportunities for applying the Hägerstrand framework at a wide range of scales. Many of these possible uses neither have immediate planning ramifications nor neatly fall within the various subdivisions of human geography as traditionally defined. Only four such possibilities are sketched briefly here.

1. The intellectual history of an entire discipline, an academic school of thought, or a school of artistic or musical creation can be depicted, at least in part, in terms of the converging and diverging "life paths" of key individuals at a particular set of universities, cities, studios, coffee-houses, or other relevant "station" types. In this particular scheme of things it would even be possible to consider the "life paths" of specific books, writings, works of art, or musical compositions.

2. Certain large-scale, historical-political developments can be reinterpreted in the context of knowledge about small-scale, time-geographic realities. For example, the failure or success of grass-roots national protest or revolutionary movements to materialize in the face of past economic adversity in specific instances may well have greatly depended upon whether or not the choreography of daily existence in many local areas permitted large numbers of people to easily assemble so as to be exposed to influential information and to spontaneously organize action.

3. The phenomenon of alienation, so widespread in modern urban–industrial societies and so complex in its origins, could become perhaps somewhat more fathomable if its time-geographic aspects were to be more deeply considered. On the surface, at least, alientation would seem to usually be partly or fully attributable to some permutation of the following interrelated circumstances: a clash between the daily time-space behavior dictated by the activity system and the biological rhythms and emotional and psychological needs of the individual [2]; the fact that a significant portion of an individual's daily choreography of existence is often no longer rooted either in a flexible (extended) familial division of labor or in locally-based institutions and organizations, but in remote and unseen seats of private-sector and governmental authority; and the fact that so much of an individual's time is spent either in filling non-family activity-system roles which have an existence of their own, or in fleeting contact with salespersons, service providers, teachers, and other people who are themselves filling self-existing activity-system roles at highly specialized "stations." Due to the latter set of circumstances, personal identification may become a matter of what one is rather than who one is, and one can become "thingified," not only in a Marxian sense by becoming an extension of the machinery of production, but also by becoming an extension of the over-all societal machine. It may also be contended that, in a rapidly changing environment, the fleeting impersonal contacts prescribed by the activity system further contribute to alienation be inhibiting the formation of lasting relationships, the cementing of effective political protest, and the accumulation of disorientation-preventing redundant information.

4. In a not unrelated matter, fresh insights into the changing role and form of the family in Western societies from before the "Industrial Revolution" to the present can be won by focussing on how changes in the activity system affect the daily path and life path of individual family members, and how, in turn, the individual taking up of new activity-system roles and tasks constrains the choreography of existence of other family members [*31*]. Such an approach can prove particularly enlightening with respect to the inequitable activity-choice options now frequently confronted by women in highly industrialized countries [*45*].

Concluding Remarks

Time-geography is not a panacea for human geographers and process–concerned biogeographers, for no single conceptual framework can be that. It is, however, a great challenge. It is a challenge to cease taking distance itself so seriously. It is a challenge to accept that space and time are universally and inseparably wed to one another; to realize that questions pertaining to human organization of the earth's surface, human ecology, and landscape evolution cannot divorce the finitudes of space and time. It is a challenge to adopt "a sensitivity to the human condition and life that too frequently is overlooked in [the prevailing] theoretical formulations" of modern human geography [*37*]. It is a challenge to turn to the "choreography" of individual and collective existence – to reject the excesses of inter- and intradisciplinary specialization for a concern with collateral processes.

Despite its tremendous promise, some will justifiably or unjustifiably point to limitations within Hägerstrand's time-geography framework. Some may mistakenly insist that its only use is as a planning tool. Some may preoccupy themselves with the "awkward problems" of data collection and statistical application associated with the framework [*1; 50*], failing to realize that the use of statistics is not precluded and that if time-geography's conceptual structure is tight enough, "a lot ought to be accomplishable even on the basis of meager empirical observations" [26]. Some committed Marxists have asserted that the emphasis on the constraints which limit individual freedom of action reflects a bourgeois capitalistic set of values, and thereby renders the framework useless. Among other things, such a doctrinaire position neglects time-geography's simultaneous concentration on the dynamics of population-system, activity-system matching, i.e., on the collective good of those who are subject to the institutions and organizations which control jobs and technology. Yet others might object to the failure of Hägerstrand's framework to consider the impact of psychological factore (or "subjective" constraints), cultural norms, and social status on the daily and life-long choreography of existence [*1; 10; 46; 49; 50*]. An awareness of these factors may be required if the *sufficient* rather than the necessary conditions of human interaction and activity sequences are to be comprehended; however, it is quite another question as to whether or not the simplicity of the time-geography construct should be sacrificed to the inclusion of these factors.

Regardless of the validity of the above limitations, it is to be hoped that the challenge of time-geography will be taken up by significant numbers of human geographers; that geography will begin "to investigate carefully the workings of collateral processes under the perspective of all thing's togetherness and to use its insights to teach the lessons of finitude" [29]. It is further hoped that those who do take up the challenge of time-geography will not allow Hägerstrand's construct to become a willfully applied plaything; but instead heed to the principle that problems should be defined before models and techniques are chosen for application.

Literature Cited

1 Anderson, J. "Space-Time Budgets and Activity Studies in Urban Geography and Planning," *Environment and Planning*, 3 (1971), pp. 353–68.

2 Buttimer, A. "Grasping the Dynamism of Lifeworld," *Annals of the Association of American Geographers, 66* (1976), pp. 277–92.

3 Carlstein, T. *Införandet av skolgång i ett agrart bysamhälle*. Lund: Lunds Universitets Kulturgeografiska Institution, 1970.

4 Carlstein, T. *Population, Activities and Settlement as a System: The Case of Shifting Cultivation*. Lund: Department of Social and Economic Geography, University of Lund, 1973.

5 Carlstein, T. "Gruppstorlek och kommunikation," *Svensk Geografisk Årsbok, 50* (1974), pp. 114–25.

7 Carlstein, T. *Time Allocation, Innovation and Agrarian Change: Outline of a Research Project*. Lund: Department of Social and Economic Geography, University of Lund, 1974.

8 Carlstein, T. *A Time-Geographic Approach to Time Allocation and Socio-Ecological Systems*. Lund: Lunds Universitets Kulturgeografiska Institution, Rapporter och Notiser, *20*, 1975.

9 Carlstein, T. *Time Allocation, Group Size and Communication*. Lund: Lunds Universitets Kulturgeografiska Institution, Rapporter och Notiser, 21, 1975.

10 Godkin, M. and I. Emker. "Time-Space Budget Studies in Sweden: A Review and Evaluation," *Time-Space Budgets and Urban Research: A Symposium*. Edited by B. P. Holly. Kent: Department of Geography, Kent State University, Discussion Paper No. 1, 1976.

11 Granö, J. G. *Reine Geographie; Eine methodologische Studie beleuchet mit Beispielen aus Finnland und Estland*. Helsinki: Acta Geographica No. 3, Finnish Geographical Society, 1929.

13 Hägerstrand, T. "Geographic Measurements of Migration: Swedish Data," *Les Dép'acements Humains*. Edited by J. Sutter, Monaco: Entretiens de Monaco en Sciences Humaines, Première Session, 1962.

14 Hägerstrand, T. *Innovation Diffusion as a Spatial Process*, Chicago: University of Chicago Press, 1967. A translation of *Innovationsförloppet ur korlogisk synpunkt* (Lund: 1953) by A. Pred.

15 Hägerstrand, T. "Tidsanvändning och omgivningsstruktur," *Urbanisering i Sverige: en geografisk samhällsanalys*. Stockholm: Statens Offentliga Utredningar *1970*:14, Allmänna Förlaget, 1970.

16 Hägerstrand, T. 'What about People in Regional Science?" *Papers of the Regional Science Association, 24* (1970), pp. 7–21.

17 Hägerstrand, T. *Om en konistent individorienterad samhällsbeskrivning för framtidsstudiebruk*. Stockholm: Justitiedepartementet, DsJu *1972:25*, 1972.

18 Hägerstrand, T. "Tätortsgrupper som regionsamhällen: Tillgången till förvarvsarbete och tjänster utanför de större städerna," *Regioner att leva i*. Edited by Expergruppen för Regional Utredningsverksamhet. Stockholm: Allamänna Förlaget, 1972.
20 Hägerstrand, T. "Commentary," on *Values in Geography*. A. Buttimer, Washington, D.C.: Association of American Geographers, Commission on College Geography Resource Paper No. 24, 1974.
21 Hägerstrand, T. *On Socio-Technical Ecology and the Study of Innovations*. Lund: Lunds Universitets Kulturgeografiska Institution, Rapporter och Notiser, *10*, 1974.
22 Hägerstrand, T. "The Domain of Human Geography," *New Directions in Geography*. Edited by R. Chorley. New York: Cambridge University Press, 1974.
23 Hägerstrand, T. *The Impact of Transport on the Quality of Life*, Lund: Lunds Universitets Kulturgeografiska Institution, Rapporter och Notiser, *13*, 1974.
24 Hägerstrand, T. "Tidsgeografisk beskrivning: Syfte och postulat," *Svensk Geografisk Årsbok, 50* (1974), pp. 86–94.
25 Hägerstrand, T. "Ecology under One Perspective," *Ecological Problems of the Circumpolar Area*. Edited by E. Bylund, H. Linderholm, and O. Rune. Luleå: Norrbottens Museum, 1975.
26 Hägerstrand, T. "Kunskap om framtiden ur det förgångna," *Lundaforskare föreläser, 7* (1975), pp. 105–14.
27 Hägerstrand, T. "Space, Time and Human Conditions," *Dynamic Allocation of Urban Space*. Edited by A. Karlqvist, L. Lundquist, and F. Snickars, Lexington: Saxon House Lexington Books, 1975.
28 Hägerstrand, T. "Survival and Arena: On the Life-history of Individuals in Relation to Their Geographical Environment," *The Monadnock, 49* (1975), pp. 9–29.
29 Hägerstrand, T. "Geography and the Study of Interaction between Nature and Society," paper presented at the 13th International Geographical Congress, Moscow, 1976.
30 Hägerstrand, T. "The Space-Time Trajectory Model and Its Use in the Evaluation of Systems of Transportation," paper presented at an international conference on transportation research, Vienna, 1976.
31 Hägerstrand, T. "Age, Sex and Gender: The Individual and Society," *Europe 2000*. Forthcoming, 1977.
33 Hägerstrand, T. and B. Lenntorp. "Samhällsorganisation i tidsgeografiskt perspektiv," *Ortsbundna levnadsvillkor*. Stockholm: Statens Offentliga Utredningar, *1974:2*, Allmänna Förlaget, 1974.
34 Holly, B. P. "Conceptual Problems and Scale Considerations in Time–Space Research," *Time-Space Budgets and Urban Research: A Symposium*. Edited by B. P. Holly. Kent: Department of Geography, Kent State University, Discussion Paper No. *1*, 1976.
37 King, L. J. "Alternatives to a Positive Economic Geography," *Annals of the Association of American Geographers, 66* (1976), pp. 293–308.
45 Palm, R. and A. Pred, *A Time-Geographic Perspective on Problems of Inequality for Women*. Berkeley: University of California, Berkeley, Institute of Urban and Regional Develop ment Working Paper No. 236, 1974.
46 Parkes, D. *Themes on Time in Urban Social Space: An Australian Study*. Newcastle, NSW: University of Newcastle, Department of Geography Seminar Paper No. *26*, 1974.
47 Pred, A. "Urbanisation, Domestic Planning Problems and Swedish Geographic Research," *Progress in Geography, 5* (1973), pp.1–76.
49 Stephens, J. D. "Daily Activity Sequences and Time-Space Constraints," *Time-Space Budgets and Urban Research: A Symposium*. Edited by B. P. Holly. Kent: Department of Geography, Kent State University, Discussion Paper No. *1*, 1976.

50 Thrift, N. "A Reply to Brian Holly's Paper: Some More Problems and a Utopian Prospectus," *Time-Space Budgets and Urban Research: A Symposium*. Edited by B. F. Holly. Kent: Department of Geography, Kent State University, Discussion Paper No. *1*, 1976.

40

DIORAMA, PATH AND PROJECT

Torsten Hägerstrand

Torsten Hägerstrand was born in Småland, Sweden, in 1916. He lived above the schoolhouse where his father taught, which was located between a farming village and a factory town. In this autobiographical essay he uses the insights of his time-geography (see **chapter 39**) to explore his own origins and at the same time gives life to some of its dry terminology. The paths and projects of individuals' daily, weekly and life-long routines are connected with situations, themselves parts of landscapes which are more than just assemblages of visible phenomena. Hägerstrand tries here to bring some sense of intention and feeling into the more mathematical structure of time-geography. This complex, synthetic approach cannot be easily classified as either spatial science or ecology, since it combines elements of both. Furthermore, Hägerstrand's intellectual influences are exceptionally wide and varied, including past-Newtonian physics, geometry, sociology and biology. Like Raymond Williams (in **chapter 19**), but also Walter Christaller and Henri Lefebvre, his thinking has been profoundly shaped by the childhood experience of a rapidly changing countryside. In smaller, more homogeneous communities, the kinds of subtle insights of which time-geography is capable carry most weight. It is less certain how they might inform the more dynamic and complex contexts of the modern metropolis.

Source: Diorama, path and project. *Tijdschrift voor Economische en Sociale Geographie* 73, 6, 323–39, 1982.

The world is highly particular on the scale of millimeters. (Philip and Phyllis Morrison Scientific American, *Dec. 1968.)*

In his 1976 essay on "Human Geography in Terms of Existential Anthropology", Christiaan Van Paassen gave me homework to do which has remained a source of concern ever since. Those familiar with the writings of Allan Pred, or with occasional translations of my own speculations, know that *path* and *project* are two of the fundamental concepts of time-geography. Having reviewed this and related ideas, Van Paassen felt compelled to ask: "Are projects autonomous? Do they originate independently from a situation?" These questions arose, I think, because in most empirical studies made within the frame of time-geography, the projects tested in given environments were selected a priori by the investigators. This procedure was deliberately chosen in order to challenge the assumption, which is widespread among economists and often applied in planning, that observed behaviour reflects free choice guided by preferences and thus can be taken as norms. In order to elucidate the 'autonomy of action' (cf. Burns 1979), observed behaviour is not satisfactory. The use of hypothetical projects instead seemed to be a means of getting away from the behavioural delusion. This choice of approach – which I still think is a helpful one – was never considered as being more than one in the range of possibilities inherent in time-geographic thinking. Seen in the wider perspective, the real-world generation of projects is clearly a fundamental issue. But it is also exceedingly difficult to cope with.

I think Van Paassen sees geography in general as the study of 'situational ecology', a formulation which has very much guided my own thoughts since I first became aware of it in the beginning of the sixties. The problem of the relation between situation and project is clearly a central part of a situational ecology. It is a central problem also in time-geography as one can imply from the way in which the two concepts of *path* and *project* ought to be understood.

The concept of *path* (or trajectory) was introduced in order to help us to appreciate the significance of continuity in the succession of situations. We have to keep in mind that it refers not only to man but to all other packets of continuants which fill up our world. It is also essential to understand it as a reminder, although very abstract, of the 'live corporeality'[1] of man and society – to use Van Paassen's expressive term – a circumstance almost totally neglected in the human and social sciences. Continuity and corporeality set limits on how and at what pace one situation can evolve into a following in a purely physical sense.

There are also other, less tangible, factors which influence the sequence of situations within the limits set by what is physically possible. Outstanding among these are human intentions. The fact that a human path in the time-geographic notation seems to represent nothing more than a point on the move should not lead us to forget that at its tip – as it were – in the persistent present stands a living body subject, endowed with memories, feelings, knowledge, imagination and goals – in other words capabilities too rich for any conceivable kind of symbolic representation but decisive for the direction of paths. People are not paths, but they cannot avoid drawing them in space-time.

The broad generic concept of *project* was introduced in order to help us as geographers to do two things. We need to rise up from the flat map with its static patterns and think in terms of a world on the move, a world of incessant permutations. We need to have concepts which are able to relate events that happen to the strivings for purpose and meaning that we know are hidden behind many of them. The word project then, with its almost unlimited range of applicability, was

[1] Van Paassen 1976, p. 332.

meant to tie together into a whole all those 'cuts' in evolving situations that an actor must secure in order to reach a goal, be it mere individual survival or luxury happenings such as putting up a fence of cloth up and down the hills of California.[2]

In a recent paper, Derek Gregory says "that there is a basic complementarity between 'projects' as conceived in time-geography and 'projects' as conceived in constitutive phenomenology". The latter is interested in intentional *constitution*, the former in practical *realization*. ". . . the two need to be brought together if we are to avoid a conceptual 'cutting into' the continuity of action. Only then, I suspect, will we grasp the full significance of reflexivity in the conduct of practical life".[3] I fully agree. There is nothing inherent in the time-geographic project concept as such which sets up a barrier between intention and realization. But I must admit that I find it difficult to see how one can deal with the matter in actual empirical research. How does one make these backward rooted, side-bound and forward moving, deeply hidden and transient, intentional energies visible?[4] The practical realizations of projects are possible to observe, at least in principle. The configurations of underlying intentions and broader meanings are not. Even if it is true as Barrett (1978, p. 170) tells us that "meanings are first and foremost not in the mind but in the world, in the linkings and interconnections of things we find there", an observer cannot entirely conclude what they are from the practical realizations he sees. Intentions have a high death rate. And the surviving ones have to adjust. Already as simple a project as a spoken sentence suffers from the limits set by the corporeal world because words have to be lined up in a queue to form sentences, while the underlying image might well be of a quite different order of synchronic richness which simply cannot be communicated while it is there. So, we find no simple and straightforward relation between intention and observable realization; perhaps we have to do with one of the most complex processes in the whole universe. Already this circumstance makes empirical studies problematic. The task is not made simpler by the understanding that intentions are bound up with past and present situations and that their realizations have to find their vulnerable tracks through situations to come. Nevertheless, I see no real difference of opinion concerning this perspective. But beyond this, I have some reservations.

In the remarks quoted from Van Paassen and Gregory the thought seems to lie hidden that it is illegitimate to study projects apart from their situational contexts, as 'physicalistic' and 'idealistic' entities (Gregory 1982). If this is really the view, I would reject it. I think both the 'situational' and the 'idealistic' approaches are important and useful. I see them as complementary to each other. Projects are going concerns in the flow of real life. This is undeniable. But I am not able to give up the idea that they also can be seen as "objective constructions of the human

[2] The case can be made for identifying projects which extend over generations and which give to history a peculiar kind of 'fibrosity' (cf. Kubler 1962).

[3] Gregory 1980, p. 337.

[4] For a well-documented discussion of these matters and their possible points of contact with time-geography, see Anne Buttimer 1976.

mind", to quote Sir Karl Popper.[5] They have then a blueprint reality, like for example mathematical theorems, or at least many of them have. If this were not the case, how could culture exist? My impression of life is that, to a large extent, we are bound to take out projects from the blue-print library more or less in the same way as a pianist picks out ready-made tones from his instrument. Therefore, I see no good reason to bracket off the study of projects as autonomous and idealistic blueprints.

As far as I can see, one should, at least for analytical purposes, make a distinction between the decision (if that is the right word; submission might sometimes be more adequate) to launch a project and the space/time/trajectory shape which subsequently must emerge for its realization. The first event is clearly understandable only in terms of the situation. The latter might also require this perspective, if we have to do with a new creation. When, on the other hand, a standard pattern is called forth, then the situation does not explain the shape per se, but knowledge of the ideal shape helps us to interpret the coalitions and conflicts that emerge when the project paves its way forwards in time, negotiating with the situations that have to be coped with.

Thus, as I prefer to understand the concept, it is possible, legitimate and useful to understand and study projects both as historical entities, rooted in the flow of life, and as ready-made blueprints, preserved in the store-house of culture. Situations, on the other hand, are different. They can hardly in any meaningful way be extricated from the flow of life. They are not creations of the human mind but emerge out from the historically given. One may say that situations contain a mixture of many actors' projects, but this mixture does not exhaustively define them. Winter, to take just one example, has thwarted the projects of many army leaders.

In ordinary language the word situation refers to "a position or condition at the moment" or "a position with regard to surroundings". Both formulations, and the second most clearly, indicate that a situation does not present itself in general but has to be seen from the vantage point of somebody or something. Even with this limitation, a broad range of meanings remains. In a very wide and abstract sense, every somebody or something is in a situation with respect to everybody and everything else. But the way in which this is the case, is beyond description. In a more limited and apprehensible sense, a situation takes shape as such only in relation to a defined direction of change or action. To take a case from inanimate nature, the same building is in two different situations depending on whether a flood or a fire is nearing. Similarly, the situation of a person comes out with one configuration when he is just hurrying on to find protection against a shower of rain, and with another when he is trying to find a new job. The change of goal perspective in time and space brings about a reformulation of the relevant situation. So, here we come across the reflexive relation between project and situation.

[5] I am particularly referring to the chapter P2 14 and 15 on "The Reality of Unembodied World 3 Objects" and "World 3 and the Mind-Body Problem".

The situation is undetermined until a project defines it. On the other hand, whether an initiator of a project can bring it to a desired end will depend on what events the subsequent situations permit from moment to moment.

Below the level of observation of (and participation in) the interplay between projects and situations, another level of reality resides which makes the interplay at all possible by its 'thereness'. Nothing can become part of a project or of a situation without first being *there* as an idea, a feeling, an organism or a thing. At any moment these existents have a finite number – although in practice uncountable – and definite locations. (Ideas and feelings are assumed to be located with their keepers.)

Ideas and feelings are divisible in the sense that they can move on to receivers and still remain in the possession of the senders. Organisms and things are different. They are indivisible – in other words, they are bound to either here or there but cannot be in both places. They are on the whole fewer in number and more durable than the combinations into which they can enter. Therefore, they stand in a similar relation to projects and situations as the tones in the musical scale to melodies and chords or the chessmen to the moves and games that can be played on the board. But an essential difference between these models and the real world is that in reality many actors try to play each their own melodies and games with the same given set of tones or pieces simultaneously. To move a project forwards, then, is to be able to hold back competing claims, to step in at gaps and to mobilize substitutes. In this context, the preexisting location of input members is a crucial part of the situation against which a project has to be pursued.

The best approximation we have in geography to a concept capable of grasping the momentary thereness and relative location of all continuants is *landscape*. So, let me take that as a vantage point. For the initiator of a project, the landscape in which he finds himself defines the grand situation which constitutes the conditions of his actions. This, however, is the case only if landscape is understood in a much wider sense than what we have been doing as a rule. Like Johannes Granö in his '*Reine Geographie*', we must include both what is very close, even what is hidden under our roofs, and what is very distant, say, the clouds and the stars. But we must take even further steps. Everything which is contained in the part of the world we consider should be included, as for example all organisms, even if they have no collected areal expression. Most important of all, the human body subjects, the keepers of memories, feelings, thoughts and intentions and initiators of projects must be accepted as elements of this living landscape. This proposition leaves us with no sharp boundary between landscape and society. Some intangible societal phenomena are durable and located like corporeal phenomena. Property boundaries are cases in point. Status positions, on the other hand, adhere to human beings and move with them as a kind of decoration. Similarly, rules and regulations receive there reality by being understood and respected as real by humans, and they are therefore present in the landscape as much as are the things we can see and touch. Perhaps one ought to mark the richness of the concept by using a word which holds it apart from the conventional idea of landscape. To my knowledge, we have no entirely satisfactory word available for the purpose. The closest approximation I have been able to find is 'diorama',[6] the term used for arrangements in museums which show animals and people suspended in their normal environments. But when borrowing this term, it must be clearly understood that the essential characteristic does not lie in the visual property, but in the *thereness* aspect. All sorts of entities are in touch with each other in a mixture produced by history, whether visible or not.[7]

Only when we have recognized the fine-grained structure of a diorama are we in a position to appreciate how situations evolve as an aggregate outcome quite apart from the specific intentions actors might have had when they conceived and launched projects out from their different positions.

In general, I think, there are more projects in the making than can possibly be accommodated in a given diorama. This is so because of the unavoidable scarcity of inputs *at hand*.

The nature of this scarcity and the consequences of it are difficult to deal with in general terms. It does not really become available for closer examination until we direct the searchlight at a real 'diorama'. We need a portrait of the grand situation before we can begin to look at the reflexivity between the more limited situations and projects which move the content of the diorama forwards in time and gradually change it to something partly or totally different. *In the configuration of grains in the diorama lies one of the keys to its subsequent transformation.*

A real-world diorama as I understand it can never be fully accessible or describable in an empirical manner. The fullness must instead be taken as the ceiling of a way of viewing the world, the geographic way in its most genuine sense. Nevertheless, it should help us to observe relations which would escape us otherwise. It should help us to ask questions which we would not ask without it. And it should help us to estimate the importance of what we have to leave out of consideration, because we know at least the locus of what is left out.

The limited ability to grasp what is there falls upon both the outside observer and the participant, the 'insider'. But the limits probably assert themselves in different ways. The outsider might be able to perceive things which for the insider are simply too familiar to be of interest. The insider, on the other hand, is involved in the network of meanings that bind the human inhabitants together, and in his own case he might even be able to trace the roots of projects back to their finer details.[8]

6 From Greek diora'n = look through.

7 Gunnar Törnqvist (1981) has authored more complete commentaries on the background to this choice of term (p. 111) and placed the corresponding perspective in its broader scientific context. To my mind 'arena' is the more general term which does not specify approach (for example, whether one is interested in variables or in events), whereas 'diorama' is suggested to be reserved for time-geography.

The arena perspective has of course very close affinity to the world-view of Vidal de la Blache: to hold "together heterogeneous beings in vital mutual relationships" (Buttimer 1978, p. 71).

8 According to Anne Buttimer (1978): "the 'outsider's trap' is that we look at places, as it were, from an abstract sky: we try to read the texts of landscapes and overt behavior in picture languages of maps and models and are therefore inevitably drawn toward finding in places what we *intend* to find in them. The 'insider's trap', on the other hand, is that we live in places and may be so immersed in the particulars of everyday life and action that we may see no point in questioning the taken-for-granted or to seeing our home place in its wider spatial or social context."

At this point, I find it difficult to proceed any further without support of a real-world diorama with non-invented situations, paths and projects to become food for further discussion. We have good reason to assume that even those scholars who prefer to talk about societal matters in very general terms, in fact have outlooks strongly dependent upon their own experience as members of society – how could it be otherwise? Rather than concealing this tendency, I will now take the liberty to make explicit use of it and try to call forth a diorama of which I once was an insider during my first formative years. This is not in order to write an autobiography but in order to paint a picture of a kind which no field expedition or documentary study could reveal.[9] At the centre of attention is still the question posed by Van Paassen about project and situation. While data accumulate, I hope he will enjoy a glimpse of a world, contemporary with his own early years, but hidden in a vastly different environment, the inner woodlands of southern Sweden.

The *locality* was a valley with wooded slopes. At the bottom of it ran three parallel lines of communication. In the middle a small river took a breath on its way to the Baltic between little waterfalls every second kilometre. On one side twisted a road, not a major one. On the other side the trunk line between Stockholm and Malmö cut off the woods with a sharp edge.

A *Bruk*, that is a foundry and a machine-shop, picked up its energy from one of the bigger waterfalls. Two and a half kilometres to the south-west, a farmers' village spread out on a low drumlin. Both settlements had about 150 inhabitants. The *Bruk* was only about sixty years old. The village had pre-historic mounds and tall menhirs in its midst. The farms were rather small, yet many farmers were relatively well-off because they also owned forest. To be a factory worker in the 1910s and 1920s was a less lucrative task and quite insecure.

Finding places for establishments[10]

The *Bruk* itself was a splendid example of a project initiated in a situation which later on turned out to be different than assumed. In the middle of the 19th century, somebody found iron ore in the rocks up on the hillside. In the general mode of

[9] I have come to be interested in the use of autobiographical material on the suggestion of Anne Buttimer. A major contribution by her, elucidating many aspects of individual and context in an autobiographical perspective is currently in press at Longman's, London, under the preliminary title of *Life Journeys in the Practice of Geography* – Cf. by the same author *On People, Paradigms, and 'Progress' in Geography* (1981). I am also in debt to her for having opened my eyes to the thereness and role of symbols and emotional loadings in every diorama populated by humans.

A scholar who is looking back on his memories of life in a period before he had been in touch with theory, could, I think, be seen as somebody sitting on the fence between the insider's and outsider's world looking in both directions.

[10] Many of the situations described in the following can be read as illustrations to the process of 'structuration' which has been discussed in general terms in a series of recent essays by Allan Pred (see references).

enterprise at that time, a few rather wealthy farmers got together and built a blast-furnace in order to mine and exploit the ore. After a few years it was discovered that the mine did not yield very much. Bog ore had to be brought in instead during some years until the blast-furnace operations had to be given up. But now the settlement and the workers were there. The foundry and machine-shop managed to continue in adversity and sometimes prosperity. In the 1920s the chief products were locomobiles, boilers and threshers. The mighty furnace got birch trees on its top and became the major show-piece for visitors.

The railroad building passed by when the *Bruk* was young. The manager turned down the offer to get a station: "The workers would just sit there and drink". The trains came to stop at the parish church instead, three kilometres away (outside our valley section). Distance minimization was not always the first priority.

Around the turn of the century, new stately school-houses had to be built, replacing earlier more primitive arrangements. The parish council judged that the factory settlement and the farmers' village taken separately had too few children for each to have its own school-house. They had to go together. But neither group was willing to let the other have it. This was understandable. To walk two and a half kilometres in the dark on snowy winter days is taxing for a child. So, the school came to be built in the woods right at the mid-point. In a community sense, it was nowhere. Tall spruces and fir trees shadowed the garden.

This place came to be my home because my father was the teacher. We lived upstairs in the school-house. My parents came from a diffferent part of the province and had no local roots. When, just married, they moved there in 1909, the shop-keeper of the *Bruk* received them on the porch with a cornet of candy. This was a kind gesture – and he very much wanted to recruit them as customers.

The pace-setters[11]

Let us now focus our attention on this valley section, interpreted as a time-geographic diorama. In order to see enough detail without losing the grasp of the whole, the ideal would have been to consider what I like to call 'pockets of local order', the smaller ones step by step embedded in the larger ones, representing for example day, week and year in household, workplace, settlement and parish. This would not be impossible but would require a book. For the present purpose I have selected a case in the middle: the valley section observed during a typical week around 1925 (Fig. 40.1). Life received its somewhat halting rhythmicity by five pace-setters, partly coordinated, but largely not: the *Bruk*, the school, the railroad, the parish church and the cows. Thus, three of them were public institutions, representing remote centres of power.

The graph, I hope, helps to elucidate the pulsations which the pace-setters gave

[11] The idea of pace-makers was introduced by Don Parkes & Nigel Thrift (1975) and subsequently developed in several studies by them. I prefer the word pace-setter, because it seems to me better to suggest the tick-speed of a metronome.

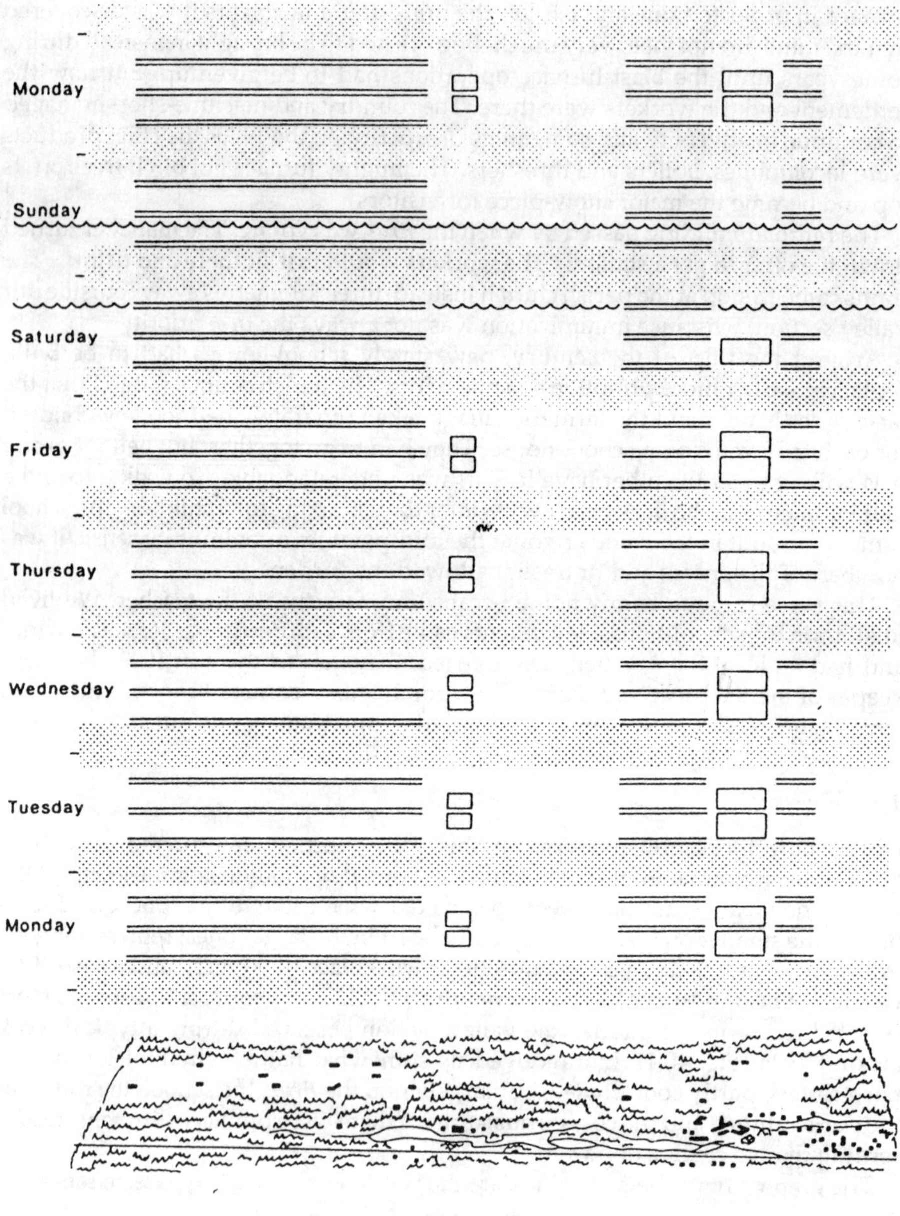

Figure 40.1 [orig. fig. 1] A simplified perspective of the valley section and its pace-setting time-schedules during a working week around 1925. The elements of the landscape are the railroad, the river, the arable islands in the woodland and the settlements, the farmers' village on the left, the 'Bruk' on the right, the school in the middle. Time/space 'boxes' indicate working hours, horizontal bars the rhythmicity of farmlife. Wavelines represent the ringing of the church bells.

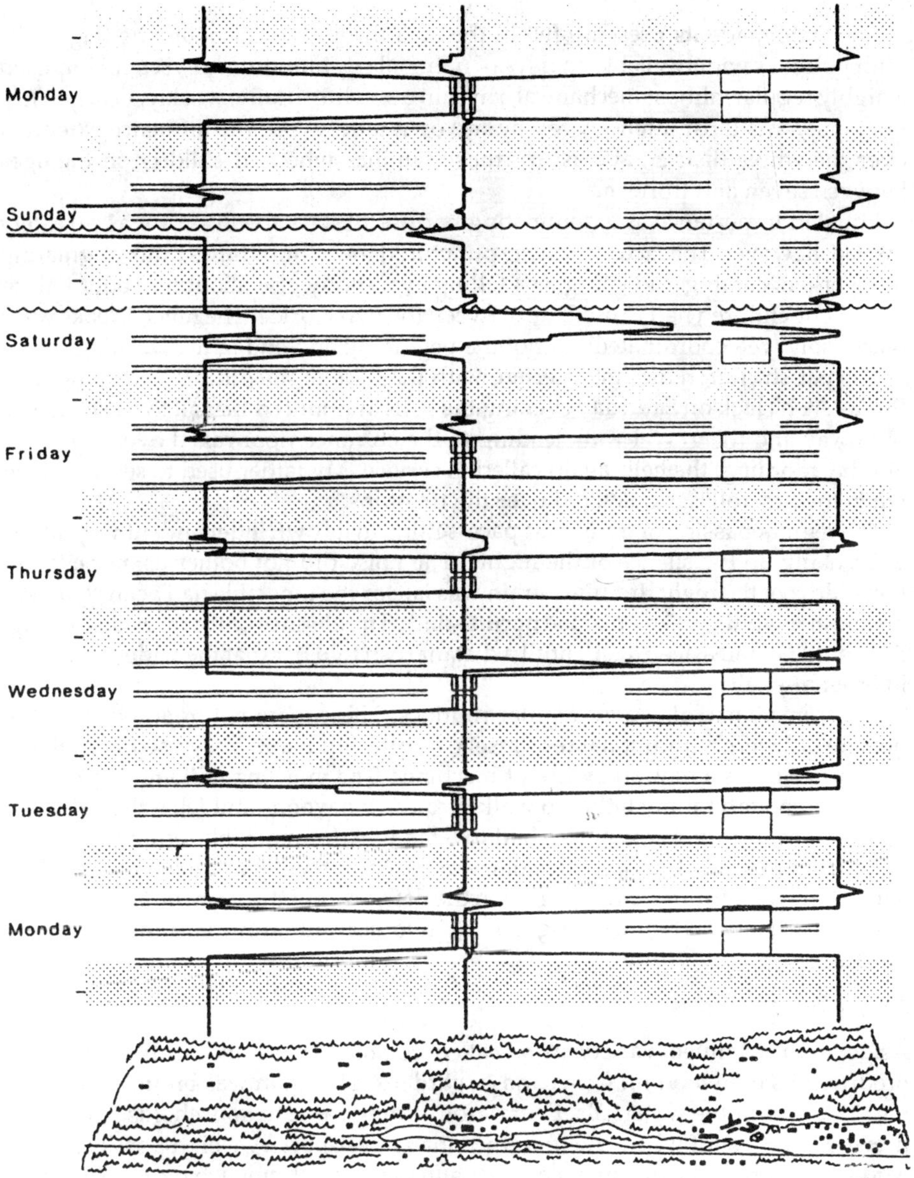

Figure 40.2 [orig. fig. 2] Three sample paths showing the movements of three schoolchildren during a week in the valley section. The small time-windows between scheduled time plus mealtimes and the night-hours had a strongly limiting effect on the individuals' reach outwards from basepoints.

rise to. (It should be read from the bottom upwards as if along a moving now-front.)

The State made its presence felt in the area through the school. The flag on its high pole was widely visible on days of national celebration. Thus, school imposed a highly regular, almost mechanical, rhythm upon life – daily, weekly, yearly. This, of course, was most intensely felt by my own family. But the influence extended over the whole district, at least for those families who had children in the ages between seven and thirteen.

Equal in importance as a dominating pace-setter was the *Bruk*. It was privately owned, however. The factory whistle punctured the air four times a day, regulating the workers coming and going and telling everybody else about it. About half of the school-children had to oscillate between the two worlds. The lunch breaks were reasonably well coordinated but not the beginning and end of the working day.

The parish church did not interfere with the pace of the ordinary working day. But by six o'clock on Saturday evening the bells announced that all tools should be put away and the gravel-walk leading to the entrance-door raked over. Then, on Sunday morning, the bells again called to service. My father used to set his watch when the first tollings quavered over the tree-tops.

The regular passing of trains was pace-setting in its own independent way, alone in breaking up the silence of the nights. The noise did not bother us, not even in the middle of the night. If a night-train was late or the timetable had been changed, my mother would wake up at the normal time. The absence of roar was disturbing. She could not fall asleep again until a distant rush told her that the wide world was in order after all.

The farmers had also their regular routines. These were not imposed from the outside but were a traditional response to nature and habit. They used to milk the cows three times a day, still without machines. The morning milking was carried out early enough for my father to walk through the woods and fetch the daily can of milk. The factory workers also had to fetch milk from neighbouring farms.

Apart from a small co-operative dairy in the church village, there were as yet no agricultural institutions intruding upon the daily lives of the farmers. For them, the household, sometimes including one or two servants, was still the dominant institution.

Projects for survival

Aside from a limited variety of so-called colonial wares and seafish, the area produced its own food on farms and in gardens. The grain was brought down to the flourmills at the waterfalls. Energy for heating came to households from local firewood, delivered when snow and ice made transport by sleigh possible. Firewood and timber were the major exports and gave a fresh smell to the station-yard. Work in field, forest, cattleshed and stable filled the days of the farmers. Mechanization was still limited to sowing-machines and threshers.

Tradition and biological necessity told the farmers what to do when and how. Few had any formal theoretical training. The major innovation of the period, which I can recall, was an ingenious crane for lifting heavy boulders. The Ice Age had left the fields full of such impediments. A major project apart from routine was to clear a field, but certainly not every year on every farm.

Given the technology of the time, acreage of arable land and woodland and number of inhabitants, it would not be too difficult to reconstruct the succession of projects during a working year and week on the farms of the area (cf. Carlstein 1981).

Work at the *Bruk* was carried on in ways which very much reminded of handicraft. The skilled workers were of course specialized as founders, turners, filers, smiths, joiners and painters, but they were all familiar with each others' tasks. The completed product was composed of parts shaped in the factory itself – the patternmaker had high status – and every delivery was a big event – just like what it still is in shipyards. The thresher or the locomobile had to be hauled along the road down to the somewhat distant railway station. The factory had to keep a large stable for the purpose. Some workers used to come along to help on the slopes. It happened that the amateur orchestra of the *Bruk* led the procession. The project structure had its own obvious rhythmicity which made achievements clearly visible to both participants and spectators.

Survival at that time required more than producing one's own food or having a money income with which to buy it. There were equally necessary household projects to care for, in particular hauling water, wood-firing and washing. All the related activities had a yearly and daily regularity which could not be changed very much. Heating, in particular, was time-consuming and had to begin in the early mornings. For the washing it was a good thing that the water in the river still was clear as drinking-water. Everybody had the right to beat the laundry at a nearby riverside washing-barge.[12] The *Bruk* granted the use of its mangle-house. A couple of women earned an income by helping households with the big laundry.

Three sample paths

Given the major time-constraints set by the dominating institutions, one can at least in the imagination, if not by pencil, sketch the generalized pattern of weekly paths of the inhabitants, all at once. This would show much of "the temporal and spatial *availability* of others" (Giddens 1979) as well as – what I think is equally important – their *non-availability*. A really complete diorama picture should include also the independent or derived trajectories of natural and fabricated things. This, of course, is impossible to achieve on paper. We have to go ahead with sampling.

For illustrative purposes, I have selected three cases, each depicting three quite different human situations (Figure 40.2). On one side is the path of a sample child from the farmers' village and on the other side that of a sample child from the *Bruk*. These two, then, would each represent around fifteen children. My own path vibrates in the middle above my home. I wish I could have attached the sound from the crowd: shouting and laughter in the yard at breaks, the rolling of clogs when

[12] The final operation in the washing procedure before hanging out the clothes in the open for drying was to dip it in running water and beat it with a batlet. There existed a bit of social control in the ways families could inspect each other's laundry.

sixty legs invaded the house. It was such a sudden change in mood every year on that spring day when everybody arrived barefoot.

Since this world is my 'Montaillou', I could easily decorate the scaffold with an endless variety of vignettes, deep-frozen in my memory or hidden in family-papers, each in its way casting light on forces at work. What follows here is just a few observations related to the question of situation and project. I do not apologize for having chosen the perspective of the young. It illustrates an essential thing: how society, largely unaware of the individual outcomes, rations out knowledge, skills, values and feelings in its coming generation.[13]

Experiences of the social and tangible worlds

All children of the valley section, the factory manager's, as well as the farmers' and workers', were bundled together day after day in the compulsory primary school. They were exposed to the same teaching. But this was not enough for providing a homogenous experience.

We all had the same amount of time free from the bounds of school – except that some might have suffered from home-work more than others, depending on their own or their family's ambitions. But already the lunch-hour made a difference. In my own case, I just went upstairs to the kitchen-table where the teacher turned into my father. Some of the others went home. The rest stayed in the entrance hall downstairs and had the sandwiches and milk they had brought with them. They used to compare their eatables and note the differences. In a subtle way, they read off the relative economic positions of their parents.

It is an axiom of time-geography that the movements of an individual are restricted by the location in time and space of fixed points which must be respected. The time-spaces left free are defined by more or less symmetrical double cones, called prisms. This means that the timetables of dominating institutions (family included) to a large extent determine indirectly where individuals, even when 'free', can act or be exposed to experience. As a consequence of this effect, the farmers' and the workers' children lived in quite different environments at the end of every day and also – although in a less restricted fashion – over the weekends. When judging the influence of distances, one must keep in mind that few children had their own bicycle. Perhaps only two families had a car.

The farmers' children dealt with animals and plants, soil and water, food-making and agricultural tools and buildings. Most of them knew how to milk a cow and handle a horse. They acquired a good grasp of the practice of farming, for they had to take part in the work. They were permitted occasionally to stay home from school in order to give a hand. The law prohibiting children's work did not really apply to them. To the extent that they were left free to play, they did so among historical monuments and farmsteads having incomprehensible names from a distant past. They literally were in touch with nature, history and technology.

13 Note, for example, in this context, Allan Pred's notion of "the life path – daily path dialectic" (1981).

The workers' children at the other end of the local world experienced an environment remote both from biological life, history and – strangely enough – also from economic production. Their parents had to buy foodstuff. Many homes had no gardens. Those with a yard of their own perhaps had chickens and a cat. Many lived in tenement houses called "Quarrel-nest", "Fall-down", "Old Corrupt" and the like, which of course degraded the residents.[14] Naturally, the children acquired some insight into the technology of the *Bruk* by watching their fathers and elder brothers at work and hearing their stories. But they were not really allowed to participate in a manner like the farmers' children. They used most of their free time for running around in crowds. Football was hardly known yet in the area.

Clearly, I know my own situation best. My existence was totally dominated by the school – in daytime as an institution and for the rest as the physical structure which contained by home. Long before I began school myself, the timetable made the place change face as a territory with a regularity like night and day. In daytime the school-children ruled the place as a group. Only after 4 p.m. and during week-ends could I consider it as belonging to me and a couple of friends of mine. This situation set me off to a certain extent both from the agricultural and industrial worlds. In conflicts between the groups, I was bound to remain neutral, an attitude encouraged by my parents.

On the other hand, I enjoyed privileges – as I learnt to see it – which my school-mates did not have. I could use the small travelling library downstairs whenever I liked without formalities – very convenient if it happened to rain. I met Jules Verne, Fenimore Cooper, Rudyard Kipling, Thomas Alva Edison. I was permitted to use for my own experiments and inventions a small room full of equipment for science teaching. The school organ was a lot more powerful than the little one my mother had upstairs. I am sure that the other children enjoyed themselves in their ways. But if only because of access to means, my experience was bound to be different from theirs in many respects.

Projects of State and Church

Nearly all matters related to school-education were regulated and standardized throughout the country. The parish could choose among a set of systems but the intellectual content of the school-work was the same as elsewhere in Sweden. The teacher had to follow a plan, prescribed by government authorities, which specified the detailed amount of reading, writing, drawing, arithmetic, natural science, geography and history which had to be covered day by day. He had a certain

[14] One can conclude from the graph that the dwellings of the *Bruk* became a women's world during the long hours while children and males were away. No work-place for women other than home existed. The tenement houses were crowded and many causes of quarrel existed around the stairs and outhouses.

freedom as to method but hardly as to subject matter.[15] The local school board could contribute little more than maintain buildings and equipment and provide firewood for the winter.

State inspectors appeared unannounced and were sometimes much feared. Ours, however, was a friendly scholar who made a point to encourage interest in archaeology and local history. A scrutiny of textbooks, particularly in reading, history and geography, and of song-books, reveals in detail much of the ways by which established society reproduced its values at that time. Many things surprise when viewed in today's perspective, for example, the very conspicuous efforts to evoke patriotic feelings. These were as a rule symbolized by the nature of the country. On the hard cover of the Swedish reader we were told above a picture with the same intent:

"Listen to the whispering of the spruce
to the root of which your home is fastened".[16]

Sometimes the whole school marched out in military order, singing with the flag leading the way, to plant trees in the forest clearings. Landowners were required by law to replant lots where timber had been cut.

The Lutheran State Church claimed a super-institutional position. This claim was recognized through its responsibility for the registration of population. In addition, it kept watch over souls and morals, partly with the school as an instrument. Schooldays began and ended with psalm-singing and prayer. On most days the first hour was devoted to biblical history.

Once a year, in the autumn, the vicar came to the schoolhouse, bringing the heavy church registers. He had called together at least one member of every household in the district in order to update the notations of births, deaths and migrations. During the first hour he acted as the arm of the State; the following hours were turned into a catechetical meeting. One person from each household was obliged to recite by heart a hymn or a passage from the Scripture assigned as homework at the meeting the year before.

At the *Bruk*, a couple of free churches were of more importance to the people than the Lutheran State Church. Laymen preached in the chapels and different songs were sung. These chapels were poor and ugly compared to the monumental medieval stone church of the parish, a white guard in the midst of all the dead, farmers and workers alike.

15 The introduction of 'timetable time' along with industrialization has been discussed at length by Thrift (1981). Among other things, he points out that the school was used for inculcating the habit of time discipline in children. My diorama clearly demonstrates the 'industrial' character of the school. The similarity goes further than to the time-discipline. Internal work had to conform to a precise design. Not even in drawing fantasy was permitted. One began with making on the right side of the paper exact copies of models drawn on the left side. Small marks were inserted to help exactness.

16 It is obvious from this example and many others that educators around the turn of the century without employing the term 'sense of place' understood how to use the phenomenon as a vehicle for nurturing feelings of national belonging. Concerning geographic thinking related to 'sense of place' and 'structure of feeling', see, for example, Anne Buttimer (1978), Yi-Fu Tuan (1977) and Allan Pred (1982).

Religion also had other more subtle ways of exerting influence. So, for example, everybody was supposed to dress up on Sundays and this set limits on many sorts of activities. Not even children were supposed to use tools. Crayon and paper were allowed but not scissors.

Expressions of authority at the 'Bruk'

A private institution like the *Bruk* – at the time a joint-stock company – did not have the legal power to force people into its orbit as had the State and Church. But entrepreneurs were free to imitate traditional symbols of power in order to have an influence on the consciousness of employees and others. The most conspicuous symbol of this kind at the *Bruk* was the white residence of the manager, the biggest dwelling-house in the area. Its exclusiveness was accentuated by the location on a small island. Everybody had to pass over a bridge in order to reach the manager and his office.

The gates to the factory area were located in front of the mansion. Four times a day workers could not avoid being reminded of the status relations they were subject to. The équipage of the manager with two horses and coachman in livery originally played a similar role but began to go out of use in the 1920s. The car took over, but could remain a symbol of distinction for only a few years.

Erosion of traditions

Up to the beginning of the 1930s, when the *Bruk* went bankrupt and years of unemployment ensued, the valley section was socially a rather quiet place. But now and then latent tensions came to the surface.

The farmers' village and the *Bruk* had really not much in common apart from the school. So, many of the tensions had no other place in which to crystallize. Some issues had national, if not international roots, others were very parochial.

Selma Lagerlöf's wellknown *The Wonderful Journey of Nils Holgersson* was only one in a series of centrally planned readers for primary school in Sweden. The series also included *From Pole to Pole*, a kind of world geography written by the great explorer Sven Hedin, who treated the Swedish language in a masterly way. But Sven Hedin was also a controversial personality in Swedish society already before the First World War. In the political fights concerning the introduction of parliamentarism and matters related to defence, a sharp dividing line had developed between conservative and radical opinions, in other words, largely between landowners and industrial workers. Sven Hedin acted on the conservative side, warning about the risk of a European war in widely spread pamphlets. Rumour told that he had authored the speech which King Gustaf V held in 1914 in the Castle courtyard to 30,000 farmers who had come up to the capital from all parts of the country – also from my homeparish – in order to express their loyalty to the constitution and more specifically to support the King's wish to strengthen the armed forces. But such direct and open communication between the King as a person and citizens was of course a project squarely against the principles of parliamentarism. The event made both social democrats and liberals furious. The government resigned. The debate came to touch all parts of the country.

The only practical outlet for their anger which the workers at the *Bruk* could find was to tell my father that they did not want to have their children exposed to Sven Hedin's geography reader. This was a hard conflict of loyalty. When he refused to give in, a school-strike broke out, and for a while only the farmers' children appeared. Finally, Sven Hedin's book was stored away for some years.

This little war mirrored the coming of new power relations in the nation as well as in the locality. At least the leading workers were fully conscious of the direction in which they wanted to move. The banishment of Sven Hedin may seem to have been a petty victory. But if the same thing happened in many schools – which it probably did – Hedin lost much of his place in the consciousness of following generations.

Another example. Once a year, on Ash Wednesday, a war broke out between the workers' and the farmers' children – the proletarians and possessors. According to ancient custom, the farmers sent their children to take eggs to the school-master's household. Parents at the *Bruk* had nothing to send of their own production. Their children were probably told that the custom was unfair. So, they hid in the woods and tried to hit the egg-bags with spruce-cones and stones. Many eggs were smashed every year. It was quite an achievement if somebody was able to sneak through with twenty unbroken eggs.

The children involved in the Easter battle were most certainly not aware of the circumstance that they participated in, namely, the fading away of the old natural economy practice whereby priest, teacher, soldiers and midwife were paid in kind. The fact that this relict survived as late as the 1920s might have had to do with the moderate amount of bribery which tradition legitimated. This probable interpretation of the custom clearly irritated those who were excluded from the game by their poorer conditions. Despite efforts of my parents to stop the traffic, it lingered on into the 1930s.

The authority of the Church was also under attack. During the yearly catechetical meeting in the school-house, senior members of the free churches at the *Bruk* used to seize the opportunity to challenge the priest in theological matters. I remember well the long debates but not what the parties actually said.

Free time projects

From what has been told before it should be clear that the inhabitants of the valley section most of their time were bound to projects which as a matter of fact were obligatory and largely beyond the discretion of the individual as far as content and succession were concerned. Disregarding the special case of school-children, people naturally did not live in villeinage. They could try to make careers by moving between livelihood positions. They could migrate out of the area. But in either case, others would take their place, and the general project pattern would remain the same. The obvious freedom accorded to everybody rested in the opportunity to develop his or her skills in doing what had to be done. It was also patently clear from conversations that the skill by which one carried out ones tasks was an important value in all the groups.

Evenings and weekends provided the only opportunity for 'freetime projects'.

Summer holidays were still a luxury, reserved only for school-children and teacher – which gave rise to some envy. Free-time projects were of two kinds, let us call them co-operative and private (which does not mean that the private ones could not be of a strong social nature).

Among the co-operative projects developed at the *Bruk*, the free churches have already been mentioned. The first nameless chapel had been built under common effort by a small group as early as 1883, the second, called Tabor, was erected by a dissenting group in 1924. Besides having religious functions, these buildings also were social centres of a kind.

A temperance lodge. 'The Guard of Honour', had come into being in the 1890s and provided room for study-groups, music and dance. An open-air dancing-floor hid at the edge of the wood. It offered entertainment on Saturday nights all summer long. A men's choir greeted spring there on Walpurgis night (April 30) while a big fire sparkled. The temperance lodge here and in other places played a tremendous role for the development of political participation in Sweden. Young persons who had only six years of primary school, taught themselves how to speak in public and how to handle meetings, minutes and accounts. This was the time when labour unions and organized political parties began to become visible. But events related to this process happened beyond my horizon.

Finally, in order to challenge the two private shopkeepers with some competition, workers got together in the 1920s to build their own co-operative shop. The founders continued to take part in its daily operations until modern ideas about 'rationality' after the Second World War led to different forms of organization.

Also a few parish-wide associations laid claims on the free time of people in the valley section. One of these, a church-based sewing society, met every second week in the home of one of its members, an occasion which caused some extra cleaning and baking in advance. This was a female preoccupation, except for the presence of the vicar who read from befitting books while the ladies worked and looked forward to coffee-time. Products were sold at an annual auction just before Christmas. The money went to missions and to the poor.

In 1914, a lecture society had been organized which invited speakers from outside to give about twelve lectures a year. History and exploration were popular topics, but also natural science, art and psychology appeared on the agenda. I used to help my father, who was the chairman, to move the heavy sciopticon between schools on bicycle or sleigh.

Common to all these co-operative ventures was that they were organized as formal institutions. This was a legal necessity, since they owned property and handled money. Some of them also enjoyed subsidies from parish or State. Thus, macro-society with its protecting hand and watching eye was indirectly present even here.

None of the voluntary institutions were genuine local inventions. They had come into being somewhere else, in Sweden or sometimes abroad, and had then spread as so-called popular movements.

Among the really private projects inhabitants engaged themselves in, one was strikingly conspicuous. Every night at eight o'clock, the year round, a crowd of people assembled at the railway station while the north-going train made a short stop. The most common excuse mentioned was the purchase of an evening newspaper or journal. But in fact, the gathering had the same meaning as the 'ramblas' in South-European cities – a time of belonging, not only to locality. One could always imagine that some well-known national figure had been reclining in a first-class compartment. When the sound of the train faded away behind the endless screens of spruce, we had once again been reconfirmed that we were anchored in an ordered, wider world.

The farming population had a calendar of feasts which arranged social life in a ritualistic manner. Parties could last for ten hours, a time devoted to consumption of an incredible amount of food in prescribed order. Two different cycles were in operation, one related to seasons and one to lifetimes. The terms of the short cycle were late summer and Christmas. The high points at the longer cycle were weddings and fiftieth birthdays.

Senior workers from the *Bruk* were frequently invited to the nearest farms, but otherwise the factory settlement was not integrated into this round dance.

Otherwise, what people actually did during their free time cannot be listed after all these years. The only pattern I can honestly describe by way of examples refers to my own family and myself.

At that time, nature played a big role as a source of recreation. One long-term project for my brother and myself was to build and maintain a boat on the river. A small woodland lake served as ice-rink in winter. Juniper bushes made strong bows. As the birch leaves began to come out in spring, we went out to cut twigs for making whisks and brooms. In passing we fabricated whistles out of mountain ash. September was the time of lingonberry picking, pleasure and profit in one stroke.

The destinations of family walks and solitary excursions were either hilltops with a wide prospect over the valley or some exceptionally large trees which had their own names and were regarded somewhat as silent friends. Some very big erratic boulders played a similar role. On the whole, nature was not just nature as an undifferentiated environment. It was a room, inhabited by personalities. For my memories of this world, images of touch and smell and sound come side by side with the visual pictures. I can still feel in my body how it was to sit on a certain stone or climb in this or that tree. This kind of familiarity applies most intensely to the nearest kilometre around my home, since this was the area I could reach and explore on my own after school-mates had disappeared to their separate worlds. This 'structure of feeling' (Pred 1982) is a uniquely private property and really beyond communication.

The integration of nature, social life and my private sphere came to a climax on the fifteenth of June, the termination of the school-year. The wooden floor smelled freshly scoured. Every child had brought a flower-garland, placed on the table to hide the hands behind. Fresh branches with leaves stuck out from the holes of the big black iron stove and from the window corners. Parents sat listening along the walls, tensions and festival spirits mingled. "Lord, bless and rule . . ." ended the year of routines.

It used to by my duty to clean up. I carried out armfuls of garlands, daisies, peonies, lilacs, and made a heap of them behind the outhouse. It looked as if somebody had just been buried. So it was. For the next six weeks the school-bell remained silent. The territory became exclusively mine and my brother's. But what I valued most was not the sudden opportunity to move away outwards as every day now put a Sunday prism at my disposal, but was, above all, the prospect of free expansion at home.

The holiday periods are interesting to consider, for then society's institutions lost their grip and one approached a utopian situation of freedom. The stage was set for total idleness apart from the few hours when garden plots had to be weeded. The opposite occurred. An autobiographer is obviously not an expert at the working of minds, but on the other hand, he knows what was in his mind. Mine was full of plans for building machines. I also know that the factual inspiration came from *The Book of Inventions.*[17] But I do not know from where the fascination came. Anyhow, over the summers I engaged myself in quite long-term projects involving the construction of a water-turbine, steam-engine, telephone, film-projector, telescope, to mention only the more complicated cases. All of it transcended any realistic possibility of my local world. Available tools were too clumsy and materials at hand little suitable. Wooden packing cases, round timbers, bobbins, tin boxes and mixed junk, found in the woods, drew up the boundaries for what could be achieved. Few things succeeded. It is not a very promising proposition to try to lead steam through a pipe made from the stem of a bush. But I thoroughly learned the principles of the various things I tried to fabricate, and I spent much exciting time looking for substitutes for material beyond my reach.

Discussion

Using path, project and diorama as ordering tools, I have rendered my story in a rather eclectic way, at times as eye-witness, at times as participant. Let me now go back to a general discussion, drawing upon observations which have been made.

The most general formulation of the meaning of project in time-geography is "the entire series of simple or complex tasks necessary to the completion of any intention-inspired or goal-oriented behavior" (Pred 1981). When combined with the idea of time/space paths (or trajectories), we might conclude that any project for its realization requires a sequence of bundles of paths, delineated by a mixed assortment of entities. Depending on the nature of the goal, these bundles must have a certain logical, consecutive order and individual duration, apart from some tolerable flexibility. One important aspect of flexibility is to what extent projects can 'survive' interruptions.

Taken in this very broad sense, projects frequently contain each other like Chinese boxes. This means that the sequences of bundles can be described at

[17] *Uppfinningarnas bok* (The book of inventions) was available to me in two versions, one six-volume series from the 1890s and one seven-volume series from the 1920s. Both were well illustrated, the oldest best suited as a source of inspiration because of its richer examples of the first efforts to solve technical problems. The enthusiasm over 'progress' was overwhelming.

various degrees of resolution. Seen in the long term and with little spatial detail, the establishment of a factory or a school is a project. So is also, seen in more detail, the fabrication of a machine or the educational program of a week. Still further down in scale, we might distinguish the casting of a cog-wheel or a lesson in history. We might go even further down in detail. It is almost like looking for smaller and smaller constituents of matter. But in the case of projects, up and down the scale, no bundle can come into being until the suitable 'path-makers' are free to join. Since in a diorama only a limited number of 'path-makers' are *there*, projects become interdependent in a situational sense, even if they belong to realms of action which per se are unrelated.

The sketch of a bygone diorama which I have drawn from memory does not describe projects in any deep and detailed way, mainly because this is impossible in verbal form. Language is discursive and cannot really reproduce the kind of constructs which are called projects in the time-geographic conceptualization. Even graphical notations would have had to leave much to the reader's imagination. But I hope enough has been indicated to serve as a basis for a general discussion of situation and project.

The first thing to note is the very considerable amount of people's daily time which was contained in, or affected by, institutions where projects to be carried out were prescribed. The factory and the school admitted no immediate, spontaneous relation between surrounding events and the initiation or completion of major projects. Both represented territorial domains, as far as possible shielded off from the local environment in order to protect a thereness of things, important to have immediately at hand – for example working machines and tools or books and instruments – and a similar thereness of people during precisely dictated hours.

The presence of a distant, powerful world is an essential feature in both cases. The *Bruk* had to adjust its projects to signals from the market, that is to say, to the fluctuations of a much wider situation than the local one. The school, on the other hand, performed a rather mechanical repetition of a program decided about years before in the remote capital under the impact of a political situation which happened to be in force at the time. Each individual farm was also a territorial domain. The farmers, however, were free from superior decision-makers. Market signals and legal rules (e.g. replanting) played a role for forestry operations. The local output of foodstuff and firewood was a matter of routine. But on the whole, masters in the farmers' world were not powers outside their own domains. They were instead immediately present in the form of biological processes and in variation of weather. The total spectrum of projects, and thus the total input of time, was probably nearly the same from year to year, but the daily choice required a sensitivity to changing conditions in a way which makes it true to say that projects were truly dependent on the day to day situations.

Territorial domains were interdependent. Some rather unavoidable projects were related to the management of material flows within the valley section. I have already mentioned the distribution of foodstuff and firewood. Other tasks had to do with the management of the river. Since water-wheels or turbines splashed in every fall, the flow of water had to be kept under surveillance in order that everybody got access to his share. Just around 1920, millers began to add small electrical generators to their equipment and households were step by step served by local grids. This, in turn, meant that the kerosene lamps could be stored away or converted and a daily family project could go to history. So, here again were some examples of the close ties between situations and projects.

The major interdependencies of projects inside the diorama, however, derived from constraints imposed on human paths inside the various territorial domains. First to be noted are certain aspects of *nonavailability*. During the larger part of the working day, the male population and the children were bound to their prescribed projects. This meant that some types of outside events were hardly worth considering. Political agitators, for example, would have had few to talk to. Travelling salesmen brought goods predominantly of interest to women, because they were the only ones at home. The mail-order catalogues had a far more important function, because they could be studied by the whole family when all were together. One should not underestimate the role of children in persuading parents to buy tempting articles.

The male adults had to postpone their free collective and private projects to the small opportunity prisms after working hours and to weekends. Therefore, their paths had to turn out very similar to those of the school-children as depicted in Figure 40.2. The few hours available in combination with low mobility limited effective reach. Institutions like the free churches, the temperance lodge and the lecture society had to survive with a very restricted population base. This fact constantly made the question of leadership acute. Intermittently their projects died off.

Only the female sewing society held its meetings in daytime. The farmers were in a similar position, autonomous enough to take days off and, for example, assemble for their feasts already by two o'clock on weekdays.

Project realization involves not only human time but also corresponding appropriation of things and room. Interdependencies related to these other inputs were mainly contained inside the various territorial domains and therefore not conspicuous. Some odd observations are perhaps worth making because of their social and cultural significance.

Concerning tools, most families owned one bicycle, if they had one at all. So, access to it was a matter of frequent negotiations. Few had a telephone at home. The factory office and later a call box were the only facilities put at public disposal. In other words, a telephone call demanded a lot of time and came to be used only for very urgent matters. To be wanted on the telephone frequently meant a disturbing message and was rather feared.

The question of room also had its humorous points. There were few places along the river suitable for swimming. Bathing suits were not yet much in use, so that families preferred to go into the water separately. On hot summer Sundays one could find family groups hiding in the slopes waiting for their turn.

The point with these remarks is to illustrate that human societies have a limited capacity to make room for projects, given certain values and a certain technology. When trying to understand what Giddens, Pred and others call 'structuration', it is therefore an essential task to study the relative strength of projects in competition. But then the factors at work can be fully appreciated only in a diorama perspective.

My starting point in this essay was the question posed by Christiaan Van Paassen concerning the project concept in time-geography and its relation to "the real life of real people". The question is fundamental but not really possible to answer in a general way until efforts have been made to carry out empirical investigations of many real cases. Thus, my rather impressionistic diorama is just a very meagre beginning. There are three points, though, that I want to stress.

The first is that without a diorama approach, the revealing power of time-geography cannot be fully explored. But this poses a tremendous problem for studies of the modern urban world, since the question of thereness is so confusing, particularly where the links between people and communication are concerned. These problems must be solved by adequate sampling procedures, whatever these are (but for goodness sake, don't believe that I am thinking of the kind of sampling modern statistics is pursuing).

The second thing is that autobiographical material, referring to the scholar himself, has value as a source of understanding beyond the normal documentary evidence one can mobilize for getting hold of unquestionably objective circumstances. Only one's own experience is able to provide the kind of intimate detail which can bring the study of project and situation into any real depth. He is after all an expert on his own networks of meaning. There are of course ambiguities of many sorts in memories, as there are in documentary sources. The remedy is to treat both residues as honestly as one possibly can.[18]

My third point is that path, project and diorama are simple concepts, readily understandable to everybody, even to a child. This means, I think, that the investigator can draw rather easily upon not only his own experience but everybody's. My hope is that we have devices which can make people's stories and even literature into productive inputs to research and also make output of research more generally understandable than is now the case.[19]

In this perspective, let me conclude by again quoting Christiaan Van Paassen's essay on human geography (1976), p. 339), where he speaks about project and situation seen in the light of history: "The items for a livable existence will change in time and place, they cannot be fixed". Does this mean that we are forever doomed to tell particular stories without ever accumulating deeper general insights into the human condition? Does the diorama perspective bring us back to the doctrine of the unique as the fate of historical and geographical studies?

I don't think so and I do not believe that Van Paassen thinks so either. If we are

[18] The ideal format of an exercise of this kind would have been to compare observations made by several contemporaries viewing events from various outlook positions.

[19] The use of literature as a source for time-geographic studies is suggested by Pred (1982). I believe that story-telling and newsreports in daily papers provide a rich source of insight, if projected onto proper time-geographic dioramas as a structuring device.

able to bring an in-depth understanding of the "live corporeality of man and society" into our scholarly consciousness, I am sure that much understanding of a lasting nature can be brought forth: how human consciousness is construed, what form (Gestalt) psychologically satisfying projects have, what form institutions ought to have in order to be able to distribute 'goods' and 'bads' in a just way, maybe even how to reduce the amount of 'bads' without creating new ones, just to mention a few problems. I think the best hope we can have as human scientists is that the result of honest research finally moves out as common sense and by so doing helps to keep human projects and situations on tracks away from disaster.

References

Barrett, W. (1978), *The Illusion of Technique: A Search of Meaning in a Technological Civilization.* Anchor Press.

Burns, L. D. (1979), *Transportation, Temporal, and Spatial Components of Accessibility.* Lexington/Massachusetts/Toronto: Lexington Books, D. C. Health & Comp.

Buttimer, A. (1976), Grasping the Dynamism of Lifeworld. *Annals of the Association of American Geographers* 66, no. 2, pp. 277–292.

Buttimer, A. (1978), Charism and Context: The Challenge of La Géographie Humaine. *In*: D. Ley and M. S. Samuels, eds., *Humanistic Geography, Prospects and Problems,* pp. 58–76. London: Croom Helm.

Buttimer, A. (1978), Home, Reach and the Sense of Place. *In: Symposia Universitatis Upsaliensis Annum Quingentesimum Celebrantis* 11, Uppsala.

Buttimer, A. (1981), On People, Paradigms, and 'Progress' in Geography. *In*: D. Stoddart, ed., *Geography, Ideology and Social Concern,* pp. 81–98. Oxford: Basil Blackwells'.

Carlstein, T. (1980). Time Resources, Society and Ecology. On the Capacity for Human Interaction in Space and Time. *Meddelanden från Lunds universitets geografiska institution,* Avhandlingar LXXXVIII, Lund.

Giddens, A. (1979), *Central Problems in Social Theory: Action, Structure and Contradiction in Social Analysis.* London: MacMillan.

Granö, J. G. (1929), Reine Geographie. Eine methodologische Studie beleuchtet mit Beispiele aus Finland und Estland. *Turun Yliopiston Maantieteelisen Laitoksen Julkaisuja,* No. 3, Helsinki.

Gregory, D. (1980), The Ideology of Control: Systems Theory and Geography. *Tijdschrift voor Economische en Sociale Geografie* 71, no. 6, pp. 327–342.

Gregory, D. (1982), Solid Geometry: Notes on the Recovery of Spatial Structure. *In*: P. Gould & G. Olsson, eds. *A Search for Common Ground,* pp. 187–219. London: Pion.

Kubler, G. (1962), *The Shape of Time. Remarks on the History of Things.* New Haven/London: Yale University Press.

Parkes, D. N. & N. J. Thrift (1975), Timing Space and Spacing Time. *Environment and Planning* A, 7, pp. 651–670.

Popper, K. R. & J. C. Eccles (1977), *The Self and Its Brain. An Argument for Interactionism.* Berlin: Springer-Verlag.

Pred, A. (1978), The Impact of Technological and Institutional Innovations on Life Content: Some Time-Geographic Observations. *Geographical Analysis* 10, no. 4, pp. 345–372.

Pred, A. (1981), Power, Everyday Practice and the Discipline of Human Geography. *In*: Space and Time in Geography. *Lund Studies in Geography. Ser. B. Human Geography,* No. 48, pp. 30–55.

Pred, A. (1981), Production, Family, and Free-Time Projects: A Time-Geographic Perspective on the Individual and Societal Change in Nineteenth Century U.S. Cities. *Journal of Historical Geography* 7, No. 1, pp. 3–36.

Pred, A. (1981), Social Reproduction and the Time-Geography of Everyday Life. *Geografiska Annaler* 63 B. No. 1, pp. 5–22.

Pred, A. (1982), Structuration and Place: On the Becoming of Sense of Place and Structure of Feeling. *Journal for the Theory of Social Behaviour* (forthcoming).

Thrift, N. (1981), Owners' Time and Own Time: The Making of a Capitalist Time Consciousness, 1300–1880. *In*: Space and Time in Geography. *Lund Studies in Geography. Ser. B. Human Geography*. No. 48, pp. 56–84.

Törnqvist, G. (1981), On Arenas and Systems. *In*: Space and Time in Geography. *Lund Studies in Geography. Ser. B. Human Geography* No. 48, pp. 109–120.

Tuan, Yi-Fu (1977), *Space and Place: The Perspective of Experience*. Minneapolis: University of Minnesota Press.

Van Paassen, Chr. (1976), Human Geography in Terms of Existential Anthropology. *Tijdschrift voor Economische en Sociale Geografie* 67, no. 6, pp. 324–341.

41

A VIEW ON THE GIS CRISIS IN GEOGRAPHY

Stan Openshaw

The superimposition of one map upon one or more others in search of patterns of correlation is a well-founded geographical technique, advocated by Hartshorne among others. Yet it has rarely been thought sufficient to define a whole discipline. Openshaw here argues that geographers should think again about this deceptively simple technique. Given the explosion of electronic information, the speed and accessibility of modern computing, and the sophistication of software to manipulate data of all kinds, Geographical Information Systems provide a potential core for geography. GIS can integrate time and space, nature and society, quantitative and qualitative data, large and small data sets in ways which far exceed the imagination of Hägerstrand in the 1950s (**chapters 39** and **40**). It can solve problems and produce the technologically-trained and useful geographers which society needs (see Mackinder, **chapter** 8). Openshaw takes a swipe at geographers who are too obsessed with theory and in this regard he is perhaps at odds with many of the authors selected in this volume. His own work has often consisted of inductive exploration of large data sets for practical purposes, on such things as modelling the consequences of nuclear attack, siting nuclear power stations and searching for childhood leukaemia clusters. Critics of GIS accuse it of being too narrowly fact-based, inclined towards managerial solutions rather than critical understanding, and too biased towards the wealthy, data-rich parts of the world. Openshaw thinks that too many geographers are technophobes.

Source: A view on the GIS crisis in geography, or, using GIS to put Humpty Dumpty back together again. *Environment and Planning A* 23, 621–8, 1991.

This editorial is for those geographers who read this journal and are interested in geographical information systems (GISs) and their relationship with geography. Some things are, I am told, best not discussed because they are potentially divisive and this is one of them. Such a discussion might also be perceived to be relevant to neither GISers or nonGISers as long as they remain separate branches of geography and are not in competition for resources or the high ground. On the other hand, they will not remain separate for long. There is seemingly also much misinformed speculation about what GIS is and does, and how it either fits or does not fit comfortably within geography; some even think that geography might be better off without it! So something needs to be said. In this commentary, I seek to anticipate the problems before they become critical, and by airing the debate I seek to divert and diffuse any subsequent impact.

Some people talk about the 'GIS Revolution' as being the 'quantitative geographer's revenge' and as a revival of positivism. Yet others are concerned about the extent to which GIS is fact rather than knowledge-based, and fear that this somehow reduces geography to a source of 'facts' and as a 'tool' that others may use rather than as a discipline in its own right. The argument is that GIS is anti-geography. Knowing little or nothing about what GIS is or does, GIS is somehow viewed as a retreat from knowledge to information. Yet without information how can there be knowledge? Indeed, the problem with much of geography is the extremely fragile nature of its knowledge base and its strong traditions of untestable theoretical speculation and descriptive storytelling! Others might well criticise GIS for the lack of any relevant inbuilt notions of the microbehaviour of people or of the social and political processes responsible for the societies that lie behind the map patterns. But how can any of this possibly be a relevant reason for throwing GIS out of geography? Only slightly less ridiculous would be to accuse GIS-literate geographers of following unsound philosophical beliefs they did not even know they possessed (or even what the words meant)! If this process continues and gets completely out of hand, then this mix of genuine ignorance and wilfully misinformed prejudice may even constitute a crisis that could infect a few more generations of young geographers; effectively blinkering their thought processes by engaging them in an essentially irrelevant and spurious philosophical debate as to why GIS is, or is not, geographically relevant. Yet the 'truth' can be quite different. The view may be expressed that the absorption of GIS into geography offers the basis for a long-overdue reconciliation between the 'soft' pseudoscience of the social sciences and the 'hard' spatial science of which GIS is part. Geography needs both. The problem is that whereas geography is characterised by pluralistic methodologies it is peopled by geographers who appear not nearly as flexible when it comes to discussing the possible role of GIS within geography or when facing the computer challenges of the 1990s, of which GIS is a manifestation.

Seemingly, revolutions in a Kuhnian sense are not rare events in subjects like geography. The last few decades have seen several 'new' geographies come and go. Each episode sooner or later creates various antifeelings and is replaced by another fashion. Although this ability continuously to mutate gives geography tremendous vitality and adaptability to changing environments, it also causes increasing and massive confusion as to what geography is really about. It is almost as if geography's Humpty-Dumpty had fallen off its wall and shattered into a thousand pieces; each relic being picked up and treasured by a handful of followers. Only rarely does this process of geographic fragmentation discover a 'new' geography that is of sufficient stature and importance to have a far-reaching, long-term, and fundamental impact on the nature of geography itself. GIS is probably one of these because it can be regarded as offering the prospect of reversing the disciplinary fissioning process and replacing it by a fusion; a drawing together of virtually all the subdisciplinary products with their multitude of conflicting paradigms created over the last thirty years, within a single (philosophy-free or philosophy-invariant or even philosophy-ignorant) integrating framework. The basis for the integration is purely, geographical. That is, GIS stresses above all else the simple holistic nature of the space–time data model that is geography. This is hardly new, it is not novel, and it is not particularly powerful in a metaphysical way. Yet suddenly there exists in GIS a language and a tool kit for manipulating the elemental space–time fabric of geography in all its forms, whether physical or human, qualitative or quantitative, and squishy or tough. This prospect of even some weak integration of the previously unintegratable is one reason why the GIS revolution looks like being important to geography. From a geographical point of view, it can be argued that GIS matters, and GIS matters because it can encapsulate (some might say imprison) the core of geography! It follows then that it is not appropriate to view the debate about GIS as being characteristic of yet another 'new' geography. Reject or accept THIS 'new' geography and it is likely that the discipline will change in a more fundamental structural way than on any previous occasion.

Amazingly, GIS appears to be starting its period of fashion by having to face criticism as to whether it is geographical and important to geography. The scale and intensity of the potential opposition could turn out to be quite unique, even for geography. There might even be some prospect for an unholy grand alliance of that motley collection of essentially noncomputerised geographical subtypes that probably previously seldom even spoke to each other let alone professed to share a common view of geography. Seemingly, all could be united in the face of a common adversary – the GIS revolution. The counterrevolutionary strategy appears to be based on building up a range of conceptio-theoretical arguments against it, express them in pseudophilosophical languages to provide a veneer of academic respectability, add a few misquotes from famous dead people who lived in a totally different world, and wait five years for the reaction to go critical. Perhaps as with the quantitative revolution before it, maybe they expect many of the leading GIS prophets to become converted to more softish and supposedly conceptually more satisfying themes. Poor fools; don't they realise that GIS is here to stay!

Regardless of whatever happens to GIS, geography and geographers are going to have to learn how to cope not just with a world full of computerised geographical data but also with the new data-driven and computer-based knowledge-creating technologies that are being developed to cope with it. GIS is useful as a tool kit, even if it never amounts to anything much more than a computerisation of previously traditional geographic map skills. However, the real crisis in geography has probably little to do with GIS. Faced with an exponential growth in available geographic information, the utility of soft and the so-called intensive and squelchy-soft qualitative research paradigms could fade into insignificance if they cannot be adequately linked into the new data and computer age that is all around us. Indeed, herein lies the source of the set of the problems presented by GIS. GIS emphasises a full-frontal and explicitly naked geographicalness at a moment in time when many geographers have seemingly forgotten what it is like to be geographical (let alone naked geographical!) and have moved away from anything to do with maps and explicit geographical data. Yet GIS emphasises a world full of digital geographical data; a particular commodity that some or many geographers seem to be trying their best to do without. Others, perhaps ashamed of their geographical map-based traditions, may choose instead to be called 'social' scientist in the hope this excuses their neglect of geographical things.

Another point to ponder is that, unlike most other 'revolutions' in geography, GIS does not seem to derive its power solely from within geography itself; most comes from outside. So if geographers decide they do not like it anymore, then it will probably be geography that will end up being impoverished. There are good grounds for believing that regardless of what geographers decide to do about it, GIS will continue to expand. On the other hand, if geographers reject GIS then it could fundamentally affect the outside world's perception of what geography is all about. Certainly, these external perceptions may well be based on a picture of geography as it once was, but nevertheless they cannot be ignored. "How could they be so foolish as to disown the very core of their discipline?", important people would probably ask and in due course would, no doubt, act accordingly. One complaint might be that because so many geographers have been so keen to get beyond the map and they have wandered off in so many different directions, often creating new colonies of geography in the process, that this is not perceived to be a problem. Certainly, few seem to return to address with any real authority the basic geographic questions that they (or in some cases their teachers or soon their teachers'-teachers) once asked. Is it possible that geography has fallen so far apart after decades of fission into more and more subspecies of ever increasing degrees of geographical irrelevancy, that most geographers can no longer recognise 'pure' geography when they see it? Sadly, the answer could be 'yes'! It should be 'no', but perhaps a good compromise would be 'maybe'.

Why might so many Geographers have Reasons to Fear GIS?

One explanation for an antiGIS reaction would be that the GIS critics have essentially become nongeographers but, like a parasite, they are trapped within a host they may despise but cannot escape, so they continue to masquerade as geographers living out their fantasies in the geographical literature and doing their best to avoid geography rediscovering its geographical roots. The 'rambling and ranting' era of so-called radical but probably second-rate philosophical thinking about geography and society might be regarded as one such device. It is all very well arguing for an holistic approach based on a synthesis of everything before anything can be studied, but how on earth do you do anything geographically relevant with such a paradigm? These and other products of modern geographic thinking may well have something important to offer but, whatever it is, it does not appear to provide any real or sound basis for geography; it does not seem to offer any basis for the future even if it might be made to retrofit the past.

An alternative and more temperate explanation would only involve having to conjure up images of basic fear and anxiety concerning the dawning of a new age of computer geography. The combination of the computerisation of most things in the world – of data, analysis, and display technologies – effectively locks out those who have no computer ID and no great knowledge of the basic computer systems that are perceived to be necessary just to survive. Combine these developments with advances in other seemingly alien and highly complex computer-science technology and the appearance of artificial intelligence methods that increasingly look likely to be practicable and useful even in a geographic domain, and it would be surprising if 50% to 80% (maybe more) of geographers did not feel threatened in some ways. To these people, GIS may look like the tip of a massive iceberg set to overwhelm them at any moment. They cannot easily participate, so they watch enviously as research resources are utilised to stimulate GIS research, that they consider irrelevant, on a scale they only ever dreamt about.

Previously, most of the technical cripples in geography seem to have survived the increasing use of computer technology by essentially ignoring most computer-based developments (word processing skills do not count). Indeed, until recently most computer developments seem to have had little impact on the nature of geography, and the area was relegated to a handful of what are often referred to as 'mindless number crunchers and mere handle crankers', the computer freaks, the left-over and born-again spatial analysts from a previous era, and mathematical modellers who live (or lived) in Leeds and a small number of other model-rich oases. This survivial-by-ignoring-computers strategy seemed to work well until the computer technologies being ignored started to be labelled explicitly as 'geographical'. It must be hard to be a 'geographer' and argue that computer technology universally labelled 'geographical information systems' has nothing whatsoever to do with geography and belongs somewhere else.

There is another underlying factor. As computer hardware becomes faster and cheap (the price of computer power has probably fallen by a factor of between a 100 and a 1000 in less than five years) it suddenly becomes feasible to do on a desktop workstation things that once required a supercomputer. This is greatly accelerating the impact and diffusion of all kinds of computer-based technologies, and geography is not exempt; and, indeed, perhaps to an extent not found in many other social sciences, much of its traditional subject matter may be fundamentally affected (some might say infected). The key question here might appear to be whether to reject the traditional map-based roots of geography in order to avoid the computers or to grasp at the new opportunities before others remove them from reach.

The GIS revolution can be viewed, therefore, as encompassing ongoing computer hardware and information developments and because of this may well become a major cause of technophobia. GIS seems to epitomise a revolution that most geographers probably think they cannot easily cope with and thus it acts as a harbinger that their worst fears about the impact of a new geography based around computer hardware and computer technologies is soon to be realised. Nothing of the old order seems to be sacred or exempt (as indeed it is not) from an emerging form of computational geography based on generic technologies. GIS brings with it application-independent tool kits able to handle and manipulate all kinds of geographic information, captured from whatever source. Post-Fordism and flexible specialisation is now reaching into the very heart of geography itself whilst also breaking down historic, well established, widely accepted, but always artificial, intradisciplinary boundaries. A geographer of the impending new order may well be able to analyse river networks on Mars on Monday, study cancer in Bristol on Tuesday, map the underclass of London on Wednesday, analyse groundwater flow in the Amazon basin on Thursday, and end the week by modelling retail shoppers in Los Angeles on Friday. What of it? Indeed, this is only the beginning.

There is a tool kit emerging of generic computer analysis methods based on neural nets and other forms of artificial intelligence that can be trained to handle both hard and soft analysis problems that occur in many contexts, including geography. New artificial-knowledge-creating technologies are to become an integral part of this wonderfully new and different era; or is it all hype and fiction? Does it matter that soon the chemical-process engineer interested in the real-time control of a bug fermenter will be using the same modelling technology as a geographer interested in studying the decisionmaking behaviour of small firms or in forecasting short-term unemployment for a set of zones? Maybe there are immense opportunities here for geographers to break free of their self-imposed disciplinary boundaries and acquire really useful computer methods that are at last able to deal with some of their hard problems. Statistical methods as currently practiced could within a time scale of five to ten years be rendered largely irrelevant. Likewise, mathematical model building tools, for example, those based on 1970s entropy-maximising procedures, could suddenly find themselves replaced by neural-net-based alternatives. The pace of change is today extremely rapid and there is every prospect that a major revolution is underway, during which computer-based technologies will increasingly replace previous manual, analytical, and hand-crafted theory-based approaches. GIS is part of a process which extends far beyond GIS and geography but which may well be perceived mainly as a GIS revolution by geographers. Maybe the 'real' revolution is not GIS at all, but the emergence of a new computational geography in the context of a world of computers and cybernetic thinking.

From a technological point of view, it is all really quite simple. The new technologies epitomised by GIS are providing tools for geographers (and others) to use on geographical information. What they are used for and how to make best use of them within geography depends on the attitudes and mind set of their users and what they want to do with them. In fact, all that is really changing is the manner by which geographers can perform some of their more explicitly geographical works and the appearance of an information framework within which all geographers should be able to work. It is true that the new tools will tend to change the substance of geography but only in a very gradual manner and mainly by intensifying the emphasis on map-based information with a growing focus on the analysis of available data resources in the context of new and more automated ways of collecting data. In time this will probably focus attention of different subject areas within geography, with a movement away from those poorly served with information. Please note! It is not necessary to declare that certain research methodologies are no longer needed or that some are 'wrong'. There is no need to be so elitist! In the new information-rich world that is emerging, researchers will make use of whatever tools of whatever sort are considered most applicable, with no concern for demarcation disputes based on narrow philosophical, or whatever, grounds.

GIS will not replace traditional tools but it does appear to offer an extremely useful complement to them. It can amplify their utility in a world that is now awash with more geographical information than ever before. It is not a matter of having to learn Arc/Info or of viewing geography as a gigantic polygon-overlay problem, but merely recognising that we are heading for an immensely data-rich but theory-poor world. New opportunities are being created for geographers to apply their essentially traditional skills to a whole new array of information resources, made accessible and infinitely manageable via GIS. Is there not a moral duty to help society and the world to unlock and understand the key patterns and relationships that may exist encrypted in these data bases for individual countries, for planet earth, and later on for other planets and other universes? Are there really geographers around who can still call themselves geographers and yet rationally argue that GIS technology offers an enabling tool kit and spatial information system framework that is not the legitimate concern of geography?

Is GIS the Glue that can be used to put Geography back Together again?

Maybe GIS is only viewed as a threat by noncomputerised geographers because it is perceived to be the tip of the computational geography iceberg. Such fears are understandable. Perhaps others do not like it because it reminds us that the core feature of geography is the map. The idea of returning geography to a map base seems to raise all sorts of philosophically induced illusions of grandeur as to what geography is about. It can also be a problem because not many geographers today will admit to being 'map based'! Maps have always been difficult things to create, manipulate, and analyse. The patterns they contain are often only capable of shallow investigation at the map level. The first generation of quantitative geographers soon discovered these limits at a time when the available geographical data sets were small (n<100) and the rich resources of the maps were locked in an analogue form and thus unavailable for computer analysis. No wonder geographers became disillusioned by the inability of the new technology to explain in a causally acceptable manner the processes that seemed to be responsible for the map patterns. It is also no great surprise that they tended to wander off in almost any direction in search of alternative paradigms. It is hardly a shock that Humpty-Dumpty fell off her wall!

It could be argued that whether they like it or not, geography needs GIS as a form of elemental super-glue in order to put the pieces of geography back together again to form a coherent scientific discipline. One problem with reconstruction is that there would no longer be any concensus image of what Humpty-Dumpty should look like or even looked like! Certainly, there is little point in glueing together the bits to recreate a 1930s or 1950s style of geography, or of using entropy-maximising methods to assemble some sort of weighted average of all the fragments (although this is a safe way of managing geographical curricula)! Maybe it is safer to have no clear image with which people may take exception. It would in any case be more relevant in the 1990s to regard geography from a cybernetic perspective and view it as part of a computer information system, based on and around GIS but which eventually goes far beyond it. Geographers can then use GIS to reassemble the bits of geography into whatever shape or form of Humpty-Dumpty they wish, using whatever methodologies they prefer and adopting whatever philosophical stance that is considered appropriate. This avoids endless debate as to the proper nature of geography but still provides some kind of explicit integrating framework which is sufficiently general as to encompass almost everything that geographers do, have done, or may want to do.

A GIS View of Geography

It would appear then that GISs can provide an information system domain within which virtually all of geography can be performed. GIS would emphasise an holistic view of geography that is broad enough to encompass nearly all geographers and all of geography. At the same time it would offer a means of creating a new scientific look to geography and confer upon the subject a degree of currency and relevancy that has, arguably, long been missing. But this GIS view of geography is also an illusion. The super-glue is geography not an information system; however, geography itself is increasingly viewable as part of an even larger computer system. The distinction between data and concepts or knowledge is arbitrary. As sixth-generation computing becomes a reality within a decade or two, so too does the appearance of a more broadly based and far more complete cybernetic view of what information disciplines such as geography seem to be becoming. GIS is only the first installment. Some of us can hardly wait for the rest but fear they may not live long enough to see it all in place.

Historically, geographers and, through them, their geographies have usually responded to the needs of society and the world around it. The problem is that for most of the twentieth-century geographers appear to have lost their ability to communicate with the public and create any kind of attractive aura. The last time geography was really famous with a high public profile was probably during the age of the great Victorian and Edwardian explorers (Africa, and the polar regions). Then, but not now, geography was 'easy'. Today, it is very hard. Digital computers promised much in the 1950s and 1960s but could not deliver; no data, no relevant methods, no GIS. Today, things are rapidly getting better. There is no shortage of data. There is no shortage of people wanting answers to geographical questions. There is also no shortage of important geographical questions to study in a multitude of different areas. Enter GIS. Suddenly, there is a geographer's equivalent to biotechnology, something that brings geography up to date. There is also now a linkage between the world of geography and many other areas of active science; namely, artificial intelligence, computer science, image processing, planetary exploration, world environmental models, global data bases, etc. Here is an opportunity to be seen to be visibly associated with some of the contemporary leading edges of science and a chance to confront some of the increasingly hard problems that the world faces today, wearing a geographical hat with some prospect of being able to provide confident answers to the questions.

GIS provides a platform for 'doing geography' in the 1990s and it does not matter one jot the precise type of style of geography you are interested in doing. Nor need you actually use it explicitly; but is it not comforting to know that your geography exists within a broader GIS environment from which help and support can be obtained? GIS provides a context, an information resource, and an environment for geographical thinking and research. Unlike other geographic philosophies, it is data based and computer based; it is open rather than closed, it can accommodate pluralistic research styles; and offers no restrictions on subject matter or approach. Its only weakness is that it emphasises the integrating and context-setting role of the map; but if you cannot live with this restriction then maybe you are not a geographer, and the problems and you go away.

GIS changes the way we can look at geography. Suddenly, geography looks like a huge integrated GIS on which various nondata layers of interpretative subjectivity have been built. No data source relevant to geography can not be included, and artificial differences between the physical and human worlds are totally transparent. Viewed in this way, GIS is no more than an information system containing data and analysis tools that underpin geography. A computerisation of the space–time data cube of old. This GIS platform provides a broad backcloth or context into which more detailed activities can be based. The objective, though, should always be to return to enrich the underlying information system. For instance, the search for describing the locational dynamics of something interesting may well focus on the need for a detailed understanding of decisionmaking by social actors. However, there is still a need to view this microbehaviour in its broader context and to return with an improved understanding back from the microlevel to the geography of the problem. The data needed to develop this understanding and the conceptual thinking that constitutes understanding can be part of the underlying information systems.

One issue here is that some, maybe many, geographers may not consider GIS to be relevant in any way to their search for an understanding of processes, a criticism that can be applied for different reasons to both human and physical domains. As a criticism of GIS, it is quite correct! However, GIS is only a part of the broader computer-based-information and knowledge-based systems that are being developed. Of course, there are limits of what can be done with purely geographical information and typically they are reached very early along the path of seeking to understand a complex world. But in searching for process understanding it is also important to be realistic and to avoid the use of misleading terminology that reflects conflicting usage of the same words with a meaning dependent on research paradigm. It is possible to indulge in so-called 'process modelling' within GIS, where it is usually termed spatial decision support systems; for instance, many of the regional models that have appeared in this journal would count in this category and might be absorbed into GIS quite readily. However, much depends on what is meant by 'process'. How many geographers will labour under the misapprehension that it is possible to tease out the causal mechanisms and the interconnections of various factors, processes, and decisions that are ultimately responsible for those features that appear as digital map data in a GIS? Yet, unless they can prove otherwise, they may need to accept that all they are doing is creating and telling realistic but not necessarily nonfictional fairy tales. This informed fiction and subjective interpretation of map patterns, their generating processes, and their changes over time may well be extremely useful mental devices for understanding geography. But if people actually believe the stories that some geographers can readily fabricate about processes and decisionmakers as 'true' representations of reality, there needs to be some hard empirical proof that they are. Geography is not like physics or chemistry where there appears to be a strong degree of universal orderliness underlying complex phenomenon. The problems of geography are in some ways far harder, especially when viewed from a normal scientific viewpoint. Yet some geographers have reacted to these problems by creating what are no more than plausible works of fiction and then attribute to them academic credibility by developing philosophical stances that render normal scientific proof unnecessary. In this way empirical verification of process predictability is deemed inadequate, insufficient, and even fatally flawed by the adoption of a philosophical paradigm that derides such notions as positivism. Again, that is fine provided it is seen in context. However, a lack of this type of process orientation cannot subsequently be used as a fundamental criticism of GIS which operates on a different philosophical plane. People who believe otherwise are deluding themselves about the nature of their work rather than criticising GIS.

GIS emphasises pattern-related description and understanding, and provided this objective is maintained it is sufficiently broad to encompass a vast range of geographical activities at many different scales. Geographic referencing is applicable to many different types of natural object, ranging from the very small-scale maps (1 : 10 000 000) to large-scale maps (1 : 50 000; 1 : 1250; 1 : 500; 1 : 50), to the microscopic world (1 000 : 1 or 10 000 000 : 1). The computer systems of the early 2000s of which GIS will be a small part will be able to combine data, information, knowledge, and concepts. The current GIS fuss is only stage 1, but even this seems to offer useful geographical benefits. Here is an emerging all-embracing implicit framework capable of integrating and linking all levels of past, present, and possible future geographies. No wonder some people get excited! There cannot be many geographers who could not live in such a world. GIS provides a means of bringing together the pieces of geography. It offers a common core not of a metaphysical nature (that has been repeatedly tried and has always failed) but as a living, dynamic, and universal information system. This view of geography as an integrated spatial information system provides a simple, weak, but all-embracing framework capable of integrating the bits and pieces of contemporary geography. There are few fragments within it that cannot be made to fit in a fairly painless fashion and there can be few activities that will not substantially benefit as a result. 'YES', the G in GIS really does stand for Geography, and geographers everywhere should be both proud and happy that it is there. If you disagree, then why not write and complain; maybe someone will reply.

A CHRONOLOGY OF GEOGRAPHY 1859–1995

Alisdair Rogers

Historical Events	Geographers' Lives	Geographical Publications
1859 *Origin of Species* C. Darwin 1861–5 US Civil War 1866 E. Haeckel coins term 'Oecologie' 1867 *Capital vol. 1* K. Marx Meiji restoration, Japan 1869 Suez Canal opens	1861 b. H. J. Mackinder 1862 J.W. Powell loses right arm at Shiloh 1863 b. E. C. Semple 1864–5 Kroptokin's Siberian expeditions 1869 Powell's 1st Grand Canyon expedition Ratzel attends Haeckel's course in Jena	1864 *Man & Nature* G. P. Marsh
1870–1 Franco-Prussian War, Paris Commune 1871 Stanley finds Livingstone at Ujiji 1872 Yellowstone national park designated 1874 1st Impressionist exhibition, Paris 1875 Bell patents telephone 1876 Battle of Little Big Horn 1878 1st telephone exchange	1871 E. Reclus captured fighting for Paris Commune & Exiled to Switzerland 1872 Vidal appointed at Nancy 1873 Ratzel travels USA 1874 Prussia decrees geography a university discipline 1874–5 G.K. Gilbert's study of Henry Mountains 1876 Kropotkin flees from Russia 1878 W. M. Davis to Harvard	1875 F. Galton's 1st weather map published in a newspaper 1876 Laws of migration, E. Ravenstein 1877 *Physiography* T. H. Huxley
1882 Britain occupies Egypt	1883 Boas's expedition to Baffin Island	1881 *Anthropogeographie vol. 1* F. Ratzel

Historical Events	Geographers' Lives	Geographical Publications
1884 Greenwich Mean Time established as world standard 1884–5 Conference of Berlin carves up Africa among European states 1887 Queen Victoria's Golden jubilee Herz identifies radio waves Trafalgar Sq. riots, London 1888 William II, emperor of Germany 1889 Paris Exhibition	1885 c. 94 geographical societies around the world 1886 Ratzel to chair at Leipzig Keltie Report on state of British geography 1887 Mackinder to readership at Oxford 1888 geography at Cambridge National Geographical Society, USA 1889 b C.O.Sauer	1885 What geography ought to be, P. Kropotkin 1886 *Elementary lessons in physical geography* A. Geikie 1887 On the scope & methods of geography, H. J. Mackinder 1887 The study of geography, F. Boas 1889 Cycle of erosion proposed by W. M. Davis
1893 World's Columbian Exposition, Chicago 1895 Roentgen discovers X-rays, Lumière brothers develop cinema 1896 H. Becquerel discovers radioactivity 1898 start of German naval build-up Spanish-American War 1899 2nd Boer War	1890s Ratzel active in Pan-German league 1891 b. J.K. Wright *Annales de Géographie* founded, Paris Semple studies under Ratzel in Leipzig 1892 John Muir helps found Sierra Club 1893 *The Geographical Journal* founded 1898 Vidal to chair at Sorbonne 1899 Mackinder climbs Mt. Kenya 1899 Oxford, 1st UK geography department	1893 Frontier in American History – F. J. Turner 1894 *Universal Geography* E. Reclus *Morphology of the earth's surface* A. Penck 1896 The territorial growth of states, F. Ratzel 1899 *Handbook of commercial geography* G. C. Chisholm
1900 *The interpretation of dreams* S. Freud 1st pan-African conference Planck's quantum theory 1901 T. Roosevelt American President 1st radio signals across Atlantic G. Marconi 1903 Wright brothers 1st flight 1905 Special theory of relativity, Albert Einstein Japanese defeat Russian army & navy	1900 Mackinder to director of London School of Economics 1901 E. Huntington travels Euphrates on a raft 1903 Chicago, 1st US geography graduate program 1904 d. F. Ratzel Association of American Geographers founded F. Younghusband expedition to Tibet	1902 *Systematic geography* W. M. Davis 1903 *Tableau de la géographie de la France* P. Vidal de la Blache *Geographic influence in American history* A. P. Brigham 1904 The geographical pivot of history, H. J. Mackinder 1905 The major natural regions, A. Herbertson

Historical Events	Geographers' Lives	Geographical Publications
1909 Model T Ford	1907 T.G. Taylor lectures in geography in Sydney 1909 K. Haushofer sent to Japan	1907 *The pulse of Asia* E. Huntington 1909 A. Weber's industrial location theory
1911 Atomic structure explained by Rutherford, Amundsen reaches South Pole 1912–3 Balkan Wars 1914 Panama canal opens 1914–19 First World War 1915 *The origin of continents and oceans* A. Wegener A. Einstein's general theory of relativity 1917 Russian Revolution 1919 Alcock & Brown fly Atlantic Versailles Peace settlement	1910–22 Mackinder elected to Parliament 1911 *Annals of the Association of American Geographers* founded 1912 W. M. Davis organises Transcontinental Expedition, USA K. Haushofer fights on western front J.K. Wright serves in infantry & intelligence E. Huntington in military intelligence 1915 1st Canadian geography course, U. of British Columbia 1918 d. P. Vidal de la Blache Bowman & Semple contribute to US preparation for Paris peace talks 1919 Mackinder high commissioner to southern Russia	1911 *Influences of geographic environment* E. Semple Les genres de vie dans la gégraphie humaine, P. Vidal de la Blache 1914 *Mutual Aid* P. Kropotkin 1915 *Cities in evolution* P. Geddes 1916 Regional environment, heredity & consciousness, A. Herbertson 1919 Human regions, H. J. Fleure Climatic cycles & evolution, T. G. Taylor *The provinces of England* C. B. Fawcett
1922 *Ulysses* J. Joyce, *The Waste Land* T.S. Eliot, *Economy & Society* M. Weber 1923 France occupies Ruhr 1925 1st surrealist exhibition, Paris 1926 General Strike, UK 1927 Stalin comes to power, USSR 1927 transatlantic telephone links 1929–33 Great Depression	1921 Semple 1st woman president of AAG I. Bowman joins Council on Foreign Relations Haushofer appointed to Munich 1st full geography course in Canada, U. of Montreal 1922 d. P. Kropotkin Michigan Land Survey 1923 Sauer to Berkeley 1925 *Economic Geography* journal founded	1922 *Principes de la géographie humaine* P. Vidal de la Blache *A geographical introduction to history* L. Febvre 1923 Geography as human ecology, H. Barrows 1925 The morphology of landscape, C. O. Sauer 1926 A plea for the history of geography, J. K. Wright

Historical Events	Geographers' Lives	Geographical Publications
	1928 T. G. Taylor leaves Australia because of his views on environmental determinism	1927 *Geography: Its history, its nature and its methods* A. Hettner 1929 Sequent occupance, D. Whittlesey Retail gravitation model, W. J. Reilly
1930 Pluto discovered 1930s Dust Bowl, USA 1931 *The logic of scientific discovery* K. Popper Japan occupies Manchuria 1932 splitting of atom, Cockroft & Walton 1933 Hitler named German chancellor 1933–45 F. D. Roosevelt, US President 1933–41 New Deal in USA 1934 purges in Germany & USSR 1936 *The general theory of employment, interest & money* J. M. Keynes, Television broadcasts, UK 1936–9 Spanish Civil War 1937 Japan invades China	1931–5 British Land Utilisation Survey under L. D. Stamp 1932 d. E. C. Semple Schaefer flees Germany 1933 Institute of British Geographers founded A. Weber attacked by Hitler youth, A. Hettner prevented from publishing by Nazis I. Bowman chair of National Research Council, USA C. Glacken works on relief effort for migrant labourers in California 1934 d. W. M. Davis Tuan's family flee Japanese invasion of China 1938–9 Hartshorne in Germany & Austria	1933 *Central Places in Southern Germany* W. Christaller *The British Isles* L. D. Stamp & S. H. Beaver 1934 *Geography in relation to the social sciences* I. Bowman *Habitat, economy & society,* C. D. Forde 1936 *An historical geography of England before AD 1800* H. C. Darby 1939 *The nature of geography* R. Hartshorne
1939–45 Second World War 1944 Bretton Woods Conference 1945 United Nations charter 1945 International Monetary Fund & World Bank	Geographers recruited to war effort for intelligence, training, air photography, meteorology etc. 1942 d. F. Boas Christaller works on planning for occupied Poland 1945 Kirk at fall of Mandalay, Burma campaign 1945–6 Glacken works in Korea	1940 Intervening opportunities, S. Stouffer 1941 A theory of location for cities, E. Ullman Foreword to historical geography, C. O. Sauer 1942 *Human adjustment to floods* G. F. White 1945 The nature of cities, C. D. Harris & E. Ullman Erosional development of streams & their drainage basins, R. Horton

Historical Events	Geographers' Lives	Geographical Publications
1947 Indian independence Marshall Aid plan 1948 Apartheid in South Africa 1949 Division of Germany People's Republic of China formed	1946 Haushofer commits suicide 1947 d. H. J. Mackinder 1948 Harvard geography closes AAG & American Society for Professional Geographers merge d. I. Bowman	1947 J.Q. Stewart's first paper on social physics 1948 *Historical geography of the United States* R. Brown 1949 *A sand county almanac* A. Leopold Principle of least effort, G. K. Zipf
1950–3 Korean War 1953 identification of DNA double helix by Crick & Watson Mt. Everest summit reached McCarthy investigations, USA *Fundamentals of Ecology* E. & H. Odum 1954 start of Vietnam War 1954–62 Algerian War of independence 1954 FORTRAN devised 1956 Hungarian uprising put down by Soviet troops, Stalin denounced in USSR, Elvis Presley 1957 Treaty of Rome leading to the European Economic Community Sputnik in orbit 1958 Fifth Republic, France; Great Leap Forward, China Silicon chip invented	1951 Canadian Association of Geographers founded L. D. Stamp appointed director of World Land Use Survey 1953 d. F. K. Schaefer 1955 Start of seminars in mathematical statistics under E. Ullman & W. L. Garrison at U. of Washington, Seattle 1958 R. Chorley to Cambridge B. J. L. Berry to Chicago Institute of Australian Geographers founded 1959 Hägerstrand visits U. of Washington, Seattle	1951 *The spirit and purpose of geography* S. Wooldridge & G. East The inadequacy of the regional method, G. Kimble 1952 The dynamic basis of geomorphology, A. Strahler 1953 Exceptionalism in geography, F. K. Schaefer Innovation diffusion as a spatial process, T. Hägerstrand 1954 *The economics of location* A. Lösch, English translation *American geography: inventory & prospect* P. E. James & C. F. Jones 1956 *Man's role in changing the face of the earth* W.L. Thomas 1959 Macrogeography & social science, J. Stewart, W. Warntz
1960 *The stages of economic growth* W. Rostow Oral contraception commercially available	1960 Anuchin's *Theoretical problems in geography* creates fierce debate in Soviet geography	1960 *Methods of regional analysis* W. Isard
1961 Vostok 1, first manned space flight, Berlin wall built	1961 IBG creates study groups AAG High School Geography Project	1961 *Megalopolis* J. Gottmann *The City in History* L. Mumford

Historical Events	Geographers' Lives	Geographical Publications
1962 Cuban Missile Crisis The Beatles *Silent spring,* R. Carson 1st geodetic satellite.		1962 *Theoretical geography* W. Bunge
1963 President J.F. Kennedy assassinated	1963 d. S. Wooldridge 1st Madingley conference on Frontiers in geographical teaching	1963 Identification of some fundamental spatial concepts, J. Nystuen Problems of geography, W. Kirk
1964 Civil Rights Act and Great Society welfare programmes, USA 1st weather satellite		1964 The decision process in spatial context, J. Wolpert
1965 Watts riot, Los Angeles 1st mini-computer	1965 L. Dudley Stamp knighted 3rd Madingley conference on Geography in a changing intellectual climate	1965 *Locational analysis in human geography* P. Haggett The Morman culture region, D. Meinig
1966 Cultural Revolution, China	1966 P. Haggett to chair at Bristol	1966 *Central places in southern Germany,* W. Christaller, English translation
1967 Six Day War, Middle East 1967–70 Biafran War, Nigeria	1967 AAG project in remote sensing *Regional Studies* founded	1967 *Traces on the Rhodian shore* C. J. Glacken *Behaviour & location* A. Pred *Models in geography* R. Chorley & P. Haggett Spatial diffusion as an innovation process, T. Hägerstrand
1968 civil unrest in Paris, Chicago, Baltimore, Mexico City and elsewhere Prague Spring uprising in Czechoslovakia Tet Offensive, Vietnam	1968 AAG annual conference moved from Chicago to Ann Arbor at protest over Chicago police tactics against protesters.	1968 *Acadia* A. H. Clark

Historical Events	Geographers' Lives	Geographical Publications
1969 Apollo 11, first humans on moon Northern Ireland, start of civil strife De Gaulle resigns as French President R. Nixon, US President; Woodstock Festival	1969 *Geographical Analysis, Antipode & Environment & Planning A* founded d. J. K. Wright, W. Christaller D. Harvey to Baltimore Detroit Geographical Expedition organised by W. Bunge	1969 *Explanation in Geography* D. Harvey *Behavioural problems in geography* K. Cox & R. Golledge On the environment as perceived, H. Brookfield
1970 Earth Day, April 22 Bangladesh Floods & famine		1970 *Geographic perspectives on urban systems* B. Berry
1971 Indo-Pakistan war leading to secession of Bangladesh (1972) Aswan High Dam opened British currency is decimalized	1971 social relevance theme of AAG annual conference The Socially and Ecologically Responsible Geographer founded by W. Zelinsky and others AAG committee on status of women geographers	1971 *Spatial Organization* R. Abler, J. Adams & P. Gould *Physical geography: a systems approach* R. Chorley & B. Kennedy *Pivot of the four quarters* P. Wheatley
1972 UN Conference on the Environment, Stockholm *Limits to growth* Club of Rome		1972 *Geography: a modern synthesis* P. Haggett
1973–4 Oil Crisis 1973 UK joins EEC Yom-Kippur War, Middle East *Small is beautiful* F. Schumacher	1973 Toronto Expedition organised by W. Bunge	1973 *Social justice and the city* D. Harvey
1974 Nixon resigns as US President Labour unrest & 3–day week in UK	1974 Relevance & public policy theme of IBG annual conference, Norwich	1974 Space and place in humanistic geography, Y-F. Tuan *Urban & Regional modelling in geography & planning* A. G. Wilson

Historical Events	Geographers' Lives	Geographical Publications
1975 Vietnam war ends New York City bankrupt Apollo & Soyuz dock in space Khmer Rouge seize power in Cambodia	1975 d. C. O. Sauer *Journal of Historical Geography* founded AAG membership peaks at 7000	1975 *Spatial Organization of Society* R. Morrill
1976 US bicentennial UK financial crisis & drought The Sex Pistols		1976 *Geographies of the mind* D. Lowenthal & M. Bowden *Place and placelessness* E. Relph
1977 New York City blackout Queen Elizabeth II Silver Jubilee Terrorist attacks in Italy & Germany	1977 *Progress in geography* splits to become *Progress in Physical Geography & Progress in Human Geography*	1977 The choreography of existence, A. Pred *Human geography: a welfare approach* D. M. Smith *The urban question* M. Castells, English translation
1978 Camp David peace accord Election of Pope John Paul II Proposition 13 cuts property taxes, California Jonestown, Guyana, mass suicide of religious cult		1978 *Humanistic geography* D. Ley & M. Samuels *The environment as hazard* I. Burton, R. Kates & G. White *Orientalism* E. Said *Ideology, Science & Human Geography* D. Gregory Paradigms and revolution or evolution, R. J. Johnston
1979 M. Thatcher elected as British Prime Minister Shah of Iran deposed Soviet invasion of Afghanistan	1979 AAG 75th Anniversary	1979 In what sense a regional problem? D. Massey
1980 R. Reagan elected as US President Solidarity formed, Poland Iran-Iraq war starts Mount St. Helens erupts, Washington, USA	1980 *Urban Geography* founded	1980 *Conceptions of space in social thought* R. Sack Geography without man, D. Ley Civilizations: organisms or systems? K. Butzer

Historical Events	Geographers' Lives	Geographical Publications
		Geography, Marx & the concept of nature, N. Smith & P. O'Keefe
1981 Columbia space shuttle launched Riots in UK inner cities IBM-PC desktop introduced	1981 U. of Michigan closes geography department Women and Geography Study Group of IBG founded	1981 *Dictionary of human geography* R. Johnston et al. Institutionalization of geography and strategies of change, H. Capel Human geography & human agency, D. Gregory
1982 British-Argentina war over Falkland Islands	1982 *Political Geography Quarterly* founded	1982 Diorama, path & project, T. Hägerstrand Musing on helicon, A. Buttimer
1983 HIV identified US invasion of Grenada	1983 *Society & Space* founded	1983 *The city & the grassroots* M. Castells On the determination of social action in space & time, N. Thrift
1984 Ethiopian famine Assassination of Indira Gandhi Bhopal gas disaster, India UK coal miners' strike	1984 25th conference of the International Geographical Union, Paris 50th anniversary of IBG	1984 *Discovering the vernacular landscape* J.B. Jackson *Spatial divisions of labour* D. Massey *Geography & gender* Women and geography study group, IBG On the history & present condition of geography, D. Harvey A woman's place? D. Massey & L. McDowell
1985 Gorbachev general secretary Soviet Communist party Mexico City earthquake Live Aid concert		1985 *The urbanization of capital* D. Harvey *Social relations & spatial structures* D. Gregory & J. Urry *Political geography* P.J. Taylor

Historical Events	Geographers' Lives	Geographical Publications
1986 Chernobyl Anglo-French agreement to build Channel Tunnel Spain & Portugal join EEC	1986 BBC Domesday project GIS Localities research programme, UK includes Changing Urban & Regional Systems initiative Chicago department downgraded to committee	1986 *The shaping of America vol. I* D. Meinig *On geography and its history* D.R. Stoddart
1987 Stock market crash Palestinian intifada Meech Lake accord, Canada Montreal protocol on ozone *Gaia* J. Lovelock	1987 National Center for Geographic Information & Analysis, USA The earth as transformed by human action, conference, Clark University National Geography Awareness Week, USA	1987 *Place, practice & structure* A. Pred *The history of cartography vol I* J.B. Harley & D. Woodward 'Localities debate' *Antipode*
1988 Australia's bicentenary Intergovernmental Panel on Climate Change	1988 H.C. Darby knighted Social and cultural geography study group, IBG	1988 *Iconography of landscape* D. Cosgrove & S. Daniels The limits to flexibility, M. Gertler The postmodern challenge to human geography, M. Dear
1989 Berlin Wall comes down Downfall of Ceausescu regime, Romania Tianenmen Square uprising, China Exxon Valdez oil disaster, Alaska	1989 d. C. J. Glacken	1989 *Postmodern geographies* E. Soja *The condition of postmodernity* D. Harvey Areal differentiation and post-modern human geography, D. Gregory Marxism, culture & the duplicity of landscape, S. Daniels The contested terrain of locality studies, P. Cooke Deconstructing the map, J. B. Harley

Historical Events	Geographers' Lives	Geographical Publications
1990 German reunification Iraq invades Kuwait Nelson Mandela released, South Africa		1990 *The making of the American landscape* M. P. Conzen *The geographer's art* P. Hagget
1991 Gulf War COMECON & Warsaw Pact disbanded Yeltsin president of Russia End of USSR War in Yugoslavia Maastricht Treaty	1991 Geography part of UK national curriculum New words, new worlds conference, Edinburgh Environmental Change Unit, U. of Oxford d. J. B. Harley	1991 *The production of space* H. Lefebvre [English tans.] Situated knowledges, D. Haraway A view on the GIS crisis in geography, S. Openshaw
1992 UN Conference on Environment & Development, Rio North American Free Trade Association Los Angeles riots & earthquake Discovery of 'cosmic ripples'	1992 J. Patten, MP, former geographer, becomes UK Education Secretary George Perkins Marsh Institute, Clark U. d. R. Hartshorne	1992 *Writing worlds* T. Barnes & J. Duncan Geography as a science of observation, G. Rose The Americas before & after 1492, K. Butzer et al.
1993 Moscow rebellion Mississippi & Missouri floods Collapse of DC-PSI coalition, Italy	1993 Geographical Association centenary	1993 *Geography & the human spirit* A. Buttimer *Eco-socialism* D. Pepper *Geography & feminism* G. Rose
1994 South African elections Chiapas rebellion Israel-PLO agreement IRA ceasefire	1994 d. J. Gottmann *Ecumene* and *Gender, Place and Culture* founded	1994 *Geographical imaginations* D. Gregory *Geography & empire* A. Godlewska & N. Smith *Technopoles of the world* P. Hall & M. Castells
1995 Oklahoma bombing Collapse of Barings bank Kobe earthquake OJ Simpson trial	Royal Geographical Society & Institute of British Geographers merger	1995 *Mapping desires* D. Bell & G. Valentine *Gender, Work & Space* S. Hanson & G. Pratt